**NATIONAL
GEOGRAPHIC**

COMPLETE

BIRDS

OF NORTH AMERICA

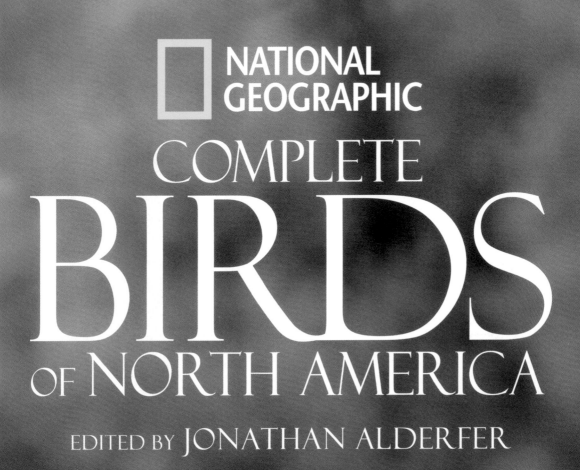

NATIONAL GEOGRAPHIC

COMPLETE
BIRDS
OF NORTH AMERICA

EDITED BY JONATHAN ALDERFER

NATIONAL GEOGRAPHIC
WASHINGTON, D.C.

CONTENTS

INTRODUCTION BY JONATHAN ALDERFER

This book is too large to be a field guide, so what is it? We envision it residing on bookshelves and car seats, ready to be consulted when a field guide doesn't provide enough information. Want to know the details of subspecies variation within Common Eider? The timing of Cerulean Warbler migration? What a Mangrove Swallow looks like? Here you'll find answers to myriad questions—in a single book: the *National Geographic Complete Birds of North America*. Here are illustrations of every accepted North American species (and a few that are waiting in the wings). You'll find in-depth information on identification, similar species, geographic variation, voice, status and distribution, population, and range—through the latest maps.

Coverage

This reference describes all species of wild birds reliably recorded in North America—the continent north of Mexico, plus adjacent islands and seas within 200 miles of the coast, excluding Greenland. With a cut-off date of September 2005, the book's last included species was Social Flycatcher. An unsubstantiated species may be included because it must be *excluded* before making an identification, such as Nazca Booby from Masked Booby on the West Coast. We include exotic species that are established or regularly observed, a subjective call in some cases, and one that will evolve.

Text The text for this guide is completely new, written by 24 of the most knowledgeable, experienced field ornithologists in North America. Each author wrote the species accounts for an entire family or for multiple families. Identification sidebars appear throughout, highlighting ID challenges. Author credits appear in the Table of Contents and after each family account.

Art and photographs Much of the artwork comes from the *National Geographic Field Guide to the Birds of North America*, 4th edition. New art was painted expressly for this book—of 73 accidental and 4 extinct species not in the 4th edition. Photographs illustrate each fam-

ily account and most of the identification sidebars. Art credits appear at the end of the book.

Maps The range maps have been updated from the 4th edition and printed in a larger format. A map key is located below. Note that boundaries are drawn where a species ceases to be regularly seen in the proper habitat. Nearly every species will be rare at the edges of its range. The range maps are augmented with a selected group of large-scale specialty maps that show long-range migration routes, vagrancy patterns, or historical data.

Fieldcraft

The art and practice of birding is a skill that develops with time. If you are new to birding, here are a few basic recommendations: First, get out in the field and

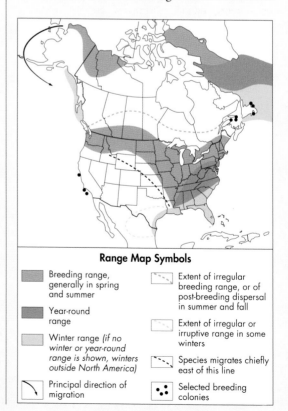

Range Map Symbols

Breeding range, generally in spring and summer	Extent of irregular breeding range, or of post-breeding dispersal in summer and fall
Year-round range	Extent of irregular or irruptive range in some winters
Winter range *(if no winter or year-round range is shown, winters outside North America)*	Species migrates chiefly east of this line
Principal direction of migration	Selected breeding colonies

look at birds with a decent pair of binoculars. Study your field guide before you go, but try leaving it behind. Instead make notes, even if they're just mental ones; soak in what you're seeing; and check the book later. Most expert birders have had a mentor—someone with great field skills who is willing to share knowledge. Great teachers are not rare in the birding community. Seek one out. Also, see Additional Reading on page 646 for books with advice on getting started.

Taxonomic Organization

This book follows the taxonomic sequence and naming conventions currently adopted by the American Ornithologists' Union (AOU) and is organized by family, genus, and species. Getting to know the latest taxonomic sequence is part of a birder's education.

Family A short essay accompanies each of the 82 families, detailing its distinctive characteristics and how those characteristics relate to field identification.

Genus Genera (pl. of genus) are groups of closely related species. The genus name is the first part of a species' scientific or Latin name: i.e., *Spizella* in *Spizella passerina,* or Chipping Sparrow. Deciding a bird's genus can be useful in identifying it. A brief text describes many of the genera, but where distinctions are less useful, genera are lumped together or have no text.

Species Taxonomists differ on the definition of "species." With new scientific information, species limits will continue to be redefined, ultimately rendering a clearer picture of the evolutionary relationships of the birds we watch. In this book, the species' accounts start with a brief overview and follow a standard layout; some accidental species have abbreviated accounts.

Subspecies (Geographic Variation). Many birders are satisfied with making identifications to the species level. Others find it challenging to look more closely, observing variation *within* the species. This book attempts to give information on many field-recognizable subspecies, or groups of subspecies. A species that shows no geographic variation is known as **monotypic.** When within-species variation forms 2 or more distinctive populations, the species is known as **polytypic.** Those populations are given a Latin subspecies name, or trinomial. *Zonotrichia leucophrys gambelii* is the trinomial for "Gambel's" White-crowned Sparrow, a distinctive, field-recognizable subspecies of the White-crowned Sparrow. In polytypic species, the first type described is referred to as the **nominate subspecies,** with a name that repeats the second part of its Latin species name. For instance, *Zonotrichia leucophrys leucophrys* is the nominate subspecies of White-crowned Sparrow. Many subspecies have no commonly used English name and are known only by their Latin epithet. When different subspecies interbreed, the result is known as an **intergrade.** When a species or subspecies varies gradually across a geographical region, it is said to form a **cline,** or to vary clinally.

Plumage Variation

The sex and age of an individual can be determined for many species, most often by observing its plumage. In many species the male and female look quite different. This book illustrates and describes most of those differences. Age determination ranges from simple to complex, depending on the species and how quickly or slowly it reaches adult plumage. Accurate age assessment requires a basic understanding of molt.

Molt describes the replacement of a bird's feathers: A fresh new feather growing from the same follicle pushes out the old worn feather. All birds molt, and a molt produces a plumage. Birds with old, abraded feathers are referred to as **worn;** birds with new feathers are **fresh.** Most birders have adopted an amalgam of terms for molt and plumage to describe what they are seeing—not a rigorous or scientific use of terminology, but a practical one. Perhaps that will change, but for now we use the same, field-tested, age and molt terminology used in the *National Geographic Field Guide to the Birds of North America.* Some of the terms used in this book are defined below.

Juvenile Juveniles (birds in **juvenal** plumage) are wearing their first true coat of feathers, the ones in which they usually fledge (leave the nest). After hatching, not all birds go through the same sequence of plumages. Some young birds (such as most wood-warblers) hold their juvenal plumage only a few weeks, then move right into adult or adult-like plumage. True hawks, loons, and many other waterbirds hold their juvenal plumage into the winter, or even the following spring.

First-fall or First-winter Most species replace their juvenal plumage in late summer or early fall with a partial molt into this plumage, usually while retaining the major, juvenal wing feathers. All plumages between juvenal and adult plumages are **immature,** an imprecise term. The sequence of immature plumages may continue for some years until adult plumage is attained.

First-summer, Second-winter, etc. These terms describe immature plumages between first-winter and adult. **Life-year** terms may be used, such as first-year, second-year, etc. These are age (not molt or plumage) terms; that is, a first-year bird is in its first 12 months of life. **Calendar-year** refers to the bird's actual calendar-year age; that is, a first-calendar-year bird becomes a second-calendar-year bird after December 31.

Adult Birds are adult when their molts produce a stable cycle of identical (or definitive) plumages that repeats for the rest of their lives. Most adult birds have either one complete molt per year *or* one partial and

Lark Sparrow

- supercilium
- postocular stripe
- ear patch (auricular)
- moustachial stripe
- submoustachial stripe
- median crown stripe
- lateral crown stripe
- supraloral area
- lores
- malar stripe

Least Flycatcher

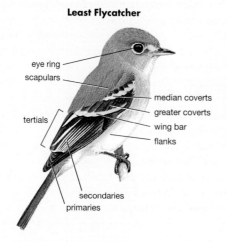

- eye ring
- scapulars
- tertials
- median coverts
- greater coverts
- wing bar
- flanks
- secondaries
- primaries

one complete molt per year. Adult birds with a single complete molt per year (usually after breeding) look the same all year, except for the effects of wear. Adults with two annual molts generally undergo a partial (prealternate) molt in late winter or early spring—often involving the head, body, and some wing coverts— into breeding (or alternate) plumage. Most of these species later undergo a complete (prebasic) molt after breeding into their nonbreeding or winter (or basic) plumage. **High breeding** refers to plumage or bare-parts colors evident only during the brief period of courtship, such as the rich colors of the bill, lores, legs, and feet of many herons. **Eclipse** plumage usually describes the briefly-held, female-like plumage of male ducks in summer, during which they molt their flight feathers and become flightless.

Other variations Two species may interbreed, producing **hybrids** that may look partly like one parent, partly like the other, or may show unexpected characteristics. For a few species this is common; we describe and illustrate these cases. **Morph** describes a regularly occurring variation, usually in plumage coloration, such as the gray-morph Eastern Screech-Owl. These terms note abnormal plumages: **Albino** birds are pure white with red eyes; **partial albino** birds have a piebald appearance with scattered white feathers, sometimes in a symmetrical pattern; **leucistic** birds have abnormally pale plumage; and **melanistic** birds have excessively dark pigmentation.

Art Labels In most cases the art labels match those in the field guide's 4th edition. In some cases, further information or clarification is added. Male (♂) and female (♀) symbols are used where the sexes are discernibly different. Many figures are labeled with an age designation. If a species shows little or no difference between ages or sexes (e.g., storm-petrels), there is no label. Some figures are simply labeled (♂) or (♀) when exact age is difficult to assess, or when juvenal plumage is briefly held. Often a subspecies or subspecies group name is included, with geographic designation.

Feather Topography

Knowing the names of the feather groups and how they are arranged is central to the language of birding. The colors and patterns of a bird's feathers are usually its most important field marks: wing bars, scapulars, eye rings, etc. Sometimes the physical proportions are equally important: primary extension past the tertials, bulging secondaries, etc. Most of the semi-bold terms below are labeled on the illustrations here.

Head A careful look at a bird's head can often provide a correct identification. At the top of the Lark Sparrow's head (top, left) there is a pale **median crown stripe**, bordered by dark **lateral crown stripes.** The line running from the base of the bill up and over the eye is the **eyebrow** or **supercilium**; in front of the eye is the **supraloral area**. The area between the eye and the bill is the **lores**. Note eye color: The pupil is always black, but the **iris** (pl. irides) can be colored. The **orbital ring** (below, left) is naked flesh around the eye; when contrastingly feathered, the area forms an **eye ring** (above, left), or **eye crescents.** A dark stripe extending back from the eye is a **postocular stripe;** when it extends through the eye it is an **eyeline.** The Lark Sparrow shows a distinctive brown patch behind and below the eye known as the **ear patch**, or **auricular.** Its lower border is the **moustachial stripe;** below that is the **submoustachial stripe;** and below that is the **malar stripe.** Most gulls (below) and some other species have a prominent ridge on their lower mandible, the **gonys,** which forms the **gonydeal angle.** The top of the bill is the **culmen.** Raptors have a bare patch of skin over part of the upper mandible, the **cere** (below). Some species, such as pelicans and cormorants, have a fold of loose

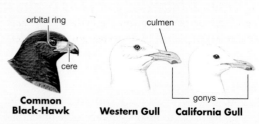

- orbital ring
- cere
- culmen
- gonys

Common Black-Hawk   **Western Gull**   **California Gull**

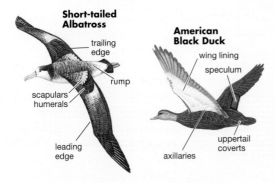

Short-tailed Albatross

trailing edge

rump

scapulars
humerals

leading edge

American Black Duck

wing lining

speculum

uppertail coverts

axillaries

skin hanging from the throat, the **gular pouch**.

Wings Folded wings and extended wings look very different, and it's useful to study both aspects. The longest, strongest feathers of the wing, the **flight feathers**, or **remiges**, are covered on both their upper and lower surfaces by shorter, protective feathers called **coverts** (right). Each feather's shaft divides its **inner web** from its **outer web**. The outermost 9 or 10 tapering flight feathers comprise the **primaries (P1-P10)**; inward from the primaries are a variable number of **secondaries**. Inside the secondaries are a group of feathers known as the **tertials**. On the folded wing, the distance the primaries extend past the longest tertial is the **primary tip projection**. Covering the area where the wing joins the body are the **scapulars**. Rows of wing coverts cover the bases of the flight feathers. From **leading edge** to **trailing edge** they are the **marginal, lesser, median**, and **greater wing coverts**. The greater and median coverts form single rows; the lesser and marginal coverts consist of multiple rows of small feathers. **Wing bars** (opposite) are formed by the pale tips of the greater and median wing coverts. On long-winged species (e.g., albatrosses, above), the **humerals** are well developed. **Mantle** refers to the overall plumage of the back and scapulars. The uniquely colored secondaries of some ducks are referred to as the **speculum** (above). A contrasting bar on the leading edge of the wing is a **carpal bar**; a bar that cuts diagonally across the inner wing is an **ulnar bar**. Dark primaries, ulnar bars, and rump may form an **M-pattern**, prominent on some seabirds. On the underwing, **wing linings** refer to the underwing coverts as a whole; **axillaries** are the feathers of the bird's "armpit."

Tail Most birds have 12 tail feathers, called **rectrices**. On the folded tail from above, only the 2 central tail feathers are visible; from below only the 2 outermost tail feathers are visible. Note the pattern of the undertail and length of the tail projecting past the undertail coverts. Some patterns and the tail's overall shape are visible only in flight.

Size All species accounts include average length, L, from tip of bill to tip of tail; some large or soaring

species also have wingspan, **WS**, measured from wing tip to wing tip. The perception of size is fraught with variables. Lighting, background coloration, and posture affects size perception, as does the use of birding optics. In identification, use size with caution, and always use multiple field marks.

Abundance

Abundance must be considered in relation to habitat. Some species are highly local, found only in specialized habitat. Here they may be common, while nearby they are rare. Ranges and abundance are detailed in the text, as well as extralimital records and population trends. The American Birding Association's *ABA Checklist* is followed for abundance terms; if unspecified, the area noted is the whole of North America.

Rare This indicates species that occur in low numbers, but annually; i.e. visitors or rare breeding residents.

Casual These are species not recorded annually, but with 6 or more total records, *including* 3 or more in the past 30 years, reflecting a pattern of occurrence.

Accidental These are species with 5 or fewer records *or* species with fewer than 3 records in the past 30 years.

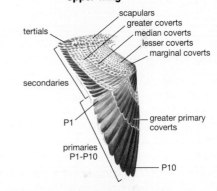

Great Black-backed Gull upper wing

tertials

scapulars
greater coverts
median coverts
lesser coverts
marginal coverts

secondaries

P1

greater primary coverts

primaries P1-P10

P10

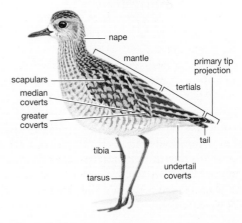

Pacific Golden-Plover

nape

mantle

primary tip projection

scapulars

median coverts

greater coverts

tertials

tibia

tail

tarsus

undertail coverts

DUCKS, GEESE, AND SWANS Family Anatidae

Black Scoters, female (second from left) with males (NJ, Mar.)

Anatids are familiar as domesticated species, and all share some basic traits that are distinctive. They have webbed feet. Most species have a standard "duck bill" that is flattened and broadened at the end; the major exception are the mergansers, which have long, thin, serrated bills. The bodies of ducks, geese, and swans are rotund, tails are usually short, while the wings are strong and generally pointed. The placement of the legs differs considerably depending on whether the species is a surface swimmer or a diver. The legs of surface species are more centrally placed and allow for a horizontal body stance, while those of divers tend be set far back on the body, making it difficult for these ducks to walk on land. Whistling-ducks, an exception, are slim and have legs placed far back, allowing them to stand more upright than other ducks.

Plumage The range in variation in plumage is huge; many are very attractive and are kept as ornamental species in captivity. Geese tend to be brownish or subdued colors, but often with attractive patterns, and there is no sexual dimorphism. Swans are often white, although 2 are black or black necked. Whistling-ducks are attractively patterned, and often show characteristic markings on the flanks; they are sexually monomorphic. Ducks are incredibly variable, but are usually sexually dimorphic, with males showing bright drake plumage with large patches of solid color or pattern; females more cryptic brown plumage. Some species of dabbling ducks, particularly those on islands, have henlike male plumages. Dabbling ducks and some other species show a colorful, and often iridescent, color patch on the secondaries known as the speculum.

Behavior This family is aquatic. Some birds feed from the surface of the water, either filtering food or tipping down to feed on vegetation, while other species are active divers ranging from piscivorous predators to species specializing on shellfish or submerged vegetation. Geese graze on open fields. Courtship behavior is well marked in ducks and is usually easy to observe during the winter and early spring. Geese and swans tend to mate for life, while ducks find new mates each year.

Distribution Anatids occur worldwide, breeding in all continents except Antarctica, where the Black-necked Swan is a vagrant.

Taxonomy This is a large family, with 49 genera and 158 species. It is divided into 5 subfamilies of which 3, Dendrocygninae (Whistling-ducks), Anserinae (true geese and swans), and Anatinae (ducks) are found in North America. The family is thought to be most closely related to the screamers (Anhimidae) and the magpie-geese (Anseranatidae); these families and the galliform families form an old lineage (Galloanserae) within modern birds (Neognathae). In fact the Galloanserae is the sister lineage to all other modern birds, the third and most basal lineage being the Palaeognathae (Tinamous and Ratites). Species level taxonomy within N.A. has been quite stable, although currently there is interest in determining adequate species level divisions within the geese. One confounding factor in waterfowl is that they readily hybridize with each other, sometimes quite commonly, and even between genera.

Conservation Six species are extinct, 6 critically endangered, 9 endangered, and 12 vulnerable. —*Jessie H. Barry, Cameron D. Cox, Alvaro Jaramillo*

WHISTLING-DUCKS Genus Dendrocygna

The 8 species of whistling-ducks are found mainly in tropical regions. Slim, long necked, and long billed, they stand rather upright. Their whistling calls inspired their name; some perch on trees, giving them the alternate name "tree-ducks." They fly with shallow wingbeats on rounded wings. The whistling-ducks comprise a subfamily of the Anatidae.

BLACK-BELLIED WHISTLING-DUCK *Dendrocygna autumnalis*

This gorgeous duck is often found perching on trees or shrubs. Polytypic. L 21" (53 cm)
Identification A long-legged, broad-winged, and long-necked duck. ADULT: Bright red bill obvious on gray face; the eye is surrounded by a bold white eye ring. Lower neck and breast tawny, with contrasting black belly and flanks. Upperparts warm brown, folded wings

adults

juvenile

show whitish shoulder/forewings, and dark primaries and tertials. Legs bright pink. JUVENILE: Similar to adult but bill grayish and body plumage much duller. Flanks brownish and belly off-white, not black. Wing pattern similar to that of adult, although duller and less extensively white. FLIGHT: A warm brown with black hindparts, including rump and lower back, with strikingly large white patch on upper wings from inner greater coverts to outer primary coverts and primary bases.
Geographic Variation Two subspecies, only *fulgens* found in our area.
Similar Species Likely to be confused only with the Fulvous Whistling-Duck, which lacks the red bill and black belly. The large white wing patch of the Black-bellied is diagnostic. Juveniles show duller plumage, but note white on the wing and gray face.
Voice CALL: A multisyllabic,

nasal whistle, *pe-che,* or a longer *pe-che-che-ne.*
Status & Distribution Fairly common, widespread in neotropics south to central Argentina. YEAR-ROUND: Wetlands, those with overhanging woody vegetation preferred. MIGRATION: A short-distance migrant, traveling only a few hundred kilometers south into northern Mexico. Arrival on breeding grounds by Apr., southbound movements noted from Aug. to Oct. VAGRANT: Casual north of regular range as far north as MN, MI, and ON and to southern CA and NM. Vagrants often appear in small flocks.
Population Both the population and range have expanded noticeably in TX and AZ in the last 3 decades.

FULVOUS WHISTLING-DUCK *Dendrocygna bicolor*

The Fulvous is a long-legged, large-winged, and long-necked largely tawny duck. Monotypic. L 20" (51 cm)
Identification Bill gray, legs blue-gray. Face, neck sides, breast and belly tawny. Throat and foreneck buffy-white, speckled with black on lower neck. Top of crown brown, continues as a brown line (broken in male, continuous in female) down the back of the neck to the upper back. Upperparts black with broad cinnamon edges to feathers. Tawny underparts accented by crisp white stripes on flanks, vent white. FLIGHT: Appears tawny with blackish wings, including underwings.

Lower back and tail black, contrasting with white rump band.
Similar Species Somewhat similar to juvenile Black-bellied, which has a gray face, and large white wing patch. Fulvous is always more tawny, with white flank stripes. In flight Fulvous shows a strong contrast between blackish underwings and tawny body, and a white rump band. In addition Fulvous is narrower winged than the Black-bellied and has a deeper wing flap.
Voice CALL: A 2-note, high-pitched, nasal, whistled call, *pt-TZEEW,* accent on second syllable.
Status & Distribution Fairly common. Widely distributed in New World tropics south to central Argentina, as well as in Africa and the Indian subcontinent. YEAR-ROUND: Freshwater grassy wetlands, rice fields commonly used. MIGRATION: A short-distance migrant, some of FL population moving south to Cuba and some of CA and TX and LA birds south into Mexico. Arrival on breeding grounds in Feb.–Mar., southbound movements Aug.–late Sept. DISPERSAL: Regular northward

dispersal after breeding. VAGRANT: Casual throughout continent, north to BC, AB, and NS. Vagrant records occur in years of increased postbreeding northward wandering. Records are concentrated in Mississippi Basin, and Atlantic Coast.
Populations have fluctuated noticeably historically, however California population and range has seriously decreased and contracted since the mid-1900s and is now basically extirpated.

adults

GRAY GEESE Genus Anser

These are the "standard" or quintessential geese. Our domesticated goose is derived from a member of this genus, the Graylag (*Anser anser*). There are 7 species in the genus, found largely in the Palearctic. These geese are brownish with a variable gray wash to the coverts. Bill color and pattern as well as leg color aid in identification.

BEAN GOOSE Anser fabalis

The Bean is a large brown vagrant from Eurasia of variable structure. Polytypic. L 31" (79 cm)
Identification Legs orange, bill black with orange subterminal area. ADULT: Brown with darker head and white belly. Tertials crisply and obviously fringed white. Flanks edged with narrow white line, which forms a separation with the folded wings. Hind flanks dark barred. JUVENILE: As adult, lacking white edge to flanks and barring on flanks. FLIGHT: Brown, showing darker flight feathers and a gray wash to the coverts. The brown upperparts contrast with the narrow white rump band, the tail is brown with a narrow white border.
Geographic Variation Five subspecies in 2 groups, the "Tundra Bean Goose" and "Taiga Bean Goose." Members of both groups have occurred in N.A. One group breeds north of the other. The Tundra birds are smaller, stockier, and shorter necked and smaller billed than the Taiga birds. Bill color also aids in separating the 2 groups. Taiga birds show an extensive orange bill with black on the nail, cutting edge, and the base reaching the nostril. The Tundra birds show a narrow, neat orange subterminal band on an otherwise black bill. There is variation in bill pattern, and it should be used in conjunction with size and structure to identify the groups. Some European authorities suggest splitting the 2 groups of Bean Goose as separate species. Largest of Taiga group (*middendorffi*) has occurred in AK, while *serrirostris* is the representative of the Tundra group.
Similar Species Juvenile White-fronted Goose is similar, but it has largely pink bill lacking black base of the Bean Goose. The Bean shows obvious white fringes on the tertials. The Bean is also very similar to the Pink-footed Goose, but the Bean has orange on bill and legs. Bean Goose browner, lacking grayish wash to upperparts of most Pink-footeds. Pink-footed smaller than the Bean Goose, with stockier shape, overlapping somewhat with Tundra Bean, but not Taiga Bean. In flight, Pink-footed Goose has a more prominent white edge to the tail.
Voice CALL: Usually silent, a nasal *gang gang;* Tundra birds higher-pitched than Taiga birds.
Status & Distribution Vagrant, breeds from Scandinavia to Siberia, wintering in various midlatitude sites from Europe to Asia. VAGRANT: Casual to Bering Sea Islands, and Seward Peninsula, AK, primarily in spring. Accidental to YK, NE, WA and QC.

serrirostris

adults

adult
middendorffii

PINK-FOOTED GOOSE Anser brachyrhynchus

A midsize brownish gray goose similar in structure to the Greater White-fronted, the Pink-footed is a vagrant from Greenland most likely to be found in the Northeast. Monotypic. L 26" (66 cm)
Identification Legs and feet pink, bill black with extensive pink on terminal half. Juveniles may show dull or even orange tone to legs. ADULT: A brownish goose with darker head and white belly. Upperparts tipped white, creating neatly barred appearance. Upperparts show gray wash, contrasting with browner underparts. Tertials crisply fringed white. Flanks edged with narrow white line, which forms a separation with the folded wings. Hind flanks dark barred. JUVENILE: As adult, but lacking white edge to flanks and barring on flanks. Legs often orange tinged. FLIGHT: A brown goose showing obvious gray wash to the upper wings. The upperparts contrast with the narrow white rump band; the tail is brown with a comparatively wide white border.
Similar Species Juvenile White-fronted Goose similar, but it has longer pink bill lacking black base. In addition, Pink-footed Geese show obvious white fringes on the tertials. Also very similar to the Bean Goose, but the Pink-footed has pink on bill and legs. The Bean Goose is browner, lacking grayish wash to upperparts of most Pink-footed Geese. Furthermore, the Pink-footed is smaller than the Bean Goose with stockier shape, overlapping somewhat with Tundra Bean, but not Taiga Bean. In flight, the Pink-footed Goose has a more prominent white edge to the tail and more gray on wings.
Voice CALL: A high-pitched *ayayak.*
Status & Distribution Vagrant, breeds in Greenland, Iceland, and Svalbard, wintering in British Isles and Low Countries of Europe. VAGRANT: Casual in QC and NF. Accidental in PA, DE, and NS.

adults

GREATER WHITE-FRONTED GOOSE *Anser albifrons*

Colloquially known as the speckle-belly due to the variable black barring on the underparts, this is a medium-size grayish brown goose. Polytypic. L 28" (71 cm)

Identification Legs and feet orange, bill pink, sometimes more orange. ADULT: Brownish with a distinctive white band around the bill base, most obvious on the forehead. The underparts are brown with black barring from lower breast to upper belly; belly and vent are white. The flanks are bordered by a white line. Above brown with paler feather tips. JUVENILE: Similar to adult, but lacks the white forehead and speckling on under-parts; bill has a dark nail. FLIGHT: Brown showing a gray wash to the coverts and a narrow white rump band.

Geographic Variation Five subspecies recognized, 3 breeding in N.A. The smaller and widespread *frontalis* and the larger "Tule Goose," *elgasi* (see sidebar below), breeding between Cook Inlet and Alaska Range, Alaska, and wintering in Sacramento Valley. The large pale *gambelli* from northern Alaska and northwestern Canada winters in Mexico to Texas. Another sub-

immature
adult
adult
taiga adult
elgasi
tundra adult
Greenland adult
flavirostris

species, *flavirostris*, the "Greenland" White-fronted Goose, is a vagrant to eastern North America. This form is larger than *frontalis*, darker brown, more heavily barred on underparts, and shows an orange bill.

Similar Species White front and barred belly diagnostic in adult. Compare immature with other "brown geese."

Voice CALL: A laughing 2- to 3-syllable *ka-yaluk* or *kaj-lah-aluk*, somewhat grating and high-pitched.

Status & Distribution Common, also in Eurasia. BREEDING: Tundra and to a lesser extent taiga wetlands. MIGRATION: Mid-continent populations move south from Aug.–Sept. to stop-over areas from eastern AB to western MB; most depart

by mid-Oct. for coastal TX, then to sites from Mexico to LA. Northward movements begin in Feb. and track snowmelt, arriving in central AK late Apr.–early May. Pacific Population of central to southwestern AK, including Tule Goose, fly south along coast eventually moving inland to stop in Klamath region of southern OR, northern CA in Sept.–Oct. More southern breeders and Tule Goose continue to winter in Central Valley of CA, while others continue to central plateau of Mexico. WINTER: Wetlands, agricultural areas, short-grass fields. VAGRANT: Rare east of range in migration and winter.

Population Generally increasing, Pacific populations declined strongly in the 1970s and '80s, but are regaining in numbers. Tule subspecies estimated at 7,500.

"Tule" Goose Subspecies of Greater White-fronted Goose

The "Tule" White-fronted Goose, subspecies *elgasi* but previously named *gambelli* or *gambeli*, is rare and range-restricted. It has been known largely from the wintering grounds, and only in the 1970s were the breeding grounds determined. More work needs to be done to clarify the status of birds breeding in the Yukon Territory, which may also be *elgasi*. In winter both the "Tule" and the "Pacific" population of Greater White-fronted

"Tule" Goose (CA)

Geese are found in the Sacramento Valley, sometimes together. It is when they are together that identification is most straightforward. The "Tule" is larger, with

a longer neck and a noticeably longer and deeper bill. In direct comparison these size and structural features should be apparent. In addition, the "Tule" is darker, particularly on the head and neck; in fact these geese often show a contrasting dark cap that extends as a dark line along the back of the neck. The speckling on the belly is less extensive on the "Tule" than on the typical White-fronted Goose. Finally, there are ecological differences. The "Tule" often feeds in marshes, eating the large tubers of tule *(Scirpus robustus)*, while other White-fronted Geese forage in open grassy fields. ■

LESSER WHITE-FRONTED GOOSE *Anser erythropus*

A medium-size brown goose, the Lesser White-fronted is accidental from the Palearctic. Monotypic. L 22–26" (55-66 cm)

adult

Identification The Lesser-White-fronted is extremely similar to the White-fronted Goose, but stockier in structure, shorter necked, and smaller billed, with longer and narrower wings. The wings extend beyond the tail when folded. The legs and feet are deep orange, bill is pink, orbital ring is yellow. ADULT: White "front" extends back beyond the eye. Brown below with minimal black barring on the belly. JUVENILE: Similar to the adult, but fresh juveniles lack the white forehead and speckling on the underparts.
Similar Species The Lesser White-front-

ed Goose is smaller, darker, longer winged, shorter necked, and smaller billed than the Greater White-fronted Goose. In adults the extensive white on the forehead and the yellow orbital are diagnostic. Juveniles may be separated from the Greater White-fronted by darker body, size and structure, yellow orbital, and bill with pale nail.
Voice CALL: Yelping and high-pitched calls.
Status & Distribution Accidental, breeds from Scandinavia to Siberia, wintering in a few midlatitude sites. VAGRANT: One specimen from Attu I., AK, June 5, 1994.

SNOW GOOSE AND ALLIES *Genus Chen*

This is a small genus of 3 species with mainly a North American distribution, sometimes incorporated into *Anser*. Two of the 3 species are polymorphic, a feature not found in other goose genera. Plumages of all Snow Geese and allies show white tails and largely white heads.

SNOW GOOSE *Chen caerulescens*

The Snow is the larger and more common white Arctic goose. Polytypic and polymorphic. L 26–33" (66–84 cm)
Identification Medium size, with a pink bill and distinctive "grin patch" along the cutting edge of the bill. Adult's legs pink, immature's legs dusky pink. ADULT WHITE: White, with black primaries. Often face is stained rust from oxides in water. JUVENILE WHITE: Similar to adult, but gray-brown wash on head, neck, and upperparts; dark centered tertials. In flight shows dusky secondaries. ADULT BLUE: Brown body, white head and neck. Wings

adults

blue-morph adults

white-morph juvenile

white morph adult

blue-morph juvenile

with gray-blue coverts, long tertials, inner greater coverts black with bold white fringes. Tail gray with white border. JUVENILE BLUE: Dull brown, including head and neck. Pattern of wing and tertials less well developed.
Geographic Variation Interior and western populations known as "Lesser Snow Goose," *caerulescens;* eastern population is the "Greater Snow Goose," *atlantica.* Size overlaps; not field identifiable. Subspecies and genetic differences do not match; perhaps better considered monotypic. Blue morph lacking in Pacific and Atlantic wintering populations.
Similar Species Most similar to Ross's Goose, but adult Snow Geese of both morphs have black

"grinning patch" on bill, are larger, longer necked, and longer billed. Blue Goose has white head and neck and blue wing panel; compare to Ross's. Immature White morph Snow extensively brownish washed above, and in flight shows brownish secondaries.
Voice CALL: A barking *whouk,* or *kow-luk.*
Status & Distribution Abundant, casual to Europe, now rare to Japan where formerly numerous. BREEDING: Moist tundra. MIGRATION: Southbound movements begin late Aug.–early Sept., arriving in wintering areas by early Oct., peaking late Oct. and Nov. Northbound movements begin in Feb., peak early Apr. in southern Canada and reach breeding areas in late May. WINTER: Wetlands and agricultural fields.
Population Growing exponentially since 1960s; they are exceeding the carrying capacity at breeding sites, overgrazing sensitive grassy tundra.

ROSS'S GOOSE *Chen rossii*

The smallest of the white Arctic geese, Ross's has a short, triangular bill. Monotypic but polymorphic. L 23" (58 cm)

Identification Stocky and short necked, with high forehead and short legs. The bill is pink and shows grayish "warts" on the base of the upper mandible. Legs pink. ADULT: Entirely white, with black primaries. JUVENILE: Similar to adult but variably washed dusky, particularly on the nape and back of neck. The tertials show dark shafts or centers. HYBRIDS: With the Snow Goose, intermediate in size and structure and grin patch, best identified by comparing with the 2 parental species. **Geographic Variation** Monotypic, but a rare blue morph exists. The origin of this blue morph is controversial and is thought to be due either to introgression with blue Snow Geese or a recurrent mutation of genes controlling feather color. Blue Ross's Geese are most frequent in wintering flocks in California's Central Valley. They are structurally like typical Ross's Geese. **Similar Species** Like the Snow Goose but smaller, shorter necked, smaller billed, and rounder headed. Ross's lacks "grin patch" but shows gray warts at bill base. In flight smaller and shorter necked with more rapid wingbeats than Snow Goose. Blue Ross's Geese differ from Blue Snow Geese in showing only a white face, with dark hind crown, nape, and neck; and extensive white on the lower breast and belly. **Voice** CALL: A high, nasal *hawhh*. **Status & Distribution** Common. BREEDING: Wet tundra. MIGRATION: Little is known about boreal staging areas in this species. However, the western population stops over in eastern AB, western SK largely in Sept. From there they move through western MT, northern ID, eastern OR into the wintering areas in CA by Oct. The eastern population moves through Hudson Bay and stages in eastern SK and MB, before moving south through

the Dakotas to wintering areas in central Mexico, eastern TX, and LA. Spring migration begins as early as Feb. and retraces the fall route, following the advance of the snowmelt. Staging in Canadian prairies takes place mid-Apr.–mid-May, and arrival in breeding grounds from end of May to early June. Lingers later in wintering grounds than the Snow Goose. WINTER: Wetlands and adjacent agricultural areas. VAGRANT: Rare but regular east of the Mississippi River; increasing.

Population Since the mid-50s Ross's Goose populations have increased dramatically, some estimates give a 10 percent annual increase from the 1950s to the 1990s.

white-morph juvenile

white-morph adult

adult

blue-morph adult

ROSS'S GOOSE

BREEDING AND WINTER RANGE EXPANSION

- Breeding range 1980
- Breeding range 2003
- Winter range 1980
- Winter range 2003

EMPEROR GOOSE *Chen canagica*

The Emperor is a gorgeous marine goose of the Bering Sea area. Monotypic. L 26" (66 cm)

Identification A small stocky goose with thick and strong legs. Bill pink with black cutting edges and nostril, and legs bright orange. ADULT: Distinctive, gray bodied, with each feather neatly tipped dark subterminally and white terminally, giving a characteristic scaly look. Head white, continuing down the back of the neck and contrasting with black throat and foreneck. Sometimes the head may be stained rust with oxides. In flight the Emperor appears gray, with white tail and white head and hind neck. IMMATURE: Browner than adult, but shows scaly appearance and

white tail although it has an entirely brown head and neck.

Similar Species Distinctive, although blue morph Snow or Ross's geese show similar dark body with white face or neck. Emperor Goose has a diagnostic pattern of white head and hind neck contrasting with black throat and foreneck. Scaly pattern to plumage and orange legs also characteristic. Barnacle Goose shares grayish scaly appearance, but it has an entirely black breast and neck with only face white and a dark tail.

Voice CALL: A hoarse and repeated *kla-ha,* although usually remains quiet.

Status & Distribution Uncommon, also breeds in easternmost Siberia. BREEDING: In coastal wetlands with

tidal influence. MIGRATION: In fall, begin staging from mid-August–Oct. on the north shore of the Alaska Peninsula, dispersing to the Aleutian Islands by Nov. Wintering areas largely in Aleutian Islands and south coast of Alaska Peninsula. Birds depart Mar.–early Apr. for staging lagoons on the north shore of the Alaska Peninsula. Birds stage until May, and then fly to nesting areas, largely in the Yukon-Kuskokwim Delta. WINTER: Intertidal habitats, from rocky coasts to eelgrass beds. VAGRANT: Casual south to CA on the Pacific coast, with few inland records in the Central Valley.

Population Appears to have decreased between 1960 and the 1980s, but has remained stable since then.

adults

juvenile

CANADA GOOSE AND ALLIES *Genus Branta*

This is a genus of 6 species found throughout the Northern Hemisphere, including Hawaii. The birds have distinctive patterns on the face, neck, or breast. Most show a black neck "sock," with contrasting white face or neck patches. All have black bills and legs. Several are high-Arctic breeders; most forage on short grass during the nonbreeding season.

BRANT *Branta bernicla*

A sea goose that forages largely on marine grasses, the Brant is known as the Brent Goose in Great Britain. Polytypic. L 25" (64 cm)

Identification A smallish, short-billed,

adults

hrota

juvenile

short-necked stocky goose. Bill and legs black. ADULT: All forms show a black head, neck, and breast; a fishbone pattern white neck collar varies in extent geographically. The upperparts are solid brown, contrasting with a white rump and vent and dark tail. Underparts variable depending on race, varying from pale brown to blackish brown with contrasting white flanks. IMMATURE: Similar to adult but lacks neck collar and shows white tips to wing coverts.

Geographic Variation There are 3 named subspecies—*bernicla,* "Dark-bellied Brant," breeding in central and western Russian Arctic and wintering in western Europe; *hrota,* "Pale-bellied Brant," breeding in eastern Arctic of N.A, Greenland, and Svalbard and wintering in Atlantic coast of U.S.,

England, and Ireland; and *nigricans,* "Black Brant," breeding from eastern Russia through western Arctic N.A. including AK to Victoria I., NU, and wintering on Pacific Coast from AK to Mexico. There is a fourth, as yet unnamed, population known as the Western High Arctic population or "Gray-bellied Brant." These birds breed mainly on Melville and Prince Patrick Is., NT, and winter in the Puget Sound area and Boundary Bay, BC. The Pale-bellied Brant has a small neck collar, divided at front, pale underparts contrasting with black neck "sock," and white belly behind legs. Black Brant is darker above and below. It shows little contrast between the dark underparts and the neck sock; pale flanks contrast with the dark underparts; the neck collar is broad and full and meets in the front of the neck. Dark-bellied Brant is a vagrant, reported from the East Coast. It is dark below, but paler than Black Brant, lacks the contrasting white flanks, and has a small and broken neck collar. Gray-bellied Brant appears to be variable, ranging from pale birds similar to Pale-bellied Brant, to birds with gray underparts and contrasting paler flanks; they have smaller, broken neck collars than the Black Brant.

Similar Species Entirely black head, neck and breast, white collar diagnostic. Cackling and Canada geese have white face patch.

Voice CALL: A quavering *crrr-oonkkk*.

Status & Distribution Common, also breeds in Palearctic. BREEDING: In salt marshes in low Arctic and moist tundra in high Arctic. MIGRATION: Four populations are treated here; 2 are part of the "Pale-bellied Brant" subspecies, the Atlantic and Eastern High Arctic population. ATLANTIC BRANT: Breed largely near the Foxe Basin, NT; stage in James Bay in Sept. and fly nonstop to coastal NY and NJ, arriving in late Oct.–Nov. They move north in Apr. Some use a coastal route to the St. Lawrence River Estuary; others move inland over Lake Ontario and up the Ottawa River Valley (late May). Both routes converge in James Bay, where they stage before heading to the breeding grounds by early June. Historically more birds moved up the coast, with important staging areas in the Maritimes; these routes have shifted westward. EASTERN HIGH ARCTIC BRANT: They leave their breeding grounds in late Aug. and stage in western Greenland in Sept. before continuing to Iceland (mid-Sept.) and wintering sites in Ireland and England by late Sept. or Oct. Spring migration begins in late Apr.; they stage for several weeks in Iceland and fly over the Greenland ice cap directly to breeding grounds by mid-June. BLACK BRANT AND "GRAY-BELLIED BRANT": They make their way from various breeding areas from the western Canadian Arctic to Wrangel I. in Siberia to congregate at Izembek Lagoon staging area on the Alaska Peninsula as early as mid-Sept. Victoria I. breeders fly a coastal route around AK and arrive at the staging grounds by mid-Oct. They then fly directly to the Queen Charlotte Is. and southern BC coast before continuing south well offshore on the Pacific coast to wintering sites, arriving late Oct.–Nov. A few migrate to Japan for the winter. Northbound migration peaks in Mar. and Apr. on California coast, with staging areas on east coast of Vancouver I. before flight to Alaska Peninsula, peaking there in mid-May, and arriving at breeding grounds mid–late June. WINTER: Coastal, primarily in large estuaries where beds of eelgrass and other intertidal plants are available for forage. VAGRANT: Casual in interior, away from eastern Great Lakes. Dark-bellied Brant has been reported but not conclusively documented from the East; it should be looked for in wintering concentrations of Pale-bellied Brant.

Population Black Brant have decreased in last several decades; Atlantic Brant have fluctuated markedly and are now stable or increasing. The "Gray-bellied Brant" population is small and of conservation concern.

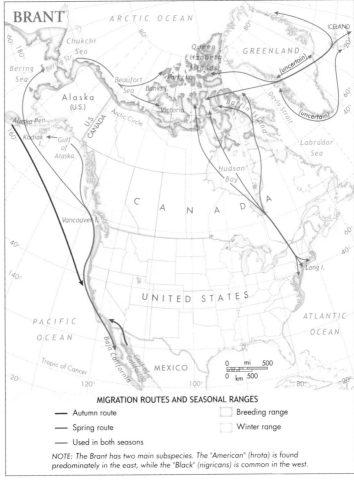

adult
hrota

adult *nigricans*
"Black Brant"

BRANT

MIGRATION ROUTES AND SEASONAL RANGES

— Autumn route

— Spring route

— Used in both seasons

☐ Breeding range

☐ Winter range

NOTE: The Brant has two main subspecies. The "American" (*hrota*) is found predominately in the east, while the "Black" (*nigricans*) is common in the west.

CANADA GOOSE *Branta canadensis*

The "honker" is the common goose in most of North America. Polytypic. L 45" (114 cm)

Identification A large and long-necked goose; legs and bill black. ADULT: Black neck and head with a contrasting white cheek patch. Body brown, paler below, often darker on rear flanks. Belly and vent white. FLIGHT: Brown above including wings, lower back blackish, as is the tail, both contrasting strongly with a white rump band.

Geographic Variation Seven subspecies in N.A. Subspecies *canadensis* breeds Ungava Bay east to Newfoundland, wintering on Atlantic seaboard; *interior* breeds west of Ungava Bay through Hudson Bay lowlands to northern Manitoba and north to southern Baffin Island and southwestern Greenland, wintering throughout the East;

canadensis
"Atlantic"

occidentalis
"Dusky"

maxima ("Giant" Canada Goose) breeds central Manitoba and Minnesota south to Kansas and western Kentucky, some resident, others short-distance migrants; *moffitti* breeds south-central British Columbia to western Manitoba south to Colorado and Oklahoma, wintering southern portion of breeding range to southern California, northern Mexico, and Texas; *parvipes* ("Lesser" Canada Goose) breeds in boreal forest zone from central Alaska to northwestern Hudson Bay, wintering eastern Washington and eastern Oregon to northeastern Mexico and eastern Texas; *fulva* ("Dusky" Canada Goose) breeds in Copper River Delta and Prince William Sound, Alaska, wintering in Willamette Valley, Oregon; *occidentalis* ("Vancouver" Canada Goose) breeds from Glacier Bay, Alaska, to northern Vancouver Island, many resident, others winter in Willamette and Columbia Valleys, Oregon. These subspecies intergrade to various extents and can be thought of as fitting 3 general groups. The subspecies *canadensis, interior, maxima* and *moffitti* are very similar, with *maxima* being largest and palest. The "Lesser" Canada Goose (*parvipes*) varies in size, but on average is smaller than all other Canada Geese. The "Vancouver" and "Dusky" Canada Geese are very dark, color saturated, the "Dusky" being smaller than the "Vancouver."

Similar Species See sidebar below.

Voice CALL: Males give a lower pitched *hwonk*, females a higher *hrink*.

Status & Distribution Abundant, the birds have been introduced to Western Europe. BREEDING: Various freshwater wetlands, golf courses. MIGRATION: Complex due to number of different populations and staging areas, however most wild populations of the Canada Goose are migratory. In modern times "feral" Canada Geese have been introduced in various parts of the continent, many of these being primarily stocks descended from mixes of "Giant" Canada Goose and others. Many of these birds are residents in urban areas, or they perform only minor migrations. Migrant geese tend to leave breeding grounds in Aug.–Sept., peak in Oct., and arrive at wintering areas from mid-Oct.–Nov. Spring movements begin in Feb., peaking in Mar. WINTER: Various grassy habitats, from urban parks to native wetlands; also agricultural fields.

Population This goose has dramatically increased in number since the 1940s; it is now estimated that nearly 5 million Canada Geese live in North America, and the birds are considered urban pests in some regions.

Small Canada versus Large Cackling Goose

Due to the split of the Cackling Goose, we have a vexing new problem in field identification, mainly that the larger Cackling Goose (subspecies *taverneri*) is close in size to the smallest Canada Goose (subspecies *parvipes*).

In the past, *taverneri* and *parvipes* were grouped together as a single subspecies; however, recent studies clearly show them to be genetically different. This issue may be due to confusion of exactly what *taverneri* is; the type specimen is from the wintering area in California rather than from the breeding area.

"Lesser" Canada Goose, parvipes (AK, May)

Therefore, smallish geese from various regions of Alaska have been called *taverneri;* no doubt some of these were really *parvipes*. As well, *parvipes* has been reported to hybridize with *hutchinsii* ("Richardson's Goose") in the eastern Arctic, as well as with *taverneri* in Alaska. However, conclusive proof of this hybridization has not yet been established. Until this confusion is clearly sorted out, identification will be problematic and often impossible as we do not know the range of variability of the 2 troubling entities.

CACKLING GOOSE *Branta hutchinsii*

leucoparenia
"Aleutian"

minima
"Cackling"

hutchinsii
"Richardson's"

River, Hudson Bay, Nunavut; may breed in western Greenland, winters from eastern New Mexico and northern Texas south into highlands of Mexico, also coastal Texas to western Louisiana and south to northern Veracruz, Mexico. "Taverner's Goose" *(taverneri)* breeds in coastal wetlands of Seward Peninsula and North Slope, Alaska, and winters in Columbia River Valley, Washington and Oregon, south to the Central Valley of California. "Cackling Goose" *(minima)* breeds in the Yukon-Kuskokwim Delta, Alaska, and winters largely from Willamette Valley, Oregon, south to Central Valley of California, previously wintered largely in California but has shifted north; "Aleutian Goose" *(leucopareia)* breeds on Aleutian and Semidi Islands, Alaska, and winters in Central Valley, California, but expanding. Some recognize the extinct *asiatica* ("Bering Goose"), which bred in Commander Island, Russia, and Kurile Island, Japan/Russia, and wintered in Japan; others consider this subspecies part of *leucopareia.* The "Richardson's" is the palest, with a pale breast form and intermediate in size but with a proportionately long bill. The *minima* is the smallest and is dark, with a dark brown breast that may only be slight-

ly paler than the neck sock; it has a stubby short bill. "Taverner's" is the largest, with a longer neck and rounder head; intermediate in darkness, but variable. The "Aleutian" is larger than *minima,* but smaller than "Taverner's"; a moderately dark form; it typically has a complete white neck collar.

Similar Species See sidebar pages 10–11.

Voice CALL: Similar in structure to Canada Goose calls, but high-pitched and cackling.

Status & Distribution Common. BREEDING: Moist coastal tundra. MIGRATION: Richardson's flies south from late Aug., staging in central and eastern prairie provinces, peaking in Oct. Northward movements begin in Feb.–Mar. Cackling *(minima)* and Aleutian stage in Alaska Peninsula into Oct., then perform nonstop (2–4 day) flight to OR and CA. They move north by late Apr. WINTER: Short-grass fields, including agricultural areas and wetlands. VAGRANT: Rare away from regular migratory areas.

Population General increase in various populations during the last decade; the Aleutian subspecies has been removed from the endangered species list.

The Cackling has only recently been split from the Canada Goose. Polytypic. L 25" (64 cm)

Identification A small, stubby-billed goose with short legs, stocky body, and short neck. Comparatively long winged, with primaries extending noticeably past the tail. Bill and legs black. ADULT: Black neck and head with a contrasting white cheek patch that wraps around the throat; typically there is a dark line along the midline of the throat, but this is difficult to see in the field. Often shows a white neck ring below the black "sock." Body brown, paler below; often darker on rear flanks. Belly and vent white. FLIGHT: Brown above, lower back and tail blackish, contrasting with a white rump band.

Geographic Variation Four subspecies recognized. "Richardson's Goose" *(hutchinsii)* breeds from Mackenzie Delta, Northwest Territories, east to western Baffin Island and south to Southhampton Island and McConnell

The extremes should be identifiable by concentrating on the following factors: size, bill proportions, neck proportions, and wing structure. On average, *parvipes* is larger than *taverneri* and has a relatively longer neck and longer bill. In general, the Cackling Goose has longer and more pointed wings than the Canada Goose, and this difference shows up as a longer primary extension (past tertials) and wing extension (past tail) in the Cackling.

Plumage color is likely not helpful in distinguishing between these 2 subspecies. "Taverner's" is supposed to be darker than *parvipes,* particularly on the breast, although such coloration is variable. Populations of *parvipes* breeding in Anchorage, Alaska, however, are quite dark, approaching the "Dusky" Canada

Goose in color. Other features, such as dark throat stripes and white neck rings, are again exhibited by both species and therefore are not useful information in identification.

The wintering range of *taverneri* is not clearly known, but it is not expected to be regular East of the Cascade Range/Sierra Nevada Mountains. So a troubling intermediate goose in the East is more likely *parvipes,* which migrates and winters largely east of the mountains. The dark-bodied *parvipes* from Anchorage, Alaska, winters in the Pacific Northwest.

In summary, until *taverneri* and *parvipes* are studied on the breeding grounds and color-banded to trace their movements, intermediate "white-cheeked geese" are best left unidentified. ∎

BARNACLE GOOSE *Branta leucopsis*

adults

Before bird migration was accepted, legends told that when these geese disappeared from wintering sites in western Europe, they turned into barnacles. Monotypic. L 27" (69 cm)

Identification A small, short-necked goose with a stubby bill. Bill and legs black. ADULT: White face and black lores contrast with black neck and breast. Underparts white with gray barring on flanks. Upperparts gray, with scaled appearance created by dark subterminal band and white terminal band on each feather. IN FLIGHT: Gray wings and back, with black neck; lower back and tail contrasting with white rump band.

Similar Species Distinguishable from Cackling Goose and Brant by white underparts and grayish wings and back;

white face a further distinction from Brant. Hybrids with Cackling or Canada geese are known.

Voice CALL: A barking *kaw.*

Status & Distribution Vagrant, status unclear as truly wild birds impossible to differentiate from escaped captives. Breeds on tundra in eastern Greenland, Svalbard, and Novaya Zemlya, winters largely in Ireland and Scotland and the Netherlands. VAGRANT: Numerous

sightings throughout continent; most or many of these pertain to escapees from captivity. Records from Maritime Provinces, NF and Labrador, and northeastern U.S. may include wild birds. Any small family group flocks during the appropriate time of year in the Northeast (Oct. to Apr.) could pertain to wild birds.

Population Has increased in last couple of decades.

SWANS *Genus Cygnus*

Of the 7 species of swans, 6 comprise the genus *Cygnus*. The genus has a worldwide distribution, but only in temperate regions. All *Cygnus* are huge birds, with long necks, long bills, and strong legs. Southern Hemisphere species are black or black necked, but all North American species are entirely white, differing from each other in subtle structural and bill pattern variations.

TRUMPETER SWAN *Cygnus buccinator*

The long-necked Trumpeter is our native swan of forested habitats. Monotypic. L 60" (152 cm)

Identification Huge swan, with a long, sloping head and bill profile, as well as a relatively thick-based neck. The bare loral skin is as wide as the eye and narrowly encircles the eye. Shape of upper edge of bill, where it meets forehead, comes forward to a create a V-shaped point along the bill's midline. ADULT: White, often stained yellowish on head and upper neck. Bill black with orange stripe on lower mandible along cutting edge. Legs black. JUVENILE: Appears dirty, pale brownish gray throughout. Bill dull pink with dark base and dark loral skin, also dark on tip and cutting edge.

Similar Species Most likely to be confused with the Tundra Swan. The Trumpeter is larger, has a longer, sloping bill with a V-shaped upper edge. The upper mandible of the Trumpeter is always black, but a few Tundras may

lack yellow bill spot. The loral skin of the Trumpeter is wide, but narrow on the Tundra.

Voice CALL: A bugling *oh-OH* like an old car horn, second syllable emphasized.

Status & Distribution Uncommon to rare, currently being stocked in various states and provinces in the East. BREEDING: Various freshwater wetlands, at least 300 feet long, needed for take-off. MIGRATION: Migrants leave north by mid-Oct., arriving in south by early Nov. or later; northbound movements begin late Feb., arriving on breeding grounds from Apr. Alaskan population winters mainly in coastal BC and western WA. YK and NT population migrates

largely east of Rockies to winter in tristate area of MT, WY, and ID. Southern breeding populations resident or make only local movements. Newly stocked populations in central and eastern N.A. largely resident, but some may move several hundred miles to south. WINTER: Freshwater wetlands to grassy and agricultural fields near water bodies. VAGRANT: Very rare to CA, casual to NM and TX.

Population Historically suffered a huge population decrease, but conservation efforts have allowed native western populations to increase. A somewhat controversial reintroduction to the central part of the continent has been successful, although former range in eastern North America is very unclear.

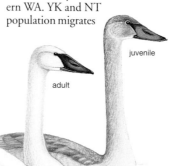

adult

juvenile

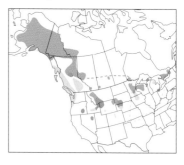

TUNDRA SWAN *Cygnus columbianus*

The Tundra is the widespread and more highly migratory swan in the continent. Polytypic. L 52" (132 cm)

Identification Large, shorter-necked swan with rounded forehead, clearly setting off bill profile. The bare skin on the lores narrows to a point before the eye. Upper edge of bill, where it meets forehead is smoothly curved—shallow U-shape when seen from front. ADULT: White throughout. Bill black with variable yellow patch at bill base, extending forward from eye; patch rarely absent. Yellowish stripe on lower mandible along cutting edge. Legs black. JUVENILE: Dull whitish gray throughout, but some become largely white by midwinter. Bill pink to base, including loral skin; this darkens from base outward as bird ages. Obvious black nostril on pink bill.

Geographic Variation Subspecies *columbianus* widespread, *bewickii* (Bewick's Swan) of Asia and Europe a vagrant to western N.A. It is differentiated from *columbianus* by having much more extensive yellow on bill

base, covering more than a third of the bill. Hybrid family groups have been seen in N.A.

Similar Species Most likely to be confused with the larger Trumpeter. Tundra has shorter bill, steeper forehead, and rounder crown. When observed from the front, the upper edge to the bill, where it meets the forehead, is shaped like a shallow U, not the sharp V of the Trumpeter. Yellow at bill base characteristic of the Tundra, and absent on the Trumpter; the loral skin of the Tundra pinches in before the eye. Immatures begin with a pink base to bill and quickly become much whiter-plumaged than most Trumpeters.

Voice CALL: A loud barking and somewhat gooselike *kwooo*.

Status & Distribution Common, a subspecies in Palearctic. BREEDING: Tundra lakes and ponds. MIGRATION: Western population stages on Great Salt Lake, then moves to more coastal wintering sites. Eastern population stages from ND to MN and flies to

Atlantic coast wintering areas. Staging areas used in Oct., arrival in wintering sites by late Oct. to mid-Nov. Northbound by late Feb. and early Mar. Eastern population stages around Lake Erie, continuing to MN and Canadian prairies, arrives in Arctic breeding grounds by mid-May. Western population retraces route through Great Salt Lake, or through Klamath region, arrives in breeding grounds of AK in Apr.. WINTER: Various wetland habitats and agricultural fields. VAGRANT: Casual to Maritimes and Gulf Coast; rare throughout interior away from regular migration routes.

Population appears stable now, but is thought to have doubled between the 1960s and '90s.

juvenile

adult

"Bewick's Swan" adult

Identification of Young Swans

In their first fall, juvenile swans migrate south in their juvenal plumage, typically accompanying their parents. Adults traveling with their young help in identifying them. During fall and early winter, juvenile swans are largely pale gray to dirty white. On average Tundra juveniles are paler than Trumpeter juveniles, although both Trumpeter and Mute Swans have a rare all-white juvenile plumage.

During winter juveniles wear somewhat and also perform a partial body molt, giving them a paler plumage as they age. By late winter Tundras are largely white; other species still grayish. Other than structure, bill patterns are the best distinctions. Juvenile Tundras have a pink bill base; Mutes and Trumpeters have a dark bill base. Mute Swans begin to develop a bill knob early. ■

Trumpeter Swan

Tundra Swan, juvenile (CA, Dec.)

Mute Swan

WHOOPER SWAN *Cygnus cygnus*

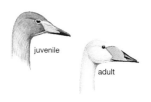

juvenile

adult

This swan is a vagrant from the Old World. Monotypic. L 60" (152 cm) **Identification** Huge, similar structurally to the Trumpeter. Bill long; sloping forehead accentuates bill length. Adults have extensively yellow bill base, covering more than half of the bill, at least to the level of the nostril. Much of the underside of the lower mandible is also yellow. The shape of the yellow comes forward to a point. **ADULT:** Body entirely white, sometimes stained yellowish on head and neck. Legs black. **JUVENILE:** Body grayish brown throughout, bill whitish gray shaped like yellow pattern of adult; nostril, cutting edge, and nail black.

Similar Species In shape and size resembles the Trumpeter, although large amount of yellow on bill easily separates the Whooper. Tundra Swan smaller, with shorter bill and steeper forehead as well as small yellow patch on bill base. However, vagrant *bewickii* subspecies, Bewick's Swan, has more extensive yellow on bill more like Whooper Swan. Note that yellow on Whooper comes forward to a point and extends past nostril; on Bewick's yellow ends more abruptly and does not reach the nostril. Immatures have a bill pattern that suggests that of the adult, helping to identify them.

Voice CALL: Bugling; often gives 3 of 4 calls in a group *kloo-kloo-kloo.*

Status & Distribution Vagrant, widely distributed from Europe to Asia, breeding in higher latitudes, wintering at midlatitudes. BREEDING: Has bred on Attu I. WINTER: Large wetlands and agricultural fields. VAGRANT: Rare in winter on central and outer Aleutians and casual elsewhere in western AK and Bering Sea islands. Casual south to OR and northern CA. Many recs. in eastern N.A. likely pertain to escapes.

MUTE SWAN *Cygnus olor*

This is the quintessential swan, a species introduced from Europe no doubt to give our local parks and ponds a royal touch. However, this species is a great ecological problem here. Monotypic. L 60" (152 cm)

Identification A huge, long-necked swan that holds its neck in a characteristic S-shape with the bill pointing downward. The wings are held partially raised, arched over the back. The bill has a prominent black knob at the base, which is larger in males than females. **ADULT:** Entirely white body, sometimes with yellowish wash to head and neck. Bill bright orange or salmon with black base, cutting edge, and nail, as well as black bulbous knob at base of culmen. Bill color of females duller. Legs black. **JUVENILE:** Entirely brownish gray; bill gray with black base and black around nostril. Older immature becomes progressively whiter, and bill becomes pale pink; black knob slowly enlarges as immature ages.

Similar Species Both Tundra and Trumpeter Swans may be found in established range of the Mute Swan. Aggressive posture with wings raised over body, and black-and-orange bill with black knob diagnostic for the Mute Swan. Immatures of all swan species more similar; Mute has black base to bill as in Trumpeter and shows distinctive S-shape to neck; bill begins grayish and turns pinkish orange later on in life, by which time growth of bill knob has started. Habitat in city parks suggestive of the Mute Swan, although reintroduced Trumpeter Swans in the East may also frequent urban parks.

Voice CALL: As its name suggests, this swan is usually silent. However, it is not mute. Usually calls heard are hisses and other soft alarm calls. Rarely it gives a resonant bugle.

Status & Distribution Common, introduced from Europe. Native from eastern Europe to western Asia. Also introduced to S. Africa, Australia, and New Zealand. YEAR-ROUND: From small urban ponds and lakes to large wetlands. MIGRATION: Mostly resident in North America, although some birds make short-distance movements to larger bodies of water in winter. WINTER: May flock together in larger bodies of water, including the Great Lakes. VAGRANT: Rare in Mississippi watershed and the southern Atlantic coast; at least some of these birds are dispersing from more northerly established sites. Most birds elsewhere are either feral or local escapees.

Population Booming in northeastern states, with substantial increases in Chesapeake Bay population and continuing expansion of the range particularly to New England. Other populations stable or increasing and of general concern as a management problem. Mute Swans can greatly alter the ecology of wetlands by uprooting emergent vegetation as they feed.

juvenile

adult

PERCHING DUCKS Genera *Cairina & Aix*

These genera are represented by 2 species worldwide. One species from each genus is present in N.A., the Muscovy (*Cairina*) and the Wood (*Aix*). Both are shy species, at home in slow-moving waters surrounded by large trees. They nest in cavities or use nest boxes and have dark glossy plumage. Otherwise, the 2 species are very different.

MUSCOVY DUCK *Cairina moschata*

This large, tropical duck is found only near Falcon Dam in southern Texas. Domestic birds are in parks throughout North America and widely established in Florida. The Muscovy is most active at dusk and dawn and perches on branches or floating debris. Monotypic. L 26–33" (66–84 cm)
Identification Adults blackish with iridescent greenish and purple highlights. MALE: Glossier than females, with dark reddish knob above bill. FEMALE: Duller and smaller; lacks knob on bill. JUVENILE: Duller, slowly acquires white wing patch during first winter. FLIGHT: Appears massive, with very broad wings with large white patches.
Similar Species Domestic Muscovies

larger than wild, usually with white blotches on head and body.
Status & Distribution Local and uncommon from Mexico to northern half of S.A. YEAR-ROUND: Wild birds from native populations in Mexico present near Falcon Dam; scarce and difficult to find. BREEDING: Nests in holes, hollow trees or earth banks.
Voice Generally silent.
Population Declining in many areas due to hunting.

WOOD DUCK *Aix sponsa*

Unlike most waterfowl, Wood Ducks are usually found in heavily wooded swamps. They are often detected by the loud squeal of the females as they take flight. Monotypic. L 18" (47 cm)
Identification Both sexes have a bushy crest that makes the head appear large and rounded. On the water they hold their heads erect and cock their long tails. MALE: Stunning, intricate plumage renders it distinctive. Most notable characteristics are red base of the bill, red eye, thick crest, and white throat patch with 2 prongs projecting up onto the face. ECLIPSE MALE: As female, but retains distinctive bill, eye, colors, and throat pattern. FEMALE: Gray-brown ghost of male, distinguished by large white eye-patch, white throat, and head shape. JUVENILES: Like females but duller, with spotted belly. FLIGHT: Dark wings with white trailing

edge to secondaries; large head held above body on slender neck; broad wings and long rectangular tails create distinctive flight profile.
Similar Species Most similar to female Wood Duck is female Mandarin, a closely related Asian species common in waterfowl collections and parks. Female Mandarin Duck lacks eye-patch of the Wood Duck.
Voice CALL: Female flight call a rising squeal, *ooEEK*. Male infrequently gives a high, thin *jeeee*.
Status & Distribution Widespread and common, generally in low densities. BREEDING: Nest in cavities in hollow trees or nest boxes in wet woods.

MIGRATION: Spring: Begins moving north in Feb.; peaking in New England in late Mar.; in the Great Lakes in mid-Apr. Fall: Many Wood Ducks disperse widely after breeding and prior to fall migration. Most begin moving south in late Sept.; peak in the Midwest in early Oct.; numbers in southern states increase steadily through Dec. WINTER: Northern migrants and local breeders gather in bottomland forests, swamps, and marshes. Uncommon to rare over much of Southwest in winter and migration. Rare to casual in southeastern AK.
Population The species faced extinction near the turn of the 20th century; it rebounded quickly after hunting restrictions and nest-box programs implemented. Currently fairly stable, expanding range across northern plains in the last 50 years.

DABBLING DUCKS Genus *Anas*

This is a large, diverse group of waterfowl, 16 species of which occur in North America; of these 10 species breed, and 6 are visitors from the Old World or the Caribbean. Structure and size vary greatly. Males have colorful plumages that are held for most of the year, except in midsummer, when bright plumage is replaced by dull, often called "Eclipse Plumage." This plumage is usually worn until early fall and helps camouflage the males as they replace their flight feathers. Females are mottled brown and show little seasonal variation. Most male dabblers and some females show a colorful speculum, an iridescent patch on the secondaries that can be useful for identification.

FALCATED DUCK *Anas falcata*

This stunning east Asian species is closely related to the Gadwall. North American vagrants often mix with flocks of Gadwall or Wigeon. Monotypic. L 19" (48 cm)
Identification Structure like that of the Gadwall but with a smaller thin bill and a shaggy head coming to a point on males. MALE: Elongated tertials trail in the water. Green-and-white striped throat often hidden; visible when the head is lifted. FEMALE: All brown with tan face, pale belly, and dull green speculum with narrow white upper border.
Similar Species Female separated from female Gadwall by longer, thinner, dark bill; crested nape, uniform head

color, and subtle dark fringes to the body feathers. Dark thin bill combined with the large head eliminate all other female dabblers.
Status & Distribution Common in eastern Asia. VAGRANT: Rare migrant to western Aleutians; casual on the Pribilofs; accidental along the West Coast south to CA. Evidence suggests that some of the West Coast records represent true vagrants, while some may be escapes from waterfowl collections. All records away from AK are likely to be treated with skepticism.
Voice Generally silent.
Population Stable.

EURASIAN WIGEON *Anas penelope*

This Old World counterpart of the American Wigeon is regular in small numbers in North America, mainly in the Pacific states and British Columbia. It is typically found in flocks of American Wigeon; individuals often return to the same location for several years. Monotypic. L 20" (51 cm)

Identification Structure is almost identical to that of the American Wigeon, though slight differences are sometimes apparent. Most useful are Eurasian's proportionally smaller head and longer wings, with primary tips that usually fall at or near the tip of the tail. In any plumage the gray axillaries and underwing coverts of the Eurasian Wigeon are diagnostic. The innermost secondary of most Eurasian Wigeons is white, not gray, and is visible as a horizontal white bar separating the tertials from the dark speculum. MALE: Distinctive, with bright chestnut head, cream-colored crown, and vermiculated gray back and sides. Some males may show small patches of green around the eye, which falls within the normal variation of the Eurasian Wigeon and does not necessarily indicate hybridization. FEMALE: Very similar to female American, but usually has warmer

brown heads; some gray morph females have dull gray heads. Females often have pale, unmarked throats and are uniformly dull with no contrast between the head and the breast. Female American often shows contrast between gray throat and warmly colored breast. IMMATURE MALE: Adult male plumage acquired slowly during first winter. Most individuals closely resemble adult male by Jan., but retain brown wing coverts. FLIGHT: Gray axillaries and underwing coverts are usually visible; white ovals on upper wings of adult males like American Wigeon. Females have uniform brown upper wing, lacking white covert bar of the female American Wigeon.
Similar Species Compare males to hybrids with the American Wigeon. Most hybrids show obviously intermediate characteristics, but some are difficult. Typical hybrids show an American Wigeon head pattern with rusty wash; flanks are a mixture of gray and pink, usually more gray. Head pattern can be variable, so the flanks are the best indication of hybridization. Any wigeon with a mixture of pink and gray flanks is almost certainly a hybrid. See the American Wigeon entry for

details on separating females.

Voice CALL: Male whistles a sharp, high-pitched, single-note, wiry *WHEEOOO,* with a distinct similarity to the Gray-cheeked Thrush flight call. The call is more attenuated than that of the American Wigeon and is clearly audible above a noisy group of American Wigeon. Female gives a harsh call like that of the American Wigeon.

Status & Distribution Small numbers winter along and near both coasts; more common in the Pacific states and BC.

In the West, fairly common in BC and the Puget Sound region; numbers peak in late Feb. and early Mar. South of Puget Sound, it is uncommon along the Pacific coast south to southern CA. Rare but regular on the Atlantic coast; generally rare to casual elsewhere, with records from almost every state and province. Regular migrant and winter visitor on the western and central Aleutians. In the lower 48, the earliest arrivals are seen in late Aug. and some individuals linger into May.

Population Abundant and for the most part stable throughout the majority of its Palearctic breeding grounds.

AMERICAN WIGEON *Anas americana*

The American Wigeon is a colorful, noisy dabbler equally comfortable on land as in the water. Large flocks are often found grazing in fields and are frequently found in flocks of American Coots, snatching food from them as they surface. Monotypic. L 19" (48 cm)

Identification The American Wigeon's large head, chunky body, short legs, and fairly long, pointed tail are characteristic of wigeon. Males have a small blue bill and females are gray. Either sex can have a black ring at the base of the bill that the Eurasian Wigeon lacks, but many female and immature Americans also lack this ring. Axillaries and underwing coverts are white, which, if visible, is a diagnostic difference from the Eurasian. Another characteristic is the color of the innermost secondary; visible just below the tertials, which is gray in the American, usually white in the Eurasian. MALE: Sports a white crown, gray face, glossy green eye stripe, pinkish breast and flanks. One common variation has variable amounts of cream on the throat and face. FEMALE: Gray-brown overall with orange or pinkish tinged flanks; brown upper wing with a white greater covert bar. FIRST-WINTER MALE: Like adult male, but more mottling on the upperwing coverts. FLIGHT: They form swift, tightly packed flocks; white

ovals on the upper wings of males are visible from a great distance. They have rounded heads and bodies and more wedge-shaped tails than any other duck except the pintail.

Similar Species Males are distinctive, but see Eurasian Wigeon account for separation of hybrids. The female is separated with caution from the female Eurasian Wigeon by gray head, speckled throat, flanks with orange or pink tones, and colder overall color with clear contrast between head, breast, and flanks. The Eurasian shows uniform coloration on throat and breast, while the American's gray throat contrasts with its warm-colored breast. Note color of innermost secondary; the American has slightly larger head and longer tail than the Eurasian.

Voice CALL: Male gives 2- or 3-part whistle, *whee-WHOO* or *whee-WHOO-who,* given in flight or on the water; call is heard constantly from any large flock. Call of the female, given infrequently, sounds like a harsh, nasal cough.

Status & Distribution Abundant and widespread, particularly in the West. BREEDING: Farther north than all other dabbling ducks except the Northern Pintail. Nests on tundra pools, river deltas, boreal lakes, and prairie pot-

holes. MIGRATION: Winter birds begin leaving in early Feb.; in most states bordering Canada it peaks in the first 2 weeks of Apr.; birds arriving on the northern breeding grounds in the first 2 weeks of May. Early fall migrant, beginning in mid-Aug. Great Lakes peak is the end of Oct., and migration is largely over by late Nov. It peaks in Nov. on coast of BC. WINTER: Widespread in winter, with scattered areas of high concentration. The central valley of CA and the panhandle of TX are the regions of greatest abundance. Found in open marshes, coastal estuaries, wet farm fields, and flocks may even gather at parks and golf courses, where they become fairly tame. Rare but a regular stray to the British Isles and a very rare vagrant to the rest of Europe and northeastern Siberia.

Population Abundant and stable.

adult ♀
adult ♂

adult eclipse ♂
adult ♂
♀

GADWALL *Anas strepera*

The Gadwall is generally thought to be nondescript, but the male's intricate plumage is stunning. Monotypic. L 20" (51 cm)

Identification Structurally similar to the Mallard but with a steep forehead and a narrow, shallow-based bill. Both sexes show a mixture of chestnut and black on the upper wing and a white square on the inner secondaries. Males have

a more colorful wing pattern than females. This is infrequently visible on swimming birds; in flight, the wing pattern is diagnostic. MALE: Tan face with darker brown crown, black-and-white scalloped breast that appears gray at a distance, gray flanks, black rump, and long scapulars with faint reddish fringes. FEMALE: Dull, mottled brown head and body, with a black bill evenly edged with orange, and a white belly.

Similar Species Female similar to female Mallard in plumage; separated by smaller bill and high, steep forehead; in flight by wing pattern and white belly. Female wigeon has shorter gray bill, rounded head, brighter flanks.

Voice CALL: Female gives a low, harsh *aack*. Male utters a soft, burping *meep*.

Status & Distribution Common and widespread across Northern Hemisphere. BREEDING: Nests on ponds, lakes, and marshes primarily in the Dakotas and prairie provinces. MIGRATION: Spring: Late migrant; many do not begin to move north until well into Apr. Numbers peak in the Great Lakes and western plains in late Apr. Fall: Migration begins in Sept.; Great Lakes peak occurs in early Nov.; OR peak mid- to late Oct. WINTER: Marshes of LA are the most important wintering area for Gadwall. Widespread in shallow lakes and marshes but tend to concentrate in coastal areas.

Population Stable and increasing. During the past century, expanded rapidly in the East.

AMERICAN BLACK DUCK *Anas rubripes*

A northeastern species, the American Black is most numerous in coastal salt marshes where few other ducks are found. Monotypic. L 23" (58 cm)

Identification Sexes similar and structurally identical to the Mallard. The 2 species are often found in mixed flocks and frequently hybridize. MALE: Body blackish with a dark crown, sharply contrasting tan face and yellow-olive bill. FEMALE: Like male but slightly paler body with duller olive bill. FLIGHT: Speculum is deep purple and can show thin white borders. Dark body contrasts with white underwing.

Similar Species Resembles female Mallard but darker, showing strong contrast between body and face, bill yellow to olive, speculum purple. Hybrids with Mallard may be paler in col-

oration overall, partially green head, brighter yellow or orange bill, white bordering the speculum, curved upper-tail coverts or paler tail feathers. Some hybrids are subtle, showing only one of these characteristics, while others more strongly resemble Mallards. Similar to western subspecies of Mottled Duck; see that entry.

Voice Like Mallard, but slightly lower and harsher.

Status & Distribution Locally common. BREEDING: Nests in a wide variety of wetlands. MIGRATION: Spring migration begins in early Feb. and proceeds gradually following the appearance of open water. Arrives in ME in early Apr., northern QC in late May.

Fall migrants peak in mid-Atlantic in early Nov., peak in the western Great Lakes in mid-Nov. WINTER: Primarily in mid-Atlantic salt marshes. Also use a variety of wetlands throughout the Northeast; some wintering as far north as NF. Casual to western gulf states and western N.A. Casual to British Isles. Accidental to Korea.

Population Serious declines; replacement by Mallards in deforested portions of its range and overhunting in past decades are the primary causes.

American Black x Mallard hybrid

MALLARD *Anas platyrhynchos*

Probably the most widely recognized and widespread duck in North America, the Mallard forms massive, noisy flocks in large marshes and agricultural fields; Mallards also make use of almost any body of water, from a roadside puddle to the Great Lakes. Polytypic. (2 ssp. in N.A., nominate *platyrhynchos* and *diazi*). L 23" (58 cm)

Identification Mallards are large dabbling ducks with heavy bodies and large, rounded heads that transition smoothly into long bills. Both sexes have bright blue speculums with bold white borders. The central uppertail coverts of the males are curled upwards; a characteristic frequently passed on to hybrid offspring. MALE: Distinctive, with bright yellow bill and metallic green head bordered by a white neck ring. Breast is deep chestnut, flanks finely vermiculated pale gray, and rump black with white outer tail feathers. The tertials are very unusually shaped, extremely broad at the base, tapering to a point. FEMALE: Nondescript medium brown overall, paler tan face with a streaked, brown crown, indistinct brown eye line, and orange bill with a black saddle. The belly is unmarked and buffy, paler than the body, and the outer tail feathers are whitish. ECLIPSE MALE: Like female but the bill remains bright yellow and the crown and breast are darker than female.
FLIGHT: Wingbeats steady and shallow, slower than other ducks, and profile resembles a miniature goose, with wings set near the rear of the bulky body, neck extended straight forward, and a short rounded tail.

Geographic Variation Two subspecies in N.A., nominate *platyrhynchos* and the southwestern subspecies *diazi,* Mexican Duck, which is found in pockets along the Rio Grande River in Texas, New Mexico, and southeastern Arizona. It is 10 percent smaller than *platyrhynchos,* and the sexes are similar, lacking the distinctive plumage of male northern Mallards. Its plumage is darker than female northern Mallards, and it has an all brown tail. The white borders to the speculum are narrower than on *platyrhynchos* but still distinct and obvious. Most *diazi* Mallards found in the Southwest have interbred with nominate *platyrhynchos.* Mexican Duck resembles Mottled Duck, but has a grayer more distinctly patterned face, streaked throat, and stronger white borders to the speculum.

Similar Species Female paler than Mottled (especially western subspecies) and Black Duck, bill brighter orange, tail and rump paler, with distinct white borders to the blue speculum. From the smaller female Gadwall by rounded head shape, lacking a distinct forehead, larger, deeper based bill, iridescent speculum with white borders. Much larger than female teal with a larger, extensively orange bill.

Voice Female gives series of loud, descending *QUACKS* for which

Mallard is known. Male less vocal; shorter, soft *quack* is often drowned out by the calls of the females.

Status & Distribution Abundant and widespread across Northern Hemisphere. BREEDING: Any place that has both water and cover. Typically nests on the ground in thick grass or shrubs, but also may build nests in hollow trees, on top of duck blinds, or use an old nest of another bird. MIGRATION: Driven by the availability of open water. In the spring it is an early migrant, along with Northern Pintail, appearing north of its winter range as soon as there is open water. Begins in early Feb.; peaks in the Midwest and Great Lakes region in late Mar.; northernmost breeders arrive in AK in early May. In the fall it is among the last to leave the north, retreating only as water freezes. Some begin moving south in Sept., however most northern breeders do not move south until Oct.; peak numbers arrive in the Great Lakes and across the northern plains in early Nov. WINTER: Spends the winter in a variety of habitats, mostly shallow freshwater. Often very mobile in the winter; moving farther north during warmer periods, then driven back south by cold fronts.

Population The most abundant duck in N.A., population more or less stable.

eclipse ♂

juvenile

"Mexican"-Mallard intergrade ♂

♀

♂

MOTTLED DUCK *Anas fulvigula*

maculosa

This southern look-alike of the American Black Duck is primarily a resident of the coastal marshes of the Gulf of Mexico and Florida. Like the Black Duck, the sexes are similar in appearance. Mottled Ducks retain their pair bond for most of the year, so are most often seen in pairs and do not form large winter flocks as many other ducks do. Polytypic (2 ssp.). L 22" (56 cm)
Identification Structure is very similar to Mallard, but slightly smaller with proportionally shorter wings. Overall color is intermediate between female Mallard and American Black Duck, *maculosa* tending toward Black Duck coloration. The blue-green speculum has very narrow white borders. ADULT MALE: Dark brown body with golden brown, V-shaped marks on interior of flank feathers. It has buffy brown face with an unmarked throat, slightly darker crown and eye line, and a yellow bill. ADULT FEMALE:

Similar to male but slightly paler, with dull orange or olive-yellow bills with black marking on the culmen. FLIGHT: The upper wing appears all dark, and underwing coverts flash bright white. Broad winged with slow wingbeats like Mallard.
Geographic Variation Two subspecies, nominate *fulvigula* in the Florida Peninsula and along the coast of Georgia and South Carolina; *maculosa* found, primarily coastally, from LA and coastal Mississippi to northern Mexico. The 2 are similar but *maculosa* is darker and more coarsely marked than nominate *fulvigula*. Some authorities consider Mottled Duck to be a subspecies of Mallard.
Similar Species Similar to female Mallard and American Black Duck. Separated from female Mallard by darker overall color; buffy, unstreaked throat; all brown tail; and narrower white border to the speculum. Frequently mistaken for American Black Duck; great care should be taken when separating these species. Compared to Black Duck it has a buffier face, no streaking on the throat, paler brown V-shaped markings on the interior of the flank feathers, and a blue-green speculum with narrow white borders. Black Duck has essentially all-dark flanks, a grayer face, streaked throat, and lacks white borders on the speculum. Some Mallard **x** Black Duck hybrids can look extremely similar to Mottled Duck, but have dull gray faces and streaked throats.

Voice Females give a loud *QUACK* like Mallard but slightly softer and not as harsh. Males infrequently give a short, soft *quack* like male Mallards.
Status & Distribution Closely tied to the Gulf Coast, where it is fairly common but rarely found in large numbers. YEAR-ROUND: Essentially nonmigratory, however individuals move in response to food resources and water levels. Large numbers move from coastal marshes to interior rice fields in fall to feed on the ripening rice. Rare away from coastal areas but known to wander and occasionally nest in the interior. Introduced to SC coast. BREEDING: Nests in cordgrass meadows, fallow rice fields, and grassy islets in marshes. VAGRANT: Rare breeder in northeastern TX, southern AR, and OK. Very rare north to KS. Accidental to KY.
Population Fairly stable, but population declines occur during droughts, rebounds occur in wet years. Also vulnerable to drainage of coastal marshes for development.

SPOT-BILLED DUCK *Anas poecilorhyncha*

This robust, dark brown duck is an Asian species and a rare vagrant to Alaska. Its structure and habits are identical to the Mallard. It is found in Southeast Asia and India on freshwater marshes and lakes, lagoons and rivers. Polytypic. (3 ssp.; *zonorhyncha* has reached N.A.). L 22" (56 cm)
Identification The diagnostic, sharply defined yellow tip on the black bill is visible at great distances. Sexes are similar, female is slightly paler. Head is pale with light gray throat and cheeks, dark crown, dark stripe through the eye, and shorter, dark stripe beginning at the base of the bill. Body is dark brown, flank feathers have dark centers with pale edges giving a scalloped impression, and speculum is bluish with white border. Diagnostic white-edged ter-

tials are readily visible when at rest. FLIGHT: Large and dark with a heavy body and broad wings, striking white underwing coverts, and dark upper wing with narrow white borders to the blue speculum.
Geographic Variation Chinese Spotbill, *zonorhyncha*, is the only subspecies that has reached N.A.; it lacks the red spots at base of bill. It is sedentary in the southern part of its range, but the northern breeders are migratory and the source of N.A. records.
Similar Species Like the American Black Duck and female Mallard; separated by distinctive bill coloration, paler head, scalloped edges to the flank feathers, and the pale-fringed tertials.
Voice CALL: Females give a loud *quack*. Male gives raspy *kreep*.

Status & Distribution Generally widespread and locally common throughout its range in Asia. VAGRANT: Casual to western and central Aleutians. Accidental to Kodiak I.
Population Due to little study true status is unknown, though it is fairly common within its range.

zonorhyncha

BLUE-WINGED TEAL *Anas discors*

This small duck is largely a summer resident; most Blue-winged Teal spend the winter in northern South America. Monotypic. L 15" (39 cm)

Identification Both sexes have black bills and a pale area at the base of the bill that is crescent-shaped in males and oval-shaped in females. The profile of the Blue-winged Teal is long and low, with a slender neck and long, thin bill. ADULT MALE: Cold blue head with large white crescent on face and white flank patch; the body is covered with black spots. ADULT FEMALE: Cold gray-brown with paler face, a distinct dark eye stripe, white eye arcs, and a pale loral spot that is connected to the throat. FLIGHT: Powder blue wing coverts and green speculums are visible; the wing-

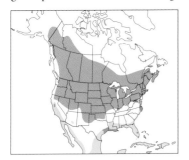

beats are rapid. Adult males have a broad white border to blue forewing. **Similar Species** The female Blue-winged Teal is smaller and grayer than the female Mallard and the Gadwall, with an all-black bill. Larger and colder gray than the Green-winged Teal, with a pale loral spot and longer bill. See sidebar below for separation from the Cinnamon Teal.

Voice Males give a high, whistled *peew;* females give a shrill *quack.*

Status & Distribution Common south to northern half of S.A. BREEDING: Nests in grassy clumps near small ponds and small flooded fields. The Blue-winged Teal is most abundant in the prairie pothole region. MIGRATION: The Blue-winged is a relatively late spring and early fall migrant. Spring: Begin arriving along the Gulf Coast in Feb.; peaking in Apr. in the Midwest; migration is largely over by the end of May, a few continuing into early June on the West Coast. Fall: Peaks in the Midwest and Southwest during late Sept.–early Oct.; peaks in the Gulf states in early Oct., but quickly

declines later in the month. By early autumn, most Blue-winged Teals have moved south of the U.S. WINTER: Although most of the birds winter in S.A., some remain in southern states, primarily in coastal areas, usually in rice fields and in brackish and freshwater marshes. VAGRANT: Annual in British Isles; numerous records from western Europe and northwestern Africa.

Population Stable or increasing, especially in the East, where it has benefited from man-made wetlands.

Identification of Female Teal: Blue-winged and Cinnamon

These 2 female teal appear much alike but with care can be identified. Although similar in size and proportion, they differ slightly in head and bill shape. The Cinnamon Teal has almost no forehead; instead the head slopes directly into the bill like that of the Northern Shoveler. The Blue-winged Teal shows a slight rising forehead, so the head appears more square than that of the Cinnamon Teal. The latter has a longer, wider bill with a spoonlike appearance. The bill of the Blue-winged Teal is smaller; it is more similar to the bills of other dabblers, lacking the spatulate look.

Overall color is also important. Blue-winged Teal tend to be pale gray-brown overall and give a cold impression. Cinnamon Teal are slightly darker brown with a strong rusty wash that gives them a much warmer look.

As for plumage, Blue-winged Teal

Blue-winged Teal, female (CA, Nov.)

Cinnamon Teal, female (CA, Dec.)

have a sharply defined face pattern, with large white eye arcs, a strong brown eye line, and a clear pale loral spot at the bill's. The loral spot is usually connected to the pale throat and is reminiscent of the male's white crescent. In contrast, Cinnamon Teal have a diffuse face pattern, usually lacking noticeable eye arcs. The eye line looks washed out, and the loral spot is buffy. Sometimes the bird completely lacks the loral spot; when present, it does not have the definition shown by Blue-winged Teal and is usually separated from the throat by some stippling across the malar area. Overall, dark facial markings are more distinct in the Blue-winged than in the browner, blended face of the Cinnamon.

Some birds with mixed features are better left unidentified. Male hybrids between these 2 species occur somewhat regularly, and there are certainly some female hybrids as well. ∎

CINNAMON TEAL *Anas cyanoptera*

This uniquely plumaged teal is exclusively a western species. Generally it does not form large flocks as other teal do, and it is usually found in small, tight groups that move and forage together. Polytypic. (5 ssp. in the Americas; only *septentrionalium* occurs in N.A.). L 16" (41 cm)

Identification The head is large and rounded, grading into a long bill reminiscent of the Northern Shoveler. Males have intense red eyes in all but first few months of life. MALE: Bright cinnamon head and body are distinctive. FEMALE: Rusty or golden brown overall with faintly scalloped flanks; variable, but usually small, pale loral spot and faint eye stripe. FLIGHT: Powder blue upperwing coverts contrast sharply with bright cinnamon plumage of male. Male has broad white border to blue coverts. Flight is swift with rapid wingbeats, bill tilted slightly downward.

Similar Species Female is smaller and darker than female shoveler with less distinctly spatulate bill. (See sidebar p. 21 for separation from female Blue-winged Teal.)

Voice Male makes dry series of *click* notes; female gives shrill *quack*.

Status & Distribution Locally common in the West. BREEDING: Unlike its close relative, the Blue-winged Teal, the Cinnamon largely avoids prairie potholes; most common in the Great Basin and mountain regions of the western U.S. Nests on marshes, ponds and shallow lakes; often uses highly alkaline water. MIGRATION: In spring, begins in mid-Jan. in Southwest; peaks in late Apr. in UT; most breeders are in place by mid-May. In fall, numbers diminish sharply after early Sept. WINTER: Uncommon to rare in Southwest. VAGRANT: Casual to eastern N.A.; some records may involve escapees.

Population Due to its limited breeding range, it is one of the least numerous species of waterfowl in North America. Little is known about population trends; it appears to be stable, however, in most of its range, declining slightly in the Pacific Northwest.

GREEN-WINGED TEAL *Anas crecca*

A tiny, Holearctic dabbler, the Green-winged Teal is frequently seen foraging on mudflats. Polytypic. L 14" (37 cm)

Identification The Green-winged Teal has a small, compact body; rounded head; and a short, thin bill. ADULT MALE: Chestnut head with large green ear patch and a vertical white bar on each flank. ADULT FEMALE: Dull brown body and head, black bill with dull orange edges, a pale line on the sides of the undertail coverts, and white belly. FLIGHT: Green-winged teals fly with very rapid wingbeats, forming tight bunches that twist and turn erratically. White restricted to central part of underwing, unlike the Blue-winged and Cinnamon.

Geographic Variation Of the 2 subspecies in North America, *carolinensis* is widespread; the Eurasian subspecies nominate *crecca* is found in the Aleutians and the Pribilofs. It has a white horizontal bar above the flanks instead of a vertical bar and more white on the face. subspecies *nimia* of the Aleutian Islands is no longer considered a valid subspecies.

Similar Species The female Green-winged has a smaller bill and white undertail coverts that separate it from other female teal.

Voice Males give a sharp, whistled *kreek* (like the Northern Pintail); females give a high, thin *quack*.

Status & Distribution Common and widespread. BREEDING: Wooded ponds, potholes, and tundra pools. MIGRATION: In spring, mid-Atlantic peak late Mar. In fall, mid-Atlantic peak mid- to late Oct. Peak late Oct.–early Nov. on BC coast. WINTER: Shallow wetlands and marshes, often in large flocks. VAGRANT: Nominate *crecca* is regular to western AK, uncommon to fairly common on Aleutians and Pribilofs, rare to St. Lawrence I. and mainland western AK, very rare on West Coast, regular to NF in winter; casual elsewhere.

Population Abundant and stable throughout its range.

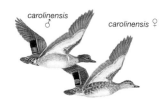

carolinensis ♂   carolinensis ♀

crecca ♂   carolinensis ♀

carolinensis ♂

NORTHERN SHOVELER *Anas clypeata*

This is an odd-looking, Holarctic species with a distinct spatulate bill. It obtains most of its food from the surface, straining it through its large bill. Often small groups of Northern Shovelers bring food to the surface by swimming rapidly in a circle while swinging their bills side to side. Monotypic. L 19" (48 cm)
Identification On the water, shovelers look front heavy and short necked, with the bill angled downward. Adult males have bright golden eyes, while eye color in young males and females ranges from dull yellow to brown. Upperwing coverts powder blue in both sexes. MALE: Distinctive, with bright green head, white breast, reddish brown flanks and belly. FEMALE: Mottled light brown head and body; some have a faint rusty wash. Most have dark bills with orange edges, but a few have all-dark bills. ECLIPSE MALE: As female, but golden eye and bright orange legs. FALL MALE: An intermediate plumage in early fall, with heavily spotted breast and flanks, dull head, and pale facial crescent.
Similar Species The long, spatulate bill is diagnostic.
Voice Generally silent, courting males give a repeated low, nasal *erp-EERP.*
Status & Distribution Common. BREEDING: Uses a wide variety of shallow wetlands for nesting, such as saline ponds and sewage-treatment plants. MIGRATION: In spring, a late migrant: begins migration in late Mar., peaks in the southern Great Lakes in early Apr., arriving on the prairie breeding grounds mid-Apr.–early May. Fall: Begins in late Aug.; peaks in BC in late Sept. or early Oct.; Great Lakes peaks mid-Oct. WINTER: Primary wintering areas CA and the Gulf Coast. Found in marshes, ponds, and bays.
Population Long trend of stability, but population has increased substantially in recent years. Breeding range expanding eastward.

GARGANEY *Anas querquedula*

The Garganey is the highly migratory Eurasian counterpart of the Blue-winged Teal. Vagrant Garganeys are often found in flocks with Blue-winged Teals. Monotypic. L 15" (39 cm)
Identification Structure is very similar to that of the Blue-winged, but the Garganey has a blockier head shape, a slightly heavier bill, and a slightly longer tail. Its wide, pale tertial edges are distinctive. BREEDING MALE: Bold white supercilium, brown breast, drooping tertials, and gray flanks. ADULT FEMALE: Pale face with strong dark eye stripe and additional diffuse dark stripe across the face starting at the lores. Pale loral spot and typically white throat. Sharply defined white belly. ECLIPSE MALE: Like the female, but it retains the paler gray upper wing of the breeding male. The Garganey holds its eclipse plumage much longer than most ducks, so that from midsummer to late January or February, the males look much like females. FLIGHT: The wing pattern is distinctive. The male has whitish gray upperwing coverts; the female's are brownish with thin white speculum borders. Silvery gray inner primary webs. The underwing is pale with a strongly con-trasting dark leading edge. FLIGHT: The Garganey is small and agile and flies with rapid wingbeats.
Similar Species Compare the female and the eclipse male to the female Blue-winged Teal. The Garganey's wing pattern is diagnostic. On the water look for its double-striped face, a pale loral spot separated from the white throat, and all dark scapulars with sharp white fringes. The Garganey is larger, with a heavier bill than on the Green-winged Teal, duller, with a pale throat, lacking a pale streak on undertail coverts.
Voice The male gives a series of dry clicking noises. The female utters a harsh *quack* like that of the Green-winged Teal.
Status & Distribution The Garganey is abundant across Europe and Asia. MIGRATION: Highly migratory, completely vacating its breeding range. VAGRANT: Regular migrant on the western Aleutians; casual on the Pribilofs and in the Pacific states; additional records are widely scattered throughout N.A. Most often found in Apr. and May, when migrating males are most easily recognizable. WINTER: West, central, and eastern Africa; in Asia from Pakistan east to southern China, and south to the Philippines.
Population Abundant and stable in the Old World.

BAIKAL TEAL *Anas formosa*

The Baikal is an East Asian teal only slightly larger than the Green-winged Teal. Populations had been declining sharply, but the bird appears to have rebounded dramatically in recent years. Most Baikal Teal winter in eastern China and South Korea. The bird favors several lakes, where counts can reach hundreds of thousands. It blends into and disappears in flocks of Green-winged Teals surprisingly well; however a glimpse of the elongated, pink-edged scapulars or yellowish cheek patch is sufficient to pick out a male. The Baikal is rare in captivity; most sightings, especially away from the West Coast, are probably escapes. Monotypic. L 17" (43 cm)
Identification Small dabbler with a proportionally large, square head and small bill. MALE: Its intricate face pattern and long, ornate scapulars are exquisite. FEMALE: Tawny brown with 2 short stripes on the face; some, which have an additional line dropping down from the eye, are called the "bridled form"; they have a pale loral spot with a brown outline and an extensive pale throat that extends up onto the face.

Similar Species The female Baikal is very similar to the female Green-winged Teal; look for the pale throat, face pattern, and a loral spot stronger than most Green-wingeds'. However, some female Green-wingeds have strongly patterned faces that appear very similar to that of the Baikal, so be cautious. Even the most strongly patterned Green-wingeds generally do not show the sharply delineated pale loral spot of the Baikal. The upperwing pattern is much like the Green-winged's, but the narrow cinnamon-buff upper border to the green speculum is straight, not wedge shaped; the white trailing edge is broader than on the Green-winged; and the under wing is more extensively gray.
Voice Male frequently gives a deep, repeated *wot-wot-wot.* Female gives a soft *quack.*
Status & Distribution Locally common in East Asia. VAGRANT: Spring overshoot to western and northern AK. Fall migrants recorded on Seward Peninsula and Pribilof Is. West Coast records

Dec.–Jan. Occur in AK in spring in May–June, and fall in Sept.–Oct.
Population Recent discovery of enormous flocks in South Korea and an increase in Alaska records perhaps indicate a rise in population.

bridled ♀

NORTHERN PINTAIL *Anas acuta*

This elegant species is as easily identified by structure as by plumage. The birds frequently gather in huge flocks to feed in grain fields. Monotypic. Male L 20–26" (51–66 cm)
Identification The thin grayish bill; long, slender neck; slim body; and long, wedge-shaped tail give pintails a diagnostic shape. MALE: Combination of brown head with white neck stripe,

white breast, and spikelike tail is distinctive. FEMALE: Mottled brown, with a plain, warm buff head. FLIGHT: Looks long and lean, with slender neck extended. The wings are thin and pointed, with bold white trailing edges to the secondaries.
Similar Species Female's combination of structure and unmarked buffy head is unlike any other female dabbler.
Status & Distribution Abundant, especially in the West. BREEDING: Holarctic species; nests on marshes, lakes and tundra pools. MIGRATION: In spring, early migrant relative to other waterfowl. Mid-Atlantic peak late Feb.; northern plains peak in early Apr.; Arctic breeders arrive in mid- to late

May. In fall, arrive in Southwest mid-Aug. Peak in the mid-Atlantic and Great Lakes late Oct.–early Nov. Pacific Northwest peak mid- to late Oct. WINTER: Prefers open marshes, agriculture fields, and tidal flats. Much of the population winters in CA; also, rarely, in southern AK and the Great Lakes region.
Voice Male gives a high, whining *mee-meee* during courtship and short, mellow *proop-proop,* like the Green-winged Teal's but lower pitched and more musical; female gives a hoarse, weak *quack.*
Population Fluctuates, low during prairie droughts. High in 1950s and 1970s; sharp decline in time of drought around 1990.

WHITE-CHEEKED PINTAIL *Anas bahamensis*

This neotropical duck is a vagrant from the West Indies, where it is casual to southern Florida. Sightings even from Florida are often of uncertain origin as the White-cheeked Pintail is popular in captivity; those away from Florida are most likely birds that have escaped from captivity. The White-cheeked Pintail is found on shallow-water habitats in salt water or fresh water, where it feeds by dabbling and tipping up. The large, white patch on the side of the White-cheeked's head and throat, for which it is named, is distinctive. Polytypic (3 ssp.; *bahamensis* has reached N.A.). L 17" (43 cm)

Identification Sexes of this pintail are similar; the female is paler than the male, with a slightly shorter tail. White cheeks and throat contrast with a dark forehead and cap; the blue-gray bill has a red spot near the base. The long, pointed tail is buffy; the underparts are tawny or reddish and and are heavily spotted. FLIGHT: The bird's slender body and long, pointed tail are evident. The White-cheeked is agile and swift, like the Northern Pintail. Both sexes of the White-cheeked show brown forewing, green speculum bordered on each side with broad buffy edge. The bird's pale, buffy rump and tail contrast with the darker brown body.

Geographic Variation Nominate *bahamensis* from the West Indies and northeastern South America occurs in North America. The *bahamensis* is brighter and larger than *rubrirostris,* which is from mainland South America, and *galapagensis* of the Galápagos Islands is the palest.

Similar Species Generally distinctive, not likely to be mistaken. Prominent white cheek patch readily distinguishes the White-cheeked Pintail from the Northern Pintail.

Voice Generally silent. Female gives weak descending *QUACK* notes. Male produces low whistle.

Status & Distribution Widespread and locally common resident in West Indies; small movements between islands occur. VAGRANT: Casual to southern FL, majority of records mid-Dec.–late Apr., with bulk of records from Everglades N.P., FL. Accidental in coastal southern TX, perhaps an escape.

Population Threatened, with moderate declines in the West Indies due to habitat loss, hunting, and introduced predators.

bahamensis

BAY DUCKS *Genus Aythya*

This genus is made up of 12 species worldwide. Five species breed in North America, and 2 are vagrants. *Aythya* are medium to medium-large diving ducks that often gather together in impressive rafts on coastal bays and large lakes in the winter. These rafts are an excellent place to check for rare species of waterfowl. *Aythya* ducks regularly hybridize with each other. Hybrid combinations are routinely detected. Hybrids often resemble other members of this genus and can be mistaken for the rare Tufted Duck or the Common Pochard. Hybrids must be considered when dealing with a potential sighting of 1 of the Eurasian *Aythya.*

COMMON POCHARD *Aythya ferina*

This Old World counterpart of the Canvasback, also similar to the Redhead, is a Eurasian species rare in western Alaska. Monotypic. L 18" (46 cm)

Identification This is a heavily built *Aythya* with a thick neck and a long sloping forehead grading smoothly into the bill. It is similar to the Canvasback, but the profile is more concave. The bill of the Common Pochard has a dark base and a black tip separated by a thick whitish blue stripe. MALE: Patterned as the Canvasback with chestnut head, black breast, and light gray body. FEMALE: Light brown head with pale throat, lores often paler than the face, fairly prominent pale eye ring, brown breast, mottled gray and brown body. FLIGHT: Wings uniform gray with no wing stripe. Appears chunkier than the Canvasback with short, rounded wings.

Similar Species Males separated from the Canvasback by shorter bill with more concave profile, more compact build, shorter neck, slightly grayer back, and lack of black crown. Separated from the Redhead by sloping forehead, bill pattern, darker eye color, and paler back. Females separated from Redheads and Ring-necked Ducks by structure and the presence of gray on the flanks and back. Differentiated from the Canvasback by structure, bill pattern, pale loral spot, and darker color. Hybrids between the Canvasback and Redhead are rare, but have occurred and do cause confusion with the Common Pochard. Such hybrids can appear very similar to the Common but lack its unique bill pattern.

Voice Generally silent.

Status & Distribution Widespread in Europe and Palearctic Asia. VAGRANT: Rare migrant to the western and central Aleutians; casual to the Pribilofs; records from St. Lawrence Is., Seward Peninsula, and coastal southern AK. Accidental to southern CA.

Population Abundant and stable in its home range in Eurasia.

CANVASBACK *Aythya valisineria*

The Canvasback is perhaps 1 of the more elegant ducks; its distinctive structure makes identification simple. Monotypic. L 21" (53 cm)
Identification Forehead slopes straight down to a long, dark bill. The largest *Aythya* species, it has a thick neck and long body. MALE: Chestnut head with a dark crown and forehead, red iris. The flanks, back, and tertials are very pale, almost white. FEMALE: Light brown head and breast with a slightly darker crown; contrasting pale gray flanks and back. FLIGHT: Wings are uniform, with only a faint gray wing stripe.
Similar Species Compare the Redhead and the Common Pochard. The Canvasback can be distinguished by its sloping forehead and long, uniformly colored bill. The forehead is straight, not concave as in similar species. In all plumages, the Canvasback has a dark bill and pale back unlike any other *Aythya* species.
Voice Generally silent.
Status & Distribution Locally common south to central Mexico; casual to Honduras. BREEDING: Uses a wide variety of freshwater wetlands, from lakes and ponds to large marshes; also found on alkali lakes. MIGRATION: Spring migration begins in early Feb.; peaks in the Midwest and Great Plains in early Apr.; most breeders have arrived by mid- to late May. Fall migration is fairly late. Most begin moving south in Oct.; peaking in the Great Lakes in early Nov.; peaks in early Dec. on the Gulf Coast. WINTER: Ranges widely in freshwater lakes and brackish bays and estuaries; south to Mexico. The largest concentrations are mainly in coastal areas. VAGRANT: Casual on the Aleutian and Pribilof Islands. Accidental to Iceland.
Population Canvasback numbers have fluctuated widely due to changing water levels on the breeding grounds and, to some degree, hunting regulations. The Canvasback population is currently rebounding from period of low numbers (1982–1995).

REDHEAD *Aythya americana*

An attractive duck usually found in small groups except in massive rafts along the barrier islands of southern Texas in winter. Monotypic. L 19" (48 cm)
Identification Large *Aythya,* slightly larger than the Greater Scaup, with a short bill, rounded head. MALE: Tricolored bill with a black tip, white subterminal ring, and pale blue base. The head is uniformly rufous with a yellow eye. The heavily vermiculated back and flanks appear smoky gray. FEMALE: Brown overall, with paler face and dark crown. The bill is tricolored with a slate gray base. FLIGHT: Brown upper wing, with a paler gray stripe on the flight feathers.
Similar Species Male separated from Canvasback by short, tricolored bill and darker back. Female from Canvasback by structure and darker color. More uniform and paler backed than Ring-necked Duck and scaup, lacking distinct paler area at the base of the bill.
Voice Generally silent.
Status & Distribution Fairly common, south to central Mexico. BREEDING: Highest concentrations in the western prairies; nesting on prairie potholes, seasonal pools, and lakes. MIGRATION: In spring, begins leaving the wintering grounds in late Jan., peaking in the southern prairies in mid-Mar. In fall, begins in late Aug., peaking in the southern prairies in mid- to late Oct., arriving on the Gulf Coast in numbers in early Nov. WINTER: Widespread but fairly sparse except along the Gulf Coast, where most of the population winters, especially the Laguna Madre of southern TX and northern Mexico. VAGRANT: Accidental in Bermuda, HI, and the U.K.
Population Stable, but eastern breeders are declining.

RING-NECKED DUCK *Aythya collaris*

This distinctive duck is usually found in marshy pools and small ponds. Monotypic. L 17" (43 cm)

Identification Angular head with a high crown, peaking near the rear with the nape slanting forward. Both sexes have a white ring adjacent to a black-tipped bill; male has an additional thin ring at base of bill. Male has a white wedge between the breast and flanks, a unique feature. ADULT MALE: In addition to the multiringed bill and white wedge on the flanks, dark purple head, gray flanks and black back. ADULT FEMALE: Gray face with a white eye ring, darker crown, and indistinct pale area at the base of the bill; some show a pale thin stripe behind the eye. FLIGHT: Rapid, showing a slight gray stripe on the secondaries. Slightly more agile than scaup; flocks form tight clumps.

Similar Species Male similar to Tufted Duck but lacks tuft, has more prominently marked bill with a second white ring at the base, gray flanks separated from breast by a white wedge, and lacking wing stripe. Female similar to female Redhead, but with an angular head, darker back and crown, and more distinctly pale face. Separated from female scaup by gray face contrasting with darker crown and white eye ring.

Voice Generally silent.

Status & Distribution Widespread and fairly common, more numerous in the East. BREEDING: Nests on freshwater marshes and shallow ponds and lakes. MIGRATION: In spring, begins early Feb., peaking in Great Lakes in early Apr.; most breeders in place by late Apr. or early May. In fall, begins in Sept., peaking on Great Lakes in late Oct., Pacific Northwest in late Nov. WINTER: Sometimes uses coastal marshes, but usually in shallow freshwater. VAGRANT: Annual in British Isles, recorded widely in western Europe.

Population Stable or increasing.

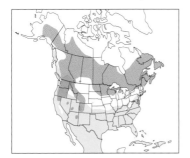

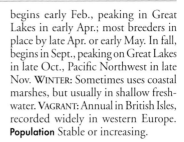

TUFTED DUCK *Aythya fuligula*

An Old World species, regular in Alaska and a vagrant to the rest of N.A., the Tufted Duck is usually found in the company of scaup or sometimes Ring-necked Ducks. Individual Tufted Ducks often return to the same locations year after year. Monotypic. L 17" (43 cm)

Identification The Tufted has a small body, with a large head and slender neck. MALE: Its long and shaggy crest is the most striking feature. The bill is similar to that of a scaup but has more black on the tip. From a distance, their black backs and gleaming white flanks are distinctive. FEMALE: Dark brown head, back, and breast, with paler mottled brown flanks. The female shows a variably sized crest and a black tipped bill. FIRST-WINTER MALE: Like the adult male, but has a shorter crest and light gray flanks. FLIGHT: The Tufted Duck shows an extensive white stripe on the wing, broader than that of the Greater Scaup. The Tufted has a deep forehead, unlike a scaup; the tuft is difficult to see in flight, even on adult males.

Similar Species First-winter males are similar to hybrids between a scaup and a Tufted Duck or a scaup and a Ring-necked Duck. Scaup x Tufted Duck hybrids are regular, almost as frequent as pure Tufted Ducks; hybrids tend to show a short crest, reduced black on the tip of the bill, a pale gray wash on the flanks, and grayish barring on the upper back; they lack the faint white spur on the flanks of the Ring-necked x scaup hybrids. The female has a completely dark head, and a slight tuft separates them from other *Aythya* species.

Voice Generally silent.

Status & Distribution The Tufted Duck is abundant and widespread, breeding across northern Palearctic Europe and Asia. WINTER: On pond, bays, and rivers; a number of records have come from ponds or lakes in city parks, where Tufted Ducks are easily observed. In southern Europe and Asia, south to Africa. VAGRANT: Regular migrant in AK; rare but regular winter visitor on the West Coast south to southern CA. Casual on the East Coast. Accidental elsewhere.

Population The most numerous of the *Aythya* in the world. The population is stable.

GREATER SCAUP *Aythya marila*

Very similar to the Lesser Scaup, the Greater Scaup often forms mixed flocks. In coastal bays and inlets or other areas of deep water, the Greater Scaup generally dominates these flocks, while the Lesser Scaup is more numerous in the interior and on shallower lakes and ponds. Polytypic (2 ssp.; *nearctica* in N.A.). L 18" (46 cm)

Identification Structure is the best way to separate and identify scaup. The Greater Scaup has a more rounded head, thicker neck, and larger, thicker bill. The Greater Scaup also has more black on the bill, covering much of the bill tip. MALE: Dark head that shows a bright green sheen in bright light. The breast is black; the back is pale gray covered with fine vermiculations; the flanks are white with very light to moderated gray vermiculations. FEMALE: Dark brown head with a slight reddish tone. There is an extensive white ring encircling the base of the bill. Females in worn plumage show a variably sized pale ear patch. The back of the female is brown, and the flanks are mottled gray-brown. FIRST-WINTER MALE: Like females in fall, but with less white surrounding the bill; acquires plumage like adult males by spring, but with more vermiculations on the flanks and heavily worn brown tail feathers. FLIGHT: The Greater Scaup has a thin, white wing stripe that extends almost to the tip of the wing.

Similar Species See sidebar below for help in identification of male scaup. Compare females to other female *Aythya*. The female Ring-necked shows a more angular head, ringed bill, and more defused pale face pattern. The female Redhead is more evenly brown, with more black on the bill, and lacks the white ring surrounding the bill. See the Lesser Scaup entry for separation from that species.

Geographic Variation North American and east Asian birds are of the subspecies *nearctica*. There is 1 specimen record of the nominate *marila* from St. Paul Is. in AK in late June.

Voice Generally silent.

Status & Distribution Widespread and abundant in the Northern Hemisphere. BREEDING: Whole-Arctic breeder; nests on tundra pools and lakes. MIGRATION: In spring, begins gradually in early Mar. Mid-Atlantic peak mid-Mar to mid-Apr. In the West, most have left the southern part of their winter range by late Mar. Peak in BC the last 2 weeks of Apr. In fall, departs breeding grounds mid-Sept.–late Oct. The bulk of the population migrates to the Atlantic coast via the Great Lakes. Peak in Great Lakes the second week of Oct.; late Oct.–early Nov. in the mid-Atlantic. Peak in southern BC mid- to late Oct. WINTER: Uses bays, estuaries, and deep inland lakes and rivers.

Population Numbers are declining for unknown reasons.

Identification of Male Scaup on the Water

Scaup rank highly on the list of most frequently misidentified birds in North America because birders often rush the identification process. While scaup are truly difficult and can cause much frustration, they can be learned, but only with patience and practice. Two keys to learning scaup are studying them carefully when you see the species together and taking time when identifying them.

The most solid field marks for scaup are subtle aspects of structure that can be altered by a bird's behavior and posture; time is often required to correctly assess structure. There are several useful plumage characteristics, but they are variable, and relying on plumage leads to errors.

Greater Scaup, male

Size can be a starting point in identification. In direct comparison, the Greater is noticeably larger than the Lesser. Head shape is often the key to identifying scaup. The Greater has a smoothly rounded head that appears large in comparison with the body; the Lesser has a smaller, more angular head shape. Start by looking at the nape, which in the Lesser is tilted slightly forward in a straight line until it meets a slight bump on the back of the crown. This bump is caused by several long crown feathers coming to an end; it is frequently referred to as the topknot. At times the topknot forms an obvious bump; in some postures the bump disappears, becoming just a few ruffled feathers on the crown. The head has a strong-

LESSER SCAUP *Aythya affinis*

The most abundant, frequently encountered *Aythya* in North America, the Lesser Scaup is smaller than the Greater Scaup and usually more common in freshwater. Monotypic. L 16.5" (42 cm)

Identification Lesser Scaup are medium size with small, narrow heads; high, peaked crowns; and thin necks. Their bills are small and thin, with only a small amount of black surrounding the nail. MALE: Dark head has a purple gloss in good light, but may also appear green. It has a vermiculated gray back and lightly vermiculated flanks that may appear light gray or white. FIRST-WINTER MALE: Like female in fall, but with no white surrounding the bill; acquires plumage like adult male's by spring, but with more vermiculations on the flanks. FEMALE: Dark brown head with a moderate white ring enclosing the base of the bill. A few females, in worn plumage, show a small, pale ear patch; back is dark brown, and flanks are a mottled mix of gray and brown. FLIGHT: White

wing stripe is strong on the secondaries and very faint on the primaries.
Similar Species See sidebar pp. 28–29 for separating males from the Greater Scaup. Compare females to other female *Aythya*. Separated from the Ring-necked Duck by uniform dark head with sharp white ring at the based of the bill. Smaller and darker than female Redhead or Canvasback. Separate with caution from female Greater Scaup by noticeably small size in direct comparison, angular head shape, usually with a slight bump (topknot) at the peak of the nape. Usually shows noticeably less white on the face enclosing the bill; also most have little or no pale ear patch. On average appears slightly more mottled and "messier" than Greater Scaup.
Voice Generally silent.
Status & Distribution Abundant and widespread in N.A., south to northern Columbia. BREEDING: Nest near lakes and pools and large, permanent potholes in the western prairies. MIGRATION: In spring, some Lesser Scaup

begin to leave their winter range in early Feb., while large numbers remain through Apr. Mid-Atlantic and Great Lakes peak early Apr., late Mar in the Pacific Northwest. In fall, they remain on the breeding grounds until Sept. South of its breeding range, in the lower 48, the fall peak occurs in the first 2 weeks of Nov. virtually everywhere. WINTER: Found on lakes, reservoirs, and coastal lagoons. The bulk of the population winters near the Gulf of Mexico in FL, LA, and TX. VAGRANT: Casual to Bering Sea, north to Greenland, and Europe. Accidental in S.A.
Population No strong population trends. Overall, the Lesser Scaup seems to be declining slightly, but the breeding range has expanded due to the creation of reservoirs.

adult ♂

adult ♂

ly peaked appearance; the highest point on the head is near the back of the crown. Viewed directly in front or behind, the head of the Lesser is very narrow. On the Greater the nape bulges out slightly near the base, then smoothly curves to a slight peak above the eye. Its head does not look as tall as that of the Lesser and has a narrow crown that expands below the eye, giving a heavy-jawed appearance. The Lesser has a small bill with parallel sides; the Greater has a proportionally longer bill that expands near the tip. The Greater tends to have more black surrounding the nail, but this is variable enough to be unreliable.

Most plumage characteristics can be used only to support conclusions drawn from structure. However,

Lesser Scoup, male (CA, Jan.)

plumage tends to be more visible than structure, making it easier to choose which scaup to concentrate on in a large raft.

The Greater tends to have gleaming white flanks, while the Lesser tends to have slightly gray flanks; a few individuals of both species, however, show the "wrong" flank color. In strong light the color of the head gloss can be obvious. The Greater has bright green gloss, but the Lesser usually has purple gloss, but it sometimes appears green. Using head gloss can often be misleading.

Even with years of practice and knowledge of all field marks, everyone will misidentify a scaup occasionally, but with care, most scaup can be correctly named. ■

EIDERS Genera *Polysticta & Somateria*

Each of the 4 species worldwide are found in North America. These large, bulky diving sea ducks have dense down feathers that help insulate them from cold northern waters. Females pluck their own down to line nests. Eiderdown is harvested and sold for pillows and blankets. Eiders generally migrate in large flocks. Spectacular movements can be witnessed at points in coastal northwestern Alaska. Most eiders head north to tundra nesting grounds as soon as sea ice breaks up. In years of late breakup in combination with severe storms, many eiders, mainly King, starve to death. In spring 1964, an estimated 100,000 King Eiders, 10 percent of the population migrating on the Arctic coast, died.

STELLER'S EIDER *Polysticta stelleri*

This small, compact sea duck seems inappropriately named as an eider. Structurally and behaviorally it is more reminiscent of a dabbling duck. It lacks the highly developed frontal lobes and bill feathering characteristic of other eiders. Monotypic. L 17" (43 cm)
Identification The head is rectangular, with a flat crown and sharply angled nape. Its long, pointed tail is generally held out of the water. BREEDING MALE: Distinctive. Appear mostly white at a distance. ECLIPSE MALE: Like adult female, but darker, retaining white in the wing and broad pale tertial tips. FEMALE: Easily overlooked in mixed flock. Plain brown face, with pale eye ring, warm cinnamon brown coloration overall. Blue speculum and white-tipped tertials diagnostic when present. JUVENILE: Gray-brown, plumage wears and fades quickly; thin white speculum borders, tertials dull and short. FLIGHT: Flies swiftly in tight flocks, with a long-winged, short-

necked, heavy-bellied appearance.
Similar Species Blue speculum with broad white boarders, like a Mallard, in combination with long, curved white-tipped tertials separate Steller's from all other sea ducks. Female distinguished from the Harlequin by pale eye ring on warm brown face and lack of white spots on head and shape.
Voice Noisy in winter flocks; females giving rapid guttural call, inciting females give loud *qua-haa* or *cooay.* Growling and barking noises given by both sexes; does not produce cooing calls like other eiders.
Status & Distribution Threatened. BREEDING: Arrive on AK breeding grounds on Arctic tundra late May–early June. WINTER: To southern Bering Sea,

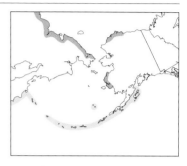

arrive late Oct.–Nov. Steller's Eider favors shallow, sheltered coastal lagoons and bays. VAGRANT: Casual outside Alaskan waters to BC, WA, OR, CA. Casual to accidental on East Coast; records from QC, ME, MA, MD, and Baffin I.
Population Marked decline in AK breeding population since 1960s for reasons largely unknown. Population estimates of wintering concentrations along Alaskan Peninsula (includes Russian breeders) are also dropping.

SPECTACLED EIDER *Somateria fischeri*

This hardy sea duck is appropriately named for its bold, pale "spectacles," which are apparent in all plumages. The Spectacled Eider has a gradually sloping forehead, with feathers extending down the bill. It lacks the highly developed frontal lobes of the Common and King Eiders. Otherwise, the Spectacled is structurally similar to the Common Eider in flight but significantly smaller, with a bit shorter neck. Monotypic. L 21" (53 cm)
Identification BREEDING MALE: Bold head pattern with big white, black-bordered goggles and orange bill; generally distinctive. ECLIPSE MALE: Resembles

breeding plumage, but white and green areas replaced with dusky gray feathers. FEMALE: The head appears light overall with dark forehead, due to pale "spectacles" and cheek. The bill is dark, blue-gray. Vertical barring on the flanks, paler body coloration overall than other eiders. FLIGHT: Male only eider with black belly extending to upper breast. Upperwing coverts all white, like on the Common. Underwing duskier than on other eiders. Female difficult to identify, but dark forehead contrasts with pale spectacles and cheek and can be useful in combination with structural characteristics.

Similar Species The Spectacled Eider is smaller than the Common and the King. Similar to the Common in flight, with triangular-shaped head, but more

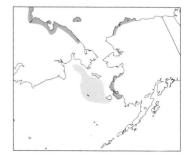

adult ♂

♀

adult ♂

adult ♀

♀

extensive dark breast on males and distinctive head pattern. The female Spectacled Eider is separated from the Common and the King Eider by pale cheek and "goggles"; feathering extends down the smaller bill, and lacks the chevron pattern on the flanks of the King.
Voice Typically silent. The male display call is a very soft *hoo-hoo.*

The female gives a short, guttural *croak* and a 2-syllable clucking call.
Status & Distribution Threatened. BREEDING: Return to AK breeding grounds, coastal tundra near lakes and ponds, first week of May. MIGRATION: Depart late June for offshore molting areas. WINTER: Bering Sea in large flocks in openings of pack ice, primarily south of St. Lawrence Island. VAGRANT: Casual on Aleutian and Pribilof Is. Not prone to wander far from breeding and wintering grounds.
Population Three distinct breeding populations in western and northern AK and in Russia. Russian population is currently much larger than Alaskan populations, which have experienced dramatic declines in the last 50 years.

KING EIDER *Somateria spectabilis*

The King Eider undergoes spectacular migrations in large flocks to arrive on the breeding grounds with enough time to breed and molt in the short Arctic summer. Monotypic. L 22" (56 cm)
Identification MALE: The King is distinctive in breeding plumage, with bright orange frontal lobes, pinkish red bill, baby blue head, and a green wash on the side of the face. FIRST-WINTER MALE: Has a brown head, pinkish or buffy bill, and lacks white wing patches. Full adult plumage is attained by the third winter. ECLIPSE MALE: Dark overall, with only a bit of white mottling on mantle and in wing coverts; pinkish bill; and a distinct head shape with thin white postocular stripe. FEMALE: Brown overall with dark chevron markings on flanks and scapulars. The bill is dark, appears stubby, with a fairly rounded head. FLIGHT: Large rectangular head and short neck; stockier than the Common, with faster wingbeats. The Common is larger, with a more horizontal body posture and triangular head. The King tends to have the rear dragging

below its rectangular shaped head and a shorter neck. The male shows a partly black back and black wings with white patches. Young males have white flank patches.
Similar Species Males in flight have more black on upperparts than the Common Eider. Females can be difficult to separate from the Common. Structurally the King is smaller, with a flatter crown, rounded nape, and slightly bulging, shorter forehead that does not slope evenly into its bill, which is relatively smaller than the Common's. At rest the bill of the King is held more horizontally than that of the Common, which is often angled down a bit. Also, note that female Kings have a crescent or V-shaped markings on the flanks and scapulars as opposed to the vertical barring on the Common.
Voice Males give a low, dovelike *urr urr urr.* Various low croaks given in flight.
Status & Distribution Fairly common. BREEDING: Common on tundra and coastal waters in northern part of range. MIGRATION: Move in impressive large

flocks at all hours. In spring, begin departing Bering Sea in Apr. and early May. Undergo molt migration 3–4 weeks after end of spring migration. Fall: Rare in MA, generally not seen before late Oct. WINTER: Very rare on the Great Lakes, except on Lake Ontario, where it is rare and increasing. VAGRANT: Casual to FL and West Coast to southern CA. Some West Coast individuals linger into summer. Accidental to Gulf Coast.
Population Declining. Food depravation during spring migration may have significant impact on numbers; large percentage of population (e.g., 10 percent) may die of starvation.

adult ♂

♀

adult ♂

1st winter ♂

adult ♂

♀

COMMON EIDER *Somateria mollissima*

adult ♂
dresseri

v-nigrum

eclipse adult
♂

♀

dresseri ♀

♀ dresseri

1st winter ♂
dresseri

adult ♂
dresseri

adult ♂ v-nigrum

This most common and widespread eider shows extensive geographic variation. Polytypic (6 ssp.; 4 in N.A.). L 24" (61 cm)

Identification ADULT MALE: Distinctive head pattern; frontal lobes and bill color vary with respect to subspecies. ECLIPSE MALE: Dark with white mottling overall. IMMATURE MALE: Dark with white breast. Full adult plumage by third year. FEMALE: Evenly barred flanks and scapulars. The "Pacific" *(v-nigrum)* is colder brown and duller overall compared to eastern subspecies, which is warm reddish brown. In the East, *dresseri* is dark and richly colored; *borealis* is reddish with dark markings; *sedentaria* palest.

Geographic Variation There are 4 subspecies: *dresseri, borealis, sedentaria,*

and *v-nigrum.* See sidebar below.
Similar Species See the King Eider entry.
Voice Male gives a ghostly *ahOOOOoo* during courtship. Female gives a grating *krrrr* and other guttural calls.
Status & Distribution Locally abundant. BREEDING: Nests in colonies along marine coasts. MIGRATION: Some populations sedentary, others long-distance migrants. In spring, Mar.– mid-June for Arctic breeders. Molt migration in June and July. In fall, peaks in MA Oct.–Nov.; late Nov.–early Dec. in NJ. WINTER: "Pacific" winters in Bering Sea to south coastal AK in N.A. VAGRANT: In East *dresseri* and *borealis* casual on Great Lakes, rare in winter on coast south to NC, casual south to FL. "Pacific" *(v-nigrum)* rare in BC; accidental to Pacific states south to northwestern CA; rare east to Greenland; *sedentaria* accidental outside Hudson and James Bays.
Population Subspecies *v-nigrum* and *borealis* are declining. On Atlantic, *dresseri* relatively stable, recovered from excessive commercial hunting in the 19th century.

Subpecies Identification of Adult Male Common Eiders

Six Common Eider subspecies are recognized, 4 of which breed in North America. They fall into 2 groups, Eastern and Pacific. The Eastern group includes *dresseri* ("Atlantic Eider"), *sedentaria* ("Hudson Bay Eider"), and *borealis* ("Northern Eider"). The Pacific group consists of *v-nigrum* ("Pacific Eider"). Nominate *mollissima,* and *faeroeensis* are found in Europe.

The "Pacific Eider," *v-nigrum,* is the largest eider subspecies. Adult males are readily distinguished from the Eastern group by a black V on the chin and a bright orange bill. The frontal lobes are narrow and pointed, and green on the head is extensive, continuing to a narrow line below the eye. In the Eastern group, *dresseri* is medium size, with an olive-green to greenish yellow bill and broad frontal lobes rounded at the top. It is distinguished from *sedentaria,* which has narrower, shorter frontal lobes. *Borealis* is found in the northernmost regions of the Atlantic and is the smallest subspecies in N.A. It has a bright yellow-orange bill; its frontal lobes are narrow, tapered, and rounded; and it has less green on the side of head than *dresseri. Borealis* resembles *v-nigrum* in bill color, but its overall bill size is smaller, and it lacks the black V on throat. However, the black V is occasionally seen on *dresseri* and nominate *mollissima.* ∎

"Atlantic Eider"
♂ *dresseri*

"Hudson Bay Eider"
♂ *sedentaria*

"Northern Eider"
♂ *borealis*

"Pacific Eider"
♂ *v-nigrum*

Genus Histrionicus

HARLEQUIN DUCK *Histrionicus histrionicus*

This small diving duck is structurally unique, with a steep rounded forehead, stubby bill, and chunky body. Males have a white crescent in front of the eye, a small white circular patch near the ear, and a white vertical stripe on the hind neck; these create the clown-like appearance for which it is named. Monotypic. L 16.5" (42 cm)
Identification BREEDING MALE: Distinctive. Dark blue-gray overall with chestnut flanks; appears dark at a distance. Scapulars and tertials white, white band on breast and neck. ECLIPSE MALE: Dark sooty brown, but still shows male characteristics. FIRST-WINTER MALE: Like adult, but duller overall. Attains adult-like features throughout winter. FEMALE: Dark brown overall, pale belly, variably sized white patch in front of the eye, white spot behind eye. FLIGHT: Small

head, steep forehead, plump body with long tail. Wings are entirely dark, but adult male has small white spots on a few coverts; whitish belly of female is not very noticeable, and it appears dark overall. Flies swiftly, low over water with rapid wingbeats; usually seen in small numbers.
Similar Species Female, compared with female Bufflehead in flight, has darker body and longer, pointed tail. Smaller overall size, smaller bill, steeper forehead than female scoters. Chunky body with proportionally tiny head and bill, round spot on face, and longer tail separate it from female Black Scoters. Darkest of female Long-tailed Ducks similar, but have different head pattern and more white on body.
Voice High-pitched, nasal squeaking; commonly a mouselike squeak, *gia.*
Status & Distribution Locally fairly common from N.A. to Iceland and Eastern Asia. BREEDING: Nests on ground, near

fast-flowing rivers, streams, lakes. MIGRATION: Not seen moving in large concentrations, short- to intermediate-distance migrant. In spring, moves inland from the coasts, departing East Coast Apr.–mid-May. West Coast departs late Mar. and largely gone by mid-May. Immature and injured birds may stay on wintering grounds. In fall, males undergo molt migration starting in late June. Rare in MA before Nov. WINTER: Rocky coastlines. VAGRANT: Rare, but increasing on Great Lakes in winter. Casual south to FL; accidental on Gulf Coast to TX. In West occurs in small numbers to northern CA, rare to southern CA, casual to Baja California. Accidental to CO and AZ.
Population Declining. Pacific population larger than Atlantic. Local extirpations contribute to range reduction. Many studies underway to better understand and conserve Harlequins.

Genus Camptorhynchus

LABRADOR DUCK *Camptorhynchus labradorius*

This wary sea duck was the first North American endemic to reach extinction. The last reliable report was a specimen collected on Long Island, New York, in 1875. Bill shape suggests the species was a food specialist, but very little is known about the Labrador's natural

history. It is believed to have foraged near sandbars for shellfish. Monotypic. L 22.5" (57 cm)
Identification BREEDING MALE: Head, neck, and chest are white; the crown has a black stripe. FEMALE: Plumage is gray-brown overall, with throat whiter than head, mantle and scapulars slaty blue, and white speculum. IMMATURE AND ECLIPSE MALE: Resemble females.
Similar Species Confusion unlikely.
Voice Unknown.
Status & Distribution Extinct. BREEDING: Remote areas, probably rocky

coasts, islands, or short distance inland, likely Labrador or farther north. WINTER: Atlantic coast from NS south possibly to Chesapeake and Delaware Bays, estuaries, and sandy bays. VAGRANT: In very poor weather, reported from rivers as far inland as Philadelphia. Accidental to Montreal, QC, spring 1862.
Population Extinct. Explanations for extinction are largely speculative. The population already was believed to be small in the 1800s. There are no published accounts of causes of mortality aside from shooting and trapping in nonbreeding season for consumption and collection.

SCOTERS Genus *Melanitta*

The AOU recognizes 3 species of scoters; Europeans split both the Black and White-winged Scoter for a total of 5. They are medium to large, with black or blackish plumage and orange or yellow on the bill. They nest in northern Canada and Alaska and winter along both coasts. While scoters migrate nocturnally when crossing land, along the coast they migrate diurnally, often in mixed flocks. During peak migration these flocks may consist of several thousand individuals. Away from the breeding grounds and the Great Lakes, scoters are primarily coastal. A handful of all 3 species, however, are scattered throughout the interior ever year. Scoters are most often found on lakes and rivers after late fall storms.

BLACK SCOTER *Melanitta nigra*

The smallest scoter, the Black is often located in spring by the male's constant whistling. In the winter, small flocks form around jetties and rocky points. The Black dives with a small leap, wings held closed, unlike other scoters. On the water, it often rears out of the water, dips its head down, and performs a rapid series of wingbeats; other scoter species hold their head up when they stretch their wings. The Black often migrates in huge, spectacular flocks in long lines, mixing with Surf and White-winged Scoters as well as other ducks, alcids, and grebes. When several lines join together, the flock becomes a seething, undulating mass of birds and 1 of the most incredible migration spectacles in North America. Polytypic (2 ssp.; *americana* in N.A.). L 19" (48 cm)

Identification Chunky body with small head and bill; at a distance the bill disappears, leaving the impression of a flat face. The tail of the Black Scoter can be cocked out of the water, like a stiff-tail duck's, or it can lie flat on the water. ADULT MALE: Uniform black plumage with a bright orange knob on the bill. ADULT FEMALE: Dark brown body with sharply contrasting pale face and throat, dark cap and nape. FIRST-WINTER MALE: Like female, but with pale belly. Slowly acquires partially black plumage and orange knob during the winter. FIRST-YEAR FEMALE: Like adult female but duller with pale belly. FLIGHT: Compared to the Surf Scoter, the Black Scoter has a potbellied appearance, shorter hand with rounded wingtips, and in good light, usually shows stronger silver flash on the underside of the primaries. However, the most reliable way to separate distant flying birds is head shape. The rounded head of the Black Scoter, which ends abruptly at a flat forehead, is quite different from the long, sloping foreheads of the other 2 scoters. As a Black Scoter's primaries wear, they become strongly translucent, a feature that is most useful in the spring, especially for adult males, and an attribute that separates the Black from the 2 other scoters.

Geographic Variation The Black Scoter, *americana*, breeds in North America and east Asia (from River Lena east); the nominate *nigra* (the "Common" Scoter) is native to Europe and east to the River Olenek in Siberia. The extent of overlap, if any, is unknown; no known intermediates. Many European authorities split these 2 subspecies. Nominate *nigra* has yet to be recorded in North America. Male nominate *nigra* has a much smaller knob on the bill that is yellow and less extensive than that of *americana*. There are also slight differences in structure, with nominate *nigra* showing more pointed wings, a thinner neck, and more rounded head than in the *americana*. Females are probably not identifiable in the field, but the base of the bill is less swollen in nominate *nigra*, and the nostril is closer to the base of the bill.

Similar Species Distinctive at close range. Distant birds in flight are difficult to separate from the Surf Scoter but, with practice, are still identifiable. Concentrate on head shape; wing shape, the appearance of the belly, the potbellied appearance of the Black (the Surf Scoter is sleeker) and the translucency of the primaries can also be helpful.

Voice By far the most vocal scoter; in late winter groups of 5–30 males follow females, giving a long, low, mellow whistle. Females are largely silent.

Status & Distribution Locally common. BREEDING: Nest on tundra pools, lakes, and rivers. MIGRATION: Usually in large flocks, more visible in fall, more nocturnal movements in spring. In spring, peak in the mid-Atlantic in early Apr., early May in Canadian Maritime Provinces, arriving on the breeding grounds in northern QC third week of May. In CA begins in early Mar. In fall, begin moving south in Sept., mid-Atlantic peak third week of Oct., in BC numbers peak in early Nov. Small numbers on Great Lakes (common on Lake Ontario, where some winter). WINTER: Found on inshore bays and inlets along both Atlantic and Pacific coasts. VAGRANT: Rare to very rare in the interior and along the Gulf Coast. Rare in southern CA, casual to Baja California. Records of *americana* from northwestern Europe. Nominate *nigra* casual to Greenland.

Population Thought to be declining, but little solid information exists.

americana

1st winter ♂

adult ♂

adult ♀

adult ♂

adult ♀

SURF SCOTER *Melanitta perspicillata*

Surf Scoters are the most common scoter in many areas. Male Surfs have a distinctive clownlike face. Monotypic. L 20" (51 cm)

Identification Forehead and bill are smoothly merged, forming a wedge-shaped head. The bill meets the face in a straight, vertical line; some feathers extend down the culmen toward the nares. Diving birds flick their wings open just as they submerge. ADULT MALE: Black with white patches on the nape, forecrown, and base of the bill. Eye pale and bill orange with a yellow tip. ADULT FEMALE: Uniform blackish brown with diffuse pale loral and postocular spots; some also have pale napes. FIRST-WINTER MALE: As female in fall, but with a pale belly; acquires much of the black-and-white plumage and orange bill during the first winter. FIRST-

WINTER FEMALE: As female but with a pale belly. FLIGHT: Large, wedge-shaped head, sleek body, and pointed wings give the Surf Scoter a unique silhouette. Forms dense flocks.

Similar Species First-winter females can have pale cheeks, like the Black Scoter but can be separated by head shape.

Voice Generally silent.

Status & Distribution Common. BREEDING: Nesting on shallow lakes, often with rocky shores. MIGRATION: In spring, begins in Mar.; peaking in CA and OR in second half of Apr.; mid-Atlantic peak in late Mar. or early Apr.; movements less noticeable in spring than fall on Atlantic coast. In fall, begins in late Aug., peaking in CA in early Nov.; mid-Atlantic peak mid- to late Oct. WINTER: In large flocks along both coasts, usually close to shore. VAGRANT: Rare in the interior, where it is primarily a migrant; rare on the Gulf Coast. Casual to U.K. and Greenland.

Population Declining for unknown reasons.

WHITE-WINGED SCOTER *Melanitta fusca*

When migrating, these (the largest and most distinctive of the 3 scoters) form smaller flocks that spread out more evenly. Polytypic (3 ssp.; 1 in N.A.). L 21" (53 cm)

Identification The white secondaries are usually obvious on close birds but disappear on distant birds in strong light. White secondaries may be visible on swimming birds, but are often hidden. When diving, they flip their wings open even more distinctly than Surf Scoters. MALE: Head, breast, and back are black; sides are dark brown. A small white comma mark surrounds the eye; orange tip on bill. FEMALE: Dark brown with 2 faint round spots on the face. FLIGHT: Broad wings and heavy flight are reminiscent of eiders; white secondaries are diagnostic.

Geographic Variation Three subspecies: *deglandi* in N.A.; records of *stejnegeri*

from St. Paul Is. and Nome have different bill color and black flanks.

Similar Species Compare females to Surf Scoter. Face pattern less distinct, feathers extend farther down bill. White secondaries distinctive if visible.

Voice Generally silent.

Status & Distribution Locally common. BREEDING: Tundra pools. MIGRATION: Early Mar.–May. In fall, peaks in the mid-Atlantic in late Nov. VAGRANT: Rare to casual in the interior and the Gulf Coast. Nominate *fusca* casual to Greenland.

Population Possibly declining.

Genus *Clangula*

LONG-TAILED DUCK *Clangula hyemalis*

winter adult ♂

1st fall ♀

This sea duck, formerly known as the "Oldsquaw," is unique in having 3 plumages a year. Monotypic. L 16–22" (41–56 cm)

Identification ADULT MALE WINTER: Long tail conspicuous. White head with gray patch around eye, black band across breast, long gray scapulars, light gray flanks. EARLY SUMMER MALE: Head black, still with eye patch, scapulars buffy with black centers. By late summer, head and neck become whiter, flanks darker gray. FIRST-YEAR MALE: Gradually attains adultlike features by second fall. FEMALE: Crown and nape blackish brown, breast grayish, flanks whitish, scapulars buff with black centers. By fall whiter head and neck. In summer head and neck dusky overall. FLIGHT: Appears very white, with uniformly dark underwings. Identifiable by swift, careening flight.

Similar Species Female similar to female Harlequin, but Harlequin's dark flanks, steep forehead, rounded head, and facial pattern are distinct. Female Steller's Eider is darker overall with plain face, white-edged speculum, curved tertials. In winter flight, guillemots can cause confusion; they have a bold white wing patch, unlike the black wings of the Long-tailed.

Voice Highly vocal. Utters nasal, loud, yodeling, 3-part, *ahr-ahr-ahroulit*. Both sexes give soft *gut* or *gut-gut* call while feeding.

Status & Distribution Common. BREEDING: Arctic tundra ponds and marshes. MIGRATION: In spring, begins east coast in late Mar.–early Apr.; West and Great Lakes in late Feb.–May. In fall, U.S. coasts and Great Lakes peak numbers in late Nov. and Dec.

Population Hard to evaluate; information is lacking.

winter ♀

winter ♀

1st winter ♂

early summer adult ♂

winter adult ♂

Genus *Bucephala*

BUFFLEHEAD *Bucephala albeola*

This diving duck has adapted to a wide variety of habitats from sheltered bays, rivers, to flooded fields. It is 1 of the smallest ducks, with a large puffy head, a steep forehead, and a short stubby bill. Its plumages are suggestive of miniature goldeneyes. It flies so quickly, with rapid wingbeats, that the wings blur; it usually seen only in small flocks. Monotypic. L 13.5" (34 cm)

Identification MALE: Glossy black back, white below, with large white patch on iridescent purple-green head. ECLIPSE MALE: Like female, but darker head with larger white patch; retains white in wing. FIRST-YEAR MALE: Like female. FEMALE: Dark gray-brown above, dusky white below. Dark head, elongated white patch under eye.

Similar Species Female's very rapid wingbeats and small size can resemble some alcids. Compare female Harlequin; Bufflehead has larger head, shorter tail, and faster wingbeats. Female and juvenile Long-tailed Ducks are larger, with slower wingbeats, longer tail, whiter head.

Voice Generally silent, except during courtship displays.

Status & Distribution Common and widespread. BREEDING: Nests in woodlands near small lakes, ponds. MIGRATION: In spring, begins in Feb., arrives on breeding grounds early Apr.–early May. In fall, begins late Oct., with numbers on wintering grounds increasing until early Dec. WINTER: Uses a wide range of open-water habitats including sheltered bays, rivers, and lakes. VAGRANT: Casual to U.K.

Population One of the few species of ducks whose numbers have increased markedly since the mid-1950s.

adult ♂

adult ♂

♀

adult ♂

1st winter ♂

♀

COMMON GOLDENEYE *Bucephala clangula*

The common and widespread Goldeneye is usually found in or near deep, clear water. Polytypic (2 ssp.; *americana* in N.A.). L 18" (47 cm) **Identification** Large triangular head, sloping forehead, and longer bill than the Barrow's, with shallower base. ADULT MALE: White circular spot on dark head distinctive. FIRST-YEAR MALE: Like female; transition to adult male throughout first winter. White loral spot develops slowly, can appear crescent shaped, causing confusion with the Barrow's. FEMALE: Dull brown head, pale gray body, and black bill with yellow tip. Rarely can have mostly yellow bill. FLIGHT: Heavy and muscular appearance. Show more white on the upper wing than the

Barrow's, but difficult to judge. **Geographic Variation** Two subspecies of the Common Goldeneye are recognized: *americana* in N.A. and the smaller nominate *clangula,* found across the Old World. **Similar Species** Males have more white on the scapulars than the Barrow's, lack the black spur on the breast of the Barrow's. Loral spot round and forehead not as steep as the Barrow's. Hybrids Common X Barrow's rare, majority of reports from the East. Male hybrids typically look almost exactly intermediate between the 2 species. **Voice** Male gives a soft, short *preent* during display. Female

occasionally gives a harsh croak: *gack.* **Status & Distribution** Common. BREEDING: Open lakes with nearby woodlands where nest holes are available. MIGRATION: In spring, departs southern part of winter range in late Feb. Peak on Atlantic coast late Mar.–early Apr. In fall, New England and Atlantic coast peaks early Dec. Pacific coast migration late Oct.–early Dec.; CA peak third week of Nov. WINTER: Coastal areas, inland lakes, and rivers. **Population** Most data suggests population is relatively stable, but effects of habitat loss and alterations are of concern.

courtship display

1st winter ♂

adult ♂

adult ♂

BARROW'S GOLDENEYE *Bucephala islandica*

In winter this North American and Icelandic species is found around jetties and old pilings, feeding on barnacles. Monotypic. L 18" (46 cm) **Identification** Puffy, oval-shaped head, steep forehead, and stubby, triangular bill. BREEDING MALE: Dark head with white crescent; black spur interrupts white breast and flanks. ADULT FEMALE: Dark brown head, gray body, yellow-

adult ♂

1st winter ♀   adult ♀

orange bill that becomes black in summer. FIRST-WINTER MALE: White facial crescent develops slowly, evident by late December. FIRST-WINTER FEMALE: Like adult, but with largely black bill. JUVENILE: Like female; dark eyes and bill, darker and browner overall; difficult to distinguish from the Common. **Similar Species** Female separated from Common by steep forehead and shorter bill. Bill usually all yellow-orange; some female Commons can have a yellow bill, but color is paler, not as orange as Barrow's. Separation of many individuals in fall very difficult; hybridization complicates. For distant males, dark spur that extends onto breast of Barrow's is useful. More extensive black on the back of the Barrow's, with spotted pattern on the scapulars.

1st winter ♂

adult ♂

Voice Generally silent. **Status & Distribution** Fairly common in West, uncommon to rare in East; northeast to Greenland and Iceland. BREEDING: Open lakes and small ponds. MIGRATION: In spring, Pacific coast mostly late Mar.–early Apr.; MA by early Apr. In fall, Pacific coast late Oct.–early Nov.; arrive late Nov–early Dec. in ME and MA. WINTER: Sheltered coastal areas, lakes, and rivers. VAGRANT: Casual away from Great Lakes and Northeast. Accidental from Southeastern states. **Population** The numbers are stable throughout most of range.

MERGANSERS Genera *Lophodytes, Mergus,* and *Mergellus*

The long, thin, serrated bills and slender, long-necked bodies of mergansers aid them in catching fish, crustaceans, and aquatic insects. There are 6 species worldwide; 4 in N.A. Fast and direct in flight, mergansers show pointed wings, shallow wingbeats, long neck and bill. They nest in tree cavities, nest boxes, and on ground sheltered by vegetation.

HOODED MERGANSER *Lophodytes cucullatus*

This small, oddly shaped diving duck is frequently found on ponds, wooded sloughs, and streams in small groups or pairs. Monotypic. L 18" (46 cm)
Identification ADULT MALE: Black-and-white fan-shaped crest, black back, chestnut flanks, white breast with black band, black bill. FIRST-YEAR MALE: Like female, but white in crest, yellow eye, sometimes dark feathers on head, bill blackens. ECLIPSE MALE: Dusky-brown crest, dark bill,

yellow eye. FEMALE: Brownish overall, paler breast, upper mandible dark, lower yellowish. FLIGHT: Very quick wingbeats, head usually held low, crest flattened, prominent tail.
Similar Species Female can be confused with female Red-breasted. Much smaller; thinner dark bill; lower mandible yellow. In flight like Wood Duck, but more slender, faster, shallower, and wingbeats are more direct.

Voice Generally silent; but froglike growl often given during courtship displays.
Status & Distribution Uncommon in West, common throughout much of East. BREEDING: Forested areas with nest cavities. MIGRATION: In spring, begin departing Southeast early Feb.; remain on coastal areas in Pacific Northwest until mid-Apr. In fall, peak mid-Nov. in New England; numbers increase by late Dec. in FL. Arriving on wintering areas late Oct. in Pacific Northwest. **Population** Stable, possibly increasing in some areas.

adult ♂

adult ♀

1st spring ♂

♀

adult ♂

RED-BREASTED MERGANSER *Mergus serrator*

This species is most often seen in flocks in coastal wintering areas. Monotypic. L 23" (58 cm)
Identification Medium size; a slim neck and smaller bill; ragged, 2-pronged crest. ADULT MALE: Green head; white collar; brown breast; gray flanks; distinctive. ADULT FEMALE: Gray-brown body with a dull reddish brown head; slender reddish bill; all-white throat and breast. FIRST-YEAR MALE: Similar to female, but paler gray with variable green on head. FLIGHT: White wing patches divided by 2 black lines; head

and neck appear flat.
Similar Species Female similar to Common, but Red-breasted is slender, with thinner neck, much thinner bill, full ragged crest, uniformly pale throat.
Voice Generally silent, except during courtship. Male gives catlike *yeow-yeow.* Female produces raspy croaking during displays.
Status & Distribution Common. BREEDING: Arrive mid- to late May. Nest in woodlands near freshwater or sheltered coastal areas. MIGRATION: Abundant on Great Lakes, where some winter. In

fall, pass through Great Lakes first 2 weeks of Nov., with numbers increasing in mid-Atlantic in early Nov. Peaks mid-Sept.–early Nov. in BC. Uncommon in interior, more common in East as migrant. WINTER: Favors salt water more than other mergansers. Common in coastal regions and Great Lakes, except Lake Superior.
Population Declining; reasons unknown.

adult ♂

♀

1st winter ♂

♀

adult ♂

COMMON MERGANSER *Mergus merganser*

This hardy merganser is regularly seen along raging streams or loafing on chunks of ice in winter lakes. It forms large single-species flocks in winter, often tightly packed and facing the same direction. Frequently it obtains food by diving in deep water; however, it also forages in shallow water by swimming with its face submerged looking for prey. Polytypic. L 25" (64 cm)

Identification One of the largest ducks, with a heavy body, thick neck, and long, slender, hooked bill. Sits low in the water, holding its large head erect. Slight crest on nape can be held close to the head so it almost disappears. Thicker bill than other mergansers, especially at base. ADULT MALE: Dark head, white breast and flanks, generally distinctive. FEMALE: Bright chestnut head and neck contrast with white chin; the bill is bright red and the body uniformly pale gray. ECLIPSE MALE: Resembles female, but retains adult male's wing pattern. FIRST-WINTER MALE: Resembles adult female, but with paler body and with variable amounts of dark green feathers appearing during the first winter. FLIGHT:

Shows large white wing patches with a single black bar across the median coverts, larger on males than females. Has bulkier body and thicker neck than Red-breasted Merganser. Flight is extremely swift, with shallow, rapid wingbeats.

Geographic Variation Three subspecies worldwide; only *americanus* regular in North America. Nominate *merganser* migrant to western Aleutian Islands, found across Eurasia. The males of the nominate race have a shallower base to the bill, larger hook on bill, and lack the black bar across the median coverts. Largest subspecies, *comatus,* found in Central Asia.

Similar Species Female can be confused with female Red-breasted Merganser, but has sharply delineated white chin surrounded by chestnut head and throat, unlike diffused pale throat and neck of Red-breasted. Bill has a heavier base than a Red-breasted that meets the head on a straight line. Tends to look paler and cleaner than Red-breasted, which appears more mottled. Robust build with a thick neck and large head, unlike slender Red-breasted.

Voice Generally silent, except during courtship or when alarmed.

Status & Distribution Common. BREEDING: Nests in woodlands near lakes and rivers. MIGRATION: Short- to intermediate-distance migrant, nocturnal overland movements and diurnal migration along coasts. In spring, leave southern part of wintering range in mid-Feb.; most birds gone by Apr. Great Lakes region, arrive late Mar., peak late Apr. In fall, on Atlantic coast, arrive mid-Nov., peak Dec.–Feb. in VA. On West Coast peak in BC in Nov. WINTER: Found as far north as there is open water; large lakes, reservoirs, rivers, sometimes on coastal bays, estuaries, and harbors. VAGRANT: In eastern N.A. regular in winter to Ohio River, casual to Gulf Coast.

Population Stable or increasing in N.A. Good indicator species to assess contamination levels.

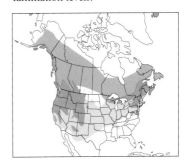

SMEW *Mergellus albellus*

This Eurasian species is a vagrant throughout N.A. Most records are from Alaska and the West Coast. The Smew is kept in captivity in U.S., therefore origin is often questioned for sightings away from Alaska and the West Coast. Monotypic. L 16" (41 cm)

Identification BREEDING MALE: White with black markings, black-and-white wings conspicuous in flight. FIRST-SPRING MALE: Dark rufous crown and nape, dark around eye, white cheek, gray body. FEMALE: White throat and lower face contrast with reddish head and nape. FLIGHT: Male and female have large white ovals on upper wing.

Similar Species White patch on lower face of females and nonbreeding males

separates all other sea ducks. Female-like plumages resemble Common Merganser, but significantly smaller; extensive white lower face and dark smaller stouter bill are distinctive.

Voice Generally silent, except during courtship. Male gives grunting and rattling calls; female's grating or rattling.

Status & Distribution Rare migrant to west and central Aleutians mid-Mar.–May and primarily Oct. to early winter, where it has been observed in small flocks. BREEDING: Northern Eurasia near rivers and small lakes in forested areas. VAGRANT: Casual on Pribilofs. Accidental on Kodiak I. and in lower 48. Most records away from AK Nov.–Mar.

Population In Europe apparently stable after long-term decline.

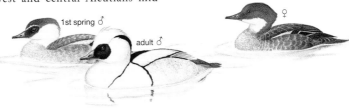

STIFF-TAILED DUCKS Genera Nomonyx and Oxyura

Long, narrow, stiff tail feathers serve as a rudder for these diving ducks. Males have a bright blue bill in breeding season. They are found in fresh and brackish water; the Masked prefer ponds with dense emergent vegetation. When actively swimming and diving, the tail is frequently laid on water, not cocked and spread as it is held when resting.

MASKED DUCK Nomonyx dominica

This small tropical stiff-tail most frequently appears in southern Texas. Shy and difficult to see even when present, it spends most of its time hidden in dense aquatic vegetation. Monotypic. L 13" (34 cm)

Identification Slightly smaller than the Ruddy, with smaller head and shorter bills. Like the Ruddy, it has a long tail that can be cocked above the body or trail behind on the water. BREEDING MALE: Black face with sky blue bill. Nape and body are dull reddish brown with black-centered flank feathers. FEMALE: Warm buffy brown, with a buffy supercilium and 2 dark stripes on the cheek. WINTER MALE: Like female, but with stronger stripes on the face. FLIGHT: Large white patches on inner wing. Unlike the Ruddy, it takes to flight easily off the water.

Similar Species Dull plumages similar to the Ruddy's, but with 2 distinct dark stripes on face. Also shows a pale supercilium, which the Ruddy lacks. Ruddy Ducks prefer more open water with less vegetation. Any stiff-tail with white wing patch can instantly be identified as a Masked Duck. Male Ruddy Ducks can show an entirely black face or heavily flecked cheek patch during molt to breeding plumage.

Voice Generally silent.

Status & Distribution Rare; sometimes occurs in small numbers after invasions in N.A. Generally local in neotropics and West Indies. BREEDING: Nests on lowland ponds, marshes, and rice fields with much floating vegetation. MIGRATION: Nonmigratory. VAGRANT: Rare in southern and southeastern TX, casual in LA and FL. Accidental in East, records from WI, MA, NC, MD, and VT.

Population Numbers fluctuate in TX, more likely in wet years. Recent invasions in 1930s, late 1960s, early 1970s, and 1990s. Due to the species' secretive nature, preference for highly vegetated ponds, and fact that it is often on private land, it is difficult to assess the population. The Masked Duck is probably not as rare as is perceived.

RUDDY DUCK Oxyura jamaicensis

The Ruddy is the only widespread stiff-tail in N.A. Bright breeding plumage is held during summer and dull plumage during the winter, unlike other ducks of N.A.. Polytypic (3 ssp.; only nominate in N.A.). L 15" (38 cm)

Identification Small, chunky duck with proportionally large head and bill. Frequently cocks long tail in a fan shape. BREEDING MALE: Bright baby blue bill, black crown contrast with white cheeks and chestnut body. Often males have black flecking or almost entirely black cheeks when molting to breeding. WINTER MALE: Retains a white cheek and black crown but body becomes dull gray-brown. FEMALE: Fairly dull gray year-round. Dark crown; a single dark line crosses buffy cheek. FLIGHT: Rarely seen, prefers to dive or run on water to avoid danger. When they do fly, wingbeats are rapid, usually barely clearing the water.

Similar Species Unique structure and plumage, most likely to be confused with the Masked Duck. Female Bufflehead is superficially similar, but has a rounded head with a high forehead and smaller bill.

Voice Generally silent.

Status & Distribution Common. BREEDING: Nests in dense vegetation of freshwater wetlands. MIGRATION: Almost exclusively nocturnal. In spring, begins in early Feb. in south; ends third week of May in northern parts of range. In fall, earlier than other diving ducks, beginning in late Aug., peaks mid-Sept.–late Oct., ending in Dec. WINTER: Lakes, bays, and salt marshes.

Population Stable or increasing in N.A.

EXOTIC WATERFOWL

Many waterfowl species are brought into North America from other continents for zoos, farms, parks, and private collections. They occasionally escape from captivity. The species shown here are among those now seen all over; some are becoming established in the wild. While some species such as the Tufted Duck, Smew, and Baikal Teal are natural vagrants to North America, they are also kept in captivity. Use caution when assessing the origin of waterfowl and look for marks of formerly captive birds such as leg bands, lack of a hind toe, notches in webbing, and unusual feather wear.

SWAN GOOSE *Anser cygnoides*

This native to eastern Asia has a domestic form commonly known as the Chinese Goose, which is the only domestic goose not of Graylag ancestry. There are 2 types: the slimmer-bodied Chinese Goose (Brown and White) and the larger, heavy-bodied African Goose. The wild form is slim; its long, swanlike bill lacks knob at base. Rear end floats higher than rest of body. L 45" (114 cm)
Identification Crown, nape, hind neck

dark brown; cheek and sides of neck white. Upperparts dusky brown with buffy edges.
Similar Species Generally distinctive. White form could be confused with other domestic white geese of the Graylag-type, but note prominent orange knob on bill of Graylag-types.
Status & Distribution Domestic forms found regularly in N.A.
Population Little is known; endangered in its native land of Asia.

domestic type

GRAYLAG GOOSE *Anser anser*

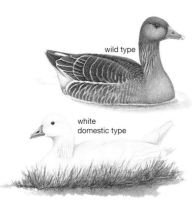

wild type

white domestic type

This native of Europe and northern Asia is the progenitor of most domestic geese. Often not shy, the domestic forms are larger and heavier bodied, with deeper bellies than their wild ancestors. Many show variable amount

of white at base of bill, like the White-fronted. When swimming, domestic's rear end floats higher than rest of body. L 34" (86 cm)
Identification Wild-type Graylag is large, with thick neck, large head, heavy, pinkish orange to pink bill, and dull pink legs. The dumpy domestic Graylag is a very large, heavy-bodied, thick-necked goose. Domestic forms range from gray-brown to entirely white or multicolored. Hybridization between domestics and sometimes with Canada Goose is frequent, producing a wide away of structures and plumages. Presumed Canada **x** domestic Graylag often has a large, buffy cheek patch, white eye ring, brown crown and neck, and some white at base of bill-suggestive of Canada **x** White-fronted hybrids.
Similar Species Wild form compared to juvenile White-fronted Goose is stock-

ier, thicker necked, and grayer overall. Compare domestics carefully to the White-fronted Goose and white forms to the Snow Goose. Graylag is larger, stockier, with deep belly, often practically dragging on the ground. Domestic Graylag bills are usually larger and thicker at base then those of White-fronted Goose. Some white forms, known as "Domestic Goose" can have relatively petite bills, but do not show "grinning patch" of the Snow Goose. Plumage of the Ross's Goose could be confused, but it is significantly smaller and lighter bodied, with a dainty bill. The Graylag is larger and stockier and lacks dark markings on bill of the Pink-footed or the Bean Goose.
Voice Loud, raw, deep *honks*. Wide repertoire of calls.
Population The Graylag is increasing in native lands of Europe.

BAR-HEADED GOOSE *Anser indicus*

This native to central Asia is known for its record high-altitude flights over the Himalaya; it was recorded above Mount Everest at 30,758 feet. It is particularly tolerant of cold climatic conditions. The Bar-headed Goose is common in captivity in N.A and Europe, where it frequently escapes. L 30" (76 cm)
Identification ADULT: Two conspicuous black bars on rear of white head; white line runs down side of gray neck. Back

is pale gray with white-edged feathers. Bill is yellow with a black nail; orange-yellow legs. JUVENILE: Less distinctive than adult, with white face, dark gray crown and hind neck, paler gray body.
Similar Species Generally not confusing. Compare the Graylag with the juvenile, which has a paler gray body and paler gray forewing.
Voice Honking flight call.
Status & Distribution Escapes can be found in N.A. and western Europe. BREEDING:

High-mountain lakes of central Asia. MIGRANT: Flies over the Himalaya to reach wintering grounds. WINTER: Mountain rivers, lakes, and grassy wetlands primarily in northern half of Indian subcontinent, west to Pakistan and east to northern Burma.

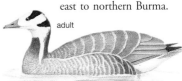

adult

EGYPTIAN GOOSE *Alopochen aegyptiacus*

This native of tropical Africa is usually found inland on freshwater. It feeds by grazing but also dabbles, swimming with rear end floating higher than rest of the body. L 27" (68 cm)
Identification ADULT: Head and neck buffy with dark brown patch around eye and base of bill. Body buffy to gray-brown, paler on flanks, whitish belly. JUVENILE: Duller than adult, with dark crown and hind neck, lacking brown eye patch. FLIGHT: Strong and quick flier with slow wingbeats, white wing coverts, green to purple speculum.
Similar Species Likely to be confused only with Ruddy Shelduck, which is smaller, shorter legged, with orange-chestnut body, and no dark eye patch.
Voice Male gives a harsh, breathing sound; female a loud, harsh quacking.
Status & Distribution An escape throughout N.A., concentration in southern CA and warm climates in U.S. Feral breeder in Britain; escape in Europe.

adults

COMMON SHELDUCK *Tadorna tadorna*

This native to Europe, Asia, and northern Africa is often known as the "Shelduck." Commonly kept in collections and reported as an escapee in N.A., the Shelduck is as at home on land as it is in water, favoring salt or brackish water. L 25" (64 cm)
Identification Sexes are similar. Bright red bill; green head; broad chestnut band across white breast and belly. ADULT: Bold black band around neck. Prominent knob at base of bill, especially on males in breeding season. JUVENILE: White face; lacks chestnut band on breast. FLIGHT: White wing coverts prominent.
Similar Species Generally distinctive.
Voice Loud calls. Males give musical whistles in flight and perched females give a low and nasal *ak-ak-ak-ak*.
Status & Distribution Abundant western Europe. BREEDING: Nests in cavities, on ground if those are unavailable.
Population Population increasing in Europe.

adult ♂

RUDDY SHELDUCK *Tadorna ferruginea*

adult ♂

This Afro-Eurasian species (popular in zoos and private collections) is mainly a nomadic species. L 26" (66 cm)
Identification Prominent white wing coverts, green speculum, and ruddy back in flight. MALE: Head and neck buffy, with thin black band around neck, buffy orange body. FEMALE: Like male, but lacks neck collar and buffier overall. FLIGHT: Upperwing coverts white, black primaries, green speculum. Underwing coverts, white, contrasting with dark flight feathers.
Similar Species Likely to be mistaken only for Egyptian (mainly brown, larger, thinner necked, and longer legged).
Voice Frequently gives a loud, nasal trumpeting call in flight.
Status & Distribution Common in captivity; reported as an escapee in N.A. Potentially has reached N.A. on its own.
Population Long-term decline until recently. In some years, trend has been variable.

MANDARIN DUCK *Aix galericulata*

This native of eastern Asia is 1 of 2 species in the genus *Aix*. The female is very similar to the female Wood Duck. One of the most popular exotic waterfowl species, it is common in collections. It favors wooded lakes and rivers, where it is often seen perching in trees. Monotypic. L 16" (41 cm)
Identification BREEDING MALE: Elaborate and ornate plumage. Pinkish red bill, white band sweeps behind eye, orange "mane," dark green crown, and orange tertial "sails." ECLIPSE MALE: Resembles female, but bill is reddish with less distinct eye ring, shaggier crest, and glossy upperparts. FEMALE: Resembles female Wood Duck. Pale and grayer overall, with shaggy hind neck. White eye ring with thin white postocular stripe. Bill grayish with pale nail. Wing coverts dull brown (glossy on Wood Duck). JUVENILE: Like female, but duller with less distinct facial pattern. Attains adult plumage throughout first winter. FLIGHT: Dark with white belly and dark upper wings.
Similar Species Thin white line behind eye, unlike broader white patch of Wood Duck. Wood Duck's head is darker, with a dark nail. Head is large and rounded with sloping forehead, more rectangular on Wood Duck.
Voice Generally silent, except during display.
Status & Distribution Eastern Asia. Established in Britain. Feral population in northern CA. BREEDING: Eastern Siberia, China, Japan, where it nests in tree cavities on forested river banks. WINTER: Lowlands of eastern China and southern Japan.
Population Declining in Asia due to habitat destruction and previous export from China in large numbers.

♂ ♀

CURASSOWS AND GUANS Family Cracidae

Plain Chachalaca (TX, May)

Cracids are a diverse family of primarily arboreal game birds, many of which have elaborate wattles and knobs. They generally feed on leaves and fruits of trees, with some species foraging on the ground for fallen fruits.

Structure They range in size from medium to large and have heavy bodies. Common characteristics include longish necks with small heads, long broad tails, and rounded wings. Their bills are rather chickenlike and their legs are fairly long and strong.

Behavior In general, cracids live in groups; the chachalacas are the most sociable. Most species are found moving through the canopy of tropical forests, but chachalacas generally stay closer to the ground.

Plumage Overall plumage varies from olive brown to black. The sexes appear similar in most species with only the curassows showing strong sexual dimorphism.

Distribution A New World family, cracids are found from south Texas and northwestern Mexico through the neotropics to northern Argentina. The family reaches its greatest diversity in northern South America. The chachalacas are very similar; they appear to occupy similar niches to the point that there is virtually no overlap in distribution between the different species.

Taxonomy The family can be informally divided into 3 major groups: curassows, guans, and chachalacas—50 species in 11 genera. The 12 species of chachalaca–characterized by small size (for the family) and plain coloration—are all in the genus *Ortalis*.

Conservation Most chachalaca species are common; none are considered of great conservation concern. Seven guan and 6 curassow species, however, are considered threatened. Small clutch sizes do not allow their populations to recover from hunting pressures as readily as temperate gallinaceous species. In addition, many of the threatened species depend on primary forest, much of which is seriously threatened by deforestation. —*Mark W. Lockwood*

CHACHALACAS Genus Ortalis

PLAIN CHACHALACA *Ortalis vetula*

breeding ♂

Although generally secretive, this south Texas bird is very vocal and has become habituated to feeding stations. The Plain Chachalaca is always found in small social groups—numbering 10–15 individuals—as it moves through the understory and on the ground in semi-tropical forests. Well adapted to these woodland habitats, it often hops from branch to branch without the use of its wings. The common name of the genus, chachalaca, is derived from the loud chorus given by groups of this species. Polytypic (5 ssp. in C.A.; *mccallii* in N.A.). L 22" (56 cm).

Identification Large with a proportionately long tail and small head. ADULT: Brownish olive above, buffy brown below. Gray head and neck. Long dark tail with a green sheen and broad white tip. Patch of bare skin on throat gray to dull pink, becoming bright pinkish red in the male during breeding season. JUVENILE: Similar to adult, but duller and often mottled brown above; tail feathers tipped with pale brown and less rounded.

Voice Noisy, especially at dawn and dusk. CALL: A raucous *cha-cha-lac* given in very loud chorus, although usually not synchronized. Female voice is higher pitched than male's. Various other guttural chatter given, including *krrr* notes.

Status & Distribution Common in limited N.A. range. YEAR-ROUND: Resident in brushy areas and riverine woodlands of south TX. Successfully introduced to Sapelo Island, GA. World range extends to Costa Rica along the Atlantic coast.

Population The population appears stable throughout its range.

PARTRIDGES, GROUSE, AND TURKEYS Family Phasianidae

Wild Turkey, males (TX, Feb.)

Phasianidae is arguably one of the more spectacular families in the world. Many species have elaborate courtship rituals. Most exhibit complex plumage variation that is still poorly understood. And, since many species require large tracts of quality habitat, looking for them takes birders to pristine and magnificent locations.

Structure Well adapted for life on the ground, all family members have strong legs with three long toes and a small hind toe. Adults of many species have one or more sharp spurs on the back of the leg to rake opponents during quarrels. The relatively short wings allow birds to explode off the ground.

Behavior Phasianids are unobtrusive. Most will fly only when danger is imminent; they spend their lives with minimal movement, both in their daily activities and seasonally. During the mating season, the males of most species, particularly those with polygynous systems where males compete for females at leks, engage in a barrage of displays that include drumming, wing whooshing, maniacal cackles, foot stomping, flight displays, and hoots.

Plumage Most species are sexually dimorphic, dramatically so in many pheasants. Males are often larger, and in many species of grouse have special adornments on their head and neck. Otherwise, most species are cryptically colored. Most appear very similar throughout the year, although ptarmigan change dramatically from their cryptic lichen-covered-rock summer plumage to nearly completely white in winter.

Distribution While members of this familiy are distributed across North America, diversity is generally higher away from the Southeast. Most species are sedentary.

Taxonomy Phasianidae includes 4 distinct subfamilies, which are sometimes designated as full families: pheasants and partridges (Phasianinae), grouse (Tetraoninae), turkey (Meleagridinae) and guineafowl (Numidinae). Of the approximately 180 species worldwide, 11 grouse and the Wild Turkey are native to North America. Attempts have been made to introduce several species of pheasants and partridges (and Helmeted Guineafowl for tick control), but only the Chukar, Gray Partridge, Himalayan Snowcock, and Ring-necked Pheasant are considered established. The sedentary nature of phasianids with little genetic mixing has given rise to extensive regional variation and subspecies. Taxonomy continues to undergo revision: The Gunnison Sage-Grouse was "discovered" only in the last few years, and at least 1 other species (Blue Grouse) is a leading candidate to be split.

Conservation Habitat loss poses the most serious threat, especially to native grassland grouse. The Wild Turkey's recovery, however, demonstrates that rebounds can occur when conservation is undertaken. —*Christopher L. Wood*

Genera *Alectoris* and *Perdix*

CHUKAR *Alectoris chukar*

This introduced Old World species can be challenging to find and is best located by call or by searching near water sources. By late summer it is not unusual to see a covey with 1 to 3 adults and 30 to 50 chicks. Polytypic. L 14" (36 cm)

Identification Resembles an overgrown short-tailed quail. ADULT: Cream-colored face and throat broadly outlined in black. Flanks boldly barred with black. JUVENILE: Similar

adult

but smaller, mottled, and no bold black markings; usually with adults. FLIGHT: It explodes into the air and then glides away; look for chestnut on spread tail just before landing.

Geographic Variation Complex; most birds in N.A. believed to be nominate subspecies, which is the darkest and brownest subspecies.

juvenile

Similar Species No similar species established in N.A., however, 2 released game birds are similar: The Red-legged Partridge has a white face and throat; its neck is conspicuously streaked with black, giving the appearance of having a "neck-shawl." The Rock Partridge has more black (less white) between the bill and the eye and a whiter throat.

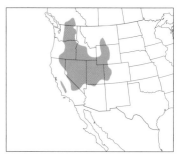

Voice CALL: A calm *chuck, chuck, chuck* that often becomes progressively louder and drawn out, culminating in a voluminous eruption of *chuckara-chuckara-chuckara*. The alarm call of flushed birds is a loud piercing squeal followed by *whitoo* notes.

Status & Distribution Uncommon to fairly common; now established in steep rocky terrain in much of the West. Released birds are possible almost anywhere, even in the East.
Population Widely released in North America starting in the 1930s, the

Chukar became established in much of the West by the late 1960s. The largest populations are in Washington, Oregon, Nevada, Idaho, Utah, and California.

GRAY PARTRIDGE *Perdix perdix*

Established as a game bird in N.A. since the early 1900s in agricultural areas, this often-evasive Old World species is best found at dawn and dusk. Polytypic. L 12.5" (32 cm)
Identification Mostly streaked brownish above, grayish below. Broad rufous bars and narrow cream-colored streaks on flanks. Contrasting rufous outer tail feathers often revealed as bird flicks its tail open. MALE: Conspicuous chestnut patch on upper belly and bright rufous-orange head and throat. FEMALE: Belly patch absent or reduced; head and throat more buff. IMMATURE: Duller in both sexes. FLIGHT:

Explodes into the air with rapid wingbeats and then alternates glides and rapid wingbeats; flights are typically low to the ground and of short distance.
Geographic Variation Clinal. Western subspecies in its native range is darker gray or rufous than subspecies in the East. Little information on introductions, but most believed to be nominate *perdix*.
Similar Species None. The Gray's broad rufous bars on the flanks and face pattern are distinctive.
Voice CALL: A harsh *kee-uck*, likened to

a rusty gate. Alarm call a rapidly repeated *kuta-kut-kut-kut*. Also various clucks.
Status & Distribution Uncommon.
Population The Gray is thought to be declining in much of its range in North America, largely due to changes in farming practices.

Genus Phasianus

RING-NECKED PHEASANT *Phasianus colchicus*

Native to Asia, the flashy Ring-necked Pheasant has been widely introduced as a game bird in North America. It is frequently seen along roadsides in agricultural areas. Polytypic. L ♂ 33" (84 cm) ♀ 21" (53 cm)
Identification Large. Very long, pointed tail; short, rather rounded wings. MALE: Iridescent bronze overall, mottled with brown, black, gray, and rufous. Head a dark glossy green to purplish, with red fleshy

eye patches and iridescent ear tufts. Most show a wide white neck ring. FEMALE: More buff colored with sparse dark spots and bars on breast and flanks. FLIGHT: When flushed, it erupts with powerful loud whirring wingbeats. The long tail is distinctive even in flight.
Geographic Variation Extensive, particularly among males. Many subspecies have been introduced in N.A.; intergrades are numerous. The male "White-winged Pheasant" has distinctive white upperwing coverts. The Japanese "Green Pheasant" is largely extirpated.
Similar Species The female resembles a Sharp-tailed Grouse, but the latter is smaller, with heavily scalloped and spotted underparts and a shorter tail with white outer tail feathers.
Voice CALL: Male territorial call is a loud,

"Green Pheasant"

penetrating *kok-cack*. Both sexes give hoarse, croaking alarm notes.
Status & Distribution Locally common to uncommon resident of open farmland and grassy fields.
Population While populations fluctuate with weather changes, pheasants are in decline. Some populations are preserved through continual introductions.

Genus Tetraogallus

HIMALAYAN SNOWCOCK *Tetraogallus himalayensis*

The central Asian Himalayan Snowcock has established a toehold in North America, but seeing this exotic is no small feat. Its numbers are small (only about 1,000 birds) and it lives only in Nevada's rugged Ruby Mountains. At dawn, the Himalayan Snowcock calls from its roost site and flies downhill. It spends the day walking back up, feeding, resting, and preening. Birds congregate just before dark, then fly or walk to roost. Polytypic (nominate in N.A.). L 28" (71 cm)

Identification The Himalayan Snowcock is large (nearly 2.5 times the size of the Chukar). It is generally grayish overall with rusty-brown streaks on upperparts. Two prominent chestnut stripes on each side of the head outline the whitish face and throat. The predominantly white primaries are conspicuous in flight. FEMALE: She is smaller and duller than the male with a buff forehead; the area around the eye is grayer. She lacks spurs. JUVENILE: It is similar to the adult female, but smaller and duller. Very young birds lack the chestnut markings on the face.

Similar Species None within restricted range.

Voice CALL: Generally similar to the Chukar; other calls surprisingly reminiscent of a Long-billed Curlew. Clucks and cackles persistently while foraging.

Status & Distribution Successfully introduced to the high elevations of the Ruby Mountains of northeast NV, where it resides in subalpine and alpine habitats. MOVEMENTS: Generally sendentary; may move slightly downslope during severe winters.

Population The Himalayan Snowcock was first released into the Ruby Mountains in 1963; the first brood was seen in 1977. By the 1980s the species was self-sustaining. Limited threats include overgrazing by sheep and pressure from hunters and birders.

Genus Centrocercus

GREATER SAGE-GROUSE *Centrocercus urophasianus*

The largest North American grouse, the Greater Sage-Grouse is a highly social denizen of aromatic sagebrush flats and foothills centered on the Great Basin. Where common, it may form flocks of several hundred birds. Impressive lekking displays begin in late February or early March and continue into early summer. Monotypic. L ♂22–28" (71 cm) ♀22" (56 cm)

Identification Distinctive dark belly and long pointed tail feathers. MALE: Yellow eye combs, black throat and bib, large white ruff on the breast. FEMALE: Similar to male but smaller. Brown throat and breast, showing only a hint of the male's pattern. JUVENILE: Resembles the female but with upperparts finely streaked. FLIGHT: Superficially suggests waterfowl, but note dark belly, long tail, and grouse shape.

Geographic Variation Some consider birds in the interior Northwest a separate subspecies (*phaios*), but differences minor and validity questionable.

It hybridizes occasionally with Sharp-tailed and Blue Grouse.

Similar Species See Gunnison Sage-Grouse. Distinguished from all other grouse by black belly and larger size.

Voice CALL: Courting male fans tail and rapidly inflates and deflates air sacs emitting two popping sounds, at times audible up to 2 miles away; also a variety of wing swishes, coos, whistles, and tail rattles. When flushed, it gives a rapid cackling *kek-kek-kek*.

Status & Distribution Uncommon to fairly common but local. MOVEMENTS: Generally resident, but may engage in local movements, particularly to find sage in times of deep snow. Movements of more than 100 miles have been noted in ID and WY.

Population The species declined during the 20th century; hunting probably reduced numbers early on, but threats to habitat pose the biggest risks today.

displaying ♂

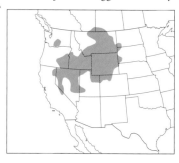

GUNNISON SAGE-GROUSE *Centrocercus minimus (E)*

displaying ♂

This bird was only recognized as a separate species by scientists in the 1990s when differences in size, plumage, and lekking displays were described. Only 2,000 to 4,000 birds remain in less than 193 square miles of land in south-central Colorado and extreme southeastern Utah. The Gunnison requires large expanses of sage with a diversity of forbs and grasses and a healthy riparian habitat, interspersed with grassy open areas, where the male performs his elaborate courtship display. Monotypic. L ♂22" (56 cm) ♀18" (46 cm)

Identification Roughly two-thirds the size of the Greater Sage-Grouse. Identify by range: Gunnison Sage-Grouse is the only sage-grouse in south-central Colorado and southeastern Utah.

Similar Species The Greater Sage-Grouse. During display, the Gunnison has pronounced, even white bands on the tail, whereas the Greater's tail feathers are more mottled; it also appears noticeably paler at a distance, almost blond in color. Gunnison males display less frequently, and produce different sounds (typically 9 air sac plopping sounds during each display, compared with 2 for Greaters). The Gunnison's longer, thick filoplumes are thrown forward over the top of the head, and then flop back down (unlike Greater, where the sparse filoplumes are held erect). The female Gunnison is nearly identical to the Greater in plumage and behavior.

Voice CALL: Similar to the Greater Sage-Grouse.

Status & Distribution Endangered. Most in Gunnison Basin of Gunnison and Saguache counties in CO; 6 smaller disjunct populations, each with fewer than 300 birds. Fewer than 150 in UT.

Population Habitat loss, degradation, and fragmentation have reduced the populations. In recent years this has been exacerbated by drought.

FOREST GROUSE Genera *Bonasa, Falcipennis,* and *Dendragapus*

Members of these genera live in relatively forested landscapes. Two of these genera are monotypic: *Bonasa* (Ruffed Grouse) and *Dendragapus* (Blue Grouse). The Spruce and Siberian Grouse of *Falcipennis* are quite similar to the Blue Grouse but lack the unfeathered neck sacs. There is considerable geographic variation among all the genera.

RUFFED GROUSE *Bonasa umbellus*

This generally solitary species is the most widespread grouse in North America. In spring, the male's deep accelerated drumming often resonates in open woodlands. Displaying males also raise their ruffs and crest. Most active in morning and evening, the Ruffed may be seen along edges of woodland road, or in winter, perched high in deciduous trees feeding on buds, twigs, and catkins. It sometimes visits feeding stations. Polytypic. L 17" (43 cm)

Identification Slim, long-tailed species with a small crest (most apparent when bird is alarmed). Black ruffs on side of neck often hard to see. Most populations have 2 color morphs, red and gray, most apparent in coloration of tail; coloration varies regionally. Barred underparts and tail with many narrow bands and a wide dark subterminal band (center of which is typically broken or blotchy on female). JUVENILE: Similar to female, but less well marked and lacks subterminal band; usually seen with female. FLIGHT: When alarmed, it explodes into the air with a roar of the wings, but even then tail pattern is usually easily seen.

Geographic Variation Complex, with 14 recognized subspecies. Birds in the Pacific Northwest average darker and richer brown; in interior West, paler gray; in the Northeast, generally grayish; in the Southeast, brownish.

Similar Species Both Blue and Spruce Grouse are uncrested. The larger Blue Grouse is more uniformly colored, without the barring on the underparts. The Spruce Grouse has a shorter tail and neck with more noticeable white spotting below. Note the tail pattern.

Voice CALL: Both sexes may give nasal squeals and clucks, particularly when alarmed.

Status & Distribution Fairly common resident of deciduous and mixed woodlands.

Population Generally stable, with populations rising and falling in regular cycles.

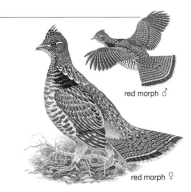

red morph ♂

red morph ♀

gray morph ♂

SPRUCE GROUSE *Falcipennis canadensis*

red morph ♀

"Franklin's Grouse"
franklinii

♂

While this species may be seen along roadsides, particularly in fall, the Spruce Grouse is often challenging to find. Typically very tame, this species is so well camouflaged that by remaining still it can remain undetected even when observers are only a few feet away. The Spruce Grouse is usually

solitary, but it will gather in small loose flocks in winter. Polytypic. L 16" (41 cm)

Identification A short-tailed compact grouse. Over most of range, both sexes have black tail with chestnut tail tip. Male has dark throat and breast, edged with white and red eye combs. Female occurs as red and gray color-morphs; in all females note the heavy dark barring and white spots below. JUVENILE: Similar to red-morph female.

Geographic Variation Two groups of subspecies: the Taiga Grouse (*canadensis, atratus, canace,* and *isleibi*) and the Franklin's Grouse (*franklinii*). Some argue that the Franklin's Grouse of the northern Rockies and Cascades should be considered a separate species from the Taiga Grouse (*canadensis*) found throughout the rest the range. The Franklin's has bold white spots on the uppertail coverts, and on males the tail is uniformly dark. Courtship displays also differ: Both give strutting displays where the male spreads his tail, erects the red combs above his eyes, and rapidly beats his wings; some give a series of low hoots. In territorial flight display, the Taiga male flutters upward on shallow wing strokes; the Franklin's, however, ends the performance by beating his wings together, which produces a loud clapping sound.

Similar Species Compared with the Blue and Ruffed Grouse, the Spruce appears to have a shorter tail.

The female Spruce is similar to the Blue, but it has more heavily marked underparts. The Ruffed has a broad black subterminal tail band.

Voice Relatively quiet outside the breeding season. CALL: Birds in foraging groups give a *sreep*. The female gives a high-pitched call that is thought to be territorial.

Status & Distribution Rare to fairly common resident of conifer forests, particularly early successional stages with young dense trees. Franklin's Grouse is also found in more open subalpine habitats. Usually found near conifers, but when dispersing in fall may be seen in deciduous woods.

Population Population declines in the southern perimeter of the species' range are possibly due to changes in habitat; populations are generally stable in the northern part of the range. Fires are important to renew the Spruce's favored habitat.

gray morph ♀

♂

BLUE GROUSE *Dendragapus obscurus*

This dusky gray grouse is highly sought after by visitors to western states and provinces. A displaying Blue Grouse is a sight particularly

northern Rockies ♂
obscurus

southern Rockies ♀
richardsonii

memorable, as it struts with tail fanned, body tipped forward, head drawn in, and wings lowered, revealing brightly colored bare skin patches on the sides of the neck. Polytypic. L 21" (51 cm)

Identification A relatively large and long-tailed grouse. MALE: Sooty gray overall. On each side of the neck, white-based feathers cover an inflatable neck sac that is either yellow or magenta. Prominent yellow eye combs become orange or red during display. FEMALE: Similar to male but more mottled brown above, with a rather uniform grayish belly. JUVENILE: Similar to female but with fine pale streaks above. Tail is heavily mottled brown.

Geographic Variation Eight subspecies are separable into 2 subspecies groups: The coastal Sooty Grouse (*fuliginosus*

group: *sitensis, fuliginosus, sierrae,* and *howardi*) and the interior Dusky Grouse (*obscurus* group: *richardsonii, pallidus, obscurus, oreinus*). The Sooty is noticeably darker than the Dusky. The male's hooting is also different: Sooty songs frequently delivered from high in tree and consist of 6 higher-pitched syllables that can be heard at distances of a quarter mile. The less vocal Dusky delivers hoots from on or near ground; the 5 low syllables are rarely audible at distances over 55 yards. Populations of Dusky in the northern Rockies (sometimes called Richardson's Grouse—*richardsonii* and *pallidus*) lack or nearly lack the tail band found on all other Blues.

Similar Species The female looks similar to the Spruce Grouse, but it has less heavily patterned underparts. The

Spruce is also smaller and has a shorter tail. The Ruffed Grouse has a broad black subterminal tail band and more

coastal ♂
fuliginosus

barred underparts.

Voice CALLS: Both sexes give various soft clucking sounds and low *gr gr gr gr*.

Status & Distribution Fairly common resident of open coniferous and mixed woodlands, brushy lowlands, and mountain slopes. In parts of range, the Dusky wanders into sagebrush flats. MOVEMENTS: Many individuals move from relatively open areas during the breeding season to dense conifer forest; depending on the location this may be downslope, but more frequently to higher elevations.

Population The Blue Grouse has declined in California and has been

extirpated from the southern portion of its range. Coastal populations apparently fluctuate more than those of the interior.

Genus Meleagris

WILD TURKEY *Meleagris gallopavo*

Writing to his daughter, Benjamin Franklin observed that the Wild Turkey would have made a better national symbol for the United States than the Bald Eagle, proclaiming it "a bird of courage." The Wild Turkey is among our best-known birds. After major declines, the Wild Turkey is once again regularly encountered in open woods bordered by clearings, particularly where oaks are prevalent. At night it roosts in trees. Polytypic. L ♂46" (117 cm) ♀37" (94 cm)

Identification The Wild Turkey is the largest game bird in North America, albeit smaller and more slender than its domesticated cousin. MALE: Dark, iridescent body, flight feathers barred with white, red wattles, blackish breast tuft, spurred legs; bare-skinned head is blue and pink.

FEMALE AND IMMATURE: Smaller, duller, and often lack the breast tuft of the male.

Geographic Variation Four of the 6 recognized subspecies occur north of Mexico. The widespread Eastern Turkey *(silvestris)* has tail, uppertail coverts, and lower rump feathers tipped with chestnut. These feathers are tipped a buff white in the Merriam's Turkey (found in the Great Plains and Rockies). The Rio Grande Turkey *(intermedia),* found from Kansas south to Mexico, is intermediate in plumage; in fall and winter it forms huge flocks of up to 500 birds (40–50 typical of other subspecies). The Peninsular Florida *(osceola)* is similar to the Eastern Turkey, but smaller. Introductions of subspecies outside of native range and presence of escaped and released domestic birds and resultant interbreeding greatly complicates regional variation.

Similar Species None.

Voice CALL: The distinctive gobble given by males in spring may be heard a mile away. Other calls include various yelps, clucks, and rattles.

♂ western
merriami

Status & Distribution Restocked in much of its former range and introduced in other areas; now found in each of the lower 48 states and southernmost Canada.

Population The Wild Turkey declined throughout its range in the 19th and early 20th century; the loss was generally blamed on overhunting and habitat loss. Since then, the species has rebounded dramatically with an estimated population of nearly 4 million. Population numbers in Mexico remain extremely low.

eastern
silvestris

PTARMIGAN Genus Lagopus

All three ptarmigan species are found in North America: The White-tailed is endemic to the mountains of the West; the Rock and Willow Ptarmigan are circumpolar. They have thickly feathered toes and tarsi, short tails, and cryptic plumages. All but the "Red Grouse" of the British Isles molt to a near completely white plumage in winter.

WILLOW PTARMIGAN Lagopus lagopus

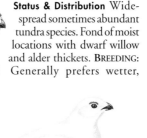

The largest ptarmigan, the circumpolar Willow is characteristic of willow flats and low dense vegetation near tree line. It has the most widespread distribution of any grouse. Polytypic (19 ssp. worldwide; 7 in N.A.). L 15" (38 cm)

Identification Both sexes have a black tail, predominantly white wings, and white feathered legs year-round. The red eye combs are more pronounced in males; they may be largely concealed or inflated during courtship or aggression. MALE: Mottled summer plumage predominately rufous. White winter plumage similar to Rock Ptarmigan but face white (without black eye line). BREEDING FEMALE: Warm brown; very similar in plumage to Rock Ptarmigan. JUVENILE: Heavily barred black and buffy yellow. Dark wings for a short period in summer.

Geographic Variation Extensive regional variation. Differences in both sex and molt complicate subspecies recognition.

Similar Species The Willow is larger than the Rock Ptarmigan and has a bigger bill. Vocalizations and habitat are helpful in identification. While the Willow will move upslope in mountains, it is restricted to relatively lush patches of vegetation. The nonbreeding male Willow's relatively uniformly patterned face and head does not have the distinctive dark eye line of the male Rock.

Voice In displays, male utters a loud raucous *go-back go-back go-backa go-backa go-backa*. CALL: Low growls and croaks; noisy cackles.

Status & Distribution Widespread sometimes abundant tundra species. Fond of moist locations with dwarf willow and alder thickets. BREEDING: Generally prefers wetter,

brushier habitat than the Rock Ptarmigan. MOVEMENTS: Vary between largely resident populations with only short shifts between breeding and wintering ranges, to relatively long-distance migrants. Thousands have been recorded in a day moving through Anaktuvuk Pass, AK. Flocks of up to 2,000 individuals have been recorded in migration. MIGRATION: Fall peak at Anaktuvuk in mid-Oct. Spring migration begins as early as mid-Jan., peaking late Apr. VAGRANT: Casual in spring and winter to southern ON, southern SK, and northern tier states (e.g., MT, ND, MN, WI, and ME).

Population Substantial cyclic ups and downs in populations over several-year periods. Little data on changes, but apparently stable. Most of range is remote, but disturbance from natural resource extraction, accumulation of toxins, and climate changes are all potential concerns.

summer ♀ · molting spring ♂ · summer ♂ · winter

WHITE-TAILED PTARMIGAN Lagopus leucura

molting fall ♂ · summer ♂ · summer ♀

The White-tailed Ptarmigan is the smallest grouse in North America, and it is the only ptarmigan regularly found in the lower 48. Its ability to blend in perfectly with its remote alpine tundra environment makes it among the most challenging resident species to find. Territorial during the breeding season, the White-tailed forms flocks of up to 80 birds from late October to late April. During winter, it roosts under the snow. The White-tailed forages largely on buds, stems, and seeds

year-round, but it augments this diet with insects in the summer. Polytypic. L 12.5" (32 cm)

Identification WINTER: Completely white except for eye combs, dark eye and bill and fine dark shaft streaks to primaries. SUMMER MALE: More white on belly than female; conspicuous coarsely barred brown and black breast feathers form a necklace. SUMMER FEMALE: More evenly patterned with barring of buffy yellow and black. JUVENILE: Heavily barred black and buffy yellow and have dark wings for a short period in summer.

Geographic Variation Clinal among 5 subspecies; average larger and grayer in the south, smaller and darker in the north.

Similar Species A white tail distinguishes it from the Willow and Rock Ptarmigan in all seasons; however, the tail feathers in all ptarmigan are typically concealed by the uppertail coverts, making it difficult to judge tail color.

Voice Males give a loud raucous flight call with 4 distinct syllables, *ku-ku-KII-KIIEUR;* also a variable chattering clucking series of calls given on the ground, *duk-duk-DAAAK-duk-duk; duk-DAK-DADAAK-duk.* CALL: Clucks, churrs, and high-pitched chirps.

Status & Distribution Endemic to mountains of the West where it is found in rocky alpine areas at or above timberline. Uncommon to locally common. Small numbers have been introduced in the Wallowa Mountains, Sierra Nevada, Pike's Peak, and the Uinta Mountains. Reintroduced into northern NM. MOVEMENTS: Depends on severity of winter and snowfall, but usually moves to lower elevations; during heavy snow years moves to streambeds and avalanche chutes dominated by willows and alders.

Population Numbers fluctuate widely among years, but there is little data on population changes. Local populations may be affected by natural resource extraction, road construction, off-road vehicles, and overgrazing by domestic livestock and elk; these activities have the greatest effect on reducing winter forage, principally willow. Population on Vancouver Island *(saxatilis)* considered vulnerable.

winter

ROCK PTARMIGAN *Lagopus muta*

The Rock Ptarmigan is the archetypal bird of the arctic. Found in cold and barren windswept tundra, it has been recorded as far north as 75° N in winter, when the region is enshrouded in 24 hours of darkness. Like other ptarmigan it has an unusual sequence of three body molts each year, generally allowing it to remain well camouflaged at all times of the year. Males molt later than females in spring. By early June many are still mostly white and can be spotted from up to a mile away; at the same time the females have completed their molts and are difficult to spot from a few feet away. Polytypic (26–30 ssp.; 14 in N.A.). L 14" (36 cm)

Identification Like the Willow Ptarmigan, both sexes have a black tail, predominantly white wings, and white feathered legs year-round. The mottled summer plumage is black, dark brown or grayish brown, the exact patterning varies with subspecies. ADULT MALE: White winter plumage is similar to the Willow Ptarmigan but the black eye line is prominent. ADULT FEMALE: She is very difficult to distinguish from a Willow Ptarmigan except by overall size and bill size. JUVENILE: It is heavily barred black and buffy yellow and has dark wings for a short period in summer.

Geographic Variation Extensive regional variation. Individual variation and complex molt complicates subspecies identification. Subspecies on the Aleutians are larger with heavier bill. Males on westernmost Aleutians are mostly blackish in breeding plumage; central Aleutian males more ocher toned.

Similar Species The Rock Ptarmigan is smaller than the Willow Ptarmigan, and with a smaller bill. Use caution when estimating bill size as the dark feathers between the eye and bill on birds in transitional plumages can give the impression that the bill is larger. The presence of dark lores is diagnostic for male Rock Ptarmigan (their absence is not diagnostic).

Voice In courtship and territorial flight displays, male utters a low rattling *ah-AAAH-ah-AAAAH-a-a-a-a.* CALL: Low growls and croaks; noisy cackles.

Status & Distribution Common. BREEDING: Generally prefers higher and more barren habitat than the Willow Ptarmigan. MOVEMENTS: May withdraw from northernmost summer range, but only irregularly south of the southern boundary of the breeding range. Most make only limited movements, which are largely altitudinal and likely influenced by weather and snow depth. Populations on the Aleutian Islands are resident. VAGRANT: The bird is accidental in Queen Charlotte Is., BC, and most remarkably northeastern MN.

summer ♀ summer ♂

Population Numbers fluctuate. Some southern populations may have contracted. Most of range is remote, but disturbance from natural resource extraction and climate changes are potential concerns. Populations in the Aleutian Islands declined as a result of non-native arctic fox introductions.

fall ♂

winter ♂

winter ♀

PRAIRIE GROUSE Genus Tympanuchus

Endemic to North America, the three species of *Tympanuchus* are found in open grasslands and brushy habitats. They are generally barred or mottled in shades of brown, black, and pale buff. The males have colorful neck sacs and tufts (pinnae) on their head that they inflate and raise during their foot-stomping springtime displays.

SHARP-TAILED GROUSE *Tympanuchus phasianellus*

Early each spring, Sharp-taileds gather at leks located on rather open elevated sites. The male inflates his purplish neck sacs, rapidly stomps his feet, bows his wings, and shakes his tail rapidly from side to side, producing a distinctive rattling sound. A variety of cackles and low coos accompany the performance. In other seasons, the Sharp-tailed is more difficult to see. During winter, look for it feeding on buds and catkins in deciduous trees early and late in the day. Where ranges overlap, it occasionally hybridizes with the Greater Prairie-Chicken and Greater Sage-Grouse; at least one record of hybridization with Blue Grouse. Polytypic. L 17" (43 cm)

Identification Similar to prairie-chickens, but underparts scaled and spotted. ADULT: Pointed tail, with central rectrices extending far beyond the others. Yellow eye combs (sometimes difficult to see). Small erectile crest most noticeable when bird agitated. Female smaller and with a less contrasting facial pattern. JUVENILE: Like female, but shorter central tail feathers and outer tail more brownish (not white).

Geographic Variation The northern subspecies (*caurus, kennicotti, phasianellus,* and *campestris*) are darker, with heavy markings below and bold pale spotting on upperparts. The southern subspecies (*columbianus,* and *jamesi*) are paler brown and more uniform.

Similar Species The Greater Prairie-Chicken is always heavily barred below; it also has a rounded tail shape and color to edge. The Ring-necked Pheasant is superficially similar but is larger with a much longer tail, unfeathered legs, and less heavily marked underparts.

displaying ♂

Voice CALL: Various clucks and peeps; also a 3-note *whucker-whucker-whucker* given in flight.

Status & Distribution Fairly common in most of range; rare in western portions of range.

BREEDING: Open and brushy habitats including grasslands, sagebrush, woodland edges, and river canyons. MOVEMENTS: Sedentary, but snowcover may induce movements to more wooded areas.

Population Habitat destruction and fragmentation led to declines throughout much of its southern range; populations generally stable in north. Extirpated from California and Oregon; reintroductions underway in some places.

GREATER PRAIRIE-CHICKEN *Tympanuchus cupido*

The once widespread Greater Prairie-Chicken is now very local in mixed-grass and tallgrass prairie. It is best found and appreciated in early spring, when males gather at hilltop leks; the sounds of their dramatic booming display may carry for nearly a mile. Polytypic. L 17" (43 cm)

Identification Heavily barred above and below with dark brown, cinnamon, and pale buff. Barring on underparts broader. MALE: Uniformly dark, short, rounded tail; yellow-orange neck sacs (inflated during the breeding season); and long pinnae, erected in displays to form "rabbit ears." FEMALE: A subtle version of the male, with smaller pinnae, indistinct eye combs, and barred tail. JUVENILE: Resembles female but is smaller with white shaft streaks on upperparts.

displaying ♂

Geographic Variation Three subspecies recognized; the 2 coastal subspecies are darker. Attwater's Prairie-Chicken (*attwateri*) of southeastern Texas is nearly extinct. The Heath Hen, nominate *cupido,* is now extinct but was once found on the coastal plain from Massachusetts to Virginia; the last record was on Martha's Vineyard in 1932. The widespread *pinnatus* is found in the rest of the species range.

Similar Species Lesser Prairie-Chicken is best separated by range. The Greater is slightly larger, with darker, broader, and more uniform barring on underparts. The Sharp-tailed Grouse is similar but is more heavily scalloped and spotted below with a pointed tail.

Voice Courting males make a deep low *ooAH-hooooom* sound known as "booming," often likened to the sound of blowing across a bottle, and also give a variety of wild frenzied cackles and yelps. CALL: Both sexes give a variety of clucking notes.

Status & Distribution Uncommon and local;

Attwater's Prairie Chicken is endangered. MOVEMENTS: Poorly understood; show no clear relationship with weather or food availability. Typically less than 25 miles between breeding and wintering areas.

Population Greater Prairie-Chickens have experienced enormous declines in much of their range. The species was extirpated from Tennesee (1850); Kentucky (1874); Arkansas (1913); Louisiana (*attwateri,* 1919); Texas (*pinnatus,* 1925); Ohio (1934); Indiana (1972); Iowa (1984); Alberta (1965); Manitoba (1970); Ontario (1975); and

Saskatchewan (1976). Some of the first conservation legislation in the United States was passed in 1791 to protect the Heath Hen from market hunting—efforts that ultimately failed. Market hunting was a major component in historic declines. Today, habitat destruction, deterioration, and fragmentation pose threats. Small isolated populations also face genetic, demographic, and environmental uncertainties. Conservation and reintroduction efforts exist in many areas. Some, such as efforts by the Colorado Division of Wildlife and local communities in northeastern

Colorado, have been extremely successful in rebuilding Greater Prairie-Chicken numbers.

LESSER PRAIRIE-CHICKEN *Tympanuchus pallidicinctus*

displaying ♂

♀

This shortgrass prairie grouse has a very limited range in the southern Great Plains. It is best looked for during early spring at leks on relatively open sites on exposed hills and ridges. During this time, the differences between the Lesser and the Greater Prairie-Chicken are best appreciated. Note the Lesser's dull orange-red neck sacs; its more maniacal wails and cackles; and slight differences in displays. Monotypic. L 16" (41 cm)

Identification Very similar to Greater Prairie-Chicken; see below for separation from that species. As with the Greater, the Lesser male has a uniformly dark tail while that of the female is barred. The Lesser juvenile is also similar to a Greater but is slightly paler.

Similar Species Best separated from Greater Prairie-Chicken by range; the two species come very close in central Kansas and Oklahoma, but do not overlap. The Lesser is slightly smaller than the Greater, with paler barring on the underparts, which is narrower and less uniform in width. The barring typically becomes paler on the center of the belly. On the Greater the barring is bold throughout the breast and

belly; the upperparts are more finely barred with black edging. There is much individual variation.

Voice CALL: Similar to the Greater Prairie-Chicken; male's courtship calls are higher, more piercing, and even more demonic than the Greater's.

Status & Distribution Uncommon and local; found in sand sagebrush-bluestem and shinnery oak-bluestem ecosystems. MOVEMENTS: Sedentary, although more likely to be found in agricultural fields during winter.

Population This species has declined by an estimated 97 percent since the 1800s, including a 92 percent reduction in range (78 percent since 1963). Conversion of native habitat to crop-

land, excessive grazing by livestock, and herbicide control of sand sagebrush and shinnery oak all contributed to habitat loss. Hunting likely played some role in early declines. Droughts have exacerbated all these factors.

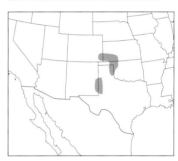

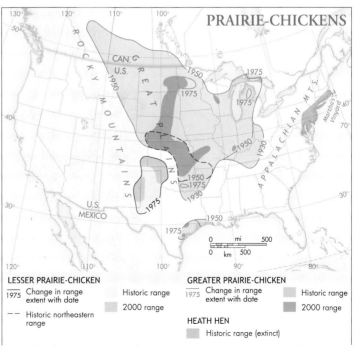

PRAIRIE-CHICKENS

LESSER PRAIRIE-CHICKEN

1975 Change in range extent with date

– – Historic northeastern range

Historic range

2000 range

GREATER PRAIRIE-CHICKEN

1975 Change in range extent with date

Historic range

2000 range

HEATH HEN

Historic range (extinct)

NEW WORLD QUAIL Family Odontophoridae

Gambel's Quail, male (center) and females (AZ, May)

This family composed primarily of terrestrial gamebirds is restricted to the New World; it includes both temperate and tropical members. Many species have crests and head plumes as well as rather ornate body plumage. Omnivorous, they feed on insects as well as mast from a variety of plants.

Structure Of small to medium size, these birds have heavy bodies and rather small heads. All have stout bills with slightly serrated cutting edges, and long toes and short tarsi, which do not develop spurs. A long tail separates the wood-partridges from the rest of the family.
Behavior In general, New World quail are found in pairs during the breeding season and in groups otherwise.
Plumage They generally exhibit sexual dimorphism, although it ranges from strong in some quail to weak in wood-quail to virtually nonexistent in the wood-partridges. Although the overall plumage of most species is dominated by grays and browns, many species are quite ornate. Most species of quail have crests or head plumes or distinctive head plumage.
Distribution Found from southwestern Canada to Paraguay, the family reaches its greatest diversity in western N.A. and Mexico, but there is excellent diversity in the Andes.
Taxonomy This family informally divides into 3 groups: wood-partridges, quail, and wood-quail. Worldwide, there are 32 species in 9 genera recognized.
Conservation Poorly studied, wood-partridges pose a conservation concern, as do at least 4 tropical wood-quail. BirdLife International lists 5 species as threatened, with 3 more as near threatened. —*Mark W. Lockwood*

Genus *Callipepla*

SCALED QUAIL *Callipepla squamata*

A bird of the desert grasslands, mesquite savanna, and thorn-scrub of the Southwest, the Scaled Quail is generally sedentary, moving short distances to form winter coveys. Fall and winter coveys can have as many as 200 individuals. It prefers to run to escape, but it will fly when startled. Hybrids with Gambel's Quail and Northern Bobwhite have been documented. Polytypic (3 ssp.; 2 in N.A.). L 10" (25 cm)
Identification This quail is plump and short-tailed and has grayish plumage. The bluish gray breast and mantle feathers are edged in black or brown giving it a scaled appearance.

ADULT: Sexes are similar. The male has a prominent white crest; the female's is smaller and buffier in coloration.
JUVENILE: Similar to adults but more mottled above and less conspicuous scaling on the underparts.
Geographic Variation The *pallida* inhabits most of the Scaled's range in N.A., whereas the *castanogastris* occurs in southern Texas, below the Balcones Escarpment. A chestnut patch on the belly and darker overall plumage, particularly on the upperparts, separates *castanogastris* from *pallida*. Some authors divide *pallida* into 2 weakly defined taxa, *pallida* and *hargravi*.
Similar Species The distinctive Scaled is unlikely to be confused with any other quail in N.A.
Voice During the breeding season, both sexes give a location call when separated, a nasal

chip-churr, accented on the second note. The male's advertising call is a rhythmic *kuck-yur,* often followed by a sharp *ching*.
Status & Distribution Fairly common year-round resident.
Population Scaled Quail has declined dramatically in the United States since the 1940s. In Texas, the species has become increasingly scarce in the Hill Country and Rolling Plains; reasons for the decline are unknown, but they are probably attributable to habitat degradation. Scaleds are still abundant in the Trans-Pecos northward to the Texas Panhandle.

pallida ♂

juvenile

South Texas ♂
castanogastris

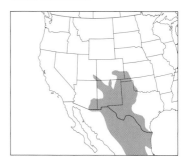

CALIFORNIA QUAIL *Callipepla californica*

Although highly sedentary, the California Quail congregates in large coveys during the fall and winter. It hybridizes with the Gambel's Quail where their ranges overlap. Polytypic (5 ssp.; 4 in N.A.). L 10" (25 cm)

Identification The California is a plump, short-tailed quail with gray and brown plumage; a prominent teardrop-shaped head plume or double plume is present in both sexes. ADULT MALE: Pale forehead with brown crown and black throat, scaled belly with a chestnut patch, brown upperparts. ADULT FEMALE: Similar to adult male but muted and lacking distinctive facial pattern; head plume smaller. JUVENILE: Grayish brown to brown overall and heavily mottled.

Belly pale and lacking the scaled appearance of the adults. Usually has a short head plume.

Geographic Variation Subspecies variation is based on differences in coloration and size, which are more pronounced in females. Adult female *canfieldae* (found in east-central CA) and *californica* (the most widespread subspecies) have grayish upperparts; adult female *brunescens* (found in the more mesic coastal mountains) have brown upperparts. The *catalinensis* subspecies is endemic to Santa Catalina Island.

Similar Species The California is similar in structure and size to the Gambel's Quail, but the Gambel's lacks the scaled underparts and brown sides and crown.

Voice CALL: An emphatic *chi-ca-go* similar to the Gambel's, but lower pitched and usually 3 notes; sometimes shortened on only 1 or 2 syllables. A variety of grunts and sharp cackles are also made.

Status & Distribution Common year-round in open woodlands and brushy foothills, usually near permanent water sources. It has adapted well to urban

♀ *californica*

coastal ♀ *brunescens*

coastal juvenile *brunescens*

♂ *californica*

development where sufficient cover is provided. This species has been introduced locally within the general boundaries of the mapped range, including UT. Successful introductions have been made in HI, Argentina, Chile, and New Zealand.

Population Since 1960, the overall population has declined in the U.S.

GAMBEL'S QUAIL *Callipepla gambelii*

juvenile

Although a common quail of the desert Southwest, the Gambel's requires a lot of water. Generally sedentary, it moves short distances in the late summer to form coveys, usually comprising several family groups. It hybridizes with both California and Scaled Quails where their ranges overlap. Polytypic (2 ssp.; nominate in N.A.). L 10" (25 cm)

Identification Plump, short-tailed quail with gray plumage; prominent teardrop-shaped head plume or dou-

ble plume in both sexes. ADULT MALE: Chestnut crown with black forehead and black throat; chestnut sides with whitish underparts with a black belly; gray upperparts. ADULT FEMALE: Similar to adult male but muted and lacking distinctive facial pattern. Head plume smaller. JUVENILE: Grayish brown overall and heavily mottled. Usually has a short head plume.

Similar Species The California is similar in structure and size, but the chestnut crown and sides and lack of scaling on

the Gambel's easily separate them.

Voice CALL: A plaintive *qua-el;* and a loud *chi-ca-go-go* similar to the California's, but higher pitched and usually 4 notes, sometimes shortened on only 1 or 2 syllables. Also a variety of clucking and chattering calls.

Status & Distribution Common year-round in desert shrublands and thickets, usually near permanent water sources. Introduced to HI, ID, and San Clemente I., CA.

Population The numbers appear to be stable over the past 60 years. The Gambel's seems to be more tolerant of habitat disturbances than other *Callipepla*.

Genera *Colinus, Oreortyx,* and *Cyrtonyx*

NORTHERN BOBWHITE *Colinus virginianus*

juvenile

"Masked Bobwhite"
♂ *ridgwayi*

The Northern Bobwhite, found in coveys except during breeding season, is the most widespread and familiar quail in North America. It exhibits the greatest range of geographic variation of any galliform. Polytypic (20 ssp.; 4 in N.A.). L 9.7" (25 cm)

Identification Plump, short-tailed quail with reddish brown plumage. ADULT MALE: Intricate body plumage of chestnut, brown, and white; blackish plumage on head; white throat and eye line. ADULT FEMALE: Similar to adult male but throat and eye line buffy and plumage on head brown. JUVENILE: Similar to adult female but body plumage browner, less rufous, and eye line less prominent. RUFOUS MORPH: Very rufous body plumage masks markings. Black face superficially resembles the "Masked Bobwhite." Extremely rare. "MASKED BOB-WHITE": Similar to eastern birds, but it has a black face with the white eye line greatly reduced and flecked with black. Underparts are entirely rufous with white markings on the flanks; the upperparts have prominent rufous markings, becoming browner on the lower back and rump.

Geographic Variation The Northern Bobwhite is remarkably complex, with differences sometimes being striking in the plumage of the adult male. The species is often broken into 4 distinct groups, 2 of which occur in the U.S. The northern group occurs in eastern N.A.; it is made up of 5 similar subspecies that are differentiated by changes in overall coloration and the width of barring on the underparts. The second group is the "Masked Bobwhite" *(ridgwayi)* found in southern Arizona and Sonora; at times it has been considered a separate species.

Similar Species The Northern Bobwhite is distinctive; no similar species exist within its range. The Montezuma Quail is superficially similar, but its range overlaps with the Northern Bobwhite's only in south-central Texas.

Voice The male's advertising call is a whistled *bob-WHITE* or *bob-bob-WHITE.* Other calls include a low whistled *ka-lo-kee* and a variety of clucks.

Status & Distribution Uncommon to common year-round in a variety of open habitats with sufficient brushy cover. Introduced to northwestern N.A., the Bahamas, several Caribbean islands, and New Zealand. The "Masked Bobwhite" is rare in the Altar Valley of southern AZ and is the result of a reintroduction effort from remaining populations in Sonora; it is federally listed as endangered.

Population Although still locally common, Northern Bobwhite has declined significantly in the U.S. Manipulation of habitat and the high populations of the introduced fire ant are believed to be key factors in the decline. Dramatic declines have left the species virtually extirpated in many areas where it was once common. The native population of "Masked Bobwhite" was extirpated from the U.S. by 1900.

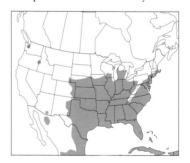

MOUNTAIN QUAIL *Oreortyx pictus*

Although fairly common in much of its range, the Mountain Quail is very shy and hard to find under most circumstances. This bird is perhaps best seen when males call from rocks or in late summer, when family groups often forage along roadsides near dense brush, which provides cover for a quick escape. This species seems to occur with greater frequency in mixed evergreen woodlands on mountain slopes than in chaparral or riparian corridors. As with other quail, the Mountain is more successful where permanent water is available. As its name suggests, this species can be found on mountain slopes at elevations as high as 10,000 feet. Winter coveys often consist of family groups numbering less than 10 birds, but they can include up to 20. Polytypic (5 ssp.; 4 in N.A.). L 11" (28 cm)

Identification Plump, short-tailed quail with gray and brown plumage. Two long, thin head plumes present in both sexes. ADULT MALE: Brown or grayish brown above; slate blue chest and chestnut belly barred with white on the flanks; slate blue crown with chestnut throat bordered in white. ADULT FEMALE: Very similar to adult male, but normally has shorter, brownish plumes and brown mottling on the hind neck in interior populations. JUVENILE: Dull version of the adult. Lacks bold flank pattern and the rich coloration of the face and throat pattern. Body more mottled with dark and light edging.

Geographic Variation Subspecies differ in general coloration of the back and breast. The interior subspecies—*plumifer, eremophilus,* and *russelli*—

are grayer above, generally lacking brown mottling in the nape and breast. The *russelli* is confined to the Little San Bernardino Mountains in California. The nominate subspecies is found in more mesic habitats and is brown on the nape with some brown mottling on the sides of the breast. This subspecies now includes *palmeri*.

Similar Species The Mountain Quail is distinctive; no similar species exist within its range. The California and Gambel's Quail share some common characteristics, but a reasonable view of the bird should provide a straightforward identification; long head plumes and chestnut throat eliminate both species. The prominent white bars on chestnut flanks are often a key mark in distinguishing this species when seen in heavy cover. A juvenile Mountain is more like a California in plumage, but its straight head plumes and less intricate belly

plumages eliminate possible confusion. **Voice** The male's advertising call is a clear, descending *quee-ark* that can carry up to a mile away. The covey call that is frequently given is an extended series of whistled *kow* or *cle* notes. **Status & Distribution** Locally common in

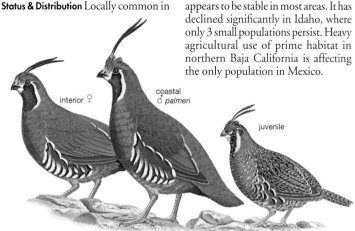

interior ♀

coastal ♂ *palmeri*

juvenile

evergreen woodlands, chaparral, brushy ravines, and mountain slopes. Nominate subspecies introduced on Vancouver I. WINTER: Some descend to lower elevations, usually on foot. **Population** The population in the U.S. appears to be stable in most areas. It has declined significantly in Idaho, where only 3 small populations persist. Heavy agricultural use of prime habitat in northern Baja California is affecting the only population in Mexico.

MONTEZUMA QUAIL *Cyrtonyx montezumae*

♂

♀

juvenile

The Montezuma Quail is perhaps the most attractive quail in North America. The elaborate plumage of the male provides a very cryptic pattern in tall grasses or in dappled sunlight under a shrub. The Montezuma has highly specialized long claws, used for digging up bulbs and tubers. It remains in pairs all summer, although nesting often does not begin until the monsoon rains of July and August. It is often seen cautiously crossing roads or in grassy areas along roadsides. When chanced upon, it prefers to crouch to remain hidden rather than run or fly away. In winter, it forms into small coveys (rarely more than 15 birds). Populations appear to be as much as 60 percent male, enhancing mate selection in females. It is more closely related to

the forest dwelling wood-quail of the neotropics than other species in N.A. Polytypic (5 ssp.; *mearnsi* in N.A.). L 8.7" (22 cm) **Identification** Plump, short-tailed, round-winged quail. ADULT MALE: Distinctive facial pattern with a rounded brown crest on the back of the head; brown upperparts, but heavily marked with black and tan; dark chestnut breast; black sides and flanks, heavily spotted with white. ADULT FEMALE: Brown overall with mostly unmarked pinkish brown underparts; upperparts heavily marked with black and tan; brown rounded crest on the back of the head; face somewhat lighter tan than remainder of the body. IMMATURE MALE: Seen only in late summer. A pale gray face; black sides and flanks, heavily spotted with white. Distinctive facial pattern appears in late fall. JUVENILE: Similar to adult female, but lighter in overall color and more heavily mottled with black.

Similar Species The Montezuma Quail is unmistakable; no similar species exist within its range. The Northern Bobwhite is superficially similar to the Montezuma, but their ranges overlap only in south-central Texas.

Voice The male's advertising call is a descending whistled *vwirrrrr*. The covey call, which is given by both sexes, is a loud descending whistle. Contact calls are a rather quiet *whi-whi*. **Status & Distribution** Uncommon, secretive and local in open juniper-oak or pine-oak woodlands on semiarid slopes.

Population The Montezuma was once much more widespread in North America. In Texas, it was found throughout all mountain ranges and in the central portion of the state east to San Antonio. In Arizona and New Mexico, it was more widespread in the mountain ranges in the southern half of each state. By 1950, the population had shrunk to its current range. Tall grasses in oak-juniper woodlands are believed to be an important part of habitat quality; when these grasses are reduced by more than half, quail no longer find the habitat suitable.

LOONS Family Gaviidae

Pacific Loon, breeding (MB, June)

L oons, usually called "divers" in the Old World, present major identification challenges in both breeding and winter plumages: Swimming birds dive frequently, making them difficult to study, and flying birds rarely allow prolonged views. On swimming birds note the bill shape (stout or slender, straight or with any uptilt), head shape, and overall head-and-bill proportions and posture. In breeding plumages, note the overall patterns, especially of the head, neck, and back. On winter and juvenal plumages, details of the dark/light patterning on the head and neck are important, in combination with bill shape and color. (See sidebar p. 60 for identification of loons in flight.)

Structure Bodies are long and heavy, with large webbed feet set well back; bills are strong and dagger-shaped. Wings are relatively small with 10 primaries and 22 to 24 secondaries; tails are small and short, with 16 to 20 rectrices. Males are up to 10 percent larger than females.

Behavior Loons are aquatic birds that swim and dive with proficiency. Birds trying to avoid predators can swim very low in the water, whereas resting birds sometimes ride quite high and buoyantly, and preening birds often roll to the side, exposing their flanks and even belly. Such differences in posture can help determine the extent and pattern of white along a bird's sides. Flight is fairly heavy and direct, with steady, measured wingbeats; the neck held outstretched and often slightly below the body plane; the large feet are visible beyond the short tail.

Plumage Plumages are mostly monochromatic, with breeding adults more boldly patterned than winter adults and juveniles; sexes look similar. Juveniles and first-summer birds resemble winter adults. Second-summer birds resemble breeding adults but with messier, less complete breeding patterns, especially on the head and neck. Adult plumage aspect is attained in the third winter. Molt occurs mostly away from the breeding grounds. Loons have high wing loading and shed their remiges synchronously, becoming flightless for a few weeks. The smaller Red-throated Loon has its complete prebasic molt in late fall, whereas the other loons split their prebasic molt: The head and body feathers are molted in late fall, and the wings in late winter or early spring (when wing molt can overlap with the start of prealternate head/body molt).

Distribution High-latitude breeders throughout the Northern Hemisphere, loons are short- to mid-distance migrants that winter south in the New World to the southern United States and northern Mexico. Nonbreeding immatures often remain south in summer.

Taxonomy Five species in 1 genus, *Gavia*, make up the modern-day loon family; all occur in North America.

Conservation Oil spills present a major threat to nonbreeding populations in marine waters. Industrial poisons (such as mercury) may affect both breeding and wintering populations. Human disturbance and acid rain affect nesting Common Loons at more southerly lakes.
—*Steve N. G. Howell*

Genus Gavia

ARCTIC LOON *Gavia arctica*

This Old World species' breeding range extends into western Alaska, where it is a prized find to be distinguished with care from the much commoner Pacific Loon. A small number of individuals have been found in winter along the Pacific coast. Polytypic (2 ssp.; 1 in N.A.). L 24–28" (61–71 cm).

Identification Resembles the Pacific Loon, but averages larger, with a longer and stouter bill, and often a more angular forehead. The Arctic's single best field mark in all plumages is the white anterior feathering of its femoral tract, which shows as a white flank patch on swimming birds and a white flank bulge on flying birds. Otherwise, all age-related variation and molts are like the Pacific, except breeding. BREEDING ADULT: Arctic's hind neck is a slightly duskier, smoky gray, and its throat patch is glossed green. WINTER ADULT AND JUVENILE: The dusky chinstrap common on the Pacific is usually lacking on the Arctic.

Geographic Variation North American records are of the eastern Eurasian subspecies, *viridigularis*, distinguished from nominate *arctica* of western Eurasia by its slightly larger size and a more greenish sheen to the breeding adult's throat patch.

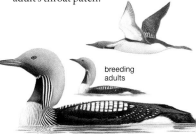

breeding adults

winter adult

Similar Species A Pacific Loon averages smaller, with a rounder head that accentuates the smaller bill, and it lacks well-defined white femoral patches, but a swimming bird can show white along the waterline. Usually this is an untidy patch at about mid-body. The Arctic has a generally neater patch that flares up at the back. A breeding Pacific has a paler crown and nape, and a purple-glossed throat patch bordered

winter adult

by less contrasting white stripes that are separated from the chest striping by a narrow black bar (stripes typically merge on the Arctic). A winter/juvenile Pacific often has a distinct dark chinstrap and averages paler on the hind neck. A winter/juvenile Common Loon is larger and bulkier with a stouter bill, a broken whitish eye ring, a more irregular dark/white border to the neck sides (suggesting the breeding pattern), and the hind neck is darker than the back, the opposite of the Arctic.
Voice: Similar to the

juvenile

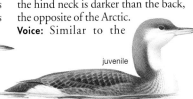

Pacific Loon, but lower pitched.
Status & Distribution Eurasia and western AK. BREEDING: Rare in N.A., small- to large tundra lakes. MIGRATION: In Bering Sea, western Aleutians. WINTER: Casual south along Pacific coast to Baja California. Accidental in CO.
Population No data.

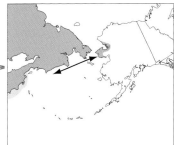

PACIFIC LOON *Gavia pacifica*

Intermediate in size between the more widespread Red-throated and Common Loons, the Pacific is best known as a migrant and winter visitor along the Pacific coast. When flocks migrate north in spring, adults are in their handsome breeding plumage. Monotypic. L 22–26" (56–66 cm)
Identification The Pacific Loon has a straight, fairly stout bill and usually a fairly smoothly rounded head and hind neck profile. In winter/juvenile plumages, note the well-defined and generally even dark/light border on the head and neck sides, and the contrast between a paler hind neck and darker back. The Pacific is told from the slightly larger Arctic Loon in all plumages by its black femoral feathering. BREEDING ADULT: Head and hind neck are ashy gray with a purple-glossed throat patch bordered by white stripes; the upperparts are boldly patterned black-and-white. Bill is black, eyes red. WINTER ADULT: Throat and foreneck are white; about 90 percent of birds have a dusky to dark chinstrap, and the blackish upperparts have very muted paler

winter adult

winter adults

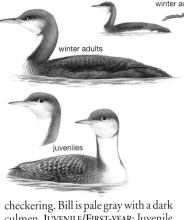

juveniles

checkering. Bill is pale gray with a dark culmen. JUVENILE/FIRST-YEAR: Juvenile resembles winter adult but paler feather tips to its upperparts create a scaly patterning; its upperwing coverts lack white spots; eyes are duller, brownish red. About half of juveniles lack the dusky chinstrap. The first prealternate molt, starting in mid- to late winter, produces limited and variable traces of breeding-type plumage, mainly on the head and neck. Many first-summers look like faded winter adults. SECOND WINTER: Produced by complete second prebasic molt in late summer, resembles winter adult but upperwing coverts lack distinct white spots. Following a molt in spring of the third year, resembles breeding adult but the head and neck can be mottled white, the white back markings average smaller, and the bill may be piebald.
Similar Species The winter adult/juvenile Common Loon is distinctly larger and bulkier, and its stouter bill has

breeding adults

a pronounced gonydeal angle. Note the Common's broken whitish eye ring, the more irregular dark/white border to its neck sides (suggesting the breeding pattern), and that its hind neck is darker than the back, the opposite of the Pacific. A Red-throated Loon is lighter in build, often has a paler face, and has an uptilted bill. Winter adults and juveniles are usually paler overall with fine white flecks on the upperparts and either a more extensive white face or (juveniles) a messier and more extensively dark face and neck than the Pacific. See Arctic Loon.
Voice Rarely vocal in winter. CALL: Includes a low, grunting *awhrr*. SONG: Loud, slightly trumpeting, melodic wailing, *hooo-AHHr-uh*, and variations.
Status & Distribution N.A. BREEDING: Fairly common on small to large lakes. MIGRATION: Mainly Apr.–early June and Sept.–early Dec. over inshore waters, often in flocks. WINTER/ VAGRANT: Rare inland throughout West, very rare in Midwest, and casual to East Coast.
Population Stable or increasing, but large interannual variation of breeding numbers in some areas.

COMMON LOON *Gavia immer*

This large and widespread species is the most familiar loon throughout N.A. Monotypic. L 26–33" (66–84 cm)
Identification Distinctive stout, dark bill with, usually, a distinct gonydeal angle; lower mandible often looks slightly recurved. Head shape fairly angular, often with a distinct forehead bump. In winter/juvenile plumages, white extends over eye and jagged dark/light borders on the neck sides. BREEDING ADULT: Head and neck oily green-black with two horizontal white neck bands striped dark; back boldly patterned black-and-white. Bill black, eyes red. WINTER ADULT: Throat and foreneck white, upperparts blackish brown with very muted paler checkering. Bill pale gray with dark culmen. JUVENILE/FIRST-YEAR: Like winter adult, but paler feather tips on upperparts create scaly effect and eyes duller. Some first-summer birds retain almost all juvenal plumage, which can become faded and pale. Other first-summers attain new head, neck, and back feathers, so their upperparts have scattered darker feathers and sometimes small white spots. SECOND-WINTER: Like winter adult, but upperwing coverts lack distinct white spots. Following molt in spring of third year, upperparts have variable, usually bold, white spotting (but smaller than adult), and head, neck, and bill variably intermediate between breeding and winter adult.
Similar Species The Yellow-billed Loon is slightly larger overall; longer bill has straight culmen, often held slightly raised, accentuating upturned shape; bill pale yellow (breeding) to creamy or pale ivory with a duskier base, but culmen always pale, at least distally (dark on Common). Winter/juvenile Yellow-billed paler

breeding adult

winter adult

above, especially face, which usually has dark auricular mark; pale upperpart scaling on juvenile Yellow-billed averages more contrasting. See Pacific and Arctic Loons.
Voice CALL: Includes a slightly manic, yelping tremolo. SONG: Loud, mournful and eerie wailing cries are far-carrying, *whoo'oo ooh-ooh* and variations.
Status & Distribution Holarctic breeder. BREEDING: Fairly common, on large lakes. MIGRATION: Mar.–May and Sept.–Nov. WINTER: Mainly coastal, also on large, inland water bodies.
Population Bulk of world population nests in Canada.

breeding adult

winter adult

juvenile

Identification of Loons in Flight

Loons are often seen in flight, particularly off coastal headlands during migration. As a group they are distinctive: Cormorants have broader wings and a heavier flight manner that lacks the fluid, sustained power of loons; Western and Clark's grebes are lighter in build with large white wing patches, and are rarely seen in prolonged flight. Flight identification of loons takes practice, and even experienced observers have a "distance threshold," beyond which they are not comfortable.

The larger loons, the Common and the Yellow-billed, usually can be distinguished by their slower, more measured (or gooselike) wingbeats, bigger "front end" (with a thicker neck and larger head and bill), and bigger feet. They tend to fly singly or in groups of 10 to 20 birds, often higher than smaller loons. Specific identification depends mainly on details of bill shape and color.

Red-throated, Pacific, and Arctic Loons are smaller,

with quicker wingbeats, have smaller feet, and tend to fly lower over water. The Red-throated often looks more gangling, accentuated by a thin neck, often held slightly drooped and then raised briefly. The Pacific has a steadier flight and looks more compact than the Red-throated, with a thicker neck, often held fairly level, but many Pacifics fly with drooped necks recalling a Red-throated. The Arctic flies like a heavily built Pacific, and has slightly slower wingbeats.

Red-throated usually flies alone or in groups of up to 10 to 20 birds; ones and twos often join flocks of Pacifics. Pacific often flies in loose flocks or lines of 10 to 50 birds, sometimes hundreds. Arctics fly alone or in pairs but also are often seen with Pacifics at St. Lawrence Island, Alaska. Specific identification is always best confirmed by plumage and bill features; beware that the Red-throated looks "white-flanked" like the Arctic. ■

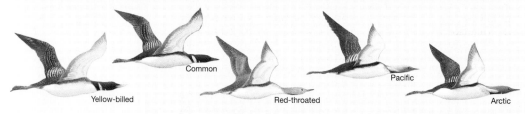

Common

Yellow-billed

Red-throated

Pacific

Arctic

YELLOW-BILLED LOON *Gavia adamsii*

This spectacular far-northern loon is being found in winter with increasing regularity in the lower 48 states, but it is still best appreciated when breeding adults are experienced on their high-Arctic summer grounds. Monotypic. L 28–34" (71–86 cm)

Identification Most Yellow-billed Loons are readily identified, but on problem birds always check the bill shape and color: This bill is long and stout with straight culmen (that is pale, at least distally) and a distinct gonydeal angle; hence the lower mandible looks slightly recurved, an effect enhanced by the bill usually being held slightly raised. Winter adults and juveniles typically have pale-faced aspect with dark auricular mark. Age-related variation and molts are much like those of the Common Loon except for bill coloration. BREEDING ADULT: Bill is straw yellow. WINTER ADULT AND JUVENILE: Bill is pale creamy yellow to ivory, sometimes with a grayish base.

Similar Species The Yellow-billed Loon resembles the Common Loon in all plumages, but winter Yellow-billed adults and juveniles are usually paler above. The Common Loon is slightly smaller overall with a smaller bill that has a decurved culmen and less exaggerated wedge shape to the lower mandible; the Common's bill is black (breeding adult) to pale gray with a dark culmen. (See the Common Loon entry for other differences.)

Voice Similar to that of the Common Loon but lower pitched and hollower; tremolo is slower paced.

Status & Distribution Holarctic breeder. BREEDING: Uncommon to fairly common on tundra lakes and rivers. MIGRATION: Apr.–early June and late Sept.–Nov. WINTER: Rare on Pacific coast south to CA, casual to very rare inland in West, and casual east to Great Lakes region, south to TX.

Population No information available on trends or reliable population estimates.

RED-THROATED LOON *Gavia stellata*

This smallest and most lightly built loon differs from other loons in its relatively subdued breeding plumage and in having a complete molt in late fall. Monotypic. L 21–25" (53–63 cm)

Identification Note slender, slightly upturned bill, often held slightly raised. Swimming birds often lack a chest bulge at the waterline, shown by other loons. BREEDING ADULT: Head and neck gray with black-and-white hind neck lines; brownish upperparts; dark red throat patch. Bill black; eyes red. WINTER ADULT: White face and neck; bill gray. Small, mainly subterminal, white spots and ovals on scapulars. JUVENILE/FIRST-SPRING: Resembles winter adult, but face and neck variably smudged dusky (not to be confused with the Pacific Loon's "chinstrap"), scapulars have nar-rower, chevronlike, subterminal whitish marks, and eyes duller, brownish red. First-summer birds range in appearance from like winter adult to having patches of adultlike gray and dark red on neck. Complete second prebasic molt in late summer produces adult-like winter plumage.

Similar Species The Pacific Loon is slightly larger and bulkier with thicker neck, straight bill, white back patches, and has a fuller-chested profile when swimming. Winter/juvenile Pacific has dark cap extending down through eye, and hind neck more extensively dark (beware juvenile Red-throated, but its dark areas are messy, not well defined).

Voice CALL: Flight call in summer a low, grunting or barking *ahrr* or *ahrk,* usually in series. SONG: A male-female duet of loud, wailing, drawn-out screams, *whEEahhr, heeAHH,* etc.

Status & Distribution Holarctic breeder. BREEDING: Fairly common, mainly on lakes and ponds. MIGRATION: Mar.–May and Sept.–Nov., mainly coastal but also overland in East, especially Great Lakes. WINTER: Casual inland and south to Gulf Coast.

Population The Alaska population declined about 50 percent between 1977 and 1993, mostly on western tundra (no decline on North Slope or in boreal forest zone).

GREBES Family Podicipedidae

Least Grebe, adult with chicks (TX, Apr.)

Grebes are fairly small to medium-large diving birds of freshwater and inshore habitats. A tailless appearance and a fairly long neck distinguish them from most swimming birds; relative to loons, note their proportionately shorter bodies and fluffy rear ends. Rarely seen in flight, grebes can be identified readily to species, given good views of head shape, face and neck patterns, and bill size, shape, and color. **Structure** Grebes are heavy bodied with longish necks and lobed feet set far back on the body. Their beaks vary from somewhat long and pointed to stout and chickenlike. The wings are relatively small and pointed, with 11 primaries and 17 to 22 secondaries; vestigial rectrices are difficult to distinguish from body feathers. Males average larger than females, especially in bill size.

Behavior Grebes dive for food. Smaller species are mostly found singly or in small groups, but Eared and *Aechmophorus* grebes occur in flocks of hundreds, sometimes thousands. They fly direct with steady, fairly quick wingbeats, the neck held outstretched and feet trailing.

Plumage Seasonally dichromatic plumage, but the sexes look similar; juveniles resemble winter adults. Generally, plumages are dark above and light below; 2 species with golden head plumes in breeding plumage. Molt occurs mostly on nonbreeding grounds, with remiges shed synchronously in fall during prebasic molt. Adult plumage aspect attained by second prebasic molt at about 1 year of age.

Distribution Cosmopolitan, with both resident and migratory species. In North America, grebes occur in all but the far northern latitudes.

Taxonomy About 22 species worldwide in 6 genera; 7 species in 4 genera in North America.

Conservation Pollution, disturbance, and draining of inland lakes affect breeding and wintering populations. Oil spills threaten nonbreeding grebes on marine waters. BirdLife International lists 4 species as threatened, with 1 as near threatened. —*Steve N. G. Howell*

Genera Tachybaptus and Podilymbus

LEAST GREBE *Tachybaptus dominicus*

breeding

winter

This well-named, diminutive, and somewhat retiring grebe of southern Texas often holds its neck retracted and its rear end puffed out. Polytypic (4 ssp.; 2–3 in N.A.). L 8.5–9.5" (21–24 cm)

Identification Bill slender and slightly uptilted. BREEDING ADULT: Black face and throat; slate gray sides of neck. Black bill finely tipped white, eyes golden. WINTER ADULT: A paler face with a blackish mottled or dusky throat; lower mandible mostly pale grayish to horn. FIRST-YEAR: Juvenile head sides striped dark gray and whitish; lower mandible mostly pale horn; eyes paler and duller. Partial molt into formative plumage similar to winter adult, but head and neck washed brownish; throat mostly whitish; less extensive and less well-defined white edging on retained juvenal remiges. Eyes develop golden color over first year. First-summer bird has throat mottled sooty gray, but lacks adult's well-defined black patch.

Geographic Variation The *brachypterus* of Texas averages slightly larger and longer billed than the *bangsi*, which is a vagrant to the Southwest from western Mexico.

Similar Species No other species should be confused with the Least in its limited North American range; the Pied-billed Grebe looks nearly twice its size and has a stout, mostly pale bill.

Voice An overall descending, purring trill, *pc, pc, purrrrrrrrrrrrrr;* often starts hesitantly. Also a quacking k*wrek,* and a slightly shrill, emphatic *ehkehr*

Status & Distribution Southern TX to S.A. BREEDING: Fairly common, but local on vegetated ponds and lakes; nests year-round in southern TX (mainly Apr.–Aug.). VAGRANT: Casual visitor to southern CA, southeastern AZ, southern FL, and the upper TX coast.

Population No data.

PIED-BILLED GREBE *Podilymbus podiceps*

winter

breeding

This widespread chunky grebe is usually found singly or in small groups on small ponds. It can hide by sinking until only its head is above water. Polytypic (3 ssp.; nominate in N.A.). L 11–13.5" (28–34 cm)

Identification The Pied-billed has a diagnostic thick bill and fairly large head, and, unlike other North American grebes, lacks distinct white upperwing patches. BREEDING ADULT: Face and throat black, neck sides grayer; bill pale blue-gray with sharply defined black medial band. WINTER ADULT: Face paler and throat whitish, neck sides warmer and browner; bill pale horn to grayish,

without black band. FIRST-YEAR: Juveniles have head sides striped dark gray and whitish, and bill pale horn. The formative plumage after molting resembles the winter adult, but the head and neck average buffier, and some birds retain vestiges of dark head striping through winter. First-summer plumage resembles a breeding adult, but it can have a less solidly black throat and the bill band may be narrower and less complete.

Similar Species Eared and Horned Grebes have slenderer bills, and a more capped appearance in nonbreeding plumages; also see the Least Grebe.

Voice CALL: Includes single clucks and

a rapid-paced, slightly nasal, pulsating chuckling chatter in interactions. SONG: A series of slightly hollow, rapid-paced cooing notes run into slower-paced, gulping clucks that can fade away or run on into more prolonged variations on a theme: *kuh, kuh-kuh-kuhkuhkuhkuh … k'owh k'owh k'owh k'owh, k'owh.*

Status & Distribution N.A. to southern S.A. BREEDING: Lakes and small ponds with emergent vegetation. MIGRATION: Mainly Mar.–Apr., late Aug.–Oct. in interior regions, less often on saltwater. VAGRANT: Casual visitor north to AK. **Population** Stable or declining locally, especially in the East.

Genus *Podiceps*

RED-NECKED GREBE *Podiceps grisegena*

1st winter

juvenile

winter adult

breeding adult

This grebe often forms flocks at favored coastal locations in winter. Polytypic (2 ssp.; 1 in N.A.). L 17–20" (43–51 cm)

Identification Distinctive thick neck and chunky head, with overall dusky to dark head and neck. White secondaries and white patagial panel visible in flight. Medium-long, pointed bill with yellow at base. BREEDING ADULT: Neck chestnut; throat and auriculars smoky gray, outlined in white. WINTER ADULT: Neck dusky; face dusky gray with paler auricular patch. JUVENILE/FIRST-YEAR: Head sides striped dark gray and buffy to whitish, neck sides washed rufous.

Fall formative plumage like winter adult, but bill often has a less well-defined dark culmen and tip. First-summer plumage like breeding adult, but crown browner and foreneck duller.

Similar Species The Eared Grebe's winter plumage is somewhat similar, but the Eared is distinctly smaller and has a slender dark bill, steep forehead, usually whiter and more contrasting auricular patches, and bright reddish eyes. Eared also often has a puffier rear end and shows more whitish along waterline. A molting Horned Grebe can suggest a breeding Red-necked, but is smaller and has a smaller blackish bill, bright-red eyes, and some indication of golden supercilium. Eareds and

Horneds also lack a clean-cut white patagial panel on the upper wings. **Voice** Mainly vocal when breeding. Low, slightly gull-like wailing cries often run into slightly metallic, pulsating bickering or chattering series. Also a clipped, harsh note, usually repeated, *kerk! kerk!*

Status & Distribution Holarctic breeder. BREEDING: Favors shallow freshwater lakes. MIGRATION: Mainly Mar.–early May, Sept.–Nov. WINTER: Rare in interior south of northern tier of states; casual to the Southwest and Gulf Coast. **Population** No clear population trend in recent decades, but declines have been noted, especially at edge of range.

EARED GREBE *Podiceps nigricollis*

winter

breeding adult

This fairly small, mostly western grebe is famed for its fall molt migrations, when tens of thousands of birds swarm at Mono Lake, California, and Great Salt Lake, Utah. It also nests colonially. Polytypic (3 ssp.; *californicus* in N.A.). L 11–12.5" (28–31.5 cm)

Identification Distinctive steep forehead and relatively thin neck. Overall dusky to dark head and neck and slender, slightly upturned bill. White secondaries visible in flight. BREEDING ADULT: Black head and neck, expansive postocular fan of golden plumes, black bill, and red eyes; body sides chestnut. WIN-

TER ADULT: Dusky head sides and neck with a whitish throat and postauricular patches; gray bill with dark culmen. FIRST-YEAR: Juvenile resembles a winter adult, but its head sides and foreneck are washed buff and the eyes are duller, orangey. In fall, the formative plumage resembles a winter adult but the upperparts average browner and the eyes are orange to orange-red. First-summer plumage resembles a breeding adult, but the head and neck average duller, with paler and less extensive head plumes.

Similar Species The Horned Grebe is more thickset and has a shallow-sloping forehead, flatter crown, and a straight, slightly thicker bill tipped white. The Horned often rides flatter on the water, without the pronounced puffy rear end of the Eared. The winter Horned is typically a much cleaner black-and-white, with a shallow black cap (beware of nonbreeding Eareds with bright whitish necks; check bill shape and depth of cap). The breeding Horned has a chestnut neck, golden superciliary "horns," and rufous lores. Molting birds of the two species can look quite similar (mainly Apr. and Sept.): Note bill shape differences and the position of yellow on the head sides. Also see the Red-necked Grebe.

Voice An upslurred, slightly reedy or plaintive *hoor-EEP* or *eeihr-EK!* Rapid-paced, high piping chittering in interactions.

Status & Distribution Holarctic breeder. BREEDING: Common (rare in eastern N.A.). Favors shallow ponds with high macroinvertebrate productivity; rarely on ponds with fish. MIGRATION: Mainly Mar.–May, Aug.–Nov. WINTER: Casual to very rare in the east.

Population No demonstrable trend apparent in N.A. over recent decades.

HORNED GREBE *Podiceps auritus*

This fairly small but stocky grebe is generally less familiar than the Eared Grebe on the breeding grounds, but it is more widespread in North America in winter, mainly on saltwater. Polytypic (2 ssp.; *cornutus* in N.A.). L 11.5–13" (29–33 cm)

Identification Medium-length straight bill with fine white tip in all ages, shallow-angled forehead, and flat crown. Undertail coverts rarely fluffed into a high rear end. White secondaries visible in flight. BREEDING ADULT: Black head with bushy postocular "horns," black bill, and red eyes; neck and body sides chestnut. WINTER ADULT: White head sides and foreneck with blackish cap extending down to

eye level; bill grayish. FIRST-YEAR: Juvenile head sides striped dark gray and whitish, lower mandible mostly pale horn. After molt into formative plumage, it is rarely distinguishable from a winter adult; however, upperparts can be mixed with worn, brownish feathers, and first-summer plumage averages duller, with paler and less extensive horns.

Similar Species The Eared Grebe is more lightly built with a thinner neck and steep forehead that create a blockier head profile; its slimmer, upturned bill lacks a white tip. The Eared often rides higher on the water, with a puffy rear end. The winter Eared is typically much dingier, with the black cap extending down well into the cheeks. Some Eareds, though, have surprisingly bright whitish necks and faces; check bill shape and depth of cap. The breeding Eared has a shaggy fan of golden postocular plumes and black lores. The bold black-and-white pattern of the Clark's and Western Grebes can suggest a winter Horned, but the former are much larger and longer necked with long and thin yellow bills. Also see the larger Red-necked Grebe.

Voice Mainly vocal when breeding. A fairly high-pitched, rapid, pulsating whinny often given in duet, and a slightly hoarse, whistled *hiki-sheihr,* repeated.

Status & Distribution Holarctic breeder. BREEDING: Favors small to medium-size lakes with emergent vegetation. MIGRATION: Mainly Mar.–early May, Sept.–Nov. Casual in NF.

Population More than 100,000 Horneds are estimated in N.A., but the numbers are apparently slowly declining with a steady northwestward contraction of breeding range.

breeding adult

winter

Genus *Aechmophorus*

CLARK'S GREBE *Aechmophorus clarkii*

winter

breeding adult

A large, striking black-and-white grebe once considered conspecific with the generally commoner Western Grebe. The two species associate readily and hybridize. Polytypic (2 ssp.; 1 in N.A.). L 18–24" (45–61 cm)

Identification This grebe has a long, slender neck and a long, slender, pointed bill (noticeably larger on males) with a distinct gonydeal angle. BREEDING ADULT: White lores and supraorbital region, bright orange-yellow bill with dark culmen, orange-red to red eyes. WINTER ADULT: White to mostly dusky lores and supraorbital region with whitish loral patch. FIRST-YEAR: Juvenile similar to winter adult but crown washed grayish and eyes duller and paler, orangey. After molt, rarely distinguishable from adult, although upperparts can be mixed with worn, brownish feathers. First summer may have dusky face, lacking bright white surround to eye, which is paler red through first year.

Similar Species The Western Grebe is best separated by its greenish yellow to yellow bill, but also note its more extensive black crown (extending down to the eyes), broader black hind neck stripe, and overall grayer flanks. The breeding Western has blackish to dusky-gray lores and surround to eye, but these areas are paler on winter birds, which can have a loral pattern similar to the Clark's. Although the upper wing of the Clark's averages more extensive white on primaries, it is not diagnostic. The range of variation within each species is not well understood, compounded by hybridization; some birds, mainly in winter, may not be identifiable. In flight, the Red-necked Grebe is more compact with a duskier neck and its upper wing has a more restricted white secondary panel and white patagial patch. Also see the winter Horned Grebe.

Voice CALL: A rather drawn-out, disyllabic *kreeeIH* or *kreeet* among others. Screechy and scratchy. Juveniles solicit adults with high-pitched whistles that can still be given in midwinter.

Status & Distribution N.A. to central Mexico. BREEDING: Fairly common. MIGRATION: Mainly Apr.–May and Sept.–Nov. Nonbreeding birds oversummer on inshore waters along Pacific coast. WINTER: Fairly common to uncommon on West Coast (only 10–20 percent of "Western Grebe" flocks in CA are Clark's). Accidental in the east.

Population From 1890s to about 1906, tens of thousands of Western/Clark's Grebes were shot for their silky white feathers; today, oil spill mortality, disturbance, habitat degradation, and pesticides continue to keep present populations below historic levels.

WESTERN GREBE *Aechmophorus occidentalis*

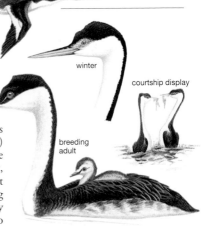

winter

courtship display

breeding adult

The Western looks similar to the Clark's Grebe, and the 2 were once considered conspecific under the name Western Grebe. Flocks in winter can number hundreds, with Clark's associating readily. Polytypic (2 ssp.; 1 in N.A.). L 19–25" (48–64 cm)

Identification Extent of white on face varies with age and season. Intermediate (and unidentifiable) birds are not rare; some may be hybrids. BREEDING ADULT: Dusky gray to blackish lores and supraorbital region, yellow bill with dark culmen, and orange-red to red eyes. WINTER ADULT: Dusky lores and supraorbital region, often with whitish loral patch. FIRST-YEAR: Aging criteria as Clark's. First summer may have pale loral spot.

Similar Species Bill color best separates the Western (greenish yellow to yellow) from the Clark's (orange-yellow). See Clark's for other differences. In flight, a Red-necked Grebe is more compact with a duskier neck; the upper wing has a more restricted white secondary panel and white patagial patch. Also see the winter Horned Grebe.

Voice Varied screechy and scratchy calls include a 2-note *kreeih chik* or *kree-kreet,* the first part upslurred. Begging calls much like Clark's Grebe.

Status & Distribution N.A. to central Mexico. BREEDING: Favors freshwater lakes with large areas of open water and bordered by reeds or other emergent vegetation. MIGRATION: Mainly Apr.–May and Sept.–Nov. Large numbers of nonbreeding birds oversummer on inshore waters along Pacific coast. WINTER: Casual in the East.

Population See the Clark's Grebe.

ALBATROSSES Family Diomedeidae

Black-footed Albatross (CA, Nov.)

Albatrosses, open ocean birds, spend the majority of their lives at sea, some wandering thousands of miles in search of food. They are characterized by their large size and long, narrow wings; the Wandering and Royal Albatrosses possess the largest wingspans of any bird, measuring just over 11 feet! While the North American species are smaller, all are strikingly large when compared to other seabirds. Although identification can be straightforward, the separation of similar species relies on observation of subtle plumage differences and bill color. Albatrosses live long lives, typically tens of years.

Structure Albatrosses are characterized by their long, narrow wings and thick, heavy bodies. Unlike the procellariids, which have a single tube on the culmen, albatrosses have very large bills with single tubes on either side of the culmen. The bills, made up of individual plates, are sharply hooked. Bill size and coloration can be critical field marks, and bill color often changes with maturation. Albatrosses have large, webbed feet, which sometimes extend past the tail in flight.

Behavior Flight style varies with wind speed and sea condition, but almost always incorporates a large amount of energy-efficient arcing and gliding, especially in stiff oceanic gales. Wingbeats are heavy and labored, and in light winds albatrosses work hard to stay aloft, often sitting on the water in calm conditions. Albatrosses typically feed by surface dipping, alighting on the water and picking prey—including squid, fish, flotsam, offal, and carrion—from the surface. Their acute sense of smell helps in detecting food; many are attracted to fishing boats and chum. Although vocal on breeding grounds, most albatrosses are silent at sea. Most species nest in large colonies on remote oceanic islands; pairs mate for life.

Plumage Albatross plumages are largely variations of black and white, with some having gray or brown tones. The contrasting patterns of black and white are important identification field marks. Some species' plumages change with maturation; others exhibit less variation. Albatrosses show little sexual dimorphism, however, more work is needed. The molt can be complex and protracted, particularly in the larger species; it is not possible to replace all the feathers between breeding cycles, hence the long maturation.

Distribution Albatrosses reach their greatest diversity in the Southern Hemisphere; the doldrums of the equatorial waters presumably represent a barrier to their northward dispersal. In the North Pacific there are 3 breeding albatrosses: Laysan, Black-footed, and Short-tailed. The Short-tailed Albatross was historically common and is slowly recovering from near extinction. All others occur as vagrants in North America. Other than when they nest, albatrosses are entirely pelagic.

Taxonomy Albatross taxonomy continues to undergo scientific debate. Some scientists believe there are only 2 genera, but more recently up to 4 have been recognized. Worldwide 13 to 24 species in 2 to 4 genera are recognized. The AOU lists 8 species in 4 genera as occurring in North America: 3 mollymawks or southern albatrosses, 1 sooty albatross, 1 great albatross, and 3 North Pacific albatrosses.

Conservation BirdLife International lists 16 species as threatened and 4 as near threatened. Threats include feral predators (esp. rats, pigs, and cats) at nesting sites; longline fishing at sea; ingestion of floating plastics by adults and the subsequent regurgitation of this material to chicks; and the human harvesting of birds and eggs for food. —*Brian Sullivan*

MOLLYMAWKS Genus *Thalassarche*

Three of the 11 mollymawk species, medium-size albatrosses of southern oceans, occur as vagrants in North American waters. All are superficially similar in plumage—largely white below with blackish brown backs and upper wings. Important distinctions are the extent of dark margins on the underwings and bill coloration. Superficially all mollymawks resemble the Great Black-backed Gull, but are much larger, and have longer wings and larger bills.

YELLOW-NOSED ALBATROSS *Thalassarche chlororhynchos*

adult

adult

chlororhynchos

juvenile

adult

The Yellow-nosed is the smallest and slimmest mollymawk occurring in North America's Atlantic waters. Polytypic (2 ssp.; nominate *chlororhynchos* in N.A. and *bassi* of the Indian Ocean). L 32" (81 cm) WS 80" (203 cm) **Identification** Small and slim, appearing rangier in the field due to its long neck, bill, and tail. ADULT: Gray headed in fresh plumage, otherwise strikingly black-and-white. Upper wings blackish with white primary shafts; back grayer; underwings white, with thin black margins, widest at the leading edge. Gray tail. At a distance, bill appears black; at close range, yellow ridge along the length of the culmen and orange-reddish tip visible. JUVENILE: All dark bill. White head, lacking the adult's grayish wash. May show wider dark margins on the leading edge of the underwing, causing confusion with adult Black-browed Albatross. **Similar Species** The Black-browed Albatross will cause the most confusion. Adults differ in structure, underwing pattern and most notably bill col-

oration. The more heavily built Black-browed has a broader dark leading edge on the underwings and a yellowish bill with an orange tip. The immature Black-browed's dark bill is actually grayish with a notably dark tip. Juvenile and immature Black-broweds appear gray-headed, often with a grayish collar, turning whiter with age. Juvenile and immature Yellow-noseds appear white-headed, becoming grayer with age. Head patterns can overlap; caution is needed. An immature Northern Gannet has a longer pointed head and tail, and a pointed, not blunt-tipped, bill.

Status & Distribution BREEDING: Islands in southern oceans; nominate *chlororhynchos* breeds on Tristan da Cunha and Gough Islands. NONBREEDING: Wanders north to subtropical and subantarctic waters of the Atlantic and Indian Oceans. VAGRANT: Casual offshore from the Gulf of Mexico to the Canadian Maritimes; several records from shore or inland.

Population The global population is apparently stable, but certain subpopulations are declining due to human exploitation and habitat alteration and loss. BirdLife International lists *chlororhynchos* as near threatened.

BLACK-BROWED ALBATROSS *Thalassarche melanophris*

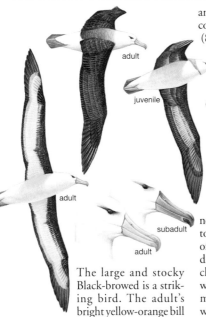

adult

juvenile

adult

subadult

adult

The large and stocky Black-browed is a striking bird. The adult's bright yellow-orange bill

and dark brow mark give it a fierce countenance. Polytypic (2 ssp.) L 35" (89 cm) WS 88" (224 cm) **Identification** Stocky and heavily built, with thick neck and large-bodied jizz. ADULT: Unique combination of yellow-orange bill with bright orange tip and whitish head with dark brow. Underwings darkest on leading edge, generally characterized by broad dark margins. JUVENILE: Grayish to dark horn-colored bill, typically with dark blackish tip. Grayish head, turning whiter with age, with darkest gray on the hind neck often connecting across the breast to form a partial collar. Underwing often darker than adult; can appear all-dark at a distance. SUBADULT: Bill changing from dark to mostly pale with dark tip. Underwing becoming mostly adultlike and head mostly white with dark brow.

Similar Species See Yellow-nosed Albatross—the major identification problem in the western North Atlantic. It is larger and bulkier than the Yellow-nosed, with differing underwing pattern and head and bill coloration. **Status & Distribution** Circumpolar in southern oceans. BREEDING: Nominate *melanophris* nests around tip of S.A. on subantarctic oceanic islands; *impavida* off New Zealand. NONBREEDING: North to waters off Peru and off Brazil. VAGRANT: Casual in N. Atlantic Ocean; most records are from European waters. Several fairly convincing sightings off the East Coast; 1 well-documented immature off VA (Feb. 6, 1999). **Population** The Black-browed is the most abundant albatross worldwide, but BirdLife International lists it as near threatened. Populations are currently stable. Incidental drowning from longline fishing is the likely cause of local declines.

SHY ALBATROSS *Thalassarche cauta*

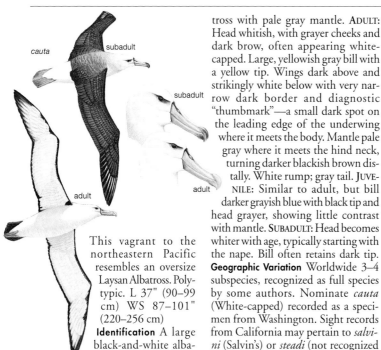

This vagrant to the northeastern Pacific resembles an oversize Laysan Albatross. Polytypic. L 37" (90–99 cm) WS 87–101" (220–256 cm)
Identification A large black-and-white alba-tross with pale gray mantle. ADULT: Head whitish, with grayer cheeks and dark brow, often appearing white-capped. Large, yellowish gray bill with a yellow tip. Wings dark above and strikingly white below with very narrow dark border and diagnostic "thumbmark"—a small dark spot on the leading edge of the underwing where it meets the body. Mantle pale gray where it meets the hind neck, turning darker blackish brown distally. White rump; gray tail. JUVENILE: Similar to adult, but bill darker grayish blue with black tip and head grayer, showing little contrast with mantle. SUBADULT: Head becomes whiter with age, typically starting with the nape. Bill often retains dark tip.
Geographic Variation Worldwide 3–4 subspecies, recognized as full species by some authors. Nominate *cauta* (White-capped) recorded as a specimen from Washington. Sight records from California may pertain to *salvini* (Salvin's) or *steadi* (not recognized by some authors); *eremita* (Chatham Island) is resident around the Chatham Islands, New Zealand. Subspecies determination depends on head and bill color, and is further complicated by age variation.
Similar Species Compared with the Laysan Albatross, the Shy is much larger, with grayer mantle, larger gray bill, and diagnostic, dark "thumbmark" on an otherwise much whiter underwing. Longer tail is gray, not blackish.
Status & Distribution Vagrant to North Pacific. BREEDING: Islands off Tasmania and New Zealand. NONBREEDING: Disperses east and west from breeding areas across southern oceans, ranging to waters off western S.A. and southern Africa. VAGRANT: Casual off Pacific coast from northern CA to WA.
Population Global populations were decimated by plume hunters in the 1800s, but they are recovering. Feral pigs threaten some breeding colonies. BirdLife International lists subspecies *salvini* and *eremita* as threatened.

SOOTY ALBATOSSES Genus *Phoebetria*

LIGHT-MANTLED ALBATROSS *Phoebetria palpebrata*

This elegant, rakish albatross with long, narrow wings flies with effortless grace. Monotypic. L 31–35" (79–89cm) WS 72–86" (183–218 cm)
Identification Very distinctive. ADULT: Large. Dark head with prominent white eye crescents. Strikingly pale mantle and body. Long, dark, and wedge-shaped tail. Bluish purple cutting edge to the upper mandible (sulcus). JUVENILE: Similar to adult, but with browner plumage, less prominent eye crescents, and gray or brownish sulcus.
Similar Species Confusion with a Black-footed Albatross is possible, but the Light-mantled has a longer tail, prominent white eye crescents, and very different jizz. Related Sooty Albatross (*P. fusca,* unrecorded in N.A.) has an all-dark body and a yellow sulcus.
Status & Distribution Circumpolar in southern oceans. BREEDING: Subantarctic islands. VAGRANT: Accidental, 1 record off northern CA (Cordell Bank, July 17, 1994).
Population Global populations appear stable, but losses occur due to drowning from long-line fishing.

GREAT ALBATROSSES Genus *Diomedea*

WANDERING ALBATROSS *Diomedea exulans*

This very large seabird's wingspan reaches over 11 feet! Polytypic (5–7 ssp.). L 42–53" (107–135 cm) WS 100–138" (254–351 cm)
Identification Massive pinkish bill and white underwings with narrow dark trailing edge and primary tips. ADULT: Extensively white back and wings. JUVENILE: Dark chocolate brown with conspicuous white face. SUBADULT: Complex plumage maturation takes up to 15 years. Becomes white first on the mantle, body, and head, eventually spreading across the upperwing coverts.
Similar Species Superficially similar to Short-tailed Albatross (see species for details). Very similar to Royal Albatross (*D. epomophora,* unrecorded in N.A.) of Southern Hemisphere.
Status & Distribution Circumpolar in southern oceans. BREEDING: Subantarctic islands. NONBREEDING: Disperses north after breeding, but typically stays south of Tropic of Capricorn. VAGRANT: Accidental; 1 record in N.A., on a CA sea cliff (Sea Ranch, Sonoma Cty, July 11–12, 1967); 5 European records.
Population The global population is slowly declining; it is especially susceptible to incidental mortality from long-line fishing.

NORTH PACIFIC ALBATROSSES Genus Phoebastria

Of the 4 species in this genus, 3 occur in the North Pacific. The Laysan and Black-footed are small for albatrosses, while the Short-tailed is much larger. The Waved Albatross breeds on the Galapagos Islands and has not been recorded in North America. All take advantage of cold, nutrient-rich waters for foraging.

SHORT-TAILED ALBATROSS *Phoebastria albatrus (E)*

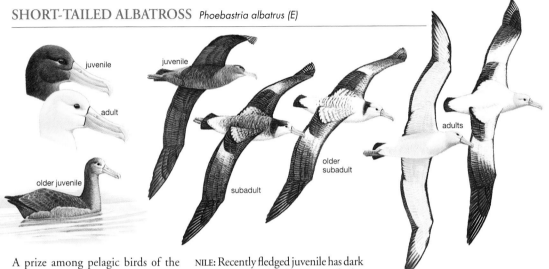

juvenile
juvenile
adult
older juvenile
subadult
older subadult
subadult
adults

A prize among pelagic birds of the west, this large albatross with its striking "bubblegum pink" bill is becoming more regular in North American waters. Once nearly extinct, the species has partly recovered in recent years and has been found with increasing regularity in North America, particularly off the coast of Alaska. Our most variably plumaged species, the Short-tailed Albatross—sometimes known as the Steller's Albatross—has a succession of age-related plumages similar to the great albatrosses found in the southern oceans. It is obviously larger and more robust than the Black-footed Albatross, with which it often appears in association off the West Coast. Most recent records off the West Coast are of chocolate brown juveniles; however, a few subadults and adults have been documented as well. Monotypic. L 36" (91 cm) WS 87" (215–230 cm)

Identification Where it occurs with other North Pacific species, the Short-tailed's large size, massive pink bill with pale bluish tip, dark humerals, and pale feet are distinctive in all plumages. ADULT: Plumage pattern similar to that of great albatrosses of Southern Hemisphere. Largely white both ventrally and dorsally with golden wash on head. White scapulars and upperwing coverts contrast with black humerals, primary coverts and outer greater upperwing coverts creating a somewhat pied pattern on the upper wing. Underwings white with narrow dark margin. JUVE-

NILE: Recently fledged juvenile has dark bill with traces of pink. Timing of color change uncertain (possibly within first 2 months at sea), but bill soon pink. Fresh plumage wholly dark brown with small variable white around eye and below bill, but often appearing cleanly dark-headed. Worn, older juveniles more white-headed overall. Underwings dark. SUBADULT: Slow change (up to 10 years) from the mostly brown juvenile-like plumage of younger subadult, to the whiter adultlike plumage of older subadult. Scapulars, upperwing coverts, and back change from brown to white as bird ages. Underwing changes from all dark to white. Older subadult can appear nearly adultlike but often retains dark nape patch on the otherwise unmarked yellowish head.

Similar Species An adult Short-tailed is not likely to be confused with any other North Pacific albatross. The combination of dark underwings in juvenile and early subadult plumages and smaller size separate it from a Wandering Albatross, though it's unlikely the species occur in the same waters. Recently fledged juveniles with dark bills are very similar to a Black-footed Albatross, and older juveniles and younger subadults are superficially similar. Note the bright pink bill on the older birds, visible at long range. On all ages note much larger size. The Black-footed always lacks white on the upper wing unlike the pied upper wing of a subadult Short-tailed. Hybrids between Black-footed and Laysan

Albatrosses can have plumages resembling a Short-tailed's; however, the hybrids are smaller and lack white on the upper wing.

Status & Distribution Rare but increasing. BREEDING: Historically multiple islands off Japan; currently restricted to Torishima and Minami-kojima. Single adults have occurred in albatross colonies on Midway; 1 breeding pair bred in 1993. NONBREEDING: Disperses to surrounding waters and follows the trade winds to the northeast Pacific and southern Bering Sea and rarely farther south off the west coast of N.A.

Population Hunting by Japanese plume hunters and several volcanic eruptions severely reduced this species by 1900; additional exploitation pushed it to the brink of extinction by the early 1930s. Now fully protected on their breeding islands—although eggs and chicks still suffer predation by introduced rats, and future volcanic eruptions threaten nesting habitat—the Short-tailed population is slowly recovering; thus the higher percentage of juveniles and subadults than in a stable population. The population has rebounded to an estimated 1,000 individuals. Records off the west coast of North America are becoming more regular; historically, large numbers of Short-taileds occurred during the nonbreeding season from the Aleutians to California.

LAYSAN ALBATROSS *Phoebastria immutabilis*

The Laysan is the only regularly occurring black-and-white albatross in the eastern North Pacific. Monotypic. L 32" (81 cm) WS 79" (200 cm)

Identification There are no age-related or sexual differences in plumage, but black areas turn paler with wear. Blackish above; white below. Distinctive dark brow above the eye; auriculars washed gray. Yellowish to pinkish bill with a dark tip. Variably dark underwings with central white area (mostly white underwings exceptional). Black tail. **HYBRID:** Rare hybrid with a Black-footed Albatross appears a darker version of the Laysan plumage pattern; often washed gray on the body and head. On darker hybrids the white facial markings of a typical Black-footed are exaggerated, giving the face a prominent white appearance.
Similar Species The Laysan is most easily confused with the larger and rarer Shy Albatross, which has a whiter underwing with a dark "thumbmark," a grayish mantle, and a longer, gray tail. The Laysan lacks the yellowish wash on the head of an adult or older subadult Short-tailed Albatross.
Status & Distribution BREEDING: Atolls in the northwestern HI islands and on Kauai; recently established in small numbers in the Revillagigedo Archipelago and Isla de Guadalupe, Mexico. Regularly ranges to cold AK waters

throughout summer. NONBREEDING: Moves mostly north and east into the Northern Pacific Gyre; found widely scattered in the eastern Pacific. Most commonly observed from CA to WA in deep water Sept.–Feb. VAGRANT: Casual in desert Southwest (southeastern CA and southwestern AZ), where (presumably) individuals traveling north up the Gulf of California continued overland.
Population The global population is stable and likely increasing, recovering from plume hunting and other human exploitation at the end of the 19th century. Threats include introduced predators at breeding colonies and the ingestion of plastic that is regurgitated to nestlings.

BLACK-FOOTED ALBATROSS *Phoebastria nigripes*

The Black-footed is the only regularly occurring dark albatross in the eastern North Pacific. Monotypic. L 32" (81 cm) WS 80" (203 cm)
Identification Typically appears overall dark brown at all ages and seasons; worn individuals can have paler brown wing coverts. Variable amounts of white at bill base and on uppertail and undertail coverts, occasionally onto the lower belly. Black tail. Grayish black bill, sometimes paler with yellow or pink tones. **ADULT:** Older bird has a whiter face, sometimes even appearing white headed due to wear and sun bleaching, and has more white on the undertail coverts. **JUVENILE:** Like adult, but generally darker in fresh plumage with less white at bill base. White typically restricted to uppertail coverts. **HYBRID:** Rarely with Laysan Albatross (see that species).
Similar Species A mostly dark-plumaged juvenile or young subadult Short-tailed Albatross differs from a Black-footed by its much larger size and large pink bill. An exceptionally pale, adult Black-footed has been confused with a subadult Short-tailed, but note the

older adult

different distribution of white plumage areas and the Short-tailed's pink bill.
Status & Distribution Uncommon to locally common year-round in northeast Pacific waters. BREEDING: Atolls in the northwestern HI islands and on islands off Japan. NONBREEDING: Disperses widely during summer. Moves largely north and east in the Northern Pacific Gyre, reaching Aleutians. Rare in Bering Sea. Most numerous in deep water off CA, OR, and WA June–Aug.
Population The global population is declining, threatened by human disturbance, habitat loss, introduced predators, long-line fishing, and oil pollution.

SHEARWATERS AND PETRELS Family Procellariidae

Pink-footed Shearwater (CA, Oct.)

The identification of shearwaters and petrels—the procellariids—is challenging. Almost all North American observations are made at sea, where rocking boats, great distances, and generally drab plumages can exasperate even an experienced seabirder. Birders should focus on the light-dark plumage patterns and the body proportions. Distant identifications of shearwaters and petrels must often be based on a bird's unique flight style and shape, and these identification skills are gained only through experience.

Structure Heavy bodies, short tails, and long, narrow wings are the standard for procellariidae. Their bills are made up of individual plates and are sharply hooked. The nostrils are situated in tubes on the upper surface (culmen) of the bill—hence the term *tubenoses*. Both bill size and color can be useful field marks. Shearwaters and petrels have webbed feet.

Behavior Shearwaters and petrels can be found singly or in large groups, with the shearwaters being more prone to flocking behavior than the others. Their flight is usually a series of wingbeats interspersed with stiff-winged glides. The speed, duration, and depth of the wingbeats and the frequency and duration of the glides define a species' flight style. Body and wing proportions are also major variables. Wind speed and a bird's activity will alter its flight style. In traveling flight, the bird's feet are often hidden, tucked into the belly feathers. Feeding styles vary from surface dipping to deep diving. Prey items range from small copepods to squid and fish, and many species are attracted to fishing boats and chum. Their acute sense of smell helps them to detect food. Procellariids are generally silent at sea.

Plumage Procellariids appear monochromatic. Their plumages are generally variations on black, gray, brown, or white; some are tinged with blue. Male, female, and immature plumages look very similar. Many species have dark upperparts and light underparts. Some species have distinct color morphs (e.g., light or dark), and several species have individuals that show intermediate characteristics between light and dark, further complicating identification. All undergo a single annual molt after breeding. In our spring, most austral breeders will be noticeably in molt; fresh-plumaged birds of the same species are likely to be juveniles. Subadults and nonbreeders may molt earlier than breeders, complicating the issue. When worn and bleached, dark colors become paler and browner. Light conditions also affect color perception.

Distribution Shearwaters and petrels reach their greatest diversity in the Southern Hemisphere, but they inhabit all oceans. With few exceptions they come ashore only to breed; most nest in colonies on remote oceanic islands. Many nest in burrows underground. Only two procellariids—the Northern Fulmar and the Manx Shearwater—breed in North America; however, all the others migrate through North American waters. A number of species are casual or accidental. Species in this family are known to wander, and many records of wayward individuals come from both the Pacific and the Atlantic Oceans.

Taxonomy Taxonomy continues to undergo revision, and ornithologists often differ on species limits, especially in the genera *Pterodroma* and *Puffinus*. Worldwide between 70 and 80 species in 12 to 14 genera are recognized. The American Birding Association lists 25 species in 5 genera as occurring in North America. Informally, they are often subdivided into 3 groups: fulmars (1 sp.), gadfly petrels (11 sp.), and shearwaters (13 sp.).

Conservation Many nesting sites are threatened by feral predators, especially rats, pigs, and cats. Long-line fishing drowns birds at sea. The human harvesting of birds and eggs for food is a threat to some species.
—*Brian Sullivan*

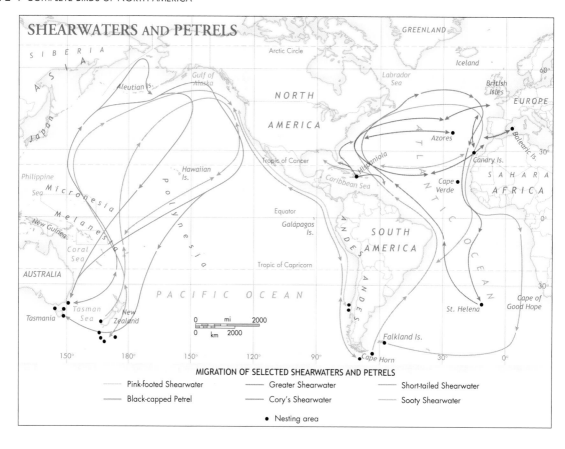

SHEARWATERS AND PETRELS

MIGRATION OF SELECTED SHEARWATERS AND PETRELS

--- Pink-footed Shearwater   --- Greater Shearwater   --- Short-tailed Shearwater

--- Black-capped Petrel   --- Cory's Shearwater   --- Sooty Shearwater

• Nesting area

FULMARS Genus *Fulmarus*

NORTHERN FULMAR *Fulmarus glacialis*

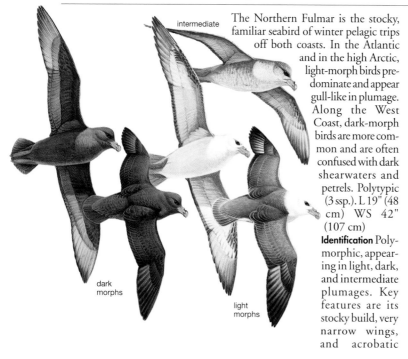

intermediate

dark morphs

light morphs

The Northern Fulmar is the stocky, familiar seabird of winter pelagic trips off both coasts. In the Atlantic and in the high Arctic, light-morph birds predominate and appear gull-like in plumage. Along the West Coast, dark-morph birds are more common and are often confused with dark shearwaters and petrels. Polytypic (3 ssp.). L 19" (48 cm) WS 42" (107 cm)

Identification Polymorphic, appearing in light, dark, and intermediate plumages. Key features are its stocky build, very narrow wings, and acrobatic flight style in strong winds. Ages and sexes alike. LIGHT MORPH: White below and gray dorsally; white head with dark eye smudge. Pale primary bases appear as wing patch on upper wing. Rump white or gray. Tail gray. Underwing mostly white. DARK MORPH: Plumage wholly chocolate brown to brownish gray, often with darker smudge around eye. Underwing coverts concolorous with body, but primaries appear paler. Upperwing may or may not have pale primary patch. INTERMEDIATE: Any shade of color between dark brown and white. Most often appears light, pearly gray with darker upperwing. Blotchy birds often seen on West Coast. FLIGHT: It flies on stiff, outstretched wings with little bend at the wrist, arcing high off the water in strong wings. In light winds, it flies direct and low to water; its stiff, short wingbeats alternate with accomplished glides.

Geographic Variation The polymorphic *rodgersii* of the Pacific has a darker tail that contrasts with the rump and a more slender bill (on average). The nominate *glacialis* describes Atlantic high-arctic breeders, predominately the light morph; the polymorphic *auduboni* describes Atlantic populations breeding in low Arctic and boreal areas. Both Atlantic subspecies have tails similar in color to the rump and the uppertail coverts.

Similar Species The light morphs are similar to large gulls. Note the fulmar's stocky overall shape; relatively short, narrow wings; and complicated bill structure with multiple plates and tube on the culmen. The dark morph can be confused with dark shearwaters, which have thinner, darker bills and longer, broader wings. Confusion with dark *Pterodroma* petrels is a problem,

but note the small, stocky, dark bills of those species and their more dynamic flight on longer, crooked wings.

Voice Generally silent at sea when alone; feeding flock can be noisy. At breeding colonies, it makes a variety of cackling and croaking sounds.

Status & Distribution Common. BREEDING: Breeds on sea cliffs along the coasts of the north Pacific and north Atlantic as well as on high-arctic islands. NONBREEDING: Moves south in most years to winter off the coast of New England and off the West Coast south to Mexico. Numbers fluctuate annually, and in some invasion years hundreds are visible from shore along the West Coast south through Baja California. Can be found year-round off the West Coast, but typically few are present

during the summer months.

Population Increasing in the Atlantic and stable in the Pacific. Thought to be benefiting from large amounts of fish refuse available in the North Sea. Breeding colonies are threatened by introduced predators, pesticides, and oil pollution.

PETRELS Genus *Pterodroma*

This wide-ranging genus includes 31 species worldwide, of which 10 occur in North America. They are characterized by robust bodies, thick necks, and large blunt heads, and they have long, often pointed, tails. In many species, a notable M-pattern appears across the upperwing, formed by dark primaries, primary coverts, greater upperwing coverts, and in some cases rump and uppertail coverts. Their unique flight style is striking at sea, typically when they cover large tracts of ocean on dynamic, high arcs over the sea. Most nest in burrows underground on oceanic islands, spending the majority of their lives at sea.

MURPHY'S PETREL *Pterodroma ultima*

The Murphy's Petrel is the dark *Pterodroma* most likely to be observed off the West Coast. Although it superficially resembles dark shearwaters and dark-morph Northern Fulmars, the Murphy's Petrel flies on stiff, angled wings with dynamic agility. Monotypic. L 16" (41 cm) WS 38" (97 cm)

Identification It is small, dark, thick-necked, and large-headed. Its bill is all-dark, slender for a *Pterodroma*, and short. Its plumage is overall gray-brown, with a subtle dark M-pattern across upperwing. It appears white-throated, with a few white feathers on the forecrown. The upperwing is grayish brown, concolorous with upperparts. The underwing is dark, with

white bases to primaries showing a white flash below. Ages and sexes are alike. FLIGHT: The Murphy's Petrel flies with dynamic arcs above the horizon with stiff wings bent back at the wrist. It often tilts to beyond vertical position at the apex of the arc. In light winds, its flight is low with stiff wingbeats.

Similar Species Similar to the Great-winged Petrel; see that species account for details. The Solander's Petrel *(Pterodroma solandri)* of the South Pacific is also very similar and should be considered. The larger Solander's shows a white flash in the underwings (similar to the Murphy's), so it is important to get a good look at the head if possible: the Solander's has a bigger, more bulbous bill, and the white on its face is more evenly distributed above and below the bill (mostly below in the Murphy's).

Voice Generally silent at sea.

Status & Distribution Rare visitor to West Coast. BREEDING: Breeds on islands in the central south Pacific. NONBREEDING: Poorly known, thought to disperse to tropical Pacific waters, but reaches waters off CA

(rare, probably annual); typically seen over deep water mid-Apr.–May. VAGRANT: Offshore north to OR.

Population Little is known about breeding populations and nesting habits. Most colonies have introduced non-native predators; more study is needed. BirdLife International considers the Murphy's as near threatened.

GREAT-WINGED PETREL *Pterodroma macroptera*

This vagrant gadfly petrel from the southern oceans has only been recorded twice, off California. It closely resembles the Murphy's Petrel. Polytypic (2 ssp.; 1 in N.A.). L 16" (41 cm) WS 38" (97 cm)

Identification Subspecies *gouldi*, which the California birds were thought to be, is described and illustrated. Large for a petrel; wholly dark except pale gray around bill and on

gouldi

chin and throat. Overall uniform blackish brown, but can appear darker on head and breast; thick, stout, black bill. Ages and sexes alike, but dark brown fades paler with wear. FLIGHT: More languid wingbeats than other pterodromas, but still performs dynamic arcs in strong winds bounding high above the ocean's surface.

Similar Species Most similar to Murphy's Petrel (rare off CA), which is smaller overall with quicker wingbeats. Murphy's has prominent pale-based flight feathers and grayer plumage. Pale feathering around the bill base is more restricted to area below bill on Murphy's. Murphy's legs and feet are pink, not black. Solander's Petrel *(Pterodroma solandri)*, of

the South Pacific, is very similar to Great-winged but has prominent whitish primary bases and a subtle M-pattern across the upperwing.

Voice Generally silent at sea.

Status & Distribution Accidental in N.A. BREEDING: Oceanic islands from Australasia to S. Atlantic; *gouldi* off New Zealand. NON-BREEDING: Movements poorly understood, in general disperses to surrounding waters. VAGRANT: Accidental off central CA (2 recs.: Cordell Bank, July 21–Aug. 24, 1996; off Point Pinos, Oct., 18, 1998).

Population Populations largely stable or increasing. Taken for food by native Maoris; commercial harvesting has been banned. Threatened at breeding colonies by introduced cats and rats.

HERALD PETREL *Pterodroma arminjoniana*

This acrobatic gadfly petrel is rare but regular in warm Gulf Stream waters off the East Coast. A medium-sized and polymorphic petrel, the Herald lacks the strong M-pattern on the upperwing shown by many congeners: Its upperparts are generally a smooth velvety brown. The Herald's dark morph is more commonly observed in North America. Polytypic (2 ssp.; nominate in N.A.). L 15.5" (39 cm) WS 37.5" (95 cm)

Identification Polymorphic; the 3 morphs vary mainly in body color; all lack bold contrasts across the upperwing. Underwing coloration is variable, but generally matches morph type (e.g., dark morph has darker underwings overall). Flight feathers whitish with dark trailing edge; underwing coverts largely blackish often with paler lesser coverts (usually lacking on dark morphs). Upperwing brown, often with subtle, darker brown M-pattern (usually absent on dark morph); brown rump and tail. LIGHT MORPH: Light morph is white below and brownish gray above; brownish head and neck sides often give dark-hooded look. Flanks dusky brownish; belly and undertail coverts bright white. DARK MORPH: Plumage wholly chocolate brown to brownish gray, often with darker head and upper breast. Underwing coverts concolorous with body, but primary bases flash white below due to pale bases of flight feathers and greater primary coverts. INTERMEDIATE: Ven-

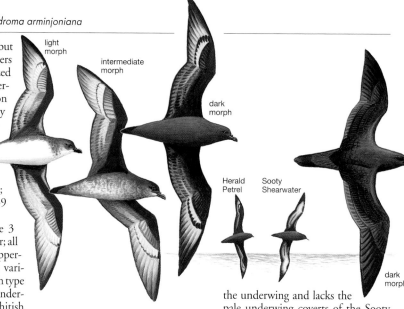

light morph

intermediate morph

dark morph

Herald Petrel

Sooty Shearwater

dark morph

trally the body can be a mix of dark brown and white, generally palest on belly. FLIGHT: Acrobatic and agile, arcing high above the water on stiff set wings, angled back at the wrist. Direct flight low with stiff, measured flapping.

Geographic Variation Nominate Atlantic population (separated from Pacific *heraldica*, which itself is sometimes split into 2 sp.) given full-species status by many authors; sometimes known as the Trinidade (or Trindade) Petrel.

Similar Species Light morph similar to the Fea's Petrel, but it lacks the bold upperwing pattern and pale tail of the Fea's. The dark morph can be confused with the Sooty Shearwater or the dark-morph Northern Fulmar, but it has white restricted to primary bases on

the underwing and lacks the pale underwing coverts of the Sooty Shearwater; also lacks the pale patch on the upperwing of the Northern Fulmar, which is a stockier bird with a pale bill.

Voice Generally silent at sea.

Status & Distribution Rare visitor to Gulf Stream. BREEDING: Nests in colonies on islands off Brazil: Trinidade and Martin Vaz Is. NONBREEDING: Disperses to surrounding waters. Rare but regular as far north as NC in deep offshore waters from May–Sept. VAGRANT: Accidental inland after hurricanes.

Population Breeding colonies suffer predation from introduced predators. Small population size and limited breeding range make nominate *arminjoniana* especially susceptible to drastic declines. BirdLife International considers the nominate vulnerable.

MOTTLED PETREL *Pterodroma inexpectata*

An elusive gadfly petrel of the north Pacific, this species is most easily identified by its striking wing pattern and its diagnostic gray belly. Given any reasonable view, this species is one of few *Pterodroma* petrels that can be considered easy to identify. Monotypic. L 14" (36 cm) WS 32" (81 cm)

Identification Medium-sized and agile; largely white below; bold black ulnar bar across the underwing; diagnostic grayish black belly patch contrasts with the white chest and paler undertail coverts. Can appear largely gray below; white throat and restricted white upperbreast; dark neck sides connect with gray

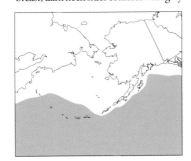

belly and flanks. Wear and molt can make dark belly somewhat paler. Underwing white; dark outer leading edge and black ulnar bar across the underwing coverts extend to the axillaries; dark trailing edge. Upperwing gray, with black M-pattern. Tail gray with white outer tail feathers. Gray head; dark eye smudge; stout black bill. Juvenile has pale-tipped upperparts, imparting a more scaled appearance. **FLIGHT:** Arcs high over the water on stiff, crooked wings bent at the wrist. **Similar Species** The dark belly patch contrasting with white chest and undertail is unique among *Pterodroma* species. The smaller Cook's lacks the contrasting pattern below, has a less distinct ulnar bar (appearing largely white on the underwings), and a bolder dark M-pattern across the upperwing. **Voice** Generally silent at sea. **Status & Distribution** Casual in N.A. BREEDING: Nests on islands off New Zealand. NONBREEDING: Transequatorial migrant. Spends nonbreeding season in the north Pacific; concentrates

off the Aleutians and in the Gulf of Alaska (mostly May–Oct.). VAGRANT: Casual further south along West Coast (mostly mid-Nov.–mid-Apr.). Almost half of those found were onshore, dead or exhausted. Remarkable specimen rec. in upstate NY (Apr. 1880). **Population** Global populations have declined due to habitat loss, human persecution, and predation from introduced predators. Considered near threatened by BirdLife International.

FEA'S PETREL *Pterodroma feae*

Part of a confusing species complex (inc. Zino's and Soft-plumaged Petrels), this infrequent visitor to Gulf Stream waters is the most strikingly plumaged tubenose in the region. Polytypic. L 14" (36 cm) WS 37" (94 cm)

Identification Small gadfly with bold dorsal M-pattern; blackish underwings; pale uppertail and rump. Upperwing grayish, often with distinct darker gray M-pattern; some have brownish tinge above. Head generally dark, imparting a grayish hooded appearance; throat pale. Tail distinctive: grayish to occasionally whitish above; pale rump typically paler than mantle. White below; dark gray sides of neck typically do not connect in breast band. Ages, sexes similar. **FLIGHT:** Typical gadfly style, arcing high over the water in strong winds; direct flight on stiff, clipping wingbeats. **Geographic Variation** Subspecies taxonomy unclear; recent information suggests that the 2 currently recognized taxa might be separate species. Nominate (nesting on the Cape Verde Is.) is characterized by its clean flanks, whereas *deserta* (nesting on the Desertas Is.) typically has barred flanks. A third nesting population (in the Azores) has yet to be assigned to subspecies but is generally thought to be *deserta*. **Similar Species** Unlike any other species in the western Atlantic, but so similar to the extralimital Zino's Petrel (*P. madeira*) that records in N.A. have only been accepted as Fea's/Zino's on the ABA Checklist. Zino's (one of the world's rarest seabirds, endemic to the island of

Madeira) is smaller overall, notably so in the field; but perhaps most importantly, it is smaller billed. The shorter, thinner-based bill helps impart a dove-like appearance to the head. (Considerable experience is needed when assessing size in the field, and very few observers have seen enough Fea's at sea to make a useful comparison.) Other field marks have been postulated, but still need field testing, including the Zino's more contrasting, dark eye patch owing to its paler forecrown, a weaker M-pattern across the upperwing, and on average a darker gray tail. **Voice** Generally silent at sea. **Status & Distribution** Rare. BREEDING: Colonies on islands in the eastern Atlantic. NONBREEDING: Disperses to surrounding waters. Rare from May–Sept. in warm Gulf Stream waters off Hatteras, NC. VAGRANT: Accidental inland after hurricanes and north in the Gulf Stream to the Canadian Maritimes (1 rec.). **Population** Global population fewer than 1,000 pairs. Suffers predation from introduced predators, direct persecution from humans, and indirect habitat loss due to feral grazers. BirdLife International considers it near threatened.

BERMUDA PETREL *Pterodroma cahow*

darker rump

Once thought to be extinct, this endangered species (also known as the Cahow) was rediscovered breeding on islets off Bermuda. In North America it has been recorded only from Gulf Stream waters off North Carolina. In recent years, records of the Bermuda (first recorded in N.A. in 1996) have increased; it is now seen annually. Its rebounding population may account for this, but increased observer awareness and identification skills are probably also factors. Monotypic. L 15" (38 cm) WS 35" (89 cm)

Identification Distinctive small, slim structure and dark-hooded appearance (typically lacking pale collar). Generally dark across the back, sometimes blackish with faint M-pattern when fresh. Pale uppertail coverts usually restricted. Dark blackish gray head, typically lacking white collar; pale throat and dark neck sides. Underparts white. Underwing white, with dark flight feathers and bold dark ulnar bar diagonally across the underwing coverts. Ages and sexes similar. FLIGHT: Dynamic high arcing flight typical of gadfly petrels, but more like the smaller western Atlantic species.

Similar Species Most similar to the Black-capped Petrel in plumage, but lacks that species' distinct white collar and bright white uppertail coverts; generally lacks the white-tailed appearance of that species when viewed dorsally. Head darker than the Black-capped's, with a more cowled appearance. In flight more like the smaller western Atlantic gadflies; overall smaller and slimmer than the Black-capped.

Voice Generally silent at sea; gives eerie nocturnal flight calls at breeding colonies.

Status & Distribution Casual in N.A. BREEDING: One of the rarest seabirds in the world, restricted to islets off Bermuda. NONBREEDING: Disperses to surrounding waters. VAGRANT: Casual in warm Gulf Stream waters off NC May–Aug. Historic at-sea range unknown.

Population Exploited as a food resource during the 17th century, leading to its near extinction. Rediscovered after a 300-year absence breeding on islets off Bermuda. World population now about 50 pairs. Threatened by introduced predators. Protection of colony on Nonsuch Is., Bermuda, largely responsible for this species' recovery. BirdLife International considers it endangered.

BLACK-CAPPED PETREL *Pterodroma hasitata*

The Black-capped is the most commonly occurring gadfly petrel in North America (found regularly in warm Gulf Stream waters off the East Coast north to VA). One can expect to encounter tens or even hundreds of these petrels on a typical pelagic trip off Cape Hatteras in May to October. Its highly acrobatic flight style is distinctive, and its bright, white plumage details make it identifiable at long range. Polytypic. L 16" (41 cm) WS 37" (94 cm)

Identification Large and stocky; especially apparent when viewed ventrally, with dark blackish upperwings and a bold white collar. Appears white tailed at a distance, but at close range the dark tips to the tail feathers become obvious. Upperwings dark blackish with indistinct, dark M-pattern. Tail and rump white, with dark tips. Head largely white; dark cap ranging from black to dark brown, occasionally restricted or lacking; dark black eye smudge and bold white collar; white forehead. Large, stocky, dark bill. White below, with white underwing and variable dark ulnar bar across the underwing coverts. Dark flight feathers. Ages

typical

darker variant

Black-capped Petrel   Greater Shearwater

and sexes similar; molt can cause unusual splotching on dark upperwing. FLIGHT: Dynamic, arcing high above the water; rarely flapping on stiff wings angled back at wrist. Arcs higher above the water than shearwaters.

Geographic Variation Two subspecies generally recognized, but some authorities consider them separate species: nominate restricted to breeding on Hispaniola, with the largest historic colonies in Haiti; recent information suggests possible breeding in Cuba and other small Caribbean islands. The all-dark *caribbaea* (the "Jamaican" Petrel), bred only on Jamaica; it was last seen in the 1800s and is now feared extinct.

Similar Species Most similar to the Bermuda Petrel, but larger and stockier with bold white collar and largely white tail. The Bermuda is generally darker headed.

Voice Generally silent at sea.

Status & Distribution Common in restricted range. BREEDING: Restricted to a few Caribbean islands (see Geographic Variation). NONBREEDING: Common over deep Gulf Stream waters off NC, May–Oct.; rare in winter. Perhaps regularly ranges to VA and FL. Disperses to surrounding waters north of the Gulf Stream, rarely to the Canadian Mari-

times, and south to Brazil. VAGRANT: Casual inland to the Great Lakes on large bodies of water after hurricanes. **Population** Global population dwindling; likely just a few thousand breeding pairs persist. Breeding areas in Haiti decimated by habitat destruction, with many petrels still being taken directly as a food resource. Predation by introduced predators (esp. rats, mongooses) is a persistent problem. Considered endangered by BirdLife International.

HAWAIIAN PETREL *Pterodroma sandwichensis (E)*

This rarely encountered gadfly petrel was recently split from the very similar Galápagos Petrel (*P. phaeopygia*). Both taxa were previously classified as a single species, the Dark-rumped Petrel. Monotypic. L 17" (43 cm) WS 39" (99 cm)

Identification Medium-sized; sleek; elegant pattern of clean white below, black above. Blackish gray, uniform upperparts; a slight darker M-pattern when fresh. Dark tail and rump; occasionally flecked white uppertail coverts. Head largely dark; white forehead; dark neck sides form partial collar. Underwing largely white; darker flight feathers; restricted black ulnar bar. Axillaries white; dark patch visible when arcing high into the wind. Ages and sexes alike. FLIGHT: Strong flight on long wings bent back at wrist; quick deep flaps followed by high arcs above the sea.

Similar Species Almost identical in the

field to the Galápagos. Note that species' lighter build, black-flecked forehead. Field criteria for their identification still being worked out; the ABA Checklist has only accepted records as Hawaiian/Galápagos Petrel.

Voice Generally silent at sea. At breed-

ing colonies, gives several call types including a resonant *A'uuuuu'A'uu'A'u-u'A'* presumably the origin of their Hawaiian name, the "'Ua'u."

Status & Distribution Casual in N.A. BREEDING: Once nested on all the Hawaiian Is. Now primarily restricted to small colonies on Maui and Hawaii; small numbers possibly remain on 3 other islands. NONBREEDING: Presumably disperses to surrounding tropical waters; pelagic range poorly known. VAGRANT: Casual off CA and the Pacific coast with about 10 recs.

Population Very small global population of fewer than 1,000 pairs. Decimated by habitat loss and predation by introduced predators (esp. mongooses, cats, rats). Prized as a food source; populations decimated by human persecution; feared extinct until rediscovery in 1948. Designated as vulnerable by BirdLife International and as endangered by U.S. government.

COOK'S PETREL *Pterodroma cookii*

The Cook's is a small, sharply patterned gadfly petrel of the Pacific. It is often grouped with the Stejneger's Petrel and several other very similar extralimital species and referred to collectively as Cookilaria petrels. Monotypic. L 10" (25 cm) WS 26" (66 cm)

Identification Combination of small size, pale gray upperparts with striking dorsal M-pattern, and clean white underparts is unlike most other pterodromas. Tail gray above with dark, central tip; white outer tail feathers difficult to see under field conditions. Head largely grayish; dark eye patch; white throat. Clean white underparts, including underwing; thin, dark mark at wrist. Ages and sexes alike. FLIGHT: Dynamic but erratic compared to other pterodro-

mas, with quick direction changes.

Similar Species In N.A., the Stejneger's Petrel is the most similar, but it is darker above with a less distinct M-pattern and a darker head, imparting a capped or hooded appearance.

Voice Generally silent at sea.

Status & Distribution Rare in N.A. BREEDING: Nests on 3 islands off New Zealand. NONBREEDING: Moves northeast to eastern Pacific. It is rare in deep water off the West Coast from spring through fall. VAGRANT: Accidental in Alaskan waters. Has been found several times at the Salton Sea in midsummer (presumably birds traveling north across the desert from north end of the Gulf of California).

Population Global population threatened from predation of introduced

mammals and from a native rail, the weka. Removal of cats and wekas from some breeding islands has produced promising results. BirdLife International designates it as endangered.

STEJNEGER'S PETREL *Pterodroma longirostris*

Similar to the Cook's Petrel in its overall appearance, the dark-capped Stejneger's Petrel (another of the so-called Cookilaria petrels, inc. the Cook's Petrel) has been recorded just a few times off the West Coast. The first North American record was made in 1979, off California. Monotypic. L 10" (25 cm) WS 26" (66 cm)
Identification A small, slim *Pterodroma* bird showing a dark M-pattern on its gray wings and upperparts, with clean white underparts. It has a notably black-capped (or half-hooded) head; the black half-hood encompasses the eye and contrasts strongly with the gray mantle and pale forehead. Normally the dark half-hood is very noticeable, but it can be difficult to see on birds flying away. The white of the throat hooks up slightly behind the eye, accentuating an intrusion of dark feathers just behind it. The tail is long and appears uniformly dark; the white in the outer tail feathers is restricted and difficult to see under field conditions. Underwings are clean white, with a thin, dark mark at wrist (similar to the Cook's Petrel). Ages and sexes are alike. FLIGHT: Dramatic and bounding, the Stejneger's Petrel arcs high off the water in strong winds. It is prone to erratic maneuvers, though it is somewhat less so than the Cook's Petrel.
Similar Species Similar to the Cook's Petrel and to other unrecorded Cookilaria petrels. When comparing it to the Cook's Petrel, note the Stejneger's Petrel's black cap, its darker gray upperparts, its blacker outer wing, and its darker tail. Structurally, the Stejneger's Petrel is slightly smaller and shorter-winged.
Voice Generally silent at sea.
Status & Distribution Vagrant to North America. BREEDING: Nests on the Juan Fernandez Is. off Chile. NONBREEDING: Disperses to surrounding waters with movements north of the equator. It has been suggested that the Stejneger's Petrel makes a loop migration through the northern Pacific, passing through waters east of Japan as it moves north, and through the eastern Pacific (closer to our West Coast) as it moves south in Oct. and Nov. VAGRANT: Accidental off CA; recorded from mid-summer through fall in deep offshore waters. More regular much further offshore, beyond the 200-mile limit, but confusion with similar species confounds status.
Population Population likely stable. Threatened at breeding colonies, mostly by feral cats. BirdLife International has designated the Stejneger's Petrel as vulnerable.

Genus Bulweria

BULWER'S PETREL *Bulweria bulwerii*

This unusual petrel—which recalls an oversized, dark storm-petrel with very long wings and an exceptionally long, pointed tail—is accidental in North American waters. The genus *Bulweria* contains only one other species, the larger Jouanin's Petrel *(B. fallax)* of the Indian Ocean. Monotypic. L 10" (26 cm) WS 26" (66 cm)
Identification A medium-sized and all-dark petrel with a long, pointed tail, recalling a large storm-petrel. The long, pointed wings are dark brown above and below, with a bold tawny carpal bar extending forward to the leading edge of the wing. The tail is long, dark, and pointed; its wedge shape is concealed except during twisting aerial maneuvers. The head and the underparts are wholly dark brown; the bill is heavy and black. The Bulwer's appears dove-headed, lacking the thick neck and heavy build of most *Pterodroma* petrels. Ages and sexes are alike. FLIGHT: Buoyant, erratic, and zigzagging with long wings slightly bowed and held well forward; usually close to the water's surface; in calm conditions, sometimes a few wingbeats then a short glide. Bulwer's has the lowest wing-loading of any tubenose. Unlike *Pterodroma* petrels, it does not normally arc high over the water, nor does it flutter like storm-petrels.
Similar Species The Bulwer's Petrel is most similar to Black Storm-Petrel, but note its larger size and medium brown coloration as well as its long, wedge-shaped tail; the Black Storm-Petrel has a deeply forked tail. The dark-morph Wedge-tailed Shearwater has a similar tail, but it is much larger and has a different flight style: slow, languid wingbeats, as well as prolonged soaring with bowed wings angled forward to the wrist, then swept back; usually stays close to the water. Surprisingly, although the various populations of the Bulwer's Petrel are separated by vast distances, no geographical variation has been detected among them.
Voice Generally silent at sea.
Status & Distribution Vagrant to North America. BREEDING: Breeds on oceanic islands in the three major oceans, including the Cape Verde Is. and the Hawaiian Is. (The majority of the world's population nests on Nihoa, in the northwest chain of HI.) These are the 2 likely sources for North American vagrants. NONBREEDING: Its at-sea distribution is poorly understood, but the Bulwer's Petrel disperses offshore to surrounding tropical waters. VAGRANT: Recorded 3 times in North America: off Cape Hatteras, NC, July 1, 1992; off Monterey Bay, CA, July 26, 1998; off Oregon Inlet, NC, Aug. 8, 1998. There are several other sight records, but none of these has been accepted by state and provincial records committees.
Population Stable, but populations are experiencing predation at breeding colonies by introduced mammalian predators. Some populations are still exploited as a food resource by humans.

LARGE SHEARWATERS Genus *Calonectris*

These Shearwaters are typically large and long-winged; their slow, languid wingbeats are quite unlike the shorter, shallow wingbeats of the *Puffinus* shearwaters. They are able to arc high off the water, when they appear uncharacteristically buoyant for their size. Only 2 species are currently recognized: the Cory's (Atlantic) and the Streaked (western Pacific).

CORY'S SHEARWATER *Calonectris diomedea*

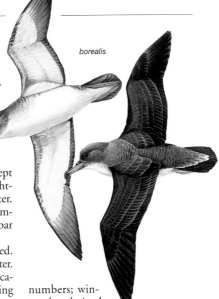

borealis

A large, familiar shearwater of the western Atlantic, this species occurs regularly offshore from spring through fall. Polytypic (2 ssp. in N.A.). L 18" (46 cm) WS 46" (117 cm)

Identification Subspecies *borealis* described and illustrated. Large; pale brownish gray upperparts; heavy yellow bill, dusky tip; strikingly white underparts. Brownish gray upperparts rather featureless, somewhat paler on the mantle; when fresh some show a darker M-pattern. Dark tail; uppertail coverts variably pale to whitish. Gray head, slightly darker around eye. Pink legs, feet. Molting birds (frequent in summer) show bluish gray, fresh flight feathers contrasting worn brownish ones;

may show whitish wing bars due to dropped coverts. Ages and sexes alike. FLIGHT: Unusually buoyant for its size, sometimes arcing high even in light winds; arcs unusually steep, often appearing to pivot on a wing tip at the apex of its arc. Intersperses slow, heavy flapping between glides, imparting the impression of an albatross. Wings usually held pressed forward in a gentle curve, then swept back; quite different from the straight-out wings of the Greater Shearwater. **Geographic Variation** Only *borealis* is common off the East Coast. See sidebar below.

Similar Species Unlikely to be confused. Compare distant birds with the Greater.

Voice Generally silent at sea; but occasionally gives a descending cackling when excited around food.

Status & Distribution Common in offshore Atlantic waters from spring through fall. BREEDING: Nests on oceanic islands in the eastern Atlantic and Mediterranean. NONBREEDING: Disperses to surrounding waters, some moving west and some south; reaches the western edge of the Gulf Stream in numbers; winters largely in the south Atlantic off the coast of west Africa. VAGRANT: Casual inland after hurricanes. Accidental off central CA (1 rec.).

Population Large global population. Breeding sites threatened by habitat loss, introduced predators, and human exploitation as a food source.

Subspecies Variation in the Cory's Shearwater

Cory's Shearwaters comprise 3 subspecies (all recorded in N.A.), and some authorities suggest that they may be distinct species based on differences in morphology and vocalizations. The familiar, "everyday" Cory's in North American waters is the widespread *borealis,* breeding on east Atlantic islands. Very similar is *diomedea* ("Scopoli's" Shearwater), breeding in the Mediterranean and known to occur in North American waters from specimen records. The distinctive *edwardsii* ("Cape Verde" Shearwater) breeds on the Cape Verde Islands in the east Atlantic. All three taxa are separable in the field. From the "baseline" *borealis,* the "Scopoli's" shows more extensive white on the underwing: the white

"Cape Verde" Shearwater (NC, Aug.)

"Cape Verde" Shearwater (NC, Aug.)

extends out onto the primaries. It also has somewhat paler upperparts and a less heavy, duller yellow bill. The "Cape Verde" is very different from the others and is relatively easy to identify. It is smaller and darker overall, with more slender wings, a longer tail, a darker cap, an often paler mantle that contrasts with its darker wings, and a slim, mostly grayish or fleshy gray bill. These differences make the "Cape Verde" somewhat similar to the Greater, but it lacks that species' bright white collar and dark marking on the underwings and belly. Recently well-documented off Hatteras, NC, the "Cape Verde" might soon see full-species status in North America: It has already been split by European ornithologists. ■

STREAKED SHEARWATER *Calonectris leucomelas*

This rare wanderer from the western Pacific is a much-sought-after specialty of West Coast fall pelagic trips. Monotypic. L 19" (48 cm) WS 48" (122 cm) **Identification** A large pale shearwater giving a dirty white-headed appearance; overall dark above and white below. Variable head pattern, but almost always appears white at a distance; at close range streaked with brown, heaviest on nape and palest around bill and eye. The bill is bluish or yellowish gray (rarely pinkish) with a darker tip. Dark brownish upperparts, often appearing scaly due to pale fringes on the upperwing coverts and mantle feathers; the upperparts become paler and browner when worn and bleached. Long, dark tail. The uppertail coverts are variable: they can be all-dark or white, forming a pale U-shape on the rump. The underwings are largely white with a broad rear border and wing tip formed by the dark flight feathers. Just out from the wrist, the mostly dark, median primary coverts form a conspicuous dark patch on the underwing. The

legs and feet are fleshy pink. Ages and sexes alike. FLIGHT: Agile, with long, broad-based wings. Flies with slow, languid wingbeats unlike most shearwaters; arcs high above the sea surface when traveling.
Similar Species Most likely to be confused with the Pink-footed Shearwater. The Pink-footeds appear dusky headed with pink bills; have dark undertail coverts and darker (not scaly) upperparts; and usually have darker underwings than those found on the Streaked.
Voice Generally silent at sea, but gives excited cackling in feeding groups.
Status & Distribution Casual off the West Coast. BREEDING: Nests abundantly on islands off Japan and Asia. NON-BREEDING: Migrates south to waters off the Philippines, Indonesia, and eastern Australia. VAGRANT: Casual in the eastern Pacific. Most records from Monterey Bay, CA (Sept.–Oct.), including the first for North America on Oct. 3, 1975. One inland record, a bird seriously off course, captured at Red Bluff, CA, Aug. 1993.

variant with white uppertail coverts

Population Large global population stable. Threatened at breeding colonies by introduced mammalian predators. Some human exploitation as food source still exists, and occasionally birds die due to fishing industry nets.

SHEARWATERS Genus *Puffinus*

This large, complex genus (15–20 sp.) comprises all the remaining shearwaters in the world. Ongoing debate has resulted in the recognition of 40–49 taxa. In N.A., the Manx is the only breeding representative; the remaining species visit offshore waters during migration or dispersal. In the eastern Pacific, 6 species occur regularly; another 4 have been recorded as vagrants. In the western Atlantic, 4 species occur regularly, and 2 have been recorded as vagrants. These species are known to wander, and individuals of several species have turned up multiple times in the wrong ocean altogether! Plumages range from all brown to black-and-white, with many muted variations. All nest in burrows and are pelagic when not breeding.

GREATER SHEARWATER *Puffinus gravis*

This strikingly plumaged large shearwater of the Atlantic often attends boats, where it forages for offal and refuse as well as for handouts. Monotypic. L 18" (46 cm) WS 44" (112 cm) **Identification** Large and dark above; more neatly patterned than other Atlantic shearwaters. Brownish black upperwings; pale tips on the upperwing coverts and mantle create a scaled appearance. Secondaries and greater upperwing coverts washed pale gray when fresh. Dark tail, with white uppertail coverts often forming a bold, U-shaped rump patch. Unique head pattern: The dark cap extends just below the eyes and is set off by white collar. The rear edge of the dark cap and a brownish half-collar near the wings frame a prominent white triangular shape on the

side of the head; often prominent on distant birds, this is completely lacking on the Cory's Shearwater. Dark bill is long and thin. Clean white underparts, with gray belly patch (often hidden, lost in shadow, or occasionally absent; but diagnostic if seen). The pale-centered underwings are broadly framed in dark with variable dark markings on the axillaries and coverts. Does not molt in North American waters. Ages and sexes alike. FLIGHT: Although a large shearwater, the Greater flies with stiff wingbeats like the smaller *Puffinus* shearwaters and unlike the slow, languid wingbeats of the Cory's Shearwater. The Greater arcs and glides on stiff wings that are not crooked back at the wrist, but held straight out, generally staying close to the water.

Similar Species Most similar to the Black-capped Petrel, but it lacks the clean white underparts and dark ulnar bar as well as the white-tailed appearance (when viewed dorsally) of that species. The black cap of the Black-capped Petrel is variable, but it is usually more restricted than on the Greater; and most Black-cappeds show

a prominent white forehead (lacking in the Greater) and a broader white collar. At a distance, the Greater often stays lower to the water than the Black-capped and, noticeably, holds its wings more straight out (not angled back at the wrist, like pterodromas). The Greater is smaller and more boldly patterned than the Cory's Shearwater, with a dark cap and pale collar. The "Cape Verde" Shearwater (a ssp. of the Cory's) lacks the pale collar and does not appear to have the Greater's clean head-pattern.

Voice Generally silent at sea, but gives a whining drawn-out call when excited during foraging. Often vocalizes upon landing among other feeding seabirds.

Status & Distribution Common off the Atlantic coast from May through late fall. BREEDING: Nests colonially on oceanic islands in the S. Atlantic Ocean. NONBREEDING: Moves north

to spend the austral winter in the North Atlantic, where large numbers congregate in late summer. VAGRANT: Casual inland after hurricanes. Accidental off central CA.

Population Large global population. Overharvesting of adults and chicks as a food resource at breeding colonies could negatively impact the population.

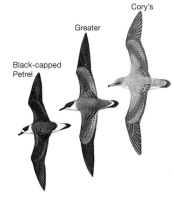

Cory's

Greater

Black-capped
Petrel

PINK-FOOTED SHEARWATER *Puffinus creatopus*

in molt

light

typical

dark

dark

The Pink-footed—the large, pale-bellied shearwater of offshore Pacific waters—is easily seen on pelagic trips from late spring through fall. Monotypic. L 19" (48 cm) WS 43" (109 cm)

Identification Large; lacks strong plumage contrasts; appears mostly grayish above and pale below. Heavy pink bill with dusky tip; legs and feet also pink, often visible against the dark undertail coverts in flight. Upperwing coloration ranges from gray to brownish, with odd white patches visible when molting. Underparts and underwings are quite variable: some authors consider it polymorphic, with light, dark, and intermediate morphs. Head generally dusky gray-brown, occasionally wholly dark on the darkest individuals; typically has a whitish throat. Whitish underparts, often dusky tinged, typically not appearing bright white below (beware strong sunlight); palest on belly. Underwing variable, but consistently shows dark flight feathers and pale underwing coverts, with variable dark markings on the axillaries. Dark individuals can have extensive grayish brown flanks and undertail coverts. FLIGHT: Generally flaps with slower, more labored wingbeats than other shearwaters, arcing and gliding high off the water in strong winds. Wings

are usually angled back slightly at the wrist, showing a long-handed appearance unlike most other *Puffinus* shearwaters.

Similar Species Darker individuals can be confused with the Flesh-footed Shearwater (esp. distant, swimming birds). The Flesh-footed is similar in shape, size, and flight style, but it never shows a pale belly or throat.

Voice Generally silent at sea.

Status & Distribution Common in offshore Pacific waters from spring through fall, rare in winter. BREEDING: Nest colonially on oceanic islands off Chile. NONBREEDING: Generally moves north from breeding areas across the Equator to spend the austral winter in North American Pacific waters.

Population Threatened at breeding sites by introduced mammalian predators, including coatis. Considered vulnerable by BirdLife International.

FLESH-FOOTED SHEARWATER *Puffinus carneipes*

This large, all-dark shearwater is uncommon during fall in the throngs of shearwaters gathering to feed in offshore Pacific waters. Some authorities consider it conspecific with the similar Pink-footed Shearwater. Mono-typic. L 17" (43 cm) WS 41" (104 cm) **Identification** Its all-dark plumage, slow-flapping, languid wingbeats, and pale bill are the first clues to its identity. Upperparts wholly chocolate brown, lacking contrasting patterns. Underparts and underwing coverts dark brown; primaries flash silvery in strong sunlight (compare to the Sooty Shearwater). Dark head, with a stout, pink to pinkish horn bill with dark tip. Pink legs and feet, visible against the dark undertail coverts in flight. FLIGHT: Flaps slowly and deliberately, lacking the hurried wingbeats of most other shearwaters. Arcs and glides high over sea surface in strong winds, with wings bent back slightly at the wrist.
Similar Species Most similar in size, shape, and flight style to the Pink-footed Shearwater, but differs in being wholly dark below. Larger than the Sooty and the Short-tailed Shearwaters, lacking silvery underwing coverts, and always showing a thick, pinkish bill. The dark-morph Wedge-tailed Shearwater is more delicately built and longer tailed, with a thinner dark bill, a wedge-shaped tail, and dark flight feathers. Also compare to the chocolate brown, first-winter Heermann's Gull.
Voice Generally silent at sea.
Status & Distribution Uncommon to rare off the West Coast. BREEDING: Nests colonially on oceanic islands off Australia and New Zealand and in the Indian Ocean. NONBREEDING: In the Pacific, moves north across the Equator. Small numbers move east to the eastern Pacific, occurring from BC to Baja California (Aug.–Dec., rarely through spring); rare south of Point Conception, CA.
Population Threatened largely by habitat loss and introduced mammalian predators. It was historically exploited as a food resource.

SHORT-TAILED SHEARWATER *Puffinus tenuirostris*

This small, dark shearwater visits the West Coast primarily during late fall and winter. Separation from the more common Sooty Shearwater is problematic. Spectacular concentrations of up to a million birds have been seen off Alaska, where this species congregates in late summer to feed in the nutrient-rich, shallow waters of the Bering Sea. Monotypic. L 17" (43 cm) WS 39" (99 cm) **Identification** Small, dark, and delicately built. Largely dark underwings and usually a pale chin. Bill structure and head shape are important identification features. Upperparts wholly chocolate brown, lacking strong contrasts. Underwings variable, typically dark brownish, but many have pale silvery underwing coverts (like the Sooty Shearwater's). Small, fine head and bill. Typically round headed, imparting a dove-like appearance. Bill short, thin, and all-dark. Head often appears dark capped due to the pale feathers around the bill, on the throat, and often on the lower face. Ages and sexes alike. FLIGHT: Flaps in short bursts, stiffly from the shoulder. Does not appear long winged; rather its wings often look short and narrow (stick-like) for its relatively bulky body. Rarely shows much angle at the wrist, usually holding wings completely outstretched. Arcs high above water in strong winds.
Similar Species Most similar to the Sooty Shearwater (see sidebar p. 83). Told from other dark shearwaters by overall shape, size, and plumage pattern.
Voice Generally silent at sea.
Status & Distribution Common off AK in summer, less common further south in winter. BREEDING: Nests colonially on islands of Australia. NONBREEDING: Moves north during the austral winter

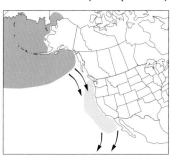

(our summer) to waters off AK, then further south along the West Coast in fall and winter where it can be found regularly off OR, WA, and CA. Scarcer in southern CA and Baja CA waters.
Population The large global population is threatened by a number of factors including human exploitation, habitat loss, predation at colonies by introduced predators, and entanglement in fishing nets.

SOOTY SHEARWATER *Puffinus griseus*

The commonest dark shearwater—in both oceans—this transequatorial migrant reaches our waters during the austral winter. Spectacular concentrations occur during mid-summer off central California, where hundreds of thousands can often be seen from shore, appearing as an endless dark cloud of birds moving over the sea surface just offshore. Common, though less concentrated, in Atlantic waters. Monotypic. L 18" (46 cm) WS 40" (102 cm)

Identification Medium-sized, heavily built, dark shearwater with silvery underwings. Upperwing wholly dark, lacking strong contrasts. Dark tail. Head pattern variable, but generally dark, sometimes with restricted pale feathering around bill. Bill long and black. Underwing pattern distinctive, with pale silvery coverts and dark flight feathers. Lighting can affect the visibility of this character: In strong morning light, underwings can appear very white, but they can appear all dark when backlit. Care is warranted. Beware that individuals in heavy molt can have variably tawny patches on upperwing and large tracts of missing feathers. Ages and sexes alike. FLIGHT: Varies with wind speed like all seabirds, but generally intersperses glides with bursts of clipped, stiff-winged flaps. Flapping often appears hurried, and wing movement seems to initiate wholly at the shoulder. Arcs high over the water in strong winds when it can be confused with dark *Pterodroma* petrels.

Similar Species Most similar to the Short-tailed Shearwater (see sidebar below). Told from other dark shearwaters by silvery underwing coverts, dark bill, and heavy structure.

Voice Generally silent at sea.

Status & Distribution Common to abundant in nearshore waters of both oceans. BREEDING: Nests colonially on oceanic islands off southern South America, Australia, and New Zealand. NON-BREEDING: Undertakes long, transequatorial migration in both oceans moving north to spend the austral winter (May–Aug.) in North Pacific and

North Atlantic waters; rare at other times. VAGRANT: Recorded 8 times at the Salton Sea during summer.

Population Large global population exploited as a food resource; still sold legally in New Zealand. Also used for soap and oil. Predation at colonies by introduced predators, habitat loss, and incidental death due to entanglement in fishing nets are ongoing problems.

Identification of Sooty and Short-tailed Shearwaters

Separating Short-tailed and Sooty Shearwaters is one of the most difficult field problems off the West Coast. Key field marks for separating the 2 are the shape and coloration of the head and bill, and the underwing pattern; however, these are not diagnostic. A combination of features is necessary to confirm identification, and typically any candidate is considered a Sooty Shearwater until proven otherwise. Probability should weigh into any identification: Sooty Shearwaters greatly outnumber Short-tailed Shearwaters during spring, summer, and early fall; but during late fall and winter, they can occur in relatively even numbers.

Note the dove-like head shape of the Short-tailed; it is more delicate, with a rounded crown and steeper forehead than the Sooty's flatter forehead. The bill of the Short-tailed is finer, shorter, and slimmer overall.

Sooty Shearwater

Short-tailed Shearwater (CA, Nov.)

The bill of the Sooty is thicker at the base and tip (with a "pinched-in" center) and longer, with a more prominent nail.

Generally, the underwing of the Short-tailed is darker than the Sooty's, and any individual with dark underwing coverts is automatically a strong candidate for the Short-tailed. But variation exists in this feature. On Short-taileds with paler underwings, there exists a subtle difference in the distribution of light and dark: typically the Short-tailed's underwing is palest in the center (on the median secondary coverts), whereas the Sooty is palest further out on the underwing (on the median primary coverts), creating a strong contrast between these pale feathers and the dark primaries. Additionally, on the Sooty, the pale feathers of the secondary coverts have dark tips that often form thin, dark rows on the inner wing. ∎

WEDGE-TAILED SHEARWATER *Puffinus pacificus*

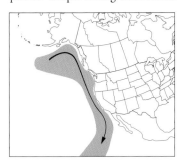

dark morphs

light morph

This rare visitor is always a surprise when encountered on West Coast pelagic trips. The provenance of individuals recorded in North America is a matter of some debate, as breeding populations exist on islands off Mexico and in Hawaii. Its graceful shape and flight style immediately separate it as something unique among Pacific shearwaters. Monotypic. L 18" (46 cm) WS 40" (102 cm) **Identification** Polymorphic, occurring in both light and dark morphs. A large,

lanky shearwater characterized by a slim build and a long, wedge-shaped tail. Head appears small; the long, thin, blue-gray bill has a dark tip. Pinkish legs and feet. LIGHT MORPH: White below and brownish above with pale tips on the upperwing coverts and scapulars giving a scaly appearance. White throat, chest, and belly, but head can appear largely dark at a distance. Underwing variable, but generally light; some with darker leading edge and dark line across the underwing coverts connecting with the axillaries. Dark flight feathers. DARK MORPH: Upperparts as in light morph, but often slightly darker. Underwing and ventral body wholly dark, with dark flight feathers. Some intermediate birds occur: dark morphs with grayer underparts or paler underwings, and light morphs with a grayish breast band or gray below with a white throat. FLIGHT: Extremely graceful, with slow, languid wingbeats; usually stays low to the water. Holds broad-based wings slight-

ly forward, bent back at the wrist and bowed down.
Similar Species The light morph is most similar to the Buller's Shearwater in size and shape, but note the Wedge-tailed's longer tail, bulging secondaries, and plainer, gray-brown back. The dark morph is similar to other dark shearwaters in plumage; note unique shape and flight style. Most similar to the Flesh-footed; note the Wedge-tailed's longer tail, lighter build, thinner black bill, and darker flight feathers.
Voice Generally silent at sea.
Status & Distribution Vagrant to North American waters. BREEDING: Nests colonially on oceanic islands in the tropical Pacific (including HI and islands off western Mexico) and Indian Oceans. NONBREEDING: Disperses to surrounding tropical waters; migration, if any, is poorly understood. VAGRANT: Casual, fewer than 10 records for the Pacific coast, most from CA; 1 inland record at the Salton Sea, July 31, 1988.
Population Global populations severely impacted historically by human exploitation, predation pressure from introduced mammalian predators, and habitat loss.

BULLER'S SHEARWATER *Puffinus bulleri*

This strikingly plumaged Pacific species can be mistaken for a rare *Pterodroma* petrel due to the bold M-pattern across the surface of its wings. Widely considered the most elegant shearwater in North America, its plumage, structure, and flight style are unusually graceful. Monotypic. L 16" (41 cm) WS 40" (102 cm)
Identification Distinctly black-capped head, with a clean demarcation between the dark cap and light sides of face and throat. Dove gray upperparts set off by a bold, blackish M-pattern, creating a black-on-gray pattern unique among shearwaters.

Gleaming white underwings and ventral body; the underwings are neatly outlined in black. Some fresh-plumaged birds have a very subdued M-pattern; worn birds are browner above. Ages and sexes alike. FLIGHT: Elegant, with smooth, unhurried wingbeats and elongated appearance. In direct flight uses slow, measured wingbeats; in strong winds arcs high like a pterodroma, flapping little, if at all.
Similar Species Most similar to pterodromas, especially the Cook's Petrel, but note the larger size and more rangy appearance of the Buller's, its slower wingbeats (if flapping), and its long, thin bill. Unlikely to be confused with other shearwaters.
Voice Generally silent at sea.
Status & Distribution Uncommon to fairly common off the West Coast. BREEDING: Nests colonially on a few islands off New Zealand. NONBREEDING: Moves north and east of breeding islands to feeding areas in the North Pacific. Uncommon; sometimes numerous or in large flocks, in late summer and fall off central CA north-

worn

ward to the Gulf of Alaska; rare south of Point Conception. VAGRANT: Accidental inland at the Salton Sea (Aug. 6, 1966); 1 rec. off NJ (Oct. 28, 1984).
Population Historic numbers impacted by human exploitation and predation by introduced predators. BirdLife International considers it vulnerable.

MANX SHEARWATER *Puffinus puffinus*

This species belongs to a group of small black-and-white shearwaters that are confusing to identify and taxonomically unsettled. Historically, the Manx

was considered a single species with many subspecies distributed. Recent authors have separated it into many distinct species. Polytypic (3 ssp., nominate in N.A.). L 13.5" (34 cm) WS 33" (84 cm)

Identification Small, stocky build; sharply demarcated black-and-white plumage. Upperwings typically blackish, occasionally fade browner. Distinctive head pattern: eye encompassed by dark cap, contrasting sharply with white throat and a pale area that wraps up behind the ear coverts (the pale "ear surround"). Clean white underparts. Underwing variable, often pure white coverts contrast with blackish flight feathers; occasionally a dark intrusion across coverts connects with axillaries. Ages and sexes alike. FLIGHT: Wingbeats stiff, hurried; in strong winds arcs high above water. Wings held straight out with little or no bend at the wrist.

Similar Species Most similar to the Audubon's Shearwater in the western Atlantic. Note the Audubon's lighter build, longer tail, whiter face, and dark undertail coverts. The Manx in the eastern Pacific (where rare) most closely resembles the Black-vented Shearwater.

Voice Generally silent at sea.

Status & Distribution Regular off the Atlantic coast; rare off the West Coast. BREEDING: Oceanic islands in the North Atlantic; in N.A. only on islands off NF and MA. NONBREEDING: In winter (Sept.–May) moves south to waters off the east coast of S.A.; some stay as far north as NC. Some birds (presumed nonbreeding) summer as far south as NC, where rare. Very rare off the West Coast (100+ records for CA); breeding unconfirmed in Pacific. VAGRANT: Casual inland to the Great Lakes and occasionally farther west (e.g., MN).

Population Large global population, but impacted by introduced predators, habitat loss, and human persecution.

BLACK-VENTED SHEARWATER *Puffinus opisthomelas*

This small shearwater occurs during the winter months in the nearshore waters off southern California. Monotypic. L 14" (36 cm) WS 34" (86 cm)
Identification Dingy; stocky build. Dark undertail coverts; individuals with white undertail coverts have been recorded. Upperwings largely brownish; can appear blackish when fresh; fade substantially with wear. Head generally dusky grayish brown, lacks strong contrast between dark cap and paler throat. Underparts variable: typically whitish, often washed on the flanks with dusky gray-brown. Ages and sexes alike. FLIGHT: In direct flight, flaps with stiff

typical

dark

light

hurried wingbeats, wings held straight out with little bend at the wrist. In strong winds, arcs high over the water.
Similar Species Distant birds resemble Pink-footed, but fly with faster wingbeats and are generally seen in flocks. Cautiously separated from much rarer Manx: note Manx's cleaner white appearance below, more contrasting black-and-white plumage, white undertail coverts, pale "ear-surround." Harsh lighting can make Black-vented appear more black-and-white. Townsend's shearwater *(P. auricularis)* is very similar, but not recorded in N.A.
Voice Generally silent at sea.
Status & Distribution Common within limited West Coast range. BREEDING: Oceanic islands off Baja California. NONBREEDING: Disperses primarily north after breeding; large numbers spend the winter (Oct.–Mar.) off southern CA; rare north to BC.
Population Small global population and restricted breeding range make it especially susceptible to drastic declines. Considered vulnerable by BirdLife International.

AUDUBON'S SHEARWATER   *Puffinus lherminieri*

This small black-and-white shearwater resides in the tropical oceans and is closely related to the Manx and Little Shearwaters. Polytypic (approx. 10 ssp.). L 12" (30 cm) WS 27" (69 cm)

Identification Small, fast flying; solidly blackish above, white below. Blackish brown upperparts; thin pale tips to greater upperwing coverts when fresh. Head variable, but typically dark capped; sharply demarcated from the white cheek and throat, bordered behind with a dark half-collar; some show white completely encircling the eye. Medium-length bill is thin, and dark. Underparts bright white, including underwings; occasionally with variable dark bar across underwing coverts to axillaries. Flight feathers grayish below, black above. Tail long and dark; undertail coverts typically blackish brown, giving a "dipped in ink" appearance; occasionally shows mixed white feathers in the undertail coverts. Legs and feet typically pink, but can be blue or a mix of both. Ages and sexes alike. FLIGHT: Generally stays low to the water interspersing hurried, stiff wingbeats with long glides; arcs modestly during strong winds.

Geographic Variation Taxonomy is still evolving and confused (2 ssp. likely occur in N.A.). The nominate, of the Caribbean, is the most likely to be encountered based on proximity; subspecific identification at sea is impossible due to lack of identification criteria. The smaller *loyemilleri,* which nests in the Caribbean off Panama, closely resembles the Little Shearwater; its status in North America is uncertain. In the Pacific, *subalaris* (smaller and darker, lacks half-collar) wanders as far as central Mexico (potential West Coast vagrant).

Similar Species Most similar to the Manx. Note the Audubon's brownish cast to the upperparts, longer tail, and dark undertail coverts. Also similar to the Little, but larger, with darker face, larger bill, longer tail, and dark undertail coverts.

Voice Generally silent at sea.

Status & Distribution Common in warm Gulf Stream waters typically along temperature breaks. BREEDING: Nearest populations nest on islands in the Caribbean. NONBREEDING: Caribbean breeders disperse north into the Gulf Stream (May–Sept.). Uncommon in Gulf of Mexico and rare off New England. VAGRANT: Casual inland after hurricanes.

Population Restricted breeding range and sedentary habits make this species susceptible to human exploitation and introduced predators.

LITTLE SHEARWATER   *Puffinus assimilis*

The Little Shearwater is known in North America from a few records off the East Coast and one off the West Coast. Polytypic (8 ssp.). L 11" (28 cm) WS 25" (64 cm)

Identification Subspecies *baroli* described and illustrated. The smallest of the black-and-white shearwaters to occur in North America. Upperparts largely blackish, but a whitish panel on the upper secondaries is usually visible. Dark-capped head; bold white face, eye completely encircled with white. Tiny, all-dark bill. White underparts, including underwing coverts and, most importantly, the undertail coverts. Blue legs and feet, difficult to see. FLIGHT: Flies low to the water on hurried wingbeats and short glides; sometimes compared to an alcid or the Spotted Sandpiper. Intersperses glides with modest arcs in strong winds; sometimes raises head upward at the end of glides.

Geographic Variation Current taxonomy undergoing revision. In the western North Atlantic, only *baroli* has occurred with certainty. It nests on the Azores and Canary Islands. The subspecies *boydi* nests on the Cape Verde Islands, and its proximity to our area makes it a likely, if not already overlooked, subspecies. Confusingly, *boydi* is often considered part of the Audubon's Shearwater complex, which it closely resembles due to its similarly dark face (lacking the white eye-surround of *baroli*). The Eastern Pacific record may pertain to the nominate, *assimilis.*

Similar Species Most similar to the Audubon's Shearwater but structurally smaller, more compact, and stockier, with shorter, more rounded wings. Subspecies *baroli* further differs from the Audubon's in having a white face and white undertail coverts; *boydi* unlikely to be separable from the Audubon's in the field based on known plumage characters.

Voice Generally silent at sea.

Status & Distribution Vagrant to N.A. BREEDING: Breeds on oceanic islands;

baroli

Cape Verde, Azore, and Canary Is. have the closest breeding colonies to N.A. NONBREEDING: Poorly known; some likely sedentary, others dispersing to surrounding waters. VAGRANT: Accidental. Recorded fewer than 6 times in N.A. (1 rec. on West Coast; several unsubstantiated reports).

Population Several small populations are declining due to human exploitation as a food resource; also impacted by habitat loss and introduced predators.

STORM-PETRELS Family Hydrobatidae

Fork-tailed Storm-Petrel (AK)

The small size, quick flight low over the water, and monochromatic, generally dark plumages of storm-petrels challenge the abilities of many birders. For identification purposes, first know that in general Northern Hemisphere storm-petrels have longer wings and shorter legs, whereas those from the Southern Hemisphere have shorter, rounded wings and long legs; there is some overlap in the tropics. Secondly, focus on the exact distribution of white on the rump and, perhaps more important, on flight style. Not all birds are identifiable, and sufficient views are a must. Many species will closely approach boats when attracted by chum and fishing refuse; they have well developed olfactory systems and use their sense of smell to locate food sources—and even individual nest burrows and crevices. At these times, close scrutiny is possible.

Structure Most storm-petrels are small birds, lightly built with long narrow wings. They have large heads, with slim bodies and tails that range from short to quite long. Some species have long legs that dangle below the body and long feet, which they patter on the surface of the water.

Behavior Flight pattern varies with each species, but most stay low to the water due to their small size and foraging techniques. They often appear swallowlike when searching for small prey items on the surface, but some of the larger species act more like small shearwaters, gliding and arcing on stiff wings. Several species have exaggerated, languid wingbeats like those of a nighthawk. Flight style changes significantly with activity and wind conditions. Many species are more dynamic in direct flight, incorporating more arcing and gliding when covering large tracts of open ocean. Mixed-species flocks of up to 10,000 birds occur off the California coast during early fall. Prey items are generally phytoplankton or other small invertebrates, but many species will occasionally take small fish if available. Most species only make nocturnal visits to their breeding colonies and are rarely observed in the immediate vicinity.

Plumage For the most part storm-petrels are dark brown to blackish, but several species are gray above and pale below. Many have extensively pale rumps, other species are all-dark. Most dark storm-petrels show a pale diagonal bar across the upper wing, formed by the buffy and often faded greater upperwing coverts; its extent and prominence can aid field identification. Ages and sexes generally look alike, but plumages fade considerably with wear. Most birds complete a single annual molt on the nonbreeding grounds at sea. One can see a wide variety of molt states within a single species in a day, presumably due to age and fitness.

Distribution Storm-petrels occur in all oceans. In North America, at least 6 species occur in the eastern Pacific; 3 white-rumped species commonly occur (Wilson's, Leach's, and Band-rumped Storm-Petrels), and at least 4 others have been recorded as vagrants, in the western Atlantic. Only the Wilson's regularly undertakes a transequatorial migration from subantarctic breeding areas into North American waters. The Black and the Least regularly migrate into the Southern Hemisphere during their nonbreeding season. Migratory routes are poorly understood. It is believed that many species disperse into surrounding waters during the nonbreeding season. Some undertake northward dispersal events in the eastern Pacific, others disperse southward from breeding colonies.

Taxonomy Worldwide there are 20 species in 7 genera; 36 taxa are generally recognized. The taxonomy of many species is still a matter of debate. The AOU lists 10 species in 4 genera as occurring in North America; we include here the Black-bellied Storm-Petrel, recently recorded off Cape Hatteras, NC.

Conservation Storm-petrels suffer little direct persecution or indirect mortality as a result of the fishing industry; however, they are subject to avian (esp. skuas) and mammalian predation. The introduction of non-native predators to breeding islands has resulted in the decimation of some breeding colonies; the nearby Mexican Guadalupe Storm-Petrel *(Oceanodroma macrodactyla)* has presumably gone extinct. BirdLife International lists 1 species as critical, 1 as vulnerable, and 2 as near threatened. *—Brian Sullivan*

Genus *Oceanites*

WILSON'S STORM-PETREL *Oceanites oceanicus*

The small, dark, white-rumped Wilson's Storm-Petrel is abundantly observed in the Atlantic. Its distinctive feeding style includes pattering on the surface with long, dangling legs and feet. Polytypic. L 7.3" (18 cm) WS 16" (41 cm)

Identification Overall dark plumage, with bold white rump extending well down onto the undertail coverts. Well-defined pale carpal bar, frosty gray when fresh, fading to pale tan when worn, on the upper wing. Tail shape variable, often appearing squared in direct flight, but can appear slightly notched or even rounded during feeding. Long dark legs with yellow-webbed feet distinctive, often visible during feeding behavior. Ages and sexes look alike. Adults undergo molt during spring and summer in North American waters. FLIGHT: Flies low to the sea surface, occasionally arcing up into the air over wave tops. Direct flight with fluttery wingbeats interspersed with short glides. Feet extend past the tip of the tail. When feeding, holds its wings above the horizontal, fluttering while pattering the surface with its feet; often appears to be "walking on water."

Geographic Variation Two subspecies recognized: nominate *oceanicus* and *exasperatus*. The latter is proportionately larger but the two are inseparable under field conditions.

Similar Species The Wilson's has a similar plumage to other North Atlantic storm-petrels, but the Leach's and Band-rumped Storm-Petrels have distinctly longer wings and different flight styles. The Leach's flight is nighthawk-like; the Band-rumped's is shearwater-like. The European Storm-Petrel is very similar, but is smaller and lacks both the foot projection and prominent pale carpal bar of the Wilson's. See the European Storm-Petrel account for more.

Voice Generally silent at sea, but gives a faint peeping call when excitedly feeding in groups.

Status & Distribution Common. BREEDING: Nests colonially on oceanic islands in the southern oceans. NONBREEDING: Common offshore in the Atlantic May–Sept.; regularly seen from shore at favored locations. Rare in the Gulf of Mexico and rare off the CA coast late summer and fall. VAGRANT: Casual elsewhere on West Coast and inland after hurricanes.

Population The global population of this species, considered one of the most abundant seabirds, is likely stable. Introduced predators affect some colonies.

Genus *Hydrobates*

EUROPEAN STORM-PETREL *Hydrobates pelagicus*

The European is small and blackish with a white underwing bar. Its feet do not extend past the rounded tail. L 5.5–6.5" (14–17 cm) WS 14–15.5" (36–39 cm)

Identification Small and dark overall with long, narrow wings. The white greater underwing coverts are best looked for when it feeds with wings held high, otherwise they are difficult to see in flight. Bold, clean, white rump patch extends marginally onto rump sides. Upper wing typically dark, lacking the pale greater upperwing coverts of other Atlantic storm-petrels; juveniles can have pale-tipped greater upperwing coverts. Head and bill are small and delicate. Feet and legs are dark. Ages and sexes look alike. FLIGHT: Flies with flexing bursts recalling a large swift or Spotted Sandpiper; changes direction frequently. Wings rarely appear to break the horizontal in direct flight.

Similar Species Most likely to be confused with the Wilson's Storm-Petrel. Smaller and darker than the Wilson's, it is most easily picked out of a flock by its smaller size and darker upper wings lacking a distinct pale bar, lack of foot projection, longer narrower wings, different flight style, and white greater underwing coverts.

Voice Generally silent at sea.

Status & Distribution BREEDING: Nests on oceanic islands in the northeastern Atlantic and Mediterranean. NONBREEDING: Transequatorial migrant; wintering largely in southwest African

waters. VAGRANT: Fewer than 10 North American records. Single 1970 specimen record from NS; recent records in late May and early June off Cape Hatteras, NC.

Population Largely stable, but introduced predators, habitat loss, and pollution are affecting some populations.

Genus *Pelagodroma*

WHITE-FACED STORM-PETREL *Pelagodroma marina*

This much sought-after species occurs rarely in the western Atlantic, where it is now seen almost annually in late summer. Polytypic. L 7.5" (19 cm) WS 17" (43 cm)

Identification Where it occurs in the western Atlantic with other dark storm-petrels, this small, dynamic bird is distinctive in having primarily whitish underparts and a bold white facial pattern with dark auriculars and dark half-collar. The clean white underwing coverts contrast with the dark flight feathers. The brownish mantle and darker upperwing coverts and remiges create a pale saddled look; contrasting pale rump. Long tarsi dangle below the body during feeding and extend past the tail in direct flight. Ages and sexes look alike. FLIGHT: Its unique foraging technique, where it appears to hop across the water in pogo-stick fashion, its long legs dipping into the water as it moves across the sea surface, is unlike any other storm-petrel. It appears to spring off the surface of the water while rapidly changing direction with its wings almost always held fully extended and often seeming slightly bowed down.

It flaps with stiff, short wingbeats, and skips across the water with short glides. It flies in direct flight with similar stiff, short wingbeats followed by long glides on outstretched wings.

Geographic Variation Worldwide, 5 to 6 subspecies are recognized; the majority of North American records are of the Cape Verde Islands *eadesi*. It has a whiter forehead and pale collar compared with the darker faced *hypoleuca* of the Salvage Islands.

Similar Species The White-faced is unlikely to be confused with any other storm-petrel in the western Atlantic due to combination of white underparts, white face with bold dark auriculars, and distinctive feeding behavior. Potentially it could be confused with a winter-plumaged phalarope while sitting on the ocean, but note the White-faced's different posture, wing shape, and flight style when flushed.

Voice Generally silent at sea.

Status & Distribution Very rare in N.A. during late summer and early fall.

eadesi

BREEDING: Widely distributed on oceanic islands across the southern oceans and, north of the Equator, in the eastern Atlantic on the Cape Verde islands and Salvages. NONBREEDING: Disperses to waters north and west of breeding grounds in the Cape Verde Islands, reaching the continental shelf of N.A. in late summer and fall.

Population The White-faced Storm-Petrel suffers predation by native and introduced predators, as well as habitat loss.

Genus *Fregetta*

BLACK-BELLIED STORM-PETREL *Fregetta tropica*

This widespread southern ocean species has a distinctive flight style and plumage. It has been recorded only once in North American waters. Despite its name, the bird's black belly can be relatively hard to see. Polytypic (N.A. record presumably of nominate *tropica*). L 8" (20 cm) WS 18" (46 cm)

Identification The Black-bellied has a black-and-white pattern. It is distinctive among other western Atlantic storm-petrels in being mostly white below. The upperparts are dark, with pale-tipped greater upperwing coverts; the rump is white. It has a variable dark line that connects the dark chest with dark undertail coverts; the dark line is absent on some birds. The white underwing coverts contrast with dark flight feathers. Long legs and feet project past the tail. Ages and sexes look alike. FLIGHT: The bird's distinctive foraging technique of splashing its breast into the water and then springing off forward with its long legs is unique. In direct flight it flies low across the water, rarely flapping.

Similar Species It is unlikely that the Black-bellied would be confused with other storm-petrels in the western

Atlantic. Its combination of white underparts, dark stripe down belly, and distinctive foraging action are quite unique. It is separated from the similar-looking White-bellied Storm-Petrel *(F. grallaria)* by its darker upperparts, typically black belly stripe, and long feet that project past the tail. Its flight style is similar to the White-faced Storm-Petrel; however, it splashes into the water with its breast and does not pogo-hop with its feet like the White-faced.

Voice Generally silent.

Status & Distribution BREEDING: Nests on subantarctic islands. NONBREEDING: Disperses to tropical seas north of breeding areas, reaching the Equator in the Atlantic. One N.A. record, May 31, 2004, off Manteo, NC.

Population It suffers predation by native and introduced predators. Habitat loss is a concern as well.

Genus *Oceanodroma*

FORK-TAILED STORM-PETREL *Oceanodroma furcata*

The Fork-tailed is found year-round in the northern Pacific, but only rarely south of central California. Polytypic. L 8.5" (22 cm) WS 18" (46 cm)

Identification The only grayish storm-petrel in the northeastern Pacific. Underparts pale gray with darker grayish black underwing coverts. Head grayish, with dark blackish mark through eye. Upperparts gray, with pronounced M-pattern across wings. Ages and sexes look alike. FLIGHT: Wingbeats shallow and measured, flight relatively direct.
Geographic Variation Two subspecies recognized: nominate *furcata* of Asia and the Aleutians; and *plumbea* of the North American west coast, which is smaller and darker than the nominate.
Similar Species In the northeastern Pacific, confusion is unlikely with other storm-petrels, which are largely blackish brown. It could be confused with winter-plumaged phalaropes while sitting on the water, but note differences in posture, structure, and flight style.
Voice Generally silent at sea. A raspy *ana, ana, ana* given at the nesting colonies.
Status & Distribution Uncommon to fairly common. BREEDING: Nests on islets from AK south to northern CA. NON-BREEDING: Disperses south and west after breeding. Rare off southern CA.
Population Some breeding islands suffer losses from native and introduced predators.

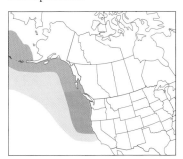

LEACH'S STORM-PETREL *Oceanodroma leucorhoa*

The widespread and variable Leach's is easily confused with several congeners. Essentially a Northern Hemisphere species, it occurs in both oceans from the Equator to the Arctic. Polytypic. L 8" (20 cm) WS 18" (46 cm)
Identification Dark brownish black below. Underwing coverts and flight feathers dark brown. Upper wing dark brown with prominent tawny carpal bar extending to the leading edge of the wing. Rump pattern variable, typically lacks a clean white appearance, often smudged gray through the middle, resulting in a "split-rumped" appearance in all Atlantic and most North Pacific populations; it can range from all-white to all-dark in more southerly Pacific breeders. Entirely dark-rumped birds regularly occur in southern California waters. Ages and sexes similar, but molt and wear can result in plumage fading. FLIGHT: Very active. Flies with deep, rowing wingbeats incorporating frequent direction changes, bounding from side to side and up and down. Arcs and glides over wave tops on bent wings. In strong winds it may fly more shearwater-like. When flushed, can give short, hurried wingbeats but quickly returns to languid deep wingbeats.
Geographic Variation Four subspecies. Nominate *leucorhoa* breeds in the North Atlantic and Pacific Oceans. It is the largest and the least variable in terms of plumage. Individuals in the southern part of its range begin to show intermediate rump characteristics, yet, totally dark-rumped individuals are rare. The subspecies *chapmani* breeds off Baja California. It has a high proportion of dark-rumped individuals, slightly rounder wing tips, and a more deeply notched tail. The subspecies *socorroensis* breeds in summer on Isla de Guadalupe, off Mexico. It is typically smaller and darker than northern populations, with a large proportion of dark-rumped individuals. The subspecies *cheimomnestes* breeds in winter on Isla de Guadalupe. It is generally larger and has a high percentage of white-rumped individuals compared with *socorroensis*. Field identification of subspecies in the Pacific is problematic, but individuals can be characterized as white-rumped, intermediate, or dark-rumped.
Similar Species Separated from other similarly plumaged storm-petrels by nighthawk-like flight style, typically split-rumped appearance, and pale carpal bars reaching the leading edge of the wing. In the Pacific, a dark-rumped individual is easily confused with Ashy and Black Storm-Petrels.

Leach's west coast
northern   intermediate   southern

Differs from the Ashy in having darker underwings, darker overall plumage, and deeper flight style; differs from the Black by smaller size, less notably forked tail that often appears shorter, and less

shearwater-like flight behavior. In the Atlantic and Gulf, see the Band-rumped Storm-Petrel. In the Pacific some dark-rumped individuals may be unidentifiable under field conditions.

Voice Generally silent at sea. Gives a series of generally eerie sounding nocturnal vocalizations including growls and grunts, as well as a low owl-like purring, at breeding colonies.

Status & Distribution Common at sea around breeding colonies; usually scarce elsewhere. Prefers deep water; rarely seen from shore. BREEDING: In burrows on offshore islets. NONBREEDING: Generally disperses to surrounding waters, but some populations undertake long migratory movements across the Equator to tropical oceans. VAGRANT: Casual inland during hurricanes.

Population Widely distributed and numerous. It suffers predation from introduced mammals at many breeding colonies.

BAND-RUMPED STORM-PETREL   *Oceanodroma castro*

This blackish, long-winged storm-petrel flies on stiff bowed wings and often glides like a small shearwater. Its distinctive clean-cut white rump patch and unique flight style are good identification clues. Monotypic. L 9" (23 cm) WS 17" (43 cm)

Identification Dark overall. Blackish brown ventrally, with uniform dark underwings. Upper wings blackish brown. Indistinct carpal bar typically does not reach leading edge of wing; worn individuals in late summer/early fall can show a more prominent bar. Shallow-forked tail, often looks square in direct flight. U-shaped rump clean white, extending partially onto rump sides. Ages and sexes similar; juveniles can have grayish upper-wing coverts. Wear and abrasion cause extensive fading. FLIGHT: Flies on shallow, steady, measured wingbeats with prominent downward stroke, often gliding and arcing over wave tops. Wings held slightly raised at the body, then drooped at the hands creating a generally bowed down appearance.

Similar Species Separation from the Leach's Storm-Petrel is problematic. It is typically darker overall than the Leach's, with a less forked tail and a pure white rump pattern (rare in the Leach's). Flight style is more direct and uses shallower, steady wingbeats. It is similar to the Wilson's Storm-Petrel in terms of plumage, but it lacks the foot projection of that species and its wings are longer and thinner. It typically glides more on bowed wings and its wingbeats are stiff and measured compared to the Wilson's fluttery flight style.

Voice Generally silent at sea. CALL: A low repetitive *kair chuk-a-chuk chuck chuck*. A low purring call from inside the burrow.

Status & Distribution BREEDING: It nests on the Azores, Cape Verde Islands, and farther south in the Atlantic; on HI and other islands in the Pacific. NONBREEDING: Disperses west from eastern Atlantic breeding colonies to the western edge of the Gulf Stream from FL to VA late May–early Sept., rarely as far north as MA. Regular in spring and summer over deep water in Gulf of Mexico. VAGRANT: Casual inland after hurricanes. Potential vagrant to west coast of N.A., but no accepted records.

Population Introduced predators account for some losses on islands in the Atlantic.

WEDGE-RUMPED STORM-PETREL   *Oceanodroma tethys*

This vagrant appears white-tailed in flight. It visits breeding colonies during the day, unlike other storm-petrels. Polytypic. L 6.5" (17 cm) WS 13.3" (34 cm)

Identification Small and dark. White rump patch extends well down upper-tail coverts and even the undertail coverts, giving bird the appearance of being white-tailed; the dark corners are visible at close range. On the water, folded wings completely hide the white rump. Underparts blackish brown; pale-centered dark underwings distinctive. Upperparts dark with pale carpal bar restricted primarily to the wing's inner half. Ages and sexes alike. FLIGHT: Deep, strong wingbeats; direct flight higher above water than most storm-petrels.

Geographic Variation Two subspecies: nominate *tethys* of the Galápagos Islands and the much smaller *kelsalli* of islets off Peru. Both disperse north after breeding.

Similar Species Separation from the Wilson's Storm-Petrel is problematic, but note the Wedge-rumped's extensive triangular white rump patch, longer, pointed wings, and lack of foot projection.

Voice Generally silent at sea.

Status & Distribution Vagrant to waters off CA. BREEDING: Nests colonially in the

Galapagos and on islands off Peru. NONBREEDING: Disperses to tropical eastern Pacific waters off Colombia and Ecuador and north to Panama. VAGRANT: 6 records from central and southern CA (July–Oct.); 1 *kelsalli* specimen (Jan.).

Population Short-eared Owls prey on the Wedge-rumpeds in the Galapagos.

ASHY STORM-PETREL *Oceanodroma homochroa*

Endemic to California and waters off northwestern Baja California, the Ashy is best identified by its direct, but fluttery flight style, plumage, and pale silvery underwings. It can be very similar to the dark-rumped Leach's Storm-

Petrel, with flight style differences and pale underwings being the key identification criteria. Monotypic. L 8" (20 cm) WS 17" (43 cm)

Identification Mid-size, all-dark storm-petrel with medium brown plumage washed gray when fresh. The unique pale underwing coverts can appear silvery at sea, but they are often difficult to see under field conditions. Overall plumage is paler than other dark storm-petrels, but difference is subtle and subject to wear and fading. Ages and sexes alike. FLIGHT: Steady, measured wingbeats, rarely raising wings above the horizontal, and rarely gliding.

Similar Species Separate the Ashy from a Leach's by its silvery wing linings and stiff, steady wingbeats and direct flight style. Compared with the Black and the Least, the Ashy has shallower wingbeats, and paler brown plumage; also note its proportionally longer tail length, especially compared with the Least.

Voice Generally silent at sea. Around breeding colonies it makes eerie barking and yelping noises and purring calls from inside burrows.

Status & Distribution Rare to locally common. BREEDING: Nests colonially on islets off the coast of CA north to the Farallon Islands and south to the Coronados Islands off Tijuana, Mexico. NONBREEDING: In early fall, it congregates in large numbers in Monterey Bay and Cordell Bank, where much of the world population stages. Main wintering area(s) unknown; rarely recorded in winter off CA.

Population This species' low numbers (approx. 5,000 pairs) and restricted range make it especially susceptible to accidental oil spills and predation from introduced predators.

BLACK STORM-PETREL *Oceanodroma melania*

The Black is the largest and darkest regularly occurring dark storm-petrel in the eastern Pacific. Monotypic. L 9" (23 cm) WS 19" (48 cm)

Identification Often appears more "sub-

stantial" at sea than other dark eastern Pacific storm-petrels. Entirely blackish brown, with extensive pale carpal bar formed by tawny greater upperwing coverts. Tail deeply forked. Ages and sexes alike. FLIGHT: Wingbeats deep and deliberate, Black Tern-like, rising high above the horizontal before each downstroke. Glides frequently and arcs over wave tops like a small shearwater.

Similar Species Separation from other dark-rumped Pacific storm-petrels is difficult, especially from the Leach's. Note the distinctive flight style of the Black, which lacks the nighthawk-like, bounding quality of the Leach's. The Black is noticeably larger than the Least at sea, and appears to have a longer tail and wings. It is darker overall than the Ashy, with longer wings and more deliberate flight style. It is similar to other potential, currently unrecorded vagrants, especially the Markham's, Tristram's, and Matsudaira's.

Voice Generally silent at sea. A shrieking repeated call given in flight over colonies at night. A purring call from inside burrows.

Status & Distribution Uncommon to common during late summer and early fall off CA coast. BREEDING: Colonially

on islands off western Mexico and in the Gulf of California. A very few nest on rocks off Santa Barbara Island, CA. NONBREEDING: Regular visitor when postbreeding dispersal brings many birds north along the CA coast in late summer, more during warm-water years, but generally not occurring farther north than central CA. Most birds winter off C.A. and south to Peru. VAGRANT: Casual to northern OR and inland at the Salton Sea and on other bodies of water in the desert southwest after hurricanes track inland from the Gulf of California.

Population Predation by cats and rats at the breeding colonies and a limited availability of breeding habitat affect the Black's population.

LEAST STORM-PETREL *Oceanodroma microsoma*

The small Least is endemic to Mexican waters and disperses northward to near-shore California waters during the late summer and early fall. Its overall appearance has been described as batlike due to its unusual shape, but its flight is direct on deep wingbeats. Monotypic. L 5.3" (13 cm) WS 15" (38 cm)

Identification Completely dark brownish black and relatively featureless in terms of plumage. Short wings. Often appears almost tail-less in flight due to short wedge-shaped tail. Dark upper wing,

with a tawny carpal bar primarily on the inner wing. FLIGHT: Wingbeats unusually deep, strong, and direct for a bird of its small size. Wings held high above body while feeding on the surface.

Similar Species The Least differs from other all-dark storm-petrels in its small size, flight style, and shorter wings and tail. It superficially resembles the Black, but it is much smaller with much shorter wings and tail. Other all-dark storm-petrels have notched tails.

Voice Generally silent at sea.

Status & Distribution Uncommon in N.A. most years; common during warm-water events. BREEDING: Colonially on islands off west coast of Baja California and on islands in the northern Gulf of California. NONBREEDING: Disperses north to southern CA waters during warm-water years (a few to central CA); in other years majority stay south of North American waters. VAGRANT: Casual inland at Salton Sea (hundreds in 1976 after Hurricane Kathleen) and other bodies of water in the desert Southwest after hurricanes move inland from the northern Gulf of California.

Population It is restricted by limited breeding habitat available on offshore islands and it suffers losses from introduced mammalian predators at breeding colonies.

TROPICBIRDS Family Phaethontidae

Red-billed Tropicbird (Galápagos Is., Jan.)

Behavior Flight is direct with species-unique, rapid, pigeonlike wingbeats; glides are usually brief. On oceangoing trips, you may see them making a brief pass over the boat, or less frequently resting on the water in the distance, with tail streamers held in a high arc. They are found singly or in small, loose groups. They plunge-dive for prey, preferring flying fish and squid.

Plumage Tropicbirds are mainly bright, satiny white with some black markings; the sexes look similar but juveniles are more heavily barred with black than adults. Molts are prolonged and poorly studied; adult tail streamers are often broken.

Tropicbirds are pelagic seabirds with long central tail streamers and direct flight styles with steady rapid wingbeats. For field identification, focus on the distribution of black on the wings (especially on the primaries and primary coverts, which are visible only from above) and flight style; the bird's size, bill color, and tail streamers can be difficult to assess from a distance.

Structure Tropicbirds have heavy, pointed red to yellowish bills and long central rectrices forming spectacular streamers in adults. The pointed wings angle back and the body appears front-heavy in flight. Small, black fully webbed feet, set well back on the body, make tropicbirds walk with clumsy lunges.

Distribution Found over most tropical and subtropical oceans, tropicbirds nest on oceanic islands or offshore islets or stacks. None nest in our area. They are uncommon to casual visitors to our southern waters, and vagrants (often storm-related) occur well north of their regular range, onshore and inland.

Taxonomy The world's 3 tropicbird species form a uniform group without close relatives within the Pelecaniformes. Geographic variation is minor.

Conservation Tropicbirds face threats from introduced predators on nesting islands. The number of birds visiting North American waters has probably remained stable, and in fact sightings tend to increase with better coverage far offshore. —*Kimball L. Garrett*

Genus *Phaethon*

WHITE-TAILED TROPICBIRD *Phaethon lepturus*

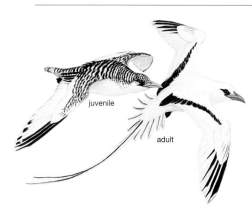

juvenile

adult

The White-tailed, the smallest and most graceful tropicbird, has the most buoyant flight of the tropicbirds. Its long, white tail streamers are especially visible, undulating and ribbonlike. The distinctive upperwing pattern is only hinted at from underneath, and can be difficult to judge from above in harsh light. Polytypic. L 15" (38 cm) Tail streamers 12–25" (30–64 cm) WS 37" (94 cm)

Identification The bill is smaller than in other tropicbirds. ADULT: The large, black diagonal upperwing bar of adults is unique; it extends from the longest scapulars and tertial centers out the wing to near the wrist joint. The outer wing is white, with black on outer 4–5 visible primaries; the black appears cut off by the white primary coverts halfway along the outer wing. The remainder of the upperparts and underparts are white with no barring; the few black flank markings are not generally visible in the field. There is a small black patch through the eye. The long to very long white tail streamers are ribbonlike (they may have a pink

or golden tinge) with black shafts. JUVENILE: It is heavily barred with black on upperparts and upperwing coverts, but still shows sharp contrast between black outer primaries and white primary coverts. Black around eye does not extend back around nape. The bill is a dull yellow. Older immatures have lost most dorsal barring and have brighter yellow bills. FLIGHT: It is more graceful and buoyant than other tropicbirds; it appears slim-bodied and flies with rapid tern-like wingbeats. The suggestion of a black W-pattern above is distinctive.

Geographic Variation Worldwide 5–6 subspecies; 2 in North America. There is slight geographic variation in size, bill color, and extent of black in the primaries. Caribbean and Atlantic records refer to *catesbyi*, with a deep orange bill (can approach red in color) and slightly more black on wing tips (showing black on 5 visible primaries). Pacific records of *dorotheae* note a greenish yellow bill and black on 4 primaries.

Similar Species Separating a White-tailed from a Red-billed Tropicbird in the Atlantic is the main problem. Bill color is unreliable, and the diagnostic upperwing pattern may be hard to see. Adult Red-billeds have barred (not white) upperparts and more black in the outer wing, extending through the primary coverts closer to the bend of the wing. Juvenile Red-billeds show an upperwing pattern like adults, but species differences are subdued by extensive dorsal barring in both species. The juvenile Red-billed also has a longer

black eye patch that extends to or across the nape. Red-billeds and Red-taileds are much larger birds, with wider wings and larger bills than the White-tailed.

Voice Generally silent at sea. Grating *keek keek* series and shrill whistled notes given mainly on breeding grounds.

Status & Distribution Rare in our area. BREEDING: Pantropical; nearest colonies on Bermuda, Bahamas, and Greater Antilles. NONBREEDING: Regular visitor (mostly adults) mainly May–Sept., to Gulf Stream off NC; also formerly around Dry Tortugas, FL; casual elsewhere off Atlantic coast north to NS and in the Gulf of Mexico. Very rarely onshore after hurricanes. VAGRANT: One onshore record from CA (only certain record of *dorotheae,* which breeds as near as HI), and inland records for AZ (likely of Caribbean origin), PA, and NY.

Population Stable. The declines on Bermuda and in the West Indies have been partly offset by conservation measures (predator control, artificial nest sites); there are now some 2,000–2,500 pairs on Bermuda and 2,500–3,500 pairs in the West Indies.

RED-BILLED TROPICBIRD *Phaethon aethereus*

The Red-billed ranges off both of North America's southern coasts, but is most numerous off CA, where it is most often seen on long-range day trips beyond the Channel Islands (Aug.–Sept.). The combination of barred upperparts, red bill, and long white tail streamers is diagnostic for adults. Polytypic (3 ssp.; *mesonauta* in N.A.). L 18" (45 cm) Tail streamers 12–20" (30–50 cm) WS 44" (112 cm)

Identification Large tropicbird with obvious black in primaries and barred

upperparts in all plumages. ADULT: Mainly white with fine black barring above from nape to uppertail coverts; extensive black in the primaries and black in the longer primary coverts of upper wing. A long black mark extends from in front of the eye to the nape. Very long, thin white tail streamers lack a black shaft. Bill bright red. JUVENILE: Finely barred with black above. Black mark through eye wraps around nape, unlike juveniles of other tropicbirds. Tail shows black tip; no tail streamers.

Bill dull yellowish to orange. Older immatures have only sparse spots

adult

adult

juvenile

nia and Puerto Rico/Virgin Is. NON-BREEDING: Regular at sea off southern (casually northern) CA, mainly May–Sept.; esp. frequent in waters off Channel Islands, CA. Rare off Southeast and in Gulf of Mexico (May–Sept.). VAGRANT: North to WA (1 record in 1945), New England, along Gulf Coast (including several storm-wrecked birds), and inland in southern CA and AZ. **Population** Worldwide, the Red-billed is the least numerous tropicbird. Nearby, some 1,800–2,500 pairs breed in the West Indies (mainly Lesser Antilles) and 500–1,000 pairs breed in the Gulf of California.

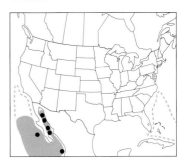

on crown and short white tail streamers. FLIGHT: Flies with rapid, stiff wingbeats, different from the more buoyant flight of the White-tailed Tropicbird and the slower more powerful strokes of the Red-tailed Tropicbird. **Similar Species** The White-tailed Tropicbird poses an identification problem in the Atlantic and Gulf of Mexico; see that species for separation. In the Pacific, a casual Red-tailed Tropicbird also has a deep red bill, but whiter plumage; all ages of Red-tailed look completely white-winged at any distance. The Red-billed superficially resembles large Royal (often seen well

at sea) and Caspian Terns; but note the tropicbird's more rapid wingbeats, elongated central tail feathers (adults), black barring on the upperparts, dark tertials, and contrasting white secondaries and inner primaries. **Voice** Generally silent at sea. Grating ternlike notes are given mainly around the nesting colonies. **Status & Distribution** Rare in our area, but double figures have been seen on long day trips off southern CA. BREEDING: Tropical and subtropical eastern Pacific, southern Atlantic, and northwestern Indian Oceans. Nearest colonies in northern Gulf of Califor-

RED-TAILED TROPICBIRD *Phaethon rubricauda*

This large, broad-winged, robust tropicbird flies with slower and more powerful wingbeats than the other tropicbirds. Casual in North America, most records are from far off the California coast. Polytypic. L 18" (45 cm) Tail streamers 12–15" (30–38 cm) WS 44" (112 cm)
Identification ADULT: The Red-tailed is entirely white (adults may show a faint rosy tinge below) except for a black mark through the eye, black centers to the tertials (a hint of which may show from below), and black shafts to the primaries (not visible from below); the black centers to some flank feathers are not usually visible in the field. The central tail feathers are very thin, stiff, and red (with black shafts); though diagnostic, they tend to disappear against a blue sky or water background. The tail streamers frequently break or are lost. The bill is bright red. JUVENILE: It is heavily barred with black above, spotted black on the crown and nape; black in the primaries extends to vanes adjacent to shafts, thus slightly more extensive than in adults. The tail appears mainly white, wedge-shaped. The bill is black, changing after fledging to yellow. Older immatures retain

juvenile

limited spotting on head and some black in the primary vanes adjacent to shaft, and show short, whitish or pinkish tail streamers. The bill becomes orange to orange-red in the second year. FLIGHT: Strikingly white in flight, it appears large, heavy, and broad winged. **Geographic Variation** Worldwide 4 subspecies. There is minor variation in size. Birds in our area are likely *melanorhynchos,* breeding in north-central Pacific Ocean. **Similar Species** The Red-tailed's at-sea distribution in eastern Pacific overlaps with the Red-billed Tropicbird's; note the Red-billed's extensive black in the primaries, long white tail streamers, and more rapid wingbeats. **Voice** Generally silent at sea. Grating *ack,* often repeated, around nesting islands.

adult

Status & Distribution Very rare (but perhaps annual) in our area. BREEDING: Tropical Indian and Pacific Oceans; nearest colonies are on HI, but a few may breed on islands far off southwestern Mexico; absent from Atlantic Ocean. NONBREEDING: Ranges widely over tropical and subtropical Pacific and Indian Oceans. Probably regular more than 100 miles off CA coast, most records Aug.–Jan. VAGRANT: One onshore record at a large tern colony in southern CA (July 1999); remains of 1 found on Vancouver I., BC (June 1992). **Population** The Pacific Ocean breeding population consists of fewer than 15,000 pairs. Exploitation for human food threatens some important central Pacific colonies. Introduced mammalian predators also impact many breeding populations.

BOOBIES AND GANNETS Family Sulidae

Brown Booby, female (center) and males (Baja California, Mexico)

Boobies and gannets are supreme plunge-divers, entering the water from great heights to catch prey up to several meters underwater. Flight silhouette is distinctive, with long pointed wings and a body pointed both fore and aft. All are generally pelagic in our area, but gannets are readily seen from shore, as is the occasional booby. For field identification note especially the distribution of dark and light in the plumage, foot and bill color, and overall size. At least some plumages of each species can resemble one or more other species.

Structure They are very large (gannets) to medium-size seabirds with long, pointed wings set well back on the body, wedge-shaped tails, and moderately long, thick necks; the pointed bills lack a hook on the tip and have serrated cutting edges. All sulids have thick, short legs and fully webbed feet. The bare gular pouch, orbital ring and loral area, and the forward-directed eyes give the birds a distinctive countenance.

Behavior The steady flap-and-glide flight may be low over water or (esp. gannets) well above the water surface. The plunge-diving foraging behavior is directed at fish and squid. Sulids ride buoyantly on the water. Masked and Blue-footed Boobies generally perch on beaches, rocks, and gravel bars; Brown and especially Red-footed Boobies perch on bare tree limbs, buoys, and ship's rigging (often riding long distances). Gannets usually roost at sea. In most boobies sexes differ in voice, with males (except Red-footed) giving wheezy whistles, and females giving quacking calls; usually silent at sea.

Plumage Most species as adults are largely white below and variably all-dark to white above. The primaries are dark; other flight feathers are variably dark to white. Juveniles are generally darker than adults; plumage maturation takes 3 years (up to 6 for gannets). The Red-footed Booby has distinct color morphs. Bare parts (facial skin and gular pouch, bill, legs, and feet) are often brightly colored, especially in breeding birds, and may differ between sexes and ages. Gannets show more extensive feathering on face.

Distribution Boobies are found in tropical and subtropical waters worldwide; gannets occupy colder waters in the North Atlantic, southern Africa, and Australasia. Nonbreeders disperse to coastal or pelagic waters. Gannets are migratory.

Taxonomy The Sulidae comprises 2 closely related genera, *Sula* (7 sp. of booby, 5 occurring in or near N.A.) and *Morus* (3 gannets, 1 in N.A.). The 3 gannets have been merged into a single species by some authors. Boobies show weak to moderate geographic variation; a population of Masked Booby was recently accorded full-species status—the Nazca Booby.

Conservation Nesting sulids have long been exploited for human food, and introduced predators may also decimate colonies. Gannets are largely protected and well-recovered from past declines, but few booby colonies enjoy effective protection. BirdLife International classifies the Abbott's Booby *(S. abbotti),* nesting only on Christmas Island (in the Indian Ocean), as vulnerable.
—*Kimball L. Garrett*

Genera Morus and Sula

NORTHERN GANNET *Morus bassanus*

adult

2nd year

1st year

This species is the only common sulid along the Atlantic coast. Readily seen from shore in winter and on migration, it often flies in low lines or may soar high above the ocean. It executes spectacular aerial feeding dives, wings folded back just before hitting the surface. Monotypic. L 37" (94 cm) WS 72" (180 cm)

Identification It is larger and has longer wings than a booby. Sexes similar, but age classes differ; adult plumage attained in about 4 years. ADULT: Mainly white with black primaries; golden buff wash on head. Pale gray bill, black facial skin, mostly black feet. JUVENILE: Slate brown, spotted

with white, with white uppertail coverts; underwings dark with white axillars. SUBADULT: Dark body, wing coverts, secondaries, and rectrices gradually replaced by white, with much variation within age classes. Third-year birds often have a checkered or "piano key" look to the wings and a yellowish head. Central tail feathers and secondaries are usually the last dark feathers replaced.

Similar Species A distant immature flying low over the water can suggest a large shearwater or

even an albatross. See Masked Booby for differences between immatures.

Status & Distribution Common to abundant. BREEDING: Colonially on uninhabited islets and rocky cliffs, mainly Gulf of St. Lawrence and off NF. MIGRATION: Atlantic coast, mainly Mar.–May, Oct.–Dec. WINTER: Atlantic coast from MA to FL, and Gulf of Mexico, mainly Nov.–Apr. VAGRANT: Casual on Great Lakes; accidental elsewhere in Northeast, Midwest, once (Sept.) on Victoria I., NT.

Population Not globally threatened.

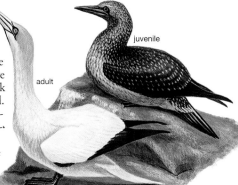

juvenile

adult

BLUE-FOOTED BOOBY *Sula nebouxii*

This aptly-named booby with sky blue feet is an inshore species. Dispersing birds from the Gulf of California are sometimes found in the interior Southwest and along the California coast, but sightings have declined since the 1970s. Polytypic (2 ssp.; nominate in N.A.). L 32" (81 cm) WS 62" (158 cm)

Identification A large, long tailed, long-billed booby with dirty brown and white patterning and distinctive blue (to blue-gray) legs and feet. Central tail feathers mostly whitish. ADULT: Streaked head and neck diagnostic. Brownish upperparts with white barring; white patches on upper back and rump. White below with brown on thighs and flanks. Underwing with white linings divided by dark median covert bar, dark primary coverts. Pale yellow eyes (dark ring around pupil in female); dark gray bill; blackish facial skin. JUVENILE: Head, neck more solidly and extensively brown than in adult, whitish dorsal patches more limited. Grayish blue feet. Dull grayish bill; gray-brown eyes.

Similar Species Compare juvenile with juvenile Brown and Masked Boobies.

The Brown is smaller and solidly dark above; the dark brown breast contrasts sharply with paler underparts; underwings lack dark median covert bar, tail all dark. A juvenile Masked usually shows a complete white collar, shorter all-dark tail, and more extensively white underwing.

Status & Distribution Irregular vagrant in N.A. BREEDING: Common on rocky or

juveniles

adults

adult

sandy deserts islets in Gulf of California, and south to the Galapagos Islands and Peru. NONBREEDING: Rare and irregular (mainly mid-July–mid-Oct.) to Salton Sea, with occasional irruptions to coastal and central CA, southern NV, and western AZ; few recent records, with only 1 "flight year" (1990) since 1977. VAGRANT: Single records to OR and WA; 1 record of a long-staying bird in central TX.

Population Not globally threatened.

BROWN BOOBY *Sula leucogaster*

adult ♂
brewsteri

adult ♀

adult ♂

subadult ♀

juvenile

A dark brown and white bird of tropical and subtropical waters, the Brown Booby occurs rarely but regularly in southern North American waters, mainly in southern Florida and California. It readily perches on buoys, towers, bare branches, and ship rigging. Polytypic. L 30" (76 cm) WS 57" (145 cm)

Identification Moderately small. Sharp contrast between dark chest and paler belly and underwing coverts; contrast subtle in the darkest juveniles. Bill and foot colors vary with population, age, and season (brighter at onset of breeding). ADULT: Upperparts, tail, head, and breast dark brown, meeting bright white underparts in a sharp line across the lower breast. Axillars and underwing secondary coverts white. Legs and feet pale green to yellowish. On female, yellow to pale flesh-colored bill, yellow facial skin, and a dark spot in front of the eye. On male, dusky yellowish bill, blue facial skin. JUVENILE: Dusky brown head, breast, upperparts; underparts dull whitish with dusky scalloping. Axil-lars and underwing secondary coverts dull whitish to mottled pale gray, but showing some contrast with remaining underwing. Bill bluish gray. SUBADULT: Increasingly white on belly, wing linings.

Geographic Variation Nominate *leucogaster* (Caribbean and tropical Atlantic) occurs in our southeastern waters. In *brewsteri* (Gulf of California to islands well off southwestern Mexico), the males are distinctive with extensive whitish frosting on the head and upper neck; juveniles are often very dark on the underparts.

Similar Species Separating juvenile sulids is not easy. A juvenile Brown, even the darkest *brewsteri,* shows a sharp line of contrast between the breast and slightly paler lower breast and belly, but it can be very subtle, even invisible on distant birds. A paler Red-footed Booby juvenile is mostly tan below with a dark band across the chest; a darker juvenile is more uniform, but it still shows a chest band. The Red-footed's underwings are uniformly dark, but at least muted whitish on Brown. The legs and feet can appear pinkish in both species, but the head shape differs sub-tly; the Brown has a more continuous contour from the culmen to the forehead, the Red-footed has a more concave culmen and more rounded forehead. Juvenile Masked and Nazca Boobies are larger than a Brown, have a dark hood limited to the head and neck, and show white on underwing primary coverts. A juvenile Northern Gannet is much larger, spotted with white, and has a dark underwing with only the axillars white.

Status & Distribution Rare in N.A.; common in most tropical and subtropical seas including Gulf of California and parts of Caribbean. BREEDING: On ground on rocky islands and coral atolls. NONBREEDING: Rare to our southern coasts; regular to Dry Tortugas, FL; very rare on TX coast. Seen most years on CA coast (70+ recs. for CA, about a fourth inland from Salton Sea and vicinity). VAGRANT: Casual on Atlantic coast (mostly July–Sept.), north to MA (twice) and NS, usually after southerly storms. Accidental to OR.

Population Not globally threatened.

RED-FOOTED BOOBY *Sula sula*

juvenile

adult white morph with black tail

This smallest and relatively graceful booby is widespread in tropical oceans, but occurs only marginally in North America. Adults show an array of color morphs, but they always have striking red feet. Polytypic. L 28" (71 cm) WS 60" (152 cm)

Identification The Red-footed is relatively slender with long, narrow wings. The forehead is more rounded than in other boobies, and the small bill is slightly concave along the culmen. ADULT: Plumage variable. In all morphs, the bill is pale blue, the facial skin pink, the orbital ring pale blue, and the feet brilliant red. WHITE MORPH: White to creamy white throughout with black primaries and secondaries (innermost secondaries white), black median primary coverts on underwing, pure white scapulars; tail white or black (tipped white). BROWN MORPH: Brown throughout, but lighter tan on head and underparts and darker dusky on flight feathers; underwings entirely dark. WHITE-TAILED BROWN MORPH: Similar, but rump, vent, tail coverts and tail white. JUVENILE: Brownish throughout, but usually paler (even creamy tan) on head, neck, and underparts, with dark chest band. Bill blackish, feet dull pinkish. SUBADULT: Approaches respective adult color morph; white morph subadult often shows brown mantle (retained in some adults). Bill pink with dark tip, gradually changing to blue-gray; feet gradually brighten; definitive adult plumage attained in third year.

Geographic Variation Caribbean birds (nominate *sula*) and eastern Pacific

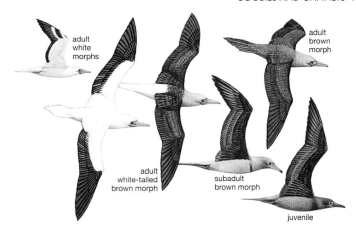

birds *(websteri)* differ little; the all-brown morph is rare in the Caribbean.

Similar Species The white morph adult with black tail resembles the much larger Masked and Nazca adults, but note the Red-footed's blue-gray (not yellow or orange) bill, pink and pale blue facial skin, and bright red feet. In flight, the black on the Red-footed's wings does not reach the body (scapulars and innermost secondaries are white) and there is a black "comma" mark on the primary coverts. See Brown Booby for juvenile separations.

Voice Generally silent in our area.

Status & Distribution Pantropical distribution. Casual in our area. BREEDING: Well-vegetated, tropical islets; nearest colonies off western Mexico and in the eastern Caribbean (off Yucatan), and rarely the Bahamas. DISPERSAL:

Nonbreeders generally well out to sea. VAGRANT: Casual but perhaps regular on Dry Tortugas Islands and Gulf Stream waters off FL; has occurred north to SC on Atlantic coast; 1 record

off upper TX coast. Casual in CA, along the coast and well offshore (±13 recs., mainly Aug.–Nov., north to San Francisco area).

Population Not globally threatened.

MASKED BOOBY *Sula dactylatra*

The Masked Booby is the largest of the boobies. It is also the most highly pelagic, staying well at sea except when breeding. The striking white adult, with its blackish flight feathers and yellow bill, is distinctive. Polytypic. L 32" (81 cm) WS 62" (158 cm)

Identification The Masked is large and has a heavy bill and relatively short tail. The facial skin is bluish black, the legs olive-yellow to blackish. ADULT: Plumage shows white with black trailing edge to wing, mostly black tail, black tips to scapulars. The bill is yellow. JUVENILE: Plumage shows dark brown hood with white collar, back and upperwing coverts brown with pale edges, and underparts and most of wing linings white. The bill is gray to dull yellowish. SUBADULT: It replaces brown body feathering with white dur-

ing its second and third years; the bill shows yellow by second year.

Geographic Variation There are 4 to 7 Masked Booby subspecies. They differ slightly in size and in bare part colors. Nominate *dactylatra*, occurring in the Caribbean Sea, is smaller than the Pacific subspecies. Birds recorded in California are likely *californica* (although the central Pacific *personata* is very similar).

Similar Species Adults can suggest a much smaller, white-morph Red-footed Booby (see species) and a larger, Northern Gannet, which lacks black on its secondaries and tail, has a blue-gray bill, and shows a yellow wash on its head and neck. Near-adult gannets with all-black secondaries have been

reported, resembling the pattern of an adult Masked, but they have had all-white scapulars and white in the tail. A juvenile Masked can be confused with a juvenile or first-winter Northern Gannet, however, note the Northern's darker underwing (only the axillars are white), lack of white collar, and feathered gular area. See Nazca Booby for separation from that species.

Status & Distribution Very rare breeder and uncommon to rare nonbreeding visitor in N.A. BREEDING: Small numbers have nested in Dry Tortugas Islands, FL, since the mid-1980s; closest large colonies in the Caribbean are off the Yucatan Peninsula, with small colonies in the northern Caribbean. A small Pacific colony is located at Alijos Rocks west of Baja California; larger colonies are on the Revillagigedo archipelago and especially Clipperton Island off southwestern Mexico. NONBREEDING: Regular at Dry Tortugas Islands, with up to double-figures in a day; rare visitor elsewhere off the Atlantic coast north to Outer Banks, NC, and in the Gulf of Mexico west to TX. VAGRANT: About 15 records for CA, plus several juvenile Masked/Nazca; recorded throughout year, but mostly in the summer.

Population The Masked Booby populations are not globally threatened.

NAZCA BOOBY *Sula granti*

adult

Recently split from the Masked Booby, this eastern Pacific endemic ranges north to Mexico; all Masked-type boobies along the West coast should be scrutinized for this species. Monotypic. L 32" (81 cm) WS 62" (158 cm)

Identification Resembles the Masked Booby in all plumages. ADULT: Orange-pink bill and more orange (not yellow) iris. JUVENILE: Extent of plumage variation unknown. The juvenile Nazca averages paler dorsally than the Masked (gray-brown, not dark chocolate brown) and lacks or has an inconspicuous white collar (most Masked juveniles show a broad white neck collar).

Similar Species Slight shape differences separate it from a Masked. The Nazca averages a shorter and thinner bill, shorter legs, and longer wings and tail. The Nazca often shows more extensive white at base of tail feathers. An adult Masked shows a yellow to yellow-green bill (not orange-pink) and a yellow (not orangish) iris.

Status & Distribution Common in its limited range. Potential free-flying vagrant to N.A. BREEDING: Main colonies are on the Galapagos and off western Colombia; about 200 breed on Clipperton Island far off southwestern Mexico, and a few breed on the Revillagigedo archipelago and possibly Alijos Rock southwest of Baja. DISPERSAL: Generally inshore, north to west coast of Mexico (a few into the Gulf of California). VAGRANT: One May record of a juvenile landing on a ship off northwest Baja California and riding into San Diego Bay, CA.

Population Not globally threatened.

PELICANS Family Pelecanidae

Brown Pelican (CA, Feb.)

Pelicans are instantly recognizable large fish-eaters with long, hooked bills and comically extensive gular pouches. In North America, the Brown inhabits subtropical and temperate coastlines and the American White breeds in the interior western and central parts of the continent and winters on the southern coastlines. Identification is straightforward, so concentrate on age determination, breeding condition, and scrutiny of flocks for individually marked birds.

Structure Pelicans are huge waterbirds with long, broad wings, short tails, long necks, and long, hook-tipped bills. The gular pouch can greatly expand as the mandibles bow outward to form a large fishing "net" or scoop. The long bill rests on the foreneck in flight and often when at rest. The legs are short and stout; the feet are webbed. The skeleton is lightweight, and pelicans ride buoyantly on the water. Despite such adaptations for weight reduction, American Whites may weigh up to 20 pounds; the smallest Browns (West Indian populations) only weigh about 8 pounds.

Behavior Pelicans spend a lot of time loafing on beaches, lakeshores, low islets or (Brown) piers, barges, rocky islets, and mangroves. They are highly gregarious, often feeding or loafing in groups of hundreds or even thousands; they breed in colonies on low islets on large lakes (American White) or rocky coastal islands, vegetated barrier islands, or mangroves (Brown). American Whites feed by swimming, often in coordinated groups, and dipping for fish with the pouched bill. Browns rarely feed this way, instead they plunge-dive from as high as 50 feet (18 m), hitting the water with a slight leftward rotation, and scoop up as much as 2–2.5 gallons of water, filling the pouch underwater. Mergansers, cormorants, and other fish-eating birds often accompany feeding flocks of Whites, and Heermann's and Laughing Gulls frequently attend diving Browns to steal captured fish. Pelicans have a distinctive flap-and-glide flight, often in lines or Vs; they can soar for long periods, and migrating flocks of American Whites are often seen high within thermals. Pelicans are generally silent, but they do hiss and grunt in breeding colonies.

Plumage Most pelican species are predominantly white, with variably dark flight feathers; the Brown is darker bodied. Molts are prolonged and complex; definitive adult plumage is reached in about 3 years. Bare parts can be brightly colored, especially during courtship season.

Distribution Pelicans are found on inland lakes and coast-lines over much of North America, southern Eurasia, Australasia, and the northern and western coasts of South America. The North American species differ in habitat; the Brown is almost exclusively marine (it is the only pelican species normally seen at sea, though generally absent from waters more than about 100 miles from land). All species undergo postbreeding dispersal, and some are truly migratory.

Taxonomy The Pelecanidae family is uniform; it only has 1 genus. Pelicans are perhaps most closely related to the shoebills (Balaenicipitidae) of Africa. There are 7 species worldwide, although the "Peruvian" or "Chilean" Pelican is often split from the widespread smaller Brown Pelican as *P. thagus*.

Conservation The fish diet magnifies problems of organochlorine contamination of aquatic environments. Evidence of Brown Pelican reproductive failures owing to eggshell thinning mediated by the DDT metabolite DDE, providing a clear cause and effect, was a key motivation in the banning of DDT and related pesticides. Populations that crashed between the 1950s and early 1970s have generally recovered, but DDT residues still linger and impact the birds. Human disturbance of nesting colonies is also an important and persistent threat.
—*Kimball L. Garrett*

Genus Pelecanus

BROWN PELICAN *Pelecanus occidentalis* (E)

The small, dark Brown Pelican of marine coasts feeds mainly by plunge-diving. Although still considered endangered in parts of its range, it has generally rebounded well from severe declines caused by pesticide residues. Polytypic. L 48" (122 cm) WS 84" (213 cm)
Identification Diagnostic typical pelican form and extensively dark plumage. Sexes look similar, but age classes differ in plumage and body feather shape (narrower and more pointed in adults). Adults have white heads and dark bellies; juveniles the opposite. BREEDING ADULT: Upperparts appear gray (feathers slaty with silvery center streaks); underparts dark brown, streaked with silver on sides, flanks. Head and neck mainly white, with dark brown to chestnut hindneck stripe and foreneck (encircling yellow or whitish chest patch) and yellowish crown. Eyes white. Gular pouch dark greenish gray (bright red at base in courting *occidentalis*); bill with extensive pink or orange toward tip, and whitish area near base during chick-feeding stage. NONBREEDING ADULT: Similar, but entire neck whitish, eyes dark by late summer, bright colors on pouch bill less evident. JUVENILE: Mainly brown

on head, chest, and upperparts, but white from breast through remaining underparts; greater underwing coverts pale grayish white, forming a long stripe below. Eyes dark. IMMATURE: Year-old birds have some pale feathering on head and neck and some dark flecking on underparts; third-year birds resemble adults but show some whitish mottling on belly and hint of pale underwing stripe.

Geographic Variation The Pacific coast *californicus* is distinguished from the Atlantic and Gulf coast *carolinensis* by its larger size and (in adults early in breeding season) the bright red rather than blackish-blue gular pouch. The small, darker-bellied nominate *occidentalis* (from West Indies) has been collected once in coastal northwest Florida.

Similar Species Unmistakable. Adults can look pale above when seen in strong lighting and momentarily may be mistaken for American White Pelicans. Even a heavily marked juvenile White is still mainly white with yellowish bill and legs, thus not likely to be confused.

Status & Distribution Common. BREEDING: Atlantic and Gulf coast colonies mainly on low vegetated islands (mangroves in FL). Northernmost colonies in MD and on northern Channel Is., CA. DISPERSAL: Postbreeding dispersal May–Oct.

north to DE, NJ, WA, then south to breeding regions by late fall. Irregular postbreeding visitor to Salton Sea (common in 1990s when some breeding attempts occurred). VAGRANT: Rare (mainly late summer, fall) to NS, BC; recorded rarely but widely in the interior to ID, ND, and Great Lakes region.

Population The species has recovered since the 1970s, but it is still listed as endangered in California. About 6,000 pairs breed in California; 40,000 in Baja California and Gulf of California; 15,000 on the Atlantic coast (from MD to FL); and 24,000 on the Gulf Coast (from FL to TX).

AMERICAN WHITE PELICAN *Pelecanus erythrorhynchos*

The huge American White Pelican has black primaries and outer secondaries and a yellow to orange bill. Breeding on inland lakes, this pelican is the only one likely to be seen away from seacoasts in most of North America. Monotypic. L 62" (158 cm) WS 108" (274 cm)

Identification Unmistakable in all plumages. ADULT: Entirely white except for black primaries and outer secondaries. Bill, gular pouch, and bare facial skin orange-yellow, brightening to deep orange-pink in breeding birds; legs and feet yellowish, becoming orange in breeding birds. Early breeding season adults have pale yellowish plumes on crest and center of breast, and a fibrous knob up to 2 inches high two-thirds of the way out the culmen; after egg-laying a supplemental molt results in dusky gray feathering on crown and nape. Sexes similar. JUVENILE: Similar to adult but head, neck, and especially upperwing coverts marked with dusky gray; bill and feet duller yellow. Older immatures resemble adults, but lack yellowish plumes and supplemental crown markings.

Similar Species A distant flying bird could be confused with the smaller Wood Stork, also largely white with black on the flight feathers. Other white-plumaged pelicans could occur as escapees; of these only the Great White Pelican (*P. onocrotalus*) shares the all-white body plumage, sharp black and white wing pattern, and yellow pouch. The Great White is even larger, has black bill sides, and always lacks the bill knob.

Status & Distribution Common. BREEDING: Lakes in inland west and prairie regions; largest colonies in western and southern Canada. Small resident population in coastal TX. MIGRATION: Arrive breeding colonies Mar.–May; fall movements protracted. WINTER: Mainly from central CA and Gulf states to southern Mexico on coastal bays and estuaries, but also on large inland lakes; nonbreeders may summer well outside breeding range. DISPERSAL: Irregular postbreeding wandering brings small numbers to much of the Northeast (to Canadian Maritimes) and Atlantic coast. VAGRANT: Accidental in southeastern AK and far northern Canada.

Population The population is stable or increasing since the 1960s. More than 20,000 pairs nest in the U.S., more than 50,000 in Canada.

immature

nonbreeding adult

chick-feeding adult

breeding adult

nonbreeding adult

CORMORANTS Family Phalacrocoracidae

The largest pelecaniform family, cormorants (including "shags") are long-necked diving birds represented in North America by the widespread Double-crested Cormorant and 5 more localized species. For identification, concentrate on shape and color of bill and gular region, overall size, tail length, neck thickness, flight silhouette, and distinctive markings of breeding adults.

Structure Cormorants have long necks, long, heavy bodies, stiff tails, and long bills strongly hooked at the tip. Their feet are fully webbed for underwater propulsion but serve also for perching on branches, cables, and cliff faces. The moderately long wings are rounded at the tip.

Behavior Cormorants pursue fish in shallows or exploit schooling fish in deeper water; they move underwater by simultaneous backstrokes of their webbed feet. The dense, wettable body plumage reduces buoyancy; after a diving bout cormorants perch with spread wings to

Double-crested Cormorant, immatures (NJ, Jan.)

dry. Flight involves steady, shallow wingbeats; cormorants briefly glide but rarely soar. They hold the neck straight out in flight, although some species elevate the head above the plane of the body. Marine species usually fly low over the water in loose lines. Perching birds stand upright. Cormorants nest in small to very large colonies on sandy or rocky islands, cliff faces, or mangroves and other shrubs or trees. Their grunting calls are usually heard only around the colonies.

Plumage North American species are mainly black as adults, often with a green or purple gloss and, in some species, scaly patterning on the upperparts; many extralimital species are white below. Cormorants variously show wispy plumes, crests, bright gular pouches, and white flank patches early in the breeding season. The sexes look similar. Juveniles and immatures are duller and browner than adults and lack ornaments. Definitive plumage is attained in 2 to 4 years.

Distribution Cormorants frequent coastlines and interior lakes and wetlands worldwide, from the tropics to subpolar regions. Some species are quite sedentary, others are somewhat migratory. Four North American species are strictly marine; 2 others also occur inland (Double-crested widely so).

Taxonomy All of the some 39 species worldwide are in the genus *Phalacrocorax*. Some authors place several natural groups in 2 subfamilies and in as many as 9 genera. The darters are the cormorants' closest relatives.

Conservation Many cormorant species have declined (1 is extinct; at least 10 are threatened), but North American populations are generally stable—in fact, expanding populations of Double-crested Cormorants have prompted some control measures. Threats include coastal oil spills, organochlorine residues, exploitation of eggs and breeding adults for human food, disturbance to colonies, and drowning in fishing nets. —*Kimball L. Garrett*

Genus *Phalacrocorax*

GREAT CORMORANT *Phalacrocorax carbo*

This species, North America's largest cormorant, has a huge worldwide range, but in N.A. it breeds only in easternmost Canada and Maine; nonbreeders occur southward along the Atlantic coast. Polytypic (at least 6 ssp.; *carbo* in N.A.). L 36" (94 cm) WS 63" (160 cm)

Identification Large size, large blocky head, short tail, and limited yellow gular pouch bordered by white feathering. BREEDING ADULT: Black with scaly upperparts; broad white throat patch bordering small lemon yellow gular pouch and facial skin; thin white plumes on sides of head and bold white patch on flanks. NONBREEDING ADULT: Similar to breeding, but white throat patch more limited and white head plumes and flank patches absent. JUVENILE: Gray-brown head, neck and breast contrast with white belly; flanks, wing linings and upperparts dusky; pale feathered border to small yellow

facial skin area. Older immatures progressively darker on body; definitive plumage attained in third year.

Similar Species The Double-crested Cormorant, the only other cormorant in the Great's N.A. range, is smaller with slightly slimmer neck and bill. A breeding adult Double-crested lacks the Great's white feathering on face and flanks and has more extensive and deeper orange-yellow facial skin. A nonbreeding adult is more similar, but note the Great's limited pale yellow facial skin is pointed, not rounded at rear, and the broad pale feathering bordering the facial skin points forward on throat toward bill. Most immature Greats are readily told from

immature Double-cresteds by 2-toned underparts: dark on breast and flanks, whitish on belly; a few Greats are more uniformly dark below and best told by facial characters (above) and grayish (not extensively orangish) bill. Also compare with much smaller and longer-tailed Neotropic Cormorant.

Status & Distribution Fairly common. BREEDING: Maritime habitats; colonially on ledges, plateaus on rocky islands, coastal points. NONBREEDING: A few immatures summer to NJ, rarely farther south. WINTER: Seacoasts, bays, and lower portions of major rivers; regular south to NC and SC, very rarely to FL. VAGRANT: Rare and irregular inland in Northeast as far as Lake Ontario. Casual in Gulf of Mexico (western FL, MS); 1 record for WV.

Population Only about 5,500 pairs breed in North America, 80 percent of these in Quebec and Nova Scotia. Largely recovered from 19th-century declines, populations are stable.

adult

1st year

2nd year

breeding adult

NEOTROPIC CORMORANT *Phalacrocorax brasilianus*

Resembling a small, long-tailed version of the Double-crested Cormorant, this aptly named, primarily Neotropical species is fairly common in North America along the Texas and western Louisiana coasts and locally inland in Texas and New Mexico (it occurs more rarely elsewhere in the Southwest and as a vagrant over the mid-continent). Polytypic. L 26" (66 cm) WS 40" (102 cm)

Identification The combination of the bird's characteristic field marks—small size, relatively long tail, short bill, black feathered lores, and dull yellow gular pouch bordered by white feathering and distinctly pointed at the rear—identify most Neotropic Cormorants. BREEDING ADULT: It is blackish throughout with a slight bluish gloss; the back feathers and wing coverts are olive-gray with black borders. The gular pouch varies from brownish to yellow, but it is always bordered at the rear by a distinct band of white feathering coming to a point behind the gape. Short, thin white plumes are concentrated on the sides of the head and neck. NONBREEDING ADULT: It resembles a breeding bird, but it lacks the white plumes, the body plumage is less glossy, and the gular pouch is a paler yellow with a less distinct white border. JUVENILE: It is brown throughout, often considerably paler on the head, neck, and breast; the wing coverts are dusky edged with paler brown. The gular pouch is a pale yellow; the white border is indistinct or absent. Older immatures gradually attain the dorsal patterning, blacker body plumage, and white throat border of adults.

Geographic Variation North American birds *(mexicanus)* are considerably smaller than nominate birds found ranging from Panama through South America.

Similar Species To distinguish an immature Neotropic from the closely similar Double-crested, see the sidebar below. It is unlikely that other small, long-tailed cormorants (e.g., the Pelagic) will be confused for a Neotropic—they do not overlap with the Neotropic, have much thinner necks and bills, and lack the yellow gular pouch.

nonbreeding adult

immature

breeding adult

immature

Identification of Immature Double-crested and Neotropic Cormorants

The Double-crested and Neotropic Cormorants are the two cormorants in North America most likely to be seen away from marine habitats, and they share many plumage and structural features. Both have thick necks and deep bills and fly with their heads elevated above the plane of the body. The Double-crested occurs widely, especially in winter, within the more limited U.S. range of the Neotropic, and vagrant Neotropics are often seen with Double-cresteds; therefore opportunities for close comparison of the two species are often available.

Some characters that readily distinguish adults, such as the shape of the gular pouch, the distinct white throat border of the Neotropic, the absence of bare yellow or orange supraloral skin in the Neotropic, and the twin curled crests of the Double-crested can be absent, obscure, or difficult to assess in juveniles and younger immatures. Thus close scrutiny of facial features in combination with careful attention to (and ideally comparison of) size and shape characters are important.

The yellowish gular pouch of the Neotropic comes to a point behind the gape of the bill, with the dark throat

Double-crested Cormorant, immature (FLA, Jan.)

Neotropic Cormorant, immature (TX, Feb.)

feathering coming forward to a point under the pouch. In the Double-crested the gular pouch is squared or rounded at the rear, with less feathering protruding forward underneath. This shape difference holds for all postnatal plumages. In all Double-cresteds, bare yellow or orange facial skin extends from above the gape to just above the eye; this area is dark and feathered in the Neotropic. (But beware: Some individuals show a thin yellowish streak above and in front of the eye.)

Double-cresteds Cormorants average larger than our *mexicanus* Neotropics in all standard measurements except tail length, but the smallest Double-crested can overlap the Neotropic in bill length. Neotropics have slightly slimmer bodies and smaller heads. The most distinctive shape difference is the relatively much longer tail of the Neotropic (the tail is 60 percent of the wing length in the Neotropic, but less than 50 percent in the Double-crested); in flight the tail length of the Neotropic roughly equals the length of the neck (with head), whereas the tail is shorter than the neck in the Double-crested. Consider these marks when separating these two cormorants in the field. ∎

Status & Distribution Fairly common. BREEDING: In main U.S. range (coastal TX and southwestern LA) found in coastal bays, inlets, and freshwater lakes and ponds. More local inland on reservoirs, lakes, and rivers; breeds in southern NM and possibly OK. NONBREEDING: Northeast and north-central TX birds withdraw south in winter. VAGRANT: Regular visitor to southeastern AZ; casual in south-eastern CA, southern NV, CO, Great Plains, and western Midwest states. **Population** The Neotropic Cormorant is common and widespread from Mexico through South America. There are about 10,000 breeding pairs in the core U.S. range in Texas and south-west Louisiana. After suffering severe declines in the 1960s, the populations in the United States have largely rebounded, but there remains strong yearly variation in colony site use and population size.

DOUBLE-CRESTED CORMORANT *Phalacrocorax auritus*

The Double-crested is North America's most widespread and familiar cormorant, found in both marine and freshwater habitats. It often flies higher than other cormorants, often in goose-like V-formations. Polytypic. L 32" (81 cm) WS 52" (132 cm)

Identification Stocky, with medium-length tail, thick neck, and moderately thick bill; yellow to orange gular pouch, rounded or square at rear; bare supraloral skin yellow to orange. BREEDING ADULT: Black; coverts and back feathers with grayish centers, black fringes. Facial skin orange. Nuptial crests black, white or peppered. Bill blackish above, spotted with pale below. NONBREEDING ADULT: Similar to breeding adult, but crests lacking and facial skin often more yellow. JUVENILE: Dark gray-brown above with paler edges to back feathers and wing coverts; underpart color varies with individual and feather wear, but breast always paler than belly. Throat and breast dark brownish gray, becoming paler, even nearly white, with wear and fading (flanks and lower belly darker). Bill extensively yellow to pale orange. Older immatures resemble nonbreeding adults but plumage duller, browner.

Geographic Variation Five subspecies, 4 in North America, differing in overall size and in color and shape of crests in breeding adults. Nominate *auritus* (widespread from the Great Basin and Rocky Mountain region east through central and eastern N.A.) is moderately large with black crests; *floridanus* (Florida) is our smallest subspecies, with dark crests; *cincinnatus* (coastal AK to northern BC) is largest, with straight white crests; and *albociliatus* (Pacific coast from southern BC to western Mexico, and presumably inland to the Great Basin) is large and usually shows white to partially white crests. Subspecies range limits in interior western North America are not clear.

Similar Species The Neotropic is similar (see sidebar p. 104) as are the Great and Brandt's Cormorants (see those species for separation). Very pale-breasted immatures might be mistaken at a distance for loons or, when perched, boobies.

Status & Distribution Common. BREEDING: A wide range of lakes, marshes, coastal estuaries, and offshore islands; colonially on rocky or sandy islands, marsh vegetation, flooded snags, waterside trees, or artificial structures. MIGRATION: Northern breeders move north mainly Mar.–Apr., return south mainly Aug.–Nov. WINTER: Mainly coastal habitats, but also on inland lakes, reservoirs, and fish farms. VAGRANT: Some summer wandering north of regular range (e.g., Great Slave Lake). Accidental in Britain and the Azores.

Population Currently there are about 350,000 breeding pairs in North America. Most populations declined greatly from the 1800s through the early 1900s because of persecution and introduced predators. Major declines occurred again from the 1950s to about 1970 because of pesticide impacts. Numbers have strongly rebounded since the 1970s in the interior and Atlantic coast regions. Some populations are now controlled through management (especially in the Great Lakes region).

juvenile

winter adult

breeding adult

western breeding adult

2nd year

1st year

1st year

BRANDT'S CORMORANT *Phalacrocorax penicillatus*

A common bird along the Pacific coast, this species is also the most numerous cormorant well offshore. Monotypic. L 35" (89 cm) WS 48" (122 cm)

Identification Fairly large with a short tail. Always shows pale buff on throat. BREEDING ADULT: Black throughout (with slight gloss) except for yellow-buff

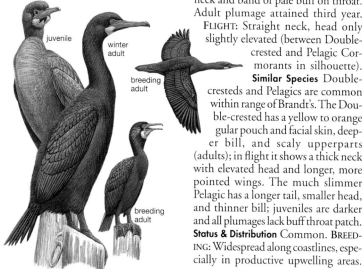

juvenile

winter adult

breeding adult

breeding adult

throat feathering; gular pouch bright blue; thin white plumes on neck, back. NONBREEDING ADULT: Similar to breeding, but no gloss or plumes and pouch dull gray. JUVENILE: Dark brown above (fringed paler brown on back and wing coverts); lighter brown below, becoming tan on breast with a darker brown neck and band of pale buff on throat. Adult plumage attained third year.

FLIGHT: Straight neck, head only slightly elevated (between Double-crested and Pelagic Cormorants in silhouette).

Similar Species Double-cresteds and Pelagics are common within range of Brandt's. The Double-crested has a yellow to orange gular pouch and facial skin, deeper bill, and scaly upperparts (adults); in flight it shows a thick neck with elevated head and longer, more pointed wings. The much slimmer Pelagic has a longer tail, smaller head, and thinner bill; juveniles are darker and all plumages lack buff throat patch.

Status & Distribution Common. BREEDING: Widespread along coastlines, especially in productive upwelling areas.

Colonially on flats, slopes, or sometimes cliff ledges on offshore islands. A few have bred near Prince William Sound, AK. NONBREEDING: General northward postbreeding move July–Oct., and southward move in fall and winter; during these seasons found north to southern AK and south through much of Gulf of California. VAGRANT: Accidental in interior CA.

Population Populations fluctuate greatly, but overall numbers are stable; there are some 75,000 pairs, mainly between Oregon and Baja California. The related Spectacled or Pallas's Cormorant, resident on Bering Island in the Bering Sea, was hunted to extinction by 1852.

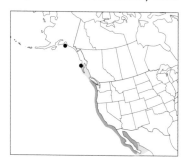

RED-FACED CORMORANT *Phalacrocorax urile*

A close relative of the Pelagic Cormorant, this species is found only from southwest Alaska west through the Pribilofs and Aleutians to the northern Sea of Japan. It is not especially gregarious and nests in small colonies on cliff faces and steep rocky islands. Monotypic. L 31" (79 cm) WS 46" (117 cm)

Identification Extensive yellow to pale yellowish gray on bill in all plumages. A bit stockier in build than Pelagic, with a slightly thicker bill. BREEDING ADULT: Glossy black with browner wings, large white flank patch; bill yellowish with blue base; bright red pouch and facial skin surrounding eyes and extending across forehead; thin white neck plumes. NONBREEDING ADULT: Similar

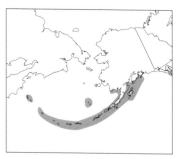

to breeding, but body less glossy, red face and blue bill base duller, and white neck plumes and flank patch lacking. JUVENILE: Dark brown, slightly paler on breast; facial skin dull yellow to pinkish (but forehead feathered); some yellow on bill.

Similar Species Closely resembles the Pelagic, but the Red-faced is about 20 percent heavier with a stockier build and slightly thicker bill. The Red-faced's bill is extensively pale (usually yellow), whereas the Pelagic's is slate-gray or blackish. In adult Red-faced dark brown wings contrast with black body (the Pelagic is more uniformly black). The facial skin of the adult Red-faced is a bright red and extends across forehead and broadly surrounds the eyes; in the Pelagic, the red is deeper in color and limited to the lower face (forehead is feathered black). Juveniles are best told apart by the pale yellowish bill and face of the Red-faced (the Pelagic is dark in these areas).

Status & Distribution Fairly common but local. YEAR-ROUND: Nests on sea cliffs with kittiwakes and alcids, most commonly on Pribilofs and westernmost Aleutians; some fall and winter dis-

persal within general breeding range. VAGRANT: Casual in AK north to Norton Sound and southeast to Sitka. Recorded twice (Apr., June) on Queen Charlotte Is., BC.; 1 May sight record in northwestern WA.

Population About 50,000 birds breed in Alaska; populations are apparently stable, but little trend data exists.

bree adult

winter adult

juvenile

breeding adult

PELAGIC CORMORANT *Phalacrocorax pelagicus*

Despite its name, this small, slender cormorant frequents rocky coastlines and is rarely seen far at sea. Polytypic. L 26" (66 cm) WS 39" (99 cm)

Identification Slender neck (held straight in flight), small head, very thin blackish bill, and relatively long tail. Plumage entirely dark, except for white flank patches of adults early in the breeding season. BREEDING ADULT: Shiny black, glossed purple and green, except for large white patch on flank and thin white plumes on the head. Short crests on crown, nape. Deep red facial skin limited around chin and eyes. NONBREEDING ADULT: Similar to breeding, but no flank patch, head

plumes, or crests. Body plumage slightly less glossy; red facial skin less evident. JUVENILE: Blackish brown above, only slightly paler on underparts; our darkest juvenile cormorant. Adult plumage attained second year.

Geographic Variation Two subspecies. Nominate *pelagicus* breeds from southern British Columbia through Alaskan and northeast Asian range; *resplendens,* from southern British Columbia to extreme northwestern Mexico, is smaller, with a more slender bill.

Similar Species See Red-faced Cormorant. Along the Pacific coast, it can be confused with the Brandt's Cormorant; the latter is larger, with a heavier body and neck, larger head, thicker and longer bill, and shorter tail. The Brandt's also shows a buff throat (dark in all Pelagic plumages).

Status & Distribution Common, but rarely in large groups. BREEDING: Colonially on steep rocky slopes or cliff faces on coastlines and islands. NONBREEDING: Generally resident, but northernmost populations withdraw south for winter. Winters south to Pacific coast of Baja California. VAGRANT: Casual on

northern coast of AK and on leeward Hawaiian Is.; 1 Dec. record east of Sierra Nevada in Mono Co., CA.

Population The North American population of about 130,000 birds (mostly in AK) is generally stable.

breeding adult

winter adult

juvenile

breeding adult

DARTERS Family Anhingidae

Anhinga, breeding male (FL, Apr.)

Darters resemble slender, long-tailed cormorants. They are often seen loafing or sunning on waterside perches, or in their flap-and-glide or soaring flight.

Structure Darters have a thin neck and small head with a pointed bill and small gular pouch; the heronlike neck is kinked between the eighth and ninth vertebrae (serving as a hinge for quick strikes at prey). The long broad wings, thin-based tail, and straight neck give flying darters a crosslike appearance. The short legs have large, fully webbed feet.

Behavior Highly aquatic, they swim with the body sub-

merged; the wettable plumage reduces buoyancy, but it requires long periods of drying and sunning with wings and tail spread. Flight consists of several flaps and short glides; darters often soar on thermals. They use their sharply pointed bills to spear fish and other prey. They are seen singly or in small, loose groups and nest in waterside trees and mangroves, often alongside herons, ibis, cormorants, and storks.

Plumage Adult males are largely black with silver-white markings on the upperwing coverts, back, and scapulars; in Old World taxa the head and neck have brown and white markings. Females and immature males are extensively gray-brown to buff on the head, neck, and breast. Unique transverse corrugations are found on the outer webs of the central rectrices and the longest scapular.

Distribution Darters occur in warmer regions of the New World from the southeastern U.S. through tropical South America, sub-Saharan Africa, South Asia, and Australia/New Guinea. Some populations are migratory or move in response to changing water conditions.

Taxonomy Darters, closely related to cormorants, consist of the Anhinga in the Americas and a widespread Old World group variously considered either 1 species or 3.

Conservation Populations are generally stable, although organochlorine residues and the draining of wetlands have caused some local declines. —*Kimball L. Garrett*

Genus *Anhinga*

ANHINGA *Anhinga anhinga*

This bird inhabits warm southern wetlands. Polytypic (2 ssp.; *leucogaster* in N.A.). L 35" (89 cm) WS 45" (114 cm) **Identification** Unique. Long, snake-like neck, small head, sharply pointed yellow bill, and long fan-shaped tail with pale tip. ADULT MALE: Black throughout with extensive silver-white panel on upperwing coverts and streaks on lance-like back and scapular feathers. Breeding birds show wispy white plumes on sides of head and neck, green lores, and orange gular pouch. ADULT FEMALE: Like male, but with grayish tan head, neck,

and breast (richer cinnamon on lower breast). JUVENILE: Similar to adult female but duller, with reduced white on scapulars, coverts.
Similar Species A soaring cormorant can suggest an Anhinga, but note Anhinga's longer tail and different bill shape. African nominate escapees (e.g., seen in southern CA) lack a pale tail tip and have brown greater secondary coverts; males have rufous throat and neck and white stripe below cheek (females hint at this pattern).
Voice Generally silent away from nesting colony. Clicking and rattling calls sometimes heard from perched birds.
Status & Distribution Fairly common. BREEDING: Wooded swamps, lakes, slow-moving rivers, and mangrove estuaries, with highest densities in FL, LA, southeast GA; formerly bred to OK, IL, MO, OK, and KY. WINTER: Northernmost populations withdraw south

breeding adult ♂

in Oct; return in Mar. Greatest U.S. winter densities in north and central FL. VAGRANT: Casual to Great Plains, Great Lakes states, southern ON, NJ, MD, CA, AZ, CO, and NM.
Population The U.S. population is generally stable, but the breeding range is contracting in the north.

FRIGATEBIRDS Family Fregatidae

Magnificent Frigatebird, male (Honduras)

C onsummate aerialists, frigatebirds are lightly built tropical seabirds with long, angular wings and distinctive, long, deeply forked tails. Only the Magnificent Frigatebird is expected in North America; 2 other species occur accidentally. Identification is fraught with difficulties.
Structure Light wing loading allows for long periods of effortless flight. The tail is deeply forked, and the small legs and feet are useful only for perching. The long bill is deeply hooked at the tip; the males' gular pouch is bare and red, and can be greatly inflated during courtship.
Behavior They soar great distances over warm waters, occasionally flapping with deep, slow wingbeats; they do not

alight on the water, but select perches such as rocks, shrubs, rigging, and guy wires. They pluck fish, squid, or offal from near the water's surface, often attending seabird feeding flocks or concentrating around fish cleaning operations. They frequently pirate prey from pelicans, boobies, gulls, terns, and other seabirds through deft aerial chases. Breeding colonies are on shrubs, mangroves on oceanic islands, or coastal bays.
Plumage Adult males are mostly black; females show more white on the underparts and juveniles more extensively white below and on the head. Plumage transitions to adult, taking 3 or more years, are complex and variable.
Distribution Frigatebirds are found throughout tropical waters, but show great potential for vagrancy well beyond their normal ranges (accidental north to NF and AK).
Taxonomy Worldwide, 5 species in 1 genus. The systematic position of frigatebirds within the large complex of penguins, tubenoses, and pelecaniform birds is unclear, but they are generally placed in the Pelecaniformes.
Conservation Destruction of or disturbance to breeding colonies by humans and exotic species has caused strong declines in many populations. —*Kimball L. Garrett*

Genus Fregata

GREAT FRIGATEBIRD *Fregata minor*

Closely similar to the Magnificent Frigatebird, Great Frigatebird vagrants have been recorded three times in North America. Polytypic (5 ssp.; N.A. ssp. unknown). L 37" (95 cm) WS 85" (216 cm)

Identification ADULT MALE: It differs from the Magnificent in the brown bar on the upperwing coverts, pinkish feet, and (often) whitish scallops on axillars. ADULT FEMALE: She has a pale gray throat (black in the Magnificent), red orbital ring, and a rounder (less tapered) black belly patch in front.

JUVENILE: It has a rust wash on head and chest. The feet are pink.
Status & Distribution Accidental. BREEDING: Extensive range in Pacific and Indian Oceans; large colonies in northwestern Hawaiian Is. and in east Pacific from off western Mexico to Ecuador. West Atlantic population (Trinidade and Martín Vaz Is.) nearly extirpated. VAGRANT: 1 specimen from OK (Nov. 3, 1975); adults have been photographed in CA in Mar. (Faral-

lon Is.) and Oct. (Monterey Bay).
Population Nearest source colonies include up to 10,000

adult ♀

pairs in Hawaiian Archipelago and about 165 pairs on Revillagigedo Islands off western Mexico; the tiny remaining population in the southwest Atlantic is endangered.

LESSER FRIGATEBIRD *Fregata ariel*

The smallest frigatebird, only a bit larger than the largest gulls, the Lesser has only been recorded once in North America. Polytypic (3 ssp.). L 30" (76 cm) WS 73" (185 cm)

Identification In all plumages, white extends from the sides into the axillars. ADULT MALE: Differs from the Magnificent Frigatebird by its much smaller size and the white flank patch that extends into the axillars. ADULT

adult ♂

FEMALE: It has a black head and chest (like the Magnificent), but the white breast sides extend into the axillars. JUVE-

NILE: It has a pale rusty head; a white axillar spur is present.
Status & Distribution Accidental; an adult male (presumably *trinitatis*) photographed at Deer Island, ME (July 3, 1960). Nearest breeding colonies are in S. Atlantic at Trinidade I. and Martín Vaz I. east of Brazil. Widespread in southwest and central Pacific and Indian Ocean, but not known from northeastern Pacific.

MAGNIFICENT FRIGATEBIRD *Fregata magnificens*

Our only "expected" frigatebird, the Magnificent is numerous in southern Florida, but occurs widely along the Gulf coast and more rarely on the Atlantic and Pacific coasts and in the interior. Monotypic. L 40" (102 cm) WS 88" (224 cm)

Identification Frigatebirds are unmistakable. ADULT MALE: He is entirely blackish overall, with a slight purple gloss; the gular pouch (inflated in display) is orange to red. The bill and feet are gray. ADULT FEMALE: The black on the head comes to a point on the chest; the lower breast is white and the upper belly is constricted in the center. The bill is gray, the feet are pink. JUVENILE: It is blackish, with a white head, chest, and belly patch, and brown wing coverts. Complex plumage maturation takes 4 to 6 years.

juvenile

adult ♂

displaying adult ♂

adult ♀

Similar Species See Great and Lesser Frigatebirds.
Status & Distribution Locally common. BREEDING: Colony on Dry Tortugas Is., FL.; nearest Mexican colonies in Baja California Sur, Sinaloa. DISPERSAL:

Along Gulf of Mexico coast and throughout Gulf of California. Rare but regular, mainly June–Sept., on CA coast and inland at Salton Sea; fewer in recent years. VAGRANT: Casual (mainly summer, fall) north on coasts to southern AK, NF, and through interior of continent.
Population There are about 200 pairs on the Dry Tortugas; large colonies exist in western Mexico.

BITTERNS, HERONS, AND ALLIES Family Ardeidae

Yellow-crowned Night-Heron (NJ, Apr.)

One of the most distinctive and graceful bird families, the Ardeidae played a major role in the formation of the American conservation movement. Wading bird populations were decimated in the late 19th and early 20th centuries, when it was fashionable for women to wear hats adorned with feathers, wings, or even entire stuffed birds. Hundreds of thousands of wading birds were slaughtered for the fine plumes—aigrettes—grown by some species for courtship displays. The loss of the adults during the breeding season meant that their nestlings starved, causing the populations of most species to plummet within a few decades. Ardeids are called wading birds in the United States, a term that should not be confused with the British term "waders," which refers to shorebirds.

Structure Some ardeid species are small and chunky, but most species have moderate to large, slender bodies with long necks and legs—the legs of most species extend beyond the tail when in flight. The wings are generally long and rounded, the tail short. The long, dagger-shaped bill aids in capturing aquatic prey. The neck, which is held in an S-curve while birds are resting, may be extended fully when foraging, and is drawn toward the body during flight.

Plumage Herons generally have a dull blue or gray plumage, while egrets typically show a plumage that is entirely white. Bitterns are plumaged cryptically, with brown or buffy streaking. Many species grow elongated plumes from the head, breast, or back that are used in elaborate courtship displays. Also associated with courtship is the intensifying of soft-part colors of the lores, bill, and legs of many species.

Behavior Most species nest colonially (bitterns are the exception); nightly roosts or breeding colonies may contain thousands of individuals of several species. Wading birds use several foraging strategies that vary greatly by species. Many species stand in or near water and wait for prey to pass by—usually fish and small crustaceans, but snakes and other vertebrates are taken by larger species. Others walk slowly, perhaps also stirring up the water with their feet to flush prey. The Reddish Egret has a particularly active foraging behavior. Cattle Egrets and occasionally other species hunt in fields or yards for insects or small vertebrates.

Distribution Cosmopolitan. The largest numbers of wading birds occur in areas with abundant wetlands and mild climate. The Everglades is perhaps the area most associated with wading birds in North America, but large populations occur along the entire Gulf Coast and in parts of California.

Taxonomy Species limits remain uncertain for many taxa. Worldwide, 60 to 65 species in 16 to 21 genera are recognized. According to the AOU, 17 species in 9 genera occur in North America. They are often divided into 3 groups: bitterns (3 sp.), herons and egrets (12 sp.), and night-herons (2 sp.).

Conservation BirdLife International lists 3 species as endangered and 5 as vulnerable—all from the Old World. In North America, the end of the millinery trade in the early 1900s allowed many wading bird populations to recover—a recovery that continues for especially sensitive species such as the Reddish Egret. Wetland loss or degradation, pollution, colony disturbance, and overharvesting of prey, however, now threaten some populations. —*Bill Pranty, Kurt Radamaker*

BITTERNS Genera *Ixobrychus* and *Botaurus*

In contrast to other wading birds, which are showy and feed in the open, bitterns are secretive marsh dwellers with cryptic, streaked plumage that allow them to blend in with their surroundings. Bitterns are solitary species, but they can be common in an ideal habitat. Three species occur in North America, 1 as an accidental.

YELLOW BITTERN *Ixobrychus sinensis*

This Old World relative of the Least Bittern has occurred once in N.A. Monotypic. L 15" (38 cm) WS 21" (53 cm) **Identification** ADULT: Sexes similar. Head and neck buffy with black cap; brown back with black tail. Underparts white with buffy streaking on neck and breast, extending to flanks. JUVENILE: Plumage browner, boldly streaked with black on upperparts (except rump); neck also streaked. FLIGHT: Black primary coverts and flight feathers. Adults with buffy wing patch on upper wing. Juveniles with brown secondary coverts heavily streaked with black.

Similar Species Schrenk's Bittern of the Far East is distinguished by its dark rufous upperparts (solid in male and light-spotted in female) and less contrasting upperwing pattern.
Voice Guttural grunt.
Status & Distribution Locally common. BREEDING: Wetlands, even tall trees. From India to Japan through Malay Peninsula. MIGRATION: Partially migratory. WINTER: Much of breeding range (withdraws from Japan and China) to New Guinea and Guam. VAGRANT: One rec. in N.A. (Attu Island, AK, May 17–22, 1989). Also accidental to Australia and Christmas I.
Population Not threatened.

adult

LEAST BITTERN *Ixobrychus exilis*

The Least Bittern, the world's smallest heron, is an easily overlooked inhabitant in the East and locally in the West. It is usually associated with cattails, bulrush, or sawgrass in freshwater marshes, but it also occurs in mangroves. It is very adept at clambering up reed stems, aided by its small size, long toes, and extremely narrow body. Like its larger cousin, the American Bittern, the Least attempts to avoid detection by "freezing" in place, with its head and bill pointed skyward. Knowledge of its vocalizations will aid in finding this secretive, solitary species. Polytypic (5 ssp.; nominate in N.A.). L 13" (33 cm) WS 17" (43 cm) **Identification** This tiny heron has bright buff wing patches, a dark crown, and 2 white or buff scapular stripes that contrast with a dark mantle. Whitish underparts are variably streaked on the foreneck with buff. The eyes, loral skin, and bill are yellow; the bill has a dusky culmen. The legs are greenish in front and yellow in back. ADULT MALE: The crown, back, rump, and tail are a glossy black. The loral skin turns reddish pink during courtship. ADULT FEMALE: Similar, but upperparts are dark brown rather than black; the foreneck has fine, dark streaking. JUVENILE: Similar to female, but colors are more muted. Streaking on foreneck is browner and bolder, extending onto sides of neck; buffy wing coverts have dark centers. DARK MORPH: Very rare; known as the "Cory's Least Bittern." It has bred at Toronto, Ontario, and Lake Okeechobee, Florida. In all ages, chestnut replaces pale areas on upperparts and wing patches, as well as on upperwing coverts. In adults, the white scapular lines are lacking. FLIGHT: It flies with quick wingbeats low over reed beds, dropping abruptly into them. All plumages except the "Cory's" morph show a large buffy patch on the upper wing that contrasts strongly with the dark flight feathers and deep rufous greater coverts.
Similar Species A juvenile Green Heron is also small with streaked underparts, but its wings are always entirely dark. Aurally the Least is very similar to a King or Virginia Rail, whose calls typically are longer with more notes.
Voice Quite vocal with a varied repertoire. ALARM: Several calls, including *quoh* and *hah*. CALL: A rail-like *tut-tut-tut* or *kek-kek-kek-kek* heard year-round (often mistaken for a King or Virginia Rail). SONG: Male only gives 3 or 4 short, low *coo* notes in rapid succession.
Status & Distribution Uncommon to locally common. BREEDING: Dense marshland vegetation, especially cattails; rare in mangrove swamps. Very local in interior West. MIGRATION: Partially migratory. Arrives in breeding areas Apr.–May; departs Aug.–Sept. WINTER: Resident in southernmost N.A. breeding areas. Majority of N.A. birds winter in C.A. and the Caribbean. VAGRANT: Casual north to southwest Canada and NF. Accidental to the Azores, Bermuda, Clipperton I., and Iceland.
Population Least Bittern numbers are probably declining with loss of wetlands, but the species is still rather common in some areas.

adult ♂

high breeding adult ♂

juveniles

"Cory's" adult ♂

adult ♂

adult ♀

AMERICAN BITTERN *Botaurus lentiginosus*

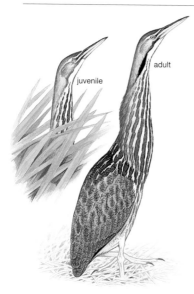

juvenile

adult

adult

Cryptic in plumage and mostly crepuscular in habits, the American Bittern is a denizen of freshwater (rarely saline) marshes with thick vegetation. It attempts concealment by pointing its bill upward; it may sway its head and neck back and forth to mimic wind-rustled vegetation. It is detected primarily by its eerie "pumping" vocalizations, given primarily on the breeding grounds. It feeds on a variety of aquatic prey. Monotypic. L 28" (71 cm) WS 42" (107 cm)

Identification A large brown stocky heron with a proportionately thick neck and short legs. ADULT: Sexes similar. Brown upperparts finely flecked with black. Brown head with darker cap, white supercilium, chin, and throat, and wide blackish malar streak. Yellow eyes and mostly yellow bill; legs and feet pale greenish or yellowish. White or pale underparts with bold rufous streaking. JUVENILE: Blackish malar stripe absent. FLIGHT: Strong and direct; may appear hunch-backed. Wings somewhat pointed. On upperwings, blackish flight feathers contrast with brown coverts; underwings sooty.

Similar Species Immature night-herons are smaller, lack the dark malar stripe, have rounded wings and reddish eyes, and are often found in open habitats. The contrasting upperwing surface of an immature Yellow-crowned Night-Heron is similar to the American Bittern, but its bill is short and black.

Voice SONG: Distinctive, resonant "pumping" *oonk-a-lunk* (rarely heard on wintering grounds). CALL: A hoarse *wok* or *wok-wok-wok* when flushed.

Status & Distribution Uncommon. BREEDING: Non-colonially in freshwater wetlands with tall emergent vegetation. Throughout southern Canada and northern U.S.; rarely in southern U.S. MIGRATION: Partially migratory; some birds probably resident along Pacific coast and in the southern portion of breeding range. WINTER: Pacific coast as far north as Puget Sound, southern U.S., Mexico, Cuba, and possibly C.A. VAGRANT: Prone to extralimital wandering; reported from Bermuda, Canary Is., Great Britain, Greenland, Iceland, Lesser Antilles, Norway, and Spain.

Population American Bittern numbers may be declining severely due to wetland loss and degradation.

Genus Ardea

GREAT EGRET *Ardea alba*

This tall, stately egret is found in a variety of freshwater, brackish, or saline habitats over much of the United States. It feeds primarily on fish and aquatic invertebrates, and can wade into deeper water than other wading birds because of its larger size. It is also found locally in fields and pastures, stalking small mammals. The plumes of Great Egrets were among the most sought after for the millinery trade, resulting in severe population declines of this once again common species. This species is known in the Old World as the Great White Egret or the Great White Heron. Polytypic (4 ssp.; *egretta* in N.A.). L 39" (99 cm) WS 51" (130 cm)

Identification The Great Egret is a large, white egret with a long, slender neck. NONBREEDING ADULT: The sexes are similar. The plumage is entirely white. The eyes, lores, and bill are yellow; the legs and feet are black. BREEDING ADULT:

It develops long, graceful plumes (aigrettes) on the back that extend beyond the tail. Unlike many other herons and egrets, there are no plumes on the head or neck. The lores flush light green and the bill turns orangish. IMMATURE: It looks similar to a nonbreeding adult.

Similar Species The Great Egret is most similar to the white morph of Great Blue Heron but it is somewhat smaller and less bulky, with thinner bill, and black legs and feet. It lacks the short head plumes of adult Great White Herons. The bill of the white morph Reddish Egret is either all dark (immature) or bicolored with a pink base (adults). Other egrets are much smaller and lack the combination of yellow bill and black legs and feet.

Voice Generally silent except when nesting or disturbed, when it may utter *kraak* or *cuk-cuk-cuk* notes.

high breeding adult

nonbreeding

Status & Distribution The most cosmopolitan egret; found on all continents except Antarctica. Common. **BREEDING:** In shrubs or trees in colonies with other wading birds. Along the Atlantic, Gulf, and Pacific coasts, the Mississippi River floodplain, and locally elsewhere in the interior. Also in extreme southern Canada, the West Indies, C.A., and S.A. **MIGRATION:** Partially migratory; birds mostly resident along coasts and in southern U.S. Postbreeding dispersal may carry birds north of regular summer range. **WINTER:** Locally in the West and throughout the Southeast; also south of U.S. **VAGRANT:** Casual to southern AK and Atlantic Canada; also to southern Africa, Britain, Canary Is., Clipperton I., and Scandinavia.

Population Great Egret numbers were decimated by the plume trade in the late 1800s and early 1900s, but they have largely recovered. Some populations are still increasing.

GREAT BLUE HERON *Ardea herodias*

The largest and most widely distributed wading bird in N.A., the Great Blue is found in a range of wetland and upland habitats. It feeds on crustaceans, vertebrates, and small mammals. The white morph, Great White Heron, is sometimes considered a distinct species. Polytypic. L 46" (117 cm) WS 72" (183 cm)

Identification BLUE MORPH: Blue-gray upperparts; grayish neck; large, daggerlike yellow bill. NONBREEDING ADULT: Sexes similar. Bluish gray back and wings with scapular plumes and a black shoulder patch; blackish tail. Neck gray or rusty gray with fine black streaking on the underside; short, gray plumes on lower neck and breast. Head and crown white, divided by a wide black stripe that extends to black occipital plumes. Yellow eyes; bluish gray lores; mostly yellow bill. Legs and feet brown, brownish green, or greenish black. Underparts blackish. BREEDING ADULT: Soft-part coloration intensifies but varies regionally. Lime green or blue lores; yellow, orange, or reddish bill; reddish or greenish yellow legs. JUVENILE: Darker overall without plumes; black crown; blackish lores and upper mandible. FLIGHT: Strong, slow, deliberate wingbeats. Grayish coverts contrast with dark flight feathers. WHITE MORPH: Size, shape, and behavior like Great Blue, but white in all plumages; legs and feet dull yellow. IMMATURE: Legs and feet dull yellowish gray; upper mandible grayish blue. INTERMEDIATE MORPH ("WURDEMANN'S HERON"): Intergrade between blue and white morphs; similar to blue morph but head white and neck pale with inconspicuous streaking on underside.

Geographic Variation The nominate subspecies is found over most of the North American range. The Pacific Northwest form *(fannini)* has darker plumage and a shorter bill; the white *("occidentalis")* and intermediate morphs are restricted to southern Florida.

Similar Species The Great Blue is distinctive. The Great White Heron is distinguished from a Great Egret by its larger size, larger, thicker bill, and entirely dull yellow legs and feet.

Voice Relatively silent away from nest. CALL: A load, hoarse *kraaank*.

Status & Distribution BLUE MORPH: Common. BREEDING: Colonially (rarely solitary) in all lower 48 states, AK, all but northern Canadian provinces, the West Indies, and American tropics. MIGRATION: Partially migratory; withdraws from northern portion of breeding range, except along coasts. WINTER: Along coasts and in southern portion of breeding range. VAGRANT: Wanders widely; casual to Arctic coast, Azores, Clipperton I., Greenland, HI, and Spain. WHITE MORPH: Uncommon. Restricted in U.S. to southern FL (±850 pairs resident). Strays along the coasts north to TX and NJ/southern NY, and inland to PA; also to the West Indies.

Population The numbers are stable.

adult

breeding adult

juvenile

"Wurdemann's Heron" adult

"Great White Heron" white morph adult

Genus *Egretta*

This genus contains 13 to 14 species. Four species (all called egrets) are white, 6 (mostly called herons) are blue or blackish, and 3 or 4 others contain both white and dark morphs. The species inhabit a variety of freshwater and saline environments.

CHINESE EGRET *Egretta eulophotes*

This elegantly plumed species is closely related to the Snowy and Little Egrets. A rare resident of Southeast Asia, it has strayed to North America once. Monotypic. L 27" (65 cm) WS 41.5" (105 cm)
Identification Similar to the Snowy Egret in size and plumage. Sexes and ages similar. Plumage entirely white. Yellow eyes; yellow-green lores; dusky bill with pale base to the lower mandible. Yellow-green legs and feet. BREEDING ADULT: Develops shaggy plumes from the nape, breast, and back. Soft-part colors intensify: yellow bill, turquoise lores, black legs, and yellow feet.
Similar Species The Snowy and Little Egrets are very similar, but the Chinese looks proportionately short-legged. In nonbreeding plumage, identify the Chinese by its yellow-green legs and feet. In breeding

plumage, the combination of its turquoise lores, entirely yellow bill, and black legs with yellow feet is distinctive.
Voice Undescribed; presumably sounds like other egrets.
Status & Distribution Considered endangered by BirdLife International, with ±1,800–2,500 birds remaining. BREEDING: Colonially on islands off Korea, China, and possibly the Russian Far East. DISPERSAL: Wanders widely from northern Japan south. WINTER: From the Malay Peninsula to the Philippines and northern Borneo. One accidental record in N.A. (Agattu I., AK, June 16, 1974); also accidental to Myanmar and Sulawesi.
Population Nearly exterminated by plume hunters, populations continue to decline, primarily from destruction of wetlands.

breeding
adult

LITTLE EGRET *Egretta garzetta*

nonbreeding
adult

breeding
adult

This Old World counterpart to the Snowy Egret inhabits a variety of freshwater and saline environments. It feeds primarily on small fish but takes other prey. It has 2 color forms, a typical white morph and a rare dark morph. Many ornithologists consider the Little Egret conspecific with the Western

Reef-Heron *(E. gularis)* and Dimorphic Egret *(E. dimorpha),* but the AOU considers each a separate species. Polytypic (3 ssp.; nominate in N.A.). L 24" (60 cm) WS 38" (91 cm)
Identification Medium-sized egret, very similar to the Snowy Egret and the Western Reef-Heron. Primarily the white morph is discussed here; dark-morph birds breed in Barbados. Sexes similar. NONBREEDING ADULT: Plumage entirely white. Yellow eyes, blue-gray lores, black legs, and yellow feet. BREEDING ADULT: Two white occipital plumes, as well as numerous plumes on lower neck and back. Lores and feet flush red. IMMATURE: Pale base to lower mandible, gray lores, brownish green legs.
Similar Species The Little is most readily told from the Snowy Egret in nonbreeding plumage by its blue-gray rather than yellow lores; in breeding plumage, it has only 2 or 3 occipital plumes. The Little also has a flatter crown, a somewhat thicker bill, duller yellow feet, and more upright, longer necked posture; the Snowy habitually forages in a hunched manner. An immature Little Blue Heron has often dark tips to the primaries, and green-

ish yellow legs and feet. A nonbreeding Cattle Egret differs by its yellow bill and dark legs and feet. The white morph is best distinguished from the very similar Western Reef-Heron by bill structure. The dark-morph Western Reef-Heron is very similar, but it has a white throat, which the Little sometimes lacks; an immature often has scattered dark flight feathers.
Voice Usually silent. CALL: A low guttural *kraak.*
Status & Distribution Common. Widespread in Eurasia and Australasia. Rare but increasing in the West Indies (±20 pairs breed at Barbados). VAGRANT: Casual along the Atlantic coast north to Maritimes, and also to Puerto Rico and Lesser Antilles. Accidental inland to QC.
Population The Little Egret is widespread in the Old World. New World populations have been increasing since the first report in the West Indies in 1954. (Colonization of the New World probably originated from birds in West Africa flying across the Atlantic Ocean.) It will presumably be found with greater frequency in the U.S. as the West Indies population increases.

WESTERN REEF-HERON *Egretta gularis*

This Old World species has recently colonized the West Indies and has strayed once to the United States, and once to Canada. It has 2 color morphs, white and dark, with rare intermediates. The Western Reef-Heron is often considered conspecific with the Little Egret. Polytypic (2 ssp.; nominate in N.A.). L 23.5" (60 cm) WS 37.5" (95 cm) **Identification** The dark morph primarily is discussed here. NONBREEDING ADULT: The sexes are similar. It shows entirely slate gray overall, with a white chin and throat. The eyes are yellow; the lores and bill dusky yellow. The legs are black, the feet yellow. BREEDING ADULT: It develops 2 long, wispy, slate occipital plumes. Soft-part colors intensify: The lores flush red and the feet turn black. IMMATURE: It shows overall brown or dark gray-brown with a white chin and throat.

Similar Species An adult Little Blue Heron is entirely dark; in breeding plumage it has a shaggy head and neck plume and entirely dark legs and feet. The Tricolored Heron has an entirely white belly. The rare dark morph of the Little Egret is very similar, but it often has a dark throat. The white morph Little Egret is best distinguished by bill structure. The reef-heron bill has a subtle decurvature toward distal portion. **Voice** Usually silent. CALL: A throaty squawk.

Status & Distribution Occurs coastally from West Africa east to India; vagrant to southern Europe, possibly from deliberate releases. Recent arrival in the New World, beginning in mid-1980s. Several records from the West Indies, primarily Barbados. Two recs. in N.A.: Nantucket, MA (Apr. 26–Sept. 13, 1983) and west NF (summer 2005).

dark morph
adult

Population Widespread in the Old World, the Western Reef-Heron is increasing in the West Indies.

SNOWY EGRET *Egretta thula*

immature

high breeding adult

breeding adult

breeding adult

The delicate and graceful Snowy Egret occurs throughout the New World. The Snowy is found in a wide range of freshwater and saline habitats. It feeds on a variety of prey such as fish, aquatic invertebrates, and even snakes and lizards. Monotypic. L 24" (61 cm) WS 41" (104 cm) **Identification** The Snowy Egret is a medium-size white heron with a slender build and a thin black bill. NON-BREEDING ADULT: The sexes look similar. The plumage is entirely white. The eyes and lores are yellow; the legs are black and the feet yellow. BREEDING ADULT: It develops elegant plumes on its crown, nape, foreneck, and back. Some soft-part colors intensify: The lores flush red, and the feet flush orange or reddish. JUVENILE: The bill has a pale gray base; the lores are a grayish green. **Similar Species** The Little Egret closely resembles the Snowy Egret. The Snowy is distinguished by its yellow lores, more rounded crown and shorter bill, narrower at the base. It also has numerous breeding plumes, compared to only the 2 or 3 occipital plumes found on the Little. When foraging, the Little's posture is more upright, in a manner similar to a Great Egret. An immature Little Blue Heron has a thicker, more bicolored bill, greenish yellow legs and feet, and often darkish tips to the primaries. **Voice** Generally silent except away from breeding colony. CALL: A harsh, raspy *aah-raarrh*.

Status & Distribution Common. BREEDING: Colonially with other wading birds. Locally from eastern OR and CA across the Interior West; primarily coastally along the Atlantic and Gulf coasts from ME south to S.A.; also in the West Indies. MIGRATION: Partially migratory; most inland breeders in northern part of range withdraw. WINTER: Coastally from OR and NJ south to S.A.; also all of FL, along the entire Gulf coast, and the West Indies. DISPERSAL: Wanders irregularly north to south Canada from BC to NF; also to HI, Bahamas, Lesser Antilles, Bermuda, and the Galápagos. Accidental to southeastern AK, Clipperton I., Iceland, and South Georgia I.

Population Its numerous breeding plumes made it among the most sought after species for the millinery trade in the late 1800s and early 1900s, resulting in the near decimation of the species, but the species has since recovered. The species' adaptability to a range of environmental conditions has allowed it to expand its range beyond its original distribution in the past several decades.

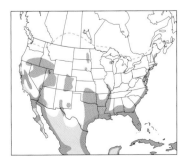

LITTLE BLUE HERON *Egretta caerulea*

Unique among herons, the Little Blue has an all-white juvenal plumage and an all-dark adult plumage. It is most often seen singly or in small groups. Found in freshwater and saline habitats, it forages for aquatic invertebrates, fish, and amphibians by walking slowly or by standing still, with neck bent forward at a 45-degree angle. Monotypic. L 24" (61 cm) WS 40" (102 cm)
Identification A medium-size bird with a dark bill and dark legs. No filamentous plumes; long lanceolate plumes develop during breeding. ADULT: Sexes similar. Dark slate blue body with purple head and neck. Yellow eyes, dull greenish lores, blue-gray bill with black tip; gray to greenish gray legs and feet. BREEDING ADULT: Bright reddish purple head and neck with long lanceolate plumes on the crest and back. Lores and base of bill turquoise; legs and feet black. JUVENILE: Entirely white, but often with dark gray tips to most of the primaries. FIRST-SPRING: Adult plumage acquired gradually by second summer or second fall, resulting in splotchy white and blue ("calico" or "pied") plumage.

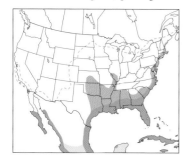

Similar Species A dark morph Reddish Egret is larger and paler overall, with shaggy head and neck plumes, and a pink-based, black-tipped bill in the breeding adult. A white

immature

molting immature

breeding adult

immature

nonbreeding adult

morph Reddish Egret is larger with pale lores and dark legs and feet; it also has a different foraging behavior. A Tricolored Heron has dark upperparts and white underparts in all plumages. An immature Little Blue is distinguished from a Snowy Egret by its stouter, more bicolored bill, gray-green lores, greenish yellow legs and feet, and usually dark tips to the primaries. A Cattle Egret has a stout yellow bill.
Voice Generally silent away from breeding colony. CALL: A harsh, croaking *aarr-aarrh*.
Status & Distribution Common. BREEDING: Colonial; in lower shrubs and small trees, often on islands. Along Atlantic coast from NY (local north to southern ME) through FL, along entire Gulf coast to northern S.A., up the Missis-

sippi River drainage to southern IL and IN, and in southern Great Plains. Along Pacific coast from Sonora and Baja California south. Locally at San Diego, CA, and north to ND and SD. MIGRATION: Partially migratory; withdraws from northern portion of breeding range. WINTER: Along entire Gulf coast, along Atlantic coast to VA, and from extreme southwestern CA south along Pacific coast; also in West Indies. DISPERSAL: Widely after breeding; casual to BC, HI, MT, NF, and WA. VAGRANT: Accidental to the Azores, Chile, and western Greenland.
Population The species escaped much of the slaughter for the millinery trade. The big threats are wetland degradation or loss and colony disturbance. Some range expansion has occurred since the 1970s.

TRICOLORED HERON *Egretta tricolor*

This colorful, slender-necked heron of southern affinity is a graceful and active hunter. When feeding, it often dashes about in the shallows pursuing prey with wings slightly raised, and may change direction swiftly and with precision; it often wades in deeper water than most other herons. It feeds nearly exclusively on small

fish, with crustaceans and frogs taken only rarely. Polytypic (2–3 ssp.; *ruficollis* in N.A.). L 26" (66 cm) WS 36" (91 cm)

juvenile

adult

Identification A medium-size bird with a long, slender neck and long, thin bill. NONBREEDING ADULT: Sexes similar. Slate-gray head, neck, back, wings, and tail; back covered with elongated purplish maroon scapular feathers. White rump, throat, and underparts; white often extends as a narrow stripe down the center of the neck to the belly. Brown eyes, yellow lores, mostly yellow bill; and grayish yellow legs and feet. BREEDING ADULT: A few long, white occipital plumes and elongated purple plumes on the lower neck. Chin, throat, and scapulars tinged with rufous. Soft-part coloration intensifies: red eyes; turquoise lores and base of bill; and maroon, orange, or pink legs and feet. IMMATURE: Rich chestnut head and neck; scapulars and wing coverts gray, edged with chestnut. FLIGHT: Swift and direct. White underparts and wing linings contrast with dark flight feathers.

Similar Species The Green Heron is similar, but the Tricolored is easily told by its larger size, longer, thinner neck, and white belly. See Little Blue Heron. **Voice** Relatively silent away from breeding colony. CALL: A raspy *aaah*.

Status & Distribution Uncommon to common. BREEDING: Colonial, usually on islands. Along the entire Atlantic and Gulf Coasts from NY (locally to southern ME) to northern Mexico, and throughout FL and most of LA, and occasionally inland to KS and AR; also

in the West Indies and along the Pacific coast from Baja California south to northern S.A.. Irregular breeder inland in SC, ND, and SD. MIGRATION: Partially migratory; withdraws from northern portions of breeding range; some U.S. breeders winter in the West Indies. WINTER: Along the Atlantic coast from VA south, peninsular FL, and the Gulf Coast; a few also in southwestern CA. VAGRANT: Casual to CA and OR, and to southern Canada from MB to NF; also to the Lesser Antilles. Accidental in the Azores.

Population Although less affected by the millinery trade than the white egrets, the Tricolored's populations were still reduced. Notable increases in breeding

and wintering populations have been recorded along the Atlantic coast from North Carolina since the 1950s. However, Florida populations are showing a recent rapid decline, perhaps due to wetland loss or degredation.

REDDISH EGRET *Egretta rufescens*

North America's rarest and most restricted heron, the Reddish Egret is confined as a breeder to the Gulf coast. It is unique among our wading birds in having 2 distinct color morphs; the dark morph predominates in North America. It is also notable for its curious, active foraging behavior, quickly pursuing fish in shallows, or "dancing" around with wings flapping. It feeds on fish and aquatic invertebrates. Polytypic. L 30" (76 cm) WS 46" (117 cm)

Identification Large wading bird restricted to shallow estuaries. ADULT: Sexes similar. NONBREEDING DARK MORPH: Entirely rufous head and neck with short, "shaggy" plumes. Pale eyes, bill entirely dark, blackish legs and feet. Remainder of body dark gray. WHITE MORPH: Plumage entirely white. INTERMEDIATE PLUMAGE: Similar to dark morph, but white feathers scattered on wings or body. BREEDING ADULT: Elongated plumes on head, neck, and back. Basal portion of bill pink, lores violet-blue, legs and feet blue (greenish blue in some white morphs). IMMATURE DARK MORPH: Plumage brownish gray; wing coverts edged with rufous. Pale eyes. Black bill. WHITE MORPH: White plumage, black bill.

Geographic Variation Two weakly differentiated subspecies. Nominate *rufescens* is found in the U.S. Southeast and the West Indies; *dickeyi*, with browner head and neck and darker plumage, is found from Baja California to Central America (it wanders north to CA and the Southwest).

Similar Species The dark morph is larger than a Little Blue Heron, with black legs and feet; the bill is pale- or violet-

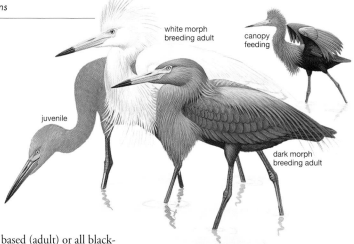

white morph breeding adult

canopy feeding

juvenile

dark morph breeding adult

based (adult) or all blackish (immature). A Tricolored Heron always has entirely white underparts. Compared to a white morph, an immature Little Blue has greenish legs and feet and grayish lores; most have dusky wingtips. It is distinguished from a Snowy Egret by its larger size, all-black legs and feet, bicolored bill and pale or pale violet lores (breeding adults).

Voice Generally silent. Low *raaaah* and other notes when foraging or disturbed.

Status & Distribution Uncommon to locally common. BREEDING: Colonially with other wading birds; typically islands in coastal estuaries. Presently ±2,000 pairs in the U.S.: AL (few), FL (±350–400), LA (±100), and TX (±1,500). DISPERSAL: Nonmigratory, but disperses along Gulf Coast and southern Atlantic coast to NC during spring and summer; some move inland. WINTER: Perhaps some withdrawal from northern parts of Gulf Coast; a few regularly move north from Baja California to southern CA.

VAGRANT: Mostly by dark morphs; casual north to NV, WY, CO, MI, IL, NY, and MA.

Population Numbers are still recovering from the millinery trade slaughter; the species continues to reclaim historic breeding range in Florida. Some colonies are threatened from disturbance by boaters; intensive coastal development has greatly reduced foraging habitats in Florida.

Genus *Bubulcus*

CATTLE EGRET *Bubulcus ibis*

nonbreeding adult

immature

high breeding adult

The most terrestrial of the herons, the Cattle Egret rarely forages in water, but is regular in marshy areas. It is appropriately named for its customary habit of following cattle and other large grazing animals to forage on insects and other invertebrates that the mammals flush up. It has adapted well to modern living by learning to follow tractors and other machinery in the same way. It may also be seen foraging for exotic lizards in Florida parking lots. Polytypic (3 ssp.; nominate in N.A.). L 20" (51 cm) WS 36" (91 cm)

Identification A small, stocky, white egret, with a short, thick neck and relatively short and stocky bill. ADULT: Sexes similar. Plumage entirely white. Yellow bill; black legs and feet. BREEDING ADULT: Bright orange-buff plumes develop on the crown, nape, lower back, and foreneck. (Aberrant individuals may be extensively peach-colored.) The bill becomes 2-toned with a reddish base and yellow distal end; the lores flush purplish pink; and the legs and feet become dark red. JUVENILE: Like nonbreeding adult, but with a black bill.

Similar Species The Snowy Egret is slim-mer with an entirely black bill and black legs with yellow feet. The Great Egret is much larger with a longer neck and bill and much longer black legs. The immature Little Blue Heron has a gray bill with a black tip, dark-tipped primaries, and greenish gray legs and feet.

Voice Silent away from the breeding colony. Emits a coarse nasal *rick-rack* greeting when returning to the nest or roost.

Status & Distribution Common to abundant. Found in much of the U.S., Mexico, C.A., and the West Indies. BREEDING: Colonially with other wading birds in shrubs or small trees, often on islands. MIGRATION: Partially migratory, withdrawing from the northern part of breeding range. WINTER: In the southern U.S., especially in southeastern CA, along the entire Gulf Coast, and throughout the FL Peninsula; also the in the West Indies and American tropics. DISPERSAL: Disperses widely. VAGRANT: To AK and the northern Canadian Provinces. Introduced to HI. One extralimital record of the Asian subspecies *coromanda* in AK.

Population The now widespread Cattle Egret has one of the most renowned and well-documented expansions of any bird into North America. First documented in the New World in the West Indies in the 1930s, the species colonized Florida by 1941. Its arrival in the New World probably originated with birds from Africa crossing the Atlantic during favorable westerly winds. By the early 1970s, Cattle Egrets had colonized most of the continental United States. Most expansion has slowed or stopped, and major population declines have been seen in the Northeast (and possibly elsewhere) since the peak in the 1970s and early '80s.

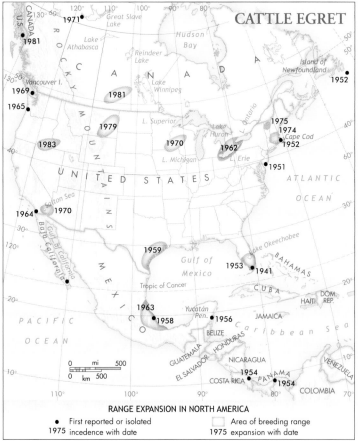

CATTLE EGRET

RANGE EXPANSION IN NORTH AMERICA

• First reported or isolated
1975 incedence with date

☐ Area of breeding range
1975 expansion with date

Genus *Ardeola*

CHINESE POND-HERON   *Ardeola bacchus*

The Chinese Pond-Heron is the most northeasterly occurring of the 3 pond-herons. Monotypic. L 18" (46 cm) WS 34" (86 cm)

Identification NONBREEDING ADULT: Short and stocky with entirely white wings, rump, and tail. Head, neck, breast, and back dark. Yellow bill with black tip; yellow eyes, legs, and feet. BREEDING ADULT MALE: Head, neck, and upper breast bright chestnut. Base of bill bluish. Lower breast slaty colored. Long plumes. BREEDING ADULT FEMALE: Like breeding male, but plumes less showy, foreneck pale; no slaty patch on breast. IMMATURE:

Head and breast buffy, streaked with dark brown; mantle brown. FLIGHT: White wings, rump, and tail contrast with a dark body.

Similar Species None; the contrasting dark body and white wings and tail are distinctive.

Voice Undescribed; other pond-herons squawk.

Status & Distribution Common. BREEDING: China and Indochina. WINTER: Throughout much of S.E. Asia. Has strayed to Japan (where increasing) and Korea. Accidental: one breeding-plumaged male reached St. Paul I., Pribilofs (Aug. 4–9, 1996).

Population It is declining in some breeding areas.

breeding adult ♂

Genus *Butorides*

GREEN HERON   *Butorides virescens*

adult

juvenile

adult

The Green Heron (found throughout N.A. and C.A.) was once taxonomically combined with the Striated Heron (found throughout S.A. and much of the Old World) as the Green-backed Heron, based on reported widespread hybridization where their ranges overlap in the southern West Indies, southern Central America, and northern South America. Their status as separate species was restored after it was learned that hybridization was not as widespread as was previously thought. The Green Heron is generally found solitary or in family groups, occurring in many wetland habitats ranging from freshwater to saline, and open to wooded. It feeds primarily on small fish, but also takes a variety of aquatic invertebrates. The Green Heron is one of the few North American birds to use tools to forage: It places a leaf, feather, piece of bread, or other object on the sur-

face of the water. When a fish swims in to investigate the item, it is captured by the heron. Polytypic. L 18" (46 cm) WS 26" (66 cm)

Identification Small and stocky, with short legs, a thick neck, and a small crest. NONBREEDING ADULT: Sexes similar. Crown and short crest blackish, sides of head and neck rufous. White chin, throat, underside of neck, and breast. Yellow-orange eyes; dark lores. Blackish yellow bill with greenish yellow base. Yellow legs and feet. Greenish gray back, wings, rump, and tail; upperwing feathers edged with buff. Gray belly and undertail coverts. BREEDING ADULT: Soft-part colors intensify: The lores flush bluish black; the bill turns largely black; the legs and feet flush orange. JUVENILE: Sides of face, neck, and breast heavily streaked with brown. Upperparts browner; upperwing feathers marked with buff edges and whitish spots at the tips. FLIGHT: Underwings of adult are uniformly dark gray; those of immature are paler with contrasting pale feather edges.

Geographic Variation Four subspecies, 2 occur in North America: The larger, paler *anthonyi* is found along the Pacific coast of Mexico and in the U.S. Southwest; the *virescens* occurs in east and central North America and Mexico, the West Indies, and all of Central America.

Similar Species The only other small wading bird regularly encountered in North America is the smaller Least Bittern, which shows white scapular lines and bright buffy wing coverts in all typical plumages.

Voice Sharp *skeow* given when migrating at night or when flushed (often accompanied in flight by defecating). ALARM CALL: A series of *kuk* notes; raises crest and flicks tail.

Status & Distribution Common. BREEDING: From ND east to southern NS south to TX through FL. Also, mostly coastally from Puget Sound south through Baja California east to western AZ. Rare and sporadic through much of the interior. MIGRATION: May be seen casually through much of U.S. WINTER: Many birds resident along coasts and in the Deep South; distribution in C.A. more widespread. VAGRANT: Has strayed to the Azores, U.K., Greenland, and HI.

Population The numbers are stable.

NIGHT-HERONS Genera *Nycticorax* and *Nyctanassa*

BLACK-CROWNED NIGHT-HERON *Nycticorax nycticorax*

This medium-sized, stocky heron feeds day and night on a range of fish and aquatic invertebrates and even upland prey. Polytypic (4 ssp.). L 25" (64 cm) WS 44" (112 cm)

Identification NONBREEDING ADULT: Sexes similar. Black back; pale gray upperwings, rump, and tail. Black crown and nape; white forehead, face, neck. Two or 3 white occipital plumes. Red eyes; black bill; yellow legs and feet. BREEDING ADULT: Legs and feet bright pink or red. Occipital plumes lengthen. JUVENILE: Dark brown above and paler below, with upperpart feathers tipped with large white spots, and underparts heavily streaked. Orange eyes; yellow bill with a dark culmen and tip. FIRST-SUMMER: Dark brown crown, back, and upperwings. Face and neck

pale with diffuse light brown streaking; belly and undertail coverts white. SECOND SUMMER: Like adult, but white forehead, hind neck, and underparts washed with brown or gray. FLIGHT: Fast and direct. Wings short and rounded; only the foot projects beyond tail.

Similar Species The larger, solitary American Bittern is rarely seen in the open. Adults have a conspicuous blackish malar stripe. In flight, they show rather pointed wings, and dark flight feathers contrast with brown coverts. The larger Limpkin has dark eyes, a long, slightly decurved bill, and blackish legs and feet. A juvenile Black-crowned is told from a juvenile Yellow-crowned

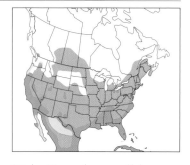

Night-Heron by overall browner plumage, paler crown color, shorter legs, and extensive greenish yellow on slightly slimmer bill. By its first summer, an immature begins to resemble an adult, and is readily told from a similarly aged Yellow-crowned.

Voice A harsh *wock,* lower pitched than the Yellow-crowned.

Status & Distribution Uncommon to fairly common, but local. BREEDING: Colonial. Also in Eurasia and Africa. MIGRATION: Partially migratory; withdraws from most of breeding range. WINTER: Along Pacific coast, entire Gulf Coast, and along Atlantic coast from MA south. VAGRANT: Casual to AK, Clipperton I., Greenland, and HI.

Population Stable or declining.

1st spring

juvenile

2nd spring

adult

juvenile

adult

high breeding adult

YELLOW-CROWNED NIGHT-HERON *Nyctanassa violacea*

Found in habitats ranging from coastal beaches to inland cypress swamps, this medium-sized, stocky bird is more likely to be found nesting alone or in scattered pairs compared to other colonial heron species. Active day and night, it forages for aquatic invertebrates. Polytypic. L 24" (61 cm) WS 42" (107 cm)

Identification Longer neck and more upright posture than the Black-crowned Night-Heron. NONBREEDING ADULT: Sexes similar. Head black with bold buffy white cheek patch, pale yellow crown, and a few wispy occipital plumes. Rest of plumage blue-gray; feathers on back and upperwings black with wide blue-gray borders. Orange eyes; short, thick, black bill; yellowish

green legs and feet. BREEDING ADULT: White crown. Eyes scarlet; lores dark green; legs scarlet or bright orange. JUVENILE: Mostly grayish brown above with small white tips to feathers on upperparts; head and neck heavily streaked. FIRST-SUMMER: Like juvenile, but darker crown and mostly brown upperparts. FLIGHT: Slower wingbeats than the Black-crowned; feet and a portion of the legs extend beyond tail.

Geographic Variation Six subspecies, 2 in N.A: The nominate occurs in central and eastern U.S. and the Atlantic coast of C.A., and *bancrofti,* which has paler plumage, narrower dorsal streaking, and a larger bill, occurs (as a vagrant) in the Southwest, along the Pacific coast

of C.A., and in the West Indies.

Similar Species A juvenile is told from a juvenile Black-crowned Night-Heron by somewhat darker and grayer plumage with less conspicuous white markings on upperparts, shorter,

slightly thicker, entirely dark bill, and longer legs.

Voice A harsh *wock,* higher pitched than the Black-crowned Night-Heron.

Status & Distribution Uncommon to fairly common, but local overall. BREEDING: Primarily coastal, from MA through FL to TX; a few inland north to MN, OH, and WI. MIGRATION: Partially migratory; withdraws from most of breeding range. WINTER: In the U.S., primarily central and south FL, but north to NC and west to TX. VAGRANT: To CA, AZ, NM, ND, and southern Canada from SK to NS; also Clipperton I.

Population Thought to be stable.

IBISES AND SPOONBILLS Family Threskiornithidae

Roseate Spoonbill (TX, Mar.)

Although easily distinguished from each other by bill shape, plumage coloration, and foraging behavior, ibises and spoonbills are closely related; hybridization between the two groups has been documented in the Old World.

Structure Threskiornithids are medium to large birds with relatively long necks and legs. Bill shape defines this family: long, downcurved, and slender in ibises, and long, straight, and flattened, with a broad, spoon-shaped distal end in spoonbills. Flight is strong and direct on moderately long, rounded wings; flocks of ibises often soar.

Plumage Species are mostly unicolored, typically white in the spoonbills (but pink in Roseate Spoonbill) and white or blackish in the ibises; the brilliant red plumage of the Scarlet Ibis is unique. Immature plumage is dusky or mottled with brown in ibises, and whitish in spoonbills.

Behavior Colonial breeders, ibises and spoonbills nest and roost with other wading birds. They tend to forage in flocks away from other species. Tactile feeders, they feed on fish and aquatic invertebrates (especially crabs) in shallow fresh or saltwater. Spoonbills feed most often by sweeping their bills back and forth, while ibises tend to probe into the substrate to locate prey. Ibises also forage visually in uplands, feeding on terrestrial invertebrates such as grasshoppers.

Distribution They are found on all continents except Antarctica, reaching their greatest diversity in the tropics. Worldwide, there are about 32 species in 13 genera (26 ibises in 12 genera; 6 spoonbills in 1 genus).

Taxonomy Ibises are often placed in the subfamily Threskiornithinae and the spoonbills in the subfamily Plataleinae, but hybridization between species in the 2 groups has led some taxonomists to reject the subfamilies. The taxonomic status of ibises in North America has been debated for centuries. Glossy and White-faced Ibises have often been considered conspecific, but hybridization has only recently been documented. Also often considered conspecific are White and Scarlet Ibises, based on hybridization in South America, where the 2 species occur sympatrically, as well as in Florida, where Scarlet Ibises were unsuccessfully introduced in the 1960s.

Conservation BirdLife International lists 4 species as critical, 2 as endangered, and 1 as vulnerable, with 2 others as near threatened. The *Plegadis* ibises are expanding beyond previous range limits, but all threskiornithids remain at risk from colony disturbance and wetland loss or degradation, as well as the threat of pesticide contamination or oil spills. —*Bill Pranty, Kurt Radamaker*

SPOONBILLS Genus *Platalea*

ROSEATE SPOONBILL *Platalea ajaja*

1st fall

breeding
adult

The Roseate Spoonbill's pink and red plumage make it perhaps the most flamboyant wading bird. Monotypic. L 32" (71 cm) WS 50" (127 cm)
Identification Unmistakable. All ages have a large, flat, spoon-shaped bill and pink wings and back. ADULT: Sexes similar. Head featherless, yellowish or greenish gray with black collar. Bill grayish with black markings; eyes, legs, and feet reddish. Neck and upper back white with red patch on breast, lower back pink; rump

breeding
adult

1st fall

red. Tail orange. Wings pink with wide red carpal bars. FIRST WINTER: Head fully feathered. Plumage white except for wings and tail, which are entirely pale pink. Yellowish bill. SECOND WINTER: Like adult, but plumage paler; wings lack red carpal bars.
Similar Species Flamingos share the spoonbill's pink plumage, but have much longer and thinner necks and longer legs, as well as very different bill shape and foraging posture.
Voice Silent except at breeding colonies; various low, guttural grunts and clucking.
Status & Distribution Locally common. BREEDING: Colonially on estuarine islands, rarely inland. ±5,000 pairs breed in FL, LA, and TX. DISPERSAL: Nonmigratory, but prone to summer-fall postbreeding dispersal along Gulf and S. Atlantic coasts; many disperse inland. Movements farther north usually made by juveniles. WINTER: Resident in coastal southern FL, LA, and

TX. VAGRANT: Disperses regularly to northeast TX, southeast OK, AR, and casually north to OH, PA, and NY and west to CO and UT. Casual to southern CA and the Southwest from colonies in northwestern Mexico, but numbers reduced in recent decades.
Population Recovering in range and numbers from declines during the millinery trade and associated disturbance at colonies.

Genus *Eudocimus*

SCARLET IBIS *Eudocimus ruber*

This wading bird graces wetlands in the New World tropics. Monotypic. L 23" (58.5 cm) WS 36" (91 cm)
Identification Unmistakable. Sexes similar. BREEDING ADULT: Entirely brilliant red with black tips to outermost 4 primaries. Red legs and bill with blackish distal half. NONBREEDING ADULT: Pinkish bill. IMMATURE: Head and neck margined brown and gray. Brown upper back and wings; white

lower back and rump tinged with pink. Underparts white tinged with pinkish buff; dark gray legs and feet.
Similar Species The Roseate Spoonbill is larger with a spoon-shaped bill; its plumage is also pink and white rather than red. Juveniles indistinguishable from juvenile White Ibis until pink feathering develops.
Voice Usually silent. FLIGHT CALL: Low, grunting *hunk-hunk-hunk.*

Status & Distribution
Common. Resident in northern S.A. and Trinidad. BREEDING: Colonial with other wading birds. DISPERSAL: Nonmigratory but prone to dispersal. VAGRANT: Perhaps to FL but issue clouded by possibility of escapees; observations elsewhere in U.S. presumed to be escapees.
Population Declining, but still common.

adult

WHITE IBIS *Eudocimus albus*

Historically one of the most abundant wading birds in North America, the White Ibis remains numerous in parts of the Southeast despite substantial declines in recent years. The White Ibis is found in virtually all wetland types, and is often seen foraging in grassy fields or along roadways. Despite often breeding in coastal habitats, it feeds primarily on aquatic crustaceans (especially crabs) in freshwater marshes, or on insects in

fields. Monotypic. L 25" (64 cm) WS 38" (97 cm)
Identification ADULT: Sexes similar. Plumage entirely white except for the black tips of the 4 outermost primaries. Soft parts orange or orangered; decurved bill with a blackish tip. Eyes pale blue. BREEDING ADULT: Softpart coloration intensification: face, bill, legs, and feet bright red or redorange. JUVENILE: Head and neck streaked with dark brown. Dark brown

mantle, upperwings, and tail; white rump. Underparts white; underwings white with blackish band on trailing half of flight feathers. FIRST SUMMER: Juvenile-like head and neck pattern with increasing white feathering on the back, wings, and finally head and neck as adult plumage acquired gradually. FLIGHT: Rapid wingbeats alternating with glides; sometimes soars at great heights. Flies in a V-formation or tight flocks.
Similar Species *Plegadis* ibises always have dark rumps and underparts.
Voice Often silent. CALL: Identical to the Scarlet Ibis.
Status & Distribution Locally common. BREEDING: Colonially, either with other wading birds or in large single-species colonies. Along Atlantic coast from VA south, and along the entire

Gulf Coast. MIGRATION: Partially migratory in northern parts of breeding range. Elsewhere highly nomadic and prone to long-distance vagrancy. Regular visitor to northern TX, OK, AR. VAGRANT: To southern CA and the Southwest and north to SD, MI, and southern Canada; also to the Bahamas, Puerto Rico, Bermuda, and Clipperton I.
Population White Ibis populations are declining due to wetland loss and hydrologic disturbances, but the species is still considered common within its range.

1st fall

breeding adult

1st fall

breeding adult

1st spring

DARK IBISES Genus *Plegadis*

GLOSSY IBIS *Plegadis falcinellus*

The predominantly eastern Glossy Ibis inhabits a variety of wetlands, from freshwater to saline, where it feeds primarily on aquatic invertebrates. Its range now overlaps with its western counterpart, the White-faced Ibis. In direct light, the plumage of the adult Glossy Ibis, with its beautiful chestnut upperparts green and bronze iridescence, is dazzling to behold. Monotypic. L 23" (58 cm) WS 36" (91 cm)

breeding adult

1st fall

1st fall

winter adult

breeding adult

Identification ADULT: Sexes similar. BREEDING ADULT: Rich chestnut on head, neck, upper back, and underparts. Lower back, tertials, and median wing coverts glossy, lesser coverts and remainder of wing mostly metallic bronzy green. Uniformly grayish bill tinged horn-colored or dull red, thin and downcurved. Dark gray facial skin bordered by pale bluish skin above and below the eye; brown eyes; dark gray legs and feet with dark maroon ankle joints. NONBREEDING ADULT: Less glossy and chestnut overall; dark brown head and neck feathers edged with white, appearing finely streaked; throat and foreneck paler brown with less streaking. JUVENILE: Chiefly sooty brown on the head, neck, and underparts with variable amounts of white splotching on the throat and chin. Less lustrous overall with less iridescence. By late fall, many juveniles have acquired the pale blue stripes bordering the facial skin. FLIGHT: Flocks fly in a weak V-formation, appearing all dark at a distance.
Similar Species The White-faced Ibis is similar. To separate the 2 species, see sidebar page 124.
Voice CALL: A sheeplike *huu-huu-huu-huu*. Flocks some-

times emit a subdued chattering or grunting, particularly on taking flight.
Status & Distribution Locally common. BREEDING: Coastally from southern ME south to VA and locally south along the Atlantic coast to coastal and inland locations in southern FL and locally along the Gulf Coast west to LA. Widespread in the Old World. MIGRATION: Withdraws from northern part of breeding range. WINTER: Mainly along the Gulf Coast, throughout FL, and along Atlantic coast north to SC. VAGRANT: A few birds now found annually far north and west to southern Canada, WY, MT, NM, AZ, CA, and WA.
Population The Glossy Ibis was rare in North America through the 1930s, but its numbers have increased since that time. Colonizing birds presumably arrived across the Atlantic from West Africa via the West Indies, in a manner similar to the Cattle Egret.

Identification of *Plegadis* Ibises

Separating the Glossy Ibis and White-faced Ibis has become even more important because both species have undergone substantial range expansions in recent years. White-faced Ibises are now annual along the Atlantic and eastern Gulf coasts, and in the Midwest, while Glossy Ibises now occur regularly to the Great Plains, and some have reached the Pacific coast. The breeding ranges of both species overlap in Louisiana and perhaps elsewhere. Hybridization in the wild has been documented; thus, the identification of *Plegadis* ibises can no longer be taken for granted. Scrutinize vagrants carefully; some cannot be identified to species with certainty.

Distinguishing *Plegadis* ibises in breeding plumage is easier than in other plumages. Breeding adult Glossy Ibises have brown eyes, dark lores with narrow pale blue borders that do not extend behind the eyes or under the chin, and gray legs and feet with contrasting reddish ankle joints. In contrast, breeding adult White-faced Ibises have red eyes, pink or red loral skin

with wide white borders that extend behind the eyes and under the chin, and more extensive pinkish legs and feet.

The identification of *Plegadis* ibises in nonbreeding and immature plumages requires close views in good light, and even then, some birds cannot be identified with certainty. Nonbreeding adult Glossy Ibises retain from breeding plumage the dark eyes and dark gray facial skin with a narrow but well-defined pale blue border above and below the eye. The legs are entirely grayish. White-faced Ibises retain their red eyes and pale pinkish facial skin, but lose most or all of the white outline around it. Juvenile *Plegadis* ibises cannot always be identified conclusively in the field. However, by their first fall, many juvenile Glossy Ibises have acquired the pale blue facial stripes, and many juvenile White-faced Ibises have acquired a reddish cast to their eyes and a touch of pink facial skin by their first fall. Leg color and bill color between the two species are too variable to be used as useful field marks. ∎

WHITE-FACED IBIS *Plegadis chihi*

The White-faced Ibis is the quite similar, western counterpart to the eastern Glossy Ibis, mostly replacing it west of the Mississippi River. Monotypic. L 23" (58 cm) WS 36" (91 cm) **Identification** A tall bird with long legs and a long decurved bill. The sexes look similar. BREEDING ADULT: In this plumage, a rich chestnut maroon colors the head, neck, upper back, and underparts. The lower back, tertials, and median wing coverts are a glossy iridescent purple; the lesser coverts and remainder of the wing are most-

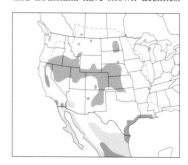

winter adult

1st fall

breeding adult

ly metallic bronzy green. The eyes are red; a narrow but prominent white band of feathering extends around the eyes and under the chin, bordering reddish or pinkish facial skin. The grayish bill has a reddish suffusion, particularly near the tip. The legs and feet are largely reddish brown. NON-BREEDING ADULT: It is less glossy than a breeding adult and chestnut overall. The dark brown head and neck feathers are edged with white, appearing finely streaked; the throat and foreneck are a paler brown with less streaking. The legs are dull brownish or brownish gray and, the bill is gray; both of these features lack the reddish tones of breeding season. JUVENILE: It is duller overall with less sheen than the adult. It shows sooty brown on the head, neck, and underparts, with variable amounts of white splotching on the throat and chin. The legs and bill are dull brownish or brownish gray.
Similar Species The Glossy Ibis looks similar; to separate the 2 species, see sidebar above.
Voice Sound identical to Glossy Ibis. CALL: A sheeplike *huu-huu-huu-huu*. Flocks sometimes emit a subdued chattering or grunting.
Status & Distribution Locally common. BREEDING: Colonially, usually in dense marsh vegetation in low shrubs or trees, often on islands. Locally from OR, ID, AB, MT, ND, and SD south to

CA, TX, and through Mexico; casual breeder in FL. The largest concentrations are found year-round near the Salton Sea, with a peak population estimated in the tens of thousands. MIGRATION: Withdraws from northern part of breeding range; migrates primarily south through the Great Basin and the Colorado River Valley; migrants in the desert southwest usually seen singly or in small groups. TX and LA populations mainly resident. WINTER: Southern CA, southwestern AZ, and coastal TX and LA. VAGRANT: Disperses widely, but casually to the Midwest and the East Coast from NY and MA to FL. Accidental to Clipperton I. and HI.
Population White-faced Ibis populations declined during the 1970s, but, in recent years, the breeding range and populations have expanded in the West, due in part to the widespread increase in favored agricultural and wetland habitats. Populations in Texas and Louisiana have shown declines.

STORKS Family Ciconiidae

Wood Stork (FL, May)

Storks superficially resemble other wading birds (especially ibises), but are larger and bulkier. They lack the breeding plumes characteristic of herons and egrets. The only species seen regularly in the United States is the Wood Stork, which forages in any freshwater habitat, even stormwater retention ponds in shopping centers and drainage ditches beside busy highways. Saline habitats are used more frequently in the northern parts of their U.S. range.

Structure Storks are large to huge birds, with long necks and legs and heavy bills that may be straight or slightly upturned or downcurved. The tails are short and the wings long and rounded.

Plumage Nearly all species have a combination of white and black feathering. Many have featherless faces or heads to aid in foraging in deeper water or scavenging at carcasses. Soft parts are reddish or orange in most species.

Behavior Most species are colonial, foraging, roosting, and breeding in flocks; the Jabiru and a few other species nest solitarily or in small groups. Tactile foragers, storks stand or walk slowly in marshes or lakes with their bills open; the mandibles close instantly upon contact with prey. Storks often stir the water with a foot, presumably to flush prey. They feed on a wide variety of aquatic animals, primarily fish; a couple Old World species also scavenge carrion. The "hunched" foraging posture is distinctive. Storks nest in a variety of sites (including trees and shrubs) and use various substrates. The European White Stork is renowned for nesting on chimneys and other artificial structures. Unlike wading birds, but similar to cranes, storks fly with the head and neck fully extended. They soar to great heights on thermals, allowing them to efficiently travel great distances from nesting colonies.

Distribution Found on all continents except Antarctica, storks number 19 species in 6 genera. They are most widespread in the Old World, especially Africa and Asia. Only the Wood Stork and Jabiru occur in North America.

Taxonomy Stork taxonomy is the subject of much debate. Although superficially very similar to other wading birds, storks are thought to be closely related to New World vultures (Cathartidae). Storks are separated into 3 subfamilies: the Mycteriini (Wood Storks and openbills; 6 sp.); Ciconini ("typical" storks; 7 sp.); and Leptoptilini ("giant" storks; 6 sp.).

Conservation BirdLife International lists 3 species as endangered and 2 as vulnerable, with 2 others as near threatened. Most species are declining due to wetland loss and degredation, pesticide contamination, colony disturbance, and direct persecution. The Wood Stork is endangered because it relies on particular hydrologic conditions to breed successfully, but it remains locally common. —*Bill Pranty*

Genus *Jabiru*

JABIRU *Jabiru mycteria*

juvenile

This huge stork—the largest flying bird in the Americas—is an uncommon resident of tropical freshwater wetlands, where it feeds on fish, mud eels, and other aquatic vertebrates. Monotypic. L 52" (132 cm) WS 90" (229 cm)

Identification Unmistakable, with a massive, upturned bill. ADULT: Sexes similar. Plumage entirely white, including wings and tail. Unfeathered head and neck black, with conspicuous red band at base of neck. Black eyes, bill, legs, and feet. JUVENILE: Downy feathers on head and neck shed shortly after fledging. Upperparts pale gray, edged grayish brown. Inner webs of primaries pale brown. IMMATURE: Scattered brownish feathers on upperparts; red

patch on lower neck paler.

Similar Species The Wood Stork is smaller, with a slightly downcurved bill, entirely black neck, and black flight feathers on the upper and underwings.

Voice Generally silent; rattles bill when disturbed, primarily at nest.

Status & Distribution Uncommon. Native from southeastern Mexico to Bolivia, Argentina, and Uruguay. BREEDING: Usually singly but sometimes loosely colonially; nest usually in crown

breeding adult

of tall palm or in mangroves. DISPERSAL: Nonmigratory, but prone to summer-fall postbreeding dispersal. VAGRANT: Casual stray to northern Mexico (Veracruz) and TX (±8 reports); accidental to OK.

Population Considered near threatened from small population sizes, hunting, and habitat destruction in Central America, the species is more numerous in South America.

Genus Mycteria

WOOD STORK *Mycteria americana (E)*

The Wood Stork is the largest wading bird regularly encountered in N.A. Flocks forage in fresh water with the bill held open, ready to close on contact with prey, primarily fish. Monotypic. L 40" (102 cm) WS 61" (155 cm)

Identification Distinctive, large white wading bird. NONBREEDING ADULT: Sexes similar. It has black flight feathers and a tail with green or purple iridescence. The head and upper neck are

juvenile

adult

featherless, "scaly," and dark gray. The dark bill is wide at the base and slightly decurved. The legs are dark; the feet are pale pinkish. BREEDING ADULT: The feet turn pink. Develops plumelike undertail coverts. IMMATURE: Adult plumage attained in fourth year. The neck and most of the head are covered with grayish feathering, which is lost by the second year. Head and upper neck become "scaly." Straw-colored bill becomes blackish. FLIGHT: Black flight feathers contrast strikingly with white underparts and wing linings; black tail partially obscured by legs.

Similar Species In flight, the Wood Stork is distinguished from the American White Pelican by legs protruding beyond tail, color and shape of head and neck, and irregular flock formation.

Voice Silent except at nests.

Status & Distribution Locally common. BREEDING: Colonially, typically in tall trees. Locally from coastal SC and GA throughout the FL Peninsula. Also in the American tropics and West Indies. DISPERSAL: Nonmigratory, but prone

adult

to postbreeding dispersal north and west. VAGRANT: Regular to the Salton Sea, where declining; casual or accidental to the CA coast, AZ, NM, BC, ID, ON, and Atlantic coast north to ME, and NB; also Grand Bahaman and Jamaica.

Population Although listed as endangered because of a sensitivity to local water levels when nesting, the species' population in the U.S. is stable at about 5,000 pairs. Colonies extirpated from Texas, Louisiana, and Alabama.

NEW WORLD VULTURES Family Cathartidae

Black Vulture (FL, Feb.)

Ew World vultures share their naked heads and the practice of feeding on carrion with Old World vultures; however, they are presently believed to be more closely related to storks. Usually found in warm climates, they have a unique habit of urinating down their legs, letting the evaporative process cool their bodies in the process. Banding and tagging studies must therefore use wing-tags instead of the standard metal or plastic leg band,

which would interfere with that cooling process, and in some cases harm the bird.

Behavior Usually solitary nesters, New World vultures are otherwise gregarious in roosting, searching for food, and gang-feeding at carcasses. A single bird spiraling down out of the sky toward food will attract the attention of other birds from a great distance. At the roost site in the morning, they often will perch spread-winged in the sun before leaving to forage.

Plumage All species are primarily black on the wings, body, and tail, with some pattern of white or silver on the underwings. All share the naked head, in order to feed on carcasses without fouling head feathers. Immatures usually have dark skin on the head, with the adult's skin lightening or becoming more colorful.

Distribution Primarily warm-weather species, New World vultures are colonizing more northerly areas, perhaps as a consequence of global warming, or perhaps due to increased availability of winter roadkills.

Taxonomy There are 7 species in the family, 3 of which occur in the continental United States.

Conservation Farmers occasionally persecute the Black Vulture for aggressive behavior toward newborn farm animals. The California Condor is on the U.S. Endangered Species List. —*Clay Taylor*

Genus *Coragyps*

BLACK VULTURE *Coragyps atratus*

The gregarious Black Vulture roosts, feeds, and soars in groups, often mixed with Turkey Vultures. A carrion feeder that will bully a Turkey Vulture away from a carcass, it occasionally kills smaller live prey. Polytypic (3 ssp.; nominate in N.A.). L 25" (64 cm) WS 57" (145cm)

Identification ADULT: Glossy black feathers can show iridescence in the right light. Whitish inner primaries often hard to see on the folded wing. Whitish legs contrast with dark gray head color.

Skin of head wrinkled; bill dark at base and tipped ivory or yellowish. JUVENILE: Black body and wing feathers usually duller, less iridescent. Skin of head smooth, darker black than an adult. FLIGHT: Conspicuous white or silvery patches at base of primaries that contrast with black wings, body, and tail. Whitish legs extend almost to tip of relatively short tail. Soars and glides with wings held in a slight dihedral. If seen at a distance, the quick, shallow, choppy wingbeats interspersed with glides are usually enough for an identification.

Similar Species The Turkey Vulture shows silvery inner secondaries and a pronounced dihedral while in flight, along with a deeper, more fluid wingbeat.

Voice Hisses when threatened.

Status & Distribution Abundant in the Southeast, expanding up the East Coast into southern New England. Less common in southern Great Plains, local in southern AZ. BREEDING: Nests in a sheltered area on the ground, including abandoned buildings. MIGRATION: Sedentary, northern breeders may migrate with Turkey Vultures to warmer winter territory. VAGRANT: Casual to CA, northern New England, and southern Canada.

Population The species adapts well to human presence, feeding on roadkills and at garbage dumps.

adults

Genus *Cathartes*

TURKEY VULTURE *Cathartes aura*

The most widespread vulture in North America, the Turkey Vulture is locally called "buzzard" in many areas. A Turkey Vulture standing on the ground can, at a distance, resemble a Wild Turkey. It is unique among our vultures in that it finds carrion by smell as well as by sight. When threatened, it defends itself by vomiting powerful stomach acids. Polytypic (4 ssp.). L 27" (69 cm) WS 69" (175 cm)

Identification Overall, it is black with brownish tones, especially on the feather edges. Legs are dark to pinkish in color, the head unfeathered.

ADULT: The red skin color of the head contrasts with the ivory bill and dark feather ruff on the neck. JUVENILE: The skin of the head is dark, the bill dark with a pale base. FLIGHT: A large dark bird that flies with its wings held in a noticeable dihedral. Usually rocks side-to-side, especially in strong winds. Underneath, the silvery secondaries and primaries contrast with the black wing coverts, giving a two-toned look to the wing. The tail is relatively long.

Geographic Variation Three subspecies are found in North America (*aura, meridionalis, septentrionalis*). Only a few minor differences in size and overall tone separate them.

Similar Species The Black Vulture has a quicker, shallow flap, shorter tail, and obvious white patches at the base of the primaries on its shorter, broader wings. The Zone-tailed Hawk and Golden Eagle will mimic the wing dihedral when hunting, and dark-morph Swainson's Hawks and Rough-legged Hawks also can fly in a dihedral, but at closer range all have feathered heads and different wing shapes. Zone-tailed also shows banded tail and yellow cere and legs.

Voice Hisses when threatened.

Status & Distribution Year-round in southern U.S., migrates into northern U.S. and Canada. BREEDING: Nests on the ground, using a shallow cave, hollow log, or thick vegetation. MIGRATION: Northern populations migratory, some heading to C.A. WINTER: Increasing numbers in snowbound states. VAGRANT: To AK, YK, NT, and NF.

Population Stable.

juvenile   adult

adults

Genus *Gymnogyps*

CALIFORNIA CONDOR *Gymnogyps californianus (E)*

The largest raptor in North America, the California Condor is unmistakable when seen flying with any other bird. It will soar for hours on thermals in search of carrion, rarely flapping, and can cover vast amounts of territory. The wingbeat is slow and deep, the wingtips appearing almost to touch at the bottom of the stroke. Monotypic. L 47" (119 cm) WS 108" (274 cm)

Identification ADULT: The body is black; the head shows bare red-orange to yellow skin. Large areas of white are visible on the underwings. Legs are whitish. JUVENILE: Body and legs are similar to adult, but the head is dark. White on the underwings is mottled, less extensive. FLIGHT: Wings held flat or with the tips slightly higher, with large splayed primaries ("fingers") evident. The dark tail is relatively short. Seen from above, the wings have a thin white diagonal line at the greater coverts.

Similar Species The Turkey Vulture is much smaller, with no white on underwings, and flies with a more pronounced dihedral. The smaller Golden Eagle has a feathered head and longer tail; the juvenile has restricted white patches at base of primaries. A juvenile Bald Eagle always flies with flat wings and shows irregular white on underwings, but is smaller and has a feathered head.

Voice Hisses and croaks.

Status & Distribution California Condor fossil evidence has been found through much of western North America and even southern Canada. By the early 1900s the species was restricted to a relatively small area in southern California. Many condors died by feeding on poisoned carcasses set out by farmers to control coyotes. Learning that a hunter's gunfire signaled a carcass, a bird flying directly toward the sound would find itself being used for target practice. The U.S. listed the species as endangered in 1967. As the population decreased, the remaining wild birds were live-trapped (the last on April 19, 1987) and placed into a captive breeding program. Released birds are gaining a toehold in ranges in both CA and the Grand Canyon area in AZ and UT, with a few wild-produced young thus far. YEAR-ROUND: Nonmigratory. BREEDING: Solitary nesters, usually on a cliff face in a shallow cave; easily disturbed by man. Fledged chicks are looked after for up to 8 months.

Population As of 2005, there were more than 100 birds in the captive breeding program and almost 100 released birds.

juvenile

adult

adult

adult

FLAMINGOS Family Phoenicopteridae

Extremely long necks, a unique bill shape, and pink plumage make flamingos among the most recognizable birds in the world. Nonetheless, flamingos are rare in the United States, occurring regularly at only one site. They are common in captivity, however, which casts doubt on many extralimital reports, and even induces identification issues—not all escapees are species native to North America.

Structure Proportionately, flamingos are the longest necked and longest legged birds in the world. The neck is so long that it must be draped over one side of the body when the bird is at rest. The bill bends down in the middle, giving the bird a distinctive "broken nose." Webbed feet provide stability on mudflats and allow the flamingos to swim in water too deep for wading.

Plumage All species are unmistakably pink or red with black flight feathers. The color of the feathers is obtained from carotenoid pigments in the food supply; it takes

Greater Flamingo (Bahamas, Mar.)

3 or more years to reach full adult plumage. Immatures are gray or brown.

Behavior Highly gregarious, flamingos nest, forage, and roost in colonies apart from other birds. Breeding takes place on mud- or marlflats near water; flamingos build unique volcano-shaped nests of mud at the top of which they lay a single egg. They use their curiously shaped bill to strain algae, diatoms, and aquatic invertebrates; when foraging, the head faces directly downward so that the distal half of the bill is parallel with the water. They usually prefer to forage in hypersaline estuaries and lakes; they feed by swinging their bill from side to side as they walk, and may even dabble like ducks in deep water. Their flight is swift and direct, with quick wing-beats and with the neck fully extended. Flocks fly in lines or in V-formation.

Distribution Flamingos are found on all continents except Antarctica and Australia. In North America, only the Greater Flamingo occurs naturally (in extreme southern Florida, but elsewhere along the Gulf and south Atlantic coasts, mostly after tropical storms); however, escapes of other species have been regularly observed.

Taxonomy Confused. Flamingos are alternately considered as a suborder of wading birds, waterfowl, or shorebirds, or as a separate order, Phoenicopteriformes. There are 5 subspecies worldwide in 1 to 3 genera; many taxonomists consider the Caribbean and Eurasian subspecies of Greater Flamingo to be separate species.

Conservation Flamingos have suffered from hunting and disturbance at nesting colonies, but they were largely spared the ravages of the late 18th–early 19th century millinery trade because their feathers fade once plucked from their bodies. Populations are recovering now that colonies are protected, but they remain at risk from wetland loss, pollution, disturbance, and other factors. —*Bill Pranty*

Genus *Phoenicopterus*

GREATER FLAMINGO *Phoenicopterus ruber*

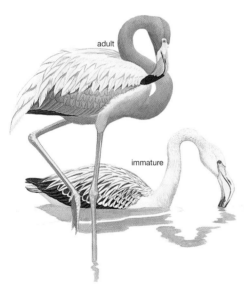

adult

immature

This well-known species is common in exhibits, but it has an extremely limited native range in the United States. In Florida Bay—an area within Everglades National Park—one small, mostly wintering flock offers the thrill of seeing flamingos in their natural habitat. At least some of these birds originate from Mexico—one fledgling color-banded in a colony at the Yucatan Peninsula was discovered recently at Florida Bay. Polytypic (2 ssp.; nominate in N.A.). L 46" (117 cm) WS 60" (152 cm)

Identification Unmistakable (except for escaped flamingos of other species).

ADULT: The sexes look similar. Plumage entirely pink (darker below); black flight feathers often not visible at rest. Pink orbital ring and yellow eyes. Tricolored bill—gray base, pink mid-section, black tip. Pink legs and feet. **JUVENILE:** Grayish white overall with blackish streaking on wing coverts. Eyes dark; mid-section of bill gray; gray or grayish pink legs and feet. Transition to adult plumage occurs gradually over 3 years, intermediate plumages not well known. **FLIGHT:** All ages show black flight feathers on both upper and lower wings.

Similar Species The Roseate Spoonbill shares the same coastal habitats and pink plumage, but its body shape and proportions and foraging behavior differ considerably. Escaped flamingos of other species are rare but present identification problems—be particularly circumspect with extralimital reports. The subspecies Eurasian Greater Flamingo *(roseus)* is mostly whitish with reddish flight feathers, and the base of its bill is pink. The Chilean Flamingo *(P. chilensis)* has very pale pink plumage except it is darker on the neck and has reddish flight feathers; its bill lacks any pink and its legs are gray with pink ankle joints. The Lesser Flamingo *(P. minor)* is smaller and has a shorter, thicker neck; the basal half of its bill is maroon, the distal half is red with a black tip.

Voice Low guttural sounds given when feeding. **FLIGHT CALL:** A goose-like honking.

Status & Distribution Rare in the U.S.; restricted to southern FL. Locally common in Mexico, Cuba, and the Bahamas. **BREEDING:** Builds a volcano-shaped mound of mud in shallow coastal estuaries. No certain U.S. nesting records. **DISPERSAL:** Prone to postbreeding and nonbreeding dispersal from colonies in Yucatan Peninsula, Cuba, and Great Inagua, Bahamas. **VAGRANT:** Individual flamingos may be carried north to Gulf or southern Atlantic coastal states by tropical storms, but many extralimital reports may refer to escaped captives. Reported north to KS, MI, ON, QC, NB, and NS. Flamingos in CA, NV, and WA presumably refer to escapes (a variety of species).

Population The species was formerly a locally abundant postbreeding visitor to Florida Bay from Mexican or Greater Antillean breeding grounds; only a small flock remains. Some populations now are increasing with protection. The species numbers some 80,000 in the West Indies; about 40 nonbreeders are semi-resident at Florida Bay.

HAWKS, KITES, EAGLES AND ALLIES Family Accipitridae

Bald Eagle, adult (left) and subadult (AK, Mar.)

Most non-birdwatchers can identify a large, hook-billed, fierce-looking bird as a "hawk" or an "eagle," even if they do not know much more than that. The North American members of family Accipitridae include a wide range of body sizes, structures, flight styles, prey selection, and habitat preference.

Structure Common features of this group are a hooked beak, strong feet with curved talons for grasping and in some cases killing, and sharp eyesight for locating prey at a distance. The buteos have long, wide, rounded wings for soaring, as do the eagles and Osprey. The kites and harrier have slimmer wings with pointed or rounded wing tips and long tails to help with hovering or maneuvering. Short, wide wings and long tails give the accipiters the ability to make quick turns in close quarters. Most juveniles have shorter wing feathers and longer tails than adults. Females are usually larger than males, and among species that inhabit a wide range of latitudes, northern breeders are usually larger than southern birds.

Behavior Not surprisingly, birds with different body and wing types employ different hunting strategies and prey selection. The soaring buteos and eagles spy prey from afar and make long glides or dives from above on small mammals, reptiles, and ground birds. The 3 pointed-wing kites actively flap and all hover—except Mississippi Kites—in search of small prey on the ground, mostly mammals, reptiles, and insects; the 2 other kites are snail-eating spe-

cialists that course low over their habitats in search of their slow-moving meals. The accipiters are bird-catchers, speeding through the trees and brush to capture their prey on the wing. All species except the harrier build a stick nest, usually in a tree, but western species may use a rock ledge. Harriers use grasses and sedges in their ground nest, which is usually concealed in longer grasses or reeds. Most breeders are site-faithful, and the larger birds will reuse a nest site for many years, adding to the nest structure. Most species are migratory, with the northern nesters following well-known migratory paths, passing regular hawk-watch sites to the delight of birders. The southwestern species are more sedentary, but may wander outside of the breeding season. Mississippi and Swallow-tailed Kites are becoming regular wanderers in late spring up to the northeastern states, and it is theorized that global warming may be contributing to possible range expansions.

Plumage Immatures are distinct from adults, with most species acquiring adult plumage in 1 year; the eagles take 4 years. Body feathers are replaced annually, as are flight feathers on the smaller hawks. The eagles and many buteos typically do not replace all their flight feathers in 1 year, creating visible patterns of old and new feathers. All show significant feather wear by spring, bleaching out colors on the upperparts.

Distribution The species in this group inhabit virtually every habitat in North America, from tundra to desert, mountain forests to coastal marshes. A species' relative abundance is usually tied to its habitat and prey preference. All are regular breeders in North America, though not necessarily abundant, except 2 of the sea-eagles, Crane Hawk, and Roadside Hawk, which are casual visitors.

Taxonomy The birds in this group comprise 14 genera. Osprey is the sole inhabitant of subfamily Pandioninae; Hook-billed Kite is the only North American example of the genus *Chondrohierax*, as are the Swallow-tailed Kite of *Elanoides*, Crane Hawk of *Geranospiza*, Harris's Hawk of *Parabuteo*, and Golden Eagle of *Aquila*. The genus *Buteo* is best represented, with 10 species.

Conservation Worldwide, 34 species are listed as threatened, including Old World vultures, 25 as near threatened. The fish-eating birds have suffered population declines in the past due to pesticide-laden food sources, with Bald Eagle and Osprey attaining federal protection. After banning most of the offending substances for use in North America, recent increases in breeding populations have allowed regulations to be relaxed, and Bald Eagles have made an impressive comeback as breeders in eastern states. Species that winter in Central America and South America, where some of these compounds are still in use, are still considered at risk, but to a lesser degree than previously. Traditionally, raptors have suffered most from indiscriminate shooting, although in recent years, statistics on banded raptors found dead have seen a drop in the percentage killed by gunshot, especially in the eastern states. —*Clay Taylor*

Genus *Pandion*

OSPREY *Pandion haliaetus*

Known to many as the "Fish Hawk," the Osprey is one of the easier raptors for the beginning birder to identify, with a unique combination of size, shape, pattern, and even voice. Whether on the breeding grounds, in migration, or wintering along southern coastlines, it is hard to miss seeing the distinctive shape or hear the whistled call coming from above. They are almost exclusively fish-eaters, capturing them by plunging into the water, either from a long glide or after hovering above the water. Their feet feature hooked talons on large toes with rough areas that allow a better grip on a slippery fish. Their wing area is very large for their body size, giving them great lifting power in order to haul their prey out of the water. Ospreys are unique in that they will migrate while holding a fish in their talons, referred to by watchers as an OPAL—"osprey packing a lunch." Polytypic (4 ssp.; *carolinensis* in N.A.). L 22–25" (56–64 cm) WS 58–72" (147–183 cm)

Identification Usually seen in the immediate vicinity of water, the Osprey is a large raptor that is dark above and white below. The head has a white crown and forehead, offset by a dark eye line that connects to the dark nape. The bill is dark and strongly hooked. The throat, neck, and underparts are white. The back and upperwings are dark brown, appearing black at a distance. The tail is barred. Mostly-dark (melanistic) Ospreys have been recorded, but are rare. ADULT: Upperparts are uniformly dark, the eyes are yellow. Most have some streaking on the upper breast, with females usually showing heavier markings, forming a "necklace." This character is variable in extent between individuals. JUVENILE: The back and wing feathers are brown with pale or buffy fringes, giving the bird a "scaly" appearance. These tips can wear off by late winter or spring, making it look more like an adult. The underwing coverts are usually buffy, not white as in adults. Eyes are orange to red in color. FLIGHT: Ospreys fly with their wings in a characteristic "W" shape, the wings held forward and bent at the wrist. Seen from below, light underwing secondary coverts contrast with a dark carpal "wrist" patch. The primaries are lighter than the secondaries, with immatures showing noticeably darker secondaries than adults. The combination of all-white body, black-and-white underwings, and the "W" shape are unique. A bird approaching head-on will show the white head and chest, with the wings dark above and light below. On migration, a gliding Osprey will droop its wing tips.

Similar Species The adult Bald Eagle has all-white head and all-dark underparts; immature Bald Eagles can show a dark-light pattern on the head and variable mottling on the belly and underwings. Their larger size, dark body, and straight-wing silhouette set the eagles apart from the Osprey. The Great Black-backed Gull has dark uppersides and white undersides, but lacks the dark carpal patch and has an all-white tail and head plus straight yellow beak.

Voice Distinctive whistles that are easy to mimic, categorized into 5 types: Guard, Alarm, Excited, Screaming, and Solicitation.

Status & Distribution Ospreys occur wherever there are fish populations throughout North America. They became the poster child for species loss due to pesticide use in the 1950s and '60s, as Osprey populations plummeted, especially along the Atlantic Coast, receiving federal protection. The banning of DDT and related substances in the U.S., along with conservation programs including nest-platform construction, have resulted in spectacular comebacks in Opsrey populations. YEAR-ROUND: Southern U.S. birds tend to be nonmigratory. BREEDING: A large stick nest is built, usually in a dead treetop, occasionally on the ground or on a fallen tree, and increasingly on man-made structures like channel markers, telephone poles, and the newest of man's structures, cellphone towers. MIGRATION: Postbreeding dispersal occurs in late summer, and migrants are common through Oct. at most hawkwatch sites. Breeders north of the winter freeze line all migrate to open water, many to the Caribbean and C.A. Juveniles occasionally winter along open rivers during northern winters, but survivorship is low.

Population North American populations have dramatically increased since 1980 and continue to grow.

adults

juvenile

adult

SEA-EAGLES Genus *Haliaeetus*

These birds are very large raptors with a preference for fish; there are 8 species worldwide, 1 breeding in North America, and 2 casual visitors. Large, wide wings allow them to soar effortlessly as they search for prey which can also include waterfowl and carrion. They are skilled at kleptoparasitism, stealing prey from Ospreys, hawks, and falcons.

STELLER'S SEA-EAGLE *Haliaeetus pelagicus*

An eagle of eastern Asia, the Steller's is a vagrant to the Aleutian Islands and Alaskan mainland. Sexes are similar; females are larger than males. Monotypic. L 33–41" (84–104 cm) WS 87–96" (221–244 cm)
Identification A huge eagle with a very long, wedge-shaped tail, wide wings, and a massive bill. ADULT: Striking white upper and lower wing coverts, tail coverts, tail, and leg feathering. Head is dark with grayish streaks; bill is bright yellow. Neck, body and flight feathers are dark brown. IMMATURE: Bill yellow with dusky tinges, head brown with pale streaking on neck

and breast. Underwing coverts brown streaked with white, white axillaries, flight feathers dark with light bases to primaries. Leg feathers and undertail dark, wedge-shaped white tail flecked with dark. FLIGHT: Soars with wings in a strong dihedral, secondaries often wider than those of other eagles.
Similar Species Adults are unique, immatures are like Bald Eagle but with longer, wedge-shaped tails and huge yellow bill.
Status & Distribution VAGRANT: Most records are from the Aleutian and Pribilof Is. An adult has been seen with a Bald Eagle south of Juneau, AK, and a probable Bald X Steller's hybrid was

photographed in BC during the winter of 2004–2005.

adult

juvenile

BALD EAGLE *Haliaeetus leucocephalus*

2nd year

juvenile

3rd year

juvenile

adults

The official symbol of the United States is most non-birder's "default" image of an eagle. While primarily fish-eaters, Bald Eagles will also take waterfowl and occasionally mammals, but most often prefer to steal kills from other raptors, as well as feed on carrion. Monotypic. L 31–37" (79–94 cm) WS 70–90" (178–229 cm)
Identification A large, dark raptor with bulky body, large head and neck. Sexes are alike, females larger than males. Adults have longer wings than immatures. Flight feathers take 2 to 3 years to replace. Head and neck project to one-half the length of the tail. ADULT: The pure white head and tail contrast with the dark brown body, wings, and legs. The bill and eyes are yellow. IMMATURE: There are 4 distinct stages, corresponding to each year of life. JUVENILE: Uniformly dark brown, with white on underwing coverts and axillaries; trailing edge of the secondaries is even. Beak and eye are dark. SECOND-YEAR: The eye turns gray-brown or whitish; the head gets a whitish superciliary line. The back and belly become speckled with varying amounts of white. Trailing edge of wings is irregular due to new (shorter) and retained older (longer) secondaries. THIRD-YEAR: The cheeks and head become whiter, with a contrasting dark eye stripe; bill becomes yellow; eye color turns yellow. Back and belly still with white mottling, under-

wing coverts not as white as before. Secondary feathers are even in length, although with an occasional retained juvenile feather. FOURTH-YEAR: Body and wing coverts mostly dark, but with white spots throughout. Head white with dark eye line, bill yellow. The tail is usually white, but often has a black terminal band. FLIGHT: Soars on flat wings, wingbeats are heavy, slow and powerful. Upstroke of the wingbeat ends above the body.

Similar Species Turkey Vulture glides in a dihedral, rocks side-to-side when turning, has 2-tone underwings when in flight. Golden Eagle at all ages has dark axillaries, dark wing linings, head and neck project less than half the tail length. Immature Golden has white at the base of the primaries, white base of tail.

Voice It has a remarkably weak call, rapidly repeated in a high, thin, hollow tone.

Status & Distribution Occurs throughout most of North America, always near water. Southern birds are nonmigratory. BREEDING: Long-lived, they build impressive stick nests in the crotch of a tall tree, adding to the structure every year. MIGRATION: They follow coastlines, rivers, and mountain ridges in fall. DISPERSAL: Southern juveniles wander to the Great Lakes in early summer. WINTER: Northern birds keep to the coastlines or south of the freeze line to find open water. Hydroelectric dams are a favorite location.

Population The species formerly was common throughout the continent; pesticides in the food chain dramatically reduced numbers in the 1950s and '60s. Subsequent conservation efforts have been exemplary, with nesting reported in most states.

WHITE-TAILED EAGLE *Haliaeetus albicilia*

This large fish-eating eagle from Eurasia most closely resembles the Bald Eagle. Females are larger than males; immatures take 4 to 5 years to attain adult plumage. Monotypic. L 26–35" (66–89 cm) WS 72–94" (183–239 cm)

Identification Sitting bird has wing tips that reach the tip of the tail. ADULT: Dark brown body and wings, white tail slightly wedge-shaped, head color creamy brown, blending into darker brown upper breast. Bill yellow. Undertail coverts are dark brown. IMMATURE: Generally follows the age patterns of Bald Eagle, but with less white on underwings and axillaries; tail longer and less wedge-shaped with variably dark feathers with white centers or white mottling. Wings are shorter and

wider than those of adults. FLIGHT: Shows 7 emarginated (notched) primaries or "fingers" in flight. Caution—raptors can occasionally have "extra" primaries, so this character should be used in conjunction with other field marks.

Similar Species Bald Eagle in flight has 6 emarginated primaries. Adult has white head, tail, and undertail coverts, dark chest. Immatures have white axillaries (wingpit), more white on underwing coverts, dark band on tip of tail.

Status & Distribution VAGRANT: Widespread across Eurasia, most N.A. records are from AK. It has also been recorded on the East Coast of the U.S., and there have been nesting records from the Aleutian Is.

juvenile

adult

EAGLES *Genus Aquila*

Worldwide, there are 10 species in this genus, only 1 of which occurs in North America: the Golden Eagle. Large raptors with wide wings, all are fierce hunters of mammals and birds, and many are prized for falconry. The human descriptive term "aquiline nose" refers to the hooked beak of *Aquila* eagles.

GOLDEN EAGLE *Aquila chrysaetos*

Large, dark eagles of open areas in the U.S. West and Canada. The Golden is a fierce hunter, preying on small to medium-size mammals but also taking ground birds, reptiles, insects, and even carrion in winter. Females are larger than males. Polytypic (5 ssp., *canadensis* in N.A.). L 30–40" (76–102 cm) WS 80–88" (203–224 cm)

Identification Overall coloration of all ages is a uniform dark brown, with varying amounts of golden feathers on nape and

crown. Legs are feathered down the tarsis to the toes. Bill appears tricolored: dark tip, lighter base, and yellow cere. JUVENILE: Has noticeable white base to tail, cleanly separated from dark terminal band, inner primaries with white patch visible in flight, sometimes even from above. The amount of white in the wing varies by individual, not simply age. Wings are wider and shorter than those of older birds. SUBADULT: Second-, third-and fourth-year plumages are distinc-

adult

tive. Second-year birds will have an irregular trailing edge to the wing as new, shorter feathers mix with the retained juvenal feathers. The new tail feathers have a less clear-cut boundary between the white tip and dark base. The upperwing coverts become tawny, giving a diagonal bar across the wing. Third- and fourth-year birds lose the white base of the tail and the white on the primaries also disappears. ADULT: All-dark plumage with no white in wings or tail. An adult male has 2 or 3 dark gray bands on the brown tail, while adult females have a single gray region in the center of the tail. FLIGHT: Powerful flaps can accelerate it surprisingly fast; it often power dives after prey. Soars with wings flat or in a dihedral, and may sometimes fly with and mimic Turkey Vultures.

Similar Species Immature Bald Eagles will always have white by the body at the base of the wing, a longer head and shorter tail projection in flight, and a larger, bicolored bill. Turkey Vulture has silvery flight feathers underneath, and a naked head.

Status & Distribution Found throughout northern Europe, Asia, and N.A. BREEDING: Builds a large stick nest on a high ledge or cliff, occasionally in a large tree. MIGRATION: Northern nesters move south late (Nov.–Dec.). Southern birds (mostly adults) are sedentary. WINTER: Casual to the Gulf Region.

Population Formerly persecuted by farmers and ranchers. Breeding numbers are thought to be slowly declining in the western U.S. but stable in Canada and Alaska.

juvenile

adult

KITES Genera *Chondohierax, Elanoides, Elanus, Rostrhamus,* and *Ictinia*

Kites" are a loosely-related group of raptors, 5 of which occur in North America. They are all of different genera, and do not share many common physical characteristics. Our kites are found in the warmer regions of North America, and 2 are long-distance migrants, with Swallow-tailed and Mississippi kites wintering south of the border. For field identification purposes, we can break them into 2 groups: pointed-wing kites and round- or paddle-winged kites.

WHITE-TAILED KITE *Elanus leucurus*

A nearly all-white bird often seen hovering above a field or marsh in the Pacific states and Texas, this bird has undergone recent taxonomic revisions

juvenile

adults

adult

(formerly called Black-shouldered Kite). Often seen perched along roadsides on telephone wires or dead snags, when hunting they slowly descend (it can hardly be considered a dive) on small rodents with their wings held up in a deep V. Polytypic (2 ssp.; *majusculus* in N.A.). L 16" (41 cm) WS 42" (107 cm)

Identification ADULT: The white head, tail, and undersides contrast with black upperwing coverts (the "shoulders"), and gray crown, back, and upper flight feathers. Below, the black carpal patch contrasts with gray primaries and white secondaries and coverts. Deep red eyes are framed with dark feathers. JUVENILE: Best told by brownish feathers on the back and crown, rufous wash across the

breast, brown to orange eye. The tail has faint gray subterminal band, flight feathers with white tips. The darker body feathers are molted within a few months, giving the bird a more adult appearance, but still with the retained flight feathers. FLIGHT: Fast, shallow wingbeats interspersed with glides, pausing to hover tail-down, wings held high when hunting. Glides with a slight dihedral.

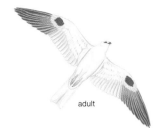
adult

Similar Species Mississippi Kites are darker on the tail and body, immatures are heavily streaked. An adult male Northern Harrier has a white rump above a darker tail, no carpal patches on underwing, and a low, swooping flight.
Status & Distribution YEAR-ROUND: Resident in coastal CA to the Sierra Nevada, grasslands of southeastern AZ and into TX, uncommon in FL, rarely in southern NM. BREEDING: Builds a small nest in a solitary tree or brushline. Feeds primarily on small rodents. VAGRANT: Casual north to BC and MN, east to the Carolinas.

MISSISSIPPI KITE *Ictinia mississippiensis*

This small, pointed-winged kite looks more like a falcon than any other of our kites. A buoyant flier, it soars on flat wings, often high up in the air on thermals, catching and eating insects on the wing. Monotypic. L 14.5" (37 cm) WS 35" (89 cm)
Identification ADULT MALE: Dark gray overall, lighter head with red eyes, dark primaries and tail. Seen from above, light secondaries form a bar across the wings. ADULT FEMALE: Like male, but darker head, whitish barring on undertail coverts. JUVENILE: Dark brown eyes in a gray-brown head, with wide, creamy superciliary line and gray cheeks. Back and wings are dark brown with buffy edges, scapulars have white spots. Underparts are heavily streaked, and the dark tail has multiple thin white bands. SUBADULT: Body plumage similar to adult's, but with a blend of juvenal and adult feathers, especially on tail and flight feathers in late summer/first summer. FLIGHT: It does not hover. The pointed wings are notable in that the outer primary is much shorter than the next one. Tail is square-tipped, usually flared in flight. Underwing coverts are gray in adults, mottled in juvenile.
Similar Species Most other kites are whiter. Adult Peregrine Falcon is larger, but shows similar silhouette in flight. Facial moustache mark and more powerful flight are diagnostic.
Status & Distribution BREEDING: Central Great Plains states, Gulf Coast, and up the Atlantic coast into the Carolinas. Isolated colonies in NM and AZ. A stick nest built in a tall tree may be part of a loose colony of up to 20 pairs. MIGRATION: Most migrate Aug.–early Sept., stragglers into Oct., often in large groups through coastal TX. Return late Mar.–early Apr. WINTER: well down in S.A. VAGRANT: Casual spring recs. in NJ (May) and southern New England (June). Summer recs. to northern MI, NF.
Population Breeding range is slowly expanding.

1st summer · adult ♀ · adult ♂ · juvenile · adult ♂

HOOK-BILLED KITE *Chondrohierax uncinatus*

A tropical hawk that is a decidedly uncommon resident in the Rio Grande Valley area in Texas, the Hook-billed is usually atop the "mostwanted" list of birders visiting the area for the first time. Most sightings are of birds taking flight in the morning; they rarely venture up in the air later in the day. During raptor migrations, it will occasionally come up to "escort" visiting hawks out of its territory. Polytypic (4 ssp.; *aquilonis* in N.A.). L 16" (41 cm) WS 33" (84 cm)
Identification Featuring a long, slim body with long, square tail, the wing silhouette is unique: Wide, rounded primaries and bulging secondaries taper down to a narrow wingbase, giving a diagnostic paddle-shaped wing. Dark morph is rare in the U.S. ADULT MALE: Dark gray with light barring across the belly, tail with 2 wide bands, white eye color. ADULT FEMALE: Brown

adult ♂ · black-morph adult · black-morph immature · immature · juvenile · adult ♀

with heavy rufous barring on underside, rufous on underwings, 2 tail bands, white eye. JUVENILE: Like adult female, but with thinner barring underneath, no rufous in wings, 3 narrow bands on tail, brownish eyes. FLIGHT: Slow, deep wingbeats for a bird of its size, will occasionally soar on thermals.

adult ♀

Similar Species Gray Hawk is not as strongly barred underneath, has dark eyes. Red-shouldered Hawk shows crescents at the base of the primaries, narrow white tail-bands. Harris's Hawk has similar wing shape, but is all-dark below with white undertail coverts and white tail tip. Roadside Hawk has orange eye, small bill, thinner wing silhouette.

Population The U.S. population is small but seemingly stable, as long as snails are available.

SWALLOW-TAILED KITE *Elanoides forficatus*

It is sheer pleasure to watch one of the most graceful, elegant flyers in the bird world cruise a tree line, soar on a thermal, or swoop in a stiff breeze. It feeds mostly on insects, lizards, snakes, and frogs, usually taken on the wing, bending its head to reach the prey. Polytypic (2 ssp.; *forficatus* in N.A.). L 23" (58 cm) WS 48" (122 cm)

Identification A unique raptor in North America, the head, neck, chest, and underparts are pure white. Seen from above, the long, pointed wings are dark, with the flight feathers, lower back, and

long, forked tail slightly lighter. The wing linings are white, flight feathers are dark. The head appears small for a raptor. ADULT: Has red eyes. JUVENILE: Brownish eyes, the shorter tail is less deeply forked, flight feathers have lighter tips. FLIGHT: Unmistakable.

Similar Species None.

Status & Distribution Very uncommon. BREEDING: Breeds in FL, along the Gulf Coast into eastern TX, up the Atlantic coast to SC. Builds a flimsy stick nest in a treetop, often exposed to view or on a lone tree. MIGRATION: Most pass through the FL Keys, increasing numbers through southern TX hawk-watch sites. WINTER: Radio-tagged individuals from the Orlando, FL area have been satellite-tracked to S.A. and back. VAGRANT: Increasing frequency of records into the upper Midwest and northeastern U.S.

Population Very small (approx. 1,000 pairs in U.S.), but appears stable. Historical range much larger (north to MN, IL, OH).

adults

SNAIL KITE *Rostrhamus sociabilis* (E)

adult ♂

adult ♀

adult ♂

juvenile

Formerly known as the Everglades Kite, this bird is a specialist that feeds on apple snails, using its hooked beak to pry open food. Another of the rounded-wing kites, it flies low over marshes in search of slow-moving quarry. Polytypic (4 ssp.; *plumbeous* in N.A.). L 17" (43 cm) WS 46" (117 cm)

Identification Long wings with rounded tips, wide secondaries, white-tipped dark tail with large white patch at base. ADULT MALE: Dark gray overall, appearing black in poor light, flight feathers darker than back and wing

coverts. ADULT FEMALE: Dark brown above, thin white streaking on underparts, white markings around red eye. JUVENILE: Brown eye, tawny markings on head and upperparts, undersides tawny with dark streaks. FLIGHT: Slow, graceful wingbeats, wings held with tips cupped.

Similar Species Female and juvenile Northern Harriers have white rump,

no white in the tail, and fly with wings in a dihedral.

Status & Distribution YEAR-ROUND: Resident in southern FL up to the Orlando area. BREEDING: Nests in low trees or bushes, often surrounded by water. Will nest colonially. VAGRANT: Records from TX may be Mexican birds.

Population Endangered and intensely managed (approx. 500 pairs in FL).

Stable, but dependent on freshwater marshes for snails.

adult ♀

ACCIPITERS Genus *Accipiter*

Three species of these short-winged, long-tailed raptors occur in North America, 46 worldwide. Primarily bird-catchers, they hunt by ambush, flying rapidly around and even through brush to grab their prey with long legs and slender toes. Females are often visibly larger than males. All start out with yellow eyes as immatures, changing to orange, then red.

NORTHERN GOSHAWK *Accipiter gentilis*

Our largest accipiter, the Northern Goshawk is found in northern forests and in the montane West. Aggressive around the nest, it noisily attacks humans that approach too closely. It preys on birds and mammals, especially chipmunks and the like. Sexes are alike, females larger; adults are distinct from juveniles. Polytypic (8 ssp.; 2 in N.A.). L 21–26" (53–66 cm) WS 40–46" (102–117 cm)

Identification A large, thick-bodied hawk with wide wings. The long tail with graduated-length feathers is wedge-shaped when folded. ADULT: Dark gray above, light gray or white superciliary line, lighter below with fine barring, fluffy white crissum. Red eye. JUVENILE: Brown above with heavy mottling, often with a checkerboard effect. Undersides light, with thick, dark streaks, including crissum. Dark tail bands are wavy, with white borders between bands. FLIGHT: From above, adult has darker flight feathers than coverts, from below looks more pointy-winged than other accipiters. White-appearing superciliary easily visible, giving head a striped appearance.

Juvenile from above has a pale diagonal band across wing coverts, irregular tail bands. From below, heavy streaking on breast and belly. When soaring, the wings taper out to the tip.

Geographic Variation The subspecies *langi*, found only on islands off British Columbia, is heavily barred and darker than widespread *atricapillus*.

Similar Species Adult Cooper's Hawk has no eyebrow, rufous barring on chest. Juvenile Cooper's has larger-appearing head, is more finely streaked underneath, and has longer, rounded tail with white tip. Flying immature Red-shouldered Hawk has buffy crescents at base of primaries.

Voice Around the nest, a loud, accelerating *kek-kek-kek-kek*.

Status & Distribution Widespread but never common in mature northern forests and mountains. Periodically "invades" to the South. BREEDING: Stick nest is placed high, usually in main fork of a deciduous tree. MIGRATION: A late-season migrant, usually along inland flight paths. Migration numbers are cyclical, dependent on food populations. WINTER: Usually only juveniles winter in the Northeast. Fall passage adults usually work their way back north before winter's end. Mountain residents head to lower altitudes. VAGRANT: During invasion years, may be found as far south as Gulf Coast.

Population In the eastern U.S., the trend toward reforestation has created more habitat, with migration counts supporting a population increase.

adult

juvenile

adult ♂

juvenile ♀

SHARP-SHINNED HAWK *Accipiter striatus*

Our smallest accipiter, the "Sharpie" is a jay-size hawk that frequents backyard bird feeders in winter, bursting from nearby bushes to snatch a small bird off a branch. Although some homeowners vilify them, Sharpies serve a needed function of keeping wild bird populations healthy and wary. Sexes look alike, females are larger than males, adults differ from immatures. Polytypic (10 ssp.; 3 in N.A.). L 10–14"(25–36 cm) WS 20–28" (51–71 cm)

Identification A small, round-winged, long-tailed hawk of woods, edges, and mixed habitat. The tip of the tail appears square, bands are wide and straight. The head is rounded, with a distinct "notch" in the profile from crown to beak. The eye appears more centered in head. ADULT: Blue-gray crown and nape are same color as the back, creating a "hooded" effect against the buffy cheeks. The eyes are red-orange (females) to deep red (males). Underparts are barred rufous; undertail is white. JUVENILE: Brown back feathers have rufous tips, white spots on wing coverts. Eye color is pale yellow. White undersides are streaked to belly with blurry brown lines. FLIGHT: Quick, choppy wingbeats interspersed with short glides. Almost no "flex" to the wing. When gliding or soaring, wings are held forward with wrists bent, the head barely projecting in front of the wings.

Geographic Variation The subspecies *velox* is common throughout most of North America; *perobscurus,* found on the islands of British Columbia, is darker and more heavily barred; *suttoni* of Mexico, into Arizona and New Mexico, is lighter, with fainter barring.

Similar Species The Cooper's Hawk is noticeably larger, although small males in western populations approach large female Sharpies in length, but have a longer, rounded tail and flatter head. An adult Cooper's has a dark cap, not hooded as in Sharpie.

Voice A high, chattering *kew-kew-kew* is heard around the nest, otherwise it is mostly silent.

Status & Distribution Widespread in northern and western forests. BREEDING: Prefers coniferous and mixed forests, makes a small stick nest usually high and close to the trunk. MIGRATION: The commonest accipiter seen at hawk-watches; adult birds prefer to follow mountain ridges, while many juveniles end up following the coasts. Juveniles migrate first, followed by adults. WINTER: Throughout much of N.A. and into Mexico.

Population Never abundant, but steady.

Juvenile Sharp-shinned versus Juvenile Cooper's

Hawk-watchers in the 1960s and 1970s would get into heated arguments over whether a passing juvenile accipiter was a Sharp-shinned or Cooper's Hawk (henceforth, Sharpie and Cooper's). Since then, watchers and hawk banders have gradually worked out many of these field-identification problems. More recently, the advent of digiscoping has made it much easier for a birder to make a positive identification.

Sharp-shinned Hawk, juvenile (NJ, Oct.)

Physically, Sharpies are grackle-size, noticeably smaller than Cooper's, which are about the length of a crow. This is handy when a bird is seen in a backyard or perched on an object of known size. Sharpies have a rounded head, with a noticeable "notch" in the profile where the forehead meets the bill. A Cooper's has a flatter crown, especially if the hackles are raised, and the profile from crown to bill is smooth and continuous. The eye of a Cooper's appears larger in the head and nearer to the bill. Both can show a pale superciliary line, both have pale yellowish eyes. Back and wing coloration are similar—brown with rufous feather tips that slowly wear down through the winter and spring. The scapulars often show large white spots. The tail is brown with dark, evenly spaced bands. The undersides are white, with Sharpie showing blurry brown streaking down through the belly, while Cooper's has thinner, darker breast streaks that thin out or stop at the belly.

COOPER'S HAWK *Accipiter cooperi*

The "chicken hawk" of colonial America, this medium-sized accipiter is a common sight at home bird feeders across the country, swooping in to nab an unwary dove or jay. Females are larger and bulkier than males, juveniles differ from adults. Monotypic. L 14–20" (36–51 cm) WS 29–37" (74–94cm)

Identification The long tail is rounded at the tip, also the relatively short wings and flat-topped head are good field marks. Eye is close to the beak. Crown merges with forehead and bill in a smooth line. ADULT: Blue-gray upperparts, the crown is darker and contrasts with the lighter nape and buffy cheeks, giving the look of wearing a "beret." Eye color is orange to red. Undersides with rufous barring, undertail is white. JUVENILE: Brown above, with rufous edges and white spots on upperwing coverts. Tail long, with straight bands and wide, white tip that wears down by spring. Head usually buffy, eyes pale yellow. Undersides are white with thin brown streaks, white undertail. FLIGHT: Wings typically held straight out from body, head, and neck projecting forward. This along with tail length make a "flying cross" appearance. Shallow, quick wingbeats alternate with short glides.

Geographic Variation Western populations hunting more open country are smaller, with longer wings, shorter legs than eastern birds. Plumages are alike.

Similar Species Northern Goshawk is usually larger, heavier appearing, and has relatively shorter tail and longer wings. Sharp-shinned Hawk is smaller and has a square tail.

Voice A low *keh-keh-keh* uttered around nest, occasionally mimicked by jays.

Status & Distribution Widespread through U.S. and southern Canada, more commonly seen in suburbs, probably due to reforestation in the East. BREEDING: Nests in a variety of forest types, preying on small- to medium-size birds and small mammals, hunting from perches under the canopy. MIGRATION: Increasing numbers at eastern hawk-watches probably due to better identification skills. WINTER: Juveniles winter farther north than adults; eastern birds move to the southern states, western birds as far south as Mexico.

Population Common and stable in the West, increasing in the East.

Both have a white undertail, although some western Cooper's show thin streaks.

When viewing a perched bird from the front, the tail can be diagnostic—Cooper's has a proportionally longer, rounded tail, created by the feathers decreasing in length from inner to outer. A Sharpie's tail feathers are almost the same length, creating a square tail tip. Seen from behind, a Cooper's tail has a broad white terminal band (usually 10–17 mm wide), while a Sharpie tail only has a thin white edge. By spring, much of the white has worn off a Cooper's tail tips, especially the longest (central) feathers. In flight, they have different characteristics, or "jizz." The shorter wings of a Sharpie allow it to flap more

Cooper's Hawk, juvenile (NJ, Sept.)

quickly in a rapid, choppy motion with almost no flexing. A Cooper's wings are much longer, and thus its wingbeats have a more fluid motion, almost like a wave traveling out the wing. Both fly in bursts of flapping and gliding. When gliding, the Sharpie pushes its wings forward, cocking the wrists. As a result, the head barely protrudes in front of the leading edge of the wing. A Cooper's holds its wings almost straight out from its body, giving it a noticeable head and neck projection. This, along with the longer, rounded tail, gives a Cooper's the appearance of a "flying cross." As in all aspects of bird identification, the more birds you see in the field, the easier it is to name them. ∎

NEAR-BUTEOS Genera Asturina, Buteogallus, and Parabuteo

These raptors are similar in appearance to those in genus *Buteo*, with long, wide, rounded wings. Some authors consider Gray Hawk to be a *Buteo*, but differences in molt timing and other factors lead others to place it in *Asturina*. All are neotropical species that are found in the arid southwestern United States.

GRAY HAWK Asturina nitida

juvenile
juvenile
adult
juvenile
adult

This bird was called the Mexican Goshawk in older literature due to its overall gray coloration, longish tail, and barred undersides. Sexes look alike; females are larger. Juveniles are different from adults. Polytypic (4 ssp.; 1 in N.A., *plagiatus*). L 17" (43 cm) WS 35" (89 cm)

Identification A small raptor with wide, rounded wings like a buteo and long tail like an accipiter; all ages have uppertail coverts forming a distinct white U at the base of the tail. ADULT: Overall gray, with fine white barring on breast and belly. White wing linings have fine gray barring, appearing whitish at a distance. Undertail coverts are white, the tail has 2 distinct white bands. JUVENILE: Has a dark brown body and a distinct head pattern with light super-

cilium and cheek contrasting with dark eye line and malar stripes. Undersides are heavily streaked; the tail has multiple stripes that grow progressively wider toward the tip. The tail is longer than that of the adult. FLIGHT: Short, choppy wingbeats are interspersed with flat glides. From underneath, adult shows black tips to primaries. **Similar Species** Adult Hook-billed Kite is barred gray but has very different wingshape. Juvenile Broad-winged Hawk lacks the face pattern and uppertail U-mark and has more pointed

wings. Juvenile Red-shouldered Hawk has buffy crescent at base of primaries. **Status & Distribution** Resident in the Lower Rio Grande Valley, it breeds in Big Bend N.P. and into southeastern AZ, rarely to southwestern NM. Nests in large trees, usually near water. **Population** Stable, possibly expanding. About 80 pairs breed in the United States. Habitat degradation and illegal shooting are ongoing threats.

COMMON BLACK-HAWK Buteogallus anthracinus

adult
juvenile
adult

This dark raptor is from the Southwest. Juveniles are different from adults; females are slightly larger than males. Polytypic (2 ssp.; nominate in N.A.). L 21" (53 cm) WS 50" (127 cm)

Identification A large, all-dark raptor with long, wide wings and a short tail. ADULT: Body and wings black, cere and legs are orange-yellow. Adult females can show some white below the eye. Tail has a broad white band and narrow white tip. JUVENILE: Dark brown overall, with rufous markings above and heavy dark streaks on buffy breast and underparts. The head is patterned with dark crown, eye line, and malar mark contrasting with buffy supercilium and throat. The tail is white with numerous dark, wavy bands, and

juvenile

is proportionally longer than in an adult. FLIGHT: Wide wings make the tail appear very short in comparison to other dark buteos. Adult has small, whitish crescent at base of primaries; tail band is very evident. Immature has large buffy patch at base of primaries; tail appears lighter with dark terminal band. All soar on flat wings.

Similar Species Zone-tailed Hawk soars with a dihedral and has a slimmer wing shape. With close views, Zone-tailed has a white forehead, gray lores. Dark-morph buteos will show an underwing contrast between flight feathers and coverts, and have longer-appearing tails.

Status & Distribution A tropical hawk of C.A. and S.A., an uncommon breeder in western TX, NM, and AZ, very susceptible to human disturbance around the nest. Always nests near water, usually a year-round stream or river. Usually hunts from a perch. VAGRANT: Casual north to CA, southern UT, southern NV, and into southern TX.

Population Probably stable. About 250 pairs breed in the United States, mostly in Arizona. The species is threatened by habitat destruction and human disturbance.

HARRIS'S HAWK *Parabuteo unicinctus*

Also known as the Bay-winged Hawk in South America, this large, dark raptor of the Southwest is noted for its habit of cooperative hunting in the deserts and scrub areas it inhabits. Working in groups of up to a dozen birds, individuals will take turns flushing prey out of heavy brush into the waiting talons of the others. A call from a perched "lookout" bird will summon others from their concealed locations. Females are larger than males; adults differ from juveniles. Polytypic (3 ssp.; 2 in N.A.). L 21" (53 cm) WS 46" (117 cm)

Identification A long-tailed, long-legged, dark raptor with long, wide wings. It is often seen on a dead snag, telephone pole, or similar open perch. The dark tail has a broad white terminal band and a white base with white undertail coverts. The wing tips reach halfway down the tail. ADULT: Uniformly dark head, body, and wings, with chestnut wing coverts and leg feathers. The facial skin, cere, and legs are yellow. JUVENILE: Dark brown body with lighter streaks on head and neck, whiter streaking on belly than on breast. The tail has fine dark barring, as do the flight feathers. The white at the base of the tail is not

as extensive as in an adult. FLIGHT: Very active hunter, flying with quick, shallow wingbeats, wings held slightly downward, often cupped. Its short, broad wings and long tail allow it to be very maneuverable; it can hover for short periods. From below, adult has chestnut coverts and dark flight feathers; immature shows barred gray secondaries, barred primaries with dark tips and lighter bases. Soars with flat wings. Wing silhouette is broad, often called "paddle shaped."

Geographic Variation The 2 North American subspecies—*harrisi* (TX) and *superior* (AZ)—are virtually identical; they are often not recognized.

Similar Species Dark-morph buteos have 2-tone underwings with silvery-tone flight feathers. Zone-tailed Hawk soars with wings in a dihedral, has dark undertail coverts, dark tail tip. Juvenile Northern Harrier at a distance, when compared to a juvenile Harris' Hawk, has slimmer, longer wings, a white rump (not the base of the tail), and glides with a dihedral.

Status & Distribution Common, permanent resident in southern TX, into southern NM and southern AZ, exceptionally, recent records and nesting in southern CA. Occasionally expands breeding range, probably in response to prey availability. BREEDING: A complex social structure including multiple adults and pairings is still being investigated by researchers. Breeding groups consist of a dominant pair, related helpers that are offspring of that pair, unrelated helpers, and sometimes additional females with an intermediate position of dominance. MIGRATION: Mostly sedentary. WIN-

TER: Often gathers in large groups to roost and hunt. VAGRANT: A popular falconer's bird, any records outside of their normal range should be treated with caution.

Population Apparently stable, but under pressure from habitat (esp. mesquite) destruction, falconry, and electrocution from power lines.

adult

juvenile

adult

BUTEOS Genus *Buteo*

Called "buzzards" in many parts of the world except North America, there are 68 species in this genus—10 in North America; all are regular breeders except Roadside Hawk, which is a casual visitor into South Texas. They soar on wide, rounded wings, hunting small mammals, lizards, snakes, and the occasional unwary bird. They also perch-hunt along treelines or under the canopy. Sexes are similar in appearance, females are slightly larger than males, and juveniles have different plumage than adults. During fall migration, buteos travel in groups, riding thermal updrafts along mountain ridges or coastlines. In late September, nearly 1 million buteos pass over Texas on their way south.

ROADSIDE HAWK *Buteo magnirostris*

adult

A small tropical hawk, the Roadside Hawk is a casual vagrant to the Rio Grande Valley of Texas, with 4 accepted records and multiple sightings during the winter of 2004–2005. Females are slightly larger than males, juveniles are slightly different from adults. Polytypic (at least 14 ssp.; *griseocauda* in N.A.). L 14" (36 cm) WS 30" (75 cm)

Identification A small, long-tailed, long-legged raptor, it frequently perches and hunts from fence posts, telephone poles, or trees alongside fields and roads. Wing tips reach halfway down the long tail, which has a buffy or whitish U along the uppertail coverts. Legs are long and slim. ADULT: Gray to brownish on head, back, and wings; large, pale yellow eyes. The long tail has 3–4 dark bands. Undersides have a brown bib and barred belly. JUVENILE: Browner than adults, with a wide superciliary line and darker eyes. The chest has vertical streaks, the belly horizontal barring. The tail has 4–6 dark bands. FLIGHT: The wings are wide and rounded, with barred flight feathers, rufous on inner primaries. Stiff, rapid wingbeats and the long tail make it look very accipiter-like; glides with wings bowed.

Geographic Variation Populations farther south show more rufous in the wings and grayer plumage.

Similar Species See Broad-winged Hawk and Gray Hawk. Barred belly and dark bib on adult, vertical streaks on breast of juvenile, plus long, evenly banded tail are distinctive.

ZONE-TAILED HAWK *Buteo albonotatus*

This dark raptor of the Southwest mimics a Turkey Vulture both in appearance and flight. Monotypic. L 20" (51 cm) WS 51" (130 cm)

Identification Appears all-dark at a distance, has barred flight feathers, and the tail shows a distinct pattern. When perched, wing tips equal or exceed tail length. ADULT: Uniformly black with a grayish cast; yellow cere and legs. Tail has 1 wide white band and additional thin white bands. JUVENILE: Black overall, dull yellow legs and cere; tail is dark from above, light below with many thin dark bands and a dark tip. FLIGHT: Long, dark wings are 2-tone, with heavily barred flight feathers. Adults show a dark trailing edge to the wing. Wing-beats are deep, but not as floppy as a vulture's. Usually glides and tips side-to-side in a dihedral, but can also glide on flat wings. Head and banded tail project farther than a vulture's.

Similar Species Common Black Hawk in flight has shorter, wider wings and a shorter tail; when perched it has longer legs, a bigger bill, and wing tips do not reach tip of tail. Juvenile dark-morph Red-tailed Hawk has light panels at base of primaries; juvenile White-tailed Hawk usually has a white chest patch and a pale crescent on the upper tail coverts.

Status & Distribution Occurs throughout C.A., into S.A. Northern birds are migratory. BREEDING: Uncommon and local in wooded hills from western TX through AZ, now also in southern CA and has bred in southern TX. MIGRATION: South into Mexico and beyond. WINTER: Rare in the Rio Grande Valley, TX, southern CA, and southern AZ. VAGRANT: Records for NV and UT, east to LA, and to NS.

Population Slowly expanding in California, northern Arizona and New Mexico declining in southern Texas, probably due to habitat changes.

juvenile

Turkey Vulture for comparison

adult ♂

adult

RED-SHOULDERED HAWK *Buteo lineatus*

A common hawk of wet deciduous woodlands, they are the noisiest of the buteos, especially during spring courtship. A perch-hunter of the forest understory, it feeds on frogs, snakes, lizards, and small mammals. Females are larger than males, sexes similar in appearance, juveniles differ from adults. Polytypic. L 15–19" (38–48 cm) WS 37–42" (94–107 cm)

Identification A medium-size buteo with rounded wing tips that do not reach the tip of the tail. ADULT: Brown above with lighter feather edges and some streaking on head. Rufous on the upperwing coverts gives the "red shoulders." The primaries are barred or checkered black and white, the dark tail has 3 white bands. Underparts are rufous with white barring. JUVENILE: Mostly brown above, with less rufous on the shoulders than an adult. Undersides are buffy with variable dark streaks, the brown tail has multiple narrow bands. FLIGHT: All ages show a distinct light crescent at the base of the primaries. Soars on flat wings held forward, glides with wings cupped, giving a "hunched" appearance. Wingbeats are quick and shallow, interspersed with quick glides.

Geographic Variation Eastern *(lineatus)* as above, with adult showing dark streaks on breast. Juvenile tail from below is light with dark bands. Southeastern *(alleni)* and Texas *(texanus)* are very similar to each other, with adults showing no dark streaks on breast; *texanus* is slightly brighter rufous. Juveniles have darker underside of tail,

heavier markings on underparts. South Florida *(extimus)* is the palest subspecies. Adults are pale gray above, pale rufous underneath, with the head appearing light at a distance. Juveniles are less rufous, have thinner streaking underneath. California *(elegans)* is the brightest subspecies, with juveniles appearing more like adults. Adults have unbarred rufous on the breast, wider tail bands. Juveniles have similar upperwings to the adult, with the most rufous on the shoulders of any subspecies, and a white crescent on the primaries. Underparts are barred rufous and buffy. The dark tail shows whitish bands.

Similar Species Broad-winged Hawk adult has rufous on breast, but no barring on primaries, only 1 or 2 tail bands, in flight shows more pointed wings. Juveniles are similar, but Red-shouldered shows 3 bands on the folded secondaries; Broad-winged lacks the pale crescent at the base of the primaries. Juvenile Northern Harrier is rufous underneath, but long tail, thin wings, and flight style are very different. Juvenile Northern Goshawk perched has heavy

streaking underneath and a long tail, but dark-banded tail pattern and shorter wings will help the identification process.

Voice A loud, repeated *KEE-ahh,* often in groups of 8–10 repetitions.

Status & Distribution A widespread breeder throughout East, into southern Canada. Found throughout the South, into eastern and southern TX. CA subspecies is coastal and in the Central Valley, up into OR and southern WA. BREEDING: Nests in deciduous woodlands, usually river bottoms, near lakes or swamps. Coexists in similar habitat with the Barred Owl. MIGRATION: Northern birds migrate to southern states and into Mexico. Southern forms are nonmigratory. VAGRANT: There are records of eastern birds west to CO, and CA birds wander casually to AZ, ID, and NM.

Population Stable, as far as is known.

adult
lineatus

juvenile
lineatus

juvenile
lineatus

juvenile
lineatus

adult
extimus

adult
elegans

juvenile
elegans

juvenile
elegans

BROAD-WINGED HAWK *Buteo platypterus*

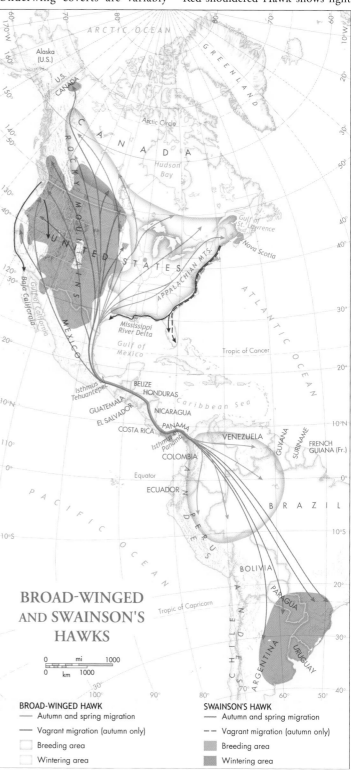

juvenile

adult

This bird made hawk-watching famous. Thousands of birders gather to watch the annual fall migration of Broad-winged Hawks. They start in September in New England, traveling down the Appalachian ridges on their way to their wintering grounds in South America. They occur in light and dark (rare) morphs, females are slightly larger than males, juveniles different from adults. Polytypic (6 ssp.; nominate in N.A.). L 16" (41 cm) WS 34" (86 cm)

Identification The smallest North American buteo. DARK MORPH: Adult has an all-dark body with dark wing coverts and silvery flight feathers, the dark tail has a wide white band. The juvenile is dark with variable light streaking on body and wing coverts. LIGHT-MORPH ADULT: Head, back, and wings are brown, throat is white, wing tips dark, dark tail with 1 wide white band. A second, thinner band may be visible on the fanned tail. Undersides are white with brown or rufous barring across breast, less on the belly. Some individuals may have a solid-colored dark breast, giving the bird a dark bib. JUVENILE: Brown above like adult, but with pale superciliary line on head, dark malar stripe; brown tail has multiple darker bands, widest band at tip. Underparts are white with dark streaking on breast and belly, but amount of streaking is highly variable, sometimes almost absent. FLIGHT: Wing tips are more pointed than those of the other common buteos, and the trailing edge is almost straight. Adult has pale wing linings and flight feathers contrasting with dark primary tips, a wide dark band along the trailing edge of the wing. Juveniles have slightly longer tails, but the same wing sil-

houette with the trailing edges not as dark. Backlit wings show a light rectangle at the base of the primaries. Underwing coverts are variably streaked, as is the belly. Wingbeats are stiff; it soars on flat wings.

Similar Species When flying, a juvenile Red-shouldered Hawk shows light

BROAD-WINGED AND SWAINSON'S HAWKS

0 — mi — 1000
0 — km — 1000

BROAD-WINGED HAWK
— Autumn and spring migration
— Vagrant migration (autumn only)
☐ Breeding area
☐ Wintering area

SWAINSON'S HAWK
— Autumn and spring migration
-- Vagrant migration (autumn only)
▨ Breeding area
▨ Wintering area

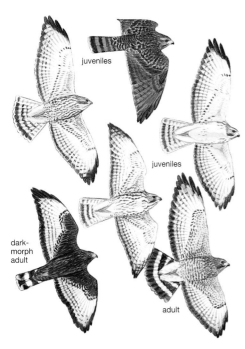

juveniles

juveniles

dark-
morph
adult

adult

crescents at base of primaries and a longer tail. Perched, it has a brown tail with dark bands, 3 bands on folded secondaries. Juvenile Cooper's Hawk can show the same overall markings, but no malar stripe; shorter, barred wings and much longer tail give a different shape.

Voice A thin, whistled *kee-eee,* rarely in migration, easily whistled by Blue Jays.

Status & Distribution Common. BREEDING: Nests in woodlands throughout eastern N.A. to eastern TX and MN, in Canada west to AB and BC. The rare dark morph nests in western Canada. MIGRATION: Famed for migrating in groups (called "kettles"), generally utilizing updrafts along mountain ridges. Reluctant to cross open water. The Great Lakes create good viewing spots in both fall (Lake Erie) and spring (Lake Ontario). During the last 6 days in Sept., typically over 700,000 Broad-wings pass over Corpus Christi, TX. WINTER: Small numbers, usually juveniles, in southern FL and southern TX, rare in CA. VAGRANT: Dark morph birds casually seen in the East, mostly in spring migration.

Population Stable, as far as is known.

SHORT-TAILED HAWK *Buteo brachyurus*

This small buteo of the tropics occurs in 2 color morphs—light and dark. Usually hunts from below the forest canopy, mostly seen in flight. Polytypic (2 ssp.; *fuliginosus* in N.A.). L 15" (39 cm) WS 35" (89 cm)

Identification Perched, the wing tips reach the tail tip. LIGHT-MORPH: Adult dark above, including head and cheeks, giving a "helmeted" appearance. Light below, usually white or creamy-white on throat, body, and undertail coverts. Tail from below has wide, dark terminal band and lighter, thin bands. Juvenile has more patterning on face, brownish secondary coverts, variable streaking on sides of breast, tail from below is light with many thin bands and narrow terminal band. Both show white underwing coverts with darker, barred flight feathers, black tips, and paler base to primaries. DARK-MORPH: Adult uniformly dark brown, flight feathers lighter than coverts, but with dark trailing edge, lighter bases to primaries. Tail is lighter than body with dark terminal band. Juveniles have heavily marked bodies and underwing coverts, tail has fine bands and dark tip. FLIGHT: A highly aerial species, the Short-tailed shows a pointed-wing silhouette, especially when gliding. It typically soars at high altitudes when hunting, and dive or glide down when prey is sighted. When wind conditions allow, it often kites for considerable periods of time. White body and wing coverts stand out from darker flight feathers. White spot on forehead and lores is often visible.

Similar Species Broad-winged Hawk is similar size, but has lighter flight feathers and shorter wings when perched. Juveniles are spotted or streaked underneath. Light-morph Swainson's Hawk is larger, has 2-tone underwing, but flight feathers are uniform in color.

Status & Distribution Widespread throughout C.A. and S.A., uncommon resident in southern FL. Formerly rare, more recently uncommon in southeastern AZ, southern TX. BREEDING: Only recorded in FL, but a recent (failed) attempt with a Swainson's

light-
morph
adult

dark-
morph
adult

light-morph
adult

Hawk in southern TX is interesting. Summer records from southeastern AZ present the possibility of breeding.

Population Stable in Florida.

SWAINSON'S HAWK *Buteo swainsoni*

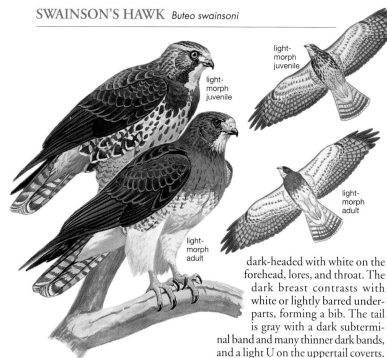

light-morph juvenile

light-morph juvenile

light-morph adult

light-morph adult

dark-morph adult

A large hawk with long, narrow pointed wings, it is found in open grasslands and agricultural areas. Widely distributed across the West and highly variable in plumage. Sexes are similar, females are larger, and juveniles and subadults differ from adults. Feeds mostly on small mammals and insects, primarily grasshoppers and caterpillars, but will also take snakes and occasionally birds. Hovers while hunting, and soars effortlessly on strong winds. Monotypic. L 21" (53 cm) WS 52" (132 cm)

Identification Individuals can grade evenly from light to rufous to dark morphs. When perched, adults have long wings that extend past the wing tips; a juvenile's wings almost reach the tail tip. In late spring, juveniles often have bleached heads that appear white at a distance. Year-old birds are similar to juveniles, but have wide subterminal bands on tail, flight feathers. LIGHT-MORPH ADULT: Dark above and dark-headed with white on the forehead, lores, and throat. The dark breast contrasts with white or lightly barred underparts, forming a bib. The tail is gray with a dark subterminal band and many thinner dark bands, and a light U on the uppertail coverts. Underwings are distinctly 2-tone with white coverts and darker gray flight feathers and dark gray trailing edges. LIGHT-MORPH JUVENILE: Dark back and wings with buffy feather edges, a buffy head with a pale superciliary line, buffy cheek, and dark malar line. The underparts are light-colored with variable streaking, also usually with dark patches on the sides of the breast. Tail is brown with narrow bands, darker tip, and white undertail coverts. INTERMEDIATE (RUFOUS) MORPH: Above, similar to light-morph adult, while the undersides are rufous below, either evenly colored or with a darker chest than the rufous underparts. The throat is white, as are the undertail coverts. Juveniles are similar to light-morph except for buffy underparts with heavier streaks. DARK MORPH: Adults are overall dark above and below, varying from black to dark brown. The undertail coverts are always lighter, and underwing coverts can feature whitish or rufous mottling, paler flight feathers with dark trailing edge. Juveniles from above are similar to other morphs, but have darker wing coverts and heavy, dark mottling on body. FLIGHT: Best told by the combination of long, slim, pointed wings with the 2-tone underwing coloration, a relatively long tail, and the dark bib on light-morph adults. They often soar with wings in a dihedral, while their wingbeats are relatively quick and light for a large buteo. They often hover in place when hunting.

Similar Species LIGHT MORPH: Short-tailed Hawk is smaller, has secondaries darker than primaries. Immature has darker head, shorter wings. Adult White-tailed Hawk has no bib, wider wings with darker primaries than secondaries, white tail with black subterminal band. Juvenile has dark body and underwing coverts contrasting with a white chest patch. Red-tailed Hawk has shorter wings, dark patagial mark on the leading edge of the evenly colored underwing, most have a dark belly band. Perched, its wing tips do not reach the end of the tail. RUFOUS AND DARK MORPHS: All other dark adult buteos have dark undertail coverts and silvery, not gray, flight feathers.

Status & Distribution BREEDING: Breeds in N.A., winters primarily in Argentina (see map p. 144). The breeding range is from the Great Plains westward to central CA, north to Canada and locally into AK and YK, and south into Mexico. MIGRATION: In fall, migrates in huge flocks through the western states, often descending into fields to feed on insect swarms. They pass through southern TX in late Sept. and early to mid-Oct. It is a rare fall migrant in the East, almost always juveniles. WINTER: A small but regular population winters in southern FL, in the Rio Grande Valley, TX—especially immatures around the sugarcane fields—and a few in Sacramento Valley, CA.

Population Habitat change has been blamed for population losses in the 1900s in some locations, but overall it seems to be stable.

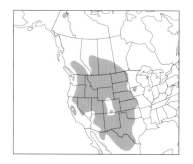

intermediate-morph adult

WHITE-TAILED HAWK *Buteo albicaudatus*

juvenile

adult

adult

juvenile

dark
juvenile

juvenile

This large, striking raptor found in open areas and scrubby habitat in southern Texas has an adult plumage and 3 immature plumages: juvenile, second-year, and third-year. A dark-morph exists in southern populations, but not in the United States. When the White-tailed Hawk is perched, the wing tips exceed the tip of the tail, even in juveniles. Females are larger than males; the sexes are similarly plumaged. It feeds on small mammals, insects, reptiles, and even birds. It will gather at a prairie fire as well as burning sugar cane fields to pursue prey that is fleeing the fire. Polytypic (3 ssp.; *hypsopodius* in N.A.). L 23" (58 cm) WS 50" (127 cm)

Identification ADULT: Uniform gray on back, head, and wings, with a rufous patch on the lesser coverts forming an easily visible shoulder patch. Throat is white, as are the underparts, though some individuals will show fine barring underneath. The white lower back and uppertail coverts lead to the distinctive white tail with a black subterminal band and multiple faint bands. JUVENILE: Above, dark brown to blackish on head, back, and wings, with rufous feather edges on upper coverts. The head is dark with whitish areas on the cheek, and a dark throat frames white on the chest with darker underparts. The amount of dark on the belly and white on the chest varies greatly among individuals, with some heavily mottled to completely dark, but with lighter undertail coverts. The tail is light gray with many fine dark bands, con-

trasting with a white U on the uppertail coverts. The wings are narrower, and the tail is longer than an adult's. SECOND-YEAR: A blend of juvenile and adult features, including the wing and tail proportions of an adult and the coloration of a juvenile. The head is more uniformly dark, the back and wings are dark with a rufous shoulder patch. The chest is whitish with variable streaking, the undersides barred with black or rufous. The uppertail coverts are white, rump is black, tail is gray with fine bands and a dark subterminal band. Below, the undertail coverts are white with variable mottling. THIRD-YEAR: Similar to adult plumage overall, but with blackish head, throat, neck, and back; tail is a mix of gray and white feathers, rump is a mix of black and white. Underneath, whitish barred with rufous. FLIGHT: The long, pointed wings pinch in at the body. In flight, often soars in a dihedral; will hover while hunting. The White-tailed's wingbeats are heavier than a Swainson's Hawk's. On adults, the white underwing coverts contrast with darker flight feathers, secondaries being lighter than primaries. Its namesake tail with wide black subterminal band is unique among buteos. All immature plumages show variable dark streaking on the underwing coverts, lighter at bases of flight feathers than at tips. A white chest spot is usually visible.

Similar Species In flight, the adult light-morph Swainson's Hawk has 2-tone underwings, but primaries and sec-

ondaries are the same color; it has uniform dark trailing edges to wing and dark bib on chest. The wing does not pinch in at the body like White-tailed's. Dark-morph Swainson's Hawk is similar to a juvenile White-tailed, but has a more noticeably barred tail with a wide, dark terminal band, and does not show the white chest patch or white uppertail coverts. Ferruginous Hawk has all-white undersides, but legs are dark, underwings are uniformly white, tail lacks dark subterminal band. All other dark buteos are distinguished from juvenile White-tailed by the silvery flight feathers and lack of white U on the uppertail coverts.

Status & Distribution The species is widespread in similar habitat throughout S.A., into C.A, and locally into coastal southern TX. Birds in TX are resident from just west of Galveston and Houston to Brownsville on coastal prairie and agricultural land, especially large private ranches. VAGRANT: Along the Gulf Coast as far as LA and inland TX.

Population The species is listed as threatened in Texas, mostly due to its limited range and lack of knowledge of its breeding dynamics. A small Texas population of 200 to 400 pairs appears to be stable.

RED-TAILED HAWK *Buteo jamaicensis*

The Red-tailed Hawk's widespread breeding range makes it the "default raptor" in most of the U.S. and Canada. It utilizes a wide range of habitats, from wooded to open areas, farmland to urban settings. Red-tails come in a variety of color morphs, from pale to rufous to dark, average size varies from north (largest) to south (smallest). Prey species include rodents and small mammals, snakes, occasionally birds, even carrion. They are prone to albinism, occasionally appearing totally white. Polytypic (13 ssp.; 6 in N.A.). L 22" (56 cm) WS 50" (127 cm)

Identification A large, chunky, short-tailed raptor, often seen hovering or kiting in a stiff breeze. All show a diagnostic dark patagial mark on the leading edge of the underwing, more easily seen in light-morph birds. The bulging secondaries give the wing a sinuous trailing edge. Juveniles have shorter wings and longer tails than adults, but when seen perched the wing tips usually fall short of the tail. Most adults have a reddish tail, varying in intensity by color morph and subspecies. LIGHT-MORPH ADULT: Occurs in all subspecies. A brown head is offset by darker malar stripe, white throat (except in some western populations and Florida). Back and wings are brown, with white spots on scapulars, giving the appearance of a whitish V on the back. Chest and underparts white, crossed by a belly band of spots or streaks (darkest in Western and Florida subspecies, missing in Fuertes'). Tail is orange to brick-red with a dark terminal band and often with multiple thinner bands (Western). LIGHT-MORPH JUVENILE: Brown head with a dark malar stripe, often with a lighter superciliary line. Throat is white (Eastern) to streaked darker (Western). Dark back and wings are mottled with white on the scapulars, forming a light V. Primaries are lighter than the secondaries, giving a 2-tone look to the wing. Below, white undersides are separated by a belly band of heavy dark streaks. Tail is brownish with multiple thin, dark bands, often with a slightly wider terminal band. Underwings are light, coverts occasionally washed with rufous (Western), flight feathers tipped dark and lightly barred, and a pale rectangle at the base of the primaries. DARK ADULTS: Darker brown above, usually without white spots on wing coverts. Dark belly is offset by rufous to black chest. Tail is rufous, with thin dark bands and wider subterminal band. On rufous morph, undertail coverts are unbanded rufous, upper-tail coverts barred brown. Underwing coverts are rufous with variable dark barring, patagial mark is visible. Darkest birds are uniformly dark, the dark undertail coverts are barred rufous. Tail is dark rufous with thin barring and a wider dark subterminal band.

eastern adult borealis

eastern adult borealis

adult krideri

eastern juvenile borealis

Head Details of Ferruginous, Red-tailed, Swainson's, and Rough-legged Hawks

When viewing a perched raptor closely through a spotting scope or digiscoping setup, here are a few ways to identify Red-tailed, Ferruginous, Swainson's and Rough-legged Hawks.

The buteos display a bewildering amount of plumage variation, so on perched birds it often helps to look carefully at structural differences rather than at feathers. Concentrate on the bird's head shape, the length and visibility of the gape (the fleshy edges of the mouth visible on the side of the head), and the bill size. Additionally, most juveniles have light-colored eyes, while adults have dark or darker eyes.

Among the large buteos, the Ferruginous Hawk has

Ferruginous Hawk

Red-tailed Hawk

the largest head and bill, and the head usually appears flat-topped. The hawk's yellow gape is very visible and long, extending past the center line of the eye. The large bill appears taller (deeper) than its length, and the cere is yellow.

DARK JUVENILES: Above, similar to light-morph with white speckles on secondaries, often darker on the head and throat. Variable below, they are heavily streaked with rufous across chest, dark belly band with white or rufous streaks. Underwing coverts are mottled rufous or dark, with patagial mark often hard to discern. Tail is brown with many darker bands, like light-morph Western. KRIDER'S RED-TAIL: Head whitish with little or no malar stripe. Back and upperwings heavily mottled with white, underparts almost pure white with reduced patagial mark on underwing. Adult has orangish tail fading to white at the base; immature has light tail banded with dark bars. HARLAN'S RED-TAIL: Light-morph (rare) adults similar to Krider's, with light head but dark malar stripe, darker wings and flight feathers. Tail has a gray subterminal band and gray mottling fading to white at tail base. Dark-morph adult is blackish, similar to other dark-morph birds, but with variable white mottling or streaking on chest and belly. Tail is

eastern adult
borealis

eastern juvenile
borealis

adult
harlani

rufous-morph
adult calurus

gray with wide, dark subterminal band. FLIGHT: Wingbeats are heavy, usually slow. Red-tails glide with wings level, occasionally soar in a slight dihedral. Immatures show a light rectangle at the base of the primaries.

Geographic Variation Eastern *borealis* is found west to the Great Plains, Western *calurus* west from the Great Plains, north into Canada, and south to the range of Fuertes' *fuertesi* in Arizona, New Mexico, southern Texas. Alaskan *alacensis* along the Alaskan coast, to the Pacific Northwest, Harlan's *harlani* from northwestern Canada into southern Alaska, and *umbrinus* in Florida.

Similar Species Red-shouldered Hawk has light crescents at base of primaries in all plumages. Adult Ferruginous Hawk has mostly white underparts with dark legs, slimmer wing silhouette. Juveniles lack patagial mark, have dark crescent at the end of underwing coverts and pale primaries. Dark Ferruginous has white comma at end of underwing coverts, unbanded tail.

Voice A husky scream, rising then dropping in pitch *shee-eeee-arrr.*

Status & Distribution Found across N. A., into Mexico, and across Carribbean. MIGRATION: Late fall along mountain ridges, the Great Lakes, fewer along the East Coast. Reluctant to cross open water, late July–Aug. movement along the south shore of Lake Ontario is primarily juveniles in postbreeding dispersal. Spring peak is Mar.–early Apr. along the south shores of the Great Lakes. WINTER: Many northern breeders winter in the southern U.S., subspecies mixing together. VAGRANT: Casual to Bermuda and NF.

Population Stable.

Swainson's Hawk

Rough-legged Hawk

The Red-tailed Hawk has a rounder forehead, but the head still has a flat crown. Its bill is slightly smaller and longer than that of the Ferruginous Hawk. The gape reaches past the leading edge of the eye. Both gape and cere range in color from greenish yellow in juve-

niles to bright yellow in adults.

The Swainson's Hawk has a rounder and smaller head than either the Ferruginous or Red-tailed Hawk. This hawk's visible gape does not reach the leading edge of the eye. The gape and cere are yellow and the lores are light. Most individuals, except dark-morph adults, have a pale throat framed in dark, and a whitish forehead.

The Rough-legged Hawk has the smallest bill and the roundest appearing head of all 4 large buteo species. The gape extends to between the leading edge and the center line of the eye. Both gape and cere are yellow in adults, grayish in juveniles. Many Roughlegs have a dark spot within a pale area located on the nape. ∎

FERRUGINOUS HAWK *Buteo regalis*

The largest of our buteos, the Ferruginous is sometimes called the Ferruginous Rough-leg for its feathered tarsi. Sexes are similar, although the females are larger. The immatures are different from adults. Their variations include light, rufous, and dark morphs, light birds being far more commonly found. Ferruginous Hawks choose open perches, both man-made and natural, while they are hunting. They generally feed on small mammals (prairie dogs are among their favorite prey), snakes, insect swarms, and occasionally birds taken on the ground. The species is notable for gathering in winter roosts. Monotypic. L 23" (58 cm) WS 53" (135 cm)

Identification The Ferruginous is a large-headed, big-chested raptor with leg feathering that reaches to the toes. The wings are long and tapered with light flight feathers. The light tail is of moderate length. Perched birds show the wing tips almost reaching the tip of the tail, shorter on juveniles. The head features a large bill and an enormous yellow gape reaching past the center line of the eye (see sidebar p. 148). LIGHT-MORPH ADULT: Head is variably colored whitish or gray with rufous streaks and dark eye line. Back and upperwings are chestnut with dark markings and primary coverts, and darker wing tips. Primaries are white at the base. Below, underparts are white with variable rufous barring on belly and flanks; legs barred rufous. Underwing coverts are variable, white to heavily barred, with light flight feathers almost unbarred, and dark crescent ("comma") at wrist. Tail is plain, varying from white to gray, often with a rufous wash. LIGHT-MORPH JUVENILE: Dark brown back and upperwings are similar to many Red-tailed juveniles, but the head shows a large gape, dark eye line, and lighter cheeks. The primaries have light bases, giving a noticeable white spot on the upper wings in flight. White undersides are usually sparsely marked, and the leg feathers are white. The underwings are mostly white with scattered dark markings, and with a dark comma at wrist. The light tail has light bands on the outer half, and a whitish base. RUFOUS AND DARK-MORPH ADULTS: Very uncommon. Individual variations are distributed evenly from rufous to very dark. Dark brown or gray head, back, and wings, outer primaries show gray. Unbanded tail is

gray above, silvery on underside. Undersides are dark, with variable amounts of white or rufous streaking. Underwings have silvery flight feathers and dark brown or rufous coverts, and white comma at wrist. Legs are dark, barred brown, or rufous. DARK JUVENILES: Dark brown above, head and breast slightly lighter and more rufous than belly, underwing coverts dark with white comma at wrist, dark primary tips, silvery flight feathers with light barring. Large gape evident on head, note the dark forehead. The tail is gray with darker bands. FLIGHT: From above, the white at the base of the primaries is very visible, as is the light tail. The long, pointed wings are often held in a dihedral. Wingbeats are slow and powerful, interspersed with gliding. Hunts by soaring at high altitudes followed by long dives or low-level pursuit-flights near the ground to flush and ambush prey.

Similar Species Light-morph Red-tailed Hawks have the dark patagial mark on the underwing that the Ferruginous Hawks lack, and they are less rufous or chestnut above. Other dark-morph buteos have different wing shapes, they lack the pale area on the upper wing at the base of the primaries, and they have more patterned tails. The Dark Rough-legged Hawk also has a light forehead.

Voice Quite vocal during the breeding season, especially when near its nesting site or during confrontations with other raptors. The hawk may call to signal alarm or location, to beg for food, or while engaged in territorial defense. The hawk gives harsh alarm calls, *kree-a* or *kaah*.

Status & Distribution Uncommon. BREEDING: Breeds in the western U.S. into Canada and south to northwestern TX, NM and AZ in open, dry country, often hilly. The large stick nest is built on a lone tree or on a rocky outcrop, and usually reused over many years. MIGRATION: Northern birds migrate into southwestern U.S., TX, and northern Mexico,

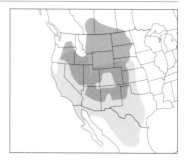

and west to CA. Fall movements are at their peak in Oct.; in spring, adults move north in Feb.–Mar., juveniles tend to migrate later. Southern breeders are more or less sedentary. VAGRANT: Casual east to IN, OH, VA, NJ, and FL, most regularly in MN and WI.

Population Never abundant, the Ferruginous Hawk is susceptible to habitat loss and to human disturbance when nesting; otherwise, it seems stable. In parts of its range it can suffer from programs to poison ground squirrels or prairie dogs.

adult

adult

juvenile

da
mo
ad

adult

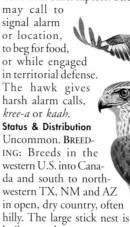

ROUGH-LEGGED HAWK *Buteo lagopus*

The most northerly of our buteos, the Rough-legged Hawk is a winter visitor to the lower 48 states from its Arctic breeding grounds. The numbers of visiting birds vary geographically and from year to year, most likely in response to the abundance or lack of prey within the birds' range. Possessing the smallest feet and toes of the large buteos, Rough-legs feed heavily on voles, lemmings, and other small rodents and occasionally on small birds captured on the ground, including Snow Buntings, shorebirds, and others. Females are larger than males, and adults have different plumage characteristics. Juveniles are different from adults; all occur in light and dark morphs. Polytypic (4 ssp.; *sanctijohannis* breeds in N.A., Asian *kamtschatkensis* was recently collected on Shemya I., western Aleutians). L 22" (56 cm) WS 56" (142 cm)

Identification All light-morph birds show a large, dark carpal patch on the underwing, all have their legs feathered down to the toes. When perched, the wing tips exceed the tip of the tail in adults, but just reach it in juveniles. Most show a white or light forehead. ADULT: All morphs have a dark trailing edge to the underwings and a subterminal band on the tail. Light-morph shows dark carpal patches on underwing and variably marked underwing coverts. A light-morph male has its breast more heavily marked than its belly (which can be almost white), dark gray back and wings, light tail with multiple dark bands and a wide, dark subterminal band. A light-morph female has a browner back and upper wings and a more heavily marked belly than the male, usually with a lighter band between breast and belly, and the undertail has a large, dark subterminal band. Dark-morph adults have a black carpal patch against dark brown coverts and silvery flight feathers with a dark trailing edge. Males are uniformly dark, with 3 or 4 light bands on a dark tail. Females show a single dark band on the light undertail. JUVENILE: Light-morph has markings similar to light adult female's, but with less dark markings on the underwing coverts, breast, and legs, including a narrower dark band on the trailing edge of the wing. The tail has a single, diffuse dark terminal band and a light base. The head often appears whitish. Seen from above, primaries have a light patch at the base; coverts are darker. Uppertail coverts are light. Dark-morphs are similar to dark adult females, with narrower dark trailing edges to the underwings and tail, sometimes with lighter heads. FLIGHT: The long wings flap slowly, and frequently are held in a dihedral. When gliding, they can push forward into a loose W-shape, like an Osprey's. Juveniles show a large white patch at the base of the primaries, especially from above. The wing tip is rather blunt and shows 5 "fingers."

Similar Species A Ferruginous Hawk light-morph lacks the dark carpal patch on the underwing and breast streaking. Dark-morph juveniles resemble Rough-legs but have a white comma at the wrist and dark foreheads. A dark Harlan's Hawk usually has white markings on the breast or head, a blurry terminal band on the undertail, and gray on the uppertail. The Northern Harrier has white on the uppertail coverts, not at the base of the tail, longer wings, and a different flight style.

Status & Distribution Fairly common. BREEDING: Occurs throughout the Holarctic region, nesting on the tundra and less commonly in subalpine forests. The nest is built on a rocky outcropping, on the ground, or in a lone tree, if present. MIGRATION: The entire breeding population leaves the tundra to winter in lower Canada and the U.S., but the timing and abundance of the migration is determined by the abundance of their food source. Few arrive in northern states as early as late Sept.; most arrive in late Oct. and Nov. Spring migration sees adults moving north first in Mar., followed by the juveniles in Apr. and into May. WINTER: Immatures often winter farther south than adults; adult males winter farther south than females. A few winter as far south as north-central Mexico, and casually to southern TX, the Gulf Coast, and northern FL.

Population Nesting is so remote that human influences are minimal on the large scale. Nesting success and density are determined by prey availability.

dark-morph adult ♂

adult ♀

adult ♂

juvenile

HARRIERS Genus *Circus*

Of the 13 species worldwide in this genus, only the long-winged, slim-bodied Northern Harrier is found in North America. Harriers have facial discs that help focus the sounds of rodents under the grasses. Adult males and females are dissimilar in coloration, but immatures look similar, with females always larger than males.

NORTHERN HARRIER *Circus cyaneus*

A long-winged, long-tailed hawk coursing low over a grassy field or marsh is likely to be this species. Females are larger, immatures are similar, adults have different plumages. Polytypic (2 ssp.; *hudsonicus* in N.A.). L 17–23" (43–58 cm) WS 38–48" (97–122 cm)
Identification Long, slim, rounded wings, and a long tail with white on the rump. The head is small, with well-defined facial discs like an owl's. ADULT MALE: Often gives the appearance of a gull, with pale gray mantle above, white wings and body below, and black wing tips. Eyes are a blazing yellow. ADULT FEMALE: Brown back and wings above, head with yellow eyes, brown on neck. Underparts are lighter brown with distinct streaking on breast and belly. JUVENILE:

Similar to adult female, with darker brown head, undersides washed with rufous, streaking less heavy and less extensive. The undersides of the secondaries are usually darker than those of the primaries. Perched at close range, immature males have yellowish to gray eyes; females' eyes are dark brown. FLIGHT: Wings held in a dihedral, they rock side-to-side as they quarter across the marshes. Occasionally soars high on set wings, at which time the long tail and slim wings are unique.

Similar Species Rough-legged Hawk has dark carpal patches on underwing, white at base of tail. Swainson's Hawk has pointed wings, shorter tail. Turkey Vulture is larger and darker,
Status & Distribution Fairly common. BREEDING: Nests on the ground in tall reeds or grasses. Nesting location and success are dependent on local rodent populations. MIGRATION: They prefer to follow coastlines, but will ride thermals along ridges. The East Coast migration is composed mostly of immature birds. Unafraid to cross open water. WINTER: Ranges from coastal and southern U.S. into Mexico. They often associate with Short-eared Owls.
Population Widely dispersed. Breeding has declined in many regions as agricultural areas have disappeared, especially in the eastern states.

adult ♀

adult ♂

juvenile

adult ♀

CRANE HAWKS Genus *Geranospiza*

Long-tailed hawks of tropical forests, Crane Hawks have long, double-jointed legs that they use to probe into holes and crevices in search of prey. There is 1 record for North America.

CRANE HAWK *Geranospiza caerulescens*

A specimen of the Crane Hawk was recorded from December 20, 1987 to March 17, 1988, at Santa Ana National Wildlife Refuge in the Rio Grande Valley, Texas. Polytypic (6 ssp.; *nigra* in N.A.). L 18–21" (46–53 cm) WS 36–41" (91–104 cm)
Identification The dark body and wings are offset by 2 bright-white tail bands; the legs are orange. When the bird is perched, the wing tips barely reach

the base of the tail. ADULT: Slate gray, often with fine barring on leg feathers and belly. JUVENILE: Overall browner than adult, white on forehead and cheeks. FLIGHT: Shows white crescent at primaries, flight feathers are darker than wing coverts.
Similar Species None.
Status & Distribution YEAR-ROUND: Prefers tropical lowlands, usually near water. Subspecies *nigra* occurs up the

eastern edge of Mexico, and is also resident on Mexico's west coast.

adult

CARACARAS AND FALCONS Family Falconidae

American Kestrel, immature male (NJ, Oct.)

The jet fighters of the bird world, falcons are flashy, flamboyant fliers that often seem to fly for sheer pleasure. For centuries captive birds have been trained by humans to hunt, leading to the term "falconry." Historically, larger falcon species were reserved for royalty, and even today they command extremely high prices. In recent times, falconers have crossbred similar species to achieve optimum size and behavioral characteristics; so escaped falconry birds may challenge birders in field identification. At hawk-watch sites across the continent, the appearance of a migrating large falcon is a thrill. The name "falcon" comes from the term "falcate," meaning sickle-shaped, which describes the bird's wing silhouette.

Structure The typical falcon is a large-headed, dark-eyed raptor with pointed wings and a square-tipped tail. Most are strong fliers and take their prey in the air. Powerful flight muscles give them a thick-chested, stout body. The beak has a notch on the cutting edge of the culmen, which severs the spinal cord of prey. The feet and toes are not designed for killing prey, but for grabbing and holding it immobile. Females outsize males, dramatically so in larger species. Differing external features are found in the forest-falcon and caracara, such as rounded or square-tipped wings.

Behavior These pointed-winged birds commonly take their prey in flight, either by diving powerfully from above, or by pursuing it from behind and below. Most falcons also hunt from an exposed perch, dropping down to pursue prey from behind. Small birds may be forced to high altitudes; then the falcon dives upon the exhausted prey. Many falcons hunt at dawn and dusk, even by city lights. Caracaras often feed on carrion and will rob food from other raptors. The *Micrastur* forest-falcons are ambush-hunters in heavy foliage, much like North American accipiters. Caracaras build stick nests in trees, whereas falcons make scrape nests on a ledge or in a shallow cave. Kestrels favor a cavity and use man-made nest boxes. The nest of another hawk may be used. Northern-nesting species are usually migratory, although the Gyrfalcon does not follow any discernable pattern of passage. Eastern migrants prefer following coastlines, preying on shorebirds and migrant passerines. They often fly in wind conditions unfavorable to other migrating raptors and are not as reluctant to cross open water. Inland migrants soar on fixed wings along mountains' thermal updrafts, like other hawks, but take a direct flight line instead of the swirling "kettles" favored by the buteos. An owl decoy placed atop a long pole at a ridgeline hawk-watch site may attract a migrating falcon to swoop down and harass its historic enemy.

Plumage Except for the kestrels and the Merlin, adult falcons and caracaras of both sexes share similar plumage, while juvenile birds have different plumages than their adults, in some cases only by degree. All are darker above and generally light below. Most falcons have moustache marks on the face.

Distribution Falcons are found worldwide, caracaras and forest-falcons only in the New World. Falcons fly at all altitudes, in open areas throughout North America; caracaras are found in open areas with warm climates.

Taxonomy Within the family Falconidae, there are 38 species of *Falco* worldwide, with 8 in North America. The AOU lists 3 forest-falcons (Micrasturinae) and 3 living caracaras (Caracarinae) under Falconidae; other sources list them differently. Some authorities place caracaras in a subfamily, Polyborinae.

Conservation Worldwide, 4 species are endangered, 6 are listed as near threatened. Pesticides and other toxins in the environment are detrimental to nesting success. The prohibition of DDT and similar chemicals in North America has allowed populations to rebuild. Loss of grassland habitat in the East due to development and reforestation of farmland is a concern. —*Clay Taylor*

FOREST-FALCONS Genus *Micrastur*

COLLARED FOREST-FALCON *Micrastur semitorquatus*

adult

Forest-falcons are tropical raptors that look decidedly unlike a falcon. The Collared Forest-Falcon looks more like an accipiter of the northern forests. There is 1 accepted North America record from Bentsen Rio Grande State Park in southern Texas. Polytypic (2 ssp. in New World, 1 reaching N.A., presumably *naso*). L 20" (52 cm) WS 31" (79 cm)

Identification Dark above and light below; short-winged, long-tailed, and long-legged. It has large eyes for hunting in dense foliage. Black above, with white cheeks, neck collar, and undersides. Cheek has black crescent some call "sideburns." Wings and back dark; tail dark with thin white bars, white tip. ADULT: Unmarked below, can be white or buff. JUVENILE: Like adult above, but browner. Undersides heavily barred, ground color has buffy wash.

Similar Species Size similar to Cooper's Hawk. Resembles nothing else common to N.A. Sharp-Shinned Hawk subspecies *chinogaster* of S. Mexico is dark above, mostly white below, but lacks "sideburns" and is far smaller.

Voice Quite vocal, especially early and late in the day. Usual call a hollow *how* or *aow*, frequently repeated, plus rapid combinations getting louder and more slurred at the end. Also repeats a whiny *keer keer keer*, which seems to be a "false alarm call" to attract small birds, similar to a birder's pishing.

CARACARAS Genus *Caracara*

Long-legged raptors of open areas throughout South and Central America, caracaras are unusual members of the falcon family. Their structure and behavior are very different from that of a true falcon, appearing more like a vulture or buteo. Nine species are found in the New World, only 1 of which reaches North America.

CRESTED CARACARA *Caracara cheriway*

adults

This large, long-legged raptor of the American Southwest is seen standing on bare ground or perched on a telephone pole. Its long, square-tipped wings are unlike a falcon's, as is its long head and neck. Its wings almost reach to its tail tip. It feeds on carrion and small prey. In flight the wingbeats are steady; gliding, the wings are held slightly downward. The bird soars on thermals with other hawks and vultures. Sexes are similar. Previously it was called Audubon's Caracara and Northern Caracara. Polytypic (3 ssp. New World; nominate in N.A.). L 23" (58 cm) WS 50" (127 cm)

Identification ADULT: At a distance, body, wings, and crown black, contrasting with white face and neck. Upper breast and back are white, finely barred with black. Tail white with dark barring and dark terminal band. Facial skin and cere are orange; legs yellow. BASIC: One-year-old birds are similar to adults, but browner above, not black; facial skin pink. JUVENILE: Similar pattern to adult, but with brownish and buffy coloration in place of black-and-white areas. Legs are gray, and facial skin is pinkish. In flight, gives a striking black-and-white look, with black cap, long white neck, dark wings with white wing panels at base of primaries, and dark body with white undertail coverts. Whitish tail is tipped in black.

Similar Species None.

Voice Generally silent.

Status & Distribution Rare to common within range. YEAR-ROUND: Resident in central FL, along TX coastal prairies, and in a small range in southeast AZ. Range is expanding into central TX. BREEDING: Inhabits bulky stick nest in treetop, often reused. MIGRATION: Generally nonmigratory, but seen annually at TX hawk-watch sites. VAGRANT: Casual to CA and NM; scattered summer reports north into MN, ON.

Population Stable in Florida and Arizona, it has been expanding in Texas since the 1980s.

adult

juvenile

FALCONS Genus *Falco*

Also known as "typical falcons" or "true falcons", there are 38 species described, 9 of which appear in North America. Six species are regular nesters here, including the re-introduced Aplomado Falcon. Known for their aggressive nature, aerial acrobatics, and spectacular dives, falcons are often a symbol of sports teams and warplanes. All true falcons typically have pointed wings, a large head, and dark eyes. They occur worldwide, nesting on all continents except Antarctica.

AMERICAN KESTREL *Falco sparverius*

Our smallest and most common falcon, it is usually found in close proximity to open fields, either perched on a snag or telephone wire or hovering in search of prey. The typical falcon-shaped wings are slim and pointed; the tail long and square-tipped. Sexes are of similarly size. Adult male plumage is easily told from adult females and juveniles of both sexes. All have 2 bold, dark moustache marks framing white cheeks on the face and have the dark eyes typical of falcons. It hunts insects, small mammals, and reptiles from a perch or on the wing. Will hover above a field on rapidly beating wings, or soar in place in strong winds above a hillside. Flight style is quick and buoyant, almost erratic, with wings usually swept back. Polytypic (New World 17 ssp.; 2 in N.A.). L 10.5" (27 cm) WS 23" (58 cm)

Identification ADULT MALE: Head has gray crown, rufous nape with black spot on either side, dark moustaches around white cheeks. Back is bright rufous with black barring on lower back. The tail is patterned with highly variable amounts of black, white, or gray bands. Wings are blue-gray with dark primaries. Underparts are white, washed with cinnamon. ADULT FEMALE: Head similar pattern to male, but more brown on crown. Back, wings, and tail are reddish brown with dark barring; subterminal tailband much wider than other bands. Underparts are buffy-white with reddish streaks. JUVENILE MALE: Head similar to adult, but less gray and with dark streaks on crown. Back is completely streaked, heavy streaks on breast. JUVENILE FEMALE:

Very similar to adult female. FLIGHT: Light, bouncy flight is usually not direct and purposeful—often with "twitches" or hesitation. Light underwings and generally light body coloration. Males show a row of white dots ("string of pearls") on the trailing edges of the underwings. Fans tail when hovering.

Geographic Variation Two subspecies occur in N.A.; widespread nominate *sparverius* is the typical migratory form. Subspecies *paulus,* from South Carolina to Florida, is smaller, the male with less barring on the back and fewer spots on its undersides, essentially nonmigratory.

Similar Species Merlin appears darker in flight due to dark underwings, shorter tail. When perched, looks darker, more heavy-bodied, lacks the 2 moustaches. Peregrine Falcon is larger, has wider wings, shorter tail, single heavy moustache. Eurasian Kestrel is slightly larger, has 1 moustache, wedge-shaped tail; males have blue-gray tail and reddish wings.

Voice Loud, ringing *killy-killy-killy* or *klee-klee-klee* used all year round. Distinctive.

Status & Distribution Common in open areas, it ranges throughout N.A., including much of Canada and into AK. BREEDING: A cavity nester, it uses dead trees, cliffs, occasionally a dirt bank, and even a hollow giant cactus in the Southwest. It will also use man-made nestboxes placed high on trees and telephone poles. Up to 5 or 6 young per brood, depending on food availability. MIGRATION: Northern breeders follow traditional fall migration routes to wintering ranges in the southern U.S. and northern Mexico. Eastern populations use the coastlines more than the inland corridors, and are not reluctant to cross water. Spring migrants are only concentrated along the Great Lakes watch-sites. WINTER: The majority of birds winter in the southern

U.S., often spaced out on every other telephone pole in agricultural areas. A small percentage winter in snow-covered states, the numbers depending on food sources.

Population Overall, numbers are stable. However, increases in the central U.S. are being offset by declines in the Northeast and the West Coast (CA and OR). Eastern populations are thought to be affected by loss of open habitat due to 2 factors; human development and agricultural abandonment leading to reforestation, with a subsequent increase in Cooper's Hawk predation.

♀

adult ♂

adult ♀

adult ♂

juvenile ♂

adult ♂

EURASIAN KESTREL *Falco tinnunculus*

Also called Common Kestrel, this small falcon is from Eurasia. A typical falcon with large head and dark eyes, slim pointed wings and a long tail, it shares many of the characteristics of the American Kestrel, but appears slightly larger and heavier and has only 1 moustache mark on its face. Undersides on all ages are buffy and streaked. In flight the tail looks slightly wedge-shaped, and from above the wing gives a 2-tone appearance. The bird feeds on small prey, including insects, small mammals, and birds, first hovering to spot its quarry, then descending in steps before stooping to the ground. Polytypic (11 ssp.; strays to N.A. are most likely all nominate). L 13.5" (34 cm) WS 29" (74 cm)

Identification ADULT MALE: Gray head and nape, with a single moustache and paler throat. The reddish back and wing coverts have black streaks, dark primaries. The gray rump and unmarked gray uppertail contrast with the wide, dark subterminal tail band and a white tip. Undersides are whitish buffy, with spots on breast, streaked flanks, plain undertail coverts. ADULT FEMALE: Head with similar pattern to male, but more rufous-brown. The back is more heavily barred, the rump gray with gray-brown barred tail and wide subterminal band. JUVENILE: Similar to female, but usually with buff tips to feathers on upperparts.

Similar Species American Kestrel is smaller, slimmer; has 2 moustache marks on face. Underparts are usually whiter, tail more rounded. Males have blue-gray wing coverts; red tail; females are less heavily marked.

Voice A repeated *kee-kee-kee.* Mostly quiet away from breeding grounds.

Status & Distribution Widespread in Old World, casual to western Aleutians and Bering Sea, accidental to East and West Coasts of U.S., most recently to FL. MIGRATION: Northern European and Asian birds are highly migratory, wintering in southern Europe, the Middle East, and southern Asia

Population The Eurasian Kestrel seems to be stable across its range, with human persecution being the most common threat. No signs of range expansion to North America.

adult ♂

juvenile

♀

adult ♂

EURASIAN HOBBY *Falco subbuteo*

juvenile

adult

adult

juvenile

Also called Hobby, Northern Hobby, and the "mini Peregrine" by raptor aficionados, this Old World species is casual in the Bering Sea region, including the Aleutians. There are additional records from ships in Alaskan waters, and 1 from waters well off Newfoundland. Polytypic (2 ssp.; N.A. records likely *subbuteo*). L 12.25" (31 cm) WS 30" (77 cm)

Identification A small falcon with long thin, pointed wings and a relatively short tail, dark above and whitish below with heavy streaking. A rapid, strong flier, it takes prey on the wing, usually small birds, but also dragonflies and other large insects. Sexes are similar in size, with females more robust, approximately 5 percent larger, but up to 30 percent heavier. ADULT: Dark-gray head and upperparts, black moustache framing white cheek, short white streak above eye, whitish throat, with whitish underparts heavily streaked. Undertail coverts and legs bright rufous, easier to see when perched. Cere and eye ring yellow. JUVENILE: Upperparts are more brownish, rufous tips to new feathers quickly wear off. Head pattern similar to adult, underside ground color may appear more buffy, tail more distinctly light-tipped, undertail coverts and legs buffy to dull-rufous. FLIGHT: Long, slim wings and a relatively short tail, it uses its speed more often than its maneuverability to catch prey. At ease in all kinds of wind conditions. The underwings are uniformly grayish with dark markings and darker wingtips. The rufous undertail of adult is visible in good light, but by the time you see that, the identification should already be clinched.

Similar Species American Kestrel is longer-tailed and shorter-winged with a lighter flight; is lighter above, has 2 moustache marks on face. Merlin is stockier, darker, less heavily streaked underneath. It resembles the far larger Peregrine Falcon in proportions, powerful flight, and dark over light plumage.

Voice Silent away from breeding grounds.

Status & Distribution Widespread in the Old World; winters in Africa and Indian subcontinent. MIGRATION: A long-distance migrant. Birds overshooting the breeding grounds in Siberia are the likely source for Aleutian records. Accidental in western WA.

MERLIN *Falco columbarius*

A small, dark falcon, most often described as "dashing," the Merlin is an active hunter, taking its prey in midair, often after spectacular chases. It primarily feeds on birds, sometimes those larger than itself, and will also take insects like dragonflies while on migration, munching on the snack while still flying. Hunting is generally on the wing, but it will hunt from a perch and ambush passing prey. It occasionally soars on spread wings, but never hovers. It shows typical falcon features of a dark eye, pointed wings, and a square-tipped tail. Its facial moustache mark is less noticeable than that on most falcons. Females are larger than males, and adults have different plumages. Polytypic (9 ssp.; 3 in N.A.). L 12" (31 cm) WS 25" (64 cm)

adult ♂

adult ♀

adult ♂

♀ *suckleyi*

adult ♂ *suckleyi*

adult ♀ *richardsonii*

adult ♂ *richardsonii*

Identification At a distance, a small, dark falcon either flying or sitting is usually a Merlin. Its wings are wider and tail much shorter than a kestrel's. Usually perches atop a dead snag, tower, or building. When perched, the wingtips do not reach the tip of the tail. The following descriptions apply to Taiga Merlin. ADULT MALE: Called "Blue Jack" or "Blue Lightning," the back and upper wing coverts are blue gray, undersides are whitish streaked with brown with an overall rufous wash to the sides and leg feathers. The tail is dark with lighter gray banding. ADULT FEMALE: Above, it has a slate-brown back and upper wing coverts. The tail bands are buffy on a dark brown tail. Below, buffy underparts are heavily streaked. JUVENILE: Apart from size, sexes very similar to each other; plumage like adult female; tail bands buffy. FLIGHT: Fast, flickering wingbeats and direct flight set it apart from American Kestrel. Usually travels close to the ground, where it can ambush flying birds from below and behind. Most photographs of flying Merlins are taken of gliding or soaring birds, when they are easier to focus on, showing the wings straight

out and the tail occasionally fanned. When in pursuit, the wingtips are swept back and the upstroke goes high above the body.

Geographic Variation Taiga Merlin *(columbarius)* from Alaska to eastern Canada is the smallest of the 3; averages darker to the east of its range; and is highly migratory, wintering down to the Caribbean, and Central America. Prairie Merlin *(richardsoni)* is largest of the 3, much paler than Taiga Merlin, especially adult females, which also have thinner streaks on body. Adult male is paler blue on back than Taiga. All have wider tail bands than Taiga. The moustache mark can be very faint. Black Merlin *(suckleyi)* is a resident of the Pacific Northwest; generally sedentary, but does wander down to California. About the size of Taiga Merlin, but much darker overall, with almost no white on face, heavy streaking on body, and tail bands are often incomplete.

Similar Species American Kestrel is slimmer, has longer tail, less direct flight style. Peregrine Falcon is much larger, has broader base of wings, large moustache mark on head. When perched, its wingtips reach or almost reach tip of tail. Prairie Falcon is larger, has a distinct moustache mark on face, dark axilliaries on underwing.

Voice Rapid *kee-kee-kee* or *klee-klee-klee* heard often around nest. Males are higher pitched than females. On migration, often heard when harass-

ing other raptors, especially Peregrines.

Status & Distribution Widespread throughout the Holarctic, they are uncommon nesters throughout range. Relatively common on East Coast during fall migration, an uncommon winter bird. BREEDING: Uses a mix of habitats in conjunction with open spaces, anything from tundra to coastline, boreal forest to Northwestern rain forest, prairie edges, and parkland. In recent years they have been increasingly found within cities in prairie states and provinces. MIGRATION: Merlins follow most traditional migratory routes, but are less likely to soar on thermals, so are usually underreported on mountain hawk-watches as they cruise by at treetop level. Along coastal routes, primary passage times in fall are mid-Sept. through late Oct., with juveniles often passing first, followed by adults. They are more active migrants during morning and late afternoon, and many hawk watches call 4 p.m. "Merlin Time." WINTER: Uncommon in northern states in winter, more likely to be found along coast feeding on shorebirds. Prairie Merlins have recently been taking to wintering in Great Plains cities, feeding on small birds and rodents.

Population Numbers are stable for Taiga and Black Merlins, while Prairie Merlins are increasing as they become more habituated to cities. There seem to be no major threats from habitat destruction or environmental factors.

RED-FOOTED FALCON *Falco vespertinus*

This medium-size falcon of Eastern Europe and western Asia is larger than the Eurasian Kestrel and Merlin. It feeds mainly on insects, hawking them from midair, often hovering above a spot in search of prey. In August 2004 the first North American record of this bird, a subadult male in heavy flight-feather molt, was found on Martha's Vineyard, Massachusetts. Numerous diagnostic photographs were taken, and thousands of birders made the trip to see the bird, which the locals christened "Red Socks."

Some proclaimed it a "miracle bird," that it was a harbinger of the October 2004 Boston Red Sox World Series win. Monotypic. L 11"(27 cm) WS 29" (73 cm)

Identification ADULT MALE: Red Socks was a SY male (in his second calendar year of life), with dark-gray head, mostly gray wings and body, and barred flight feathers and tail. ADULT FEMALE: Very different from male, with slaty-gray back and wings; brown head with black moustache; and white cheek and side

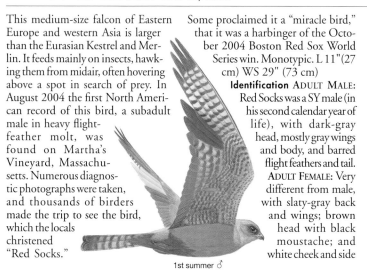

1st summer ♂

of neck. Underparts are buffy with thin streaking. JUVENILE: Back and wings browner, with light feather edges. Head pattern similar to adult female. Female and juveniles would be unique in North America.

Similar Species Mississippi Kite is all gray with pointed wings, but does not hover when foraging. In Old World, see Amur Falcon.

Status & Distribution VAGRANT: A long-distance migrant between Europe and Africa. There are vagrant records to Iceland. The bird found on Martha's Vineyard was possibly storm-driven or ship-assisted in crossing the Atlantic. There is no evidence to suggest whether it arrived in MA from the north or the south.

APLOMADO FALCON *Falco femoralis*

This medium-size falcon is a neotropic species whose range barely reaches into North America. Birders visiting the Laguna Atascosa National Wildlife Refuge in the area of Brownsville, Texas, usually have a good chance of spotting one. However, at this time, the South Texas Aplomado Falcon is not yet considered established. It is often seen perched atop a single tree, cactus, etc., as it scans for prey. Polytypic (5 ssp. New World; *septentrionalis* in N.A.). L 15–16.5" (38–42 cm) WS 40–48" (102–122 cm)

Identification A slim, long-winged, long-tailed falcon, the tail extending well past the wingtips on a perched bird. Adults and juveniles have slightly different plumages. All show a distinctive head pattern of dark eye line and moustache mark, dark crown, and contrasting buffy cheeks and buffy superciliary line that meets at the nape. ADULT MALE: Head as described above. Dark-gray back and upper wings contrast with buffy chest, black belly band, and rufous belly, undertail coverts, and legs. Flight feathers and tail are blackish, with 6 or more narrow white bands on the tail. The black underparts are often finely barred in white. Eye ring and cere are yellow. ADULT FEMALE: Like the male, but buffy chest has black streaking that is usually lacking in males. Females are noticeably larger than males. JUVENILE: Shows a similar pattern to adults, but with brownish back and wings, buffy tail bands, buffy underparts, legs, and undertail coverts. The buffy breast is more heavily streaked with black. Cere and eye ring are bluish gray. FLIGHT: Shows deep, rapid wingbeats. It is highly maneuverable, able to turn and

adult

juvenile

adult ♂

juvenile ♀

swoop in pursuit, and will continue flapping wings even when diving on prey. Can also hover and buoyantly soar. The combination of slim wings and long tail, plus the light-dark combination of chest and underparts make it fairly distinctive in flight.

Similar Species Larger than American Kestrel, slimmer and more buoyant than Merlin. Adult Peregrines have a dark moustache on the face and dark back and wings, but are much larger, more stocky, and shorter-tailed. Peregrine and Prairie Falcon lack black underparts.

Voice Most typically a fast *ki-ki-ki-ki-ki-ki* sound, males higher-pitched than females. Also with single notes and a sharp scream around the nest.

Status & Distribution Uncommon, local from Mexico to Argentina. Formerly bred in open country from south TX to AZ. Listed as endangered in 1986. Reintroduced into southern TX, nesting has occurred with unbanded (presumably wild) birds, but unbanded young from a nest of released birds is also possible. BREEDING: Historically on ground, rock outcropping, or in old raven or raptor nest. One known nest in southern TX was an old raven nest in a radio tower. DISPERSAL: Has occasionally been recorded on hawk-watch sites up the TX coast, but most birds appear to stay within their natal range.

Population Very little data on Mexican populations, U.S. numbers slowly continue to grow, including a few pairs in southern New Mexico and a recent record in the Davis Mountains, Texas.

GYRFALCON *Falco rusticolus*

A visitor to the lower 48 states from its breeding grounds in arctic Alaska and Canada, the Gyrfalcon is the largest falcon in the world, capable of taking down flying geese and cranes. It is a powerful flyer, with deceptively slow wingbeats and the longest tail of the large falcons. Gyrfalcons occur in 3 color morphs—white, gray, and dark (black). Juveniles are different from adults; sexes are similar, but females are larger. The Gyrfalcon is typically seen in the lower 48 states during fall migration and winter, an individual bird may take up winter residence and remain there for a period of months. A bird seen daily around the Boston, MA, harbor was determined to be one that was banded in the area more than 5 years earlier. In medieval Europe, the Gyrfalcon was highly prized as a falconry bird. Monotypic. L 20–25" (51–64 cm) WS 50–64" (127–163 cm)

Identification A large, bulky falcon, with thick pointed wings wide at the base, giving a fatter wing silhouette than most large falcons. Females are larger than males. Perched, they sit with an upright posture on cliffs, towers, buildings, and other man-made structures. The wings extend about two-thirds of the way down the tail. ADULT LIGHT MORPH: All white with varying amounts of dark markings above, blackish primary tips; dark bands on tail often incomplete. Occasionally shows a faint moustache. ADULT GRAY MORPH: Dark gray to gray-brown ground color on back and wings is patterned with lighter gray to blue-gray feather tips, giving a scaled pattern. Tail strongly barred. Head can appear lighter than the back, with a dark eye line and paler supercilium, moustache usually visible. Underparts with barred flanks and spots on breast and belly. ADULT DARK MORPH: Blackish brown above with less obvious barring on back and tail; head usually with a "hooded" appearance; moustache usually lost in the overall pattern. Underneath, overall dark with some whitish streaks on breast and barring on flanks, belly, and undertail. JUVENILE LIGHT MORPH: Similar overall color to adult, but more heavily marked above with black or brown. The primaries are blackish with complete barring. Tail bands are complete, heavier than adults. JUVENILE GRAY MORPH: Darker gray-brown than adult, with back and wing coverts finely edged or spotted in lighter brown. Head color as dark as back, but still showing faint moustache and supercilium. The underparts are heavily streaked with brown, lightest on throat and undertail. JUVENILE DARK MORPH: Overall dark brown with heavy streaking underneath, barred undertail coverts. FLIGHT: A large falcon with heavy chest, wide pointed wings that are blunt on the tips. The long tail is wide-based and tapers down to the tip when folded. Its wingbeats are slow and relatively stiff, yet the bird flies with great speed. Gray- and dark-morph birds show lighter flight feathers that contrast strongly with dark wing coverts, giving a strong 2-tone look.

Similar Species White morph Gyrfalcon is unmistakable. Albino or pale morph Red-tailed Hawk may look similar, but wing shape and tail differences are easy to spot. Peregrine Falcon is slimmer, shorter-tailed, shows heavier moustache, usually darker crown. Adult Peregrine is horizontally barred across breast; juveniles show uniformly dark underwings. Peale's Peregrine of the Pacific Northwest resembles dark morph. Prairie Falcon is lighter underneath, has dark axiliaries contrasting with light underwing, white spot behind eye. Northern Goshawk has the same bulk, but differs with blunt rounded wings, wide secondaries, 2-tone upperwings; and strong eye line.

Voice Usually silent.

Status & Distribution An uncommon species, it is a widespread breeder in the Holarctic. BREEDING: Nest scrape usually on a cliff, but also uses old Raven nests in a suitable location. MIGRATION: Gryfalcon sightings along traditional hawk migration sites are usually late in the season—Nov.–Dec. There are enough late-Oct. records to make it a species to watch for. WINTER: There seem to be no real patterns in wintering birds, but individuals have shown that they will return to the same general area in succeeding years. A favored roost site will be used for the night, with the bird leaving in the morning and arriving in the evening with sufficient fidelity to afford birders a "viewing schedule." Most wintering birds are found above 40° N. VAGRANT: Casual to northern CA, OK, northern TX, and east to the mid-Atlantic states.

Population Circumpolar and out of the range of most habited areas, populations are thought to be stable.

gray morph juvenile

gray morph adult

dark morph juvenile

white morph adult

PEREGRINE FALCON *Falco peregrinus*

The Peregrine Falcon is world-renowned for its speed, grace, and power in the air. It is distributed across the world, found on every inhabited continent, and on many islands. Formerly called the "Duck Hawk" in North America. It can occur in almost any habitat in North America, but is frequently seen around water—lakes, rivers, or coastal shorelines. Peregrines feed primarily on birds taken in flight, along with the occasional bat or rodent. Its large hind talon (the hallux) is anchored by heavy tendons, allowing it to use the force of its dive to kill its prey on contact. The true velocity of its high-speed dive has been the subject of much debate over the years, with some observers claiming speeds of up to 200 miles an hour. Recently a falconer's Peregrine was outfitted with a skydiver's altimeter and data recorder and trained to chase down a lure released by the skydiver. The bird easily dove to a speed of 247 miles an hour, and the feeling is that it could still go faster! Polytypic (at least 16 ssp.; 3 in N.A.). L 16–20" (41–51 cm) WS 36–44" (91–112 cm)

Identification The Peregrine is a raptor with long pointed wings and a medium-length tail. All ages have a dark moustache mark on the face. When sitting the wings extend almost to the tip of the tail. They favor an exposed perch, natural or man-made, to scan for prey. The majority of successful kills are made with high-speed dives that overtake from above or behind. Females are larger than males; sexes appear similar. ADULT: A dark head and nape, with dark moustache and white cheek. The cere and eye ring are yellow. Tundra shows the thinnest moustache, whitest cheek, and often a light forehead. Some Anatum have a dark cheek, blending with the moustache. The upperparts are dark gray, underparts are whitish, with clear breast and barring on belly and flanks. Subspecies *anatum* often shows a salmon wash on the breast. Peale's is without the salmon color and has streaking on the breast. JUVENILE: Browner above than the adults, with brown streaking on buffy underparts. Cere and eye ring are blue-gray. Tundra has a light forehead, often a light crown (giving a "blonde" look), and the thinnest moustache. Subspecies *anatum* shows a darker head, thicker moustache, thicker streaking on underparts. Peale's is overall very dark with a small cheek patch; underparts heavily streaked or almost uniformly dark. FLIGHT: Capable of swift level flight, power dives, and soaring on outstretched wings, the Peregrine can fly in virtually any wind and weather condition. Typical flight is a smooth, quick, rhythmic, shallow wingbeat. With deeper wingbeats, it gains speed and dives, whereas it executes quick turns after fleeing prey with a fanned tail and choppy wingbeats. When soaring, the wing silhouette tapers smoothly from body to tip, like a dipped candle. The underwings are barred on both flight feathers and coverts, giving a uniformly dark appearance.

Geographic Variation Tundra *(tundrius)* nests on the Alaskan and Canadian tundra, is overall the lightest N.A. subspecies, and is the longest-distance migrant. Peale's *(pealei),* the darkest and most sedentary, is found along the coast of the Pacific Northwest. Continental-breeding *anatum* is intermediate, but variable in features, while movement is on a smaller scale than Tundra. The release of mixed-subspecies birds as part of the North American reintroduction program has resulted in many eastern birds showing characteristics of Peale's, selected in hopes that the newly hacked birds will remain in the vicinity of their release points.

Similar Species Gray and dark-morph Gyrfalcon is usually larger and darker, with smaller moustache, wider wing bases with 2-toned underwing, and a longer tail that tapers from base to tip. Some small, dark males can appear similar to dark juvenile female Peale's. Prairie Falcon is lighter overall, has a thin moustache and dark axiliaries contrasting with light underwing. When perched, wingtips do not reach the tip of the tail.

Voice A rapid *kak-kak-kak,* not often heard away from the nesting area.

Status & Distribution The widespread continental form was decimated by the use of pesticides in the 1950s and 1960s, placing it on the Endangered Species List by 1970. A reintroduction program begun in the late 1970s has helped to restore Peregrine numbers throughout. Wintering Peregrines may be found in large cities throughout the southern U.S. Recently taken off the

adult

juvenile pealei

adult pealei

adult anatum

juvenile anatum

Endangered Species List, the Peregrine is a showpiece for the ability of a species to rebound from the effects of pesticides in the environment. Most major cities in the eastern U.S. now host Peregrine nests, often equipped with web-cams to follow the progress of the nestlings. Populations of Tundra were never in real danger, but concern continues due to their wintering in countries where DDT use is still allowed. BREEDING: Historically nesting in a scrape atop cliffs, they have taken well to man-made structures like tall buildings, bridge beams, and towers, and even use old Osprey and Bald Eagle nests in coastal locations. MIGRATION: During the 1970s and early 1980s, a single Peregrine passing by a hawk watch site was cause for celebration. A site in the Florida Keys now records single days with more than 350 Peregrines passing by. Fewer fly the inland ridges, often soaring in with kettles of other raptors to the delight of hawk watchers. Prime fall dates in the East are early to mid-Oct., spring dates in late Apr. Recent surveys of offshore oil-rigs in the Gulf of Mexico found that Peregrines pick off exhausted migrants, with any 1 rig hosting up to a dozen falcons. WINTER: Usually found along the coast or around cities, wherever food is available.

Population Slowly increasing in North America.

juvenile *tundrius*

adult *tundrius*

PRAIRIE FALCON *Falco mexicanus*

The large, light-colored falcon of the arid western United States, it inhabits foothills, grasslands, and other open country. While it primarily feeds on birds, especially flocking species in winter, it also takes ground squirrels when they are abundant. It takes birds on the wing, usually while flying low to the ground and surprising its prey as they take off. It can also dive down on prey from above. Monotypic. L 15.5-19.5" (39–50 cm) WS 35–43" (89–109 cm)

Identification A large raptor with pointed wings and a wide, square tail. When perched, the wingtips fall noticeably short of the tip of the tail. The birds have a large head, a light spot behind the eye, and a thin, dark moustache mark. Sexes appear similar, but females are larger. ADULT: The upperparts are brownish with pale barring on wing coverts and back; tail and flight feathers are lightly barred. The underparts are whitish with dark spots on sides and belly. Cere, legs, and eye ring are yellow. JUVENILE: Darker brown above than adults with less light barring on wing coverts and back, they appear darker at a distance. Underparts are more buffy and thinly streaked. Cere and eye ring are blue-gray. FLIGHT: Wingtips are not as sharply pointed as those of other large falcons, underwings feature light-colored flight feathers and outer wing coverts contrasting with dark axilliaries, forming a dark "wingpit" that makes it look broader-winged. Females show more dark feathers on innerwing coverts than males.

Similar Species Peregrine Falcon shows more contrast between dark above and light below, a thicker, darker moustache, and uniformly darker underwings. Flight style is similar to Prairie, but hunts less often at low altitudes. A light-colored juvenile Tundra Peregrine does not have the Prairie's white spot behind the eye. Juvenile Swainson's Hawk can show a similar coloration and contrasting facial pattern, but the small head and wingtips that reach the tip of the tail aid in identification. Light-colored Prairie Merlins have similar shapes and colorations, but are much smaller with faster wingbeats, show a faint moustache mark, and lack the dark axilliaries of the underwing.

Voice A loud *kik-kik-kik* around the nest, usually silent at other times.

Status & Distribution Widespread throughout acceptable habitat from Canada to Mexico, but never abundant. BREEDING: Uses a small scrape on a cliff or ledge, high above the ground. It will also use the old nest of another raptor or raven, almost always on a cliff, rarely in a tree or on a building. MIGRATION: No particular pattern of movements, with some individuals wintering in Canada, while others migrate into the Southwest, with regular records at Corpus Christi, TX. DISPERSAL: Prairie Falcons, both adults and juveniles, are noted for their post-breeding dispersal, wandering west to the Pacific and east to the plains states. Prey availability is probably a factor. WINTER: Found along the West Coast from WA to CA and into Baja CA, Mex., and inland as prey availability dictates. VAGRANT: Records as far east as WI, IL, OH, KY, and AL. The farther away from traditional ranges, the greater the suspicion that the individual might be an escaped falconer's bird. **Population** Stable, adapting more and more to the spread of cities and western development.

adults

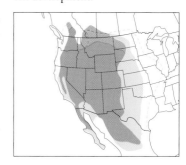

RAILS, GALLINULES, AND COOTS Family Rallidae

Purple Gallinule (FL, Mar.)

One of the most widely distributed families of terrestrial vertebrates, this group includes some of our most familiar birds as well as some of our most mysterious and difficult to observe species. Most are small- to medium-size ground dwellers and are easy to identify if well seen or heard. However, because rails are secretive and often inhabit dense, relatively inaccessible, wetland vegetation, observation can be difficult and requires patience. Typically, an observation involves a brief glimpse as a bird runs, jumps, or swims or is accidentally flushed. Coots and gallinules tend to be less secretive, more ducklike, and often frequent open water or marsh edge.

Structure All species have proportionately short and rounded wings, short tails, and strong legs and feet. Laterally compressed bodies allow rails and gallinules to move effortlessly, almost rodentlike, through dense vegetation. Long slender toes help distribute weight and allow some species to walk on floating vegetation. The more aquatic coots are ducklike, heavier, wider bodied, with lobed toes for swimming. Bill shapes vary from short, stubby, and chickenlike to long and slender, mainly reflecting diet: more herbivorous/omnivorous (taking vegetation, seeds, or snails) versus taking a higher proportion of invertebrates such as crabs, respectively.

Behavior Most rails are adapted to living in low, dense vegetation on moist substrates. Thus, most occur in association with water: Fresh water or brackish, salt marshes, mangrove swamps, bogs, wet meadows, or flooded fields. All species can swim; some can sink beneath the water's surface. Most can dive and use their wings underwater to escape predators. Coots and moorhens are the most aquatic, forage while swimming, and must patter across the water to get airborne. Rails rarely forage in the open, bur when they do they can be surprisingly tame and oblivious. Most rails and gallinules prefer to run to avoid danger, but if startled will flush, fly a short distance with legs dangling, then drop back into cover. Once airborne, most species are remarkably strong fliers, and many are capable of sustained long-distance migration or vagrancy. As a group rails are very vocal, especially during the breeding season and at night. Vocalizations are usually loud and diagnostic. Calls vary from soft cooing to harsh and monotonous series of mechanical sounds; some species engage in duets.

Plumage Somber, cryptic colors provide camouflage; a few species are brightly colored. Sexes are usually similar, and plumage generally does not vary seasonally, although some species have a slightly brighter breeding plumage. Chicks are covered in black down, some adorned with colorful plumes or naked skin on the head. Down is replaced by juvenal plumage while birds are still substantially smaller than adults, and juvenal plumage is fairly quickly replaced by first basic plumage. These immatures resemble adults, but typically have duller plumage and soft parts. The postbreeding molt is complete; the rapid loss of flight feathers results in temporary flightlessness in some species.

Distribution Worldwide except polar regions and waterless deserts. Many oceanic islands have been colonized by rails, many of which have evolved into new species, and some of which have become flightless.

Taxonomy About 133 extant species. Family relationships have undergone a number of reclassifications; genetic studies are ongoing.

Conservation About 25 percent of extant species are globally threatened; 17 species are almost certainly extinct since about 1600. Many oceanic species and populations, especially flightless species, are extinct or seriously threatened by introduced predators. Habitat loss has caused declines in many continental species.
—*Donna L. Dittmann, Steven W. Cardiff*

Genera *Crex, Coturnicops, Laterallus*

CORN CRAKE *Crex crex*

Once a regular vagrant, it has been recorded only 5 times in N.A. since 1928, most recently in 2002. Secretive, it prefers dense grass, runs to avoid danger, and is not easily flushed. Monotypic. L 10.8–12" (27–30 cm) **Identification** Relatively large. Bill stubby, pale. Shoulders chestnut, back feathers blackish brown broadly edged buff, flanks banded reddish brown and buff. **MALE:** Gray breast and superciliary stripe. **FEMALE AND IMMATURE:** Similar, browner, less gray on face, breast. **Similar Species** Yellow Rail smaller with white-tipped secondaries, lacks chestnut shoulders. **Voice** Loud, rasping *crex crex*. **Status & Distribution** Common but increasingly localized. BREEDING: Meadows; northern Europe to Siberia. MIGRATION: In fall, Aug.–Nov. In spring, late Mar.–May. WINTER: Eastern Africa. VAGRANT: Casual/accidental (fall), northeastern N.A. coast (Baffin I. to MD); recent records in Bermuda and Guadeloupe. **Population** Vulnerable.

YELLOW RAIL *Coturnicops noveboracensis*

This secretive and mysterious species is rarely found away from dense cover and is not easily flushed, preferring to run and hide. It relies on its cryptic plumage for camouflage. It is seen in fall, when rice combines flush rails. Polytypic (2 ssp.; nominate in N.A., also has been considered conspecific with Swinhoe's Rail, *C. exquisitus* of Japan, eastern Russia, China). L 6.4–7.6" (16–19 cm)

Identification ADULT: Small. Sexes similar. Back feathers black broadly edged yellow-buff with narrow white terminal crossbars. Crown and nape blackish, dark stripe below eye. Broad supercilium; rest of face, with darker brown feather tips. Throat and belly white, sides and flanks black with narrow white bars; undertail coverts rufous. White distal portions of coverts and trailing edge of inner wing extensively white. Nonbreeding males and most females have blackish olive bill; breeding males, some breeding females have paler yellow bills; legs brownish to greenish. IMMATURE: Darker; face, neck, breast, and sides less buffy, with heavier blackish brown and white barring, white spots on crown.

Similar Species Sora similar in shape but larger and underwing barred with gray; no white in secondaries. Corn Crake much larger, no white in secondaries. Black Rail smaller, more uniformly dark, grayer, no white in wing.

Voice Sounds like 2 stones tapped together, *tic-tic tic-tic-tic,* 4 or 5 notes repeated. Usually vocalizes only on breeding grounds, mainly at night.

Status & Distribution Uncommon, local. BREEDING: Sedge- or grass-dominated fresh water or brackish marsh. MIGRATION: Nocturnal. Spring: Apr.–May. Fall: Sept.–Nov. WINTER: Marsh, grassy fields, and rice fields along S. Atlantic and Gulf coastal plains, NC to TX. VAGRANT: Casual/accidental from southeastern AK and BC south to CA, AZ, NM; also Labrador, NF, Bermuda, Bahamas.

Population Probably declining; secretive behavior complicates estimates.

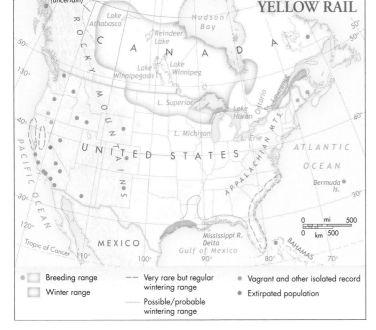

juvenile

YELLOW RAIL

Breeding range
Winter range

–– Very rare but regular wintering range

······ Possible/probable wintering range

Vagrant and other isolated record

Extirpated population

BLACK RAIL *Laterallus jamaicensis*

Our tiniest rail is rare, local, and usually only heard. If flushed, it flies a short distance then drops out of sight. Best chance of viewing this secretive bird is during unusually high tides in some California salt marshes, when flooding forces rails to marsh edge. Polytypic. L 4–6" (10–15 cm)
Identification ADULT: Generally dark gray, with short black bill, red eyes, dark brown hind crown, dark chestnut nape, white speckling on upperparts, white barring on flanks, lower belly, undertail coverts, and underwing coverts.

Female paler gray throat and breast. IMMATURE: Similar to female but more brownish, less dorsal spotting.
Geographic Variation Five subspecies, 2 breed in N.A., 3 others resident in S.A. Smaller, more brightly colored *coturniculus* occurs year-round in California, southwestern Arizona, and northwestern Baja California. Larger, duller nominate occurs in eastern U.S., eastern Mexico, and C.A.
Similar Species Downy chicks of other rail species are small and uniformly black, but have disproportionately large legs and feet. Yellow Rail, almost as small, is blackish above but more patterned and paler below, with extensive white on wing. Sora larger, paler, browner, with stouter, paler bill, and extensive white on leading edge of wing and under wing. Small passerines may look rail-like in certain situations.
Voice *Kik-kee-do, kik-kee-derr,* or *kik-kik-kee-do,* mainly at night during breeding season.
Status & Distribution Rare to locally uncommon. BREEDING: Shallow freshwater or salt marshes, wet meadows. MIGRATION: In spring, arrives Mid-Mar.–mid-May. Departs early Sept.–early Nov., peak mid-Sept.–mid Oct. WINTER: Local along southern Atlantic and Gulf coasts, NC to TX, casual north to NJ and south to Greater Antilles (may breed Cuba), C.A., S.A. VAGRANT: Rare to casual inland in eastern N.A. north to CO, MN, Great Lakes region, ON, QC, ME, CT, RI; accidental to Bermuda.
Population Declining. Generally considered threatened, but the species is endangered in Arizona.

TYPICAL RAILS *Genus Rallus*

Considerable size variation exists among the 6 New World species, but all have relatively long, slender, slightly decurved bills and rusty breasts; most have barred flanks. All have adapted to a semiaquatic existence and are often seen foraging along habitat edge.

VIRGINIA RAIL *Rallus limicola*

Almost as widespread as the Sora, the Virginia is seen less frequently. It forages in dense vegetation. Polytypic (4 ssp.; nominate in N.A.). L 8.8–10.8" (22–27 cm)
Identification ADULT: Sexes similar. Relatively small with reddish-brown eye, long reddish bill, reddish legs, and rusty chest and belly. Crown and nape brown, contrasting with gray cheek. Upperparts brown edged with rufous. Throat white, flanks black barred

white, undertail coverts mottled black, rusty, and white. JUVENILE: Similar but duller above, underparts extensively mottled blackish or brownish, legs and iris brown. IMMATURE: Like adult but buffy-white on lower breast and belly.
Similar Species King and Clapper Rails generally similar but much larger.
Voice Year-round, descending series of *oink* notes; breeding calls include *kid-kid-kiDik-kiDik-kiDik-kiDik.*
Status & Distribution Common. BREED-

ING: Primarily freshwater marsh, less frequently brackish or salt marsh. Other populations resident in southern Mexico, C.A., northwestern S.A. MIGRATION: Mostly migratory. Arrives in spring Mar.–May, peak early Apr.–early May. Departs mid-Aug.–Nov., peak mid-Sept.–mid Oct. WINTER: Western and southern U.S. south to central Mexico; regular in salt marshes. VAGRANT: Rare to Bermuda, casual/accidental to AK, Cuba, and Greenland.
Population Possibly declining. Game bird in many states.

juvenile

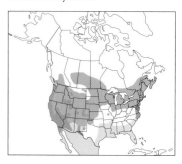

CLAPPER RAIL *Rallus longirostris*

crepitans

scottii

yumanensis

levipes

The clapper call is a familiar sound of our coastal salt marshes, and this large rail can occasionally be observed foraging for crabs, other invertebrates, and seeds along the edges of tidal channels, mudflats, or ditches. It prefers to run into vegetation rather than fly when startled, but will readily flush, fly a short distance with legs dangling, then drop back into cover. It swims across deeper tidal channels. Polytypic. L 12.8–16.4" (32–41 cm)

Identification ADULT: Sexes similar in plumage, but males about 20–25 percent larger. Bill long, dark, with paler reddish to brown base of lower mandible (brighter on male), eye reddish brown, legs long and brownish red to gray. Dark brown crown and nape, brown to blackish back feathers edged with gray, olive, or brown. Cheek gray, sometimes bordered brownish gray. Throat white. Color of breast varies geographically from buff to deep rufous to olive-gray. Flanks and undertail coverts gray to black, heavily barred with white. Plumage is darker and brighter in fall when fresh, becomes progressively paler and duller into spring and summer. Some subspecies exhibit considerable individual color variation, referred to as olive and brown morphs to describe color of feather edges on back. JUVENILE: Similar to adult but center of breast more extensively white contrasting with darker gray sides, white barring on flanks less conspicuous, and underparts varyingly mottled with blackish gray feather tips. Fully feathered juveniles can be considerably smaller than adults.

Geographic Variation Up to 21 subspecies can be broken into 3 groups based on size and coloration. Four western subspecies included in *obsoletus* group have richly colored plumage, bright rufescent brown underparts, and a brownish gray cheek; three in U.S. include California Clapper Rail, *obsoletus* of San Francisco Bay (largest); the slightly smaller Lightfooted Clapper Rail, *levipes,* of coastal southern CA south into Baja California; and the Yuma Clapper Rail, *yumanensis,* of the lower Colorado River drainage and Imperial Valley (dullest of western group). The *crepitans* group includes 12 subspecies, 5 in the U.S., which intergrade with each other along the Atlantic and Gulf coasts: Northern Clapper Rail, *crepitans,* of the northern Atlantic Coast from New England to North Carolina (grayest on chest and back); Wayne Clapper Rail, *waynei,* of the southern Atlantic Coast from North Carolina to northeastern Florida (slightly smaller and darker); Florida Clapper Rail, *scottii,* along most of the mainland Florida coast (darkest upperparts); Mangrove Clapper Rail, *insularum,* of the Florida Keys (smaller, paler); and Louisiana Clapper Rail, *saturatus,* of the Gulf Coast from western Florida to Mexico (more rufescent below and most similar to King Rail). Remaining subspecies of the *crepitans* group occur in eastern Mexico, northern C.A., and the West Indies. Some authors consider the Clapper to be conspecific with the King; hybrids have been reported on the Atlantic and Gulf Coasts. Some subspecies formerly recognized as full species.

Similar Species Virginia Rail smaller and more delicate even compared to half-size juvenile Clapper. Some Clapper subspecies very similar to King Rail, but King larger, overall browner, has browner cheeks, back edgings, and brighter chestnut wing coverts.

Voice CALL: Most typically a series of ten or more loud *kek* notes, accelerating then slowing (King Rail similar but series usually deeper, shorter, slower, more evenly spaced); also shorter *kek-kek-kek,* other squawks, grunts. Calls day or night, but most vocal at dawn and dusk during breeding season.

Status & Distribution Uncommon to common. YEAR-ROUND: Coastal salt marsh, mangroves; freshwater marsh in interior Southwest. Also patchily distributed West Indies, Mexico, C.A., northern S.A. MIGRATION: Northern Atlantic Coast populations at least partially migratory, generally scarce in winter north of NC. Arrives north Atlantic Coast mid-Mar.–Apr. Departs late Aug.–Nov. Other populations considered nonmigratory, but individuals will undertake erratic post-breeding movements. VAGRANT: Western subspecies casual to south-central AZ, Farallon Is., extreme northwestern coastal CA, and inland away from breeding areas. In East casual to NE, TN, WV, central VA, western PA, central NY, NH, VT, ME, NB, PE, NS, NF, and Bermuda.

Population Western subspecies is endangered. Eastern populations are stable but have experienced declines, vulnerable to wetlands loss. It is a game bird in many states.

Atlantic and Gulf Coast Clapper Rail Versus King Rail

Along the Atlantic and Gulf coasts, Clapper and King Rails breed in close proximity. The King prefers freshwater habitats; the Clapper prefers salt or brackish marshes. Vegetation type offers a clue to salinity and, thus, which rail is likely to occur at a site. Grasses, sedges, and especially cattails are indicators of the freshwater haunts of the King. Mangroves, cordgrass, needle rush, and pickerel weed are the preferred saline habitats of the Clapper. In some areas the King inhabits one side of a road and the Clapper the other. In addition, in some areas King Rails breed in brackish marsh, and the occasional Clapper has been found in freshwater marsh. Wanderers/migrants of both species can be found away from typical habitat, and hybrids have been reported from DE to LA. Atlantic Coast *crepitans* (New England to northeastern NC) and *waynei* (southeastern NC to northeastern FL) are largely gray breasted, and more easily distinguished from the King. However, Gulf Coast subspecies *insularum* (FL Keys), *scottii* (most of FL coast), and *saturatus* (central and western Gulf Coast) have cinnamon brown chests and are more similar to the King. Some individuals are grayer chested like Atlantic Clappers; whether grayness is age-related or a plumage polymorphism is not known. Considering the potential for individual or regional variation, identifications should be based on a combination of characters. The King averages larger, more brightly colored, and overall browner. The Clapper averages smaller, grayer, and shows a greater degree of individual, seasonal, and regional vari-

"Gulf Coast" Clapper Rail (TX, Apr.)

King Rail (TX)

ation. The King's bright chestnut upperwing coverts stand out compared to the browner coverts of the Clapper. The pale edges of back feathers are more consistently brown in the King and gray to olive in the Clapper. The Clapper has extensively gray cheeks; gray is more limited in the King. The King tends to have a cleaner white throat, sharply contrasting with rusty breast; the Clapper averages less contrast. Adult Kings never have grayish wash on sides and across the breast that is typical of Clappers. Juveniles of both species grayer below and almost identical on the underparts, but dorsal coloration is similar to adult. The barring pattern on the flanks is variable between species, individuals, and ages, and although the King tends to be more conspicuously barred black and white, some individuals are duller. Dark and pale morphs have been described for the King, darker birds with more olive-edged back feathers, which could

further complicate identification. Consider lighting, distance, and seasonal changes in plumage that occur due to wear and fading. Rails occupying "wrong" habitat for their appearance or lacking definitive identification characters are sometimes referred to as "Cling" Rails. First generation hybrids intermediate in size and coloration would be difficult to distinguish with certainty from the Clapper. Variation shown by the Clapper may be the result of introgression with the King, and some authorities consider them conspecific. Much needs to be learned about the extent of hybridization and range of normal variation within these species. ∎

KING RAIL *Rallus elegans*

The largest rail is generally secretive and heard more often than seen, but is observed relatively frequently for a rail. King Rails occasionally forage in the open along marsh edge or in roadside ditches; in spring and summer

parents venture into the open with their downy chicks in tow. If startled, individuals run with head lowered in line with the body and disappear into vegetation. The birds flush when nearly underfoot, fly with legs dangling,

then drop into vegetation out of sight. Polytypic (3 ssp.; nominate in N.A.). L 15.2–19.2" (38–48 cm)

Identification ADULT: Sexes similar in plumage but males average larger. Very large, heavy rail, but there is considerable individual size variation. Bill long with yellowish orange base, eye orange-brown, legs and feet grayish brown to grayish olive. Plumage overall rusty-brown in coloration, mantle heavily streaked brownish black and edged with brown to olive. Upperwing coverts conspicuously chestnut on folded wing. Crown dark brown, cheek mostly brown or with a small patch of gray. Throat white contrasting with bright rusty breast, belly buffy white, flanks blackish to dark brown

juvenile

barred with white, undertail coverts mottled dark brown and white. Plumage is brightest in fall, and becomes much duller, paler, and abraded by spring and summer. JUVENILE: Heavily mottled with gray below and is darker and less conspicuously striped above. Downy chick like the Clapper Rail, black with a bicolored bill, pale at tip and around nostril.

Similar Species Virginia Rail superficially similar but much smaller and has pure gray face. Briefly glimpsed chicks might be confused with the Black Rail, but have disproportionately large legs and feet and downy plumage. (For separation from Clapper Rail, see sidebar p. 166 and Clapper Rail account.)

Voice CALL: Most typically a series of 10 or fewer loud *kek* notes, fairly evenly spaced; also shorter *kek-kek-kek,* other squawks, grunts. Calls day or night, but most vocal at dawn and dusk during breeding season.

Status & Distribution Common. BREEDING: Freshwater and brackish marshes, rice fields. Other subspecies are resident in Cuba and interior central Mexico. MIGRATION: Nocturnal, partial migrant. Spring: Apr.–May. Fall: Sept.–Oct. WINTER: Mainly near Gulf Coast, coast of eastern Mexico south to Veracruz, and Cuba, occasionally farther north within the breeding range; typically absent from areas with regular freezes. VAGRANT: Casual/accidental west and north to western TX, southeastern NM, CO, ND, MN, ME, MB, ON, QC, NB, NS, NF, and PE.

Population Serious declines in northern breeding range since mid-1900s blamed on combinations of habitat degradation, pesticides, accidental trapping (for furbearers), and collision mortality during migration and with vehicles. Vulnerable in Canada; considered endangered, threatened, or of concern in 12 states. Game bird in many eastern states.

Genus *Porzana*

SORA *Porzana carolina*

The calls of the Sora are some of the most familiar sounds of the freshwater marsh, and with patience or luck one can occasionally be observed as it ventures into the open to forage along marsh edges or the shoreline of a ditch, walking deliberately with bobbing head and cocked tail. The Sora runs to avoid danger, but will also flush when nearly under foot, fly a short distance, and then drop from sight into dense vegetation. Soras commonly cross deeper channels by swimming and will occasionally even forage coot-style in the water. Monotypic. L 7.6–10" (19–25 cm)

Identification ADULT: Stubby yellow bill with black around base and on throat to center of upper breast. Breast gray barred white, belly white, sides barred white, brown, and black, undertail coverts buffy-white. Crown and nape rich brown with black center, contrasting with gray face and neck, and white spot behind eye. Rest of upperparts brown, back and tail with black feather centers and white fringes. In flight, leading edge of inner wing conspicuously white, underwing coverts barred gray and white. Legs and feet yellowish-green, toes long. Female similar but bill duller, black on face and throat less extensive, slightly smaller. JUVENILE: Paler with white throat, buffier face and breast, lacks black on face, bill darker; immature gradually acquires black on face and throat, and gray on neck and breast.

Similar Species Duller, buffier juvenile superficially similar to Yellow Rail.

Sora is larger, upperparts have white streaks (not buffy stripes and white bars) and in flight, lacks white on trailing edge of wing. Black Rail smaller, uniformly darker, with all-dark bill.

Voice Year-round, descending whinny, *Whee-hee-hee-hee-hee-hee,* and a sharp *keek*; breeding, an upslurred *soo-rah.*

Status & Distribution Common. BREEDING: Shallow freshwater marsh; occasionally brackish or salt marsh. MIGRATION: In spring, late Mar.–mid-May, peak mid-Apr.–early May. In fall, late July–early Nov., peak Sept.–Oct. WINTER: Vegetated shallow wetlands, CA and southern Atlantic coasts and extreme southern U.S. to northern S.A. VAGRANT: Accidental east-central AK, Queen Charlotte Is., southern Labrador, Bermuda, Greenland, western Europe, and Morocco.

Population Generally stable, but declining in central U.S. from habitat loss. Game bird over much of the East.

Genera Neocrex and Pardirallus

PAINT-BILLED CRAKE *Neocrex erythrops*

This secretive and poorly known vagrant from South America has been encountered only twice in North America, both times in the 1970s during winter. Polytypic. L 7.2–8" (18–20 cm)
Identification ADULT: Superficially like a small, uniformly colored Sora. Most of upperparts dark olive-brown. Forecrown, supercilium, and face gray. Throat whitish, rest of underparts dark gray; sides, flanks, undertail coverts, and underwing coverts barred white. Bill yellow-green with bright orange base, legs red. JUVENILE: Duller.
Geographic Variation Two subspecies, nominate *erythrops* of coastal Peru and the Galapagos Is. is a vagrant to TX. A Virginia specimen is tentatively identified as *olivascens,* patchily distributed in S.A. east of the Andes; darker, with less white on throat.
Similar Species Sora more patterned above and below, lacks orange base to bill, has yellow-green legs. Black Rail smaller, has dark bill and legs, chestnut nape, white spots on upperparts.
Voice Guttural, froglike *qur'r'r'rk,* or *pip* notes.
Status & Distribution Poorly understood, secretive; abundance varies locally from rare to common. Also recorded from Costa Rica and Panama, but status unclear. YEAR-ROUND: Marsh, pasture, rice fields, overgrown drainage ditches, damp thickets in scrub or woodland. MIGRATION: No clear migratory pattern. VAGRANT: Accidental in TX, VA.
Population Unknown.

SPOTTED RAIL *Pardirallus maculatus*

This amazing tropical rail vagrant was detected in the U.S. twice in the 1970s. Polytypic (2 ssp.; northern *insolitus* in N.A.). L 10–11.2" (25–28 cm)
Identification ADULT: Somewhat larger and heavier than Virginia Rail. Upperparts blackish brown with white spots, head and breast blacker with white spots, remainder of underparts black banded with white. Bill long, slender, greenish yellow with red spot at base of lower mandible; eyes, legs, and feet red. JUVENILE: Polymorphic. All have duller legs and bill, brown eyes. Dark morph is plain dark brown above, sooty gray below; pale morph has pale grayish-brown throat and breast with fine white bars on breast; barred morph has gray throat with white spots, breast and belly heavily barred white.
Similar Species Virtually unmistakable based on size, plumage pattern, soft parts colors. Beware juvenile Virginia, King, and Clapper, which have varying amounts of blackish or gray plumage.
Voice Sharp *geek,* a screech preceded by a grunt, and a series of pumping *wumph* sounds, like a starting motor.
Status & Distribution Common. YEAR-ROUND: Vegetated wetlands; patchily distributed southern Mexico to Costa Rica, Cuba, Jamaica, Hispaniola, and Colombia to Argentina. VAGRANT: Accidental in PA (Nov. 12, 1976), TX (Aug. 9, 1977), Juan Fernandez Is. off Chile, and at sea in S. Atlantic off Brazil.
Population Unknown.

Genus Porphyrio

PURPLE SWAMPHEN *Porphyrio porphyrio*

First detected in 1996, this species is quickly spreading in southern Florida after escaping from captivity. Some censuses have exceeded 100 individuals. Polytypic (13 ssp.). L 18–20" (45–50 cm)
Identification ADULT: Sexes similar, females somewhat smaller. Unmistakable. Suggestive a huge Purple Gallinule, with thick, reddish bill, broad reddish frontal shield, red eye, massive reddish legs. Body plumage generally purplish blue, lower throat, upper breast paler greenish blue, sides of head, neck, upper throat gray, tinged light blue. Undertail coverts white. JUVENILE: Duller, grayer plumage; bill, frontal shield, and legs darker grayish.
Geographic Variation Most Florida individuals resemble gray-headed *poliocephalus* group, occurring from Turkey to southern Asia, which includes subspecies *poliocephalus, caspius,* and *seistanicus.* Some Florida individuals have bluer heads and may represent other subspecies.
Similar Species Adult Purple Gallinule smaller with azure frontal shield and yellow legs.
Voice Dull moans or mooing.
Status & Distribution Common in native range. FL status uncertain, but locally uncommon to fairly common. YEAR-

adult
poliocephalus

ROUND: Shorelines of artificial lakes and natural marshlands.
Population Initially increased dramatically; current trend uncertain.

PURPLE GALLINULE *Porphyrio martinica*

This colorful rail prefers floating or emergent vegetation, using long toes for balance or climbing. More secretive than the Common Moorhen, it spends less time in the water. Monotypic. L 13" (33 cm)
Identification ADULT: Sexes are similar. Purplish-blue head and underparts. Upperparts green, wing coverts turquoise. Undertail coverts bright white. Bill red with yellow tip; frontal shield pale blue; legs, feet yellow. JUVENILE: Upperparts brownish to greenish, underparts buffy, whiter on throat, belly, undertail. Bill greenish brown; legs, feet dull greenish. Downy chick black, legs and feet dark, bill red, tip black, black and pink subterminal bands.
Similar Species Coots and Common Moorhen blackish gray, larger, spend more time on water. Purple Swamphen much larger with red shield and legs.
Voice Sharp *puckk;* cackling, grunting.
Status & Distribution Common. BREEDING: Freshwater marsh with dense floating or emergent vegetation. Breeds casually north to IL, OH, MD, DE. MIGRATION: Primarily a trans-Gulf spring migrant, late Mar.–May, peak mid-Apr.–early May; occurs rarely north of breeding range. Migrates in fall late Aug.–Oct., peak Sept., stragglers into Nov. WINTER: Primarily areas of year-round occurrence, peninsular FL, eastern and central-western Mexico to S.A.; also, northern Yucatan Peninsula, northern C.A. Rare Gulf Coast. VAGRANT: Many records well north of eastern breeding range to southern Canada; casual to Southwest, accidental to U.K.
Population Stable. Game bird in some states, but most depart before season.

juvenile

Genus Gallinula

COMMON MOORHEN *Gallinula chloropus*

Almost ducklike, Common Moorhens typically forage while swimming, picking at vegetation. Sometimes Common Moorhens are tame and confiding; family groups will feed in the open. Polytypic (12 ssp.; *cachinnans* in N.A.). L 12.8–14" (32–35 cm)
Identification ADULT: Sexes are similar. Head, neck, and breast are blackish gray, underparts paler gray with white stripe down side, rest of upperparts dark brown. Undertail coverts black and white. Bill is red tipped with yellow, frontal shield and eyes are red. Legs yellow with basal red patch. JUVENILE: Paler gray below, throat and belly white, color retained into winter. Bill, legs are greenish. Downy chick is black, with yellow and orange head plumes; frontal shield is red, orange-yellow bill is red tipped.
Similar Species See American Coot, Purple Gallinule.
Voice Cackling *ka-ka-ka-ka-ka-kee-kree-kree-kree-kree,* rasping *krraaaaaaa,*

breeding

juvenile

winter

a sharp *puck,* or softer *took-took-took-took-puk.* Noisy.
Status & Distribution Common; nearly worldwide distribution. BREEDING: Fresh to slightly brackish marshes with emergent vegetation. MIGRATION: Partial migrant, mainly in East. In spring, mid-Mar.–mid-May. In fall, mid-Aug.–early Nov. WINTER: Generally vacates eastern N.A. to southeastern coast and south. VAGRANT: Casual in southern Canada beyond breeding range; accidental in Greenland.
Population Generally stable, but threatened or of concern in some northern states due to local declines. Considered a game bird in many states.

COOTS Genus *Fulica*

AMERICAN COOT *Fulica americana*

immature

variant

Whether swimming on a lake, grazing on a golf course, diving for submerged vegetation, or wading along a pond, this comical, chickenlike rail is one of our most familiar waterbirds. Coots have to run along the surface to take flight, but once in the air flight is strong and fast. Can occur in large flocks. Polytypic (2 ssp.; nominate in N.A., sometimes considered conspecific with Andean Coot). L 12.8–17.2" (32–43 cm)

Identification ADULT: Sexes similar, males slightly larger. No other species has a short, whitish, chickenlike bill, overall gray coloration and, in flight, white trailing edge to secondaries. Head and neck black, body somewhat paler blackish gray, center of belly usually paler, undertail coverts black with white outer patches. Bill and frontal shield mostly white with brownish-red partial ring on bill and spot in center of frontal shield. Size and coloration of frontal shield variable: Some individuals have more yellowish white shield without darker center. Eyes red, legs and lobed toes greenish yellow. JUVENILE: Duller and paler, with more whitish underparts. Bill dusky, legs more olive. Downy chick is black above, dark gray below, with stiff curly orange and yellow fluff on forehead, chin, and lores, fleshy red skin on crown, blue skin above eye, and bright red bill with black tip.

Similar Species Immature Common Moorhen similar but smaller, more slender, has white stripe along sides, browner back, and more slender bill. Caribbean Coot (*F. caribaea*) of West Indies more uniformly blackish below, has larger, broader, yellowish-white frontal shield. Some American Coots lack brownish red center in frontal shield and may suggest Caribbean Coot based on coloration of frontal shield alone. Caribbean Coot, sometimes regarded as conspecific, not satisfactorily documented in our area. European Coot similar but averages larger, overall blacker, and has entirely black undertail coverts.

Voice Assortment of grunting and cackling notes, including an emphatic *puck,* crowing *croooah,* and *punk-unk-punk-uh-punk-unk-uh.* Vocal day or night.

Status & Distribution Abundant. BREEDING: Freshwater wetlands with emergent vegetation, occasionally slightly brackish marshes. Breeds south through most of Mexico and locally in C.A., Colombia, and West Indies. MIGRATION: Northern populations migratory; others resident, may migrate during severe winters. Spring: Feb.–May. Fall: Late Aug.–Nov. WINTER: Northern interior populations move to coasts and southern half of continent. Occurs on brackish estuaries in winter. VAGRANT: Rare in HI; casual to western AK, northern and eastern Canada, Greenland, Iceland, and Ireland.

Population Currently stable, but has declined historically. Considered a game bird in many states.

EURASIAN COOT *Fulica atra*

This vagrant to the far northern corners of North America looks and acts very much like our American Coot. Polytypic (4 ssp. ; nominate in N.A.). L 14.4–15.2" (36–38 cm)

Identification ADULT: Larger than the American Coot. Upperparts, head, chest are black with white trailing edge to secondaries. Remainder of underparts are slightly paler grayish black, undertail coverts entirely black. Bill and frontal shield are white; legs and feet greenish. JUVENILE: Similar, but much paler below.

Similar Species The American Coot averages smaller, is less uniformly blackish with more head-body contrast, has white on undertail coverts, partial dark ring on bill, and usually has a dark spot on its frontal shield.

Voice *Kowk* and double *kek-wock.*

Status & Distribution Common and widespread in Old World. BREEDING: Freshwater marshes. MIGRATION: Northern Eurasian populations migratory. In fall, migrates mid-Aug.–Nov. In spring, migrates late Feb.–May. VAGRANT: Casual to Greenland, accidental in fall and winter in AK, QC, Labrador, and NF.

Population Stable.

LIMPKINS Family Aramidae

Limpkin (FL)

This family consists of a single large, wading-type species, limited in North America to Florida. The Limpkin superficially resembles herons and ibises, but it is only distantly related to them—its closest relatives are the cranes.

Structure The bird has a long neck, bill, and legs, a short tail, and long, rounded wings.

Behavior The Limpkin is loosely colonial, perhaps in part due to clumped distribution of prey abundance or availability. Active throughout the day and night, it forages by slowly walking in water; prey is detected either visually or by contact with bill. It nests in a variety of freshwater sites, ranging from mounds of vegetation built in marshes to stick nests built high in trees. Despite its name, the Limpkin does not limp; rather, it walks slowly while flicking its tail. It flies with its neck fully extended and held below the body plain, creating a distinctive hunch-backed profile. Its flight style—quick upstrokes followed by slower downstrokes—is similar to cranes. When flying short distances, the Limpkin dangles its legs below the body, but in sustained flight it draws the legs up.

Distribution The Limpkin is restricted to the New World, primarily the tropics.

Taxonomy The Limpkin's taxonomy is much debated. It is currently placed within the order Gruiformes, which comprises 10 families, including rails and cranes. The Limpkin formerly was considered 2 species: One found in North America, Central America, and the Caribbean and the other in South America.

Conservation Populations in Florida are apparently stable; status elsewhere is unknown. —*Bill Pranty*

Genus *Aramus*

LIMPKIN *Aramus guarauna*

This Florida species feeds nearly exclusively on freshwater mollusks, primarily apple snails and clams. The tip of the Limpkin's lower mandible is curved to the right to facilitate extracting snails from their shells. Polytypic (4 ssp.; *pictus* in N.A.). L 26" (66 cm)

Identification The Limpkin is a large, brown, heronlike bird with dense streaking over much of its body. The long, slender, slightly downcurved bill is yellow with a blackish culmen and tip. ADULT: The sexes look similar—wholly dark brown, paler on face, chin, and throat. Most feathers, especially those on the neck, have white markings; those on the upper back and upperwing coverts show large white triangles. Dark eyes; blackish legs and feet. JUVENILE: White markings are narrower, appearing more streaked than spotted.

Similar Species American Bittern adults have a conspicuous dark malar streak, and they have more pointed wings in flight. Immature night-herons have orange or red eyes, shorter, straight bills, shorter necks, and yellow legs. *Plegadis* ibises have wholly darker plumage.

Voice Loud, varied, and distinctive; mostly by male except when breeding pairs duet. Most common calls are a drawn-out *kreow* and a *kow.*

Status & Distribution In the U.S., restricted to FL, where generally sedentary. Uncommon and local. VAGRANT: Casual throughout Southeast and accidental along the Atlantic and Gulf states from TX to NJ and NS.

Population Hunting nearly extirpated the Florida population by the early 1900s. The population has since recovered to about 5,000 pairs and is apparently stable, despite continuing wetland loss. Recent extirpation from the state's eastern panhandle is unexplained and alarming.

CRANES Family Gruidae

Sandhill Cranes (NM, Oct.)

Cranes are evocative of wild and open habitats in temperate regions around the world. In North America they present limited identification challenges, although distance and lighting can play into determining features accurately. Note overall plumage coloration and contrasts, details of head pattern, and the extent and contrast of any black on the remiges (best seen in flight); with experience, voice can be useful, but be aware that vocal variation can also be related to age and, in Sandhill Cranes, to subspecies.

Structure Cranes are large, heavy-bodied, and long-necked. They have a distinct tertial bulge, or bustle, which is conspicuous when they stand. Their wings are long and broad, with 10 primaries and 18 to 21 secondaries (including 4–5 elongated tertials); their short, square tails have 12 rectrices. Their bills are moderately long, straight, and pointed, and their legs long and sturdy, with unwebbed feet. Males average 5 to 10 percent larger than females. Juveniles do not attain full growth until nearly a year old; they often look noticeably smaller than adults.

Behavior Cranes are terrestrial and social birds of open habitats, where they pick and probe for food in soil and marshes; they are not known to perch in trees. Their flight is graceful. With their necks and legs outstretched and holding their wings mostly above the body plane, they fly with stiff wingbeats with a relatively quick and slightly jerked upstroke. Migrating cranes are diurnal and often fly high, typically in V-formations or well-spaced lines, and they frequently glide and sail on fairly flat wings, without flapping. Cranes are perennially monogamous; courtship involves spectacular leaping and "dancing" by pairs and groups, accompanied by much calling. Extended parental care means that families remain together for 9 to 10 months, through migration and winter. Although cranes nest in territorial pairs, they form large flocks in migration and winter, when they commute from safe roost sites to feeding areas. They often feed in agricultural land, and roost on islands or gravel bars in lakes and rivers. Their far-carrying calls are loud cries with a distinctive

rolled or throaty quality, sometimes likened to bugling. Cranes show strong site fidelity to their migration staging grounds and to their wintering grounds.

Plumage Their plumage is gray to white overall, usually with darker to blackish primaries, and often with variable rusty blotching on the neck and upperparts. Adults have bare forecrowns patterned red and black; juveniles have mostly cinnamon-brown feathered heads and necks. Adult prebasic molts occur mostly on or near the breeding grounds, whereas first-cycle preformative molts take place on nonbreeding grounds. Cranes have high wing loading and shed their primaries synchronously to become flightless for a short period—adults do this while nesting; prebreeding immatures also molt their remiges during the summer months, in remote areas with adequate food. Adult plumage aspect is attained by the second prebasic molt at about 1 year of age, although second-year birds are often distinguishable by their less developed and duller bare crowns and the presence of a few retained and worn juvenal feathers, such as secondaries.

Distribution Cosmopolitan, with both resident and migratory species.

Taxonomy Worldwide, there are 15 species in 4 genera, in North America, 3 species (2 breeding, 1 vagrant from Asia) in 1 genus. Another species, the Demoiselle Crane (*Anthropoides virgo*), is hypothetical in North America.

Conservation Several crane species rank among the world's most threatened birds due to habitat modification, pollution, and hunting. Their faithfulness to traditional sites in migration and winter makes them particularly vulnerable to localized habitat loss (e.g., 80 percent of the mid-continent Sandhill Cranes stage in spring along Nebraska's Platte River). Most populations of Sandhill Crane are stable or increasing—some states even permit hunting. The Whooping Crane, however, is one of the rarest birds in North America; conservation measures have brought the species back from only 15 to 16 birds in the 1940s to more than 200 individuals today. —*Steve N. G. Howell*

Genus *Grus*

SANDHILL CRANE *Grus canadensis*

This crane, the only one seen in most of N.A., is largely unmistakable. Northern populations are migratory; the sight of many thousands staging in spring along the Platte River in Nebraska is one of the great wildlife spectacles in N.A. Polytypic (6 ssp.; 5 in N.A.). L 34–48" (86–122 cm) WS 73–90" (185–229 cm)

Identification ADULT: Gray overall with variable rusty blotching on neck, body, and upperwing coverts. Naked forecrown dark red; amber eyes. JUVENILE/ FIRST-WINTER: Feathered head, neck, and upperparts cinnamon to rusty; eyes dusky. Preformative molt changes over first winter, with forecrown becoming unfeathered midwinter through summer, neck and upperparts become var-

iegated with newer gray and rusty feathers. SECOND YEAR: After second prebasic molt in first summer, resembles an adult, but some may have a partially feathered forecrown and retain some abraded juvenal wing coverts or secondaries; eyes duller, dusky amber.

Geographic Variation Six subspecies generally recognized; only extremes separable in the field. See sidebar below.

Similar Species Unlikely to be confused. The Whooping Crane is larger and mostly white with contrasting black wing tips; in bright light, a Sandhill can look silvery, but not the true, egret white of the Whooping. The Common Crane averages larger and slightly heavier in build (esp. compared with the Lesser Sandhill). The adult has a broad white postocular stripe contrasting with black foreneck and crown; remiges are extensively black and contrast more strongly with pale-gray coverts. A juvenile/first-winter Common is best told from a Sandhill by its wing pattern. The Great Blue Heron, often referred to by non-birders as a "crane," is rare in groups of more than 10 to 20 birds, usually flies with its neck pulled in (occasionally outstretched for short periods), and flies with steady down-

beats of arched wings. A distant resting heron has a longer neck, often kinked; longer bill; and lacks a bustle; often alight in trees.

Voice Deep, far-carrying, rolled or rattled honking cries, *k'worrrh, grrrowh* or *grrrah-uu,* and *ah grruu.* In duets of mated pairs, female calls higher and shriller. Lessers average higher-pitched calls, *oohrr'ah* and *ooh'uhrr-rr,* but much variation. Immatures have very different, high, slightly reedy trills through at least first year; voice presumably "breaks" in first summer.

Status & Distribution BREEDING: Common to locally rare (Apr./May–Sept.), in a variety of open, undisturbed habitats in N.A., Siberia, and Cuba (where resident). MIGRATION: Mainly Feb.– Apr./May and Sept.–Nov. WINTER: Farmland and open country, usually near marshes and lakes in N.A. and south to northern Mexico. Very rare on East Coast. VAGRANT: Accidental in Eur. and HI; casual Japan.

Population The Mississippi *pulla* is on the federal list of endangered species; its population is 75 to 80 percent captive-produced.

adult

adult

juvenile

stained adult

Subspecies Variation in Sandhill Cranes

Six subspecies of Sandhill Crane are recognized, the northern populations being migratory and the southern ones resident. The smallest subspecies is nominate *canadensis*—the Lesser Sandhill or Little Brown Crane— which breeds from Alaska (and eastern Siberia) across Arctic Canada to Baffin Island, and winters mainly from California to Texas. All other populations (collectively termed Greater Sandhills) are larger, but *rowani* of Canada bridges the size difference between *canadensis* and the largest subspecies, *tabida,* which breeds from the prairie provinces through the West and the central interior. Two large subspecies are resident locally in the Southeast: the paler *pratensis* in southeast Georgia and

Florida, and the darker *pulla* in southern Mississippi.

The most obvious field distinction of the subspecies is their size, however, males of a given population average 5 to 10 percent larger than females. Furthermore, a large-scale study of mid-continent populations found traditional criteria for distinguishing *canadensis, rowani,* and *tabida* to be unsatisfactory. Therefore, although size differences among Sandhill subspecies can be quite striking, as within wintering flocks in California, only extremes may be safely identifiable. Other features of Lesser Sandhills—which have occurred casually east to the Atlantic Maritimes and Florida—are their blacker primaries and higher pitched calls relative to Greaters. ■

COMMON CRANE *Grus grus*

This Old World species, a vagrant to North America, is usually found with migrant Sandhill Cranes. Monotypic. L 44–51" (112–130 cm) WS 79–91" (201–231 cm)

juvenile

adult

adult

Identification Average larger and slightly heavier in build than the Sandhill Crane. Distinctive black-and-white head-and-neck pattern on adult; contrasting black remiges on all ages. ADULT: Gray overall, sometimes with pale cinnamon wash to chest and back. Naked crown black with red band behind eye; black foreneck, which contrasts with white auriculars and hind neck. JUVENILE/FIRST-WINTER: Feathered head, neck, and upperparts extensively cinnamon. Preformative molt changes appearance, with forecrown becoming unfeathered midwinter through summer, head and neck develop muted adult pat-tern. SECOND-YEAR: After second prebasic molt in first summer, resembles an adult, but some may have a partially feathered forecrown and retain some abraded juvenal wing coverts and remiges.

Similar Species See Sandhill Crane.

Voice The adult has far-carrying, trumpeting *krooh* and *krooah*, and a harsher *kraah*. The immature gives high reedy *peep* or *cheerp* calls through its first year.

Status & Distribution Eurasia. VAGRANT: Casual in migration and winter from AK to Great Plains and to IN and QC; of about 15 records, some may pertain to escapes. Mixed Common and Sandhill Crane pairs with hybrid offspring have been seen in eastern N.A.

WHOOPING CRANE *Grus americana* (E)

This large, tall-standing, white icon of endangered species management is best known on its winter grounds in coastal Texas. It breeds in northwestern Canada. Monotypic. L 50–55" (127–140 cm) WS 87" (221 cm)

Identification Occasional cinnamon-tipped upperwing coverts may be shown by birds of any age. ADULT: Large, white overall with naked red crown, black face, dark red malar. Has dark greenish bill with orange-yellow base; pale yellow eyes. Black wing tips, usually concealed at rest, contrast strikingly in flight. JUVENILE/FIRST-WINTER: Feathered head, neck, and upperparts are extensively cinnamon; eyes are olive. Protracted preformative molt changes appearance over first win-ter, with the forecrown becoming unfeathered from midwinter through summer, and the neck and upperparts variegated with growth of new white feathers. SECOND-YEAR: After second prebasic molt in first summer, the Whooping resembles an adult, but some second-winter birds may have a duller and partially feathered forecrown and retain some abraded juvenal wing coverts or secondaries. The eye averages duller, and the bill base is a duller yellow. Occasional cinnamon-tipped underwing coverts may be shown by birds of any age.

adult

juvenile

adult

Similar Species Unlikely to be confused. The Wood Stork, rare on the Whooping's winter grounds along the Texas coast, is smaller with a longer, decurved bill and a blackish head and neck; in flight it also has black secondaries and lacks the distinctive stiff upstroke of the crane's wingbeats. Be aware that in some light the Sandhill Crane can look silvery, almost white, but not the true, egret white of the Whooping Crane.

Voice Has loud, trumpeting or bugling cries that carry more than a mile: *k'raah-hu k'raah*, and *k'raah kah, kah*. These are higher pitched and less throaty than the Sandhill's cries. In duets of mated pairs, female calls are higher and shriller. Immatures have strikingly different, reedy whistles through at least their first winter; their voice presumably "breaks" in their first summer.

Status & Distribution North America, formerly wintered south to central Mexico. BREEDING: Rare (May–Sept.), in freshwater marshes found in boreal forests. MIGRATION: In spring, mainly late Mar–early May; in fall, mid-Sept.–mid-Nov. Flight path is along a 50- to 100-mile-wide corridor in a fairly direct route across the Great Plains between breeding and wintering grounds. Includes brief fall staging in southern SK, and irregular spring and fall stopovers in central NE, KS, and OK. Casual recently in migration west to southeast BC and CO, and east to IL and AR. WINTER: Restricted to estuarine marshes and shallow coastal bays in southeast TX, arriving late Oct.–mid-Nov., departing late Mar.–Apr.

Population Endangered (extirpated as a breeder in U.S.). The only self-sustaining population breeds in and around Wood Buffalo N.P., Alberta, and winters in coastal Texas in and around Aransas N.W.R. A cross-fostering attempt (using Sandhills) to establish a second migratory flock (breeding in the Rockies, wintering in NM) failed. An attempt to establish a resident population in Florida is still in progress.

THICK-KNEES Family Burhinidae

Double-striped Thick-knee

Thick-knees are large shorebirds with a unique cryptic plumage. Their crepuscular and nocturnal habits are also different from other shorebirds. They earned their name for rather thick intertarsal joints (knees).

Structure Thick-knees are large and heavily built like plovers. The head and eyes are large and the bill is stout and straight. Wings and tail are fairly long and the legs are exceptionally long.

Behavior Thick-knees are terrestrial and can run quite fast. Their typical gait is ploverlike with runs punctuated by abrupt stops. Flight is typically low over the ground with long legs projecting well beyond the tail. Wingbeats are silent and rapid. During the day they often sit or stand in the shade of a bush or tree, often with other thick-knees. Most of their activity is between dusk and dawn. They feed on insects, reptiles, and amphibians. Their nests are simple scrapes on the ground.

Plumage The sexes look alike, although the females average slightly smaller than the males. Their highly cryptic plumage camouflages them while they rest during the day. Juveniles are duller and can be separated from adults; adult plumage is achieved in approximately a year.

Distribution The Burhinidae family is composed of 9 species that are found primarily in the tropics and the Old World. Two species live along rivers or coastlines, while the other species typically nest in savanna or other grassland habitats.

Taxonomy There are 7 species in the genus *Burhinus*; 2 species are from the New World, but only 1 is found in the Northern Hemisphere. Thick-knees were once thought to be more closely related to the bustards (Otididae) of the Old World, and indeed they superficially resemble bustards, but skeletal, biochemical, and other studies have proved thick-knees to be shorebirds.

Conservation More information is needed, although some species might actually benefit from forest destruction as it opens habitats they could not otherwise use. BirdLife International lists 1 species as near threatened. —*Matthew T. Heindel*

Genus *Burhinus*

DOUBLE-STRIPED THICK-KNEE *Burhinus bistriatus*

The large head and eye, cryptic plumage, and unique behavior separate this accidental species from all other shorebirds. The terrestrial Double-striped Thick-knee can run quite fast; indeed, it seems to prefer running over taking flight. When it does fly, it is fast and low to the ground, with legs stretched behind the tail, showing white in the wings. The Double-striped becomes most active after sundown; its large eyes enable it to hunt in the dark for insects and other animals. Polytypic. L 16.5" (42 cm)

Identification The Double-striped has brown upperparts; a gray-brown face, neck, and chest; a white belly; and a brown tail. A dark lateral crown stripe borders the top edge of its bold white supercilium. ADULT: The brown upperparts are edged cinnamon or buff in fresh plumage. Its face, neck, and chest are gray-buff and streaked darker. Its yellow bill has a dark tip. The legs and eyes are bright yellow. JUVENILE: It is duller and grayer overall than an adult with greenish yellow legs. The streaking along the neck is narrower and darker. In addition to the white supercilium and dark lateral crown stripe, a dark stripe below the supercilium extends to the nape. FLIGHT: Striking. The upper wing is dark with the outer primaries marked with a short white bar. A second white bar covers the base of the inner primaries. The underwings are white.

Similar Species The Double-striped is unique and offers no identification challenge. Other congeners are unlikely to occur here naturally.

Voice CALL: A loud and far carrying, barking or cackling *kah-kah-kah.*

Status & Distribution Fairly common to common. BREEDING: Arid and semiarid savannas and grasslands from Mexico to Brazil. VAGRANT: One record for U.S. (Dec. 5, 1961, King Ranch, TX). A tame individual in AZ was determined to have been transplanted from Guatemala.

LAPWINGS AND PLOVERS Family Charadriidae

Black-bellied Plover (NY, Nov.)

Birds of wetlands, grasslands, and shorelines, plovers are gregarious. They are known for undertaking long migrations, but some species are sedentary.

Structure Plovers have medium to long legs, a rather sturdy frame, a short neck, and a round head. The bill is short; thick at the base, it usually narrows and then expands at the tip. Most plovers have long, pointed wings, excellent for rapid flight and energy-efficient for long migrations. The less migratory lapwings have more rounded wings. The pectoral muscles of plovers are relatively large; this fact and their ability to store large amounts of fat allow them to migrate long distances over the ocean.

Behavior Plovers hunt by running and abruptly stopping. After a few seconds, if no prey is taken, they run again. They pick small invertebrates from either wet or dry surfaces. They rarely perch; most plovers lack the hind toe that would help them do so. Flight is generally rapid for "true" plovers, but floppy in the broad-winged lapwings. The nest is typically a scrape, and the precocial young feed themselves. Some species have exaggerated "broken-wing" displays to distract potential predators. Quite gregarious, they form flocks for migration and roosting; however, they are very territorial during breeding season. Some species will defend feeding territories in winter and during migration.

Plumage Sexual differences are slight, with males usually brighter than females. Plovers typically molt their contour-body feathers in spring. Most species are in breeding plumage when they migrate, a few start in basic and molt on the way north. Many species have black facial markings, which are boldest during breeding season and may play a role in territorial displays. Most Arctic breeders start molting head feathers when incubation begins. Fall migrants usually show some signs of molt, but some species start migrating before much molt is evident. Juveniles do not distinctly differ from basic-plumaged adults, other than look far more crisp in early fall. Some first-summer birds look similar to breeding adults, whereas others look like basic-plumaged birds. First-years have varying migration strategies, sometimes remaining on the wintering grounds, moving north to an intermediate point, or, moving all the way to the breeding grounds.

Distribution Worldwide the family numbers more than 65 species—17 have been recorded in North America—inhabiting the tropics, mountains, deserts, and a variety of wetlands. Plovers are both resident and some of the longest-distance migrants in the avian world.

Taxonomy Generally the family is divided into lapwings and "true" plovers, but some work suggests that the 4 Arctic-breeding *Pluvialis* species belong in their own subfamily. The 10 genera include some rather unique plovers; however, North American birds are quite similar. There are few controversial placements at the species level. The largest remaining uncertainty surrounds the Snowy Plover, which is usually placed with the Kentish Plover of the Old World.

Conservation Historically, plovers were hunted in large numbers (with tens of thousands killed on a spring migration day); they are now protected. Today, loss or degradation of habitat and human disturbance are the biggest threats. —*Matthew T. Heindel*

LAPWINGS Genus *Vanellus*

Lapwings are generally more strikingly colored than other plovers. Their large, boldly marked, broad wings often have spurs at the carpal joint. While most lapwings are sedentary and found in the tropics, some species live at higher latitudes and are migratory. They are quite noisy when approached, particularly during breeding.

NORTHERN LAPWING *Vanellus vanellus*

A vagrant from Eurasia, the Northern Lapwing is closely tied to wet or dry fields. Monotypic. L 12.5" (32 cm)
Identification Black and white from a distance, it is actually quite colorful. The face, throat, and upper breast are black; the back has a glossy green sheen. Most of the auriculars and adjacent areas are gray; the remaining underparts are white, with pale cinnamon undertail coverts. The wings are broad with white tips, obviously rounded; the wing linings are white. Flight is slow and floppy. The white rump and base of tail contrast with the tail's black tip. The wispy but prominent crest is unique. NON-BREEDING ADULT: Most of the gray near the face of a breeding adult is replaced with buffy tones; the black is reduced and the throat is white. The upperparts have pale buff edges to the feathers. JUVENILE: It is duller than an adult, with a shorter crest, and bolder edges to the upperparts. Legs are gray.
Similar Species None. It is unique.
Voice CALL: A whistled *pee-wit*, with the second note higher.
Status & Distribution Eurasian species. Casual in the Northeast and Atlantic provinces in late fall and winter. Accidental elsewhere in the east and at other seasons; recorded south to FL, west to OH.

Genus *Pluvialis*

The largest North American plovers, members of this tundra-breeding group are plump and tall. Their breeding plumage is impressive—black bellies (less black in females) with white- or gold-spangled upperparts—whereas their basic plumage is dull (usually grayish or dingy brown). They feed in the typical plover fashion and usually fly and roost in flocks.

Judging Shape and Proportions on *Pluvialis* Plovers

With experience and caution, most juvenile *Pluvialis* plovers can be identified to species. Key characters to understand are bill size, leg length, and where the tertials and primaries fall in relation to each other and the tail. (The species accounts cover body plumage, face pattern, and call.)

For identifying a Black-bellied, the most likely challenge is separation from a juvenile American Golden-Plover, but the plumages are distinct. The Black-bellied's bill is larger, with a bulbous tip; and its overall size is larger, more robust.

Golden-plover identifications create different challenges, depending on plumage; the plumage might affect feather proportions, due to molt status. See the species accounts.

Proportions in golden-plovers are subtly different. Both North American species are smaller than the Black-bellied; the Pacific is slightly smaller than the American, but it

American Golden-Plover, juvenile

Pacific Golden-Plover, juvenile

looks to have longer legs and a longer and heavier bill. The Pacific's long legs project behind the short tail in flight; if the American shows this, it is minimal.

The tertials are long in the Pacific and the primary extension is shorter, whereas the tertials are shorter in the American, with a long primary projection. The tertials of the Pacific often end near the tail tip, but might extend only halfway out. The American tertials often reach only the base of the tail, but also might reach halfway out. Judging primary extension can be difficult and is complicated by birds molting their tertials or primaries, which render judgments useless. If one has a fresh juvenile for example, the Pacific shows 1 to 3 primaries extending beyond the tertials, whereas the American shows 4 or 5. As the winter progresses, and in particular in the subsequent spring, molt makes this a problematic feature. ∎

AMERICAN GOLDEN-PLOVER *Pluvialis dominica*

bright juvenile

juvenile

April ♂

breeding ♀

juvenile

breeding ♂

Voice CALL: A common shrill 2-note *queedle* or *klee-u*, with the second note shorter and lower pitched.

Status & Distribution Common. BREEDING: Dry tundra. MIGRATION: In spring, primarily through interior U.S. Early arrivals late Feb., but more typically Mar. in southern states, late Mar. in southern Great Lakes, with peak late Apr.–mid-May. Fall migrants typically off the Atlantic coast. Adults detected early July, but more typically late July–mid-Aug, peak into Sept. Juveniles peak Sept.–mid-Oct., smaller numbers into Nov., and exceptionally Dec. WINTER: Primarily in S.A., winter status in U.S. uncertain; some records likely pertain to very late migrants or misidentifications. VAGRANT: Casual spring migrant and rare fall migrant in the West; fall records are nearly all juveniles.

Population Hunting in the 19th century took a heavy toll on this species; the numbers have rebounded but current studies are needed.

Golden-plovers are most frequently seen as migrants, often in flocks. Monotypic. L 10.3" (26 cm)
Identification The American is plump, but not as large as the Black-bellied Plover. Early spring arrivals are in nonbreeding plumage; they molt over the course of spring, sometimes not finishing until they reach the breeding grounds. The primaries on the long wings extend noticeably beyond the tail and tertials, the latter usually end closer to the base of the tail. BREEDING MALE: Gold spotting on most upperpart feathers. White forecrown extends into the supercilium and then broadens into a neck stripe, which wraps to the sides of the breast, extending slightly toward the breast's center, but goes no farther down the lower sides and flanks. Underparts are usually all black. BREEDING FEMALE: She is like the male, but duller. White flecks may be present throughout the underparts. NONBREEDING ADULT: It molts on its way south, but early arrivals in southern Canada and the lower 48 are likely to be in partial breeding plumage; later in fall, it usually retains some black flecks below and more heavily gold notched feathers above. Basic plumage

is dull brown above and dingy below, with minimal marking, except for the supercilium. JUVENILE: It is rather grayish, with a bold whitish supercilium. Upperparts are gray with gold notched feathers. Underparts dingy, with pale brown barring or mottling on the sides of breasts and flanks. Postocular spot is dark, but diffuse at its edges. FLIGHT: Rather uniform brown above, including the rump; indistinct white wing stripe. From below, underwings pale gray with no black in axillaries.

Similar Species The American is similar to the basic and juvenile Black-bellied Plover and all plumages of the Pacific Golden-Plover (see sidebar p. 177). Compared with the Black-bellied, the American is smaller, with a bolder supercilium and darker crown; in flight, it appears uniform brown above, and the pale gray underwings lack black axillaries. The Pacific poses somewhat of a problem since there is an overlap potential. In spring, a nonbreeding American could be confused with a Mountain Plover; however, note the American's dark legs, darker and patterned upperparts, lack of breast pattern, and the fact that few Mountains linger on wintering grounds into spring.

PACIFIC GOLDEN-PLOVER *Pluvialis fulva*

The Pacific Golden-Plover, a powerful flier, is known for long, transoceanic migrations. It prefers sandy beaches more than the American Golden-Plover; on migration, an interior bird is most likely encountered in fields or around ponds. Monotypic. L 9.8" (25 cm)
Identification The primaries do not extend much beyond the tertials; the latter are long and often extend near the tip of the tail. Adults in spring are usually in breeding plumage; only second-year birds are expected in nonbreeding

juvenile

juveniles

winter

breeding ♂

breeding ♀

breeding

breeding ♂

plumage in early to mid spring. Migrant fall adults in July already show signs of molt. BREEDING MALE: The white forecrown extends into the supercilium and then becomes a stripe that extends to the neck and along the flanks, where black spots or stripes mix with the white. The underparts are black from face and throat through to belly, but not the undertail coverts. BREEDING FEMALE: Similar to the male, but duller, with black more limited and mottled. NONBREEDING ADULT: Grayish brown above with yellowish edges to feathers, and pale yellow supercilium; dingy whitish or with buff tones below. JUVENILE: It is rather bright, with distinctly buffy-yellow tones. Spots on upperparts; brown streaks on breast and neck. Bold, dark postocular spot. FLIGHT: From above, uniform brown, including rump and tail, and indistinct wing stripe; pale gray underwings from below. Feet usually project noticeably beyond tail.

Similar Species The American Golden-plover is similar; however, breeding American males have a broad white stripe that stops at the sides of the breast, and wholly black underparts—a plumage unmatched by the Pacific. A female American, which is slightly duller and has the white flecks along the flanks, can be similar to a male Pacific, but the Pacific has black markings in these white flanks, and the American has white flecks in the remaining black underparts. Juvenile and winter Pacifics typically appear brighter than juvenile and winter Americans, which are grayish with a bold white supercilium and a dusky, rather poorly defined postocular spot. The American has dusky barring or mottling on dingy white underparts; this barring can extend well past the legs. The Pacific is buffy, almost yellow in some cases, with a bold buffy supercilium and a dark, but small postocular spot. Below, the Pacific is buffy yellow with streaks on the neck and upper breast; this can turn to

mottling along the flanks (see sidebar p. 177).

Voice CALL: A loud, rich *chu-weet* with the last note higher pitched, like a Semipalmated Plover.

Status & Distribution Common breeder, rare transient. BREEDING: Prefers moister habitats than the American Golden-Plover, including the coast and river valleys. Northern Siberia to western AK. MIGRATION: Movement from wintering grounds typically mid-Apr.–mid-May, with arrivals on breeding grounds late May, or June where snowmelt is later; arrivals into southwestern AK as early as late Apr. In fall, adults migrate primarily July–Aug., with lingerers into Sept. Juveniles are most numerous Sept.–Oct., lingerers into Nov. WINTER: Primarily southern Asia to Pacific islands; small number on West Coast and in central CA. VAGRANT: A few recent late summer records on the East Coast.

Population Studies are needed as some southern wintering populations (e.g., in Australia) are thought to have recently declined.

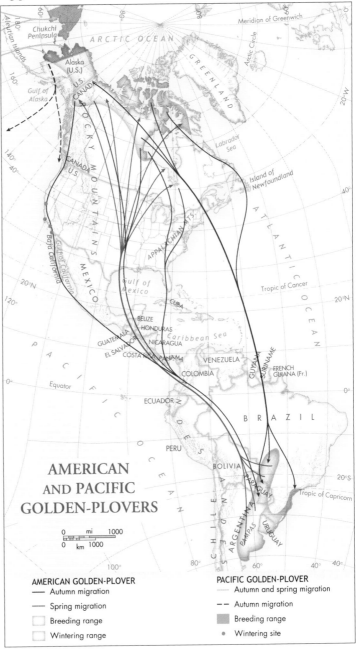

AMERICAN AND PACIFIC GOLDEN-PLOVERS

0 mi 1000
0 km 1000

AMERICAN GOLDEN-PLOVER
— Autumn migration
— Spring migration
☐ Breeding range
☐ Wintering range

PACIFIC GOLDEN-PLOVER
--- Autumn and spring migration
-- Autumn migration
▦ Breeding range
• Wintering site

BLACK-BELLIED PLOVER *Pluvialis squatarola*

bright juvenile

winter

breeding ♀

juvenile

juvenile

breeding ♂

While lacking the more colorful tones of the related golden-plovers, the Black-bellied Plover is a handsome bird in breeding plumage. It feeds singly or somewhat spread out, but collects into flocks for roosting. Polytypic (2 ssp. in N.A.; no plumage features separate them). L 11.5" (29 cm) **Identification** Larger plover than its congeners. Bill bulky. BREEDING MALE: Frosty crown and nape, black-and-white barred upperparts and tail. Black face, throat, and breast to belly; remainder of underparts white. BREEDING FEMALE: Less black; varies from rather dull to almost as bright as males. NON-BREEDING ADULT: Drab gray-brown above, with only a hint of a supercilium; dingy below, with grayish brown streaks on neck and streaks or mottling on sides of breast and flanks. JUVENILE: Like adult, but upperparts spotted whitish, with buff tone; fresh juvenile

can have pale buff spots. Breast more heavily streaked. FLIGHT: White upper-tail coverts, barred white tail, and bold white wing stripe from above; black axillaries from below.
Similar Species The winter and juvenile American Golden-Plover and, to a lesser extent, the Pacific Golden-Plover are similar. See those species.
Voice CALL: A drawn out, 3-note whistle, *wee-er-ee;* the second note is lower pitched. It carries some distance.
Status & Distribution Common. BREEDING: Dry Arctic tundra. MIGRATION: In spring, southern states (where they also winter) peak mid-Apr.–early May; late Apr. peak in NW; Great Lakes peak mid to late May; lingerers into June, nonbreeders linger all summer. In fall, adults early July, typically late July–Aug., some linger to late Sept.; juveniles first arrive late Aug. (exceptionally earlier), and peak mid to late

Sept., lingerers to mid-Nov., exceptionally later. WINTER: Common on coasts to S.A., Central and Willamette Valleys in CA and OR, and Salton Sea. Otherwise, rare to accidental elsewhere in the interior.
Population The numbers are generally stable, with little fluctuations. Nineteenth-century hunting did not victimize the Black-bellied Plovers as it did the American Golden-Plovers.

EUROPEAN GOLDEN-PLOVER *Pluvialis apricaria*

The European Golden-Plover, as its name suggests, is a vagrant from the Old World. Monotypic. L 11" (28 cm) **Identification** Short tertial extension emphasizes long primaries. BREEDING MALE: White sides of breasts quite broad; sides, flanks, and

undertail coverts more purely white, and gold spotting denser than on the Pacific Golden-Plover. BREEDING FEMALE: Duller than male; less black below. NON-BREEDING ADULT: Brownish, with yellow-gold spangles above;

dingy whitish below. JUVENILE: Super-cilium and auriculars rather indistinct; heavily barred below. FLIGHT: Uniform brown upperparts, including rump and tail; bright white underwings distinctive.
Similar Species See other golden-plovers.
Voice CALL: A mournful, evenly pitched 2-note whistle.
Status & Distribution Eurasian species. BREEDING: Greenland to western Siberia. VAGRANT: Irregular spring migrant to NF; casual elsewhere in Atlantic Canada. WINTER: Europe to N. Africa; 1 exceptional record for southeastern AK.

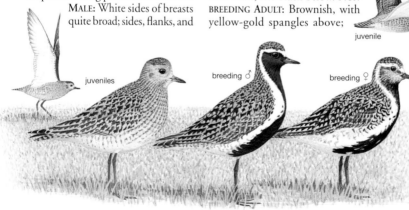

juveniles

breeding ♂

breeding ♀

juvenile

RINGED PLOVERS Genus *Charadrius*

Charadrius contains the most species of plovers. Ringed plovers are brown or sandy-colored above and white below, and often have one or two breast bands. Many species have a white collar and/or black face markings during the breeding season. Many species reside in the tropics, while others breed at high latitudes and migrate long distances.

LESSER SAND-PLOVER *Charadrius mongolus*

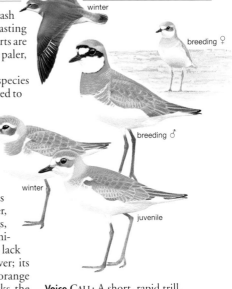

winter

breeding ♀

breeding ♂

winter

juvenile

The Lesser Sand-Plover's breeding plumage differs substantially from its nonbreeding plumage—quite unlike most of the smaller plovers. A vagrant from Asia, the Lesser was formerly called the Mongolian Plover. Always a welcome sight, it is likely found on a beach or mudflat, as opposed to an irrigated field, like larger plovers. Polytypic. L 7.5" (19 cm)
Identification The Lesser is only a mid-size plover, but it is larger than the plovers with which it would most likely associate in the United States. The Lesser lacks a pale collar, and has a dark bill and dark legs. BREEDING MALE: Unmistakable. A bright rufous breast extends more broadly at the sides, usually bordered above by a narrow black line. The facial pattern is bold—black mid-crown, cheek, and lores contrast with a white forecrown and throat. BREEDING FEMALE: She is duller than the male, but still colorful. The facial markings are brown instead of black. NONBREEDING ADULT: It lacks the rufous breast band and black facial markings. Most birds show a white supercilium and have broad grayish patches on the sides of the breast.

JUVENILE: It has a broad, buffy wash across the breast, sharply contrasting with the white throat. Upperparts are edged with buff. Legs might be paler, greenish gray.
Geographic Variation Five subspecies recognized. N.A. records believed to be nominate *mongolus,* which has a white forehead and breeds farther northeast than others.
Similar Species The Lesser presents no identification challenge when it is in breeding plumage. In other plumages it might recall a Wilson's Plover, but note the Wilson's pale legs, pale collar, and longer bill. A Semipalmated Plover can appear to lack a collar when it is hunched over; its soft parts often retain some orange color, it is smaller, and it lacks the broad patches at the sides of the breast. The Greater Sand-Plover, an unlikely vagrant, can be very similar to the Lesser in nonbreeding plumages. Most Lessers have dark legs, but juveniles can be quite pale-legged; the larger bill of the Greater is always the best distinguishing feature.

Voice CALL: A short, rapid trill.
Status & Distribution Asian visitor. Rare but regular in migration in western and northwestern AK, casual in summer and it has bred. Casual along West Coast in fall. Accidental elsewhere, primarily eastern North America (recorded in ON, RI, NJ, LA).
Population Stable.

GREATER SAND-PLOVER *Charadrius leschnaultii*

Closely related to the Lesser Sand-Plover, the Greater Sand-Plover is a most unexpected vagrant from the Old World. Polytypic (3 ssp. in Asia). L 8.5" (22 cm)
Identification BREEDING MALE: It is like the Lesser, but the rufous breast band is not as broad or intense. It has black facial markings, but it lacks the dark border to the upper breast, and there's

not as much contrast with the crown and throat. BREEDING FEMALE: She is like the male but duller, and lacks black. NONBREEDING ADULT: The rufous and black colorations are absent, like a dull breeding female. A brown breast band can be complete or incomplete. JUVENILE: Like a basic adult, but it has pale fringes on the upperparts. FLIGHT: Broad wing stripe is visible, and the toes project beyond the tail tip.
Similar Species It can be difficult to separate the Greater from the Lesser Sand-Plover, particularly from juvenile Lessers that have pale legs. The Greater is a larger version of the Lesser: Its bill is up to 50 percent larger; its body is 10 percent larger than the average Lesser, with legs 20 percent longer. In combination, it looks more elongate, with a long bill. The legs are pale greenish gray, sometimes yel-

lowish green; only a juvenile Lesser will show pale legs. The Greater's larger bill, broader white wing stripe, and toes projecting beyond the tail in flight are the best features. And lastly, the Greater's underwings are a cleaner white; the Lesser has a dark mark in the under primary coverts.
Status & Distribution Accidental, 1 record from CA (Jan. 29–Apr. 8, 2001). Given the breeding range for this species (Middle East to Central Asia) and that it winters in coastal areas of eastern Africa and Southeast Asia to Australia, a record in N.A. is remarkable.
Population The nominate subspecies appears stable, while other subspecies have shown local declines due to wetlandss destruction, and runoff from irrigation impacting breeding grounds.

winter

COLLARED PLOVER *Charadrius collaris*

The Collared Plover is common from Mexico to South America; the presence of one in inland Texas was unexpected. Monotypic. L 5.5" (14 cm)
Identification This small plover is pale brown above and white below. It lacks

adult

the white collar that most small plovers have. A black breast band is complete and narrow. The black bill is small and notably thin and the legs are pinkish, or dull flesh, and proportionately long. ADULT: The forecrown is dark, often with a rusty border; the auriculars, nape, and sides of the breast often have distinct rusty tinges, especially in males. JUVENILE: The breast band is incomplete. The upperparts have pale rusty edges. FLIGHT: A white wing stripe and white edge to outer tail are visible.
Similar Species The Collared is most similar to a Snowy Plover, but it lacks

the white collar. An adult Collared has a complete breast band, is slightly darker above, and has proportionately longer, pinkish legs, whereas a Snowy has a partial breast band and dark legs.
Voice CALL: A sharp *pit,* sometimes repeated.
Status & Distribution Generally resident from S.A. to Mexico, as far north as southern Tamaulipas and Sinaloa, where it inhabits coastal and inland regions. VAGRANT: Accidental, with 1 record from Uvalde, TX (May 9–11, 1992).
Population Stable, although the population appears to be expanding in South America.

SNOWY PLOVER *Charadrius alexandrinus*

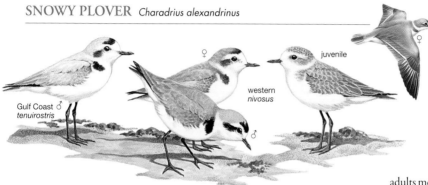

Gulf Coast ♂
tenuirostris

♀

western
nivosus

juvenile

♂

♀

The Snowy Plover might be the most overlooked shorebird. In addition to being rather pale, it blends in with its surroundings. When running across a salt pan, it seemingly disappears. And on beaches, it often rests in furrows, cryptically hidden in the sand. A fast runner, it will run to escape disturbances before it will take flight. It generally eats invertebrates that it picks off the sand. Polytypic. L 6.3" (16 cm)
Identification The Snowy Plover is pale sandy brown above, with a dark ear patch, and a partial breast band that extends from the sides of the breast. The white collar on the nape is complete. The bill is thin and dark. The legs are dark or grayish. BREEDING MALE: The ear patch, partial breast band, and forehead are black. The crown and nape may have a buffy orange tint. BREEDING FEMALE: Where the breeding male is black, the breeding female is often brown, and she lacks the warm buff tones to the crown and nape. NONBREEDING ADULT: It looks like a dull breeding female, with no black in the plumage. JUVENILE: It looks like a nonbreeding adult, with pale edges to the upperparts; it quick-

ly fades and looks like an adult. The legs are pale and have a greenish hue. FLIGHT: A white wing stripe is often conspicuous. The outer tail has bold white edges, and a dark subterminal bar on the tail contrasts with a paler base and rump.
Geographic Variation Gulf Coast birds from Florida, *tenuirostris,* are paler dorsally compared with *nivosus,* the darker subspecies from the interior west to the Pacific. Those from farther west on the Gulf Coast, from Texas for example, while classified as *tenuirostris,* look more like *nivosus.* Some authors consider these the same subspecies, but differences are usually apparent. Old World subspecies differ by call; they might be distinct species.
Similar Species Females and juveniles resemble a Piping Plover, the only plover that shares the Snowy's pale coloration, although the Piping is paler than western Snowies. Note the Snowy's thinner, black bill and darker legs.
Voice CALL: A low *krut* or *prit,* which can be rolled into a trill. Also a soft, whistled *ku-wheet,* the second note higher.

Status & Distribution Uncommon and declining on Gulf Coast. BREEDING: Barren, sandy beaches and, inland, alkali playas and marsh edges. MIGRATION: Some populations resident, others migrate short to medium distances. In spring, arrive early Mar.–Apr. in CA; slightly later in TX. In fall, adults move from July, more frequently Aug., migration completed by early Sept., with stragglers into Oct. WINTER: Primarily coastal, but irregularly in winter in southeastern CA, southern AZ, NM, western TX. Recently found in the Rio Grande Valley of south TX in relatively large numbers. VAGRANT: Accidental in western AK; records across much of N.A., including the Great Lakes and along the southern Atlantic coast.
Population The U.S. federal list of endangered species officially lists the western *nivosus* as threatened. Snowy populations are also under threat in the Southeast. Human disturbance, as well as habitat loss and degradation, play a role in the diminished numbers of this species.

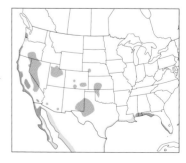

WILSON'S PLOVER *Charadrius wilsonia*

The Wilson's Plover is often encountered during a stroll on the beach. Polytypic. L 7.8" (20 cm)

Identification The forecrown is white, with a narrow supercilium; the dark lores are continuous with the ear patch. The upperparts are brown, with a broad, white collar; the underparts are white, except for a broad breast band. The bill is long, very heavy, and black. The legs are pale, but occasionally have yellow or orange tones. BREEDING MALE: The breast band is black, and there is some black in the lores and on the crown; the ear patch is cinnamon-buff. BREEDING FEMALE: The black parts of the male are usually replaced by brown.

NONBREEDING ADULT: It looks like a dull breeding female. JUVENILE: It resembles a female, but note the scaly-looking upperparts, and the breast band is usually incomplete. FLIGHT: The white wing stripe is indistinct, particularly on the inner wing.

Geographic Variation Nominate *wilsonia,* occurring on the Atlantic and Gulf coasts, has a broader white forehead and narrower breast band compared with the *beldingi* of Mexico's Pacific coast.

Similar Species A large Semipalmated Plover is similar, but it has a much smaller bill. The Wilson's could be confused with a juvenile Killdeer, which only has one breast band early in its life, but its downy plumage and different shape should be readily apparent. See the sand-plover species.

Voice CALL: A sharp, hard *whit,* sometimes repeated.

Status & Distribution Fairly common, but declining on barrier islands. BREEDING: Sandy beaches and mudflats, although has occurred inland in south TX and

once at Salton Sea. MIGRATION: Where summer resident, arrivals generally Mar., but as early as Feb. Fall departures usually in Sept., but lingerers into Nov. WINTER: FL, otherwise rare along southern Atlantic coast and Gulf Coast, most likely in south TX. VAGRANT: Casual to CA, OR, on Atlantic coast north to the Maritimes, and inland to the Great Lakes and Great Plains.

Population Development, disturbance, and habitat destruction are known to impact this species.

PIPING PLOVER *Charadrius melodus (E)*

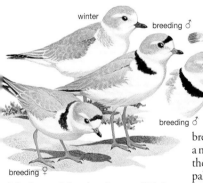

The beautiful and endangered Piping plover is primarily found on beaches. Pale above, it blends well with its sandy home and is often not detected until it runs. Polytypic. L 7.3" (18 cm)

Identification Pale sandy brown above, with white collar and forecrown. Coloration sufficiently pale to make contrast with white throat and underparts rather muted; supercilium generally indistinct. The orange legs are often the field mark most likely to bring attention. BREEDING MALE: Black, narrow breast band wraps around the back, below the white collar. Black bar bordering the forecrown nearly connects

between the eyes. Obvious orange base to short black bill. BREEDING FEMALE: Like the male but collar and bar on crown are paler, usually not black. NONBREEDING ADULT: Bill is black, and the black from the breeding plumage is lost. JUVENILE: Like a nonbreeding adult with pale edges to the upperparts, difficult to see against pale upperparts. FLIGHT: Distinct white wing stripe; conspicuous white rump.

Geographic Variation The breast band is variable, can be incomplete, especially in eastern populations. The inland subspecies *circumcinctus* has darker facial features than the nominate *melodus.*

Similar Species The Piping's breeding plumage is unique. In nonbreeding plumage, distinguish it from a Snowy Plover by its thicker bill and orange legs.

Voice CALL: A clear *peep-lo.* And high-pitched piping notes during flight display.

Status & Distribution Endangered, generally uncommon. BREEDING: Sandy

beaches, lakeshores, dunes. Rare and declining breeder around the Great Lakes. MIGRATION: Rare between breeding and wintering ranges. Departures from winter range peak early Apr.–early May. Arrivals in north Atlantic and Great Plains mid-Apr.–mid-May. Departures from breeding ground as early as July, but mostly Aug.–early Sept., lingerers to Nov. WINTER: Atlantic and Gulf coasts. VAGRANT: Accidental to OR in fall, and in winter to coastal CA.

Population Only a few thousand Pipings are thought to remain. Development, habitat degradation, and water management practices contribute to their decline.

COMMON RINGED PLOVER *Charadrius hiaticula*

The Common Ringed Plover is an Old World species, but its breeding range extends into North America. This species is highly sought-after due to its rarity; most observations are from St. Lawrence Island, Alaska. Its behavior and preferred habitat are like those of the Semipalmated Plover, to which it is closely related. It frequents beaches and mudflats, and runs in typical plover fashion in search of food. It migrates longer distances than its congeners. Polytypic. L 7.5" (19 cm)

Identification Brown upperparts from crown to back, except for white collar. Dark lores and auriculars offset by white forecrown and throat, the latter continuous with the white collar. Rather distinct white supercilium. Pale yellow eye ring incomplete, or missing entirely. White underparts, except for a broad breast band. Webbing, while difficult to assess in the field, is important: The Common Ringed has no webbing between the outer two toes, and only slight webbing between the inner toes. **BREEDING MALE:** Mid-crown bar, lores, auriculars, and breast band black. Black of lores joins bill at or just below gape. The bill has extensive orange to the base. **BREEDING FEMALE:** Generally paler than male with black parts often replaced partly with brown, but can be difficult to sex. **NONBREEDING ADULT:** Like a dull adult female, with no black on the head. Breast band possibly incomplete. Duller legs. Bill mostly black. Supercilium broader and more likely to extend in front of the eye than in breeding plumage. **JUVENILE:** Like a nonbreeding adult, except duller. Obvious pale edges and darker submarginal lines create a scaly appearance above though, at least, early fall. **FLIGHT:** White wing stripe quite obvious (much more so than in the Semipalmated).

Geographic Variation Nominate *hiaticula* in northeast Canada; *tundrae* in western Alaska. Although *tundrae* averages smaller and darker, there is overlap: Northern birds of the two subspecies look more like each other than

northern and southern birds of the same subspecies.

Similar Species Almost identical to the Semipalmated Plover (see sidebar below).

Voice CALL: A soft, fluted *pooee*, lower pitched and less strenuous than the Semipalmated's; repeated in a series of notes during display flight.

Status & Distribution BREEDING: Occasionally on St. Lawrence Island, AK; regularly on Baffin Island, as well as throughout Eurasia. **MIGRATION:** A long-distance migrant, wintering to Africa. Very rare migrant on western AK islands, and casual to eastern Canada and New England. There is little doubt this species is more numerous than this pattern suggests. While conceivable that most of the breeding birds that creep into North America retrace their steps and winter in the "correct" hemisphere, it is also conceivable that this species passes through either coast annually, only to be overlooked.

Population The populations of both subspecies are stable.

breeding ♂

breeding ♀

juvenile

Common Ringed Versus Semipalmated Plover

These two plover species are very similar. Undoubtedly the Common Ringed Plover appears in North America more frequently than it has been detected; however, the subtle nature of this identification requires caution. Only consider a vagrant plover if the diagnostic calls are noted. Ideally, use a combination of other characters to confirm the identification.

The calls are straightforward. The Semipalmated gives an emphatic, upslurred *chu-weet*, with the emphasis on the second syllable. The Common Ringed gives a more plaintive, flute-like *poo-ee*. Both species have minimal webbing between the inner toes; the Semi has fairly obvious webbing between the outer toes, the Common Ringed lacks

Semipalmated Plover, breeding adult

webbing between the outer toes. If you see webbing in the outer toes, identification is straightforward, but if you do not see webbing, is it because there was no webbing, or was the view insufficient? Verifying this mark is difficult.

Other than calls and webbing, identification is much more complex. The key characters to look at are the supercilium, orbital ring, lore-gape junction, white forecrown, bill, and breast band.

1. Supercilium. In adult males, the Common Ringed has a more distinct white supercilium than the Semi. It is important to know the bird is a breeding male, however, as a female Semi shows a less distinct supercilium than the female Common Ringed.

SEMIPALMATED PLOVER *Charadrius semipalmatus*

One of our most common plovers, the Semipalmated is sometimes seen in large flocks during migration. It prefers wet fields and is often found in freshly irrigated fields that attract large numbers of shorebirds. It flocks when roosting, but the flock spreads out when the birds feed, so the birds seem less numerous than some of the other birds present. Monotypic. L 7.3" (18 cm)

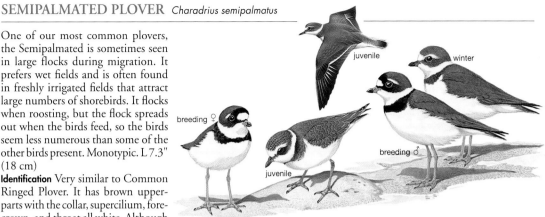

Identification Very similar to Common Ringed Plover. It has brown upperparts with the collar, supercilium, forecrown, and throat all white. Although difficult to assess under most field conditions, this species shows obvious webbing between its two outer toes (and a little webbing between the other toes). The bill is short and has an orange base. The legs are orange. BREEDING MALE: The lores, auriculars, and midcrown bar are all black, as is the breast band; soft part colors are bright orange. The dark of the lores joins above the gape. The eye ring is usually obvious, orange or yellow in color. A supercilium is usually not present in this season. BREEDING FEMALE: It is like the male, but the facial markings and breast band might be brown. It is more likely than the male to have a partial supercilium. NONBREEDING ADULT: It is like a dull female with no black on facial markings; the breast band might be brown or incomplete. The bill is all dark and the legs are duller. JUVENILE: Pale fringes and dark subterminal marks give bird a scaly appearance; darker legs than in adults.

Similar Species The Semipalmated's dark back separates it from the Piping and Snowy Plovers; its much smaller bill separates it from a Wilson's Plover. It is almost identical to a Common Ringed Plover (see sidebar below).
Voice CALL: Distinctive. A whistled, upslurred *chu-weet,* the second syllable higher pitched and emphatic; repeated in a series during breeding.
Status & Distribution Common. BREEDING: Beaches, lakeshores, rivers, tidal flats. MIGRATION: A broad-front spring migrant on both coasts and through the center of the continent. Migration generally starts mid-Mar., but usually early Apr. before southern states see a lot of migration. Most migration is mid-Apr.–mid-May in southern and middle latitudes; peaks at Great Lakes mid to late May. Lingers to June and some nonbreeders stay south of the breeding range, complicating departure dates. In fall, much of the eastern movement take place to the northeast

Atlantic and then south. First arrivals usually detected in mid-July, but can be earlier. Most adults move through late July–mid-Aug., when the juveniles start migrating in numbers. Most states have passed the peak by early Sept., with mostly juveniles through that month. Lingerers occur into Oct., and in some cases Nov. WINTER: A coastal bird, with only a few inland locales where it is rare; accidental elsewhere. Winters to S.A.
Population The numbers are stable.

2. Orbital ring. The Semi shows an obvious yellow, or almost orange, orbital ring. The Common Ringed shows either a faint yellow orbital ring or none at all.

3. Lore-gape junction. A very difficult mark to accurately assess in the field (it is hard enough with pictures!). In the Common Ringed, the white from the throat meets the black of the lores at the gape, whereas in the Semi, this junction is above the gape. An important note on this character is its apparent utility in several plumages.

4. White forecrown. The white forecrown shape is subtly different on the two species. The rear border is rather straight in the Semi and pointed toward the nape on the Common Ringed. Furthermore, the white usu-

Common Ringed Plover, breeding adult

ally runs to the eye on the Common Ringed; the eye sits well within the dark area on the Semi.

5. Bill. The Common Ringed has a bill that is a little longer and of more even thickness throughout its length (i.e., thinner at the base) than the Semi. Furthermore, the adult Common Ringed has a more extensive orange base.

6. Breast band. It is thicker on the Common Ringed and, while variable, normally thinner on the Semi. Posture affects this character, so its use should be as supportive evidence, not definitive.

Unless the diagnostic calls are heard, a claim of a vagrant will likely not pass muster without using multiple characters for confirmation. ∎

LITTLE RINGED PLOVER *Charadrius dubius*

This Old World plover has been recorded as a vagrant in North America. The Little Ringed Plover is rather solitary. Polytypic (3 ssp.; only *curonicus* recorded in northeast Asia and AK). L 6" (15 cm)

Identification A small plover, notably smaller than Semipalmated Plover. Brown upperparts; white collar. Lores, forehead, auriculars, and breast band dark, contrasting with white forecrown and white bar behind the dark crown. Conspicuous yellow orbital ring in all seasons. Rather dull yellow legs. On a standing bird, note the long tertials, which almost reach the tail tip. BREEDING MALE: Facial markings black; pale base to the lower mandible. BREEDING FEMALE: Like male, but auriculars brown. NONBREEDING ADULT: Dull brown above; no black facial markings. JUVENILE: Often a yellow-buff tint to paler areas on head and throat. Scaly appearance due to pale edges and dark subterminal marks. Dull yellow orbital ring. FLIGHT: Uniform brown above; no wing stripe.

Similar Species The Little Ringed most closely resembles a Semipalmated Plover, but it is smaller, with a yellow orbital ring, and it lacks a wing stripe in flight.

Voice CALL: A descending *pee-oo* that carries a long way.

Status & Distribution Vagrant from the Old World, breeds from U.K. to Siberia, and into southern Asia. Winters from Africa to southern Asia. Casual spring vagrant to western Aleutians.

Population The population is generally expanding as Little Ringeds are opportunistically able to take advantage of man-made developments—more than offsetting declines resulting from habitat loss or agricultural runoff.

breeding

juvenile

breeding ♂

KILLDEER *Charadrius vociferus*

The Killdeer is North America's most well-known plover, although many people know the Killdeer without understanding its family affiliation. The Killdeer can be common around human developments, frequently seen on playing fields, parking lots, and other unnatural habitats. Its "broken-wing" display is famous and known by many non-birders. The Killdeer often forms flocks after breeding in late summer. It feeds in fields and in a variety of wet areas, but rarely along the ocean shore, and in general, it is not prevalent on mudflats. It is noisy. It reacts quickly to any perceived disturbance. Polytypic (3 ssp.; nominate in U.S.). L 10.5" (27 cm)

Identification The brown upperparts turn orange at the rump and upper tail coverts, but this only shows in flight, or during its "broken-wing" display. The forecrown is white, as is a short but distinct supercilium, and there is a white collar. The lores are dark; this coloration continues and broadens at the auriculars. The underparts are white, except for 2 bold black breast bands. The legs are pale, usually flesh tones, but sometimes with a yellow-green cast. The orbital ring is narrow, but a bright orange-red. The Killdeer is the largest of the "ringed" plovers and looks long-tailed. The sexes generally look similar in adult plumage, and there is little seasonal change. Males average more black on the face than females, but this is variable. Fresh feathers, typically in late summer, have rusty edges to them. JUVENILE: Its plumage is paler than an adult's, with pale edges to the upperparts. Downy young have only one breast band, but they quickly grow out of this plumage. FLIGHT: A particularly bold white wing stripe marks the inner wing. In addition, the bright reddish orange rump is visible and the tail has obvious white corners, with dark central rectrices.

Similar Species The Killdeer's double breast band is distinctive; as is its loud, piercing call. Downy young Killdeer have one breast band and might be identified as Wilson's Plovers by overeager birders.

Voice CALL: Loud, piercing *kill-dee* or *dee-dee-dee*.

Status & Distribution Common. BREEDING: Open ground, usually on gravel, including in cities. MIGRATION: Early spring migrants show up in the middle latitudes with the first bit of warmth after mid-Feb. Peak in Great Lakes mid to late Mar., with most migrants having passed through by mid-Apr. In fall, numbers build July–Aug., sometimes as early as late June. Migration peaks Aug., with numbers decreasing during Sept. Many birds will linger until Nov., or later if warm weather persists. WINTER: While most winter populations are well established, some vary according to the extent of snow cover. VAGRANT: Can occur north of breeding range.

Population Stable. The Killdeer seems to adapt to human disturbance.

MOUNTAIN PLOVER   *Charadrius montanus*

winter

breeding

winter

juvenile

The unique Mountain Plover is appreciated for its scarcity and barren habitats more than for its plumage. Birders usually make specific efforts to find this bird as it is usually hard to find and is found in areas that are likely to have few other species. Its coloration blends in with its environment; if not for the white underparts, usually noted only when it moves, sightings would be few indeed. It is gregarious in winter, and is usually found in short grass or bare dirt fields. Monotypic. L 9" (23 cm)
Identification Uniform brown upperparts from collar through rump. White forecrown and narrow, somewhat indistinct whitish supercilium. Underparts generally whitish, brightest near the belly; the breast has a dingy brown wash. Black bill. Pale pinkish to gray legs. BREEDING ADULT: Black lores and forecrown. Underparts mostly white. NONBREEDING ADULT: In fresh plumage (seen on

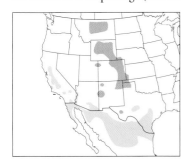

early fall migrants), rufous edges to scapulars and coverts, fading by early winter in most birds. Buffy tinge on breast more extensive at this season, as is the supercilium. JUVENILE: Paler than adult with buff edges to the scapulars and coverts. FLIGHT: Brown above, with a hint of a white wing stripe, particularly toward the middle of the wing. Underwing white, visible as bird banks low above the ground. Tail has a pale tip and a dark subterminal bar.
Similar Species Except for the closely related Caspian and Oriental Plovers from Asia, no other species quite looks like a Mountain Plover, but inexperienced birders might mistake a Mountain for one of the more numerous American Golden-Plovers when that species arrives in early spring. In nonbreeding plumage in early spring, Americans share a rather brown-and-white plumage, but they are darker above, with pale spots and a bolder supercilium, and have gray underwings and dark legs.
Voice CALL: A harsh *krrr* note.
Status & Distribution Local and declin-

ing. BREEDING: Plains and shortgrass prairies. MIGRATION: Wintering populations thin out late Feb., and withdrawal usually complete by late Mar., early Apr. in TX and CA. First CO arrivals early Mar., those in MT to mid-Apr. Fall dispersal starts July and ends by Nov. Winter populations generally do not arrive until late Oct. WINTER: Primarily southern CA, southern AZ, southern and central TX, and Mexico. VAGRANT: Rare to Pacific coast, except for favored locations in central CA; accidental in eastern N.A.
Population Numbers have declined severely with the conversion of grasslands to farmland.

EURASIAN DOTTEREL   *Charadrius morinellus*

breeding ♂

breeding ♀

winter

juvenile

A unique vagrant from Eurasia, the Eurasian Dotterel is interesting for its beauty and biology. Rather tame, it allows bird-watchers to approach quite closely. Unlike other plovers, the female Eurasian Dotterel has the bolder plumage and males tend the nest. Typically, the female only helps rear the young when gender ratios are out of balance. Monotypic L 9" (23 cm)
Identification This mid-size plover has a small bill and, in all plumages, a bold white supercilium. BREEDING ADULT: The gray upperparts have buff edges. The dark crown sets off a bold white line that starts above and extends well behind the eye, wrapping around to the back of the head. A white bar separates the neck from reddish brown to dark underparts. NONBREEDING ADULT: It looks similar to a breeding bird, but the underparts are paler, grayish throughout;

the white line at the breast is less distinct. JUVENILE: It is like a nonbreeding adult, but has bold, colorful edgings to many feathers above and is buffy below; the breast band is somewhat obscured. The bold white supercilium extends around the entire head.
Similar Species The Eurasian Dotterel recalls the golden-plovers, but the supercilium that wraps around the head and the white line on the breast are diagnostic, and the Eurasian Dotterel also has pale legs.
Voice CALL: A soft *put, put,* repeated.
Status & Distribution Eurasian species; very rare, sporadic breeder in northwestern AK on open, rocky tundra; rare late spring migrant to western AK. VAGRANT: Casual to Aleutian Islands and along West Coast in the fall. Accidental in winter in CA and 1 record in adjacent Baja California.

OYSTERCATCHERS Family Haematopodidae

American Oystercatcher, adult (left) with juvenile (NY, July)

Oystercatchers are large, chunky birds usually tied to the coast. Their bills, which they use like a chisel during feeding, are long and bright orange or red.

Structure These are bulky shorebirds, larger than most species. The stout and straight bill flattens laterally toward the tip. Oystercatcher legs are short and thick, and typically pink or red.

Behavior Oystercatchers frequent sandy beaches or rocky shores. Their gait alternates between a steady walk and short bursts of a fast run; they tend to run rather than take flight to escape danger. When they stand upright, they often tuck the neck in and they hold the bill below horizontal. Their flight, usually low to the surface, is powerful and direct on deep, rapid wingbeats with rounded wings. To feed, the oystercatcher plunges its bill into the sand for prey or uses its bill to chisel mollusks off surfaces and pry them open. The birds feed singly, or in small, noisy flocks on coastal beaches and mudflats. Unlike most shorebirds, they feed their young, and the young often stay with the parents through the first winter. Oystercatchers often form pair-bonds.

Plumage Oystercatchers are black or pied (black and white). Closer views show substantial brown in the plumage, with only the European adult being wholly black. Juveniles are paler, with duller soft part coloration. Those soft parts typically brighten over the first year of life.

Distribution Oystercatchers live around the world's coasts. Some species are less tied to the immediate shore; most are not expected away from the ocean. There are 11 species currently recognized, 2 mostly resident in the U.S.

Taxonomy A debate rages about the number of species in *Haematopus*: as few as 4 or as many as 11. While the pied and black species look very different, hybridization occurs in northwest Baja California, resulting in intermediate plumages. Some taxonomists consider *frazari* a hybrid and do not give it species status. The 3 North American species represent a superspecies.

Conservation Beach development impacts oystercatchers, as do spills of harmful pollutants (e.g., the *Exxon Valdez* spill in AK); yet, they quickly colonize dredged areas. BirdLife International lists 1 species as threatened and another as near threatened. —*Matthew T. Heindel*

Genus *Haematopus*

EURASIAN OYSTERCATCHER *Haematopus ostralegus*

The Eurasian is an unexpected vagrant from the Old World. Polytypic. L 16.5" (42 cm)

Identification The black head, neck, and upperparts contrast with the white rump, wing stripe, and remainder of the underparts. The eyes, eye rings, and bill are bright red. ADULT BREEDING: The legs are pinkish red. ADULT NONBREEDING: A white bar extends across the lower throat. JUVENILE: It is browner above, with a narrower tail band, than the adult. It has a dark-tipped bill, brown eyes, and grayish legs; the bare parts get brighter over first year. FLIGHT: The white wing stripe extends almost to tip, with pale primary shafts on outer primaries. The base of the tail is white, with the distal tail black.

Geographic Variation Subspecies include nominate *ostralegus* of W. Europe and *osculans* of Siberia (a possible vagrant to the Pacific Coast); *osculans* has a slightly shorter wing stripe and dark outer primary shafts.

Similar Species It is similar to the American Oystercatcher but the adult Eurasian is black above, lacking brown, its eyes red, and its legs brighter.

Voice CALL: A series of loud, piercing whistles, similar to congeners.

Status & Distribution Accidental. BREEDING: Eurasia, from Iceland to Kamchatka, more local in Asia. MIGRATION: Southern populations largely resident, but northern populations move south.

breeding adult

WINTER: Southern Europe, N. Africa, Arabian Peninsula, and coastal Asia. VAGRANT: Two spring records from NF; casual to Greenland.

AMERICAN OYSTERCATCHER *Haematopus palliatus*

This species is typically seen along sandy beaches, oyster bars, bays, and mudflats. Polytypic. L 18.5" (47 cm)

Identification Striking. A black head with contrasting brown back, white underparts, large red-orange bill, flesh-colored legs, and yellow eyes. JUVENILE: Whitish fringes on upperparts give a scaly appearance. Duller bill with a dusky tip, dusky eyes, and grayish flesh-colored legs. FLIGHT: A bold white wing stripe and white base of tail.

Geographical Variation Up to 5 subspecies, including nominate *palliatus* (along the Atlantic coast) and *frazari* (casual in southern CA from nearby breeding grounds in Baja California). Some *frazari* appear identical to *palliatus,* but most show some dark mot-

adults

juvenile

tling on the lower breast and uppertail coverts (white on *palliatus*) and the white wing stripe on the inner part of the wing does not reach the primaries. Some authors speculate that these two are one subspecies, but most current authors treat them separately.

Similar Species See Eurasian Oystercatcher. Hybridization between a *frazari* and a Black Oystercatcher creates a variety of plumages; a bird that shows too much dark on the rump or barely has a white wing stripe should not be considered a pure *frazari.*

Voice CALL: A loud *wheep* or *whee-ah,* often rising into an excited chatter.

Status & Distribution Fairly common. BREEDING: Populations extend south through both coasts of Mexico, C.A, and S.A. Expanding northward in the East. MIGRATION: Poorly understood but some northern Atlantic populations withdraw in Sept., returning Mar.–Apr. Populations south of VA are resident, and augmented in winter by northern populations. Casual in southern CA. VAGRANT: A record from ON, a flock of 3 immatures at Salton Sea, and a sight record from ID.

Population Recent expansion in the Northeast, but development and disturbance are of concern.

BLACK OYSTERCATCHER *Haematopus bachmani*

adult

The Black Oystercatcher is a dark, large, chunky shorebird likely to be seen only along the rocky coastline of the Pacific. It is typically found hunting for food on tide-exposed rocks, where it blends into the dark rocks, only to be revealed by its large, red-orange bill. It demonstrates tremendous site fidelity, with pairs typically returning to the same territory for many years. Monotypic. L 17.5" (45 cm)

Identification The Black Oystercatchers's all-dark body is washed with brown on the upperparts and belly. The eyes are yellow, with a red eye

ring, and the legs are pinkish. Sexes similar, except females are slightly larger and bill is slightly more orange than male's. While subtle, these differences might be evident in pairs. JUVENILE: The outer half of the bill is dusky, the legs are grayish pink, and the eyes are dusky. Fine, pale edges to the upperparts in fresh plumage.

Similar Species This oystercatcher cannot be confused with any other species. Beware of hybrids between Black and American Oystercatchers in Baja California: The resulting offspring can look similar to either parent. See the American Oystercatcher account for more detail.

Voice CALL: Similar to the American Oystercatcher. Its loud, piercing *wheep* or *whee-ah* notes can accelerate into an excited chatter.

Status & Distribution Common. BREEDING: Rocky shores and islands along the Pacific coast from the Aleutians to Baja California. MIGRATION: Largely resident, but some local movements, not

all of which are understood. Many northern populations are abandoned as some birds move south. Autumn numbers in BC peak in Nov., with vacated territories reoccupied in Mar.–Apr. WINTER: Territories are abandoned and flocks are formed during winter, but range largely within breeding range. VAGRANT: A Jan. record of a "distressed" bird found at 3,400 feet in the Washington Cascades is hard to explain.

Population Human disturbances have eliminated local populations in the Pacific Northwest.

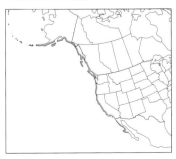

STILTS AND AVOCETS Family Recurvirostridae

Black-necked Stilt, female (CA, Apr.)

Stilts and avocets are found around the world, primarily in warmer climates. Typically pied black-and-white, they walk gracefully on long legs, particularly the stilts.

Structure These large shorebirds are slender. The bill is long and thin, and typically black; the bill of the avocet is thicker at the base and upturned. The neck is often held in a gentle curve, or pulled into the shoulders. Wings are long and pointed; in flight, the neck is outstretched and the legs trail behind the tail. Males are larger than females in stilts and equal in size in avocets.

Behavior The birds typically feed along the water's edge or in deeper water beyond the reach of other shorebirds. They pick at the surface, but they can also grab invertebrates well below the surface. On land, their gait is typically graceful when walking (it can be brisk with long strides), but they do appear gangly when they run. Their flight is direct and avocets appear to be stronger fliers than stilts. Both genera swim; avocets do so well and more frequently than stilts. These are highly social birds, particularly so in the nonbreeding season, when they might form large flocks. They are usually colonial nesters and mob predators with a zeal beyond most shorebirds. Unlike most shorebirds, they are quite conspicuous when breeding, out in the open and very noisy instead of the more common cryptic strategy.

Plumage Both stilts and avocets have a striking black-and-white pattern. Differences between the sexes are slight, but noticeable. Seasonal differences are marked in avocets, but slight in stilts. The wings are dark in stilts, and mixed black-and-white in avocets.

Distribution The species are scattered around the world, primarily in warmer climates. Most breeding populations withdraw to (or close to) the coasts in winter.

Taxonomy The systematics of this family continue to be debated. The stilts *(Himantopus)* have been placed into as few as 1, and as many as 8 species; most authors follow the current treatment, which includes 4 species. Avocets *(Recurvirostra)* have also been subject to taxonomic revision, but the acceptance of 4 species spread across the world is generally accepted. The stilts and avocets share behavioral traits, and the third genus in the family *(Cladorhynchos)*, with 1 representative from Australia, is intermediate between the 2 genera. Stilts and avocets have hybridized in captivity and recently in the wild in California.

Conservation Hunting and trapping sharply reduced populations in the 19th century, but populations are in the process of reclaiming some of the former breeding areas along the mid-Atlantic coast. Pollutants and habitat loss remain threats. BirdLife International lists the Black Stilt as threatened. —*Matthew T. Heindel*

Genus *Himantopus*

BLACK-WINGED STILT *Himantopus himantopus*

A vagrant from the Old World, the Black-winged Stilt picks at the water with its needlelike bill for prey. Polytypic (several ssp. thought to belong to the same sp. found in the Old World). L 13" (33 cm)

Identification Black back and wings; white underparts; long, bright pink legs. ADULT: Head and neck vary from entirely white to extensively black, although a portion of the hind neck will remain whitish or pale gray-brown. Extent of black on head and neck not diagnostic of sex, although males tend to be more white headed. BREEDING MALE: Back glossy, pink flush to underparts at onset of breeding season. FEMALE: Duller than male, lacking gloss and pink flush. JUVENILE: Gray-brown back; thin, white trailing edge to wing (visible in flight); legs duller and paler. **Similar Species** Black-necked Stilt always has entire hind neck black and has white spot above and behind eye. **Voice** CALL: A repeated *kik, kik, kik* like the Black-necked. **Status & Distribution** Accidental. BREEDING: Nominate subspecies breeds in Europe and locally in Asia and the Middle East. VAGRANT: Three spring records for western Aleutians and Pribilof Is. This species increasingly occurs in Japan and Korea, with rising breeding records, and there have been a few extralimital records in northeastern Siberia.

adult

BLACK-NECKED STILT *Himantopus mexicanus*

juvenile

♂

This graceful wader with an elegant posture is highly social, but is less gregarious than the avocet. Polytypic (nominate in N.A.). L 14" (36 cm)
Identification Boldly pied, black above and white below; long pink or red legs. The dark head has a white spot, above and behind the eye. BREEDING MALE: Glossy black back, red legs, and occasional pink flush at beginning of breeding season. NONBREEDING MALE: Duller legs; gloss and pink flush absent. FEMALE: Back has brown tones. JUVENILE: Paler than adult. Buffy edges to upperparts; grayish pink legs. Inner primaries and secondaries tipped white, visible in flight.
Similar Species See Black-winged Stilt.
Voice CALL: A loud, piercing *kek kek kek,* particularly when disturbed while breeding. A loud *keek,* recalling a Long-billed Dowitcher, is a common contact note.
Status & Distribution Locally common. BREEDING: Marshy areas and shallow ponds, including sewage and evaporation ponds, with emergent vegetation. Range is spreading north in interior western states and along Gulf and Atlantic coasts. MIGRATION: Short to medium-distance migrant, usually away from inland areas during winter. Spring migrants primarily Mar.–Apr., but locally as early as late Feb., and into May. Fall migration protracted with many areas seeing movement in July, but most areas peak Aug.–Sept., trickling into early Nov. WINTER: Central and southern CA, Gulf and Atlantic coasts, and southern FL. VAGRANT: Rare or casual across southern Canada and various places in the Northeast and Great Lakes.
Population Despite recent expansions, the species has not recovered from 19th-century losses.

Genus *Recurvirostra*

AMERICAN AVOCET *Recurvirostra americana*

Avocets feed in water by sweeping their bills back and forth, and on mudflats, where they peck at the surface for prey. Monotypic. L 18" (46 cm)
Identification Black scapular stripes on upperparts; white underparts; black-and-white wings. The long, thin bill is recurved; the male's is longer and straighter, while the female's has more of an upward tilt. Bluish gray legs. BREEDING: Rusty colored head and neck, with a white eye ring and white at the base of the bill. NONBREEDING: Pale gray head and neck. JUVENILE: Pale cinnamon wash on head and neck; pale fringes on tertials and coverts.

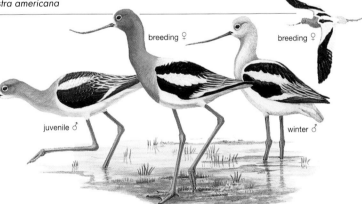

breeding ♀
breeding ♀
juvenile ♂
winter ♂

Similar Species Not likely to be confused with any North American species.
Voice CALL: A loud, piercing *wheet* or *kleep,* usually repeated when agitated, higher pitched than the call of a stilt.
Status & Distribution Fairly common. BREEDING: Shallow ponds, marshes, and lakeshores. MIGRATION: Anywhere in the West and along the Atlantic (mostly DE and south) and Gulf coasts. Spring migration primarily mid-Mar.–May. Great Lakes usually in small numbers with arrivals mid-Apr.–mid-May, but dozens occur in exceptional years. Fall migration July–Oct. with adults expected first, through early Aug., followed by juveniles mid-Aug.–mid-Oct. Lingerers annually into Nov. WINTER: Coastal and locally, inland CA, locally along Gulf Coast, and southern FL. Rarely inland near more northerly breeding sites (e.g., UT, NV, OR). VAGRANT: North to southern AK and various points in southern Canada.
Population Wetland losses have led to local population declines.

JACANAS Family Jacanidae

Northern Jacana (Costa Rica)

J acanas are atypical shorebirds; they look more like rails. Their bold plumage, unique behavior, and rarity in the United States make them a sought-after species. They are easy to identify; the only difficulty posed is pronouncing the name. Most people prefer ZHA-sah-na, from a local tribe in Brazil (from where Linnaeus named it in 1758). Other common pronunciations include ha-KAN-ah, ja-KAN-ah, and YAH-sa-nah.

Structure Their long legs and very long toes and toenails are unique. The wings are rounded; some species have a pointed spur at the carpal joint, used for displays and fighting. The bill has a frontal shield.

Behavior Jacanas walk with a high-stepping gait, and frequently do so across floating vegetation. Their long toes and toenails distribute their weight over the vegetation so that they do not sink. They can also swim. Jacanas are quite conspicuous and do not hide in vegetation. Weak fliers, jacanas usually fly only for short distances; in flight, their necks are outstretched and their legs trail behind their tails. They often raise their wings upon landing or in various displays. Jacanas are fiercely territorial. In most species, the female is polyandrous, taking several males in her territory. While the female may help with nest building (on floating vegetation), the males sit on the eggs and care for the young. Jacanas usually feed on aquatic insects, but they also eat small fish and plants.

Plumage The sexes look alike, although the females are larger than the males.

Distribution Eight species of jacanas are found worldwide, primarily in the tropical regions. Of the 2 New World species, the Northern Jacana of Mexico barely reaches our area.

Taxonomy New World jacanas are in the genus *Jacana*. Some authors consider the Northern Jacana to be conspecific with the Wattled Jacana (*Jacana jacana*) of Central and South America; they overlap in Panama.

Conservation The destruction of wetlands through drainage or overgrazing has eliminated populations. No species are threatened currently. —*Matthew T. Heindel*

Genus *Jacana*

NORTHERN JACANA *Jacana spinosa*

The Northern Jacana is unique. This conspicuous bird walks on long legs and is as adept at walking along ditches and grassy lakeshores as across lily pads. It often raises its wings, revealing yellow flight feathers; a spur sticks out from the middle of the wing and is occasionally visible during these displays. The Northern Jacana flies with stiff wingbeats and short glides. Monotypic. L 9.5" (24 cm)

Identification ADULT: It is chestnut with a glossy black head, neck, breast, and upper back. A pale blue cere separates the yellow frontal shield and yellow bill. The yellow underwing is visible in flight and during display. JUVENILE: It is white below and brown or olive-brown above with cinnamon edges in fresh plumage. The dark hind neck and crown and dark postocular stripe con-

trast with a whitish buff supercilium. The frontal shield and spur are tiny. One-year-olds are mottled with chestnut, brown, and black. The dark bill has a yellow base.

Similar Species No other North American species looks like the Northern Jacana. An immature gallinule, perhaps the closest confusion species, has a different shape and coloration.

Voice CALL: A cackling, harsh sound often given in a series *ka-ka-ka-ka* or *jik-jik-jik-jik;* similar to a large rail.

Status & Distribution Rare and irregular visitor. BREEDING: Common nesting species in Mexico and C.A.; has bred in TX, but not recently. MIGRATION: Over 30 records, most from the coastal marshes of southern TX, primarily Nov.–Apr. A few records are well inland. Accidental near Marathon,

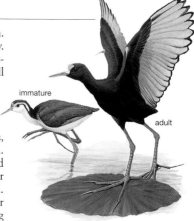

immature

adult

TX, and in southern AZ.

Population Although there was a resident population in Texas last century, the United States currently does not have a stable population.

SANDPIPERS, PHALAROPES, AND ALLIES Family Scolopacidae

Long-billed Dowitchers (far right and lower center) and Short-billed Dowitchers (NJ, May)

The large, diverse Scolopacidae family represents the heart of the shorebirds. The general similarity of shorebirds and the inherent identification difficulties keeps many birders from enjoying their distinctive traits. Most sandpiper identifications can be simplified once their basic structure and plumage are understood.

Structure This group has a great variety of shapes, from the large, long legs and long bills of a curlew to the short bills and short legs of sandpipers. Scolopacids are distinct from plovers in having longer bills. Most sandpipers forage primarily by feel; their bills have many receptors to aid in the location of prey. The males are larger than the females in some species, while in other species the females are slightly larger than the males. Transequatorial migrants have long wings and primary projection.

Behavior Most sandpipers feed and roost in or near water. They often migrate and winter in mixed-species flocks. During breeding season, however, they are territorial with little tolerance for perceived intruders; some sandpipers are territorial in migration also. Many species perform breeding displays that seem unusual for shorebirds. These displays might include slow, floppy flights with rather well-developed songs and perching in tops of trees. Feeding behavior varies, depending on shape and length of bills and legs. Most scolopacids pick at or near the water's edge, some feed in the water, and others forage in forest litter. Most sandpipers eat invertebrates, such as worms or small bugs, and some swallow mollusks whole—their strong gizzards break up the shell—and yet others eat small fish. The family as a whole is highly migratory; some species migrate long distances over the ocean, but most follow coasts, major waterways, or simply move over land. When sleeping, shorebirds typically stand on 1 leg and tuck the other into their feathers.

Plumage Understanding molt and plumages is the key to identifying difficult shorebirds. Shorebirds have at least 3 distinct plumages: breeding, nonbreeding, and juvenile. Transitional or second-year plumages are more complex, but these 3 plumages provide a good baseline. Some species show sexual dimorphism, but many show little or none. The species have different molt strategies. (The timing of molt might serve as an identification clue.) After breeding, adults generally molt into their winter plumage; most species will be pale and more unmarked below and plainer above. As spring approaches, many species begin to molt into a more colorful plumage, often with red and orange tones and streaks, spots, or splotches on the underparts. Birds less than a year old molt into their first breeding plumage. It is quite variable; sometimes they look like alternate adults, but more frequently they have a dull, incomplete plumage, with a mix of new and old feathers, closer to basic plumage. In most species juveniles leave their natal grounds in a fresh plumage that is quite distinct from either adult plumage, but a few species molt out of many juvenal feathers before moving south. Most sandpiper species retain a few juvenal feathers for months, allowing birds to be aged well into late fall or winter; seeing these feathers can be accomplished under good viewing conditions.

Distribution Of the almost 90 species worldwide, most breed in the Northern Hemisphere and migrate to temperate or tropical areas or, often, well into the Southern Hemisphere. Species nest in a variety of habitats, such as marsh, prairies, tundra, and boreal forests; in winter, most species take advantage of exposed mudflats at intertidal wetlands, although a few use bogs and marshes.

Taxonomy There is little controversy in most of the sandpiper family; however, discussions are ongoing relative to the recognition of various subspecies. Most species of sandpipers are monotypic.

Conservation All shorebirds face the continuing loss of wetlands habitats. Many species have narrow breeding ranges, and many use key staging areas as feeding stops on migration. In the event of some catastrophe, such as an oil spill, or the degradation of a habitat that impacts food sources at staging areas, populations could be rapidly put at risk. —*Matthew T. Heindel*

TRINGINE SANDPIPERS Genera *Tringa, Catoptrophorus, Heteroscelus, Actitis,* and *Xenus*

This tribe of the Sandpiper family includes the genera *Tringa, Catoptrophorus, Heteroscelus, Actitis,* and *Xenus.* Most of these birds are of medium size, although they range from small to rather large. Most of them feed by picking, but those with longer legs will wade in water to probe or take small fish. Many of these sandpipers have gray or gray-brown as their primary color, but breeding and juvenile plumages can be attractive. A majority of these birds breed in the northern latitudes, typically in marshy openings within boreal forests; only the Willet is a common breeder in the Lower 48. Most *Tringa* sandpipers migrate long distances, wintering as far south as South America and Australasia.

GREATER YELLOWLEGS *Tringa melanoleuca*

breeding

winter

winter

juvenile

The tall and somewhat robust Greater Yellowlegs is a common bird, and it is easily studied as a migrant or wintering bird. It serves as an excellent example to learn about shorebird plumages. It feeds along the water's edge, although it will partially submerge itself and feed in belly-deep water. On shore, it may walk and pick at the surface, or it may run short distances when in an active feeding mode. It often bobs the front part of its body. Monotypic. L 14" (36 cm)

Identification Long yellow legs, a long neck, and a rather thick and often upturned dark bill. BREEDING ADULT: On a whitish background, the throat and breast are heavily streaked and the sides and belly are spotted and barred with a dark blackish. On the upperparts, many feathers are black centered, and the tertials have dark barring. The legs might tend to bright yellow with orange tones. The bill is usually dark, but it can have a slightly paler base to the lower mandible. NONBREEDING ADULT: It is rather pale and uniform, being gray above and white below. The upperparts have dark notches on the outer edges of feathers and pale fringes; neither are seen easily from a distance or if worn. The legs are paler and the bill usually has an obvious pale base. JUVENILE: It is like the nonbreeding, but the upperparts have bold white spots on scapu-

lars and coverts and lack the dark marks of adult; the neck has dark streaking. The bill base averages more pale gray than in adults. FLIGHT: It has rather plain upperparts with gray wings and a white rump and whitish gray tail; the legs and feet stick out beyond the tail.

Similar Species The Greater is quite similar to the Lesser Yellowlegs, but they are usually easy to distinguish when together. The Greater has 50 percent more bulk, so it is a little taller and more robust. The bill is also thicker and longer (longer than the head) and often upturned, compared to a narrower, shorter, and straighter bill of the Lesser. The adult Greater molts earlier in fall, so early migrants might have dropped flight feathers; the Lesser does this after migration. The Greater is more heavily marked below in breeding plumage. Structure and the differing calls are the best methods of identifying these species. A Greater usually uses 3 or more *tew* notes, but a Lesser more commonly uses 2; the tone is more important than the number of notes. The Common Greenshank, a vagrant from the Old World, is similar in size and shape.

Voice CALL: A loud, slightly descending series of 3 or more *tew* notes. This ringing call can be heard for long distances. SONG: A rolling *whee-oodle;* the song might be heard on migration.

Status & Distribution Common. BREEDING: Muskeg and open or sparsely wooded areas. MIGRATION: Migrates on a broad front, but in most areas, in smaller flocks than the Lesser Yellowlegs. In spring, usually a week or so earlier than the Lesser. More southerly states see peak passage late Mar.–mid-Apr., but numbers seen into early May. Great Lakes and mid-Atlantic peak mid-Apr.–mid-May, might be seen as early as early Mar. First breeding arrivals late Apr. or early May, depending on latitude. In fall, the migration is protracted late June –late Nov. First adults arrive in late June, but most adults arrive late July–late Aug., although southern states (e.g., TX) are a little later. Juveniles account for the majority of migrants by late Aug., peaking most areas late Aug. into early Oct. Stragglers linger into Dec. if conditions mild. WINTER: Coastal and, unlike the Lesser, some inland areas in the U.S. south to S.A. VAGRANT: North of breeding grounds. Casual in Europe, primarily in fall, Japan, and S. Africa.

Population It appears stable. The species has recovered from hunting pressures.

LESSER YELLOWLEGS *Tringa flavipes*

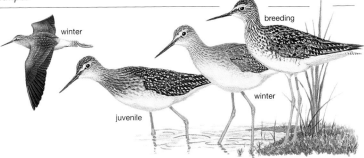

This dainty version of the Greater Yellowlegs looks almost delicate in comparison. It picks its way along the edge of the water, taking prey with its thin, straight bill. It often bobs the front part of its body in a jerky fashion. Monotypic. L 10.5" (27 cm)

Identification Long yellow legs and a short, thin, dark bill. Generally gray above, white below. BREEDING ADULT: The breast is finely streaked and the sides and flanks show fine, short bars. The legs might have an orange tone in high breeding plumage. NONBREEDING ADULT: The upperparts are gray or gray-brown, with alternating dark and light notches on the feather edges; these are difficult to see from a long distance or when worn. The underparts are white, except for the dingy breast, which has obscure streaks. JUVENILE: Similar to the nonbreeding, except the upperparts have bold white spots on coverts and scapulars. FLIGHT: The gray wings are rather uniform, with a white rump and whitish tail. The legs and feet stick out well beyond the tail.

Similar Species Similar to the Greater Yellowlegs but smaller—a comparison easily made when the 2 are together. The Lesser's all-dark bill is shorter, thinner, and straighter. The calls are different: the Lesser utters fewer notes, which are, more importantly, not as long or as piercing as the Greater's. The Stilt Sandpiper can look similar in flight, but its bill is longer and curved. The Wilson's Phalarope can be superficially similar outside of breeding plumage, but it has smaller, shorter legs, is paler above, and has a white breast.

Voice CALL: *Tew* notes, higher and shorter than the Greater's; notes usually given singly or double, but can be given in threes. SONG: *Wheedle-ree,* given with an undulating flight display.

Status & Distribution Common. BREEDING: Tundra or taiga woodland openings, generally farther north than the Greater Yellowlegs. MIGRATION: Common in the Midwest and fairly common in the East; uncommon in far West. More likely to be seen in large numbers (e.g., hundreds) than the Greater, especially during spring. In spring, it follows a pattern similar to the Greater, but usually a week later in most areas. Southern states peak in Apr.; Great Lakes and mid-Atlantic peak late Apr.–mid-May. In fall, the first adults move south in late June and peak late July–mid-Aug. Juveniles generally first arrive in early Aug. and peak late Aug.–Sept. More numerous in fall than in spring along the Pacific coast.

Lessers have a more defined peak than Greaters and have generally left by mid-Oct., with lingering birds into Nov., exceptionally later. WINTER: Most winter in S.A. or C.A. Local along the coasts, especially in TX, but always outnumbered by Greaters. Away from the coast, use caution when identifying winter Lessers. VAGRANT: North and west of breeding range, primarily May–June; annual to Europe, primarily Aug.–Oct.; fall records from Japan and China, winter records from New Zealand and Australia.

Population The numbers have stabilized since hunting was stopped.

COMMON GREENSHANK *Tringa nebularia*

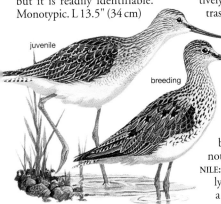

This species is a vagrant from the Old World. It might be overlooked since it is similar to the Greater Yellowlegs, but it is readily identifiable. Monotypic. L 13.5" (34 cm)

Identification A rather large and robust *Tringa*, the Greenshank has a long neck. The black tip of the relatively long, slightly upturned bill contrasts with a gray base. Greenish legs. BREEDING ADULT: Brownish gray above, with black centers to many scapulars. White underparts, with light to moderate streaking on the breast and neck. NONBREEDING ADULT: Streaking absent or restricted, with a rather pale head and foreneck. Upperparts lack black; feathers have dark and light notches on outer feather edges. JUVENILE: Like the nonbreeding, but boldly marked above; white edges create a distinctly striped appearance.

FLIGHT: A white rump and a wedge continuing up into the lower back is distinctive.

Similar Species Looks similar to the Greater Yellowlegs, but the adult is less heavily streaked and the juvenile has striped, not spotted, upperparts. In all plumages, the legs are greenish, and in flight, a white wedge extends up to middle of back.

Voice CALL: A loud *tew-tew-tew* on same pitch.

Status & Distribution Eurasia. Rare migrant to Aleutian and Pribilof Is., very rare to St. Lawrence I., casual to eastern Canada, and 2 CA records Most records from spring, but some in fall and winter.

MARSH SANDPIPER *Tringa stagnatilis*

juvenile

The Marsh Sandpiper is a vagrant from the Old World, recorded to date in N.A. only on the Aleutian Islands. It is the most delicate *Tringa*, with long legs and a long, thin bill. Its gait is rather deliberate as it picks its way around water, and it is more stiltlike in many ways. Monotypic. L 8.5" (21 cm)
Identification Gray-brown above and white below; greenish legs; long, thin, dark bill, almost needlelike. Face pattern different from most *Tringa*, lacking a distinct loral stripe

and having a supercilium that extends beyond the eye. BREEDING ADULT: Irregular dark markings on plain brown scapulars create somewhat mottled upperparts, alternating black and brown. The tertials and many wing coverts are brown, with black barring. The head, neck, and breast are liberally streaked or spotted with brown, largely eliminating the supercilium. The remaining underparts are white, although some light spotting or barring might be present on the flanks and undertail coverts. NONBREEDING ADULT: Plain gray-brown on the upperparts, with the head and back slightly paler than the wings. The scapulars and wing coverts have thin, whitish borders when fresh. The underparts are white below, generally lacking streaks. JUVENILE: Similar to the nonbreeding, except for darker upperparts, with bold white or buff spots on scapulars and coverts. FLIGHT: Gray upperparts, with slightly darker wings, contrast with the white

tail, rump, and lower back. The legs extend well beyond the tail in flight.
Similar Species Only vaguely similar to the Lesser Yellowlegs, but the 2 species share long legs and straight, thin bills. The Marsh has a thinner, longer bill, giving it a more dainty look. In flight, the white on the lower back is more like that of the Common Greenshank, whereas the Lesser has white restricted to the rump and tail. Somewhat similar to both the Stilt Sandpiper and the Wilson's Phalarope in nonbreeding plumage. The Stilt has an obviously curved bill and, in flight, a white wing stripe and no white on the back. The Wilson's has a rather needlelike bill and no wing stripe, but it has a dark back. It also looks more compact as its legs are much shorter than those of the Marsh; as a result, its legs do not extend as far beyond the tail in flight.
Voice CALL: *Tew*, repeated like a Lesser Yellowlegs.
Status & Distribution Vagrant. Three recs. from western and central Aleutians.

SPOTTED REDSHANK *Tringa erythropus*

The Spotted Redshank, an Old World vagrant to North America, is unique among the *Tringa* for a molt of its underparts to dark feathers and for its bill that droops toward the tip. Its behavior involves the expected picking and probing near the water's edge, although this species is an impressive wader and seems to take to swimming more readily than its congeners. Monotypic. L 12.5" (32 cm)

winter

juvenile

breeding

winter

Identification The long, mostly dark bill droops at the tip. BREEDING ADULT: It has a dark plumage overall with white spots on dark brown upperparts; black below, with females more likely to have a black breast or belly interrupted with white spots. The legs are long and dark red, although they can be almost black. The bill is long and black, with red at the base. NONBREEDING ADULT: Upperparts a rather uniform gray with a dingy whitish breast; the remaining underparts are white. The red-orange to red legs are much brighter than in a breeding bird. JUVENILE: It has darker upperparts than a nonbreeding bird, and is somewhat variable. Most juveniles are dark brown with white spots on the upperparts and underparts that are brownish gray; some juveniles can be quite dark, almost approaching breeding females in coloration. The supercilium is bold and the legs are paler than on

a nonbreeding bird. The base of the mandible is orange-red, not as bright as in a nonbreeding bird. FLIGHT: Dark above, with a white wedge on the back, and a barred rump and tail; light or dark below, depending on the plumage; and white wing linings. The legs and feet extend well beyond the tail.
Similar Species It is unlikely that you would confuse the Spotted Redshank with other waders. Its drooping bill, red legs (orangish in some yellowlegs), and the white wedge up the back are unlike any other species. The Common Redshank, a less likely vagrant, other than having red legs, looks little like the Spotted: It is shorter, smaller billed, and browner above, and has a bold white secondary patch in flight.
Voice CALL: A loud rising *chu-weet*. Similar to the Pacific Golden-Plover's, more strident than the Semipalmated Plover's.
Status & Distribution Breeds on tundra and northern boggy or marshy openings within open forests in Eurasia. A very rare spring and fall visitor to Aleutian and Pribilof Islands. Casual on both coasts in migration and winter; accidental elsewhere with scattered records across N.A.

COMMON REDSHANK *Tringa totanus*

juvenile

juvenile

breeding

This species is a vagrant from the Old World. Multiple birds occurred during a season, suggesting that the right weather pattern will deposit more Commons in the future. Polytypic (probably *robusta* in N.A.). L 11" (28 cm)

Identification The Common Redshank is slightly smaller than its relative, the Spotted Redshank. Its bill is short and straight, almost stout, and red at the base. Its legs are of medium length and vary from orange to red. The Common is generally brownish above and white with streaking below. BREEDING ADULT: It is brown above with heavy streaking; it has a whitish background below, usually with streaks on the breast that turn into barring on the flanks. A white eye ring is usually evident, but the dark lores are obscured. NONBREEDING ADULT: It is rather plain brown above, with some feathers having dark notches on the feather edges; these notches are less evident than on other *Tringa* and might not be visible without good views. The breast and sides are brownish, with some spots or streaks. The belly and undertail coverts are white, with some barring. JUVENILE: It is similar to a nonbreeding, but it is more heavily marked above, with the scapulars and coverts having bold white spots. The breast is whiter with breast streaking; the remainder of the underparts are paler. The legs are paler, with more of a yellow tone to the orange. The bill has minimal color to the base of the mandible. FLIGHT: A white dorsal wedge is visible in flight, as are a distinctive broad white trailing edge to the secondaries and inner primaries that looks like a white patch.

Similar Species Given a good view, no other species looks like a Common Redshank.

Voice CALL: A loud *twek-twek* and a mournful, liquid whistle, *teu,* with a distinctly lower ending.

Status & Distribution Breeds in Eurasia, as close as Iceland. The Common's breeding range is more southerly than its congeners', and its wintering range is more northerly; the combination makes the Common a less likely candidate for a wide pattern of vagrancy; however, it is casual to NF (5 recs.; 4 in spring 1995). Numerous records for Greenland indicate a pattern of short-distance vagrancy.

WOOD SANDPIPER *Tringa glareola*

The Wood Sandpiper is a vagrant from the Old World, somewhat intermediate between the Lesser Yellowlegs and the Solitary Sandpiper. Along with the Green and Solitary Sandpipers, the Wood is a more compact *Tringa,* with obviously shorter legs. It frequents edges of wetlands, often where there is grass. Its methodically picks food from the surface as it ambles along. Monotypic. L 8" (20 cm)

Identification The dark upperparts are heavily spotted, and the underparts are white, with brownish streaks on the breast and neck. It generally has a prominent whitish supercilium, particularly bold in front of the eye, which contrasts with a dark lore. An eye ring is usually obvious. The bill is rather short and dark; the legs vary from yellow to greenish yellow. BREEDING ADULT: The upperparts are boldly checked with white; the breast and neck are heavily streaked. The bill often shows a pale base; legs more often with yellow tone. NONBREEDING ADULT: It is duller than a breeding bird, with upperparts lacking the black-centered feathers. In fresh plumage, there are pale fringes on most scapulars and white spots on the coverts. JUVENILE: It is like a nonbreeding adult, but the upperparts are darker, with more extensive spotting and more streaking on the breast. The crown is distinctly dark, set off from the supercilium. The legs are paler, more greenish. FLIGHT: It looks brown above and whitish below, with plain wings, a white rump and a whitish tail, moderately barred, including the outer tail feathers. The wing linings are pale gray.

Similar Species The Wood's plumage is closer to the Lesser Yellowlegs, but its shape is similar to the Green and Solitary Sandpipers. The Solitary has dark central rectrices and is also darker, more gray, or grayish olive, as opposed to brown. The Wood is distinguished from the Green by paler wing linings, a smaller white rump patch, and a more densely barred tail. Compared to the Lesser Yellowlegs, note the Wood's eye ring, shorter bill, and the presence of a supercilium. In addition, Lessers are taller, with more leg extending beyond the tail in flight.

Voice CALL: A loud, sharp whistling of 3 or more notes. Similar to the call of the Long-billed Dowitcher.

Status & Distribution Eurasia. Casual breeder on the outer Aleutian Islands. MIGRATION: Fairly common spring migrant to the outer Aleutians; uncommon on the Pribilof Islands; rare on St. Lawrence I. Rare in fall. Casual to BC and northeastern N.A.

breeding

juvenile

juvenile

breeding

GREEN SANDPIPER *Tringa ochropus*

The Green is a vagrant from the Old World. Monotypic. L 8.8" (22 cm) **Identification** Dark above with variable spotting; white below, with breast streaking. Straight, dark bill of medium length; greenish legs. BREEDING ADULT: Dark olive-gray tone to upperparts, with white spots on many scapulars and coverts. NONBREEDING ADULT: Brown tone to upperparts, less spotting above; neck and breast brown with indistinct streaks. JUVENILE: Like nonbreeding adult, but more heavily spotted above, streaks on breast on white background. FLIGHT: Blackish wing linings, white rump, with barring primarily near tips of tail; outer rectrices with little or no barring.

Similar Species The Green resembles a Solitary Sandpiper in plumage, behavior, and calls. Note the Green's white rump and uppertail coverts, with less extensively barred tail; darker wing linings; and lack of solidly dark central tail feathers. The similar Wood Sandpiper has more spotting above, more barring on tail, and paler wing linings.

Voice CALL: *Peet-o-weet.* Like Solitary's, but mixes notes with different pitch.

Status & Distribution Eurasian breeder. Casual in spring on outer Aleutian Islands; accidental to Pribilof Islands and St. Lawrence Island.

breeding

juvenile

juvenile

SOLITARY SANDPIPER *Tringa solitaria*

This mid-size sandpiper is usually seen singly or in small groups. Typically encountered around small pools, wet grassy areas, or creeks, it bobs its entire body or, more rarely, just the tail. It calls frequently as it flies overhead and is reliably vocal when flushed. Upon landing it often holds its wings up, as if getting its balance, allowing looks at the underwings. Polytypic. L 8.5" (22 cm)

Identification Dark brown above, with spots, and white below; the lower throat, breast, and sides streaked with blackish brown; the undertail coverts might be streaked. Dark bill, often with a pale base. Yellowish to greenish legs. White eye ring in all plumages; bold white supraloral line does not extend beyond the eye. BREEDING ADULT: Dark brown, with extensive spotting on upperparts and streaks on the neck and breast. Pale base to the bill can make the bill look 2-toned. Legs more likely to be yellow. NONBREEDING ADULT: Duller, with streaking more obscure, and fewer pale spots above. Bill usually dark; greenish legs. JUVENILE: Dark upperparts, with bold white spots, more marked than nonbreeding adult. Plain brown head and breast, with minimal or no streaking. FLIGHT: Dark central tail feathers, white outer feathers barred with black, darkish underwing.

Geographic Variation Two subspecies. Nominate *solitarius* breeds from interior British Columbia to Labrador; it is more common in the East as a migrant. The adult has dark lores and the juvenile's upperparts are spotted white. The *cinnamomea* breeds from Alaska to Hudson Bay; it is more common in the West. It is larger and paler; the adult has streaked lores and the juvenile's upperparts are spotted buffy.

Similar Species Most similar to Green and Wood Sandpipers. Bolder white eye ring, shorter olive legs, tail pattern, and call distinguish it from a Lesser Yellowlegs.

Voice CALL: A shrill *peet-weet,* sometimes 3 notes, higher pitched and more emphatic than calls of the Spotted Sandpiper.

Status & Distribution Fairly common. BREEDING: Shallow backwaters, taiga pools, and bogs. Uses abandoned passerine nests in small trees, unique for North American shorebirds. MIGRATION: Journey in spring starts late Mar., but migrants have been noted late Feb. Peak mid-Apr. in TX, late Apr.–mid-May in Great Lakes, mid-Atlantic, etc. Stragglers seen late May south of Canada. In fall, adults arrive late June–early July in Great Lakes and mid-Atlantic, mid-July in TX, etc. Juveniles predominate in West during fall, peak in Aug. Numbers drop in Sept., with most gone by early Oct., stragglers to Nov. WINTER: Primarily the tropics but rarely in the U.S., primarily southern TX. VAGRANT: W. Europe, Bering Sea, and S. Africa.

Population Studies are needed; there is remarkably little data, perhaps owing to the largely remote breeding grounds and the bird's solitary nature.

juvenile

Solitary Sandpiper breeding

Green Sandpiper breeding

breeding

juvenile

WILLET *Catoptrophorus semipalmatus*

western
inornatus

winter

winter

breeding

juvenile

returns to breeding areas in mid-Atlantic mid- to late Apr. In fall, *inornatus* starts moving in late June; adults peak mid-July–mid-Aug., juveniles numerous by late July; most migrants through by early Sept., with stragglers into Oct., rarely later. Most *semipalmatus* depart early, and arriving *inornatus* outnumber them by Aug. WINTER: Coastal beaches and Salton Sea. VAGRANT: Casual to YK, northern BC, Hudson Bay, and southern QC. Accidental to Europe.

Population Hunting in the 1900s devastated Atlantic populations, but they seem to have rebounded.

The Willet's shape—large, plump, rather long legs, a thick bill—is unique for a shorebird. It picks and probes for prey, feeding along the shore, sometimes in the water. It often bobs its body, like a yellowlegs. It often occurs in small flocks during migration or while feeding; it roosts in large groups with other large shorebirds. Polytypic (2 ssp; see sidebar below). L 15" (38 cm)

Identification Generally gray or brownish gray above and whitish below. Stout, straight, dark bill, gray or brown at base. Gray legs, with possible dull olive or blue tones. BREEDING ADULT: Heavily streaked on neck, barred on breast and sides; white belly. The upperparts might have extensive black feathers. NONBREEDING ADULT: In general, unmarked gray above and white below. JUVENILE: Brownish upperparts, with obvious white or buff spots and fringes. FLIGHT: Striking black-and-white wing pattern diagnostic in all plumages.

Similar Species Unmistakable in breeding plumage and in flight. A roosting nonbreeding bird might recall a yellowlegs, but the Willet's legs are always dull, the bill larger, and the shape plumper.

Voice CALL: In nesting areas, a *pill-will-willet,* higher and faster in eastern birds. Also a *kip* or *yip,* sometimes repeated.

Status & Distribution Fairly common. BREEDING: Freshwater and alkaline marshes in the West; salt marshes in the East. MIGRATION: In spring, "western" Willet *(inornatus)* occurs by late Mar. in inland parts of southern states. Peak late Apr.–early May at Great Lakes. The "eastern" *(semipalmatus)* generally

Separation of Eastern and Western Willets

Some birders believe that the 2 Willet subspecies—the western *inornatus* and the eastern *semipalmatus*—may be different species. Separating them is not always easy.

In general, the eastern Willet is smaller by approximately 10 percent. It also has a shorter bill and shorter legs, by up to 15 percent. Easterns are more heavily barred below in breeding plumage than the western Willet; they also have more gray on the breast in nonbreeding plumage. A juvenile eastern's wing coverts are less noticeably marked, compared to a western.

The western is paler in all plumages. With its longer legs, the western is more apt to be seen wading in belly-deep water. The bill is longer, slightly thinner at the base, and more likely upturned; the combination of longer legs, wading in water, and an upturned bill might recall

"Eastern" Willet, breeding (NY)

"Western" Willet, breeding (TX, Apr.)

a godwit more than eastern birds. The white wing stripe is broader in the *inornatus.*

Subspecies can be differentiated by their songs; all calls and songs are lower pitched in the western.

And finally, distribution is important: eastern Willets are not recorded inland, nor are they expected in winter; their winter range is poorly known. ∎

WANDERING TATTLER *Heteroscelus incanus*

breeding

breeding

winter

juvenile

One of the shorebirds of the rocky Pacific coast, the Wandering Tattler is admired more for its habits than for its coloration. A chunky gray bird, it can easily go unnoticed as it feeds on rocks exposed by the tide; it bobs as it feeds. Its call can be heard over crashing waves, and it is often a clue in detecting the bird. It is generally seen singly or in small groups. Monotypic. L 11" (28 cm)

Identification Long wings and short legs contribute to a horizontal look. The wings extend noticeably beyond the tail tip. The bill is rather long and black, at times showing a pale base; the nasal groove is often visible, extending more than halfway to the tip. The legs are dull yellow, sometimes with a greenish tone. The bird is uniformly dark gray above and white below. BREEDING ADULT: The underparts are heavily barred, all the way through the sides to the undertail coverts. The white supercilium is flecked with gray and is most prominent in front of the eye. Legs are at their brightest, usually yellow. Some first-year birds, with an incomplete plumage, can be difficult to age. NONBREEDING ADULT: It is unbarred below with a gray wash on breast, sides, and flanks; uniform gray above. Legs are duller, more greenish yellow. JUVENILE: Like the nonbreeding bird, but it has pale fringes on upperpart feathers, sometimes with alternating light and dark spots along those feathers.

Similar Species The Wandering closely resembles a Gray-tailed Tattler and is best distinguished from it by voice. In breeding plumage, the Gray-tailed's finer barring does not extend beyond the flanks; it has a few bars on undertail coverts and flanks. A juvenile Gray-tailed is more heavily marked above, with more extensive spotting and notches. In all plumages there is a difference in the length of the nasal groove; the Wandering's extends more than half way to the bill tip. Use caution in assessing this feature—it is hard to see on some individuals.

Voice CALL: A rapid series of clear, hollow whistles, *twee, twee, twee;* all on one pitch.

Status & Distribution Fairly common. BREEDING: On or near gravelly stream banks. MIGRATION: Mostly along the coast or over the ocean. In spring, peaking early Apr.–mid-May in southern CA, mid-Apr.–early May on Pacific islands. Common by early May in southern AK, on breeding grounds by late May. In fall, adults depart July, peak late July–mid-Aug. in OR. Juveniles predominate late Aug.–Sept. Smaller numbers move through Oct. WINTER: CA to Ecuador, Pacific islands, and in Australasia. VAGRANT: Casual inland during migration, with a few records east of the Rockies (e.g., TX, MA, and ON).

Population No recent data.

GRAY-TAILED TATTLER *Heteroscelus brevipes*

This vagrant from Asia is very similar to the Wandering Tattler in behavior and preferred habitat, but it is more likely to be found on sandy beaches, ponds, or mudflats. Monotypic. L 10" (25 cm)

Identification The Gray-tailed is generally similar to the Wandering Tattler in plumage and structure, although it has slightly shorter wings, with the primaries barely extending beyond the tail. The whitish superciliums are more distinct and meet on forehead. The dark bill might have a pale base; the nasal grooves usually do not extend more than halfway to the tip. BREEDING ADULT: The upperparts are pale gray and unmarked. The underparts have fine barring that is not extensive beyond the flanks; there are a few bars on the undertail coverts. NONBREEDING ADULT: Pale gray above, and unmarked white below, except for grayish on the sides and breast. JUVENILE: Similar to a nonbreeding bird, but with a white belly and sides, and pale spots on the upperparts, almost like a *Tringa*.

Similar Species The Gray-tailed closely resembles the Wandering, however, its upperparts are slightly paler gray and the barring on the underparts is finer and less extensive in a breeding adult. A juvenile has less extensive gray on the sides and belly and is more heavily marked above; some are tinged brownish above. The shorter nasal groove of the Gray-tailed can be difficult to accurately assess in the field. Best distinction is voice.

Voice CALL: A loud ascending *too-weet,* similar to the Common Ringed Plover.

Status & Distribution Breeds in Asia. Regular spring and fall migrant on outer Aleutians, Pribilofs, and St. Lawrence Is. Casual visitor to north AK; accidental in fall to WA and CA.

breeding

juvenile

COMMON SANDPIPER *Actitis hypoleucos*

The Old World equivalent to Spotted Sandpipers, this vagrant has not been recorded away from Alaska. Monotypic. L 8" (20 cm)

Identification This species is a small, short-legged sandpiper with a long tail, which it bobs. Typically seen near

freshwater, its flight is low over the water, with shallow, flicking wingbeats. The bill is gray and the legs are greenish. BREEDING ADULT: Brown above, with dark streaks on the upperparts and dark spots along the edge of the tertials; it is white below, with brown on the upper breast, which is finely streaked. NONBREEDING ADULT: Similar to breeding birds, but it lacks extensive streaking. JUVENILE: Similar to nonbreeding birds, but the upperparts are well marked; pale fringes and dark subterminal lines give a scaled effect; and tertials have barring around the entire feather. FLIGHT: A broad white wing stripe extends to the base of the

juvenile

wing and is adjacent to a bold white trailing edge to the inner secondaries.

Similar Species Juvenile and nonbreeding plumages resemble the nonbreeding and juvenile Spotted Sandpiper. Note the Common's longer tail; on juvenile, the barring on the edge of the tertials extends along the entire feather. In flight the Common shows a longer white wing stripe and longer white trailing edge.

Voice CALL: A piping *twee-wee-wee*, higher than the Spotted Sandpiper.

Status & Distribution Breeds in Eurasia. Rare but regular migrant, usually in spring, on the outer Aleutians, Pribilofs, and St. Lawrence Is. Accidental to Seward Peninsula.

breeding

SPOTTED SANDPIPER *Actitis macularius*

North America's most widespread breeding sandpiper, the Spotted is found on freshwater, typically rivers, streams, and lakes. It has a unique and bold breeding plumage and an interesting biology. Its flight is low to the water, on shallow, flicking wingbeats that seem jerky. It bobs and teeters constantly, whether walking along the shore or just standing. The polyandrous females arrive early, find and defend territories, and attract males, who take the lead parental role. Generally seen singly, they may form small flocks in migration. Monotypic. L 7.5" (19 cm)

Identification This short-legged, horizontal-looking sandpiper is brown above and white below. The bill is pale at the base, varying from flesh to yellow. The legs vary from greenish to yellow. BREEDING ADULT: Unmistakable. It has bold spotting throughout underparts, and dark bars or streaks above. The bill is nearly entirely pale; the legs

are more yellow. NONBREEDING ADULT: It has dark patches on the sides of the breast; the white of the underparts forms a wedge above the dark wing. The spots are absent or reduced; often only a few spots on undertail coverts or, rarely, elsewhere. The bill and legs are duller; the barred wing coverts contrast with the rather uniform brown back. JUVENILE: Similar to nonbreeding birds, with faint edges to the upperparts, but barred wing coverts still contrast with back. The barring on the edge of the tertials, absent on some juveniles, extends no farther than halfway along each feather. FLIGHT: A white wing stripe is evident, but it does not extend to the base; there is also a narrow trailing edge to the wing.

Similar Species Compared to the Common, the Spotted has a shorter tail, and in flight it shows a shorter white wing stripe and a shorter white trailing edge. Also the Common's shallow wingbeats are not as exaggerated as the Spotted's. On juveniles, the Spotted shows a

greater contrast between the wing coverts and the scapulars, which are more boldly marked on Common. The Common's tertials are barred; if bars are present on Spotted, they do not extend around the entire feather.

Voice CALL: A shrill *peet-weet;* a series of *weet* notes in flight. Lower pitched than calls of the Solitary Sandpiper.

Status & Distribution Common and widespread. BREEDING: Sheltered streams, ponds, lakes, or marshes. MIGRATION: In spring, peak late Apr. in the southern states (e.g., FL, TX), first 3 weeks of May in Great Lakes. Females arrive mid-May in MN, a week before males. In fall, some adults leave late June, peak mid- to late July through Aug. Juveniles predominate in Sept., with stragglers Oct.–mid-Nov. WINTER: Most winter in C.A. and S.A. Uncommon to fairly common in coastal southern states; rare to southern edge of breeding range. VAGRANT: Eastern Siberia and Europe.

Population The Spotted's population is stable, but the birds are sensitive to the health of rivers and lakes.

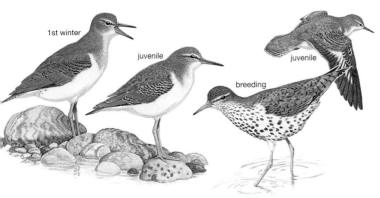

1st winter

juvenile

juvenile

breeding

TEREK SANDPIPER Xenus cinereus

The Terek Sandpiper, a vagrant from the Old World, has a unique, frenetic personality. When hunting, it uses a jerky, start-and-stop run to cross mudflats. It teeters like a Spotted Sandpiper. Monotypic. L 9" (23 cm)

Identification Gray or brownish upperparts; white underparts. Long upturned bill. Short orange-yellow legs. BREEDING ADULT: Dark-centered scapulars form 2 dark lines on the back; faint streaking on the breast. NONBREEDING ADULT: Reduced black lines on back and breast streaking. Dark lores and faint supercilium both bolder. JUVENILE: Like nonbreeding, but darker brown above, with buffy edges to most of the upperparts.

breeding

FLIGHT: Distinctive wing pattern with dark leading edge, grayer median coverts, dark greater coverts, and broad white tips to the secondaries.

Similar Species Unmistakable. A roosting bird might present a challenge, but the Terek's short legs and thick-based upturned bill are unlike any other species.

Voice CALL: A series of shrill whistled notes on 1 pitch, usually in threes.

breeding

juvenile

Status & Distribution Rare migrant on outer Aleutians. Casual on Pribilofs, St. Lawrence Is., and in Anchorage area; accidental to coastal BC, CA, and MA (June rec.).

CURLEWS Genera Bartramia and Numenius

These waders have long legs and, usually, long bills. Most plumages are brown with little change between seasons, ages, or sexes. Females tend to be larger than males in most species, with larger bills. The bills grow over the first year. Most species stay near water (less so during breeding season), feeding on crabs, worms, and more, but insects are also a key part of the diet for some species.

UPLAND SANDPIPER Bartramia longicauda

The Upland Sandpiper is typically found in fields, where its head and neck are visible above the grass; on the breeding grounds, it perches on posts. It often bobs the rear portion of its body, and, upon landing, will typically hold its wings up momentarily. The Upland is one of few shorebirds that seems disinterested in water. Monotypic. L 12" (31 cm)

Identification This small, aberrant curlew is an elongate species with a long, thin neck; long legs; long tail; and long wings. It has a short, straight bill. The legs and bill are yellow; the bill is dark at the tip and atop the ridge. The head is small and dove-like, with large, dark eyes. It is generally brown; the upperparts are dark with buff edges and brown streaks on the foreneck, which turn into chevrons on the breast and flanks. The belly and undertail coverts are white. ADULT: The upperparts look barred, whereas the tertials are entirely barred. JUVENILE: It can look very similar to the adult. The upperparts look less barred due to pale fringes on dark feathers; the tertials are edged in buff. Some juveniles have a rich tawny color to the sides of the neck in fresh plumage. FLIGHT: Blackish primaries contrast with mottled brown upperparts.

Similar Species The unique shape and plumage of the Upland eliminate most confusion with other waders.

Voice CALL: A rolling, bubbling *pulip, pulip.* A "wolf whistle," given on breeding grounds, sounds distinctly human.

Status & Distribution Rare to fairly common. BREEDING: Tallgrass prairies (less common in short-grass prairies), increasingly restricted to airports in the East. MIGRATION: More likely found in dirt or short grassy fields, including sod farms. In spring, the first arrivals appear mid-Mar., with peak late Mar.–mid-Apr. in south, mid-Apr.–early May farther north. Fall movement begins in July, with peak late July–mid-Aug. in north, Aug.–mid-Sept. farther south, stragglers to Oct., rarely to Nov. WINTER: Primarily southern S.A. VAGRANT: Casual on West Coast and in the Southwest in migration; casual in Europe in fall. Accidental in Australia and Guam.

Population Upland numbers are seriously declining in the eastern parts of the bird's range. The loss of habitat due to grassland conversion to agricultural fields has had a greater impact on the population than the hunting pressures of the 19th century.

adult

juvenile

juvenile

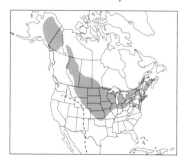

LITTLE CURLEW *Numenius minutus*

adult

adult

This aptly named, diminutive curlew is a vagrant from Asia. Monotypic. L 12" (30 cm)

Identification This small curlew has a short, dark bill that is only slightly curved; it has a pale base. Its legs are grayish but variable; they can be flesh-colored or greenish. The dark crown (occasionally showing pale mid-crown) is offset by a pale buff supercilium. A dark line or patch behind the eye is interrupted in front of the eye, leaving the lores at least partial-ly pale. The upperparts are composed of dark scapulars and coverts that are broadly edged buff. Below, there are faint streaks on a buff breast, and slight barring on the sides and flanks. It is very difficult to age this species other than in fall, when assessing the degree of feather wear will reveal juveniles, who look fresh in early fall. On adults, the tertials are usually distinct, showing brown with narrow, dark bars, whereas juveniles show dark feathers, almost black, with buff notches along the edge of the feather. But this feature appears suf-ficiently variable to limit its use as a diagnostic tool. FLIGHT: It appears uni-form brown above, with only slight-ly darker primaries. The underwings are brown. The toes barely extend beyond the tip of the tail.

Similar Species The Little Curlew is similar to the less diminutive Whim-brel, but with a shorter and only slight-ly curved bill, mostly pale lores, and buffy tones. The Little's size and short bill are like the Upland Sandpiper's, but note the curve to the Little's bill and the Little's stronger head pattern. If you are lucky enough to encounter the Little, you must con-sider the probably extinct Eskimo Curlew. The Eskimo has a bolder head pattern, including dark lores, heavier dark chevrons on flanks, and cinna-mon wing linings.

Voice Vagrants here are mostly silent. CALL: A musical *quee-dlee* and a loud *tchew-tchew-tchew.*

Status & Distribution Breeds in central and northeast Siberia. Casual fall vagrant to coastal CA; 1 spring record for St. Lawrence I. and 1 sight record for WA. WINTER: Mainly northern Australia.

Population Small and disjunct; threat-ened due to habitat loss in migration and winter range.

ESKIMO CURLEW *Numenius borealis* (E)

The Eskimo Curlew is probably extinct; the last confirmed record was of a bird shot by a hunter in Barba-dos in 1963. There have been several sightings in the intervening years, but none with definitive documentation. Given the species' remote summer and winter habitats, it is conceivable, but not likely, that the Eskimo still exists. Monotypic. L 14" (36 cm)

Identification The Eskimo is similar in looks to the Little Curlew or a small Whimbrel, but its head pattern is more muted than the Whimbrel's and the central crown stripe is indistinct or lacking entirely. The lores are entire-ly dark, like the Whimbrel, but unlike the Little. The Eskimo's upperparts are dark with buff edges; the underparts are buff, with streaks on the neck and dark chevrons down the sides. The wings are long and project past the tail. FLIGHT: It appears entirely brown above, with slightly darker primaries. The underwing is cinnamon but looks darker in flight.

Similar Species The Eskimo differs from the Whimbrel and a buffy Bristle-thighed Curlew in its smaller size, smaller, less curved bill, more muted head pattern, and cinnamon under-wings. (The Bristle-thighed has a cin-namon-rust rump and tail.) This identification would be more prob-lematic with a fresh juvenile Whim-brel, as its bill can be substantially shorter than an adult's. In compari-son with the Little Curlew, the Eski-mo is slightly larger, with a more curved bill, completely dark lores, more heavily marked flanks, and dark-er underwings.

Voice CALL: Poorly known, but includes clear whistles.

Status & Distribution This species is prob-ably extinct, although it is federally list-ed as endangered. It nested on Arctic tundra and wintered in S.A., but its full, former breeding range is not known. MIGRATION: This species used to be found in large flocks, with north-bound migration being primarily mid-continent, and southbound birds being largely transoceanic, taking the Atlantic Ocean to S.A. Their stopover points hosted large numbers. During spring movements, migrants were found Mar.–Apr. In fall, Eskimos would stage along Canada's Atlantic coast, fatten-ing up on berries for their transocean-ic flights, typically Aug.–Sept. Records on the U.S. Atlantic coast were rather sparse, particularly south of New Eng-land. VAGRANT: Records from Russia and from the British Isles in the 19th century.

Population This species, once so numer-ous, has declined so precipitously as to be probably extinct. The 2 primary reasons for its decline are 19th-cen-tury hunting pressures, which impact-ed almost all shorebirds, and, uniquely for the Eskimo Curlew, the disap-pearance of a key prey item (a grasshopper). Most of the breeding grounds are hard to access, as are much of the wintering grounds. The 2 most likely places to search for this bird are along the upper Texas coast from late March through mid-April and along the Labrador coast August through September. However, given the high-ly social nature of this species during migration and winter, it is unlikely that the species has survived.

adult

adult

WHIMBREL *Numenius phaeopus*

variegatus

phaeopus

hudsonicus

The Whimbrel is most frequently encountered along the coasts during migration. It forms large flocks away from the breeding grounds. The Whimbrel picks at the ground for food while walking. It often forms large flocks with other large shorebirds, such as godwits and curlews. Polytypic. L 17.5" (45 cm)

Identification The Whimbrel is a medium-size curlew, rather cool brown in color, with bold head stripes. The black bill, a little pale at the base, is moderate in size and curvature; the legs are blue-gray. The crown has a broad dark lateral stripe, with a pale midcrown stripe. A dark eye line, including the lores, sets off the paler supercilium. The upperparts are dark brown with pale notches along many of the scapulars and coverts. The neck and breast are lightly streaked, with barring on the sides; the remainder of the underparts are dingy whitish buff. JUVENILE: It can be difficult to age this species, but juveniles typically have more extensive pale edging and notches on the upperparts and a shorter bill. There is often a greater contrast between the scapulars and coverts on young birds compared to adults. FLIGHT: Uniform cool brown above, including dark rump; from below,

hudsonicus

juvenile

adult

dark underwings. Feet do not project beyond the tail.

Geographic Variation The North American *hudsonicus* is described above. The European nominate *phaeopus,* a casual vagrant to the East Coast, has a white rump and underwings and coarser dark markings on the breast; the Asian *variegatus,* a regular migrant in western Alaska, with a few Pacific coast records farther south (and 1 interior rec.), has a whitish, variably streaked rump and underwings. On some *variegatus* the rump can be very white, on others the entire area is boldly barred. Both *phaeopus* and *variegatus* share a whiter ground color to the underparts, compared to the browner ground color of *hudsonicus.* They also average grayer on the upperparts, with greater contrast between the wing coverts and scapulars. Many characters overlap within the Eurasian subspecies; identification should be made carefully and include a component of geographic probability until more is learned about separating these taxa. Unless the plumage is at one of the extremes, presume that birds on the East Coast are *phaeopus* and those on the West Coast are *variegatus.*

Similar Species The Long-billed Curlew, given its status and distribution, could cause confusion, but identification is usually straightforward. The Whimbrel is smaller, with a smaller bill and bold head stripes, and its plumage never matches the warmth of the Long-billed. In Alaska, less likely elsewhere, the Bristle-thighed Curlew is similar. It has a bold head pattern and, when worn, might lose some of its buff coloration on the body as well as the buff notches to the upperparts, increasing the potential for con-

fusion with the Whimbrel. But even a worn Bristle-thighed has a distinctively buffer tail and rump than the uniform brown of a *hudsonicus* Whimbrel, or compared to the dull gray-and-white barring of a *variegatus* Whimbrel. The Little Curlew, a possible vagrant, is smaller, with a smaller bill and has pale lores; it could be confused with a young Whimbrel, which has a small bill—assess other characteristics to make sure.

Voice CALL: A series of hollow whistles on 1 pitch, *pi-pi-pi-pi.*

Status & Distribution Fairly common. BREEDING: Open tundra. MIGRATION: Starts late Mar., exceptionally in early Mar. Peak in most southern states from mid- to late Apr.; peak in mid-Atlantic and Great Lakes states mid-May; western states slightly earlier. In fall, adults move first, typically early to mid-July. Juveniles peak mid-Aug.–mid-Sept., stragglers in Great Lakes and mid-Atlantic to mid- or late Oct. WINTER: Beaches and coastal wetlands from CA and VA south to S.A. VAGRANT: N.A. *hudsonicus* is casual in Europe, Africa, and Australasia. Records of non-*hudsonicus* Whimbrel recorded from ON and OH.

Population The numbers are stable and no recent trend data is available.

BRISTLE-THIGHED CURLEW *Numenius tahitiensis*

Lucky is the birder who finds the Bristle-thighed Curlew on migration, as it is rarely found away from its remote Alaskan breeding grounds or its winter home on ocean islands. In addition, this curlew is unique in being completely flightless during its molt on Pacific islands. The species'

common name derives from the bare shafts on the thigh feathers; reasons for this characteristic are not clear. Monotypic. L 18"(46 cm)

Identification The medium-sized Bristle-thighed is like a bright Whimbrel. Bold head stripes include a dark eye line that connects to the bill and a pale

supercilium, bordered above by a broad, dark lateral crown stripe. The upperparts are dark brown with bold, buff edges and notches on the scapulars and coverts. The underparts are buff, rather bright, with streaking on the neck and breast, and bars on the sides. The tail and rump are strong buff, with dark bars on the tail. Worn adults can lose much of the buff edges to the upperparts, and the underparts can become faded; however, the rump and tail remain distinctly buffy. The bill is dark, but it is much paler on the lower mandible than on most curlews, extending almost to the tip; the legs are blue-gray. The stiff feathers on the thighs and flanks are hard to see in the field except at close range and in good light. JUVENILE: It is similar to an adult except in early fall, when its plumage will be uniform and fresh, compared to the more worn appearance of the adult. As winter progresses, juveniles look darker than adults, retaining buff coloration on only their rump and

tail. They generally do not return to the breeding grounds for 3 years. FLIGHT: It appears brown above, with noticeable buff edges. More important, the bright buff rump and tail are usually evident.

Similar Species Overeager birders will most likely confuse a Whimbrel with a Bristle-thighed; while not a particularly difficult identification, poor lighting can make it more challenging. The Bristle-thighed is a brighter buff above and below and has a bright buff rump and tail. Calls are different.

Voice CALL: A loud whistled *chu-a-whit*, somewhat recalling a Black-bellied Plover, but louder, with more-distinct syllables; somewhat humanlike. On the breeding grounds, loud, sharp whistles accompany impressive display flights.

Status & Distribution Local and uncommon. BREEDING: Uneven, hummock tundra. MIGRATION: Spectacular flights covering 2,000–4,000 miles with minimal or no stops. In spring, through the Pacific islands in Apr., clearing out of HI early to mid-May on average. Arrive in AK early to mid-May,

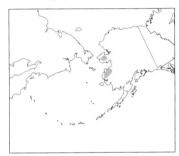

adult

but as early as late Apr. In fall, adults stage July–Aug. in AK, where they fatten up on berries prior to moving south. Juveniles move south mid-Aug.–early Sept. WINTER: Pacific islands. VAGRANT: Casual to the Pacific coast. A weather-related occurrence accounted for the 13 birds found May 6–25, 1998, in northern CA, OR, and WA; prior to this event, there were 9 records (6 spring, 3 fall) for OR, WA, and BC.

Population The population is vulnerable because of its relatively small size, restricted range, and flightless period. Introduced mammals on some Pacific islands could pose a threat to populations.

FAR EASTERN CURLEW *Numenius madagascariensis*

The Far Eastern Curlew, a vagrant from Asia, is the largest curlew. Monotypic. L 25" (64 cm)

Identification The Far Eastern has a dull coloration, generally brown with streaks, but its size, and extremely long, curved bill are noteworthy. The face pattern is indistinct, with a slightly darker lore being the most noticeable feature. The upperparts are grayish brown with warmer tints on occasion; the neck and crown

are streaked. The underparts are pale brown with dark streaks on the neck and breast, extending down the sides. JUVENILE: Fresh birds differ from adults by their buffier breast and belly, with less streaking, and they are also more boldly marked above, with buffy fringes to all feathers. As feathers wear, juveniles can be difficult to separate from adults. FLIGHT: The wing linings are dingy

adult

with dark barring, but in many lights they look gray or gray-brown. The upperparts are uniform brown with the rump the same color as the back.

Similar Species The Far Eastern's large size and lack of head pattern leave the Long-billed and Eurasian Curlews as the only identification challenges. The more likely problem is the Long-billed along the Pacific

coast, where a vagrant Far Eastern is most likely to occur. The Long-billed is slightly smaller, with warm cinnamon tones on the body and, in flight, on the underwings. The Far Eastern has heavier streaking than the Long-billed. Compared to the Eurasian, note the Eurasian's white rump and lower back, and the white underwings.

Voice CALL: A *curlee,* similar to other curlews.

Status & Distribution Breeds in Asia. Casual in spring and early summer on the Aleutian and Pribilof Islands. Accidental in coastal BC in fall. WINTER: Southeast Asia and Australasia.

Population The numbers are probably declining due to loss of habitat during migration and winter.

SLENDER-BILLED CURLEW *Numenius tenuirostris*

This Old World species is near extinction; future records are most unlikely. Monotypic. L 15" (39 cm)

Identification The Slender-billed is the size of a Whimbrel, but its plumage is more like a Eurasian Curlew, except for the chevron-shaped marks on the Eurasian's flanks. The rump is white; the tail is white with dark bars. White underwings are visible in flight. The bill is slender, even at the base.

Similar Species The Slender-billed Curlew would not be confused with either the Whimbrel or the Long-billed Curlew—the expected North American curlews. The Slender-billed's short bill and bright white underparts are similar to a Eurasian Curlew, but the Eurasian has a longer and thicker bill, and has chevrons on its sides instead of spots and streaks.

Status & Distribution Thought to breed in western Siberia, but few nests actually located. WINTER: Thought to be near Mediterranean, to include Morocco, Tunisia, and points east. VAGRANT: A record in southern ON, on Lake Erie, around 1925.

adult

Population The species is critically endangered, if not already extinct, due to habitat loss and hunting.

LONG-BILLED CURLEW *Numenius americanus*

The Long-billed Curlew is typically seen in large roosting flocks along the coast or feeding in fields. It often roosts with other large shorebirds, such as godwits and willets. The Long-billed's habitat and diet are quite different between breeding and nonbreeding seasons; in the former it inhabits grasslands and shrub-steppe and eats insects and birds, in the latter it largely moves to water and eats crabs and worms. Polytypic. L 23" (58 cm)

Identification The Long-billed is a large, warm brown shorebird—not well marked, but distinct. The upperparts are cinnamon-brown, with a slightly darker crown due to faint streaking. The upperpart feathers have dark stripes or bars. The face is rather uniform with only a hint of a buff supercilium and slightly darker lores. The underparts are buffy, with streaking on the neck and breast. The wing coverts are warm cinnamon with fine bars. The very long bill curves strongly down; the basal half is pale. The long legs are gray. JUVENILE: It has a shorter and less curved bill. Dark wing coverts with broad buff edges result in a striped look. FLIGHT: Cinnamon-buff wing linings are distinctive in all plumages. The toes extend slightly beyond the tail.

Geographic Variation Nominate *americanus* breeds in the southern part of the species' range, north to Nevada, Idaho, Wyoming, and South Dakota. The slightly smaller *parvus* breeds north of *americanus;* these size differences are difficult to appreciate in the field.

Similar Species The Long-billed is most likely to be confused with a Whimbrel, but it is larger, warmer brown, with buff and cinnamon tones, and lacks the dark head stripes of the Whimbrel. The Long-billed's bill is also longer and more curved, but be aware that the juveniles have smaller bills. The Eurasian Curlew has white on the rump, tail, and lower back, in addition to white underwings. The Far Eastern Curlew presents more of a problem, but it is even larger, and is plain brown above, lacking any cinnamon tones. The plain brown underwings of the Far Eastern will look dull in comparison to those of a Long-billed. The Far Eastern's bill is long, even in comparison to the Long-billed. A Marbled Godwit, roosting with its bill tucked, will look smaller with unmarked or barred underparts. In addition, the Marbled has dark legs, but the Long-billed has paler, gray legs.

Voice CALL: A loud, musical, ascending *cur-lee.* On breeding grounds it repeats *cur-lee,* followed by sharp, descending whistles.

Status & Distribution Fairly common. The southernmost breeding curlew, and the curlew with the northernmost winter range. BREEDING: Nests in wet and dry uplands. MIGRATION: Found on wetlands, grainfields, and coasts. In spring, migrants as early as mid-Feb., but more typically Mar. Peak mid- to late Apr. for UT and the Northwest. Most migrants leave wintering grounds by early May. In fall, first arrivals occur in July, occasionally late June. In most areas they peak in Aug., and almost all birds are gone from their breeding grounds by this time, peaking in southern states in Sept. WINTER: Pacific, Gulf, and Southeast coasts, Central and Imperial Valleys of CA, southern AZ, central TX, and Mexico. VAGRANT: Casual to mid-Atlantic and Great Lakes in late spring (late May–mid-June) and fall (mid-July–Oct.).

Population The numbers have declined locally, particularly in eastern parts of the Long-billed's range, due to habitat loss.

juvenile ♂

adult ♀

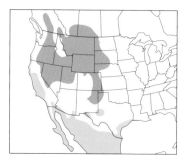

EURASIAN CURLEW *Numenius arquata*

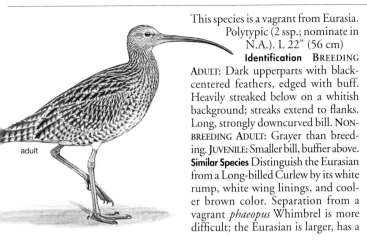

adult

juvenile

This species is a vagrant from Eurasia. Polytypic (2 ssp.; nominate in N.A.). L 22" (56 cm)

Identification BREEDING ADULT: Dark upperparts with black-centered feathers, edged with buff. Heavily streaked below on a whitish background; streaks extend to flanks. Long, strongly downcurved bill. NON-BREEDING ADULT: Grayer than breeding. JUVENILE: Smaller bill, buffier above.

Similar Species Distinguish the Eurasian from a Long-billed Curlew by its white rump, white wing linings, and cooler brown color. Separation from a vagrant *phaeopus* Whimbrel is more difficult; the Eurasian is larger, has a longer bill, and lacks the dark head stripes. The Far Eastern Curlew is similar, but the Eurasian is paler and has more heavily streaked sides and a white rump.

Voice CALL: A sharp *cur-lee*.

Status & Distribution Breeds in Eurasia. WINTER: Southern Europe, Africa, and Asia. VAGRANT: Casual on East Coast, primarily fall and winter, from NF to NY. One summer rec. from NU.

Population Local declines are a result of habitat loss and hunting pressures.

GODWITS Genus *Limosa*

Godwits are large with long legs and long, usually upturned bills. Most godwits undergo a substantial change from breeding to nonbreeding plumage, with some sexual dimorphism. They feed by probing and stitching while standing in water or along its edge; they roost with other large shorebirds. All 4 godwits occur in North America.

MARBLED GODWIT *Limosa fedoa*

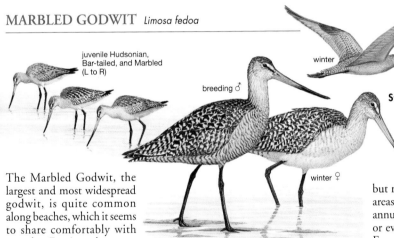

juvenile Hudsonian, Bar-tailed, and Marbled (L to R)

breeding ♂

winter

winter ♀

The Marbled Godwit, the largest and most widespread godwit, is quite common along beaches, which it seems to share comfortably with people. During the non-breeding season it roosts in coastal wetlands with other large shorebirds, typically Willets and curlews. It feeds by probing into mud. Polytypic. L 18" (46 cm)

Identification Large, tawny-brown bird. Long, slightly upcurved, bicolored bill. Brown-streaked crown. Upperparts have dark feather centers, with buff bars and spots, providing a mottled appearance. Breast and sides variably barred. NONBREEDING ADULT: Bill with brighter, more extensive pink base. Much less barring than on breeding bird. JUVENILE: Like nonbreeding, no trace of barring below. Wing coverts less heavily marked, contrasting with upperparts. FLIGHT: Distinctive cinnamon wing linings and cinnamon on primaries and secondaries.

Geographic Variation Nominate *fedoa* is the interior breeder; the slightly smaller *beringiae* has an isolated breeding population in Alaska and migrates south as far as California.

Similar Species The Marbled, particularly a worn Marbled that loses some of its color, is most similar to a Bar-tailed Godwit. However, the Marbled has longer legs and a duller face pattern. If seen in flight, the striking Hudsonian Godwit should pose no serious challenge (see Hudsonian Godwit). A roosting Long-billed Curlew with its bill tucked has a similar coloration, but the Marbled is smaller and is either unmarked or has some barring on the sides, versus the breast streaking of the curlew.

Voice CALL: A loud *ker-ret;* also *widica widica widica.*

Status & Distribution Common. BREEDING: Grassy meadows, near lakes and ponds. MIGRATION: In spring, peak mid-Apr.–mid-May in most areas, a little earlier farther south. In fall, adults seen mid-June, but more typically during July. Most areas peak Aug.–mid-Sept., lingerers annually to Oct., exceptionally to Nov. or even Dec. Rare but regular in the East, primarily late July–late Sept. WINTER: South to S.A. Casual to southwest BC and Central Valley of CA. VAGRANT: Rare, but annual in Great Lakes; casual in mid-Atlantic in spring, late Apr.–late May, more numerous in fall. Also to HI.

Population The numbers seem stable.

BLACK-TAILED GODWIT *Limosa limosa*

The Black-tailed is a vagrant from the Old World. Polytypic (3 ssp.; 2 in N.A.). L 16.5" (42 cm)
Identification Straight, or only slightly upcurved, long, bicolored bill. Tail mostly black to tip, white uppertail coverts. Buff or whitish supercilium and dark loral line. Diagnostic flight pattern. BREEDING MALE: Chestnut head, neck, and breast; black upperparts with warm rufous edges to scapulars and coverts. White belly and undertail coverts; heavily barred sides and flanks. BREEDING FEMALE: Similar to male but paler, sprinkled with white. NONBREEDING ADULT: Gray or grayish brown above; grayish breast but otherwise whitish below, lacking barring. JUVENILE: Brown upperparts, with warm cinnamon edges to feathers; pale orangish hindneck and streaked crown. The dark tertials are

notched with buff. Pale cinnamon neck and breast; remainder of underparts white. FLIGHT: Broad wing stripe across all secondaries and most primaries; conspicuous white wing linings.
Geographic Variation Three subspecies. The *melanuroides* (from Asia) and *islandica* (breeds in Iceland) are similar in breeding plumage, but the *islandica* breeding male has a deeper and more extensive reddish color below; *melanuroides* is darker above in nonbreeding plumage, with a shorter bill and tarsus. Alaska and West Coast birds are likely *melanuroides;* Atlantic birds are likely *islandica.*
Similar Species The Black-tailed shares a bold white

wing stripe and black-and-white tail with the Hudsonian Godwit; however, note the Black-tailed's more extensive wing stripe on the inner portion of the wing and white underwings (black in Hudsonian). In breeding plumage, the Hudsonian has dark streaks and lacks reddish color on the hindneck. On juveniles, the Black-tailed is warmer colored, with an orange-reddish tint to the hindneck.
Voice CALL: Generally silent.
Status & Distribution Wet meadows from Iceland to Russia. MIGRATION: Rare, but regular spring migrant on western Aleutians; casual to Pribilofs and along Atlantic coast. WINTER: Southern Europe to Australia. In N.A., a winter rec. of a Back-tailed Godwit is more likely than a winter rec. of a Hudsonian Godwit. VAGRANT: Casual on Atlantic coast in migration and winter, exceptionally inland to ON and south to LA.
Population Stable.

BAR-TAILED GODWIT *Limosa lapponica*

The Bar-tailed is primarily an Old World godwit. It has an impressive migration: the Alaska-breeding *baueri* stages near breeding grounds and flies nonstop, thousands of miles, to its wintering grounds in New Zealand. Polytypic (3 ssp.; 2 in N.A.). L 16" (41 cm)
Identification Slightly upcurved, long, bicolored bill; brown crown and hindneck, with dark streaks; pale supercilium and dark eye line.

Distinctive black-and-white barred tail. BREEDING MALE: Reddish brown underparts with some white near the belly, no barring; streaks limited to sides of breast. Dark scapulars with rufous edges. BREEDING FEMALE: Larger and paler than male; some females mostly whitish below. NONBREEDING ADULT: Gray-brown upperparts with paler buff edges, giving a striped appearance.

Grayish brown on foreneck and breast, otherwise whitish below. JUVENILE: Like nonbreeding, but more obviously marked: buffy spots and notches on upperparts; wing coverts with dark streaks. Neck and breast with buff tones and light streaks; barring might be present on sides. FLIGHT: Weak wing stripe; tail barring visible. White or barred underwings.
Geographic Variation Nominate *lapponica*, a vagrant on the Atlantic coast, has a white rump, white wing linings, and brown-barred axillaries; Alaska-breeding *baueri* has brown-and-white barring on rump and underwing. Also, the *baueri* is more boldly marked, and the female is more likely to be richly colored in breeding plumage.

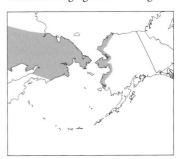

Similar Species The Bar-tailed resembles a Marbled Godwit but lacks the cinnamon tones. (Some worn winter *baueri* Marbleds can be more problematic, but they still retain cinnamon flight feathers.) Note the Bar-tailed's shorter bill, shorter legs, bolder face pattern, white or barred underwing coverts, and barred tail. The Bar-tailed's rufous breeding plumage might recall a Hudsonian Godwit, but the Hudsonian's underparts are more heavily barred and males have much deeper chestnut. **Voice** CALL: Generally silent.

Status & Distribution Tundra from Scandinavia to AK. MIGRATION: In spring, AK arrivals mid- to late May, with earliest arrivals late Apr., and arrivals to north AK into early June. In fall, adults typically depart breeding grounds late July–mid-Aug. Juveniles generally depart by Sept. WINTER: Europe, Africa, Asia, and Australasia; a few records for the Pacific coast. VAGRANT: Rare to casual in spring and, mostly, fall on Pacific coast, particularly in Pacific Northwest. Casual along Atlantic coast in spring, summer, and fall.

Population The population is stable, but the Bar-tailed is vulnerable due to its limited staging and wintering sites.

HUDSONIAN GODWIT   *Limosa haemastica*

juvenile

juvenile

molting fall adult ♂

breeding ♂

breeding ♀

The striking Hudsonian is a particularly sought-after godwit. Its breeding grounds are remote, and it has few reliable migration stopovers. Monotypic. L 15.5" (39 cm)
Identification Long, slightly upcurved, bicolored bill. Black tail, tipped white, with white uppertail coverts. Pale supercilium and dark loral line. BREEDING MALE: Dark upperparts, with buff edges; dark chestnut underparts, finely barred. BREEDING FEMALE: Larger and grayer, with reduced chestnut below. Tertials less patterned than on male, often with small notches. NONBREEDING ADULT: Rather plain, with gray-brown upperparts, lighter on the breast. JUVENILE: Like nonbreeding, but darker above, with buff feather edges to mantle and upper scapulars; lower scapulars and tertials with buff notches. FLIGHT: Bold white wing stripe, thin on the secondaries and broader on inner primaries; black underwing coverts.
Similar Species A nonbreeding adult Hudsonian resembles a Black-tailed Godwit but has dark wing linings and a narrower white wing stripe. A breeding Hudsonian is chestnut below with barring, whereas a Black-tailed has chestnut on the hindneck, with minimal barring below. Barred underparts on breeding Marbled Godwit might recall Hudsonian. In flight, the Hudsonian's striking wing pattern might recall a Willet, but the Willet has a shorter bill and a paler tail.
Voice CALL: Generally silent.
Status & Distribution Uncommon and local. BREEDING: From AK to the Hudson Bay, but in very disjunct pockets. MIGRATION: Spring route primarily through central and eastern Great Plains. Migrate generally Apr.–May. Peak migration in TX and KS second half of Apr.–early May. Arrival on AK breeding grounds peak late May; in Churchill, ON, peak early to mid-June. In fall, migrate much farther east; large staging areas from SK to James and Hudson Bays, with most birds flying southeast to the Atlantic and then to S.A. Adults generally leave mid- to late Aug. Great Lakes and mid-Atlantic coast to New England peak late Aug.–early Oct., lingerers to Nov., exceptionally to Dec. WINTER: Southern S.A., unexpected in N.A.; 1 sight rec. for GA. Any winter rec. should eliminate Black-tailed Godwit, which is more likely in midwinter. VAGRANT: Casual Great Lakes and mid-Atlantic in spring (mid-May–early June); casual in western states in spring (mid-May–mid-June) and fall (mid-Aug.–mid-Oct.); annual in New Zealand; casual HI, Australia. Accidental in Europe and S. Africa.
Population The Hudsonian is considered a near-threatened species. There is an incomplete understanding of its breeding range; population studies are needed.

TURNSTONES Genus *Arenaria*

Turnstones are named for their habit of flipping over stones and other material with their short, pointed bills in search of food. These short-legged, almost chunky birds are quite social, chattering as they feed and flock along the coasts. In flight, the black-and-white pattern on the back, wings, and tail is impressive.

RUDDY TURNSTONE *Arenaria interpres*

breeding ♂

The Ruddy Turnstone frequents the shore, picking through rocks, shells, seaweed or other flotsam in search of food. Polytypic. L 9.5" (24 cm)
Identification Dark breast and neck on otherwise white underparts; demarcation from black to white on bib uneven, more extensive toward the sides; white throat. Median coverts quite long, hanging down over the wing, like long scapulars. BREEDING MALE: Striking, bold black-and-chestnut upperparts; mostly white head, with dark streaks on crown. Bright orange legs. BREEDING FEMALE: Duller and browner than male; less rufous in the upperparts. NONBREEDING ADULT: Dull brown above and relatively unmarked. JUVENILE: Like nonbreeding, but with pale edges on upperparts that give the back a scaly appearance. Once edges wear, remaining upperparts look darker than non-

breeding. Legs paler orange, some near flesh-toned. FLIGHT: Complex pattern on back and wings: white wing stripe, white back, and white scapular bar separated by rufous or brown patches. Dark tail has white base.
Geographic Variation Nominate *interpres* breeds from Greenland eastward to northwest Alaska; it averages more black and less rufous than *morinella,* which breeds from northeast Alaska through Canada.
Similar Species The Black Turnstone is similar, particularly in flight, but it has more contrast, lacking brown or rufous patches. The bright orange legs of a breeding Ruddy are diagnostic, but this mark is less reliable in winter. Use instead the white in the throat, brown in the plumage, or an uneven dark breast bib to identify a Ruddy.

Some juvenile Ruddies look fairly dark overall.
Voice CALL: A low-pitched, guttural rattle.
Status & Distribution Common. BREEDING: Coastal tundra. MIGRATION: Generally rare inland, except Great Lakes region and Salton Sea. In spring, western populations (primarily *interpres*) peak mid-Apr.–mid-May, with some lingering to June. Eastern populations *(morinella)* move primarily from late Apr., with peak mid-May–early June along mid-Atlantic and Great Lakes. In fall, adults seen in late July, primarily Aug. Juveniles arrive mid- to late Aug., peak in Sept., with most gone by early or mid-Oct, depending on region, lingerers to Nov., exceptionally later. WINTER: Along the coasts, south to S.A. Accidental to Great Lakes.
Population Stable. Old World populations show slight increases.

juvenile

winter

breeding ♂

BLACK TURNSTONE *Arenaria melanocephala*

A dichromatic bird from the rocky shores of the Pacific coast, the Black Turnstone is social outside of the breeding season, wintering in small flocks. It has a restricted range, in contrast to the circumpolar Ruddy Turnstone. Monotypic. L 9.3" (24 cm)
Identification Dark upperparts, dark throat and upper breast, and white underparts found in all plumages. The legs are reddish brown; some birds show pinkish brown. BREEDING ADULT: Head and entire upperparts are black; the eyebrow and lore spot are white. White spotting is visible on sides of neck and breast; the dark breast is separated from the white underparts in a

rather even line. Black median wing coverts are long, hanging over the edge of folded wing, edged with white. NONBREEDING ADULT: Browner, but generally looks black. Some scapulars and coverts are edged white; the white on

the breast, neck, and head is absent. JUVENILE: Like nonbreeding; median coverts are not as large and are edged with white. Legs are often paler, with more of a flesh or orange tone. FLIGHT: Striking black-and-white pattern:

winter

breeding

winter

white wing stripe, white back, and white scapular bar separated by black. Tail is black, with white base and tips.

Similar Species The Black's wing pattern and habits recall a Ruddy Turnstone, but the Ruddy has brown or rufous upperparts, an uneven black bib, a white throat, and, usually, bright orange legs. A Surfbird, with which the Black is often seen, shares the Black's general dark coloration above, white below, with black-and-white tail; however, it is paler above, lacks the white patches on the back and scapulars, and has a thicker bill and yellow legs.

Voice CALL: Includes a guttural rattle, higher than the call of the Ruddy.

Status & Distribution Locally common. BREEDING: Coastal tundra. MIGRATION: In spring, movement on the Pacific coast Mar.–early May; peak in southern AK mid-May, arriving on breeding grounds mid-May–early June. First fall migrants appear early July in BC, generally mid-July in OR and WA; adults move earlier, with juveniles arriving in early Aug., peaking late Aug.–Sept. WINTER: On rocky coasts from southern AK south. VAGRANT: Casual in eastern WA, eastern OR, and interior CA, primarily May and late Aug.–early Sept. More regular at Salton Sea. Acciden-

tal records east to AZ, AB, MT, and WI. Extralimital records from western Mexico and eastern Russia.

Population Stable, but the species is potentially vulnerable due to its restricted range.

CALIDRINE SANDPIPERS   Genera *Aphriza, Calidris, Eurynorhynchus, Limicola, Philomachus,* and *Tryngites*

Calidrine sandpipers—the smallest are commonly referred to as peeps or stints—make up this varied group. Plumages tend to be bright in breeding and juvenal birds, rather colorless and unmarked in nonbreeding birds. Most species are rather small with little difference in size or plumage between the sexes. Identifications within this group can be difficult. Most species pick along the shore and mudflats or in shallow water; some species feed in slightly deeper water. Although many species migrate and roost in large flocks, they can be very aggressive and territorial. Most species undergo long migrations, breeding in the Arctic and wintering to South America.

SURFBIRD   *Aphriza virgata*

A Pacific coast rocky shorebird, the rather chunky Surfbird is often seen in the company of Black Turnstones. It picks invertebrates from rocks, although rarely it will feed on mudflats and sandy beaches. Monotypic. L 10" (25 cm)

Identification Generally gray above and on the throat, white below. Stout dark bill with a yellow base. Short yellowish green legs. BREEDING ADULT: Head and underparts heavily streaked and spotted with dusky-black. Upperparts edged with white and chestnut; scapulars rufous and black. NONBREEDING ADULT: Gray spots along the sides. White edges to wing coverts. JUVENILE: Like nonbreeding, but upperparts have pale edges and darker subterminal markings, creating scaled appearance. FLIGHT: White wing stripe and con-

spicuous black band at end of white tail and rump.

Similar Species A breeding Surfbird could be taken for a Great Knot; however, the Great has a longer, more typical sandpiper bill and dark legs. The Surfbird's short, thick bill and bold flight pattern are unique.

Voice CALL: Generally silent, but chatter notes, like those of a turnstone, often given in flight.

Status & Distribution Fairly common. BREEDING: Mountain tundra in AK and YK. MIGRATION: Spring northward movement noted Mar. to early May along coast, with most birds departed by the end of Apr. Prince William Sound (AK) is a major staging area early to mid-May. In fall, adults first noted south of breeding areas in late June or early July; most adult movement July–early Aug. Juveniles start moving early Aug.; most movement from BC south is over by late Sept. WINTER: Reefs and rocky beaches from southern AK to Chile. VAGRANT: Casual in spring on TX coast, Salton Sea, and points east from FL to AB; accidental inland in fall (e.g., sight record Aug. 18,

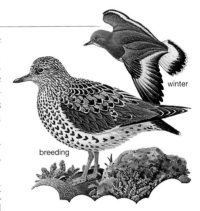
winter

breeding

1979, at Presque Isle, PA).

Population Stable, but vulnerable since a high percentage of the population uses Prince William Sound as a staging area, an area that narrowly escaped the *Exxon Valdez* oil spill in 1988.

winter   juvenile

Calidris Plumage and Structural Details

At first glance, *Calidris* sandpipers seem incredibly difficult to distinguish. Indeed, a sure sign that birders have truly become enthralled with identification is their love for this particular group of shorebirds. Part of the learning process for correctly identifying *Calidris* sandpipers is refining the identification keys. Instead of looking at the bird as a whole, it is helpful to focus instead on specific characteristics to guide the identification. Three critical aspects in identifying *Calidris* are the bird's structure, the bird's feather topography, and the proper aging of sandpipers.

Begin by considering the bird's structure. Most of the *Calidris* species have a subtly unique structure. The key characters to study to assess structure are bill length and shape, leg length, and primary length. Most sandpipers share a medium-length bill that is relatively straight and which thins toward the end. However, the bill's length relative to the head is variable, as is its thickness and the amount of droop toward the tip. Leg length on its own would not be a good identification mark since it only varies a little; however, used in combination with other features, one can assess whether a sandpiper is shorter, chunkier, or more elongate. Primary projection is also only subtly different, but it helps in both the objective assessment of whether the primaries project past the tail, as well as the subjective determination of the shape of the bird.

The second characteristic to take careful note of when attempting to identify *Calidris* sandpipers is the bird's feather topography. Identifications within this genus will greatly accelerate once there is a working knowledge of the various feather groups. While patterns on the crown, breast, and elsewhere are important, the key patterns to look for and understand are those on the mantle, the scapulars (both upper and lower), the upperwing coverts, and the tertials. You also need to understand what happens to these feathers over the course of the year. The mantle is the upper back; the small feathers here often have bright colors or edges. Near the edge of the mantle, many *Calidris* species have a row of feathers that are boldly edged white, creating a mantle line. The adjacent feather group is the upper scapulars. Starting at the top, many species have the first row of upper scapulars edged white, creating a scapular line. Some species show both of these lines boldly, creating a V along the sides of the upperparts. The lower scapulars are usually marked slightly differently than the upper scapulars, depending on the plumage. These scapulars often hang down and cover the wing coverts, a critical feather group when trying to determine the identification of our smallest sandpipers, the peeps or stints.

Finally, be careful to determine the proper aging of the sandpipers present. Aging a *Calidris* sandpiper is typically easy and necessary before one can hope to identify it. There are straightforward, basic age guidelines. Most identification problems occur in fall. In most species, we see juveniles from the end of July through most of October in crisp, often bright plumage. The feathers are fresh and uniform, often with bright rusty or buff edges and often appearing scaly. In contrast, adults in fall have passed their peak appearance, although those seen in July and early August might still be mostly in breeding plumage. By late summer, most adult sandpipers are molting to nonbreeding plumage, and many of their more colorful breeding feathers on the upperparts are wearing off the bright edges. This wearing results in a darker, more blotchy appearance, in contrast to the uniform appearance of juveniles. When adults complete their molt, most species go into a drab, rather unmarked nonbreeding plumage. Juveniles also molt later in fall (a few species molt earlier) and look very similar to adults; however, close views of the coverts or tertials usually betray their youth. Sandpipers molt into their breeding plumage in the spring. Some do so before migrating; others do so during the passage. Many birds that are less than a year old do not migrate all the way north and do not molt into a pristine breeding plumage. Instead, these birds molt into their first alternate (breeding) plumage. ■

Least Sandpiper, juvenile (NJ, Aug.)   Baird's Sandpiper, juvenile (CA, Sept.)

GREAT KNOT *Calidris tenuirostris*

The Great Knot is a vagrant from Asia. Monotypic. L 11" (28 cm)
Identification Large and chunky. Generally gray above; white and spots below. BREEDING ADULT: Black breast with large spots extending to flanks. Extensive rufous on scapulars. NON-BREEDING ADULT: Gray-brown above; white with limited streaks or spots below. JUVENILE: Dark back feathers edged with brown and white; buffy wash and distinct spotting below. FLIGHT: Faint wing stripe; dark primary coverts and white uppertail coverts. **Similar Species** Larger than the Red Knot, with longer bill; less rufous on back, none on head and breast on breeding birds. In flight, wing stripe is fainter, and uppertail coverts are whiter than in the Red Knot. Remark-

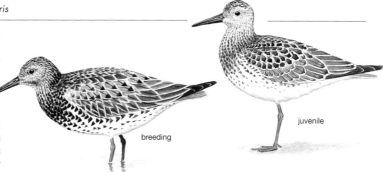

breeding

juvenile

ably similar in breeding plumage to the Surfbird, but it has a longer, thinner black bill, as well as dark gray or green legs, not yellowish as in the Surfbird. **Voice** CALL: Generally silent.
Status & Distribution Breeds in Siberia. Casual spring migrant in western AK; accidental in fall. Accidental in OR in fall. Vagrant to western Palearctic. WINTER: Primarily Australia through Indonesia; smaller numbers in southeast and south-central Asia.
Population Stable, but there is major concern over hunting and habitat loss in China and Korea, which the Great Knot uses on migration.

RED KNOT *Calidris canutus*

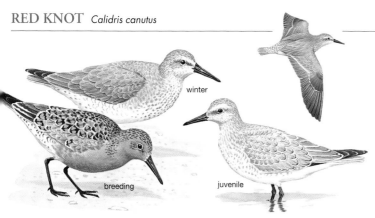

winter

breeding

juvenile

Thousands of Red Knots collect at staging areas during migration. The Red Knot feeds along sandy beaches and mudflats, often with dowitchers. Polytypic. L 10.5" (27 cm)
Identification Chunky and short-legged for a *Calidris*. Medium-length black bill. Legs vary from black to olive or gray. BREEDING ADULT: Dappled brown, black, and chestnut above, with buffy chestnut face and breast; entirely or mostly chestnut below. Males average brighter and females average more white on the belly, but there is overlap. Worn adult looks darker above, once paler chestnut edges wear. NONBREEDING ADULT: Pale gray upperparts and head; white underparts, except breast, which has grayish wash or spots, and fine markings along sides. JUVENILE: Like nonbreeding, but with more distinct spotting below and scaly-looking upperparts. Pale fringe and a dark subterminal line on the scapulars and coverts. Fresh juveniles often

have a buff wash on the breast. FLIGHT: White wing stripe and paler rump, which has gray barring.
Geographic Variation Work continues on this taxa; there is uncertainty over the winter distribution of some subspecies and the subspecific limits in the Alaska populations. Of the 5 subspecies, *islandica,* which breeds in Greenland and northern Canadian islands and winters in Europe, is more chestnut above and below. Breeding south of *islandica* in Canada, the *rufa* has less chestnut above, and is paler below. It is believed to winter in South America and possibly the southeast United States. The Alaska *roselaari* is similar to the *rufa,* only darker. It winters from the southern United States to South America.
Similar Species In breeding plumage, the Red Knot's uniform color is similar to a dowitcher's, but the knot has a shorter bill, paler crown, and (in flight) a whitish rump, finely barred with gray. In non-breeding plumage, the Red Knot differs again by structure, bill, and tail pattern.
Voice CALL: Generally silent, but *cur-wit* sometimes given when taking flight.
Status & Distribution Uncommon to fairly common. BREEDING: Dry tundra. MIGRATION: Rare to casual migrant in the interior. Often missed in coastal areas not used as staging grounds; may be common in 1 place, but only in small numbers between the staging area and the next stop. In spring, earlier in the West than in the East, peaking on Pacific coast late Apr.–mid-May. Mid-Atlantic peak mid-May–early June. In fall, adults seen mid-July, peak late July–mid-Aug. Juveniles peak late Aug.–Sept. Smaller numbers to mid-Oct.; lingerers into Nov. WINTER: Coasts, south to Argentina. VAGRANT: HI.
Population Declines in *rufa* noted in the mid-Atlantic during migration. Species is at some risk using staging areas where it relies on a single food source (e.g., horseshoe crab eggs at Delaware Bay).

SANDERLING *Calidris alba*

The Sanderling is the familiar sandpiper watched by beachcombers. It seemingly chases waves out to sea, only to be chased back by the next wave, its legs blurring in speedy retreat. Monotypic. L 8" (20 cm)

Identification Larger than other peeps. Black bill and legs. Lacks hind toe. Prominent white wing stripe in flight; black primary coverts contrast with remainder of wing. BREEDING ADULT: Not acquired until late April or later; head, mantle, and breast are rusty or mottled brown. Tertials often with markings inside the edge, unlike any other peep. NONBREEDING ADULT: Palest sandpiper in winter; pale gray above, white below. JUVENILE: Blackish above, with pale edges near tip; looks checkered. Breast washed buff when fresh.

Similar Species Rather distinct compared to other small *Calidris*. Bright breeding plumaged birds have been mistaken for the Red-necked Stint, but the Sanderling is larger, with bolder wing stripe, and lacks dark necklace of streaks below rusty breast. Nonbreeding birds are paler than any congener and larger, with a larger bill, than the other peeps.

Voice CALL: A sharp *kip,* often given in a series.

Status & Distribution Common. BREEDING: Dry tundra of Canadian islands, Eurasia, and, rarely, AK. MIGRATION: In spring, peak on Pacific coast late Apr.–late May; Great Lakes and mid-Atlantic 2 weeks later. In fall, adults arrive south mid-July, peaking late July–Aug.; juveniles late Aug.–Sept.; stragglers noted into Nov. WINTER: Coastlines to southern S.A.

Population Recently noted declines might be tied to prolonged severe weather on the breeding grounds.

SEMIPALMATED SANDPIPER *Calidris pusilla*

The Semipalmated is an abundant shorebird. During migration it congregates in large flocks at wetland habitats in the eastern half of the continent. Monotypic. L 6.3" (16 cm)

Identification Short to medium length, tubular-looking bill with rather blunt tip; female's bill larger than male's. Black legs; webbing on toes visible under ideal conditions. BREEDING ADULT: Dark upperparts, a mixture of black and brown, with only a tinge of rust on crown, auriculars, and scapular edges; usually lacking spotting on flanks. NONBREEDING ADULT: Gray-brown above; white below, with faint streaks on sides of breast. JUVENILE: Strong supercilium; dark crown. Uniform brown upperparts, typically edged buff, giving a slightly scaled appearance, but variably brighter, edged with rufous. White scapular lines, if present, narrow and usually indistinct.

Similar Species Separating a juvenile Western from a juvenile Semipalmated can be difficult (see sidebar p. 215). The process of identifying juvenile Little and Red-necked Stints must first eliminate the more likely Semipalmated; see those species accounts.

Voice CALL: A short *churk,* very different from a Western Sandpiper.

Status & Distribution Abundant. BREEDING: Tundra from west AK to Atlantic. MIGRATION: In spring, first arrivals late Mar., but most in southern states April–mid-May. Peak in mid-Atlantic and Great Lakes mid-May–early June. Rare in West late Apr.–late May. In fall, adults as early as late June, peaking mid-July–mid-Aug., very rare in West south of WA; juveniles peak in Aug., with numbers declining by early Sept., and largely departed by early Oct. Migration a little later in eastern N.A. A few linger into early Nov. WINTER: Mexico to S.A. Casual in southern FL. VAGRANT: Casual in Europe.

Population Local declines noted.

WESTERN SANDPIPER *Calidris mauri*

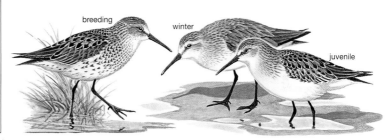

winter

The Western Sandpiper is the abundant western counterpart of the Semipalmated Sandpiper. It is found in large flocks during migration. Monotypic. L 6.5" (17 cm)

Identification Black legs; tapered bill, of variable length, with a slight droop at the tip. BREEDING ADULT: Bright rufous wash on crown and auriculars; rufous base to scapulars. White underparts, with streaks and arrow-shaped spots across the breast and along sides and flanks. NONBREEDING ADULT: Gray-brown above and white below, with faint streaks on breast. JUVENILE: Extensive rufous edges on upper scapulars. Gray-brown wing coverts with pale edges. Somewhat distinct head pattern of dark lores, pale super-

cilium, and darker crown.

Similar Species The Western is easily confused with the Semipalmated in basic plumage, but a Semipalmated is most unexpected in winter. The Semipalmated has a shorter, more tubular bill, and its face shows slightly more contrast. Juveniles of these species are also similar (see sidebar below). Some breeding Semipalmateds show tinge of rust to head and back. Winter Westerns might recall a Dunlin as both share a bill that droops toward the tip; however, the Dunlin has a bigger bill, with a more pronounced droop, is browner, and is more heavily marked on the throat and breast. A winter Least Sandpiper is browner and smaller, with a darker throat and upper breast and yellowish or greenish legs.

Voice CALL: A high, raspy *jeet*.

Status & Distribution Abundant. BREEDING: Wet Arctic tundra from east Siberia to northwest AK. MIGRATION: Throughout N.A., except very rare to casual in ND, MN, and eastern Canada. Movement in spring by late Mar., peaking in WA early Apr.–early May, with lingerers to late May. Casual on East Coast in spring. In fall, first adults late June, most July. First juveniles arrive late July (later in the East), peak Aug.–early Sept., lingerers into Nov. WINTER: Primarily coastal to S.A. VAGRANT: Europe and Asia.

Population Stable, but vulnerable given a majority of the population uses the Copper River in Alaska as a staging area.

breeding   winter   juvenile

Separation of Juvenile Semipalmated and Western Sandpipers

Many birders forsake identifying juvenile Semipalmated and Western Sandpipers since separating them can be complex. Nevertheless, given good views and a reasonable understanding of their character differences, almost all of them can be identified.

A feature useful in separating them is the size and shape of the bill. Typically, Semipalmateds have an obviously short, tubular bill, whereas Westerns have a long bill, noticeably drooped, with a narrow tip. While there is overlap—and eastern Semipalmateds have longer bills than western Semipalmateds—eastern female Semipalmateds that have long bills still have a stubbier tip. Another good character is the subtle difference in head pattern. The Semipalmated's bold supercilium contrasts with darker auriculars and a darker crown, imparting a capped appearance. The Western has dark lores, but the crown and auriculars

Semipalmated Sandpiper, juvenile (Sept.)

Western Sandpiper, juvenile (Sept.)

are not as dark, nor the supercilium typically as pale.

The scapulars and coverts also subtly differ. Most Semipalmateds look brown above, with pale edges giving them a buffier, more uniform look. Westerns look lighter above and have bold rufous edges to the upper scapulars. The Western's lower scapulars are gray with dark "anchors" near the tip, whereas the Semipalmated's are more uniform. Bright Semipalmateds can cause a problem, as some of them have brighter rust edges to the upper scapulars; worn or duller Westerns duplicate the problem, but, in both cases, the anchors on the wing coverts, head pattern, and bill shape are consistent characters.

Finally, keep in mind that Western Sandpipers molt early in fall, while migrant Semipalmated Sandpipers maintain their juvenal plumage and that the species have different calls. ∎

RED-NECKED STINT *Calidris ruficollis*

The Red-necked is an Old World vagrant. Monotypic. L 6.3" (16 cm) **Identification** Small peep. Black legs, feet unwebbed. Rather short black bill. Primaries extend slightly beyond tail tip. BREEDING ADULT: Rufous throat, upper breast, head, and mantle can be bright; paler in some birds, to pinkish orange, with throat entirely white. Below, the necklace of dark streaks extends below the color onto the white lower breast, with a few spots or streaks on the sides. NON-BREEDING ADULT: Gray-brown above with dark shaft streaks on scapulars. White below, with some streaks at sides of breast. JUVENILE: Scapulars vary from bright to pale rufous, with white tips. White scapular and man-

tle lines. Drab tertials, edged in pale buff, some with a faint rust tinge. Plain brown wing coverts with dark anchor-shaped shaft streaks. Crown seems darkest in the center; partial, indistinct forked supercilium.
Similar Species A breeding Little Stint has breast spotting contained within the color of the breast and always has a white throat, usually with extensive rufous-edged tertials and upperwing coverts. Distinguish a juvenile Red-necked from a juvenile Little Stint by its plainer gray wing coverts and tertials, dusky streaks rather than darker spots at breast sides, and less distinct mantle and scapular lines. Separate it from the Semipalmated and shorter billed Western by its plainer coverts and

tertials; the Semipalmated also has a darker crown and less contrast between the scapulars and wing coverts. No certain records of juveniles away from Alaska. See the Sanderling.
Voice CALL: A squeak somewhat like that of a Western Sandpiper.
Status & Distribution BREEDING: Northeast Siberia to (rarely) west AK. MIGRATION: Regular migrant on western AK islands. VAGRANT: Breeding adults casual on both coasts and interior late June–late Aug.; lack of juvenile records in this area, although some probably pass through undetected. Accidental in CA and DE in spring. WINTER: Australasia and S.E. Asia.
Population Stable or declining somewhat due to habitat loss.

juvenile

breeding breeding

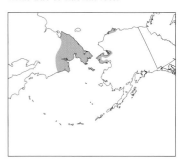

LITTLE STINT *Calidris minuta*

This Old World vagrant peep is likely found with congeners during fall migration. Monotypic. L 6" (15 cm) **Identification** The short, black bill has a fine tip. The legs are black; the feet do not have webbing. Primaries clearly extend beyond the tail tip. BREEDING ADULT: Bright, with dark upperparts brightly fringed with rufous. Yellowish mantle lines appear whitish when worn. The throat and underparts are white; a warm brownish orange wash on the breast contains bold spotting, particularly on the sides of the breast. NONBREEDING ADULT: It is gray-brown above, with some scapulars having dark feather centers. It is white below, with some light streaks on the sides of the breast. JUVENILE: Most juveniles average brighter than other peeps. The upper scapulars are edged rufous, the lower scapulars are dark, usually black, with paler edges. The tertials are dark, typically with bright rufous edges. Both mantle and scapular lines are bold. The crown is dark with a distinctly forked supercilium. Streaking and spotting on the sides of the breast is distinct.

Similar Species See the Red-necked Stint for separation of breeding birds. A breeding Sanderling is superficially similar and the only North American peep that would have such a colorful throat and breast combo; since this plumage is seen infrequently away from the breeding grounds, unsuspecting birders might jump to a Red-necked, but the Sanderling is bigger, bulkier, with a longer bill and dark, boldly marked tertials. It also lacks a hind toe. Juveniles must be distinguished from the Red-necked and Semipalmated. It is best distinguished from juvenile Red-neckeds by its extensively black-centered wing coverts and tertials usually edged with rufous, but it is also usually brighter with bolder mantle lines, and the dark markings on sides of the breast tend to be sharper and more spotted than streaked. The Semipalmated has a darker crown and unforked supercilium and is usually paler than the Little. On a bright Semipalmated, also note its

more tubular bill; in comparison, the Little has sharper breast markings, and bolder mantle and scapular lines. Although not as similar, the first fall juvenile Least Sandpiper can often confuse birders due to its bright plumage (see the Least Sandpiper).
Voice CALL: A single *kip*, often given when flushed.
Status & Distribution BREEDING: Eurasia. MIGRATION: Very rare on islands in western AK in spring and fall; casual to AK mainland. WINTER: Africa and Asia. VAGRANT: Casual, primarily on East and West Coasts June–Sept.; both adults and juveniles recorded. Accidental in spring.
Population Stable.

breeding

juvenile

TEMMINCK'S STINT *Calidris temminckii*

juvenile

juvenile

breeding

The Temminck's Stint, an Old World vagrant, has a preference for freshwater habitats with vegetation. It is usually found singly or in small numbers, even where it is common. Monotypic. L 6.3" (16 cm)

Identification The Temminck's is a rather brown, horizontal-looking peep, with subtle, but attractive plumage. The white outer tail feathers are distinctive in all plumages, but they are hard to see. The bill is dark and short, with a slight droop; the legs are yellowish, sometimes with a green tint. The tail is quite long, extending past the wings. BREEDING ADULT: Brown upperparts are more beautiful than a first glance suggests. The scapulars and coverts are dark with rufous or buff edges; although appearing uniform from a distance, they can be colorful. There is little of a face pattern, with no supercilium and only slightly darker lores; a white eye ring is usually rather distinct. The breast is brown with dark streaks. Worn adults are brown with dark splotches above. NONBREEDING ADULT: The upperparts and breast are plain graybrown; the remainder of the underparts are white. Some shaft streaks are visible on the scapulars. JUVENILE: Like nonbreeding, but feathers of upperparts have dark, subterminal edges and buffy fringes.

Similar Species The breeding adult Temminck's resembles in plumage and shape the larger Baird's Sandpiper; however, note that the Temminck's has yellow or greenish yellow legs and its tail extends beyond the primaries, whereas the Baird's has dark legs and its primaries project past the tail and tertials. Eager birders might focus on the white outer tail feathers, but this mark, while diagnostic, must be used with caution. Outer tail feathers of other *Calidris* can appear pale and lead a birder to the wrong conclusion. Instead, focus on the plumages, which are distinctive in their own right.

Voice CALL: A repeated, fast, dry rattle, almost recalling a longspur; routinely calls when flushed. Its call might be the first clue to its identity.

Status & Distribution BREEDING: Eurasian species in wet tundra from Scandinavia to Siberia. A rare spring and fall migrant on the Aleutians and Pribilofs; very rare on St. Lawrence Is. One Sept. record of a juvenile from BC. WINTER: Mediterranean, Africa, and southern Asia.

Population Stable, with large winter populations in south-central Asia.

LONG-TOED STINT *Calidris subminuta*

This Old World vagrant prefers freshwater with vegetation and is often seen singly or in small numbers, even where common. It often appears erect, highstepping on mudflats. Its long legs and toes, however, are of marginal use in the field. Monotypic. L 6" (15 cm)

Identification Brown peep with a reduced wing stripe. Short and slightly drooped black bill, usually with a pale greenish base. Yellow legs, with either brown or green tones at times; relatively long, so toes extend beyond tail in flight. Dark underwings, unique among stints. BREEDING ADULT: Bright above, recalling a miniature breeding Sharp-tailed Sandpiper. Crown, auriculars, mantle, scapulars, and tertials with rufous edges; lower scapulars often edged white. Greater wing coverts edged buffy. Breast usually buff with fine dark streaks. Rather bold face pattern, with dark lores and a split supercilium. In early fall, when edges worn, bird looks dark brown above. NONBREEDING ADULT: Gray-brown above, looking mottled with dark centers to some scapulars and streaks on the crown and neck. Graybrown breast with faint streaking. Face pattern stays bold. JUVENILE: Upperparts and scapulars edged broadly with rufous and white. Bold white mantle line; less distinct scapular line. Median wing coverts edged white. Breast is streaked, but usually on a grayish, less frequently buffy, background. Supercilium stops short of the bill, resulting in a noticeably dark forehead.

Similar Species The Long-toed is most likely to be confused with the much more expected Least Sandpiper. Distinguish it in all plumages by its dark forehead and region above lores; bolder, split eyebrow, broadening behind eye; white-edged median coverts; pale base to the mandible; and darker underwing coverts. Also, the Long-toed's breast is often grayish or whitish with fine streaks, whereas the Least's is brown or buff with streaks. Variation occurs: claim of a Long-toed should rest on a combination of characters.

Voice CALL: *Purp,* lower pitched than the Least Sandpiper's.

Status & Distribution Asian breeder. Casual in spring to Pribilofs and St. Lawrence Is.; can be fairly common on the western Aleutians. Casual in fall. WINTER: Australasia and southeast Asia. VAGRANT: Accidental elsewhere on the west coast in fall.

Population Believed to be stable, but poorly studied.

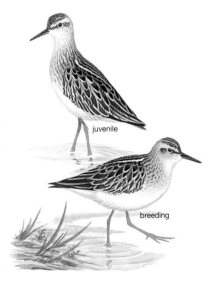

juvenile

breeding

LEAST SANDPIPER *Calidris minutilla*

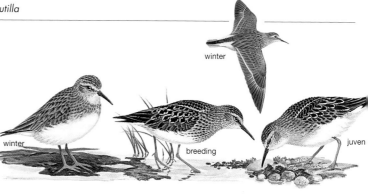

winter

winter

breeding

juven

A common peep throughout the continent, the Least Sandpiper prefers freshwater habitats with vegetation. While common in winter, including in inland habitats, this species does not amass in the large flocks of Western and Semipalmated Sandpipers. Monotypic. L 6" (15 cm)

Identification This brown peep should look smaller and darker than the Western and Semipalmated, the other 2 common peeps. The bill is dark, short, and obviously drooped. The yellow legs can be dull or obscured by mud. BREEDING ADULT: It is black and brown above, with rufous and buffy edges to the scapulars and coverts; some feathers are tipped white. The breast is brown with conspicuous streaks; the remaining underparts are white. The supercilium is bold and meets the base of the bill, so that its forehead is white. NONBREEDING ADULT: The upperparts and breast are brown, with some dark centers to the scapulars. The supercilium, while present, is less distinct than in breeding plumage. JUVENILE: Like breeding plumage, but very crisp; the upperparts are edged rufous and buff, some

feathers are tipped white. The white mantle line is bold; the scapular line is less distinct. It usually has a strong buffy wash across the finely streaked breast.

Similar Species The Least Sandpiper is not too similar to the Western and Semipalmated Sandpipers; however, these 3 species are the common peeps and the first step in learning sandpiper identification. Beginning birders often emphasize the yellow legs of the Least, compared to the darker legs of the other 2 species, but the identifications are sufficiently straightforward to eliminate the need to base an identification on a mark that can be altered by mud, lighting, or something else. The Least is darker above than the Western and Semipalmated and noticeably smaller when seen with either. In non-breeding plumage, the Least has a prominent brown breast band. The Long-toed Stint, a potential vagrant from Asia, is similar; see that species account. In fall, the first arrival of juveniles and their crisp, bright plumage might suggest vagrant stints to the eager birder, but their upperpart pat-

tern, drooped bill, yellow legs, and buffy, streaked breast should cinch the identification.

Voice CALL: A high *kree* or *jeet*.

Status & Distribution Common. BREEDING: Moist tundra and wet habitats in boreal forest; breeds farther south than other peeps. MIGRATION: Spring movement in the West starts in late Mar., peaks in Apr. (CA) to as late as mid-May (WA). Migration in the East averages 1–2 weeks later. In fall, adults move as early as late June, and are common on both coasts and the Great Lakes by mid-July. Most have migrated by the end of Aug. Juveniles first appear in late July, but more typically there is a push in mid-Aug.; they can remain common through Sept. Where they do not winter, stragglers seen into Nov., rarely later. WINTER: Across southern U.S., as far south as Chile. VAGRANT: Europe, northeast Siberia, Azores, and HI.

Population Stable, but the numbers are hard to assess given the Least's remote breeding areas and the lack of large migrating or winter flocks.

WHITE-RUMPED SANDPIPER *Calidris fuscicollis*

juvenile

The White-rumped Sandpiper's larger size and longer wings separate it from the smaller peeps. It is often seen along shore edges or on mudflats. Monotypic. L 7.5" (19 cm)

Identification Long wings, with primaries extending noticeably beyond the tertials and tail. Black bill, noticeably pale reddish at the base. White, unmarked rump typically only visible during

breeding

juvenile

fall molting adult

flight; some birds hold their wings lower, allowing a view on a perched bird. BREEDING ADULT: Gray-brown upperparts with pale edges on the scapulars and coverts. Distinct whitish supercilium. Crown, auriculars, mantle, and upper scapulars might have some rufous tones. Mantle and scapular lines, if present, are indistinct. Black streaks on breast extend to the flanks. Worn fall birds are remarkably plain; they usually have only remnant streaking along the flanks. NONBREEDING ADULT: Gray-brown above and on neck, giving it a hooded look; upperparts have shaft streaks or dark inner markings. Whitish below, with indistinct breast streaks that extend along flanks. JUVENILE: Upperparts brighter than breeding adult, with rather broad rufous edges to crown, mantle, scapulars, and tertials. White mantle and scapular lines rather distinct. Breast, cheek, and throat are streaked. Rather bold white supercilium, contrasting with dark lores.

Similar Species The White-rumped is similar to the Baird's Sandpiper in structure, but is grayer overall, has an entirely white rump, a bolder, whiter supercilium, and a pale base to the lower mandible. In flight, the Curlew and Stilt Sandpipers both show a white rump; however, both species show longer legs sticking out past the tail, and larger, more curved bills.

Voice CALL: A high-pitched *jeet*.

Status & Distribution Fairly common. BREEDING: Moist tundra from north AK to Baffin Island. MIGRATION: A late spring migrant, with the majority of the population moving through the middle of the U.S. and southern Canada. Although first arrivals reach southern states after mid-Apr., they peak late May–early June in most of the country; small numbers are still moving through southern states in early June, the Great Lakes area in mid-June, with a few to late June. In fall, most birds take an Atlantic route to their wintering grounds, moving east to Atlantic Canada or the northeast U.S. Adults are found south of the breeding grounds in late July, but most adults migrate Aug.–early Sept. Juveniles are very late migrants, rarely recorded south of Canada before Sept.; they peak in Oct., and are seen regularly into Nov., strays into Dec. Juveniles yet to be doc-umented in the western states. WINTER: Southern S.A. VAGRANT: Casual in the West, late May–mid-June, and adults July–Oct. Casual in Europe; regular in Britain and Ireland (with more records than Pacific states).

Population Stable. The use of staging areas between long-distance flights places importance on the maintenance of these sites.

BAIRD'S SANDPIPER *Calidris bairdii*

This long-winged sandpiper often feeds up from the shoreline, on dryer surfaces, where it pecks for food. Monotypic. L 7.5" (19 cm)

Identification Long primary tips, projecting beyond the tail and tertials when standing. Brown upperparts; breast a lighter brown, with light streaks. Thin dark bill; dark legs. BREEDING ADULT: Mixture of brown and buff on dark scapulars and coverts; plain tertials. Rather indistinct pale supercilium; dark lores. In worn plumage, adults look blotchy black and brown above. NONBREEDING ADULT: Paler than breeding plumage; rather nondescript light brown on upperparts, slightly paler brown (or gray-brown) on breast. JUVENILE: Pale edgings on back give a distinctly scaled appearance. No mantle or scapular lines. Light brown or buffy breast contrasts with white belly.

Similar Species The Baird's is distinguished from the Least Sandpiper, our other brown sandpiper, by its larger size, longer wings, longer and straighter bill, lack of rufous in the plumage, and black legs. Some juvenile Semipalmated Sandpipers can recall a Baird's with their brown plumage and pale feather edges, but Semipalmated are less elongated, lacking the obviously long wings of Baird's, and their breast is not as notably brown. In flight, the Pectoral Sandpiper can look and sound somewhat like a Baird's. The Pectoral has bolder white sides to the rump and a clearer demarcation at the breast;

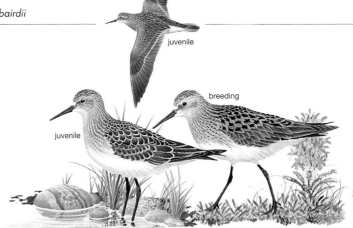

juvenile

breeding

juvenile

also, the brighter edges to its upperparts are often visible.

Voice CALL: A low, raspy *kreeep*.

Status & Distribution Fairly common. BREEDING: Dry tundra from northeast Siberia and west AK to Baffin Island and Greenland. MIGRATION: In spring, through midcontinent, from TX north through the Great Plains; rare in spring west of the Rockies, east of western Great Lakes. Early birds documented in early Mar. (exceptionally Feb.), but most pass late Mar.–mid-May. Lingerers found to early June. In fall, most migration is midcontinent, but uncommon at this season to both coasts, usually juveniles. Adults first noted early to mid-July, a few in late June. Many adult Baird's fly thousands of miles in just 5–6 weeks, so they are less likely encountered than juveniles, although adults do pass through the Plains. The majority of fall Baird's are juveniles, which peak mid-Aug.–mid-Sept. Numbers drop until rare after early Oct. on West Coast, after late Oct. elsewhere, lingerers to Nov. or even later on occasion (with a few Dec. records and a Jan. record). WINTER: S.A. VAGRANT: HI, Europe, Australasia, and South Africa.

Population Stable.

PECTORAL SANDPIPER *Caldiris melanotos*

A favorite among most birders, the Pectoral Sandpiper is found in wet fields, marshy ponds, and similar wetlands. It is often seen in small groups, and its migration is quite long. Monotypic. L 8.8" (22 cm)

Identification Unique within the genus *Calidris,* the male Pectoral is notably larger than the female. This upright sandpiper has a dark bill with a pale base and yellow legs that might have

breeding ♂

juvenile

breeding ♀

juvenile

greenish tones. BREEDING ADULT: The upperparts are brown, with rufous or buff edges. Below, prominent streaking on the breast, darker in male, contrasts with a clear white belly. NONBREEDING ADULT: The plumage is paler and more nondescript than the breeding plumage. JUVENILE: It is brighter above than the breeding plumage, with bold white mantle and scapular lines; the scapulars and coverts are broadly edged in rufous and white. The buffy breast is lightly streaked. FLIGHT: It shows a weak wing stripe but bold white uppertail coverts, separated by a black bar.

Similar Species Especially compare the Pectoral with the juvenile Sharp-tailed Sandpiper (see that account). See also the Baird's Sandpiper. In flight, the Pectoral's bold white sides of the rump recall a Ruff, but they are not as extensive and not oval-shaped (see Ruff for more detail).

Voice CALL: A rich, low *churk.* SONG: A deep hoot, with chest distended.

Status & Distribution Fairly common to common (Midwest). BREEDING: Moist tundra from central Siberia to Hudson Bay. MIGRATION: Common in Midwest; fairly common on East Coast; scarcer from western Great Plains to West Coast. In spring, although the majority of migrants do not reach us until Apr.,

they are numerous in Mar. in several states, and as early as late Feb. Peak migration late Apr.–early May in Great Lakes and mid-Atlantic coast (where less numerous), with lingering birds to late May. Very rare west of Rocky Mountains. In fall, they are more numerous along both coasts than in spring, with juveniles accounting for most West Coast records. Adults first arrive early to mid-July but have been seen in late June. Adults decline by early Aug., when juveniles arrive, peaking late Aug.–Oct. This species often lingers, with a few noted into Nov. and later, even to Dec., in Great Lakes area. WINTER: Casual in the southern states; most winter southern S.A., annual in Australasia. VAGRANT: Annual in northwestern Europe; casual elsewhere in Europe, south to Africa.

Population Stable.

SHARP-TAILED SANDPIPER *Caldiris acuminata*

The Sharp-tailed is an Old World vagrant. Monotypic. L 8.5" (22 cm)

Identification Similar to the Pectoral Sandpiper, and often seen with that species during migration. Dark bill might have pale base; legs greenish. BREEDING ADULT: Rufous crown and edges to scapulars and tertials. Buffy breast, spotted below with dark chevrons on flanks, usually extending to undertail coverts. Distinct white eye ring, rather indistinct supercilium, and dark lores. NONBREEDING ADULT: Paler than breeding adult, lacking most rufous and buff tones. Some spots and chevrons on underparts. JUVENILE: Like breeding adult on upperparts, with rufous cap and edges to scapulars and tertials; bold supercilium. Bold white mantle and scapular lines. Underparts more lightly marked than on a breeding bird; rich buff breast lightly streaked on upper breast and sides; streaked undertail coverts.

Similar Species Most sightings are of juveniles, distinguished from the juvenile Pectoral by a bolder white supercilium that broadens behind the eye; bright buffy breast lightly streaked on upper breast and sides only; streaked undertail coverts; brighter rufous cap and edging on upperparts; and call.

Voice CALL: A mellow 2-note whistle, *to-wheet.*

Status & Distribution Breeds in Siberia, where adults migrate inland and juveniles move to the coast. Casual spring, and irregularly fairly common fall migrant in western AK. Rare in fall and casual in spring along entire Pacific coast, with a few inland records from YK south to CA. Accidental in spring, and casual in fall across rest of continent. WINTER: Australia.

Population Stable.

juvenile Sharp-tailed (center)
with juvenile Pectorals

juvenile

breeding adult

juvenile

PURPLE SANDPIPER *Calidris maritima*

winter

juvenile

breeding

winter

The stocky Purple is primarily noted in the Northeast, along rocky coastline. Monotypic. L 9" (23 cm)
Identification Long, slightly curved bill, with an orange-yellow base. Yellow legs. BREEDING ADULT: Seen only occasionally. Tawny crown streaked with black. Mantle and scapulars edged from white to tawny-buff; rufous usually restricted to scapulars. Breast and flanks spotted with blackish brown. NONBREEDING ADULT: Dark gray or slate upperparts, throat, and breast; blurred spots along sides and flanks; white belly. Purple tinge to upperparts often more easily imagined than actually seen. JUVENILE: Like breeding, but less streaked on head

and neck, more gray. Upperparts edged buffy or white. Completes molt prior to arriving on wintering grounds.
Similar Species In flight and in winter, the Purple resembles a Rock Sandpiper. Separate by range; the Rock has more distinct spotting on the breast and sides, less colorful base to the mandible.
Voice CALL: A low, rough *kweet* or similar note, given in flight.
Status & Distribution Fairly common. BREEDING: Tundra, often with gravel. MIGRATION: Typically reach wintering grounds in the Northeast in late Oct., peak Nov.–Mar. Can linger in spring,

well into May. Return to breeding grounds late May–early June. The few Great Lakes spring records range late Mar.–mid-May. WINTER: Rocky shores and jetties, often with Ruddy Turnstones and Sanderlings. VAGRANT: South of normal winter range along the coast, and scattered inland areas of the eastern U.S. Fall records can be surprisingly early (mid-Sept.), but most records are Nov.–Feb. Southern birds (FL, TX) have been recorded through Apr.
Population Declines have been noted in Quebec; studies are needed to determine if this decline is local.

ROCK SANDPIPER *Calidris ptilocnemis*

winter

tschuktschorum

winter

breeding

juvenile

breeding Pribilofs
ptilocnemis

from a Surfbird by its longer bill, smaller size, and different tail pattern.
Voice CALL: A rough *kreet,* like a Purple's.
Status & Distribution Fairly common. BREEDING: Tundra from west AK to Siberia. WINTER: Most birds arrive WA, OR, and northern CA late Oct.–late Nov. Generally leave vicinity of breeding grounds Sept.–Oct. Wintering birds depart by late Apr.–mid-May. Nominate subspecies winters Cook Inlet, AK.
Population Stable.

This western counterpart of the Purple Sandpiper is usually seen on rocky shores, often with Black Turnstones and Surfbirds. Polytypic (4 ssp.; 3 in N.A.). L 9" (23 cm)
Identification Shape like Purple Sandpiper; dark bill with pale yellow-green at base; yellow-olive legs. BREEDING ADULT: Rufous crown and edges to mantle and scapulars. Supercilium and dark on head variable. Black patch and gray streaks on lower breast; spots on flanks and belly. NONBREEDING ADULT: Dark gray upperparts and breast, with distinct spotting on flanks. JUVENILE: Like breeding, but paler, with buffy edges to scapu-

lars and coverts; buff color to breast. Molts prior to reaching wintering grounds. FLIGHT: White wing stripe and all-dark tail.
Geographic Variation Nominate *ptilocnemis* (Pribilofs) is larger and has paler chestnut above, less black below, and a bolder white wing stripe. The Aleutian *couesi* has a darker head and breast and more obscure auricular patch. The brightest breeding bird is the *tschuktschorum,* from St. Lawrence Island, the Seward Peninsula, and elsewhere.
Similar Species Separate a winter Rock from a Purple Sandpiper by its range and duller bill base and legs. Separate

DUNLIN *Calidris alpina*

winter

molting juvenile

winter

breeding

The Dunlin frequently flocks in large groups on the coasts during winter and migration. It often feeds in water, although it will also feed along the shore, probing into the mud for prey. Polytypic. L 8.5" (22 cm)

Identification The Dunlin is a mid-size sandpiper with a short neck; it appears hunchbacked. It has a sturdy, black bill, curved at the tip, and black legs. BREEDING ADULT: The reddish back is distinctive. It has whitish, finely streaked underparts with a conspicuous black belly patch. NONBREEDING ADULT: Gray-brown above and on the breast; the remainder of the underparts are whitish. The molt takes place prior to arrival on winter grounds. JUVENILE: Like the nonbreeding plumage, but with rufous on crown and edges of upperparts; a bold white mantle line is usually evident. The neck and breast are buffy with dark streaks that extend to the belly, where there is often a par-

tial belly patch. This plumage is not expected south of the breeding range, as molting occurs near the breeding grounds prior to migration. FLIGHT: There's a dark center to the rump and a white wing stripe.

Geographic Variation Nine subspecies. The *hudsonia* breeds in the Canadian Arctic and winters in eastern North America; it is marked by streaks along its sides. The *pacifica* breeds in western Alaska and winters primarily in the West. Asian and Greenland subspecies have visited our coasts on rare occasion; the Asian *articola* is regular in western Alaska.

Similar Species The Rock Sandpiper in breeding plumage has a similar black patch, but it is on the chest, not the belly. Also, in nonbreeding plumage, see Curlew and Western Sandpipers.

Voice CALL: A harsh, reedy *kree*.

Status & Distribution BREEDING: Abundant. MIGRATION: Peak in spring early

to mid-May in mid-Atlantic and Great Lakes, 1–2 weeks earlier in the West; lingering birds into early June. Generally a late fall migrant, perhaps in part due to its molt prior to migration. Early arrivals usually in early Sept., only rarely earlier, with peak numbers mid-Oct.–mid-Nov. Rare on Great Plains. WINTER: On both coasts, across the Southeast, and south to Mexico. VAGRANT: To S.A.

Population Local declines are suggested.

CURLEW SANDPIPER *Calidris ferruginea*

The Curlew is a vagrant from the Old World. Monotypic. L 8.5" (22 cm)

Identification More elegant than somewhat similar Dunlin. Long, black legs. Medium-length, black, rather evenly downcurved bill. BREEDING MALE: Distinctive rich chestnut underparts and mottled chestnut back; grayish wing coverts. Scattered bars on sides and across uppertail coverts; white where bill joins face. BREEDING FEMALE: Slightly paler.

Many birds show patchy spring plumage or molt to winter plumage, showing grayer upperparts and partly white underparts. NONBREEDING ADULT: Gray-brown above, with white edges when fresh. White uppertail coverts unbarred. JUVENILE: Appears scaly above; shows rich buff across breast. FLIGHT: White rump conspicuous; white wing stripe rather distinct.

Similar Species In fall, young

juvenile

juvenile

breeding ♂

birds are in full juvenal plumage; compare with young Dunlins, which are mostly in winter plumage. The Dunlin has a dark line on the upper tail, and its bill is unevenly curved at the tip. In flight, the White-rumped has less white on rump and in wing stripe, and a smaller bill. The Stilt Sandpiper has paler legs, more leg extending beyond the tail, and less of a wing stripe.

Voice CALL: A soft, rippling *chirrup*.

Status & Distribution BREEDING: Siberia; has bred in northern AK. WINTER: Africa, Asia, Australasia. VAGRANT: Rare on East Coast (primarily mid-Atlantic), casual elsewhere. Spring records primarily late Apr.–late May. In fall, adults most likely encountered mid-July–mid-Aug., juveniles mid-Aug.–mid-Oct, a few records into Nov.

Population Threats due to loss of habitat in migration and winter.

STILT SANDPIPER *Calidris himantopus*

juvenile

juvenile

juvenile

winter

molting
juvenile

breeding

The Stilt Sandpiper frequently feeds with dowitchers in belly-deep water, its head down and rear end up, as it probes into the mud for food. Monotypic. L 8.5" (22 cm)

Identification The Stilt is a long-legged sandpiper with a long, slightly downcurved bill; its legs are yellow-green. BREEDING ADULT: Chestnut patches on sides of head and rear of crown contrast with dark gray upperparts and pale eyebrow. Heavy barring on the breast thins out somewhat on the belly and lower flanks. Males average brighter than females. NONBREEDING ADULT: Gray-brown above including crown, auriculars, and lores, contrasting with white supercilium. The underparts are mostly whitish, with some gray on the breast. JUVENILE: Plumage similar to nonbreeding plumage, but scapulars and coverts have broad pale edges. When plumage

is fresh, a buff wash might be present on the breast; dusky breast streaking, and some spotting on the flanks is possible, too. Migrants are often seen with molted scapulars. FLIGHT: White uppertail coverts (except in breeding plumage), weak white wing stripe, and legs extend noticeably beyond tail.

Similar Species The Curlew Sandpiper is similar, but the Stilt has a somewhat straighter bill and yellow-green legs that are noticeably longer. Also, in flight the Stilt lacks a prominent wing stripe. See dowitchers.

Voice CALL: A low, hoarse *querp,* but often silent.

Status & Distribution Common. BREED-ING: Tundra from AK to Hudson Bay. MIGRATION Primarily migrates mid-continent in spring; first arrivals late Mar., but typically peak in southern states mid-Apr.–early May; closer to mid-May in KS, and the latter half of May in the Prairie Provinces. Very rare in the West, except at Salton Sea. Common in fall on East Coast; rare but regular in West, primarily juveniles. Adults first seen early or mid-July, peak in KS late July, generally completing migration in early Aug. Juveniles first arrive in early Aug., peaking mid-Aug.–early Sept. Small numbers into Oct., rarely into Nov. WINTER: Scattered areas in southern U.S. (inc. Salton Sea, southern TX, southwestern LA, and southern FL); Mexico to S.A. VAGRANT: Europe, Asia, and Australia.

Population Stable. Possible recent western shift of breeding range.

SPOON-BILLED SANDPIPER *Eurynorhynchus pygmeus*

This Asian vagrant is perhaps the most sought-after sandpiper due to its rarity and distinctive bill structure. It molts into breeding plumage late, so spring migrants are typically pale. The Spoon-billed is stintlike in its behavior, although it sometimes walks with a stumbling gait. It often forages in shallow water. Monotypic. L 6" (15 cm)

Identification The spoon-shaped bill is diagnostic, but the shape is hard to see at some angles; the bill is longer than that of most peeps. BREEDING ADULT: Rufous head, throat, and upper breast; reddish edges to upperpart feathers. Dark spotting along lower edge of orange breast color, spreading onto the white lower breast and sides. NON-BREEDING ADULT: Pale grayish above, paler than most congeners. White supercilium forked and quite broad in front of eye; darker auriculars. JUVE-

NILE: Supercilium forked, as in nonbreeding, leaving white forehead that contrasts boldly with dark cheek patch and lores. Upperparts edged white or buff, sometimes rufous. Mantle and scapular lines, if present, usually indistinct. White underparts, although a buff wash across the breast expected in fresh plumage.

Similar Species Similar in breeding plumage to a Red-necked Stint, which usually has a hint of a white supercilium, although the Spoon-billed averages more spotting on the underparts. A juvenile Spoon-billed has a darker cheek patch than a juvenile Red-necked, emphasized by its forked supercilium. While no other sandpiper has a similar-looking bill, beware of mud

creating a misleading blob.

Voice CALL: A quiet *wheet.*

Status & Distribution Endangered. BREEDING: Tundra in northeast Siberia. MIGRATION: Casual migrant in AK; 1 fall record of an alternate adult from coastal BC. WINTER: Southeast Asia.

Population Declining and endangered; only a couple thousand birds are thought to remain. Low population, narrow breeding habitat, and habitat loss create a tenuous position for this species.

breeding

juvenile

BROAD-BILLED SANDPIPER *Limicola falcinellus*

breeding

juvenile

The Broad-billed is an Old World vagrant. Polytypic. L 7" (18 cm)
Identification The plump body, short legs, and long bill form a distinctive profile. The thick bill droops noticeably at the tip; at times the distal portion of the bill looks like it has an unnatural kink. The Broad-billed is more likely to probe for food than peck, but it does both. The split supercilium is present in all plumages. The legs vary from olive to almost black. BREEDING ADULT: Black scapulars edged buff or rufous; the coverts typically edged buff. Underparts white except for the brownish and heavily streaked breast; streaks extend down the sides. NONBREEDING ADULT: Gray-brown above with some scapulars having dark centers, giving a somewhat mottled look. White below with variable breast streaking. JUVENILE: Scapulars and coverts edged buff or rufous, with bold mantle and scapular lines. Breast lighter, more lightly streaked than breeding plumage.
Geographic Variation Two subspecies. Nominate *falcinellus* from Europe and west Russia perhaps pertains to the Atlantic record. *Sibirica* from Asia, which averages more rufous above, is thought to pertain to Alaska records.
Similar Species While the Dunlin is superficially similar—it shares a rather plump appearance, with a downcurved bill—no species matches the Broad-billed's combination of plumage and structure.
Voice CALL: Ascending trill, *brreeet*.
Status & Distribution Breeds in Eurasia. Casual fall migrant on the Aleutians; accidental in fall in coastal NY. All sightings so far juveniles. WINTER: Arabian Peninsula to Australia.
Population Stable.

RUFF *Philomachus pugnax*

The Ruff male has a spectacular breeding plumage. The males gather in leks and display for females. Monotypic. L 10–12" (25–31 cm)
Identification Tall with long legs, plump body, small head, and small bill. Scapulars often stick out from the back when the bird is standing. BREEDING MALE: Neck ruff colors black, rufous, or white. Legs may be yellow, orange, or red; bill has pale base, black tip. BREEDING FEMALE: The "Reeve," as the female is called, lacks the ruff, is smaller, and has a variable amount of black below. Some females can become very bright, almost matching males. NONBREEDING ADULT: Legs and bill usually duller than in breeding, but some birds still with bright tones. Scapulars and coverts dark, with thin, pale edges; tertials often with bars or internal markings. Underparts dingy whitish with mottling sometimes present on the neck and sides of the breast. Typically, with white feathering at base of bill. JUVENILE: Like nonbreeding, but bolder edges to the upperparts, buffy breast, and tertials lack internal markings. FLIGHT: Distinctive U-shaped white rump band in all plumages; white underwings.
Similar Species The Ruff's combination of small bill, long legs, and plump body is distinct. The Upland Sandpiper is superficially similar, but it is more marked on the upperparts, has streaks on the neck and a straight bill, and lacks the white ovals on the sides of the rump. Compare the juvenile Ruff with the Sharp-tailed Sandpiper, which has a different face pattern. The Buff-breasted is smaller and less erect and lacks any facial markings (juvenile Ruffs usually have a postocular line or mark) and the rump ovals.
Voice CALL: Silent away from breeding grounds.
Status & Distribution Old World species; has bred in AK. MIGRATION: In spring, rare in western AK and on Atlantic coast, casual elsewhere, primarily late Mar.–late May, into June in AK. In fall, as above, but more regular in West, primarily late July–Aug. (adults), and Sept.–early Nov. (juveniles); juveniles more numerous than adults in West, opposite in East. WINTER: Rare CA, accidental OR.
Population Some local population declines appear to be offset by local increases.

juvenile ♀

breeding males

♀

summer molting ♂

juvenile ♀

summer molting ♀

winter ♂

BUFF-BREASTED SANDPIPER *Tryngites subruficollis*

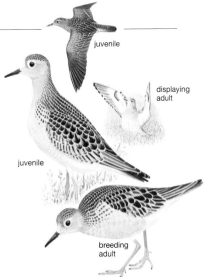

juvenile

displaying adult

juvenile

breeding adult

A rather elegant sandpiper, most likely encountered in plowed or grassy fields. Males join leks in search of mates, using bold wing displays. Monotypic. L 8.3" (21 cm)

Identification Dark eye prominent on buffy face; underparts paler buff. Pale orange-yellow legs. Dark bill. ADULT: Dark scapulars and coverts, with rather broad buff edges when fresh. Bright legs, almost orange. JUVENILE: Like adult, but scapular edges duller and more narrow, look distinctly scaled. Wing coverts with dark subterminal marks, in addition to the pale fringe. Pale buff breast. Notably paler belly than adult. Legs not as bright as adult. FLIGHT: Bright white wing linings; darker underwing primary coverts.

Similar Species Unique, but see the Ruff species account.

Voice CALL: Generally silent, but utters a low *tu*.

Status & Distribution Locally fairly common. BREEDING: Tundra. MIGRATION: Via interior of N.A. in spring. Arrivals typically early Apr., with peak late Apr.–mid-May, peak in northern Great Plains mid-May. Only a few records to Great Lakes and Atlantic, or in the West. In fall, adults reverse migration through midcontinent; juveniles more likely to wander, very rare on the West Coast, very uncommon to the East, at both drying wetland edges and sod farms. Migrate from late July, but peak late Aug.–late Sept., lingerers through Oct. WINTER: Southern S.A. VAGRANT: Europe, Africa, Asia, and Australia.

Population Hunted to dangerously low levels in the early 20th century. Present numbers appear stable.

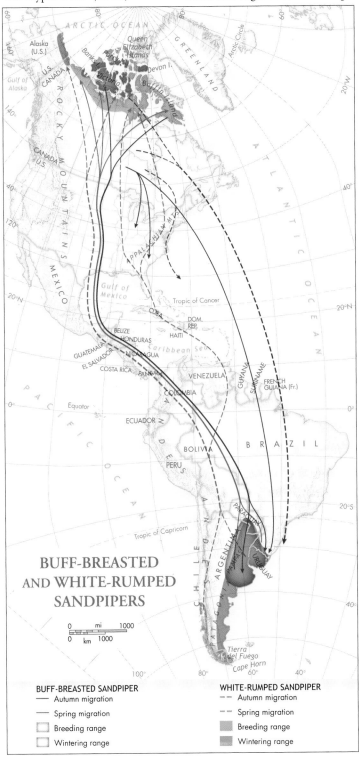

BUFF-BREASTED AND WHITE-RUMPED SANDPIPERS

0   mi   1000
0   km   1000

BUFF-BREASTED SANDPIPER
— Autumn migration
— Spring migration
☐ Breeding range
☐ Wintering range

WHITE-RUMPED SANDPIPER
-- Autumn migration
-- Spring migration
▨ Breeding range
▨ Wintering range

DOWITCHERS Genus *Limnodromus*

The dowitchers are medium-size, chunky, dark shorebirds, with long, straight bills and distinct pale eyebrows. They feed in mud or shallow water, probing with a rapid jabbing motion. In flight they show a white wedge from barred tail to middle of back. Separating the species is easiest with juveniles, difficult with breeding adults, and very difficult in winter.

SHORT-BILLED DOWITCHER *Limnodromus griseus*

The Short-billed Dowitcher is often encountered in large flocks along the coasts during winter or migration. The Short-billed and the Long-billed Dowitcher present very difficult identification challenges. Polytypic. L 11" (28 cm)

Identification Rather long, gray bill (shorter in eastern birds); females have longer bills. Alternating light and dark bars, usually more light than dark, on tail. Primaries usually extend a bit past the tail. BREEDING ADULT: Dark upperparts with orange feather edges. Underparts a mixture of orange and white, with spots and bars (vary by subspecies). NONBREEDING ADULT: Uniform brownish gray above, feathers without darker center. White below with barring on the sides that contrasts with upperparts; gray breast with fine speckling visible at close range. JUVENILE: Dark scapulars and coverts, boldly edged orange; tertials, and some coverts, with intricate internal markings and loops. Dark crown contrasts boldly with white supercilium. Orange-buff neck and upper breast; color sometimes extends farther through the underparts. FLIGHT:

White trailing edge to the secondaries, white wedge from tail through lower back. Tail barred dark gray and white.

Geographic Variation Three subspecies: nominate *griseus* (breeds northeast Canada), *hendersoni* (central and western Canada), and *caurinus* (AK). Most Short-billeds show some white on the belly, especially *griseus*, which also has a heavily spotted breast and may have densely barred flanks. The Pacific *caurinus* is intermediate, but more similar to *griseus*. In *hendersoni*, which may be mostly reddish below, foreneck is much less heavily spotted than in the other subspecies. The tertials and greater wing coverts have broad reddish buff and internal bars, loops, or stripes. In juveniles, *caurinus* averages duller, with more narrow markings, although *griseus* is quite similar. Both are duller than *hendersoni*, which can be quite rufous, with broad edges and more buffy below.

Similar Species See the Long-billed Dowitcher and the Red Knot.

Voice CALL: A mellow *tu tu tu*, repeated in a rapid series as an alarm call. More likely to remain silent than the Long-billed Dowitcher. SONG: A rapid *di-di-da-doo* year-round.

Status & Distribution Common. BREEDING: Muskegs in boreal forest. MIGRATION: Common along the Atlantic coast *(griseus);* from the eastern Plains to Atlantic coast from NJ south *(hendersoni);* and along the Pacific coast *(caurinus);* a few *griseus* are seen on eastern Great Lakes in late spring, and a few *hendersoni* move through western states. Spring movement for *griseus* begins mid-Mar., peaks late Apr.–early June, particularly mid-May. In the interior, *hendersoni* peaks on the Great Lakes and Great Plains mid-May; *caurinus* a bit earlier, with CA peak mid-Apr, WA late Apr., and southern AK ±10 May. Fall migration begins earlier than for Long-billed; in 3 distinct waves, led by adult females, as early as late June; then adult males (adults complete most of migration by Aug.), followed by juveniles, typically arriving in early Aug., peaking through early Sept., with small numbers into early Oct.; lingerers to early Nov. They molt when they reach wintering grounds; late juveniles still in their juvenal plumage. WINTER: Coastal habitats to S.A., almost unknown away from the coasts. VAGRANT: One definite rec. for Europe; other dowitcher species from that area.

Population There are indications of a decline in *griseus*.

LONG-BILLED DOWITCHER *Limnodromus scolopaceus*

The Long-billed Dowitcher, like the Short-billed Dowitcher, can be seen in large flocks in winter and on migration. It has a preference for freshwater, although it does frequent coastal estuaries. Monotypic. L 11.5" (29 cm)

Identification The size of the bill is not a particularly helpful feature for identification purposes since all dowitchers have rather long bills. In addition, the female Long-billed's bill is notably longer than the Short-billed's, but the male's bill is not. The tail is barred dark and white, with the dark bars wider than the white bars; the primaries do not extend beyond the tail. BREEDING ADULT: The underparts are entirely reddish below, except for whitish edges to fresh feathers that wear off in early spring. The foreneck is heavily spotted and the sides are usually barred. The black scapulars have rufous markings and show white tips in spring. As this plumage wears, usually in July and August, the bird looks uniform rufous below and a mixture of rufous and black above, making identification difficult. NON-BREEDING ADULT: The scapulars have dark centers, giving a more mottled appearance; the upperparts are gray-brown. The breast is rather dark gray and is unspotted. JUVENILE: It is dark above; the dark crown moderately contrasts with the supercilium. The tertials and greater wing coverts are plain, with thin gray edges and rufous tips; some birds show 2 pale spots near the tips. The underparts are gray, with only hints of warmth on the breast.

Similar Species Separating the Long-billed from the Short-billed Dowitcher ranges from the straightforward to the very difficult. A familiarity with variation, molt, and vocalizations is needed and will result in a high percentage of identifications; many dowitchers, however, will likely be left unidentified. Start with the age, and consider which Short-billed subspecies need to be eliminated. In full breeding plumage, the rufous underparts of a Long-billed are easy to distinguish from those of a breeding *griseus* and *caurinus*, but they are similar to those of *hendersoni*. Look for white tips to the scapulars of the Long-billed and small dots restricted to the neck of *hendersoni*, whereas the Long-billed has spots and bars on the underparts. Other clues for intermediate plumages are the short primary projection, visible in the Short-billed and absent in the Long-billed, and the lighter tail in the Short-billed, owing to the wider white bars. This tail feature is hard to assess, further compounded by *griseus* having wider dark bars than the other Short-billed subspecies; *griseus*, however, also shows wavy internal bars on rectrices that are lacking on the Long-billed. Breeding Long-billeds have rufous on their central tail feathers, unlike any Short-billed Dowitcher. Adult Long-billeds go to favored locations in late summer to molt; Short-billeds molt when they reach winter grounds. In non-breeding birds, Long-billeds are darker, more mottled above, with a darker breast, lacking the fine spotting that Short-billeds show. Juvenile Long-billeds are darker above and grayer below than Short-billeds; they also lack the internal feather markings found on the tertials and greater coverts of Short-billeds. One other species could cause some confusion: the Red Knot in breeding plumage. It has a shorter bill and shorter, darker legs, however, and lacks the white wedge up the back.

Voice CALL: A sharp, high *keek*, given singly or in a rapid series. SONG: Like the Short-billed Dowitcher.

Status & Distribution Common. BREEDING: Tundra from northeast Siberia to northwest Canada; a restricted and more northerly range than Short-billed. MIGRATION: Common in western half of continent; generally uncommon in the east in fall, rare in spring. Spring migration is earlier than the Short-billed's, arriving in nonwintering areas late Feb.–mid-Mar., peaking Great Plains and Great Lakes late Mar.–early May, before most Short-billeds. Arrive breeding grounds mid to late May. Fall migration begins later than Short-billed's, in mid-July (West) or late July (East). Juveniles migrate later than adults; rare before Sept. Dowitchers seen inland after mid-Oct. are almost certainly Long-billed. WINTER: South to C.A., casual to northern S.A. VAGRANT: Europe, Asia, and HI.

Population The populations are stable. Appear to be expanding west in Siberia.

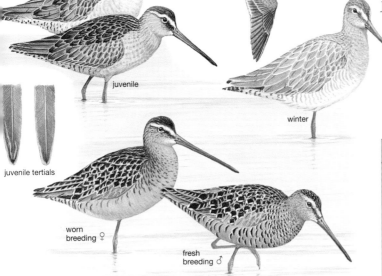

molting juvenile

winter

juvenile

juvenile tertials

worn breeding ♀

fresh breeding ♂

winter

SNIPES Genera *Lymnocryptes* and *Gallinago*

Snipes are stout, long-billed shorebirds that frequent bogs, marshes, and other similar wetlands. Some of the 19 species are poorly known, isolated on islands around the world. Snipes are generally solitary, but they can collect into flocks during migrations. Their heavily striped, cryptic patterns allow them to blend into their surroundings. They probe the mud for food, and the males' display flights during breeding season are spectacular.

JACK SNIPE *Lymnocryptes minimus*

The Jack Snipe, a Eurasian vagrant, is most frequently detected by hunters. Monotypic. L 7" (18 cm)
Identification The Jack Snipe is small and chunky. Secretive, it is reluctant to flush. Its flight is low, short, fluttery, on rounded wings; it is more rail-like. It bobs while feeding. The short bill has a pale base. The tail is dark and wedge-shaped. It has a bold head pattern with a split supercilium; no median crown stripe. The broad, buffy back stripes are striking. The underparts are pale, with streaking on both the breast and flanks; there is no barring.

Similar Species The Jack Snipe has the general coloration and the shape of a snipe, but it is more likely confused with a rail, given its size (only half that of other snipes) and its flight characteristics.

Voice CALL: Generally silent.

Status & Distribution BREEDING: Forest bogs of northern Eurasia. MIGRATION: A vagrant migrant. Hunters have shot a few Jack Snipes, which suggests that they are more frequent than the few records would suggest. But their secretive behavior, resistance to flushing, and immediate return to cover once they are flushed make detection difficult. Furthermore, most birders likely do not consider this species when they are flushing snipes and might overlook the occasional vagrant. Three late-fall records for CA and Labrador, along with 1 sight record for WA in Sept.; 2 spring records from the Pribilof Is. WINTER: Africa and Asia.

Population Declines in the 20th century that resulted from habitat degradation appear to have stabilized.

WILSON'S SNIPE *Gallinago delicata*

The Wilson's is generally seen singly, standing in wet, grassy habitats, although flocks of dozens can be encountered during winter. It probes the mud with its long bill, much like a dowitcher. This species was called the Common Snipe until the recent decision to re-split Wilson's from that species. Monotypic. L 10.3" (26 cm)
Identification The Wilson's is a stocky shorebird with a very long dark-tipped bill, pale at the base; the legs are greenish gray. The head is boldly striped with pale lines above and below the auriculars and in the middle of the crown, all separated by dark brown. The upperparts are dark brown with pale buff or white lines. Below, the breast is brown with dark streaks, and the flanks are heavily barred. The outer rectrices are barred black-and-white, with no trace of orange. FLIGHT: It often explodes from the ground straight up into the air. The general impression is a brown breast and white underparts, along with dark gray underwings. The toes do not extend beyond the tail in flight.

Similar Species It is very difficult to separate the Wilson's from a Common Snipe; see that species account. More likely to be confused with dowitchers in most of North America, as they share a chunky, long-billed profile. Dowitchers, however, do not share the extensive head stripes or light buffy lines on the upperparts, and snipes lack the dowitcher's white wedge up the back.

Voice CALL: A raspy, 2-note *ski-ape*, given in rapid, zigzagging flight when flushed. On nesting grounds, the male delivers loud *wheet* notes from perches. In swooping display flight, vibrating outer tail feathers make quavering hoots, commonly referred to as "winnowing," similar to the song of the Boreal Owl.

Status & Distribution Common, but overlooked. BREEDING: Marshes. MIGRATION: In spring, southern states see movement in late Feb.–early Mar. Peak Pacific Northwest to Great Lakes late Mar.–late Apr., lingerers recorded to June. Fall migration begins as early as mid-July, but peak mid-Sept.–late Oct. WINTER: To northern S.A.

Population There have been local declines, but the population appears stable overall.

underwing

displaying

COMMON SNIPE *Gallinago gallinago*

The Common Snipe, a vagrant from the Old World, is so similar to the Wilson's Snipe that it could easily be overlooked. In fact, the species formerly included the Wilson's until taxonomists split them into separate species. Polytypic (2 ssp.; 1 recorded from N.A.). L 10.5" (27 cm)

Identification The long bill has a black tip and a pale base; the legs are greenish gray. The bold head pattern has alternating light and dark lines from the light midcrown stripe through the auriculars. The upperparts are dark, with buffy lines running along the back from the head toward the tail. The tertials are heavily barred, all the way to the base. The tail is composed of 14 feathers, the outer feather on each side is broad, and the inner web of these feathers has an orange coloration. Below, the breast is brown with dark streaks; the flanks are barred. FLIGHT: Like the Wilson's, the Common is likely to explode up from the ground and fly straight up in the air. As it flies overhead, it gives the impression of a dark-breasted bird with a white belly. The underwing has substantial white, although juveniles have more gray than adults. There is a rather broad white

trailing edge to the secondaries, easily visible in flight.

Similar Species The Common is very similar to the Wilson's; close scrutiny is needed. There are features that average different between the 2 species. The Common has a paler, buffier color overall than the Wilson's and slightly fainter flank markings; however, sufficient variation renders these marks suggestive, not diagnostic. The broader white trailing edge to the secondaries and paler white-striped underwings are consistent features separating the 2 species. The outer tail feathers are also diagnostic, but you'll need great views of a preening bird or a well-timed photograph; the Common has 1 broad feather, with orange on the inner web, versus the Wilson's 2 narrower feathers, the outer of which lacks orange.

Voice CALL: A 2-note *ski-ape,* similar to the Wilson's. SONG: Male flight display notes distinctly lower pitched than the Wilson's.

Status & Distribution BREEDING: Throughout northern Eurasia; it has bred in western Aleutian Is. MIGRATION: Regular migrant to the western

underwing

Aleutian Is., where it has also been found casually in winter; rare to the central Aleutian and Pribilof Is.; casual to St. Lawrence I.; and 1 rec. from Labrador. Given the difficulty in identifying this species, a review of hunters' snipe collections might prove valuable to assess whether this species is more numerous in N.A. WINTER: Southern Europe, Africa, and S.E. Asia. VAGRANT: Rarely to HI.

Population Stable.

PIN-TAILED SNIPE *Gallinago stenura*

underwing

tail

The Pin-tailed Snipe is a vagrant from Asia. Monotypic. L 10" (26 cm)

Identification The Pin-tailed's bill is relatively short and thick for a snipe. It has a bold head pattern with alternating dark and light bars from the pale midcrown stripe through the auriculars. The expansion of the buff supercilium in front of the eye is

broad, leaving a small dark lore stripe, and a small dark stripe at the top of the bill. The upperparts are dark with rufous internal markings and rufous-and-white edges. There is a bold white mantle line; it does not have a series of parallel lines. Many of the scapulars and coverts have white around the tip of the feathers, extending to both sides, leaving a slightly more scaled look. In hand, the razor-thin outer tail feathers are diagnostic; this feature is very difficult to see in the field, except perhaps on a preening bird. FLIGHT: There is a fairly obvious buffy secondary covert patch; while not the intensity of the patch of a Least Bittern, for example, it is unlike that of the other 2 snipe species. The secondaries lack pale edges. Below, the underwings are uniformly dark, and the foot distinctly projects past the tail.

Similar Species The Pin-tailed most likely needs to be separated from the Common Snipe in western Alaska.

The Pin-tailed is chunkier, shorter billed, and shorter tailed. On a perched bird, note the barred secondary coverts and even-width pale edges on the inner and outer webs of the scapulars that give a scalloped look. Also, the Pin-tailed's face pattern subtly differs with a particularly broad supercilium in front of the eye. The underwing is the same between the Pin-tailed and the Wilson's Snipe, but the Wilson's lacks toe projections in flight; the buffy patch on the upper wing of the Pin-tailed is unmatched by any snipe. Typically found in more upland habitats than the Common and the Wilson's, and often flushes only a shorter distance ahead.

Voice CALL: A high *squak,* sounding more like a duck or a pig.

Status & Distribution The Pin-tailed breeds in Siberia. Two certain records from western Aleutian Is.; birders in AK and along Pacific coast should be aware of its potential to occur. WINTER: Primarily S.E. Asia.

Population Stable.

Genus *Scolopax*

EURASIAN WOODCOCK *Scolopax rusticola*

A vagrant from Eurasia, the Eurasian Woodcock is likely to be found on moist forest floors, probing into the leaf litter with its long, sensitive bill. Monotypic. L 13" (33 cm)

Identification The Eurasian is a chunky, large-headed bird, with a long, dull pinkish bill that has a darker tip. Its unique shape is completed by short wings and a short tail. It is cryptically colored: earthy brown, combined with bars and stripes that allow it to blend into the forest floor. The hindcrown is barred with black; the lores are dark. The upperparts are dark brown, with paler brown markings and tips; there are pale lines on the mantle. The underparts are heavily barred, particularly the breast and flanks. The wing coverts and neck are also barred.

Similar Species The Eurasian is similar to the American Woodcock, which is far more expected. The Eurasian is larger, with heavily barred underparts. The pale lines on the mantle and scapular do not contrast on the Eurasian to the extent that they do on the American. Superficially, woodcocks look like snipes, sharing their general chunky shape as well as their feeding style. But snipes have stripes on the head, compared to the crossbarring on woodcocks.

Voice CALL: Generally silent.

Status & Distribution Eurasian breeder. WINTER: South to N. Africa and southeast Asia. VAGRANT: A few records, mostly old, primarily from northeast N.A., inland to QC, PA, and, remarkably, AL. A skeleton from OH was incompletely assessed, but is likely correctly assigned to Eurasian.

Population Millions of Eurasian Woodcocks are hunted annually in Eurasia, yet there is no clear trend in the Eurasian Woodcock population.

AMERICAN WOODCOCK *Scolopax minor*

A bird of moist woodland floors and brushy marsh and field edges, the American Woodcock is usually found singly as it probes and picks through soil and leaves for worms or other prey. It is typically nocturnal, although it may feed during the day as well. It is secretive and is seldom seen until flushed; it flies up abruptly and the wings make a twittering sound. The males have a spectacular display flight, typically performed at dawn and dusk. Monotypic. L 11" (28 cm)

Identification The American is a chunky, atypical shorebird with rounded wings and a short tail. The long bill is dull pink with a darker tip. The large eyes stand out on a rather buffy face. Bold crossbars mark the hindcrown. The upperparts are dark with obvious pale mantle lines and upper scapulars with pale pinkish or buff edges. The wing coverts are brown with orange-buff markings. The underparts are buffy

and unmarked. JUVENILE: It is very much like an adult; it is only separable early in its plumage, when the juvenile has a gray-brown throat and neck that contrasts with the white chin. FLIGHT: A stubby bird in flight with a long bill held downward, round wings, and a short tail. It looks dark brown above and warm buffy-orange below.

Similar Species Most North American birders will likely need to separate the American Woodcock from the Wilson's Snipe. Both species are chunky, with long bills; they share a generally brown coloration and feed by probing in wet, vegetated areas. The snipe has stripes along its head, as opposed to the bars that cross the head of a woodcock. The American's eyes are large and isolated on a pale, buff face; the eyes of a dowitcher do not stand out. The Eurasian Woodcock, if one is lucky enough to chance upon it, is more similar, but does not present a tough identification challenge. The American is smaller, more colorful with cinnamon and buff tones, and unbarred below.

Voice CALL: A nasal *peent,* heard mainly in spring. Gives twittering notes in display flight.

Status & Distribution Common but local. BREEDING: Moist woodlands. MIGRATION: In spring, woodcocks move early; they are the earliest arriving and breeding northern shorebirds. First departures from southern states as early as late Jan., with most having left nonbreeding areas of southern states by late Feb. Mid-Atlantic birds peak late Feb.–mid-Mar.; peak in Great Lakes during latter half of Mar. The first fall migrants are detected late Aug.–early Sept., but most migration is noted in Oct.–Nov. A juvenile banded in AL in Mar. and found in MI in Oct. stresses the fact that movements of this species are not well understood. WINTER: Mostly southern U.S. VAGRANT: Casual in West to MT, eastern CO, eastern NM. Accidental in southeastern CA.

Population Recent declines might be a result of the loss of second-growth forests.

PHALAROPES Genus *Phalaropus*

These elegant shorebirds have partially lobed feet and a dense, soft plumage. Feeding on the water, phalaropes often spin like tops, stirring up larvae, crustaceans, and insects. Females are larger and more brightly colored than males, and the sexes reverse roles: females do the courting and males incubate the eggs and care for the chicks. In fall, they rapidly molt to winter plumage (esp. Wilson's and Red); many are seen in transitional plumage farther south. All species are pelagic to a certain extent, with the Red and Red-necked spending most of their lives at sea. Although some phalaropes stay farther north, most migrate to the tropics, and many winter well south of the Equator.

WILSON'S PHALAROPE *Phalaropus tricolor*

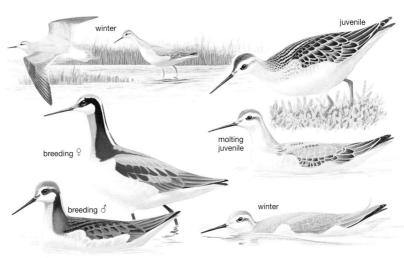

winter

juvenile

breeding ♀

molting juvenile

breeding ♂

winter

winter

The Wilson's Phalarope is a splendid species with beautiful breeding plumage and an impressive biology. Large flocks are encountered during migration. It is the only phalarope that breeds south of Canada. This species is the largest and most terrestrial of the phalaropes. It will swim in circles on shallow ponds, evoking laughter or surprise from those that have not seen it before; this spinning creates a vortex that delivers food to the surface. It also feeds on land, where it is even more humorous when it walks in circles. Monotypic. L 9.3" (24 cm)

Identification The Wilson's long, thin bill is black and almost needlelike. BREEDING FEMALE: Has a bold black and rufous stripe on the face and neck. The warm orange breast contrasts with the white throat. The mantle and lower scapulars are rufous, separated by gray upper scapulars. The crown is whitish or pale gray; the whitish supercilium usually does not extend beyond the eye. BREEDING MALE: Like the female, only usually duller; the crown is dark gray. The upperparts have less contrast and are more mottled, having often dark centered feathers with pale or rufous edges. Some males are quite dull, almost like nonbreeding plumage, except for the mottled upperparts and the dark, almost black legs. NONBREEDING ADULT: The legs are paler, olive to yellow. It is gray above, including gray crown and gray postocular

stripe. The upperparts are edged white in fresh plumage. JUVENILE: Resembles a nonbreeding adult, but its back is browner with buffy edges to feathers and its breast is buffy. It quickly molts out of this plumage; most juveniles seen south of breeding grounds are gray backed and are identifiable as juveniles by the broad buffy edges to the dark wing coverts and tertials. FLIGHT: White uppertail coverts, whitish tail, and the absence of a white wing stripe are important characters.

Similar Species The lack of the "phalarope mark" through the eye; the long, thin bill; and the white uppertail coverts, whitish tail, and absence of white wing stripe distinguish juvenile and winter Wilson's from other phalaropes. They are more easily confused with a nonbreeding Stilt Sandpiper, but phalaropes have a straight (not curved) bill and less of a wing stripe, and their legs do not extend well beyond the tail, as they do on the Stilt. The Lesser Yellowlegs, occasionally noted swimming, is larger and its bill is thicker, and the Wilson's has a notably whiter breast. The Marsh Sandpiper, a vagrant from Eurasia, has a longer bill and longer legs; in flight it shows a white wedge up the back.

Voice CALL: A hoarse *wurk* and other low, croaking notes.

Status & Distribution Common. BREEDING: Grassy borders of shallow lakes, marshes, and reservoirs. MIGRATION: Common to abundant in western N.A.; uncommon to rare in the east. Mid-Mar.–mid-May, spring migrants pass through CA, peak late Apr.–early May. Farther north and East, extending to the Great Lakes, peak is mid-May, although they are rare, and uncommon at best. Adult females are the earliest fall migrants, with the first arrivals in early June. Large flocks stage at key areas (e.g., Mono Lake, CA, and Great Salt Lake, UT), where hundreds of thousands molt into nonbreeding plumage. Adults fly to S.A. over the Pacific, bypassing western Mexico and C.A. Juveniles, seen as early as early July, peak mid-July–Aug., lingerers into Oct., exceptionally later. WINTER: Casual in southern CA; recently found in southern TX, sometimes in small flocks. Most winter in S.A., on alkaline lakes in the Andes. VAGRANT: Annual in western Europe; casual to S. Africa, Australasia, the Galápagos, and the Falklands.

Population Declines due to habitat loss and drought.

RED-NECKED PHALAROPE *Phalaropus lobatus*

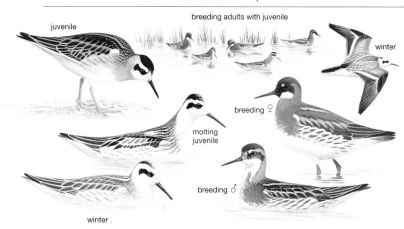

breeding adults with juvenile

juvenile

winter

breeding ♀

molting juvenile

breeding ♂

winter

The Red-necked Phalarope winters at sea, but flocks occur at inland locales. Monotypic. L 7.8" (20 cm)
Identification Small, relatively thick, dark bill. BREEDING ADULT: Dark back with bright buff stripes along sides. Chestnut on front and sides of neck distinctive in female, less prominent in male. More prominent supercilium, often rufous behind the eye, on male. NON-BREEDING ADULT: Blue-gray above with whitish stripes on the upperparts. Dark patch extending back from eye. JUVE-NILE: Like winter adult but darker above, with bright buff stripes. Dark crown and dark tertials separate juvenile from non-breeding adult. FLIGHT: White wing stripe, whitish stripes on back, and dark central tail coverts.
Similar Species The Red is similar outside of breeding plumage. The Red-necked has pale stripes on the slightly darker upperparts (visible with good views) and a thinner, all-black bill, compared to the slightly thicker bill of a Red, which might retain a pale base.

Voice CALL: A high, sharp *kit*, often given in a series.
Status & Distribution Common. BREEDING: Tundra. MIGRATION: Common inland in West and off West Coast; rare in Midwest and East; uncommon off East Coast; more numerous off ME and Maritimes. In spring, peaks first half of May, although might appear by late Mar. and linger to June. In fall, early July–mid-Oct., earlier than the Red Phalarope. WINTER: Chiefly at sea in Southern Hemisphere, but records in southern CA, southern TX, and off-shore southern coasts.
Population The reasons for major declines in autumn staging population at Bay of Fundy are unknown.

RED PHALAROPE *Phalaropus fulicarius*

Highly pelagic away from breeding grounds, this phalarope is rare inland. Monotypic. L 8.5" (22 cm)
Identification Short bill, thickest of 3 phalarope species. BREEDING FEMALE: Black crown; white cheek patch. Neck and entire underparts rich chestnut. Upperparts black with buff or whitish lines. Bill mostly yellow, with a dark tip. BREEDING MALE: Duller; not as crisp. NONBREEDING ADULT: Pale gray above; white below. Bold dark eye patch. Dark bill with small pale base. JUVENILE: Like nonbreeding adult, but dark upperparts with buffy edges and streaks, peachy buff wash on neck. Juveniles seen in southern Canada and U.S. already molting. FLIGHT: Bold white wing stripe and dark central tail coverts.
Similar Species Similar to the Red-necked Phalarope; see that species.
Voice CALL: A sharp *keip*.
Status & Distribution Common. BREEDING: Tundra ponds. MIGRATION: In spring, Pacific migration from mid-Apr., but peaks mid-May. Generally uncommon off East Coast, peaking late May. In fall, adult females as early as late July, stages Aug.–Sept. (e.g., Bay of Fundy); juveniles migrate into Nov. Movements in late fall and early winter off both coasts irregular. WINTER: At sea to S.A. VAGRANT: Rare to casual inland, mostly in late fall.
Population The Red needs study, but its pelagic range makes this difficult. The population from eastern N.A. to Greenland is thought to have declined.

molting fall adults

winter

breeding ♀

juvenile

molting juvenile

breeding ♂

winter

PRATINCOLES Family Glareolidae

Oriental Pratincole, nonbreeding (Japan, Sept.)

Although ternlike in many aspects, pratincoles are indeed shorebirds. This family, which includes long-legged terrestrial coursers of deserts and brushlands, is unlike any North American family.

Structure Generally mid-size shorebirds, they have long, pointed wings; long, forked tails; and short legs. The combination with the three gives them a very horizontal, elongated look when perched. The bill is short.

Behavior Pratincoles are highly aerial, much more so than other shorebirds; unusual for waders, they rarely enter the water. Their flight is ternlike and can be high and fast. Quite gregarious, they often migrate in large flocks and nest colonially. They nest on bare ground, frequently in plains or desert-like habitats. They feed on insects (their main source of food) in the air, although they will chase insects on the ground. Their gait is ploverlike, alternating running and abruptly stopping.

Plumage Both sexes look alike with only modest differences in plumage during the year. They molt prior to fall migration, leaving a more muted plumage, blurring the more crisp pattern present in spring. Adult plumage is reached in approximately 1 year.

Distribution This Old World family is found primarily in southern Europe, Africa, and Asia, with 1 aberrant pratincole in Australia. There are only 3 records of this family from the Americas.

Taxonomy The 17 species in this family are predominantly coursers and pratincoles. There are no coursers in the New World. There are 7 pratincoles in the genus *Glareola;* you are unlikely to encounter more than 2 species in any one area.

Conservation Land reclamation, pesticides, and development have had an impact on some members of this family. BirdLife International lists the Black-winged Pratincole as near threatened. —*Matthew T. Heindel*

Genus *Glareola*

ORIENTAL PRATINCOLE *Glareola maldivarum*

The Oriental Pratincole is an unexpected vagrant from the Old World. Its graceful and unique flight would be a welcome sight to any North American birder, particularly given the few records to date. Where common, it is often seen in flight, as it does most of its feeding on the wing; its flight is powerful, very much like a tern, or even a large swallow or martin. On the ground, the Oriental might chase insects in ploverlike fashion, but more likely it will sit or stand rather motionless until it takes flight. Monotypic. L 9" (23 cm)

Identification Adults are not particularly colorful. They are generally brownish above and on the breast, but their white rump and deeply forked black tail make for an impressive sight. When there is adequate light, the chestnut underwing coverts may be viewed, but when shaded they look dark. BREEDING: Both sexes usually have a warmer orange tint to the brown. A black line extends below the eye and frames the buffy throat with a semicircle. The bill is black, with red restricted to the base. NONBREEDING: The colors are all muted. The breast is a duller brown. The bill base is a duller red. The black frame to the throat is more diffuse. JUVENILE: It looks similar to the winter adult, but it is duller still, with a pale pink base to the mandible, a whitish throat, and pale edges to most of the upperparts.

Similar Species The Oriental is unlike any bird expected in this hemisphere, but there is 1 record of the similar Collared Pratincole (*Glareola pratincola*), a bird that wintered in Barbados. Adult Orientals lack the white trailing edge on the secondaries, have darker upperparts (so the outer primaries do not boldly contrast), have less red on the bill, and have a shorter tail, with a shallower fork. Juveniles are harder to separate.

breeding
adult

Voice CALL: A harsh *kik-kik-kik* or *chik* notes that recall a *sterna* tern.

Status & Distribution Fairly common, but some local populations declining. BREEDING: Much of Asia to northern and northeastern China, and southeastern Siberia. WINTER: In southern part of breeding range south to northern Australia. VAGRANT: Two spring records from islands in western AK.

SKUAS, GULLS, TERNS, AND SKIMMERS Family Laridae

Black-headed Gull (center) with Bonaparte's Gulls, nonbreeding adults (NJ, Feb.)

Highly successful and cosmopolitan, gulls are very well known as a group. Even people with scant interest in birds can identify a "seagull." The other subfamilies (terns, skuas, and skimmers) are less well known, but their relationship to the gulls is not difficult to ascertain. Easily identified to family, they are not so easily identified to species. Discussions of the identity of a gull, tern, or jaeger are classically lengthy. The difficulty in species-level identification is due in part to similarity among closely related species, but also to complex age-related changes and to hybridization in gulls. Species identification is achieved by looking at structure. Soft-part colors are also important.

Structure All show webbed feet, but they vary in wing structure and bill shape. Gulls are medium to large in size, with longish blunt-tipped bills. They have long pointed wings, short square tails, and strong, medium-length legs. The narrow-winged terns are smaller, usually with notched or strongly forked tails, sharply pointed bills, and short legs. Jaegers and skuas have a more powerful, raptor-like look: they have stronger bills with a well-developed hook and elongated central tail feathers (short on skuas, long on jaegers). The skimmers are the most specialized of the group. They are very long-winged and short-legged, but they have a laterally compressed bill, in which the lower mandible is much longer than the upper.

Behavior Flight is direct and strong, with much gliding in some species. Ocean-going gulls, skuas, jaegers, and some terns may arc up over the waves, especially under windy conditions, as tubenoses do. Gulls, terns, and skimmers roost in flocks, often mixed-species flocks. Gulls, jaegers, and skuas swim well, as do some species of tern, although terns prefer to perch on floating material. Skimmers can't take off from a swimming position, so they roost only on land. All members tend to breed in colonies, although some are solitary. Foraging varies, with the skimmer having the most impressive strategy: It flies over calm water, trailing its lower mandible in the water. When it senses a fish, it slams its bill closed, capturing the prey. Large gulls tend to be generalists, and a scavenging nature has allowed them to do well in urban areas. Smaller gulls specialize in seizing small prey on the surface. The terns fish, usually by plunge diving and spearing fish with their pointed bills. Skuas and jaegers may resort to stealing food from other seabirds during the non-breeding season and are carnivorous and predatory during summer.

Plumage Gulls and terns are usually gray above and white below, with notable exceptions. In summer, terns have black caps; large gulls have white heads, and small gulls, black heads. Soft-part colors vary. Skuas and jaegers all show a characteristic white flash at the base of the primaries, best developed on the skuas. The jaegers are pale below, dark above, and dark-capped, with elongated central tail feathers. The skuas are dark throughout (streaked or mottled in some plumages) and have only short rounded extensions on the middle tail feathers.

Distribution This family is as cosmopolitan as they come. There are Arctic and Antarctic species, tropical and temperate species, and pelagic to montane species. Gulls are more diverse in temperate zones, while terns vary more in tropical and subtropical areas. Arctic Terns and South Polar Skuas have record-long migrations.

Taxonomy Recent genetic work shows that the Charadriiformes divide into 3 groups, one of these being the Lari, which includes the gulls, terns, skuas, and skimmers as well as the alcids and pratincoles. The skuas and jaegers are found to be more closely related to the alcids than to the gulls! Genetic work suggests that the broad genera *Larus* (gulls) and *Sterna* (terns) are not adequately showing relationships and should be subdivided. In the gulls, suggested changes are to separate the Little in the genus *Hydrocoleus* while giving the Bonaparte's, Black-headed, and Gray-hooded the genus *Chroicocephalus*. It is also suggested that the "crested terns" (e.g., the Elegant and Royal) be divided as *Thalasseus;* the Least and all other small terns as *Sternula;* the Bridled, Aleutian, and Sooty as *Onychoprion;* the Gull-billed as *Gelochelidon;* and the Caspian as *Hydroprogne.* Species-level taxonomy is equally complicated, and several gulls may be split in the future: for example, the Herring and perhaps the Mew.

Conservation BirdLife International classifies 5 species as vulnerable, including the Red-legged Kittiwake; 3 as endangered; and the Chinese Crested Tern as critically endangered. In California the Least Tern is given legal protection. —*Steve N. G. Howell, Alvaro Jaramillo*

SKUAS AND JAEGERS Genus *Stercorarius*

This subfamily comprises the larger skuas (4 sp.; 2–3 in N.A.) and smaller jaegers (3 sp.). Well known for pirating food from other birds at sea, they also scavenge (esp. skuas) and hunt (esp. jaegers). Their slightly hook-tipped bills have a sheath covering the nostrils; they also have strongly hooked claws and white flashes on the primary bases. Sexes look alike but, unlike gulls, females are larger on average. Skuas' overall dark-brown plumage suggests bulky, immature gulls. Jaegers are more ternlike in build; they are also polymorphic and show strong age variation. Adult jaegers have pronounced, elongated central rectrices.

GREAT SKUA *Stercorarius skua*

This sought-after visitor to the North Atlantic is often associated with winter mid-Atlantic pelagic trips (where it associates with feeding assemblages around fishing boats), but it can also be found in the western North Atlantic in summer, especially off Canada. Monotypic. L 21–24" (53–61 cm) WS 51–55" (130–140 cm) **Identification** Large, bulky; stout bill, broad wings, barely (or not) projecting central rectrices. ADULT: Ginger-brown overall; buff streaking on face and neck; rufous to buff mottling and streaking on back, and, to a lesser extent, upperwing coverts; often slightly darker cap or face. Underwing coverts mottled dark brown; white flash across primary bases usually bold and striking in flight. Blackish bill and legs. Primary molt mainly Sept. to Mar. JUVENILE AND FIRST-YEAR: More uniform overall and often darker. Head and body vary from dark rufous-brown (as shown) to fairly cold brown (suggesting juvenile South Polar, but fresh in fall), without pale neck streaking; head sometimes contrastingly darker. Note pale tips or U-shaped subterminal markings on scapulars and upperwing coverts. Paler grayish bill base; legs blotched whitish. Protracted molt in first summer (primaries Apr.–Sept.) runs into complete second prebasic molt (primaries Sept.–Apr.). First-year birds in May–June can be largely in bleached juvenile plumage and look paler and more uniform than winter birds, inviting confusion with the South Polar. SECOND-YEAR: Resembles adult, but pale markings on head, neck, and scapulars sparser and reduced in extent.
Similar Species The South Polar averages smaller and is more lightly built, with more slender bill and narrower wings. Differences difficult to judge at sea, as all skuas are "big" and are not always seen well. Adult South Polar's wing molt mainly May–Sept. and first-year's July–Feb., thus similar to "opposite ages" of the Great. Adult and older immature South Polars differ from adult Greats in uniformly dark upper wings

and cold-brown, usually fairly dark head and body, with paler hind neck. Main problem is the bleached first-summer Great from the South Polar: note the Great's evenly worn (and more tapered) juvenal outer primaries, which can be very bleached at tips; dark brown (vs. blackish) underwing coverts, and any remaining juvenal upperwing coverts, with bleached U-shaped markings. Also check for whitish tarsus markings. Adult South Polars generally colder brown on head and body; contrasting pale hackles on neck (less uniformly bleached on head and neck than on the Great); blunter primaries. Still, many birds not seen well should be recorded as "unidentified skua species." With aseasonal, atypical-looking, or vagrant individuals, consider the possibility of other skua species from Southern Hemisphere, especially the Brown Skua (a few recs. from Maritimes and mid-Atlantic coast probably are this species). Also see the smaller Pomarine Jaeger.
Voice Likely to be silent in N.A.
Status & Distribution Breeds in northwestern Europe; ranges in north and tropical Atlantic; winters south to Brazil.

MIGRATION AND WINTER: Uncommon; offshore, rarely in sight of land. Occurrence patterns clouded by confusion with the South Polar Skua. Some Great (from Iceland) occur off Atlantic Canada mainly Sept.–Mar.; smaller numbers June–Aug. Farther south, off East Coast of U.S., recorded mainly Dec.–Feb./Mar., south regularly to NC, possibly to FL. Northbound first-summers (from tropical winter grounds) probably also occur May–June, during same time as migrant South Polars.
Population Increased in Britain through 1900s; probably stable (around 6,000 pairs) in Iceland, following a rapid increase there and then a decline, apparently linked to fisheries industry.

dark adult

typical adult

pale adult

juvenile

SOUTH POLAR SKUA *Stercorarius maccormicki*

This polymorphic bird breeds closer to the South Pole than any other. It is highly migratory, however, and visits both of our coasts, allowing us a glimpse of this attractive southerner. Monotypic. L 21" (53 cm) WS 52" (132 cm)

Identification The smallest of the skuas, its small size can allow for confusion with larger female Pomarine Jaegers, particularly dark juveniles. Stocky, thick necked, potbellied. Thick, strong, hook-tipped bill. In many respects, intermediate between the Great Skua and the Pomarine Jaeger, although clearly a skua, with characteristic short-tailed appearance, broad wings, and large white primary flash visible from above and below. Typically, older ages show a contrasting pale nape; paler birds have a small pale blaze at the base of the upper mandible. PALE ADULT: Distinctive, pale golden brown ("blonde") on head and body, contrasting with dark brown wings and mantle. Narrow golden streaks on back. Face darker, contrasting with pale golden nape. Often strongly developed pale blaze at bill base. Black bill and legs. In flight, pale body contrasts strongly with dark underwings. From above, pale nape and upperback contrast with darker rear quarters and wings. This look (pale in front and dark at back) is characteristic of this morph. DARK ADULT: Dark brown throughout; uniform, lacking much streaking on upperparts. Cold brown, lacks rufous or warm tones. Dark, unicolored face contrasts with paler nape, which is narrowly streaked golden. Body dark, so there is no contrast with dark underwing; paler nape most obvious area of any contrast, other than the wing flash. INTERMEDIATE ADULT: Intermediate between the 2 extremes. Body somewhat paler than dark underwings. JUVENILE: Similar to dark adult, but gray bill base contrasts with blackish tip; tarsus also gray. Plumage crisp and evenly worn; lacks streaking or other markings. Nape paler but lacks golden streaking. Unicolored, as in dark adult; lacks warm tones; evenly colored. Body slightly paler than dark underwings. HYBRID: Frequently hybridizes with the Antarctic (Brown) Skua in the Antarctic Peninsula. Distribution of these hybrids during the nonbreeding season is not known. They are intermediate between the 2 parental species.

Similar Species The Great Skua is extremely similar to the juvenile and dark-morph adult South Polar Skua. South Polars lack rufous or cinnamon tones on plumage and look more uniform in general pattern, but they show a pale nape. Paler South Polars show contrast between pale body and darker underwings. While in our waters, South Polars tend to be in obvious molt, whereas adult Great Skuas molt later (starting Sept.). However, young Great Skuas molt in spring to summer, so lack of midsummer molt is useful only for identification of adult Great.

Voice LONG CALL: A harsh series of low-pitched notes, approximately 3 per second for at least 4 seconds. Lower-pitched and faster than the Great Skua's. During its long call, it raises its wings over its body and throws its head back—farther back than other skuas. Silent while in our region.

Status & Distribution Uncommon on Atlantic and Pacific Oceans; more frequent on Pacific. Strongly pelagic, extremely unlikely to be seen from shore. BREEDING: Breeds in Antarctica. MIGRATION: Hypothesized clockwise migration: arriving earliest on west side of northern oceans, moving later to the east side, before moving south. On Pacific, rare in spring; numbers increasing through summer, peak Aug.–Oct. On Atlantic side, most common May–July, numbers dropping later on in summer and autumn. Unclear whether all age groups move into the Northern Hemisphere; evidence suggests that only younger birds arrive here. Pale-morph adults, or similarly plumaged birds, are extremely rare in N.A., most being darker individuals. WINTER: Breed during our winter (southern summer), so winter here during our summer months. They seem to always be on the move during their nonbreeding season, thus they really migrate through our area. VAGRANT: Casual in AK. Accidental in interior with 1 record in ND.

intermediate-morph adult

light-morph adult

dark-morph adult

juvenile

light-morph adult

juvenile

POMARINE JAEGER *Stercorarius pomarinus*

This bulky brute with a commanding presence is the largest jaeger. Large individuals recall skuas, while smaller ones are deceptively similar to the Parasitic Jaeger. Monotypic. L 21" (53 cm) WS 48" (122 cm)

Identification A large, broad-winged, pot-bellied, polymorphic jaeger with a thick bull-neck—a Rottweiler among the jaegers. Adult central tail extensions are broad and twisted, with distinctive spoon-shaped tips. The bill is thick and strong. Outer 4–6 primaries have white shafts. Upper wings unicolored; no contrast between wing coverts and secondaries. SUMMER PALE -MORPH ADULT: Dark brown above; wings with variable pale flash at base of primaries. Black cap contrasts with yellow neck; breast white with broad, dark mottled breast band and dark mottled flanks. Males show reduced breast band, rarely lacking it altogether. White underparts and dark vent. Bicolored bill with orange-pink base and dark tip. SUMMER DARK-MORPH ADULT: Chocolate throughout; slightly blacker cap, pale wing flash. WINTER ADULT: Pale birds show dark cap; variably barred underparts; coarsely black-and-white barred rump. Tail streamers lacking or less well developed than in summer. JUVENILE AND FIRST-YEAR: Variable. Brownish, barred below and on underwings. Lacks capped effect. Juveniles are brown to chocolate, lacking warm tones. Head unicolored, not streaked; nape unstreaked. Primaries dark to tip. Tail shows short, broad, rounded extensions on central rectrices. All juveniles (even dark birds) show pale uppertail coverts. On the underwing, juveniles show the white primary flash; they also sport a second white flash at the base of the greater primary coverts. IMMATURE: Similar to winter adult, but underwings with variable amount of white barring.

Similar Species Most similar in size to the Parasitic Jaeger, but shapes differ: The Pomarine appears broader-winged, more potbellied, thicker-necked, and shorter-tailed (not including streamers). Breeding pale-morph adult Pomarines easily identified by spoon-tipped, twisted central tail feathers; generally more mottled and broader breast band; bicolored bill; extension of dark cap below bill base; brighter yellow face coloration. Dark morph adults separated by structure and tail spoons. In fall, the Pomarine is the only jaeger expected to show wing molt while in our waters; the

light-morph breeding adult

dark-morph breeding adult

light-morph 1st summer

juvenile

more highly migratory small species tend to molt south of N.A. and later in the season. In winter, the adult Pomarine is separable from the Parasitic by shape, more heavily barred body plumage, and thicker barring on rump. Growing broad-tipped tail streamers are not pointed as on the Parasitic. Juvenile and first-year Pomarines are also similar to young Parasitics. The Pomarine shows a second flash on the underside of the primary coverts (the "double wing flash"); this is typical in juveniles and some adults. Overall it is less warmly colored than the Parasitic, it lacks head streaking, and it consistently shows coarse black-and-white barring on rump; this is less obvious on Parasitics and is not present in the darker morphs. Pomarines have dark primary tips, while Parasitics' primary tips are fringed with pale. Long-tailed Jaegers are much smaller and slimmer, with a proportionately narrower and longer wing as well as a longer tail. Adult Long-taileds lack a dark morph, and they show long and pointed tail streamers as well as a small, crisply demarcated black cap. Pomarines at all ages show at least 4 white shafts on outer primaries; only 2 on Long-tailed Jaegers. Juvenile Long-taileds are paler and grayer than the Pomarines: The palest extremes are contrastingly white-headed, whereas Pomarines are solidly dark-headed. Other than the dark extremes, juvenile Long-taileds show an unbarred white belly, but Pomarines are consistently barred on the belly.

Voice LONG CALL: A series of *yowk* notes, roughly 2 per second, given for several seconds. Not heard south of the breeding areas.

Status & Distribution Common in our area. Numerically it is more common than the Parasitic Jaeger, but it is less likely to be seen from land and is therefore encountered less often. BREEDING: Nests in wet tundra, often near coast. MIGRATION: Pelagic on both coasts. Adults move south before juveniles. First arrivals in July; peak movements Sept.–early Oct., with some wintering in North American waters. Juveniles arrive after Oct. Northbound birds peak late Apr.–late May, arriving in Arctic early to mid-June. Rare in autumn migration on Great Lakes. WINTER: Most common wintering jaeger, found as far north as central CA, central FL, and the Gulf of Mexico. Main wintering areas farther north than either of the other 2 jaegers, with concentrations in the Caribbean and northern S.A. VAGRANT: Casual throughout interior of continent, mainly juveniles in fall.

Population No estimates of population or trends in N.A. However, population estimated to be 10,000 to 20,000 pairs from Barrow to Inaru River, Alaska.

PARASITIC JAEGER *Stercorarius parasiticus*

This is the standard jaeger, the one to learn as a basis for comparison. It is the one most likely seen from land during migration, often harassing terns. Monotypic. L 19" (48 cm) WS 42" (107 cm) **Identification** Polymorphic; medium size; intermediate between the other species. Slim yet powerful. Adult central tail extensions are narrow and pointed, not long ribbon-like streamers. Narrow, long bill. Outer 3–5 primaries have white shafts. Upper wings unicolored; no contrast between wing coverts and secondaries. SUMMER PALE-MORPH ADULT: Dark brown above, pale below with dark vent. Black cap; paler forehead; contrasting pale yellow neck. Breast white (male) or with breast band. DARK MORPH: Chocolate overall with a blacker cap. WINTER ADULT:

Shows dark cap; variably barred breast and flanks; complete breast band. Tail streamers less well developed than in summer. JUVENILE AND FIRST-YEAR: Variable. Brownish; barred below and on underwings. Lacks dark cap. Juveniles light brown to blackish with cinnamon fringes, but usually cinnamon brown. Streaked pale nape patch. Densely barred throughout; pale primary tips. Paler juveniles show pale uppertail coverts. IMMATURE: Similar to winter adult, but underwings barred white. **Similar Species** Compared to the Long-tailed, not as slim and ternlike; has shorter tail, longer bill. Compared to the Pomarine, slimmer, longer tailed, narrower winged. Breeding pale adults identified by short, pointed tail extensions; narrow, even (unmottled) breast band; black bill. In all ages upper wings evenly dark above; coverts not paler than secondaries. Parasitics show 3 or more white primary shafts on outer wing.

Juvenile Parasitics are warm colored, showing rusty or rufous tones, unlike the more chocolate Pomarine or the colder gray-brown Long-tailed. Nape paler than head and shows streaking, unlike the Pomarine. Above, paler individuals showing pale barred rump have narrower, wavier bars than the Pomarine. Primaries pale fringed, unlike the other species. **Voice** LONG CALL: A series of 3–4 bisyllabic notes, roughly 1 per second, rising in pitch. Only in breeding areas. **Status & Distribution** Common in our area. BREEDING: In Arctic, wet and moist tundra, and coastal wetlands. MIGRATION: Pelagic. Small number through the Great Lakes in autumn. Adults move south before juveniles. First arrivals July; peak late Aug.–late Sept. Juveniles arrive late Aug. Northbound birds peak late Apr.–late May; arrive in Arctic early to mid-June. WINTER: Rare in southern CA, FL, and Gulf of Mexico; most winter in S.A. Found closer to shore than other jaegers. VAGRANT: Casual throughout interior of continent.

dark-morph breeding adult

light-morph breeding adult

light-morph 1st summer

light-morph juveniles

How to Look at Jaegers

Jaegers breed in the Arctic or alpine tundra, and they are pelagic during the nonbreeding season. They are strong and powerful on the wing—falconlike—flying lazily along and suddenly bursting quickly to high speed for a chase. In aerial pursuit they are relentless and maneuverable. Given their aerobatics and highly aerial nature, shape and size are important in separating the 3 Jaeger species. But this is confounded by the fact that females

Long-tailed Jaeger, juvenile (Europe, Aug.)

are substantially bigger and bulkier than males in all species, causing a certain amount of overlap in size. Even so, in shape the 3 differ on average.

The Pomarine Jaeger is the bulkiest and appears potbellied and very deep at the chest. The wing is broad,

the tail is short, and the head is big. Often it appears as if there is more body before the wing than behind the wing. The Parasitic is slimmer and longer, and its wing base is nearly equal to the tail length, with roughly equal amounts of bulk before and after the wing. The Long-tailed is petite, with a long and narrow wing. Its wing base is less than the tail length, and there is less in front of the wing than behind the wing. A Long-tailed in flight may remind the observer of a tern, which is graceful in nature. The bill is long and thin in the Parasitic; the Long-tailed has a short bill, which makes it appear thick; while the Pomarine has a thick, stout bill that is pale at the base.

LONG-TAILED JAEGER *Stercorarius longicaudus*

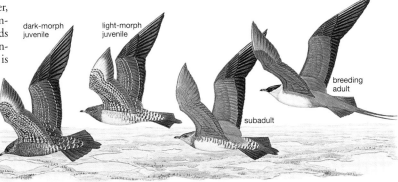

dark-morph juvenile

light-morph juvenile

subadult

breeding adult

The smallest and most elegant jaeger, the Long-tailed Jaeger is locally common on its northern breeding grounds (where it has been nicknamed the "tundra kestrel" for its hovering) and is sought after on pelagic trips in the lower 48. Its flight is relatively buoyant and graceful. Unbroken tail streamers add 6–8" (15–20 cm) to length of breeding adult. Monotypic. L 14.5–16" (37–41 cm) WS 37–41" (94–104 cm)

Identification Wings relatively narrow based; tail projection behind wings usually longer than width of wing base, even without streamers. Bill relatively small; legs have pale markings at all ages (dark on adults of other species). Wing molt occurs south of N.A. On upper wing of all ages, outer 2–3 white primary shafts most prominent (typically only the outer 2 shafts). Adult lacks dark (or intermediate) morph. BREEDING ADULT: Neat black cap; no breast band; belly to vent dusky. On upper wing, blackish remiges contrast with medium brown-gray coverts; no white flash on

underwing. Tail streamers long and finely pointed (often shed in fall). WINTER ADULT: Unlikely in N.A. Dusky chest band (partially shown by some fall migrants); barred tail coverts; short tail streamers. JUVENILE AND FIRST-SUMMER: Polymorphic. Underwing has bold white flash lacking in older ages. Most show bold pale barring on underwings, bold whitish barring on uppertail coverts. Juvenile has bluntly pointed tail streamers; primary tips (at rest) with little or no whitish edging; pale tips to upperwing coverts. First-summer is more capped and lacks pale tips to upperwing coverts; tail streamers have needle-like tips. Dark morph blackish brown overall, usually with bold whitish bars on tail coverts. SECOND-SUMMER: Resembles adult but tail streamers average shorter, underwing with variable pale barring; a few have dark body and messy whitish belly. **Geographic Variation** Breeding adults from N.A. average less extensive dusky

on belly than those in northern Europe. Previously considered polytypic.

Similar Species See the other jaegers. As a rule, the Long-tailed may be likened to the Mew Gull; the Parasitic likened to the Ring-billed Gull; and the Pomarine likened to the California Gull. Juvenile Long-taileds lack the warm reddish tones often shown by the Parasitic.

Voice Shrill, mewing chippers *kyi-kyi-kyik,* etc., and high, clipped yelps. Mostly silent away from breeding grounds.

Status & Distribution Holarctic breeder, winters mainly off S.A. and S. Africa. BREEDING: Common on dry tundra, late May–Aug. MIGRATION: Mostly well offshore and not likely to be seen from land. Mainly May and late July to early Oct., stragglers into Nov.; immatures off coasts June–July. Casual to rare inland (mainly fall) and off the Gulf Coast.

Population Most abundant and widespread jaeger in Arctic.

Identifying jaegers is tricky—sometimes impossible. Age adds to the variability, and thus far we know little about aging jaegers, as they are difficult to study when out at sea. There appear to be 4 general age types: juvenile/first-year, second-year, third-year, and adult. Adults show entirely dark underwings. Juveniles/first-years have variable tones of brown, they show strong barring on the underwings, and they lack dark caps. Second-year

Long-tailed Jaeger, juvenile (CA, Sept.)

immatures show some barring on the underwing, particularly on the axillaries, and a dark cap; their body plumage is browner than adults'. Third-year immatures are often indistinguishable from adults, but they show a few barred feathers on the wing linings.

Polymorphism as well as the complexity of maturation creates a bewildering array of plumages, often shared by the different species. Note the following highly useful or diagnostic features. When encountering an adult jaeger, look for tail streamers, cap shape, number of white primary shafts, presence and strength of breast band, color of bill and legs, contrast between coverts and secondaries, and strength of yellow on face. On first-year birds, look for overall warmth of plumage color, pale-headed look, presence of white tips on primaries, shape of central tail feather tips, contrast of pale nape, streaked or unstreaked nape, number of white primary shafts, and presence of pale bases to under primary coverts. ■

GULLS Genera Larus, Xema, Rissa, Rhodostethia, and Pagophila

Gulls comprise a familiar subfamily of the Laridae. Recent studies divide gulls into 2 groups: the smaller, ternlike gulls (in N.A., the *Xema, Rissa, Rhodostethia,* and *Pagophila,* plus the Bonaparte's, the Black-headed, and the Little) and the larger, "typical" gulls (most species now in the genus *Larus*). The presence of a dark hood is not a taxonomically informative character. Males are larger overall and bigger-billed than females; this can be striking in large white-headed gulls and is an important consideration in identification. An understanding of molt is helpful for identification, as gulls can have up to 4 years of immature plumages: e.g., a 4-cycle (or 4-year) gull is one that attains adult plumage by its fourth prebasic molt.

LAUGHING GULL Larus atricilla

This dark-hooded species is the common and familiar "parking-lot gull" of Atlantic and Gulf coast beaches. Polytypic (2 ssp.; 1 in N.A.). L 15–17" (38–43 cm) WS 38–42" (97–107 cm) **Identification** Medium-size, 3-cycle gull with long, pointed wings. Relatively long bill often looks slightly droop tipped. BREEDING ADULT: Blackish hood, white eye crescents. Upperparts slaty gray with black wing tips; small white outer primary tips worn off by summer. WINTER ADULT: Whitish head, dusky auricular smudge. JUVENILE AND FIRST-WINTER: Juvenile head, neck, chest, and back brown; upperparts with scaly buff edgings. Broad black distal band on tail; underwings dusky brownish. Back, neck, and chest molt to gray in fall; head to whitish with a dark mask. First-summer can attain partial hood. SECOND-WINTER: Resembles winter adult, but more black in wing tips, often some black on tail, neck sides grayish.

Geographic Variation North American populations are subspecies *megalopterus,* larger than *atricilla* of Caribbean.
Similar Species The Franklin's is slightly smaller, with a shorter, undrooping bill; all plumages have bold white eye crescents. The adult Franklin's has a white medial band inside black wing tip. In spring, adult Franklin's bright pink flush is often striking among white-breasted Laughings. Winter Franklin's have a blackish half-hood. The first-winter has whitish underwings; its narrower black tail band does not reach tail sides. First-summer Franklin's can suggest adult Laughing, but the Franklin's smaller black underwing tip contrasts with pale gray primary bases.
Voice Laughing and crowing calls.
Status & Distribution N.A. to Caribbean, winters to northern S.A. BREEDING: Common (Apr.–Aug.), colonial on sandy and rocky islands, salt marshes. Attempted southern Great Lakes region, where it has hybridized with the Ring-billed Gull. MIGRATION AND DISPERSAL: In Northeast, peak movements late Aug.–Sept. (lingerers Dec.), and Apr.–early May (arrivals Mar.); rare north to NF. Casual Pacific coast states. Fairly common (mainly May–Nov.) at Salton Sea, CA (has bred there), and casual inland elsewhere in West. WINTER: Aug.–Apr. (some oversummer in much of winter range). Casual inland in Midwest. VAGRANT: To Europe, Africa, Japan, and Australia.
Population East Coast colonies rebounded after near extirpation in late 1800s by eggers and plume hunters. U.S. population fairly stable in late 1900s at around 250,000 pairs.

winter adult

1st winter

breeding adult

breeding adult

2nd winter

winter adult

1st winter

juvenile

FRANKLIN'S GULL Larus pipixcan

Sometimes known as the "prairie dove," this dark-hooded gull is mainly a bird of the midcontinent. It is unusual in having 2 complete molts a year. Monotypic. L 14–15" (36–38 cm) WS 35–38" (89–97 cm)

Identification Medium-size, 2-cycle gull. BREEDING ADULT: Blackish hood with thick white eye crescents; slaty gray upperparts. Black subterminal band on outer primaries is framed by large white primary tips and a white medi-

al band. Red bill; dark reddish legs. WINTER ADULT: Head is whitish with a blackish half-hood and thick white eye crescents. Black bill has an orange tip. JUVENILE AND FIRST-WINTER: Note its hood, like that found on the winter adult. Juvenile has brown hind neck and back; back has pale edgings. Tail has black distal band not extending to sides of tail; underwings whitish overall with blackish wing tips. Back molts to gray in fall, hind neck to whitish. After complete molt in winter, the first-summer resembles winter adult, but its wing tip lacks white medial band; usually looks like winter adult after complete second prebasic molt in fall.

Similar Species See Laughing Gull.

Voice Pleasant yelping and laughing chatters often heard from migrant flocks.

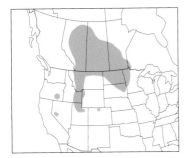

Status & Distribution Breeds interior N.A., winters Pacific coast of S.A. BREEDING: Common (May–Aug.) in N.A., colonial in freshwater marshes. MIGRATION: In fall mainly Aug.–Nov., south through Great Plains to TX, lingerers into Dec. First spring arrivals Mar., peak movements late Apr.–early May. Uncommon to very rare to Pacific coast; casual north to Bering Sea. Uncommon to rare in Midwest and ON, casual to very rare along Atlantic coast from NF to FL. WINTER: Rare to casual north to TX. Occasional winter recs. elsewhere in U.S. VAGRANT: To Europe, Africa, Japan, and Australia.

Population Breeding range shifted west and south through 1900s, which—in combi-

nation with interannual colony fluctuations—makes population trends difficult to ascertain.

LITTLE GULL *Larus minutus*

This is the smallest gull, most often seen with flocks of Bonaparte's Gulls. In its fluttery and ternlike flight, it dips down to pick from the water's surface. Monotypic. L 11–11.5" (28–29 cm) WS 27–29" (69–74 cm)

Identification Small, 3-cycle gull; slender bill, fairly short legs. BREEDING ADULT: Black hood lacks white eye crescent. Pale gray upper wings, smoky gray underwings; note white trailing edge out to tips. Red legs. WINTER ADULT: White head with dark cap and ear spot. JUVENILE AND FIRST-WINTER: Juvenile has blackish brown hind neck collar and back; pale-edged scapulars. Soon molts pale gray back of first-winter. Upper wings have bold blackish M-pattern, dark secondary bar. Tail white with black distal band. First-summer can attain partial dark hood and white tail. SECOND-WINTER: Resembles winter adult, but some have black wing-tip markings.

Similar Species The Bonaparte's is slightly larger and longer-billed, with longer and more pointed wings; first-winter lacks dark cap, has upper wings with white leading wedge and bolder black trailing edge. The Ross's is similar to the Little in most plumages, but has shorter bill, long and graduated tail; winter adult lacks dark cap; first-winter has bright white trailing edge on upper wing, black tail tip prominent on long central rectrices. The first-winter Black-legged Kittiwake shares bold black M-pattern on upper wings, but is markedly larger, with longer, more pointed wings, bigger bill (pale based by winter), dark legs. Note the kittiwake's whitish secondaries and lack of dark cap, often with blackish collar through winter.

Voice Nasal *kek* occasionally given in migration and winter.

Status & Distribution Eurasia and eastern N.A. BREEDING: Rare and local (May–Aug.), solitary pairs or small groups in marshes from Great Lakes region to Hudson Bay. MIGRATION: Mainly Aug.–Nov. and Mar.–May, primarily Great Lakes region, rare New England. WINTER: Nov.–Mar., mostly mid-Atlantic coast; movements closely tied to the Bonaparte's Gull. Casual north to Maritimes and in Southeast. VAGRANT: Casual west to Pacific coast, annual to CA.

Population Colonization of N.A. in the 1900s (first bred 1962) mirrored by expansion in western Europe. In N.A., population is in low hundreds, stable or increasing.

BLACK-HEADED GULL *Larus ridibundus*

This Old World counterpart of the Bonaparte's Gull (with which it is often found) is generally rare in N.A. Polytypic (2 ssp.; both in N.A.). L 15–16" (38–41 cm) WS 35.5–39" (90–99 cm) **Identification** Medium-small, 2-cycle gull. Medium-long red to pink bill; dark underside to middle primaries. BREEDING ADULT: Chocolate brown hood. Bold white leading wedge on pale gray upper wing; dark middle primaries on underwing, narrow white wedge on outer primaries. Deep red bill and legs. WINTER ADULT: White head, dark ear spot; paler red bill and legs. JUVENILE AND FIRST-WINTER: Juvenile has mottled cinnamon-brown hind neck and back, soon molting to pale gray in fall. Upper wing has cinnamon-brown ulnar bar, dark trailing edge, less prominent white leading wedge than on adult. Pale peach to pinkish-orange bill and legs; black-tipped bill. First-summer head plumage variable: some like winter adult's; others with a solid dark-brown hood, like breeding adult's; legs and bill pink to reddish.
Geographic Variation Often con-

sidered monotypic. Breeding populations in N.A. presumably nominate (Europe). *Sibiricus* (eastern Asia) ranges to western N.A., averages larger (esp. longer bill) and molts later.
Similar Species A reasonably distinctive species. Only likely to be confused with the smaller and much commoner Bonaparte's Gull. Attention to a few key points (e.g., bill size, bill color, pattern on the underside of the primaries) should separate these species. The Bonaparte's is smaller and daintier with relatively narrower wings; a more slender black bill; appreciably shorter legs; white underwings with translucent primaries; and slightly darker upperparts—thus white leading wedge on adult upper wing contrasts more. The breeding adult Bonaparte's has a blackish hood (attained a month or so later than the Black-headeds attain hoods in the east), orange-red legs; the winter adult has a darker smoky-gray hindneck wash, peach-pink legs. The first-winter Bonaparte's averages a darker ulnar bar and has dark streaks on outer primary-coverts (mostly white on the Black-headed).

Voice Varied screams and a grating *meeahr,* higher and less buzzy than the Bonaparte's Gull's.
Status & Distribution Eurasia and eastern N.A.; winters to Africa and northern S.A. BREEDING: Rare (May–Aug.) in N.A., where first found in 1977. Colonial or in solitary pairs; on open or partly vegetated ground near water, usually in association with other water birds. Mainly NF; smaller numbers in Gulf of St. Lawrence region, QC; has nested, or attempted to, in NS, ME, MA; also possibly northwest IA or adjacent MN. MIGRATION & DISPERSAL: In western AK, rare in spring (mainly May– June, a few into summer) and casual in fall (late Aug.–Oct.), mainly to the western Aleutians and Pribilofs. Casual in the Great Lakes region and west to the Great Plains. WINTER: Mainly Oct.–Apr. Locally fairly common in NF; uncommon to rare along the St. Lawrence Seaway and the Atlantic coast south to NJ; very rare in NC; casual farther south along the Atlantic coast to FL and (mainly Nov.–Mar.) from TX east through the Gulf Coast states. VAGRANT: Casual (mainly Sept.–Apr.) along the Pacific coast from south-coastal AK to CA. Accidental to HI.
Population Marked increase in Europe from 1800s; especially in 1900s, when spread across north Atlantic. First bred in Iceland in 1911; has bred in western Greenland since the 1960s.

breeding adult

1st summer

1st winter

winter adult

winter adult

1st winter

BONAPARTE'S GULL *Larus philadelphia*

This attractive gull is the only small gull that is common and widespread in North America. In migration and winter, it occurs in flocks of up to a few thousand birds, feeding over tidal rips, power station outflows, sewage ponds, and so on. The Bonaparte's has a graceful, buoyant flight, which is rather tern-like. Monotypic. L 13–13.5" (33–34 cm) WS 31.5–34" (80–86 cm)

Identification Small, 3-cycle gull with slender black bill, white leading wedge on upper wing, and translucent underside to primaries. BREEDING ADULT: Slaty black hood. Bold white leading wedge on pale gray upper wing; underwing has translucent primaries with narrow black tips. Black bill, orange-red legs. WINTER ADULT: White head with dark ear spot; legs

paler, flesh-pink to reddish pink. JUVENILE AND FIRST-WINTER: Juvenile's hind neck and back are mottled cinnamon-brown, soon molting to pale gray in fall. Upper wing has dark brown ulnar bar, black trailing edge, and less prominent white leading wedge than adult's, with mostly dark outer primary coverts. Pale flesh legs; bill black or with dull flesh base (not striking);

legs pink to orange. First-summer has variable head plumage: some are like winter adult, others attain a partial blackish hood. SECOND-WINTER: Resembles winter adult, but with black marks on primary coverts, alula, and sometimes on tertials and tail; legs often paler in early winter.

Similar Species Distinctive and generally common; note wing pattern, fine black bill. See the rare Black-headed Gull and the Little Gull, often found among flocks of Bonaparte's Gulls.

Voice Chatters and single *mew* calls all have relatively low, rasping, or buzzy tone; distinct from other gulls' calls.

Status & Distribution N.A.; winters to northern Mexico. BREEDING: Common (May–Aug.), in solitary pairs and loose colonies, around lakes and marshes in boreal forest zone; nests usually placed in conifers. Has nest-

ed locally in eastern QC, probably ME. MIGRATION: In fall, first birds reach Great Lakes region and Bay of Fundy in July–Aug., but main passage in east late Sept.–Nov., when rare north to NF. On Pacific coast, a few early migrants occur late July–Aug.; main migration Oct.–Nov. In spring, mainly Mar.–May. Northbound influxes typically start late Mar. on Great Lakes, mid-May in Prairie Provinces. On Pacific coast, northbound influxes start late Mar.; peak movements Apr.–mid-May. Nonbreeders oversummer irregularly in Great Lakes region, locally in New England and Pacific states. WINTER: Bulk of population spends winter period (Oct.–Mar.) on Lake Erie and Lake Ontario and along

Atlantic coast from MA south through mid-Atlantic states. During early winter most birds are on Great Lakes, but once lakes start to freeze, birds move toward coast. Casual north to NF. In the west, fairly common but local (Nov.–Mar.) in Pacific states, casual to southeastern AK. VAGRANT: Casual (late May–June, Aug.) to Bering Sea islands. Also Europe, Africa, HI, Japan.

Population No data on trends. This species' largely inaccessible breeding range makes it difficult to survey.

GRAY-HOODED GULL *Larus cirrocephalus*

This gull has occurred once in North America. The adult has a gray hood. Also known as Gray-headed Gull. Polytypic (2 ssp.). L 16" (41 cm) WS 43" (109 cm)

Identification A slim, 3-year gull. Large for a hooded gull, but much smaller than, say, the Ring-billed. Longish bill, long legs. SUMMER ADULT: Hood distinctive: pale gray with darker border. Medium gray mantle; otherwise body white, tail white. Whitish eye, red orbital ring. Dark red bill, orange-red legs. Wing pattern distinctive: white wedge on outer primaries interrupted by large black wing tip; large mirrors on P9 and P10. Dark gray underwing; blacker on primaries with the obvious mirrors showing. WINTER ADULT: Hood replaced by dark ear spot and smudgy area around eye, both connected by stripes on crown. Bicolored bill: red base, black tip. FIRST-YEAR: Dark ear spot, smudgy area around eye as in winter adult. Medium gray mantle; gray wings,

dark tertials; brown centers to lesser and median coverts. Pinkish yellow bill with dark tip; brownish orange legs. In flight, outer wing as in adult: white outer wedge with large black wing tip, but no mirrors. Inner wing gray, brown bar diagonally across inner wing, contrasting darker secondary bar. Tail white with black tail band. SECOND-YEAR: As adult, but smaller primary mirrors.

Geographic Variation Subspecies *cirrocephalus* in South America and *poiocephalus* in Africa.

Similar Species Summer adult easily identified by gray hood and wing pattern. First-year easily confused with the Black-headed Gull of similar age. The Gray-hooded is larger, with a longer bill and longer legs; shows slightly darker mantle. In flight, the Gray-hooded has a solid black wing tip. The Black-headed shows white on primaries, reaching slot-like toward the tips. The Gray-hooded's primaries are entirely dark on under-

side. The outer 2 primaries are white on the Black-headed, producing long white underwing stripes.

Voice Similar to the Black-headed Gull, but deeper and rougher.

Status & Distribution Accidental to N.A. Native to Africa and S.A. YEAR-ROUND: Estuaries and coastal concentrations of small gulls. VAGRANT: One record: Apalachicola, FL (Dec. 26, 1998).

Population Combined African and South American population estimated to be 50,000 pairs.

HEERMANN'S GULL *Larus heermanni*

winter adult

breeding adult

breeding adult

2nd winter

1st winter

A striking Pacific gull, entirely dark-bodied and white-headed when breeding—like a photo negative of our smaller dark-hooded and pale-bodied gulls. Monotypic. L 19" (48 cm) WS 51" (130 cm)

Identification A medium-size, 4-year gull, neither stocky nor slim, neither large-billed nor small-billed. Bill slightly drooped. SUMMER ADULT: Dark body, paler on underparts. Snow-white head contrasts strongly. White head obtained in late fall to early winter and lost by midsummer. Tertial and scapular crescents narrow, but obvious. Deep red bill with black tip; eyes dark with red orbital ring; black legs. In flight, all dark gray, but slightly paler on secondary coverts than flight feathers; shows a narrow white trailing edge extending to inner primaries. No mirrors or white primary tips. Black tail has white tip and contrasts with pale gray rump and uppertail coverts. WINTER ADULT: Crisply streaked head; otherwise similar to summer adult. JUVENILE AND FIRST-YEAR: Dark brown; scaly above due to pale feather edges; older birds gray-brown on mantle. Dull pink bill with dark tip. In flight, wings are brown with darker secondaries and primaries. SECOND-YEAR: Body dark gray; wings may be washed brown. Dark brown hood shows white eye crescent. Tertial crescents white; bill reddish at base. THIRD-YEAR: Much like adult, but head with more extensive brown wash.

Similar Species First-year birds may be confused with young California Gulls, but the Heermann's is much more uniform above and has blackish legs. Young often mistaken for juvenile jaegers. Ironically, some Heermann's

Gulls show a white patch on the greater primary coverts, not the primaries as on jaegers. Heermann's Gulls separated by slower, less powerful flight; unbarred body and underwings; and lack of primary flash.

Voice CALL: A nasal *ahhh*. LONG CALL: Short, deep, and nasal.

Status & Distribution Common. Over 90 percent breed on Isla Raza in the Gulf of California, so essentially it is a Mexican breeding species that migrates north to our region. YEAR-ROUND: Coastal, preferring sandy beaches. BREEDING: Very rare breeder in CA. MIGRATION: In central CA appears as early as late May in some years, late-June in others; reaching Pacific Northwest in July, peaking late July–Sept. During warm-water years arrival is earlier and birds travel farther north. Moves south

Sept.–Nov.; largely absent north of Monterey, CA, Jan.–May. VAGRANT: Very rare in lower Colorado River Valley, into AZ. Casual farther east, records from NV, NM, UT, WY, OK, TX, MI, OH, FL, and ON.

Population Estimated at over 300,000 breeding individuals, populations increased steadily from the 1970s to the 1990s.

BELCHER'S GULL *Larus belcheri*

This attractive gull was previously known as the Band-tailed Gull. It was lumped with the threatened Olrog's Gull of coastal southeastern S.A. Monotypic. L 20" (51 cm) WS 49" (124 cm)

Identification A medium-size, stocky, 4-year gull with long thick legs. Long, thick, parallel-sided bill lacks an expansion at the gonydeal angle. SUMMER ADULT: Black mantle; white head, underparts; pale gray neck; white tail with wide black tail band, narrow white

tip. Tertial, scapular crescents narrow but obvious. Bright yellow bill; black subterminal bar on both mandibles; red tip, rarely missing or restricted to

breeding adult

2nd winter

1st winter

winter adu

breeding
adult

upper mandible. Dark eye, red orbital ring; bright yellow legs. In flight shows extensive black underwing tip. WINTER ADULT: Similar to the summer adult, but with dark hood and white eye crescents. JUVENILE AND FIRST-YEAR: Brown with contrasting dark head, neck, breast; white eye crescents; white belly and undertail coverts. Juveniles with pale-fringed mantle feathers;

older birds' mantle gray-brown. Uniform, dark brown wings. Blackish tail contrasts with whitish rump and uppertail coverts. Dull pink legs. Distinctive bill: pinkish or yellowish white with crisp black tip (outer third of bill); red nail. SECOND-WINTER: Blackish mantle, like adult. Browner wings, often with blackish inner median covert bar. Extensive brownish hood extends to lower breast. Tail band (like adult's) developed by this age. Bill characteristically bicolored; red tip now obvious. Bright yellow legs. SECOND-SUMMER: Similar, but white head and neck. THIRD-YEAR: Very like adult, but brownish wash to wings.

Similar Species Adults identified by crisp black tail band. The Black-tailed shows pale eyes, dark gray mantle,

thinner bill, slimmer body, longer wings. In comparison to the Lesser Black-backed or the Yellow-footed, the Belcher's has a red-tipped bill, darker mantle, dark eye, no white primary tips. Strongly hooded look of first-year plumages distinctive. Second-year told from same-aged Kelp by brighter yellow legs, red bill tip, and structural differences.

Voice Undescribed.

Status & Distribution Casual in N.A., native to Humboldt Current. YEAR-ROUND: Strictly a coastal species, often on rocky coastlines. VAGRANT: One rec. from CA and 4 from FL. The FL recs. are unusual as this is a Pacific Gull, suggesting that vagrants cross over C.A.

Population Estimated to be fewer than 100,000 pairs.

BLACK-TAILED GULL *Larus crassirostris*

This Asian vagrant has the potential to occur nearly anywhere. Adults are slim, with a black tail band and a characteristic red-tipped bill. Monotypic. L 18" (46 cm) WS 47" (119 cm)

Identification A medium-size, long-billed 4-year gull with long, narrow wings. Long bill is characterized by being nicely parallel-sided, lacking an expansion at the gonydeal angle. This gull typically looks attenuated, with the long wings trailing back well behind the tail. SUMMER ADULT: Dark gray mantle. White head, neck, and underparts; white tail has a wide black tail band and narrow white tip. Tertial and scapular crescents narrow but obvious. Bright yellow bill, black subterminal bar on both mandibles, red tip. Yellow eye, orange-red orbital ring. Bright yellow legs. In flight shows extensive black wing tip, to P5 or P4;

there are no mirrors on the outer primaries. WINTER ADULT: Similar to summer, but head and neck crisply streaked on face and nape, not extending much onto the foreneck; some show white eye crescents. JUVENILE AND FIRST-YEAR: Chocolate brown with paler facial area at bill base; contrasting white undertail coverts and belly; contrasting white eye crescents. Coverts and tertials brown with fine buffy edgings; juvenile scaly-looking mantle due to crisp buff edges; first-winter birds more gray-brown above with darker feather centers. Unicolored dark brown wings. Blackish tail contrasts with whitish rump and uppertail coverts. Bill distinctive: pale pink with crisp black tip (outer third). Pinkish legs. SECOND-YEAR: Dark gray mantle; browner wings; gray inner median coverts. Brown head with white eye crescents and face.

Black tail with crisp white tip. Bill characteristically bicolored, but greenish at the base. THIRD-YEAR: As adult, but black on tail more extensive.

Similar Species Adults are identified by their crisp black tail band and their pale eyes. The vagrant Belcher's Gull also has a tail band; however, it shows dark eyes, blacker mantle, thicker bill, and bulkier body. Can be told from the adult California Gull by a red-tipped bill, darker mantle, pale eye, and very small white primary tips. The first-year Black-tailed resembles both the California and the Laughing Gulls. The California shares the bicolored bill, but the Black-tailed is more uniformly colored and has a contrasting and nearly unmarked white rump, well-defined white eye crescents, and a longer and slimmer shape. The first-year Laughing Gull shares the long and slim shape, eye crescents, and uniform-looking plumage, but it has a dark bill and dark legs.

Voice LONG CALL: Mewing and deep.

Status & Distribution Casual in N.A. Native to temperate Asian coast. YEAR-ROUND: Prefers rocky coastal habitats, but should be looked for any place where medium-size gulls congregate. Most recs. in N.A. Mar.–Aug. VAGRANT: Over 20 recs., most in AK. Other records in BC, WA, CA, MB, TX, several sightings around Lake Michigan, MD, VA, NJ, NY, RI, VT, NS, and NF. Other records include Sonora, Mexico, and Belize. This gull can truly show up anywhere!

breeding
adult

winter
adult

breeding
adult

1st
winter

2nd
winter

MEW GULL *Larus canus*

The Mew Gull is the smallest white-headed gull in N.A. Polytypic (4 ssp.; 3 in N.A.). L 16–17" (41–43 cm) WS 41–44" (104–112 cm)

Identification Medium-small, 3-cycle gull with rounded head, relatively small and slender bill, dark eyes in all ages. Adult has large white mirrors on P9–P10. North American Mew Gull described first; other subspecies ("Common" and "Kamchatka" Gulls) follow. BREEDING ADULT: Upperparts medium gray; yellow legs and unmarked bill. WINTER ADULT: Head and neck with smudgy dusky mottling and streaking. Duller bill sometimes has dusky ring; legs can be yellowish green. JUVENILE AND FIRST-WINTER: Fresh juvenile has neat, scaly upperparts; back becomes gray in first winter. Tail mostly dark brown (variable); uppertail coverts barred brown; underwing coverts brownish overall. Flesh bill with dark tip; flesh legs. SECOND-WINTER: Resembles winter adult, but more black on wing tips; tail usually with black markings; legs and black-tipped bill flesh to greenish. "COMMON"

GULL: Average larger, longer billed. ADULT: Slightly paler gray upperparts, more black on wing tip than on the Mew (but much variation); winter head markings more spotted; bill usually has dusky ring. JUVENILE AND FIRST-WINTER: Whiter on head, body, and underwing coverts than the Mew; uppertail coverts and tail base mostly white with clean-cut black tail band. "KAMCHATKA" GULL: Largest and bulkiest subspecies, with longer and stouter bill than the Mew's. Adult upperparts average darker, wing tip with more black (but much variation), and eyes often pale (can be pale on the Mew); coarser winter head markings. JUVENILE AND FIRST-WINTER: Mostly white uppertail coverts and tail base; clean-cut black tail band narrowest at sides. Tail typically paler at base; broad, cleaner-cut blackish distal band (pattern matched by some Mews).

Geographic Variation Population in N.A. is subspecies *brachyrhynchus* (Mew Gull), which is smaller than nominate *canus* group ("Common" Gull, inc. slightly larger *heinei*) of Eurasia, and

kamtschatschensis ("Kamchatka" Gull) of eastern Asia.

Similar Species Distinctive in its normal range. The Ring-billed is larger with flatter head and deeper, blunter bill; adult pale gray above with pale eyes, neat black bill ring. Juvenile and first-winter paler and more contrasty overall, with whitish underparts (variably spotted dusky) and underwings, whiter tail base, and clean-cut blackish tail band (variable). "Common" and "Kamchatka" Gulls more similar to Ring-billeds: on first-year Ring-billeds, upperwing coverts have broader, pale-notched tips (often creating a more checkered, rather than scaly, pattern); tertials tend to be darker with wider and more notched pale edgings; note tail patterns. Also see California Gull, page 248.

Voice Slightly shrill mewing calls in series can suggest the Red-shouldered Hawk. Also a clipped *kehk,* often given in winter.

Status & Distribution Following refers to the North American Mew Gull unless noted. Holarctic breeder, winters south to midlatitudes. BREEDING: Common (May–Aug.), from tundra and inland marshes to sea cliffs, usually colonial. MIGRATION: Mainly Aug.–Nov. and Mar.–Apr. WINTER: Mainly coastal, also inland, commonly (Oct./Nov.–Mar./Apr.) from eastern Aleutians south to central CA, uncommon to southern CA. Locally inland in BC and Pacific states. Casual (mainly Nov.–Mar.) in interior west, Great Plains, TX, and Great Lakes region. VAGRANT: Mew Gull casual on Bering Sea islands, accidental on Atlantic coast. "Common" Gull rare in Atlantic Canada (mainly late Oct.–Apr.), most frequent to NF; casual south to mid-Atlantic coast. "Kamchatka" Gull rare spring and casual fall migrant in western Aleutians; casual on Bering Sea islands.

Population Mew Gull: No data. "Common" Gull: European range increasing in past 50 years (Iceland colonized in 1955).

RING-BILLED GULL *Larus delawarensis*

This is the common and familiar "seagull" across much of North America—from coastal beaches to malls in the middle of the continent—yet it is rarely seen offshore. This notably adaptable and bold feeder takes bread from children, soars to catch insects, scavenges at dumps, and even plucks berries from trees! Monotypic. L 17–20" (43–51 cm) WS 44.5–49" (113–124 cm)

Identification Medium-size, 3-cycle gull with sloping head, medium-size bill. On adult, note yellow legs, pale eyes, and neat "ring bill." BREEDING ADULT: Pale gray upperparts; black wing tip with white mirrors on outer 1–2 primaries. Staring pale-yellow eyes set off by red orbital ring; yellow legs and bill; bill with a clean-cut black subterminal ring. WINTER ADULT: Head and neck with fine dusky streaking and spotting. Slightly duller bill and legs; dark orbital ring. JUVENILE AND FIRST-WINTER: Fresh juvenile has neat, scaly upperparts; back usually becomes pale gray by late fall. White head and underparts with coarse dark spots and chevrons, variably lost over winter by molt and bleaching; underwings mostly white. White uppertail coverts with sparse dark bars. Tail variable: base whitish (bleaching to white); broad blackish distal band; often dark wash basally (most heavily marked birds look dark-tailed); tail band sometimes broken subterminally by whitish marks. Dark brown eyes, flesh-pink bill with dark tip, flesh-pink legs. SECOND-WINTER: Resembles winter adult, but has more black (less white) on wing tips (wing tips at rest usually all black); tail sometimes has black markings (but often all white), head and neck more heavily marked dusky. Legs and bill flesh to yellowish; bill with broad black tip or ring; eyes pale to dark.

Similar Species The Ring-billed is distinctive, but variable, and should be learned well as a reference point for less common species. The larger California (commonly occurs alongside the Ring-billed in the west) is a 4-cycle gull with

breeding adult

2nd winter

1st winter

2nd winter

winter adult

breeding adult

juvenile

1st winter tail

1st winter

1st winter tail

a stouter bill and dark eyes in all ages. The adult California has slightly darker medium gray upperparts (white scapular and tertial crescents contrast, unlike the Ring-billed); a red gonys spot as well as a black bill band. Legs often duller and more greenish in winter. The California has relatively longer and narrower wings, which from above have a larger and blunter-based black wing-tip area and larger white mirrors; in flight from below, slightly darker tone of the California's upperparts apparent as a dusky-gray subterminal secondary band that offsets white trailing edge (underwings more evenly white on the Ring-billed). The first-year California is brownish overall, unlike the Ring-billed; but the second-winter California is similar to the first-winter Ring-billed: In addition to noting size and structure, note the California's medium gray back; dark brownish greater coverts (pale gray on the Ring-billed); and paler legs, often with a greenish hue. The second-winter Herring can also suggest a first-winter Ring-billed, but is much larger (not always easy to judge on lone birds) with stouter bill, dark brownish greater coverts, more finely peppered whitish tertial markings, more extensively dark tail, and usually messier and browner appearance overall. Also see the smaller Mew Gull.

Voice Mewing calls and laughing series,

higher pitched and less crowing than the California Gull's.

Status & Distribution Midlatitude N.A., winters to Middle America. BREEDING: Common and usually colonial, on low, sparsely vegetated islands in lakes. Arrives late Mar.–May, departs July–Aug. DISPERSAL: Postbreeding dispersal begins by late June, with juveniles recorded by mid-July as far south as Salton Sea, CA. Casual north to central AK, accidental Arctic coast of AK. MIGRATION: Nearly throughout N.A. where common to abundant in many regions. Mainly Aug.–Oct. and Mar.–mid-May. Oversummering nonbreeders regular along Pacific, Atlantic, and Gulf coasts, local elsewhere. WINTER: Main arrival in most of U.S. Sept.–Oct., with most departing Feb.–Apr. Rarely north to NF, casually to south-coastal AK. VAGRANT: Casual Europe, W. Africa, HI; accidental to Amazonian Brazil.

Population Largely disappeared from the Great Lakes region and other areas during late 1800s due to human persecution. Recolonization occurred by 1920s, and populations in the Great Lakes/St. Lawrence River region exploded during 1960s and 1970s. Range still expanding in many areas, and today the Ring-billed may be the most populous gull in N.A., with an estimated 3 to 4 million individuals (70 percent nesting in Canada).

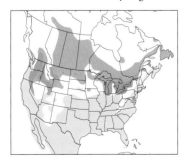

CALIFORNIA GULL *Larus californicus*

A midsize gull of the Western interior, the California is closely tied to saline lakes. Polytypic. L 21" (53 cm) WS 54" (137 cm)

Identification A medium- to large-size, long-legged, long-billed, and long, narrow-winged 4-year gull. Bill characterized by being nicely parallel sided, lacking an expansion at the gonydeal angle. SUMMER ADULT: A dark gray mantled gull, darker than the Ring-billed Gull. White head, neck, underparts, and tail. Bright yellow bill with a red gonys spot and a black subterminal band. During breeding period the black bill band is reduced in size; on some birds it may be nearly absent. Eye dark, with bright red orbital ring, carmine gape. Greenish yellow legs. The wing pattern is distinctive: this gull shows extensive black on the primaries, particularly so on P8 and P7, giving the black wing tip a nearly square-cut shape. The mirrors on P9 and P10 are large. WINTER ADULT: Similar to breeding adult, but head and neck streaked brown, concentrated on back of the neck, nape, and lower neck sides; often with a dark postocular streak. Throat and front of neck are unstreaked. JUVENILE: Usually dark, grayish brown, although some cinnamon brown, and often whitish on the center of the breast and belly. Bill all dark. The wings lack paler inner primaries, and they show dark-based coverts. The tail is largely dark, and the legs are pink. FIRST-YEAR: Like the juvenile, but bill bicolored with pink base and black tip. Juvenal scapulars replaced by variable patterned feathers, but tend to show a solid gray-brown center and shaft streak and a

large buffy gray tip with a narrow blackish terminal fringe. Summer birds with whiter head and worn and faded wings, contrasting with newer mantle. SECOND-YEAR: Dark gray mantle; browner wings with marbled pattern on coverts and tertials, often some gray inner median coverts present. White head, neck, and underparts with streaks concentrated on ear coverts, nape, and particularly the breast sides. Bicolored bill, with grayish to gray-green base; legs similarly greenish gray. Wing pattern at this age shows blackish outer primaries clearly contrasting with paler gray inner primaries; dark secondary bar. Tail remains blackish, but now contrasts with white rump and upper-tail coverts. In second-summer, head and body much more whitish; may obtain more adultlike soft-part colors. THIRD-YEAR: Like adult, but retains dark on greater primary coverts and tail. White mirrors on primaries not as well developed.

Geographic Variation Nominate subspecies breeds east to Colorado, Utah, and Idaho. Subspecies *albertaensis* farther east and north in Northwest Territories, Alberta, Saskatchewan, Manitoba, North and South Dakota; intermediates in Montana. It is larger, larger-billed, and paler on mantle than *californicus*, and it has a tendency to show less black on the primaries and larger mirrors, with that of P10 often with entirely white tip.

Similar Species Distinguished from the adult Herring Gull by darker mantle, dark eyes, greenish legs, and black and red on bill tip. Second-year birds similar, but note the California's darker

mantle, dark eyes, grayish bill base and legs, as well as structural differences. (See sidebar p. 249.) First-year Californias can be told from first-year Lesser Black-backeds by their more extensively dark tail, bicolored bill, and blotchy, pale tipped scapulars.

Voice LONG CALL: A series of *kyow* notes; the first 2 are longer and more drawn out. Call is higher pitched than corresponding call of the Herring Gull.

Status & Distribution Abundant. BREEDING: Colonies on flat islands, some on saline lakes. MIGRATION: Moves to coast after breeding. In summer and early fall, shows a generally northward movement. Southward movements begin in fall and winter, reaching southernmost winter range in midwinter, before moving north again. Interior birds, *albertaensis,* appear to move farther south than *californicus* and return slightly later in spring. WINTER: Shifts to Pacific coast and interior near coast during winter. VAGRANT: Casual throughout interior to East Coast, appears to be increasingly regular as a vagrant to east.

Population Estimated between 500,000 and 1 million individuals. Population in U.S. estimated to have doubled since 1930. Increases ongoing: for example, in San Francisco Bay, California breeders increased from 400 to over 21,000 in last 20 years.

Large White-headed Gull Basics

The best way to learn these gulls is to spend time looking at the common species and study how they change throughout the year. Learning the variations caused by age, molt, wear, and plain old individual variation of the common species is key in gaining the confidence to tackle finding the less common species.

Consider these 3 general topics: structure, adult features, and age-related changes. Structure is shorthand for saying shape and size. Relative size can be assessed by comparing the gull to well-known and wide-ranging standard species such as the Ring-billed Gull and the Herring Gull, the first being a medium-size gull and the latter a large gull. Shape is also best learned by comparison. For example, a Lesser Black-backed Gull is a long-winged species. You could quantify this by looking at comparative lengths on the bird, such as how far the primaries extend past the tail, and compare this to a fixed length, like the tarsus or bill length. In general, however, the best way to assess shape differences is to compare the gull in question to the common species around it. Gulls are seldom by themselves, so it is not difficult to make comparisons. When a gull is called "bulky" or "big-billed" in the accounts, these qualitative descriptions are in reference to other gull species of similar size.

Herring Gull, juvenile (NJ, Jan.)

Learning the adult features of the gulls in your area is important for 2 reasons. First, adults can often be identified by simple features such as leg color, mantle color, and so forth. In general, adults are not as difficult to separate, and they are less variable than other ages. Learning the structure by looking at the easier-to-identify adults simplifies identification of the more variable immatures. Second, as immatures age, they become more and more like adults, so knowing the terminal features allows you to interpret the field marks on an immature more clearly. Apart from noting structure when looking at adult gulls, one should concentrate on the mantle shade, eye color, orbital ring color, leg color, wing-tip pattern (with particular reference to the extent of black and the number and size of mirrors), and streaking pattern (on winter birds). Underwing pattern is also useful.

Herring Gull, winter adult (NJ, Feb.)

The third topic to try to master—and it is the most difficult—is how gulls change due to age. To understand these changes, study the beginning stage (the juvenile) and the end point (the adult, as noted above). All other plumages are intermediate between the end points. Juveniles are generally brown, with paler markings and edgings on the mantle and wings. Unlike all other age classes, they show thinner and more pointed primaries; this can be seen in the field through a scope and is a very useful feature. On juveniles and first-year birds, concentrate on bill pattern, tail pattern, presence of secondary bar and paler inner primaries, underwing pattern, extent of banding on greater coverts, and extent of pale markings on tertials. Note that while leg colors vary from pinks to yellow in adults, juveniles of even the yellow-legged species show pink legs. The juvenal is the first plumage obtained after the down, and it all grows in at the same time. This gives the juvenile an even appearance, for all feathers are the same age. In older age classes, newer and fresher feathers always contrast with older and more worn feathers.

Plumage maturation is caused by molts, which can be complete (all feathers replaced) or partial (largely body feathers with no wing and tail feathers). Adult gulls have a complete molt after breeding and a partial molt before breeding. During the complete molt, the first feathers to change are the median coverts, inner greater coverts, and inner primaries. The tail and secondaries change when primaries are half done. Molt ends with outer primaries, inner secondaries, and subscapulars. In larger gulls, the molt out of the juvenile plumage lasts a long time—often into the first spring—and it is a partial molt that involves the head, underparts, and mantle. Most noticeable is the change of the upperparts, with new scapulars replacing the juvenal feathers. Note that early molted feathers are more juvenal-like (brown) and late-molted feathers are more adult-like (gray-brown). By spring, the second molt starts with new median coverts, inner greater coverts, and inner primaries. This is a complete molt. After the first year, the immature bird's molts match up to the adult's. There is a complete molt in summer/fall and a partial molt in late winter.

Here are some key points to remember: First-year gulls are generally brownish and have the juvenal wings and tail. Second-year birds have gone through a complete molt, so they have a new wing and tail, patterned closer to an adult's. In the 3-year gulls (which obtain adult plumage in the third year), this second-year plumage is adultlike with some immature features. In 4-year gulls, second-year immatures have an adultlike mantle contrasting with a browner wing. Third-year plumage is obtained through a complete molt, and it looks often very much like an adult except for minor features, such as showing some black on the tail or on the greater primary coverts, smaller primary mirrors, more extensive black on primaries, and smaller white primary tips. Plumage changes owing to the partial molts of immatures are minor. Mainly, the head whitens out in spring. Finally, hybridization, feather wear, and bleaching can confound these issues, and not all immature gulls will be identifiable. ∎

HERRING GULL *Larus argentatus*

The most widespread pink-legged gull in N.A, the Herring is common in the east and mainly a winter visitor in the west. Hybrids can be locally common (mainly in the west). Polytypic. L 22–27" (56–69 cm) WS 53.5–60" (136–152 cm)

Identification Large gull with 4 plumage cycles; sloping head and fairly stout bill with distinct (but not bulbous) gonydeal expansion. Pink legs at all ages. Subspecies *smithsonianus* described unless otherwise noted. BREEDING ADULT: Pale gray upperparts; black wing tip with white mirrors on outer 1–2 primaries. (In West, most have mirror only on outermost primary.) Pale-yellow eyes (can be dusky, esp. in west); yellow-orange orbital ring; yellow bill, reddish gonys spot. WINTER ADULT: Dusky streaking and smudging on head and neck. Duller bill and legs; bill often develops black subterminal mark; orbital ring can be dark to pinkish. JUVENILE AND FIRST-WINTER: Fresh juvenile sooty brown overall; neat, scaly upperparts; strong dark barring on tail coverts. Inner primaries form pale panel on upper wing. Tail is mostly blackish (but some with extensive whitish hue at base). VARIABLE FIRST-WINTER MOLT: Some (esp. East Coast breeders) soon attain new barred and mottled back feathers; others (esp. west coast winter populations) retain most or all juvenal plumage through winter. Head often bleaches to whitish. Blackish bill soon develops dull flesh color on base; rarely flesh-pink with clean-cut black tip by midwinter. SECOND-WINTER: Resembles first-winter, but back usually with pale-gray feathers (from none to a solid pale-gray saddle); tail mostly black. Pink bill with black distal third (more adultlike in second summer); eyes sometimes become pale. In second-summer, head and body whiter; bill rarely like adult, but usually with black distal mark. THIRD-WINTER: Highly variable. Some resemble second-winter; others resemble winter adult, but have more black on wing tips, some black on tail. Best aged by adultlike pattern of inner primaries. (Second-winter's inner primaries resemble first-winter's.) Bill usually pink with black distal band; eyes pale. In third-summer, head and body mostly white like breeding adult; bill like adult's or with some black marks. ADULT *VEGAE*: Upperparts medium gray; eyes dark (mostly) to pale (rarely); reddish

orbital ring; rich pink legs. JUVENILE AND FIRST-WINTER *VEGAE:* Head and body paler overall than *smithsonianus,* with sparser dark barring on tail coverts; tail whitish based with broad blackish distal band. Older ages best distinguished by medium gray tone of upperparts. ADULT *ARGENTATUS:* Some have darker, medium gray upperparts; but many not safely told from *smithsonianus.* JUVENILE AND FIRST-WINTER *ARGENTATUS:* Resembles *vegae,* from which perhaps not safely told except by (presumed) distribution.

Geographic Variation Recent work indicates species status warranted for several taxa subsumed into traditional Herring Gull complex, including the "American Herring" Gull *(smithsonianus),* the "European Herring" Gull *(argentatus)* of northwest Europe, and the "Vega" Gull *(vegae)* of east Asia.

Similar Species Adult fairly distinctive, but see the Thayer's, which is smaller with more slender bill, shorter legs; eyes often dark; wing tips slaty blackish at rest and mostly pale from below, showing much more white on outer primaries than do Herrings in the West. Beware "diluted" adult Herrings, which may be hybrids with the Glaucous-winged or the Glaucous. Juvenile and first-winter Herrings are extremely variable, but not like any other regular large gull in the East. Main problem in the west is separation of small female Herrings from dark Thayer's, besides different structure, Thayer's outer primaries are more extensively pale on inner webs, creating venetian-blind pattern on spread outer primaries; unlike Herring's more solidly dark

wing tip. (Some Herring x Glaucous-winged hybrids very like Thayer's in plumage, but bigger-billed.) The Western is stockier and broader-winged, with a more bulbous-tipped black bill; lacks pale inner primary panel. See sidebar (p. 251) for separation from the California. On older immatures, note overall shape, bill structure, and upperwing pattern. Some Herring x Glaucous-winged hybrids look like adult "Vega" but are often bulkier, with slightly paler upperparts and wing tips. First-year "Vegas" are told from bulkier Slaty-backeds by more solidly blackish outer primaries; narrower, blacker tail band. Bleached first-summers not always identifiable.

Voice Varied. Long call has slightly honking or laughing quality. The "Vega" Gull's call is lower pitched, harsher.

Status & Distribution The following refers to *smithsonianus* unless otherwise noted. BREEDING: Breeds N.A. Common (May–Aug.); colonial or in

breeding adult

1st winter

smithsonianus

juvenile

3rd winter

2nd winter

winter adult

1st winter

1st wir

scattered pairs on coastal islands, islands in lakes, on buildings. Since late 1980s has bred in LA, TX. Subspecies *vegae* is fairly common on St. Lawrence I. (May–Sept.). MIGRATION: Nearly throughout N.A. where common to abundant in many regions. Mainly Aug.–Oct. and Feb.–Apr. Subspecies *vegae* rare to casual in Aleutians. DISPERSAL: Ranges (mainly June–Sept.) to

Arctic coast of AK and Bering Sea islands. Subspecies *vegae* uncommon (esp. Aug.–Sept.) to Seward Peninsula. WINTER: South to Middle America. Coastal, inland, and offshore. In west, uncommon along much of immediate coast in range of the dominant Western and Glaucous-winged Gulls. Wintering birds arrive continentwide by Oct., with marked increase during

mid to late Oct. Departs most regions by May, but some nonbreeders oversummer along Pacific, Atlantic, and Gulf coasts; locally elsewhere. VAGRANT: Casual to Europe and HI. Subspecies *vegae* accidental in TX and apparently also CA. Subspecies *argentatus* rare to casual (mainly Nov.–Apr.) in the east, most records from NF; casual west to ON, south to mid-Atlantic coast.

Population In N.A., recovered after egging and feather hunting in late 1800s. (U.S. pop. only 8,000 pairs in 1900.) East coast population greater than 100,000 pairs in mid 1980s and spreading south. Numbers in Northeast and Atlantic Canada now declining; linked to egging and competition with expanding Great Black-backed Gull populations.

1st winter *argenteus*

breeding adult *vegae*

1st winter *vegae*

winter adult *vegae*

1st winter *vegae*

Separating First-winter Californias from First-winter Herrings

First-winter California and Herring Gulls look quite similar—specifically Herrings that show a crisply bicolored bill. They share a brown body plumage, dark tail, and pink legs. Though they overlap in size, these gulls do consistently differ in structure. The long-winged California is slimmer, with a long, even-sided tubular bill. The Herring is bulkier, showing a deeper belly, thicker neck, and proportionately shorter, broader wings; the bill tends to expand a bit at the gonydeal angle. Most first-winter Herrings have a dark bill or a variable, but ill-defined pinkish base to the bill; very few show a crisply set-off black tip on a pink bill, like the California's. Any black "bleeding" back toward the gape along the cutting edge suggests a Herring. In flight the wing patterns differ. Californias do not show strikingly paler inner primaries, thus they look more evenly patterned. They also show dark greater coverts with paler

California Gull, juvenile (CA, Sept.)

Herring Gull, 1st winter (CA, Nov.)

tips, creating a second dark bar on the wing—the other dark bar being the secondaries. Herrings have strikingly paler inner primaries; and due to more banding on the greater coverts, they lack the second dark bar. Many first-winter Herrings show a whitish head that contrasts with the dark body. Californias that have a whitish head also show a similarly pale neck and breast, with contrasting dark streaks on the breast sides and nape. At rest, the California's dark greater coverts, with their whitish markings concentrated at the tip, create a whitish "skirt" pattern. The white markings also concentrate on the inner greater coverts, forming a "covert crescent" inside of the tertial crescent. These patterns are not shown by most Herrings. Finally, mantle molt begins early on the Californias, and by the first winter they show a complex, messy mosaic of feather patterns. Herrings more often look less messy above. ∎

YELLOW-LEGGED GULL *Larus cachinnans*

This vagrant from Europe has recently been recognized as a distinct species within the Herring Gull complex, and its status in N.A. is masked by identification difficulties. Polytypic. L 21–26" (53–66 cm) WS 52–58" (132–147 cm) **Identification** Large gull with 4 plumage cycles; intermediate between the Herring and the Lesser Black-backed. Fairly stout bill, slight to distinct (but not bulbous) gonydeal expansion. BREEDING ADULT: Medium gray upperparts; black wing tip with white mirrors on outer 1–2 primaries. Yellow legs; pale lemon eyes, reddish orbital ring. Orange-red gonydeal spot often extends to upper mandible. WINTER ADULT: Dusky head and neck streaking concentrated in half-hood and on lower hind neck. Streaking most distinct in late fall; by midwinter most birds are white-headed. Bill quite bright yellow, rarely with black subterminal marks. FIRST-WINTER AND SUMMER: Brownish overall; whitish ground color to head and underparts. Head, neck, and chest often bleach to mostly whitish with variable dusky-brown streaking and spotting by spring. White tail coverts sparsely barred dark brown. Bright white base to tail, with sparse blackish markings and broad blackish distal band—striking in flight. Slightly paler inner webs to inner primaries form an indistinct paler panel on spread upper wing. Blackish bill can show dull flesh base by spring; legs flesh-pink. SECOND-YEAR: Second-winter resembles first-winter, but back usually has some medium gray feathers; tail ranges from extensively black to variably mixed with white; inner primaries average slightly paler, but do not form an obvious pale panel. In second-summer, head and body whiter; usually a solid medium gray saddle. Brownish to pale lemon eyes; reddish orbital ring in summer. Through winter, bill typically pinkish basally, blackish distally, with a pale tip and sometimes a blush of red at gonys. In summer, bill typically yellow with reddish gonydeal smudge and black distal band. Legs flesh in winter, yellowish by second summer. THIRD-YEAR: Resembles winter adult, but more black (less white) on wing tips; some have black on tail.
Geographic Variation Taxonomy complex, but AOU treatment anachronistic. Two widely recognized taxa in western Europe: smaller and shorter-legged *atlantis* of Azores; and larger, longer-legged *michahellis* of Mediter-ranean region; both may reach N.A. Other populations in western Europe may deserve recognition as subspecies, but more study is needed. Adult *atlantis* is darker-backed, and immatures are more brownish overall, suggesting the Lesser Black-backed. Adult *michahellis* is paler-backed, and immatures are more whitish on the head and body, suggesting the Great Black-backed. Recent work indicates that *cachinnans* is a species distinct from the Yellow-legged, and most authors now treat it as the Caspian (or Pontic) Gull *(Larus cachinnans)*, which is unrecorded N.A.
Similar Species Note adult's medium gray upperparts (intermediate between the Herring and the Lesser Black-backed) and yellowish legs. Be aware that Herrings can have yellow legs (mainly in spring) and that Herring X Lesser Black-backed hybrids may closely resemble the Yellow-legged. (Hybrid adults typically have extensive dusky head streaking in winter, unlike the Yellow-legged.) The Lesser Black-backed averages a more slender bill, has narrower and relatively longer wings, and is slightly to distinctly darker above; it has less contrasting and slightly less extensive black wing tips (longer gray basal tongues on P8 and P9) and heavier dusky head and neck streaking in winter. The Herring has less extensive black wing tips that often have more white (at least in the Northeast, where Yellow-leggeds are most frequent), flesh-pink legs, and yellow-orange orbital ring; in winter, the Herring has heavier dusky head and neck streaking and often a duller and more pinkish bill, with more distinct dark distal marks, but no red on the upper mandible or gape (shown by many Yellow-leggeds). The California is on average smaller and lighter in build with more slender bill, dark eyes; winter adult typically with heavier dark hindneck markings, often more greenish legs. First-winter Yellow-leggeds are most similar to Lesser Black-backeds, and perhaps not always separable. The *michahellis* is larger and bulkier than the Lesser Black-backed, with blockier head, stouter bill, and longer legs; tail base averages more extensively white (and less barred) at sides; and head and underparts often whiter overall. Also see the Great Black-backed. The *atlantis* is structurally more similar to the Lesser Black-backed, but is on average bulkier and broader-winged; outer rectrices usually unbarred at base (usually barred on the Lesser Black-backed). Herrings generally darker and browner overall with heavy dark barring on tail coverts, mostly black tail, pale inner primary panel, and often paler-based bill. On older immatures, note overall shape, bill structure, medium gray tone of upperparts, and upperwing pattern.
Voice Harsher and more grating than the Herring's; more similar to the Lesser Black-backed's.
Status & Distribution Western Europe to N. Africa. VAGRANT: Casual (mainly Oct.–Apr.; also June and Aug. recs. from QC) to eastern N.A., from Atlantic Canada (mainly NF) south to mid-Atlantic coast. Accidental to TX. Specimen from QC referred to *atlantis;* provenance of other birds uncertain.
Population In western Europe, *michahellis* has increased since 1970s; no trends reported for *atlantis* (more than 8,000 pairs in 1990s).

breeding adult

1st winter

michahellis

1st winter

winter adult

LESSER BLACK-BACKED GULL *Larus fuscus*

This European species has "colonized" North America in the last 50 years, although breeding birds have yet to be found here. It can occur anywhere large gulls congregate and is often seen with Herrings. Polytypic (3 ssp.; 2 in N.A.). L 21–25" (54–64 cm) WS 52–58" (132–147 cm)

Identification Subspecies *graellsii* described and illustrated. Large 4-cycle gull slimmer in build than the Herring, with relatively longer and narrower wings and more slender bill (with depth at base often slightly greater than depth at gonys). BREEDING ADULT: Slaty gray, upperparts; black wing tip with white mirrors on outer 1–2 primaries. Yellow to orange-yellow legs; pale lemon eyes; reddish orbital ring. Bright yellow bill with orange-red gonydeal spot. WINTER ADULT: Dusky head and neck, streaking often concentrated around eyes. Duller bill often pinkish at base, with blackish medial or subterminal marks. FIRST-WINTER AND SUMMER: Brownish overall; whitish ground color to head and underparts. Many with whiter head and underparts that contrast with dark upperparts. White tail coverts sparsely barred dark brown. Tail has bright white base with blackish barring and variable, clean-cut blackish distal band. Inner primaries on upper wing not appreciably paler than outers; dark-based greater coverts often form a dark band. Dark eyes; blackish bill can show dull flesh-hued

base by spring; flesh-pink legs. SECOND-WINTER AND SUMMER: Second-winter resembles first-winter, but some feathers on back are medium gray; tail ranges from extensively black to variably mixed with white. In second-summer, head and body whiter; usually a solid slaty gray saddle. Brownish to pale lemon eyes; reddish orbital ring in summer. Through winter, bill typically blackish with pale creamy tip; in summer, often brightens to yellow with a reddish gonydeal smudge and black distal band. Legs flesh-hued in winter, yellowish by second summer. THIRD-YEAR: Resembles winter adult, but more black (and less white) on wing tips; some have black on tail; bill blacker in winter.

Geographic Variation Records in N.A. refer mainly to paler-backed *graellsii* of western Europe, with fewer records of darker-backed *intermedius,* which breeds in northwest Europe. Many birds intermediate in appearance, however, and not safely assigned to subspecies.

Similar Species Adult and older immature Lesser Black-backeds in the East are distinctive among the Herring and larger Great Black-backed Gulls. First-winters, however, can be overlooked easily among Herrings. Note the Lesser Black-backed's smaller size, relatively longer and narrower wings, more slender black bill, and whiter ground color to head and underparts (esp. tail coverts, which have sparser dark barring); in flight,

upperwing pattern and tail/uppertail-covert pattern distinctive. Primary molt in first summer is later than Herring's. (Some Lesser Black-backeds in June are just starting primary molt, when Herrings are well advanced.) Main problems arise with separation from rarer species and hybrids. The Kelp is larger and bulkier with broader wings and a stouter bill (deeper at gonys than base, the reverse of a typical Lesser Black-backed). Adult Kelps are blackish above; legs often more greenish yellow. The first-winter Kelp perhaps not distinguishable from the Lesser Black-backed by plumage, but tail often has broader blackish distal band; note also bill shape, broader wings. Kelp x Herring Gull hybrids can resemble the Lesser Black-backed closely, but are bulkier in build with a stouter bill (deepest at gonys); black underwing tip of hybrid adult contrasts more. Yellow-footeds larger and bulkier with much deeper, bulbous-tipped bill and broad wings; adults lack distinct dusky head markings in winter. The adult California is paler above, but structure similar to a small Lesser Black-backed; note the California's dark eyes, often more greenish legs, wing-tip pattern; the first-winter California has black-tipped pink bill, dark tail. Also see the Yellow-legged Gull.

Voice Deeper, hoarser than Herring's.

Status & Distribution Northwestern Europe, wintering to Africa. Has increased dramatically in N.A., especially since 1980 and continues to do so; first N.A. record in 1934 in NJ. MIGRATION: Mainly Aug.–Oct. and Mar.–May; oversummers on Atlantic coast, casually Gulf Coast. WINTER: Rare to locally fairly common in east (mainly Sept.–Apr.); max. counts are from mid-Atlantic region south to FL. VAGRANT: Casual to rare (mainly Sept.–Apr.) in interior and to West Coast, north to AK.

Population Large increase in *graellsii* and *intermedius* populations since the mid-1900s.

breeding adult

winter adult

winter adult

1st winter

graellsii

2nd winter

1st winter

THAYER'S GULL *Larus thayeri*

The identification and taxonomy of the Thayer's—a high Arctic gull that winters mainly on the Pacific coast—has been, and remains, controversial. Sometimes the Thayer's is lumped with the Iceland Gull. Monotypic. L 23" (58 cm) WS 55" (140 cm)

Identification A 4-year, medium-size, short-legged, small-billed, potbellied, and somewhat long-winged gull. Relatively thin bill, even in width; not expanding at the gonydeal angle. In all ages shows a largely pale underwing, with dark trailing edge of outer primaries. SUMMER ADULT: Medium gray mantle; white head, neck, underparts, and tail. Dull yellow bill, sometimes with greener base; red gonys spot. Eye color is variable: most are dark-eyed, yet a few are pale-eyed, particularly in sunny conditions; dark red to purplish orbital ring. Bright pink legs. Distinctive variable wing pattern: Outer 5–6 primaries are black (or blackish) with extensive white tongues on inner and sometimes outer vanes, which breaks up the black into thin strips—a venetian-blind effect. The mirror on P9 is confluent with the white tongue; the mirror of P10 is large and separate or extends to the primary tip. WINTER ADULT: Like summer adult, but head and neck streaked. JUVENILE: Retains full juvenal plumage through most of the winter. Variable, ranging from dark, Herring-like birds to lighter extremes; exacerbated by bleaching and wear by late winter and early spring. Classic juvenile evenly warm brown, with mantle and wings checkered with pale buff or whitish markings. Primaries dark brown but not blackish; show crisp pale fringes. Dark-centered tertials with variable pale markings on the tips. Typically the body is palest, tertials darker, and wings and tail darkest; this stepped gradation is distinctive. Dark bill. In flight, there is a noticeable dark secondary bar as well as paler inner primaries. Bright pink legs. FIRST-SUMMER: Similar to juvenal, but has a ten- dency to bleach out and become very pale, contrasting with newer mantle. SECOND-YEAR: Medium-gray mantle; browner wings; greater coverts and tertials marbled or vermiculated. Extent of blackish primaries maximal at this age, contrasting with paler inner primaries. Tail mostly dark but contrasts with whitish rump and uppertail coverts. Bill usually bicolored with pinkish base and dark tip; some retain darker bill. THIRD-YEAR: Very much as adult, but some dark on greater primary coverts and tail. HYBRIDS: Thayer's and Iceland Gulls are in a complex relationship and hybridize extensively; the "Kumlien's" Iceland Gull could be thought of as intermediate population between the Thayer's and the Iceland Gull. Hybridization between the Thayer's and the "Kumlien's" is also frequent. As such, many intermediate birds cannot be identified.

Similar Species The Thayer's Gull is most often confused with Herring Gulls of corresponding ages. Structural differences are useful: the Thayer's shows a smaller bill, steeper forehead, shorter legs, and more potbellied appearance. Adult Thayer's identified by reduced black on upper wings, extensive white tongues, extensively pale underwings, darker eye when present, reddish orbital ring, greener bill, pinker legs, and often slightly darker mantle. Pale underwings are a reliable feature to separate second- and third-year birds. First-year Thayer's are paler than Herrings, and they have paler underwing with dark trailing edge, more uniform upperwing pattern, noticeably paler tertials than primaries while perched, and buff-fringed primaries. First-year Thayer's intergrade in these characters with "Kumlien's," and some individuals can't be identified. However, typical adult Thayer's show black, not gray, on outer primaries; black reaches to P5. First-year Thayer's show dark-centered tertials and solidly dark tail and secondary bar. Glaucous-winged x Herring Gull hybrids similar to the Thayer's at all ages, but best told by larger and bulkier structure, particularly the large bill which tends to expand at the tip on the hybrids. First-year hybrids typically start molt out of juvenal plumage by late fall or early winter; Thayer's retains juvenal plumage until late winter.

Voice Long call higher pitched and quicker than that of the Herring Gull.

Status & Distribution Common Pacific coast, some adjacent valleys in winter; rare in continental interior. BREEDING: Colonial, on steep coastal cliffs in western Arctic. MIGRATION: Fall migrants reach central CA by late Oct., larger numbers present Dec. and remain until early Apr. WINTER: Variety of habitats, from coastal beach and estuaries, to inland garbage dumps and lakes. VAGRANT: Casual to easternmost N.A.

Population Estimated at 6,300 pairs; one of North America's least common gulls.

winter adult

1st winter

2nd winter

winter adult

breeding adult

1st winter

1st winter

ICELAND GULL *Larus glaucoides*

Best known as a bird of Atlantic Canada and the Northeast in winter, the Iceland is an extremely variable-looking gull whose taxonomy remains unclear: most North American records are of the subspecies *kumlieni,* commonly known as the "Kumlien's" Gull. Its behavior is much like other large gulls', but it also forages around sea ice in the northern parts of its winter range. Polytypic (2 ssp.; both in N.A.). L 20–24" (51–61 cm) WS 51–56" (130–142 cm)

Identification A medium-large 4-cycle gull with a relatively small and slender bill; all ages have flesh-pink legs and lack black in the wing tips. BREEDING ADULT: Clean white head and neck. "Kumlien's" wing-tip pattern highly variable: most birds have dark gray markings on the outer 4–5 primaries and a large white tip to P10. Birds with reduced gray markings are not rare, though, and a few birds even appear to have all-white wing tips. (Darker gray restricted to outer webs of P9–P10 often not discernable in the field.) Birds with darkest and most extensive wing-tip markings approach the Thayer's in pattern, and some may be hybrids with that species. The nominate has white wing tips that lack gray markings, and its upperparts are slightly paler than the "Kumlien's" (and more like the Glaucous's). Eyes usually pale but can be dark; orbital ring reddish pink to purplish. Yellow bill with orange-red gonys spot. WINTER ADULT: Head and neck

variably mottled and streaked dusky; duller bill often greenish-based, rarely with dark subterminal marks. FIRST-WINTER: Pale overall; wing tips vary from medium brown to whitish; upper wing lacks contrasting dark secondary bar. Bill black or with variable dull flesh-hue basally. Upperparts, including tertials, finely patterned. (Much juvenal plumage retained into winter.) SECOND-WINTER: Resembles first-winter, but back often has some pale gray; bill usually flesh with broad black distal band; eyes can be pale. THIRD-WINTER: Resembles winter adult, but upper wings and tail usually washed brownish; bill duller, flesh to yellow with a black subterminal band; often some reddish on gonys.

Geographic Variation Breeding population in N.A. is *kumlieni* ("Kumlien's" Gull, which may be specifically distinct). Adult *kumlieni* typically have variable gray wing-tip markings, unlike pure white wing tips of nominate *glaucoides* (known as the "Iceland" Gull, which, ironically, breeds in Greenland). "Kumlien's" and Thayer's Gulls purportedly hybridize; details are unclear.

Similar Species Separating dark-winged "Kumlien's" from Thayer's is compounded by presumed hybridization between them (and some birds are best left unidentified). The Thayer's is on average slightly larger and longer-billed, and most are readily distinguished from "Kumlien's." Adult Thayer's have slightly darker upperparts, blackish gray (not slaty gray) wing-tip markings; first-winters have dark brown (not medium brown) wing tips and secondary bar, coarse-patterned tertials. Some bleached first-years in spring are mostly white, but note dark secondary bar (usually protected from bleaching). The Glau-

cous is usually much larger, with bigger and deeper bill and relatively short wing projection beyond tail; wing tips always white or with faint dusky subterminal marks in first winter. First-winter Glaucous has brightly bicolored pink-and-black bill. Adult Glaucous has yellow to orange orbital ring (which can be flesh-pink in winter). Hybrid Glaucous x Herrings and Glaucous-winged x Herrings can be very similar in plumage to "Kumlien's" in plumage but are larger, bulkier, and bigger-billed.

Voice Shriller than Herring Gull's; rarely vocal in winter.

Status & Distribution Subspecies *kumlieni* breeds in eastern Arctic Canada, winters northeast N.A. Nominate breeds Greenland, winters to northwest Europe. Following applies to *kumlieni* unless stated. BREEDING: Fairly common, but local (June– Aug.) on sea cliffs. Presumed to hybridize locally with Thayer's and possibly with nominate. WINTER: Fairly common Atlantic Canada (arriving Oct.–Nov., departing Apr.–May; very rare in summer), smaller numbers south to NJ, inland to eastern Great Lakes. Rare (mainly Dec.–Mar.) south to NC; casual to FL, Gulf Coast, Great Plains. VAGRANT: Casual (Sept.–Oct.) along Arctic coast of AK and south (mainly Dec.–Mar.) into the Northwest. Nominate probably rare but regular (Nov.–Mar.) in Atlantic Canada (few recs.), accidental (Oct.–Jan.) in the west (AK, YK, CA).

Population Estimates of 5,000 pairs of *kumlieni* and 40,000 pairs of nominate *glaucoides,* but no data on trends.

1st winter

ter adult

breeding adult

kumlieni

winter adult

winter adult

1st winter

2nd winter

1st winter

SLATY-BACKED GULL *Larus schistisagus*

This marine gull of the Asian North Pacific regularly visits Alaska. Monotypic. L 25" (64 cm) WS 58" (147 cm)

Identification A large, long-necked, short-legged, potbellied, 4-year gull. Strong bill is even in thickness, not showing a bulge toward the tip. Paradoxically, immature plumages show some resemblance to pale-winged gulls such as the Thayer's and Glaucous-winged Gulls, although adults have dark backs and wings. SUMMER ADULT: Slate gray, appearing blackish in some lights. Dark mantle is a colder gray than the Western's blue-gray mantle. White head, neck, underparts, and tail. Yellow bill, red gonys spot. Gleaming yellow eye with a red orbital ring. The legs are pink, often bright bubble-gum pink. Wing pattern distinctive: Slate gray of primary bases separated from black primary tips by a series of white tongues or spots, which begin at P4 or P5 and extend to P8; this line of white spots is referred to as the "string of pearls." Outer primaries are black to the base; mirrors on both or missing on P9. The underwing is similarly distinctive, appearing tricolored. White wing linings contrast with dark gray (or in some lights pale gray) underside of the secondaries and primaries and a restricted black area at the tip of the primaries separated from the gray underwing by the "string of pearls." The white trailing edge on the secondaries is broad, with the inner secondaries often looking entirely white. WINTER ADULT: Head and neck are densely but crisply streaked, concentrating around the eye and also the lower nape. JUVENILE AND FIRST-WINTER: Variable and difficult to characterize at this age. Tend to look uniform, lacking contrast; in this way they resemble young Glaucous-wingeds, although primaries, tail, and secondaries are darker than the rest of the plumage. Pale underwings show a dark trailing edge to the primaries. Upper wings show a large pale inner primary patch, which extends out at least to P8, unlike on other similar large gulls. Other features include uniform or poorly marked greater coverts,

dark centered tertials without much pale patterning, a dark tail, black bill, and bright pink legs. FIRST-SUMMER: Similar to first-winter, but has a tendency to bleach out and become very pale, with darker tertials, tail, and primaries. SECOND-WINTER: At this age the dark slate-gray of the mantle is obvious, contrasting with the pale brownish wings. Coverts are uniform and pale brown; folded wing shows very little contrast or pattern whatsoever. Tertials are dark-centered, with a well-developed white tertial crescent; folded primaries are blackish, contrasting with the paler coverts. In flight, underwings are still pale, with a contrasting dark trailing edge to the primaries. Dark tail contrasts with white uppertail coverts and rump. The head streaking is as on adults, concentrated into a dark patch around the eye and highlighting the now obviously pale eye. Bill shows a pale base, but it is still largely dark. SECOND-SUMMER: Similar, but body, head, and neck average whiter; wing coverts are often incredibly bleached, whitish, and contrast strongly with the dark mantle. THIRD YEAR: Looks much as adult, but retains some dark on tertials, greater primary coverts, and tail.

Similar Species Adults likely to be confused with the Western, but the Slaty-backed has a darker, cold-gray mantle and a strongly streaked head, especially around the gleaming yellow eye. The wing pattern of the Slaty-backed—particularly the tricolored nature of the underwings—is not found on the Western, which is more evenly dark below. The Slaty-backed is also shorter-legged, potbellied, and longer necked and lacks a blob-ended bill. Identification of first-year Slaty-backeds is still uncertain, but useful features are structure, uniform greater coverts, and extensive pale on primaries and underwings. Immature Herring x Glaucous-winged hybrids may show some or all of these features. After the second year, the dark mantle, pale eye, and streaking pattern make identification more straightforward.

Voice LONG CALL: Slower and deeper than the Western's, resembling the Glaucous-winged's.

Status & Distribution Breeds in Asia; rare in western AK; casual south of AK, although recs. throughout continent. BREEDING: One rec. from Cape Romanzof, AK. VAGRANT: Annual to Pacific Northwest; other recs. from YK, AB, CA, CO, ID, WI, MO, ON, NY, TX, and FL.

breeding adult

1st summer

winter adult

1st summer

2nd summer

YELLOW-FOOTED GULL *Larus livens*

A marine gull endemic to the Gulf of California, the Yellow-footed shows a very thick bill. Monotypic. L 27" (69 cm) WS 60" (152 cm)

Identification A large, stocky, dark-backed gull with a thick and extremely blob-ended bill shape. A 3-year gull, unlike other gulls of its size. ADULT: White head, neck, and body contrasting with a dark gray mantle. Bright yellow bill with a reddish gonys spot. Yellow eye with yellow to orange-yellow orbital ring; yellow legs. In flight it shows a broad white trailing edge to the wing and 1 mirror on P10. JUVENILE: A gray-brown gull, brownish above with contrasting white belly and vent. White head and neck with fine but blurry streaking throughout. Dark bill with yellow patch at base of lower mandible; dull pink legs. Dark tail contrasting with whitish rump and uppertail coverts. Wings brownish and uniform, lacking pale inner primary panel; secondaries are neatly tipped white, creating a noticeable but narrow whitish trailing edge. FIRST-WINTER AND FIRST-SUMMER: Wings and tail as in juvenile, but head and body showing more white, less streaking. Obtains a largely solid, dark-gray mantle starting in the first winter, unlike other large gulls; mantle is well-developed by the summer. First-summer birds may begin showing yellow tones to the legs. SECOND-WINTER: Similar to adult, with solid slate-gray mantle and wings; dark on tail; often

a darker secondary bar. The head is variably streaked; bill is pale pinkish yellow with a dark terminal third. The legs are yellowish by this stage. SECOND-SUMMER: Similar, but body, head, and neck average whiter.

Similar Species Most likely to be confused with the Western Gull, particularly the darker *wymani* of the South. The adult Yellow-footed Gull differs from the Western in its generally thicker bill and yellow legs. Once first-year Yellow-footeds obtain a gray back, they closely resemble second-year Westerns. These are perhaps best separated by looking for any yellow tones that may be present on the legs and for the Yellow-footed's generally thicker bill. In addition, the Yellow-footed's dark bill tends to show a distinctive yellow patch at the base of the lower mandible. The second-year Western shows a strongly bicolored bill, with an extensive pinkish yellow base and a dark terminal (half to third). The vagrant Kelp Gull is similar, but records of its appearance are farther east than the range of the Yellow-footed Gull. Adult Kelp Gulls can be differentiated by their blackish mantle, reddish orbital ring, greener (often olive) legs, and a strong bill not so obviously blob-tipped as on the Yellow-footed Gull. First-year Kelp Gulls are not so contrastingly white below

and have thinner bills, and any adult-type mantle feathers are blackish, not slate-gray.

Voice LONG CALL: A series of *keow* notes, starting with a slower and longer note and speeding up somewhat toward the end of the series; typical of a large *Larus*. Slower tempo and lower frequency than the Western Gull's corresponding call.

Status & Distribution Uncommon. Breeds in Mexico, restricted to the Gulf of California. In the U.S. only as a nonbreeding visitor. BREEDING: Breeds on various rocks and small islands in the Gulf of California (from 31° N to 24°30' N). DISPERSAL: Largely resident, but disperses north to the Salton Sea, CA, mainly June–Oct. Disperses south as far as Oaxaca during this period as well. Flocks in the Salton Sea may number in the hundreds. VAGRANT: Casual to CA coast in Orange, Los Angeles, and San Diego (several recs.) Counties. Otherwise, there are 2–3 recs. from NV and Mono Co., CA.

Population Estimated to be 20,000 pairs, and no population trends exist from Mexico. The Yellow-footed Gull was first recorded from the Salton Sea in the mid 1960s. The numbers built up to about 50 by 1970, and now the non-breeding visiting population is in the hundreds, confirming a recent expansion to this nonbreeding site.

1st summer

adult

2nd winter

juvenile

adult

1st summer

GLAUCOUS-WINGED GULL *Larus glaucescens*

This thick-billed Pacific gull is the only large gull that shows primaries similar in darkness to the body. Monotypic. L 26" (66 cm) WS 60" (152 cm) **Identification** A large, stocky, pale-winged 4-year gull with broad wings, longish legs, and a thick, blob-ended bill. SUMMER ADULT: Gray primaries nearly unicolored with the gray upperparts. White head, neck, body, and tail. Dark eyes, pinkish orbital rings, pink legs, and a yellow bill with red spot at the gonys. In flight, wings look gray above; primaries slightly darker, showing white tongues, a "string of pearls," and a mirror on P10. WINTER ADULT: Heavily marked head, most typically finely barred or vermiculated with dark. Often bill becomes a duller yellow. JUVENILE AND FIRST-WINTER: Pale and uniform, with grayish brown primaries similar in darkness to upperparts. Markings on coverts and tertials reduced, often looking vermiculated. Black bill, dusky pink legs with dark anterior tarsus. In flight looks uniform, lacks darker secondary bar or contrasting pale rump; dark tail. Underwings pale, primaries translucent. FIRST-SUMMER: Much paler, bleached, worn than first-winter. Primaries may appear whitish at this age. New scapular and upperparts feathers gray. SECOND-WINTER: Gray mantle contrasts with browner wings. Coverts and tertials often very uniform dull brownish gray, lacking obvious pale patterning. Gray-brown tail now contrasts with whiter rump and uppertail coverts. Bill begins to show a pink base at this time,

but many retain largely dark bill into older age classes. SECOND-SUMMER: Similar, but body, head, and neck average whiter. THIRD-WINTER AND THIRD-SUMMER: Much as adult, but retains some dark on tertials, wing coverts, greater primary coverts, and tail. Primaries tend to have small or no white tips. Bill has at least a dark subterminal band; sometimes the terminal half is dark. HYBRIDS: Hybridizes commonly with the Western (in WA) and also with the Herring (in southwest and south-central AK). **Similar Species** No other large graymantled gull shows primaries that are uniform in darkness with the upperparts. Some "Kumlien's" Iceland Gulls may show similar grayish primaries, but the petite-billed Iceland is much smaller and longer-winged than the Glaucous-winged. In addition, older Icelands tend to show pale eyes. Hybrids with the Western, informally known as "Olympic" Gulls, range from nearly identical to the parental types to intermediate in appearance. A Glaucous-winged that shows a yellow orbital ring, noticeably darker primaries than upperparts, a darker than average mantle color or, in younger ages, a dark secondary bar, and contrasting paler rump or well-marked coverts is likely a hybrid. Hybrids with the Herring may resemble the Thayer's in plumage features, but note that they are larger-billed, bulkier, and longer-legged, and often show barred or vermiculated head markings in winter. Juvenile hybrids begin molting their upperparts early in winter;

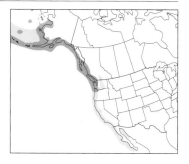

Thayer's retains full juvenal plumage into late winter or early spring.
Voice LONG CALL: A typical loud series of evenly spaced *haaaw* notes. Slower pace and lower pitch than the Western's.
Status & Distribution Abundant. Also breeds in Asian Pacific, south to Japan. YEAR-ROUND: Rocky coasts preferred. BREEDING: Colonial, often uses small rocky islands, or rooftops in Seattle and Vancouver, BC. MIGRATION: Migrates south after breeding; first adults arriving in central CA as early as late Aug. Numbers peak in midwinter; most are gone from central CA by early Apr. First-year birds migrate longer distances than adults. WINTER: Some winter near breeding areas; others move south as far as Baja California Sur, Mexico. VAGRANT: Casual to interior with recs. east to IL; accidental in NF, Canary Islands, and Morocco, so its occurrence is possible anywhere.
Population Estimated 200,000 breeders in N.A.; increase in last 50 years likely due to garbage dumps and waste from industrial fishing.

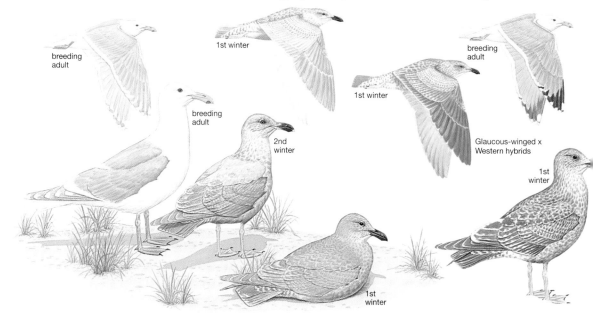

breeding adult

1st winter

breeding adult

2nd winter

1st winter

breeding adult

Glaucous-winged x Western hybrids

1st winter

1st winter

GLAUCOUS GULL *Larus hyperboreus*

This northern gull basically looks like a larger white-winged Herring. Even more aggressive than that species, it scavenges at dumps and harbors, often with gatherings of other large gulls. Polytypic (3 ssp.). L 22–29" (56–74 cm) WS 56–63" (142–160 cm)

Identification A large 4-cycle gull. Stout but not bulbous-tipped bill often expands slightly at culmen base; can be relatively parallel-edged and "slender" on immature females. All ages have flesh-pink legs and lack black in the wing tips. BREEDING ADULT: Clean white head and neck. Pale gray upperparts; pure white wing tips. Pale yellow eyes (dusky flecking on some may indicate hybridization); orange-yellow orbital ring can be orange-red on *pallidissimus* subspecies. Yellow bill; orange-red gonys spot. WINTER ADULT: Light to moderate dusky mottling and streaking on head and neck. Duller bill often has pinkish base and dark subterminal marks; orbital ring often fades to flesh-pink. FIRST-WINTER: Whitish overall; variable pale-brownish patterning. Wing tips white to creamy, often with neat dusky subterminal spots or chevrons on outer primaries. Flesh-pink bill with clean-cut black distal third; dark eyes. Often retains most or all of juvenal plumage through winter; it can be bleached white overall by spring, when newly molted body feathers look contrastingly dark. SECOND-WINTER: Resembles first-winter, but back usually with some pale gray by spring; bill usually has distinct pale tip; eyes can be pale. THIRD-WINTER: Resembles winter adult, but upper wings and tail usually washed brownish. Bill duller, flesh to yellowish with a black subterminal band; often some reddish on gonys.

Geographic Variation Smallest and darkest-backed *barrovianus* (AK); larger and paler-backed nominate (Canada, northern Eurasia); largest and palest-backed *pallidissimus* (northeast Asia). The *pallidissimus* occurs in northwestern Alaska and breeds on St. Lawrence and St. Matthew Islands, where it can be seen with the *barrovianus*. Immatures not identifiable to subspecies in field.

Similar Species Glaucous is mostly distinctive, but smaller females may be confused with the Iceland. Also beware leucistic or albino individuals of other species (check structure, bill pattern). The Iceland's bill is smaller, shorter, and more slender (often greenish-based on winter adult); relatively longer wing projection beyond tail: At rest, the Glaucous's tail tip usually falls between tips of P7 and P8, the Iceland's between tips of P6 and P7. The adult Iceland has a reddish to purplish pink orbital ring. The first-winter Iceland lacks the Glaucous's clean-cut, pink-and-black bill, but second winter Iceland's bill can be similar. Glaucous-winged has a more bulbous-tipped bill and darker wing tips. Bleached first-year Glaucous-winged can be whitish overall, including primaries. Note the blackish bill on the Glaucous-winged (second-winter Glaucous-wingeds can have a Glaucous-like bill, but wing tips are grayish). The adult Glaucous-winged is slightly darker above, with gray wing-tip markings. Southern sightings of the Glaucous should be double-checked for hybrids with the Herring or Glaucous-winged; good views often needed for this. (Flight views

of a "classic" Glaucous at even medium range are insufficient to establish purity.) Herring hybrids can look very like a Glaucous, but their outer primaries have dusky markings (a ghosting of the Herring's pattern). Glaucous-winged hybrids can look even more like a Glaucous; some not safely identifiable in field. On first-winters, a bulbous-tipped bill and messy bill pattern are clues; on adults, check eye color and orbital-ring color. (Faint gray wingtip markings may be visible only in the hand.)

Voice Similar to the Herring's, but slightly hoarser and lower pitched.

Status & Distribution Holarctic breeder, winters to midlatitudes. BREEDING: Common on coastal islands, sea cliffs, tundra lakes. Arriving late Apr.–June; mostly departing through Sept. Hybridizes with the Herring in AK and Canada and with the Glaucous-winged in western AK. MIGRATION: Mainly late Aug.–Nov., Feb.–Apr.; some linger through summer in Canada. WINTER: Mainly Nov.–Apr. Rare (mainly late Dec.–Mar.) south of northern tier of states; very rare to southern CA and Gulf states.

Population Poorly known (AK population perhaps more than 100,000 individuals); may be fairly stable in North America.

breeding adult

2nd winter

winter adult

winter adult

1st winter

1st winter

1st winter

GREAT BLACK-BACKED GULL *Larus marinus*

The largest gull in the world, the Great Black-backed is an efficient scavenger and predator. It commonly preys on ducklings and can snatch adult puffins in flight! Monotypic. L 25–31" (64–79 cm) WS 60–65" (152–165 cm)

Identification A huge 4-year gull with very long, broad wings and a low-sloping forehead. Its very stout bill (which is notably smaller on females) has a swollen gonys. BREEDING ADULT: Slaty blackish upperparts (browner when worn, in summer) blend into black wing tips; large white tip to P10 merges with a large white mirror on P9. Pale flesh to flesh-pink legs; olive to dull, pale-yellow eyes; a reddish orbital ring. Yellow bill with an orange-red gonydeal spot. WINTER ADULT: Inconspicuous, fine dusky head and neck streaking concentrated mainly on the hind neck; birds look white-headed at any distance. Bill is duller than in summer, often pinkish at the base and with blackish subterminal marks; orbital ring can be pinkish. FIRST-WINTER AND SUMMER: Head and underparts whitish overall (often bright white by spring) with relatively sparse brownish mottling and streaking. Upperparts contrasty and checkered. Often retains most juvenile plumage through winter. White uppertail coverts and tail; broad black distal tail band typically broken up by internal, narrow white barring; tail base and uppertail coverts with fairly sparse dark bars. Poorly to moderately contrasting pale panel on inner primaries on upper wing. Dark eyes; dull, flesh to flesh-pink legs. By spring, black bill usually develops a dull, flesh base. SECOND-WINTER AND SUMMER: Second winter often looks very similar to first-winter, but primary tips more rounded; greater coverts plainer and browner, typically with fairly fine markings (unlike boldly barred first-cycle coverts); and bill has large pale tip. A few slaty back feathers appear on some birds. By spring, back has some to many slaty feathers; eyes paler brown. In summer, orbital ring can brighten to orange; some birds develop yellow bill with reddish gonydeal smudge and black subterminal band. THIRD-WINTER AND SUMMER: Some third-winters resemble second-winters (but note bill pattern and adultlike inner primaries); others much more adultlike, but with black on tail, less white in wing tips, some brownish on wing coverts. In winter, bill typically flesh-pink with broad black

subterminal band and creamy tip. In summer, bill usually brightens and may be indistinguishable from adult's, but typically has dark distal marks.

Similar Species Note very large size and stout bill with swollen gonydeal expansion. First-winter and second-winter separated from the smaller first-winter Herring by much whiter head and underparts and more boldly checkered upperparts; in flight, note white rump and tail base with broken black tail band. On older immatures and adults, note slaty blackish on upperparts and pale, flesh legs. The adult Kelp has blacker upperparts, limited white in wing tip, and yellowish legs. Adult Great Black-backed x Herring hybrid has been mistaken for the Western, but that species is relatively bulkier and broader-winged, with a more rounded head and a more bulbous-tipped bill.

Voice Very deep calls, much lower-pitched than the Herring Gull's.

Status & Distribution Northeast N.A., northwestern Europe. BREEDING: Common (Apr.–Aug.); in small colonies or scattered pairs on rocky islands, beach barriers, locally on rooftops; fairly common on eastern Great Lakes, rare on western. MIGRATION: Mainly late Aug.–Nov. and Mar.–Apr.; small numbers of nonbreeders oversummer in winter range. WINTER: Mainly Oct.–Mar., at beaches, fishing harbors, dumps, etc. VAGRANT: Casual to very rare (mainly Nov.–Mar.) on Great Plains, and north (May–July) to Hudson Bay and NV. Accidental (Dec.–Feb.) in southern AK and the Northwest.

Population Dramatic increase in North America since early 1900s, with range expansion both south along Atlantic coast and inland through Great Lakes. Increased in U.S. by about 17 percent per year 1926–1965.

1st winter

winter adult

3rd winter

breeding adult

2nd summer

1st winter

WESTERN GULL *Larus occidentalis*

A bulky, dark-backed Pacific coast gull with a bright banana-yellow bill. Polytypic. L 25" (64 cm) W 58" (147 cm)
Identification A stocky, 4-year gull with moderately long legs; relatively short, broad wings; and a bill that expands noticeably at the gonydeal angle to give a "blob-ended" appearance. ADULT: White head, neck, and body contrast with a dark gray mantle. Consistently darker-mantled than commonly occurring large gulls on the West Coast. Bright yellow bill with a reddish spot on the gonydeal angle. Eye varies from yellow to heavily speckled with dark; yellow orbital ring; and pink legs. In flight shows a broad white trailing edge to the wing and 1 mirror on P10. JUVENILE AND FIRST-WINTER: Dark and uniform-looking, with dark tail and underparts as well as a solid, unstreaked dark mask. Typically shows a paler area behind the dark ear coverts, which extends forward to the neck sides. Pale rump contrasts with the darker tail and mantle. Dusky pink legs, with dark on front of tarsi. Dark inner primaries; no pale inner wing panel; secondaries neatly tipped white, creating a noticeable but narrow whitish trailing edge to the wings. FIRST-SUMMER: Similar to first-winter, but more uniform and gray-brown on upperparts; slightly paler on head, neck, and underparts. SECOND-YEAR: Whitish head and body with darker streaking on nape and breast sides and a dark wash on the belly. Dark gray mantle, contrasting with browner wings, although median coverts usually gray at this age. Tertials have wide white tertial crescent. Black tail contrasts with white rump and uppertail coverts. Usually pink-based bill color, with darker subterminal band and white tip. Dull pink legs. THIRD-YEAR: Much as adult, but retains some dark on tertials, greater primary coverts, and tail. Primaries tend to have small or no obvious white tips; head streaking is noticeable. Dark subterminal band on the bill.
Geographic Variation The Western comprises 2 subspecies: *occidentalis*, breeding north from Monterey County, California; and *wymani*, breeding south of Monterey County. The more southern *wymani* differs in having darker upperparts and a tendency to show pale eyes; other ages are not separable.
Similar Species The adult Yellow-footed has yellow legs; a thicker, even more blob-ended bill; and darker upperparts than *occidentalis*. The first-year Yellow-

southern 3rd winter *wymani*

southern winter adult *wymani*

1st winter

southern breeding adult *wymani*

southern 2nd winter *wymani*

1st winter

footed resembles the second-year Western, but its head and underparts are whiter, its bill shows a yellow base to lower mandible, and its legs begin showing yellow tones. The adult Slaty-backed is darker above and more slate-gray than *occidentalis*, lacking the blue-gray of the Western. Winter head streaking on the Slaty-backed is extensive, particularly around its bright yellow eye. The Slaty-backed shows a complex wing pattern with a "string of pearls" on primaries to P8, dividing the gray primary bases from the black wing tip. The Western has a darker underwing than the Slaty-backed. The first-year Slaty-backed has pale inner primaries and pale underwings with narrow dark trailing edge to wing tips, whereas the Western is an even brown. Hybrids with the Glaucous-winged are common and intermediate in appearance. Individuals that look like the Western with odd features may be hybrids. Hybrid features include pinkish orbital rings, a paler mantle, and markings on head in winter.
Voice LONG CALL: Typical of a large

Larus, but faster-paced and higher-pitched than the Glaucous-winged's.
Status & Distribution Abundant. YEAR-ROUND: Strongly coastal, venturing inland in the San Francisco Bay Area, but otherwise nearly always on the ocean. BREEDING: Colonial, usually on rocky islands. DISPERSAL: Western Gulls of all ages disperse north after breeding season, as far as BC. Movements begin in July, peak Aug.–Sept., with some remaining into winter. Southbound movements peak in Mar. VAGRANT: Very rare in AK; accidental to IL and TX.
Population No data available.

KELP GULL *Larus dominicanus*

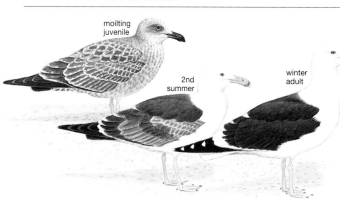

moilting juvenile

2nd summer

winter adult

breeding adult

white rump. THIRD-YEAR: Much like adult, but it retains some dark markings on the greater primary coverts and sometimes on tail.

Similar Species The adult Great Black-backed is larger and has dull pink legs, and large white tip to P10, and a second mirror on P9. First-year Kelp Gulls differ from Great Black-backeds of similar age by their largely dark tail, more uniformly patterned upperparts, and dark-based greater coverts. Lesser Black-backeds (*graellsi* and *intermedius*) are smaller, slimmer, thinner billed, and much longer winged; adults are paler above than the Kelp, which retains its unstreaked head all year long. First-year birds separated on structure and Kelp's darker tail. Kelp x Herring hybrids are similar in mantle color to the Lesser Black-backed, but they differ in stockier structure and larger bill.

Voice LONG CALL: Similar to Herring Gull's, although faster in tempo.

Status & Distribution Casual in N.A., widespread in Southern Hemisphere. BREEDING: Colonial; has bred and hybridized with Herrings on the Chandeleur Islands of LA. VAGRANT: Casual in eastern N.A. (inc. breeding recs. off LA coast). Otherwise, records have been accepted from TX, IN, and a now famous long-staying individual in MD.

Population No estimates exist from S.A., but recent range expansion northward suggests an increasing population.

This stocky, longish-legged, black-backed gull from S.A. has bred in Louisiana and has hybridized with the Herring Gull, complicating identification. Polytypic (5 ssp.; nominate in N.A.). L 23" (58 cm) WS 53" (135 cm)

Identification A 4-year gull that shows an advanced maturation schedule: Blackish upperparts come in as early as the first summer, and the gull becomes entirely blackish above by the second summer. Bulky, large bill, and long greenish legs. Kelps have thick bills that lack an obvious expansion at the gonydeal angle. Adults have a black mantle, showing little difference in darkness of the primaries and mantle; only the Great Black-backed approaches this darkness. ADULT: Adults show a mix of blackish upperparts; bright yellow bill with red gonys spot; reddish orbital ring; variable but usually pale eye; greenish to yellow-green legs; and 1 mirror on P10. White head, neck, underparts, and tail. Legs vary in color, being yellow-green during the breeding season but becoming olive to olive-gray when not breeding. FIRST-YEAR: Brownish, with well-streaked whiter head and underparts. Juvenile mantle brown with neat pale fringes, many of which are replaced in first-winter by dark gray-brown feathers with darker shaft streaks; extent of gray-brown back and lightening of head and underparts continues into first summer. Tertials are dark with narrow paler fringes; greater coverts dark at bases. Tail is entirely dark. In flight, wings lack paler inner primaries and have dark secondaries and greater coverts. SECOND-YEAR: Upperparts blackish by this age, contrast with browner wings. White head and body; moderate streaking on face, breast sides, flanks. Dark postocular line retained in even the whitest individuals. Pale pink-based bill by this age; dark eyes; grayish pink to grayish green legs. The tail is largely blackish or white with a broad black terminal band, contrasting with

SABINE'S GULL *Xema sabini*

This striking gull often occurs with the Long-tailed Jaeger and the Arctic Tern. The Sabine's tern-like flight is buoyant and graceful. Polytypic (2–4 ssp.) L 12.5–14" (32–36 cm) WS 33.5–35.5" (85–90 cm)

Identification Small, 2-cycle gull; slender bill, forked tail. Striking upperwing pattern at all ages. BREEDING ADULT: Dark slaty hood; black neck ring; lacks white eye crescents; hood often spotted white in fall migrants. Bright white triangle on trailing edge of upper wings; whitish underwing; contrasting black outer primaries; medium-gray inner coverts; dusky secondary bar. Underparts often flushed pinkish. Yellow-tipped black bill; blackish to dusky flesh-hued legs. WINTER ADULT: Unlikely in N.A. White head;

slaty hind collar; ear spot; dark mottling on nape; neck sides washed smoky. Dusky flesh legs. JUVENILE AND FIRST-SUMMER: Juvenile (plumage kept through fall migration) has dark gray-brown crown, hind neck, upperparts; scaly

molting adult

breeding adult

juvenile

breeding adult

breeding adult

juvenile

pale-edged back feathers with dark subterminal crescents. Wing pattern like adult's, but with dark brown coverts; tail has black distal band. Black bill, flesh legs. Complete preformative molt in winter produces plumage like winter adult's; initially gray back contrasts with brown upperwing coverts. After partial first prealternate molt, first-summer notably variable: Some have slaty-gray hind neck, mostly white head with dark ear spot; others have dark-slaty hood with whitish spotting. Black bill usually has variable yellow tip.

Geographic Variation Nominate (breeds northern Alaska, Arctic Canada, to Greenland; migrant off both coasts) is smallest, palest subspecies; *woznesenskii* (breeds western AK; migrates off Pacific Coast) larger, upperparts average darkest. Two other described subspecies (breeding northern Russia; possibly migrating off Pacific coast) intermediate. Fall migrants (off CA) include small-

er, paler adults and larger, darker adults; appreciably different when seen together. Sometimes considered monotypic.

Similar Species Distinctive, but see first-year kittiwakes. Rarely seen juvenile Ross's have dark-brown upperparts and bold white trailing edge to upper wing similar to the Sabine's, but tail strongly graduated with black-tipped central rectrices, bill smaller, white postocular area more extensive. Some heavily pigmented juvenile Franklin's (mainly July–Aug.) have dark brownish head and hind neck, but larger; stouter bill; blackish legs; bolder white tips to primaries; different wing pattern in flight.

Voice Grating ternlike *kyeerr,* mainly given on summer grounds.

Status & Distribution Holarctic breeder, winters mainly off S. Africa and western S.A. BREEDING: Fairly common (late May–Aug.) in N.A., on low-lying tundra and marshy areas, often near coast. MIGRATION: In fall, mainly late July–

Oct.; stragglers into Nov., exceptionally Dec. Main passage off west coast mid-Aug.–late Sept.; rare in interior (mainly Sept.); rare to casual off Atlantic coast. In spring, mainly late Apr.–May off west coast; casual at best in interior; casual off Atlantic coast (late Apr.–mid-June). Nonbreeders oversummer locally off west coast, rarely in northwest Atlantic. WINTER: Accidental Lake Erie and FL.

Population Few data; difficult to survey remote nesting populations.

ROSS'S GULL *Rhodostethia rosea*

This sought-after "pink gull" of the high Arctic rarely graces the lower 48. Vagrants are usually found with flocks of Bonaparte's. Its flight is buoyant and strong, with deep wing beats; it dips down to pick food from water. Monotypic. L 12.5–14" (32–36 cm) WS 32–34" (81–86 cm)

Identification Small, 2-cycle gull; long, graduated tail; small bill. All postjuvenal plumages can be strongly flushed pink on head and underparts. BREEDING ADULT: Narrow black neck ring. Pale-gray upper wings; smoky-gray underwings, broad white trailing edge to secondaries and inner primaries. Orange-red legs. WINTER ADULT: White head with dark ear spot; sometimes broken neck ring; duller legs. JUVENILE AND FIRST-WINTER: Juvenile has sooty-brown crown, hind neck, and back; pale-edged scapulars. Soon molts into adultlike head and pale-gray back of first-winter. Upper wings have bold blackish M-pattern, broad white trailing edge. White tail, black tips to elon-

gated central rectrices. Flesh legs. First-summer can attain black neck ring, all-white tail; orange-red legs.

Similar Species Distinctive, but at a distance might be confused with the Little, which is similar in most plumages. The Little has slightly longer bill; shorter, blunter wings; and "normal" squared tail. The adult Little has narrower white trailing edge to wings extending to wing tip; winter adult has dark cap. The first-winter has duller and less extensive whitish trailing triangle on upper wing (with dark secondary bar); black tail tip forms an even band. See the juvenile Sabine's. Most small gulls can attain a pink flush on their head and underparts, but rarely as intense as most Ross's.

Voice Vagrants usually silent. In summer, a mellow yapping *p-dew* and ternlike chitters.

Status & Distribution Holarctic breeder, wintering near pack ice. BREEDING: Rare and local (June–Aug.); solitary pairs and small colonies at marshes and small tundra lakes. First confirmed N.A.

breeding in late 1970s. MIGRATION AND DISPERSAL: Postbreeding dispersal starts July–Aug. from breeding grounds in Siberia; move east to western Beaufort Sea by late Sept.–early Oct.; followed by late Oct.–Dec. passage south into Bering Sea. Best known in fall from Point Barrow, AK (peak numbers late Sept.–mid-Oct.). In spring, small numbers range east irregularly (late May–June) to northeast Bering Sea. WINTER: Distribution probably linked to pack ice; main winter grounds (Dec.–Apr.) apparently Bering Sea south to waters north of Japan. VAGRANT: Casual central Canada (mainly spring) from southern MB east to ON and in lower 48 (mainly winter), mostly in Midwest and Northeast. Accidental in winter south to CO, MO, and DE and in the Northwest, south to OR and ID.

Population Estimated 20,000–40,000 birds occur in northern Alaska waters in fall. No data on trends.

breeding adult

1st winter

winter adult

BLACK-LEGGED KITTIWAKE *Rissa tridactyla*

juvenile

winter adult

breeding adult

juvenile

This gull is buoyant and agile. It feeds mainly in flight by shallow plunge dives or by picking from the surface. Polytypic (2 ssp.). L 17–18" (43–46 cm) WS 37–41" (94–104 cm)

Identification A 3-cycle gull. Medium-length bill; slightly cleft tail; short legs. BREEDING ADULT: Medium gray upperparts; upper wing's paler primaries contrast sharply with black wing tip (lack white mirrors); whitish underwing, contrasting black wing tip. Plain yellow bill; black legs. WINTER ADULT: Attains dark ear spot, dusky washed hind neck (sometimes on nonbreeding summer adults); primaries molted June–Jan. JUVENILE AND FIRST-SUMMER: Juvenile has smoky-gray washed nape, blackish ear spot, blackish hind collar (often lost by midwinter on Atlantic birds). Note black M-pattern on upper wings, whitish trailing edge; black tail band. By spring, dark bill mostly yellow; dusky flesh-hued legs blackish. Unlike most juvenile gulls, upperparts gray. Primaries molted late May–Oct. SECOND-YEAR: Resembles adult, but more extensive black on outer primar-

ies' outer webs; usually some black on alula; bill sometimes dark tipped.

Geographic Variation Nominate breeds in North Atlantic; *pollicaris* in North Pacific. The latter averages larger, longer-billed, darker above, more extensive black wing tip, and later molt.

Similar Species Adult distinctive. Note medium gray upperparts, paler primary bases accentuating "ink-dipped" black wing tips, short black legs, plain yellow bill. In Bering Sea, see Red-legged. Distant first-year's upperwing pattern could suggest a Sabine's Gull, but note kittiwake's black ulnar bar, white underwings with small black wing tip. Juvenile Sabine's has brownish hind neck and back; older plumages lack black tail band. Similar upperwing pattern on a first-year Little Gull, but it is much smaller with shorter wings; slender bill; relatively longer, pinkish legs. Note Little's dark secondary bar and cap, and lack of black hind collar.

Voice Named for rhythmic *ketewehk ketewehk* call; flocks' laughing or honking calls can suggest small geese.

Status & Distribution Holarctic breeder,

winters in northern seas. BREEDING: On sea cliffs. Returns Apr.–May, departs Aug.–Sep. MIGRATION AND WINTER: Rarely seen from shore. Marked year-to-year variation in southward movements; winter wrecks periodically, with birds blown onshore and inland. Peak fall movements off BC in Sept.; off CA in mid-Nov. First arrivals to New England usually Oct., most Nov.–Dec. Northbound Pacific movement mainly mid-Mar.–Apr. In Atlantic, moves north from southern areas Feb.–Mar.; most depart New England mid-Apr. Very rare on Gulf Coast in winter. Nonbreeders oversummer irregularly south to CA and New England. VAGRANT: Rare to casual (mainly late Oct.–Jan.) in interior.

Population Atlantic populations increased and range expanded since 1960s. Populations in N.A. Arctic show no trends.

RED-LEGGED KITTIWAKE *Rissa brevirostris*

This attractive local gull of the Bering Sea region is best known (and readily seen) as a summer resident on the Pri-

bilof Islands. Monotypic. L 15.5–17" (39–43 cm) WS 33–35" (84–89 cm)

Identification A 3-cycle gull with a relatively short, stubby bill; short legs; big dark eyes. Tail slightly cleft (most marked on juvenile). BREEDING ADULT: Pale, slaty-gray upperparts; upper wing with narrow white trailing edge, black wing tip (lacking white mirrors); underwings with dusky-gray primaries, black wing tip. Clean

white head. Plain yellow bill, bright red legs. WINTER ADULT: Attains dusky ear-spot, hind-neck collar (sometimes on summer adults); primaries molted July–Feb. JUVENILE AND FIRST-SUMMER: Juvenile has smoky-gray wash to nape, blackish ear spot, mottled slaty hind collar. Note upper wings' broad white trailing edge. Dark bill mostly yellow by spring; dusky flesh legs, orange-red by spring. Unlike most juvenile gulls, upperparts gray; lacks black on tail; primaries molted late May–Oct. SECOND-YEAR: Resembles adult, but black on outer webs of outer primaries more extensive; bill sometimes tipped dark.

Similar Species Black-legged slightly larger, more sloping forehead, longer bill,

breeding adult

juvenile

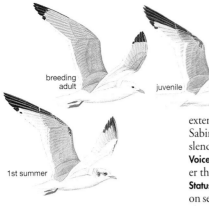

breeding
adult

juvenile

1st summer

legged has a black ulnar bar and tail band. Upperwing of first-year Red-legged suggests a Sabine's Gull, but white trailing triangle less extensive, bases of outer primaries gray. Sabine's is smaller and tern-like, with slender bill.

Voice Laughing calls distinctly squeakier than the Black-legged's.

Status & Distribution BREEDING: Very local, on sea cliffs in Bering Sea region; often alongside Black-leggeds. Returns to colonies Apr.–May; departs Sept.–Oct. WINTER: Presumed (Oct.–Mar.) offshore in North Pacific and north to pack ice in Bering Sea. VAGRANT: Casual (late Nov.–Mar., late June–mid-Aug.)

paler upperparts. Adult has black legs, whitish underwings; hence, black wing tips contrast more above and below. Head-on in flight, the Black-legged's white marginal coverts show up, unlike the Red-legged's gray. First-year Black-

south to WA and OR, also Japan; exceptionally to YK (Oct.), CA (Feb.), and NV (July).

Population In 1970s, estimated 232,000 birds worldwide. Since the 1970s populations of Red-leggeds have declined on Pribilof Islands and increased on Aleutian Islands.

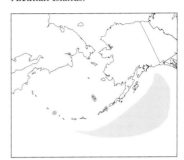

IVORY GULL *Pagophila eburnea*

This sought-after icon of the high Arctic (*Pagophila* means "ice-loving") strays very rarely into the lower 48. It can be confiding and usually associates only loosely with other gulls except when scavenging. Rarely, and only very briefly, it alights on water. Monotypic. L 17–19" (43–48 cm) WS 36–38" (91–97 cm)

Identification Medium-size bill slightly tapered; well-developed claws; fairly short legs. ADULT: Wholly ivory-white; no seasonal variation. Primaries molted Mar.–Sept., mostly before breeding (when molt suspended). Dark eyes; narrow orbital ring black to red in winter (rarely noticeable), red on breeding birds. Gray-green bill, orange to yellow-orange tip; black legs, feet. JUVENILE AND FIRST-WINTER: Variable sooty blotching on face and throat; scattered dusky spots on rest of head, back, underparts. Highly variable blackish distal spots on upperwing coverts, tertials, flight feathers. Some mostly white overall with dark face, black spots largely restricted to flight feathers; others have extensive dark spotting on upperparts. Grayish orbital ring; bill darker gray-

green basally than adult's, with yellow-orange tip and often dusky distal marks from late winter to spring. Attains all-white plumage by complete second prebasic molt (mainly Apr.–Aug.).

Similar Species Unmistakable. Beware leucistic or albino individuals of any gull species. Some first-summer Glaucous and Iceland Gulls can bleach to almost all-white but are larger with longer pink legs, larger bills (pink-and-black on Glaucous, dark with a flesh base on Iceland), and typical large-gull structure.

Voice Rarely heard away from breeding grounds. Ivory calls include high, shrill to slightly grating whistles, unlike other gulls.

Status & Distribution Holarctic breeder on bare ground in high Arctic; mainly around pack ice in winter. BREEDING: Uncommon and local (June–Sept.); in N.A. (Canada) breeds on Ellesmere, Seymour, Devon, Baffin, and Perley Is. MIGRATION AND WINTER: Tied to pack ice. Main passage late Oct.–Dec. south into Bering Sea and Davis Strait, where most winter

(Dec.–Mar./Apr.); irregularly NF. Moves north from Bering Sea late Mar.–Apr.; immatures linger through May in most years (when seen, St. Lawrence I.). VAGRANT: Southern occurrences mainly Dec.–Feb. In West, casual BC, exceptionally southern CA and CO. Better known in East, where casual through Great Lakes region, exceptionally TN. Casual from Maritimes south to NJ.

Population Late-winter counts of over 35,000 birds in Davis Strait suggest that the estimate of 2,400 breeding birds in Canadian Arctic is low, although the origin of former numbers not known (may include Greenland and Old World birds). Recent data suggest major declines in Canadian populations, perhaps linked to shrinking extent of pack ice.

1st winter

adult

adult

TERNS Genera *Sterna, Phaetusa, Chlidonias,* and *Anous*

Terns resemble angular gulls with pointed bills, shorter legs, and forked tails. Several breeding plumages have outermost rectrices attenuated into streamers. Typical terns are pale gray to black above and white below, often with a black cap. Marsh terns are more compact, with dark underparts in breeding plumage. Noddies are tropical terns with dark plumage, white caps, and graduated tails. Typical terns' fresh outer primaries have a pale bloom that covers the dark feather bases; when this is lost, worn feathers look darker than newly molted feathers. In typical and marsh terns, first-summer birds resemble winter adults. Second-summers are variable: Some look like first-summers, others like breeding adults.

GULL-BILLED TERN *Sterna nilotica*

This distinctive, medium-size tern of salt marshes and beaches has a smooth flight as it sweeps over open areas such as fields or salt flats, picking its prey (insects, small crabs, etc.) from the ground or the water's surface. It does not hover and dive into the water. Polytypic (6 ssp.; 2 in N.A. weakly defined). L 13–14" (33–36 cm) WS 35–38" (89–97 cm)

Identification All plumages have ghostly pale-gray upperparts, lacking a contrasting white rump and tail. The stout bill and relatively long legs are black. BREEDING ADULT: The black cap becomes spotted white in late summer. WINTER ADULT: Note the distinctive white-headed appearance with dark postocular mask or smudge; primaries in molt July–Feb. JUVENILE AND FIRST-YEAR: Resembles winter adult, but juvenile in fall is fresh plumaged, with variable buff wash and brownish subterminal marks on back; the dark mask is often less distinct; and bill can have pinkish base into fall. Protracted complete molt (with primaries molted Jan.–Aug.) produces first-summer plumage, much like winter adult's. SECOND-YEAR: Second prebasic molt averages later than in adults, so outer primaries fresher and paler in second summers than in adults.

Similar Species Unlikely to be confused; note the Gull-billed's behavior. Winter and juvenile Forster's Terns have a bolder black mask, are smaller and slimmer in build, and dive in the water for food; on perched birds, note the Forster's short, orange-red legs.

Voice Nasal but mellow laughing and barking calls, usually 2–3 syllables: *keh-wek* or *ku-wek,* and *keh-w-wek* or *kit-u-wek;* sharper than calls of the Black Skimmer. Juvenile has high piping whistles given into first winter.

Status & Distribution Warmer climates worldwide. BREEDING: Fairly common but local in N.A., present Mar./Apr.–Aug. at most colonies. MIGRATION: Mainly Mar.–Apr. and Aug.–Sept. WINTER: Casual north to NC. VAGRANT: Casual in interior N.A. except Salton Sea, CA, where it breeds. **Population** Locally erratic, but overall population in N.A. probably stable, although western population perhaps fewer than 600 pairs (inc. Mexico). In San Diego, CA, preys on chicks of the endangered Snowy Plover and the Least Tern, hence Gull-billeds have been shot in attempts to adjust the "balance" of nature.

juvenile

breeding adult

winter adult

CASPIAN TERN *Sterna caspia*

This, the largest tern in the world, is widespread in interior and coastal habitats but is rarely seen offshore. Its graceful flight is steady and powerful, with fairly shallow wing beats and wings not held strongly crooked. Monotypic. L 20–22"

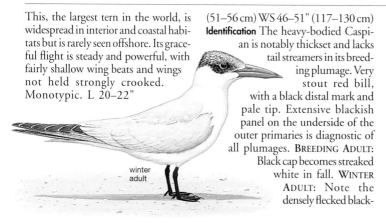

winter adult

(51–56 cm) WS 46–51" (117–130 cm)

Identification The heavy-bodied Caspian is notably thickset and lacks tail streamers in its breeding plumage. Very stout red bill, with a black distal mark and pale tip. Extensive blackish panel on the underside of the outer primaries is diagnostic of all plumages. BREEDING ADULT: Black cap becomes streaked white in fall. WINTER ADULT: Note the densely flecked black-and-white crown, which blends into a broad black auricular mask; primaries molted Aug.–Feb. JUVENILE AND FIRST-YEAR: Resembles winter adult, but juvenile fresh-plumaged in fall, with variable blackish subterminal marks on back and tail. Paler bill, orange to orange-red, with a dark subterminal mark; legs often yellowish, becoming dark by winter. A protracted complete molt (primaries molted Jan.–Aug.) produces first-summer plumage much like winter adult's. SECOND-YEAR: Second prebasic molt averages later than in adults, so outer primaries fresher and paler in

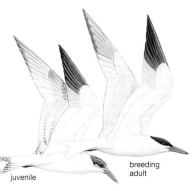

juvenile

breeding adult

second summers than in adults; forecrown often streaked whitish.

Similar Species Distinctive. The Royal is coastal, smaller, and more lightly built; its more slender (but still stout) bill is orange, without a dark tip (rarely orange-red in spring). In flight, note the Royal's narrower wings, often held more crooked; its deeper wing beats; a mostly whitish underside to the primaries; and a more deeply forked tail (with streamers in breeding plumage). Winter and immature Royals have an extensively white ("bald") forecrown never shown by the Caspian.

Voice Adult has a distinctive, loud rasping *rraah* or *ahhrr* and a drawn-out, upslurred *rrah-ah-ahr* in chases and when diving at colony intruders. Begging young (into first-winter) give a high whistled *ssiíuuh*.

Status & Distribution Worldwide except S.A. BREEDING: Common in N.A.; arrives at southern nesting sites Mar.–Apr. and northern sites (Canada, Great Lakes) mainly mid-Apr.–May, departs mainly Aug.–Sept. MIGRATION: Mainly Mar.–May and late July–Oct.; stragglers occur through Nov. WINTER: Uncommon southern CA.

Population Stable or increasing. Major increases on Pacific coast, in interior West, and in Great Lakes region have taken place in last 50 years.

ROYAL TERN *Sterna maxima*

A large tern of southern coasts, the Royal is rarely seen inland. It nests in dense colonies, often with other species. Its flight is strong and graceful, the wings held somewhat crooked. Unbroken tail streamers add 2 inches (5 cm) to the length of breeding adults. Polytypic (2 ssp.; nominate in N.A.). L 17–19" (43–48 cm) WS 41–45" (104–114 cm)

Identification Note the stout orange bill of all ages. BREEDING ADULT: Black cap solid in Jan.–May, becoming spotted white in early summer. Bill deep orange, rarely orange-red; legs black. WINTER ADULT: Extensive white forecrown often has a white postocular crescent separating the eye from the black crest; primaries molted July–Feb. JUVENILE AND FIRST-YEAR: Resembles winter adult, but juvenile is fresh-plumaged in early fall, with dark gray centers to greater coverts and tertials, dark subterminal tail marks, dark secondary bar. Bill paler orange; legs often yellowish, becoming dark by winter. Protracted complete molt (primaries molted Nov.–Aug.) produces first summer plumage much like winter adult's. SECOND-YEAR: Second prebasic molt averages later than in adults, so second-summers' outer primaries fresher and paler than adults'. White spotting on the forecrown of breeding-plumaged spring birds may occur in all ages.

Geographic Variation California populations average larger; they breed and molt earlier, and are mostly resident or short-distance migrants. Atlantic coast populations average smaller, breed and molt later, and are medium- to long-distance migrants.

Similar Species See sidebar (p. 268) for separation from the Elegant Tern. The Caspian is larger, more heavily built, and broader winged, with a stouter red, dark-tipped bill; in flight, note the Caspian's diagnostic dark underside to the outer primaries. Winter and immature Caspians have dark-streaked crowns and never show the extensive white forecrown typical of Royals.

Voice A fairly deep grating *ehrreh* and *rreh'k* or *rreh-eh*, lower and less shrieky than the calls of Elegant and Sandwich Terns; a higher and shriekier *krriéh* or *rriehk;* a yelping or clucking *krehk* and *kehk;* and a more laughing *kweh-eh-eh.* Begging young (into first-winter) give a high whistled *see-ip.*

Status & Distribution Mainly New World, also W. Africa. BREEDING: Common in N.A. MIGRATION AND DISPERSAL: Spring migration mainly late Feb.–Apr.; post-breeding northward movement and fall migration on East Coast mainly late June–Nov., regularly to New England, casually Atlantic Canada. VAGRANT: Casual in interior, and to northern CA.

Population Generally holding constant. Formerly common into early 1900s as nonbreeding visitor (mainly Sept.–Mar.) north to San Francisco Bay (from Mexican colonies). Conversely, has colonized southern California as a breeding bird since 1959.

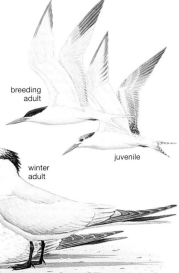

breeding adult

juvenile

winter adult

juvenile

Identifying Royal versus Elegant Terns

Although similar in plumage, these orange-billed terns are not difficult to identify when other terns are present for comparison: Royal and Caspian Terns standing together don't look greatly different in size, and both have stout bills and black caps that do not droop down the nape. But when an Elegant is with a Caspian, it is strikingly smaller, standing little more than half the Caspian's height. With Royal and Elegant Terns together, it is clear the Royal is larger and stands taller.

Bill shape is probably the most important character. Although the Royal's and Elegant's bills are the same length, the Royal's is much thicker, and its gonydeal angle is farther out. The Royal's large, stout bill recalls the Caspian Tern's. The Elegant, however, has a slender bill that varies from being longer, with

Royal Tern, winter adult (FL, Feb.)

Elegant Tern, winter adult (CA, July)

a slightly drooped tip, to being notably shorter and straighter, without any droop. This variation is due mainly to sex: Males average longer bills. The Royal's bill is uniform orange—paler orange on first-cycle birds and orange-red on some spring adults. The Elegant's bill varies in color from reddish orange with a yellowish tip, to uniform orange and bright mustard-yellow.

Other pointers include the bright-pink flush that Elegants of any age can have on their underparts (which are lacking or faint on the Royal); the Elegant's longer crest (beware that apparent crest length can vary with posture); and its winter head pattern. The Royal typically has a distinct white break separating the eye from the black postocular, whereas any break on the Elegant is usually small and inconspicuous. ∎

ELEGANT TERN *Sterna elegans*

This medium-size Pacific-coast tern nests in dense colonies and disperses north in late summer after breeding, with largest movements in warm-water years. Its flight is strong and graceful, with the wings held somewhat crooked. Unbroken tail streamers add 1.5 to 2 inches (4–5 cm) to the length of breeding adults. Monotypic. L 14.5–16" (37–41 cm) WS 37–39.5" (94–100 cm)

Identification Note the slender bill, which sometimes looks almost droop-tipped, and the long, shaggy crest. All plumages can be flushed strongly pink on under-

parts. BREEDING ADULT: Black cap solid Jan.–June; spotted white in summer. Orange bill varies from bright orange-red with paler tip to uniformly mustard-yellow. Black legs rarely mottled or solidly orange. WINTER ADULT: Extensive white forecrown rarely has thin white postocular crescent separating eye from black crest; primaries molted July–January. JUVENILE AND FIRST-YEAR: Resembles winter adult, but juvenile fresh plumaged in early fall, with dark gray centers to greater coverts and tertials, dark subterminal tail marks, and dark secondary bar. Legs are often yellowish, usually becoming dark by winter. Protracted complete molt (primaries Oct.–July) produces first-summer plumage much like winter adult's. SECOND-YEAR: Second prebasic molt averages later than adult's, so outer primaries fresher and paler in second-summer than in adult. White spotting on forecrown of breeding-plumaged spring birds may occur in all ages.

Similar Species See sidebar above for separation from Royals. Some Elegants' bills have dark smudging; this pattern rarely suggests the Sandwich. These may be hybrids with the Sandwich or normal variants of the Elegant.

Voice A slightly screechy *rreeah* or *rreahk,* and *krreéh* or *krreíhr;* and a rough,

grating *ehrrk.* Calls scratchy and grating; given incessantly by flocks of hundreds. Similar to the Sandwich's, but higher and screechier than the Royal's. Begging young (into first-winter) give high, piping *sii, siip-siip.*

Status & Distribution Breeds northwestern Mexico and southern CA. Winters Pacific coast of S.A. BREEDING: Local southern CA, Mar.–July. MIGRATION AND DISPERSAL: Common postbreeding visitor (mainly July–Oct.) to central CA, irregularly to BC. WINTER: Casual southern CA. VAGRANT: Casual inland in Southwest, accidental on Atlantic and Gulf Coasts, where it has hybridized with Sandwich in FL.

Population Increase on U.S. Pacific coast since 1970s may reflect changing ocean conditions rather than population change. Colonized in southern California since 1950s. Considered near threatened by BirdLife International.

breeding
adult

juvenile

winter
adult

SANDWICH TERN *Sterna sandvicensis*

This medium-size tern nests in dense colonies. Its flight is strong and graceful, with wings held slightly crooked. Unbroken tail streamers add 1 inch (3 cm) to a breeding adult's length. Polytypic (3 ssp.; 2 in N.A.). L 13.5–14.5" (34–37 cm) WS 34–36" (86–91 cm) **Identification** Slender, yellow-tipped black bill, black legs, shaggy crest. Breeding Adult: Black cap solid mainly Mar.–June, spotted white late summer.

breeding adult

juvenile

winter adult

juvenile

Winter Adult: White forecrown, primaries molted mainly Aug.–Mar. Juvenile and First-year: Like winter adult, but in fall juvenile has variable blackish subterminal marks on back, dark secondary bar. Black bill may have yellowish side patches (soon lost); develops yellow tip by spring. Complete molt (primaries Dec.–Aug.) produces first-summer plumage like winter adult's. Second-year: Second prebasic molt averages later than adult's, so second summer's outer primaries fresher and paler. White-spotted forecrown of breeding spring birds may occur in all ages. **Geographic Variation** "Cayenne" Tern *(eurygnatha)* of Caribbean and S.A. averages larger, longer billed than *acuflavida* of N.A., which is distinguished by its yellow to yellow-orange bill (occasionally with dusky patches on the sides).

Similar Species In West and on Gulf Coast, beware hybrids with the Elegant. **Voice** Scratchy, penetrating *kree-ik* or *krrík;* slightly sharp, yelping *kehk;* and slightly reedy *ki-i wii-wii.* Begging young (into first-winter) has high, whistled *sree* or *sri-sree.* **Status & Distribution** Europe, eastern N.A., eastern S.A. Breeding: Common in N.A., arriving colonies Apr.–early May, departing Aug.–Sept. Migration: Spring mainly Apr.–May. Fall and postbreeding movement north on East Coast mainly Aug.–Oct. Vagrant: Casual southern CA (where hybridized with the Elegant), north to Atlantic Canada, inland to Great Lakes. The "Cayenne" accidental NC. **Population** U.S. populations apparently stable or even increasing.

ROSEATE TERN *Sterna dougallii*

This tern feeds offshore; flies with fairly stiff, almost hurried wingbeats; is distinct from other like-size terns; and is reminiscent of the Least. Unbroken tail streamers add 2 inches (5 cm) to breeding adult's length. Polytypic (5 ssp.; nominate in N.A.). L 12–13" (30–33 cm) WS 26–28" (66–71 cm) **Identification** Relatively short wings; long tail. Breeding tail streamers project well beyond the wing tips at rest. Bill black most of year. Breeding Adult: Solid black cap; bill develops red basally in summer, can be red with black tip by August; rosy underpart flush usually subtle. Dark primary wedge on resting

birds. Juvenile and First-summer: Juvenile has variable blackish subterminal marks on back and tail (recalls the Sandwich); forehead often dusky. Protracted complete molt produces first-summer plumage with white forehead, pale-gray upperparts, dark patagial bar. **Similar Species** Breeding adult in flight quite distinct from Arctic, Common, Forster's. Note Roseate's dark upperwing wedge on outer few primaries, lack of dark trailing edge to primaries, whitish underparts. Juvenile patterned like Sandwich. First-summer Roseate, from first-summer Common, by lack of dark secondary bar, finer bill. **Voice** A scratchy *krrízzik* or *kír-rik,* often doubled, suggesting the Sandwich; a rasping *rrahk* or *ahrrr;* a mellow *ch-dik* or *ch-weet;* and a chippering *cheut cheut.*

Status & Distribution Atlantic, Indian, western Pacific Oceans. Breeding: Uncommon and local in N.A., arriving colonies Apr.–May. Departs breeding areas through Sept. Migration: Rare recs. Atlantic coast south of NJ, mostly off NC (late May, late Aug.–Sept.). Winter: Mainly northeast coast of S.A. **Population** Atlantic subspecies declining. Northeast breeding population endangered (U.S.) and threatened (Canada).

juvenile

1st summer

breeding adult

breeding adult

juvenile

FORSTER'S TERN *Sterna forsteri*

This medium-size tern is rare offshore, but a familiar sight in interior and coastal habitats. Its flight is steady and graceful with strong, smooth wing beats, hovering briefly before plunge diving for fish. Unbroken tail streamers add 2.5 inches (6 cm) to breeding adult's length. Monotypic. L 12.5–14" (32–36 cm) WS 30–33" (76–84 cm)

Identification Slightly bulkier, heavier billed, and longer legged than the Common. It is the only medium-size "white tern" likely seen molting its outer primaries in N.A. Breeding tail streamers project well beyond wing tips at rest (but

1st winter

winter adult

breeding adult

juvenile

often broken in midsummer). BREEDING ADULT: Solid black cap, orange-red bill with large black tip, orange-red legs. White underparts, contrasting pale-gray upperparts; pale-gray tail has white outer edges. WINTER ADULT: Note diagnostic bold black auricular mask with limited dusky wash on nape; blackish bill. Primaries molted July–Nov. JUVENILE AND FIRST-WINTER: Resembles winter adult, but fresh juvenile has gingery wash and barring on head, back; first-winter has dark tertials, duskier uppersides to primaries, duskier legs than adult. In first-summer, legs brighter orange-red; bill can be orange-red with blackish culmen, tip. First-summer's protracted complete molt (primaries Apr.–Sept.) produces second-winter plumage. SECOND-YEAR: Resembles adult, but some second-summers have white-spotted forecrown; outer primaries darker and more worn than on adults, often forming an upperwing wedge recalling the Common.

Similar Species Common is slightly smaller and slimmer with more slender bill and appreciably shorter legs; all Common plumages have white tail with contrasting dark outer webs to outermost rectrices. Breeding adult Common pale gray below; tail streamer tips fall about equal with, or shorter than, wing tips at rest; deeper red bill with smaller black tip; upper wing often shows dark wedge or contrast on trailing edge of duller primaries (but beware second-summer Forster's). Juvenile and first-summer Commons have dark patagial bar on upper wing; black partial cap extends solidly around nape. Arctics smaller with shorter neck, smaller bill,

short legs, relatively longer and narrower wings, and quicker, more clipped wing beats; all Arctic plumages have white tail, contrasting dark outer webs to outermost rectrices. Breeding adult Arctic smoky gray below, all-red bill, primaries translucent but not silvery above. Juvenile Arctics have dark patagial bar on upper wing; black partial cap extends solidly around nape. First-summer Arctics have fresh primaries (replaced in winter); cap extends solidly around nape. Also see the Roseate.

Voice Hard, clipped dry *kik* or *krik;* slightly grating, shrill *krrih* or *kyiih* and *kyerr kyerr;* in breeding-season chases, gruffer, slightly shrill rasping series of *zzhi-zzhi-zzhi.*

Status & Distribution N.A. south to northern Mexico. BREEDING: Common, arrives southern breeding sites Apr., northern sites (Canada, Great Lakes) mainly late Apr.–May. Departs northern breeding areas through Sept. MIGRATION AND DISPERSAL: Fall migration mainly Aug.–Oct., ranging north to Maritimes. WINTER: Southern U.S. south to Middle America and Caribbean. VAGRANT: Increasingly detected in Europe since 1980s.

Population Apparently fairly stable.

LEAST TERN *Sterna antillarum (E)*

Colonies of this tiny tern "compete" with humans for beach space. Consequently, the species is declining in much of its range. Its very small size is diagnostic among North American terns. Its flight is fast and direct, with fairly deep, hurried wing beats and frequent hovering before plunge diving for fish. Polytypic (4–5 ssp.; 3 in N.A.). L 8–9" (20–23 cm) WS 19–21" (48–53 cm)

Identification The smallest tern, with a relatively long bill and forked tail. All plumages have a pale smoky-gray rump and tail. BREEDING ADULT: Black cap has clean-cut white forehead chevron;

outer 1–3 primaries form a contrastingly blackish upperwing wedge against fresher, pale gray middle primaries. Yellow legs; yellow bill tipped black. WINTER ADULT: Seen (Aug.–Sept.) before birds leave U.S. Lores and crown become white, with variable dark streaking on crown; bill becomes black. Dark-mottled lesser coverts form patagial bar on upper wing. Best told from first-summer (and juvenile) by strong contrast of old outer 1–3 primaries on upper wing. (Adult prebasic primary molt mainly June–Dec., followed by prealternate primary molt including 7–9 inner pri-

maries). JUVENILE AND FIRST-SUMMER: Resembles winter adult, but fresh-plumaged juvenile has variable brownish barring and tipping on back and upperwing coverts; bill base often flesh to yellowish; black auricular mask stronger. They undergo variably extensive primary molt in first winter and spring, followed by prealternate molt in spring that includes inner primaries. First-summer plumage variable, ranging from similar to winter adult's to almost as bright as breeding adult's. Most frequent first-summer plumage resembles winter adult's, but with darker, blackish patagial bar and blackish outer 4–5 primaries, forming a contrasting upperwing wedge suggesting the Sabine's Gull; bill usually black. Some birds resemble breeding adults, but less clean-cut chevron on forehead, forecrown speckled white, and yellow bill more extensively black distally.

Geographic Variation Nominate *antillarum* (breeds on East Coast and Gulf Coast) averages larger and paler than both *browni* (of CA) and, especially, *anthalassos* (of the interior).

Similar Species Should be unmistakable by virtue of its small size: When perched it can hide behind a Sanderling! The Little Tern, its Old World counterpart, is very similar to the Least and should be sought on East Coast; all Little plumages have contrasting white rump and tail, unlike the pale smoky gray of the Least.

Voice High reedy chippering; chatters with frequent disyllabic calls: *chi-rit* and *k-rrik;* a reedier *kree-it* or *kreet;* a clipped *k'rit;* and longer series, *kik kirvee,* etc.

Status & Distribution U.S. south to Mexico and Caribbean. BREEDING: Fairly common but local, arriving at southern breeding areas late Mar.–Apr., northern sites through May; fall movements start June–Aug. MIGRATION AND DISPERSAL: Most birds move south through Sept. and depart U.S. by late Oct. Casual north to southern Canada. WINTER: Poorly known, presumably off coasts from Mexico and Caribbean to northern S.A. VAGRANT: Accidental HI.

Population Pacific coast *(browni)* and interior *(anthalassos)* populations are endangered in U.S.; the main threats being habitat modification and human disturbance.

breeding adult

juvenile

breeding adult

1st summer

ALEUTIAN TERN *Sterna aleutica*

This handsome tern is a sought-after summer resident of western Alaskan coasts. Its calls are quite unlike those of other terns, and it could be passed off as a songbird. In flight and behavior, the Aleutian recalls the Common Tern. Unbroken tail streamers add 1 to 1.5 inches (3–4 cm) to the length of a breeding adult. Monotypic. L 11–12" (28–30 cm) WS 29.5–32" (75–81 cm)

Identification Slender and relatively small bill; deeply forked tail. On all plumages, note dark secondary bar on underwing. BREEDING ADULT: Black cap has clean-cut, V-shaped white forehead patch, and upperparts are medium gray. In flight, smoky gray underparts contrast with whitish underwings, which have a diagnostic dark secondary bar; upper wing has wedge as on the Common Tern. Black legs and bill. JUVENILE AND FIRST-SUMMER: Fresh juveniles are relatively dark above, with cinnamon to rufous edging and barring on upperparts; cinnamon wash bleeds onto chest and sides (soon fades to whitish). Bill pinkish with dark culmen and tip; legs pinkish. Presumably undergoes complete molt in first winter (similar to the Common Tern); and first-summers may reach Alaskan waters but go unreported. First-summers probably resemble the winter adult in having white lores and white forecrown; note dark underwing secondary bar and medium gray upperparts.

Similar Species Arctic Tern is smaller and paler overall, but distant, flying birds might be a challenge: Broader-winged Aleutians have smoother, less snappy wingbeats; note white forehead, shorter tail streamers, and voice. Breeding adult Common Terns of the Siberian subspecies *longipennis* are slightly slimmer in build with a longer bill; they lack a black underwing secondary bar and have a full black cap. Second-summers can have the white forehead, but theirs is more rounded and irregular than the neat V found on the adult Aleutian.

Voice Adult's piping whistled calls have a mellow to slightly rolled quality: *piiu* and *piirr-i-u* or *piiu-pi-pip,* and so on.

Status & Distribution BREEDING: North Pacific. Fairly common, but local; arriving southern AK late Apr.–May; in Aleutians and Bering Sea mid-May–early June. Departs colonies Aug.–mid-Sept. MIGRATION: Casual off Queen Charlotte Is., BC (mid-May–early June). WINTER: Winter grounds unknown, possibly in western tropical Pacific (recently found in autumn off Hong Kong). VAGRANT: Accidental to Europe.

Population Locally erratic and no clear trend. Ironically, not known to breed in the Aleutians before 1962, with subsequent increases there perhaps due to the removal of non-native foxes from the islands.

breeding adult

juvenile

COMMON TERN *Sterna hirundo*

Fairly common along coasts, offshore, and inland, the Common Tern is steady and graceful in flight, with smooth wing beats, hovering briefly before plunge diving for fish. Unbroken tail streamers add 1.5 inches (4 cm) to breeding adult's length. Polytypic (3 ssp.; 2 in N.A.). L 11.5–12.5" (29–32 cm) WS 29.5–32.5" (75–83 cm)

Identification Medium size; medium-long bill; forked tail. Breeding tail streamers fall about even with wing tips at rest. BREEDING ADULT: Solid black cap; black-tipped red bill (mostly dark on early spring migrants, rarely all-red in late summer); red legs. Pale smoky gray underparts; white rump and tail with dark outer web to outer rectrices. Pale-gray upper wings usually have distinct dark wedge on trailing edge of primaries. JUVENILE AND FIRST-FALL: Fresh juveniles have variable gingery wash and barring on back and upperwing coverts (often fading by fall); pinkish red legs, bill base. Upper wing has contrasting blackish patagial bar, dusky gray secondary bar. Protracted complete molt in first winter (primaries Jan.–July) produces first-summer. FIRST-SUMMER: Rare in N.A. Forecrown, underparts white;

black bill. Note dark patagial bar, dark secondaries. SECOND-SUMMER: Some resemble first-summer, but lack worn juvenal outer primaries; bill usually reddish basally. Others resemble breeding adult, but forecrown white or spotted white, underparts paler, tail streamers shorter, bill duller.

Geographic Variation Nominate in N.A., with red bill and legs. Breeding *longipennis* adults (Siberia) have darker plumage overall; bill and legs blackish.

Similar Species The Arctic is slightly smaller with shorter neck, slightly more rounded crown, narrower wings, shorter bill, much shorter legs (striking on birds at rest). Primaries are evenly translucent when backlit (only inner primaries look translucent on the Common); outer primaries have narrower blackish tips, never show a dark wedge like the Common. In flight, the Arctic has narrower, proportionately longer wings; shorter head-and-neck projection forward of the wings; generally snappier, less floppy wing beats. Breeding adult Arctic has all-red bill, duskier gray underparts, tail streamers that project beyond wings at rest. Juvenile Arctics have

a less contrasting dark patagial bar, which on upper wing, blends into gray coverts and whitish secondaries. First-summer Arctic best told by structure. Also see the Forster's and Roseate; compare *longipennis* with the Aleutian.

Voice Calls include a sharp *kik* and *kik-kik;* a grating *krrrih;* slightly drawn-out, disyllabic *eeeahrr;* also a rapidly repeated, grating *kehrr kehrr kehrr* in breeding-season chases.

Status & Distribution Holarctic breeder. BREEDING: Common in N.A., arrives at colonies Apr.–May, departs Aug.–Sept. MIGRATION: Mainly Apr.–May, July–Oct. Subspecies *longipennis* rare (mainly spring) on islands of western AK. WINTER: Off coasts from Middle America to S.A. Very rare Gulf Coast, southern CA. **Population** Historical fluctuating trends difficult to assess.

breeding adult

breeding adult

1st fall

2nd summer

breeding adult *longipennis*

1st summer

juvenile

ARCTIC TERN *Sterna paradisaea*

This medium-small, northern-breeding tern winters in Antarctic waters (see map) and migrates mainly well offshore, with birds rarely seen on coasts and inland. The Arctic's flight is quick and graceful, with snappy wing beats. It hovers briefly before plunge diving for fish. Unbroken tail streamers add 1.5 to 2 inches (4–5 cm) to the length of breeding adults. Monotypic. L 11.8–13" (30–33 cm) WS 30–33" (76–84 cm)

Identification Medium-small tern with a fairly short and slender bill, deeply forked tail, and notably short legs. Breeding adults' tail streamers project well beyond the wing tips at rest. BREEDING ADULT: Solid black cap; red bill and legs. Smoky gray underparts may offset white cheeks; has white rump and tail with dark outer webs to outer rectrices. Pale gray upper wings with translucent primaries, narrow dark trailing edge to the outer pri-

maries. JUVENILE: Fresh juveniles have variable brown wash and barring on back and upperwing coverts (often fading by fall). Upper wing has contrasting dark gray patagial bar and whitish secondaries and inner primaries. Protracted complete molt in first winter (primaries Jan.–May) produces first-summer plumage. FIRST-SUMMER: Forecrown and underparts white, or the underparts have gray smudging; upper wing has dark gray patagial bar; bill black to dull reddish.
Similar Species See the Common Tern; see also the Aleutian, Roseate, and Forster's Terns. Best distinguishing features for a perched Arctic are its relatively small bill and very short legs. On flying birds, note the Arctic's short neck, its long and narrow wings, its evenly translucent primaries with narrow blackish tips, and its generally snappy flight.
Voice Calls include a high, clipped *kiip;* a shrill grating *keeahr,* higher and drier than the Common's; and

a shrill, rapid-paced *ki-ki-kehrr* by scolding birds at colony.
Status & Distribution Holarctic breeder. BREEDING: Common in N.A., arriving at colonies from mid-May (New England, southern AK) to late June (high Arctic), departing late July–Aug. MIGRATION: Mainly late Apr.–early June, late July–Oct. Rare to casual inland. WINTER: Antarctic pack ice and adjacent waters, where rich food enables rapid complete molt.
Population Recent declines in many areas, from Alaska to New England, perhaps linked to food shortages in northern oceans and reflecting the combination of changing ocean conditions and human over-exploitation of fisheries.

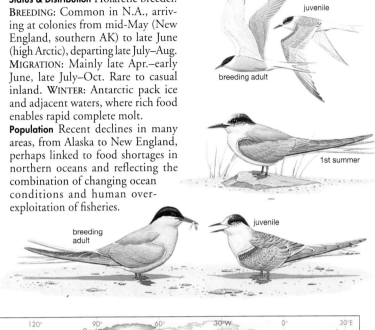

juvenile

breeding adult

1st summer

juvenile

breeding adult

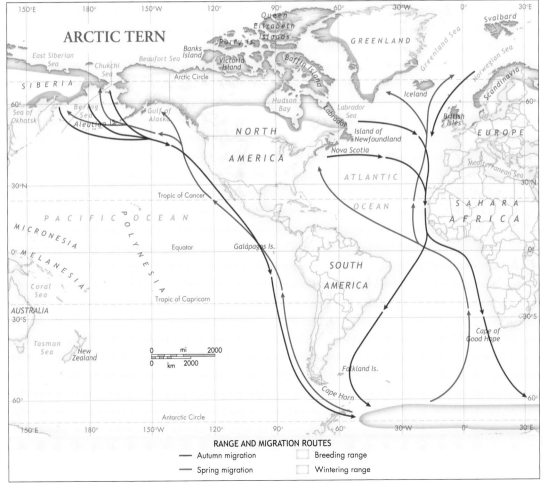

ARCTIC TERN

RANGE AND MIGRATION ROUTES
— Autumn migration   ☐ Breeding range
— Spring migration   ☐ Wintering range

SOOTY TERN   *Sterna fuscata*

This handsome, colonial-nesting tropical tern is largely pelagic and comes ashore only to breed. Banding recoveries have shown that the Florida population spends most of its nonbreeding time off West Africa, where young birds remain for their first 1 to 2 years of life. Sooty Terns have a graceful, buoyant flight and swoop down to pick food from the surface; they do not plunge dive. They will rest on the sea, often in flocks, but seem less prone to perch on driftwood, which Bridled Terns do regularly. Unbroken tail streamers add 2.5 to 3 inches (6–8 cm) to the length of a breeding adult. Polytypic (8+ ssp.; 2 in N.A.). L 14–15.5" '36–39 cm) WS 34–36.5" (86–93 cm)

Identification Medium size with fairly broad wings and a deeply forked tail. BREEDING ADULT: Deep black crown, hind neck, and upperparts, with a broad, triangular white forehead patch; white underparts have variable pale-gray clouding (often not apparent in bright sunlight). Tail black with a white outer edge. In flight, note the dark underside to the remiges contrasting with white underwing coverts; note also that in bright light the upperside of the remiges can look paler and browner than the back and coverts. Black bill and legs. Prebasic molt occurs at sea between breeding seasons. WINTER ADULT: Not illustrated, but may be encountered in fall (esp. storm-blown birds). Resembles breeding adult, but hind neck mottled pale gray, back feathers often have broad whitish tips, and forehead patch less neatly defined. The less deeply forked tail is black overall, with white-tipped outermost rectrices. JUVENILE: Sooty brownish black overall with white-spotted back and upperwing coverts; white vent to undertail coverts. In flight, note the contrast between the white underwing coverts and the dark body. A protracted complete molt in first winter and summer produces first-summer plumage. FIRST-SUMMER: Not illustrated; rarely

found in North America. Appearance variably intermediate between juvenile and non-breeding adult. Lacks juvenile's whitish spotting, but back feathers often tipped whitish, and underparts have variable dusky mottling and smudging. Subsequent immature plumages poorly known.

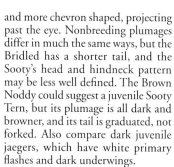
juvenile

breeding adult

Geographic Variation Atlantic breeding populations are the nominate subspecies *fuscata,* the breeding adults of which have white underparts with little or no smoky clouding on the belly and vent. East Pacific breeding populations (casual in southern CA) are the subspecies *crissalis;* there, breeding adults average smaller and have pale-gray clouding on their underparts.

Similar Species The Bridled Tern is slightly smaller and lighter in build, with narrower wings, a longer tail, and a more buoyant and lighter flight; it often stands on driftwood, weed patches, and other floating objects but rarely alights on the sea (which the Sooty does). Only the adultlike plumages of the Bridled are likely to confused with the Sooty's, and then only if birds are distant or not seen well. Breeding adult Bridleds are dark brownish gray above, with the remiges often appearing the darkest part of the upperparts (the opposite of the Sooty's) and with the long tail looking mostly white (striking even at long range). Also note that the underside of the primaries are white based on the Bridled (all dark on the Sooty); the Bridled's paler hind neck often appears as a hind collar, separating the black cap and dark back; and its white forehead patch is narrower

and more chevron shaped, projecting past the eye. Nonbreeding plumages differ in much the same ways, but the Bridled has a shorter tail, and the Sooty's head and hindneck pattern may be less well defined. The Brown Noddy could suggest a juvenile Sooty Tern, but its plumage is all dark and browner, and its tail is graduated, not forked. Also compare dark juvenile jaegers, which have white primary flashes and dark underwings.

Voice Adult has a nasal barking or laughing *ka-waké* or *ke wéh-de-wek* given year-round; also varied shrill and grating cries mainly given at colonies. Juveniles give high reedy whistles into their first-winter: e.g., *wheeir.*

Status & Distribution Pantropical. BREEDING: Large colony on Dry Tortugas, FL, where birds arrive by Mar., depart late July–Sept.; also nests on islets off LA and TX. DISPERSAL: Regular in summer (esp. July–Sept.) north to NC. VAGRANT: Casual to southern CA. Storm-blown birds (mainly late summer and fall) to Great Lakes and north to Maritimes; accidental to Gulf of Alaska.

Population World population perhaps declining due to introduced predators, trapping, and egg harvesting, but protected Dry Tortugas colony seems fairly stable.

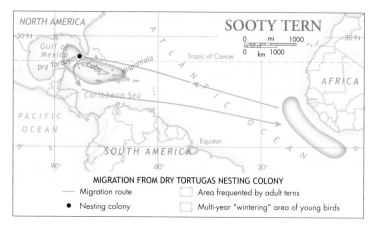

NORTH AMERICA

SOOTY TERN

0   mi   1000
0   km   1000

Gulf of Mexico
Dry Tortugas
Cuba
Hispaniola
Tropic of Cancer

AFRICA

Caribbean Sea

PACIFIC OCEAN

ATLANTIC OCEAN

Equator

SOUTH AMERICA

MIGRATION FROM DRY TORTUGAS NESTING COLONY

— Migration route   ☐ Area frequented by adult terns

● Nesting colony   ☐ Multi-year "wintering" area of young birds

BRIDLED TERN   *Sterna anaethetus*

This handsome tropical tern occurs in North America. mainly as a non-breeding pelagic summer visitor to warm offshore waters. Bridleds have a graceful, buoyant flight and swoop down to pick food from the surface; they do not plunge dive. Often found resting on driftwood, sargassum weed mats, and even the backs of turtles, they rarely if ever alight on the sea. Unbroken tail streamers add 2 to 2.5 inches (5–6 cm) to length of a breeding adult. Polytypic (6+ ssp.; 2 in N.A.). L 12.5–14" (32–36 cm) WS 31–33.5" (79–85 cm)
Identification Medium size; medium-length, slender bill; long, deeply forked tail. BREEDING ADULT: Black crown; chevron-shaped white forehead patch; gray-brown upperparts; whitish hind collar; outer rectrices mostly white (often striking at long range). In flight,

breeding
adult

juvenile

upperwing remiges often look darker than coverts, and underwings whitish overall with a dark trailing edge. Black bill, legs. Prebasic molt occurs at sea (with primaries molted Aug.–Feb.). WINTER ADULT: Not illustrated, but may be encountered in fall (esp. storm-blown birds). Resembles breeding adult, but back feathers tipped pale gray to whitish; forehead patch less neatly defined; whitish streaking in forecrown; lores can be white. Less deeply forked tail; outer rectrices' tips washed dusky. JUVENILE: Pattern overall resembles adult's, but much less well-defined. White forehead and short supercilium are framed by black auricular mask and dark-streaked crown; upperparts boldly barred pale buff to whitish; neck, chest sides washed buff in fresh plumage. Protracted complete molt in first winter and summer (primaries molted Apr.–Aug.) produces first-summer plumage. FIRST-SUMMER: Not illustrated, but commonly seen in waters of N.A. Variable appearance intermediate between juvenile and winter adult. Upperparts have little or no whitish barring; head ranges from whitish overall, with an indistinct blackish auricular mask, to a messy dark cap and poorly defined white forehead chevron. SECOND-SUMMER: Not illustrated. Resembles breeding adult, but outer primary molt may not complete until May; forehead chevron less neatly defined; tail streamers average shorter.
Geographic Variation East Coast birds are of subspecies *recognita,* breeding adults of which have white underparts. East Pacific breeding populations (accidental in southern CA) are presumed to be subspecies *nelsoni,* breeding adults of which average larger than *recognita* and have pale-gray clouding on their underparts.
Similar Species Distinctive appearance unmatched by other terns in its range. At a distance, especially when remiges are seen in bright tropical light, a breeding adult Bridled might be confused with the Sooty Tern. See Sooty Tern.
Voice Not especially vocal except around the nest, where adults give a mellow *kowk-kowk* or *kwawk kwawk,* and a harder *kahrrr.*
Status & Distribution Pantropical. BREEDING: Very local in FL Keys (Apr.–Aug.). DISPERSAL: Regular offshore visitor (mainly May–Oct.) in Gulf of Mexico and shoreward edge of Gulf Stream north to NC, rarely to NJ. VAGRANT: Storm-blown birds (mainly late summer and fall) north to Atlantic Canada. Accidental to southern CA and AR.
Population Caribbean populations fluctuate widely, so trends not apparent. More frequent records off southeastern U.S. likely reflect increased coverage rather than any population increase.

LARGE-BILLED TERN   *Phaetusa simplex*

This striking, aptly named species nests in freshwater habitats of South America and moves to coastal regions there in the non-breeding season. Its occurrence in North America is accidental, although vagrants have also been found in Bermuda and the Caribbean. They have a graceful flight and feed by plunge diving and hawking for insects in flight. Polytypic (2 ssp.). L 14–15" (36–38 cm) WS 36–38" (91–97 cm)
Identification Proportionately long bill is stout and yellow; legs are medium length and olive to greenish yellow; relatively short tail is shallowly forked. BREEDING ADULT: Black cap separated from bill base by a white forehead band. At rest, the upperparts are dusky gray,

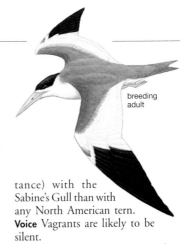

breeding
adult

with black primaries and a broad white band along the bottom edge of the wing. In flight, upperparts display a striking pattern recalling the Sabine's Gull: Bold white triangular panels on the wings set off by the dusky-gray lesser upperwing coverts and the black primaries and greater primary coverts (the inner primaries are whitish). The underwings are mostly white, with dark wing tips. NONBREEDING ADULT: Resembles breeding adult, but forecrown mottled white. JUVENILE AND FIRST-YEAR: Resembles adult, but back and upperwing coverts mottled brownish, cap mottled whitish, and bill is duller yellowish.
Similar Species Should be unmistakable. More likely to be confused (at a distance) with the Sabine's Gull than with any North American tern.
Voice Vagrants are likely to be silent.
Status & Distribution VAGRANT: Accidental (late May–July); 3 recs. from Great Lakes region and mid-Atlantic coast.

WHISKERED TERN *Chlidonias hybridus*

breeding
adult

This Old World marsh tern is an accidental visitor to eastern North America. As its scientific name suggests, the Whiskered Tern is somewhat intermediate in appearance between typical terns (such as the Common) and marsh terns. Its flight is similar to the Black Tern's but somewhat heavier, with less floppy wing beats. Like the Black Tern, the Whiskered swoops down to pick food from the water, rather than diving. Polytypic (6 ssp.; presumed nominate in N.A.). L 9.5–10" (24–25 cm) WS 26.5–28.5" (67–72 cm)

Identification Medium-size tern with a medium-short and relatively stout bill and medium-length legs. The wings are fairly broad and bluntly pointed; the tail is shallowly cleft. BREEDING ADULT: Black cap and smoky-gray underparts strongly set off the white cheeks (or "whiskers"). Underparts are similar in tone to the upperparts, except the undertail coverts are whitish and the rump and tail are smoky gray. In flight, the upperside of the remiges often contrasts paler and more silvery than the smoky-gray wing coverts, and the smoky-gray underbody contrasts with whitish underwings and undertail coverts. The bill and legs are deep red. Prebasic molt usually starts in fall, later than most of other marsh terns'. WINTER ADULT: The head and underparts are white with a black postocular patch that merges into blackish streaking on the hind crown; note the pale gray rump and tail. The bill and legs are blackish. JUVENILE: Unlikely in North America. Resembles winter adult, but

the wings are uniformly fresh in fall and it has a dark brown saddle with broad cinnamon bars and pinkish legs. A protracted complete molt in the first winter produces first-summer plumage. FIRST-SUMMER: Resembles winter adult, but primaries in molt mainly January through August.

Similar Species Separated from Commons and Arctics by typical marsh-tern flight; smaller size; and more compact shape, with a pale gray rump and shallowly cleft tail. Also, breeding adult Whiskereds have darker body plumage and more contrasting white cheeks. Winter adult White-wingeds are smaller and more lightly built, with narrower wings and a shorter, finer bill; their black ear-spot is often more distinct and separate from the dark cap.

Voice Vagrants are usually silent; flight call a rasping *krehk*.

Status & Distribution VAGRANT: Accidental (July–Aug.), with 2 recent records from mid-Atlantic coast.

WHITE-WINGED TERN *Chlidonias leucopterus*

This small tern of Eurasia (where it is more evocatively called the White-winged Black Tern) is a casual visitor to North America, and the breeding-plumaged adults are among the most handsome of birds. White-winged Terns might be found anywhere Black Terns occur and readily associate with them. (The 2 species have hybridized in QC). The Whited-winged's flight is similar to the Black Tern's, swooping down to pick food from the water as well as soaring to catch insects in flight. They perch readily on posts and wires. Monotypic. L 9–9.5" (23–24 cm) WS 22–23" (56–59 cm)

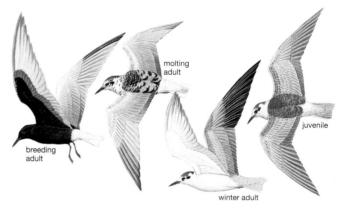

molting
adult

juvenile

breeding
adult

winter adult

Identification Small with a fairly short, slender bill and medium-length legs. Wings are slightly more rounded than the Black Tern's, and the tail has only a shallow cleft. BREEDING ADULT: Unmistakable: Black head, body, and underwing coverts contrast with the white "wings," tail coverts, and tail. The outer 2–3 primaries are dark (basic) feathers that contrast with the newer middle primaries attained by the prealternate molt. The bill is blackish to dark red; the legs and feet are orange-red. Prebasic molt starts in midsummer, when white spots appear on the head and body. Molting adults in fall often lack most or all the black,

except for some underwing coverts. WINTER ADULT: Head, underparts, and underwings are white with a dark-streaked cap and a blackish ear spot often separated from the cap by a white supraorbital area; the back and tail are pale gray. Note the dusky secondaries contrasting with whitish upperwing coverts. JUVENILE: Not recorded in North America. Resembles winter adult, but the wings are uniformly fresh in fall; its dark-brown saddle contrasts with the pale upperwings and uppertail coverts, and it has duller, pinkish legs. A protracted complete molt in the first winter (primaries molted Jan.–Aug.; sometimes

later on vagrants) produces first-summer plumage. FIRST-SUMMER: Not illustrated, but resembles winter adult. SECOND-SUMMER: Not illustrated, but resembles breeding adult. Some have white spots on underwing coverts, and others have strongly piebald head and body in spring.

Similar Species The Black Tern is slightly larger with more pointed wings, a slightly more cleft tail, a slightly longer bill, and slightly shorter legs. All plumages of the Black Tern have smoky-gray underwing coverts; its upper wings, back, and tail are essentially concolorous dusky-gray, but the marginal coverts of breeding adults can be paler and look whitish in some lights. Confusion is most likely in winter plumages, but note the White-winged's paler upperwings with contrasting dark secondaries, its pale gray rump and tail, its whitish underwings, its lack of a dark mark on the neck sides, and its lack of dark mottling on the flanks. On perched birds, note the Black Tern's dark mark on the neck sides and its smokier-gray upperparts; in direct comparison, the Black Tern's slightly longer (and thus finer-looking) bill and shorter legs may be appreciated. The overall pale-gray winter plumage of the White-winged recalls many typical terns, but note its small size, short bill, marsh-tern flight, and shallowly cleft tail. If a suspected White-winged does not show the classic suite of features, the possibility of a hybrid with the Black Tern should be considered. Also see the Whiskered Tern.

Voice Mostly silent away from the breeding grounds, the White-winged Tern may give a hoarse *kesch,* slightly deeper and harsher than the Black Tern's call.

Status & Distribution VAGRANT: Casual visitor (mainly late May–Aug.) to widely scattered locales in the eastern half of North America, especially the along the Northeast and mid-Atlantic coast. Accidental in the West (AK and CA).

BLACK TERN   *Chlidonias niger*

This handsome small tern occurs widely as a migrant and summer visitor at lakes and marshes across North America, where it breeds in freshwater habitats. Its winter range is pelagic. Black Terns have an easy, slightly floppy flight as they patrol back and forth and swoop down to pick food from the surface; they also soar like giant swallows and catch insects in flight, but they do not dive like typical terns. Migrants occur singly or, locally, in flocks of hundreds. Black Terns perch readily on posts and wires, and their nests are mats of floating vegetation. Polytypic (2 ssp.; 1 in N.A.). L 9–9.7" (23–25 cm) WS 23.5–25.5" (60–65 cm)

Identification Small with a fairly short, slender bill and medium-length legs; tail with shallow cleft. BREEDING ADULT: Distinctive, with a black head and body, slaty-gray upperparts, and white undertail coverts. The marginal upperwing coverts are sometimes pale gray; when seen head-on, they can sometimes flash whitish. The underwing coverts are smoky gray. The bill is blackish, the legs dark reddish. Prebasic molt starts in midsummer, when white spots appear on the head and body; the underparts of fall adults are mostly white or blotched black and white. WINTER ADULT: The head and underparts are white with a dark-streaked cap connected to a blackish ear spot and forming "headphones"; note the dark bar on the chest sides and slaty-gray mottling on the flanks. JUVENILE: Resembles winter adult, but the wings are uniformly fresh in fall, the back and tertials have variable dark-brown distal markings that create a subtly mottled aspect, and the legs are often dull pinkish. A protracted complete molt in the first winter (primaries Jan.–Aug.) produces first-summer plumage. FIRST-SUMMER: Resembles winter adult, but the underparts of some birds have scattered black spots. SECOND-SUMMER: Not illustrated. Most resemble the breeding adult, but some have white spotting on the head and underparts in spring; others resemble first-summers, but have heavier black blotching on the underparts. Not safely distinguished after adult prebasic molt starts in June–July.

Geographic Variation North American birds comprise New World subspecies *surinamensis,* which differs from nominate *niger* of the Old World (possible vagrant to the east) in deeper black head and body of breeding adults and in slaty-gray mottling on sides and flanks of winter adults and immatures.

Similar Species Distinctive; often strikingly small when seen perched among other terns, being barely larger than a Least Tern. See vagrant White-winged and Whiskered Terns.

Voice A piping, slightly reedy *peep* or *pseeh* and a quiet *kriih* given by birds in feeding flocks; a quacking *kek* in alarm; and a shrill, slightly grating *kehk* given by birds scolding near the nest.

Status & Distribution North America and western Asia. BREEDING: Generally common, arriving on nesting grounds late Apr.–May, departing late July–Aug. MIGRATION: Mainly mid-Apr.–May and late July–Sept. Uncommon to rare along and off Pacific coast. Casual visitor north to AK and Atlantic Canada. WINTER: Over Pacific Ocean waters from southern Mexico to Peru. Casual to CA. VAGRANT: Accidental to Europe *(surinamensis).*

Population Declining in most areas, mainly because of habitat degradation and loss. North American population in early 1990s was a third of what it was in late 1960s.

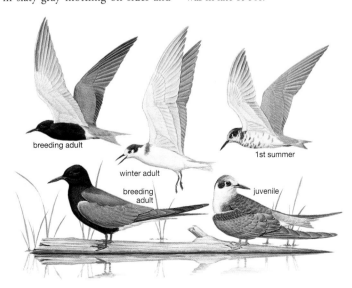

breeding adult

winter adult

breeding adult

1st summer

juvenile

BROWN NODDY *Anous stolidus*

In North America, this distinctive all-dark tern nests only on the Dry Tortugas, Florida, where it builds a nest in low bushes. Its flight is steady and graceful, typically low over the water. Here flocks often feed with other tropical seabirds, milling and swooping to pick food from the surface. The Brown Noddy does not usually dive for food and rarely alights on sea. Polytypic (5 ssp.; nominate in N.A.). L 14–16" (36–41 cm) WS 31–35" (79–89 cm) **Identification** Medium-size with medium-long bill and long, graduated tail. No seasonal variation in appearance (unlike most terns). ADULT: Plumage dark brown overall (inc. underwings) with contrasting ashy-white forecrown offset by black lores and narrow white subocular crescent; ashy-gray hind crown and nape. On resting birds, primaries contrastingly blacker than upperparts, which, in fresh plumage, have gray cast often lost by summer. Black bill; dark gray legs. Prebasic molt begins April to June, then suspends during breeding, and is completed at sea by March, in time for return to colonies. IMMATURE: Juveniles dark brown overall with a neat white supraloral line that continues over the bill base; the forecrown is dull ashy gray, and the brownish hind crown does not contrast with the hind neck. Fresh fall birds have subtly paler brown tips to the upperwing coverts and scapulars. Protracted complete postjuvenal molt starts in fall and continues into the following summer (primaries molted mainly Feb.–Aug.). FIRST-SUMMER: Not illustrated. Forecrown mostly ashy

white, often with some brownish smudging. Some birds' crown mostly ashy white; others still show a contrasting white supraloral line and have little ashy white on crown. Brownish to gray-brown hind crown merges with nape. Many spring birds still have some contrastingly pale, bleached (juvenal) upperwing coverts.

Geographic Variation Birds in N.A. are of nominate subspecies, *stolidus*. Subspecies *ridgwayi* of west Mexico (not separable in field from *stolidus*) is a potential hurricane-assisted vagrant to the West Coast or the Southwest.

Similar Species Unlikely to be confused when in the Tortugas, but vagrants elsewhere may be puzzling. Juvenile and first-year Sooty Terns are slightly bulkier overall with a forked tail, fine pale spotting on the upperparts in fresh plumage, contrasting white underwing coverts, and a white central belly and undertail coverts. The Black Noddy is smaller and blacker overall (primaries not contrastingly blacker at rest) with a more extensive and contrasting white cap on adults and immatures; its bill is distinctly thinner (obvious in direct comparison), and its white subocular crescent is shorter (lying mostly behind the eye's midpoint). At sea, the Bulwer's Petrel (accidental in N.A.) can suggest a small noddy, with its dark brown plumage, long wings and tail, and low flight over the water; it lacks any pale

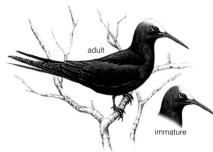
adults
immature

head markings, but has a pale-brown ulnar bar on the upper wing. Its wing-beats are stiffer, and its flight is more wheeling, with frequent weaving glides. Also compare dark juvenile jaegers, which have white primary flashes.

Voice Mostly silent except around colonies, where it gives varied guttural barks and a braying *keh-eh-eh-ehr*. First-year birds give higher, whistled calls.

Status & Distribution Pantropical. BREEDING: Fairly common but very local, arriving (at first nocturnally) at colony mid-Jan.–Feb. and departing through Oct., with breeding season mainly May–July. DISPERSAL AND VAGRANT: Casual in summer along Gulf Coast and north to Outer Banks, NC; accidental north to New England. WINTER: FL population presumably winters at sea in tropical Atlantic.

Population Florida population is believed to be stable, fluctuating between 1,000 and 2,000 pairs.

BLACK NODDY *Anous minutus*

adult

immature

In North America, this all-dark tern is a sought-after vagrant on the Dry Tortugas, where it associates with Brown Noddies, usually on the colony island. Its flight is typically low over

the water, but is often quicker than the Brown Noddy's, with more fluttery wing beats. Polytypic (7 ssp.; 1 in N.A.). L 12–13.5" (30–34 cm) WS 26–29" (66–74 cm) **Identification** Medium-small bird with a proportionately long and distinctly slender bill and a long, graduated tail. No seasonal variation in appearance (like the Brown Noddy). ADULT: Plumage blackish overall (inc. underwings) with a contrasting white crown offset by black lores, and a narrow white subocular crescent; hind neck is ashy gray. On resting birds, primaries not contrastingly blacker than upperparts, which, in fresh plumage, have a gray cast often lost by summer.

The upperside of the tail can look paler and grayer. Black bill; dark gray legs. Molts poorly known, but likely similar to Brown Noddy's. IMMATURE: Resembles adult, but worn first-summer birds often slightly browner overall, sometimes with bleached (juvenal) upperwing coverts. The rear border to the white cap is often messier than on adults, but contrasts more sharply with the blackish hind neck.

Geographic Variation North American birds are presumably of the subspecies *americanus*, which breeds on islands off the north coast of Venezuela.

Similar Species The Brown Noddy is larger and bulkier with a thicker (and thus often slightly shorter-looking) bill and dark brown plumage overall. (Its primaries are contrastingly blacker at rest.) However, plumage tones can be difficult to evaluate in bright sunlight: On adults, look for the Black Noddy's smaller size and, especially, its long, slender bill; also note the more extensive white cap (beware that bright light can cause the Brown Noddy to show a large white cap), shorter white subocular crescent, and grayish tail. The immature Black Noddy is more distinctive, with a large and contrasting white cap unlike any plumage of the Brown Noddy's.

Voice Rarely vocal away from colonies; likely to be mostly silent in North America. Calls include guttural growls, *ahrrr* and *garrr;* first-year birds have a high, piping *swee.*

Status & Distribution Tropical Atlantic and Pacific oceans. VAGRANT: Rare or casual spring-summer visitor to Dry Tortugas, FL; accidental TX coast (mid-Apr.–July).

SKIMMERS Genus Rynchops

This pantropical genus (3 sp.) is sometimes treated as a separate family, Rynchopidae. Resembling large, angular terns, they are distinguished by long, laterally compressed bills with projecting lower mandibles. They feed in flight, mostly at night, by skimming with an open bill, then snapping it shut on contact with fish and crustaceans.

BLACK SKIMMER Rynchops niger

This species favors coasts with sandy beaches and lagoons, but it has also colonized the Salton Sea. Its flight is strong and buoyant, with smooth wing beats mainly above the body plane. Flocks often fly in fairly tight formation, at times wheeling like shorebirds. Males are larger than females and often noticeable in the field (male bills average 10–15 percent longer). Polytypic (3 ssp.; nominate in N.A.). L 17–18" (43–46 cm) WS 45–49" (114–124 cm)

Identification Striking. Long, laterally compressed bill; fairly short legs; very long wings; fairly short, forked tail. BREEDING ADULT: Crown, hind neck, and upperparts solidly black, contrasting sharply with white forehead, lores, foreneck, and underparts. Black upper wings have a white trailing edge to the secondaries and inner primaries; tail is mostly white with a black central stripe. Whitish underwings grade to dusky on the remiges, with blacker wing tips. Black-tipped, bright red bill; red legs. Prebasic molt starts in late summer on the breeding grounds (when a few inner primaries may be replaced before suspending molt for migration) or on the winter grounds. Primary molt completes Mar.–May, overlapping with prealternate molt of hindneck feathers. WINTER ADULT: Resembles breeding adult, but white hind neck, sometimes with a little dusky mottling, and bleached upperparts can look brown-

er in early winter. JUVENILE AND FIRST-YEAR: Juvenile crown and hind neck heavily streaked buffy and whitish; back and upperwing coverts blackish brown; broad buff to whitish edgings create a bold, scaly pattern. Bill duller, less extensive red basally; legs paler, flesh to pale orange-red. Protracted, complete molt starts Sept.–Dec. (primaries molted mainly Jan.–Aug.); produces plumage resembling the winter adult's by end of the first summer. Crown is dark sooty-brown to blackish with paler feather edgings; hind neck is white or mottled blackish; bill and legs average paler than on adults.

Geographic Variation Birds in N.A. are of the nominate subspecies, with white underwings and an extensively white tail. The nomadic Ama-
 zonian-breeding *cineras-
 cens,* a potential vagrant to N.A., has dusky-gray underwings, reduced white on the trailing edge of the wings, and a dark tail.

Similar Species Unmistakable.

Voice A nasal, slightly hollow laughing *kyuh* or *kwuh* and a disyllabic *k'nuk* or *k'wuk,* with calling flocks producing chuckling choruses at times; alarm call a more drawn-out *aaawh.* Juvenile call higher pitched and squawkier than adult's.

Status & Distribution Warmer regions of the Americas. BREEDING: Fairly common to common but local, arriving at northern colonies late Apr., departing Aug.–Sept. MIGRATION: Mainly Mar.–Apr. and Sept.–Nov. WINTER: Southern U.S. to S.A. DISPERSAL AND VAGRANT: Casual inland in coastal states, also (mainly summer) casual in the Southwest, Great Plains, Great Lakes region, and (mainly after storms) Atlantic Canada.

Population Atlantic, Gulf Coast colonies fluctuate greatly: Was considered declining in 1970s; some evidence of recent stabilization. West Coast population has increased markedly in last 30 years.

juvenile

breeding adult

winter adults

AUKS, MURRES, AND PUFFINS Family Alcidae

Atlantic Puffin, breeding (ME, July)

Spectacular and easily observed at their remote breeding colonies, alcids pose a challenge to scrutinize and identify at sea, where they spend most of their time—much of it submerged. A typical birder's view is of distant birds in flight, often in rough sea condition. Swimming birds can be hidden in wave troughs and many species are difficult to approach closely. Identifications are best based on pattern of dark and light colored plumage, bill shape (if visible), and subtle differences in body shape and flight style.

Structure Heavy compact bodies, dense waterproof plumage, very short tails, and small, short wings are the standard. Bills are highly variable in shape and coloration, from dagger-shaped in murres, guillemots, and some murrelets, to hatchet-shaped (puffins), to tiny (auklets, dovekie, and some murrelets). The legs are short and the feet, which lack a hind toe, are fully webbed; they are brightly colored in some species.

Behavior Alcids normally fly close to the sea surface in a very rapid and direct manner with continuous rapid wingbeats; a few of the smaller species zigzag among wave tops. Most species (except *Cepphus* guillemots and *Brachyramphus* murrelets) usually remain well offshore except when attending breeding colonies. Solitary sick, weak, or oiled birds sometimes enter bays and harbors. Large numbers occasionally fly by headlands, especially just after dawn, driven close to land during onshore winds. "Wrecks," in which hundreds of birds occur far

inland, sometimes take place after late fall and early winter storms. Alcids forage by wing-propelled pursuit diving with 3 feeding preferences: schooling fish (murres, puffins), bottom fish (*Cepphus* guillemots), and zooplankton (murrelets, auklets, puffins). The clutch consists of 1 or 2 eggs. Alcids are extraordinarily variable in breeding habits: Chicks may depart the colony 2 days after hatching (*Synthliboramphus* murrelets), when half grown (murres), or remain in their burrows until full size (puffins, auklets). Adults of some species may be seen at sea with small chicks that resemble miniature adults. Most species breed colonially (except *Brachyramphus* murrelets) on cliff ledges, rock crevices, earth burrows, surface scrapes (Kittlitz's Murrelet), and even mossy tree limbs (Marbled Murrelets)—invariably in areas where terrestrial predators are absent or scarce. A few species have entirely nocturnal colony attendance. Dexterity on land varies, with some species clumsy and unable to stand upright (murrelets), and others agile (auklets and puffins).

Plumage Alcids have black-and-white, or dull gray-and-brownish plumage. A few display spectacular nuptial plumes during the breeding season. The sexes look alike. Most undergo minor seasonal changes in coloration, some change drastically between winter and summer (*Cepphus* guillemots and *Brachyramphus* murrelets), and a few look the same year-round (auklets). The Least Auklet is strikingly polymorphic.

Distribution Alcids are restricted to the cold seas of the Northern Hemisphere, with the notable exception of 2 *Synthliboramphus* murrelet species that inhabit the warm subtropical waters off southern California and Mexico. Most alcids come ashore only to breed on remote islands and exposed headlands. The Long-billed Murrelet is a casual vagrant to North America from Asia.

Taxonomy Worldwide there are 23 living species. Twenty species in 10 genera breed in North America, with diversity highest in the North Pacific. The Long-billed Murrelet was recently split from the Marbled Murrelet, but otherwise alcid taxonomy has been stable.

Conservation Most species' breeding areas are protected in parks and nature reserves. The greatest threat has been the introduction of predators (rats and foxes) onto breeding islands (now diminishing due to management). Increasing frequencies of both chronic and catastrophic oil pollution events affect all species. Healthy alcid populations are not compatible with intensive gill net fisheries. Three species have experienced severe declines and have threatened or endangered status: Marbled Murrelet (loss of old-growth nesting habitat, gill netting), Xantus' Murrelet (introduced predators on breeding islands), and Kittlitz's Murrelet (oil spills, gill netting, and unknown factors). Most Atlantic species have been depleted by hunting, drowning in gill nets, and oil pollution at sea. Great Auks were hunted to extinction by the mid-19th century. —*Ian Jones*

DOVEKIES, MURRES, AND AUKS Genera Alle, Uria, Alca, and Pinguinus

Crisp black-and-white plumages characterize this group, which includes the largest alcids and a small planktivorus species. There were 5 species; one was extinct by the mid-19th century. All genus members occur in the Atlantic (murres also in the Pacific). Males leave the breeding colonies with their single, partly grown chick and provision it at sea.

DOVEKIE Alle alle

breeding adult

breeding adult

winter

winter

The Dovekie is by far the smallest alcid in the North Atlantic—nearly half the size of the Atlantic Puffin. A swimming bird typically adopts a distinctive neckless posture with its head held low to the water. An active bird often "drags" its wings on the surface between dives. Monotypic. L 8.8" (21 cm)

Identification Entirely black and white. Upperparts are black, with distinctive scapular stripes, formed by narrow white margins on scapulars; underparts are white. Bill is short, blending evenly with forehead to give a bull-headed look; at close range, the bill shape is noticeably short, deep, and broad with a strongly curved culmen.

Feet are blackish. BREEDING ADULT: Face, throat, neck, nape, and upper breast (bib) are entirely black, except for a small highly contrasting white spot "headlight" above eye. WINTER ADULT: White extends to throat, sides of nape, and neck, forming an incomplete white collar. FLIGHT: Football-shaped body, small size, and rapid "buzzing" wingbeats are distinctive. Secondaries are tipped with white; underwings are blackish. Flies low over sea, zigzagging among waves.

Similar Species Given a decent view, it is unlikely that the Dovekie will be confused with any Atlantic alcid. Starlinglike in size, it is closest in

appearance to a juvenile Atlantic Puffin, which is 50 percent larger and has a different bill and head shape, and a dark face, throat, and neck. The Dovekie's body shape is like the Thick-billed Murre's, but tiny. In the Bering sea, where it occurs in summer with Least, Parakeet, and Crested Auklets, the Dovekie is closest in size to the latter 2 species, but differs in body shape and crisp black-and-white plumage. The Parakeet has broad wings, a pot-bellied body shape, a large red bill, and a shallow fluttering wingbeat. The Dovekie is more than twice the size of the Least.

Voice Highly vocal. A high-pitched *ha-keek,* frequently given at sea when flocks are present. At breeding colonies, a variety of maniacal laughlike chattering and screeching, given when perched and in flight.

Status & Distribution Millions breed in high arctic Greenland, Norway, and Russia. In N.A. a few hundred breed along the Canadian side of the Davis Strait and presumably in AK near the Bering Strait (Little Diomede Island). Rare summer visitor to other Bering Sea islands. BREEDING: Colonially in crevices on scree slopes on high Arctic islands. MIGRATION: Moves away from breeding areas in Sept.; returns in June. WINTER: Abundant off Atlantic Canada, especially on Grand Banks, arriving Nov. Occasionally large "wrecks" of hundreds of birds are blown inland (usually late fall). Uncommon and irregular off New England (occasionally in large numbers) to NC, Dec.–Mar. VAGRANT: Casual south to FL and inland to Great Lakes and bodies of water near the coast.

Population No trends are apparent.

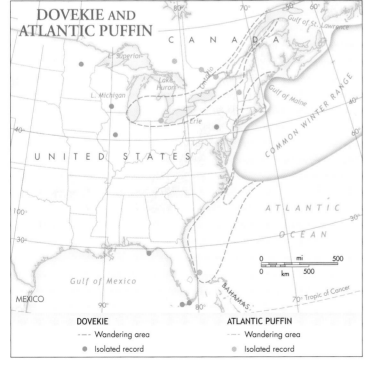

DOVEKIE AND ATLANTIC PUFFIN

DOVEKIE
--- Wandering area
● Isolated record

ATLANTIC PUFFIN
--- Wandering area
● Isolated record

COMMON MURRE *Uria aalge*

The Common Murre is the largest living alcid. Its flight is rapid and direct, usually close to the sea surface. Small flocks of Common Murres moving to and from feeding locations often fly in lines or "trains." On land, the Common Murre stands nearly vertically upright, but it rests its weight on the full length of the tarsi. It swims buoyantly, when not foraging, with head erect and tail cocked. Polytypic. L 18" (46 cm)

Identification It has a long dagger-shaped bill, slender neck (contracted in flight), and distinctive head profile of nearly a straight line from the crown through the culmen (the angle of the gonys is not prominent). The upperparts are nearly uniform dark brown; the underparts are white except for sparse dark streaking on the flanks. The trailing edge of the inner wing is white. The underwing is white, variably mottled with brown on tips of greater underwing coverts; the axillaries are usually heavily marked with brown. The bill, legs, and feet are blackish. The eyes are dark brown. BREEDING ADULT: The head and neck are blackish brown. The shape of the black-and-white border on the neck forms a smooth, U-shaped curve. Bridled morph birds, which vary in numbers at different Atlantic colonies, have a prominent white spectacle-like facial mark. WINTER ADULT: A winter bird looks similar to a breeding bird, except that its throat, sides to neck, sides of nape, and face are white, save for a dark streak extending from behind the eye toward the nape. A first-winter bird has a shorter bill and mottled, less contrasting, facial plumage.

Geographic Variation There are 5 subspecies; nominate *aalge* is widespread in the Atlantic. The Pacific subspecies (*inornata* and *californica*) are larger and lack the bridled morph. Two additional subspecies occur in the western Atlantic.

Similar Species The Common Murre differs strongly from sea ducks, loons, and grebes in its distinctive symmetrical artillery shell-like flight shape, with trailing feet. All plumages of the Common Murre appear brownish dorsally (especially in strong light), whereas the Thick-billed Murre and the Razorbill have blacker backs. Bill shape (long and pointed, lacking a prominent gonydeal angle in the Common Murre) is useful in close views, but first-winter Thick-billeds and Commons have more similar bills. The presence of obvious flank streaking—visible on swimming birds—is a good indicator of the Common Murre. In winter, distinguish the Common from a Thick-billed by its pale face with white extending onto sides of nape, crossed by a prominent dark line extending from behind the eye. Molting and subadult Commons may have freckled throats and intermediate head patterns; the best way to separate them from Thick-billeds is by assessing structural differences. Most populations of Common Murre attain breeding plumage earlier (often by late winter) than Thick-billeds, and this difference can be helpful in picking out the unusual bird. In breeding plumage, the Thick-billed has a prominent white gape stripe, which the Common Murre lacks; the Thick-billed's neck border of black-and-white is V-shaped, whereas the Common's neck border is U-shaped. And lastly, the Common has a more upright stance when

standing and a thinner head and neck than the Thick-Billed.

Voice Highly vocal near breeding colonies, giving a variety of harsh grating *arggggh* calls. Not usually vocal at sea and in winter.

Status & Distribution Common on both coasts, never seen inland. BREEDING: Nests in dense colonies on bare cliff ledges and rocky shelves on islands. MIGRATION: Moves offshore after departing from breeding colonies Aug.–Sept. WINTER: Occurs farther offshore than the Thick-billed Murre. VAGRANT: Casual on Atlantic coast south of Cape Cod, MA, and much rarer than the Thick-billed Murre in those areas; on the Pacific coast recorded rarely as far south as Baja California.

Population Various pressures—gill net fishing, oil spills and chronic petroleum pollution, toxic chemicals, and introduced predators (e.g., foxes) on breeding islands—continue to severely affect some Common Murre populations on the Pacific coast.

breeding adult

breeding adult

bridled breeding adult

winter

juvenile

THICK-BILLED MURRE *Uria lomvia*

The Thick-billed Murre is a large black-and-white alcid restricted to cold seas. Its flight is rapid and direct. On land, it stands nearly upright but leans forward slightly, usually resting its weight against a cliff face (it breeds on narrow cliff ledges). Polytypic. L 17" (43 cm) **Identification** Bill relatively thick with curved culmen and noticeable angle of gonys, thick neck, and head shape with relatively prominent forehead. Upperparts nearly blackish, head, and neck very dark brown, underparts immaculate white. Secondaries white tipped. BREEDING ADULT: Prominent white stripe along gape. Upward, V-shaped point at center of neck formed by black-and-white border. Underwing white, variably mottled with dark gray on underwing coverts. Bill and feet blackish. Irises dark brown. WINTER ADULT: Similar to breeding, except that throat and front of neck white with mottled border of entirely dark face. Gape stripe less prominent. A shorter

bill and mottled, less contrasting facial plumage on first-winter birds.
Geographic Variation The Pacific *arra* has a proportionately longer bill with a less strongly curved culmen.
Similar Species The Thick-billed's distinctive, bulky, thick-necked artillery shell-like flight shape, with trailing feet, differs strongly from sea ducks, loons, and grebes. It is similar to the Common Murre, but in winter it is distinguished by its darker face, with dark mottling extending well below the eye and onto sides of neck, and blacker back. In summer, the Thick-billed has a prominent white gape stripe and a V-shaped white point in the black center of the neck, both lacking in the Common. In flight, the Thick-billed is noticeably blacker above than the Common. A first-winter bird resembles a juvenile Razorbill, but it lacks that species' pointed tail and more extensive white on face. In flight at a distance, the Thick-billed is confusable at all ages and seasons with the Razorbill, which has a deeper bill (usually visible) and much longer, graduated tail (surprisingly hard to see).
Voice Highly vocal near breeding colonies, giving a variety of harsh grating *argggggh* calls. Not usually vocal at sea and in winter.

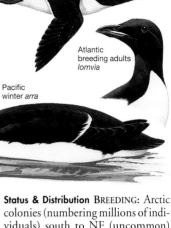

Atlantic breeding adults *lomvia*

Pacific winter *arra*

Status & Distribution BREEDING: Arctic colonies (numbering millions of individuals) south to NF (uncommon) and BC (rare). Nests colonially on narrow cliff ledges. MIGRATION: Moves mainly south after departing colonies Aug.–Sept., returning May–June. WINTER: Atlantic birds winter farther south than Pacific birds, occurring regularly to mid-Atlantic states (where they are much more likely than Common Murres). VAGRANT: In Atlantic, casual south as far as FL, and inland on Great Lakes. On Pacific coast, casual south of Canada to southern CA (many records from Monterey Bay).
Population Although the Atlantic populations are large (numbering in the millions), hunting and oil pollution do affect them.

GREAT AUK *Pinguinus impennis*

The Great Auk was the original "penguin"—a massive, flightless, black-and-white Atlantic alcid. It was hunted to extinction in the 19th century. It had a rapid, wing-propelled underwater flight. On land it was fearless, stood upright, and bred in large colonies on a few low islands. Its weight is estimated at about 10 pounds. Monotypic. L 31" (80 cm)
Identification Black and white. Resembled a giant Razorbill, with similar deep, laterally compressed bill with numerous concentric grooves. Wings tiny. BREEDING ADULT: Face and throat black, oval white face patch between eye and bill. Faint white stripes on grooved bill. WINTER ADULT: Similar to summer, but face patch absent.
Status & Distribution Extinct; about 80 extant specimens of birds and eggs.

Only 3 known breeding sites in N.A.: Funk (the largest colony) and Penguin Islands, NF, and Bird Rocks, Gulf of St. Lawrence. Five colonies in eastern Atlantic (2 in Iceland, 1 in the Faeroes, 1 on St. Kilda, and 1 on Orkney). Highly colonial, forming tightly packed colonies; a single egg laid on bare rock. WINTER: Atlantic Canada south to New England, mostly offshore, casual to SC. Remains have been found in prehistoric middens as far south as FL.
Population The Great Auk was slaughtered for food, oil, bait, and feathers. The last birds at Funk I. (where an estimated 100,000 pairs bred) were killed in about 1800. Grassy patches on the island still outline where thousands of carcasses enriched the barren rock. The last pair was collected at Eldey Stack, Iceland, in 1844.

breeding adult

RAZORBILL *Alca torda*

breeding adult

immature

winter adult

breeding adult

The Razorbill is a large Atlantic alcid with a massive head accentuated by a thick neck and an extraordinary, deep, laterally compressed bill with curved culmen. Its flight is rapid and direct, usually close to sea surface. On land, it stands nearly upright and walks like a penguin. Compared to a murre, it breeds in a wide variety of habitats and regularly forages closer to shore in bays and estuaries. It swims with its head and long tail angled up. Polytypic (2 ssp.; nominate in N.A.). L 17" (43 cm)

Identification Long graduated tail, extending beyond wing tips on swimming bird, unique among alcids. Upperparts jet black; underparts white. Trailing edge of secondaries white. White flanks extend onto sides of rump. Underwing mostly white. Mouth interior yellow; bill and feet blackish; eyes dark brown. **BREEDING ADULT:** Face and throat black. Narrow white stripe from top of bill base to eye. Prominent vertical white stripe on grooved bill. **WINTER ADULT:** Similar to breeding, except that throat, front of neck, and sides of nape white, bill stripe less prominent, and face darker. Unmarked, short bill on first-winter birds.

Similar Species The Razorbills' bulky flight shape distinguishes it strongly from sea ducks (beware Long-tailed Duck). It is similar to a Thick-billed Murre, but in winter it can be told by its large bill and paler face, with white extending well above and behind eye onto sides of nape. The Razorbill's facial plumage resembles a Common Murre in winter, but the Razorbill always has a much deeper bill. In summer, the Thick-billed has a prominent white gape stripe and the Common entirely lacks white marks on its bill. A first-winter Razorbill has a small bill and resembles a juvenile Thick-billed, but it has a pointed tail and more extensive white on its face. In flight at a distance, a Razorbill can be confused with a murre, but its bill is deeper (usually visible), white extends onto sides of rump, and its graduated tail is longer (surprisingly hard to see), with feet tucked underneath.

Voice Highly vocal near breeding colonies, giving a variety of harsh growling calls.

Status & Distribution Locally common at colonies in Gulf of St. Lawrence, NF, and Labrador. BREEDING: Variety of habitats, including rock crevices and cliff ledges on coastal islands. WINTER: Most of Atlantic population winters on Grand Banks and in Gulf of Maine. Occurs regularly to Long Island; rare off mid-Atlantic states. VAGRANT: Casual south as far as FL and inland on Great Lakes.

Population The Razorbill is the least common Atlantic alcid, having been depleted by drowning in gill nets, illegal hunting, and oil pollution; populations are now recovering.

GUILLEMOTS *Genus Cepphus*

Medium-size alcids, guillemots show a conspicuous white wing patch year-round. Thin necks and relatively small bills and heads make them look delicate. They fly low with shallow fluttering wingbeats, rather rounded wings, and a heavy-sterned appearance. They usually forage in shallow waters year-round, but some species move offshore in winter.

BLACK GUILLEMOT *Cepphus grylle*

The Black Guillemot's distinctive features include white, oval wing patches with a smooth outline and gleaming white underwings. Brilliant red feet set off a stunning black-and-white summer plumage. Agile on land, it stands upright and walks on tarsi and toes or on toes alone. Polytypic. L 13" (33 cm)

Identification Black and white; underwings white. Legs and feet bright red (pink in winter). Eyes dark brown; bill black with mouth interior red. BREEDING ADULT: Unmistakable. Complete-ly sooty black except for a broad, crisply defined white patch on the greater and lesser coverts and white underwings, excepting the tips of flight feathers. WINTER ADULT: Very different. Underparts, uppertail coverts, rump, neck, and head white, with sparse dusky streaking and mottling around eye, on crown, and on back of neck. Mantle, scapulars, and uppertail coverts variably mottled. Individuals with patchy, mixed breeding and winter plumage occur late fall and early spring.

arcticus

winter adult

breeding adult

JUVENILE: Similar to winter adult, but more extensively mottled with grey-brown overall; dull-colored feet.

Geographic Variation Five subspecies worldwide, 2 in North America. Variation is most notable in winter plumage. In N.A., the Arctic *mandtii* shows much whiter overall than the east coast breeding *arcticus*. There are 3 additional subspecies from Iceland, the Faroe Islands, and the Baltic Sea.

Similar Species In all plumages, the Black's distinctive upperwing patch separates it from all other alcids except the Pigeon Guillemot (in the northern Bering Sea, the small area of overlap); however, the Black lacks the dark bar seen in the Pigeon's patch. The Black's smaller size and faster wingbeat also may be useful identification cues to separate it from a Pigeon, as well as its white underwings and axillaries. A distant bird might be confused with a White-winged Scoter, but a Black Guillemot has faster wingbeats, a pear-shaped silhouette, and is smaller.

Voice A variety of peeping and thin high-pitched screams and whistles, given near breeding colonies.

Status & Distribution Common and widespread. BREEDING: Small colonies in rock crevices on low rocky islands and in coastal cliffs. MIGRATION: Most birds move only short distances from breeding areas. WINTER: Wherever ice-free water, even in high Arctic. Occurs regularly south to Long Island. VAGRANT: Casual on Atlantic coast south of New England and in AK south of the Bering Strait. Also casual inland (Great Lakes).

Population No trends are apparent.

arcticus

winter adult

juvenile

PIGEON GUILLEMOT *Cepphus columba*

This Pacific species is similar to the Black Guillemot, but it has a dark bar in its white wing patch. Like the Black, it is often seen from shore. It breeds in small colonies in crevices on low rocky islands and in coastal cliffs, sometimes under wharves, and forages in shallow waters year-round. Polytypic. L 13.5" (34 cm).

Identification Black and white. A conspicuous white wing patch has a black, wedge-shaped intrusion on its lower (or outer) edge. On a flying bird, the patches appear almost divided into 2 white crescents. Some birds, particularly in western Alaska, have an additional dark wing bar. The underwing, including underwing coverts, axillaries, and flight feathers, is uniformly dark. Eyes are dark brown; bill is black; mouth interior is bright red. Legs and feet are bright red (pink in winter). BREEDING ADULT: Plumage is completely sooty black except for the wing patch. WINTER ADULT: Very different. Underparts, uppertail coverts, neck, and head are white, with dusky streaking and mottling on face, on crown, and on back of neck. Individuals with patchy mixed summer and winter plumage occur late fall and early spring. JUVENILE: Similar to winter adult, but it is more extensively mottled with grey-brown overall and has dull grayish pink feet.

Geographic Variation Five subspecies worldwide; 4 in North America. Nominate *columba* (Bering Sea, coast and islands) and *kaiurka* (central and outer Aleutians) have more extensive dark feathering on their wing patches. Some authorities merge *eureka* (CA to OR) and *adianta* (WA to central Aleutians) with nominate *columba*. Extralimital *snowi* (Kuril Islands) is darkest, sometimes lacking white wing patches.

Similar Species In all plumages the Pigeon is distinguished from a Black Guillemot by its dark underwings and axillaries, and its oval wing patch always has a dark bar, which the Black lacks. In the northern Bering Sea, where it overlaps in distribution with the Black, its larger size and slower wingbeat might be apparent.

Voice A variety of thin high-pitched screams and whistles, normally given near breeding colonies.

Status & Distribution Common and widespread near rocky Pacific coastlines. BREEDING: In cavities under rocks and driftwood, and in cliff crevices. MIGRATION: Mostly resident, but retreats from areas of heavy ice in Bering Sea. WINTER: CA and OR populations apparently move north.

Population No trends are apparent.

juvenile

winter adult

winter adult

breeding adult

MURRELETS Genus *Brachyramphus*

These murrelets are unique among alcids in having a cryptic summer plumage, which camouflages them at their open solitary nests on tree limbs and mountaintops. In fall they molt into black-and-white plumage. A streamlined body form and long, slender wings give them a very fast, direct flight style. They lack agility on land and cannot stand upright.

LONG-BILLED MURRELET *Brachyramphus perdix*

winter

breeding adult

winter

This enigmatic Asian species has occurred as a vagrant in widespread, inland locations across North America and along the Pacific coast. In 1997, it was split from the very similar Marbled Murrelet. Monotypic. L 11.5" (29 cm)

Identification Like a large, long-billed Marbled Murrelet. In all plumages, underwing coverts whitish, eyes dark brown, and bill, legs, and feet black. BREEDING ADULT: Extensively mottled dark grayish brown overall except for

whitish throat, with the mantle feathers and scapulars thinly edged with buff. WINTER ADULT: Black-and-white plumage similar to that of murres, however, conspicuous white scapular patches contrast strongly with the otherwise dark upperparts. Blackish brown cap over most of the face to well below the eye. Nape, sides, and back of neck, mantle, rump, and upperwing coverts blackish, except for faint pale oval patch on side of nape. JUVENILE: Similar to winter adult, but dusky brownish barring on breast and flanks for months after fledging.

Similar Species Along the Pacific coast, the Long-billed must be carefully separated from a Marbled Murrelet. The Long-billed is 20 percent larger and has a longer and thinner bill. In winter, it has more extensive dark plumage on lores, nape, and back of neck—entirely lacking the pale collar of a winter Marbled. It also lacks the dark barring on the sides of the breast that forms a projecting bar in the Marbled

and has whitish underwings (dark in Marbled). The Long-billed's summer plumage is generally less rufous, more grayish brown overall than the Marbled's, with a whiter throat. All *Brachyramphus* murrelets show high seasonal variability in plumage; more study of variation in field characters is needed. Beware of confusing Long-billeds with guillemots (especially juveniles), which are larger and have longer bills and white wing patches.

Voice Needs study.

Status & Distribution Asian species. BREEDING: Northern Japan, Sea of Okhotsk, and Kamchatka Peninsula; nests in trees. MIGRATION: Highly migratory. WINTER: Normally near Japan. VAGRANT: Casual in N.A. (late summer–early winter) with more than 50 records. Has strayed as far as NF, MA, NC, and FL. Accidental in Europe (Switzerland). With increased observer awareness, a growing proportion of sightings are from the Pacific coast, but why this species occurs so widely far inland in N.A., while the Marbled Murrelet shows no inclination, is a remarkable unsolved mystery.

Population Trends are unknown.

MARBLED MURRELET *Brachyramphus marmoratus* (T)

The small, slender-bodied, fast-flying Marbled has a cryptic, speckled breeding plumage adapted to its atypical solitary nesting habits. At sea, it keeps its head tilted up and its tail cocked nearly vertical; its long-necked profile is accentuated by a shallow sloping forehead. It is fequently seen in "pairs" at sea. Monotypic. L 10" (25 cm)

Identification. Bill longish, slender and pointed. Wings narrow and pointed, seeming to blur with high wingbeat frequency; underwings blackish; tail entirely blackish year-round. Eyes dark brown; bill, legs, and feet black. BREEDING ADULT: Extensively mottled overall with dark chocolate brown. Mantle feathers thinly edged with rufous; scapulars fringed with white and rufous. Some birds paler with extensive white spotting—pairs often differing in plumage. WINTER ADULT:

Black and white, recalling a miniature murre. Blackish cap over most of the face to well below eye, except for a white loral spot. Neck and lower sides of nape white, giving a white-collared appearance, accentuated by dark barring on side of breast. Whitish scapulars contrast with dark upperparts. Some birds (presumably immatures) in winter-like plumage during sum-

mer; others intermediate between typical summer and winter coloration. JUVENILE: Similar to winter adult, but dusky brownish barring on breast and flanks for months after fledging.

Similar Species The buffy, breeding-plumaged Kittlitz's Murrelet has a paler, gray-brown mottling that does not extend onto the lower belly, vent, or undertail coverts and in all seasons shows a pale face with a contrasting dark eye, tiny bill, and hard-to-see white outer tail feathers.

juvenile

breeding adult

winter

The Kittlitz's also has a similar black-and-white winter plumage, but its black cap is more restricted, giving the impression of a much whiter face from a distance. An Ancient Murrelet lacks the white scapulars, shows more extensive black on the head and neck, and has bright white underwing coverts. **Voice** Easily identifiable, loud penetrating *keer* calls, especially at dusk, dawn, and at night near suitable nesting habitat. Noisy at sea, with a complex vocal repertoire.

Status & Distribution Locally common in AK and BC, less numerous south of Canada. BREEDING: South of AK in large old-growth stands, sometimes far inland. In coastal southern and southwestern AK on the ground on steep mountainsides. Often seen close to land, frequenting fjords, deep bays, saltwater lagoons, and even coastal

winter

breeding adult

lakes. MIGRATION: Some movement away from breeding areas; no evidence of long-distance migration. WINTER: Most birds remain near breeding areas, some movement offshore in winter. VAGRANT: Very rare to casual south of breeding range to northern Baja California. Apart from regular use of inland lakes near breeding areas, no confirmed records far inland. Formerly thought to be casual inland eastward to Great Lakes, but

most inland *Brachyramphus* records now confirmed or suspected to be Long-billeds.

Population Numbers are rapidly declining in the southern part of the breeding range due to the loss of old-growth nesting habitat. Salmon gill nets also pose a threat. The U.S. and Canada list the species as threatened. BirdLife International lists it as vulnerable.

KITTLITZ'S MURRELET *Brachyramphus brevirostris*

The Kittlitz's appears similar to a short-billed Marbled Murrelet—especially in wing and body shape and behavior—but it has a grayish breeding plumage and is more extensively white in winter. It is frequently seen in "pairs" at sea. Monotypic. L 9.5" (24 cm)

Identification Outer tail feathers white year-round. Underwing coverts dark brownish gray. Bill very short, almost invisible; eyes dark brown; bill, legs, and feet black. BREEDING ADULT: Buffy upperparts and breast extensively mottled with grayish brown; mantle feathers and scapulars thinly edged buff. Face pale, with distinct dark eye. Belly, vent, and undertail coverts white. WINTER ADULT: Black and white. Blackish cap restricted to crown and forehead only. Face, neck, and nape white, giving a white-headed appearance. Blackish barring across breast, forming a nearly complete band. Back blackish, slaty gray appearance in good light, with contrasting whitish scapulars. Some birds (presumably immatures) in winter-like plumage during summer, others intermediate between summer and winter plumage. JUVENILE: Similar to winter adult, but upperparts grayer, with dusky barring on breast and flanks for months after fledging.

Similar Species In breeding plumage, the Kittlitz's is similar to a Marbled Murrelet, but it has paler gray-brown mottling that does not extend onto the lower belly, vent, or undertail coverts, and in all seasons it shows a short bill

and a paler face with a contrasting dark eye. The white outer tail feathers are hard to see—beware of the white overlapping upper and undertail coverts on the Marbled. Dark underwings contrast more with pale underparts on the Kittlitz's than on the Marbled. An

winter

breeding adult

breeding adult

juvenile

winter

Ancient Murrelet lacks white scapulars, shows more extensive black on the head and neck, and has white underwing coverts.

Voice Typical call is a nasal grunt. Apparently less vocal than Marbled Murrelet.

Status & Distribution Uncommon to common, declining in N.A. BREEDING: Solitary ground-nester on high mountainsides among glaciers and snowbeds; often seen close to land, frequenting fjords, deep bays, and saltwater lagoons. MIGRATION: Some movement away from breeding areas; no evidence of long-distance migration. WINTER: Poorly known; many birds apparently winter offshore. VAGRANT: Accidental southwestern BC and southern CA.

Population Kittlitz's numbers are rapidly declining in southeast and south-central Alaska, possibly due to climate change and competition with hatchery-enhanced salmonid populations. It is likely the bird species most seriously affected by the massive *Exxon Valdez* oil spill in 1989; many birds also drown in salmon gill nets.

MURRELETS Genus *Synthliboramphus*

Of the 4 species in this genus, 2 warm-water species occur off California and Mexico, 1 is widespread in the North Pacific, and 1 is restricted to waters around Japan. All have slender bodies and relatively long, pointed wings. They lay a clutch of 2 eggs and take their precocial chicks to sea 2 days after hatching.

XANTUS'S MURRELET *Synthliboramphus hypoleucus*

Superficially, the small, slim, black-and-white Xantus's resembles a tiny murre. The Xantus's is difficult to approach in a boat and is able to leap directly into flight. It often flies directly away, but usually not for long distances. It is normally seen singly or in small groups at sea, sometimes with very young (flightless) chicks that must attempt to escape by diving. At night it is attracted, often fatally, to bright lights at sea. Sometimes it adopts a nearly horizontal posture on the water, with head held low. Like other *Synthliboramphus* murrelets, it lacks agility on land and cannot stand upright. Polytypic. L 9.8" (25 cm)
Identification It is black with a slight grayish cast above and white below. The black cap extends on face to gape, auricular area, nape, and back and sides of neck *(scrippsi)*. The underparts, including the sides of the breast, are immaculate white. The underwing coverts and the underside of the flight feathers are white. The eyes are dark

brown. The eye crescents are faint and whitish *(scrippsi)*. The slender, pointed bill is black. The gray legs and feet (with black webs) sit far back on the body. The wings are narrow and pointed; it flies with fast wingbeats. No seasonal variation. JUVENILE: Tiny, downy black-and-white chicks are taken out to sea (move away from breeding colonies) by adults at 2 days of age. Fully grown juveniles resemble adults.
Geographic Variation The California *scrippsi* has black lores and auricular area with faint white crescents above and below the eye. Nominate *hypoleucus* (rare in fall off CA), breeding on islands off west coast of Baja California, has more extensive white on its face, including lores, auricular area, and more prominent eye crescents.
Similar Species The Xantus's is only similar to a Craveri's Murrelet. The Xantus's has a slightly less extensive black cap, less extensive black on sides of breast, whitish underwings, and a shorter bill, all of which are difficult to see. The Xantus's is best identified at sea during the stereotyped comfort behavior in which it raises its body vertically and flaps its wings, showing pale underwings. A winter-plumaged Marbled Murrelet is black-and-white, but it is differently patterned and with

conspicuous white scapular patches.
Voice Vocal at sea. Typical call is a repeated twittering whistle, also high-pitched chips.
Status & Distribution Uncommon to rare. Never seen in numbers except when gathering near colonies during breeding season. BREEDING: Colonially on arid islands in rock crevices and under dense shrubs. DISPERSAL: Some movement north after breeding season, thus rare in late summer and fall in northern CA, OR, and WA. VAGRANT: Casual as far north as Queen Charlotte Sound, BC.
Population The species is listed as threatened in California—where populations have declined historically, mainly due to introduced predators (cats, rats) on breeding islands—and as vulnerable by BirdLife International.

CRAVERI'S MURRELET *Synthliboramphus craveri*

The Craveri's Murrelet, the very similar, but smaller Mexican sister species to Xantus's Murrelet, occurs as a rare

postbreeding visitor to California, where it is more regularly observed in warm-water years. Good looks are necessary to separate the Craveri's from the Xantus's. In California it is normally seen singly at sea. Like other murrelets,

it lacks agility on land and cannot stand upright. Monotypic. L 8.5" (22 cm)
Identification Black, with slight brownish cast above and white below. Black cap extends on face below gape onto throat immediately underneath bill. Auricular area, nape, and back and sides of neck are black, extending onto sides of lower breast and giving a partial collared appearance. There are faint white crescents above and below the eyes. The underparts, except the sides of the breast, are immaculate white. The underwing coverts and the under-

side of the flight feathers are dark brownish gray. The eyes are dark brown. The slender, pointed bill is black. The gray legs and feet (with black webs) sit far back on the body. The wings are narrow and pointed; it flies with fast wingbeats. No seasonal variation. JUVENILE: Tiny, downy black-and-white chicks taken to sea by adults at 2 days of age. Fully grown juveniles resemble adults.

Similar Species It is similar only to the Xantus's Murrelet. The Craveri's has a more extensive black cap, black on sides of breast forming a partial collar, blackish to grayish underwings (sometimes with a whitish center, but never as white as that of the Xantus's), and a relatively longer and thinner bill—all

difficult to see. It is best identified at sea during wing-raising behavior. All black-and-white murrelets off the West coast require close scrutiny to confirm identification: A Marbled is differently patterned black-and-white in winter, with conspicuous white scapular patches; an Ancient has a short pale bill, lacks white scapulars, and shows more extensive blue-gray upperparts.

Voice Vocal at sea. Typical call is apparently a cicada-like rattle, rising to reedy trilling when agitated; also high-pitched chips.

Status & Distribution Generally rare. BREEDING: Nests colonially on arid islands off both sides of Baja California, in rock crevices and under dense shrubs. DISPERSAL: Some movement

north after breeding season, thus rare in late summer and fall off southern and central CA, especially in El Niño years. VAGRANT: Casual as far north as WA.

Population Introduced predators (cats, rats) threaten breeding populations on islands, depleting their numbers.

ANCIENT MURRELET *Synthliboramphus antiquus*

The Ancient is a strikingly marked, active, social murrelet with strictly nocturnal activity ashore at breeding colonies. Like other *Synthliboramphus* murrelets, it has an elongate cylindrical body and narrow, pointed wings. In flight, it holds its head above the plane of its body during taking off and maneuvering; it tumbles abruptly into sea when alighting. It flies with fast wingbeats. It normally stays in small groups offshore, sometimes coming close to land in bays and harbors. On water, it often appears neckless and flat-crowned. It lacks agility on land and cannot stand upright. Monotypic. L 10" (25 cm)

Identification Ornate. Entire back, rump, uppertail coverts, and upperwing coverts are blue-gray, contrasting with jet-black flanks and hood and immaculate white underparts. The distinctive short, laterally compressed bill has a black base and yellowish pink tip. The eyes are dark brown. Legs and feet gray (with black webs) sit far back on body. BREEDING ADULT: The black hood extends across the upper breast, form-

breeding adult

breeding adult

immature

winter adult

ing a distinctive bib that contrasts with the white sides of the neck. Variable, silvery white plumes edge the crown and nape (hence the name Ancient), with a second narrow band of similar plumes crossing the upper back from the sides of the breast. The underwing coverts are white. WINTER ADULT: White plumes on crown and upper back are reduced, and black bib is smaller, less distinct with light flecking or barring. JUVENILE: Tiny, gray-and-white downy chicks are taken to sea by adults at 2 days of age. Fully grown juveniles resemble winter adults, but bib is less distinct.

Similar Species The Ancient is easily identified by its size, shape, and coloration. Marbled and Kittlitz's Murrelets have different bill shapes; show distinct black-and-white appearance in winter, dark underwings, white scapular patches; and lack the black bib.

Voice Vocal at sea, typically a loud *chirrup*. A varied repertoire of chattering, chip, and harsh calls given nocturnally at breeding colony. In British Columbia, males give elaborate song-like vocal displays from tree perches.

Status & Distribution Common, especial-

ly when gathering near breeding colonies and at favored wintering areas. BREEDING: Colonially on predator-free islands in earth burrows (rarely rock crevices) on forested (BC and southeast AK) and grassy (Aleutian Islands) slopes. MIGRATION: Some movement south after breeding season. WINTER: Generally rare but regular off WA, OR, and northern CA; very rare and irregular to southern CA. VAGRANT: Casual inland on large lakes in late fall and winter, east to MA and as far south as LA, but most records are from the northern tier of states, many centered around the Great Lakes. Accidental off northwestern Baja California. One record from U.K.

Population Numbers are declining drastically due to introduced predators (rats, raccoons, foxes) on breeding islands. The population is recovering rapidly in the Aleutian Islands owing to the removal of foxes. Raccoons and rats seriously threaten the population in the Queen Charlotte Islands, British Columbia. Canada lists it as a species of special concern.

AUKLETS Genera *Ptychoramphus* and *Aethia*

The 5 small alcids in these genera have chunky bodies and short wings; they are not agile on land. Most species are restricted to the Bering Sea and attend colonies (some of millions of birds) in daylight; the Cassin's Auklet is more widespread and nocturnal. All species are planktivorous and raise a single chick to full-size in a crevice or burrow.

CASSIN'S AUKLET *Ptychoramphus aleuticus*

adults

The Cassin's is a medium-size, short-necked auklet with a dull plumage that remains fairly uniform at all ages and seasons. Its flight appears weak; it usually takes off from sea with difficulty at the approach of a vessel. Strictly nocturnal at breeding colonies, the Cassin's otherwise seldom comes close to land. Its short legs are placed relatively far back on the body, so it has a forward-leaning posture and clumsy gait on land. Monotypic. L 9" (23 cm)
Identification Dark brownish gray, except for white or grayish white belly and undertail coverts. Face and crown slightly darker than rest of upperparts. Small white crescents above (larger) and below (smaller) each eye. Black bill

larger relative to other auklets' bills; triangular in profile with a straight or even slightly concave culmen, a sharp-pointed tip, and a broad base, with a pale gray base to lower mandible. White eyes. Blue-gray feet with blackish webs. JUVENILE: Very similar to adult, but brown or brownish gray eyes.
Similar Species The Cassin's pale lower mandible, white iris, and white eye crescents are visible only at close range. It co-occurs with the Ancient Murrelet, which differs greatly in shape (relatively long pointed wings and slender body) and coloration, and with the Rhinoceros Auklet, which is much larger and has a massive, usually light-colored bill. Near the Aleutians, the Cassin's may be seen with other similar auklets. The Cassin's relatively large pointed bill, dull coloration, and chunky body shape are good marks. The Whiskered Auklet is smaller and darker (nearly black), and its red bill is much shorter. The Crested Auklet is larger and evenly dark colored, and has longer, more pointed wings and a blunt, orange bill. The Parakeet Auklet is also larger, shows a bright red bill, and has a more contrasting dark-gray and white body coloration.

Voice Not vocal at sea, but sometimes makes a grating *krrrk* when alarmed. A variety of loud, nocturnal, grating screeches from burrows and grassy slopes of breeding colonies.
Status & Distribution Common, the most widespread auklet. BREEDING: Colonially on predator-free islands in earth burrows (also rock crevices). DISPERSAL: Moves offshore during non-breeding season. WINTER: Mostly offshore, near breeding areas. Some southward movement along west coast. VAGRANT: No inland records.
Population Once decimated by introduced predators (rats, foxes), the Cassin's is now recovering rapidly in the Aleutians since the removal of foxes. Rats and raccoons still threaten the species in British Columbia.

PARAKEET AUKLET *Aethia psittacula*

One of the larger auklets, the Parakeet is vaguely cootlike, with a chunky body shape, long neck, rounded wings, and relatively large feet. It breeds in small colonies. At sea it is normally seen singly or in small groups. Its wings appear broad and rounded compared to other auklets; its flight is strong and direct. Monotypic. L 10" (25 cm)
Identification Blackish above and white below; minimal seasonal variation. Bill bright red, with oval upper mandible and upcurved lower mandible. White eyes, giving face a blank expression. Underwing dark gray. Large bluish gray feet with a greenish tinge and black webbing. BREEDING ADULT: Upperparts blackish gray, with blackish barring variably extending onto throat, neck, and upper breast, so when

resting on sea can appear dark overall. Slender white plumes extend from behind eye. WINTER ADULT: Underparts uniformly white, extending onto center of breast and throat. Bill dull-colored, white facial plumes reduced. JUVENILE: Similar to winter adult, but blackish bill and grayish blue eyes.

dark

juvenile

breeding adults

Similar Species Unmistakable when observed ashore, where facial ornaments and bill shape are visible. In the Gulf of Alaska (off southeastern AK and coastal BC), the Parakeet could be mistaken for a Rhinoceros Auklet, which has a longer, pointed bill, a less chunky body shape, and more blended (not black-and-white) plumage. The Parakeet somewhat resembles a Least Auk-

let, but it is twice as large. It is closest in size to a Crested Auklet, but it is easily distinguished by its white underparts and rounded wings. In flight, it resembles the Least and Cassin's Auklets, but size, bill shape, slower wingbeat, lack of white scapulars, and broader wings are useful characters. Compared to a Dovekie, it has broad wings, slow, fluttery wingbeats, and prominent red bill. **Voice** Highly vocal. At sea, bird taking flight gives a short high-pitched squeal. At colony, bird gives repetitive high-pitched whinnying calls.
Status & Distribution Locally common on Bering Sea and south-central AK islands. BREEDING: Colonially in rock crevices, often along clifftops. MIGRATION: Moves south to avoid winter ice in Bering Sea, dispersing farther offshore than other auklets.

WINTER: Most birds well offshore in North Pacific, regularly to latitude of central CA. VAGRANT: Casual in winter near coast from BC to CA. Accidental in HI and Europe (Sweden).
Population No trends are apparent.

breeding adult

winter adults

LEAST AUKLET *Aethia pusilla*

light

breeding adults

dark

breeding adults

winter adults

juvenile

The Least Auklet is a tiny, chubby alcid, barely larger than a sparrow. Gregarious, active, and noisy, it breeds in a few large colonies. Although capable of rapid takeoff from sea, it flies in a characteristic side-to-side weaving style. On land, it stands erect, usually on its toes; it is very agile on rocky breeding habitat. Monotypic. L 6.3" (16 cm)
Identification Polymorphic. Variable seasonally. Short, rounded wings. Upperparts blackish with white patches on scapulars. Underwing coverts pale. Bill small, nearly black to bright red with a black base, usually with a straw-colored tip; small knob-shaped bill ornament on adult. White eyes. Bluish gray feet with black webbing. BREEDING ADULT: Underparts variably marked with irregular dark spotting, from almost black to nearly unmarked white,

throat white with small black chin, scapulars variably white. Short, evenly scattered, white plumes on forehead, extending onto crown and lores and from behind eye. WINTER ADULT: Underparts uniformly white; no ornaments (bill black, no bill knob, only a trace of white facial plumes); and white scapular patches more prominent. JUVENILE: Similar to winter adult, but eyes grayish and scapulars less white. IMMATURE: Brown forehead with sparse plumes. Dull colored bill and smaller bill knob than breeding adult. Usually heavily spotted throat.
Similar Species The Least's tiny size and dumpy body shape easily eliminates all other alcids, except other auklets. The Least usually shows white scapulars, which are lacking in all other auklets. It is closest in size to the Whiskered Auklet, which is blacker, slightly larger, has somewhat longer wings, and shows pale feathering only on vent (only the darkest Leasts approach the

Whiskered's dark coloration). Superficially, the Least is most similar to the Parakeet Auklet, which is much larger and has slower wingbeat.
Voice Highly vocal. At sea, bird taking flight gives a short high-pitched squeak. At colony gives a variety of high-pitched, high-frequency chattering.
Status & Distribution Locally abundant in Bering Sea. BREEDING: Nests colonially in rock crevices on boulder beaches, talus slopes, boulder fields, lava flows, and cliffs. MIGRATION: Moves south to avoid winter ice in Bering Sea. WINTER: Poorly known, probably well offshore. VAGRANT: Rare inland in western AK in late fall and winter after storms. Accidental in Arctic Canada and on West Coast south of AK (1 rec. from central CA).
Populations No trends are apparent. Introduced rats at Kiska Island threaten the species' largest colony.

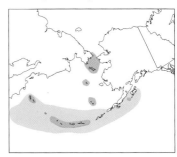

WHISKERED AUKLET *Aethia pygmaea*

Although relatively small—only the Least Auklet is smaller—the Whiskered Auklet is perhaps the most ornamented, living seabird while in breeding plumage. This sought-after species is most often seen at sea, where it flocks together in tidal rips near colonies. Its wings are relatively pointed, allowing for a strong and direct flight style. It breeds at many small colonies throughout the Aleutian Islands, where activity is mainly nocturnal. On land, it has a forward-tilting posture. Monotypic (Asian ssp. *camtschatica* is sometimes recognized). L 7.8" (20 cm)

Identification Uniformly dark appearance on water. Upperparts blue-black; underparts blackish gray, except for the light gray or whitish lower belly and vent. Flight feathers blackish; underwing coverts dark gray. White eyes. Bluish gray legs and toes, with black webbing. BREEDING ADULT: Unmistakable at colonies. A slender, highly variable, forward-curving black forehead crest, and white facial plumes including a showy V-shaped, antenna-like

ornament originating on the lores, and long, white auricular plumes—all difficult to observe at sea. Bright red bill with a straw-colored tip. Although bird appears small and black at sea, white vent is visible when bird takes flight. WINTER ADULT: Identical to the summer (breeding) plumage, but ornaments much reduced and the bill a dull red. JUVENILE: Similar to a winter adult, but feather ornaments absent, bluish gray eyes, and a blackish bill.

Similar Species The Whiskered most resembles the Crested Auklet, which is larger and grayer above with a more prominent bill. The Crested is the only other small alcid that is similarly dark in overall coloration, but it lacks whitish vent region. The Whiskered is closest in size to the Least and Cassin's Auklets, which have whiter underparts and dumpier body shapes. Compared to the Least, the Whiskered lacks white on the scapulars and underparts.

Voice Highly vocal. At sea and at breeding colonies, gives a thin kittenlike *mew*. At breeding colony, gives a variety of high-pitched mewing and trilling calls.

Status & Distribution Locally common on Aleutian Is. only. BREED-

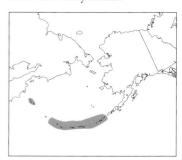

breeding adults

ING: Colonially in rock crevices on coastal cliffs, beach boulders, and talus slopes on predator-free islands. DISPERSAL: Resident near breeding islands. WINTER: Mostly in large flocks in Aleutian inter-island passes. VAGRANT: In AK, casual outside of breeding range.

Population Once decimated by introductions of exotic mammalian predators onto Aleutian Islands, the species is now recovering since the removal of foxes from many islands.

breeding adult

winter adult

juvenile

winter adult

CRESTED AUKLET *Aethia cristatella*

breeding adult

1st summer

juvenile

winter adult

The extremely gregarious Crested occurs in large flocks year-round; it is rarely seen alone. It breeds in a few large colonies on Bering Sea islands. Its wings are relatively long and pointed compared to other auklets; its flight is strong and direct. On land, it stands erect and is very agile. It has a distinctive citrus-like plumage odor, which is sometimes noticeable at sea.

Monotypic. L 9" (23 cm)

Identification Uniformly dark. White eyes. Legs and toes bluish gray; black webbing. BREEDING ADULT: Spectacularly ornamented. Bright orange bill with peculiar, curved gape plates, white auricular plumes, and forward-curving, black forehead crest. Larger, more strongly hooked bills on males, thus the sexes are distinguishable in the field,

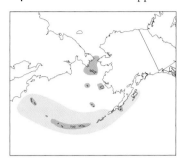

breeding adult

winter adult

unlike other alcids. WIN-TER ADULT: Bill plates shed during breeding season, leaving a small dull orange bill by late summer. Black crest and white plumes reduced. JUVE-NILE: Similar to winter adult, but black-ish bill, tiny crest, and bluish gray eyes. **Similar Species** The Crested most resembles the Whiskered Auklet, which is smaller, blacker above, and shows pale feathering on belly and vent, as does the Cassin's Auklet. The Crested is closest

in size to the Parakeet Auklet, which has white underparts, a chunkier body shape, and less pointed wings. It is often seen with Least Auklets, which are much smaller and usually show white on scapulars and underparts. Compare first-summer birds, with reduced bill and feather ornaments, to Whiskered. **Voice** Highly vocal. At sea, gives a sharp bark like the yap of a small dog. At breeding colony, gives a variety of trumpeting, cackling, and hooting calls. **Status & Distribution** Locally abundant in Bering Sea. BREEDING: Colonially in rock crevices and caves on talus slopes, lava flows, and cliffs on volcanic islands. MIGRATION: Moves south to avoid heavy ice in Bering Sea. WINTER: Mostly in a

few food-rich Aleutian passes. VAGRANT: Rare in Gulf of Alaska east of Kodiak I.; casual inland in western AK and along West Coast to northwestern Baja California. Accidental to Iceland. **Population** No trends are apparent.

PUFFINS & RHINOCEROS AUKLET Genera *Cerorhinca* and *Fratercula*

Puffins (3 sp.) are medium-size alcids with big heads, elaborate facial ornamentation, and short, rounded wings. The Rhinoceros Auklet has attributes intermediate between puffins and auklets. All are colonial and carry multiple fish externally in their bill to a single chick, which is raised to full-size in a burrow or rock crevice.

RHINOCEROS AUKLET *Cerorhinca monocerata*

immature

winter adult

breeding adult

winter adult

Although related to the puffins, this alcid's body shape, different facial ornaments, and posture give it an auklet-like appearance. Often seen in large numbers close to shore, it is nocturnal or crepuscular at colonies. On land, it walks with a clumsy horizontal gait. Monotypic. L 15" (38 cm)
Identification Upperparts grayish brown with faint paler barring. Underparts similar with indistinct grayish brown barring, except for whitish belly and undertail coverts. Yellowish eyes. Dull yellowish legs and feet. BREEDING ADULT: Two sets of prominent, somewhat unkempt-looking, white facial plumes, 1 extending from gape, the other from above the eye. Thick, dagger-shaped, orange bill, with decurved culmen, and single, whitish "rhino" horn at the base. WINTER ADULT: Very similar, but facial plumes much reduced or almost absent. Bill horn shed in fall, leaving birds with smaller, dull orange

bill with blackish base. JUVENILE: Similar to winter adult, but no head plumes, darker eyes, and smaller, shallower bill, blackish initially, gradually changing to dull yellowish orange.
Similar Species The Rhinoceros recalls a murre as much as a puffin, having a smaller head and more symmetrical body than a puffin. The larger Tufted Puffin lacks white underparts in all seasons, but compare with paler form of a juvenile Tufted, which can show a pale belly. The Horned Puffin always has pure white underparts. In direct flight, the Rhinoceros appears somewhat like a grayish and white murre, but its head and bill are proportionately larger. Both Pacific puffins look much bigger headed and more front-heavy in flight. The Cassin's Auklet is smaller and paler with a dumpier body shape, has a more wobbly flight style, and is less approachable.

Voice At and near breeding colony at night, gives sonorous *arr-aarrrgh* calls. **Status & Distribution** Common and widespread along west coast. BREEDING: Colonially in earth burrows on grassy and forested slopes of predator-free offshore islands. Center of breeding abundance is BC; also breeds in Japan. MIGRATION: Moves south along west coast Sept.–Oct.; returns to breeding colonies Mar.–Apr. WINTER: Along entire west coast, regularly south to southern Baja California. VAGRANT: Casual near central Bering Sea islands in summer.
Population No trends are apparent.

ATLANTIC PUFFIN *Fratercula arctica*

This medium-size, large-headed Atlantic alcid has a remarkably ornamented face and bill. It flies direct, and it easily lands on and takes off from flat ground. Very agile on land, it stands erect and on toes, rather than on tarsi like most large auks; it walks with a hunched posture. Its short neck and heavy, rounded body give it an overall chubby appearance. Polytypic (3 ssp.; nominate in N.A.) L 12.5" (32 cm)
Identification Upperparts blackish with lighter-colored facial "disk," black neck collar; underparts immaculate white. Deep, laterally compressed bill with multiple concentric grooves (1–5, increasing with age). BREEDING ADULT: Colorful bill with dark bluish gray crescent-shaped base outlined with pale yellow stripes, the remainder bright reddish orange. Pale orange rictal rosettes at gape. Dark eye surrounded by thin red eye ring, within a clownlike triangular dark gray wattle. Bright reddish orange legs and feet. White facial disks with silvery gray clouding, upperparts silky black fading to brownish black during breeding season. Dark faces and winter-type bills on some (first-summer?) birds.

Second- and third-summer birds have less brightly colored, more triangle-shaped bills with fewer grooves, and duller orange feet, compared to adults. Leucistic birds occur. WINTER ADULT: Very similar to breeding plumage, but bill plates, rosette, and eye ornaments shed in fall, leaving birds with smaller, dull reddish bill with constricted base and blackish face. Feet yellowish or orange-brown. JUVENILE: Similar to winter adult, but bill black, gradually changing to dull reddish, smaller, much shallower and daggerlike.
Geographic Variation Northward cline of increasing body size.
Similar Species Unmistakable in summer. In winter, its dirty blackish face, blackish underwings, short, triangular bill, and front-heavy flight shape, resulting from its large head and short neck, distinguish it from murres and guillemots. Superficially, it is similar to the much smaller Dovekie, which has a weaving flight style and a very short, stubby bill.
Voice At breeding colony, gives a variety of low sonorous growling calls, mostly from within burrows.

breeding adult

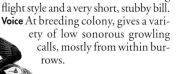

breeding adult

winter adult

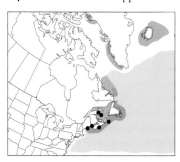

juvenile

Status & Distribution Locally abundant in Atlantic Canada. BREEDING: Colonially in burrow networks on grassy slopes of offshore islands. MIGRATION: Moves south out of Arctic Sept.–Oct.; returns to breeding areas in late Apr. WINTER: Offshore to Grand Banks, far off Canadian Maritime provinces. VAGRANT: Rare in coastal waters south to New England, casual south of VA and inland on Great Lakes.
Population No trends are apparent.

HORNED PUFFIN *Fratercula corniculata*

The Horned Puffin is a sister species to the Atlantic Puffin, only it is larger, with even more exaggerated bill and facial ornaments. Its flight is direct, typically high (50–150 ft.) above the sea surface, and its feet are prominent. Agile on land, it stands erect and on toes, walking with a forward-hunched posture. Its short neck and heavy, rounded body give it an overall stocky appearance. Monotypic. L 15" (38 cm)
Identification Upperparts blackish; underparts immaculate white. Bill very large and deep, laterally compressed. BREEDING ADULT: Bill mostly bright lemon yellow with bright reddish orange tip. Pale orange rosettes at gape. Dark eye surrounded by thin red eye

ring, within clownlike black wattle that includes a "horn" extending vertically from top of eye. Gleaming white facial disks, upperparts satiny black fading to brownish black during breeding season. Dark faces and winter-type bills on a few birds at colonies. Bright reddish orange legs

and feet. Second- and third-summer birds have shallower, triangular bills, and duller orange feet, compared to older birds. WINTER ADULT: Bill plates, rosette, and eye ornaments shed in fall, leaving bill with smaller dull, greenish brown base, reddish tip, and grotesquely constricted

juvenile

winter adult

breeding adult

base. Plumage relatively unchanged, but face becomes grayer, sooty black on lores. Yellowish or orange-brown legs and feet. JUVENILE: Similar to winter adult, but bill black, gradually changing to dull reddish, smaller, much shallower, and more daggerlike. **Similar Species** The Horned Puffin is unmistakable in summer. In winter, its large head and short neck produce a front-heavy flight shape, which together with its dirty blackish face, blackish underwings, and triangular bill, identify it as a puffin. The larger Tufted Puffin lacks pure white underparts in all seasons. The Rhinoceros Auklet also lacks pure white underparts, being more indistinctly mottled grayish

brown except for whitish belly; it also has a smaller head and more symmetrical body shape in flight.
Voice At breeding colony, gives low sonorous growling calls, mostly from within breeding crevices.
Status & Distribution Abundant and widespread in western AK; locally common in southeastern and south-central AK; rare breeder in BC. BREEDING: Colonially in rock crevices (less commonly in earth burrows) on cliffs and rocky slopes of remote islands. MIGRATION: Moves out of northern Bering Sea Sept.–Oct., disperses widely offshore into N. Pacific; returns May–June. WINTER: Almost entirely far offshore in N. Pacific, south to latitude

of CA. VAGRANT: Casual, mainly in late spring, along west coast to southern CA. Casual in summer along Arctic coast east of Barrow, AK. Casual in HI. Accidental inland.
Population No trends are apparent.

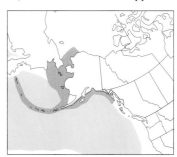

TUFTED PUFFIN *Fratercula cirrhata*

juvenile

juvenile

winter adult

breeding adult

The large, dark Tufted Puffin has a huge bill and spectacular golden-blond head tufts in summer. It takes flight from sea with difficulty, sometimes paddling across surface with wings, feet trailing, to escape approaching vessels; once airborne, though, its flight is direct, typically high (50–150 ft.) above the sea surface, and its feet are very prominent. Its huge head, short neck, and heavy body give it a burly appearance. Social on land, it breeds in large colonies. Agile on land, it stands erect and on toes, walking with a forward-hunched posture. Monotypic. L 16" (40 cm)
Identification Entirely sooty brownish black except for pale face. Deep, laterally compressed bill, with deep grooves (2–4, increasing with age). Yellowish white eyes; red eye ring. BREEDING ADULT: Colorful bill, the basal half olive green, the remainder bright reddish orange, and orange gape rosettes. Face gleaming white, with long, blond, tuft-

like plumes that curve backward. Plumage fades to brownish black during season. Second- and third-summer birds have shallower bills with fewer grooves, and duller orange feet. WINTER ADULT: Bill plates, rosette, and eye ornaments shed in fall, leaving bill with smaller blackish base, reddish tip, and grotesquely constricted base. Plumage similar to breeding, but head completely blackish, except for hint of pale buff behind eyes and along rear edges of crown. JUVENILE: Similar to winter adult, but underparts not as dark, with indistinct light brown areas on belly and throat (variable). Bill blackish, changing to dull orange, smaller than winter adult's.
Similar Species The Tufted Puffin is unmistakable in summer. In winter, its huge head and heavy body create a ponderous, front-heavy flight shape, which together with its dirty blackish face, blackish underwings, and triangular

bill, identify it as a puffin. The smaller Horned Puffin has a crisp black-and-white body in all seasons. The Rhinoceros Auklet also has whitish underparts, but it is paler and more grayish brown overall than a juvenile Tufted; it also has a smaller head and a more symmetrical body shape in flight.
Voice At colony, gives low sonorous growling calls, most from burrows.
Status & Distribution Abundant and widespread breeder in western AK; locally common in south-central and southeast AK and BC; uncommon to rare and local south to CA. BREEDING: Colonially in earth burrows (less commonly rock crevices) on grassy slopes and vegetated cliffs of remote islands. MIGRATION: Moves out of N. Bering Sea in Oct., disperses offshore mainly into N. Pacific; returns May–June. WINTER: Mostly offshore, less pelagic than Horned Puffin. VAGRANT: Accidental in HI. Single specimen from ME, apparently shot during winter of 1831–32 (accepted by AOU), used by J. J. Audubon to paint illustration in his *Birds of North America*.
Population Decreasing in California, otherwise no trends are apparent.

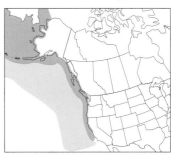

PIGEONS AND DOVES Family Columbidae

Inca Dove (TX, Mar.)

Species in this family are familiar to birders and non-birders alike. The larger species are usually called pigeons, the smaller ones doves; there is no scientific or taxonomic distinction between the 2 groups. Pigeons and doves feed chiefly on grains, seeds, and fruits. Nests are usually flimsy structures, and most clutches are limited to 2 white eggs.

Structure This group varies in size from the huge crowned-pigeons of New Guinea to the towhee-size ground-doves of the Americas. Most are plump with short, round-tipped wings and have tails varying from short and square-tipped to long and pointed. All have small rounded heads, and virtually all have short legs and similarly shaped short bills.

Behavior Pigeons and doves are strong, fast fliers (although a few species fill a terrestrial role in dense jungles and fly less frequently); only a few species are long-distance migrants, but many disperse randomly in search of food. While most eat various forms of vegetable matter—primarily seeds and fruit, but also leaves and flowers—some species have been known to eat invertebrates, such as worms or insect larvae. The species covered herein feed primarily on the ground; many species in other parts of the world are arboreal. Their nest-building skills seem poor, but such untidy nests, usually appearing to be little more than several sticks connecting tree branches, might allow them to rebuild quickly in the event of a nesting failure.

Plumage Pigeons and doves vary in color from the near patternless grays of some Old World pigeons to the highly patterned oranges and greens of fruit-doves.

Many species show iridescence on the hind neck; many also show a pinkish suffusion to the underparts. Most juveniles have pale-fringed feathers and lack the neck markings of adults. Some species have spectacular head plumage, such as elaborate crests and long, pointed feathers.

Distribution Except for Antarctica, pigeons and doves are present on all continents, with the greatest variety in the tropics. Most are found in woodlands varying from open to dense, but members of this family have evolved to exploit habitats from rather barren deserts to sea cliffs and areas near the tree line in high mountain ranges.

Taxonomy As with all large families, the taxonomy is in a constant state of change, evident from the fact that the AOU as recently as 2003 recognized the "splitting" of the American pigeons, *Patagioenas,* from the Old World pigeons, *Columba.* About 310 species in 40 genera are recognized worldwide, with 20 species in 8 genera recorded in the United States and Canada.

Conservation Almost a third of the world's pigeons and doves are threatened to some degree, with a few already extinct. Predators, particularly rats, threaten island species, such as some of the fruit-doves or large terrestrial pigeons, which evolved with little competition and few natural enemies. Wholesale clearing and fragmentation of forests eliminates cover and food for many species, though a few may benefit. Overhunting, for food and for sport, has played a major role in some extinctions, such as the extermination of the Passenger Pigeon. Surprisingly, trapping for the pet trade appears to have little or no impact. —*Guy McCaskie*

OLD WORLD PIGEONS Genus *Columba*

ROCK PIGEON *Columba livia*

This highly variable city pigeon is familiar to all urban dwellers. Multicolored birds were developed over centuries of near domestication. Polytypic (12 ssp.; nominate in N.A.). L 12.5" (32 cm)
Identification A medium-size compact pigeon with long wings and a short tail. Birds most closely resembling their wild ancestors are gray with head and neck darker than back, and a prominent white rump. Black tips on the greater coverts and secondaries form bold black bars on inner wing, and there is a broad black terminal band on the tail. ADULT MALE: Metallic green and purple iridescence on the neck and breast; iris orange to red; orbital skin blue-gray; bill grayish black; and feet dark red. ADULT FEMALE: Like male, but iridescence on neck and breast

more restricted and subdued. JUVENILE: Generally browner, lacks iridescence; orbital skin and feet gray.
Voice CALL: A soft *coo-cuk-cuk-cuk-cooo*.
Status & Distribution The Rock Pigeon was introduced from Europe by early settlers; it is now widespread and common throughout the U.S. and southern Canada, particularly in urban settings. Gregarious and forming large flocks, it feeds on handouts and grains during the day in city parks and open fields; roosts on buildings at night.

Flocks or otherwise displaced pigeons can be found far from civilization. BREEDING: Nest is loosely constructed of twigs and leaves, primarily on structures such as window ledges, bridges, and in barns; has 2 white eggs.
Population Primarily associated with human development and dependent on people for food and shelter.

color variations

AMERICAN PIGEONS Genus *Patagioenas*

SCALY-NAPED PIGEON *Patagioenas squamosa*

A large dark pigeon of the West Indies, with two historical records in North America; larger than a Rock Pigeon. Monotypic. L 13.8" (35 cm)
Identification This species appears entirely dark slate-gray when seen perched or in flight from a distance; there are no obvious markings on the

adult ♂

wings or tail. ADULT MALE: Head and upper breast dark maroon; the feathers on the sides of the neck are more reddish, tipped black, forming diagonal lines and creating the scaled appearance that gives this species its name. Iris orange red; orbital skin orange; bill dark red with pale yellowish tip; and feet dark red. ADULT FEMALE: Same as male, but slightly subdued. JUVENILE: Duller with rusty-brown fringes on scapulars.
Similar Species The White-crowned Pigeon is slightly smaller, a little darker, and normally shows white on the head; however, the white on young birds is reduced, and washed with grayish brown, so could be overlooked. The Red-billed Pigeon is similar, also with a red-based, 2-toned bill. But Red-billed lacks any trace of the dark-edged nape feathers, and the ranges of the 2 species are widely separated.

Voice CALL: An emphatic *cruu, cruu-cru-cruuu*, the first syllable soft with a pause before the last three syllables, which sound like "who are you?"
Status & Distribution A resident, primarily arboreal, throughout much of the West Indies and islands off the north coast of Venezuela, but absent from the Greater Antilles, and now uncommon to rare in Cuba. Occurs individually or in small flocks. BREEDING: Nest is loosely built of twigs lined with grass and found in trees, including palms, but occasionally on the ground. Usually has 1 white egg. VAGRANT: Single birds collected at Key West, FL, Oct 24, 1896, and May 6, 1929, are the only 2 recorded in N.A.
Population While some have adapted to more urban areas, the overall population is declining, with threats of local extinctions, due to deforestation and intensive hunting.

WHITE-CROWNED PIGEON *Patagioenas leucocephala*

The White-crowned Pigeon is the large, dark pigeon seen in the Florida Everglades and Florida Keys. Flocks of varying sizes commute daily from nesting colonies in coastal mangroves to feed inland, at times flying many miles. Monotypic. L 13.5" (34 cm)

Identification A large, square-tailed slate-black pigeon with a conspicuous white crown. ADULT MALE: Crown is pure white; the sides of the neck are iridescent green merging into an iridescent purple on the hind neck. The iris is whitish, with pale blue-gray orbital skin. The bill is dark reddish with a white tip; feet are dull red. ADULT FEMALE: Like male, but slightly duller. JUVENILE: Browner; rusty brown fringes on coverts and scapulars. The white on the crown is reduced and washed with grayish brown; it can be difficult to see at times. The iris is brownish, with brownish gray orbital skin.

Similar Species Some Rock Pigeons can appear black, but will normally show white on the rump and lack white on the crown.

Voice CALL: A loud, deep *coo-cura-coo,* or *whoo-ca-cooo* repeated several times; a soft *coo-crooo* is believed to be given from the nest.

Status & Distribution Fairly common, but declining throughout the West Indies and the east coast of the Yucatan Peninsula. In Florida, a fairly common resident in the Keys and Everglades. Casual north to St. Lucie and Lee Counties. BREEDING: A colonial nester. Nest is a loose platform of twigs, normally in mangroves, but sometimes in dry scrub and trees, and occasionally on the ground; bears 1 or 2 white eggs. VAGRANT: A sight record for TX.

Population This species is declining dramatically throughout much of the West Indies due to clearing of hardwood forests, severe overhunting, harvesting of nestlings for food, and introduced predators.

RED-BILLED PIGEON *Patagioenas flavirostris*

The Red-billed Pigeon is the large, all-dark pigeon seen flying in pairs or in small groups along the Rio Grande in southern Texas. Polytypic (4 ssp.; nominate in N.A.). L 14.5" (37 cm)

Identification The species generally appears entirely dark when seen from any distance. ADULT MALE: The head, neck, most of the underparts, and lesser wing coverts are dark maroon; the rest of the plumage is dark blue-gray, with a blackish tail. Narrow, pale-gray tips on the greater coverts form a thin, indistinct wing stripe that might be visible in flight. The iris is reddish orange, with bordering red orbital skin. The bill is pale yellow, or whitish with a dark red at base. The feet are dark red. ADULT FEMALE: The female's coloring is similar to the male's, but generally duller. JUVENILE: Like the female, but its maroon feathering is rustier and paler.

Similar Species Within its expected area of occurrence, there are no likely identification problems. Other Columbids do not have the rather uniform blue-gray plumage, as they have bars on the secondaries or tail. In addition, they lack the distinctly two-toned bill of Red-billeds.

Voice CALL: A distinctive long, high-pitched *cooooo* followed by 2–5 loud *up-cup-a-coo*'s given in the early spring and summer; also a single, swelling *whoo* often repeated several times.

Status & Distribution Widespread throughout the lowlands of Mexico and C.A. Uncommon, local, and declining along the lower Rio Grande in TX; rare in winter. Casual north to Nueces and Kerr Cos. Arboreal; perches in tall trees above brushy understory; seldom comes to the ground except to drink. BREEDING: Nest is a loose platform of twigs built well above the ground; normally has 1 white egg.

Population Deforestation along the Rio Grande in the 1920s greatly reduced the Red-Billed Pigeon's numbers there, and the species is now protected in the state of Texas.

BAND-TAILED PIGEON *Patagioenas fasciata*

The large, heavily built gray pigeon frequents the forests and woodlands of the West; most often seen in flocks of varying sizes in rapid flight. Wings make a loud clapping sound when flushed. Polytypic. L 14.5" (37 cm)

Identification Larger, with a longer tail than a Rock Pigeon; blue-gray on the upper parts with contrasting blackish gray flight feathers; a blackish gray tail with a broad, pale gray terminal band. Paler-gray greater coverts show as a broad wing stripe when in flight. ADULT MALE: Gray on the head, and breast tinged pinkish; narrow white half-collar across the upper hind neck, with iridescent greenish below. Narrow orbital skin purplish; bill yellow with a black tip; and feet yellow. ADULT FEMALE: Like male, but pink color somewhat subdued, and with less iridescent green. JUVENILE: Paler than the adults, with narrow whitish fringes on the breast and coverts; half-collar reduced or obscured.

Geographic Variation At least 8 subspecies. Nominate *fasciata* breeds in the Southwest from Utah and Colorado south into Mexico; and *monilis* breeds in the Pacific states from British Columbia, uncommonly in southeast Alaska, to Baja California, Mex. Subspecies are not separable in the field.

Similar Species Rock Pigeons have blackish tails; most have black markings on the wings and conspicuous white rumps; at close quarters the bill lacks yellow; and the feet are reddish rather than yellow.

Voice CALL: A low-pitched *whoo-whoo* delivered several times.

Status & Distribution Locally common in low-altitude coniferous forests in the Pacific Northwest, and in oak or oak-conifer woodlands in the Southwest; presence dependent on availability of food; increasingly common in suburban gardens and parks. BREEDING: Nest is a platform of twigs lined with grasses placed in a tree well above the ground; bears 1 white egg. MIGRATION AND WINTER: Most birds breeding in the Southwest winter in Mexico, and most breeding in the Pacific Northwest move south into CA in winter. VAGRANT: Casual across southern Canada east to Nova Scotia and New England; also along the Gulf Coast from TX to western FL.

Population Pacific population formerly threatened by overhunting, but with the introduction of controls, population is recovering.

OLD WORLD TURTLE-DOVES Genus *Streptopelia*

ORIENTAL TURTLE-DOVE *Streptopelia orientalis*

This large, heavy dove of Asia, appearing almost pigeonlike when in flight, has strayed to North America. Polytypic. L 13.5" (34 cm)

Identification Generally ashy gray, but with warm brown scaly pattern above, formed by broad chestnut fringes on the blackish tertials and wing coverts. Flight feathers blackish; underside of wings dark gray; and blunt-tipped tail blackish with broad gray terminal band.

orientalis

ADULT MALE: Crown pale gray; underparts grayish brown merging into gray on the undertail coverts; conspicuous black-and-white stripes on sides of neck; iris orangish; orbital skin purplish; bill blackish with a trace of dark purple at base; feet dark reddish. ADULT FEMALE: As male, but slightly duller and browner on underparts. JUVENILE: Paler; fringes on tertials and coverts narrower; neck markings obscured.

Geographic Variation Six subspecies, but only the larger and highly migratory nominate subspecies *orientalis,* breeds in eastern Siberia. It is known to have reached North America.

Similar Species European Turtle-Dove is smaller, overall paler, and has a white terminal band on tail.

Voice CALL: Nominate birds give a 4-

orientalis

phase *deh-deh co-co*, with the last 2 notes lower-pitched.

Status & Distribution Present throughout much of Asia; northern birds highly migratory, withdrawing to S.E. Asia and India in winter. Casual to western Aleutians and Bering Sea in spring and summer; one record each for Vancouver I. and CA.

RINGED TURTLE-DOVE *Streptopelia risoria*

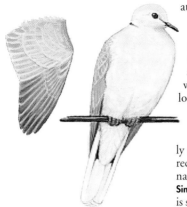

A domesticated form of the African Collared-Dove, *S. roseogrisea,* the Ringed Turtle-Dove is encountered as an escape almost anywhere. Monotypic. L 10.5" (27 cm)
Identification A very pale Mourning Dove-size bird with a blunt-ended tail. It has a whitish head and neck, and is pale buff above with an obvious black collar on the hind neck. Whitish below, including the undertail coverts. There are many color vari-

ations in adults; a pale buff variant is commonly encountered, but others, including peach-colored and rather uniform whitish birds, are also seen. The primaries are only slightly darker than the rest of the wing, providing a more uniform look. The tail is black at the base, visible from below; the black typically falls short of the longest undertail coverts. The tail has an entirely white outer web on the outermost rectrices, and a broad whitish terminal band.
Similar Species Eurasian Collared-Dove is superficially similar, but most birds can be identified with reasonable views. Given the expansion of the collared-dove, combined with the generally poor ability of the Ringed Turtle-Dove to survive in the wild, most encounters away from known Ringed Turtle-Dove populations will likely pertain to collared-doves. Beware of hybrids between the 2 species, which may show a mixture of plumage characters. Otherwise, Ringed Turtle-Doves are smaller and paler. Their primaries are paler, contrasting less with the rest of the

wing and adjacent coverts. In addition, the inner wings, visible in flight, are rather uniform in the Ringed, versus the contrasting gray secondaries of the Eurasian Collared-Dove. The undertail coverts of the Ringed are white, versus gray, and the outer webs of the outer rectrices are white in the Ringed, versus black in the Eurasian Collared-Dove. The black at the base of the tail, visible from below, falls short of the longest undertail coverts and is generally hard to see in the Ringed, whereas it extends beyond the longest undertail coverts and is quite evident to observers looking up at a perched Eurasian Collared-Dove.
Voice CALL: A rolling bisyllabic *kooeek-krrroooo,* noticeably softer than that of the Eurasian Collared-Dove.
Status & Distribution An escapee that can be locally common. Small populations have persisted where fed, but they do not do well in the wild; no known viable wild populations are known in North America. They can be encountered well away from cities, but these are presumably birds that have recently escaped or been released.

SPOTTED DOVE *Streptopelia chinensis*

This Asian dove was introduced into urban areas of southern California about 100 years ago. Polytypic (7 ssp.; nominate in N.A.). L 13" (31 cm)
Identification This is a large and dark dove with broad, rather round-tipped wings. The tail is long, dark, and broad at the end with white tips on the outer 3 to 4 rectrices. ADULT MALE: The gray on top of the head bleeds into the face. The dark brown upperparts have feathers finely fringed with pale brown, and the flight feathers are black. The underparts are a warm dark pinkish brown, merging into gray on the undertail coverts. The upper wing in flight has gray secondaries; below, the underside of the wings are dark. The broad black collar has prominent white spots. The iris is reddish orange, bordered by narrow, dark red orbital skin. The bill is blackish, and the feet are reddish. ADULT FEMALE: Same as male. JUVENILE: Browner with broader, buffer fringes on feathers of upperparts; collar obscured or missing.
Similar Species The Spotted Dove is unique, at least compared to the regular doves of its area. In most cities, it will most likely be compared with the

chinensis

juvenile

Mourning Dove, and it differs in the following ways: The Spotted is a large, chunky dove, with broad, round wings and a broad, squared-off tail. In contrast, the Mourning has a more slender look, with a more pointed wing and a thinner tail, with an obviously pointed central tail. Also, the Spotted is a dark brown bird, lacking the paler buff and sandy tones of the Mourning. If the distinctive black nape, pitted with white spots, is visible on the Spotted, the identification is simple.
Voice CALL: A rather harsh *coo-coo-crooo* and *coo-crrooo-coo,* with the emphasis respectively on the middle and last notes of the calls.

Status & Distribution The Spotted Dove occurs naturally throughout southeast Asia and India; it was introduced into Los Angeles in the early 1900s, then spread throughout much of urban southern California from Santa Barbara and Bakersfield south to Baja California. It is now declining, and gone from most areas it formerly occupied. BREEDING: The nest is a flimsy platform of twigs, usually built in a tree or shrub, but occasionally found on buildings or even on telephone poles; 2 white eggs.

EURASIAN COLLARED-DOVE *Streptopelia decaocto*

A fairly recent arrival to North America, this large pale dove can now be found across the U.S. It flaps on broad wings, and often soars briefly, with wings extended slightly above horizontal as it seemingly floats down to a landing. Polytypic (2 ssp.; nominate in N.A.). L 12.5" (32 cm)

Identification A large, pale gray-buff dove with a black collar, noticeably larger than the Mourning Dove. There is also a naturally occurring cream-colored variant, and this species is known to hybridize with the Ringed Turtle-Dove, so plumage variation will occur. The tail is fairly long and blunt-ended. ADULT MALE: The head is an unmarked, pale buff-gray, while the upperparts are a darker buff-brown, tinged gray; a conspicuous black collar can be seen on the hind neck. The primaries are noticeably darker than the rest of the wing, appearing blackish; the secondaries are gray and contrast with the blackish primaries and the brown wing coverts in flight. The undersides of the wings are pale. The underparts are a paler buff-gray merging into gray on the undertail coverts. A dark gray tail has obvious black at the base when seen from below; the black extends beyond the undertail coverts. This black includes the outer webs of the outer rectrices, and the tail has a broad, pale buff-gray terminal band. A reddish brown iris borders narrow grayish-white orbital skin. The blackish bill has gray at the base, and the feet are dull reddish. ADULT FEMALE: Similar. JUVENILE: Paler; buff fringes on feathers of the upperparts; black collar obscured or missing.

Similar Species The Ringed Turtle-Dove is smaller, shorter-tailed, and noticeably paler; it has far less contrast between the flight feathers and the rest of the wing; undertail coverts are white with black at the base of the tail more restricted, and the outer webs of the outer rectrices white. In addition, the call is different.

Voice CALL: A monotonous repeated, trisyllabic *kuk-koooo-kook,* slightly nasal, with the emphasis on the middle note; also a harsher *kwurrr* sometimes given in flight.

Status & Distribution A Eurasian species introduced to the Bahamas, which spread to Florida in the late 1970s. It was quickly established there, then spread westward in the 1990s, and it has now reached the Pacific coast. The population is anticipated to increase and spread northward into Canada. Its westward expansion follows a similar expansion from its original range in Asia all the way to the Atlantic coast of Europe. BREEDING: Nest is a flimsy construction of twigs placed in trees, particularly palm trees, but occasionally on manmade structures; normally 2 white eggs, occasionally more; 3 to 6 broods a year from the same nest. MIGRATION: Not a migrant in the true sense, in that individuals are not known to return to breeding or wintering grounds. But individuals move great distances, thus enabling the species to quickly expand its range across North America.

Population The 2004–2005 Audubon Christmas Bird Count showed dramatic evidence of the Eurasian Collared-dove's explosive expansion across the continent in a quarter century. The species was listed in 32 states and 4 Canadian provinces (British Columbia, Alberta, Saskatchewan, and Ontario). Small numbers present in some areas may have escaped or been released from captivity by dove breeders, but most birds are thought to represent genuinely wild colonizers.

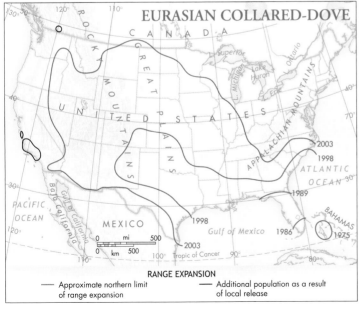

EURASIAN COLLARED-DOVE

RANGE EXPANSION
— Approximate northern limit of range expansion
— Additional population as a result of local release

AMERICAN DOVES Genus Zenaida

WHITE-WINGED DOVE *Zenaida asiatica*

Flocks of these doves, with large white wing patches, and short square-ended tails, are a common sight in summer in many areas near the Mexican border. Polytypic. L 11" (29 cm)

Identification A little larger than the Mourning Dove; generally brownish gray above and a paler gray below; white ends on the greater coverts form prominent patches on the wings, contrasting sharply with the blackish flight feathers; blackish square-ended tail with prominent white terminal band. Prominent black crescent framing lower edge of auricular. On perched bird, wing patch shows only as a thin white line along the leading edge of the folded wing. ADULT MALE: Grayish or grayish brown head and neck, with neck and breast washed lightly with pink; iris reddish brown; orbital skin bright blue; bill black; and feet bright red. ADULT FEMALE: Similar to male. JUVENILE: Paler on the head; narrow pale gray fringes on the scapulars and wing coverts.

Geographic Variation Most recent treatment recognizes 2 subspecies, but there have been varied interpretations, with several subspecies previously considered in this complex. Until recently, it was considered conspecific with West Peruvian Dove, *Z. meloda* of South America. The 2 subspecies are nominate *asiatica* from western Texas eastward along the Gulf Coast to Florida, and *mearnsi* in the Southwest, east to New Mexico. Differences are weak and clinal, with *asiatica* on average showing a less grayish tone to the brown plumage; but the subspecies are likely not separable in the field.

Voice CALL: A drawn-out *who-cooks-for-you* cooing; has many variations.

Status & Distribution Breeds in the southern tier of the U.S., from southeastern CA to the Gulf Coast of TX, and from southern FL south through C.A. to Panama. BREEDING: Nest is a fragile platform of twigs in medium-height brush; nominate birds typically nest in colonies, while the western birds are more solitary; bears 2 white eggs. MIGRATION: Primarily a summer resident in the U.S., with most migrating into Mexico in winter. Increasing numbers are remaining through the year, establishing isolated resident populations scattered across the U.S. from southeastern CA to FL; regular visitor to the Gulf Coast from LA to FL. VAGRANT: Casual on the East Coast north to the Maritime Provinces, in the interior to the Canadian border, and along the West Coast north to extreme southeastern AK.

ZENAIDA DOVE *Zenaida aurita*

This shorter-tailed and somewhat darker version of the Mourning Dove is found throughout the West Indies. Polytypic (3 ssp.; nominate in N.A.). L 10.5" (27 cm)

Identification About the same size as a Mourning Dove; warm brown above, with black spots on scapulars and tertials, and slightly paler cinnamon-brown below. A black crescent frames the lower edge of the auricular. The flight feathers are blackish; the secondaries are tipped white, creating a white trailing edge on the inner wing in flight, showing as a white patch on the inner secondaries on the folded wing. The short tail has a narrow blackish subterminal band and pale gray terminal band. ADULT MALE: Bronze iridescence on hind neck; iris dark brown; orbital skin pale blue; bill black; and feet bright red. ADULT FEMALE: Slightly paler with much less iridescence on hind neck. JUVENILE: Duller with buff fringes on both scapulars and coverts.

Similar Species Differs from the Mourning Dove in having white on the trailing edge of the secondaries, and in having a shorter, rounded, gray-tipped tail. Also, the brown of the back and tail is a darker, warmer shade on the Zenaida Dove.

Voice CALL: A gentle cooing, very similar to that of the Mourning Dove: *coo-oo, coo, coo, coo,* with the second syllable rising sharply.

Status & Distribution A common resident of open woodlands throughout the West Indies and along the east coast of the Yucatan Peninsula. BREEDING: Nest is usually found in a bush or tree; may have up to 6 broods per year. VAGRANT: Said to be resident on small islands off the Florida Keys during the time of Audubon, but only 2 extant 19th-century specimens. Strictly accidental in the U.S. since 1900, with up to 2 on Plantation Key (Dec. 18, 1962–63; Mar. 1963) and singles on Key Largo (June 19–22, 1988 and May 3–6, 2002) being the only unequivocal records.

MOURNING DOVE *Zenaida macroura*

juvenile

This familiar medium-size dove, with its slim body and tapered tail, is the most common and widespread dove in most of North America. Wings make a fluttering whistle when the bird takes flight. Polytypic. L 12" (31 cm)

Identification Head and underparts unmarked pale pinkish brown, but with black crescent framing lower edge of auricular; upper parts darker and grayer brown; prominent black spots on coverts and tertials, and flight feathers contrasting darker; long pointed tail dark, with black subterminal spots and bold white tips on all but the central rectrices. ADULT MALE: Iridescent blue and pink on hind neck, with pinkish bloom extending onto breast; iris blackish;

orbital skin pale blue; bill dark; and feet red. ADULT FEMALE: Similar to adult male, but with reduced iridescence and pinkish bloom. JUVENILE: Generally darker and browner; pale buff-gray fringes on most of the feathers give the bird a "scaly" appearance; dark crescent below auricular extends forward toward the base of the bill; cheek area pale.

Geographic Variation Five subspecies; 3 in North America, with *carolinensis* breeding in the East, and *marginella* breeding in the West, and nominate *macroura* from the West Indies recently invading the Florida Keys; not separable in the field.

Voice CALL: A mournful *oowoo-woo-woo-woo*.

Status & Distribution Common throughout the U.S. and southern Canada south through C.A. Prefers open areas, including rural and residential areas, avoiding thick forests; normally feeds on the ground. BREEDING: Nest is a loose platform of twigs placed at various heights above the ground, flimsy enough that the eggs are frequently visible from below. MIGRATION: Highly migratory, with birds breeding at the northern limit of the range believed to winter in Mexico, but those breeding farther south moving less, with birds present all year in the southern half of the U.S. VAGRANT: Casual to AK and northern Canada; once in Great Britain.

Population The species is a well-managed game bird, with about 45 million killed by hunters in North America each year.

PASSENGER PIGEON Genus *Ectopistes*

PASSENGER PIGEON *Ectopistes migratorius*

This large edition of the Mourning Dove is extinct. Formerly believed to be the most abundant bird in North America, it occurred in huge flocks said to "blacken the sky" in the early 1800s. By the 1870s breeding numbers had been reduced to small scattered colonies, and the last wild bird was recorded in Ohio in 1900. The species became extinct when the last remaining bird in captivity at the Cincinnati Zoo died in 1914. Monotypic. L 15.8" (40 cm)

Identification Like the Mourning Dove, this species had long, broad wings and a very long graduated tail, but it was substantially larger. ADULT MALE: Generally blue-gray above and pinkish below, brightest on the breast, with black markings on the coverts, and contrasting darker primaries and secondaries; white in the tail restricted to the outer pair of remiges; bill black;

and the tarsi and feet coral-red. ADULT FEMALE: Browner above and paler below than the adult male, lacking the pinkish coloration on the breast; bare-part colors as in the male, but duller. JUVENILE: Similar to the female, but black markings on the wings are obscured or lacking, with the feathers of the head, breast, and mantle fringed with buff-gray.

Voice CALL: Variously reported to give a series of harsh *keek* notes, often ending with a *keooo*.

Status & Distribution Extinct. BREEDING: Formerly in vast colonies in the deciduous woodlands stretching across the northern U.S. and southern Canada from the Great Plains east to the Atlantic. WINTER: The woodlands of the southeastern U.S., south along the Gulf Coast of Mexico. VAGRANT: Casu-

adult ♂

al in Cuba during the middle of the 19th century; also north to northern Canada, and west to BC and NV; records from Great Britain and France possibly involved genuine vagrants.

Population The conversion of woodland habitat to farmland, along with overhunting, led to the rapid decline and eventual extinction of this once-abundant dove.

GROUND-DOVES Genus *Columbina*

INCA DOVE *Columbina inca*

The conspicuously long-tailed, small dove is encountered in urban areas of the Southwest near the Mexican border. Monotypic. L 8.3" (21 cm)
Identification A small gray dove with black fringes on the feathers of both the upper and underparts forming an obvious "scaled" appearance. In flight, shows chestnut on the upper and underside of the wing like Common Ground-Dove; however, also shows prominent white edges on the long tail. ADULT MALE: Crown and face pale blue-gray and breast tinged lightly with pink; iris reddish; narrow eye ring blue-gray; bill blackish; and feet bright red. ADULT FEMALE: Similar, but duller on head and breast. JUVENILE: Duller with a slight brownish tinge overall, and "scaling" less noticeable.
Similar Species Its long tail provides a very different shape from that of the ground-dove, but beware of the Inca Dove's regrowing lost tail; it can be mistaken for a ground-dove, and the dark bill along with black on the underwing coverts could lead the unwary to identify such a bird as a Ruddy Ground-Dove. The scaling of the upperparts is unique.
Voice CALL: A long series of disyllabic *kooo-poo* that can be interpreted as "no hope."
Status & Distribution Common resident across the southern U.S. from southern NV to western LA; primarily around human habitation and in city parks. Terrestrial, feeding on the ground; fairly tame, and easily observed. BREEDING: Nest is a small fragile floor of twigs placed in a low bush or shrub; bears 2 white eggs; 2–3 broods each year. MIGRATION: Resident, but species expanding range northward, especially in the far west. VAGRANT: Casual to southern UT, NE, and AR; also recorded in ND and ON.

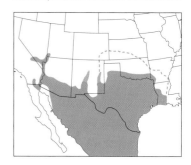

COMMON GROUND-DOVE *Columbina passerina*

This very small, short-tailed dove lives in open areas throughout most of the southern United States. Polytypic. L 6.5" (17 cm)
Identification The smallest of the doves, with short rounded wings and a short, square-ended tail; generally grayish brown above, with underparts paler and washed with pink; prominent blackish spots on the coverts and tertials; dark centers to the feathers on the head and breast create a "scaled" effect; short, square-ended tail blackish; fine white tips on the outer 2–3 rectrices; bright chestnut panel in the primaries and entirely rufous underwing all visible in flight. ADULT MALE: Crown paler and grayer than the rest of upper parts, with iridescent blue-gray on nape and hind neck; face decidedly pinkish, with pinkish tone extending down onto the flanks and belly; blackish spots on wings show iridescent maroon sheen; iris reddish brown; orbital ring blue-gray; bill blackish with bright pink on the basal third; and feet bright red. ADULT FEMALE: Similar to adult male, but lacking the iridescence on the hind neck, and pale gray-brown below instead of pinkish; colors on soft parts less intense. JUVENILE: Noticeably browner; scapulars and wing coverts fringed buff-gray; black spots on wings obscured or missing; and pink at base of bill far less noticeable.

Geographic Variation Eighteen subspecies; 2 in North America: nominate *passerina* in the Southeast, and *pallescens* in the West; pinkish on underparts and pink at the base of the bill more intense on nominate race, but generally not separable in the field.
Similar Species Similar to Ruddy Ground-Dove (and see that account), but note Common's scaled head and breast, pale base to the bill, and different wing markings.
Voice CALL: A repeated soft, drawn-out and ascending *wah-up* double note given every 2–3 seconds.
Status & Distribution Common resident in open areas along the southern border of the U.S., but declining along the Gulf Coast. Prefers open areas and feeds on the ground. BREEDING: Nest is a flimsy collection of twigs on the ground or low in dense shrubs; normally 2 white eggs; 2–3 broods each year. MIGRATION: Although considered resident, some disperse northward in fall. VAGRANT: Casually north to OR, SD, MI, MA, and NS.

RUDDY GROUND-DOVE *Columbina talpacota*

This small, short-tailed dove is widespread throughout the lowlands of Central and much of South America, and is expanding its range northward. It often associates with Inca Doves. Polytypic. L 6.8" (18 cm)

Identification Similar in shape to Common Ground-Dove, but slightly larger and sexually dimorphic; wings with bright rufous panels in primaries, and underwing coverts black; tail black with narrow whitish tips on outer 2–3 rectrices; black spots on wings form vertical lines that extend up onto the scapulars. ADULT MALE: Head unmarked pale grayish with blue-gray on crown and hind neck; upper parts rufous, most intense on lower back and rump; underparts unmarked rufous; iris reddish brown; orbital ring pale blue-gray; bill gray with black tip; and feet bright red. ADULT FEMALE: Head unmarked pale gray-brown; upper parts gray-brown, and underparts paler and grayer; most have whitish fringes on tertials and greater coverts; soft parts as on male. JUVENILE: Similar to female, but males show varying amounts of rufous; black spots on wings obscured or missing.

Similar Species Separating adult male Ruddy Ground-Doves from Common Ground-Doves poses no problem. Female Ruddy Ground-Doves show no "scaling" on the head and breast; no reddish coloration at the base of the bill; and invariably show white fringes on the tertials. The underwing coverts are mostly black.

Geographic Variation Four subspecies; 2 in North America: *rufipennis* of eastern Mexico and *eluta* of western Mexico. Adult males of *rufipennis* are a rich rufous above and below, more so than the adult males of *eluta,* and tips of their outer rectrices are rufous instead of whitish. Females and immatures are probably inseparable in the field.

Voice CALL: A monotonous series of evenly pitched disyllabic *ca-whoop* notes given at 1-second intervals.

Status & Distribution Common to abundant throughout the lowlands of Mexico south to northern Argentina, frequenting open and semi-open woodlands. The western Mexican population is expanding northward, and a few are found annually, primarily in fall, in southeastern CA, southern AZ, southern NM, and western TX east to Big Bend N.P.; now resident at isolated locations within this area. Casual west to coastal southern CA, southern NV, and southwestern UT. BREEDING: Nest similar to that of Common Ground-Dove, but always off the ground; bears 2 white eggs. VAGRANT: Birds from the eastern Mexican population *rufipennis* are casual to accidental in southern TX.

NEOTROPICAL FOREST DOVES *Genus Leptotila*

WHITE-TIPPED DOVE *Leptotila verreauxi*

This plump, short-tailed terrestrial dove with broad, rounded wings is found in forested areas of southern Texas, often on the ground. It jerks its tail when alarmed. Polytypic. L 11.5" (29 cm)

Identification Head gray, palest on the face; upper parts unmarked, faintly bronzed olive-brown, and under parts unmarked pale gray; short, square-tipped tail blackish with prominent white tips on outer 3 rectrices; underwings rufous. ADULT MALE: Iridescent green and maroon wash on hind neck; iris yellow; orbital skin red; bill entirely dark; and feet coral-red. ADULT FEMALE: Like male, but iridescence on hind neck reduced. JUVENILE: Duller; fine buff fringes on scapulars and coverts; lacks iridescence.

Similar Species Most of the doves in this genus are similar, but differ in the amounts of white in the tail; any *Leptotila* found away from southern Texas should be identified with care.

Geographic Variation Depending on the authority: 1 species with at least 14 subspecies, or 2 species, with multiple subspecies. The subspecies *angelica* is resident in southern TX.

Voice CALL: A low-pitched *waa-woooo,* like the sound produced by blowing across the top of a bottle.

Status & Distribution Common throughout lowlands of C.A. and S.A.; resident in southern TX north to Dimmit and Refugio Co.; expanding northward; casual north to the Edwards Plateau. BREEDING: The nest is a bulky flat of twigs lined with grasses, normally in dense brush close to the ground; typically 2 creamy-white eggs. VAGRANT: Two in Dry Tortugas, FL (Apr. 2–8, 1995; Apr. 19–May 3, 2003). **Population** Appears to adapt well to fragmentation of forests, so is increasing in numbers.

QUAIL-DOVES Genus *Geotrygon*

KEY WEST QUAIL-DOVE *Geotrygon chrysia*

Although named Key West, this most widespread and common of the quail-doves in the West Indies is but a casual stray to Florida. It is rather secretive and is usually found singly, even where it is common, although pairs are also frequently encountered. It feeds on the forest floor, primarily on seeds and fruit. Quail-Doves will tend to walk from danger, as opposed to taking flight. The male will perch on low branches, from which it makes its territorial calls. Monotypic. L 12" (31 cm)

Identification The Key West is one of the larger quail-doves. It is bicolored with a prominent white facial stripe; rich chestnut-brown above, and grayish white below. ADULT MALE: The crown, nape, and hind neck are washed with iridescent blue-green. A white face is bordered below by a narrow dark chestnut malar stripe. The breast is pale grayish white, merging into white on the belly, with pale olive-brown on the flanks and undertail coverts. An orange iris is bordered

by red orbital skin. The dark red bill has a brownish tip. The feet are bright coral-red. ADULT FEMALE: Duller brown above than the adult male, with less iridescence and with a less obvious facial stripe. JUVENILE: Duller still than the adult female, generally lacking the rich chestnut tones, and lacking any hint of iridescence. The scapulars and wing coverts are fringed cinnamon; the feet are a much duller red than on the adults.

Voice CALL: A low moaning ventriloquial *ooooo* or *oooowoo,* with the second part accentuated and slightly higher; very similar to the call of the White-tipped Dove.

Status & Distribution Fairly common to uncommon, primarily resident in arid and semiarid woodlands and scrub thickets on the Bahamas, Cuba, and Hispaniola, and locally on Puerto Rico. BREEDING: The nest is a fragile platform of twigs

lined with dead leaves built in low undergrowth or on the ground; normally has 2 creamy-buff eggs. VAGRANT: Possible former resident, prior to about the mid-19th century, on the Florida Keys. Now a casual mid-Oct.–mid-June straggler to the Florida Keys and southern FL, with at least 15 records since 1964, the northernmost being in Palm Beach County. Single birds have been reported in residential areas of southern FL, where they frequented roadways in Everglades N.P. in 1979 and Boot Key in 1987.

RUDDY QUAIL-DOVE *Geotrygon montana*

montana

As is typically the case for this genus, the Ruddy Quail-Dove is secretive and quite terrestrial, frequently running rather than flying when alarmed. It is normally encountered on the forest floor in Central and South America. Males readily fly to low branches to vocalize, but otherwise flight is infrequent, except during the courting process. The Ruddy Quail-Dove feeds on seeds, fruits, and more so than most congeners, on a regular diet of invertebrates, such as beetles. Poly-

typic (2 ssp.; nominate in N.A.). L 9.8" (25 cm)

Identification One of the smaller but most widespread of the quail-doves, most often encountered walking on the forest floor. A plump, shortish-tailed dove, reddish brown above with buff underparts and a pale stripe through the face. While the bird has subtle colors, it gives the general impression of a dark reddish brown, stocky dove. ADULT MALE: The reddish brown on the upper parts is washed with iridescent purple. Chin, throat, and sides of the face are pale buff; cheeks are separated from the throat by a broad, reddish brown malar stripe. Iris is yellow-orange; orbital skin red; bill dark reddish with dusky tip; feet bright coral-red. ADULT FEMALE: Smaller; darker olive-brown above and below, lacking iridescence; facial stripe less obvious. JUVENILE: Coloration like the female, but has rufous fringes on the feathers.

Voice CALL: A series of very deep, resonant, monosyllabic coos, *waooo* or *wooo* repeated every 3–4 seconds, trailing off at the end. In his classic *Birds*

of the West Indies, James Bond described the call as "reminiscent of the doleful sound of a fog buoy."

Status & Distribution Uncommon to locally common, largely resident in lowland humid forests of the West Indies and Mexico southward through C.A. to southern Brazil. BREEDING: The Ruddy Quail-Dove's nest is a platform of twigs lined with dead leaves, built low in a bush or tree, but sometimes on the ground; normally has 2 creamy-buff eggs. MIGRATION: Much remains to be learned abut the movements of this species. It is partially migratory or nomadic, but specific patterns and causes of migration are undiscovered. Numbers vary from year to year, even where the species is common; but the extent and regularity of the bird's movements remain unknown. As an example of the significant travel that can take place, this species has been recorded at sea in the Caribbean. VAGRANT: Eight recorded on the Florida Keys, including the Dry Tortugas, and 1 at Bentsen-Rio Grande Valley S.P. in TX.

PARAKEETS, MACAWS, AND PARROTS Family Psittacidae

Monk Parakeets (IL, Feb.)

Throughout tropical and subtropical (rarely temperate) areas of the world live 322 species of these colorful birds. Hundreds of thousands of them were imported into the U.S. during the late 1960s through early 1990s. Numerous species are now at liberty (primarily in CA and FL) as a result of accidental or deliberate releases.

Structure Psittacids are large-headed birds with no necks and short legs. Parakeets and macaws are slim with long tails; parrots are chunky, with short tails. Psittacids are primarily arboreal. Their bills are short, thick, and curved, with a powerful, articulated tongue that aids in processing palm nuts and other plant food. In all species, 2 toes face forward and 2 backward. Psittacids show the greatest size diversity of all the world's bird families, ranging from 3.7 to 39 inches (8–100 cm).

Behavior Most species are social, gathering in large mixed flocks at nighttime roosts or when foraging; some species are communal breeders. Virtually all nest in cavities in palms, trees, or termite mounds; the Monk Parakeet is the sole exception. Psittacids forage primarily for seeds, nuts, and fruit and often visit bird feeders. Typically noisy in flight, they often grow quiet when feeding or roosting. They can be difficult to locate then, as their plumage blends into the vegetation. Flocks can be identified to group fairly easily—based on shape and flight style—but multiple species are often present.

Plumage Psittacids are primarily green, especially in the New World, but usually show some red, orange, or yellow on the head or in wings or tail. Some species are entirely red, blue, or yellow. Sexes are usually similar, but many parrots take more than 2 years to reach adult plumage, resulting in confusing immature plumages. Aviculturists have created numerous artificial color morphs that may be seen outside of captivity.

Distribution Widespread. Greatest native diversity is in the tropics; greatest exotic diversity is in southern Florida.

Taxonomy Confused, especially for the New World, the result of insufficient studies from much of the tropics. Species limits are unknown for many genera; more than 700 species and subspecies are recognized.

Conservation Capture for the pet trade during the late 1960s to early 1990s was vast. Unregulated capture and the massive degree of habitat destruction have endangered dozens of species. All psittacids in the U.S. currently are exotic and unprotected. The potential impacts of exotic psittacids in the U.S. on native species, habitats, or agriculture are largely unknown. BirdLife International lists 94 species as threatened and 30 others as near threatened. —*Bill Pranty*

Flight Silhouettes of Various Psittacid Genera

The flight patterns of psittacid genera differ.

Brotogeris. These small parakeets have moderately long, pointed tails. In flight several rapid wingbeats are followed by brief closure of bowed wings. Flight is rapid, but seems halting and undulating from wing closures and side-to-side twisting of body.

Psittacula. The Rose-ringed Parakeet is of medium size and has a markedly long, slender tail. It appears relatively small headed, thus does not seem "front-heavy." Its wingbeats are deeper and more sweeping than those of other parakeets.

Aratinga, Nandayus, and *Myiopsitta.* These medium-size parakeets have long, pointed tails. Bills are moderate to large, giving them a more "front-heavy" look. Flight is rapid and constant; wingbeats are fairly shallow, with wings bowed slightly below the body plane. There is some side-to-side body-twisting.

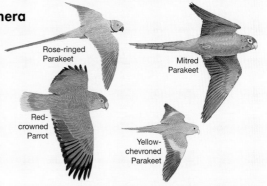

Amazona. These medium to large parrots seem large headed and markedly "front-heavy" in flight. The tail is squared and moderately short. Wings are bowed down; wingbeats are stiff, continuous, and fast, but flight is slower than in parakeets. ∎

AUSTRALIAN PARAKEETS Genus *Melopsittacus*

This genus consists of a single species, the Budgerigar. One of the world's most abundant psittacids, it numbers perhaps 5 million individuals. These birds breed communally in cavities, or—as in Florida—in nest boxes, raise multiple broods annually, and feed extensively on grass and other seeds obtained from the ground, and on birdseed in Florida.

BUDGERIGAR *Melopsittacus undulatus*

variants

Perhaps the most popular cage bird in the world, the budgerigar has been bred in captivity since the mid-1800s. A wide variety of artificial color morphs exist, including white, yellow, or blue plumages. Monotypic. L 7" (18 cm)

Identification This is a tiny parakeet—the size of a warbler if the tail is excluded. Sexes are similar. ADULT: Head is mostly yellow with black barring on the auriculars, hind crown, and nape. Two black spots on each side of the throat, with a small purplish patch on the malar. Eyes are yellow; bill, legs, and feet grayish. Back and wing coverts are yellow, barred with black. White or yellow wing stripe in flight. Rump green. Tail equal to length of body, with blue central rectrices. Underparts wholly lime green. JUVENILE: Forehead barred, throat unspotted, eyes dark. **Similar Species** None; much smaller than any other psittacid found in N.A. **Voice** A series of pleasant high-pitched chittering or chirping; some notes reminiscent of House Sparrows. **Status & Distribution** Exotic in the U.S. Common to abundant in native Australia. YEAR-ROUND: Nonmigratory. In U.S. restricted to FL, where a breeding population along the central Gulf Coast since the early 1960s is nearing extirpation. Escapees are possible anywhere. **Population** The Florida population has declined more than 99 percent since the late 1970s, from perhaps 20,000 individuals to fewer than 100. Nesting competition with House Sparrows thought to be the primary cause of the decline. Now limited to residential areas at Hernando Beach and Bayonet Point.

TYPICAL PARROTS Genus *Psittacula*

Thirteen species make up this Afro-Asian genus. *Psittacula* species possess extremely long tails—equal to or greater than their body length. Most species have reddish bills and black chins and throats. Only one species, *P. krameri*, breeds in North America, but several others similar in appearance may be observed.

ROSE-RINGED PARAKEET *Psittacula krameri*

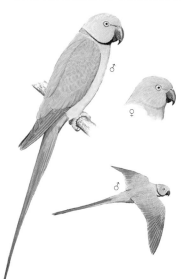

The Rose-ringed Parakeet is the only representative of the North American psittacid fauna native to Africa and India. It is established in a few restricted areas of Florida and California. The species is known as the Rose-necked Parakeet in the Old World. Polytypic. L 15.8" (40 cm)
Identification Overall, the Rose-ringed Parakeet is yellowish green. It has a slender tail with very long central feathers. A narrow, red orbital surrounds the pale yellow eye. The upper mandible appears bright red, but the lower mandible is mostly or completely black. Remiges are darker green, contrasting with yellowish green coverts. ADULT MALE: The chin and throat are black. The black extends backward to encircle the head; the back end of the collar is tinged with rose pink. The nape is pale azure. ADULT FEMALE AND JUVENILE: The bird's chin and throat are yellow-green, the collar is lacking, and the nape is green.
Geographic Variation There are 4 subspecies worldwide. The North American subspecies—*manillensis*, possibly also *borealis*—are both native to the Indian subcontinent.
Similar Species Green Parakeets and immatures of other birds of the genus *Aratinga* may be mostly or entirely green, but these birds lack the red bill and extremely long central tail feathers of the Rose-ringed Parakeet. The collar of the adult male Rose-ringed is diagnostic.
Voice Highly vocal at roosts. CALL: A loud flickerlike *kew* is common, along with various high, shrill notes uncharacteristic of most psittacids.
Status & Distribution Exotic in the U.S. The most widespread Old World psittacid, the Rose-ringed Parakeet, is native to Africa and India. YEAR-ROUND: Nonmigratory. In the U.S. the Rose-ringed is restricted to CA and FL. Common to abundant in its native range.
Population The California population is currently increasing. Trends in Florida are unknown; some populations are now extirpated. Rose-ringed Parakeets number about 200 in Florida, at Fort Myers and Naples. A population at Bakersfield, California, numbers about 1,000 birds, with less than 100 at Los Angeles.

NEW WORLD PARROTS Genera *Myiopsitta, Conuropsis, Aratinga, Nandayus, Rhynchopsitta, Brotogeris,* and *Amazona*

This diverse group of about 148 species ranges from northern Mexico to the southern tip of South America. New species are still being discovered in the tropics. Many species with allopatric native ranges occur sympatrically in California and Florida (e.g., the Red-masked Parakeet). As a result, some field marks remain to be worked out. Some psittacids in California and Florida may hybridize, creating additional undescribed plumages, which further complicates identification. Many species not included in this guide may be encountered outside captivity.

MONK PARAKEET *Myiopsitta monachus*

This most widespread and numerous psittacid in North America, the monk survives frigid New England and Illinois winters by feeding on birdseed and sheltering in its bulky stick nest. Polytypic (3–4 ssp.). L 11.5" (29 cm) **Identification** Sexes similar. ADULT: Green, with forepart of head grayish. Orbital ring inconspicuous, eyes dark, bill pinkish orange, legs and feet gray. Breast scalloped grayish and white; belly yellowish, merging with green undertail coverts. Remiges and lesser primary coverts blue, remaining coverts green. Rump and tail green.

IMMATURE: Forehead tinged with green. **Similar Species** None; gray hood and nest-building behavior unique among N.A. psittacids. **Voice** Highly vocal, a variety of loud, harsh notes or quieter chattering. **Status & Distribution** Exotic in U.S. and many other countries. Native to lowlands of southern S.A. YEAR-ROUND: Nonmigratory. Builds stick nests in trees, on poles or other objects. Locally common in CT and FL Peninsula. Smaller numbers in several other states including IL, NY, OR, and TX. **Population** Expanding; many N.A. pop-

ulations doubling every 5 to 6 years. Eradicated in some states (e.g., CA, GA) due to exaggerated reputation as a crop pest; also destroyed in huge numbers in native range.

CAROLINA PARAKEET *Conuropsis carolinensis*

adult

North America's only native breeding psittacid became extinct about 70 or more years ago. Its stronghold was the great river basins of the Midwest and Deep South, where it favored cottonwoods, cypress swamps, and old-growth bottomlands and fed on a variety of fruits and seeds. The exact reasons for the bird's demise are not well understood. Polytypic (2 ssp.). L 13.5" (32 cm) **Identification** Sexes similar. ADULT: Green body with yellow head and reddish orange face. Bill and orbital ring pale, eyes brownish, legs and feet pale pink. Yellow and/or orange patches on shoulders, "thighs," and vent. Blackish primaries with yellow to green edges on outer webs; green coverts, greater coverts yellower. Long green tail, yel-

lower below. IMMATURE: Entirely green except for orangish patch on forehead. **Similar Species** None in former range, early 20th-century reports from FL or GA possibly misidentified exotics. **Voice** Vocal, especially in flight. CALL: A loud and harsh *qui* or *qui-i-i-i.* **Status & Distribution** Formerly locally common throughout eastern U.S. YEAR-ROUND: Nonmigratory but evidently some movements based on availability of food resources; occurred north at least occasionally to MN, MI, and NY, and west to central CO. **Population** Last captive died in 1918.

BLUE-CROWNED PARAKEET *Aratinga acuticaudata*

This parakeet is identified by its blue head and pinkish bill. Polytypic (5 ssp.; nominate in N.A.). L 13.3" (35 cm) **Identification** Mostly green overall, with a long tail. Sexes similar. ADULT: Most of head dull blue; may appear green from a distance or in bad light. Prominent white orbital ring, eyes orange (often appear dark), upper mandible pinkish orange, lower mandible dark. Flight feathers dull yellow-green. Reddish inner webs and dull yellow outer webs of tail feathers visible from below. JUVENILE: Blue on head restricted to forehead and forecrown.

Similar Species The Dusky-headed Parakeet is superficially similar, but its head is purplish and "scaly," its bill, black. **Voice** A loud *cheeah-cheeah,* often repeated. **Status & Distribution** Exotic in the U.S. Widely distributed and common in 3 regions of S.A. YEAR-ROUND: Nonmigratory. In U.S. restricted to CA and FL; ±100 in CA at San Francisco, Los Angeles, and San Diego; ±125 in FL, at Fort Lauderdale, Upper Keys, and St. Petersburg. **Population** Increasing in California and Florida.

GREEN PARAKEET *Aratinga holochlora*

This Mexican parakeet is most common in the U.S. in Texas. Breeding colonies are found throughout several large and small towns along the Rio Grande. Polytypic (3–4 ssp.; uncertain which occur in N.A.). L 13" (33 cm)

Identification Green overall, slightly yellower below, with a long tail. Sexes similar. ADULT: Head often with scattered orange feathers. Wide white or beige orbital ring; dull red in some Texas birds. Eyes orange, bill beige, legs and feet gray. May have scattered orange feathers on breast. Underparts paler green. Undersurface of flight feathers pale yellow; coverts yellow-green. JUVENILE: Similar to adult; eyes brown.

Similar Species Juveniles of other *Aratinga* such as the White-eyed or Crimson-fronted Parakeet may be encountered in Florida. These have entirely green bodies but reportedly have at least scattered red, orange, or yellow feathers on the underwing coverts. Otherwise, the only entirely green parakeet in the United States.

Voice Various chattering calls. In flight, harsh screeches.

Status & Distribution Exotic in the U.S. Native to Mexico and C.A., where fairly common. YEAR-ROUND: Nonmigratory, but some movement of native birds in response to food supply. In U.S. restricted to FL and TX; ±2,000 in TX, along the Lower Rio Grande Valley. Some also in FL at Fort Lauderdale and Miami, where juveniles of other *Aratinga* species complicate identification.

Population Increasing in Texas and probably also in Florida.

MITRED PARAKEET *Aratinga mitrata*

Mitred and Red-masked Parakeets, along with other species not included here, represent a great identification challenge in California and Florida, where several species may co-occur. Mitred Parakeets in Florida roost—and apparently breed—in cavities and chimneys of buildings. Polytypic (2 ssp.; nominate in U.S.). L 15" (38 cm)

Identification Large, with variable red facial markings. Sexes similar. ADULT: Body green. Head has variable amount of red spotting; forehead dusky. Wide, white orbital ring; orange eyes; pale bill; pink legs and feet. Red spotting often on shoulders. Flight feathers yellowish below, green above—like other *Aratinga*. Underparts often with random red breast feathers. Juvenile: Less red on cheeks and head; eyes brown.

Similar Species Smaller Red-masked Parakeet usually has more extensive, solid red hood, red shoulders, and gray legs and feet. Juvenile Mitred resembles other *Aratinga* not included here.

Voice Strident *scree-ah* and other shrieking calls.

Status & Distribution Exotic in the U.S. Native to Andes of Peru, Bolivia, and Argentina, where common. YEAR-ROUND: Nonmigratory. In U.S. restricted to CA and FL.

Population Populations stable or increasing in California and Florida. Some local declines in native range; prior to 1990, exported in great numbers.

RED-MASKED PARAKEET *Aratinga erythrogenys*

Like most other exotic parakeets, but unlike the similar Mitred Parakeet, this species nests singly in natural cavities in oaks and palms. It flocks and roosts with other *Aratinga* species. Monotypic. L 13" (33 cm)

Identification A medium-size parakeet with a red hood and shoulders and a green body. Sexes similar. ADULT: Extent of bright red hood variable, may end near mid-bill or extend to throat. Wide white orbital ring; orange eyes; pale bill; gray legs and feet. Wings show red shoulders. Underwings are yellowish with red on the lesser coverts. "Thighs" often red. JUVENILE: Red on head and underwing coverts much reduced; "thighs" green.

Similar Species Mitred Parakeet larger (conspicuous in mixed flock) has much less red on head (forehead dusky) and crown, and little or no red on shoulders. Mitred has pink legs and feet rather than gray. Confusion possible with immatures of other *Aratinga*.

Voice Strident *scree-ah* or *skreet* calls, higher pitched than Mitred Parakeet.

Status & Distribution Exotic in the U.S. Native to western Ecuador and northwestern Peru YEAR-ROUND: Nonmigratory. In U.S. restricted to CA, ±300, and FL, perhaps ±200.

Population Populations stable or increasing in California and Florida. Declining and near threatened in limited native range from extensive capture for the pet trade.

DUSKY-HEADED PARAKEET *Aratinga weddellii*

This species is limited in the U.S. to one Miami neighborhood. It has persisted for about 20 years and visits bird feeders regularly, but otherwise nothing is known about its natural history here. Monotypic. L 11" (28 cm) **Identification** Sexes and ages similar. A small green *Aratinga* with a purplish gray head that appears "scaly" due to bluish feather tips. The gray head contrasts prominently with the white orbital ring and shiny black bill. White eyes; gray legs and feet. Breast and undertail coverts light green; belly and "thighs" yellow. FLIGHT: Unlike other *Aratinga,* its dark remiges contrast with yellow-green underwing linings—resembling the Black-hooded Parakeet's underwing pattern.

Similar Species The larger Blue-crowned Parakeet is somewhat similar, but the head is not "scaly" and the upper mandible is pinkish orange.

Voice CALL: A nasal *jee-eek,* but the Dusky-head is mainly silent, especially when perched.

Status & Distribution Exotic in the U.S. Native to lowlands of northwestern S.A., where common. YEAR-ROUND: Nonmigratory. In U.S. restricted to FL, where ±50 occur at Miami Springs.

Population Perhaps declining in Florida.

BLACK-HOODED PARAKEET *Nandayus nenday*

This large parakeet is one of the most successful psittacids in North America.

It has bred in sycamore woodlands in California, but prefers palm snags and telephone poles in urban areas in Florida. It is also known as the Nanday Parakeet. Monotypic. L 13.8" (35 cm)

Identification Sexes similar. ADULT: Prominent blackish hood with an inconspicuous red or brown border on the hind crown; black bill and dark eyes. Light green body with powder blue breast patch. Bright red "thighs" distinctive. Lower half of upper tail bluish, undersurface of tail blackish. Orbital ring gray and inconspicuous. IMMATURE: Blue breast patch smaller; red "thighs" paler. FLIGHT: Primaries and secondaries dark blue above and blackish below, contrast with yellow-green wing linings.

Similar Species The Dusky-headed Parakeet shares a darkish head, black bill, and dark primaries contrasting with light green coverts, but note the purplish gray head and bold white orbital ring.

Voice A harsh *kee-ah,* often doubled, or *chree, chree, chree;* Vocal, especially in flight.

Status & Distribution Exotic in the U.S. Native to interior of central S.A., where common. YEAR-ROUND: Nonmigratory. In U.S. restricted to CA and FL.; ±200 birds in southern CA, mostly coastal Los Angeles, Huntington Beach, and San Gabriel Valley. Established in FL, ±1,000 individuals, primarily in the central Gulf Coast.

Population Increasing in Florida and California.

THICK-BILLED PARROT *Rhynchopsitta pachyrhyncha*

adults

This majestic psittacid wandered infrequently from its Mexican haunts to the southwestern U.S. until about 70 years ago. An attempt to introduce a flock into the Chiricahuas of southeastern Arizona in the 1980s was unsuccessful. Monotypic. L 16.2" (41 cm) **Identification** A large green psittacid with a long, pointed tail and large, black bill. Sexes similar. ADULT: Red forehead extending in a broad line over the eyes; red shoulders. Underparts wholly green with red "thighs." Orange eyes and dull yellow orbital ring. IMMATURE: Bill dusky; red on head limited to forehead; no red on wings. FLIGHT: Pattern unmistakable from below. A prominent yellow stripe (greater coverts) is set off by dark green wing linings and blackish flight feathers. Underside of tail also blackish; leading edge of the wing is red.

Similar Species No other psittacid within former North American range. Distinguished from *Amazona* by dark bill and long, pointed tail. Paler-billed immature similar to smaller, white-billed Mitred or Red-masked Parakeet but orbital ring gray and inconspicuous.

Voice Screeches, screams, and squawks.

Status & Distribution Uncommon to rare in old-growth pine forests in the Sierra Madre Occidental of northwestern Mexico. YEAR-ROUND: Nonmigratory but wanders in response to pine crop success.

Population Endangered, presumably still declining due to forest destruction.

WHITE-WINGED PARAKEET *Brotogeris versicolurus*

In size, *Brotogeris* parakeets fall between Budgerigars and *Aratinga* parakeets. They are mostly green with moderately long, pointed tails. White-winged and Yellow-chevroned parakeets formerly were considered conspecific under the name Canary-winged Parakeet, a name still sometimes used for the White-winged Parakeet. Monotypic. L 8.75" (22 cm)

Identification Sexes and ages similar. Perched birds often show little or no white in wings—only yellow of the greater coverts. Body and tail entirely dull green. An inconspicuous gray orbital ring merges with unfeathered gray lores. Dark eyes; pale yellow bill; pink legs and feet. FLIGHT: Large white areas—formed by the white secondaries and inner primaries—conspicuous in flight. Outer primaries bluish. **Similar Species** Yellow-chevroned Parakeet very similar. The primary field mark on a perched White-winged Parakeet is the unfeathered gray lores and orbital ring. In flight, white secondaries diagnostic, but note that hybrids with Yellow-chevroned Parakeet apparently occur at San Francisco and Fort Lauderdale.

Voice Perched birds give various chattering calls. Flight call of *chree* or *chree-chree* richer and slightly lower-pitched than that of the Yellow-chevroned. **Status & Distribution** Exotic in the U.S. Native to the Amazon Basin of northern S.A., where common. YEAR-ROUND: Nonmigratory. In U.S. restricted to CA, ±50 at San Francisco and Los Angeles, and to FL, ±200 mainly in Fort Lauderdale, smaller numbers at Miami. **Population** U.S. populations have declined considerably since the 1970s.

YELLOW-CHEVRONED PARAKEET *Brotogeris chiriri*

The Yellow-chevroned was formerly considered conspecific with the White-winged and known as the Canary-winged Parakeet (see account above). In Florida both species nest in living date palms by burrowing into the insect debris surrounding the trunks. Polytypic (2 ssp.; apparently nominate only in N.A.). L 8.75" (22 cm)

Identification Sexes and ages similar. Perched birds show a yellow wing bar—similar to the White-winged. The body and tail are entirely light green. The green lores are fully feathered, and there is a narrow white orbital ring. Dark eyes; pinkish yellow bill; pink legs and feet. FLIGHT: Yellow wing bar prominent in flight. The primaries and secondaries are green. **Similar Species** White-winged Parakeet is very similar. Fully feathered lores of Yellow-chevroned Parakeet best field mark when perched. In flight, shows no white in wings. **Voice** Calls are similar to White-winged Parakeet but higher and scratchier. **Status & Distribution** Exotic in the U.S. Native to central S.A., where common. YEAR-ROUND: Nonmigratory. In U.S. restricted to CA, ±650 primarily in Los Angeles with a few at San Francisco (where hybrids with the

White-winged reported) and FL, ±450 mainly at Miami with some at Fort Lauderdale (hybrids also reported). **Population** In U.S. stable or increasing.

RED-CROWNED PARROT *Amazona viridigenalis*

adult ♂

The Red-crowned is the most widespread and common parrot in North America and the second most successful psittacid overall. It roosts in large, noisy flocks with other species and nests singly in cavities in palms or other trees. Monotypic. L 13" (33 cm)

Identification Chunky green psittacid with variable amount of red on forehead and crown. Pale orbital ring, bill, and cere; yellow eyes. ADULT MALE: Extensive red forehead and crown; blue hind crown and nape. ADULT FEMALE AND IMMATURE: Red on head restricted to forehead; crown bluish. FLIGHT: Upper wings have a red patch on the secondaries and a dark blue trailing edge. Underwings green. Yellowish band across tip of tail. **Similar Species** Similar to the Lilac-crowned, which has a burgundy forehead and purplish blue crown and nape, extending farther onto the auriculars. Longer tail of the Lilac-crowned Parrot noticeable in flight. **Voice** Loud grating and cawing calls, a distinctive rolling, descending whistle. **Status & Distribution** Exotic in the U.S. Native to northeastern Mexico, where endangered; ±3,000–6,500 remaining. YEAR-ROUND: Nonmigratory, but may wander in response to food availability. In U.S. restricted to CA, FL, and TX. Largest numbers in southern CA, ±2,600; ±400 in FL. Hundreds in TX. **Population** Expanding in California and Texas; stable or perhaps declining in Florida due to capture for local pet trade. Native population in Mexico endangered and declining.

LILAC-CROWNED PARROT *Amazona finschi*

A close relative of the Red-crowned Parrot, with which it flocks, the Lilac-crowned roosts and rarely hybridizes in California. Monotypic. L 13" (32 cm) **Identification** Adult: Sexes similar. Body green, head green with burgundy forehead and purplish blue crown and nape that curves downward behind the auriculars. Gray orbital ring, red-orange eyes, dark cere, and pale bill. IMMATURE: Eyes brown. FLIGHT: Upper wings green with blackish blue primaries and secondary tips; red outer secondaries. Underwings green. Yellowish band across tip of long tail. **Similar Species** Very similar to the Red-crowned Parrot. The primary differences are the lilac crown and nape versus the red crown (adult male) and bluish

nape. Note also the dark cere and reddish eyes of the Lilac-crowned Parrot. In flight, its longer tail is apparent. **Voice** Various loud grating and cawing calls indistinguishable from those of the Red-crowned Parrot, but also utters, especially in flight, a distinctive, squeaky, ascending whistled *ker-leek?* **Status & Distribution** Exotic in the U.S. Native to northern Pacific coast of Mexico. YEAR-ROUND: Nonmigratory. In U.S. restricted to southern CA, where ±500 occur at Los Angeles and San Diego, nesting in cavities in trees and telephone poles. Escapees seen in southern FL. **Population** Increasing in California. Native populations considered near-threatened from habitat loss.

YELLOW-HEADED PARROT *Amazona oratrix*

This species (or 1 among a complex of species) native to the tropics is often considered conspecific with the Yellow-naped *(auropalliata)* and Yellow-crowned *(ochrocephala)* under the combined name of the Yellow-crowned Parrot. Polytypic. L 14.5" (36 cm) **Identification** A green parrot; head largely or entirely yellow, depending on subspecies. ADULT: White orbital ring, eyes orange, bill pale. Red and yellow markings on shoulder; yellow on "thighs." IMMATURE: Head mostly green with yellow crown and face, green wings; dark eyes. FLIGHT: Wings green with bluish tips to remiges. Red patch on outer secondaries. Underwings green. Tail green with yellow outer rectrices. **Geographic Variation** Three subspecies:

oratrix (head yellow, but nape and breast green), apparently in California and Florida; *belizensis* (green nape and breast); *tresmariae* (yellow head and breast and greater amount of yellow at the shoulders). The Yellow-naped Parrot breeds in very small numbers in southeastern Florida; the Yellow-crowned is seen there occasionally. **Similar Species** Yellow-headed, pale-billed adults unmistakable. Immature similar to adult Yellow-crowned Parrot but has dark eyes. **Voice** A variety of shrieks, squawks, and whistles; excellent mimic. **Status & Distribution** Exotic in the U.S. Native from Mexico to northern Honduras. YEAR-ROUND: Nonmigratory. In U.S., restricted to CA and FL.

Population Declining in California and Florida; apparently extirpated as a breeding species. Subspecies *oratrix* and *belizensis* endangered due to habitat destruction and capture for the pet trade.

ORANGE-WINGED PARROT *Amazona amazonica*

The Orange-winged is one of several *Amazona* species breeding in small numbers in Florida. Little is known of its natural history in the United States, but nests in royal palm snags have been found. It feeds on native and exotic fruits, nuts, and flowers. Monotypic. L 12.3" (31 cm) **Identification** A small, green parrot. Sexes similar. ADULT: Yellow face and crown divided by azure stripe above and through each eye, extending on to the nape. Orange eyes with narrow, purplish orbital ring; pale bill with blackish edges; gray legs and feet. IMMATURE: Brown eyes. FLIGHT: Upper wings have a small orange-red patch on the

outer secondaries and a dark blue trailing edge. Underwings green. Tail has a yellowish band with orange stripes on the outer tail feathers. **Similar Species** None; yellow and azure head pattern distinctive. **Voice** CALL: A shrill *kee-ik, kee-ik,* as well as various squawks, and whistled notes. **Status & Distribution** Exotic in the U.S. Native to lowlands of northern S.A., where common to abundant. YEAR-ROUND: Nonmigratory. In U.S., restricted to FL, where ±100 are found at Fort Lauderdale and Miami. **Population** Stable or increasing in Florida. Native birds are heavily trapped for the pet trade and shot for sport.

CUCKOOS, ROADRUNNERS, AND ANIS Family Cuculidae

Almost all of the species in the Cuculidae family are arboreal, inhabiting forests and well-wooded areas. Cuckoos form a remarkably variable family, which is well known for having members that are brood parasitic. Various species are known as "rain birds" throughout the world because they are very vocal at the beginning of the rainy season.

Structure Cuckoos have slender bodies and long tails. All species in the family have zygodactyl feet, where the outer toes point backward and the two inner toes point forward. The bill is usually long with a curved culmen. The wing length varies depending on whether the species is a long-distance migrant or a more sedentary species. Terrestrial species—such as the Greater Roadrunner—have long, strong legs.

Behavior Many cuckoos are solitary and are more often heard than seen. Although mostly diurnal, many species call at night. Up to 53 species of cuckoos are brood parasites; their cryptic plumage allows the females to surreptitiously approach the nests of hosts. Black-billed and Yellow-billed Cuckoos are nest builders, but they have been documented as brood parasites. Unlike cuckoos, anis live in noisy social groups and are often cooperative breeders with several females using the same nest and multiple adults feeding the nestlings. Because of the texture of their plumage, many cuckoos, when wet or in the early morning, dry their bodies by sitting on an open perch with their wings and tail spread and often with their back feathers raised to expose the skin to the sun.

Plumage For most Cuculidae species the plumage is soft and is a brown, gray, or black color, often streaked or barred. A few species exhibit bright green, rufous, or even purple plumage. The tail is generally tipped in a different color, often white. The sexes are similar in plumage in almost all species, with some size dimorphism—the females being larger.

Distribution The species of this widespread family occur in tropical and temperate regions worldwide; however, the family reaches its greatest diversity in the Old World. Most species are nonmigratory or short-distance migrants; a few species are long-distance migrants, including the Yellow-billed and Black-billed Cuckoos of North America, whose numbers may vary from year to year in response to local prey abundance. Vagrants may turn up far out of range.

Taxonomy The family divides into six subfamilies: Old World cuckoos, coucals, malkohas and cauas, American cuckoos, New World ground-cuckoos, and anis. Some taxonomists suggest that these groups represent

Groove-billed Ani (left) and Smooth-billed Ani (FL, Mar.)

distinct families. Worldwide, there are 138 species in 35 genera recognized. In North America, 6 species regularly occur, while 2 additional species are rare visitors, primarily to western Alaska.

Conservation Several species in the family rate conservation concern. Most of them occur in tropical forests and on islands; however, the populations of the Smooth-billed Ani in Florida and the Yellow-billed Cuckoo in western North America are also on the list. One species in the family has been extinct since 1850 and two others have not been reported since the early 1900s. Pollution could be a contributing factor—it appears that cuckoos are heavily impacted by pollutants. Studies have shown that chlorinated hydrocarbons build up in their tissues. —*Mark W. Lockwood*

OLD WORLD CUCKOOS Genus *Cuculus*

In this genus composed of 15 or 16 species—with most species found in southern Asia and Africa—the most well-known and widespread species is the Common Cuckoo. All species share the same basic plumage of uniform-colored upperparts and paler, often barred, underparts. They have slender bodies and long, graduated tails.

COMMON CUCKOO *Cuculus canorus*

The Common Cuckoo is well known as a brood parasite, affecting a very wide variety of hosts and occurring in numerous habitats ranging from woodlands to farmlands. Polytypic (4 ssp. worldwide; 1 recorded in N.A.). L 13" (33 cm)

Identification The Common Cuckoo has a slender body, a long rounded tail, and pointed wings. In flight, it has a falconlike appearance; its wings rarely rise above the body. It often perches in the open; when perched, it often droops its wings. It closely resembles the Oriental Cuckoo. ADULT MALE: Pale gray above and paler below with a white belly narrowly barred with gray. The undertail coverts are white and lightly barred. He has a prominent yellow orbital ring. GRAY MORPH FEMALE: Difficult to separate from the adult male, but often has a rusty buff tinge on the breast. HEPATIC MORPH FEMALE: She is rusty brown above and on breast and heavily barred—the black bars are narrower than the brown ones. Her lower back and rump are a lighter brown and either unmarked or lightly spotted.

Geographic Variation Variation in subspecies is slight and possibly clinal. All records in North America likely refer to nominate *canorus*. Subspecies identification is difficult and is based on variation in plumage coloration.

Similar Species The Common Cuckoo is very similar in appearance to the Oriental Cuckoo, and the identification of silent birds is difficult. The Common is ever so slightly larger with a proportionally heavier bill and is generally slightly lighter in overall color. The Oriental has a bolder pale marking on the underwing and buffy undertail coverts. Hepatic morph birds can be identified by their paler unmarked rumps.

Voice The male's call is a disyllabic *cuc-oo*, with emphasis on the first syllable. The female utters a load bubbling trill.

Status & Distribution Very rare spring and summer visitor to central and western Aleutian, St. Lawrence, and Pribilof Islands in Alaska. Casual to mainland. BREEDING: Palearctic, ranging from western Europe to eastern Russia. WINTER: Primarily in southern Africa, but also in India and southeast Asia. VAGRANT: Accidental to Martha's Vineyard, MA, and Lesser Antilles.

Population Stable.

hepatic morph ♀

hepatic morph ♀

♂

ORIENTAL CUCKOO *Cuculus saturatus*

hepatic morph ♀

♂

hepatic morph ♀

As with other *Cuculus,* the Oriental Cuckoo is a brood parasite. It is encountered in North America only as a casual visitor to western Alaska. Polytypic (3 ssp. worldwide; *optatus* recorded in N.A.). L 12.5" (32 cm)

Identification The Oriental closely resembles the Common Cuckoo. It has a slender body, long rounded tail, and pointed wings. In flight it resembles a small falcon. ADULT MALE: Medium gray above and paler below with a white belly barred with gray. The buffy undertail coverts are generally sparsely barred or unmarked. Prominent unmarked whitish wing linings are visible in flight. The orbital ring is bright yellow. GRAY MORPH FEMALE: Difficult to separate from the adult male, but often has a rusty buff tinge on the breast. HEPATIC MORPH FEMALE: Rusty brown above and on breast and heavily barred overall, including rump—the black bars are wider than the brown bars.

Geographic Variation Complicated. The Oriental Cuckoo is sometimes split into 2 species with the northern populations *(optatus)* separate from those in southern Asia *(saturatus* and the smaller *lepidus).* To further confuse matters, the northern population is often called *horsfieldi,* although *optatus* appears to have priority.

Similar Species It is very similar in appearance to the Common Cuckoo and the identification of silent birds is difficult. The Oriental is very slightly smaller, and gray morph birds are generally somewhat darker in overall color with slightly broader barring on the belly and buffy undertail coverts. The Oriental's prominent pale wing linings (contrasting with a solid dark underwing coverts patch) are a good field character when seen in flight. Hepatic morph birds are easily separated from the Common based on the broad black barring and barred rump.

Voice The male's call is a series of hollow notes usually given on the same pitch and in groups of four. The female's call is very similar to the trill of a Common.

Status & Distribution Casual spring, summer, and fall visitor to western Aleutian, St. Lawrence, and Pribilof Islands, AK. BREEDING: Primarily Palearctic, ranging from eastern Europe to eastern Russia and China, but with populations in S.E. Asia and Indonesia. WINTER: Primarily in S.E. Asia and Australia.

Population Stable.

NEW WORLD CUCKOOS Genus *Coccyzus*

Nine species, primarily neotropical, make up this genus. The 2 most common species in North America are long-distance migrants to South America. Most New World Cuckoos share a basic plumage pattern that consists of brown or gray upperparts with buffy or white underparts. They have slender bodies and long, graduated tails.

MANGROVE CUCKOO *Coccyzus minor*

The Mangrove Cuckoo is more often heard than seen as it often perches quietly in a tree. It is widespread in the Caribbean and in coastal habitats from northern Mexico to northern South America. Monotypic. L 12" (31 cm)
Identification It has a slender body, a long tail, and rounded wings. ADULT: It has grayish brown upperparts with a grayer crown. The throat and upper breast are white or buffy with the remainder of the underparts buffy.

The long tail is graduated with brown central rectrices tipped in black, the remaining tail feathers are black and broadly tipped with white. The bill is strongly curved with a black upper mandible and a black-tipped yellow lower mandible. IMMATURE: The black mask is faint to near absent.
Geographic Variation Up to 14 subspecies have been described, but the species is now considered monotypic. Previously the Florida population was placed in *maynardi* and the vagrants to the western Gulf Coast in *continentalis*. The birds found farther west tend to be darker in overall plumage.
Similar Species The Mangrove most closely resembles the Yellow-billed Cuckoo, but it is distinguished by the black mask, buffy underparts, and lack of rufous primaries. The voice is

continentalis

very different as well.
Voice CALL: A very guttural *gaw gaw gaw.*
Status & Distribution Uncommon. BREEDING: Nests in mangrove swamps and low canopy tropical hardwood forests. WINTER: Withdraws from northern portions of its range in FL. VAGRANT: Casual, presumably from northern Mexico, along the Gulf coast from TX to northwestern FL.

maynardi

BLACK-BILLED CUCKOO *Coccyzus erythropthalmus*

The Black-billed Cuckoo regularly feeds on caterpillars, and it also greedily consumes tent caterpillars and gypsy moth larvae during outbreaks of those insects. Monotypic. L 12" (31 cm)
Identification The Black-billed Cuckoo has a slender body, a long tail, and rounded wings ADULT: It has grayish brown upperparts and whitish under-

parts. The long tail is graduated; it is predominantly brown above, narrowly tipped with white, while the undertail is patterned in gray. It has a prominent red orbital ring. The bill is strongly curved and all dark. IMMATURE: It looks similar to the adult, but it has a buffy throat and undertail coverts. This coloration sometimes extends in the remainder of the underparts. The undertail pattern is muted and the tips of the rectrices are buffy and not as prominent. The orbital ring is buffy as well.
Similar Species The Black-billed Cuckoo most closely resembles the Yellow-billed Cuckoo, but it is distinguished by its red orbital ring, lack of rufous primaries, different undertail pattern, and narrower dark bill.

Voice CALL: A monotonous *cu-cu-cu* or *cu-cu-cu-cu* phrase.
Status & Distribution Uncommon. BREEDING: Deciduous and mixed forests to open woodlands and brushy habitats. MIGRATION: Trans-Gulf migrant, rare in the U.S. after mid-Oct. WINTER: Northern S.A. VAGRANT: Casual visitor west to the Pacific coast.
Population The Black-billed has shown a substantial decline and is considered a species of conservation concern in many areas of the United States.

juvenile

YELLOW-BILLED CUCKOO *Coccyzus americanus*

juvenile

Generally shy and elusive, the Yellow-billed Cuckoo can be easily overlooked. Its calls are usually loud and often provide the best evidence to the presence of the bird. It favors eating caterpillars and seems to respond well to outbreaks of tent caterpillars. Monotypic. L 12" (31 cm)

Identification It has a slender body, a long tail, and rounded wings. ADULT: It has grayish brown upperparts with whitish underparts. The crown can be noticeably grayer than the rest of the upperparts on some individuals. The rounded wings have reddish primaries. The long tail is graduated with brown central rectrices tipped in black; the remainder are black and broadly tipped with white. It has a yellow orbital ring. The bill is curved with a black culmen extending over much of the upper mandible; the lower mandible is yellow with a black tip. IMMATURE: It looks similar to the adult but has buffy undertail coverts. The undertail pattern is muted and the tips of the rectrices are buffy and not as prominent. The orbital ring is a dull yellow.

Geographic Variation Presently considered monotypic; however, there have been 2 subspecies described: *americanus* in eastern N.A. and *occidentalis* in the Southwest. The differentiation of these taxa is weak and limited in the contact zone.

Similar Species The Yellow-billed Cuckoo most closely resembles the Black-billed Cuckoo, but it is distinguished by the yellow orbital ring, rufous primaries, more prominently white-tipped tail, and the yellow lower mandible. Some calls, however, are quite similar.

Voice CALL: A rapid staccato *kuk-kuk-kuk* that usually slows and descends into a *kakakowlp-kowlp* ending; sounds hollow and wooden.

Status & Distribution Common in eastern N.A., becoming increasingly rare and local in much of the West. BREEDING: Open woodlands with dense undergrowth, riparian corridors, and parks. Southwestern populations increasingly limited to riparian corridors. MIGRATION: Trans-Gulf migrant as well as southeastward over Caribbean Islands. In spring, the Gulf Coast peak occurs ±1 May; southern Great Lakes ±10 May. In fall, it wanders up eastern seaboard as far north as NF. Southern Great Lakes peak ±20 Aug; Gulf Coast peak ±10 Sept. Rare in the U.S. after 1 Nov. Southwestern populations arrive late May–early June. WINTER: Casual to accidental along Gulf Coast, these records could pertain to lingering fall migrants. The majority of population winters in northern S.A., as far south as northern Argentina.

Population Populations in the western United States are declining fairly rapidly and are of considerable conservation concern. These populations depend on riparian corridors, which are under increasing pressure from exotic plants, water impoundment, and other factors. The validity of *occidentalis* may become of greater importance because some conservation groups would like to have the population considered for federal protection under the Endangered Species Act. Populations elsewhere are declining at a less precipitous rate.

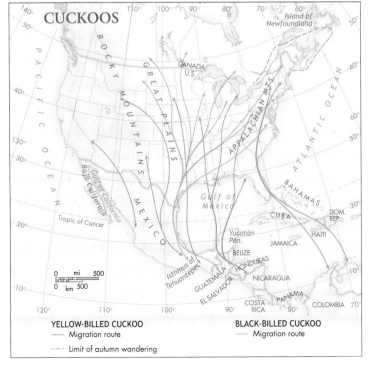

YELLOW-BILLED CUCKOO
— Migration route
- - - Limit of autumn wandering

BLACK-BILLED CUCKOO
— Migration route

ROADRUNNERS Genus *Geococcyx*

Worldwide there are 2 species in this genus, the Greater and Lesser Roadrunners. These large terrestrial cuckoos are very similar in appearance and are found primarily in arid and semiarid habitats. Roadrunners can run at speeds of up to 15 miles an hour pursuing prey or to escape predators.

GREATER ROADRUNNER *Geococcyx californianus*

The Greater Roadrunner is omnivorous, although the majority of its diet includes insects, birds, reptiles and rodents. Monotypic. L 23" (58 cm)

Identification The Greater Roadrunner is a large ground-dwelling cuckoo with a bushy crest. It is brown overall and streaked with brown and white. It has short rounded wings with a white crescent in the primaries. Its long tail has rectrices edged in white. Note the bird's long, heavy bill.

Similar Species Unmistakable. No real contenders for misidentification.

Voice CALL: A descending series of low coos.

Status & Distribution Uncommon. BREEDING: Nests in low woody plants in open scrub habitats, including chaparral, and in open woodlands. WINTER: Some local movements away from nesting habitat.

ANIS Genus *Crotophaga*

The 3 species in this genus—the Great, Groove-billed, and Smooth-billed Anis—exhibit complex social behavior and are cooperative breeders. They share a loose black plumage and a laterally compressed bill.

SMOOTH-BILLED ANI *Crotophaga ani*

The Smooth-billed Ani is most often encountered in small social groups, which normally fly in single file from one bush to the next. The flight often looks labored and weak. The Smooth-billed rarely perches high off the ground and is often quite tame. Monotypic. L 14.5" (37 cm)

Identification The Smooth-billed's plumage is entirely black, but with some purplish or greenish iridescent edges to the feathers, and it has a shaggy or disheveled appearance. The long tail is frequently held down and

wagged. The large, laterally compressed bill often has a high curve to the culmen.

Similar Species A vagrant Groove-billed Ani can be very difficult to distinguish; it is best identified by voice and close examination of the bill shape (see Groove-billed Ani). Grackles are the only other species likely to cause confusion with the Smooth-billed. The shaggy plumage and large bill are key features to use in identification.

Voice CALL: A whining, rising *quee-lick.*

Status & Distribution Very rare, perhaps on the verge of extirpation. Year-round resident in southern FL, widespread in the neotropics. Occurs in brushy or weedy habitats, most often close to water. VAGRANT: Accidental north along Atlantic coast and inland to OH.

Population The Smooth-billed's range in Florida has shrunk by two-thirds

since the mid-1970s. The reasons for this precipitous decline are unknown. Urbanization of the Florida Peninsula may be a factor, as the Smooth-billed appears to be well adapted to disturbances that result in open habitats.

GROOVE-BILLED ANI *Crotophaga sulcirostris*

The gregarious Groove-billed Ani is most often found in vocal groups of 4 to 10 birds. It typically roosts with other anis in tight bunches on vines and other protected perches. It (and the Smooth-billed Ani) has a very distinctive flight—weak flaps on rounded wings interspersed with glides. It feeds by gleaning insects off leaves but is often seen chasing grasshoppers on the ground through high grass. Nests may be single breeders to fairly large communal nests of up to 4 pairs. In these large nests, 2 or 3 females may brood the eggs simultaneously and the eggs on the bottom rarely hatch. Both males and females defend the territory and care for the young. Throughout most of its range, the Groove-billed Ani is frequently seen around cattle feeding on insects stirred up by the livestock. This aspect of its life history is rarely observed in Texas. Formerly polytypic (2 ssp. worldwide, 1 extinct; nominate in N.A.) L 13.5" (34 cm)

Identification The plumage is entirely black with iridescent purple and green overtones; the overall appearance is often shaggy or disheveled. The bird usually holds its long tail, which appears loosely joined to the body, down. The Groove-billed Ani frequently wags its tail when on open perches. The large, laterally compressed bill has a curved culmen. Adults normally have easily observed grooves on the upper mandible; on juveniles the upper mandible might be unmarked. The Groove-billed's bill shape is similar to the Smooth-billed Ani's, but the curvature of the culmen does not extend above the crown.

Geographic Variation The Groove-billed was formerly polytypic, but *pallidula* of southern Baja California is now extinct.

Similar Species A vagrant Groove-billed is a rare visitor to Florida and can be difficult to distinguish from the resident Smooth-billed Ani. Both ani species have occurred far out of range. The species identification between the two is best distinguished by voice and close examination of bill shape (particularly the bill ridge). The Groove-billed is also slightly smaller. Grackles are the only other species likely to cause confusion with the Groove-billed. The shaggy plumage and large bill are key features to use in identification.

Voice CALL: A liquid *tee-ho*, with the accent on the first syllable. This call is given raucously in quick succession at dawn when groups leave the roost. FLIGHT CALL: Soft clucking or chuckling notes.

Status & Distribution Widespread in the neotropics from southern TX to northern S.A., and south along the Pacific coast to northern Chile. BREEDING: Uncommon to locally common late Apr.–late Sept. Nests in scrub or low-canopied woodlands and in riparian corridors. Occasionally is found in more open habitats. Breeding also occurs in more open scrub, not necessarily near water. WINTER: Rare and local as majority of population has withdrawn, presumably into northeastern Mexico. Wintering populations very localized and primarily found along the Texas coast and in the lower Rio Grande Valley. VAGRANT: Wanders regularly, most often summer through winter, east along the Gulf Coast to FL. Casual throughout remainder of TX and north to CO and the Midwest. Accidental elsewhere in the eastern U.S., and has occurred as far north as southern ON. Casual to southern AZ, southern NV, and southern CA.

Population The Groove-billed Ani populations in Texas appear stable. The species is not of conservation concern anywhere in its range.

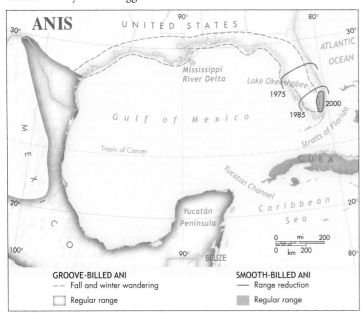

GROOVE-BILLED ANI
– – Fall and winter wandering
☐ Regular range

SMOOTH-BILLED ANI
— Range reduction
▨ Regular range

BARN OWLS Family Tytonidae

Barn Owl

Tytonidae owls share many characteristics with owls of the larger Strigidae family (see p. 321). **Structure** Tytonids differ from the Strigidae by having a heart-shaped facial disk; relatively small eyes; a short, squared tail; and serrated central claws. Their legs are long and feathered, and their toes are bare.

Behavior These owls are essentially nocturnal and sedentary. Their habitats vary, from grasslands and open areas to closed forests. They hunt small mammals and other vertebrates from a perch or in low, quartering flights over open areas; sometimes they hover in place. Voices include shrieks, whistles, hisses, and screeches, unlike the resonant hooting of Strigids.

Plumage Plumage is similar across ages and sexes, but females are generally darker and larger than males. Upperparts range from pale gray and rust through orange-red to sooty blackish, often with sparse contrasting spots. Underparts are often paler, and the facial disk is paler still.

Distribution Tytonidae is a mainly tropical family reaching its greatest species diversity in Australasia, with about 13 species present there. North America's sole representative, the Barn Owl, is the most widely distributed nocturnal raptor, resident on every continent except Antarctica.

Taxonomy The Tytonidae family comprises 2 genera (*Tyto* and *Philodus*), and about 16 species are recognized.

Conservation Species inhabiting tropical forests are threatened by the logging of large trees, which reduces their forest-dependent food supply as well as the number of large tree cavities available for nesting. The restricted range of island-dwelling species renders them particularly vulnerable to habitat destruction. BirdLife International currently lists 2 species as vulnerable and 3 as endangered.

—*David E. Quady*

Genus *Tyto*

BARN OWL *Tyto alba*

By night, an unearthly shriek may alert a birder to a ghostly white Barn Owl flying overhead. By day, whitewash on the edge of a natural cavity or pellets on the ground may indicate a nest or roost. The Barn Owl nests and roosts in dark cavities in city and farm buildings, cliffs, and trees; it hunts small rodents in low, quartering flights and from perches. Polytypic (approx. 30 ssp.; 1 in N.A.). L 16" (41 cm) WS 42" (107 cm)

Identification Flight features shallow, slow wingbeats, often with long legs dangling. May hover in place while hunting. ADULT: A very pale nocturnal owl with a white, heart-shaped facial disk. Dark brown eyes; horn-colored bill. Head and upperparts mottled rusty-brown and silvery gray, with fine, sparse black streaks and dots. Underparts vary from cinnamon to white. MALE: Palest birds are males. FEMALE: Darkest birds are always females; average larger than males. JUVENILE: Acquires complete set of fresh flight feathers within about 2 months; adults have variably worn primaries.

Similar Species Other than the Snowy Owl, this is the palest North American owl. Its flight and wing shape suggest the Long-eared Owl, but the paleness of the Barn Owl's plumage is usually evident.

Voice Male's territorial song is long, raspy, hissing shriek, *shrrreeee!* Often given many times in sequence, usually in flight and near the nest. Female's vocalization similar.

Status & Distribution Rare to fairly common. YEAR-ROUND: Occupies low-elevation, open habitats, urban and rural. Density very low in more northerly areas. WINTER: Withdraws in winter from colder areas.

Population Has suffered sharp declines in eastern North America. Canada lists it as endangered in the east and of "special concern" in the west. More than a dozen states in the Midwest and Northeast list it as endangered, threatened, or of "special concern."

TYPICAL OWLS Family Strigidae

Great Gray Owl (MN, Jan.)

Owls are chiefly nocturnal predators, ecological counterparts of the diurnal birds of prey but most closely related to nightjars (Caprimulgiformes). Being chiefly nocturnal, they are difficult to detect, identify, and study. In the daytime, a collection of regurgitated pellets on the ground or a noisy mob of songbirds will often point a birder to a roosting or nesting owl. At night, voice is the best means to detect an owl and usually the best way to identify it.

Structure All owls have a relatively large head with immobile eyes that face forward to provide binocular vision and good depth perception. Acute hearing complements owls' keen eyesight. Most have a prominent facial disk formed of stiff feathers whose shape can be altered to help focus sounds. In some genera, ear openings are asymmetrically located in the skull, improving their ability to distinguish the direction and distance to a sound source. Asymmetric external ear structures on many genera provide further discrimination based on the frequency of the emitted sound. Some owl species can detect and capture prey in total darkness, by sound alone. Feather structure contributes to quiet flight. Velvety pile on flight feathers and soft body feathering absorb sound, while comb-like fringes on the leading edge of the outermost primaries reduce the sound of wings cutting the air. Some largely diurnal owls lack these fringes; their flight is not as quiet as that of nocturnal owls. Owls' bills are strongly curved, with a sharp point for tearing prey. They can position their toes 2 forward and 2 backward for seizing prey, and their long claws are needle-sharp for clutching and quickly dispatching it. Unlike Tytonidae, Strigids generally have circular facial disks, relatively large eyes, and rounded tails; in addition, their central toe's claw is not serrated.

Behavior Most owl species forage by perching and watching for prey. They nest in natural or human-made cavities or in old woodpecker holes; some use old tree nests of raptors, crows, or squirrels. The larger owls prey mainly on mammals and the smallest on insects, with fish and small birds taken by some owls. Owls consume small prey whole but tear apart larger prey before consumption. They periodically regurgitate a dense pellet containing indigestible parts such as bones, chitin, hair, and feathers.

Voice The most commonly heard vocalization is a species-specific territorial song, delivered mainly in the month or 2 during which male owls establish a territory, locate potential nest sites, and attract a mate. This period of active singing varies among species: it begins about November for the early nesting resident Great Horned Owl and about April for the migrant Flammulated Owl. Owls also utter a variety of hoots, whistles, screams, whines, screeches, barks, or rasps when threatened, alarmed, or begging, for example. Sometimes these cannot be pinned down to a particular species; indeed one of the charms of nighttime owling is hearing a new, unidentifiable sound.

Plumage Owl plumage is similar between sexes, but females are generally larger and sometimes darker than males. Downy young of most species molt directly into adultlike plumage; only a few hold a distinctively colored juvenile plumage for an appreciable period. Owls lack a distinctive breeding plumage, so after first attaining adultlike plumage, an owl's appearance changes little during its lifetime. Most adult Strigids are cryptically patterned in shades of brown, though their facial disk may be quite distinctive. Many have erectile feather tufts at the sides of their crown, called "ear tufts," although they are unrelated to the bird's ears or their hearing; their function is not known for certain.

Distribution Owls occur worldwide in virtually all terrestrial habitats, from the tropics to the Arctic, from below sea level to elevations above 14,000 feet. Most species are mainly resident and sedentary.

Taxonomy Worldwide, about 190 Strigid species in about 25 genera are currently recognized. New species are still being described—about 10 in the last 20 years—as their voices (which are innate, rather than learned) and other attributes become better known.

Conservation Four island-dwelling Strigids are known to have gone extinct since 1600. BirdLife International currently considers 5 species critically endangered, 7 endangered, and 11 vulnerable; more than half of these are restricted to islands, where habitat loss is their greatest threat. —*David E. Quady*

SCOPS-OWLS Genus *Otus*

These are small to medium-size, mainly nocturnal Old World owls. Most have ear tufts and short, rounded wings. They inhabit forests and semi-open areas with scattered bushes or groups of trees. All have only 1 song type. About 41 species are currently recognized (1 breeding and 1 vagrant in N.A.), but more than half are confined to one or a few islands.

FLAMMULATED OWL *Otus flammeolus*

grayish type

reddish type

Once considered rare, the strictly nocturnal, insectivorous Flammulated Owl may actually be the most common owl in its breeding habitat. Its cryptic plumage provides excellent daytime camouflage, but a persistent flashlight-bearing birder tracking a singing owl at night may eventually be rewarded with deep red eye shine returned from a pine cone–sized shape perched close to a tree trunk. The Flammulated Owl nests and roosts in old woodpecker holes or natural tree cavities, sometimes in loose colonies. Monotypic. L 6.7" (17 cm) WS 20" (51 cm)

Identification Flight is nervous, darting, sometimes jerky, interspersed with occasional hovering as it pauses to check for prey. ADULT: Small; dark brown eyes; small and often indistinct rounded ear tufts; and variegated rufous and gray plumage. Pale grayish facial disk with variable rufous wash strongest around the eyes. Rufous-tinged creamy spots form bold line on scapulars. Grayish brown bill; feathered legs, bare toes.

Geographic Variation Plumage and size vary clinally. Birds in the northwestern part of the range are the most finely marked; those in the Great Basin mountains are grayish and have the coarsest markings; those in the southeast are reddish. Wingspan and weight increase from southeast to northwest, presumably correlated with migration distance. Three or more subspecies have been named, but most authors consider it monotypic.

Similar Species The Flammulated Owl resembles screech-owls, but it is smaller; it also has dark eyes, shorter ear tufts, and relatively longer, pointier wings.

Voice The male's advertising song is a series of single or paired soft, deep, hollow, short hoots repeated every 2–3 seconds, lower-pitched than a screech-owl's. Single hoots are often preceded by 2 grace notes at a lower pitch. Hoots resemble a distant Long-eared Owl's. Female's hoots are higher pitched and more quavering. Ventriloquial; difficult to localize and usually closer than the listener estimates.

Status & Distribution Uncommon to common during breeding season, but overlooked. Silent and little known the rest of the year. BREEDING: Inhabits primarily open montane coniferous forest, especially with ponderosa pine, mixed with oaks or aspen. MIGRATION: Highly migratory; winters in Central America. North American breeders depart Aug.–Nov., return beginning late Mar.–late May. Rarely detected during migration. WINTER: Range, diet, and habits are little known. VAGRANT: Accidental in FL, AL, LA, east TX, and 120 km offshore in the Gulf of Mexico.

Population Canada considers it a species of "special concern" because of its small population and vulnerability to habitat alteration by forest harvest.

ORIENTAL SCOPS-OWL *Otus sunia*

The Oriental Scops-Owl is a small, nocturnal, primarily insectivorous owl of Asia's southeast rim. Its geographically variable vocalizations suggest that perhaps more than one species is involved. Polytypic (7 ssp.; 1 vagrant in N.A.). L 7.5" (19 cm) WS 21" (53 cm)

Identification ADULT: Fine dark streaks on head; dark shaft streaks and thin horizontal pencil-lines on

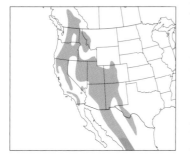

japonicus rufous morph

breast; short ear tufts. Gray-brown, reddish gray, and rufous morphs exist. Yellow eyes; horn-green bill with blackish tip. Legs only partially feathered.

Similar Species No other small owl is likely to occur on islands far offshore mainland Alaska.

Voice On the breeding grounds, the territorial song of *japonicus* (the vagrant found in N.A.) is a rather low, whistled *tu-tu-tu*, repeated monotonously at short intervals. Probably silent on migration.

Status & Distribution Uncommon on breeding grounds in Japan. BREEDING: Favors deciduous and mixed forest, from Pakistan and India through China to eastern Siberia and the main islands of Japan. MIGRATION: Four northerly subspecies, including *japonicus,* are largely migratory, wintering mostly in southern China, Thailand, and Malaysia and returning about May. Southerly subspecies are resident. VAGRANT: Rufous morph *japonicus* found June 5, 1977, and June 20, 1979, on Aleutian Islands, AK, provide the only two North American records.

Population Not globally threatened.

SCREECH-OWLS Genus Megascops

Most of these small to medium-size nocturnal owls of the New World have ear tufts and short, rounded wings. They inhabit forests, open woodlands, parks, and arid open and semi-open areas. All have more than 1 song type and are best identified by voice, combined with habitat and range. This genus (24 sp.; 3 in N.A.) recently split from the genus *Otus*.

EASTERN SCREECH-OWL Megascops asio

rufous morph

gray morph

gray morph juvenile

maxwelliae

In eastern wooded suburbs, this small, owl is often the most common avian predator, emerging from its nest or roost hole at dusk to hawk insects or hunt other small prey, including songbirds and rodents. Its whinnying and trilling songs are familiar, but its vocalizations also include rasps, barks, hoots, chuckles, and screeches. Its hunting is mostly nocturnal but often crepuscular and occasionally diurnal; it nests in old woodpecker holes or natural tree cavities and readily uses properly sized and positioned nest boxes. Courtship occurs late January through mid-March, with the male advertising its presence and also potential nest sites. Eggs are laid beginning in early March; fledging begins mid- to late May. The juvenile remains dependent on parents for another 8 to 10 weeks. The Eastern was formerly classified with the Western as a single species; range separation is not yet fully known. Polytypic (5–6 ssp.; all in N.A.). L 8.5" (22 cm) WS 21" (53 cm)

Identification ADULT: Small; yellow eyes; bill yellow-green at the base with a paler tip. Ear tufts are prominent if raised; when flattened the bird has a round-headed look. Facial disk is prominently rimmed dark, especially on the lower half. Underparts are marked by vertical streaks crossed by widely spaced dark bars that are nearly as wide as the streaks. Scapulars have blackish edged white outer webs, forming a line of white spots across the shoulder. Feet are proportionately large. Occurs in rufous and gray morphs as well as intermediate brownish plumages; plumages are alike, but the female is larger. Markings on underparts are less distinct on rufous morph birds. JUVENILE: Similar to adult in coloration, but indistinctly barred light and dark on head, mantle, and underparts; ear tufts not yet fully developed.

Geographic Variation Body size and intensity of markings vary clinally: smaller and darker in the south and east, larger and lighter in the north and west. Color morph distribution is more complex. In most areas intermediate brownish birds compose less than 10

percent of the population; but in Florida, gray, rufous, and brownish birds are evidently about equally common. The rufous morph becomes more common in the Southeast and outnumbers the gray morph in some areas. Normally only gray morph birds are found on the Great Plains and in southernmost Texas. The large northwest subspecies *maxwelliae* is the palest and most faintly marked.

Similar Species The Western Screech-Owl's bill is blackish or dark gray at the base, but gray-plumaged individuals are otherwise nearly identical in appearance and habits to the Eastern gray morph birds. Where their ranges overlap, the two species are best identified by voice.

Voice The territorial defense song is a strongly descending and quavering trill up to 3 seconds long, reminiscent of a horse's whinny. The contact song (3–6 secs.) is a single low-pitched quavering trill of about 14 notes per second that may rise or fall slightly at the end. The male utters this sound when advertising a nest site, courting, and arriving at the nest with food. Both sexes sing each song; the female's voice is slightly higher pitched. Both adult females (during courtship) and juveniles beg for food with a rough, grating rasp, usually falling in pitch.

Status & Distribution Common. Range now overlaps that of the Western Screech-Owl in eastern CO, along the Cimarron River, in extreme southwest KS, and in TX east of the Pecos River to near San Angelo. Both species are found at Big Bend N.P. in TX, where the Western is uncommon and the Eastern is rare; hybrids are known from there and from eastern CO. YEAR-ROUND: Resident in a wide variety of tree-dominated habitats: woodlots, forests, river valleys, swamps, orchards, parks, suburban gardens below about 4,500 feet. May make local or altitudinal movements in severe winters or during food shortages.

Population Generally thought to be stable.

WHISKERED SCREECH-OWL *Megascops trichopsis*

After hiding by day close to a tree trunk or in dense foliage, the nocturnal, mainly insectivorous Whiskered Screech-Owl becomes active at dusk. At the onset of the breeding season, the pair's duets reveal their presence, and imitating their song will often bring them into close view. They nest in natural tree cavities or abandoned woodpecker holes. Polytypic (3 ssp.; 1 in N.A.). L 7.2" (18 cm) WS 18" (46 cm)

Identification ADULT: Small, gray overall with yellow eyes; bill yellowish green at the base with pale tip. Facial disk feathers at the base of the bill have whisker-like extensions. Ear tufts prominent if raised; when flattened, bird looks round headed. Small feet.

Similar Species Very similar to the Western Screech-Owl (see below).

Voice Territorial song a series of 4–8 equally spaced notes, *po po PO po po po,* mostly with emphasis on the third note, falling slightly in pitch at the end. Courtship song a syncopated series of hoots, like Morse code: *pidu po po, pidu po po, pidu po po* (pitch same as the Western Screech-Owl's), often in a duet with the slightly higher-pitched female.

Status & Distribution Common. YEAR-ROUND: Inhabits dense oak and oak-conifer woodlands in the mountains of southeast AZ and adjacent NM, generally at higher elevations than the Western Screech-Owl. Found at 4,000–6,000 feet, but mostly around 5,000 feet. WINTER: May move to lower elevations.

Population Trends not known.

WESTERN SCREECH-OWL *Megascops kennicottii*

northwest coast
kennicottii

This small, widespread, eared owl of the West inhabits a broad range of semi-open, low-elevation habitats. At dusk it may be seen as it emerges from its roost cavity to perch and look for prey; or it may be heard at the onset of breeding season giving its familiar "bouncing ball" song. Courtship begins in January and February, with male singing near nest. Eggs are laid between late March and late April. It preys on a wide variety of small animals, especially mammals, birds, and invertebrates, and nests in old woodpecker holes or natural tree cavities. It is nocturnal and somewhat crepuscular, becoming active shortly after sunset.

Polytypic (8 ssp.; 6 in N.A.). L 8.5" (22 cm) WS 21" (53 cm)

Identification ADULT: Small, with yellow eyes; bill blackish or dark gray at the base with pale tip. Ear tufts prominent if raised; when flattened, bird looks round headed. Underparts marked by vertical streaks crossed by much narrower and more closely spaced dark bars. Feet are proportionately large. Sexes alike in plumage; females average slightly larger than males.

Geographic Variation Plumage generally monomorphic in a given area: brown or gray-brown in the Northwest, gray in southern deserts. Northwest coastal *kennicottii* more variable; generally dark brownish gray, but a small percentage are reddish. Size increases from south to north and from lowland to higher elevations. Toes feathered in northern populations, bristled in southern deserts.

Similar Species The Whiskered is slightly smaller, with proportionately smaller feet, different colored bill, and usually bolder cross barring below. Where ranges overlap, the Western is generally found at lower elevations. The Eastern's bill is greenish. Best separated from other screech-owls by voice. The Flammulated Owl has dark eyes, is much smaller, and generally occupies higher elevations in areas where the species overlap.

Voice Two songs; both are common. A 2-part tremulous whistled trill, first part short and second long, dropping slightly near the end: *dddd-dddddddr;* also a short sequence of 5–10 hesitating notes, accelerating in "bouncing ball" rhythm, ending in a trill: *pwep pwep pwep pwep pwepwepwepepepep.* Both sexes sing each song; the female's voice is higher pitched.

Status & Distribution Common. YEAR-ROUND: Inhabits open woodlands, streamside groves, deserts, suburban areas, and parks. Range has expanded eastward along the Arkansas River in CO, along the Cimarron River into extreme southeast KS, and across the Pecos River in TX, increasing its area of sympatry with the Eastern; slow eastward expansion may also be underway north to AB. Hybrids are known from CO and from Big Bend N.P., TX.

Population No data, but probably declining slowly as habitat is lost.

EAGLE-OWLS Genus *Bubo*

These nocturnal owls, most of which possess prominent ear tufts and powerful talons, are found in Eurasia, Indonesia, Africa, and the Americas. They occur in virtually all habitats except the densest forests and the largest deserts. About 18 species are currently recognized (2 in N.A.). Some authorities include Asia's Fish-Owls (genus *Ketupa*) in *Bubo*.

GREAT HORNED OWL *Bubo virginianus*

Many birders first meet this formidable owl in late winter by finding a female sitting in a large stick nest in a leafless tree. Others are introduced to it as a hulking, eared shape atop a power pole at dusk—perhaps a male bending nearly horizontally as it sings. Primarily a nocturnal perch hunter, the Great Horned Owl is a fierce predator that takes a wide variety of prey, but most commonly mammals, up to the size of a large hare. It favors disused tree nests of other large species, such as the Red-tailed Hawk, for nesting but also uses cavities in trees or cliffs, deserted buildings, and artificial platforms. It breeds early, with first eggs laid by January in Ohio, later farther north. Young climb onto nearby branches at 6 to 7 weeks and fly well from approximately 10 weeks. It often spends its daylight hours dozing in a tree, where the raucous cawing of a chorus of crows may lead one to the bird. Polytypic (approx. 12 ssp.; 7 in N.A.). L 22" (56 cm) WS 54" (137 cm)

subarcticus

Identification In flight, wings are broad and long, pointed toward the tip; ear tufts are usually flattened and the head is tucked in, producing a blunt profile. Flight is direct; wingbeats are stiff, steady, and mostly below the horizontal. ADULT: A very powerful, bulky owl with a broad body. Females larger than males and generally darker. Large head, stout ear tufts, and staring yellow eyes create a catlike appearance. Broad facial disk rimmed with black; whitish superciliary "eyebrows." White foreneck often conspicuous and ruff-like, especially when vocalizing. Upper chest coarsely mottled; rest of the underparts crossbarred. Gray bill; densely feathered legs and toes. Plumage and size vary geo-

graphically. JUVENILE: Downy plumage grayish to buff, with dusky barring. By about October, young birds acquire a complete set of flight feathers and tail feathers that differ in pattern, shape, and wear from those of adults: they have broader and more numerous crossbars, wings with uniformly fresh-looking rather than variably worn flight feathers, and tail feathers tapered rather than blunt ended.

Geographic Variation In general, birds of the eastern subspecies (inc. nominate) are medium sized and brownish, with medium pale feet. Birds of the Pacific coast subspecies group are small and dark, with dusky feet. Birds of the interior western subspecies group are large and variably pale, with whitish feet. The palest subspecies, *subarcticus,* is resident across the far north-central portion of the range and has wandered southeast in winter as far as New Jersey.

Similar Species The Long-eared Owl is smaller and more slender and weighs much less; it has a dark vertical stripe through its eye and longer, more closely set ear tufts; it also lacks the white

throat. Its flight is floppier, and its voice is different. All other large North American owls lack ear tufts. Female and young Snowy Owls somewhat resemble *subarcticus,* but they have a white face and lack ear tufts.

Voice SONG: Territorial song is a series of 3–8 loud, deep hoots in a rhythmic series; the second and third hoots are often short and rapid: commonly *hoo hoo-HOO hoooo hoo;* often longer, *hoo huhuHOO hooooo hoo.* Mostly heard near dusk and dawn. Male territorial singing begins about November. Duetting commonly begins 1–2 months before the first egg is laid. Female's voice is higher pitched, closer to a Mourning Dove's.

Status & Distribution Common and widespread. YEAR-ROUND: Resident, sedentary, and territorial within the varied habitats of its breeding range, from forest to city to open desert. Irruptions from northern regions can occur in winter (esp. in response to population crashes of snowshoe hares).

Population Robust and reasonably stable within limits of annual fluctuations related to prey availability.

SNOWY OWL *Bubo scandiacus*

During winter, this ground-nesting, charismatic owl might appear far to the south. It will forage at all hours during continuous summer light, mainly from a perch. Lemmings and voles are its main prey. Monotypic. L 23" (58 cm) WS 60" (152 cm)

Identification Flight strong, steady, direct, jerky. Often glides on horizontal wings. ADULT: White, large; rounded head; small yellow eyes; blackish bill; heavily feathered legs, feet. Females larger than males. Male's plumage usually broken with narrow, sparse

immature

dark bars or spots. Female's markings larger, darker. Markings less intense as birds age; old males may be pure white. IMMATURE: More heavily marked than adult females.

Voice Fairly vocal when breeding, otherwise largely silent. Male's song a far-carrying series of 2–6 deep, low hoots, last often the loudest; higher-pitched female rarely hoots. When disturbed, either sex may utter a repeated *kre* call. High-pitched, drawn-out scream protests intrusion into winter territory.

Status & Distribution Uncommon to fairly common. BREEDING: Open tundra. Nomadic; breeds only where prey abundant. WINTER: Retreats from northernmost part of its range. Irruptive; plummeting lemming populations may drive birds as far south as central CA and northern TX, AL, and FL. Accidental on Bermuda.

Population Overall numbers are presumed to have changed little in North America.

HAWK OWLS Genus *Surnia*

NORTHERN HAWK OWL *Surnia ulula*

This largely diurnal Holarctic owl is often seen perched atop a conifer in a mostly open area, watching for voles or other prey. Its flight is low and fast (with quick, stiff wingbeats) and highly maneuverable; it occasionally hovers. It stoops onto nearby prey with a smooth, gliding dive off its perch. Nests are found in cavities atop broken trunks, natural tree holes, and old holes of large woodpeckers. Polytypic (3 ssp.; 1 in N.A.). L 16" (41 cm) WS 32" (81 cm)

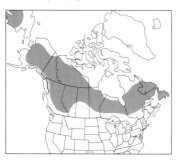

Identification ADULT: Has a long, graduated tail; a falconlike profile; and a black-bordered facial disk. Its underparts are barred brown.

Geographic Variation Eurasian nominate is paler overall than the North American *caparoch;* 2 supposed Alaskan nominate records may pertain instead to pale *caparoch.*

Similar Species The much smaller Boreal Owl is strictly nocturnal, has short wings and tail, and is streaked below.

Voice Male's song is a trilling, rolling whistle, *ulululululululul . . . ,* ±12 notes per second, lasting up to 14 seconds, then repeated. Heard mainly at night, reminiscent of the Boreal's song, but longer, higher pitched, sharper.

Status & Distribution Uncommon. BREEDING: Across taiga belt, from the edge of the forested steppe north to timberline. Nomadic; breeds only where prey abundant. WINTER: Retreats slightly from northernmost part of mapped range. Irruptions probably

tied to vole population cycles, which occasionally send large numbers of birds farther south. Has reached OR, NE, OH, PA, and NJ in winter; accidental on Bermuda.

Population Thought to be stable in N.A.

PYGMY-OWLS Genus *Glaucidium*

These small but aggressive long-tailed owls (approx. 30 sp.; 2 in N.A.) lack ear tufts; many are mainly diurnal. Best identified by voice where ranges overlap, they inhabit deserts, deciduous bottomlands, wooded foothills, and high-elevation coniferous forests; they occur on all temperate continents except Australia. Many prey mainly on other birds.

NORTHERN PYGMY-OWL *Glaucidium gnoma*

Rockies type

Pacific coast type

This aggressive diurnal predator sometimes catches birds larger than itself. Mobbing songbirds may lead a birder to the owl. Chiefly diurnal, it is most active at dawn and dusk. It makes its nests in natural tree cavities and old woodpecker holes. Polytypic (7 ssp.; 5 in N.A.). L 6.7" (17 cm) WS 15" (38 cm)

Identification ADULT: Long tail, dark brown with pale bars; rusty brown or gray-brown upperparts; spotted crown;

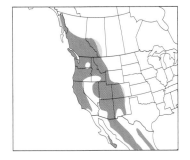

underparts white with dark streaks; prominent "false eyes" on nape. Females average redder or browner, males grayer. JUVENILE: Crown spots indistinct or lacking; other whitish markings indistinct. Flight is undulating, with bursts of quick wingbeats; not as quiet as nocturnal owls.

Geographic Variation Birds of the interior west subspecies *pinicola* are the grayest; Pacific birds are browner.

Similar Species Other small owls within the Northern Pygmy-Owl's geographic and elevation range have short tails, lack nape marks, and have different general plumage patterns.

Voice SONG: A mellow, whistled, *took* or *took-took,* repeated in a well-spaced series. (See sidebar below.) Songs of interior subspecies are lower pitched and faster than those of the coastal subspecies. Also gives a rapid series of *hoo* or *took* notes followed by a single *took.*

Status & Distribution Uncommon. YEAR-ROUND: Dense woodlands in foothills and mountains. In colder areas of its range, descends downslope in winter.

Population No data on historical changes.

Identification of "Mountain Pygmy-Owl"

Many authorities treat *Glaucidium gnoma gnoma* as a species distinct from the Northern Pygmy-Owl, calling it the "Mountain Pygmy-Owl." It ranges from the densely-wooded foothills and forests of mountains in southeastern Arizona, south through Mexico's thick interior highland forests. In plumage, the "Mountain Pygmy-Owl" closely resembles the slightly larger *pinicola,* a subspecies of Northern Pygmy-Owl found in the interior west. Their ranges may overlap. Like the *pinicola,* the "Mountain Pygmy-Owl" is grayer than other Northerns, which often have rusty-brown upperparts; and it has a spotted crown; white, dark-streaked underparts; and yellow eyes. Also, its black nape spots look like eyes on the back of its head. In the field, the "Mountain" and the *pinicola* can be separated reliably only by voice.

The "Mountain Pygmy-Owl's" song is a series of mellow, whistled,

"Coastal" Northern Pygmy-Owl (CA, Jan.)

"Mountain" Northern Pygmy-Owl (AZ, May)

and paired *took-tooks,* about 1 pair per second on about the same pitch as *pinicola's* single *tooks;* it often starts hesitantly and then runs into prolonged song, mostly of paired *took-took* notes, but with single notes occasionally thrown in.

Owl vocalizations are inherited, not learned. In recent years, vocalization differences noted in the field have led many ornithologists to recognize new species after confirming other differences from sister taxa. Within the Northern Pygmy-Owl complex, some authorities elevate *hoskinsii* of southern Baja California—with its slower, paired *took-took* notes—to species status, calling it the "Cape (or Baja) Pygmy-Owl." Some also suggest species status for *cobanense,* the "Guatemala Pygmy-Owl" of Chiapas to Honduras, in which a reddish morph predominates; its voice is apparently still undescribed. ∎

FERRUGINOUS PYGMY-OWL *Glaucidium brasilianum*

The Ferruginous Pygmy-Owl is scarce at the northern limit of its range. Still, a birder walking its arid habitat in the springtime might hear its sharp, seemingly endless song ringing through the predawn darkness. One might chance upon it hunting quietly during the day; it hunts from a perch and by inspecting tree cavities. It roosts in crevices and cavities and nests chiefly in old woodpecker holes or natural tree cavities. Polytypic (approx. 12 ssp.; 2 in N.A.). L 6.7" (17 cm) WS 15" (38 cm)

Identification Not as quiet in flight as nocturnal owls. Flight over larger distances is rather straight, with several rapid wingbeats alternating with glides; like a woodpecker. ADULT: Long tail, reddish with dark or dusky bars. Gray-brown upperparts; faintly streaked crown. White throat puffed out and more apparent when bird sings. Yellow eyes; prominent "false eyes" on nape. White underparts streaked reddish brown. JUVENILE: Like adults, but crown streaking very indistinct or lacking.

Geographic Variation Arizona's *cactorum* is slightly grayer than Texas's *ridgwayi*. Some authorities treat the 2 as belonging to a separate species, "Ridgway's Pygmy-Owl" *(Glaucidium ridgwayi)*.

Similar Species The much smaller, nocturnal Elf Owl is short tailed and lacks false eyes. The Northern Pygmy-Owl's range overlaps in Arizona, but it inhabits higher elevations, its crown and breast are spotted, and it has fewer, more-whitish tail bands.

Voice The male's territorial and courtship song is a series of upslurred, high-pitched whistled *pwip!* notes, monotonously delivered at about 2.5 notes per second. Phrases of about 10 to more than 100 notes are repeated for minutes at a time, spaced 5–10 seconds apart. Female's voice is higher and wheezier.

Status & Distribution Rare sedentary resident in southeast AZ; uncommon sedentary resident in south TX. Common throughout most of its range south of the U.S. YEAR-ROUND: Inhabits live oak-honey mesquite woodlands, mesquite brush, and riparian areas in TX, where insects are its main prey. In AZ, inhabits riparian woodlands and Sonoran desert scrub, hunting mainly reptiles, birds, and small mammals.

Population Much reduced, probably because of loss and fragmentation of habitat. The "Cactus Ferruginous Pygmy-Owl," *cactorum,* is federally listed as endangered in Arizona.

Genus Micrathene

ELF OWL *Micrathene whitneyi*

This is the world's smallest owl. The song of this strictly nocturnal, insectivorous owl is a familiar sound on moonlit spring evenings. It nests and roosts in old woodpecker holes or other cavities in saguaros and trees. Polytypic (4 ssp.; 2 in N.A.). L 5.8" (15 cm) WS 14.7" (37 cm)

Identification Flight composed of uniformly rapid wingbeats in straight-line hunting strikes; less quiet than other nocturnal owls. Occasionally glides and hovers while feeding. ADULT: Tiny; round head; yellow eyes; lacks ear tufts. Wings fairly long, tail very short. Upperparts grayish brown to brown with buff to cinnamon spots on widespread southwest *whitneyi;* face and underparts with substantial cinnamon. JUVENILE: Like adults, but head and back markings slightly less distinct.

Geographic Variation Weak; clinal where ranges meet. Upperparts of *idonea* (south TX) are grayish, with little or no brown; face and underparts have little or no cinnamon.

Similar Species Pygmy-owls are chiefly diurnal, with long tails and "false eyes." The larger screech-owls have ear tufts and streaks below. The Terrestrial Burrowing Owl is long legged, much larger, with bold brown and whitish spots.

Voice The male's territorial and courtship song is an irregular series of usually 5–7 high-pitched *churp* notes, delivered at ±5 notes per second. Both sexes utter a short, soft, whistle-like contact call, *peeu;* sometimes precedes male's song.

Status & Distribution Fairly common to common. BREEDING: Inhabits desert lowlands, foothills, and canyons, especially among oaks and sycamores. MIGRATION: Northern populations migrate to southern Mexico by Oct. and return by Mar., males first. Casual in winter in southernmost TX.

Population Numbers reduced where habitat has been destroyed or degraded. State-listed as endangered in CA; probably already extirpated there, as in southern NV.

Genus *Athene*

BURROWING OWL *Athene cunicularia*

juvenile

western *hypugaea*

During daylight, this owl often perches conspicuously at the entrance to its burrow nest or on a low post. It bobs its head to better gauge an intruder's distance. Primarily nocturnal, it hunts insects, small mammals, and birds from a perch or in low, ranging flights; it nests singly or in small colonies. Polytypic (approx. 20 ssp.; 2 breeding in N.A.). L 9.5" (24 cm) WS 23" (58 cm)
Identification Ground dweller; long legs, unlike all other small owls. Flight is low and undulating, with long legs trailing behind; often hovers like a kestrel. ADULT: Round head lacking ear tufts. JUVENILE: Plain brown upperparts with little or no distinct marking; dark brown chest; pale buff underparts.
Geographic Variation Western *hypugaea* is pale brown with buff mottling and spotting. Slightly smaller *floridana* is darker brown, with whitish mottling and spotting, and less buffy below. The *hypugaea* associates with burrowing mammal colonies and usually occupies a disused mammal burrow; *floridana* usually excavates its own burrow.
Voice Male's primary song is a soft, repeated *coo-cooooo*, reminiscent of the Greater Roadrunner; also gives a chat-

tering series of *chack* notes. When disturbed in their nest, young birds utter a dry rasping rattle very like the sound of a threatening rattlesnake.
Status & Distribution Still fairly common in some areas. BREEDING: Open country, grasslands, golf courses, airports. MIGRATION: Most northerly populations migrate or disperse, probably southward; information is scant. VAGRANT: Casual in spring and fall to west and south ON, south QC, ME, and NC; to AL and northwestern FL on the Gulf Coast. Either subspecies might be found along the Atlantic coast.
Population Greatly reduced in much of the northern Great Plains by extermination of prairie dogs, conversion of

prairies to cultivation, pesticide use, and habitat destruction. Declines continue. Many states list it as endangered or of "special concern"; endangered in Canada, with fewer than 1,000 pairs thought to remain.

WOOD OWLS Genera *Ciccaba* and *Strix*

Medium-large to large nocturnal owls with large eyes and large, rounded heads, lacking ear tufts. Their plumage is mostly cryptic; several species have different color morphs. They occupy wooded habitats in much of the world and prey mainly on small mammals and birds. (*Ciccaba* often merged in *Strix*; approx. 20 sp.; 3 resident, 1 accidental in N.A.)

MOTTLED OWL *Ciccaba virgata*

This medium-sized, very vocal nocturnal owl inhabits a variety of wooded habitats in Central and South America. Polytypic

(7 ssp.; 1 accidental in N.A.). L 14" (36 cm) WS 33" (84 cm)
Identification ADULT: Round head, no ear tufts; dark brown eyes. Light morph in mostly drier areas (e.g., northern Mex.) has brown facial disk with bold white brows and whiskers; dark brown above with faint brownish barring; mottled dark brown on chest, rest of underparts streaked dark brown. Morph in more humid areas is somewhat darker all over, underparts a deep buff ground color; some individuals very black.
Geographic Variation Northerly subspecies are smaller, with fine distinct barring above; those in the Amazon region are larger and more reddish brown.
Similar Species Closely related, larger Barred Owl has prominent barring

across upper chest and paler facial disk.
Voice Territorial song deep, gruff to resonant hoots: a single *wh-OWH* and *WOOH*, and longer series, typically 3–10 hoots, often accelerating and becoming stronger before fading.
Status & Distribution Common. YEAR-ROUND: Subspecies *squamulata* resident from southern Sonora south to Guerrero; *tamaulipensis* in central Nuevo León through southern Tamaulipas; other subspecies south through Middle and South America to northeastern Argentina. An apparent roadkill found in Feb. 1983 in south TX represents the only accidental record in N.A. Subspecies not known, but likely *tamaulipensis*.
Population Not globally threatened.

SPOTTED OWL *Strix occidentalis*

This gentle-looking owl can be quite confiding when found dozing on a shaded limb during the day, perhaps alongside its mate. Imitating its call at dusk in a mature western forest may summon a mellow, echoing response from a far-away owl, but sometimes a Spotted will fly in silently and unseen and then announce its presence with hair-raising barks. From a perch, it seeks wood rats, flying squirrels, and other small mammals. It nests mainly in tree cavities but also in debris on tree limbs or in old nests of other species. In the southwest, it also uses cliff ledges and caves. Polytypic (3–5 ssp.; 3 in N.A.). L 18" (46 cm) WS 41" (104 cm)

Identification Flight is slow and direct, with methodical wingbeats interspersed with gliding. ADULT: Brown overall with round, elliptical or irregular white spots on its head, back, and underparts; lacks ear tufts. Indistinct concentric circles set in a rounded facial disk emphasize its dark eyes. Central tail feathers expose 3–6 pale bars between their tips and the tips of the uppertail coverts. Sexes alike in plumage; female larger. Strictly nocturnal. JUVENILE: By about September, young birds acquire a complete set of fresh flight feathers that are narrower and more tapered than the adult's variably worn ones. Central tail feathers are pointed, not blunt tipped as on adults, and expose 5–7 pale bars.

Geographic Variation Three subspecies generally recognized in N.A. vary in color (dark to light) and spots (small to large) from north to south. The "Northern Spotted Owl" *(caurina)*, which resides from Marin County, California, to British Columbia, is the largest. The "California Spotted Owl" (nominate) is resident in California in the Sierra Nevada and from Monterey County southward. The "Mexican Spotted Owl" *(lucida,* or *huachucae,* according to some authorities) is resident in the Southwest and in Mexico. Some authorities recognize up to two additional subspecies in Mexico.

Similar Species The slightly larger Barred Owl is barred and streaked below, not spotted. Hybridization has occurred. See the Barred Owl.

Voice A series of usually 4 nearly monotonic doglike barks, *hoo! hu-hu hooooh,* is used by either sex to proclaim and defend territory. Female's is higher pitched. Variants include ending with a sharper, louder bark, *hoo! hu-hu ow!,* and renditions of 7–15 notes in a series. Contact call, given mainly by females, is a hollow, upslurred whistle, *cooweeeeip!* Females use a rapid series of 3–7 loud barking notes, *ow!-ow!-ow!-ow!-ow!,* during territorial disputes.

Status & Distribution Uncommon resident; decreasing in number due to habitat destruction. Further threatened by predation and hybridization as the Barred Owl expands into its range in the Northwest and CA. YEAR-ROUND: Inhabits mature coniferous and mixed forests and wooded canyons, usually with multileveled, closed canopies and uneven-aged trees. Some individuals descend to lower elevations in winter. **Population** Relatively widespread within ranges that are presumed to have changed little overall, but numbers probably have declined dramatically within specific habitats because of clear-cutting and even-aged forest management. The "Northern Spotted Owl" is listed as threatened in the U.S. and endangered in Canada, where it is estimated that fewer than 100 pairs remain. The "Mexican Spotted Owl" is also considered threatened in the U.S.

BARRED OWL *Strix varia*

This widespread woodland owl dozes by day on a well-hidden perch but seldom relies on its good camouflage to avoid harm. Instead, it flies away at the least disturbance, seldom tolerating close approach. But where foot traffic is heavy, such as along boardwalks in southern swamps, the Barred Owl may sit tight and provide good views at close range. It hunts mainly from a perch but will also hunt on the wing, preying on small mammals, birds, amphibians, reptiles, and invertebrates. It prefers to nest in a natural tree hollow, but it will also use an abandoned stick nest of another species. Polytypic (4 ssp.; 3 in N.A.).

L 21" (53 cm) WS 43" (109 cm)

Identification Flight is heavy and direct, with slow, methodical wingbeats; occasionally makes long, direct glides. ADULT: Chunky, dark brown barring on its ruff-like upper breast; rest of underparts are whitish with bold, elongated dark brown streaks; lacks ear tufts. Central tail feathers expose 3–5 pale bars between their tips and the tips of the uppertail coverts. Sexes alike in plumage; female larger. Chiefly nocturnal. JUVENILE: By about September, young birds acquire a complete set of fresh flight feathers; may be variably worn on adults. Central tail feathers expose 4–6 pale bars.

Geographic Variation Weak to moderate; clinal where ranges meet. The southeastern subspecies, *georgica*, is darker brown than the widespread nominate subspecies, *varia*. Subspecies *helveola* of southeast Texas is paler.

Similar Species The underparts of the slightly smaller Spotted Owl are spotted overall, not barred and streaked. Hybridization has occurred where ranges overlap; the hybrids' plumages, voices, and sizes were intermediate between the two species.

Voice Highly vocal, with a wide range of calls. Much more likely than other owls to be heard in the daytime. Its most common vocalization is a rhythmic series of loud *hoot* or *whoo* notes:

who-cooks-for-you, who-cooks-for-you-all. Also often heard is a loud, drawn-out *hoo-waaah* that gradually fades away; it is sometimes preceded by an ascending agitated barking. Often a chorus of two or more owls will call back and forth with these and other calls; the female's voice is higher pitched.

Status & Distribution Common in eastern N.A. Has expanded its range north and west through Canada's boreal forest and then southward into MT, ID, and CA. YEAR-ROUND: Resident in mature mixed deciduous and uniform coniferous forests, often in river bottomlands and swamps; also in upland forests. BREEDING: Proba-

bly in southeastern AK. MIGRATION: More northerly populations may drift south during late autumn if prey are scarce. Accidental on Bermuda.

Population Stable to increasing in North America.

GREAT GRAY OWL *Strix nebulosa*

Surprisingly, our largest owl is far from our heaviest: the Great Gray Owl's uncommonly dense, fluffy feathering creates an illusion of great bulk. This Holarctic owl is most often found perched low on the edge of a clearing, listening and looking intently for the small rodents on which it preys. It hunts from dusk to just before dawn from a low perch overlooking an open area; during breeding season, it may also hunt in the daytime. The Great Gray Owl is able to take prey moving unseen beneath snow by plunge-diving feet first into shallow snow, or head-first into deeper snow, before thrusting its legs to grasp its target. It favors the abandoned nests of other birds of prey, but it also uses broken tops of large trees, preferring shaded locations. Polytypic (2 ssp.; nominate in N.A.). L 27" (69 cm) WS 55" (140 cm)

Identification Its flight is heronlike, with slow and deep wingbeats and very little gliding. It often hovers above a suspected prey location before pouncing. ADULT: Relatively long tailed, with a disproportionately large head; lacks ear tufts. Pale gray facial disk with (usually) five distinct dark gray concentric

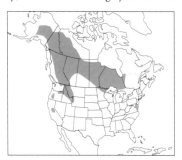

circles around each yellow eye, making the eyes seem particularly small. Black-and-white "bow tie" pattern beneath the bill. Plumage largely gray, subtly patterned with combinations of whites, grays, and browns. Upperparts marked with dark and light; underparts boldly streaked over fine barring. Yellowish bill; legs and toes heavily feathered. Sexes alike in plumage; female distinctly larger. JUVENILE: Downy plumage is cryptic gray and white. By about August, young birds acquire a complete set of uniformly fresh flight feathers, not variably worn as on adults; terminal bands on flight feathers and tail feathers are whitish when present.

Similar Species The Great Gray Owl is unlikely to be mistaken for any other species. The smaller Barred and Spotted Owls have dark eyes, browner plumage overall, and different patterns on their underparts. The similar-sized Great Horned Owl has prominent ear tufts and larger yellow eyes set in an orangeish facial disk that lacks concentric circles.

Voice The male's courtship song is a series of 5–10 deep, resonant, muffled *whoo* notes that are longer and higher pitched than the Blue Grouse's; they gradually drop in frequency and decelerate toward the end of the series. The song may be repeated as many as 10 times. The female may answer with a soft, mellow *whoop.*

Status & Distribution Uncommon. Inhabits boreal forests and wooded bogs in the far north, dense coniferous forests with meadows in mountains farther south. BREEDING: Nomadic; breeds

where it finds abundant prey and may not breed in years that prey is scarce. WINTER: Withdraws downslope or southward, where it is a rare and irregular visitor to the limit of the dashed line on the map. Extreme prey shortages in the north may cause tens or hundreds of owls to winter in areas where normally few are seen. An unprecedented 1,700 Great Gray Owls were recorded in northern MN during the 2004–2005 irruption.

Population Seems to be stable, notwithstanding wide annual fluctuations caused by prey availability.

EARED OWLS Genus *Asio*

Most of these medium-size owls have prominent ear tufts, long wings, well-developed facial disks, bold streaking below, and cryptic plumage. Some are open-country specialists; others occupy wider habitat ranges (e.g., forests, forest edges, shrubby growth, and open country). They occur on all temperate continents except Australia (6 sp.; 3 in N.A.).

LONG-EARED OWL *Asio otus*

The Holarctic Long-eared Owl is occasionally seen on its day roost in a dense tree or thicket. If it does not flush immediately, the owl may try to hide, stretching into an unbelievably slim, erect profile, often with a wing cloaking its body. With its facial disk narrowed, its eyes reduced to vertical slits, and its ear tufts raised like little twigs, it can look remarkably like a broken or decayed limb. It hunts small rodents nocturnally, coursing low over the ground, and may occasionally hover before pouncing. It makes a nest in another bird's abandoned stick nest, preferably in a clump of trees rather than in an isolated tree. Polytypic (4 ssp.; 2 in N.A.). L 15" (38 cm) WS 37" (94 cm)
Identification Ear tufts flattened in flight, not visible. (See sidebar p. 333.) ADULT: Slender; medium sized; long, close-set ear tufts. Rusty facial disk; yellow eyes set in vertical dark patches. Upperparts a mix of black, brown, gray, buff, and white. Bold streaks and bars on breast

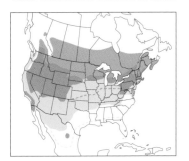

and belly. Central tail feathers expose 5–7 dark bars between their tips and tips of the uppertail coverts. Females average darker, richer buff, more heavily streaked. JUVENILE: Tail feathers have more exposed dark bars. By about October, it acquires a set of uniformly fresh flight feathers; adults' secondaries and outer primaries may be variably worn.
Geographic Variation Weak and clinal in North America where widespread *wilsonianus* meets the smaller and paler *tuftsi* of western Canada south to northwest Mexico.
Similar Species The larger, much heavier Great Horned Owl has a white throat; its eyes lack dark vertical patches. The Short-eared Owl's ear tufts are tiny; its underparts are boldly streaked.
Voice Generally silent except in breeding season. Male's advertising song is a series of 10 to more than 200 low, soft *hooo* notes, evenly spaced about 2–4 seconds apart, each note resembling the cooing note of a Band-tailed Pigeon. The female's answering call is a softer, higher-pitched *whoof-whoof-whoof.* The alarm call is a harsh, barking *ooack ooack ooack.*
Status & Distribution Rare in Southeast; uncommon elsewhere in N.A. BREEDING: Densely wooded areas in lowlands and mountains with nearby open foraging areas having fertile, boggy, or arid sandy soil. MIGRATION: Those breeding in northern parts of the range with heavy winter snow cover migrate south to areas with more favorable climates; casual on Bermuda, Cuba. WINTER: Day-roosting groups of 10–100 or more cluster close together in one or a few neighboring trees.
Population Numbers much reduced in some areas. State-listed as endangered in Illinois, threatened in Iowa, and a species of "special concern" in California, five north-central states, Montana, and all New England states except Maine.

STYGIAN OWL *Asio stygius*

This is a medium-size, strictly nocturnal forest-dwelling owl. Polytypic (6 ssp.; at least 1 accidental in N.A.). L 17" (43 cm) WS 42" (107 cm)
Identification ADULT: Deep chocolate-brown overall, with long, close-set ear tufts. Whitish forehead contrasts with blackish facial disk. Upperparts blackish brown, barred and spotted buff. Underparts dirty buff, with bold dark brown streaks and crossbars. Legs feathered; toes bristled.
Similar Species The closely related Long-eared Owl lacks bold white forehead; rusty facial disk contrasts with brown-ish plumage; underparts less boldly patterned; legs and toes fully feathered.
Voice Male's song is a series of deep, emphatic *woof* or *wupf* notes spaced 6–10 seconds apart.
Status & Distribution Little known. Resident in Mexico (within 200 mi. of U.S. in Sierra Madre Occidental) and the Caribbean locally to northern Argentina. Accidental Dec. occurrences in 1994 and 1996 at Bentsen-Rio Grande S.P. in southern TX provide the only records in N.A. Subspecies not known.
Population Considered endangered by the Mexican government.

SHORT-EARED OWL *Asio flammeus*

There is no more captivating springtime sight on the western prairies than a male Short-eared Owl in courtship song high overhead and then dropping toward the ground with wing claps that sound like a flag flapping in the wind. It hunts voles and lemmings at any time of the day but is usually crepuscular, coursing low over open areas. Its nest is a shallow ground scrape, usually under a protective cover of grass or low vegetation. Polytypic (10 ssp.; 2 in N.A.). L 15" (38 cm) WS 39" (99 cm)

Identification MALE: Holarctic *flammeus* has a boldly streaked tawny breast, paler and more lightly streaked belly. Large, round head; closely spaced ear tufts barely visible; yellow eyes in blackish patches. Upperparts mottled brown

and buff, appearing distinctly striped; tawny uppertail coverts. FEMALE: Larger, generally darker: upperparts browner; underparts rustier, heavier streaking.
Geographic Variation Both sexes of smaller *domingensis* ("Antillean Short-eared Owl") resemble female *flammeus*, but underparts buffier overall with very fine or no streaking on belly; upperparts and uppertail coverts dark brown.
Similar Species Northern Harriers display white uppertail coverts in flight. They compete with Short-eared Owls for prey during daylight hours and sometimes rob them.
Voice Male's courtship song is a series of 13–16 rapid, deep hoots. Both sexes give hoarse *cheeaw* calls when disturbed at any time of year.
Status & Distribution Nominate still fairly common in much of the northern part of its N.A. range. Rare visitor *domingensis* occurs on the Florida Keys and Dry Tortugas in spring and summer. Most appear to be juveniles, probably dispersing from Cuba, where locally common. BREEDING: Tundra, prairie, coastal grasslands, and marshes. MIGRATION: Southward to escape areas with complete snow cover. Numerous records far at sea and colo-

nization of distant islands attest to the species' propensity to wander; very rare on Bermuda. Nomadic in search of prey. WINTER: More gregarious; flocks may roost together, occasionally in trees, often with Long-eared Owls.
Population Has declined in many areas. Canada lists it as a species of "special concern" because of loss of habitat. Listed as an endangered, threatened, or "special concern" species by seven northeastern states, where it is all but eliminated as a breeder.

Flight Identification of Long-eared and Short-eared Owls

The Long-eared Owl and the Short-eared Owl appear very similar in flight. They hunt by coursing low over open ground in slow, moth-like flight. The Short-eared generally hunts during crepuscular hours, and the Long-eared generally hunts at night. Their upper wings have a broad tawny patch at the base of the outer primaries. Their underwings show a distinct carpal mark ("wrist mark"), formed by dark brown to black tips on the outermost under primary coverts. Both marks are usually more prominent on the Short-eared, but differences are not diagnostic. Identification can be made, however, by noting underwing details in flight.

The Short-eared Owl's outer 4 or 5 primaries are broadly tipped dark brown (with small buffy spots intruding). Slightly nearer the bases of the primaries, a single dark brown band cuts across the outer primar-

Short-eared Owl

Long-eared Owl

ies, separated from the dark tips by an equally wide buffy band. Two or three narrower, indistinct dark bands cut across the secondaries and the inner primaries near their tips. The overall impression is of a pale underwing with a dark wrist mark, broad dark outer primary tips, and a single dark band in between, close to the dark tips.

The Long-eared Owl's outer 4 or 5 primaries are crossed by 5 or more pairs of alternating dark and light gray-brown bands of varying width. Five or more narrower dark gray-brown bands cut across the secondaries and the inner primaries, separated by bands that are pale gray-brown near the feather tips and tawny near the feather bases. The overall impression is of a mainly pale, but patterned, underwing with a dark wrist mark and a series of dark bands extending more than halfway from the primary tips to the wrist mark. ■

FOREST OWLS Genus *Aegolius*

Small and nocturnal, with large, rounded heads that lack ear tufts, forest owls have well-developed, rounded or square facial disks. They have yellow or orange-yellow eyes and relatively long wings, and they reside in extensive forests, where they mainly prey on small rodents and shrews. One species is Holarctic; the others reside in the Americas (4 sp.; 2 in N.A.).

BOREAL OWL *Aegolius funereus*

juvenile

To see this Holarctic owl (or "Tengmalm's Owl" in the Old World), check nest boxes in late spring or search in the snow on a cold, late winter night until you hear a lovelorn male's far-carrying song. Strictly nocturnal, it hunts small rodents in direct glides from a perch and roosts by day in dense cover, usually close to tree trunk. A cavity nester, it uses mainly woodpecker holes. Polytypic (7 ssp.; 1 accidental, 1 resident in N.A.). L 10" (25 cm) WS 23" (58 cm)

Identification ADULT: Resident *richardsoni* has white underparts broadly streaked chocolate brown; whitish facial disk with distinct black border; umber-brown crown densely spotted white; pale bill. Female noticeably larger. JUVENILE: Chocolate-brown plumage held about June to September.

Geographic Variation Eurasian subspecies (e.g., Siberian *magnus*) are paler than *richardsoni*.

Similar Species Northern Saw-whet Owl is smaller; adult has streaked crown, buffy facial disk with no dark border, dark bill, and cinnamon-brown breast streaks; juvenile tawny rust below.

Voice Male's territorial song is about a 2-second-long series of 11–23 low, whistled *toot* notes, repeated after a few seconds' silence; like a winnowing Wilson's Snipe's, but does not fade at the end.

Status & Distribution Uncommon to rare. YEAR-ROUND: Inhabits boreal forest belt, also subalpine mixed conifer-deciduous forests in the high Rockies and mountains of the Northwest. MIGRATION: Adult males usually sedentary, females nomadic; juveniles disperse widely. Casual to northern IL, northern OH, New York City. Prey shortages periodically drive large numbers south, to winter in areas where normally few are seen. The unprecedented irruption of 2004–2005 saw more than 400 in the upper Midwest. One *magnus* reached St. Paul Is., AK, in Jan. 1911.

Population No reliable information on trends.

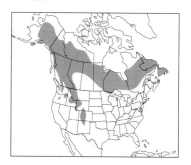

NORTHERN SAW-WHET OWL *Aegolius acadicus*

This widespread owl responds well to imitations of its song. Whether located at night or on a day roost, it usually tolerates close approach without flushing. Strictly nocturnal, it hunts rodents from a perch and roosts by day in thick vegetation, often near the end of a lower branch. Nests in a woodpecker hole or a nest box. Polytypic (2 ssp.). L 8" (20 cm) WS 20" (51 cm)

Identification ADULT: Reddish brown above with crown streaked white; white below with broad reddish streaks; dark bill; reddish facial disk, without dark border. JUVENILE: Plumage held about May to September. Dark reddish brown above, tawny rust below.

Geographic Variation Distinctive subspecies *brooksi*, endemic to the Queen Charlotte Islands, British Columbia, is much darker and buffier on facial disks and belly than nominate described above; white only on eyebrows.

Similar Species The Boreal Owl is larger; adult has a spotted crown, whitish facial disk with black border, pale bill, chocolate-brown breast streaks; juvenile chocolate brown below.

Voice Male's territorial song is a monotonous series of single, low whistles, about 2 per second, on a constant pitch. A 2- to 3-second-long rising nasal whine and a high-pitched *tssst* call are also heard.

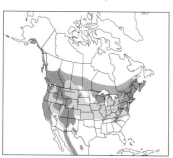

juvenile

Status & Distribution Fairly common in breeding range; uncommon to rare over much of winter range. BREEDING: Dense coniferous or mixed forests, wooded swamps, tamarack bogs. MIGRATION: Some remain year-round on breeding range, but considerable numbers migrate south or downslope in autumn. Casual on Bermuda. WINTER: Wide range of habitats with perches for foraging, dense vegetation for roosting.

Population No data, but probably declining slowly as habitat is lost.

NIGHTHAWKS AND NIGHTJARS Family Caprimulgidae

Common Nighthawk (TX)

Caprimulgids occur worldwide except in the polar regions and occupy a wide variety of habitats. They collectively are referred to as "goatsuckers," the translation of the family name. According to folklore, nightjars suckled nursing goats during the night. In reality, most species are insectivorous, but because of their nocturnal and secretive habits, strange vocalizations, huge mouth, and, in some species, tendency to forage in areas where livestock occur, this superstition became nearly as widespread as the family. **Structure** Goatsuckers are superficially reminiscent of owls because of their large head, large eyes that shine when illuminated at night, cryptic plumage, and largely nocturnal behavior. But instead of capturing and eating prey with sharp bills and talons, goatsuckers are the nocturnal counterpart of swifts and swallows. The bill is tiny, but the gape is exceptionally wide and reveals a cavernous mouth. Insect prey are literally engulfed and swallowed whole rather than being seized and manipulated with the bill. Most nightjars have elongated rictal bristles along the edges of the mouth that presumably help a nocturnal species detect and guide an insect into its mouth; these are not elongated in the more diurnal nighthawks. Caprimulgids have proportionately long wings; nighthawks' are more pointed and falconlike, nightjars' more rounded. In most species the tail is usually fairly long and provides added maneuverability. Short legs and small feet reflect mostly aerial habits, but all can grip perches or walk short distances if necessary. Virtually all species have cryptically colored plumage with complex patterns to provide camouflage in daylight. Most species are small to medium in size.

Behavior Nightjars roost by day on ground, rocks, or branches, usually in dense vegetation, and are most frequently observed during twilight hours or after dark. All species are ground nesters. Loud, distinctive calls during the breeding season usually alert observers to their presence. Nighthawks and nightjars are impressive aerial foragers. Nighthawks forage during long sustained flights; nightjars make short sallies from an exposed perch or ground. Common prey of North American species include moths, beetles, and cicadas. Drinking is usually accomplished on the wing. Most species in North America are highly migratory, but some can survive periods of cold weather by lowering their metabolism and going into torpor—the Common Poorwill, for example.

Distribution North American species occupy a diversity of habitats. All but the Common Pauraque are migratory to some extent, but the most widespread species, the Common Nighthawk, is the champion long-distance migrant, traveling from as far north as northern Ontario to as far south as central Argentina.

Taxonomy Two subfamilies: Chordeilinae (nighthawks: 4 genera, 10 species), with a strictly New World distribution; and Caprimulginae (11 genera, 79 species) occurring virtually worldwide. Relationships to other birds and within and among family members are not yet well established by phylogenetic analyses.

Conservation Nocturnal habits of most species make study difficult; much remains unknown. Habitat deterioration or destruction and pesticides present the greatest threats, but only 2 species are listed as critically endangered; 7 species listed as threatened (none in N.A.).
—*Donna L. Dittmann, Steven W. Cardiff*

NIGHTHAWKS Genus *Chordeiles*

A New World genus, 3 of 6 species occur in North America. Nighthawks are partially diurnal, open-country birds, thus easier to observe and more frequently encountered than other nightjars. All species have relatively long, pointed wings, notched tails, conspicuous pale wing patches, and a patch of puffy white feathers at the bend of the wing when perched.

ANTILLEAN NIGHTHAWK *Chordeiles gundlachii*

Formerly considered a Caribbean subspecies of the Common Nighthawk, this Florida Keys specialty was elevated to full species status following evidence there that both Commons and Antilleans nested without interbreeding. Polytypic (2 ssp.; *vicinus* in N. A.). L 8.6" (21.5 cm)

Identification Relatively small nighthawk. Upperparts generally blackish, darkest on crown and upper back, varyingly mottled with whitish gray to buff, pale markings more concentrated on upperwing coverts, scapulars, and tertials. Upper breast and malar region blackish spotted with buff or grayish white; lower breast barred dull black and grayish white, belly with pale buff. Under-

tail coverts buffy and sparsely to heavily barred dark brown. Tail brownish black, narrowly barred buff or white, slightly notched. ADULT MALE: White throat, white subterminal tail band, and uniformly dark primaries except for white patch about halfway between bend of the wing and wing tip on 5 outer primaries. ADULT FEMALE: Similar but throat patch buffy, white primary patch smaller, and lacks tail band. JUVENILE: Plumage paler and buffier, dorsal pattern with fine vermiculations or small spots; primaries and secondaries with distinctive pale edges.

Similar Species Voice best identification character. Sight identifications of silent individuals and, especially out of range, should be made with caution and may not be possible. Antillean virtually identical to southeastern subspecies *chapmani* of Common Nighthawk but averages smaller, shorter winged, and buffier on belly and undertail coverts. However, there is size overlap with Common, and some Commons have buffy underparts. Identification during migration more problematic due to the substantial geographical and individual variation within Common Nighthawk,

and because migrants are usually silent. Lesser Nighthawk overall very similar and buffy below, but has generally paler upperparts, breast, and primaries; paler, buffier underwing coverts; slightly more rounded wing tips. Antillean and Common have more pointed wing tips. Lesser has primary patch positioned about two-thirds of the way out from bend of wing to wing tip; and buffy spots on primaries and secondaries, usually visible when perched. Female Lesser has buff-and-white or completely buffy primary patch.

Voice CALL: (Males only) *pity-pit, chitty-chit,* or *killikadik;* also a Common Nighthawk-like nasal *penk-dik.* During male courtship dive, air rushing through primaries at the terminus of a dive produces hollow, roaring "boom."

Status & Distribution Uncommon. BREEDING: Open or semi-open habitats. MIGRATION: Highly migratory. Arrives in Apr.; departs Aug.–Sept. WINTER: Unknown, presumably S. A. VAGRANT: Spring and summer, rare to mainland FL, Dry Tortugas, Virginia Key; accidental LA, NC.

Population Stable; expanded breeding range to FL Keys beginning in the 1940s.

LESSER NIGHTHAWK *Chordeiles acutipennis*

This bird's trilling twilight call is a familiar spring and summer sound of the desert. It often congregates at water sources morning and evening, rarely active during midday. It is the only breeding nighthawk across most of the extreme southwestern United States lowlands, but limited overlap with the Common presents an identification challenge. Polytypic (7 ssp.; *texensis* in N.A.). L 8–9.2" (20–23 cm)

Identification Generally dark gray to brownish gray above mottled with black, grayish white, or buff; crown and upper back darkest, paler markings more concentrated on upperwing

coverts, scapulars, tertials. Secondaries and primaries dark brownish gray, secondaries and basal portions of primaries spotted with buff. Underparts generally buffy, finely barred dark brown; chest and malar area darker and grayer with whitish to buff spotting. Underwing coverts buff mottled with brown. ADULT MALE: White throat, subterminal tail band, and primary patch about two-thirds out from bend of wing to wing tip. ADULT FEMALE: Buff throat and wing patch; tail band reduced or absent. JUVENILE: Upperparts uniformly buffy-gray with fine dark markings and spots.

Similar Species Some Common Nighthawks essentially identical in general coloration and size, but have proportionately longer, more slender, more pointed wings, and primary patch is farther from wing tip. Most Commons lack buff spotting on secondaries and primaries, do not have buffy underwings.

Voice CALL: (Males only) whistled trill, in short isolated bursts or longer series of bursts. Flight dis-

play a bleating *bao-b-bao-bao.*

Status & Distribution Common. BREEDING: Arid lowland scrub, farmland. MIGRATION: In spring, arrives early Mar.–mid-May, peak in Apr.; departs early Aug.–late Oct., peak mid-Aug.–mid-Sept. WINTER: Occurs year-round from northwestern and central Mexico south to northern S.A.; rare in extreme southern U.S., including FL. VAGRANT: Casual/accidental to AK, CO, OK, ON, WV, Bermuda.

Population Stable.

COMMON NIGHTHAWK *Chordeiles minor*

This goatsucker performs flight displays and roosts conspicuously. Normally solitary, it sometimes forages or migrates in loose flocks. Polytypic. L 8.8–9.6" (22–24 cm)

Identification Varies geographically. Upperparts black to paler brownish gray; crown and upper back darkest; paler markings concentrated on upperwing coverts, scapulars, tertials. Underparts barred blackish brown and white or buff, chest and malar area darker, spotted with buff or dull white. ADULT MALE: White throat patch, subterminal tail band, and primary patch about halfway between bend of wing and wing tip. ADULT FEMALE: Throat patch buffy, primary patch smaller, tail band reduced or lacking. JUVENILE: Generally paler, more uniform above with finer spotting and vermiculations.

Geographic Variation Nine subspecies, 7 in N.A. Eastern birds darkest, blackish above, less mottling on back; nominate *minor* (large), *chapmani* (smaller). Great Plains-Great Basin-Southwestern birds paler, grayer; *henryi* (medium size), *howelli* (large), *sennetti* (large), and *aserriensis* (small). Western *hesperis* relatively dark, grayer, large. Juvenile *minor* and *chapmani* blackish; *sennetti* palest; *hesperis*, *howelli*, *aserriensis* intermediate; *henryi* rusty.

Similar Species Position of wing patch, lack of buff spotting on primaries, pointier wing, and darker underwing coverts eliminate Lesser. Separation from Antillean problematic; best told by voice, but Antillean also usually smaller, shorter winged, and buffier on belly and undertail coverts.

Voice CALL: Nasal *peent* by male in flight; multiple-syllable variation may suggest Antillean. Male courtship dive vibrates primaries, producing "boom."

Status & Distribution Common. BREEDING: Open habitats. MIGRATION: In spring, arrives early Apr.–mid-June, peak May, arrival later in North, West; departs late July–Oct., peak Sept., stragglers into Nov. WINTER: S.A.; casual Gulf Coast. VAGRANT: Casual/accidental, mainly fall, HI, northern Canada, and U.K.

Population Some declines in parts of East.

juvenile *sennetti*

COMMON NIGHTHAWK

0 mi 1000
0 km 1000

GRADUAL SPRING MIGRATION

☐ Breeding range — Approximate spring arrival date

☐ Wintering range –/● Very rare vagrant

NIGHTJARS Genus *Nyctidromus, Phalaenoptilus,* and *Caprimulgus*

Caprimulgus, with cryptic plumage patterns and proportionately long, rounded wings and tails, are typical nightjars. Only 6 of 56 species found almost worldwide occur in N.A. *Nyctidromus* and *Phalaenoptilus* are monotypic New World genera. *Nyctidromus* is similar to nightjars in appearance. *Phalaenoptilus* is distinguished by proportionately short tail.

COMMON PAURAQUE *Nyctidromus albicollis*

This beautifully patterned tropical nightjar is often detected by its golden-red eyeshine along roadsides at night, where it waits to sally after insects. By day it roosts on the ground in thickets, perfectly camouflaged in leaf litter. Polytypic (7 ssp.; *merrilli* in N. A.). L 11.2–12" (28–30 cm)
Identification Upperparts brownish gray finely vermiculated with black, crown coarsely streaked with black, back and upper wings crisply and complexly mottled with black and buff spots. Auriculars chestnut, stripe below eye (in some birds) whitish. Underparts buffy with narrow dark bars, chest, chin, malar area darker grayish brown. ADULT MALE:

Throat patch and large patch across outer primaries white, extensive white on third and fourth pairs of tail feathers. ADULT FEMALE: Can be less prominently marked on upperparts, reduced, buffier throat and wing patches, and less white in tail (restricted to feather tips). JUVENILE: Similar, but browner, less heavily patterned; lacks throat patch, wing patches smaller and buffier.
Similar Species Chuck-will's-widow and Whip-poor-will lack white primary patch, have proportionately shorter tail and longer wings, and are more uniformly colored. Nighthawks have longer, more pointed wings, and shorter, notched tails.

Voice CALL: *Whip* or *wheeeeeeer.* SONG: Buzzy whistle, *pur pur perp pur-wheeeeer.*
Status & Distribution Common. YEAR-ROUND: Mesquite- or ebony-dominated scrub and mesquite-live oak savanna in southern TX. VAGRANT: Casual in TX north of breeding range to northern Maverick, Bastrop, Grimes, Calhoun Counties.
Population Stable.

COMMON POORWILL *Phalaenoptilus nuttallii*

The smallest nightjar is more typically heard giving its forlorn song or found by its eyeshine at night. Polytypic (5 ssp.). L 7.6–8.4" (19–21 cm)
Identification ADULT MALE: Proportionately large head; short, rounded tail. Paler/gray and darker/browner morphs occur throughout distribution. Upperparts dark brown to pale grayish brown, mottled pale gray and black, especially on crown, scapulars, upperwing coverts. White throat bordered by blackish brown chin, malar area, and chest; belly pale buff finely barred blackish brown, undertail coverts buff. Blackish brown

wings broadly banded with buff. All but central tail feathers tipped white. ADULT FEMALE: Similar but can have narrower or buffier tail tips. JUVENILE: Similar.
Geographic Variation Four subspecies in N.A., distinguished by size and dorsal coloration (beware color morphs). Two low-desert subspecies palest: *hueyi* of southeastern California smallest, *adustus* of southern Arizona larger. Widespread northern nominate *nuttallii* and *californicus* of western California relatively large, darker brown above.
Similar Species Whip-poor-will and Buff-collared Nightjar larger with longer tail, less white on throat. Nighthawks larger, longer, with longer wings; longer, notched tail with subterminal band; white or buff primary patch.
Voice SONG: Plaintive whistled *poor will up,* last note heard at close range.
Status & Distribution Uncommon to locally common. BREEDING: Low-middle elevation dry, rocky, open, shrubby habitats. MIGRATION:

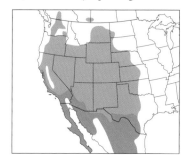

Northern populations apparently migratory, southern populations partially migratory or move to lower elevations in winter. Arrives Feb.–Mar. south, late Apr.–late May north. Departs Sept. north, Oct.–Nov. south. WINTER: Southern areas of breeding range (CA, AZ, TX) to central Mexico. VAGRANT: Accidental southwestern BC, southern MB, ON, MN, MO.
Population Possibly expanding Northeast.

CHUCK-WILL'S-WIDOW *Caprimulgus carolinensis*

As with most other nightjars, the distinctive and familiar song of the Chuck-will's-widow is heard much more often than the bird is seen. Widespread in open forest and woodlands of the Southeast, our largest nightjar is most frequently glimpsed as a silhouette at dawn or dusk as it sallies across openings in search of insects. During the day the Chuck-will's-widow roosts on or near the ground. A "Chuck" can be quite startling when flushed at close range. It flies up in a burst of brown, accompanied by loud grunting notes, before zigzagging from view. The dark, menacing, hawklike appearance of a roosting or flushed individual can result in mobbing by smaller birds. Monotypic. L 11.2–12.8" (28–32 cm)

Identification ADULT: Large nightjar, males are larger than females. Large, flat-topped head. Generally dark grayish brown, but considerable individual variation exists, from paler and rustier to darker and browner. Crown and upper back darkest; scapulars

palest, with heavy black streaks or spots on these areas. Wings blackish and heavily barred rufous. Tail long, broad, rounded, buffy to rufous, and with black bars and vermiculations. Chin and upper throat brown with fine dark bars. Whitish buff to buff patch on lower throat, contrasting with dark brown to blackish malar area and breast. Belly and undertail coverts pale buff to dark rufous, barred with blackish brown. MALE: Extensive subterminal whitish buff inner webs of outer 3 pairs of tail feathers. FEMALE: Buffy tips to tail feathers. JUVENILE: Superficially similar to female.

Similar Species The Whip-poor-will smaller, has shorter, narrower, more round-tipped wings, averages grayer tones, has dark throat, and male has different tail pattern. The Common Pauraque and nighthawks are smaller and more slender, have pale primary patch, and different pattern, proportions, and shape to tail.

Voice CALL: A single or a series of grunting notes, *quaah.* SONG: Whistled *chuck-weo-WID-ow;* the first note is rapid, the *weo* is drawn out, and the song is concluded by a rapid *WIDow.*

Status & Distribution Common. BREEDING: Variety of riparian, deciduous, evergreen, or mixed forests and woodlands with edges or gaps. MIGRATION: Spring migration Mid-Mar.–mid-May, stragglers into late May–early June. Depart Mid-Aug.–Oct., stragglers into Nov. WINTER: Southern FL, northern West Indies, and east-central Mexico south to Colombia; rare in northern FL and along Gulf Coast. VAGRANT: Rare, mainly spring and summer, north of breeding range as far as SD, MN, WI, MI, and southeastern Canada. Casual/accidental west to NM, NV, and coastal northern CA.

Population Stable; has slowly expanded range north, west, and southwest since the mid-1900s.

BUFF-COLLARED NIGHTJAR *Caprimulgus ridgwayi*

The Buff-collared Nightjar is primarily a west Mexican species that has expanded its range northward into southeastern Arizona. Polytypic (2 ssp.; nominate in N. A.). L 8.8–9.2" (22–23 cm)

Identification ADULT: Upperparts brownish gray with black blotches on crown and scapulars, head and back separat-

ed by distinct pale buff collar. Upperwing coverts spotted with buffy-white, primaries brownish black banded with cinnamon-buff. Upper throat dark grayish brown, breast somewhat paler, and belly paler tan barred with dark brown; throat and breast separated by whitish buff to buff foreneck collar. JUVENILE: Similar.

Similar Species Whip-poor-will almost identical but slightly larger, darker and browner, and lacks distinct pale buff hind neck collar. Common Poorwill smaller, shorter tailed. Lesser Nighthawk has pale primary patches, different proportions.

Voice CALL: Series of *tuk* notes. SONG: Rapid, accelerating series of 5–6 *cuk* notes, concluding with rapid *cuk-a-CHEE-a,* somewhat

reminiscent of the dawn song of the Cassin's Kingbird.

Status & Distribution Uncommon to rare and irregular in U.S. BREEDING: Local in desert canyons dominated by mesquite, acacia, and hackberry. MIGRATION: In U.S. extreme dates Apr. 17–Aug. 28; presumably migratory based on lack of winter records, but no specific information. WINTER: Western Mexico. VAGRANT: Accidental in summer to south-central NM and to coastal southern CA.

Populations Generally stable. The range in the United States has expanded since the first records in 1958–60; this peripheral population has been designated by state wildlife agencies as endangered (NM) and "of special concern" (AZ).

WHIP-POOR-WILL *Caprimulgus vociferus*

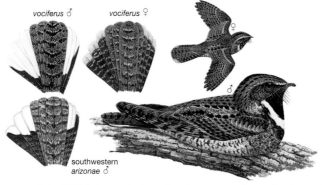

vociferus ♂   vociferus ♀

southwestern
arizonae ♂

The song of the "Whip" sounds in summer evenings across eastern forests and in wooded southwestern canyons. Daytime encounters are usually by chance when a roosting or nesting bird is flushed. Occasionally a bird roosting in a tree, especially eastern birds, will allow fairly close approach. Polytypic. L 8.8–10.4" (22–26 cm)

Identification ADULT: Relatively long, rounded wings and tail. Generally grayish brown above with black, pale gray, and buff spotting and vermiculations, thicker black streaks and blotches on crown and scapulars, indistinct rusty hind neck collar. Wings heavily barred with buff. Blackish brown throat and dark brown upper chest separated by white to buff foreneck collar, rest of underparts buffy with fine dark bars. Male has thick, white tips on outer 3 pairs of tail feathers; female has smaller, buffy tail tips and buffier foreneck collar. JUVENILE: Similar to adult.

Geographic Variation Six subspecies, 2 in N.A. Breeding range of eastern nominate *vociferus* widely separated from Southwestern *arizonae* (and remaining subspecies in Mexico and C.A.), and these 2 groups may represent separate species. In addition to vocal differences, eastern birds average smaller, shorter rictal bristles, more extensive white or buff in tail, and more barred undertail coverts.

Similar Species Chuck-will's-widow is larger, with bigger, flatter head, broader and more pointed wings; it averages darker and browner, has buffy brown throat, and male has different tail pattern. Buff-collared Nightjar is slightly smaller, paler and grayer, has more prominent pale buff collar across hind neck. The Common Poorwill is smaller with shorter tail. The Common Pauraque and nighthawks have pale primary patch, different tail pattern and shape, and pale throat.

Voice CALL: Year-round, Hermit Thrush-like *took* or *quirt,* usually at dusk and dawn. SONG: Melodious, repeated *WHIP poor WILL; arizonae* song "burrier," lower pitched, slightly slower *whirr p WIIRR.*

Status & Distribution Common. BREEDING: Nominate in variety of dry deciduous or mixed forest with open understory; *arizonae* in mixed coniferous-oak or dry coniferous woodland with brushy understory. MIGRATION: Arrives in spring mid-Mar.–mid May, peak Apr., stragglers to late May–early June. Departs late Aug.–Oct., peak mid-Sept.–mid-Oct., stragglers to Nov.–early Dec. Movements of *arizonae* similar, but typically arrives somewhat later (peak late Apr.–early May); departure may start by early Aug. WINTER: FL and northern Mexico south to Honduras; rare elsewhere along southern Atlantic and Gulf coasts (some designate these areas part of main winter range). VAGRANT: Nominate casual/accidental to coastal CA, southeastern AK, CO, east-central QC, NF, Bermuda, Cuba, Jamaica; *arizonae* casual/accidental to coastal CA, AB, SK, MT, CO.

Populations Some local declines and breeding range contractions in the East; western populations have expanded northwest to southern California, southern Nevada, and central New Mexico.

GRAY NIGHTJAR *Caprimulgus indicus*

Also known as the Jungle Nightjar, the Gray is an Asian stray to Alaska's Aleutian Islands. Common name change reflects the anticipated split from mostly sedentary Indian subspecies. Polytypic (5 ssp. worldwide; N.A. record pertains to northernmost, migratory *jotaka*). L 11–12.8" (28–32 cm)

Identification Upperparts generally brownish gray, patterned with black, buff, and grayish white spots, streaks, and bars. Primaries and secondaries dark brown (contrasting with grayer mantle); secondaries and inner primaries banded tawny buff, outer webs of outer primaries spotted with buff. Face brown, submoustachial stripe and patches at sides of throat white. Underparts grayish brown, barred with paler gray, buff, or brown. ADULT MALE: Large subterminal white patch on outer primaries and white tips to all but central pair of tail feathers. ADULT FEMALE: Tawny primary patch and brownish white or brownish buff tail tips.

Similar Species North American goatsuckers either lack primary patches or have different wing, tail, and throat patterns.

Voice CALL: Loud, rapid series of down-slurred *schurks.*

Status & Distribution Common in eastern and southern Asia. BREEDING: Variety of forest, woodland, and scrub habitats. MIGRATION: Northern populations migrate. Arrive presumably Mar.–May; depart Sept.–Nov. WINTER: Southern breeding range south to East Indies. VAGRANT: One accidental in N.A. (Buldir I., AK, May 31, 1977).

Population Stable.

jotaka ♂

SWIFTS Family Apodidae

White-throated Swift (MT, Aug.)

Superficially swallowlike with their aerial habits, small bills, and long, narrow wings, swifts differ from swallows in their wing structure (the wrist joint is closer to the body), stiff wingbeats (the wings are not swept back against the body), and more rapid flight. Swifts are usually observed in flight because they generally only perch at nests and nocturnal roost sites, which are well hidden in hollows and crevices. Most species forage at high altitudes during the daylight hours and can be hard to observe. Watch for swifts over freshwater, along bluffs and ridge tops, and near roost and nest sites. For species identification, concentrate on overall size, wing and tail shape, dark-and-light patterning on the body, and flight style (wingbeat rate, gliding, etc.).

Structure Swifts are small- to medium-size, long-winged aerialists. The largest (up to 180 g) are 20 times the weight of the smallest. *Apodidae* literally means "without feet," a reference to the swift's tiny (but strong) feet. The "hand" portion of the wing (carpal bones and digits) is quite long relative to the "arm" (humerus and forearm bones); thus the primaries dominate the flight feathers, with the secondaries short and bunched together. There are 10 rectrices; spinelike protrusions are formed by the tip of the rachis (a feather's central shaft) in some species and are used as props. The strongly clawed toes assist in clinging to vertical surfaces, the only kind of perching of which true swifts are capable. The bill is small, with a large gape.

Behavior The most aerial of birds, swifts feed throughout the day and sometimes even "roost" on the wing. Some species can attain very high speeds as they cut through the air. The swift's nest is usually a shallow open cup, with materials glued together and to a vertical substrate with saliva; some extralimital species build a larger nest with plant fibers. Their diet consists of aerial arthropods, principally small insects and spiderlings, and they may forage dozens of miles from the nest site. Large numbers of swifts may gather together before dusk around roost sites, often coming together in very vocal, swirling flocks.

Plumage Swifts are generally clad in blackish to gray-brown plumage, usually with contrasting paler and darker regions and sometimes with bold white markings. Most species show short, dense blackish feathering in front of the eyes. Tail shape varies greatly among genera and can also vary with the degree of closure or spreading of the tail: for example, swifts with deep tail forks may hold the tail closed so that it appears as a single point. Sexes are similar, but juveniles are usually distinguished by duller patterning, pale feather fringes on the body, and pale tips to the secondaries and the tertials.

Distribution True swifts are found worldwide in temperate and tropical regions; many species are highly migratory. Being wide-ranging, strong fliers, swifts have a considerable potential for vagrancy: Five of our 9 species occur only as vagrants, and the Alpine Swift, an additional European/African species, has occurred twice in the Lesser Antilles.

Taxonomy Swifts comprise 95 to 100 species, in 19 genera. These are often placed in 3 subfamilies: the more primitive Cypseloidinae (now limited to the New World) and the widespread Chaeturinae and Apodinae. Four species breed in N.A.; 5 others occur as vagrants. A closely related family, Hemiprocnidae, contains 4 Southeast Asian tree-swifts, and these 2 families are generally grouped along with hummingbirds in the order Apodiformes.

Conservation Some swift species have increased with the availability of human-built nest substrates, whereas other species are highly specialized in their nesting habits and have suffered local declines. —*Kimball L. Garrett*

CYPSELOIDINE SWIFTS Genera *Cypseloides* and *Streptoprocne*

These are primitive swifts, medium-small to very large in size, with all modern species restricted to the New World. Unlike other swifts, they do not use saliva in their nest construction. Most species nest near waterfalls or other damp, shaded sites, but they can cover huge distances while foraging.

BLACK SWIFT *Cypseloides niger*

juvenile

soaring

immature

Our largest regularly occurring swift, this species is associated with waterfalls and other damp cliff habitats in western mountains and rugged northwestern coastlines. It is generally scarce as a migrant. Polytypic (3 ssp. worldwide). L 7.3" (19 cm)

Identification A large, blackish swift with long, broad-based wings that show a distinct angle at the wrist joint and a rather long, broad, shallowly forked tail (usually held partly to widely spread, when it appears squared). The tail notch is shallowest in juveniles and deepest in adult males. ADULT: Sooty black throughout except for frosted whitish chin, forehead, lores, and thin line over the eye. In fresh plumage, some thin white fringing is also seen on the lower underparts. JUVENILE: Resembles adult, but body plumage, coverts, and flight feathers are narrowly fringed with white; this pale scalloping is especial-

ly evident on the belly and undertail coverts. FLIGHT: The wingbeats of the Black Swift can appear relatively languid, but its flight can nevertheless be exceedingly fast; it usually flies with short bursts of wingbeats interspersed with long, twisting glides on slightly bowed wings. Individuals are wide ranging and fly very high, and they are most likely to be observed lower on overcast days.

Geographic Variation The North American subspecies is *borealis*. The smaller nominate subspecies of the West Indies is a potential vagrant to the Southeast.

Similar Species The Black Swift most commonly occurs with Vaux's and White-throated Swifts. The Vaux's is much smaller and paler and has shorter wings, with rapid wingbeats and little gliding. The White-throated can appear all blackish in poor light, but it has a thinner tail (often carried in a point), slimmer wings with less of an angle at the wrist joint, and a more rapid wingbeat.

Voice The Black is relatively silent for a swift, occasionally giving bursts of low clicking or chipping notes.

Status & Distribution Generally uncommon; locally much more numerous in coastal BC. BREEDING: Locally distributed within its general breeding range, concentrating around steep mountain cliffs with a damp microclimate (often from waterfall spray) and available moss for nest material. Also nests locally in sea cliffs and caves from central CA north. MIGRATION: Spring migrants first appear at the end of Apr., but are most numerous in May; fall migrants occur mainly Sept.–mid-Oct., casually into Nov. Generally scarce away from breeding grounds, although concentrations of migrants sometimes noted during fronts and overcast weather. WINTER: Wintering range not known; presumed to be in South America. VAGRANT: Casual northern to coastal southern AK.

Population Apparently stable, as most of the nest sites are inaccessible.

WHITE-COLLARED SWIFT *Streptoprocne zonaris*

The neotropical White-collared Swift has occurred casually but widely in North America. Our largest swift, it has a distinct white collar and soaring flight, which help to identify it. Polytypic. L 8.5" (22 cm)

Identification Very large (larger and longer-winged than a Purple Martin), with slightly forked tail. Prolonged soaring flight with wings bowed downward. ADULT: Blackish throughout, with a bold white collar, broader across chest and narrower on hind neck. JUVENILE: Resembles adult, but plumage is sooty with indistinct pale fringes and collar is less distinct.

Geographic Variation Two subspecies

are documented in North America. Most records are of the large, nominate Mexican subspecies, but a Florida specimen is of the smaller West Indian *pallidifrons*.

Similar Species The Black Swift is smaller and lacks a white collar.

Status & Distribution Vagrant to North America. Widespread from eastern and southern Mexico (north to south Tamaulipas) to northern Argentina. VAGRANT: Casual vagrant, recorded widely across North America. The 4 TX records are from Mar., May, and Dec.; the 2 FL records are from Sept. and Jan. There are also single records for CA and MI, both in May.

SPINE-TAILED SWIFTS Genera *Chaetura* and *Hirundapus*

The subfamily Chaeturniae includes small to large spine-tailed swifts found in both the New and Old Worlds. It also includes the familiar Chimney Swift, the needletails, and the southeast Asian and Pacific swiftlets, which can echolocate in caves and whose saliva is the source of "bird's nest soup."

CHIMNEY SWIFT *Chaetura pelagica*

A small, dark "cigar with wings," this is the common swift of the eastern half of N.A. Its original nest sites (hollow trees, cliffs) have largely been substituted with human-built structures such as chimneys or building shafts, so it is especially common in urban areas. Monotypic. L 5.3" (13 cm)
Identification Small, dark; squared, spine-tipped tail; narrow-based wings often appear markedly pinched at the base during secondary molt in late summer, early fall. ADULT: Brownish black overall; paler chin, throat; slightly paler rump. Plumage can appear browner with wear or appear blacker from contact with chimney soot. JUVENILE: Nearly identical to adult, but with whitish tips to the outer webs of the secondaries, tertials. FLIGHT: Usually rapid, fairly shallow wingbeats, including quick turns, steep climbs, short glides. V-display of pairs involves long glides with wings raised in a V-pattern and some rocking from side to side.
Similar Species The Vaux's is very similar but is slightly smaller, paler; differs subtly in shape; has higher-pitched calls.

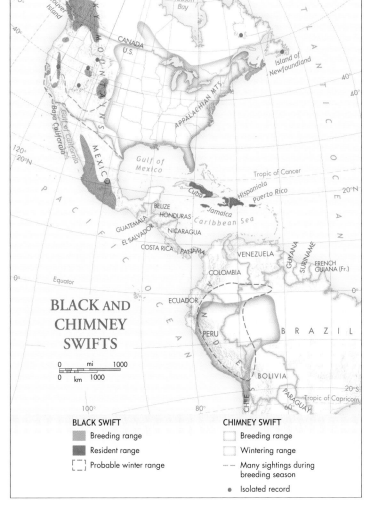

soaring

Voice CALL: Commonly heard; quick, hard chippering notes, sometimes run together into rapid twitter.
Status & Distribution Common. BREEDING: Widespread in variety of habitats; most abundant around towns, cities. Possibly breeds north to NF. Small numbers summer regularly in southern CA (though fewer since 1990s), with breeding documented; possibly also bred in AZ. MIGRATION: Migrates in flocks during the day, mainly along the Atlantic coastal plain, Appalachian foothills, and Mississippi River Valley. Large concentrations may appear during inclement weather; hundreds may roost in chimneys. First spring arrivals are in mid-Mar. in southern states; peak arrivals in northernmost breeding areas are late Apr.–mid-May. Most have departed breeding areas by late Sept.–mid-Oct; latest fall migrants occur in early Nov. WINTER: Most or all winter in Upper Amazon Basin of S.A.; unrecorded in N.A. in mid-winter, but records as late as Dec. VAGRANT: Casual away from CA in West, mainly May–Sept.; accidental on Pribilof Is., AK, and in western Europe.
Population Numbers probably increased greatly with the availability of urban nesting sites and with forest clearing, but population declines have been noted since the 1980s.

BLACK AND CHIMNEY SWIFTS

BLACK SWIFT
▨ Breeding range
▨ Resident range
[⌐ ¬] Probable winter range

CHIMNEY SWIFT
☐ Breeding range
☐ Wintering range
– – Many sightings during breeding season
• Isolated record

VAUX'S SWIFT *Chaetura vauxi*

This is the counterpart of the Chimney Swift in western N.A., occurring almost exclusively west of the Rocky Mountains. Only rarely does it overlap with the Chimney Swift; identifications of out-of-range-birds should be made carefully. The Vaux's also appears to be the only *Chaetura* to winter north of Mexico, though it is scarce and local at that season. Polytypic. L 4.8" (12 cm)

Identification Our smallest regularly occurring swift, it is very similar to the Chimney Swift in all respects. Distinctions from Chimney are fairly evident on the rare occasions the 2 species can be directly compared, but lone birds or single species flocks are more difficult to identify. ADULT: Dark brown on crown, back, and wings; short tail; pale gray-brown chin, throat, and breast, grading into darker belly; pale gray brown rump and uppertail coverts, contrasting with back. JUVENILE: Similar to adult, but secondaries and tertials are narrowly tipped white. FLIGHT: Very rapid, twinkling wingbeats are inter-

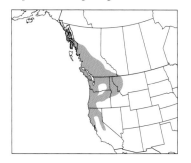

rupted by only brief glides; many quick turns and climbs when foraging, as in the Chimney. Rocking V-display also similar to the Chimney Swift's.

Geographic Variation Our birds are nominate *vauxi,* the northernmost subspecies. Five more subspecies are found from Mexico to Venezuela, one of which (*tamaulipensis* of eastern Mexico) has been collected once in Arizona; it is slightly darker and glossier black than the *vauxi.* Dark birds from southern Mexico to Venezuela (*richmondi* group) and small birds on the Yucatan Peninsula (*gaumeri* group) are sometimes treated as separate species.

Similar Species The very similar Chimney Swift shows a gray-brown throat contrasting with darker remaining underparts; In the Vaux's, the throat is paler, and this pale color extends through the breast. The Chimney is more uniform above, with a gray-brown rump only slightly paler than back; the Vaux's rump and uppertail coverts are paler, showing more contrast to back. Structural characters are subtle but important: the Chimney is larger and appears relatively longer winged; its bill is slightly deeper and its culmen is more sharply curved; its rear body appears slightly longer, thus wing placement appears slightly farther forward. Flight differs subtly, with the Chimney gliding more and flap-

ping slightly more slowly. Use the above plumage and shape characters in conjunction with important vocal distinctions.

Voice High insectlike chipping and twittering notes, often run together into a buzzy trill. Vocalizations resemble those of the Chimney, but are considerably higher pitched, more rapid, and more trilled.

Status & Distribution Common. BREEDING: Heavily forested lowland and lower montane areas; old standing snags generally required, but the Vaux's will also nest in chimneys. MIGRATION: Spring migrants arrive in the Southwest by early April, and the northernmost breeding areas are occupied by late May; fall migration is mainly late Aug.–early Oct. (to late Oct. in south). Fall migrants occur east to UT, eastern AZ. Huge postbreeding and migrant roosts sometimes noted from WA to southern CA. WINTER: Small flocks winter annually but in variable numbers in coastal central and southern CA. A few late fall and winter records for LA and FL, including some small flocks, suggest occasional wintering in the Southeast. Most Vaux's winter from central Mexico south through Central America, but details of winter range are poorly known because of the presence of resident subspecies or closely related species. **Population** Although Vaux's have become familiar sights in some urban areas—where late summer and migrant roost flocks can be very large—overall numbers have declined with loss of old growth forests in the Northwest.

WHITE-THROATED NEEDLETAIL *Hirundapus caudacutus*

This distinctly marked, large Asian swift occurs casually on the western Aleutian Islands in spring. Polytypic (2 ssp. worldwide). L 8" (20 cm)

Identification Unmistakable, large swift with stubby spine-tipped tail, broad-based wings, and large head. Remarkable high-speed flight consists of rapid and powerful wingbeats; glides on bowed wings. ADULT: Uniquely patterned: white throat, dark brown breast and belly; extensive white undertail coverts and flanks form a large U-shaped patch; white spot on the forehead, lores; white on the inner webs of

the tertials. Upperparts show pale brown saddle, contrasting with the green-glossed black crown, wings, tail. JUVENILE: Similar to adult, but lores grayish, white of lower underparts scalloped with dark.

Geographic Variation The more northerly subspecies *caudacutus* has been recorded in N.A.

Similar Species The Fork-tailed has a long notched tail, a white rump, and dark underparts.

Voice Common call is a soft, rapid insectlike chattering.

Status & Distribution Vagrant to westernmost AK. BREEDING: Nests in

hollow trees in eastern Asian forests from southern Siberia to northeastern China, Korea, Sakhalin I., and northern Japan. WINTER: Northern populations migrate to New Guinea, eastern Australia. VAGRANT: Casual on the outer Aleutian Is., AK (4 recs. from late May).

TYPICAL SWIFTS Genera *Apus, Aeronautes,* and *Tachornis*

This widespread group of typical swifts ranges in size from tiny to quite large. Most have forked tails, and many species show white patterning on the rump, throat, or belly. Nests, which are generally made of feathers and plant material, are cemented with saliva to a vertical wall, tree hollow, palm frond, or other protected site.

COMMON SWIFT *Apus apus*

The Common Swift is a familiar and well-studied swift of Eurasia, but it is recorded only casually in North America, with late-June records in the far northwestern and northeastern corners of the continent. It is a moderately large and very dark swift, with a paler throat and a strongly forked tail. Polytypic. L 6.5" (17 cm)
Identification The Common is dark nearly throughout, with a long and obviously forked tail. In flight the rapid, frenzied wingbeats alternate with long glides. ADULT: The adult's plumage is entirely blackish brown, with slight scaled effect to body feathering. The pale throat contrasts to the remaining underparts. The upperwings are uniformly dark throughout; and on the underwings the flight feathers are only slightly paler than the wing linings. JUVENILE: Similar to adult, but its plumage is blacker and more scaly, with whitish fringes on the forehead and pale tips to the flight feathers.

Geographic Variation The subspecies *pekinensis,* of the eastern half of the breeding range, is slightly paler and browner, with a more extensive whitish throat patch; the Alaska specimen is of this subspecies. Nominate European birds are the likely source of the St. Pierre and Miquelon record.
Similar Species See the Fork-tailed, which is casual in western Alaska. Compared to the Black Swift, the Common Swift has a narrower and more deeply forked tail, narrow-based and more pointed wings, and a pale throat patch. Adult Common Swifts have dark foreheads, but pale fringes on the forehead of juveniles recall the Black Swift. (Note the pale throat of the juvenile Common.) The

flight of the Black is more leisurely, whereas the Common flies with rapid wingbeats interspersed with glides. Several related Old World species (e.g., the Pallid Swift) are closely similar but not likely to occur in North America.
Voice A wheezy, screaming *sreeee* or *shreeee;* very vocal in pre-roosting gatherings.
Status & Distribution Vagrant in North America. Common breeder from Europe eastward through northern China, migrating south to winter in the southern half of Africa. VAGRANT: Three late-June records: 1 specimen from the Pribilof Is., AK, June 28, 1950; 1 photographed there June 28–29, 1986, and 1 photographed on Miquelon Island (off NF) June 23, 1986. There have been other possible sightings along the Atlantic coast; also recorded in Bermuda.

FORK-TAILED SWIFT *Apus pacificus*

This is a high-flying, large, fork-tailed Asian swift recorded casually in western Alaska. It is also known as the Pacific Swift. Polytypic. L 7.8" (20 cm)
Identification This is a large but slender, blackish brown swift with a white rump; it has a long, forked tail, but the tail's deep fork is not always apparent. ADULT: The Fork-tailed Swift is dusky black above with a white band across the rump and contrastingly black uppertail coverts and tail. The underparts appear scaly, with dusky black feathering fringed with whitish feathers; the throat is paler. The underwings have dark linings, white-fringed underwing coverts, and somewhat translucent flight feathers. JUVENILE: Similar to adult, but its flight feathers are fringed with white.
Geographic Variation Four subspecies worldwide; nominate recorded in Alaska. This is the northernmost breeder (to central Siberia) and highly migratory, moving as far south as New Zealand in winter. The other 3, more southerly

subspecies are smaller and darker; they are short-distance migrants and possibly resident in some areas.
Similar Species No species of swift occurs regularly in western Alaska. The Common Swift of Eurasia, recorded in western Alaska, is smaller and lacks the white rump. The Common is more uniformly dark, whereas the Fork-tailed has a 2-tone appearance from below: its blackish body and wing linings contrast with its silvery flight feathers. The vagrant White-throated Needletail has a short rounded tail and white undertail coverts; it also has pale upperparts without a white rump patch.
Voice Screaming *sre-eee* resembles calls of the Common Swift, but it is slightly softer and more disyllabic.
Status & Distribution Casual vagrant. Breeds in eastern Asia, northwest to the Kamchatka Peninsula (Rus.); southern Asian populations are sedentary, whereas northern birds winter in southeast Asia and Australia. VAGRANT: Casual in AK, mainly in the western

Aleutian and Pribilof Is., but also on St. Lawrence I. and Middleton I. Most records are mid-May–June and Aug.–Sept.

soaring

WHITE-THROATED SWIFT *Aeronautes saxatalis*

The White-throated Swift is a common and characteristic swift of western canyons, cliffs, coastal bluffs, and even urban areas, seemingly equally at home over the remotest desert mountains or around busy urban freeway interchanges. Its bold patterning, streaking flight, and staccato vocalizations attract attention wherever it occurs. Polytypic (2 ssp.; nominate in N.A.). L 6.5" (17 cm)

Identification The White-throated Swift is a fairly slender swift with long, scythe-like wings. Its moderately long, notched tail is usually held in a tight double-point but can be widely fanned in maneuvering birds. The bold black-and-white patterning is unique among our regularly occurring swifts. ADULT: Blackish to blackish brown on crown, upperparts, flanks, undertail coverts, and flight feathers; paler gray on the forehead, lores, and narrow supercilium. White chin, throat, and chest; white continues more narrowly to the belly. There is also a large white spot on the flanks, extending up toward the sides of the rump, and distinct white tips to the secondaries and tertials. Sexes are similar, but females have a slightly shallower tail fork and less white on secondary and tertial tips. JUVENILE: Closely similar to adult, but it appears paler and browner due to the indistinct pale fringing on forehead, crown, and undertail coverts. The flight feathers are narrowly edged with white, but the white tertial tips are indistinct.

Similar Species Beware that with distant views or poor lighting, the White-throated Swifts can often appear all dark. The Vaux's and Chimney Swifts have shorter wings and shorter, squared tails; compared with these *Chaetura,* the White-throated's long wings appear to be attached farther forward (probably due to longer rear body and tail). See also the Black Swift, which is distinguished by its broader, more shallowly forked tail, crook at the wrist joint of the wings, and generally more languid flight with long periods of soaring. In distant birds, the white rump, sides, and throat may suggest a Violet-green Swallow, but the White-throated Swift's long, stiff wings, blackish sides and undertail coverts, and long pointed tail make this distinction straightforward.

Voice Often quite vocal, giving a loud, rapid, shrill *tee-dee, dee, dee, dee …* or *jee-jee-jee-jee …* series that drops slightly in pitch.

Status & Distribution Common. BREEDING: In the interior West, the White-throated is mostly found in canyons, river gorges, and other areas of high relief, with records as high as 13,000 ft. It is also found on coastal cliffs and lowlands in southern and central CA and increasingly in urban regions where crevices in buildings, highway overpasses, and other human-built structures provide nest and roost sites. Foraging birds can wander widely over lowland areas, and like most wide-ranging swifts, their local abundance can shift with changes in wind patterns, clouds, and weather fronts. MIGRATION: Withdraws from northern part of the breeding range, where present mainly Apr.–Sept. WINTER: Most birds winter from central CA, southern NV, central AZ, and western TX southward. Numbers often more concentrated in winter when large communal roosts may be used. On colder winter days activity may be curtailed; some birds may even become torpid. VAGRANT: Casual east (mainly in fall) to central and coastal TX and northwest to Vancouver I.; recorded exceptionally in west and central OK (Apr.–May), MO (Nov.), AR (May, Dec.), and MI (Aug.).

Population Numbers generally appear stable; some declines (e.g., as suggested by the Breeding Bird Survey) may be offset by the White-throated Swift's increasing use of human-built nesting substrates, even in urban areas.

ANTILLEAN PALM-SWIFT *Tachornis phoenicobia*

A tiny Caribbean swift with a forked tail, a dark-capped appearance, and a distinctive white rump and belly

patch, the Antilliean Palm-swift was recorded once during summer in Florida. Polytypic (2 ssp.). L 4.3" (11 cm)

Identification The very small size, white rump, shallowly forked tail, and low, batlike flight combine to make this swift distinctive. ADULT: Blackish above with broad white rump; white throat and center of belly; blackish breast band, sides, and undertail coverts. IMMATURE: Similar to adult, but duller; white areas of underparts buffy. FLIGHT: Batlike, with rapid wingbeats and short glides and twists; generally flies low, among trees and around palms.

Geographic Variation The Cuban subspecies *iradii* is likely the source of the Florida record.

Similar Species The white rump and longer, slightly forked tail eliminates all dark Chimney Swifts; see the Bank Swallow (which lacks a white rump). The much larger White-throated Swift, which lacks a dark band between the white throat and belly, is very unlikely to occur in the Southeast.

Voice Weak twittering calls.

Status & Distribution Vagrant. YEAR-ROUND: Greater Antilles, including Cuba. VAGRANT: Two were present and photographed at Key West, FL, in July–Aug. 1972.

HUMMINGBIRDS Family Trochilidae

Black-chinned Hummingbird, male (AZ, Apr.)

Hummingbirds, or "hummers" as they are often known, are the smallest of all birds. Solely inhabiting the New World, they are very tiny and have incredible flight powers and brilliant, iridescent colors. These characteristics make field identification problematic, but hummers are readily attracted to sugar-water feeders, where they can be studied. In general, head and tail patterns, bill shape and color, and vocalizations are the best markers. Some birds will remain unidentified. Relatively frequent hybridization among species adds a cautionary dimension.

Structure Hummingbirds have relatively long wings, with 10 primaries but only 6 secondaries; their usually ample tails have 10 rectrices; and their feet are tiny. Bills are slender, pointed, and proportionately long, varying from straight to distinctly decurved or arched in profile.

Behavior Flight is fast and acrobatic; the wings beat so fast that they are a blur to the naked eye. Hummingbirds can reverse their primaries while hovering, in effect rotating their wings through 180 degrees and enabling them to fly backward. Aggressive for their size, several species have spectacular dive displays related to the defense of feeding territories and perhaps to courtship. They hover at flowers (or feeders) where they probe for nectar (or sugar water); they dart, spritelike, in pursuit of flying insects, which they sometimes pirate from spider webs. All hummers lay 2 unmarked white eggs; the male plays no part in nesting. Voices are unmusical and include the simple chip call (given by perched and feeding birds), the warning call, and the flight chase call. Some species are migratory (including most populations in North America).

Plumage North American hummingbirds have dichro-matic plumage related to both age and sex; adult males are more brightly colored than females. Juveniles typically resemble adult females, but their upperparts have buff tipping in fresh plumage, and the sides of the upper mandible have tiny scratches, or grooves (adult bills are smooth), that banders use for in-hand aging. Almost all species are metallic green above, but underparts vary greatly in color and pattern. The most common and widespread North American species are often termed the small gorgeted hummingbirds, for the iridescent throat panels, or gorgets, of the adult males, which vary from ruby red and magenta rose to violet and flame orange. Some of the large species have emerald green or royal blue gorgets. Molt occurs mostly on the nonbreeeding grounds. Thus, immature males of the small gorgeted species migrate south in female-like plumage and return in adultlike plumage. Because flight is integral to their existence, hummingbirds need to molt their wing feathers gradually. Thus, molt of the primaries may require 4 to 5 months. The ninth (next-to-outermost) primary is molted last, rather than the straight 1-to-10 sequence typical of most birds. Iridescence is due to the interference of reflected light; a gorget can change in appearance from blackish to flame orange in a split second. Many species show discolored (usually yellow or whitish) throats or crowns from pollen gathered during feeding.

Distribution Hummingbirds achieve their greatest diversity in the Andes of South America, from Colombia to Ecuador. At least 1 species can be found almost anywhere between southern Alaska and Tierra del Fuego. The birds occur in basically all habitats that support flowering plants; 17 species have nested in North America. Six other species have occurred in North America as rare to accidental visitors from Mexico and the Caribbean.

Taxonomy Species-level and especially genus-level taxonomy needs critical revision. Worldwide, 320+ species are recognized, but much remains to be learned about many taxa in South America. Within Middle and North America, there are 105 to 115 species depending on taxonomy, with 23 species in 15 genera reported from North America.

Conservation Feral predators such as cats can impact local populations. However, long-term data on populations of North America are sparse, because hummingbirds are hard to observe and census. Especially in the West, variations in annual rainfall (and subsequent flower abundance) confound attempts to determine population sizes and trends. —*Steve N. G. Howell*

Introduction to Hummingbird Identification

Perhaps more so than with most groups of birds, the field identification of hummingbirds usually requires a good view to confirm what species you are looking at. However, hearing a diagnostic call in a split-second view can convince an experienced observer of a species' identity. And many of the finer points can be appreciated after you have gained a degree of comparative experience—for example, are the primaries relatively tapered, or relatively blunt? At first, the frenetic behavior of hummingbirds may seem overwhelming and the differences between species almost esoteric, but with patience and practice, it is possible to identify most birds you see. And many hummingbird species are distinctive, even unmistakable.

The small gorgeted hummers include some of the greatest bird identification challenges in North America, so you're not alone if you have difficulty with them. Still, males are mostly distinctive: Check their gorget color and tail shape details to help with harder identifications. Females and immatures are undeniably problematic, and it can be helpful to start by deciding if your bird is one of the gray-and-

Anna's Hummingbird, female

Black-chinned Hummingbird, female

green species or one of the rufous-and-green species. The latter group shows distinct rufous coloration on the body sides and tail base; the former group lacks rufous tones except as a flank wash on some individuals. In gray-and-green species (the genera *Archilochus* and *Calypte*), head and body proportions, tail length and shape, and voice differences are helpful characters. And details of primary shape are diagnostic: The inner 6 primaries of *Archilochus* are disproportionately narrow, and the shape of the primary tips is diagnostic within *Archilochus*. Among the rufous-and-green species (*Stellula* and *Selasphorus*), check tail length relative to wing tip length on perched birds, the brightness and contrast of rufous coloration on the body sides, relative bill length, and tail pattern details. Even after narrowing your choices, some birds will defy specific identification, and this might be true even if an expert examined the birds in the hand (so don't be discouraged). Time and the associated experience you gain will make hummingbirds more manageable, and soon you will be able to discern more and more refined characters. ■

Genus Colibri

GREEN VIOLET-EAR *Colibri thalassinus*

♂

immature

This fairly large and overall green hummingbird is a rare visitor to the United States from the pine-oak highlands of Mexico. Polytypic (4 ssp.; nominate in N.A.). L 4.2–4.7" (11–12 cm) Bill 18–22 mm

Identification The Green Violet-ear has a proportionately short and slightly decurved bill (about the same length

as its head) and a fairly long, broad tail that is slightly notched. The size, shape, and overall color of the Green Violet-ear, in combination with its violet-blue auricular patches, are distinctive. ADULT MALE: Brighter overall with an extensive, purplish blue chest patch and auricular patches, a golden green crown, a longer, more strongly notched tail. ADULT FEMALE: Duller overall than the male, with a smaller and less purplish chest patch and smaller auricular patches, a bronzy green crown, and a shorter, less notched tail. IMMATURE: Distinguished from adult by its duller upperparts (with fine cinnamon tips when fresh), and the dull bluish green throat and chest with patchy iridescent green and blue feathers.

Geographic Variation North American records are of the nominate *thalassinus*, distinguished from southern populations (sometimes considered a separate species, the Mountain Violet-

ear—*cyanotis*) by its larger size and violet-blue chest patch.

Similar Species The Green Violet-ear is unlikely to be confused with other North American hummingbirds but, as with all extralimital hummers, beware the possibility of hybrids that might resemble violet-ears, or escapees of the southern subspecies, or similar species.

Voice CALL: Hard short rattles and clipped chips, both given from a perch and in flight. SONG: A metallic, mostly disyllabic chipping, often repeated tediously with a jerky cadence from an exposed perch; immatures may give more varied series, including buzzes and rattles.

Status & Distribution Mexico to S.A. VAGRANT: Casual to rare (mainly May–Aug., extremes Apr.–Dec.) in central and eastern N.A., with 30 of approximately 50 N.A. records from TX; accidental in NM, AB, and ON.

Genus Anthracothorax

GREEN-BREASTED MANGO   *Anthracothorax prevostii*

immature

This striking and ostensibly unmistakable large hummingbird is a casual visitor to the United States from eastern Mexico. Polytypic (4 ssp.; nominate in N.A.). L 4.5–4.8" (11.5–12 cm) Bill 24–30 mm

Identification The Green-breasted Mango has a thick and arched black bill and a broad tail. This species' size, bill shape, and overall plumage patterns are unlike any other North American hummer. ADULT MALE (AND SOME FEMALES): Plumage is distinctive: Deep green overall with a black throat and mostly purple tail. ADULT FEMALE: Note the blackish median throat stripe, becoming deep green on the white underparts and purple tail base. IMMATURE: Resembles female but has cinnamon mottling on the sides of the throat and chest.

Similar Species Unlikely to be confused, but beware the possibility of other mango species wandering from the Caribbean, or escapees of the similar Black-throated Mango (*nigricollis*).

Voice Not very vocal. CALL: A high, sharp *sip,* as well as fairly hard, ticking chips, and shrill tinny twitters in interactions.

Status & Distribution Mexico to northern S.A. VAGRANT: Casual visitor (mainly in autumn and winter) to coastal lowlands of south TX (12+ records); accidental in NC (Nov.–Dec.).

Genus Cynanthus

BROAD-BILLED HUMMINGBIRD   *Cynanthus latirostris*

immature ♂

This medium-size, lightly built hummingbird of desert canyons and low mountain woodlands is an inveterate tail wagger. It often attracts attention through its dry chattering calls. Polytypic (5 ssp.; 1 in N.A.). L 3.5–4" (9–10 cm) Bill 18.5–23.5 mm

Identification The Broad-billed has a fairly broad, cleft tail that is often wagged persistently in flight and a medium-long bill that is reddish basally. ADULT MALE: Distinctive, with deep green plumage overall, a blue throat, white undertail coverts, a cleft blue-black tail, and a bright red bill, tipped black. ADULT FEMALE: Note the broad dark auricular mask offset by a whitish to pale-gray postocular stripe that is often whitest immediately behind the eye. The throat and underparts are pale gray with limited green spotting on the body sides. The blackish tail has variable greenish basally and distinct white tips to the outer rectrices. The lower mandible is reddish basally. IMMATURE MALE: Resembles female but plumage fresh in fall with buff-tipped upperparts. The throat usually has some blue blotching or a solid blue patch, and older birds are extensively mottled green on the underparts. Red on the bill base often extends to the upper mandible, and the tail is more extensively blue-black, with smaller white corners. IMMATURE FEMALE: Resembles adult female but plumage fresh in fall, buff-tipped on upperparts, the underparts have reduced or no green mottling on the sides, and the lower mandible base averages paler, more pinkish.

Geographic Variation North American birds are of the nominate subspecies group, *latirostris.* Two other subspecies groups in Mexico (*lawrencei* and *doubledayi*) may be specifically distinct.

Similar Species Immature males with a blue throat patch might suggest the larger and heavier Blue-throated Hummingbird, which has an all-black bill, a very large blue-black tail with bold white corners, and a high-pitched squeak call. A female might be confused with a female White-eared Hummingbird, which is stockier and proportionately shorter billed, with a bold black auricular mask, an even more flagrant white postocular stripe, and a hard chipping call suggesting Anna's Hummingbird. The dullest females could suggest a Black-chinned Hummingbird, but note their reddish bill base, broad inner primaries, and call.

Voice CALL: Often gives a dry *cht,* singly or in short series, *ch-ch-cht,* etc., when the chattering cadence suggests the common call of the Ruby-crowned Kinglet; also a high squeaky chippering in interactions. SONG: A high, sharp song, repeated from a perch.

Status & Distribution Mexico to southwest U.S., winters mainly in Mexico. BREEDING: Fairly common (mainly Mar.–Sept.), in brushy woodland, desert washes, gardens. WINTER: Uncommon and local in southern AZ, casual to rare west to southern CA and east to Gulf Coast. VAGRANT: Accidental as far north as OR, MI, and NB.

Genus Hylocharis

WHITE-EARED HUMMINGBIRD *Hylocharis leucotis*

This medium-size, stocky hummer is common in Mexico's pine-oak highlands. Polytypic (3 ssp.; N.A. recs. are *borealis*). L 3.5–4" (9–10 cm) Bill 15–18.5 mm

Identification The bill is medium-length and red basally. In all plumages the bold white postocular stripe contrasts with the broad blackish auricular mask. ADULT MALE: Head often looks black with flagrant white stripe. ADULT FEMALE: Throat and underparts whitish, extensively spotted green; lower mandible reddish basally. IMMATURE MALE: Resembles female; throat usually has some blue and green. Red on

bill extends to upper mandible. IMMATURE FEMALE: Resembles adult; throat has sparser and more bronzy spotting. **Similar Species** Unlikely to be confused. See Xantus's Hummingbird and Broad-billed Hummingbird.

Voice CALL: A clipped, fairly hard ticking chip, singly or often doubled or trebled, *ti-ti-tik* or *chi-tik chi-tik*. SONG: Rapid, rhythmical chipping interspersed with squeaks and gurgles.

Status & Distribution Mexico to Nicaragua. SUMMER: Rare and local visitor (mainly Apr.–Oct.) in pine-oak of southern AZ mountains. VAGRANT: Casual east to TX, accidental in CO and MS.

XANTUS'S HUMMINGBIRD *Hylocharis xantusii*

This unmistakable vagrant shares the congeneric White-eared Hummingbird's bold face pattern. Monotypic. L 3.3–3.8" (8–9 cm) Bill 16–19 mm

Identification The bill is medium length and red basally. In all plumages a bold white postocular stripe contrasts with a broad blackish auricular mask. ADULT MALE: Unmistakable. ADULT FEMALE: Throat and underparts cinnamon, lower mandible reddish basally. IMMATURE: Resembles adult female but fresh plumage has broadly buff-tipped

crown feathers. Males usually have some blue-green throat spots, and red on bill base extends to upper mandible. **Similar Species** Should not be confused.

Voice CALL: Most often gives a low, fairly fast-paced rattled *trrrrr* or *tur-rrt*. SONG: A quiet, rough, gurgling warble interspersed with rattles and high squeaky notes.

Status & Distribution Endemic to Baja California, Mexico. VAGRANT: Accidental in winter to southern CA (2 recs.) and southwest BC (1 rec.).

AMAZILIA HUMMINGBIRDS *Genus Amazilia*

Of about 30 species in this genus, 4 have occurred north of Mexico: 2 regular breeders, a casual breeder, and an accidental visitor. The sexes look generally similar. *Amazilia* may represent two genera: A slender-billed species with a dark upper mandible, including *Berylline* (subgenus *Saucerottia*) and typical *Amazilia*, with broader red bills.

BERYLLINE HUMMINGBIRD *Amazilia beryllina*

This common Mexican hummingbird of foothill oak woodlands ranges north on an annual basis. Polytypic (5 ssp.; N.A. recs. are *viola*). L 3.7–4" (9.5–10 cm) Bill 18.5–21 mm

Identification This medium-size hummer has a slender, medium-length bill with red on at least the base of the lower mandible. Diagnostic bright-rufous wing patch of all plumages noticeable in flight. ADULT MALE: Beryl green throat and chest contrast with dusky buff belly; crown green; coppery purple tail often looks rufous. ADULT FEMALE: Similar to male but duller, with whitish mottled chin, bronzy-

green crown, and more grayish belly. IMMATURE: Resembles female but throat and chest dingy buff to whitish, mottled green.

Similar Species Buff-bellied Hummingbird (normally no overlap in range) lacks a rufous wing patch, has a pale eye ring and a broader bill that, in adults, is bright red above.

Voice CALL: A fairly hard, buzzy *dzirr* or *dzzrit*. A higher and more trilled *siirrr* is given in warning; in flight chases a high, slightly buzzy chatter. SONG: Short, jerky and squeaky phrases,

repeated, to prolonged squeaky warbling.

Status & Distribution Mexico to Honduras. SUMMER: Rare to casual visitor (Apr.–Oct., mainly June–Aug.) in oak zone of southern AZ mountains. VAGRANT: Casual in summer to southwestern NM and western TX.

BUFF-BELLIED HUMMINGBIRD   *Amazilia yucatanensis*

This fairly large hummer is found in south Texas. Polytypic (3 ssp.; N.A. records are *chalconota*). L 3.8–4.3" (10–11 cm) Bill 19–22 mm
Identification Medium-length bill; broad, cleft tail; buffy belly; pale eye ring; and mostly rufous tail in all plumages. ADULT MALE: Throat and chest iridescent green, contrasting with buffy-cinnamon belly. Mostly rufous tail tipped bronzy green,

most broadly on central rectrices. Bright red bill tipped black. ADULT FEMALE: Similar to male but duller, with whitish mottled chin, a shallower tail cleft, and mostly green central rectrices. IMMATURE: Like female but throat and chest dingy buff to whitish, mottled iridescent green, belly paler buff, upper mandible mostly blackish, developing red over first year.
Similar Species The Berylline (normally no overlap in range) has a distinct rufous wing patch, a slender bill black above, and a different voice.
Voice CALL: A clipped to slightly smacking chip, *tik* or *tk*, at times run into a rolled *tirr* or *tsirrr*. In warning, a slightly buzzy *ssir*. In chases, variable and usually fast-paced series of buzzy

to lisping calls. SONG: A varied arrangement of chips alternating with slurred whistles and wheezy notes.
Status & Distribution: South TX to Guatemala. BREEDING: Fairly common (mainly Apr.–Aug.). WINTER: More widespread in TX, rare to casual (mainly Oct.–Mar.) along Gulf Coast to north FL. VAGRANT: Casual in south FL.

CINNAMON HUMMINGBIRD   *Amazilia rutila*

This medium-large hummer is a vagrant from the tropical lowlands of west Mexico. Polytypic (4 ssp.; N.A. recs. probably *diluta*). L 4–4.5" (10–11.5 cm) Bill 20.5–23.5 mm
Identification All plumages solidly cinnamon throat and underparts. ADULT: Sexes similar. Black-tipped, bright-red bill. IMMATURE: Resembles adult but upperparts tipped cinnamon when fresh; upper mandible mostly blackish, developing red over the first year.

Similar Species Should be unmistakable. See Xantus's Hummingbird.
Voice CALL: A hard, clipped tick with a buzzy or rattled quality, *tzk* or *dzk*, can be run into buzzy rattles. In interactions, high squeaks run into excited chatters. SONG: A short, varied arrangement of slightly squeaky chips.
Status & Distribution Mexico to Costa Rica. VAGRANT: Accidental (2 recs.; July–Sept.) to southeastern AZ and south-central NM.

VIOLET-CROWNED HUMMINGBIRD   *Amazilia violiceps*

An unmistakable hummer of western Mexico, with local summer populations in southeastern Arizona and southwestern New Mexico. Polytypic (2 ssp.; 1 in N.A.). L 4–4.5" (10–11.5 cm) Bill 21–24 mm
Identification The bill is medium-long and straightish, and the tail is broad and squared to slightly cleft (averag-

ing more so on males). The bright white underparts are unique among North American hummingbirds. ADULT: Sexes similar. Crown and auriculars are violet-blue (rarely appearing turquoise) and the tail bronzy greenish to brownish. Bright red bill is tipped black. IMMATURE: Resembles adult, but the throat and underparts are dingier whitish. The crown is oily bluish (can look simply dark, with no obvious blue) with buff feather tips in fresh plumage; the upperparts and tail are tipped buff in fresh plumage; and the upper mandible is mostly blackish, developing red over the first year.
Geographic Variation North American birds are of northern subspecies, *ellioti*. Nominate from central Mexico has a brighter, coppery-bronze tail.
Voice CALL: A hard chip, *stik* or *tik*, often

run into rattled short series; in flight chases gives a rapid-paced, hollow, and slightly squeaky chatter. SONG: Apparently a single plaintive chip, repeated from perch, *chieu chieu chieu*.
Status & Distribution Mexico to southwest U.S., winters Mexico. BREEDING: Uncommon (mainly Apr.–Sept.) in arid to semiarid scrub, riparian woodland, and gardens. WINTER: Rare in southeastern AZ. VAGRANT: Casual northwest to northern CA, east to TX.

Genus Lampornis

BLUE-THROATED HUMMINGBIRD *Lampornis clemenciae*

The largest hummingbird in North America, the Blue-throated favors shady understory and edge in watered pine-oak and oak canyons. Polytypic (2 ssp.). L 4.8–5.3" (12–13.5 cm) Bill 21.5–26 mm

Identification The Blue-throated has a proportionately short black bill. Its very large tail often looks slightly rounded. The whitish face stripes, bold white corners on tail, and high-pitched call are good field marks. ADULT MALE: Blue gorget well defined but can be hard to see. Outer two pairs of rectrices have large white tips. ADULT FEMALE: Throat plain dusky gray, white tips to outer three pairs of rectrices; some birds have a few blue throat feathers. IMMATURE: Resembles female but upperparts have buffy-cinnamon edgings in fall, and lower mandible base often pinkish on younger birds. Males have irregular blue gorget patch restricted to central throat.

Similar Species Female and immature Magnificent Hummingbird longer billed with a greenish tail that has only small white corners; more mottled underparts; and a smacking chip call. Magnificent's face pattern typically dominated by a bold white postocular spot, but some can be similar to poorly marked Blue-throated. See immature male Broad-billed Hummingbird.

Voice CALL: A high, penetrating *siip* or *siik,* given from perch and in flight; less often a fuller *tsiuk.* SONG: Apparently a repetition of call, *siip siip siip,* though more complex vocalizations have been reported.

Status & Distribution Mexico to southwest U.S. BREEDING: Uncommon to fairly common (mainly Apr.–Sept.) in humid mountain forests. WINTER: Mexico. Casual in southeastern AZ. VAGRANT: Casual west to CA, north (mainly late summer) to UT and CO, east (mainly winter) to southern LA.

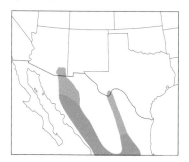

Genus Eugenes

MAGNIFICENT HUMMINGBIRD *Eugenes fulgens*

This large hummer of southwestern mountains often perches prominently on high twigs. Polytypic (2 ssp.; nominate in N.A.). L 4.7–5.3" (12–13.5 cm) Bill 27.5–30 mm

Identification Magnificent has a long black bill and a slightly notched tail. ADULT MALE: Distinctive; often looks all-dark, since violet crown and green gorget rarely seem to catch the light. ADULT FEMALE: Throat and underparts pale gray, mottled green on the sides. IMMATURE MALE: Resembles female but throat and underparts strongly mottled green, the white malar

streak more distinct, and the central throat usually has a large iridescent-green blotch. IMMATURE FEMALE: Resembles immature male but throat lacks iridescent green patches.

Similar Species Note large size, long bill, and face pattern. Plain-capped Starthroat has proportionately longer bill, dark throat patch bordered by whitish malar, and white rump patch. See the Blue-throated Hummingbird.

Voice CALL: A fairly loud, sharp *chik* or *tsik,* given from perch and in flight. Also a higher *piik,* and males, at least, give fairly hard, short rattles, *trrirr* and *trrrr ch-chrr* that may run into prolonged squeaky chattering. Aggression call a squeaky, slightly bubbling, accelerating chatter. SONG: A fairly soft, slightly buzzy gurgling warble.

Status & Distribution Southwest U.S. to Panama. BREEDING: Fairly common (Mar.–Oct.) in pine-oak and oak highlands. WINTER: Rare, mainly southeast AZ. VAGRANT: Casual west to CA, north (mainly late summer) to UT and WY, exceptionally MI, and east (mainly winter) to Gulf states, exceptionally GA and VA.

Genus *Heliomaster*

PLAIN-CAPPED STARTHROAT *Heliomaster constantii*

This large vagrant from Mexico often makes prolonged flycatching sallies over streams. Like many tropical hummers it shows little age/sex variation. Polytypic (3 ssp.; N.A. recs. are *pinicola*). L 4.7–5" (12–13 cm) Bill 33–37 mm **Identification** Very long, straight black bill; note throat pattern, white rump patch, and Black Phoebe-like call. ADULT: Throat patch is dark sooty with iridescent reddish mottling on lower portions (often hard to see). Tail has white tips to all but the central pair of rectrices. IMMATURE: Resembles adult but throat patch has little or no red, white tail tips average wider. **Similar Species** Compare with female Magnificent Hummingbird. **Voice** CALL: A sharp, fairly loud *peek!*, given from perch and especially in flight. SONG: A series of chips interspersed with varied notes.

Status & Distribution Mexico to Costa Rica. VAGRANT: Casual visitor (May–Nov., mainly late summer) to southern AZ.

Genus *Calliphlox*

BAHAMA WOODSTAR *Calliphlox evelynae*

immature ♂

There are few well-documented records of this vagrant from the Bahamas. Polytypic (2 ssp.; nominate in N.A.). L 3.4–3.7" (8.5–9.5 cm) Bill 16–17 mm **Identification** Bill slightly arched; fairly long, forked tail, projecting past the wing tip on perched birds. ADULT MALE: Unmistakable. ADULT FEMALE: Outer rectrices have cinnamon bases and tips. IMMATURE MALE: Like adult female, but throat usually has some magenta-rose spots; tail slightly longer, more forked. **Similar Species** Distinctive but might be confused with female or immature *Selasphorus* hummingbirds, which have straighter bills, dark throat markings, and shorter tails with bold white tips to the outer rectrices. **Voice** CALL: A high, fairly sharp chipping *tih or chi,* often doubled when repeated from perch, *chi chi chi-chi chi.* **Status & Distribution** Endemic to Bahamas. VAGRANT: Accidental to south FL (4 recs. 1961–1981; Jan, Apr.–Oct).

Genus *Calothorax*

LUCIFER HUMMINGBIRD *Calothorax lucifer*

immature ♂

This small hummer is a summer inhabitant of mountain desert canyons, especially in west Texas. Monotypic. L 3.5–4" (9–10 cm) Bill 19–23 mm **Identification** Bill is proportionately long and arched; the fairly long, forked tail (usually held closed) projects past the wing tip on perched birds. The dusky auricular stripe on the buff face of females is diagnostic. ADULT MALE: Expansive magenta gorget; longer tail than female. ADULT FEMALE: The throat is pale buff to whitish, rarely with 1 or a few magenta spots; outer rectrices have rufous bases and bold white tips. IMMATURE MALE: Resembles adult female but the upperparts in fall are fresher, with fine buffy tips; throat usually has more magenta rose spots. Tail is slightly longer and more forked with narrower outer rectrices. **Voice** CALL: A fairly hard, slightly smacking *chih or chi,* at times run into a rolled *chi-ti.* Varied, rapid-paced chippering in interactions. Male makes a fairly loud wing buzz in displays. **Status & Distribution** Mexico to southwest U.S. BREEDING: Uncommon and local (mainly Apr.–Oct.) in arid mountain canyons. VAGRANT: Casual visitor away from traditional sites in AZ, NM, and TX.

"BLACK-CHINNED" HUMMINGBIRDS Genus *Archilochus*

Eastern and western counterparts are the Ruby-throated and Black-chinned. Diagnostic of the genus are the relatively narrow inner 6 primaries. Adult males have shield-shaped gorgets with black chins. Females/immatures have mostly plain underparts with little or no buff wash, no rufous in tail. Primary molt typically starts in fall or later (Sept.–Jan.).

RUBY-THROATED HUMMINGBIRD *Archilochus colubris*

adult ♀ wing

immature ♂

♀

immature ♂

The Ruby-throated is the only hummer seen regularly in much of the East. Monotypic. L 3.2–3.7" (8–9 cm) Bill 14–19 mm
Identification Primaries relatively tapered. Tail forked to double-rounded. ADULT MALE: Solid ruby red gorget with black chin and face. ADULT FEMALE: Throat

whitish, often with lines of dusky flecks, rarely 1–2 red spots. Sides often washed buff, often brightest on rear flanks. IMMATURE MALE: Resembles adult female but upperparts in fall fresher, with fine buff tips; lores often darker; throat usually with ruby spots; tail slightly longer and more forked. Complete molt in winter produces plumage like adult male. IMMATURE FEMALE: Resembles adult female but fall plumage fresher; throat lacks red spots.
Similar Species Black-chinned has blunter primaries. Adult male has black throat with violet lower band, shorter tail. Females and immatures similar to Ruby-throated but generally duller green above (especially crown) and dingier below (Ruby-throated bright emerald above and whiter below). Black-chinned tail less forked; often pumps tail strongly while feeding (Ruby-throated usually holds tail fairly still). Problem identifications best confirmed by checking details of primary shape. See Costa's and Anna's

hummingbirds under Black-chinned.
Voice CALL: A slightly twangy or nasal chips, *chih* and *tchew,* given in flight and perched. Also varied twittering series. Indistinguishable from Black-chinned, but generally lacks strongly buzzy or sharp, smacking quality of Anna's and *Selasphorus,* and distinct from high, tinny chips of Costa's.
Status & Distribution Breeds N.A., winters Mexico to Panama. BREEDING: Common in woodland, gardens, etc. MIGRATION: Mainly Mar.–May, Aug.–Oct. WINTER: Rare (mainly Nov.–Mar.) in the Southeast. VAGRANT: Casual in the West.

BLACK-CHINNED HUMMINGBIRD *Archilochus alexandri*

The western counterpart of the Ruby-throated, the Black-chinned regularly pumps its tail. Monotypic. L 3.3–3.8" (8.5–9.5 cm) Bill 16–22 mm
Identification Best marks for all ages are narrow inner primaries and blunt primaries. Double-rounded tail. Age/sex differences as Ruby-throated except as noted. ADULT MALE: Black throat with violet-blue lower band. ADULT FEMALE: Black-violet spots rare on throat. IMMATURE MALE: Throat usually has black-

violet spots.
Similar Species The Black-chinned is often confused with Anna's and Costa's, which are chunkier and proportionately bigger headed, shorter billed, and shorter tailed; lack the narrow inner primaries of *Archilochus;* and molt wings in summer. Female/immature Anna's slightly larger; underparts more mottled, including undertail coverts (mostly whitish on Black-chinned); throat often with rose-red spots; wags tail infrequently. Female/immature Costa's slightly smaller; face often plainer; wing tips often fall beyond tail tip at rest (shorter than tip on Black-chinned). Anna's call is a smacking chip, Costa's is a high, tinny *tik,* both distinct from Black-chinned. See Ruby-throated.
Voice CALL: Indistinguishable from Ruby-throated but distinctive male wing-buzz in flight louder (and lower

immature ♂

♀

♀

adult ♀ wing

pitched than *Selasphorus*).
Status & Distribution Western N.A. to northwest Mexico. BREEDING: Common in riparian woodlands, foothills. MIGRATION: Mainly Mar.–May, Aug.–Sept. WINTER: Mexico. Rare (mainly Oct.–Mar.) in Southeast; casual in Northeast (fall).

"HELMETED" HUMMINGBIRDS Genus *Calypte*

This genus comprises 2 western species of scrub habitats: Anna's and Costa's. Small, fairly chunky hummers with relatively large heads and short tails; adult males have an iridescent helmet (i.e., gorget and crown), with gorgets elongated at corners. Females and immatures have dingy underparts with no buff wash on the sides, no rufous in tail.

ANNA'S HUMMINGBIRD *Calypte anna*

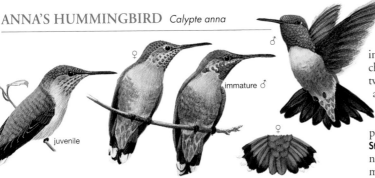

This hummer is a familiar species in West Coast gardens, where it is present year-round. Monotypic. L 3.5–4" (9–10 cm) Bill 16–20 mm

Identification Tail slightly rounded to double-rounded. ADULT MALE: Rose (fresh) to orange-red (worn) gorget and crown. ADULT FEMALE: Throat and underparts spotted and mottled dusky to bronzy green, median throat blotched rose-red. IMMATURE MALE: Resembles adult female but upperparts fresher in February to June, with fine buff tips; throat and crown usually with more scattered rose spots; white tail tips narrower. Complete summer molt produces plumage like adult male by late fall. IMMATURE FEMALE: Resembles adult female but upperparts fresher in February to June; throat often lacks rose spots.

Similar Species Costa's smaller (obvious in direct comparison), and males readily identified (beware occasional hybrids, which look more like male Costa's, sound more like Anna's). Female/immature Costa's proportionately longer billed but shorter tailed, often best told by call: high, tinny *pit* call and twitters distinct from Anna's. Costa's generally plainer on throat and underparts, without dusky throat spotting. See Black-chinned.

Voice CALL: A slightly emphatic to fairly hard *tik* or *tih* and a more smacking *tsik*, in flight and perched. In flight chases, a rapid-paced, slightly buzzy twittering, *t-chissi-chissi-chissi*, and variations. SONG: A high-pitched, wiry to lisping squeaky warble from perch, often prolonged and repeated with pulsating succession. Year-round.

Status & Distribution Western N.A. to northern Mexico. BREEDING: Common (Dec.–June) in scrub, gardens, etc. DISPERSAL/MIGRATION: Some late summer movement upslope to mountains. Local movements complex. WINTER: Casual (mainly fall and winter) north to AK and in the East.

COSTA'S HUMMINGBIRD *Calypte costae*

The Costa's is a spectacular small hummer of southwest deserts. Monotypic. L 3–3.4" (7.5–8.5 cm) Bill 16–20 mm

Identification Tail rounded to slightly double-rounded. ADULT MALE: Violet gorget and crown, tail lacks white tips. ADULT FEMALE: Throat and underparts dingy white to pale gray, throat sometimes blotched violet. IMMATURE MALE: Like adult female but upperparts fresher February to July, with fine buff tips; auriculars darker; white tail tips narrower. Complete summer molt produces plumage like adult male by early winter. IMMATURE FEMALE: Like adult female but upperparts fresher February to July, with fine buff tips; throat plain whitish.

Similar Species Anna's larger (obvious in direct comparison); males readily identified (beware occasional hybrids; see Anna's). Female/immature Anna's proportionately shorter billed but longer tailed; often best told by call, a smacking chip and buzzy twitters. Anna's generally more spotted on throat and underparts. See Black-chinned. Problem identifications best confirmed by using primary shape and voice.

Voice CALL: A high, slightly tinny, fairly soft *tik* or *ti*, often run into short, slightly liquid or rippling twitters suggestive of Bushtit chatter. Warning call a high, slightly squealing *tssirr*, singly or run into slightly buzzy series in interactions. SONG: A very high-pitched, thin, drawn-out, whining whistle, *tsi ssiiiiiiu*, given from perch and, more loudly, in looping display dives.

Status & Distribution Western U.S. to northwest Mexico. BREEDING: Fairly common (Feb.–July) in desert washes, dry chaparral. DISPERSAL/MIGRATION: Mainly Feb.–May and June–July; local movements complex. WINTER: Uncommon to rare and local north to southern NV. VAGRANT: Casual north to southern AK and MT, east to KS.

Genus Stellula

CALLIOPE HUMMINGBIRD *Stellula calliope*

The smallest breeding bird in North America, the Calliope Hummingbird is a summer resident of western mountain meadows, especially along wooded streams. Monotypic. L 3–3.2" (7.5–8 cm) Bill 12.5–6 mm

Identification Note the relatively short and squared tail, which means that the Calliope's wing tips often project slightly beyond its tail when perched; the bill is medium-short. Adult males are distinctive, females and immatures are rufous-and-green and best identified by their small size, and relatively short, mostly black tail. Note the whitish lores on many birds. ADULT MALE: The elongated "gorget" of rose stripes rarely looks solid; note the white lores and eye ring. ADULT FEMALE: The throat is whitish with

variable lines of bronzy-green flecks and rarely 1 or more rose spots. The sides of the neck and underparts are washed cinnamon and lack a distinct white "forecollar." The tail is slightly rounded (appears squared when closed). IMMATURE MALE: Resembles adult female but has fresher upperparts in fall, with fine buff tips. The throat is usually flecked more heavily with bronzy green and often has 1 or more rose pink spots or streaks; the white bill-lip line is often reduced or absent. A complete molt in winter produces an adultlike male plumage. IMMATURE FEMALE: Resembles adult female but the upperparts are fresher in fall, with fine buff tips, and the white bill-lip line is reduced or absent.

Similar Species Note the short tail. Female/immature *Selasphorus* are larger (obvious in direct comparison), with longer and slightly thicker bills, longer and distinctly graduated tails that project beyond the wing tips on perched birds. They are more aggressive, often uttering their louder calls and chasing other hummingbirds. However, the female Broad-tailed is remarkably similar in plumage to the Calliope; other than in size and bill length, note the Broad-tailed's longer tail, which is mostly green above. Rufous/Allen's

Hummingbirds have brighter and more contrasting rufous body sides and more rufous in the tail than the Calliope. **Voice** Often fairly quiet and inconspicuous. CALL: A relatively soft, high chip, often doubled, *chi* and *chi-ti;* often repeated steadily from perch, less often when feeding. High, slightly buzzier chippering in interactions. Male's wing buzz can attract attention during flight displays.

Status & Distribution Breeds western N.A., winters Mexico. BREEDING: Fairly common (Apr.–Aug.) in mountain meadows and open forest. MIGRATION: Mainly late Mar.–early May, July–Sept.; in fall, ranges east to western Great Plains and western TX. WINTER: Rare (mainly Oct.–Mar.) in the Southeast. VAGRANT: Casual in late fall as far northeast as MN and MA.

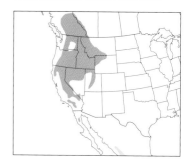

Genus Atthis

BUMBLEBEE HUMMINGBIRD *Atthis heloisa*

This tiny hummingbird is endemic to montane forests of Mexico, where it feeds inconspicuously with a relatively slow and deliberate, insectlike flight. Some authors place this species and the closely related Wine-throated Hummingbird (*A. ellioti*) of northern Central America in the genus *Selasphorus*. Polytypic (2 ssp.; N.A. recs. unclear). L 2.7–3" (7–7.5 cm) Bill 11–13 mm

Identification The bill is medium-short, and the rounded to double-rounded tail projects beyond the wing tips on perched birds. Both sexes have a femalelike tail with rufous bases and white tips to the outer rectrices. ADULT MALE: Distinctive, with an elongated magenta-rose gorget. ADULT FEMALE: The throat is whitish with lines

of bronzy-green flecks, and a whitish forecollar contrasts variably with the cinnamon sides. The white tail tips are bolder than the male. IMMATURE MALE: Resembles adult female but throat flecked more heavily with bronzy green, often with rose-pink spots or streaks. IMMATURE FEMALE: Resembles adult female but throat has finer dusky spots. Tips of outer tail feathers washed buffy cinnamon when fresh.

Similar Species Female and immature *Selasphorus* hummingbirds are larger with longer bills, more graduated tails, quick flight, and louder and harder calls. The Calliope Hummingbird is slightly larger with a short, mostly black tail that falls equal with or shorter than the wing tips at rest, and a quicker, darting flight.

Voice Quiet and inconspicuous except for the strong wing buzz of adult males; at times gives quiet, high chips when feeding. Female wing buzz is soft but stronger and buzzier than Calliope Hummingbird and easily overlooked.

Status & Distribution Endemic to Mexico. VAGRANT: Accidental in southeastern AZ (2 enigmatic specimens in July 1896).

"RUFOUS" HUMMINGBIRDS Genus *Selasphorus*

In North America this genus comprises 3 western species: Broad-tailed, Rufous, and Allen's. These small hummers have fairly long, graduated tails that project beyond the wing tips at rest. Males have solid gorgets slightly elongated at the corners; their power-dive displays from heights of 10 to 30 feet are spectacular and species-specific. Females are green-and-rufous, with cinnamon body sides and tail bases.

BROAD-TAILED HUMMINGBIRD *Selasphorus platycercus*

A common species of western mountains, where the male's diagnostic, cricketlike wing trill is a characteristic sound. Like many "western" hummingbirds, the Broad-tailed is increasingly found in late fall and winter in the Southeast. Polytypic (2 ssp.; nominate in N.A.). L 3.5–4" (9–10 cm) Bill 16–20 mm

Identification Tail weakly graduated. Pale eye ring in all plumages. ADULT MALE: Rose-red gorget with pale chin and face. Often detected by wing trill. ADULT FEMALE: Throat whitish with variable lines of bronzy-green flecks, sometimes 1 or more rose spots; sides of neck and underparts variably washed

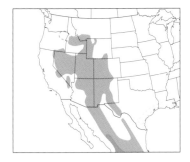

cinnamon. IMMATURE MALE: Resembles adult female but upperparts fresher in fall, with fine buff tips; throat usually flecked fairly heavily with bronzy green, often with rose-pink spots; tail averages more rufous at base. Complete molt in winter and spring produces plumage like adult male. IMMATURE FEMALE: Resembles adult female, but upperparts fresher in fall, with fine buff tips; tail averages less rufous at base.

Similar Species Female/immature Rufous/Allen's hummingbirds are slightly smaller and slimmer in build (noticeable in comparison) with more strongly graduated tails that have a more tapered tip. Rufous/Allen's typically have a whiter forecollar contrasting with brighter rufous sides, and lack the whitish eye ring often shown by the Broad-tailed; their uppertail coverts and tail base have more rufous (adult female Rufous can be all-green); and their chip calls are slightly lower pitched. Also see female and immature Calliope Hummingbird.

Voice Generally higher pitched than Rufous/Allen's. CALL: A slightly metal-lic, sharpish *chip* or *chik*, often doubled, *ch-chip* or *chi-tik,* and at times repeated steadily from perch. Warning call a fairly abrupt, clipped *buzz, tssir,* and squeaky chippering. Adult male's wing trill diagnostic.

Status & Distribution BREEDING: Western U.S. to Guatemala. Common (Apr.–Aug.) in mountains. MIGRATION: Mainly Apr.–May, Aug.–Sept. (a few to western Great Plains). WINTER: Mainly Mexico. Casual to very rare (mainly Nov.–Apr.) in the Southeast. VAGRANT: Casual north to BC, west to Pacific coast.

RUFOUS HUMMINGBIRD *Selasphorus rufus*

green-flecked ♂   immature ♂

This common summer hummingbird of the Northwest is the western species most often found in the East (in fall and winter). Note that all except (most) adult male Rufous are rarely separable in the field from Allen's Hummingbird, so many observations are best termed "Rufous/Allen's." In dive display (also given in migration, and by immatures) male climbs to a start point, then dives with a slanted J-form trajectory, typically followed by a short, horizontal fluttering flight before climbing to repeat the dive. Monotypic. L 3.2–3.7" (8–9 cm) Bill 15–19 mm

Identification Adult males often detected by wing buzz, which, like other *Selasphorus,* is produced only in direct flight, not when hovering. ADULT MALE: Flame orange gorget; rufous back often has some green spotting, can be solidly green. ADULT FEMALE: Throat

whitish with lines of bronzy-green flecks strongest at corners, and typically a central splotch of red. IMMATURE MALE: Resembles adult female but upperparts fresher in fall, with fine buff tips; throat usually flecked fairly heavily, and with red spots. Rectrices average narrower and with more rufous at bases, and white tips to outer rectrices narrower. Complete molt in winter produces plumage like adult male. IMMATURE FEMALE: Resembles adult female but upperparts fresher in fall, with fine buff tips; rectrices average broader; throat evenly flecked and with no (rarely a few) red spots.

Similar Species Female and immature

Allen's Hummingbird safely distinguished only in the hand by narrower outer rectrices relative to age and sex. Adult male Allen's has green back (like very small percentage of Rufous). Male Allen's display dives are U-shaped, not

J-shaped, and can be given by immatures in fall and winter. Females of resident southern California subspecies of Allen's have paler and strongly green-mottled flanks, unlike the Rufous. See female and immature Broad-tailed. **Voice** CALL: A fairly hard ticking or clicking *tik* or *chik,* often doubled or trebled, *ch-tik* or *ch-ti-tik.* ALARM CALL: A slightly squeaky buzz, *tssiur* or *tsirr,* and squeaky chippering in interactions. Adult male's wing buzz often draws

attention; stuttering *ch-ch-ch-ch-chi* at pullout of dive is diagnostic. Immature males make species-specific dives without the sound effects. **Status & Distribution** BREEDING: Northwestern N.A. Common (Mar.–July) in open woodlands and parks. MIGRATION: Mainly late Feb.–early May, late June–Sept. Rare (mainly July–Nov.) in the East. WINTER: Mexico. Rare (mainly Oct.–Mar.) in the Southeast and southern CA.

ALLEN'S HUMMINGBIRD *Selasphorus sasin*

Virtually endemic to California as a breeding bird, this stunning gem is 1 of the earliest migrants in North America: Males return from Mexico in January and head south in June! In dive display (also given in migration, and by immatures) male climbs to start point and then makes repeated, often fairly low, U-shaped dives followed by a single high climb and steep dive. Polytypic (2 ssp.). L 3.2–3.5" (8–9 cm) Bill 15–21 mm
Identification Rarely separable in field from the Rufous Hummingbird except by breeding range (in which Rufous is a common migrant), and many birds are best termed "Rufous/Allen's." Age-related variation and plumage sequences are as the Rufous Hummingbird (see account) with some exceptions. ADULT MALE: Back always green, with rufous uppertail coverts. ADULT FEMALE: Uppertail coverts typically rufous (ironically, often green on Rufous). Flanks paler and mottled bronzy green on *sedentarius* subspecies.
Geographic Variation Migratory subspecies *sasin* breeds from southwestern Oregon to southern California. It

may intergrade with expanding population of slightly larger and longer-billed resident subspecies *sedentarius,* originally confined to California's Channel Islands, but now breeding on mainland. Males of the 2 subspecies are identical in the field, but female *sedentarius* have paler cinnamon and extensively green-mottled sides that create a less-demarcated vest (*sasin* females have brighter rufous, well-demarcated sides).
Similar Species See Rufous Hummingbird. The very fine, almost wirelike outer rectrices of adult male Allen's may be appreciated in good views (e.g., when aggressive males spread their tail at a feeder), but identification best confirmed by photo or in-hand examination. See female and immature Broad-tailed Hummingbird (which

rarely overlap in range with Allen's).
Voice CALL: Not distinguishable in field from the Rufous (see account). However, high, drawn-out, shrieky whine at pullout of adult male Allen's power dive is diagnostic (unlike stuttering of Rufous); immature males make species-specific dive displays but without the sound effects.
Status & Distribution Breeds western N.A., winters Mexico (nominate *sasin*). Subspecies *sedentarius* is a fairly common but local resident in southern CA and Channel Is. BREEDING: Common (Feb.–July) in open woodlands of coastal belt. MIGRATION: Mainly Jan.–Mar., June–Aug., in fall, ranging east to southeastern AZ. WINTER: Casual to rare (mainly Aug.–Feb.) in the Southeast. VAGRANT: Casual (mainly July–Jan.) in the East.

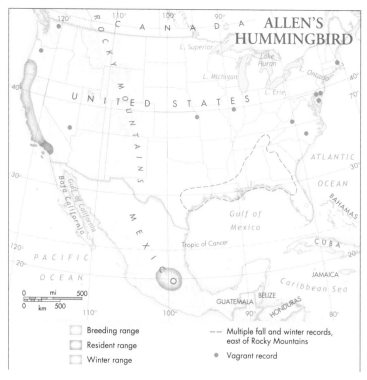

TROGONS Family Trogonidae

Trogons are stunning tropical birds with bright parrotlike colors. Their plumages and rarity in the United States place them among the most sought-after birds.

Structure Their unique profile consists of a long, relatively broad tail; a large, rounded head with large eyes; a small, broad, notched bill; a short neck; and a compact body.

Behavior Trogons sit upright and motionless for extended periods, making them hard to find. Their calls are often the easiest method of locating them, but the calls can carry some distance and have a ventriloquial quality. Flights are usually short; the flash of color gives their presence away. They primarily eat large insects and fruit. Food is taken on the wing, either "fly catching" or, more typically, via sallies where the bird plucks an item from the end of a branch without landing. They are usually seen singly or in small groups, and nest in tree cavities.

Plumage Trogons have soft, dense plumage. Males are brilliantly colored, females more subdued. Males of the two species seen in the U.S. are green and red. The metallic green upperparts occasionally appear greenish blue. Juveniles slowly molt into adultlike plumage over their first year. Adults typically molt in late summer.

Distribution A pantropical family of some 40 species, trogons reach their greatest diversity in the Neotropics. Nine

Elegant Trogon, male (AZ)

species occur in Mexico; 2 barely reach the U.S.

Taxonomy The 25 neotropical trogon species are placed in 4 genera, from the large quetzals *(Pharomachrus)* to the largest genus, *Trogon*, which includes all the similar, smaller-size birds.

Conservation Habitat destruction and human development threaten some species. Birder disturbance at well-known breeding locations in Arizona may result in nest failures. —*Matthew T. Heindel*

Genus *Trogon*

ELEGANT TROGON *Trogon elegans*

This trogon was formerly named the Coppery-tailed Trogon. Polytypic. L 12.5" (32 cm)

Identification Both sexes have a white breast band that borders a red belly; a yellow bill; and a red orbital ring. MALE: Bright green head, chest, and back. Very fine barring on the underside of tail, each feather with a broad white tip; above, tail gold to greenish copper, with 2 central rectrices tipped broadly with black. FEMALE: Gray-brown where male is green. A broad, white teardrop below and behind the eye. Rufous-brown upper tail with a black tip; underside has slightly coarser barring. JUVENILE: Like female, but lacking red. Large whitish buffy spots above.

Geographic Variation Two subspecies. The *ambiguus* occurs in Texas; the male has deeper and more extensive red underparts, the female has a brownish tinge; the *goldmani* occurs in Arizona.

Similar Species The Eared Quetzal is only superficially similar. It is larger and has a thicker body; its bill is black or gray; and it lacks a white breast band and barring on undertail. The Mountain Trogon, resident as far north as Chihuahua (Mex.), is a possible vagrant.

Voice CALL: Varying croaking or *churr* notes. SONG: A series of croaking *co-ah* notes.

Status & Distribution Fairly common, but local, in southeastern AZ. Rare in south-western NM. BREEDING: Pine-oak woodlands, in association with streamside woodlands, primarily sycamores, mostly at elevations of 4,000–6,500 feet. MIGRATION: Routes, duration, and distances largely unknown. In spring, arrives Apr.–early May. Departs in fall by early Nov. WINTER: Withdraws from most of AZ, although still annual at that season. VAGRANT: Western and southern TX, several in winter.

Population The breeding population fluctuates depending, in part, on drought conditions. Arizona lists the bird as a candidate species on its Threatened Native Wildlife list.

Genus *Euptilotis*

EARED QUETZAL *Euptilotis neoxenus*

This large, showy bird from western Mexico is rarely seen in our area. Monotypic. L 14" (36 cm)

Identification Formerly called the Eared Trogon, for the wispy, postocular plumes. MALE: Dark face and crown, almost blackish. Bright green lower throat, upper breast, and most of upperparts; bright red belly. Tail steely blue above, mostly white from below. FEMALE: Like male but head, throat, and most of breast gray; belly paler red. JUVENILE: Like female, but duller and with more black at the base of the underside of tail.

Similar Species Only superficially similar to Elegant Trogon (see that species). **Voice** CALL: A long upslurred squeal ending in a *chuck* note. And a loud, hard cackling *ka-kak*, sometimes given in flight. SONG: A long, quavering series of whistled notes that increase in volume.

Status & Distribution Casual in mountain woodlands of southeastern AZ; 1 record in central AZ (Mogollon Rim). Most records from late summer and fall, but some from winter. Its preference for obscure canyons might result in underreporting.

HOOPOES Family Upupidae

Eurasian Hoopoe (Oman)

A unique family composed of a single, flashy and unforgettable species—the Eurasian Hoopoe. **Structure** It has a long, curved bill, a head crest, a rather chunky body, and rounded wings. **Behavior** Hoopoes feed primarily on the ground, where they can be unobtrusive. They nest in cavities, either on the ground, in rocks, or in trees. The slow and undulating flight style is reminiscent of a large butterfly. The crest is held back along top of crown; the bird expands it fully when excited or briefly upon landing.

Distribution This Old World species breeds from central Europe and central Asia, through Africa and continental Asia. Northerly populations are migratory; most European breeders winter in sub-Saharan Africa, while central Asian breeders winter in southern Asia. **Taxonomy** Most authorities recognize 1 species with 9 subspecies. Some authors elevate the Madagascar and African subspecies to species status. *—Matthew T. Heindel*

Genus *Upupa*

EURASIAN HOOPOE *Upupa epops*

The Eurasian Hoopoe is an Old World vagrant to North America. Polytypic (9 ssp.). L 10.5" (27 cm)
Identification The sexes look similar, but some

adult
saturata

adult males have a pink tinge to the brown head, neck, back, and breast. The crown is a warmer brown, with black tips to the crest feathers. The back stripes alternate black and creamy white, and are continuous with the black-and-white stripes on the wings. JUVENILE: It resembles an adult female, but the brown plumage is grayer and duller. FLIGHT: Very striking. The secondaries and secondary coverts are boldly striped black-and-white, while the black primaries have

a broad white band near the tip and the black tail has a white band near the base.
Similar Species None.
Voice CALL: A high-pitched *scheer.* SONG: A low resonant *poo-poo-poo,* from which the name hoopoe derives.
Status & Distribution Accidental, 1 record of the most northerly Asian subspecies, *saturata,* in western AK (Yukon Delta, Sept. 2–3, 1975).
Population Most populations are stable, but hunting in southern Europe and Asia is of concern.

KINGFISHERS Family Alcedinidae

Green Kingfisher, female (TX, Dec.)

In general, kingfishers sit on low perches watching for prey below them. Their flight is direct and strong, with rapid wingbeats.

Structure Tremendous variation in size exists within the family. The majority of species are small to medium size. All kingfishers have large heads with long, strong beaks and short legs. Tail length varies from very short and stubby to long with streamers.

Behavior Most species are solitary except during the breeding season. The exception is the large Kookaburra of Australia, which is more social. Kingfishers nest in burrows and usually defend territories all year round. Kingfishers in North America hunt from low perches over water. Many forest species elsewhere hunt primarily for terrestrial vertebrates. Species on the smaller end of the spectrum feed primarily on invertebrates.

Plumage Almost all species are dark above, most commonly blue, green or brown. Underparts are normally white or rufous, with a few species exhibiting banding or barring. For most species the sexes are similar. Sexual dimorphism is normally expressed with minor differences, including the pattern of the underparts or changes in throat or tail color.

Distribution Kingfishers are found on all continents except Antarctica. They are also absent from the northernmost reaches of North America and most of Russia and central Asia. The family reaches its greatest diversity in an area encompassing Southeast Asia to Australia.

Taxonomy This family is divided into 3 subfamilies, only 1 of which occurs in the New World. Worldwide, there are 91 species in 17 genera recognized. There are 3 regularly occurring species in North America.

Conservation Many species of kingfisher live in primary forest and are therefore subject to pressures from deforestation. There are 12 species of kingfisher of conservation concern; most are found on islands, and 1 is considered endangered. —*Mark W. Lockwood*

Genera *Ceryle* and *Chloroceryle*

RINGED KINGFISHER *Ceryle torquatus*

The largest of North American kingfishers, the Ringed normally frequents larger rivers but can also be found around ponds and lakes. It typically perches higher than the other, smaller kingfishers found in North America and often flies at surprisingly high altitudes. Polytypic (3 ssp. worldwide; nominate in N.A.). L 16" (41 cm).
Identification Large with a big-headed appearance, short crest and long, heavy bill. ADULT MALE: Slate blue above with a prominent white collar and rufous underparts. White underwing coverts easily visible in flight. Massive bill is gray at the base, becoming black on the distal half. ADULT FEMALE: Similar to adult male, but with an obvious slate blue breast band and rufous underwing coverts. JUVENILE: Similar to adults, but male has a narrow slaty band across upper breast that is mixed with cinnamon brown. Slaty breast band of juvenile female is also mixed with cinnamon brown.
Similar Species Distinctive. The smaller Belted Kingfisher has predominantly white underparts.
Voice CALL: A harsh rattle that is slower and lower than a Belted Kingfisher's. Also a single *chack* note, primarily given in flight.
Status & Distribution Locally common in the Lower Rio Grande Valley, becoming uncommon and local farther north. BREEDING: In burrows close to or along rivers. WINTER: Wanders from nesting areas during the winter, including farther up the Rio Grande and its tributaries. VAGRANT: Some regularity to the Texas Hill Country east of current breeding distribution. Accidental to OK and LA.
Population The population in the U.S. appears to be continuing to increase, with a reflected expansion in range.

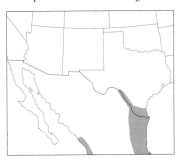

BELTED KINGFISHER *Ceryle alcyon*

The Belted Kingfisher is the most widespread and abundant kingfisher in North America. These birds need clear, still water for fishing, with elevated perches from which to hunt. Monotypic. L 13" (33 cm)

Identification Medium size with a big-headed appearance, prominent shaggy crest, and long, heavy bill. ADULT MALE: Slate blue above with a prominent white collar. Underparts white with a single blue breast band. Large bill has a gray base with a black outer half. ADULT FEMALE: Similar to adult male, but with an obvious rufous band across the upper belly. The rufous also extends down the flanks. JUVENILE: Very similar to adults in both sexes. Juvenile male has a tawny breast band

that is mottled. Juvenile female also has a much reduced rufous belly band.
Similar Species Distinctive. For most of its distribution there is nothing that can cause confusion. In southern Texas, the much larger Ringed Kingfisher has rufous underparts.
Voice CALL: A loud, dry rattle. Belted Kingfishers also make harsh *caar* notes while perched and in flight.
Status & Distribution Common and conspicuous. BREEDING: In burrows close to or along water. MIGRATION: A partially migratory species, with the northernmost populations completely

leaving the breeding grounds. The Belted Kingfisher is resident through much of the U.S., but most of the birds in this area leave to wintering grounds in the extreme southern U.S. and south through C.A. and the Caribbean. WINTER: Rare along the Pacific Coast from southeastern AK through BC. Uncommon through the northern and central U.S., becoming common in the southern third. VAGRANT: Accidental on the Azores, Iceland and western Europe.
Population Stable.

GREEN KINGFISHER *Chloroceryle americana*

Smallest of the North American kingfishers, the Green Kingfisher frequents clear streams and ponds, often perching very close to the surface. The presence of a Green Kingfisher is often betrayed by its nervous calling when approached. Polytypic (5 ssp.; 2 in N.A.). L 8.75" (22 cm)
Identification Small with a big-headed appearance, an inconspicuous crest, and long, fairly heavy bill. ADULT MALE: Green above with a prominent white collar. Underparts white with a wide rufous band across the chest. The wings are heavily spotted with white. The tail is green with

white outer rectrices that are spotted with green. ADULT FEMALE: Similar to the adult male, but with a green breast band that is mottled with white. There is also green mottling along the flanks and across the upper belly. Some individuals have a buffy wash across the throat and chest. JUVENILE: Very similar to the adult female but with buffy spotting on the crown and upperparts. FLIGHT: Direct and very fast; the bird's white outer tail feathers are conspicuous in flight.
Geographic Variation Differentiation of the 2 subspecies that occur in the U.S. is weak. Birds occurring in Texas belong to *hachisukai* and are more heavily spotted with white on the lesser wing coverts. Individuals occurring in southeastern Arizona are placed in *septentrionalis* and lack the white spotting on the lesser coverts.
Similar Species Unmistakable. Both of the other North American kingfishers are much larger and slate blue in color.

Voice CALL: Recalls 2 pebbles knocked together. Another call is a long series of rapid, but subdued *tick* notes. A squeaky *cheep* is given in flight.
Status & Distribution Uncommon and often inconspicuous. BREEDING: In burrows close to or along rivers. WINTER: Susceptible to very cold weather, withdraws from northern portion of its range during severe winters. VAGRANT: In TX accidental outside normal range north to the panhandle. In AZ occurrence primarily in the San Cruz and San Pedro River drainages.
Population Stable, but there are possible declines in Arizona.

WOODPECKERS AND ALLIES Family Picidae

Red-headed Woodpecker (ON)

Field identification of woodpeckers is generally straightforward except within a few close species pairs or groups such as the Yellow-bellied Sapsucker complex. These cases are compounded by hybridization, and not all individuals can be identified to species. Twenty-five species occur in North America, 2 as vagrants and 1 virtually extinct.

Structure Woodpecker structure and posture render them instantly recognizable (but see creepers and nuthatches). Our species vary from large sparrow to crowsize. Adaptations for trunk foraging and excavation include a chisel-like bill, skull and neck muscle adaptations to reduce brain impacts from blows with the bill, stiffened rectrices, and strong claws. Woodpeckers have short legs; their feet have 2 toes forward and 2 (rarely 1) back-ward. The extensible tongues are housed in a sling that wraps over the skull to (or nearly to) the nostril.

Behavior Woodpeckers perch along trunks and limbs, moving up in jerky "hitching" movements, using the stiff tail feathers as a prop. The flight of most species is strongly undulating. They hop when on the ground. Foraging often involves drilling into or flaking bark and dead wood for grubs, but the diverse feeding repertoire includes gleaning, lapping ants from the ground, consuming and storing acorns and other mast, excavating seeds from cones, drilling into living plant tissue for sap, and aerial sallies for insects. Most species are quite vocal, but song is replaced by drumming. Woodpeckers excavate nest cavities in trunks or branches, usually in dead wood, that are later used by a variety of birds and other animals.

Plumage Most of our woodpeckers are black and white, often in striking pied or barred patterns. Red adorns the plumage of nearly all our species, but is is usually limited to the head (and frequently present only in males).

Distribution Woodpeckers occur on most major continents. They are most diverse in wooded regions, but some species have adapted to arid scrub, grassland, and alpine tundra. Most populations are sedentary; a few species (notably sapsuckers and Northern Flickers) can be strongly migratory, and other species move short distances or are nomadic depending on food availability.

Taxonomy There are about 220 species of woodpeckers worldwide. These include the 2 wrynecks of the subfamily Jynginae, the 31 small piculets (subfamily Picumninae), and roughly 185 "true" woodpeckers (subfamily Picinae). Within the true woodpecker subfamily, several smaller groupings ("tribes") are recognized.

Conservation Some woodpeckers are among our most familiar birds. Almost universally they require standing snags for nest sites. Species requiring tracts of old-growth forests have generally declined, most strikingly the endangered Red-cockaded and the virtually extinct Ivory-billed. Worldwide, BirdLife International lists 7 woodpecker species as vulnerable, 1 as endangered, and 3 as critically endangered. —*Kimball L. Garrett*

Genus *Jynx*

EURASIAN WRYNECK *Jynx torquilla*

The Eurasian Wryneck, a vagrant from the Old World, hardly resembles a woodpecker. Patterned in browns and grays, it perches horizontally and has a long, squared tail without stiffened rectrices. Polytypic (4 ssp.; nominate vagrant to N.A.). L 6" (17 cm).

Identification Cryptic patterning, broad gray mantle stripes, buff throat, dark line through eye, sharply pointed bill, and long tail distinctive; sexes similar. **Similar Species** Unlike any other woodpecker; at a glance it can suggest a songbird such as a thrush or sparrow. **Status & Distribution** Breeds widely across temperate and boreal Eurasia from Great Britain to northern Japan; highly migratory, wintering in sub-Sahara and from India through southeastern Asia. VAGRANT: Two records for western AK (Cape Prince of Wales

Sept. 8, 1945 and Gambell, St. Lawrence I. Sept. 2–5, 2003); 1 found dead in Feb. 2000 in southern IN was probably artificially transported.

adult

Genus *Melanerpes*

The varied diets of these generalized New World woodpeckers include seeds and fruit; many take flying insects on the wing, and some store acorns and other nuts. Their tails are flat and only moderately stiffened, and the bills are medium to long and very slightly curved. Some species are highly social.

LEWIS'S WOODPECKER *Melanerpes lewis*

juvenile

adults

This distinctive large, glossy black woodpecker flies with slow, steady wing beats, recalling a crow in flight. It typically perches openly and makes long and often acrobatic aerial sallies for insects; in fall and winter it eats and stores acorns and other seeds. Most populations are migratory, and large irruptions sometimes occur within the winter range. Monotypic. L 10" (27 cm)

Identification The sexes are similar.

ADULT: Unmistakable glossy greenish black on the upperparts, wings, and tail. There is a broad pale gray breast-band that extends around the hindneck as a distinct collar; the belly is pinkish and the face is deep red. JUVENILE: Head, face, and foreparts dusky, with no gray collar. The adultlike basic plumage is attained from late fall through winter.

Similar Species Unmistakable. Acorn and Red-headed Woodpeckers show conspicuous white patches on wings and much white on the underparts. Distant flying Lewis's can appear all black and strongly suggest small crows.

Voice Generally silent for a woodpecker. CALL: Soft calls, including a series of short, harsh *churr* notes and clicking, squeaky *yick* notes. DRUM: Infrequent; a weak roll followed by a few individual taps.

Status & Distribution Uncommon to fairly common; often gregarious. BREEDING: Open arid conifer, oak, and riparian woodlands in the interior West; rare in coastal areas. MIGRATION: Large diurnal flights are sometimes noted. Arrives in northern interior breeding areas during first half of May; most have departed these areas by mid-Sept. WINTER: Open conifer and oak woodlands, oak savannas, orchards, shade trees in towns. Fall and winter movements are irregular, depending upon the availability of acorns, conifer seeds; large flights sometimes occur into the southern portions of CA, AZ, and NM. Winters irregularly north to WA, BC. VAGRANT: Recorded casually through the upper Midwest and Great Plains to southwestern TX; a few records east to NF, New England, mid-Atlantic states and south to the northern tier of Mexican states.

Population Largely eliminated from coastal Northwest due to degradation of pine, oak, and riparian woodlands.

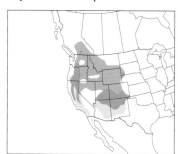

RED-HEADED WOODPECKER *Melanerpes erythrocephalus*

This flashy, distinctive woodpecker is a familiar sight over much of eastern and central North America but can be surprisingly inconspicuous at times. It occupies a variety of semi-open woodlands. Monotypic. L 9" (24 cm)

Identification All ages show white secondaries and a white rump, contrasting with dark remaining upperparts. ADULT: The bright red head, neck, and throat contrast with the black back and pure white underparts; a narrow ring of black borders the red throat. The sexes are similar. JUVENILE: Brownish on the head and upperparts, with blackish bars through the white sec-

ondary patch and some brown streaking and scaling below; adultlike plumage is attained gradually over the first winter; most first-spring birds retain some black in secondaries.

Geographic Variation Although generally considered monotypic, birds west of the Mississippi River Valley (*caurinus*) average larger and sometimes show a tinge of red on the belly.

Similar Species See the Red-breasted Sapsucker, which shares the all-red head, but with red extending through the breast, white on the wing coverts (not secondaries), and barred upperparts; note its typical retiring sapsucker

habits. The Red-bellied Woodpecker commonly co-occurs and has somewhat similar calls, but has a whitish face and throat, barred upperparts, and

very different wing pattern.
Voice CALL: A loud *queark* or *queeah,* given in breeding season, is harsher and sharper than rolling *churr* of the Red-bellied Woodpecker; also a dry, guttural rattle and, in flight, a harsh *chug.* DRUM: A simple or 2-part roll, lasting about a second and consisting of 20–25 beats.
Status & Distribution Uncommon to fairly common; sometimes perches openly and sallies for insects, but often surprisingly inconspicuous for such a flashy bird. BREEDING: Occupies a variety of open woodlands, orchards, and open country with scattered trees. Summers rarely in northeastern UT. MIGRATION: Small parties of migrants noted in early fall and late spring. WINTER: Withdraws southward from most

adults

juvenile

of the breeding range in the Great Plains and Great Lakes regions. Unrecorded in Mexico. VAGRANT: Casual west to BC, ID, CA, NV, AZ. Scarce vagrant to New England, mainly in fall.
Population New England breeding populations are nearly gone, and strong declines have been noted in the mid-Atlantic states, some Great Lakes states, FL, and elsewhere.

ACORN WOODPECKER *Melanerpes formicivorus*

♀

♂

♂

This conspicuous clown-faced woodpecker of western oak woodlands is remarkable for its social habits, living over much of its range in communal groups of up to 4 or more breeding males and as many as 3 breeding females. These groups maintain and protect impressive granaries in which thousands of acorns are stored in holes drilled in tree trunks or utility poles

for future consumption; in a study a single tree contained more than 50,000 acorn-storage holes. Acorn Woodpeckers also feed by sallying for flying insects and gleaning trunks, and they often eat ants (as reflected in the species' scientific name). Polytypic. L 9" (23 cm)
Identification A boldly patterned black-and-white woodpecker with a white patch at the base of the primaries, a white rump, black chest, streaked black lower breast, and white belly. The head pattern is striking, with a ring of black around the base of the bill, a red crown patch, a white forecrown narrowly connected to the yellow-tinged white throat, and black sides of the head setting off a staring white eye. ADULT: Iris white. Adult male has white forehead meeting the red crown. The adult female is similar, but the white forehead is separated from the red crown by a black band. JUVENILE: Resembles adult but black areas are duller and the iris is dark; juveniles of both sexes have a solid red crown like that of the adult male.
Geographic Variation Pacific coast birds, *bairdi,* have slightly longer and stouter bills than nominate birds of the interior West. There is considerable additional variation in the remaining range south to Colombia, with 5 additional subspecies.
Similar Species Unmistakable given its group-living habits and loud calls. White-headed Woodpecker has similar white wing patch and black back, but lacks white rump and belly; Lewis's

lacks white areas in plumage.
Voice The Acorn is noisy and conspicuous in communal groups, with raucous "Woody Woodpecker" calls. CALL: Loud *wack-a, wack-a* or *ja-cob, ja-cob* series. Also, a scratchy, drawn-out *krrrrit* or *krrrit-kut,* and a high, cawing *urrrk.* DRUM: A simple, slow roll of about 10–20 beats.
Status & Distribution Common. YEAR-ROUND: Oak woodlands and mixed oak-conifer or oak-riparian woodlands. Most abundant where several species of oaks co-occur. Isolated breeding populations are found on the east side of the Sierra Nevada, CA; on the central Edwards Plateau, TX; and possibly in far southern CO. VAGRANT: Found rarely or casually, primarily in fall and winter, away from woodland habitats along the immediate Pacific coast and in western deserts; accidental north to BC and east to the Great Plains states from ND south to coastal TX.
Population Stable, apart from some local declines resulting from degradation of oak woodlands.

GILA WOODPECKER *Melanerpes uropygialis*

The Gila is a zebra-backed woodpecker of southwestern desert woodlands, where it can be noisy and conspicuous in tall cactuses such as saguaros. Its U.S. range does not overlap that of the similar Golden-fronted and Red-bellied Woodpeckers. Polytypic (nominate in U.S., with 2 additional subspecies in Baja California and several more sometimes recognized in mainland western Mexico). L 9" (24 cm).

Identification Within its range, the Gila Woodpecker's barred black-and-white upperparts, pale, grayish tan head and underparts (with a touch of pale yellow on the belly), and broken white patch at the base of the primaries are diagnostic. The rump and uppertail coverts are barred with black, and the central tail feathers are white with black bars. ADULT: The male Gila Woodpecker has a round red cap on the crown, absent in the female. JUVENILE: Resembles adult but slightly paler and duller.

Similar Species The Gila's range does not overlap with that of the Golden-fronted (except at southern end of range in Jalisco, Mexico), but potential vagrants of either species (e.g., in southern NM) would need to be carefully documented. The Golden-fronted has extensive solid white on the rump, solid black central rectrices, and yellow-orange nape patch and nasal tufts. The immature female Williamson's Sapsucker is superficially similar to the Gila, but the pale bars on the back are tan rather than white; the chest and sides are barred with blackish; the head is darker gray-brown; and the bill is shorter. Note also the sapsucker's more retiring behavior. See also Northern and Gilded Flickers, which are larger, show solid white rumps, yellow or red color in the wings and tail, and a black crescent on the breast.

Voice CALL: A loud, rolling *churrr* or *whirrrr*, often doubled. Also an insistent, laughing *yip, yip* series. DRUM: Infrequent drum is a steady, loud roll.

Status & Distribution Fairly common. YEAR-ROUND: Desert woodlands, including cactus country, mesquite woods, riparian corridors, and lower canyon woodlands; often common in residential areas, date palm groves. Range extends west in CA to the Imperial Valley, east to southwestern NM, and at least formerly barely into southern NV. DISPERSAL: There is some movement into wooded foothills in southeastern AZ in fall and winter. VAGRANT: Accidental west to eastern San Diego County and on coastal slope in San Bernardino and Los Angeles Counties, CA.

Population Some declines have occurred with clearing of cottonwood-willow riparian associations, as along the lower Colorado River; colonization of the Imperial Valley occurred in the 1930s.

GOLDEN-FRONTED WOODPECKER *Melanerpes aurifrons*

A close relative of the Red-bellied Woodpecker, the Golden-fronted Woodpecker largely replaces that species from central and southern Texas south into Central America. Polytypic. L 9" (24 cm).

Identification All show a yellow area on the nasal tufts just above the bill, as well as a golden yellow to orange nape and hindneck. The rump is extensively pure white, and the central rectrices are solidly black. The underparts are pale grayish white, with black barring on the lower flanks and undertail coverts and a touch of yellow on the lower belly. ADULT MALE: Orange-yellow nasal tufts, red crown patch, and mixed red and orange-yellow nape patch. ADULT FEMALE: Similar to male, but red crown patch is absent and nasal tufts and nape are purer yellow, less orange. JUVENILE: Duller than adults, with less distinct back barring; yellow or orange lacking on nasal tufts and nape, but males (and some females) show a small red crown patch.

Geographic Variation Nominate *aurifrons* in U.S., but considerable geographic variation, with at least 10 subspecies in remainder of range. Appearance differs greatly in southern Mexico; birds from southeastern Mexico to Honduras have fine white barring on back, continuous red from crown through nape, and some red on belly.

Similar Species The Red-bellied Woodpecker overlaps marginally with the Golden-fronted from east-central TX to southwestern OK, with hybridization frequent in the latter area. The Red-bellied differs in its extensive red rear crown and nape (extending to the bill in males), white bars on the central rectrices (solidly black in the Golden-fronted), and pink or red tinge on the belly (yellow in the Golden-fronted). Rare individual Red-bellieds can show yellow or orange on the crown and nape (see the Gila Woodpecker account).

Voice CALL: A rolling *churrr* and cackling *kek-kek,* both slightly louder and

raspier than the calls of the Red-bellied; also a scolding *chuh-chuh-chuh*. DRUM: A simple roll, often preceded or followed by single taps.
Status & Distribution Fairly common. YEAR-ROUND: Dry woodlands and brushlands such as oak-juniper savannas and mesquite thickets; also riparian corridors, pecan groves, suburban areas. VAGRANT: Wanders casually to northeastern TX, eastern OK, and southeastern. NM. Accidental in MI

and FL; the latter record, at least, may pertain to an aberrant Red-bellied, and SC reports of the Golden-fronted have conclusively been shown to be abnormal Red-bellieds.
Population Apparently stable. The largest concentrations are in mesquite brushlands of southern TX. Colonized southwestern OK in the 1950s and now hybridizes there with the Red-bellied. Common in the Big Bend region of TX only since the 1970s.

RED-BELLIED WOODPECKER *Melanerpes carolinus*

The Red-bellied Woodpecker is the familiar zebra-backed woodpecker of eastern woodlands and towns. Monotypic (or up to 4 weakly defined ssp. sometimes recognized). L 9" (24 cm).
Identification All Red-bellied Woodpeckers show a black-and-white barred back, white uppertail coverts, grayish white underparts, black chevrons on the lower flanks and undertail coverts, and barred central tail feathers. In flight a small white patch shows at the base of the primaries. ADULT MALE: Entire crown, from bill to nape, is red; there is a suffusion of pink or red on the center of the belly. ADULT FEMALE: Red on the head is limited to nasal tufts (just above the bill) and nape; wash of color on the belly is paler, less extensive. In rare individual females, the nape and nasal tufts can be yellow-orange instead of red. JUVENILE: Resembles adults but duller, with red nasal tuft and nape patches lacking; bill is brownish (black in adults).
Similar Species Compare with the Golden-fronted Woodpecker, which has solid black central rectrices, lacks pink or red on the belly, and has a different pattern of color on the head.
Voice In breeding season, the Red-bellied gives a rolling *churrr; it also gives* also a conversational *chiv chiv;* softer than calls of the Golden-fronted Woodpecker. DRUM: A simple roll

of up to a second, with about 19 beats per second.
Status & Distribution Common in the Southeast, uncommon to fairly common in the Northeast, Midwest, and Great Plains. YEAR-ROUND: Pine and hardwood forests, open woodlands, suburbs and parks. Small populations exist west to southeastern ND, central SD, and northeastern CO. DISPERSAL: Not migratory, but at least some individuals in northern range withdraw southward in fall. VAGRANT: Wanders casually north to central ON, southern QC, ME, and the maritime provinces of Canada and west to eastern NM; accidental in southeastern WY, ID, and SK.
Population Generally stable. The Red-bellied has expanded its range northward in the Great Lakes region and

New England over the last century and is also expanding northwestward in the Great Plains.

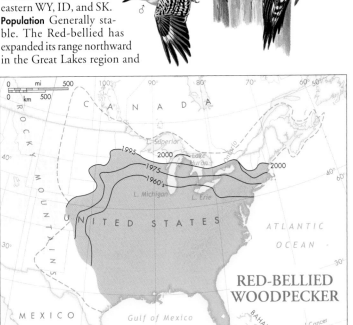

RED-BELLIED WOODPECKER

1975 Historic range limit with date
-- Limit of fall and winter wandering
Modern resident range

SAPSUCKERS Genus *Sphyrapicus*

The 4 North American sapsuckers are distinctive relatives of *Melanerpes* that feed on insects but most characteristically on living plant tissue and sap obtained from rows of drilled holes. Bills are broad based, slightly flattened, and of medium length. Sapsuckers are long winged, with strong undulating flight; all species are partially to highly migratory.

YELLOW-BELLIED SAPSUCKER *Sphyrapicus varius*

adult ♂

adult ♀

juvenile

The only sapsucker normally found in the boreal and eastern parts of the continent, this species is our most highly migratory woodpecker. Monotypic (smaller, darker resident birds in southern Appalachians sometimes separated as *appalachiensis*). L 8" (22 cm)

Identification Shows less red on head than related Red-naped and Red-breasted, and the back is more extensively scalloped with yellow-buff. ADULT MALE: Forecrown, chin, and throat red, outlined completely in black; red normally lacking on nape. ADULT FEMALE: Similar to male, but the chin and throat are entirely white. JUVENILE: Head and underparts pale brownish barred with dusky black; upperparts extensively pale buff with dusky barring, becoming white on the rump. Unlike the Red-breasted and the Red-naped, this juvenal plumage is retained well into the winter, with the red coloration of adult plumage gradually acquired through the fall but the black-and-white head and chest pattern not appearing until late winter.

Similar Species See the very similar Red-naped Sapsucker (formerly, along with the Red-breasted, considered conspecific with the Yellow-bellied).

Voice This species, the Red-breasted, and the Red-naped are similar in calls and drums. CALL: A nasal *weeah* or *meeww*; on territory a more emphatic *quee-ark*. DRUM: A distinctive rhythm of a short roll of several beats, a pause, then 2 to several brief rolls of 2–3 beats each.

Status & Distribution Common. BREEDING: Deciduous forests, mixed hardwoods and conifers of boreal regions and the Appalachians. MIGRATION: Main fall movement is Sept.–Oct.; spring migrants arrive in the Upper Midwest and Northeast during mid-Apr., and the northernmost breeding populations arrive late Apr., early May. WINTER: Widespread in the East south of New England and Great Lakes states, south to West Indies and Panama. VAGRANT: Rare but regular west to CA in fall and winter, with a few records north to WA. Accidental in Iceland, Britain, and Ireland.

Population: Generally stable.

RED-NAPED SAPSUCKER *Sphyrapicus nuchalis*

The Rocky Mountain and Great Basin representative of the Yellow-bellied Sapsucker complex, the Red-naped Sapsucker closely resembles the Yellow-bellied Sapsucker, and the 2 hybridize in southwestern Alberta; the Red-naped also hybridizes with the Red-breasted from British Columbia south to eastern California. Monotypic. L 8" (22 cm)

Identification Very similar in all plumages to the Yellow-bellied, but with slightly more red on the head. ADULT MALE: The red crown is bordered by black, with a small red patch below black nape bar; the chin and throat are red, with the red color partially invading the black malar stripe

that outlines the throat; the breast is black. ADULT FEMALE: Similar to male, but the chin is white (red on rare individual females), and the red on crown and throat is slightly less extensive, more completely bordered by black; red on nape may be nearly or completely absent. JUVENILE: Closely resembles the juvenile Yellow-bellied, but adultlike face pattern is attained by beginning of October (brown may be retained on the breast into mid-winter).

Similar Species Male Yellow-bellied Sapsuckers can rarely show some red on the nape. In the Red-naped the red throat invades or completely covers the black border along the malar, and

adult ♂

adult ♀

the pale markings on the back are whiter and more restricted. Female Red-napeds with maximal red on the chin and throat closely resemble the male Yellow-bellied, but usually have white on uppermost chin and a hint of red on the nape; note also back pattern differences. The male Red-naped Sapsucker, with maximal red invading the auricular and malar regions, may not be distinguishable from Red-breasted X Red-naped hybrids; such hybrids usually have only limited black on the breast, auriculars, and sides of crown.

Status & Distribution Common. BREEDING: Aspen parklands and deciduous groves within open coniferous woodlands or adjacent to montane forest. Breeding range narrowly overlaps that of the Yellow-bellied Sapsucker in AB, with some hybridization. WINTER: Riparian and pine-oak woodlands, orchards, and shade trees south to northwestern and north-central Mexico. Winters rarely north on the Pacific coast to WA, and BC. VAGRANT: Casual east to KS, NE, OK, southern TX, and southeastern LA.
Population Generally stable.

RED-BREASTED SAPSUCKER *Sphyrapicus ruber*

The Pacific coast representative of the Yellow-bellied Sapsucker complex, the Red-breasted Sapsucker differs from other sapsuckers in its almost entirely red head and breast. Identification is complicated by frequent hybridization with the Red-naped from British Columbia south to eastern California, as well as by more limited hybridization with the Yellow-bellied in British Columbia. Polytypic. L 8" (22 cm)
Identification The head and breast are almost entirely red, and the black breast patch is lacking. The back shows 2 rows of whitish or yellow-buff spots or bars, but this patterning is very limited in northern birds. ADULT: Red head and breast, pale yellow belly, back black with geographically variable yellow-buff to white barring on the sides of the back and lower back; white rump and white patch on wing coverts resemble other sapsuckers. The sexes are similar, but females (at least in southern populations) tend to show more pale markings on the rectrices. Many birds, especially when worn, show a ghost of underlying black in the auriculars and chest and black-and-white patterning in the malar region; the red of worn birds may appear paler and more orange-red. JUVENILE: Brown head and extensive brown mottling below; darker than both the juvenile Red-naped and Yellow-bellied, with less facial patterning. Adultlike plumage attained by September, though underparts are duller and mottled with brown.

Geographic Variation Two subspecies. Nominate *ruber* breeds from southern OR northward; *daggetti* occupies the remainder of the range. Nominate birds show deeper and more extensive red on the breast, which is more sharply delineated from the pale belly; more limited white spotting on the flight feathers; a deeper yellow wash on the belly; and a more extensively black back with limited yellowish buff cross bars.

Similar Species Compare with the Red-naped Sapsucker; extensive hybridization renders many individuals with intermediate head patterns unidentifiable.

Status & Distribution Common. BREEDING: Moist coniferous forests, mixed oak-conifer riparian woodlands in coastal mountain ranges, usually in lower and wetter habitats than Williamson's. Subspecies *daggetti* is largely limited to montane habitats from about 4,000 to 8,000 feet. The Red-breasted Sapsucker hybridizes frequently with the Red-naped in the Cascades and eastern Sierra Nevada. WINTER: Northernmost populations (e.g., in southeastern AK, BC) withdraw southward (though resident on Queen Charlotte Is.), and higher-elevation breeders generally withdraw to lower elevations. Winters widely around deciduous trees, orchards, and parks in lowlands adjacent to breeding range from southwestern BC to southern CA and south to northwestern Baja California. Northern nominate birds have been found as far south as San Diego, CA, and southern AZ. VAGRANT: Casual east to AZ, NM, central TX, Sonora, and northwest to Kodiak I., AK.
Population Generally stable.

ruber

daggetti

ruber

daggetti

WILLLIAMSON'S SAPSUCKER *Sphyrapicus thyroideus*

This sapsucker of western montane conifer and aspen forests is notable for its extreme sexual dimorphism. Polytypic. L 9" (23 cm)

Identification Slightly larger than other sapsuckers. ADULT MALE: Largely black, with white rump, white postocular and moustachial stripes, large white wing patch, red chin and throat. The belly is bright yellow; flanks scalloped black and white. ADULT FEMALE: Head gray-brown; black back has fine pale grayish tan bars; rump white. No white wing patch. Chest black, belly yellow, sides and flanks tan, barred with black. JUVENILE: Like respective adults, but duller; male has white throat, female lacks black breast patch.

Geographic Variation Nominate *thyroideus* breeds from south-central BC to northern Baja California; more easterly *nataliae* from southeastern BC to AZ, NM, has smaller, narrower bill.

Similar Species Males unmistakable; females suggest flicker, but Williamson's is smaller, shorter billed, lacks red or yellow in flight feathers, has yellow belly. See the Gila Woodpecker. Juvenile lacks large white wing covert patch of other juvenile sapsuckers.

Voice CALL: A strong, slightly harsh *cheeur* or *queeah*. DRUM: Short roll followed by several shorter rolls; slower and more regular than other sapsuckers.

Status & Distribution Fairly common. BREEDING: Dry pine, spruce or fir forests, often where mixed with aspen groves. MIGRATION: Most move south in Sept.–Oct. and return Mar.–Apr.; in CA, AZ, NM sedentary or make short altitudinal movements. WINTER: Dry conifer or pine-oak woodlands from CA and southwestern U.S. to central Mexico. Casual north to OR, WA, CO; very rare in lowlands of CA, AZ in planted conifers. VAGRANT: Casual in fall, winter to TX and LA.

Population Some declines, especially in Pacific Northwest.

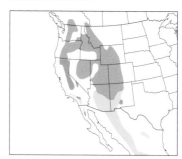

Genus *Picoides*

These woodpeckers are small to medium in size. Most are bark foragers, with chisel-shaped bills and stiffened rectrices. Distributed in the New World, except 1 "three-toed" species across Eurasia. Males of most species have red on rear crown, lacking in females and juveniles. Males and juveniles of "three-toed" species have yellow crown patches.

NUTTALL'S WOODPECKER *Picoides nutttallii*

Endemic to oak and missed woodlands in California and northwestern Baja California, the Nuttall's is closely related to the Ladder-backed. Monotypic. L 7" (19 cm)

Identification "Ladder-back" pattern; spotted sides; barred flanks; auriculars almost wholly black; uppermost back black. Sexes similar but females lack red patch on nape and hindcrown.

Similar Species Compared with Ladder-backed, Nuttall's shows more black on face; white bars on back are narrower; more extensive black on upper

back below nape; white outer tail feathers sparsely spotted rather than barred. Nuttall's underparts are purer white below, more cleanly spotted and barred with black; Ladder-backed's underparts are washed with buffy, and markings are finer but often extend across the breast as short streaks. Nuttall's nasal tufts are usually white (buffy to dusky in Ladder-backed). Red of male is restricted on Nuttall's; in Ladder-backed red covers most of crown, but is spotted with black and white on forecrown. Calls differ markedly.

Voice CALL: A short, rolling *prrt* or *pitit* that may be followed by a longer trill, *prrt prrt prrrrrrrrrrrr;* also a loud *kweek kweek kweek* series. DRUM: A steady roll of about 20 taps over a second.

Status & Distribution Common. YEAR-ROUND: Oak woodlands, mixed oak-conifer and oak-riparian woodlands, and tall dense chaparral; sea level to about 6,000 feet. Small populations extend onto deserts along riparian corridors. VAGRANT: A few wander to deserts of south-central CA, casually to Imperial Valley; southwestern OR, western NV.

Population Generally stable.

LADDER-BACKED WOODPECKER *Picoides scalaris*

This common desert woodpecker replaces the closely-related Nuttall's in arid regions; the 2 species are known to hybridize at a few localities in southern California. Polytypic (about 8 ssp. in North and Middle America; birds north of Mexico are *cactophilus*). L 7" (18 cm)

Identification The barred black-and-white back pattern of the Ladder-backed Woodpecker extends up to the hindneck, with very little solid black on the upper back. The underparts are tinged creamy or buffy, with spots on the sides, thin bars on the flanks, and sparse, short streaks across the breast. The outer tail feathers are barred with black. There is as much white as black in the face pattern, with the lower auriculars being white. The sexes are similar, but the male Ladder-backed Woodpecker has extensive red on the crown, which is lacking in the females. **Similar Species** See the closely similar Nuttall's Woodpecker. The Gila also has barred back pattern and is often common in the same habitats, but the Gila is larger than the Ladder-backed, has a plain gray-brown head and breast (with small red cap in males) and very different calls; shows white wing patches and a white rump. **Voice** CALL: A fairly high, sharp *pik;* it suggests the Downy but is louder, sharper, and slightly lower in pitch. The Ladder-backed also gives a slightly descending *jee jee jee* series and a louder, slower *kweek kweek kweek.* DRUM:

A simple roll like that of Nuttall's, but longer, averaging 1.5 seconds. **Status & Distribution** Common; extensive range south of U.S. to Nicaragua, El Salvador. YEAR-ROUND: Dry desert woodlands with yuccas, agaves, cactuses; piñon-juniper foothills; mesquite woodlands; and riparian corridors. Often common in southwestern towns. Overlaps (and sometimes hybridizes) with the Nuttall's very locally on the western edge of the California deserts from Inyo and Kern Counties south to northwestern Baja California. VAGRANT: Casual east to vicinity of Houston, TX, and on the Pacific coast near San Diego, CA. **Population** Generally stable, though declines have been noted in TX.

ARIZONA WOODPECKER *Picoides arizonae*

This brown-backed species of pine-oak woodlands in the Southwest borderlands was formerly considered conspecific with Strickland's Woodpecker *(stricklandi),* a localized species of the high mountains surrounding the Mexican Plateau, with the combined species called "Strickland's" or "Brown-backed" Woodpecker. Polytypic (3 ssp.; nominate in U.S.). L 7" (19 cm) **Identification** The solidly brown back is unique among our woodpeckers; a few individuals show limited white barring on rump and scapulars. Within shady pine-oak woodlands Arizonas can appear quite dark overall because

of extensive brown spotting and barring on the underparts. ADULT: Upperparts dark brown, underparts white with heavy brown spotting on breast and barring on flanks, belly. Brown crown, auricular, and malar contrast with large white patch on sides of neck. Male has red nuchal patch, absent in female. **Similar Species** Our other brown-backed woodpeckers (flickers, female Williamson's Sapsucker) are barred above with black, have white rumps, and lack strong face patterning. **Voice** CALL: Sharp, high *peeek* call is higher and hoarser than similar call of the Hairy. DRUM: The rapid roll is like that of the Hairy, but longer. **Status & Distribution** Fairly common, but usually wary, inconspicuous. YEAR-ROUND: Dry pine-oak woodlands and oak-riparian canyon woodlands from 4,000–7,000 feet. Found east to Peloncillo and Animas Mountains, NM; and southwest to Santa Catalina and Pinaleño Mountains, AZ; a few birds may move into lower foothill oak woodlands in winter.

DOWNY WOODPECKER *Picoides pubescens*

Rockies
leucurus ♂

Our smallest woodpecker, the Downy is also among our most widespread and familiar species; it is a confiding bird that often visits feeders. In all respects it suggests a small version of the Hairy Woodpecker, both differing from our other species by the broad white stripe down the back. Polytypic. L 6" (17 cm)

Identification The small size and often acrobatic foraging on small branches and twigs are distinctive, and the plumage pattern can be confused only with the Hairy. Has hybridized with the Nuttall's. ADULT: Black crown, auricular and malar; upper back, scapulars and rump black, but a broad white stripe extends down the center of the back. Underparts unmarked white (to grayish buff in some populations). Outer tail feathers white with limited black spotting; variable white spotting on the upperwing coverts and barring on the remiges. Male has a small red nuchal patch, lacking in the female. JUVENILE: As in other pied woodpeckers, both sexes have a pale red patch in the center of the crown, more extensive in male.

Geographic Variation The 7 subspecies differ mainly in size (northern birds generally larger), underpart color (white to gray tinged), amount of black in rectrices, and amount of white spotting in wings. Southeastern birds are smaller and slightly grayer below than boreal and northeastern birds. Pacific coast birds have reduced white spotting on the wing coverts and secondaries; such white spotting is most highly developed in birds east of the Rockies. Birds of the Pacific Northwest are tinged gray on the back and gray-buff below.

Similar Species Nearly identical in patterning to the Hairy Woodpecker. The Downy is much smaller, with a short bill (much shorter than head); outer tail feathers usually show black spots (but these can be lacking, and darkest Hairy subspecies may show a few spots). Pale nasal tuft of the Downy is relatively larger than in the Hairy. The Hairy shows a larger wedge of black from the rear of the malar stripe onto the breast. Note differences in calls.

Voice CALL: *Pik* call is higher and much softer than Hairy's sharp, ringing *peek*. Commonly gives a distinctive high, slightly descending and accelerating whinny, *kee-kee-kee-kee*. DRUM: A soft roll, slightly slower than that of Hairy; about 17 beats a second, with drum lasting 0.8–1.5 seconds.

Status & Distribution Common; uncommon in northern boreal regions. YEAR-ROUND: Resident in a variety of deciduous woodlands and, more sparsely, in coniferous forests; also found in parks, gardens, and orchards, even in urban regions. Absent from most of the lowlands of the desert Southwest. DISPERSAL: This species is not migratory, but some individuals can disperse long distances. Casual in southern AZ, Queen Charlotte Is.

Population Generally stable or increasing, but some declines have been noted in the Southeast.

HAIRY WOODPECKER *Picoides villosus*

Like a large, long-billed version of the Downy Woodpecker, the Hairy is a widespread generalist of a variety of forests and woodlands over most of the continent. Polytypic. L 9" (24 cm)

Identification Plumage pattern is nearly identical to the Downy's, with long white patch down the back, variable white spotting on the wing coverts and flight feathers, and mostly unmarked underparts. The outer tail feathers are usually unmarked white. ADULT: Male shows red nuchal bar, often divided vertically by black (especially in some eastern populations); red is lacking in female.

Geographic Variation Variation is extensive but generally clinal. About 17 subspecies, 11 north of Mexico. Nominate *villosus* is widespread in the East; southeastern birds *(audubonii)* are smaller, buffier (less pure white) below, and with less white on the back. Boreal *septentrionalis*, from interior Alaska east to Quebec, is the largest, whitest subspecies. Newfoundland *terranovae* is distinctive, with white back reduced and barred (especially in immatures), some black spotting on outer rectrices, and often with fine black streaking on the sides and flanks. In the West, *picoideus* of the Queen Charlotte Islands is most distinctive, with gray-brown underparts; black markings in the white back stripe, sides, and flanks; and strong black bars on the outer rectrices. Northwestern *harrisi* and *sitkensis* have gray-

Rockies
orius ♂

Maritimes
juvenile
terranovae ♂

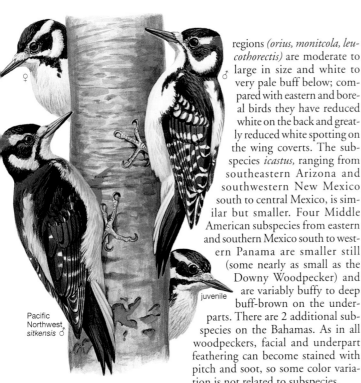

Pacific Northwest *sitkensis* ♂

juvenile

♀

♂

brown underparts and face and reduced white on the wings. *Hyloscopus* of California and northern Baja California is smaller, paler (light gray-buff) below, and whiter on the head. Three additional subspecies of the Great Basin and Rocky Mountain regions *(orius, monitcola, leucothorectis)* are moderate to large in size and white to very pale buff below; compared with eastern and boreal birds they have reduced white on the back and greatly reduced white spotting on the wing coverts. The subspecies *icastus,* ranging from southeastern Arizona and southwestern New Mexico south to central Mexico, is similar but smaller. Four Middle American subspecies from eastern and southern Mexico south to western Panama are smaller still (some nearly as small as the Downy Woodpecker) and are variably buffy to deep buff-brown on the underparts. There are 2 additional subspecies on the Bahamas. As in all woodpeckers, facial and underpart feathering can become stained with pitch and soot, so some color variation is not related to subspecies.

Similar Species The Downy Woodpecker is similar in pattern but much smaller, with a small, short bill (much smaller than half the length of the head). Beware a recently fledged Hairy with much a shorter bill than adult's; black bars on the outer tail feathers distinguish a Downy from a Hairy. See the American Three-toed Woodpecker. Note that some populations of Hairy (especially in Newfoundland) can show barred backs (especially as juveniles), and some Three-toed populations have nearly pure white backs.

Voice CALL: A piercing, sharp *peek* or *pee-ik.* The rattle call ("whinny") is a fast, slightly descending series of these *peek* calls. DRUM: Rapid roll of about 25 beats in 1 second.

Status & Distribution Fairly common; uncommon to rare in the South and FL. YEAR-ROUND: The Hairy occupies a wide range of coniferous and deciduous forests from sea level to tree line; such habitats are usually densely wooded, but in some areas are more open and parklike. DISPERSAL: Although generally nonmigratory, individuals can disperse long distances, and small irruptive movements sometimes occur. Larger, more northerly birds regularly occur in the Northeast in fall and winter. Recorded in fall and winter on the southern plains and Pacific coast lowlands well away from breeding habitats.

Population Declines that have been noted in many areas are thought to be due to fragmentation of forests, loss of old-growth trees, and nest site competition with European starlings.

RED-COCKADED WOODPECKER *Picoides borealis (E)*

This species has a highly fragmented distribution in southeastern pinewoods, especially old-growth longleaf pine. Living in family groups, or "clans," its territories can be identified by distinctive nest and roost cavity trees: large living pines with heartwood disease and with abundant resin flowing from holes drilled around the cavity entrance. This oozing pitch protects nests from snakes and other predators. Monotypic (slightly smaller Florida peninsula birds have been separated as *hylonomus*). L 8" (22 cm)

Identification Unique face pattern, with black crown and nape, long black malar, and extensive white auriculars and sides of neck; sides and flanks with short streaks. Adult Male's red "cockade" is virtually invisible in the field.

Similar Species Unmarked white face is diagnostic from Downy, Hairy, and Ladder-backed Woodpeckers. Larger Red-bellied Woodpecker shares barred back pattern but has an extensive red nape and lacks black on the head.

Voice CALL: A raspy *sripp* or *churt* and high-pitched *tsick* or *sklit* are the most frequent and distinctive calls. DRUM: Quiet and infrequently heard.

Status & Distribution Rare and local. YEAR-ROUND: Mature lowland woods of longleaf, loblolly, or other pines with open understory and suitable cavity trees afflicted with heartwood disease. Core remaining populations occur from eastern TX and adjacent OK, AR, LA, and from MS east to FL, the Carolinas and southern VA. Populations in TN, KY, MD, and MO have disappeared in

♂

recent decades. VAGRANT: Accidental in northern IL, and twice in south-central OH.

Population Endangered. Some 3,000–3,500 colonies estimated to exist, with 2–5 adults per colony. Most colonies are on federal lands, where management strategies have had mixed results, with declines continuing in many areas.

WHITE-HEADED WOODPECKER *Picoides albolarvatus*

A striking bird of far western pine forests, the White-headed Woodpecker is unique among our species in its white head and solid black body. It often forages on pine cones, extracting seeds; otherwise it mainly flakes away bark on trunks or branches of conifers. Polytypic. L 9" (24 cm)

Identification A solid black body, mostly white head, and large white wing patches make this bird unmistakable. ADULT: Red nuchal patch, lacking in females. JUVENILE: Resembles adult, but both sexes have a pale red wash on the crown, and the white wing patch is often more interrupted with black spots.

Geographic Variation Birds of the southern California mountains, *gravirostris,* are slightly larger billed than the northern nominate subspecies.

Similar Species The Acorn Woodpecker, largely black above with white wing patches, may suggest the White-headed dorsally, but the Acorn's white rump and belly and black in the face simplify identification.

Voice CALL: Distinct call is a sharp, 2 or 3 syllable *pitik, pee-dink,* or *pee-de-dink,* dropping slightly in pitch; 1- and 3-syllable notes are also given. Also a longer series of these notes, a slower *kweek kweek kweek* series, and various softer calls. DRUM: A 1–1.5 second roll with about 20 beats a second; probably not distinguishable from drum of the Hairy.

Status & Distribution Fairly common in CA; generally uncommon from OR and western NV north. YEAR-ROUND: Montane coniferous and mixed forests usually dominated by ponderosa or Jeffrey pines, but also sugar pine, white fir, Douglas fir, and incense cedar. Very rare in northwestern WY, adjacent MT. VAGRANT: Rare in fall and winter at lower elevations adjacent to breeding mountains, and casual in lowlands along CA coast and deserts.

Population Generally stable in California, but many populations, especially from Oregon north, are decreasing because of logging, even-age stand management, and long-term forest changes.

AMERICAN THREE-TOED WOODPECKER *Picoides dorsalis*

This species is 1 of 2 "three-toed" woodpeckers in N.A. This stocky, large-headed, pied woodpecker has 2 forward-facing toes and just 1 rear-pointing toe. It sports a yellow crown patch in males and forages on dead or dying trees, often in burned-over areas. The back pattern varies geographically, from solid white to heavily barred with black. Formerly known simply as Three-toed Woodpecker, it has been split into our North American species and an Old World species now called the Eurasian Three-toed Woodpecker, *tridactylus.* Polytypic. L 8" (22 cm)

Identification A "three-toed" woodpecker with white patch or barring on

the otherwise black upperparts; underparts white with black barring on sides and flanks. White spots on primaries, outer secondaries, and tertials. Tail black with white outer rectrices. ADULT: Male has yellow crown, becoming spotted with black and white on forecrown; female lacks yellow. JUVENILE: Duller than adult; both sexes show some yellow on crown, reduced in female.

Geographic Variation The 3 subspecies differ in back pattern and size. Density of barring on the back is greatest in eastern *bacatus* of eastern Canada south to New England and the Adirondacks; this is the smallest subspecies. Dorsal barring and size are intermediate in *fasciatus* of boreal regions from AK to SK, and in the Cascades south to OR. The Rocky Mountain subspecies *dorsalis* has a pure white center of the back with irregular barring on sides of back; it is also slightly larger than the other subspecies.

Similar Species See Black-backed. Can be mistaken for the Hairy, especially in Rockies region, where back is almost solidly white. Three-toed has heavily barred sides and flanks; Hairy is pure

fasciatus

dorsalis ♂   bacatus ♂

whitish. Face pattern of Hairy shows more white on sides of neck and supercilium. Male Three-toeds have yellow crown patch; crown of juvenile Hairy can be pale red, but not yellow. Beware some juvenile Hairies (e.g., in NF), which show barring on the back.

Voice CALL: *Pik or kik,* higher than call of Black-backed, less sharp than Hairy's;

also a longer rattle. DRUM: Deep, resonant drums frequent and variable, range from 11–16 beats a second.

Status & Distribution Uncommon. YEARROUND: Coniferous forests of spruce and fir, especially where there are large stands of dead trees in burned areas. Has bred south to western SD, MN, Upper Peninsula of MI, and MA. DIS-

PERSAL: Small numbers move irruptively to areas adjacent to breeding range in winter, usually after early Oct.; irruptions generally more minor than in Black-backed. VAGRANT: Casual south to KS (summer), NE, IA, RI, NJ, DE.

Population Generally stable, northerly range makes monitoring difficult.

BLACK-BACKED WOODPECKER *Picoides arcticus*

This is 1 of 2 "three-toed" woodpeckers in North America. These are stocky, large-headed pied woodpeckers that have 2 forward-facing toes and but just 1 rear-pointing toe (usually held out to the side). Its range overlaps extensively with that of the similar American Three-toed Woodpecker. Both species feed in dead or dying conifers and can be especially prevalent in burned-over forests; they flake away sections of loose bark to obtain insects and their larvae. Worked-over trees can be quite evident. Monotypic. L 9" (24 cm)

Identification A very dark woodpecker with solid black upperparts and heavy black barring below. The outer tail feathers, throat, and central underparts are white; the head pattern shows

long white submoustachial stripe, broadening at the rear; there is only a hint of a short white postocular mark. The primaries are spotted with white. ADULT MALE: Roundish yellow patch on crown. ADULT FEMALE: Similar but crown all black. JUVENILE: Black areas duller than in adults; females have a few yellow feathers on the crown; males have extensive yellow on crown.

Similar Species: Most similar to darkest eastern subspecies *bacatus* of the American Three-toed Woodpecker, which has extensive black barring on the back. The Black-backed is told by its solid black upperparts, lack of white postocular streak, and bolder white submoustachial stripe; it is also larger overall, with a longer, stouter bill.

Voice CALL: A single sharp *pik* or *chik,* lower and sharper than call of American Three-toed. DRUM: As in American Three-toed, the deep and resonant drum roll speeds up and trails off slightly toward the end. The Black-backed drums average slightly faster and longer than those of the American Three-toed.

Status & Distribution Uncommon, but can be locally fairly common when responding to insect outbreaks in burnt or otherwise stressed forests. YEARROUND: Conifer forests of spruce, fir

or pine. South of boreal regions and the northern Rockies, the Blackbacked is found locally in the Adirondacks of NY, Black Hills of SD and adjacent WY, and the Cascades and Sierra Nevadas from WA to central CA. DISPERSAL: Occasional irruptive movements south of regular range into New England, Great Lakes, and Canadian maritimes, taking advantage of outbreaks of wood-boring beetles. Exceptional irruptions have brought birds as far south as IL, OH, PA, NJ; records at the southern periphery of range have decreased in recent decades. VAGRANT: Casual in winter south of resident and irruptive range.

Genus Dendrocopos

GREAT SPOTTED WOODPECKER *Dendrocopos major*

This Eurasian woodpecker is a casual vagrant in western Alaska. Polytypic (14–24 ssp. in Old World; AK specimen *kamtschaticus*). L 9" (25 cm)

Identification Large size, white auriculars, black back bordered by large white scapular and covert patch, and red undertail coverts. Females lack red nape patch; juveniles have red in crown.

Similar Species The Hairy and Downy have white backs, black auriculars, and

lack red undertail coverts and solid white wing patch. The Yellow-bellied Sapsucker is patterned below and on back, lacks red undertail coverts, differs in head pattern. See American Three-toed and Black-backed Woodpeckers.

Voice CALL: Sharp *kix, kick* or *chik.*

Status & Distribution Resident nearly throughout Eurasia from Great Britain and northwestern Africa east to Japan, Kamchatka; northern populations may migrate irruptively.

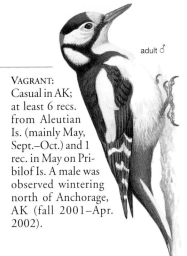

adult ♂

VAGRANT: Casual in AK; at least 6 recs. from Aleutian Is. (mainly May, Sept.–Oct.) and 1 rec. in May on Pribilof Is. A male was observed wintering north of Anchorage, AK (fall 2001–Apr. 2002).

Genus Dryocopus

PILEATED WOODPECKER *Dryocopus pileatus*

Our largest woodpecker (other than the near-extinct Ivory-billed), the Pileated is a crow-size, crested woodpecker of forested areas that feeds largely on carpenter ants and beetles extracted from fallen logs, stumps, and living trees. Foraging birds excavate large, rectangular holes in trunks and logs. Polytypic. L 16" (42 cm)

Identification Mostly black, with a slaty-black bill, white chin, white stripe from bill down neck to sides of breast, a white patch at base of primaries, and extensive white on the underwing linings. Flight consists of deep, irregular crowlike wing beats with little or no undulation. ADULT MALE: Red crown, crest and malar mark. ADULT FEMALE: Forecrown mottled black, malar black.

Geographic Variation Two to 4 subspecies recognized, but differences are minor; northern birds average larger.

Similar Species See Ivory-billed Woodpecker; virtually all Ivory-billed reports turn out to be Pileateds. Crows with aberrant white wing patches can momentarily suggest a Pileated.

Voice CALL: A long, flickerlike series *kee kee kee kee*, often slightly irregular in cadence. Also, single *wuk* or *cuk* notes. DRUM: Loud and resonant, lasting 1–3 seconds with about 15 beats a second; beat rate accelerates slightly, often trails off at very end.

Status & Distribution Common and widespread in Southeast; uncommon and more localized in the Great Lakes region, boreal areas, and the Pacific coast. YEAR-ROUND: Dense coniferous and deciduous forests and woodlots, with suitable presence of large older trees, snags, and downed wood. VAGRANT: Wanders casually slightly away from resident range, with documented records in CA from coastal Los Angeles County and the San Joaquin Valley; there are also unsubstantiated reports for east-central AK, CO, UT, northwestern AZ, and southern NM.

Population Generally stable.

Genus Campephilus

IVORY-BILLED WOODPECKER *Campephilus principalis* (E)

This spectacular bird of old southern bottomland forests was thought long extinct, but recent reports from eastern Arkansas suggest that it still survives. Polytypic (2 ssp.; nominate in U.S., extinct or nearly extinct *bairdii* in Cuba). L 19" (50 cm)

Identification The largest woodpecker in the U.S. and the third largest in the world. Mostly black with a massive creamy white bill, a large crest (male's is red and curves back, female's is black and curves forward), a striking flight pattern with completely white secondaries and white tips to the inner primaries, and long white stripes on the sides of the back. Legs and feet light gray, eyes yellow. Flight is direct with relatively rapid and shallow, continuous wing beats. Juvenile has shorter crest, browner plumage, and brown eyes.

Similar Species The Pileated Woodpecker is common in any potential area for Ivory-billed and can easily be mistaken for it, but the Pileated is 10 to 20 percent smaller, lacks white secondaries, has more extensive white on the underwing linings, lacks the white back stripes, and has a white (not black) chin. The bill of the Pileated is gray or blackish, not ivory.

Voice CALL: Tinny, toy trumpetlike *kent* or *yank* calls. DRUM: A strong double rap, typical of the Ivory-billed's genus (*Campephilus*).

Pearl River area of southeastern LA sparked an intensive search, with no subsequent sightings. A recording of calls from eastern TX in 1968 was probably of an Ivory-billed. Otherwise the bird had not been found in the U.S. since 1944, when a small population in northeastern LA lost its habitat to logging and subsequently disappeared. Formerly resident in lowland pine, hardwood, and cypress forests in the southern Mississippi River Valley, Gulf Coast, and southern Atlantic states from NC to FL. Forages by stripping bark from recently dead trees to reach beatle larvae, its primary source of food. Recent sightings in the Big Woods were in tupelo, oak, hickory, and bald cypress bottomland forests.

Population The logging of old-growth bottomland forests throughout the southern U.S. and the control of river flooding led to the decline of the Ivory-billed by the mid-1800s and its virtual extinction by the 1940s; a tiny Cuban population was well-documented as late as 1948 but not reported since the 1980s.

Status & Distribution Virtually extinct. Several recent sightings and recordings that may pertain to only 1 or 2 birds were made in the Big Woods of the White River–Cache River system of eastern AR in 2004 and 2005. An unconfirmed sighting in 1999 in the

FLICKERS Genus *Colaptes*

Largely terrestrial ant-eating woodpeckers of the New World, flickers have long, thin, slightly curved bills; large rounded wings; and flat tails that are only minimally stiffened. Plumage is barred olive to (in our area) brown on the back, spotted below, with colorful shafts on the wings and tail. Our species show a bold white rump and black chest crescent.

GILDED FLICKER *Colaptes chrysoides*

This "Yellow-shafted" flicker of southwestern desert woodlands was recently re-split from the Northern Flicker complex because of the very limited extent of interbreeding. Polytypic (*mearnsi* in U.S., with 2 more ssp. in Baja California). L 11" (29 cm)

Identification A small flicker with yellow wing flash and yellow tail base; distal half of tail black from below; chest patch deeper and more rectangular than in other flickers, and the black spots on the lower underparts expand to bars or crescents. Crown and nape are rich brown, contrasting with the gray face. Adult male has a red malar.

Similar Species Some hybrid "Yellow-shafted" x "Red-shafted" Northern Flickers approach the Gilded in looks, having yellow in wings and tail but lacking a red nuchal crescent. Note Gilded's smaller size, more extensive black on undertail, paler more finely barred back, deeper chest patch, and brown crown.

Voice CALL: High descending *klee-yer* and territorial *wick wick wick;* calls higher pitched than Northern Flicker. DRUM: Like other flickers.

Status & Distribution Fairly common. YEAR-ROUND: Desert woodlands, esp. where dominated by saguaro. Rare in limited range in CA and NV. Limited hybridization with Northern in AZ. VAGRANT: Casual to southwestern UT.

Population Presumably stable, though westernmost populations in California have declined.

NORTHERN FLICKER *Colaptes auratus*

"Yellow-shafted" ♂

"Yellow-shafted" ♂

"Red-shafted" ♂

"Red-shafted" ♂

This familiar large woodpecker and the closely related Gilded Flicker show flashy color in the wings and a bold white rump in flight. Polytypic. L 12" (32 cm)

Identification All Northern Flickers show a bold black chest crescent, a white rump, and bright color (salmon-red or yellow) in the shafts and much of the vanes of the flight feathers and on the underwing coverts. All Northern Flickers are pale buffy white to rich buff below with black spotting and have brown to gray-brown backs with black barring. **ADULT:** Sexes are similar, but males have a malar mark (red in the "Red-shafted," black in the "Yellow-shafted") that is lacking in females. The Yellow-shafted has a gray crown with a red crescent on the nape, a tan face and throat, and rich buff underparts with a relatively narrow chest crescent. The flight feathers and underwing linings are golden yellow. The Red-shafted has a grayish head and throat with pale brown on the forecrown and loral region, lacks red on the nape, and has paler buff to creamy underparts with broader chest crescent; the flight feathers and underwing linings are salmon pink.

Introgressant individuals that combine characters of both groups are widely seen. Examples include a "typical" Red-shafted with 1 or more yellow wing feathers and/or a touch of red on the nape, or a "typical" Yellow-shafted with gray in the face or throat, 1 or more red wing feathers, and/or the absence of the red nape crescent. Many males show mixed red and black malars.

Geographic Variation The "Red-shafted" and "Yellow-shafted" groups, formerly considered separate species, are easily distinguished, but identification is complicated by the wide occurrence of intergrades showing intermediate or combined characters of both groups. In an extensive hybrid zone on the Great Plains and northern Rocky Mountains from northeastern New Mexico and the Texas Panhandle north to Alberta, British Columbia, and southeastern Alaska, a large percentage of individuals encountered show traits of both groups; intergrades are frequently seen through the entire range of both groups. Within the Red-shafted group, northwestern *cafer* (southern AK to northwestern CA) is darker than remaining *collaris* group. There is slight size variation within the "Yellow-shafted" group. Birds of the Central American highlands (*mexicanoides* group) and the Cuba–Grand Cayman region (*chrysocaulosus* group) are distinct representatives of the Red-shafted, and the Yellow-shafted groups, respectively.

Similar Species The Gilded Flicker closely resembles the Northern Flicker and combines some features of the Yellow-shafted (yellow wings and tail base) and the Red-shafted (head pattern). The Gilded Flicker is smaller and shows black on the distal half of the undertail; Northern Flicker undertails are black on about the distal third (note that all flicker tails look mostly black from above). The crown of the Gilded is more exten-

sively brown than in the Red-shafted Northern, and the back is paler, more gray-brown, with narrower and more widely spaced black bars (but note that interior western Red-shafted are paler backed than northwestern birds). The black crescent on the chest of the Gilded is thicker and more truncated on the sides. The spotting on the underparts is broadened into short bars or crescents on the flanks of the Gilded; Northerns have round spots throughout the underparts.

Voice CALL: A piercing, descending *klee-yer* or *keeew* is given year-round; also a soft, rolling *wirrr* or *whurdle* in flight and a soft, slow *wick-a wick-a wicka* given by interacting birds. On the breeding grounds a long, long *wick, wick, wick, wick* series. DRUM: A long, simple roll of about 25 beats over a second, often interspersed with long *wick wick wick* series.

Status & Distribution Common. BREEDING: Found widely in open woodlands, parklands, suburban areas, riparian and montane forests. MIGRATION: Northern populations of Yellow-shafted Flickers and northern interior Red-shafteds are highly migratory. Small flocks of migrants and even large flights are evident from late Sept. through Oct. and in spring in late March and April. WINTER: Uncommon to rare north to southern Canada (but common in southwestern BC). VAGRANT: The Yellow-shafted is accidental in western Europe, where the 2 or 3 records represent known or possible ship-assisted birds. Yellow-shafted Flickers winter regularly to the Pacific coast, though outnumbered there by hybrids and intergrades. Red-shafted is casual east to MB, western MO, eastern TX, AR, LA; possibly also farther east, but most or all may not be pure Red-shafted.

Population Significant declines have occurred over much of the continent.

TYRANT FLYCATCHERS Family Tyrannidae

Gray Kingbird (FL, Apr.)

With some flamboyant exceptions, flycatchers are characterized by shades of brown, yellow, and olive. Several, like many *Empidonax* and *Myiarchus,* present some of the greatest identification challenges in North America.

Structure Tyrant flycatchers tend to perch upright and have a rather broad, flattened bill with a bit of a hook on the tip. They usually have rictal bristles at the base of the bill; the one exception in North America is the Northern Beardless-Tyrannulet. There is considerable variation in structure, and understanding it is a critical part of flycatcher identification. Overall shape, head shape, bill structure, primary projection, and wing formula are particularly important.

Behavior Tyrant flycatchers generally eat insects, but many at least occasionally eat small fruits, usually in migration or on the wintering grounds. Most sit on a perch and wait until they spot an insect, at which point they will go after it. Some species, such as most species in the genus *Contopus,* sally out to grab a flying insect and return to the same or another prominent perch. Others, like the Gray Flycatcher and the Least Flycatcher, often fly from a perch, hover, and strike prey. Vermilion Flycatchers frequently fly from a perch and pounce on or capture prey on the ground. Northern Beardless-Tyrannulets use their short warbler-like bill to glean stationary prey from foliage and branches, more in the manner of a vireo than a typical flycatcher. These differences in foraging style can be very helpful in identifying birds.

Plumage Flycatcher plumages are often studies in subtleties. Males and females are usually identical in plumage. Juveniles and immatures are similar to adults, with subtle differences in color and feather shape. Molt timing differs between some species and provides an excellent way to distinguish some difficult species in fall.

Distribution This is a large, exclusively New World family that reaches its greatest diversity and abundance in the New World tropics: 208 species have been recorded in Ecuador alone. Of some 425 species, 45 are known from North America. Thirty-five species of 10 genera are native breeders; the other 10 are vagrants. Most species in the U.S. and Canada are highly migratory.

Taxonomy Passerines are classified into 2 suborders: oscines and suboscines. The tyrant flycatchers are the only suboscines that occur north of Mexico. All have simpler syringeal morphology, which results in less impressive vocalizations than other North American passerines. Relationships among some species, such as becards and tityras, are poorly understood.

Conservation The most threatened North American flycatcher is the southwestern subspecies of the Willow Flycatcher, which is a federally listed endangered subspecies. *Contopus* may also have a relatively high risk of decline, in part because it has the lowest reproductive rate of all North American passerine genera. Loss of habitat, habitat fragmentation, and habitat degradation pose the biggest threats for most flycatchers. —*Christopher L. Wood, Donna L. Dittman, Steven W. Cardiff*

TYRANNULETS AND ELAENIAS Genera *Camptostoma, Myiopagis,* and *Elaenia*

Birds of this large, diverse group of small- to medium-size flycatchers generally feed on insects, but many at least supplement their diet with fruit. Only the Northern Beardless-Tyrannulet is regularly encountered in N.A.; 2 others have occurred as vagrants. They are best found by listening for their vocalizations and best identified by differences in facial pattern.

NORTHERN BEARDLESS-TYRANNULET *Camptostoma imberbe*

worn adult

fresh

Otherwise easily overlooked, this small flycatcher is almost always first detected by its plaintive whistled vocalizations. Its foraging behavior is very different from any other flycatcher regularly found north of Mexico. It hops through foliage, frequently flopping its tail up and down, like a vireo. Polytypic (3 ssp.). L 4.5" (11cm)

Identification Grayish olive above and on breast, fading to dull white or pale yellow below. Short pale eyebrow contrasts with dark eye line. Darker crown often raised, giving a bushy-crested appearance. Darker wings and tail, with 2 indistinct pale buffy wing bars; very short primary projection. Short blunt-tipped bill has bright pinkish orange base and dark culmen. JUVENILE: Similar to adult but with cinnamon-colored wing bars and edging to secondaries. **Geographic Variation** Two subspecies reach the U.S. Widespread nominate (southern TX) averages smaller, with smaller bill, more grayish wash to olive upperparts, and less yellow on underparts than *ridgwayi* (southeastern AZ, southwestern NM, northwestern Mexico). Differences clinal and obscured by individual variation.

Similar Species Dull but relatively distinctive. Note small crest and tail-dipping behavior. Juvenile Verdins have a stout, sharply pointed bill and are hyperactive. The Ruby-crowned Kinglet has buffy wing bars, very different posture, and behavior and lacks bold eye ring. **Voice** CALL: An innocuous, whistled *peeuuuu;* also a similar shorter call often followed by high trill: *peeut di-i-i-i.*

SONG: A somewhat variable series of loud, clear, downslurred notes, typically with 1 or 2 loudly stressed notes (e.g., *dee dee dee DEE DEE dee*).

Status & Distribution Uncommon. BREEDING: Often found near streams in sycamore, mesquite, and cottonwood groves. Occurs from Southwest U.S. to Costa Rica. MIGRATION & WINTER: Most depart northern breeding grounds by Oct., return by Mar.; but small numbers apparently winter throughout northern breeding areas. VAGRANT: Casual to western TX and outside mapped range in southern TX.

Population Unknown. Apparent increase in Pinal County, Arizona, may reflect observer effort.

GREENISH ELAENIA *Myiopagis viridicata*

This accidental, pewee-size bird usually perches vertically. Polytypic (10 ssp.) L 5.5" (14 cm)

Identification ADULT: Flat head; small, slender blackish bill (often flesh-colored at base below); long tail; very short primary projection. Mostly olive above, head more grayish; short white eyebrow; dark eye stripe. Wings and tail darker, noticeable olive edging, rather bright yellowish edging to secondaries. No wing bars. Olive breast; yellow belly, undertail coverts. JUVENILE: Similar but with brownish head and upperparts. **Similar Species** Face pattern recalls the Orange-crowned Warbler, but structure and habits very different. **Voice** CALL: High and thin, somewhat burry, descending *seei-seeur* or *sleeryip*. **Status & Distribution** Accidental in U.S. Fairly common to common in resident range. YEAR-ROUND: Forest and woodlands, often in more open areas from northern Mexico to northern Argen-

tina. VAGRANT: Accidental in Galveston County, TX, May 1984. **Population** Unknown.

CARIBBEAN ELAENIA *Elaenia martinica*

The Caribbean Elaenia is a pewee-size flycatcher, which looks somewhat like an oversized Northern Beardless-Tyrannulet. It may perch conspicuously on shrubs and low trees, or it may be hidden in the forest canopy. It feeds on fruiting trees.

Polytypic (7 ssp.) L 5.5" (14 cm)

Identification ADULT: Fairly chunky; short crest rarely raised to expose white-based feathers. Note short, pale gray supercilium and dusky lores. Pale yellowish wing bars and edging to secondaries; bill appears dark above, orangey-pink below. JUVENILE: Similar but wing bars washed cinnamon-buff, crest is shorter; it has no patch on crown.

Similar Species The Yellow-bellied Elaenia (unrecorded in U.S.) is larger with a prominent crest and more yellow on the belly.

Voice CALL: Clear whistled *wheee-u*, often repeated.

Status & Distribution: Fairly common to common in resident range. YEAR-ROUND: Woodlands and second growth on Caribbean islands and eastern Yucatan Peninsula. VAGRANT: Accidental on Santa Rosa I., FL, April 1984. (AOU does not consider this record to be definitive.)

Population Unknown.

Genus *Mitrephanes*

TUFTED FLYCATCHER *Mitrephanes phaeocercus*

This distinctive flycatcher acts like a pewee, perching on conspicuous branches. After sallying, it may return to the same group of favored perches. Polytypic

(4 ssp). L 5" (13 cm)
Identification ADULT: Obvious tufted crest. Bright cinnamon face, underparts; upperparts generally more brownish olive. Brownish olive wings; dull cinnamon wing bars; pale edges to tertials and secondaries. JUVENILE: Similar but with pale cinnamon-tipped feathers on upperparts; broader, brighter wing bars. Plumage held briefly.
Geographic Variation Texas records presumably *phaeocercus* (eastern Mexico to El Salvador); Arizona record presumably *tenuirostris* (western Mexico).
Similar Species Nearly unmistakable. Buff-breasted is much paler; lacks tuft;

has more-contrasting wing bars, blacker wings, and empid-like behavior.
Voice CALL: A whistled burry *tchurree-tchurree,* sometimes given singly. Also a soft *peek,* similar to the Hammond's.
Status & Distribution Common to fairly common in resident range. BREEDING: Favors somewhat-open areas in pine-oak and evergreen woods from Mexico to Bolivia. WINTER: Some move to lower elevations; often found in a greater variety of habitats in winter. VAGRANT: Big Bend N.P., TX, winter 1991–1992; near Ft. Stockton, TX, Apr. 1993; White Rock Canyon, AZ, Mar. 2005.
Population Unknown.

PEWEES Genus *Contopus*

These rather plain, dark olive, medium-size flycatchers (14 sp. in the Americas; 3 breed north of the Mexico border; 1 vagrant to FL) have poorly contrasting wing bars and long wings. They sit motionless on fairly high, conspicuous perches, sallying forth to catch insects.

OLIVE-SIDED FLYCATCHER *Contopus cooperi*

Olive-sided Flycatchers are usually easy to find, perching conspicuously on the top of a snag or on high dead branches or giving far-carrying vocalizations. Polytypic (2 ssp.). L 7.5" (19 cm)
Identification ADULT: Large and proportionately short tailed, with a rather large blocky head. Brownish gray-olive above. Distinctive whitish tufts on the side of the rump, often hidden by wings. Dull white throat, center of breast, and belly contrast markedly with dark head. Brownish olive sides and flanks appear streaked, giving a heavily vested appearance. Mostly black bill; the center and sometimes the base of the lower mandible are dull orange. All molting occurs on wintering grounds. JUVENILE: During fall separated from worn adults by fresh plumage, buff-brown wing bars, and brownish wash to the upperparts.

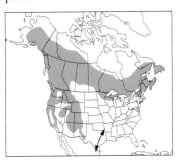

Geographic Variation Subspecies differ subtly, and many regard the species as monotypic. Breeders of *majorinus* (southern CA) differ from widespread nominate in averaging slightly larger, with a large bill.
Similar Species Wood-Pewees and Greater Pewees are similar in shape, but their underparts are less strongly patterned; they lack a sharply defined "vest" and are also relatively longer tailed. The Greater Pewee also has an orange lower mandible. Eastern Phoebes are sometimes mistaken for this species, but they also lack the strong vested appearance, tend to perch lower to the ground, and frequently dip tail downward.
Voice CALL: A repeated *pep,* often repeated in groups of 3 or 2: *pep-pep-pep pep-pep;* sometimes given singly. SONG: A far-carrying, distinctive, clear, whistled quick *THREE-BEER!;* second note higher pitched.
Status & Distribution Uncommon to common. BREEDING: Boreal forest, subalpine forest, spruce bogs, and mixed conifer or mixed conifer-deciduous forest; prefers relatively open areas, particularly burned areas. More common in the west. MIGRATION: In Southwest mostly mid-Apr.–mid-May; in Great Lakes May 10–mid-June. Generally rare migrant in East. WINTER: Mostly in Andes of western S.A.; smaller numbers

in southern Mexico and C.A. VAGRANT: Casual in winter on coastal slope of southern CA (and outside Andes in S.A.).
Population The Olive-sided is listed as near threatened on BirdLife International's IUCN 2004 Red List and is included in the U.S. Fish and Wildlife Service's Bird of Conservation Concern list. Widespread decline detected throughout most of range, including core range in Northwest. Once common in West Virginia, they are now scarce to absent as breeders; extirpated from southern New England, and locally in the West (e.g., Sequoia National Forest, CA). Threats include loss of habitat within breeding and wintering range, fire suppression, and possibly pesticides.

GREATER PEWEE *Contopus pertinax*

While restricted in the U.S. to pine and pine-oak woodlands of Arizona and adjacent New Mexico, this species is not hard to find. It perches conspicuously near the top of a tree, often larger trees than those frequented by Western Wood-Pewees. Its distinctive song carries well. Birds outside of range are often identified by *pip* notes. Polytypic (2 ssp.). L 8" (20 cm)

Identification ADULT: Large; usually shows a short spiky, tufted crest. Large bill with a dark upper mandible and a distinctive bright yellowish orange lower mandible. Generally dark olive above and on the face with somewhat paler lores. Darker wings and tail, with indistinct wing bars. Paler underparts, especially on throat, which contrasts with grayish breast. Worn summer birds are paler overall, more grayish olive above. Adults molt on the breeding grounds. JUVENILE: Similar to adult but with cinnamon wash to upperparts and buffy-cinnamon wing bars. More difficult to separate from adults

than other North American *Contopus* due to adult prebasic molt that occurs on breeding grounds.

Geographic Variation The nominate subspecies is larger than *minor* of C.A. Tendency for southern Arizona birds to average paler and grayer, but differences are minimal and broadly clinal; sometimes considered a separate subspecies, *pallidiventris*.

Similar Species Larger than wood-pewees, with more noticeable tufted crest and larger bill that is bright orange below. (Even the brightest-billed Eastern Wood-Pewees do not have such a bright orange lower mandible.) Note vocalizations. The Olive-sided Flycatcher shows distinctive "vest," is shorter tailed, and lacks crest. The Eastern Phoebe is generally paler with a darker bill, tends to perch lower to the ground, and often dips tail downward. Smaller *Empidonax* have more contrasting wing bars and usually more of an eye ring, and they typically flick their tails.

Voice CALL: *Puip* or *beek* notes, often repeated in groups (e.g., *puip-puip-puip*); very similar to the Olive-sided Flycatcher's call but averages somewhat higher pitched and softer. SONG: A far-carrying, distinctive, plaintive *ho-SAY ma-RE-ah*. Song often begins with series of repeated introductory *whee-de* or *wee-de-ip* phrases.

Status & Distribution Fairly common. BREEDING: Pine or pine-oak forest; in U.S. often found in riparian areas in

summer

steep-sided canyons where pine-oak habitat borders canyon. Ranges south to Nicaragua and El Salvador. MIGRATION: Most return to AZ in mid-Apr. and leave by mid-Sept. Rarely noted in migration. WINTER: Most withdraw from northern portion of range and from higher elevations. VAGRANT: Casual: TX 15+ records, southern and central CA 35+ records (mostly winter); also casual in winter in southern AZ.

Population No data.

WESTERN WOOD-PEWEE *Contopus sordidulus*

adult

This species is extremely similar to the Eastern Wood-Pewee and is best identified by range and voice. Vagrants should be identified with great care and preferably documented with recordings of vocalizations, photos, or video.

This is the only exclusively western-breeding passerine that winters almost entirely in S.A. Polytypic (5 ssp. north of Mexico). L 6.3" (16 cm)

Identification ADULT: Extremely similar to Eastern Wood-Pewee, with long wings that extend one-third of the way down the tail. Average differences listed below, but plumage somewhat variable. Western Wood-Pewee tends to be slightly darker, browner, and less greenish than Eastern Wood-Pewee, with complete grayish breast band, darker centers to undertail coverts, less pale nape contrast, and duller back. Wing bars, on average, are narrower and more grayish, contrasting less with wings. The base of the lower mandible is primarily dark (usually darker than the Eastern Wood-Pewee's) but usually shows some dull

orange. Adults molt on the wintering grounds, and worn summer birds (and fall birds in N.A.) are essentially identical to the Eastern Wood-Pewee in appearance. JUVENILE: During fall separated from worn adults by fresh plumage, buff-gray wing bars, and brownish wash to the upperparts. Many have more extensive pale coloration on lower mandible than adults (i.e., more like the Eastern Wood-Pewee's). On average, the wing bars contrast less than on the juvenile Eastern Wood-Pewee; also note that the lower wing bar is broader and more defined than the upper: the paler tips on the greater coverts are broader and more defined than those on median coverts.

Geographic Variation Differences minor and clinal. Compared to widespread *veliei*, coastal breeders from southeastern Alaska through central Oregon *(saturatus)* usually have more of a yellow wash to flanks, a browner breast, and a duskier crown that contrasts more with brownish or olive back. Mexican and Central American subspecies are darker and larger, except for southern Baja California's *peninsulae,* which are paler with a larger bill.

Similar Species Extremely similar to the Eastern Wood-Pewee and best separated by range and voice. (Average visual differences compared above.) Most often confused with the Willow Flycatcher; note the Willow's (and the Alder's) relatively short primary projection, smaller size, and tendency to wag tail. Compare with the Greater Pewee, the Olive-sided Flycatcher, and the Eastern Phoebe.

Voice CALL: A harsh, slightly descending *peeer;* a short, even, rough *brrt;* and clear descending whistles similar to the Eastern's upslurred *pwee-yee.* SONG: Has 3-note *tswee-tee-teet,* usually mixed with peer notes; heard mostly on breeding grounds.

Status & Distribution Common. BREEDING: Open woodlands. MIGRATION: In spring, AZ and CA mid-Apr.–mid-June. From CO to OR, first individuals generally appear in early May, with peak in mid- to late May. In fall, primarily Aug. and Sept. Most have left U.S. by early Oct. WINTER: Mostly northwestern S.A. No valid U.S. winter records. VAGRANT: Casual in East to IA, MN, WI, IL, IN, LA, MS, FL, MD, MA, ON, and QC, and north to western and northern AK and YK.

Population Breeding Bird Survey trends show widespread declines throughout most of range north of Mexico, but species not classified as threatened, vulnerable, or of "special concern." Causes likely include loss and deterioration of habitat on both breeding and wintering grounds.

EASTERN WOOD-PEWEE *Contopus virens*

This species is extremely similar to the Western Wood-Pewee and is best identified by range and voice. Vagrants should be identified with great care and preferably documented with recordings of vocalizations, photos, or video. Monotypic. L 6.3" (16 cm)

Identification ADULT: Plumage generally dark grayish olive above with dull white throat, darker breast; whitish or pale yellow underparts. Bill has black upper mandible and dull orange lower mandible, usually with a limited black tip. Long wings extend one-third of the way down the tail. Very similar to the Western Wood-Pewee, but spring and early summer adults are usually more olive with less extensive breast band (often produce vested appearance) and a pale smooth gray nape that contrasts slightly. The wing bars are often broader and more contrasty. Adults molt on the wintering grounds, and worn summer birds (and fall birds in N.A.) are essentially identical to the Western Wood-Pewee in appearance. JUVENILE: During fall separated from worn adults by fresh plumage, buff-gray wing bars, and brownish wash to the upperparts. Many have more extensive dark coloration to lower mandible and appear more like the Western Wood-Pewee. On average, the wing bars stand out more than on the Western Wood-Pewee, with the upper and lower wing bars the same color and prominence (unlike the Western, which usually has a less noticeable upper wing bar).

Similar Species Extremely similar to the Western Wood-Pewee and best separated by range and voice (see species). Most often confused with the Willow and the Alder Flycatchers. Note the Willow's and Alder's relatively short primary projection (barely reaching beyond base of tail), smaller size, brighter wing bars, and tendency to wag its tail. Woodpewees also forage from higher prominent perches, to which they repeatedly return. Compare with the Greater Pewee, the Olive-sided Flycatcher, and the Eastern Phoebe.

Voice CALL: A loud, dry *chip plit* and clear, whistled, rising *pawee* notes; often given together: *plit pawee.* SONG: A clear, slow plaintive *pee-a-wee;* second note is lower; often alternates with a downslurred *pee-yuu.*

Status & Distribution Common. BREEDING: Variety of woodland habitats. MIGRATION: Primarily circum-Gulf migrant. Most return mid-Apr. (southern TX) to mid.-May (Great Lakes); remain later than the Western, regularly into early Oct. WINTER: Mostly northern S.A. No valid U.S. winter records. VAGRANT: Casual in West to western TX, western OK, western KS, eastern CO, southeastern WY, western NE, western SD, western ND, eastern MT, south-central SK, NM, southern NV, southern AZ, southeastern OR, and CA (10 recs., mostly late spring singing birds).

Population Breeding Bird Survey shows widespread declines, particularly in central N.A., but species not classified as threatened, vulnerable, or of special concern. Causes for decline unknown.

CUBAN PEWEE *Contopus caribaeus*

This Caribbean species is accidental to south Florida. It typically forages from low perches and is relatively tame and, usually, easily approached. Also called the Crescent-eyed Pewee, it was formerly treated as conspecific with the Hispaniola and Jamaican Pewees, as the Greater Antillean Pewee. Polytypic (4 ssp.). L 6" (15 cm)

Identification Appears relatively small for a *Contopus*, with upright posture and erectile crest and large bill. Best told by the conspicuous white crescent behind the eye. Brownish gray above, darker on head. Noticeably paler underparts, especially belly and undertail coverts. Wing bars relatively weak.

Geographic Variation U.S. records likely

bahamensis of the Bahamas.

Similar Species Wood-Pewees lack bold white crescent behind the eye; Eastern and Western Wood-Pewees have longer primary projection. *Empidonax* have more uniform eye ring, prominent wing bars, and smaller bill.

Voice CALL: Repeated *wheet* or *dee;* also a *vi-vi* similar to the call of the La Sagra's Flycatcher. SONG: A long thin descending whistle, sometimes likened to the sound of a bullet flying through the air: *wheeeooooo.*

Status & Distribution Common in resident range. BREEDING: Pine and other woodlands, forest edge, brushy scrub edges; Bahamas and Cuba. VAGRANT: Two recs.: Boca Raton, FL (Mar. 11–Apr.

4, 1995), Key Largo Hammocks State Botanical Site, FL (Feb. 16, 2001). Several other FL observations either undocumented or not accepted by Florida Ornithological Records Committee.

Population Unknown.

EMPIDS Genus *Empidonax*

Eleven of the 14 species of empids breed in N.A. These relatively small, drab birds are notoriously difficult to identify. Their plumages are characterized by shades of green, brown, buff, and off-white, with darker wings and tails. Most have wing bars and eye rings. Most species are long-distance migrants. Note that plumages become duller with wear.

Identification of an Empid

First, make sure you are really looking at an empid. *Empidonax* are frequently confused with wood-pewees and are best separated by structure and behavior. *Empidonax* are active birds that frequently change perches and flick their wings or tail, whereas pewees sit still for long periods of time. While they may spread their wings and tail after landing or to preen, they do not engage in the quick flicks that are characteristic of empids. As can be seen on this Western Wood-Pewee, pewees also have longer wings. To learn *Empidonax,* watch birds that have been identified by song on the breeding grounds. Watch them for long periods of time under a variety of lighting conditions, and look at many different individuals. Pay attention to the exact shape of the bill. Some species (e.g., the Willow) have broad bills, while others (e.g., the Hammond's) have narrow bills. The pattern of the lower mandible is often important: the Hammond's lower mandible is mostly dark; the Least's is mostly pale. Study the wings, particularly the primary projection. Eastern species tend to have brighter tertial edges and wing bars. Note the Hammond's pri-

Western Wood-Pewee (CA, May)

Hammond's Flycatcher (CA, Apr.)

Dusky Flycatcher (AZ, Feb.)

Willow Flycatcher (CA, May)

mary projection is longer than the Least's. Eye ring, throat color, and upperparts coloration are also important. Listen to any vocalizations, particularly call notes. Appearance (e.g., bill color) changes based on age, molt,

and season, as well as individual variation. Breeding habitat is also an important clue. Most importantly, remember that some individuals appear intermediate and others are poorly seen. ∎

YELLOW-BELLIED FLYCATCHER *Empidonax flaviventris*

Even in migration, these birds favor shady forest interiors. They are usually detected by their vocalizations or by their active foraging with tail and wing flicking. Monotypic. L 5.5" (14 cm)
Identification Appears short tailed, with a large head and rounded crown that appears slightly peaked at the back; moderate primary projection. Broad-based bill may appear somewhat large; entirely pale yellow-orange or pink lower mandible. ADULT: Mostly olive above; much more yellow below with a fairly extensive olive wash across the sides of the breast. Olive color from the sides of the face blends smoothly into the more yellow throat. Conspicuous bold eye ring is relatively even, often yellowish, and often slightly thicker behind eye. Wings appear very black with bright white wing bars (less so on worn birds). Worn fall migrants are grayer above and paler below, occasionally nearly grayish white below. Molt occurs on wintering grounds. FIRST-FALL: Similar to spring adults but with bold buffy wing bars.
Similar Species Compared to the Acadian Flycatcher, note the Yellow-bellied's smaller size, shorter primary projection, smaller bill, shorter and narrower tail, olive wash on breast, and molt timing. Very worn fall adults approach the Least Flycatcher in appearance, but note the Yellow-bellied's more blended throat, uniformly pale lower mandible, and call. See the Pacific-slope Flycatcher for differences with that species; see also the Cordilleran Flycatcher.
Voice CALL: Includes a sharp whistled *chiu,* similar to the Acadian's. SONG: A hoarse *che-bunk* similar to the Least's, but softer, lower, not as snappy.
Status & Distribution Common. BREEDING: Northern bogs, swamps, and other damp coniferous woods. MIGRATION: Circum-Gulf migrant. Late in spring, early in fall; e.g., southern Great Lakes

1st fall

worn fall adult

spring

mostly May 15–June 5, early Aug.–late Sept. WINTER: Eastern Mexico to Panama. VAGRANT: Casual mostly in fall to west TX, NM, AZ, NV, and CA.
Population Stable.

ACADIAN FLYCATCHER *Empidonax virescens*

all

worn summer adult

spring

The Acadian has a calm, even languorous look, with often-drooped wings and a minimum of wing and tail flicking. However, its vocalizations are delivered with force and it frequently perches relatively high in trees. Monotypic. L 5.5" (14 cm)
Identification A large empid with long primary projection and a broad tail. There is usually a peak at the back of the head. The bill is the largest of any empid: long and broad based with an almost entirely yellowish lower mandible. ADULT: Generally bright olive above and pale below. Usually with pale grayish throat, pale olive wash across upper breast, white lower breast, and faint yellowish belly and undertail coverts. Usually narrow, yellowish, and sharply defined eye ring (but may be faint on some birds). Quite dark wings with prominent wing bars. Acadians typically appear very worn by mid-summer, almost white below. Molt occurs on breeding grounds. FIRST-FALL: Similar to adults but with bold buffy wing bars and more extensive yellow coloration throughout.
Similar Species Compare with the similarly structured Alder and Willow Flycatchers and the smaller Yellow-bellied and Least Flycatchers.
Voice CALL: *Peek,* similar to the first part of its song; louder and sharper than other empid call notes. On breeding grounds gives *pwi-pwi-pwi-pwi-pwi,* flicker like, but softer. SONG: An explosive *PEE-tsup.*
Status & Distribution Common. BREEDING: Mature forest, prefers larger tracts. MIGRATION: Mostly trans-Gulf migrant. In spring, arrives Gulf Coast in Apr.; southern Great Lakes, May 10–20. In fall, departs quickly after molting, July– late Sept.; rare in U.S. after early Oct. WINTER: Mostly Panama to Ecuador. VAGRANT: Casual in QC, NB, and NS. Least likely eastern empid in West. Accidental in NM, AZ, SK, and BC.
Population Stable.

ALDER FLYCATCHER *Empidonax alnorum*

Until the early 1970s, the Alder Flycatcher was considered the same species as the Willow Flycatcher. Even today, Alders are often not separable from eastern Willows without hearing their distinctive vocalizations. Many birders refer to unknown birds of this species pair by their old name, the "Traill's Flycatcher." Alders do not do as much tail and wing flicking as some empids. Monotypic. L 5.8" (15 cm)

Identification A large empid with moderately long primary projection and a fairly broad tail. Moderately long and broad-based bill; almost entirely pinkish lower mandible, sometimes with a dusky area at the tip. All molts occur on wintering grounds. ADULT: Most have strongly olive-green upperparts. Usually dark head, often with a grayish tone; contrasts with the white throat. Paler underparts washed with olive across the breast. Usually narrow and well-defined eye ring, but may be almost absent. Quite dark wings with prominent wing bars and tertial edges. Alders usually appear quite worn by mid-summer and during fall migration, with paler upperparts and reduced wing bars and eye ring. JUVENILE: Similar to adults but with buffy wing bars. First prebasic molt occurs on wintering grounds.

Similar Species Extremely similar to the Willow Flycatcher; should be identi-

fied by voice. On average, the Alder has a slightly shorter bill, a more distinct eye ring, and a greener back. It usually has a darker head with a more contrasting white throat than the nominate eastern Willow Flycatcher. The western subspecies of the Willow Flycatcher appears less like the Alder than do the eastern Willows; note the western Willow's less well-defined tertial edges, weaker wing bars, shorter primary projection, and less-distinct crown spots. The Acadian is also very similar, but it has longer primary projection, and its white throat contrasts less with the paler face. Compared with wood-pewees, note the Alder's relatively short primary projection (barely reaching beyond the base of the tail), smaller size, brighter wing bars, and tendency to flick tails.

Voice CALL: A loud *pip* similar to the Hammond's Flycatcher but more robust. SONG: Harsh and burry *rrree-bee-ah;* the last note is almost more of an inflection and may be inaudible at a distance. Sings occasionally on spring migration.

Status & Distribution Common. BREEDING: Damp brushy habitats and wet woodland edges; bogs; birch and alder thickets. MIGRATION: Circum-Gulf migrant. Spring is late; rare in south

worn
fall
adult

spring

TX before early May; southern Great Lakes peak in late May. Fall is primarily Aug. and Sept. Most have left U.S. by early Oct. WINTER: S.A. VAGRANT: Casual to CO, WA, and CA.
Population Unknown.

WILLOW FLYCATCHER *Empidonax traillii*

This is the more southerly "Traill's" species. Willow subspecies in eastern U.S. and Canada (nominate *traillii* and *campestriss,* merged by some

1st
fall
traillii

worn
fall adult
traillii

spring
traillii

authorities) are more similar to an Alder Flycatcher than to a "Southwestern" Willow. Separating Willow and Alder often requires hearing vocalizations. Polytypic (5 ssp.). L 5.8" (15 cm)

Identification Almost identical in structure to the Alder. Bill averages slightly longer in western subspecies; primary projections in western subspecies is shorter than Alder's, but in eastern subspecies equal to Alder's. All molts occur on wintering grounds. ADULT: Regional variations in plumage. Eastern subspecies' features overlap almost completely with Alder, but upperparts average less strongly olive; head is usually paler and contrasts slightly less with white throat; eye ring is less prominent. As with the Alder, the Willow often appears quite worn by mid-summer and during fall migration (paler upperparts and wing

bars; eye ring usually absent). JUVENILE: Similar, but with buffy wing bars.
Geographic Variation Subspecies fairly well defined but intergrade where ranges meet. Compared to eastern, all western subspecies have shorter primary projection; more blended tertial edges; and duller, buffy, wing bars. (They also differ from the Alder in those characteristics.) The northwestern *brewsteri* has a darker brownish head and upperparts and a brownish breast band. *Adastus* (southwestern Canada to eastern CA and southern CO) is similar to *brewsteri,* but its upperparts and head average paler brownish olive to grayish olive; it also has a more extensive yellow wash to flanks and vent. Southwestern *extimus* (generally in lower elevations near range of overlap with *adastus*) has more grayish head, contrasting with olive-tinged grayish brown back and wing bars (averages paler than other western subspecies).

Similar Species See the Alder Flycatcher. Also often confused with woodpewees; note Willow's short primary projection, smaller size, more contrasty plumage, and tendency to flick tail upward. The Least has a bold white eye ring and appears relatively large headed and smaller billed.

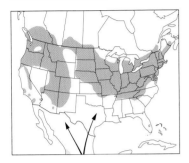

spring
extimus

spring
brewsteri

Voice CALL: Thick, rich *whit,* like the Least's or the Dusky's but more resonant. SONG: Harsh, burry *fitz-bew* with variations. Sometimes only a husky, rough *rrrrUP.* Often sings on spring migration, sometimes early in fall migration. Songs of the "Southwestern" lower pitched, more drawn out (esp. second phrase).
Status & Distribution Fairly common; "Southwestern" uncommon and local. BREEDING: Damp brushy habitats, edges of pastures and mountain meadows. MIGRATION: Nominate circum-Gulf migrant. Late in spring; rare in south TX before early May; arrives in southern Great Lakes mid-May. Fall primarily Aug., Sept. Most leave east by early Sept., west by early Oct. Casual migrant in Southeast. WINTER: Western Mexico to Venezuela; nominate believed to

winter farther south.
Population "Southwestern" subspecies is endangered. The species faces widespread decline in North America, largely due to loss and degradation of habitat.

LEAST FLYCATCHER *Empidonax minimus*

1st
fall

worn fall
adult

spring

This active species frequently flicks its wings and tail upward, changes perches, and calls. Monotypic. L 5.3" (13 cm)
Identification This is the smallest eastern *Empidonax*. Primary projection usually appears short. Short, broad-based bill with a mostly pale lower mandible, often with a small dusky area at the tip. Usually appears large headed with short, narrow tail. ADULT: Bold white eye ring. Grayish brown above with olive wash to back. Underparts pale with gray wash across breast; belly and undertail coverts pale yellow

on fresh plumaged birds. Wings usually quite dark with contrasting wing bars. By late summer, usually appears quite worn, with paler upperparts and typically reduced wing bars, tertial edges, and eye rings. Adult's prebasic molt may begin on breeding grounds but occurs mostly on wintering grounds. A partial prealternate molt begins on the wintering grounds but regularly continues into spring migration. FIRST-FALL: Similar but with buffy wing bars. First prebasic molt occurs primarily on breeding grounds.
Similar Species May be confused with almost any other empid. In the east, only the Willow Flycatcher has a similar *whit* note. Compared to the Willow, the Alder, and the Acadian, the Least is smaller, with a narrower tail, a smaller bill, and shorter primary projection; it also usually has a conspicuous eye ring. It is similar to Dusky, Gray, Hammond's, and Willow Flycatchers in the west. The Hammond's often appears similar because both have a relatively large head and a narrow tail; note the Hammond's smaller, narrower bill; longer primary projection; and usually darker underparts. Dusky and Gray Flycatchers usually appear longer tailed with duller wings; they usually have more extensive dark on the underside of the mandible. The Gray is most easily separated by its tendency to dip its tail downward. The "Western Willow Flycatcher" usually has a reduced eye ring, a larger bill, and duller wing bars; and it is usually less active.
Voice CALL: A sharp *whit,* very similar

to, but usually sharper and louder than, the Dusky's; not as thick as the Willow's. Given frequently even in migration. SONG: A snappy *che-beck, che-beck,* usually given in a rapid series. Similar to the Yellow-bellied's *che-bunk* but snappier, higher, more accentuated, and usually quickly repeated. Sings regularly on spring migration.
Status & Distribution Common, more local in west. BREEDING: Mature deciduous woods, orchards, parks, brushy understory important. MIGRATION: Circum-Gulf migrant. Spring to southern TX, mostly mid-Apr.–early May; southern Great Lakes late Apr.–early June, peaking in mid-May. In fall, adults leave very early (e.g., peak at Long Point, ON, mid- to late July). First-fall birds generally early Aug.–mid-Oct., depending on latitude. Rare migrant through most of west. WINTER: Mexico to Costa Rica. Rare but regular south of Lake Okeechobee and northwest of Orlando in FL. VAGRANT: Casual to AK. Accidental to Iceland.
Population No significant continental change.

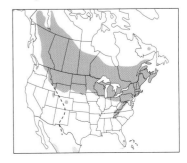

HAMMOND'S FLYCATCHER *Empidonax hammondii*

The Hammond's Flycatcher is usually quite active, flicking its wings and tail upward at the same time. The *pip* call note is distinctive, but many Hammond's are relatively quiet in migration. Monotypic. L 5.5" (14 cm)

Identification This relatively small *Empidonax* usually appears large headed and short tailed. Its short notch-tailed appearance is accentuated by the long primary projection. (The tail is actually of medium length.) Short, very narrow bill, with a mostly dark lower mandible (may be extensively pale on young birds). ADULT: Bold white eye ring, usually expands behind eye. Grayish head and throat; grayish olive back; gray or olive wash on breast and sides; yellow-tinged belly. Adult prebasic molt occurs on breeding grounds. Fall birds are much brighter olive above and on sides of breast, much more yellow below. The pre-alternate molt is variable, so some spring birds appear much brighter than others. FIRST-FALL: Similar to adults but with buffy wing bars. First prebasic molt occurs primarily on breeding grounds.

Similar Species Overall, the Hammond's is quite distinctive, with long wings, a tiny dark bill and, in fall, very bright plumage. It is most often confused with the Dusky and most easily separated by its *pip* call note if vocalizing. Experienced observers will note the Dusky's relatively short primary projection and its bill, which is wider, longer, and usually with more pale coloration to the base of the lower mandible. The Gray can be eliminated by these same characteristics and by its tendency to dip its tail, like a phoebe. The Least has a larger, more triangular bill that is usually extensively pale; much paler underparts; shorter primary projection; more contrasting dark wings with prominent wing bars and tertial edges; and frequently given *whit* call note.

Voice CALL: A *pip*, similar to the Pygmy Nuthatch's and very different from the calls of the Dusky, the Gray, and the Least. SONG: The first element of song suggests the *che-beck* of the Least and may be given alone, particularly late in breeding season. Similar to the Dusky but hoarser and lower pitched, particularly on the second phrase. Phrases tend to be more 2-parted. Also lacks the high, clear notes that are typical in the Dusky's song.

fall

spring

Status & Distribution Fairly common. BREEDING: Coniferous forest usually without shrubby component; often found at higher elevations than the Dusky, but overlaps. MIGRATION: Spring is mostly early Apr.–early June. Fall is late Aug.–mid-Oct. Throughout most of the West, the Hammond's is the most likely empid to be seen in Oct.; regular in CA into late Oct. WINTER: Southeastern AZ to western Nicaragua. VAGRANT: Mostly in fall. Casual to Great Plains (more frequent than the Gray and slightly more frequent than the Dusky). Accidental in late fall and winter to eastern N.A. **Population** No significant continental change.

GRAY FLYCATCHER *Empidonax wrightii*

This empid has the distinctive habit of slowly dipping its tail downward, like a phoebe. Monotypic. L 6" (15 cm)

winter

spring

Identification The Gray Flycatcher is a medium-size empid with short primary projection and a fairly long tail. The head often appears proportionately small and rounded. The straight-sided bill is narrow and averages slightly longer than the Dusky Flycatcher's. Most Gray's bills have a well-defined dark tip to the lower mandible that contrasts with the pinkish orange base; but some have an entirely pinkish orange lower mandible. Molting generally occurs on wintering grounds. ADULT: Gray above, sometimes with a slight olive tinge in fresh fall plumage (usually only seen in southeastern AZ, where Gray Flycatchers winter). The white eye ring is inconspicuous on the pale head. Adult prebasic molt occurs on wintering grounds. JUVENILE: Similar to the adult but more

brownish gray overall with buffy wing bars and somewhat-fresher plumage in summer and early fall. First prebasic molt usually occurs on wintering grounds but may begin on the breeding grounds.

Similar Species This species is very similar to the Dusky Flycatcher in terms of plumage and structure. The slightly longer, more 2-toned bill of the Gray Flycatcher is superfluous because the Gray Flycatcher is easily separated from the Dusky Flycatcher and all other *Empidonax* by its distinctive phoebe-like tail dipping. Make sure that the tail is really dipping downward; if the dipping happens too fast to tell or if it is accompanied by wing flicking, the observed bird is not a Gray Flycatcher, because Grays dip their tail rather slowly. Compare with the Eastern Phoebe.

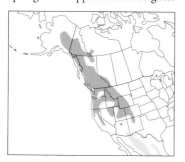

Voice CALL: A loud *wit,* very similar to the Dusky Flycatcher's; averaging somewhat stronger. Also very similar to the calls of the Least and the Willow Flycatchers. SONG: A vigorous *chi-wip* or *chi-bit,* followed by a liquid *whilp,* trailing off in a gurgle.

Status & Distribution Fairly common. BREEDING: Dry habitat of the Great Basin, usually in pine or pinon-juniper. MIGRATION: An early spring migrant; the only western empid likely to be seen away from the southwest or Pacific coast in Apr.; usually arrives on breeding grounds mid-Apr.–mid-May. Fall is primarily mid-Aug.–early Oct. Regular migrant on CA coast. WINTER: Southern AZ to central Mexico. VAGRANT: Mostly in fall. Casual to Great Plains. Accidental to OH, MA, DE, ON, SK, and AB.

Population The Breeding Bird Survey indicates that this species is experiencing an overall increase.

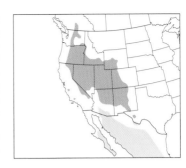

DUSKY FLYCATCHER *Empidonax oberholseri*

1st fall

worn fall adult

winter

spring

This is a relatively sedate species; it occasionally flicks its tail or wings upward. Dusky Flycatchers are generally intermediate between Hammond's and Gray Flycatchers, and many resemble the Least Flycatcher. Monotypic. L 5.8" (15 cm)

Identification A medium-size empid with short primary projection and a long tail. The straight-sided bill is intermediate in length between the Hammond's and the Gray's; it is extensively pale at the base, fading to a dark tip. Most molting occurs on the wintering grounds. ADULT: Generally drab. Grayish olive upperparts, with little contrast between the head and mantle. More yellowish below, with a pale gray or whitish throat and pale olive wash on upper breast. Usually well-defined white eye ring may not stand out against the head. Lores are often paler than on other empids. Adult prebasic molt occurs on the wintering grounds. During fall migration, these birds should not be confused with the much brighter Hammond's Flycatchers. Fresh late-fall birds appear quite bright with flanks and undertail coverts strongly washed yellow, but in the U.S. these birds are usually only seen in southeastern Arizona, where they winter. JUVENILE: Similar to adults but somewhat fresher plumage in summer and early fall with buffy wing bars. First prebasic molt usually occurs on the wintering grounds; occasionally begins on breeding grounds.

Similar Species In terms of structure and plumage, Dusky Flycatchers are very similar to Gray Flycatchers; but Grays have the distinctive habit of dipping the tail downward, like a phoebe. The Dusky Flycatcher is also often confused with the Hammond's Flycatcher. In addition to noting different molt timing, observe the Hammond's longer wings; shorter, thinner, darker bill; and eye ring that expands behind the eye. Also note vocalizations. Many Dusky Flycatchers appear similar to Least Flycatchers, particularly worn fall birds. The Dusky has a slightly longer and narrower bill, which often has more extensive dusky coloration to the lower mandible; the tail usually appears longer; the wings are usually not as black and have low contrast wing bars and tertial edges; and the eye ring is usually narrower and less pronounced. The Least is also paler below. Some heavily worn birds may be impossible to separate. The "Western Willow Flycatcher" has a wider bill with an entirely pale lower mandible and, usually, a whiter throat.

Voice CALL: A *whit* usually softer than the Gray's. Frequently gives a mournful *dew-hic* on breeding grounds, particularly early and late in day. SONG: Several phrases consisting of a quick, clear high *sillit;* a rough, upslurred *ggr-reep;* another high *sillit* that may be omitted; and a clear, high *pweet,* which is reminiscent of the male Pacific-slope Flycatcher's contact note. This song is often confused with that of the Hammond's Flycatcher, but the Hammond's song never has the high, clear notes characteristic of the Dusky's song.

Status & Distribution Common. BREEDING: Open woodlands and brushy mountainsides. MIGRATION: Spring is mostly early Apr.–early June; most arrive on breeding grounds mid-May. Fall is mostly late July–late Sept. WINTER: Mostly Mexico (southern AZ south to Isthmus of Tehuantepec, Mexico). VAGRANT: Casual to Great Plains and AK. Accidental to DE, AL, WI, and NS.

Population The Breeding Bird Survey shows a significant increase in North America.

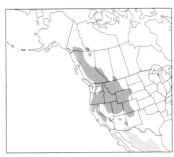

PACIFIC-SLOPE FLYCATCHER *Empidonax difficilis*

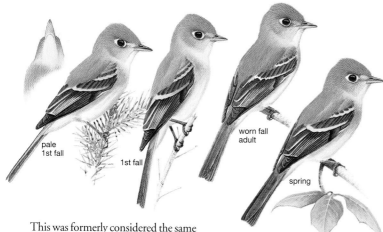

pale
1st fall

1st fall

worn fall
adult

spring

This was formerly considered the same species as the Cordilleran Flycatcher, known as the "Western Flycatcher." The 2 species are extremely similar and all but impossible to identify away from the breeding grounds. "Western Flycatchers" are usually found in shaded areas, even in migration. They tend to be quite active, often flicking the wings and tail. Polytypic (3 ssp.). L 5.5" (14 cm)

Identification Medium-size empid; fairly short primary projection; tail may appear relatively long. Wide bill; entirely yellow-orange to pinkish lower mandible, usually appearing very bright. Most molting on wintering grounds. ADULT: Brownish green above, yellow below, brownish wash across breast. Broad pale eye ring often broken or very narrow above; expands behind eye, giving it an almond shape. Adults usually appear quite worn by mid-summer and during fall migration, with paler upperparts and wing bars and typically reduced eye ring. JUVENILE: Similar but with buffy wing bars, variably pale underparts. Some quite whitish; may be confused with the Least. First prebasic molt on wintering grounds.

Geographic Variation Ranges well defined, but differences in size and plumage weak. Average differences presented, but variation makes it very difficult to identify any one bird in the field. Wide-spread nominate (south to southern CA) has relatively small bill; relatively pale dull olive and yellow plumage with pale lemon wing bars (ochre-buff in juvenile and first-year). *Insulicola* (endemic to Channel Is.) has been suggested as a separate species: relatively dull; relatively long bill; whitish wing bars (buffy in juvenile and first-year); lower-pitched song; male's position note a rising *tsweep,* unlike more slurred mainland vocalizations. The longer-billed, smaller *cineritius* (vagrant to AZ, breeds in southern Baja California) is dingy whitish in color with lemon tone.

Similar Species Virtually identical to the Cordilleran (see species). The Pacific-slope's extensive yellow throat and bright orange-yellow or pink lower mandible are different from those of other western *Empidonax.* The Yellow-bellied is quite similar, but usual range of overlap (AB) is narrow. The Yellow-bellied usually has blacker wings; bolder wing bars and tertial; shorter tail; longer and more staggered primary projection; more uniform, round eye ring, rarely broken above; and more greenish upperparts. Its head tends to be rounder and not as peaked; calls are most reliable characteristic. The Acadian rarely overlaps, but has much longer primary pro-jection, longer and broader bill, narrower eye ring, and more grayish-colored throat. Even a dull fall Pacific-slope is still almost always more yellow below than an Acadian.

Voice Very similar to the Cordilleran's; some vocalizations indistinguishable in the field. CALL: Male's position note in mainland populations is a slurred *tsee-weep;* male's position note on the Channel Islands is rising *tsweep.* Neither as 2-parted as the typical male Cordilleran's position note. SONG: A sharp *tsip;* a thin, high slurred *klseeweee;* a loud *PTIK!* Usually contains 3 separate phrases (usually repeated), all of which are higher pitched and thinner than for other *Empidonax* (except the Cordilleran).

Status & Distribution Common. BREEDING: Moist woodlands, coniferous forests, shady canyons. Often builds nests on human-made structures. MIGRATION: Thought to move more frequently in lowlands during migration than the Cordilleran. Spring is early Mar.–mid.-June. Fall is primarily Aug. and Sept., some into Oct. WINTER: West Mexico, usually at lower elevations than the Cordilleran and closer to the coast. VAGRANT: Out-of-range birds very similar to the Pacific-slope, so identification is extremely difficult and true status as a vagrant is unresolved. Except under exceptional circumstances, vagrants are best considered "Western Flycatchers." Accidental to PA, LA. Some eastern records (e.g., 1 from AL) identified only as "Western Flycatchers."

Population Little information.

CORDILLERAN FLYCATCHER *Empidonax occidentalis*

This was formerly considered the same species as the Cordilleran Flycatcher, known as the "Western Flycatcher." The 2 species are extremely similar and all but impossible to identify away from the breeding grounds. Polytypic (2 ssp.; 1 in N.A.). L 5.8" (15 cm)

Identification Essentially identical to the Pacific-slope Flycatcher, the Cordilleran Flycatcher is only readily identifiable by range and by the male's 2-note *tee-seet* contact call. Average differences in the song and other call notes are described below, but these may be matched by the Pacific-slope Fly-catcher. Some Cordilleran Flycatchers at least occasionally give contact notes that are indistinguishable from classic position notes of the Pacific-slope Flycatcher. In most cases, male Cordilleran Flycatchers will eventually give more classic 2-part calls. On average, the Cordilleran Flycatcher is

spring

slightly larger, darker, more green above, and more olive and yellow below, with slightly shorter bill. As with the Pacific-slope Flycatcher, most molting takes place on the wintering grounds. The first prebasic and pre-alternate molt averages more extensive in the Cordilleran Flycatcher, but this not evident in the field. (The only ssp. in N.A. is *helmayri*.)

Similar Species Essentially identical to the Pacific-slope Flycatcher. Average differences presented above, but individual variation makes it impossible to identify any one individual by anything other than range or vocalizations. See the Pacific-slope Flycatcher for separation from other *Empidonax*.

Voice Extremely similar to the Pacific-slope Flycatcher's. CALL: In the Cordilleran, usually a 2-note *tee-seet*. The male's position note is the most distinctive difference between the Pacific-slope and the Cordilleran Flycatchers. A minority of Cordillerans give position notes, at least occasionally, that are extremely similar to those given by Pacific-slope Flycatchers from the Channel Islands or the mainland. The whistled *seet* note often seems sharper in the Cordilleran than in the Pacific-slope. SONG: Very similar to the Pacific-slope Flycatcher's song, but the first note of the first phrase is higher than the second note.

Status & Distribution Common. BREEDING: Coniferous forests and canyons of the west. Often nests on cabins and other human-made structures. MIGRATION: Generally considered rare in lowlands during migration, even within core breeding range. Spring migration is late Apr.–early June; fall is primarily Aug. and Sept., some into Oct. WINTER: Mexico, usually in foothills above 600 meters. VAGRANT: Extreme similarity to the Pacific-slope makes the identification of out-of-range birds extremely difficult, so true status as a vagrant is unresolved. Thought to be casual on Great Plains, mostly in fall; however many of these records could pertain to the Pacific-slope. Except under exceptional circumstances, vagrants are best considered the "Western Flycatcher." Accidental to LA.

Population Little information.

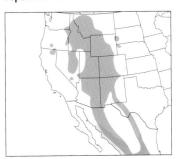

BUFF-BREASTED FLYCATCHER *Empidonax fulvifrons*

worn summer adult

fresh

The Buff-breasted Flycatcher, the most distinctive *Empidonax*, reaches north of the Mexico border, where it is found locally in southeastern Arizona. Polytypic (6 ssp.). L 5" (13 cm)

Identification Smallest empids in N.A. Short, small bill; appears entirely pale orange from below; fairly long primary projection. Birds molt before leaving for wintering grounds. ADULT: Warm brown above with bright cinnamon buff wash to breast; throat paler, but blends into face. Whitish eye ring often somewhat almond shaped; pale wing bars. Worn summer birds paler, more grayish above, usually with at least a hint of buff across breast. JUVENILE: Similar but with duller upperparts, well-defined buffy wing bars. First prebasic molt occurs mostly on breeding grounds.

Geographic Variation The *pygmaeus* (AZ and NM) has relatively dark brownish upperparts, often tinged with gray. The larger nominate (a vagrant to south TX) has pale brownish upperparts, often washed with olive.

Similar Species Distinctive. Even dullest birds usually have a light buff wash to breast. Vagrant Tufted is much richer and deeper cinnamon in color and has a distinctive crest.

Voice CALL: A soft to sharp *pwic* or *pwit*, sharper and higher than casual whit of the Dusky. SONG: Jerky, with 2 phrases that are repeated one after the other: *chiky-whew, chee-lick.*

Status & Distribution Very local in Huachuca and Chiricahua Mountains of AZ. Now casual in U.S. outside AZ, but recently recorded in Peloncillo Mountains, NM. A small outpost also found at Davis Mountains Preserve, TX, where breeding has been detected annually since first TX record was established here in 2000. Northern limit in eastern Mexico is in mountains near Monterrey (within 100–120 mi. of TX). BREEDING: Dry pine and oak woodlands, usually near openings with scattered shrubs. MIGRATION: Casual in migration. Spring migration in AZ early Apr.–mid-May. Fall departs in Aug.–mid-Sept. WINTER: Mexico to central Honduras. VAGRANT: Accidental: accepted sight record from El Paso Co., CO (May 1991).

Population Formerly bred north to central Arizona and west-central New Mexico. No information on trends south of the United States.

PHOEBES Genus *Sayornis*

These plump flycatchers have a distinctive trait of dipping their tails downward. Relatively short-distance migrants, they are found in open habitats, often near water or near human structures and sometimes nesting under overhangs on houses or barns or under bridges. The Vermilion Flycatcher is very closely related and shares many traits with the phoebes.

BLACK PHOEBE *Sayornis nigicans*

juvenile

A distinctive black-and-white phoebe of the southwest, the Black Phoebe is almost always found near water. Polytypic (5 ssp.). L 6.8" (17 cm)

Identification Black head, upperparts, breast; contrasting white belly, undertail coverts. JUVENILE: Plumage briefly held; similar to adult's, but browner, with 2 cinnamon wing bars, cinnamon tips to the feathers on the upperparts.

Geographic Variation. North American *semiatra* (south to western Mexico) has duller and duskier head; birds south of Isthmus of Panama have extensive white in wings.

Similar Species Distinctive. Has hybridized with the Eastern Phoebe (CO); offspring appear intermediate.

Voice CALL: Includes a loud *tseew* and a sharp *tsip*, similar to the Eastern Phoebe's but sounding more plaintive and whistled. SONG: Thin whistled song consists of 2 different 2-syllable phrases: a rising *sa-wee* followed by a falling *sa-sew;* usually strung together one after the other.

Status & Distribution Uncommon to common. BREEDING: Woodlands, parks, suburbs; almost always near water. MIGRATION: Resident over much of range. Breeders return to CO late Mar.–mid-Apr.; depart early Sept. Fall migrants detected on Farallon Islands (CA) early Sept.–late Nov. VAGRANT: Casually appears north and east to northern OR, WA, ID, northern and eastern UT, northern AZ, central TX, OK, and KS. Accidental to FL, southwestern BC, and south-central AK.

Population Increasing, with range slowly spreading north.

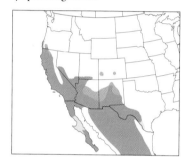

EASTERN PHOEBE *Sayornis phoebe*

The Eastern Phoebe is a rather dull phoebe found in the east and across central Canada. It frequently nests under eaves, bridges, or other overhangs on human-made structures. The Eastern Phoebe is most easily separated from other dull flycatchers by its characteristic habit of dipping its tail in a circular motion. Monotypic. L 7" (18 cm)

Identification The Eastern is brownish gray above; darkest on head, wings, and tail. Its underparts are mostly white, with pale olive wash on sides and breast. Fresh fall adult Easterns are washed with yellow, especially on the belly. Molt occurs on the breed-

worn summer adult

fresh fall

ing grounds. JUVENILE: Plumage is briefly held and similar to the adult's but browner, with 2 cinnamon wing bars and cinnamon tips to the feathers on the upperparts.

Similar Species Pewees are darker and they have longer wings, but they are most easily separated from phoebes by the phoebes' distinctive tail wagging. *Empidonax* flycatchers have eye rings and wing bars, which are absent in the Eastern Phoebe. An *Empidonax* flycatcher flicks its tail upward; only the Gray Flycatcher dips its tail downward.

Voice CALL: Typical call is a sharp *tsip*, similar to the Black Phoebe's. SONG: Distinctive, rough whistled song consists of 2 phrases: *schree-dip* followed by a falling *schree-brrr;* sometimes strung together one after the other.

Status & Distribution Common. BREEDING: Woodlands, farmlands, parks and suburbs; often near water. MIGRATION: Breeders return to the Midwest mid-Mar.–late Apr. and depart late Sept.–early Oct. Rare in fall and winter to CA. VAGRANT: Casual west of the Rocky Mountains and northwestern Great Plains. Accidental to southern YK and northern AK; sight record for England.

Population Apparently stable.

SAY'S PHOEBE *Sayornis saya*

This widespread western species is frequently seen perching on bushes, boulders, fences, and utility wires. Polytypic (4 ssp.; 3 in N.A.). L 7.5" (19 cm)

Identification Grayish brown above; darkest on wings and head, especially lores and behind eye. Breast and throat are paler, more grayish; contrast with tawny-cinnamon belly and undertail coverts. Contrasting black tail is particularly obvious in flight. JUVENILE: Plumage is briefly held. Similar to adult but browner, with 2 cinnamon wing bars and cinnamon tips to the feathers on the upperparts.

Geographic Variation Variation is complicated by individual variation and wear. Compared to more widespread nominate, northwestern breeding *yukonensis* (AK and NT to coastal OR) is smaller billed, with deeper orange underparts and deeper gray upperparts. Resident *quiescens* (deserts of southeastern CA and southwestern AZ) is paler brownish gray above and paler tan or buff on belly.

Similar Species Yellow-bellied kingbirds can appear similar in bright light (esp. the Western Kingbird), but all have a heavier bill, dark mask, yellow belly, and olive upperparts; unlike phoebes, they do not dip the tail. Female and immature Vermilion Flycatchers have a white throat and white chest with brown streaks; most show pale supercilium contrasting with dark auriculars.

Voice CALL: Typical call is a thin, plaintive, whistled, slightly downslurred *pee-ee*. SONG: A fast whistled *pit-tsear,* often given in flight.

Status & Distribution Common. BREEDING: A variety of open and dry habitats from tundra to desert, usually with cliffs, canyons, rocky outcroppings, or human-made structures for nesting. MIGRATION: Early in spring, late in fall. Bulk of migrants arrive from CO to east of the Sierra Nevada in CA late Mar.–mid-Apr.; southern BC late Mar.–mid-Apr.; and AK early to mid-May. In fall, most depart AB late Aug.–early Sept.; CO and OR late Aug.–Sept. VAGRANT: Casual over most of the East (late fall–early winter) with records for every state and province except DE, DC, MD, NH, WV, NU, and PE.

Population Apparently stable.

Genus *Pyrocephalus*

VERMILION FLYCATCHER *Pyrocephalus rubinus*

This stunning bird is usually tame and approachable, frequently pumping and spreading its tail like a phoebe. Polytypic (13 ssp.; 2 in N.A.). L 6" (15 cm)

Identification Striking adult males red and brown. Adult females grayish brown above, darker tail. Note pale throat and supercilium. Streaked pale breast; tawny belly and undertail coverts. JUVENILE: Similar to adult female but spotted below; belly often has yellowish tinge. Immature male begins to acquire red feathers no later than mid-winter.

Geographic Variation Southwestern *flammeus* has paler brown upperparts with a grayish tinge. Head and breast of adult

immature ♀

immature ♂

adult ♀

adult ♂

juvenile

male average more orange-red in color, often with pale mottling. Adult male *mexicanus* (TX) has deep, bright red underparts and darker brown upperparts without grayish tinge.

Similar Species Compare an immature with the Say's and Eastern Phoebes, noting white throat and streaked breast.

Voice CALL: A sharp *pseep.* SONG: A soft tinkling repeated *pit-a-set, pit-a-see, pit-a-see;* often given in fluttery fight display. Also sings while perched.

Status & Distribution Common. BREEDING: Woodlands, parks, suburbs; almost always near water. MIGRATION: Usually returns to northern breeding areas by late Apr.; most depart Sept.–Oct. VAGRANT: Casual, mostly in fall, throughout most of lower 48 (fewest along Canadian border and in northeast) and to ON, NS, and QC. Has bred in CO and OK.

Population Apparently stable.

Genus Myiarchus

These rather big-headed, bushy-crested, relatively slim-bodied, moderately long-tailed flycatchers (22 sp.; 4 breed in U.S.; 2 more occur as vagrants) are easy to recognize by virtue of their upright posture, large all-dark bill, grayish brown upperparts, gray chest, yellowish belly, and often rufous-edged primary and tail feathers. Dark brown wings have 2 pale wing-bars; rufous-edged primaries give the folded wing a prominent rusty wing panel. Moving from perch to perch, they sally to foliage (in wooded habitats, primarily subcanopy) or ground for insects or fruit. Distinctive vocalizations include many daytime calls, which can also be repeated or combined to form male's dawn song.

Identification of *Myiarchus* Flycatchers

The largest and smallest of these species differ in size substantially, but size overlap among most species and overall similar structure and coloration make identification challenging. Overall, males are slightly larger, but this is not appreciable in the field; the sexes are otherwise identical. *Myiarchus* do not have seasonally variable plumage; but because they have only 1 complete molt per year (during late summer or fall), their plumage can become considerably duller and paler during the spring and summer from wear and bleaching.

Great Crested Flycatcher (TX, Apr.)

Young birds leave the nest while growing their juvenal plumage. This first plumage is superficially similar to the adult's but typically paler and of a softer, more delicate feather structure. It may include a more extensively rufous tail (incl. rufous on the outer edges of the feathers) and rusty-edged upperwing and uppertail coverts; secondaries have rusty or buffy edges (adults generally have white or yellow), making the rusty "primary" panel less well defined. In some species, coloration of the secondary edges is an important adult field mark, so individuals must first be correctly aged.

Great Crested Flycatcher (TX, Jun.)

Juvenal plumage is quickly replaced by a more adultlike first basic plumage. Identifications should be made using combinations of characters. Especially important are tail pattern, mouth color, and vocalizations. Determining the extent and pattern of dark brown versus rufous on the tail is vital, particularly for identifying silent individuals in areas of overlap. In adults, the central tail feathers and outer webs of the remaining pairs of feathers are dark brown, so that viewed from above, the closed tail above appears all brown. Depending on species, the inner webs of the outer 5 pairs have varying amounts of rufous and might have a dark "shaft stripe" of varying width along the feather shaft; the rufous is best studied on a perched bird from below, where the pattern of the outermost pair is visible even when the tail is closed. The color of the inside

Ash-throated Flycatcher (CA, May)

of the mouth (mouth lining) is difficult to see in the field but with patience can sometimes be viewed when a bird calls, yawns, or feeds. *Myiarchus* call frequently during the breeding season, and key vocalizations are diagnostic; migrants and wintering birds call much less frequently. Overall size, bill size and proportions, and subtle differences in plumage coloration are important but much more subjective. Species that vary greatly in size or color will be easily distinguishable from each other, but there is extensive overlap among most species. Distance and lighting are also important with such subtle differences; distribution and breeding habitat can also be helpful in elimination.

In general, vagrants are less likely in spring and summer, so identifications are usually safe based on probability during the breeding season in areas where only 1 species normally occurs. This approach works best with the Ash-throated and the Great Crested, which are the only species present across much of the west and east, respectively. All *Myiarchus* breeding in North America are migratory and normally winter south of the U.S. border, except for small numbers of Ash-throateds in the extreme Southwest and the Great Cresteds in southern Florida. Vagrants should be identified with extreme caution. A high percentage of vagrant *Myiarchus* are found during fall and winter, usually in coastal regions. Species normally found in an area as breeders or migrants are not necessarily more likely to occur at the wrong season (e.g., the Great Crested Flycatcher is virtually unrecorded in winter in the east outside of FL). The vast majority of vagrant *Myiarchus* are Ash-throateds, the only vagrant species that has occurred in Canada, most of the interior U.S., and along the Atlantic coast north of Florida. Thus, the Ash-throated should be the first option when trying to identify a vagrant or an out-of-season *Myiarchus*. ∎

DUSKY-CAPPED FLYCATCHER *Myiarchus tuberculifer*

Widespread in the neotropics, our smallest *Myiarchus* barely enters the U.S. Its plaintive call signals its presence in the leafy subcanopy of lower montane forests and woodlands. Range and habitat can overlap with Ash-throated and Brown-crested Flycatchers. Polytypic (13 ssp.). L 6.4–7.3" (16–19 cm) **Identification** ADULT: Grayish brown crown and cheeks contrast somewhat with more grayish olive back. Outer and middle secondaries edged rufous to rusty-yellow; inner secondaries whitish. Upperwing coverts tipped pale

grayish brown, making wing bars less conspicuous than in other species. Gray throat and breast; yellow belly, with relatively sharp gray-yellow contrast; olive-suffused sides. Black, proportionately long, slender bill; paler base of lower mandible. Orange mouth lining. JUVENILE: Similar but duller overall; tail broadly edged rufous on inner webs. **Geographic Variation** Two subspecies reach the U.S.: *olivascens,* described above (southeastern AZ, extreme southwestern NM, and northwestern Mexico), and *lawrenceii* (vagrant from eastern Mexico). The latter is slightly larger and darker above (overall) with contrasting blackish cap, rufous-edged secondaries and upperwing coverts, and more extensive rufous inner edges of tail feathers. **Similar Species** Other superficially similar mainland species are slightly or much larger and have proportionately shorter or thicker bills and more rufous in tail. Ash-throateds and Brown-cresteds have flesh-colored mouth linings, more conspicuous wing bars, and different calls. The La Sagra's has whiter belly, secondary edges, and wing bars. **Voice** CALL: Mournful, descending whistled *peeeeuuuu,* sometimes preceded by *whit* note. DAWN SONG: A continu-

ous series of mixed *whit* notes, whistles, and trills. **Status & Distribution** Fairly common. BREEDING: Lower- and middle-elevation montane riparian, oak, or pine-oak woodlands. MIGRATION: Migrants seldom detected in lowlands. In spring, exceptionally, arrives late Mar.–early Apr., more typically mid-Apr. In fall, most have departed U.S. by mid-Aug., stragglers recorded to mid-Oct. WINTER: Mexico. VAGRANT: Subspecies *olivascens* is a rare migrant and breeder in mountains of western TX; casual to accidental in late fall and winter to coastal CA and OR, in spring to CO; *lawrenceii* is casual in winter in extreme southern TX. **Population** Stable.

ASH-THROATED FLYCATCHER *Myiarchus cinerascens*

This is the "default" *Myiarchus* throughout much of the west. Monotypic. L 7.6–8.6" (19–22 cm) **Identification** ADULT: Relatively small, slender; moderately long tailed. Whitish gray throat, pale gray breast with whitish transition to pale yellow belly. Brown crown and brownish gray back separated by subtle gray collar. Blackish brown wings with 2 whitish wing bars; rufous-edged primaries; secondaries edged white to pale yellow. Outer pairs of tail feathers extensively rufous on inner webs; dark shaft stripe flares at tip so that rufous does not extend to feather tips. Some lack typical tail pattern,

and pattern can vary among feathers. All-dark bill is relatively thin, short to medium length. Mouth lining flesh-color. JUVENILE: Duller and paler; browner above; belly more whitish yellow; rufous-edged secondaries; tail predominantly rufous with dark shaft stripes on outer webs. Some juvenile middle secondaries or tail feathers can be retained into first basic plumage. **Similar Species** Superficially identical to the Brown-crested, which averages darker gray and brighter yellow below, is larger in all aspects, lacks typical Ash-throated tail pattern, and has different voice. Juvenile Ash-throated tail suggests the Great Crested, but size, shape, and plumage should make identification easy. Nutting's best separated by voice, mouth color. **Voice** CALL: *Ka-brick,* soft *prrrrt* (nonbreeders less vocal). DAWN SONG: A repeated series of *ha-wheer* and other notes. **Status & Distribution.** Common. BREEDING: Desert scrub and riparian, oak, or coniferous woodland. MIGRATION: In spring, mid-Mar.–mid-May. In fall,

juvenile

adult

juvenile

Aug.–mid-Sept.; stragglers Oct.–Nov. WINTER: Extreme southwestern U.S. to Honduras. VAGRANT: Rare/casual north to southwestern BC, east to southeastern Canada and to Atlantic and Gulf coasts in the U.S., mainly in fall and winter. **Population:** Stable.

NUTTING'S FLYCATCHER *Myiarchus nuttingi*

This vagrant from Mexico closely resembles the Ash-throated Flycatcher in size, structure, and coloration. It is also superficially very similar to the larger Brown-crested Flycatcher in overall plumage coloration. Identifications are best confirmed by calls and orange-colored mouth lining. Vagrants to the U.S. have occurred in winter, when confusion would be most likely with wintering Ash-throated or Dusky-capped Flycatchers. In Mexico, distri-bution and habitat overlap extensively with Ash-throated and Brown-crested Flycatchers and, to a lesser extent, with Dusky-capped Flycatchers. Polytypic (3 ssp.; *inquietus* in U.S.). L 7.2" (18 cm)

Identification ADULT: Relatively small; small billed. Pure gray breast and bright yellow belly, with abrupt gray-yellow transition. Dull brown face and crown blend to grayish brown back. Outer-most secondary edge is rufous; remaining secondaries range (moving inward) from pale rufous or brownish white to white or grayish white. Tail pattern is variable; typically, the inner webs of the outer 5 pairs of feathers are extensively rufous with a dark shaft stripe of variable width (as in the Ash-throated and the Brown-crested), but the rufous may or may not extend to the feather tip. JUVENILE: Essentially identical to the Ash-throated; some rusty-edged juvenile middle secondaries can be retained in the first basic plumage.

Similar Species Brown-crested (esp. *magister*) and Great Crested Flycatchers are larger and have more extensively rufous tails. The Brown-crested has a flesh-colored mouth lining, a dusky cap, and little or no rufous in its tail; and it is smaller and proportionately longer billed. The Ash-throated, which averages slightly larger, has a flesh-colored mouth lining; longer and more pointed wings; paler underparts with a whitish area between the whitish gray breast and the pale yellow belly; a subtle grayish collar across hindneck; grayer auriculars; and whitish or yellowish white secondary edges. Nutting's Fly-catchers that share the typical Ash-throated pattern on the outer (sixth) pair of tail feathers (e.g., feather tips dark, no rufous to tip) also have a dark shaft stripe on the inner webs of the second pair of feathers (lacking in the Ash-throated).

Voice CALL: A sharp, whistled *wheep* (suggesting the Great-crested) or *peer;* also a *pip.*

Status & Distribution Common in normal range. YEAR-ROUND: Thornscrub and open tropical deciduous forest, from northwestern and central-eastern Mex-ico south to northwestern Costa Rica. VAGRANT: Accidental, 3 recs.: Roosevelt Lake, AZ (Jan. 8, 1952); Patagonia Lake S.P., AZ (Dec. 14, 1997–Mar. 21, 1998); Irvine, CA (Nov. 11, 2000–Mar. 26, 2001).

Population Presumably stable.

GREAT CRESTED FLYCATCHER *Myiarchus crinitus*

This is the "default" *Myiarchus* of east-ern North America. A large, stout-bod-ied species, it is usually heard more frequently than seen as it forages high in the canopy or subcanopy. Mono-typic (previously considered polytyp-ic). L 6.8–8.4" (17–21 cm)

Identification Key characters include a broad white stripe on the innermost secondary, mostly rufous inner webs of tail feathers, and overall darker plumage. Longer winged than other *Myiarchus,* it appears proportionately shorter tailed. ADULT: Dark gray face and breast (slightly paler throat) con-trasts sharply with bright yellow belly;

these colors blend at sides of breast to form olive-green patches. Brown crown blends to olive-brown back. Bill, pro-portionately long and thick, is black with a pale brown base to the lower mandible (most individuals). The mouth lining is bright orange-yellow, occasionally flesh-colored or dull yel-low. JUVENILE: Similar but duller and paler below; olive breast patches less obvious; has rusty secondary edges (but innermost 2–3 edged white) and wing bars. Immature brighter, like adult, but wing bars and most secondary edges still rusty.

Similar Species Pale or bleached Great Cresteds are superficially similar to Brown-cresteds or Ash-throateds, but they still exhibit key field marks. Tails of juvenile Brown-cresteds and Ash-throateds are like the Great Crested's but overall paler and lack broad white stripe on innermost secondary.

Voice CALL: Most familiar is an ascend-ing *whee-eep* but also gives *purr-it* and series of *whit* notes. DAWN SONG: A continuously repeated series of modi-fied *whee-eeps.*

Status & Distribution Common. BREEDING: Deciduous or mixed for-est. MIGRATION: In spring, primarily western circum-Gulf, but some trans-Gulf, mid-Mar.–early June. In fall, both circum- and trans-Gulf, mid-July–mid-Oct. WINTER: Southeastern Mexico to Colombia and Venezuela; also southern FL. VAGRANT: Rare to casual/accidental, mainly in fall, to West Coast, AK, NT, NF, Bermuda, Bahamas, Cuba, and Puerto Rico.

Population Stable.

BROWN-CRESTED FLYCATCHER *Myiarchus tyrannulus*

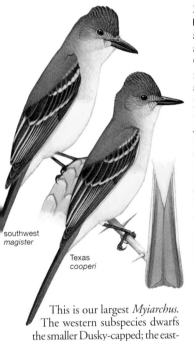

southwest
magister

Texas
cooperi

This is our largest *Myiarchus.* The western subspecies dwarfs the smaller Dusky-capped; the eastern subspecies is closer in size to the Great Crested and the Ash-throated. Brown-cresteds prefer more mature, undisturbed habitats where larger nest cavities are available. Polytypic (7 ssp.; 2 in N.A.). L 7.2–9.2" (18–23 cm)

Identification ADULT: Gray and yellow areas of underparts fairly bright, with abrupt gray-yellow contrast on breast. Outer pairs of tail feathers extensively rufous on inner webs; dark shaft stripes and rufous extend to feather tips. Bill proportionally long, heavy, and black. Mouth lining typically flesh-colored. JUVENILE: Similar, but secondaries (except whitish inner 2) and wing bars are rusty edged and inner webs of tail feathers are more extensively rufous (dark shaft stripe mostly lacking).

Geographic Variation Larger *magister* breeds in Southwest south through western Mexico; smaller *cooperi* breeds in southern Texas and eastern Mexico south to Honduras.

Similar Species The Great Crested has a darker gray face and breast; olive wash on sides of breast; broad white edge to innermost secondary; all-rufous inner webs of tail feathers; orange-yellow mouth lining; and paler base to lower mandible. The smaller, paler Ash-throated has whitish transition between gray and yellow on underparts, and its tail tip is usually dark not rufous. The smaller Nutting's and Dusky-capped have orange mouth lining; the Dusky-capped has much less rufous in tail.

Voice CALL: A sharp *whit.* Breeding, a rough, descending *burrrk* (or rasp) or *whay-burg.* DAWN SONG: Repeated *whit* notes, vibrato whistles, *burrrk* notes, and other complex phrases.

Status & Distribution Common. BREEDING: Riparian forest, thorn woodland, columnar cactus desert. MIGRATION: In spring, arrives in TX exceptionally by mid- to late Mar., more typically early to mid-Apr.; arrives in Southwest late Apr.–early May. In fall, generally departs Aug., rare after mid-Sept. WINTER: Mexico to Honduras. VAGRANT: Casual, mainly fall-winter, to coastal CA *(magister)* and to coastal TX, LA, and FL *(cooperi,* but 1 LA rec. of *magister).*

Population Stable.

LA SAGRA'S FLYCATCHER *Myiarchus sagrae*

A rare visitor to our area from the northern West Indies, the La Sagra's was formerly considered the same species as the Stolid Flycatcher (Jamaica and Hispaniola). More secretive and sluggish than our other *Myiarchus,* it prefers to forage in dense second growth. At first glance, its coloration and more hunched posture may suggest an Eastern Phoebe. Polytypic (2 ssp.). L 7.5–8.5" (19–22 cm)

Identification ADULT: A relatively small *Myiarchus* with a proportionally long, thin, black bill. Pale gray on throat and breast; whitish on belly and undertail coverts, sometimes with a faint tinge of yellow. Pale underparts contrast with relatively dark upperparts; very dark brown crown contrasts slightly with dark grayish brown back. Dull gray wing bars contrast less. Rufous edges to primaries reduced or absent, resulting in less conspicuous rufous primary panel; secondaries thinly edged white. Tail mostly blackish brown; extent of rufous on inner web of outer pairs of feathers ranges from a very narrow fringe to a fairly broad stripe along inner edge. Pale yellow mouth lining. JUVENILE: Very similar to adult; secondaries and tail feathers edged with rufous.

Geographic Variation Both subspecies have occurred in the U.S. At least some (and presumably most) FL records pertain to *lucaysiensis* of the Bahamas, which is larger, with more rufous in tail. The *sagrae* (Cuba and Cayman Is.) is slightly smaller, with less rufous in tail, and has occurred once in Alabama.

Similar Species Other *Myiarchus* are yellower on belly or have more rufous in tail. Size, structure, and tail pattern suggest the Dusky-capped Flycatcher (e.g., relatively small overall, proportionately long bill, and reduced amount of rufous in tail). The smaller-billed Eastern Phoebe lacks rufous in tail and has less conspicuous wing bars.

Voice CALL: High-pitched *wheep, whit,* or *wink,* sometimes doubled; also loud *teer teer,* softer *quip quip quip.* DAWN SONG: A repeated whistle, *tra-hee.*

Status & Distribution Common in normal range. YEAR-ROUND: Pine or mixed woodland, dense scrub and second growth, mangroves; in FL almost always on or near immediate coast. VAGRANT: Casual in southern FL, mainly along extreme southeastern coast and Keys. First recorded in FL in 1982; now about 25 records between late Oct. and mid-May, most during winter. Accidental in inland southwestern AL (Orrville, Sept. 14, 1963).

Population Stable.

Genera *Pitangus, Myiozetetes, Legatus, Myiodynastes,* and *Empidonomus*

GREAT KISKADEE *Pitangus sulphuratus*

This widespread, spectacular neotropical species barely reaches the United States. Its large size, chunky shape, massive black bill, loud voice, and striking plumage of black, white, rufous, and yellow make it unmistakable. Noisy and conspicuous, it employs many foraging tactics (inc. aerial hawking, sallying to foliage, even plunge-diving for aquatic prey); it builds a bulky domed nest with a side entrance, usually situated in the fork of a tree or on a utility pole. Polytypic (10 ssp.; 2 in U.S.). L 9.6" (24 cm)
Identification ADULT: Sexes similar. Black crown surrounded by white; central orange-yellow crown patch (larger in males; not often visible in

the field). Black face contrasts with white supercilium and throat. Rest of underparts bright yellow. Brown back; wings and tail extensively edged rufous.
JUVENILE: Similar but duller; lacks central crown patch; has rustier brown back and more extensive rufous tail and wing edgings.
Geographic Variation *Texanus* breeds in Texas; vagrants to Arizona and New Mexico reported as *derbianus,* which has a more grayish brown back. Record of nominate (CA, 1926) considered unacceptable.
Similar Species This combination of size, shape, and plumage coloration and pattern is unique in North America. The Social Flycatcher has superficially similar plumage but is much smaller and less chunky, with a much smaller bill and less contrasting head pattern; it also lacks rufous on tail and wings.
Voice CALL: Year-round, a loud *crear;* named for breeding season's *KIS-ka-dee;* also a loud, somewhat rising *reeee, chick-weer.* DAWN SONG: A repeated series of typical calls, uttered during twilight.

Status & Distribution Common. YEAR-ROUND: Lowland thorn forest, riparian forest, woodland, desert scrub, even suburban or urban situations; usually near water. Occurs from southern TX and northwestern Mexico to central Argentina. Introduced in Bermuda. VAGRANT: Rare beyond normal range in TX. Casual/accidental in southeastern AZ, southern NM, OK, southwestern KS, and southern LA. Some "vagrant" records involve breeding attempts or single birds that remain in an area for months or years and construct a nest. **Population** Stable; slowly expanding breeding range northward in Texas.

SOCIAL FLYCATCHER *Myiozetetes similis*

This bird has only recently wandered to extreme southern Texas. Polytypic (7 ssp.; 1 in N. A.). L 6.7–7.2" (17–18 cm)
Identification ADULT: Medium size; short black bill. Gray crown; white forehead, eyebrows connect indistinctly across nape; concealed reddish orange central patch; rest of face dark gray. Brownish olive back; blackish brown wings, tail faintly edged yellow. White throat; rest of underparts bright yellow. JUVENILE: Similar but duller; no crown patch;

rusty-edged wings and tail.
Similar Species See the Great Kiskadee for differences.
Voice CALL: Strident *chee cheechee cheechee cheechee;* also harsh *cree-yooo.*
STATUS & DISTRIBUTION Common, Mexico to northeast Argentina. YEAR-ROUND: Open woodland, forest edge, second growth. VAGRANT: Accidental; 1 well-documented rec. in Bentsen-Rio Grande S.P., TX (Jan. 7–14, 2005). **Population** Presumably stable.

PIRATIC FLYCATCHER *Legatus leucophaius*

This neotropical species often chooses a high, conspicuous perch. It bears a superficial resemblance to a miniature Sulphur-bellied Flycatcher and has been detected only a few times in the U.S. Polytypic (2 ssp.). L 6" (15 cm)
Identification ADULT: Sexes similar. Dark brown crown has semiconcealed yellow central crown patch (larger in male) and is bordered by white eyebrows thinly connecting across nape. Blackish brown face; whitish throat with dark

malar streaks. Rest of underparts progressively yellower toward lower belly and undertail coverts; breast and sides have extensive smudgy brown streaks. Dark brown wings and tail; slightly paler back. Wing coverts, secondaries, and tail thinly edged white to pale yellow. JUVENILE: Similar, but lacks crown patch; edges of wing and uppertail coverts tinged rusty.
Geographic Variation Both subspecies at least partially migratory. Most U.S.

records probably pertain to northern *variegatus* (described above), which breeds from southeastern Mexico to Honduras; nominate, breeding from Nicaragua into South America, is smaller and whiter on central underparts.

variegatus

Similar Species The Variegated is larger, with a proportionately longer, narrower bill; pale-based lower mandible; somewhat more well-defined breast streaks; and conspicuously rufous-edged uppertail coverts and tail. The much larger, heavier-billed Sulphur-bellied has an extensively rufous tail. **Voice** CALL: Trilled, often repeated, *pi ri ri ri ri ri.*

Status & Distribution Common. BREEDING: Open woodland, forest edge, clearings. WINTER: S.A. VAGRANT: Accidental (spring, fall records) to FL, NM, TX. **Population:** Stable.

SULPHUR-BELLIED FLYCATCHER *Myiodynastes luteiventris*

This handsome flycatcher reaches its northern breeding limit in the mountain canyons of southeastern Arizona. A cavity nester that mainly forages in the canopy, the Sulphur-bellied Flycatcher is often more easily located by its squeaky call. It usually stays within the canopy, rather than using exposed perches, but will engage in vigorous aerial pursuits of prey. Monotypic. L 7.2–8" (18–20 cm)

Identification ADULT: Sexes similar. Moderately large overall with heavy, long, mostly black bill and proportionately short tail. Strikingly patterned head: dark mask and malar stripes contrast with whitish superciliary, moustachial stripes, and throat; grayish brown

crown and back have blackish streaks; yellow concealed central crown patch. Uppertail coverts and tail extensively rufous. Dark brown wings with whitish edgings. Blackish chin, connecting malar stripes. Throat lightly streaked blackish. Rest of underparts pale yellow, heavily streaked blackish on breast and sides. JUVENILE: Similar to adult but duller and paler; upperparts more brownish buff; wing feathers edged with cinnamon-buff; yellow crown patch small or absent.

Similar Species Piratic and Variegated Flycatchers are similar but smaller, with proportionately much smaller bills, less distinctly streaked and duller yellow underparts, and less rufous in tail. The very similar Streaked Flycatcher, with migratory northernmost (southern Mexico to Honduras) and southernmost (Argentina and southern Bolivia) populations, is a potential vagrant to N.A. The Streaked Flycatcher lacks the dark chin connection between malar stripes, has a slightly heavier bill with more extensively pale base to lower mandible, and is whiter on belly. **Voice** CALL: Loud *squeez-za* recalls a squeaky toy; also a rasping screech or *weel-yum.* Migrants usually silent. DAWN SONG: Repetitive, warbled *tre-le-re-re* or combinations of other notes.
Status & Distribution Fairly common. BREEDING: Mature sycamore-walnut

dominated riparian forest at lower elevations in mountain canyons. Breeds south to Costa Rica. MIGRATION: Seldom detected in AZ lowlands. For spring, arrives in AZ exceptionally by early–mid-May, more typically late May–early June; typically about 1 month earlier in northeastern Mexico than in northwestern Mexico and AZ (e.g., spring vagrants in TX as early as Apr. 5). For fall, breeders depart AZ by early to mid-Sept. Fall vagrants have been recorded into Oct. and early Nov. WINTER: S.A., along eastern base of Andes from Ecuador to northern Bolivia. VAGRANT: Casual in spring and summer to southern TX (inc. breeding recs.), southeastern CO, southern NV, coastal LA, and the Gulf of Mexico off LA. Casual in fall west to coastal CA and north and east to ON, NB, NL, MA, and along the Gulf Coast in TX, LA, and AL.
Population Stable.

VARIEGATED FLYCATCHER *Empidonomus varius*

This "austral migrant" from S.A. occasionally strays to N.A., where it might be confused with the Sulphur-bellied Flycatcher or the Piratic Flycatcher. Polytypic (2 ssp.; nominate in N.A.). L 7.3" (19 cm)
Identification ADULT: Relatively small, proportionately long tailed. Black crown and mask; crown encircled by white and with concealed yellow central patch. Dark grayish brown back with subtle pale mottling. Blackish brown upper tail coverts; tail conspicuously edged rufous. Blackish brown wings; coverts and secondaries edged white; primaries faintly edged rufous. Dingy white throat, faintly mottled with gray and bordered

by dark malar stripes. Rest of underparts gradually blend to pale yellow on belly and undertail coverts; breast and sides heavily streaked with blackish brown. JUVENILE: Similar, but duller below, browner above; wings extensively edged rufous; lacks crown patch.
Similar Species The Piratic Flycatcher is smaller overall, with a shorter, broader, all-black bill; a shorter tail; more uniform brown back; little rufous in wings or tail; and blurrier breast streaks. The Sulphur-bellied and Streaked Flycatchers are larger overall, heavier billed, more distinctly streaked below, and more extensively rufous on tail. Sulphur-bellied Flycatchers are also more

varius

yellow below.
Voice CALL: High, thin *pseee.*
Status & Distribution Common. VAGRANT: Accidental in ME and ON (late fall), and in TN (spring).
Population Unknown.

KINGBIRDS Genus Tyrannus

These large, open-area birds (9 sp.) are conspicuous and noisy. Often seen on exposed perches or sallying to capture flying insects, they will also hover-glean fruit during migration or winter. They may be solitary or in loose flocks. Divided into 3 basic groups (white-bellied, yellow-bellied, and long-tailed), most are easily identifiable. Only the male sings a dawn song, and only the adults have a colorful, semiconcealed, central crown patch and notched outer primaries. Juveniles have duller, paler, more delicately structured body plumage; and rusty-edged upperwing and uppertail coverts, secondaries, and tail. They molt to more adultlike body plumage by fall but retain juvenile wing and tail feathers.

TROPICAL KINGBIRD *Tyrannus melancholicus*

adults

adult ♂

spring adult ♂

adult ♂
primary tips

This wide-ranging neotropical species has northern breeding limits in southeastern Arizona and in the lower Rio Grande Valley in Texas. Its deeply notched tail, and relatively heavy bill distinguish it from most other yellow-bellied kingbirds. The Couch's (southern TX and eastern Mexico) is virtually identical to the Tropical; voice is the best way to distinguish between them. Extralimital records of silent birds (esp. in the east, where the Couch's is as likely to occur) are difficult to resolve. Polytypic (3 ssp.). L 7.4–9.2" (19–23 cm)
Identification ADULT: Relatively large. Gray head, dark mask; orange-red central crown patch usually not visible. Olive back; blackish brown wings and tail; tail conspicuously notched. White throat blends to olive-yellow on upper

chest and bright yellow on lower chest and belly. JUVENILE: Similar; upperwing and uppertail coverts and tail edged pale cinnamon.
Geographic Variation Slight differences in coloration and wing, tail, and bill length; not safely separable in the field. U.S. breeders and, presumably, most nonbreeding records involve northernmost *satrapa*.
Similar Species The Couch's is slightly larger, slightly shorter; has broader bill, different call, slightly shallower tail notch. On folded wing, Tropical's primary tips visible beyond secondaries appear unevenly spaced (adults). Fresh-plumaged Couch's tends to have a more olive back, paler brown wings and tail (these are subjective and not diagnostic). Other yellow-bellied kingbirds differ in smaller bill; less extensively yellow below, darker above; or more square-ended, differently colored tails.
Voice CALL: High-pitched rapid trill or twitter. DAWN SONG: A repeated combination of 1–2 short *pip* notes followed by a trill.

Status & Distribution Uncommon in U.S., common elsewhere. YEAR-ROUND: Open areas with scattered trees, riparian woodland, forest edge and clearings, even open suburban situations; often near water. MIGRATION: Northwesternmost (AZ, Sonora) and southernmost (southern Bolivia and southeastern Brazil to Argentina) populations migratory. In spring, arrives AZ mid-May. In fall, rare in AZ after mid-Sept.; West Coast vagrant recs. mainly mid-Sept. into winter. WINTER: West-central and east Mexico south; southern TX breeding population present year-round. VAGRANT: Rare to casual but increasingly regular, mainly fall and winter, to West Coast (mainly CA but north to southwestern BC); less frequently inland in southern CA, western AZ, and TX away from areas of local breeding. Accidental in NM, LA, ME, southeastern AK, and Bermuda (May rec. of nominate).
Population Stable or increasing. Slowly expanding breeding range northward; first bred in Arizona in 1938, southern Texas beginning in 1991, and western Texas in 1997.

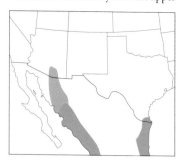

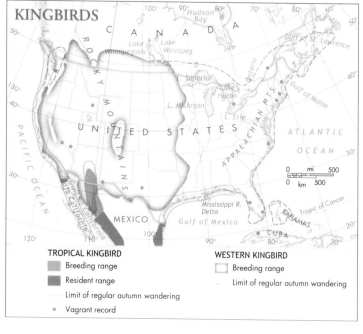

KINGBIRDS

TROPICAL KINGBIRD
- Breeding range
- Resident range
- --- Limit of regular autumn wandering
- • Vagrant record

WESTERN KINGBIRD
- Breeding range
- - Limit of regular autumn wandering

COUCH'S KINGBIRD *Tyrannus couchii*

spring adult ♂

adult ♂

adult ♂ primary tips

This southern Texas specialty was formerly combined with the Tropical Kingbird, with which it coexists in eastern Mexico and northeastern Central America. Virtually identical to the Tropical, it is best confirmed by voice in the field. Most Tropical-type kingbirds found in southern Texas will be Couch's based on probability, whereas breeding birds in Arizona and most western vagrants will almost certainly be Tropicals. During most of the year, both Couch's and Tropicals almost exclusively take aerial prey from exposed perches, but during fall and winter they will also sally to foliage for fruit. Monotypic. L 8–9.6" (20–24 cm)

Identification ADULT: Gray head, with blackish mask and concealed reddish orange central crown patch. Olive-gray back. Blackish brown wings and tail; tail prominently notched. White throat blends to olive-yellow breast and bright yellow belly and undertail coverts. JUVENILE: Similar but with buff tips to upperwing and uppertail coverts.

Similar Species Combination of distinctly notched brownish black tail and olive-yellow breast separate the Couch's from other yellow-bellied kingbirds (except the Tropical). On adult's folded wing, primary tips visible beyond secondaries are evenly spaced (uneven in Tropical). See the Tropical account for other differences.

Voice CALL: Single or slow series of *kip* notes; also *queer* or slurred *chi-queer.* DAWN SONG: A repeated *tuwit, tuwit, tuwitchew.*

Status & Distribution Common. YEAR-ROUND: Thorn and riparian forest, clearings, forest edge, woodland, overgrown fields with scattered trees, even suburban situations. MIGRATION: Partial migrant, with part of northernmost population moving south during winter. In spring, influx of migrants augments the overwintering southern TX population during mid-Mar.–early Apr.

In fall, some of the southern TX population retreats south from late Aug.–mid-Oct., with migratory flocks occasionally seen. VAGRANT: Mainly fall and winter but occasionally spring and summer. Rare in TX outside breeding areas. Casual east to southern LA, including breeding record southwest; accidental to eest in NM, CA, to north in AR and east in FL.

Population Stable or increasing. Since the mid 1900s, the Couch's has expanded range in Texas from immediate vicinity of extreme Lower Rio Grande north to Del Rio, to near San Antonio, and to Calhoun County on coast, with isolated breeding records from Brewster, Bexar, and Travis Counties.

CASSIN'S KINGBIRD *Tyrannus vociferans*

adults

juvenile

worn fall adult

spring adult ♂

adult ♂

The Cassin's is fairly widespread at middle elevations in the southwestern and west-central U.S., where it overlaps extensively with the Western Kingbird. Monotypic. L 8.4–9.2" (21–23 cm)

Identification ADULT: Dark gray head and nape (mask less obvious); semiconcealed orange-red central crown patch; dark grayish olive back, brownish wings. Dark gray chest contrasts with white chin, blends to yellow belly and olive flanks. Tail squared or slightly notched; brownish black with an indistinct pale gray terminal band. Relatively small bill. JUVENILE: Similar but wings edged pale cinnamon and pale tail tip less obvious.

Similar Species The Western has paler upperparts and chest; much less chin-breast contrast; and darker wings and black tail with white outer web of outer feather pair (but beware Westerns completely lacking outer tail feathers or with worn-off outer webs). The Cassin's has pale (but not pure white) outer web. The Thick-billed, Tropical, and Couch's have paler or yellower breasts, uniformly brown tails, and heavier bills; Tropical and Couch's also have paler backs and deeply notched tails.

Voice CALL: Single or repeated, strident *kaBeeR;* rapidly repeated *ki-dih* or *ki-dear.* DAWN SONG: A repeated *rruh rruh rruh-rruh rreahr, rruh ree reeuhr* (poss. confused with the Buff-collared Nightjar's).

Status & Distribution Common. BREEDING: Open, mature woodlands, including riparian, oak, and pinyon-juniper. MIGRATION: Relatively infrequently detected away from breeding sites. In spring, mid-Mar.–early June, peak Apr.–May. In fall, departure late July–Oct., peak Sept. WINTER: Western to central-southern Mexico. Locally resident in coastal southern CA. VAGRANT: Casual/accidental to OR, ON, MA, VA, AR, LA, and FL.

Population Stable.

WESTERN KINGBIRD *Tyrannus verticalis*

juvenile

adults

spring
adult ♂

worn
fall adult

The Western is the "default" breeding yellow-bellied kingbird across vast areas of the west (esp. arid lowlands); but its distribution and habitat overlap with other yellow-bellied kingbirds (the Cassin's, Thick-billed, Tropical, and Couch's) as well as with the Eastern and Scissor-tailed Flycatchers. From exposed perches on trees, shrubs, or wires, it chases and captures flying insects; it will also sally to vegetation or the ground and will take fruit during fall and winter. Monotypic. L 8.1–9.6" (21–24 cm)

Identification ADULT: Pale gray head; darker mask; concealed orange-red central crown patch. Pale grayish olive back. Plain brownish black wings, contrasting paler back. Square-tipped, black tail; white outer webs of outer pair of feathers. White throat subtly blends to pearly gray chest and yellow belly. Relatively small, black bill. JUVENILE: Duller, paler.

Similar Species Typical tail pattern unmistakable, but individuals with worn or missing white outer tail feathers might be mistaken for other yellow-bellied species. The Cassin's is overall much darker on chest, upperparts; has contrasting white chin, paler wings, gray tail tip. The Tropical and Couch's have heavier bills; olive-yellow chests; and dark brown, deeply notched tails. The Cassin's, Tropical, and Couch's also have pale-edged upperwing coverts with a more scalloped appearance. The Thick-billed has much heavier bill, darker upperparts, yellow central crown patch, paler underparts. (Juvenile's underparts yellower, more Western-like.) Superficially similar to juvenile or immature Scissor-tailed, immature white-bellied kingbirds with tinge of yellow on underparts, *Myiarchus*, or Say's Phoebe; but key field marks should still be apparent.

Voice CALL: Single or repeated sharp *kip* notes; also a staccato trill. DAWN SONG: A repeated series of *kip* notes and long trills.

Status & Distribution Common. BREEDING: Open country with scattered trees or shrubs; will nest on human-made structures (e.g., utility poles). MIGRATION: Mid-Mar.–early June; late July–mid-Sept.; scarce after early Oct, stragglers into Nov. WINTER: Central-western Mexico to Costa Rica; also southern FL. VAGRANT: In summer, casual/accidental to AK, central and northern Canada; in winter, rare/casual on Pacific coast to central CA, on Gulf and Atlantic coasts, and to Panama, West Indies, and Bermuda.

Population Stable or increasing.

THICK-BILLED KINGBIRD *Tyrannus crassirostris*

1st fall

1st fall

worn
summer
adult

First recorded in the U.S. in 1958, this West Mexican species now regularly breeds in southeastern Arizona and extreme southwestern New Mexico. Generally stays high in the canopy and sallies after insects from exposed perches. Monotypic. L 8.8–9.6" (22–24 cm)

Identification ADULT: Proportionately long, thick-based bill; pronounced hook. Blackish brown head; slightly darker mask; concealed yellow central crown patch, paler olive-gray back. Dark brown wings; pale-edged upperwing coverts. Dark brown tail, squared or notched slightly. White throat blends to pale gray chest, pale yellow belly, undertail coverts; belly fades to whitish yellow by spring and summer. JUVENILE: Similar but paler above, more prominent mask.

Similar Species Massive bill, white throat, contrasting dark head, and pale yellow to whitish yellow belly make identification easy. Other yellow-bellied species slightly or much smaller billed, with more extensively yellow belly, and different tail patterns and shapes.

Voice CALL: Loud, whistled *kiterREer;* also a rapid trill similar to the Eastern's.

DAWN SONG: Two repeated phrases, *T-t-t-t, t-T-t-tt-rwheeuh-t-tt.*

Status & Distribution Uncommon. BREEDING: Canopy of mature sycamore-cottonwood dominated riparian forest. MIGRATION: In spring, arrives late May–early June. In fall, departs in Sept., rare by Oct. WINTER: Western Mexico. VAGRANT: Casual to accidental, mainly in fall and winter, in western AZ, CA, southwestern BC, northern TX, Baja California; casual in summer to western TX (inc. breeding records) and CO.

Population Stable; range is expanding.

EASTERN KINGBIRD *Tyrannus tyrannus*

This small, white-bellied, conspicuous species has the largest distribution of any North American kingbird. Monotypic. L 7.8–9.2" (20–23 cm)
Identification ADULT: Black head blends to slate gray back; central crown patch varies from red to yellow. Dark gray wings; narrow white edgings to upperwing coverts and secondaries. Black tail with conspicuous white terminal band. White underparts; gray patches on sides of breast, paler gray wash across middle of breast. Extensively gray underwing coverts. JUVENILE: Generally similar but paler grayish brown upperparts contrast with blackish mask; white tail tips narrower.
Similar Species Adults in reasonably fresh plumage are virtually unmis-

juvenile

takable. Immatures and worn adults, both of which can have somewhat paler or browner upperparts and reduced white tail tips, can be superficially similar to Gray or Thick-billeds but would still be overall smaller and smaller billed. Immature Fork-taileds are also superficially similar but have more head-back contrast, a longer tail, and a whiter center of breast.
Voice CALL: Single or variety of *zeer, dzeet,* or trilled notes. DAWN SONG: A series of complex notes and trills, which are repeated over and over, *t'i'tzeer, t'i'tzeer, t'izeetzeetzee.*
Status & Distribution Common. BREEDING: Open areas in a variety of habitats that have trees or shrubs for nest sites. MIGRATION: Diurnal migrant, often observed in loose flocks; at least some trans-Gulf movement. In spring, mid-Mar.–mid-June, peaks mid-Apr.–mid-May; in west mid-May-June. In fall, late July–mid-Oct., peaks mid-Aug.–early Sept.; mostly gone by end of Sept., rare after early Oct. WINTER: S.A., mainly western Amazonia (eastern Ecuador and Peru,

western Brazil), but also casually as far south and east as northern Chile, Argentina, Paraguay, eastern Brazil, and Guyana. VAGRANT: Rare during migration to Pacific coast, southwestern states, Bermuda, Bahamas, Cuba; casual to AK, southern YK, Hudson Bay, central QC, NF, Greenland.
Population Generally stable; relatively tolerant of human disturbances.

GRAY KINGBIRD *Tyrannus dominicensis*

This mainly West Indian species is a conspicuous summer resident of coastal Florida and, locally, along the eastern Gulf Coast, where it overlaps with the Eastern Kingbird. Monotypic. L 9.2–9.6" (23–24 cm)
Identification ADULT: Relatively large and large billed. Uniformly gray head and back except for contrasting dark mask and orange to reddish orange central crown patch. Blackish brown upperwings and tail; upperwing

coverts edged pale gray to grayish white; and secondaries edged white to yellowish white. Tail distinctly notched. Underparts white with grayish wash across chest and down sides; lower belly and undertail coverts sometimes tinged pale yellow. JUVENILE: Similar but more brownish gray on back, with rusty-edged upperwing and uppertail coverts and tail feathers.
Similar Species The Eastern is overall smaller and darker above, has obvious white tail tip, and lacks tail notch. The yellow-tinged immature Gray is superficially similar to the Thick-billed, but the latter would be heavier billed, yellower below and darker above, without the notched tail. The Loggerhead Shrike has a shorter, hooked bill and white on wings and tail.
Voice CALL: *Pe-CHEER-ry;* also a rapid trill similar to the Eastern's. DAWN SONG: Poorly known; described as "complex chatter."
Status & Distribution Rare to fairly common. BREEDING: Mangroves, open woodland, second growth, forest edge, mainly along immediate coast, includ-

ing suburban situations. MIGRATION: In spring, arrives southern FL mid-Mar., elsewhere along Gulf and southern Atlantic coasts mid-Apr.–early May; stragglers into June. In fall, departs mid-Sept.–Oct. WINTER: Central and southern West Indies, central and eastern Panama, and extreme northern S.A.; rare southern FL, northern West Indies. VAGRANT: Casual, mainly in spring, west to LA (recent breeding recs.) and TX, north to Canadian Maritimes; accidental to southwestern BC, WI, IL, MI, ON, and central NY.
Population Stable; expanding breeding range westward along Gulf Coast.

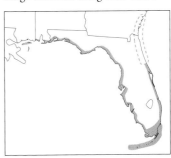

SCISSOR-TAILED FLYCATCHER *Tyrannus forficatus*

The striking Scissor-tailed Flycatcher is our only regular "long-tailed kingbird." It is not only graceful and beautiful, but also common and easy to observe. Monotypic. L 10–14.8" (25–38 cm)

Identification ADULT: Medium-size with a long, forked tail. The male's tail is longer than the female's. Entirely pale gray head and back; extensive white in outer tail contrasts with blackish upperwings and central tail. Whitish underparts; pinkish wash on belly. Salmon to salmon-pink sides, flanks, and underwing coverts; bright red axillaries. Female duller; red crown patch reduced or absent. JUVENILE: Duller yellowish pink on underparts; tail much shorter. Immature generally similar to adult female.

Similar Species Adult is unmistakable. Immature is superficially like the Western Kingbird, but it lacks pure yellow tones on belly and its tail is proportionately longer, narrower, forked, more extensively white.

Voice CALL: Sharp *bik* or *pup;* also a chatter. DAWN SONG: A repeated series of *bik* notes interspersed with *perleep* or *peroo* notes; given when perched or during display flight.

Status & Distribution Common. BREEDING: Open country with scattered trees and shrubs. MIGRATION: In spring, arrives mid-Mar.–early Apr., peaks Apr.–early May, stragglers to June. In fall, begins early Aug., peaks mid-Sept.–late Oct., stragglers into Nov. WINTER: Southern FL, southern Mexico to central Costa Rica, occasionally southwestern Panama. Rare in TX, LA; even locally regular central-south TX, extreme southeastern LA. VAGRANT: Rare to casual, mainly in spring, to Pacific coast, southeastern AK, southern Canada, Atlantic coast.

Population Stable; gradual range expansion to North and East.

juvenile

juvenile

adult ♂

adult ♂

FORK-TAILED FLYCATCHER *Tyrannus savana*

This distinctive, handsome, common neotropical counterpart of the Scissor-tailed Flycatcher is a much sought-after vagrant to North America. Polytypic (4 ssp.; 2 in N.A.). L 14.5" (37 cm)

Identification ADULT: Unmistakable. Overall relatively small bodied compared to other kingbirds, with a proportionately short, thin, narrow bill and a proportionately very long, narrow, forked, mostly black tail. Black head contrasts with pale gray back and white underparts. Yellow central crown patch. JUVENILE: Similar but much shorter tail, duller black head; upperwing and uppertail coverts and central tail feathers edged with rufous. Immature similar.

Geographic Variation Most of the more than 100 records in N.A. pertain to nominate *savana* (illus. and described above), which has on average a darker back and less head-back contrast. Presumably, these records represent "overshooting" northbound austral migrants from southernmost South American breeding populations (occurring here May–July) or "reverse" spring austral migrants (originating from northern S.A. and occurring here late Aug.–early Dec.). Northern *monachus,* occurring from southeastern Mexico to Panama, has been documented at least twice in early winter in southern Texas; it has a somewhat paler gray back, and its more distinct white collar separates the crown and back, resulting in more head-back contrast. There are also subspecific differences in the notching pattern of the outer primary tips (adults).

Similar Species The structurally similar Scissor-tailed Flycatcher lacks the black cap and has salmon-pink on underparts and extensive whitish in tail. The superficially similar Eastern Kingbird is larger and uniformly dark above and has a shorter, broader, white-tipped tail.

Voice CALL: A sharp *bik* or *plick* and a chattering trill.

Status & Distribution Common. YEAR-ROUND: Open grassland, scrub, farmland, pine savanna. Generally present year-round from southeastern Mexico to central S.A. Breeds as far south as central Argentina during austral summer; generally absent as a breeder across Amazonia, but widespread during austral winter. Locally migratory or nomadic in Mexico and C.A. VAGRANT: Casual/accidental, scattered records north to CA, WA, ID, AB, MN, WI, MI, ON, QC, NB, NS; majority of records from eastern N.A.

Population Stable.

adult

BECARDS Genus Pachyramphus

Becards (16 sp.) are sometimes placed with cotingas. Small- to medium-size, they are chunky, slightly crested, and proportionately large headed and short tailed. Typically found in forest or woodland canopy, they are sluggish, almost vireo-like, and perch with an upright posture and sally short distances with fluttery flight for fruit or insects.

ROSE-THROATED BECARD Pachyramphus aglaiae

A widespread tropical lowland species found in the U.S. only in southeastern Arizona and, occasionally, southern Texas, this canopy dweller is sometimes easier to find by locating and staking out its peculiar, globular nest suspended from the tip of a high branch. Polytypic (8 ssp.; 2 in N.A.). L 7.3" (19 cm).
Identification ADULT: Relatively small; short, thick, dark bill. MALE: Black crown; remainder of upperparts plain dark gray; light gray underparts with pink throat patch. FEMALE: Slate gray cap; pale rufous hindneck collar; brownish gray back; light buffy underparts. JUVENILE: Similar to female. First-year male more patchy gray and brown; has smaller pink throat patch.

Geographic Variation Subspecies *albiventris* (northwest Mexico; described above) breeds north to Arizona; *gravis* (eastern Mexico; stray and irregular breeder in southern TX) is larger. Male overall substantially darker, with more extensively black crown and more extensive, darker pink throat patch; female with rufous back, upperwings, and tail; more intensely rufescent below.
Similar Species None.
Voice CALL: Plaintive, descending *tseeeuuuu*, also a *pik* or *pidik* and a trill. DAWN SONG: A repeated, plaintive *see-cheew, wee-chew*.
Status & Distribution Rare to uncommon in U.S. BREEDING: Mature riparian forest in lowlands and lower mountain canyons. MIGRATION: In AZ seldom recorded away from known breeding localities; earliest arrivals mid-May, depart by mid-Sept. WINTER: Northernmost populations move south into areas of year-round occurrence, from southern Sonora and Nuevo Leon south to northwestern Costa Rica, rarely to western Panama. VAGRANT: Casual in

extreme southern TX, mainly in winter, but a few unsuccessful summer breeding attempts; a few records north to Jeff Davis, Kenedy, and Aransas Counties.
Population Presumably stable; peripheral U.S. populations very small and local.

1st fall ♂

♀

albiventris

adult ♂

gravis adult ♂

gravis ♀

TITYRAS Genus Tityra

These cavity-nesting neotropical species are sometimes considered cotingas. Large, chunky, and boldly patterned, they have relatively short tails, heavy hooked bills, and bare reddish facial skin (2 sp.). There is some sexual dimorphism. *Tityra* are usually observed on exposed perches or in fruiting trees in the canopy of lowland forest and woodland.

MASKED TITYRA Tityra semifasciata

Common to our south, this unmistakable species has been found only once in the U.S. Polytypic (8 ssp.; *personata* in N.A.). L 9" (23 cm)
Identification MALE: Generally pale gray above (inc. inner secondaries, tertials, and upperwing coverts). Whitish gray below, including underwing coverts. Starkly contrasting black on face, most of wings, and thick subterminal tail band. Bare-skinned facial spectacles and base of heavy bill are pinkish red; tip of bill is black; eye is red. FEMALE: Darker and browner on head and back; darker gray tail contrasts less with black subterminal band; lacks black face.

JUVENILE: Like female but with subtle darker streaks on crown and back, and whitish edges to inner secondaries, tertials, and upperwing coverts.
Similar Species No other passerine with similar plumage pattern or soft-part colors.
Voice CALL: A double, nasal grunt, *zzzr zzzrt*, given when perched or in flight; reminiscent of Dickcissel's call.
Status & Distribution Common. YEAR-ROUND: Lowland tropical forest and woodland from northern Mexico (southern Sonora and southern Tamaulipas) to S.A. VAGRANT: Accidental, 1 rec., Bentsen-Rio Grande

adult ♂

S.P., TX (Feb. 17–Mar. 10 1990).
Population Presumably stable.

SHRIKES Family Laniidae

Loggerhead Shrike (CA, Apr.)

W hat could be more incongruous than predators that attack mice, bats, birds, and insects, yet sing a soft catbird-like song? Add to this their habit of impaling prey and one gets extraordinarily fascinating birds.

Structure Shrikes' morphology is designed for carnivorous, raptor-like capturing and killing: broad wings and a long tail combine for speed and maneuverability; large jaws and powerful, hooked bills enable them to break the necks of their prey and carry them away. The legs and feet of shrikes are much weaker than those of true raptors and are of little use in hunting, although they occasionally do grab and carry small prey with their feet.

Behavior From an elevated perch, a shrike may watch attentively over long periods for prey. It strikes in a smooth movement, swooping down, attacking quickly, and carrying its quarry to another perch. Impaling prey on sharp objects may serve various purposes, including storage for a later meal, holding the food to tear it apart, and perhaps marking territory.

Plumage The Northern and Loggerhead Shrikes (residents of North America) are patterned distinctively in black, gray, and white with black masks. Both are gray above and paler below, with black wings marked by white patches and long, black, white-edged tails.

Distribution Of the 100 Laniidae species worldwide, about 30 are "true" shrikes. These are distributed mainly in the Northern Hemisphere, although the ranges of some extend well south in Africa.

Taxonomy Shrikes are so different from other birds that their placement within the passerine order has been unsettled. Previously placed between waxwings and starlings, they were moved more recently to a position between flycatchers and vireos. There is no consensus in classification within species; most ornithologists have recognized 2 subspecies of Northern, and 9 or 10 of Loggerhead, in North America.

Conservation Many species around the globe are in trouble, some seriously. Suggested causes include loss of habitat, elimination of prey by pesticides, warming climate, and trapping for food in Southeast Asia. In the United States and Canada, 2 Loggerhead subspecies are listed as endangered and 1 as threatened. —*Paul Hess*

Genus *Lanius*

BROWN SHRIKE *Lanius cristatus*

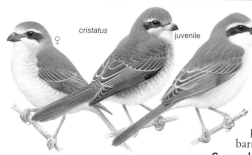

cristatus   juvenile   ♂   ♀

This small Asian vagrant usually perches on the side of a bush or tree and feeds primarily on insects, worms, and spiders. Polytypic (4 ssp.). L 7" (18 cm)

Identification No white patch on wings. ADULT MALE: Warm brown upperparts; brighter rump and uppertail coverts; buffy underparts; narrow black mask; white supercilium. ADULT FEMALE: Mask less distinct; sides, flanks barred pale brown. JUVENILE: Mask limited to brown ear coverts; upperparts, sides, flanks faintly barred; wings edged whitish.

Geographic Variation Given its range, nominate most likely to occur in N.A.

Similar Species Juvenile Northern (only brownish shrike in N.A.) is larger, longer billed, distinctly barred across underparts. Three other Old World shrikes *(tigrinus, collurio, isabellinus),* though not recorded in N.A., should be separated when identifying this species.

Voice CALL: Harsh *chacks* and *churucks.* SONG: Soft warbles interspersed with sharp notes.

Status & Distribution Common in Asia. BREEDING: Forest edges and open areas with bushes in Siberia, China, and Japan. WINTER: Similar habitats in India, Southeast Asia, and East Indies. VAGRANT: Casual in N.A. (5 recs. in AK, 2 in CA, 1 in NS). Of 6 fall records, all but the NS bird were juveniles. Accidental in Europe

Population Declining. Causes unclear, although habitat loss and trapping for food may account for declines in Southeast Asia.

NORTHERN SHRIKE *Lanius excubitor*

At a distance this hunter may appear kestrel-like, but it perches more horizontally and ceaselessly bobs its tail. It is usually seen during large winter irruptions as it scans from a treetop or shrub. Spotting a small bird, mammal, or insect, it swoops in a short burst or makes a long aerial pursuit to catch prey in its bill or feet. It occasionally prowls in bushes. Long flights are marked by fast wingbeats sometimes interspersed with short glides; undulating. Polytypic. L 10" (25 cm)

Identification ADULT: Pale gray upperparts; long, heavy, sharply hooked bill; black, narrow mask, tapering on lores; white forehead; black wings with white patch across base of primaries; grayish white underparts; long, black, white-edged tail. FIRST-WINTER: Slight brownish tint, grayish as season pro-

adult

immature

juvenile

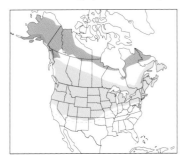

gresses; mask indistinct; underparts barred pale brown. JUVENILE: Brownish overall; dark brown patch behind eye; underparts conspicuously barred.

Geographic Variation Seven Eurasian subspecies (known as the Great Gray Shrike) and one generally recognized in North America *(borealis)* vary in size, plumage coloration. Populations breeding from Iberia and North Africa to China and India have been split as the Southern Gray Shrike *(meridionalis)*.

Similar Species The Loggerhead is smaller, smaller billed, darker on back; its mask extends thinly across forehead. In flight, either might be mistaken for the Northern Mockingbird. The shrike's white wing patch is confined to pri-

maries; the mockingbird's is larger and includes greater coverts.

Voice CALL: Loud *keek, shak,* other sharp sounds. SONG: Soft, catbird-like trills, twitters, whistles, warbles, mews, squeaks, and harsh notes.

Status & Distribution Uncommon. BREEDING: On taiga and edge of tundra. MIGRATION: Regularly moves short distances south of breeding range; irregularly invades northern U.S. in late fall and winter. WINTER: Regular in northern AZ, NM, and TX. Has occurred to southern CA, and to TN and NC. Casual in Bermuda.

Population The trend in North America is unknown because of remote breeding range, but declines in Europe.

LOGGERHEAD SHRIKE *Lanius ludovicianus*

juvenile

adults

This lively little predator occurs in many habitats, from remote deserts to suburban areas, where it perches on trees, shrubs, poles, fences, and utility wires. It captures small rodents and birds but favors large insects, typically swooping down smoothly, cruising low, and then flying up abruptly to another perch. Polytypic (7–9 ssp.). L 9" (23 cm)

Identification ADULT: Medium-gray upperparts; stubby bill; wide black mask extends thinly across forehead; black wings, white patch across base of primaries; grayish white underparts; black tail, edged white. JUVENILE: Paler gray with slight brownish tint; faintly barred overall; scapulars, wing feathers edged pale.

Geographic Variation Subspecies differ slightly in bill shape and overall coloration; *mearnsi* (San Clemente Is., CA) has darkest gray upperparts.

Similar Species The Northern is larger, paler, and larger billed; its mask does not extend across forehead. In flight, either might be mistaken for the Northern Mockingbird. (See the Northern Shrike.)

Voice CALL: Harsh *kee, kaak,* and *chek* sounds. SONG: Repeated chirps, squeaks, warbles, buzzes, and chips.

Status & Distribution YEAR-ROUND: Open country with scattered trees and shrubs, desert scrub, grasslands, farms, parks, suburban neighborhoods. MIGRATION & WINTER: Northernmost birds move into southerly portions of range.

Population Declining rapidly in most regions. Still fairly common over much of range, but *migrans* is rare to very rare in eastern Midwest and Northeast. In U.S., *mearnsi* is listed as endangered; in Canada, *migrans* is endangered and *excubitorides* is threatened.

VIREOS Family Vireonidae

Bell's Vireo (IL, June)

Vireos are known more for their vocal repertoire than their fancy plumage. Fairly small birds, they have green or gray plumage that vaguely resembles that of warblers. A few vireos are colorful, but most blend with their environs—thickets, dense brush, and trees—or have a preference for skulking. As a result, vireos are more often heard than seen.
Structure Vireos are heavily built for a small songbird; some species are almost stocky. Vireo bills are rather thick and blunt, with a hook at the end of the upper mandible. Their legs are thick and strong, usually blue-gray tones.
Behavior The movements of vireos are deliberate. Upon landing, a vireo is likely to hold its position for a few seconds or longer. It frequently cocks and twists its head, scanning its surroundings for food or potential predators. Some species move along branches with tail cocked in the air. Food is mostly insects on the summering grounds, although fruit and seeds are taken; in winter many species eat primarily fruits and seeds. Vireos glean prey from the underside of leaves and limbs and while hovering. They sometimes use their strong legs to hold prey while they eat. Vireos can sing continuously. Some are great mimics; since their songs are learned in the months after hatching, many develop notes from nearby breeding birds (e.g., White-eyed Vireos interjecting notes from Acadian Flycatcher and Western Scrub-Jay). Some species sing for hours, their songs appreciated more for their variation and length than for their melody.
Plumage The sexes look generally alike with differences readily apparent only in the Black-capped Vireo. Some species have more subtle differences between the sexes. Plumages are usually similar all year, although most species are brighter in fresh fall feathers after molting (which occurs on the breeding grounds). Vireos are typically gray or green above, white or yellowish below. Keys to identification are: the presence or absence of wing bars, distinctiveness of wing bars; presence of an eye ring and spectacles, presence of supercilia, and presence and boldness of adjacent eye lines or lateral crown stripes.
Distribution Widely distributed across the United States and Canada; nearly all vireos are migratory. Some species undertake short migrations; others move from Canada to the Amazon Basin.
Taxonomy Approximately 50 species of vireos, a New World family, have been described, but vireo taxonomy is evolving. Work is ongoing to determine if some species might involve multiple species (e.g., Hutton's). The North American species are all currently placed in the genus *Vireo*. While superficially similar to warblers, vireos are most closely related to shrikes (Laniidae).
Conservation Many vireo species are susceptible to Brown-headed Cowbird parasitism; local programs to prevent such parasitism have resulted in strong population rebounds. Habitat changes or losses impact several species. BirdLife International lists 3 species as threatened and 2 others as near threatened. —*Matthew T. Heindel*

Genus *Vireo*

THICK-BILLED VIREO *Vireo crassirostris*

crassirostris

This Caribbean species is a casual visitor to southeastern Florida from the Bahamas. Polytypic (all FL records presumably of nominate *crassirostris*). L 5.5"(14 cm)
Identification Bigger than White-eyed Vireo, with larger, slightly stouter and grayer bill. Thick-billed is olive-brown above, occasionally showing some grayish olive on sides of neck or auriculars. The yellow eye ring is broken above the eye, and the yellow supraloral mark is particularly thick. There are 2 bold whitish wing bars. The underparts are dull and rather uniform pale olive-brown, with whitish undertail coverts.
Similar Species Many reports from southeastern Florida are probably misidentified White-eyed Vireos. Note the Thick-billed Vireo's broken eye ring, pale olive throat, lack of gray on nape, and lack of contrasting yellow on flanks. The iris is darker than on the adult White-eyed, but similar to darker-eyed, young White-eyed Vireos.
Voice CALL: Slow and harsh *sheh*, or *chit* notes. SONG: Similar to that of the White-eyed, but harsher.
Status & Distribution Casual in southeastern FL; accidental in Florida Keys. BREEDING: Mangroves and, more commonly in the Bahamas, thickets.

WHITE-EYED VIREO *Vireo griseus*

adults

Florida Keys
maynardi

Explosive song from a thicket or tangle of vines usually announces the White-eyed. Polytypic. L 5" (13 cm)
Identification ADULT: Bold face pattern with yellow spectacles and white iris. Grayish olive above, gray neck and 2 whitish wing bars. Whitish below, washed grayish throat, pale yellow sides and flanks. IMMATURE: Gray or brown iris through fall, rarely longer.
Geographic Variation Three subspecies in North America. Compared to the widespread nominate subspecies, *maynardi* (Florida Keys) is grayer above, with

less yellow below and a larger bill. Subspecies *micrus* (southern TX) is smaller than *maynardi* but similar in color.
Similar Species It can be confused in worn plumage with eastern subspecies of the Bell's; it is smaller, has fainter wing bars and face pattern, and a dark iris. The Thick-billed Vireo is also similar.
Voice CALL: A raspy *sheh-sheh,* often repeated, suggestive of a House Wren. SONG: Loud, often explosive, 5- to 7-note phrase; usually begins and ends with a sharp *chick*. Great mimic.
Status & Distribution Common. BREEDING: Secondary deciduous scrub, wood mar-

gins. MIGRATION: Two southern subspecies largely sedentary. Northernmost breeders of nominate subspecies migratory; southern populations probably resident. In spring, birds wintering in southern states depart Mar., arrive Great Lakes late Apr.–late May. Most fall migrants gone by early Oct., stragglers to early Nov. WINTER: Mexico, Caribbean, and swath of southeastern U.S., with highest density in TX, LA, and central FL. Attempted wintering recorded as far north as southern ON into Dec. VAGRANT: Casual to the West; rare to the Maritimes and NF, primarily in the fall.
Population Cowbird parasitism suspected in current decline in parts of western range.

BELL'S VIREO *Vireo bellii*

Bell's is usually located by its distinctive song, often given from inside dense vegetation. This rather plain, short-winged vireo skulks in low and mid-level thickets frequently bobbing its long tail. Polytypic. L 4.7"(12 cm)
Identification Plumage coloration varies with subspecies. All have 2 ill-defined white wing bars (the lower one more prominent), indistinct white spectacles that are broken in the front and back, and dark lores.
Geographic Variation Four subspecies become progressively greener above and yellower below from west to east. Endangered West Coast *pusillus* is gray-

ish above, whitish below, with a trace of green or yellow in fresh fall birds. Nominate eastern subspecies is greenish above, yellowish below. Southwestern *arizonae* and *medius* are intermediate.
Similar Species Hutton's Vireo is chunkier, with broad wing bars and a kingletlike face pattern. The larger Gray Vireo has a longer tail, poorly defined wing bars, and an eye ring without a hint of spectacles.
Voice CALL: A somewhat nasal, wrenlike *chee*. SONG: Many birds alternate—*cheedle-ee, cheedle-ew;* notes may be sharp or slurred, often delivered in couplets, ending with ascending or descending notes.
Status & Distribution Uncommon to locally common. BREEDING: Moist woodlands, bottomlands, mesquite, and, in Midwest, shrubby areas on prairies. MIGRATION: Seldom seen on migration. First spring arrivals to southern breeding range in late Mar., May to northern breeding locales. Fall migrations occur Aug.–Sept. WINTER:

bellii

west coast
pusillus

Not well known, but primarily Mexico; scattered records for southern tier of states. VAGRANT: Casual north to OR and in Midwest to ON and along Gulf and Atlantic coasts north to NH.
Population Declines in eastern Texas, southern California *(pusillus)*, and Arizona populations due to habitat loss and cowbird parasitism. Recent expansion in northern and eastern portions of range.

BLACK-CAPPED VIREO *Vireo atricapilla (E)*

This endangered, highly sought-after species is arguably our most stunning vireo. Only in the Black-capped do clear differences exist between the plumages of male and female vireos. Its restricted range and its penchant for thick scrub make viewing this species difficult. Small and very active, Blackcaps are unforgettable when viewed. Monotypic. L 4.5" (11 cm)

Identification Both sexes have prominent white spectacles on which the eye ring is broken at the top. Other field marks include 2 yellowish wing bars, a greenish back, and reddish eyes. MALE: Glossy black cap. FEMALE: Slaty gray cap; back and flanks average paler. IMMATURE: Cap gray, with males molting in some black dur-

ing the first year. Eyes brown. Females are more buffy below.

Similar Species Prominent spectacles, smaller size, and secretive behavior distinguish immatures from the Blue-headed Vireo. Some worn immatures might approach dull plumage of the Hutton's, but Black-capped spectacles are much bolder.

Voice CALL: *Tsidik,* recalling Ruby-crowned Kinglet, and *zhree,* like Bewick's Wren. SONG: A hurried, restless *which-er-chee, chur-ee;* 2- or 3-note phrases, repeated with variations. Can be crisp and emphatic, or wren-like chatter. Whisper songs are softer, less warbled. Persistent vocalizer,

adult ♀

adult ♂

immature ♀

singing through the day March through August.

Status & Distribution Endangered. BREEDING: Scrubby deciduous vegetation, usually oaks, in rocky hill country. MIGRATION: Spring migration occurs late Mar. in TX (earliest 13 Mar.), mid to late Apr. in OK. Fall migration occurs Aug.–Sept.; most birds depart by early Sept. WINTER: Pacific slope of Mexico. No U.S. records. VAGRANT: Eastern NE, east-central NM, and southern ON.

Population The species was eliminated from Kansas in the 1930s and now is nearly gone from Oklahoma. Major factors include habitat destruction or deterioration and brood parasitism by Brown-headed Cowbird. Overgrazing removes key vegetation and attracts cowbirds; fire suppression adversely impacts the species.

GRAY VIREO *Vireo vicinior*

The Gray, drab as it may be, is a highly sought-after species. It is an easy bird to miss due to its choice of rather warm, out-of-the-way habitats and its penchant for hiding in undergrowth. It is best located by its persistent vocalizations. The Gray is an active forager and constantly flicks and whips its tail in a manner reminiscent of a gnatcatcher. Monotypic. L 5.5" (14 cm)

Identification Seemingly featureless, the upperparts are gray and the under-

parts are whitish. The Gray has a thin white eye ring and variably pale lores. The wings are brownish gray, with wing bars when fresh, the lower one more prominent. The long tail is gray and edged white. The bill is short and thick, even for a vireo. In fresh fall plumage, the Gray can show the slightest hint of green to the rump and uppertail coverts and a slight yellowish wash along the flanks.

Similar Species The Plumbeous Vireo is similar, especially when worn, but is more boldly marked, has a longer primary projection, and a shorter tail. Compared to the West Coast subspecies of the Bell's *(pusillus),* the larger Gray has a slightly bolder eye ring, heavier bill, and different vocalizations.

Voice CALL: Shrill, descending whistled notes, sometimes delivered in flight. SONG: A series of *chu-wee chu-weet* notes, faster and sweeter than Plumbeous.

Status & Distribution Fairly common, but local. BREEDING: Semiarid foothills and

mountains with a variety of thorn scrub, junipers, or oaks. MIGRATION: Almost never seen. In spring, arrive CA and TX mid–late Mar.; early May in CO. Some fall migrants depart by late Aug., most by early Sept. WINTER: Mostly northwestern Mexico, local in western TX, southern AZ, and a few have recently been discovered in southern CA (Anza-Borrego S.P.). VAGRANT: Casual along southern CA coast and offshore islands, 1 remarkable specimen record for WI (Oct.).

Population Texas population expanding over past 30 years; California's fragmented and reduced in size.

YELLOW-THROATED VIREO *Vireo flavifrons*

This is a large, colorful vireo and a strong, though slow-paced, singer. It moves sluggishly, which combined with its camouflaged coloration, can make it difficult to locate high in the leaves of the tall shade trees it favors. The Yellow-throated often cocks its head as it surveys its surroundings or methodically searches for insects. Monotypic. L 5.5" (14 cm)

Identification The bright yellow spectacles, throat, and breast of this vireo are distinctive. Its wings are dark gray, with 2 bold, white wing bars. The crown and back are olive, rather bright, contrasting with a gray rump. Immature plumage is similar to that of the adult but paler yellow, sometimes with a slightly buffy throat.

Similar Species Unlike other vireos, but compare with Pine Warbler, with which it is confused, particularly in winter. Pine Warbler has a greenish yellow rump, streaked sides, thinner bill, and less complete and distinct spectacles. Vocalizations of the 2 are different—Pine Warblers often give a high, thin note when moving between branches. The Yellow-breasted Chat, a particularly bulky warbler with a bill more suited to a vireo, has white spectacles and lacks wing bars.

Voice CALL: Includes a rapid series of harsh *cheh* notes, similar to those of the "Solitary" Vireo complex. SONG: Slow repetition of *de-a-ree, three-eight;* burry, low-pitched 2- or 3-note phrases separated by long pauses: It often gives a whisper song, which is more warbled and less burry.

Status & Distribution Fairly common. BREEDING: Deciduous and mixed deciduous-coniferous habitats. MIGRATION: Long-distance, trans-Gulf migrant. Early spring migrant, with arrivals in southern states mid–late Mar., mid Apr. farther north, early May in Great Lakes. Fall migrations Aug.–Sept. (migrants noted as early as late July). Latest records are mid-Oct. in northern and middle latitudes, early Nov. in south. WINTER: Tropical lowlands of C.A., Bahamas, and Caribbean to northern S.A. More scarce in U.S. than the numerous reports would suggest. Most reports are misidentified Pine Warblers or Yellow-breasted Chats. Rare in southernmost FL, casual in southern CA, southern TX. VAGRANT: Very rare in the West, more in spring than fall.

Population Apparently stable, with some local fluctuations.

PLUMBEOUS VIREO *Vireo plumbeus*

Formerly part of the "Solitary" Vireo complex—along with Blue-headed and Cassin's—Plumbeous is the grayer, Rocky Mountain species. Appearing large and bulky, the bird moves through trees in a deliberate manner foraging for insects and sings frequently, even in nonbreeding seasons. Polytypic. L 5.3" (13 cm)

Identification A rather colorless species, but with a strong pattern composed of bold white spectacles and wing bars contrasting with lead gray upperparts. Generally white below, except on the sides of breast, which are gray, sometimes tinged olive. The outer tail feathers are broadly edged white, visible from below; the tail looks long on this species. In fresh fall plumage, yellow, if present on the underparts, is restricted to the flanks, and the rump might show a greenish tint.

Similar Species Larger and bigger billed than the Cassin's, with sharper head and throat contrast and gray upperparts. Avoid confusion with worn spring Cassin's, which can be dull gray above and seemingly lack green or yellow. Compare worn summer Plumbeous to the Gray. The Gray has a complete eye ring, but lacks the supraloral mark that completes the spectacles, has a shorter bill, and waves its longer tail like a gnatcatcher. Grays also have short wings and a shorter primary projection.

Voice CALL: *Cheh* notes similar to the Blue-headed. SONG: Burry notes almost indistinguishable from Cassin's, but usually starts with clear notes; more burry sounding than the Blue-headed.

Status & Distribution Fairly common. BREEDING: Montane forests of pine,

and oak-juniper, locally in deciduous woodlands. MIGRATION: Late spring migrant, primarily May. In fall, migrates Sept.–mid-Oct., with stragglers to Nov. WINTER: Primarily Mexico. Rare in southern coastal CA, south-central AZ, casual southern NM, TX. VAGRANT: Spring records from ND, MA, and ON. Fall records from NJ, LA, AB, and NS.

Population Recently found breeding in northwest Nevada, northeastern California, and southeastern Oregon.

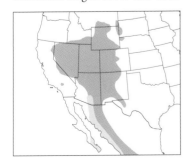

CASSIN'S VIREO *Vireo cassinii*

Cassin's Vireo is the western counterpart of—and formerly considered conspecific with—the Blue-headed Vireo. Cassin's, very similar to the Blue-headed Vireo in both plumage and behavior, is routinely heard singing on the breeding grounds, often throughout the day. The movements and behavior of the Cassin's are like those of the Blue-headed. Occasionally, the Cassin's flicks its wings like a kinglet. Polytypic. L 5" (13 cm)

Identification The olive gray head of the Cassin's contrasts slightly with its greenish back. There is a strong pattern of white spectacles and wing bars (the latter can be yellowish) contrasting with dark upperparts. The bird's flanks are heavily washed with olive-yellow; the throat and breast are whitish, typically dingy. The tail is dark blackish brown above, with olive or gray edges. From below, the outer tail feathers are edged with white when fresh. Sexes generally look alike, although the plumage of males is slightly brighter than that of females. The plumage of immature Cassin's vireos is duller, especially that of females, which can have entirely green heads and lack any white in the tail.

Similar Species Cassin's Vireo is similar to the Blue-headed (see sidebar below). Compare the all-green head of the immature female Cassin's to that of Hutton's Vireo. Note the difference in eye ring, subtle difference to underparts, and vocalizations.

Voice CALL: The call of the Cassin's consists of scold notes similar to those of the Blue-headed. SONG: Jerky 2- to 4-note song almost identical to the song of the Plumbeous; more burry than the Blue-headed. Also very similar to the song of the Yellow-throated Vireo.

Status & Distribution Common. BREEDING: Coniferous and mixed forest. MIGRATION: Early spring migrations typically occur in Mar., peak in late Apr. west of the Sierra Nevada in CA, a little later east of the mountains; early May near Canada east of the Cascades. Fall migrations are more protracted: Aug. (northern populations) to Sept. is the bulk of passage. Lingerers through Oct., particularly on the coast, a few through Nov. Migration is more likely throughout the southwestern and the western Great Plains in fall than in spring. WINTER: Primarily Mexico. Rare in coastal CA, casual in interior CA, southern AZ, NM, and western TX. VAGRANT: The Cassin's is casual north to AK; accidental in the East.

Population Recent increases have been noted in some western populations of Cassin's Vireo.

Cassin's Vireo versus the Blue-headed Vireo

Field identification of these vireos is complex; some birds must be left unidentified. Two main problems exist. First, the Blue-headed in the westernmost part of its range is said to look and sound a bit more like the Cassin's. Second, with both species, adult males are the boldest and brightest, immature females the dullest. While the Blue-headed is more colorful—richer greens, brighter yellows, and more—these characters are not reliable for specific identification. Focus on the following key marks:

1. If the head has a distinct blue cast, it is a Blue-headed. Even bold Cassin's have a lead-gray to olive-gray head. If the head is green, lacking any gray, it is an immature female Cassin's. Any other head color can be matched by both species.

2. While all "Solitary" Vireos are whitish below, many Blue-headed appear brighter white, whereas most Cassin's appear dingy.

Cassin's Vireo, male (CA, Apr.)

Blue-headed Vireo, female/immature (TX, Apr.)

3. All birds show contrast, but on the Blue-headed the transition from dark head to white throat is crisp, particularly noticeable at the lower edge of the auriculars. In the Cassin's these transitions are more blended. This mark takes experience to assess; the differences can be minor.

4. Both species can show white in the tail, but the Blue-headed has more, and all ages and sexes have white. In adult males, the entire outer web of the outermost tail feather is white (with fairly extensive white on the penultimate rectrix), with white wrapping around the tip and forming a broad edge on the inner web. Adult male Cassin's have white; it often covers much of the outer web, but is not as extensive. White is less evident in other age/sex classes.

A combination of marks, studied in good light, is necessary to tell these vireos, as is the ability to leave some unidentified to species. ∎

BLUE-HEADED VIREO *Vireo solitarius*

solitarius ♂

The Blue-headed Vireo is typically found in late spring or summer by its song. It forages at mid-level, yet can be difficult to find among the leaves. In summer it primarily eats insects and appears quite inquisitive, frequently cocking its head as it slowly forages in the branches of a tree. Polytypic. L 5" (13 cm)

Identification The bright blue-gray to gray hood clearly contrasts with a bright olive back and the white spectacles and throat. The wing bars and tertials are yellow-tinged, and the dark secondaries have greenish yellow edges. The tail is dark above, with greenish edges, and white is easily seen in the outer tail from below. The underparts are clean white with bright yellow (sometimes mixed with green) on the sides and flanks. Sexes mostly look alike, but some variation, with adult males being most colorful. IMMATURE: Like adult, but some females are duller. **Geographic Variation** Larger Appalachian *alticola* has more slaty back; only flanks are yellow.

Similar Species Identification is complex; compare to the Plumbeous Vireo and especially the Cassin's (See sidebar, p. 412).

Voice CALL: A nasal *cha-cha-cha-cha*, given as a single *cha* or repeated; a typical vireo scold. SONG: Short, clear notes with various intervals, similar to the Red-eyed, but slower. The Blue-headed Vireo can sing the song of a Yellow-throated Vireo (with which it has hybridized) and is a good mimic (e.g., singing a White-eyed Vireo song or giving a Yellow-bellied Flycatcher call).

Status & Distribution Common BREEDING: Mixed woodlands. MIGRATION: Short-distance (*alticola*) to medium-distance migrant. Earliest vireo to move north in spring, to mid-Atlantic and southern Midwest by mid-Apr.; higher elevations or latitudes not until May. Latest vireo to depart in fall, more protracted migration in fall. Most migration starts mid to late Sept. away from Appalachians. Not expected in southern states until Oct. Midwest peak late Sept.–early Oct., some remain into Nov. WINTER: Winters in southern states south to northern C.A. Rare north of mapped range. VAGRANT: Annual to the West, primarily CA in fall (most records Oct.), casual there in winter and spring. Casual in other western states.

Population Overall increases in recent years, with some local declines due to habitat destruction.

HUTTON'S VIREO *Vireo huttoni*

This active vireo often flicks its wings in a kingletlike manner. Its thicker bill is the first clue that this is not a kinglet; otherwise, the 2 can be confused. Quite vocal, the Hutton's is often heard before seen as it forages in thick trees and shrubs. Outside the breeding season, Hutton's vireos form mixed-species flocks. Polytypic. L 5" (13 cm)

Identification Similar to Ruby-crowned Kinglet. The Hutton's is greenish to olive gray above, with an eye ring broken above eye; pale lores. Two whitish wing bars; the bright, greenish yellow edges of the secondaries and primaries connect to the lower wing bar.

Geographic Variation Eight named subspecies in North America are divided into Pacific Group and Interior (or Stephen's) Group. Pacific Group birds are smaller and greener. Interior Group birds are larger, paler, and grayer. More than one species might be involved. See map for separate (allopatric) ranges.

Similar Species Most likely to be confused with the Ruby-crowned Kinglet; identify the Hutton's by its larger size, thicker bill, paler lores, and lack of dark area below lower wing bar; darkest part of its wing is between the wing bars. Immature female Cassin's Vireo can be greenish, but has prominent white spectacles and whitish throat.

Voice CALL: Low *chit* and raspy *rheee,* often followed by nasal, descending *rheee-ee-ee-ee.* SONG: Pacific Group birds give a repeated or mixed rising *zu-wee* and descending *zoe zoo.* Interior Group, a harsher *tchurr-ree.*

Status & Distribution Uncommon to fairly common. BREEDING: Mixed evergreens and woodlands, particularly live oaks. YEAR-ROUND: Largely resident, some seasonal dispersal. A larger number of migrant records in fall, as early as July in CA to coastal wintering sites, to lower elevations in the Southwest from early Aug., and to OR valleys Oct.–Feb. VAGRANT: Casual in southeastern CA and southwestern AZ; accidental in western NV.

Population Recent expansion to the Edwards Plateau in Texas.

west coast
huttoni

southwest
stephensi

WARBLING VIREO *Vireo gilvus*

spring
gilvus

fall
gilvus

fall
swainsoni

An unmarked vireo, the Warbling is most often located by its song, which it delivers for hours. The birds tend to work mid and top parts of broad, leafy trees. Polytypic. L 5.5" (14 cm)

Identification Among the dullest of vireos, lacking wing bars and spectacles; gray with brownish or greenish tones to the upper parts. The face pattern is ill-defined, with a dusky postocular stripe and pale lores; white eyebrow lacks a dark upper border. The underparts are typically whitish. FALL: In fresh plumage, greener above with yellow wash on flanks and undertail coverts.

Geographic Variation Two western subspecies, especially *swainsoni,* are smaller than the nominate eastern subspecies, have a slighter bill, and tend to be more olive above with a grayer crown. Eastern and western birds might represent 2 separate species. Two additional subspecies in Mexico.

Similar Species Fall birds greenish above, often with extensive yellow below, and can be confused with the Philadelphia. Yellow on the Warbling restricted to flanks; it lacks dark lores of the Philadelphia and is more likely to be heard calling, particularly in flight.

Voice CALL: A nasal *eahh* mobbing call; typical vireo. Note commonly uttered in flight. SONG: Eastern *gilvus* song is delivered in long, melodious, warbling phrases. Song of western *swainsoni* similar but less musical, higher tones.

Status & Distribution Common. BREEDING: Deciduous woodlands, primarily riparian areas. MIGRATION: Western birds have prolonged spring migration (early Mar.–late May). Eastern subspecies a circum-Gulf migrant, rare on eastern Gulf Coast; arrives mid-Apr. in TX, by early May to Great Lakes. Peak fall migration in northern U.S. late Aug.–mid-Sept. Mostly gone from U.S. by mid-Oct.; stragglers at southern areas to Nov., rarely Dec. WINTER: Mostly Mexico and C.A. Casual to southern CA, southern AZ, and southern LA. VAGRANT: Western AK.

Population Cowbird parasitism implicated in decline of some western populations. Ontario population has recently increased.

PHILADELPHIA VIREO *Vireo philadelphicus*

Not prone to flocking, this smallish green bird is usually seen singly amidst tall, leafy trees. In fresh plumage, this vireo is bright and may suggest a warbler to many birders. Monotypic. L 5.3" (13 cm)

Identification FACE PATTERN: Dull white eyebrow and dark eye line. Green above, with contrasting grayish cap and variably yellow below; palest on belly. No wing bars or spectacles. FALL: Fresh plumage, usually brighter green above and brighter yellow below.

Similar Species The Warbling Vireo is very similar. Note the Philadelphia's dark eye line extending through lores,

darker cap, darker primary coverts, and yellow continuing to center of throat and breast. Some spring Philadelphias can be very dull with detectable yellow only with the best of views. The Tennessee Warbler, superficially similar, has a thinner bill, white undertail coverts (usually), and usually utters high-pitched flight notes while it forages.

Voice CALL: A nasal *ehhh*. Seldom heard away from nesting areas but will respond to "pishing" while on migration. SONG: Resembles that of the Red-eyed Vireo but is generally slower, thinner, and higher-pitched.

Status & Distribution Uncommon. BREEDING: Most northerly breeding vireo; open woodlands, streamside willows and alders. MIGRATION: In spring first arrivals usually mid-Apr. (TX), and early May (Great Lakes); peak late Apr.–early May, and mid-May, respectively. Broad fall migratory path; more numerous in East and Southeast than in spring. Movement late Aug.–mid-Oct.; arrivals in southern states not expected until late Sept.

fall

spring

Lingering birds casual to Nov. WINTER: Southern C.A. Accidental in southern CA. VAGRANT: Casual to mostly rare in the West; primarily in fall (>130 CA records). Two Oct. records for Europe.

Population Disappearance from late successional forest suggests dependence on forest disturbance.

RED-EYED VIREO *Vireo olivaceus*

A large vireo, the Red-eyed is one of the most common songbirds in eastern woodlands. It moves sluggishly through the canopy of broadleaf forests, making it hard to detect, and often picks food by hover-gleaning. It sings incessantly, often throughout the day. Polytypic. L 6" (15 cm)

Identification Bold face pattern with white eyebrow, bordered above and below with black. Ruby red iris of adult visible at close range. Gray to blue-gray crown contrasts with olive back and darker wings and tail. Lacks wing bars. FALL: Flanks and undertail coverts usually washed olive or olive-yellow. IMMATURE: Brown iris; often extensive yellow or olive-yellow wash on undertail coverts and flanks, which

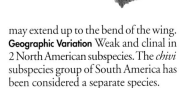

breeding

1st fall

may extend up to the bend of the wing. **Geographic Variation** Weak and clinal in 2 North American subspecies. The *chivi* subspecies group of South America has been considered a separate species.

Similar Species Resembles the Black-whiskered Vireo, but the Red-eyed has a bold, black lateral crown stripe above its white eyebrow; more green above, less brown; red eye (adult); and will not show the diagnostic black whisker. The Yellow-green Vireo can be similar.

Voice CALL: A whining, down-slurred *myahh*. SONG: A deliberate *cheer-o-wit, cher-ee, chit-a wit, de-o;* a persistent singer of a variable series of robinlike short phrases

Status & Distribution Common. BREEDING: Woodlands. MIGRATION: Long-distance migrant. First spring arrivals on Gulf Coast by late Mar., late Apr. in East/Midwest; peaks during Apr. on Gulf Coast, mid-May in East/Midwest. Migration continues into June farther north. Fall migration peaks late Aug. through Sept., most depart by early Oct., some linger to Nov. Southern peak is early Sept.–early Oct. WINTER: Winters in northern S.A. No documented winter records for N.A.—reports at this season suspect. VAGRANT: Rare but annual across Southwest; small numbers annually along CA coast. More than 75 records for Europe, primarily late Sept.–mid-Oct. **Population** Stable. Expanded into Oregon, Utah, and then Newfoundland in the mid-20th century.

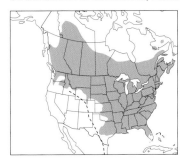

BLACK-WHISKERED VIREO *Vireo altiloquus*

Florida
barbatulus

This Caribbean counterpart of the Red-eyed Vireo is a summer visitor along the Florida coast. Territorial birds are vocal throughout the day, but are heard much more often than seen. Polytypic. L 6.3" (16 cm)

Identification The dark malar stripe can be quite evident at times, but often hard to see, owing to lighting, angle, and wear. The white eyebrow is prominent, bordered below by the black eye

line and above by the gray crown and, sometimes, a faint black border. The bill is large, and the eye is amber. Lacks wing bars and is whitish below, with variable, pale yellow wash on the sides and flanks. IMMATURE: Duller than adult, with buffier underparts.

Geographic Variation Four to 6 subspecies; 2 have occurred in North America. The common breeding subspecies is *barbatulus; altiloquus* (Greater Antilles) is a vagrant with an indistinct, brownish gray eyebrow and even larger bill.

Similar Species Most similar to the Red-eyed Vireo. Compare also to the Yellow-green Vireo and the Yucatan Vireo.

Voice CALL: A thin, unmusical *mew.* SONG: Deliberate 1- to 4-note phrases (most typically 2 to 3 notes); notes are loud and clear, separated by a distinct pause, less varied and more emphatic than the Red-eyed.

Status & Distribution Common. BREEDING: Coastal mangrove swamps and, less commonly, to a few miles inland. MIGRATION: Spring migrants arrive late

Mar.–mid-Apr. Harder to assess fall migrants as males not as vocal. Most depart by early Sept. WINTER: Mostly Amazonia, but limits of subspecies' winter ranges poorly known. VAGRANT: Many vagrant records (and some specimens) pertain to nominate *altiloquus.* NC, VA, but mostly along rest of Gulf Coast from eastern TX to northwestern FL, where casual (some 20 TX recs., mostly from early Apr.–late May). Two TX fall records.

Population: Most Florida populations are stable; the Tampa Bay population has been adversely affected by cowbird parasitism.

YELLOW-GREEN VIREO *Vireo flavoviridis*

The Yellow-green is primarily a Central American and Mexican species sighted along the U.S. border, particularly southern Texas. Behavior and general appearance are similar to the Red-eyed, including the ability to blend into the leaves through which it forages. When agitated, it often cocks its tail and raises its crown feathers. The Yellow-green was split from the Red-eyed taxon in 1987. Polytypic. L 6" (15 cm)

Identification Typically yellowish green above, with rather bold, yellow edgings to the flight feathers; lacks wing bars or spectacles. The head pattern is similar to that of the Red-eyed but more blended—a gray crown blends into the back, and the pale supercilium is bordered by rather indistinct lines. The dark line above the supercilium is often very faint or absent. Underparts are whitish, with a yellow wash to sides and undertail coverts. The yellow continues up the sides of the breast and blends into the ear coverts. The iris is ruby red, and the bill is long, often with pale coloration on the upper mandible as well as the lower. **FALL:** Brightest in fresh plumage, with more extensive yellow ventrally. **IMMATURE:** Similar to adult but iris is brown.
Geographic Variation Subspecies are weakly differentiated. Nominate *flavoviridis* breeds sparingly in southern Texas and is a vagrant to the eastern Gulf Coast; *hypoleucus* is a vagrant to the West Coast. Other subspecies in Mexico and Central America.

Similar Species Similar to the Red-eyed, but bill longer. Strong yellowish wash on flanks extends to sides of face, while the yellow of the Red-eyed is usually restricted to the flanks. The Yellow-green has a more diffuse face pattern; dark borders to the supercilium reduced or absent. The bill has pale tones (pink, blue) versus the black bill of Red-eyed. Upperparts are more yellowish green, with brighter edges to the remiges. The Black-whiskered is duller, with less green above, substantially less yellow below, and a longer, dark bill. Compare to the Warbling and the Philadelphia.

Voice CALL: A soft, dry *rieh;* chatter often repeated. SONG: A rapid but hesitant series of notes suggestive of a House Sparrow.

Status & Distribution Rare to casual. BREEDING: Very rare, but probably annual breeder in southern TX (Rio Grande Valley). Main breeding range is Mexico south to Panama, primarily utilizing lowland forests and forest edges. MIGRATION: Casual in spring on the upper Gulf Coast (mid-Apr.–May). Now recorded annually from coastal CA (mid-Sept.–Oct.). VAGRANT: Casual to southern AZ and southern NM in summer.

Population Stable, but current studies needed. Reliance on forest edge, in part, protects populations from effects of deforestation.

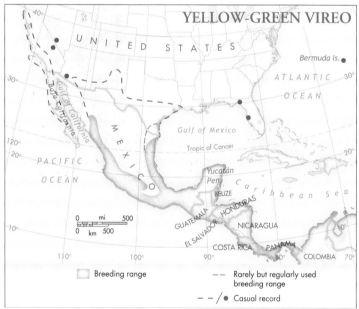

YELLOW-GREEN VIREO

☐ Breeding range

– – Rarely but regularly used breeding range

– – / ● Casual record

YUCATAN VIREO *Vireo magister*

A large brown vireo from the Yucatan Peninsula, it is accidental in the United States. Monotypic. L 6" (15 cm)
Identification Perhaps the most noticeable features are the brown plumage and the large, heavy bill. A broad pale supercilium contrasts with a dark eyeline. Throat and underparts are dull whitish, sometimes tinged buff; sides and flanks are washed with grayish brown. No spectacles or wing bars. Short primary projection, as one would expect with a generally sedentary species.
Similar Species Like a large-billed Red-

eyed that lacks olive tones. Its shorter wings and overall structure give it an ungainly look—very different from the more streamlined Red-eyed. The Yucatan's bill is much larger, and the bird lacks the dark lateral crown stripe and has a brownish (not gray) crown.
Voice CALL: Sharp, nasal *benk* notes, often strung together in a series; also a softer, dry chatter. SONG: Rich phrases, delivered hesitantly.
Status & Distribution Fairly common within home range. YEAR-ROUND: Resident on Yucatan Peninsula and some nearby islands; also Grand Cayman.

VAGRANT: Accidental in TX—1 remarkable record from the upper TX coast, Apr.–May 1984.
Population Current data needed; no indications of concern.

JAYS AND CROWS Family Corvidae

Northwestern Crow (AK, Mar.)

Identification of many species is remarkably easy, but crows and ravens present some of the greatest identification challenges in North America. These problems are often complicated by distant views of birds in flight. Where 2 or more species overlap, birders should focus on bill size and structure, tail shape, and overall proportions. Vocalizations are often the best way of separating similar species. Because everyone hears vocalizations differently, it may be helpful to transcribe your own depictions of vocalizations, noting different calls at different times of year (e.g., juvenile begging calls) and between different populations. Much remains to be learned about regional variation in many species of corvids (e.g., American Crow, Gray Jay), and detailed observations and photographs will aid in our understanding.

Structure Corvids vary considerably in size, but all species have strong legs and feet and a straight bill. Males are generally larger than females. Size differences may occasionally be helpful in sexing paired breeders but are otherwise of little help in sexing birds in the field.

Behavior Corvids are omnivorous, and many species store seeds, nuts, and other foods for consumption during winter months. Some corvids gather in large flocks, particularly during the nonbreeding season. Several species are cooperative breeders, with helpers that assist with nest rearing. Corvids tend to have a diverse array of vocalizations. Most species give a few vocalizations most frequently, but do not be surprised to hear calls not described in this guide. Corvids can also mimic sounds. While jays are most known for hawk imitations, several species give very soft songs into which they incorporate a variety of mimicked sounds.

Plumage Coloration varies considerably, from the brightly colored Green Jay to the grayish coloration of the Clark's Nutcracker and the Gray Jay. Many North American jays are blue, and all crows and ravens are entirely or mostly black. Most corvids appear very similar throughout the year. Sexes are identical. Juvenile plumage is held only briefly and is generally duller but similar to that of the adult. Juveniles and immatures of some species have pale coloration to the bill that they may hold for one or more years. All corvids undergo a single annual (prebasic) molt after breeding. The first prebasic molt is usually partial; adult prebasic molts are complete. In some species first-year birds may be aged by looking for differences in wear in the wing coverts. Crows and ravens retain juvenal flight feathers for one year. By spring immatures are often quite worn, and retained brownish flight feathers can contrast markedly with fresher, replaced black wing coverts.

Distribution Corvids are found on all continents except Antarctica. In North America these birds range from the high Arctic to the Sonoran desert and utilize nearly every habitat in between. Migration and dispersal is diurnal, but most corvids are nonmigratory or engage in limited movements. Some species stage occasional irruptions, during which time individuals can be far from their normal range. Migration and dispersal tendencies may vary between different populations of the same species.

Taxonomy Corvid taxonomy continues to undergo revision. Worldwide there are between 115 and 120 species in the family Corvidae. There are 20 species recognized in North America, but a strong case could be made for splitting the Western Scrub-Jay and placing the Northwestern Crow with the American Crow. Corvids are believed to have arisen from an Australian ancestor that gave rise to a large group of some 650 species, which includes such diverse Old World groupings as the birds-of-paradise, Old World orioles, wood-swallows, and Paradise Flycatchers. The only other families from this assemblage that are found in North America are the vireos and the shrikes.

Conservation Some species are quite adaptable and do well near humans. Habitat destruction and fragmentation pose the most serious threats to this family, with additional mortality caused by pesticides and traps. Populations of many corvids declined dramatically with the spread of the West Nile virus, but initial evidence suggests that populations rebound after several years.
—*Christopher L. Wood*

CRESTED JAYS Genus *Cyanocitta*

Two species of relatively small northern jays have conspicuous crests. The upperparts are blue, and the wings and tail are barred with black. Unlike other North American jays, Blue and Steller's Jays use mud to build their nests, usually placing the mud between the large sticks on the outside of the nest and fine rootlets or similar material that line the nest.

BLUE JAY *Cyanocitta cristata*

The Blue Jay is a familiar and widespread bird throughout the East. Generally loved or hated, it has acquired a Jekyll-and-Hyde reputation. It is a frequent visitor to backyard feeding stations, where its raucous and rambunctious behavior is well known, but this adaptable jay is equally at home stealthily moving through the forest, plundering other birds' nests, searching for nuts, or quietly raising its young. Polytypic. L 11" (28 cm)

Identification The Blue is a nearly unmistakable crested jay with black barring and white patches on blue wings and tail; its underparts are paler with a dark necklace. Juveniles are more grayish above with gray lores and more limited white markings on the wings.
Geographic Variation Minor, obscured by broad overlap. Three subspecies are generally recognized. Northern *bromia* average the largest and brightest. Southeastern *cristata* generally show a subtle violaceous wash and are smallest. Western *cyanotephra* are generally duller and paler blue.
Similar Species Nearly unmistakable. Occasionally hybridizes with the Steller's Jay; hybrids appear intermediate between the 2 parent species.
Voice Vocal with a diverse array of vocalizations. CALL: A piercing *jay jay jay;* a musical *yo-ghurt;* frequently imitates raptors, particularly the Red-shouldered Hawk. Actively migrating birds are typically silent.
Status & Distribution Common. BREEDING: A variety of mixed forests, woodlands, suburbs, and parks. MIGRATION: Diurnal migrant. Northern populations move south in varying numbers from year to year. During flight years, large loose flocks can fill the sky, particularly along the shores of the Great Lakes and other northern locations known for raptor concentrations. In fall, first detected away from breeding grounds as early as July (typically earliest in big flight years); peaks in Great Lakes late Sept.–mid-Oct. WINTER: Distribution generally similar, but departs from northernmost breeding locales. VAGRANT: Casual chiefly in fall and winter west of the Rockies, recorded most frequently in the Northwest. Accidental to Bermuda.
Population Numbers are increasing in parts of the West. Domestic cats are likely the most significant human-caused source of mortality.

STELLER'S JAY *Cyanocitta stelleri*

The Steller's Jay is a bold and aggressive species frequently found scavenging in campgrounds, picnic areas, and feeding stations in the West. The bird's flight is strong and steady, with wings rarely flexed above horizontal. Polytypic. L 11.5" (29 cm)
Identification A nearly unmistakable dark blue, black-crested jay with variable white or blue markings on the head. The wings and tail are a vivid blue, with fine black barring. The head, including the crest; back; and throat are blackish. Juveniles are washed with brownish or grayish to the upperparts and are duller below.
Geographic Variation Extensive among the 17 subspecies from Alaska to Nicaragua, but more limited and clinal among the 8 subspecies north of Mexico. The most distinctive subspecies in North America is *macrolopha* of the central and southern Rockies, which has a long crest, paler back, and white streaks on the forehead and over the eye. Other North American subspecies are short crested and generally intermediate, differing primarily in size, head patterning, and overall coloration. Some, including the nominate *stelleri* (Pacific coast from AK to southwestern BC) are darker backed and have blue streaks on forehead. The largest subspecies, *carlottae,* from the Queen Charlotte Islands off British Columbia, is almost entirely black above.
Similar Species Nearly unmistakable. The crest, shorter tail, and lack of white in the body separate Steller's Jays from the scrub-jays.

stelleri

southern
Rockies
macrolopha

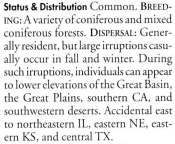

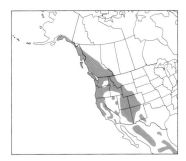

The Blue Jay, our other crested jay, has white in the wings, tail, and face, as well as pale underparts.

Voice Vocal with a diverse array of squacks, rattles, harsh screams. CALL: A piercing *sheck sheck sheck* and a descending harsh *shhhhhkk*. The Steller's Jay frequently mimics other species, particularly raptors, and also incorporates calls of squirrels and household animals, such as dogs and chickens.

Status & Distribution Common. BREEDING: A variety of coniferous and mixed coniferous forests. DISPERSAL: Generally resident, but large irruptions casually occur in fall and winter. During such irruptions, individuals can appear to lower elevations of the Great Basin, the Great Plains, southern CA, and southwestern deserts. Accidental east to northeastern IL, eastern NE, eastern KS, and central TX.

Population Apparently stable.

Genus Perisoreus

GRAY JAY *Perisoreus canadensis*

northwest
obscurus

southern
Rockies
capitalis

boreal
canadensis

juvenile

Bold and cunning, Gray Jays usually travel in pairs or family groups, but they often stay in cover and remain fairly quiet. They feed on the ground and in trees. While many corvids store food, the Gray and its Asian counterpart, the Siberian, are the only ones known to produce a saliva that allows them to "glue" food together for storage. They sometimes visit feeders. Polytypic. L 11.5" (29 cm)

Identification This is a fluffy, long-tailed jay with a small bill and no crest. ADULT: Grayish above, paler below, usually with variable dark markings on back of the head and pale tip to the tail. JUVENILE: Sooty-gray overall, with a faint white moustachial streak. They have molted by early fall, after which they closely resemble adults. FLIGHT: Typically a burst of wingbeats, followed by slow unsteady glides.

Geographic Variation A highly variable species, but variation is somewhat clinal and many intermediate individuals occur where subspecies meet. Six subspecies now generally recognized. Plumage variation is complicated by the rapid deterioration of specimens. Nominate *canadensis* (boreal forest from NT and northern AB to NF and PA) is intermediate in overall coloration, with a white collar and forehead and medium-gray hindcrown

and nape; upper parts only slightly paler than the hindcrown nape, with prominent dark shaft streaks; the wings are moderately edged with white; *capitalis* (southern Rockies from AZ and NM to eastern ID and WY) has an extensive pale crown that makes the head appear mostly white; upperparts considerably paler than *canadensis*; wings edged with frosty white. The *bicolor* (western MT to southeastern BC and northeastern OR) is intermediate between *capitalis* and *canadensis*, with the mostly whitish crown and frosty white wing edges of *capitalis* but with darker upperparts that have dark shaft streaks; *albescens* (east side of Rockies from southeastern YT and east-central BC to the Black Hills east to central MB and northwestern MN) is also intermediate between *capitalis* and *canadensis*, but darker coloration on nape and hindcrown is more extensive than on *bicolor*. Subspecies *obscurus* (Pacific coast from southwestern BC

to northern CA) has dark brownish gray upperparts (with white shaft streaks), with extensive brownish gray on crown and nape and paler underparts than other subspecies. The *pacificus* (AK to YT and northwestern BC) similar to *obscurus* with brownish-gray upperparts, but the underparts heavily washed brownish gray.

Similar Species Clark's Nutcracker has longer bill, black-and-white wings and tail, lacks dark coloration on head. Juveniles distinctive; usually seen with adults.

Voice Relatively quiet. CALL: A whistled 2-part *wheeoo* and a low *chuck*. Also a screeching *jaaay*.

Status & Distribution Common. BREEDING: Takes place in late winter in northern and mountain coniferous forests; less commonly in mixed forest. DISPERSAL: This species only infrequently strays south in the East, and to lower altitudes in the West; accidental to northeastern IA, MA, and southern NY.

Population Birds on the south edge of range may be declining. Vulnerable to traps for smaller fur-bearing mammals.

TROPICAL JAYS Genus *Cyanocorax*

This large genus includes 17 species of tropical jays, only 2 of which are found north of Mexico—the Green Jay and the Brown Jay. These are generally stocky species, with fairly prominent frontal tufts. They are generally found in the lowlands, and those species that have been studied have social breeding systems.

GREEN JAY *Cyanocorax yncas*

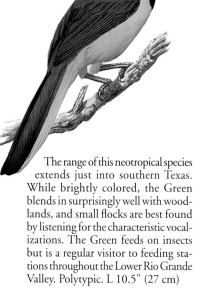

The range of this neotropical species extends just into southern Texas. While brightly colored, the Green blends in surprisingly well with woodlands, and small flocks are best found by listening for the characteristic vocalizations. The Green feeds on insects but is a regular visitor to feeding stations throughout the Lower Rio Grande Valley. Polytypic. L 10.5" (27 cm)

Identification Unmistakable long-tailed jay with short rounded wings, blue crown, complex black-and-blue face pattern, and black breast. The upperparts are bright green; the underparts are paler and tinged with yellow; bright yellow on undertail coverts and outer tail feathers. Plumage becomes bluer with wear. Juveniles are duller with brownish-olive head and throat, dull green upperparts, and paler yellow underparts. FLIGHT: Quick wingbeats interspersed with short glides; generally prefers to fly in forest interior. **Geographic Variation** All birds north of Mexico belong to northern *glaucescens.* Eleven subspecies worldwide; the 5 Andean subspecies are sometimes considered a separate species. **Similar Species** Unmistakable. **Voice** An array of chatters, clicks, mews, rattles, squeaks, and raspy notes are frequently given, although generally quiet when feeding and less vocal during the breeding season. CALL: A series of 4 or 5 harsh electric calls, *jenk jenk jenk jenk,* and a dry scolding *cheh-chech.*

Status & Distribution Locally common resident in brushy areas and streamside growth of the Lower Rio Grande Valley as far west as Laredo and north to Live Oak County and sporadically north to San Antonio. Found in suburbs (e.g., McAllen, Brownsville), where habitat is suitable. DISPERSAL: Sedentary; not known to wander. **Population** Status is unknown. Some speculate that habitat changes in southern Texas may have reduced breeding habitat. In the United States, the species is vulnerable to traps set for other birds and mammals.

BROWN JAY *Cyanocorax morio*

The range of this neotropical species barely extends into southern Texas. Brown Jays usually travel in boisterous flocks of 5–10 birds. In Texas most are found at feeding stations. When Brown Jays are nearby, they almost always reveal themselves with their incessant calls. Polytypic. L 16.5" (42 cm)
Identification A very large jay with long broad tail. Dark sooty-brown overall except for dirty whitish belly and undertail coverts. Juvenile has a yel-

low bill, yellow legs, and narrow yellow eye ring, all turning black by the second winter. Transitional birds have bills that are blotched with yellow and black. FLIGHT: Slow and unsteady, with heavy wingbeats interspersed with short glides.
Geographic Variation Six subspecies. All birds north of Mexico belong to *palliates,* characterized by uniformly brown tail and whitish belly with sooty wash.
Similar Species Nearly unmistakable; crows and ravens uniformly black.
Voice Noisy; less varied than most other jays. CALL: A loud, displeasing *KAAH KAAH* or *KYEEAH,* similar to the Red-shouldered Hawk's but higher and more offensive; usually given endlessly. Also produces a less voluminous popping or hiccuping sound.
Status & Distribution Uncommon and very local in woodlands and mesquite along the Rio Grande Valley in the vicinity of Falcon Dam. DISPERSAL:

adult

juvenile

Sedentary; not known to wander.
Population Common and increasing in much of its range, but local along the Rio Grande.

SCRUB-JAYS Genus Aphelocoma

Of the 5 species in *Aphelocoma,* all but the Uniform Jay are found north of Mexico. Generally medium or small in size, they have relatively long tails, are predominately blue above and gray below (or uniformly blue), and lack a crest. Species limits (esp. with the Western) are poorly understood. They are generally social, and 1 Mexican group is a social breeder.

FLORIDA SCRUB-JAY Aphelocoma coerulescens

The Florida Scrub-Jay is the only bird endemic to Florida, where it has been the subject of intense study since the late 1960s. These birds are cooperative breeders and are usually encountered in small family groups. While they are often hidden in scrub, flock members share sentinel duty in which individuals perch up on exposed perches and scan for predators. Many Florida Scrub-Jays are extremely tame and are well known for taking food from the hand. Monotypic. L 11" (28 cm)

Identification Similar to other scrub-jays, with blue head, wings, and tails, and pale underparts. But this species is slightly longer tailed, with a shorter and broader bill, and has blue auriculars. The forehead is whitish, blending into the eyebrow; the back is distinctly paler gray-brown, grayer than other scrub-jays; and the slightly grayish belly and flanks are faintly streaked. Juvenile is duller with a sooty grayish or brownish wash on the head and back.

Similar Species The only scrub-jay found in Florida. Blue Jay has black and white wings and tail, and is usually crested.

Voice CALL: Raspy and hoarse calls are reminiscent of the Western Scrub-Jay but lower and harsher.

Status & Distribution Fairly common, but local. Resident in scrub and scrubby flat woods of FL. Optimal habitat is produced by fire, consisting of scrub, mainly oak, about 10 feet high with small openings. Also found along roads and

vacant lots near overgrown scrub habitat. MIGRATION: Nonmigratory. Most travel only a few kilometers during their entire life, making it extremely unlikely for an individual to show up out of range.

Population Declined by some 90 percent during the 20th century due to habitat loss and fire suppression.

ISLAND SCRUB-JAY Aphelocoma insularis

The Island Scrub-Jay is restricted to Santa Cruz Island in the Channel Islands south of Santa Barbara, California. Its behavior is quite similar to that of the Western Scrub-Jay, and like that species, pairs actively defend year-round territories. Island Scrub-Jays forage at all levels of foliage and forage on the ground more regularly than the Western Scrub-Jay. As with many island endemics, this species has a more varied diet than the similar mainland representative. It regularly caches acorns, lizards, and even deer mice. Monotypic (formerly considered conspecific with Western and Florida Scrub-Jays; Island afforded species status based on morphological characters and genetic analysis). Monotypic. L 12.5" (31 cm)

Identification ADULT: Very similar to coastal populations of the Western Scrub-Jay but 15 percent larger, 40 percent heavier, and with a heavy bill that is up to 40 percent larger than the largest-billed mainland scrub-jays. The Island Scrub-Jay is darker blue above, with a darker brown back, blacker auriculars, and bluish undertail coverts.

JUVENILE: Duller, with a sooty-brown wash and little blue coloration.

Similar Species The only scrub-jay found on Santa Cruz Island; no scrub-jays have been found on any of the other Channel Islands.

Voice CALL: Very similar to calls by Pacific populations of Western Scrub-Jays, perhaps louder and harsher.

Status & Distribution Locally common on Santa Cruz I., where it is found in a variety of habitats; optimal habitat consists of oak chaparral. Approximately half of the adults on Santa Cruz I. are nonbreeding "floaters" that are generally found in marginal habitat, including pine and riparian scrub. MIGRATION: Nonmigratory; unrecorded away from Santa Cruz I.

Population Approximately 12,500 individuals were recorded on Santa Cruz Island in 1997, a large number for the size of the island. Population trends unknown; much remains to be learned about this restricted species.

WESTERN SCRUB-JAY *Aphelocoma californica*

interior juvenile
woodhouseii

interior
woodhouseii

coastal
californica

Plumage and behavior differ greatly between interior and coastal populations. Coastal populations of the Western Scrub-Jays are confiding, tame, and easily seen. Interior populations are more secretive and often are seen darting from bush to bush or are simply heard giving their harsh calls. Pairs of all North American subspecies hold territories year-round. Polytypic. L 11" (28 cm)

Identification This is a long-tailed jay with a small bill and no crest. ADULT: Generally bluish above, gray below with a contrastingly paler throat and upper breast, and a variable bluish band on the chest. JUVENILE: Much grayer overall, showing very little blue on the head. FLIGHT: Usually undulating with quick deep wingbeats.

Geographic Variation The subspecies of Western Scrub-Jays form 3 well-defined subspecies groups that may represent separate species: the coastal *californica* group; the interior *woodhouseii* group; and the *sumichrasti* group confined to southern Mexico. Subspecies groups occurring north of Mexico are discussed below. Formerly grouped with Florida and Island Scrub-Jays and considered one species, the Scrub-Jay.

Similar Species Both the Steller's Jay and the Blue Jay have conspicuous crests and wings and tail barred with black. See also the Florida Scrub-Jay and the Island Scrub-Jay (which do not overlap in range).

Voice CALL: Gives a variety of harsh calls, most frequently a raspy *shreeep*, often repeated in a short series of shorter notes: *shuenk shuenk shuenk shuenk*. Interior vocalizations are rougher and lower pitched.

Status & Distribution Common. BREEDING: Scrubby and brushy habitats, particularly with oak, pinyon, and juniper; also found in gardens, orchards, and riparian woodlands. DISPERSAL: Largely resident, but prone to occasional irruptions, particularly members of the *woodhouseii* group. Irruptions often coincide with movements of Pinyon Jay, Steller's Jay, and Clark's Nutcracker. VAGRANT: Casual to southwestern BC, eastern WA, southeastern CA, central KS. Accidental to southern MB, northeastern IL, and northwestern IN.

Population Breeding Bird Survey and Christmas Bird Count data indicate a gradual increase in populations north of Mexico.

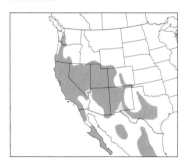

Subspecies Variation in the Western Scrub-Jay

In North America, the Western Scrub-Jay forms 2 distinct subspecies groups. The taxonomic status of the 2 groups in North America (and the isolated group in Mexico) is unresolved. Along with the plumage and behavioral differences described below, there appears to be little, if any, contact between the subspecies groups during the breeding season. Full species status may be warranted, but further research is necessary.

The "California" Scrub-Jay (or *californica* group) consists of 3 subspecies: *californica, superciliosa,* and *obscura*. As a whole, this group ranges from Washington, Oregon, and western Nevada south to southern California along the coast; west of the Sierra Nevada it ranges north to about Mono Lake. These birds are deeper blue with bright contrasty plumage and paler underparts. A brownish patch on the back, white supercilium, and blue breast band are distinctive. Undertail coverts are generally whitish but are usually tinged with blue in *obscura* (coastal southern CA) and occasionally in *californica* (interior southern OR and western NV to south-central CA). The "California" Scrub-Jay is found more frequently in suburban areas than the "Woodhouse's" Scrub-Jay and is usually very tame and confiding.

The interior "Woodhouse's" Scrub-Jay (or *woodhouseii* group) consists of 3 subspecies: *woodhouseii, suttoni,* and *texana*. This group is restricted to the interior west of the Rocky Mountains and Great Basin, including the mountains of southeastern California. Birds in this group are more dully marked than coastal birds and have straighter and thinner bills. The grayish blue back and faint blue breast band are less prominent. The underparts are more dirty gray in color, and the undertail coverts are bluish. Birds of *texana* (central TX) are stouter-billed and bluer than others in this group; *suttoni* (southeastern ID and southern WY to southern NM and southwestern TX) are intermediate between *texana* and *woodhouseii* (southeastern OR and southeastern CA to southern ID and southwestern NM). All the subspecies that comprise "Woodhouse's" Scrub-Jay are relatively shy and unapproachable. The differences in voice are described in the species account. ■

MEXICAN JAY *Aphelocoma ultramarina*

This species travels in large, raucous flocks and has a cooperative breeding system like the Florida Scrub-Jay; it regularly visits bird feeders. Polytypic. L 11.5" (29 cm)
Identification A relatively thick-bodied, broad-tailed, broad-winged jay with a large bill and no crest. ADULT: Generally bluish on the face and above, with a slight grayish cast to the back and a brownish patch on the center of the back. Underparts pale gray. JUVENILE: Much grayer overall, very little blue on the head. Juvenile *arizonae* has a yellowish bill that gradually turns black by the third year. All

ages of *couchii* have black bills.
Geographic Variation Two well-defined subspecies in N.A., with some clinal variation in Mexico. Arizona and New Mexico *arizonae* is larger with dull pale grayish blue upperparts and a uniformly gray throat and breast. Texas *couchii* has a blue head and whitish throat that contrasts with grayish underparts.
Similar Species May be confused with scrub-jays. Western Scrub-Jay best distinguished by its slimmer body, thinner tail, contrasting dark cheeks, white eyebrow, whitish throat offset by at least a faint blue breast band, and gray back. Western Scrub-Jays tend to flock less.
Voice Relatively limited. CALL: Most common is a rising *week*, often repeated in a short series; calls generally less raucous than scrub-jay's, but may be heard more frequently as they travel in family groups. Texas birds less musical, somewhat more like the Western Scrub-Jay. Texas birds also

give a mechanical rattle.
Status & Distribution Common. RESIDENT: Pine-oak canyons of southwestern mountains. DISPERSAL: Largely resident; does not wander like Western Scrub-Jay. VAGRANT/ACCIDENTAL: extreme western TX; record from central KS based on lost specimen.
Population Not threatened; no long-term trends.

Genus Gymnorhinus

PINYON JAY *Gymnorhinus cyanocephalus*

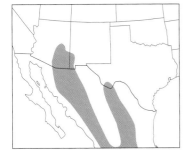

Finding this social species is usually feast or famine. Listen for the Pinyon Jay's far-carrying calls and scan for roving flocks of a few individuals to several hundred birds. Pinyon Jays nest in loose colonies beginning in winter. Polytypic. L 10.5" (27 cm)
Identification A short-tailed blue jay with a long spikelike bill. ADULT: Blue overall with white streaks on throat. JUVENILE: Ashy-gray underparts without much blue coloration. FLIGHT: Direct with rapid wingbeats, unlike the scrub-jay's undulating flight.

Geographic Variation Three subspecies are all very similar, and field separation is not possible. Birds from the northeastern portion of the range, *cyanocephalus,* have a shorter, more decurved bill, with pale plumage. Western *cassini* (from north-central OR and southern ID to southern NV and central NM) average darker with straighter bill; *rostratus,* in the southwest portion of range, has a longer and wider bill and intermediate plumage color.
Similar Species Scrub-Jays and Mexican Jays have paler underparts that contrast with bluer upperparts; shorter, thick bills; and much longer tails. The smaller Mountain Bluebird is often found in similarly large flocks but has a much shorter bill, thrush shape, and white undertail coverts.
Voice Suggestive of the Gambel's or the California Quail, or nasal like a nuthatch. CALL: Most commonly heard call, frequently given in flight, is a soft *hwaau* given repeatedly, or a single *hwauu'hau.*

Status & Distribution Common. RESIDENT: Pinyon-juniper woodlands of interior mountains and high plateaus; also yellow pine woodlands. DISPERSAL: Generally nonmigratory. When cone crop fails, may irrupt outside of normal range. VAGRANT: Casual: chiefly in fall to the Plains states, southwestern deserts, and coastal CA; irregular to western TX. Accidental to southern WA, western IA, southwestern SK, northwestern Mexico.
Population Major declines may have occurred with loss of piñon-juniper woodlands in the mid-20th century. Not threatened or endangered.

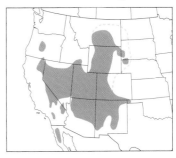

NUTCRACKERS Genus Nucifraga

CLARK'S NUTCRACKER Nucifraga columbiana

While generally found far from most human habitations, nutcrackers are very adaptable and are commonly seen at scenic overlooks and picnic grounds in the West. During summer and fall, nutcrackers store thousands of pine cone seeds, which they eat during winter and feed to their offspring during the very early nesting season (most have laid eggs by March or early April). Monotypic. L 12" (31 cm)

Identification A short-tailed, long-winged corvid with a long bill. Head and body pale grayish overall with boldly contrasting black-and-white wings and tail. ADULT: Paler whitish area on throat, forecrown, and around eyes. JUVENILE: More uniform face and generally washed with brown. FLIGHT: Direct, with deep crowlike wingbeats.

Similar Species Gray Jay has much shorter bill and more uniform grayish wings and tail, without boldly contrasting black-and-white wings.

Voice Quite varied; most are nasal and harsh, but some with clicks and cackles. CALL: Commonly gives a very nasal, grating, drawn-out *shra-a-a-a;* a nasal *whaah* similar to that of the Pinyon Jay; and a slow rattle sometimes likened to the croaking of a frog.

Status & Distribution Locally common. BREEDING: Prefers forests dominated by at least one species of large-seeded pine. In summer, often found in higher coniferous forests near timberline. MIGRATION AND DISPERSAL: Generally resident, but some populations regularly move to lower elevations in fall. In late spring, following breeding, most birds move upslope to higher elevations. Nutcrackers irrupt out of core range and into nearby deserts and lowland areas of the West following major cone crop failures. Most individuals are seen in late Sept. and Oct., but may appear as early as late July or early Aug. Major irruptions generally occur every 10–20 years and are thought to follow 2 or more years of good cone production immediately followed by a failure of all seed sources. VAGRANT: During irruptions casual to the Plains states, southeastern AK, southern YK, and coastal CA, including offshore islands. ACCIDENTAL: As far east as western ON, central MB, northeastern MN, northern IL, AR, and LA, and north to the central NT. Most extralimital records are Aug.–Nov.

Population Breeding Bird Survey suggests populations generally increased from 1966 to 1996.

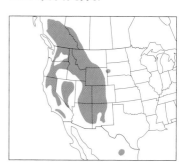

MAGPIES Genus Pica

Two members occur in N.A.; at least 1 other occurs in the Old World. That species was split from the Black-billed Magpie. All species are patterned in black and white and have long tails. They build stick nests and are usually found in open habitats with scattered trees. Less social than some species, many magpies still form larger flocks during fall.

BLACK-BILLED MAGPIE Pica hudsonia

With their large size, bold pied plumage, and fondness for open areas, Black-billed Magpies are easily seen. They hop and walk on the ground with a swaggering and confident gait. Monotypic. L 19" (48 cm)

Identification An unusually long-tailed black-and-white corvid with a black bill. In good light, black on wings and tail shine with iridescent green, blue, and violet. Juvenile has milky grayish-colored iris and fleshy pinkish gape. The upperparts are washed dull brownish, and the belly is more cream-colored. Immatures have narrower and more pointed outer tail feathers. FLIGHT: Relatively slow, with steady, rowing wingbeats, but the birds are easily able to quickly change direction in flight. Magpies usually swoop up or down to perch.

Geographic Variation While monotypic, birds in the south average smaller and tend to show bare dark grayish

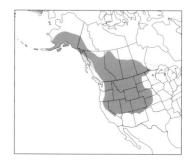

skin below eye (similar in shape to the yellow skin on Yellow-billed Magpie). **Similar Species** Black bill and range distinguish this species from the Yellow-billed Magpie; larger size of the Black-billed Magpie sometimes appreciable in the field. Until recently, the Black-billed Magpie was lumped with the widespread Magpie *(Pica pica)* of Eurasia and northwestern Africa, but all evidence suggests a much closer relationship with the Yellow-billed. **Voice** Quite varied, but most vocalizations are rather harsh. All are very similar to that of the Yellow-billed Magpie. They are strikingly faster and lower pitched than Old World populations of magpie. CALL: Frequently gives a whining, rising *mea;* sometimes these are more drawn out and questioning: *meeaaah.* Also a quickly repeated *shek-shek-shek* with each phrase repeated 3–5 times (not as

harsh or piercing as analogous vocalization of Steller's Jay). **Status & Distribution** Common. Resident of open woodlands and thickets in rangeland and foothills; nests along watercourses and other areas with trees and shrubs, but foraging birds use very open areas. MIGRATION AND DISPERSAL: Generally considered to be nonmigratory, but varies regionally and by year. Dispersing flocks form as early as July and typically consist of a few to a hundred birds; occasionally forms flocks of several hundred. Movements may be upslope, downslope, or in any direction. Banding recoveries have shown atypical movements of more than 500 km. Most birds are thought to return near where they hatched to breed. VAGRANT: Casual to Pacific

coast, western WI, IA, and northern TX, mostly in fall. In summer found north as far as northern AK, northeastern NT. Other sightings occur casually throughout the East and may pertain to escaped cage birds. **Population** Declined throughout the Great Plains with the slaughter of bison and targeted eradication. Adapting and now found in many suburban areas.

YELLOW-BILLED MAGPIE *Pica nuttalli*

This highly-prized California endemic is quite gregarious; roosting and feeding in flocks, it usually nests in small colonies. The range does not overlap with that of the Black-billed Magpie. Monotypic. L 16.5" (42 cm)
Identification Similar to the Black-billed Magpie but with yellow bill and yellow skin below the eye. The extent of yellow is variable, sometimes fully encircling eye, sometimes confined to below the eye. Differences may be related to age, state of molt, individual variation, or some combination thereof. Smaller than the Black-billed. JUVENILE: Milky grayish iris with brownish wash, most noticeable on the belly. IMMATURE: Differs as in Black-

billed Magpie. Also note that the inner tail feathers are sometimes replaced and contrast with dull retained outers. FLIGHT: Very similar to that of Black-billed Magpie; wingbeats are somewhat faster due to Yellow-billed Magpie's smaller size.
Similar Species The yellow bill and yellowish skin below the eye should easily distinguish this species from the Black-billed, which is also larger. Beware of Black-billed Magpies carrying twigs, food items, or other pale or yellowish objects—such sightings have resulted in many erroneous reports of the Yellow-billed Magpie. **Voice** Very similar to that of the Black-billed Magpie, perhaps higher pitched and clearer.

Status & Distribution Common, but distribution somewhat clumped. BREEDING: Prefers oaks, particularly more open oak savanna; also orchards and parks. Found in rangelands and foothills of central and northern Central Valley, CA, and coastal valleys south to Santa Barbara County. MIGRATION AND DISPERSAL: In late summer forms flocks that may wander short distances; these almost always remain within the breeding range. VAGRANT: Casual north almost to OR. Yellow-billed Magpies are not prone to wandering, and observations away from the breeding range may pertain to escapes.
Population Apparently stable. Loss of habitat poses the most significant risk. Some populations have been locally extirpated (e.g., western L.A. Co. and Ventura Co., western portions of Monterey Co.), and others have become fragmented due to habitat loss. Pesticides targeted at small mammals and traps pose additional threats.

CROWS AND RAVENS Genus Corvus

Crows and Ravens form the largest group of corvids. Generally considered intelligent and adaptable, *Corvus* includes some of the best studied and most well-known species. Of the 41 species worldwide, 7 are found in the continental U.S. and Canada. Crows and ravens are large, with mostly black plumages, sometimes with grayish or whitish markings on the head or neck. Ravens are larger than crows with a bigger bill and deeper vocalizations. Crow and raven identification presents some of the greatest identification challenges, complicated by variation within the species. Focus on structural differences (particularly the bill and nasal bristles) and vocalizations, and beware of regional differences.

EURASIAN JACKDAW Corvus monedula

The Eurasian Jackdaw is a widespread Eurasian and north African species that is strictly a vagrant to North America. During the 1980s, it staged a small invasion into the Northeast, with singles and small groups found in several northeastern states and provinces. Some (or all) of these these birds may have been assisted by ships. Bold and inquisitive. Polytypic. L 13" (33 cm)

Identification A small, mostly black crow with pale gray nape wrapping around the sides of the head. ADULT: Eerie pale gray iris. JUVENILE: Similar to adult but with dark iris and darker nape and side of head.

Geographic Variation No information on subspecies that appeared in North America; presumably *monedula* of Scandinavia or *spermologus* of western and central Europe.

Similar Species Other crows and ravens are larger without pale area to nape.

Voice CALL: A sharp, abrupt *chjek,* typically repeated several times.

Status & Distribution Widespread Old World species from British Isles and northwestern Africa east to Siberia and Kashmir; generally sedentary. Within native range found in a variety of open habitats. VAGRANT: Casual in Iceland and aboard ships in the mid-North Atlantic; 2 records for Greenland.

Other records from Faroes, Canary Islands, and Japan. First recorded in N.A. at Nantucket, MA, in late Nov. 1982; this bird was joined by another in July 1984; at least 1 remained until 1986. During the mid- and late 1980s found at several locations in the northeast, including a flock of 52 near Port-Cartier, QC; others at Miquelon, NS, ON, ME, RI, CT, and PA. A pair at the Federal Penitentiary at Lewisburg, PA, from May 1985 through at least 1991 nested or attempted to nest several times. The CT, RI, and PA records were ultimately rejected by state records committees, and it is generally thought that many (or all) North American records may pertain to ship-assisted birds.

Population Abundant and increasing throughout most of Old World range. Vagrants to Quebec were poisoned or shot by the Quebec Fish and Game Department.

AMERICAN CROW Corvus brachyrhynchos

The American Crow is the "default" crow across most of N.A. It overlaps broadly with the Common Raven, and to a lesser extent with the Chihuahuan Raven, Fish Crow, and Northwestern Crow. Study of vocalizations, bill structure and size, tail shape, and overall structure of this species will greatly aid in the identification of other crows and ravens. Regional variation in size of the American Crow poses challenges, particularly in the northwest. Polytypic. L 17.5" (45 cm)

Identification Largest crow in North America, with uniformly black plumage and fan-shaped tail. Bill is larger than other American crows, but distinctly smaller than either raven. On rare occasions individuals show white patches in wings. JUVENILE: Brownish cast to feathers; grayish eye, and fleshy gape (quickly darkening after fledging). IMMATURE: Tends to show worn brownish wings that contrast with fresher black wing coverts.

FLIGHT: Steady, with low rowing wingbeats. Does not soar.

Geographic Variation Four poorly defined subspecies generally recognized. While variation is largely clinal, differences between extremes are apparent. Northern *brachyrhynchos* and eastern and southern *palus* are essentially inseparable. Florida Peninsula *pascuus* has relatively long bill, long tarsus, and large feet. Also differs in behavior, never forming flocks; not found in urban areas and has more extensive vocal repertoire. The smaller western subspecies *hesperis* has been suggested to be more closely related to the Northwestern Crow than to subspecies of American Crow—the entire relationship between the American and Northwestern Crow remains unclear.

Similar Species Compare with very similar Fish Crow and nearly identical Northwestern Crow (both most easily separated by voice), Common and Chihuahuan Ravens.

Voice CALL: Adult's familiar *caw* generally well known. Voice of *hesperis* generally lower pitched than other subspecies. Juvenile's begging call is

higher pitched, nasal, and resembles the call of the Fish Crow.

Status & Distribution Common to abundant. BREEDING: A variety of habitats, particularly open areas with scattered trees. MIGRATION AND DISPERSAL: Diurnal migrant. In spring, arrive mid-Feb.–late Apr. Fall migration generally more protracted than in spring. Most depart north-central BC and AB by late Sept; peak in Great Lakes early Oct.–mid-Nov. Uncommon to rare migrant and winter visitor in deserts of the West. WINTER: Throughout much of the lower 48. VAGRANT: Casual to southwestern AZ, southwestern TX, northwestern Sonora, Mexico. **Population** Expanded with clearing of forests and planting of woodlots in prairies. Many populations experienced dramatic declines with the spread of West Nile virus early this century. Nevertheless long-term populations generally stable.

NORTHWESTERN CROW   *Corvus caurinus*

This small crow of the Pacific Northwest (see photograph p. 417) is virtually identical to *hesperis* American Crows. Field identification within the suspected range of overlap in WA is probably impossible. Many authorities consider the Northwestern Crow a subspecies of the American Crow. Monotypic. L 16" (41 cm)

Identification Virtually identical to the American Crow. The Northwestern averages smaller, with quicker wing flaps than most American Crows. Unfortunately, *hesperis* found in the Pacific Northwest are identical. A tendency for the nasal bristles to be placed along the sides of the bill on American Crow versus more on the top of the culmen in Northwestern Crow has been suggested, but there is considerable overlap, and this is unreliable. Voice often reported to be the most useful characteristic in separating this species from American Crows, but *hesperis* American Crows are so similar as to render this nearly impossible to use.

Similar Species Over most of range, likely to be confused only with Common Raven, which is much larger, with large heavy bill, and wedge-shaped tail. Separated from American Crow by range.

Voice CALL: Distinctly lower and more nasal than most populations of American Crow; *hesperis* American Crows also have lower and more nasal calls similar to Northwestern Crows.

Status & Distribution Resident of coastal areas and islands in Pacific Northwest. Common from south-coastal AK (Kodiak I.) to southern BC. Once a coastal resident in WA south through Puget Sound to Grays Harbor. Deforestation in late 1800s allowed American Crows to invade southern portions of this region by the early 1900s. Puget Sound population now generally considered to be small *hesperis* American Crows or hybrids. Within WA, birds thought most likely to be phenotypicly pure Northwestern Crows are limited to western Olympic Peninsula and San Juan Islands. MIGRATION AND DISPERSAL: Generally sedentary with local movements within breeding range.

Population Stable or increasing.

TAMAULIPAS CROW   *Corvus imparatus*

The range of this species barely extends into southern Texas near Brownsville; in recent years it has become rare and irregular in the U.S. It does not overlap with any other crow. It was formerly considered the same species as the Sinaloa Crow *(C. sinaloae)* of northwestern Mexico, then called the Mexican Crow. Monotypic. L 14.5" (37 cm)

Identification A small, very glossy crow with a short, small bill. Recalls the Fish Crow, but glossier; no range overlap. JUVENILE: Duller than adult, but still glossier than adults of other North American crows.

Similar Species The only crow regularly found in southern Texas. Chihuahuan Raven is common in the same habitat, but is larger, stockier, with larger and heavier bill. May be confused with male Great-tailed Grackle, particularly molting individuals that can have short tails. Still readily separated by crow's larger bill, stockier build, and thicker legs and dark eyes. Also note distinctive vocalizations.

Voice CALL: Rough, nasal, froglike croaking *ahrrr,* typically repeated several times and sometimes doubled, *rah-rahk.* Juvenile's begging call reportedly similar to that of the Fish Crow.

Status & Distribution Common to fairly common in northeastern Mexico; now casual or very rare in U.S. at 1 or 2 favored locales. RESIDENT: Northeastern Mexico to northern Veracruz. In the U.S. confined to Brownsville area. BREEDING: Variety of open habitats, often near dumps, cell towers and outskirts of towns.

Population Invaded Brownsville area in late 1960s; hundreds present into 1980s; declined greatly in 1990s. Not seen at Brownsville dump since late 1990s. Presumably stable in Mexico.

FISH CROW *Corvus ossifragus*

This glossy, gregarious corvid replaces the American Crow in coastal and tidewater regions of the Southeast. Its range is expanding up the Mississippi River Valley, its tributaries, and elsewhere away from the coast. While subtle structural differences exist, the most reliable way to identify this species is by call. Monotypic. L 19" (48 cm)

Identification Very similar to the American Crow but with proportionately longer tail and longer wings. Fish Crows have a bluish-violet or greenish gloss over most of the wings and body (less so on lower underparts) that is more extensive than in the American. The bill is usually more slender, but female crows have smaller bills and small-billed female Americans may have bill that appears very similar to the Fish's. JUVENILE: Brownish cast to feathers; grayish eye, fleshy gape (quickly darkening after fledging).

IMMATURE: Tends to show worn brownish wings that contrast with fresher black wing coverts. FLIGHT: Similar to American Crow but with slightly stiffer and quicker wingbeats. When gliding, wings often appear swept back at tips, creating a less-even trailing edge to wing than American Crow. The small-headed and long-tailed appearance is often most noticeable in flight. Apt to hover and soar, unlike American Crow.

Similar Species The American Crow averages somewhat larger with proportionately shorter wings and tail, but such differences difficult to use in the field; best identified by call. Note that some juvenile begging calls of American Crow resemble Fish Crow vocalizations. Closely related to Tamaulipas Crow, but does not overlap in range; Tamaulipas glossier, smaller, with proportionately even longer tail. Rarely overlaps with Common Raven, but raven much larger with very large bill and wedge-shaped tail.

Voice Possibly more limited repertoire than American Crow. CALL: Typically a high nasal *ca-hah,* second note lower; has a similar inflection and emphasis to American's sometimes casual dismissal of something with an audible *uh-uhh.* Also gives low, short *awwr.* Begging calls of Fish Crow similar in quality to American's begging calls, but are shorter and cut off abruptly.

Status & Distribution Common. Resident Usually near fresh and salt water lakes, rivers, beaches, marshes, or estuaries. MIGRATION AND DISPERSAL: In many regions (e.g., MD, TN, central NY), spring migration/return of breeders appears to peak in mid-Mar.–Apr. Fall migration more protracted: AR late Aug.–early Nov; departs central NY Sept.–Oct; MD mid- or late Sept.–mid- to late Dec. (peaks Oct. 20–Dec. 10). VAGRANT: Casual: southern ON, southern FL peninsula and Keys, NS, and Bahamas. WINTER: Becomes more localized throughout range as species gather in large flocks. Because birds become less vocal in winter, the northern limit of wintering birds is somewhat uncertain. Withdrawal from northern portions of range, particularly in the interior.

Population Increasing in abundance, and populations spreading northward. First recorded OK in 1954; KY 1959; MO 1964; ME 1978; KS 1984; IN 1988; VT 1998.

CHIHUAHUAN RAVEN *Corvus cryptoleucus*

Separating the smaller Chihuahuan Raven from the Common Raven is exceptionally difficult, if relying on subtle differences in size, bill and tail shape, and vocalizations. White bases to the neck feathers are the most reliable field mark, but these are usually hidden. Chihuahuan Ravens are very gregarious, particularly during the winter, when they often form large flocks (occasionally up to several thousand birds). Where trees are lacking, they will nest on utility poles, windmills, abandoned buildings or under bridges. Monotypic. L 19" (48 cm)

Identification Very similar to Common Raven. Major difference is the white (not gray) bases to the neck feathers. The bill is slightly shorter; the tail is slightly less wedge shaped and shorter; the nasal bristles on top of bill

extend farther out onto the bill; throat feathers are less thick and shaggy. JUVENILE: Brownish cast to feathers; grayish eye, fleshy gape (quickly darkening after fledging). IMMATURE: Tends to show worn brownish wings that contrast with fresher black wing coverts. FLIGHT: Very similar to the Common Raven, but less wedge-shaped tail often most easily seen on soaring birds.

Geographic Variation Birds of central and southern TX average smaller, but more study required to determine if slight differences warrant subspecies status.

Similar Species The Chihuahuan Raven is extremely similar to the Common Raven. The most reliable difference is the white-based feathers to the neck, often visible only under windy conditions. Additional clues include shorter bill with longer nasal bristles; less

"shaggy" throat feathering; smaller size; shorter, less wedge-shaped tail; and, on average, slightly higher-pitched vocalizations. All these characteristics are subjective, and where range overlaps some birds should probably be left unidentified, particularly given distant or brief views. Heavier bill and wedge-shaped tail distinguish the Chihuahuan Raven from crows.

Voice Less varied than that of Common Raven. CALL: The drawn-out croak is usually higher pitched and more crow-like than most Common Raven vocalizations. Common Ravens may give Chihuahuan Ravenlike vocalizations. Listening to a bird (or a flock of birds) for a period of time is preferable in order to hear full variety of calls given.

Status & Distribution Uncommon to common. Resident of desert areas and dry open or shrubby grasslands, usually with scattered trees or shrubs. MIGRATION AND DISPERSAL: Generally considered to be nonmigratory, but forms large roaming flocks in winter. Birds in northern portion of range are thought to withdraw, but this may vary between years. In some years, local movements through much of the range.

Population Declined in eastern Colorado, western Kansas during the late 1800s and early 1900s; extirpated from southeastern Wyoming. Now strictly casual in Nebraska.

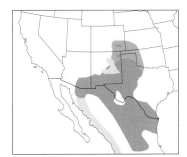

COMMON RAVEN   *Corvus corax*

This large raven found throughout much of the Northern Hemisphere is more frequently found singly, in pairs or small groups, but in many regions is sometimes found in foraging or roosting flocks of several hundred, even several thousand, birds. Polytypic. L 24" (61 cm)

Identification Largest corvid in the Americas, with uniformly glossy black plumage, long, heavy bill, and long wedge-shaped tail. The bases of the neck feathers are gray. Nasal bristles on top of bill cover the basal third to half of the bill. The throat is covered by thick and shaggy feathers. JUVENILE: Brownish cast to feathers, grayish eye, and fleshy gape (quickly darkening after fledging). IMMATURE: Tends to show worn brownish wings that contrast with fresher black wing coverts. FLIGHT: Wingbeats shallower than crows. Frequently soars; pairs frequently engage in a variety of aerial acrobatics, sometimes even turning upside down. Glossy black plumage is often most apparent in flight, when ravens often appears "greasy," as if covered with oil.

Geographic Variation Roughly 11 subspecies worldwide; 4 in North America. While variation is largely clinal, differences between extremes sometimes apparent. Northern and Eastern *principalis* large with long bill of medi-

um depth. Residents of western Alaska to northeastern Siberia are the largest, with the broadest and longest bill. Western *sinuatus* and particularly southwestern *clarionens* smaller, with smaller bill, shorter wings and tail.

Similar Species See Chihuahuan Raven, which can be extremely similar. Crows are much smaller with much smaller bills and fan-shaped tails.

Voice Extremely varied, with local dialects and individual specific calls reported. CALL: Common call is a low, drawn-out croak *kraaah;* also a deep, nasal and hollow *brooonk.* Juvenile begging calls are relatively high-pitched, but there is much individual variation. Calls can be similar to the Chihuahuan Raven.

Status & Distribution Generally common, but more local on southern periphery of range. BREEDING: Diverse array of habitats. Tends to prefer hilly or mountainous areas, but found on tundra, prairies, grasslands, towns, cities, iso-

lated farmsteads, forests, even Arctic ice floes. MIGRATION AND DISPERSAL: Generally considered sedentary, but poorly understood. Regular spring passage noted along Front Range of Colorado late Jan.–late Mar. VAGRANT: Casual chiefly in winter to Great Plains, southern Great Lakes, and lower elevations of Atlantic coast states.

Population Declined greatly in the 19th and early 20th centuries due to loss of habitat, shooting, poisoning, and disappearance of bison on the Great Plains; extirpated from Alabama, North Dakota, South Dakota, and the southern Great Lakes. Populations are now expanding into some of their former territory in parts of the East, Great Lakes, and northern Plains. Listed as endangered in Tennessee and Kentucky. Shooting, trapping, and habitat degradation continue to pose threats for this species, but it is becoming more tolerant of humans; birds are often found in cities and towns in the West.

LARKS Family Alaudidae

Horned Lark (UT, June)

Larks—small, generally cryptically colored terrestrial passerines—number some 96 species worldwide. They occur on all continents except on Antarctica.

Structure Bill shape varies from long and decurved to thick and conical. The hind toe is usually long and straight. The tertials are unusually long, often completely covering primaries on folded wing; 9 primaries are visible (the tenth is vestigial or reduced).

Plumage Larks are generally dull-colored, in browns, rufous, buff, black, and white, with many species streaky or with nondescript uniform plumage. Most species are cryptically colored; some species are more boldly marked.

Behavior These ground-dwelling birds walk or run rather than hop. Most give complex songs in display flight.

Distribution Larks reach their greatest diversity in Africa, where 80 percent of species occur, and lowest in South America, where they are represented by an isolated breeding population of Horned Lark *(E. a. peregrina)* near Bogotá, Colombia. Two species occur in North America: the Horned Lark (naturally) and the Sky Lark (introduced and also as a vagrant). The Horned Lark is the most widely distributed species in the family, with 42 subspecies occurring across North and South America, Eurasia, and North Africa.

Taxonomy Relationships remain unclear. Historically the alaudids are thought to be the most primitive of the oscine passerines despite their complex songs. Some DNA evidence places the larks near the Old World sparrows, while recent genetic studies place them closer to the Old World warblers, bulbuls, and swallows. Various authorities recognize 7 to 16 subspecies of the Sky Lark, and sometimes lump one, or all, subspecies of the Oriental Skylark with the Sky Lark.

Conservation Lark habitat in general is threatened by human agricultural activities, as well as by urbanization. Many species have very restricted ranges and habitat requirements. —*Allen T. Chartier*

Genus Alauda

SKY LARK *Alauda arvensis*

The Sky Lark raises a slight crest when agitated. It nests among short grasses or low vegetation, laying 1 to 4 eggs. Polytypic. L 7.2" (18 cm)

Identification Plain brown with pointed, slender bill. Upperparts heavily streaked, pale supercilium; buffy white underparts with necklace of fine dark streaks on breast and throat. Narrow white trailing edge on the secondaries and inner primaries and white outer tail feathers visible in flight. ADULT: Sexes similar; no seasonal, but some individual variation. JUVENILE: Less distinctly marked than adult. Upperparts spotted and speckled, throat less streaked. Distinctive buff fringes on wing coverts and outer webs and tips of flight feathers. Marbled outer tail feathers.

Geographic Variation Western European nominate *arvensis* is described above. The northeastern Asian *pekinensis* is more richly colored on the breast, darker and more heavily streaked above, and has longer wings.

Similar Species Pipits have thinner bills; sparrows, longspurs, and buntings have thicker bills. They all lack the white trailing edge on the wing.

Voice FLIGHT CALL: A liquid *chirrup* with buzzy overtones. SONG: A very long (2–4+ min.) series of buzzy, trilling, churring notes, given from the ground or in aerial display flight.

Status & Distribution Locally introduced population *(arvensis)* on Vancouver I., BC, sedentary. Asian subspecies *(pekinensis)* rare in spring to Aleutians and Pribilofs (casual in summer, has bred), casual in spring north to St. Lawrence I. BREEDING: Open habitats with short grasses and low herbs in BC; alpine tundra on Pribilofs. MIGRATION: Breeding birds on Pribilofs migratory, AK records primarily May–early June. WINTER: Sedentary population in BC uses wide variety of open habitats. VAGRANT: Record from CA likely *pekinensis;* records from WA and Queen Charlotte Is. may have been *pekinensis.* Nominate *arvensis* introduced on Hawaiian Is. Casual to Leeward Is. *(pekinensis).*

Population Introduced population in British Columbia has declined from about 1,000 in the 1950s to 100 in 1995, attributed to urbanization.

pekinensis

arvensis

Genus Eremophila

HORNED LARK *Eremophila alpestris*

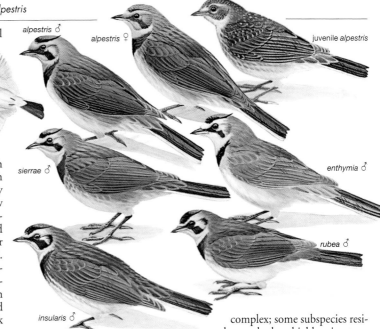

alpestris ♂
alpestris ♀
juvenile alpestris
sierrae ♂
enthymia ♂
insularis ♂
rubea ♂

The head pattern is distinctive in all subspecies: black "horns" and white or yellowish face and throat with broad black stripe under eye. The Horned usually nests on bare ground, including plowed fields, and lays 2 to 5 eggs (mid-Mar.–mid-July). Polytypic. L 6.8–7.8" (17–20 cm)

Identification Nape, back, rump, and wing brown streaked with dusky to black. Black bib. Tail black with two outer tail feathers edged light gray on outer web. Breast and belly yellow to white, breast patch black. Head boldly marked with black lores, cheek, and ear tufts; white to yellow eyebrow, ear coverts, and throat. Short, stout bill. Black legs. ADULT: No seasonal variation. Sexes similar, but males generally larger and darker. Female duller on head and face, cheek patch; breast band smaller and gray instead of black; back may be more striped; "horns" smaller and rarely erected. JUVENILE: Lacks black facial and breast markings of adult, making dark eye more conspicuous on brownish head. Back spotted with whitish to gray, giving a mottled appearance. Underparts generally creamy-buff with streaking on sides and breast. Tail as adult. Bill and legs paler yellowish to flesh in younger birds.

Geographic Variation In North America, 21 subspecies are recognized, with most intergrading. Migratory subspecies have longer wings, and birds in hotter environments have longer legs. Subspecies are mainly distinguished by plumage. Back color matches the color of the soil in local habitat; face and throat varies from yellow in Northeast to whitish or white in prairie and desert subspecies. Nominate *alpestris* of the Northeast is the largest and darkest of 5 eastern subspecies, and has a yellow throat. The white-throated "Prairie" subspecies

(praticola) is widespread in the upper Midwest. Ten subspecies, generally pale, are western in distribution; one of the palest is the Great Plains subspecies *enthymia*. Another western group consists of 6 small subspecies that are largely rufous on the upperparts. Restricted to northeastern California, the subspecies *sierrae* is very yellow below and russet above. Confined to the Channel Islands, California, the *insularis* is rather streaked above and below. The ruddy-colored *rubea* is found in central California.

Similar Species An adult Horned Lark is distinctive. Compared to an American Pipit, the Horned in flight is broader chested and broader tailed, and forms much looser flocks. A juvenile Horned is frequently mistaken for a Sprague's Pipit. Note the thicker bill, longer tail and wings, and pale spotted upperparts of the Horned, and the paler buffy face and head of the Sprague's.

Voice CALL: Includes a high-pitched *tsee-titi,* given from ground or in flight. Flight call resembles the American Pipit's, but softer. SONG: Typically, 2 or 3 thick introductory *chit* notes, followed by a high-pitched, rapid, jumbled series of tinkling notes rising slightly in pitch, given from ground or in display flight.

Status & Distribution Common and widespread in open country. Movements complex; some subspecies resident and others highly migratory. BREEDING: Open, barren country, avoiding forests. Prefers barren ground and shorter grasses, deserts, brushy flats, and alpine habitat. MIGRATION: In spring, diurnal migrant in flocks. Over much of Midwest, winter birds are largely nominate *alpestris,* but the *praticola* returns to more northern breeding areas in the East by early Feb. in southern ON to early Apr. in MB. Timing is complex in much of the West, including altitudinal movements by alpine subspecies. Arrive in AK generally by mid-Apr. In fall, peak movements in the East late Oct.–Nov. Begin departing from AK in Aug. In Southwest, move as early as mid-June–Sept. WINTER: Occur in similar habitat to breeding grounds, including beaches, sand dunes, and airports. VAGRANT: Casual to southern FL; one Palearctic subspecies *(flava)* casual to west, southwest, and south-central AK.

Population Deforestation in the late 1800s in midwestern and eastern North America provided good nesting habitat, resulting in dramatic population increases. Numbers are currently stable or declining slightly due to reforestation. Slight increases in the Southeast. Central Prairie Provinces showed significant declines from 1968–1975. Many western states show declines. Pesticide poisoning has occurred, and likely has contributed to declines.

SWALLOWS Family Hirundinidae

Cliff Swallows (CA, Apr.)

This family consists of a group of accomplished aerial-foraging songbirds. The terms "swallow" and "martin" are used fairly interchangeably, with the square-tailed species generally being referred to as martins and the fork-tailed species as swallows. In the Old World, the Bank Swallow is called the Sand Martin.

Structure Hirundinidae is a very homogeneous family of birds, all with very similar body structures, and generally unlike any other passerines. Swallows have long pointed wings with 10 primaries (the tenth extremely reduced); small compressed bills with a wide gape, sometimes with rictal bristles; short legs; and square to deeply forked tails. Feathers of the lores are directed forward, which shades the eyes, a useful adaptation for aerial insectivores. The structure of the syrinx (vocal apparatus) is well differentiated from other passerine families, though for the most part, swallows are unremarkable singers.

Plumage Swallows and martins have variable plumage on the whole, but with much consistency within genera. The birds often are iridescent blue or green above, and dark, white, or rufous below. Many species show pale rumps or dark breast bands, and a few Old World species are striped below. Sexual dimorphism is weak, with the New World martins (genus *Progne*) a notable exception.

Behavior All species are insectivorous, though one species (Tree Swallow) is able to feed on wax myrtle berries in winter, allowing it to winter farther north than most species. Swallows feed on the wing, and all are very accomplished fliers. Many temperate species undergo long-distance migrations, some among the longest of any passerines. Many species, including all those breeding in North America, are social in the breeding season, some nesting in colonies and sometimes with other swallow species. Some species are less gregarious or solitary. Nests are built either of mud—sometimes reinforced with vegetation and attached to vertical faces of natural and man-made structures—or within cavities excavated by other species. The Bank Swallow is the only cavity-nesting species that excavates its own nest. The rare Blue Swallow *(Hirundo atrocaerulea),* from southern Africa, is the only species that nests belowground, using potholes or aardvark burrows in open grassland.

Distribution About 90 species are found worldwide, except in Antarctica and the high Arctic, with the greatest diversity in Africa (29 breeding sp.), and secondarily in Central and South America (19 sp.). Eight species breed in North America and 7 additional species have been recorded as vagrants.

Taxonomy Swallows are well differentiated from other passerine families, and within the family there is little variation. Two species of river-martin, one occurring in West Africa and the other (possibly extinct) occurring in Thailand, form the subfamily Pseudochelidoninae. All other swallow species are placed in the subfamily Hirundininae. Although swallows were formerly considered to be most closely related to Tyrant Flycatchers (Tyrannidae), recent DNA evidence suggests that they are actually more closely related to Old World Warblers (Sylviidae), Babblers (Timaliidae), White-eyes (Zosteropidae), Chickadees (Paridae), and Long-tailed Tits (Aegithalidae).

Conservation Many species, including all North American breeding species, have adapted well to the influence of humans on their environment. In fact, some species now rarely nest in natural situations, preferring to nest on man-made structures. A few species have very restricted ranges and are considered threatened or endangered. —*Allen T. Chartier*

MARTINS Genus *Progne*

These largest swallows, with broad-based wings, moderately forked tails, and strongly decurved upper mandibles, are the only swallows of N.A. showing obvious sexual dimorphism. Taxonomy of this genus is unsettled, with at least 8 species described. All members of *Progne* are called martins but are not directly related to martins of the Old World.

PURPLE MARTIN *Progne subis*

adult ♂

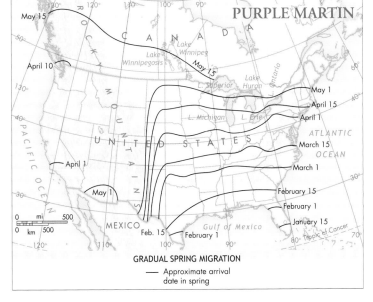

1st spring

adult ♂

adult ♀

The Purple Martin is the largest swallow in North America. Males are all dark, glossy blue-black; females and immatures duller above and grayish below. The Purple Martin is an extremely popular and well-known bird due to its willingness to nest in structures provided by humans. Polytypic. L 7.5" (19 cm)

Identification ADULT MALE: All glossy blue-black above and below, wings and tail dusky black, distinctly notched tail. In hand, small concealed white tuft on sides of rump and sides of body are visible. ADULT FEMALE: Duller above than male, with more scattered patches of blue-black above. Grayish collar

on hind neck. Throat, breast, and flanks dusky brown, paler on center of belly. Undertail coverts grayish with dusky centers. IMMATURE: Similar to adult female; young males show some blue-black on head and underparts, dark shaft streaks on ventral feathers, and sometimes a less distinct collar on hind neck; females, paler below and browner above, and lack dusky centers on undertail coverts. FLIGHT: Somewhat starlinglike shape. Graceful, liquid wingbeats interspersed with gliding and soaring.

Geographic Variation Females of western *(arboricola)* and desert *(hesperia)* subspecies with whiter underparts and forehead. Immature males tend to look more like females of eastern subspecies *(subis)*.

Similar Species Very similar to, sometimes indistinguishable from, other martins except the Brown-chested. Female Purple Martin is the only species with contrasting gray collar on hind neck and pale forehead. Mottled undertail coverts.

Voice CALL: Most frequently gives a *chur* call in many situations. When alarmed or excited, gives a *zwrack* or *zweet* call. SONG: Usually a series of chortles, gurgles, and slightly harsher croaking phrases. Also gives a churring, chortling "dawn song" around potential nest sites upon arriving on the breeding grounds in early spring.

Status & Distribution Fairly common but a local and declining summer res-

ident. BREEDING: In the East, colonially almost exclusively in artificial sites near human habitations. In the West, frequently solitarily, more often in natural cavities in forested areas, and in saguaro cactus in desert Southwest. NEST: In cavity excavated by another species, or in artificial structures; 3–6 eggs (late Mar.–late May). MIGRATION: In spring, arrives as early as mid-Jan. in TX, FL, and Gulf Coast; early Mar. in VA and KS, mid-Apr. in southern Canada, May in AZ, early May in MT. During fall, in the East, very large aggregations of thousands of birds form locally in late summer. Passage peaks late July–Sept., beginning as early as late May, with stragglers until early Oct. In Southwest, scarce Aug.–late Sept. WINTER: South American lowlands east of the Andes south to northern Argentina (rarely) and southern Brazil. VAGRANT: Accidental in Bermuda and U.K.

Population Causes of long-term declines unknown. Competes for nest cavities with the introduced European Starling and House Sparrow. In the West, logging has reduced availability of natural nest cavities. Increased availability of human-provided nest sites has had a positive effect on populations. Sharp declines in southern California.

PURPLE MARTIN

GRADUAL SPRING MIGRATION
— Approximate arrival date in spring

CUBAN MARTIN *Progne cryptoleuca*

This vagrant from the Caribbean has been confirmed only once in North America. Monotypic. L 7.5" (19 cm) **Identification** ADULT MALE: Like Purple Martin. ADULT FEMALE: Similar to the Purple, with darker upperparts, duskier brown throat, breast, and flanks contrasting with unmarked white belly and undertail; lacks paler grayish collar. IMMATURE: Similar to adult female. **Similar Species** Male indistinguishable from Purple Martin in field; in hand shows some concealed white feathers on

belly, longer more deeply forked tail. See above for female. May be conspecific with Caribbean Martin *(dominicensis)* and Sinaloa Martin *(sinaloae),* which show clean, white underparts in adult. **Voice** CALL: Gurgling; a high-pitched *twick-twick.* SONG: A strong, melodious warble close to that of Purple Martin. **Status & Distribution** Common and endemic on Cuba and Isle of Pines. Nonbreeding (Sept.–Feb.) range unknown, presumably S.A. VAGRANT: Key West, FL (specimen, May 9, 1895).

adult ♀

GRAY-BREASTED MARTIN *Progne chalybea*

adult ♀

This swallow has occurred in N.A. twice, both in TX. Monotypic. L 7" (18 cm) **Identification** ADULT MALE: Steel blue or purple glossed upperparts. Face, breast, sides, and flanks gray-brown or sooty gray; chin and throat paler. Belly and undertail coverts pure white. ADULT FEMALE: Duller than adult male with paler chin and throat; whiter below, browner forehead. IMMATURE: Duller than adult female with little gloss above. **Similar Species** Female Purple Martin has

distinct gray collar; female Southern Martin has mostly or entirely dark underparts; female Cuban Martin has more contrasting white belly. **Voice** CALL: In contact, a *cheur.* Alarm and aggressive calls include *zwat, zurr,* or *krack.* SONG: A rich, liquid gurgling. **Status & Distribution** Lowland resident, southern Mexico to northern Argentina. VAGRANT: Two TX specimens, Starr Co., 25 April 1980 and Hidalgo Co., 18 May 1889.

SOUTHERN MARTIN *Progne elegans*

This species of S.A. has occurred once in N.A. Monotypic. L 7" (18 cm) **Identification** ADULT MALE: Upperparts and underparts glossy dark, violet blue. Wings and tail black with slight bluish green gloss. Tail slightly forked. ADULT FEMALE: Smaller than male. Sooty black above, glossed blue on back; dusky brown below, often with pale edgings giving a scaly look. Uppertail coverts sometimes with narrow pale terminal margins. Most uniformly dark below. IMMATURE: Similar to adult female.

Similar Species Male slightly smaller than the Purple, with a slightly longer and more forked tail. In hand, lacks concealed white patch on sides and flanks. Female darker below than any other female martin. **Voice** CALL: A harsh contact call and a high-pitched alarm call. SONG: A short warbling. **Status & Distribution** Breeds in southern S.A.; migrates north in Austral winter to western Amazon Basin. VAGRANT: 1 specimen in Key West, FL (Aug. 14,1890).

adult ♀

BROWN-CHESTED MARTIN *Progne tapera*

adult *fusca*

This most distinctive species in the genus is reminiscent of an oversize Bank Swallow. Polytypic (2 ssp.; *fusca* in N.A.). L 6.5" (16 cm) **Identification** ADULT: Upperparts pale brown with extensive pale edgings, lores and ear coverts slightly darker. Wing coverts, inner secondaries, and tertials narrowly edged white. Chin, throat, and abdomen white. Pale brown band on upper breast; sides brownish. Undertail coverts white. IMMATURE: Like adult, with sides of throat gray-brown and

slightly squarer tail. IN FLIGHT: Closer to the ground more often than the Purple. **Similar Species** Bank Swallow much smaller, no pale edgings on upperparts. **Voice** CALL: Gives a *chu-chu-chip* call when in flocks. SONG: Series of harsh gurgling, rising and falling phrases. **Status & Distribution** S.A. from Colombia to northern Argentina. Southern subspecies *(fusca)* is an Austral migrant to northern S.A. VAGRANT: Monomoy I., MA (June 12, 1983), Cape May, NJ (Nov. 6–15, 1997).

Genus *Tachycineta*

These swallows are mainly iridescent blue or green above and white below. The genus contains 8 or 9 species depending on taxonomy, all occurring in the New World. Two species breed in North America, and 2 species have been recorded as vagrants. The tails of *Tachycineta* are shallowly notched to deeply forked.

TREE SWALLOW *Tachycineta bicolor*

Familiar denizens across North America, Tree Swallows nest in abandoned cavities in dead trees or nest boxes provided for them by admiring humans. These birds are hardier than other swallows and can feed on seeds and berries during colder months. Monotypic. L 5.8" (15 cm)

Identification SPRING ADULT: Upperparts iridescent greenish blue. Wings and tail dusky blackish, underparts entirely clean white. Lores black, ear coverts blue-black. Tail slightly forked. A few females retain brown back of immature into first spring, possibly longer. FALL ADULT: Upperparts sometimes appear more greenish than in spring. Tertials and secondaries edged pale grayish. IMMATURE: Upperparts gray-brown, with pale grayish edges on tertials and secondaries. Underparts clean white with indistinct dusky brown wash across breast, faintest in the center. FLIGHT: Small but chunky swallow with a shallowly forked tail and broad-based triangular wings. Glides more than other swallows.

Similar Species Smaller Violet-green Swallow has white of cheek extending behind and above the eye, and has white patches on sides of rump. Bank Swallow similar to immature, but smaller and with distinct, clean-cut brown breast band, different face pattern (white behind ear), and paler brown rump.

Voice SONG: An extended series of variable chirping notes—*Chrit, pleet, euree, cheet, chrit, pleet.*

Status & Distribution Common. BREEDING: Open areas, usually near water, including marshes, fields, and swamps. NEST: Brings a few pieces of vegetation to nest cavity and often includes feathers; 2–8 eggs (May–July). MIGRATION: In spring, arrives earlier in north than other swallows, usually mid-Mar.–early Apr. Departs later than other species, peaking late Sept. in MO and VA, lingering until late Nov. as far north as the Great Lakes. WINTER: Southern U.S., south through C.A. and the Caribbean. Open areas near water and nearby woodlands. VAGRANT: Casual in Bermuda, accidental in Guyana, near Trinidad, Greenland, and England.

Population The breeding range is expanding southward; the population is increasing in eastern and central United States.

MANGROVE SWALLOW *Tachycineta albilinea*

A very small swallow, the Mangrove is never found far from water, frequently in coastal areas. Monotypic. L 5.2" (13 cm)

Identification ADULT: Crown and back iridescent greenish, auriculars and lores black. Narrow white line above lores usually meets on forehead. Rump white, uppertail coverts dark. Wings and slightly forked tail dusky blackish, underwing coverts clean white. Tertial and inner secondary edges white. Underparts white, extending onto the side of the neck as a partial collar, sometimes with a dark diffuse wedge on the sides of the upper breast. JUVENILE: Gray-brown where adults are greenish blue. FLIGHT: Small size evident, with short, broad wings and short tail. Rapid, shallow wingbeats.

Similar Species Tree Swallow is noticeably larger, lacks white rump and supraloral. Common House-Martin is larger, bluish above, lacks white supraloral, and has a more deeply forked tail. White-rumped *(T. leucorrhoa)* has not been recorded from N.A., but is larger, bluish above, and has narrower white edges on tertials.

Voice SONG: A series of *chrit or chriet* notes mixed with buzzier chirps.

Status & Distribution Common nonmigratory resident of lowlands, especially near water, in Mexico and C.A. VAGRANT: One adult in Brevard Co., FL (Nov. 18–25, 2002).

VIOLET-GREEN SWALLOW *Tachycineta thalassina*

The western counterpart of the Tree Swallow, the Violet-green Swallow has narrower wings and a shorter tail. This species frequently uses nest boxes. Polytypic (3 ssp., none separable in the field; *lepida* in N.A.). L 5.3" (13 cm)

Identification ADULT MALE: Upperparts of male are dark velvet green, more bronze on the crown, becoming purple on rump and uppertail coverts. Underparts are white, extending onto cheek, to behind and above the eye. Lores are dusky. White of flanks extends onto the sides of the rump, forming 2 white patches from above in flight. Wings and short, slightly forked tail are black. Underwing coverts grayish. ADULT FEMALE: Somewhat duller than the male, browner on the head, face and ear coverts. Throat is washed slightly with ashy brown. JUVENILE: Similar to adults, but green and purple are replaced with brownish. White on cheek and behind eye is much less extensive. Slight pale brownish wash on breast. Tertials and inner secondaries are very narrowly edged pale grayish. FLIGHT: Longer, narrower wings and shorter tail than the Tree Swallow; the Violet-green has a more fluttering flight style.

Similar Species The Tree Swallow is larger, entirely greenish blue above, and lacks white around the back of the eye and on the sides of the rump. The larger White-throated Swift has narrower pointed wings and black-and-white underparts.

Voice CALL: Various short notes, including a twitter, and *chee-chee* notes. Alarm call is a *zwrack* similar to that of the Purple Martin.

Status & Distribution Common. BREEDING: Occurs in a variety of habitats, including open areas in montane coniferous and deciduous forests, coastal regions, and even in higher elevation desert areas. NEST: It brings a variety of grasses and stems, as well as feathers, to an abandoned cavity in trees, rock crevices, dirt banks, or columnar cactuses; 4–6 eggs (Apr.–May). MIGRATION: In spring, arrives in southern AZ and southern CA by late Feb., AK by early May. Departs AK by mid-Aug., lingering into mid-Oct. in BC and WA. In the Southwest departs late Sept.–late Oct. WINTER: Tidal flats to interior mountains. A few birds in southern CA, but most from Mexico south to Guatemala, El Salvador, and Honduras. VAGRANT: Casual in western AK and east of the Rockies, with most sightings in the East Sept.–Nov.

Population There is no documented effect of human activity on numbers; the introduction of the House Sparrow and European Starling may have reduced populations in urban areas of southern Canada.

adults ♂

juvenile

adult ♂

BAHAMA SWALLOW *Tachycineta cyaneoviridis*

Endemic to the northern Bahamas, this species has one of the most restricted ranges of any swallow species in the world. Monotypic. L 5.8" (15 cm)

Identification ADULT MALE: Iridescent green upperparts, dusky lores. Underparts, including lower cheek to below eye and underwing coverts, white. Wings and deeply forked tail dusky bluish black above. Margins of outer tail feathers sometimes whitish. ADULT FEMALE: Slightly duller than the male, with some slaty brown on ear coverts and breast washed with pale, sooty brown. Shorter tail. JUVENILE: Duller than adults, upperparts brownish with greenish mainly on mantle and wing coverts. Underparts white washed with sooty brown on breast. Shorter, less forked tail. FLIGHT: Resembles Barn Swallow in shape, but Tree Swallow in plumage.

Similar Species The Tree Swallow has a much less forked tail; the Barn Swallow is blue above and buffy and white below; the Violet-green Swallow has large white spots on sides of rump.

Voice CALL: A metallic *chep* or *chi-chep*.

Status & Distribution Uncommon to fairly common. BREEDING: Pine forests in the northern Bahamas (Grand Bahama, Abaco, Andros). Uses abandoned cavities in trees and sometimes on buildings; 2–4 eggs (Apr.–July). WINTER: Some winter on the breeding grounds, with some moving south to the southern Bahamas and rarely to eastern Cuba (Nov.–Mar.). VAGRANT: Casual in southern FL (9+ records).

Population Species is vulnerable due to small geographic range, and world population estimated at approximately 2,500 pairs.

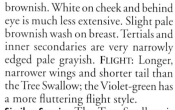

adults

Genus *Stelgidopteryx*

NORTHERN ROUGH-WINGED SWALLOW *Stelgidopteryx serripennis*

adult

adult

adult

juvenile

Named for the inconspicuous serrations on the first primary feather on the wing, this swallow is unique among birds of N.A. Polytypic (4–5 ssp.; 2 in N.A.). L 5" (13 cm)
Identification ADULT: Upperparts brown, with rump slightly paler; throat and breast pale brownish; underparts dirty white. Square tail. JUVENILE: Similar to adults, bright cinnamon-edged tertials and wing coverts. FLIGHT: Deliberate, floppy wingbeats. Broad-based triangular wings and broad chest.
Geographic Variation Southwestern sub-

species *(psammochrous)* is paler.
Similar Species Bank Swallow has clean white throat and belly, distinct brown breast band. Immature Tree Swallow has white throat and dusky on breast usually not meeting in center.
Voice CALL: Series of loose, low-pitched, upwardly inflected *brrt* notes, a buzzy *jrrr-jrrr-jrrr-jrrr, or a* higher pitched *brzzzzzt.*
Status & Distribution Fairly common over a wide altitudinal range. BREEDING: Open areas; often near rocky gorges, road cuts, gravel pits, or exposed sand banks. NEST: Singly or in small colonies in natural burrows or crevices, and on man-made structures; 4–8 eggs (May–June). MIGRATION: In eastern N.A. arrives in early Mar. in FL to mid-Apr. in MI. In West, arrives in mid-Feb. in southern CA to mid-Apr. in OR and WA. In eastern N.A. fall migration prolonged, late July–early Oct. Trans-Gulf migration suspected but not proved. In West, mainly in

Aug. with some into Sept. WINTER: Lowlands and foothills from Mex. to C.A., with small numbers in the Caribbean. Some winter in U.S. along Gulf Coast from TX to FL Panhandle and in southeastern CA and southern AZ. VAGRANT: Rare in YK; casual northern AK.
Population No serious threats identified, and species adapts well to nesting on man-made structures.

Genus *Riparia*

BANK SWALLOW *Riparia riparia*

Our smallest swallow, the Bank is one of the few passerines with nearly worldwide distribution. Polytypic (3–5 ssp.; *riparia* in N.A.). L 4.8" (12 cm)
Identification ADULT: Upperparts

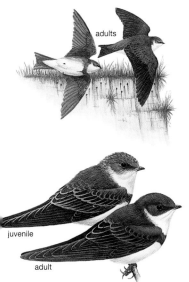

adults

juvenile

adult

brown, underparts clean white with distinct brown breast band. Slightly forked tail. JUVENILE: Similar to adult. Wing coverts and tertails narrowly edged buff. FLIGHT: Sweeps wings backward with quick flicking wingbeats. Narrow, pointed wings, slim body. Flight feathers contrastingly dark from above.
Similar Species Northern Rough-winged Swallow is larger, has a dusky throat gradually blending into dirty white underparts. Immature Tree Swallow is larger, shows an incomplete breast band.
Voice CALL: Most frequently heard is a series of buzzy *trrrt* notes.
Status & Distribution Locally common. BREEDING: Lowland areas along coastlines, rivers, lakes, and other wetlands; also in gravel quarries and road cuts. Small to large colonies in burrows in sand banks or cliffs; 1–9 eggs (Apr.––June). MIGRATION: Departs S.A. in Feb., through U.S. from early Mar. in South to late May in North. During fall migration, often in large flocks.

Among the earliest to depart in the East, with most birds departing the Great Lakes by early Sept.; late July to early Nov. in FL; peak in late July and Aug. WINTER: Most often in wetlands areas, nearly throughout S.A. as far south as central Chile and northern Argentina, Pacific slope of southern Mexico, rarely in eastern Panama and in the Caribbean. Rare in southern CA, southern TX.
Population Road building and quarries have changed breeding distribution in many areas. Erosion negatively affects breeding colonies.

Genus Petrochelidon

Two of the 3 species in this New World genus are found in North America. Four Old World species are sometimes included in this genus. Characterized by square tails, some rufous on the head, orangish or chestnut rumps, and white-striped dark backs, all build mud nests. This genus is sometimes merged with the more widespread *Hirundo*.

CLIFF SWALLOW *Petrochelidon pyrrhonota*

southwestern
melanogaster

Look for their large nesting colonies on cliffs as well as on buildings and under bridges. Polytypic. 5.5" (14 cm)

Identification ADULT: Square tail; orangish buff rump; dark cap extending below eye; chestnut cheeks, sides of neck, and throat; bluish black on lower throat; cream to buffy forehead patch. Underparts, including flanks, whitish. JUVENILE: Similar to adult, but entire head usually dark brownish black, sometimes with small pale grayish, whitish, or rusty forehead patch. Rump paler buff. Chin and upper throat pattern quite variable, some mixed with white, full black, gray, or cinnamon. FLIGHT: Short triangular wings and square tail. Whitish underparts and paler underwings contrast with dark head and

juvenile

throat. HYBRID: Very rare; hybrids with the Barn Swallow and Tree Swallow (once) known. Cave Swallow hybrids possible but not confirmed.

Geographic Variation Considerable intergradation between 4 recognized subspecies. Western *(hypopolia)* similar to nominate Eastern *(pyrrhonota)* subspecies, but larger, with larger, paler forehead, whiter breast, grayer flanks, paler rump, more rufescent underparts. Two southwestern subspecies, *tachina* and *melanogaster*, are smaller, show darker cinnamon to chestnut foreheads.

Similar Species Cave Swallow (see sidebar below).

Voice CALL: A subdued squeaky twittering given in flight and near nest.

Status & Distribution Locally common. BREEDING: Various habitats, including grasslands, towns, open forest, and river edges wherever there are cliff faces or escarpments for nesting. Small to large colonies, on cliff faces and on man-made structures (sometimes with Barn Swallows), rarely at cave entrances. A gourd-shaped structure built entirely of mud and saliva; 1–6 eggs (Apr.–June). MIGRATION: Always via C.A. Departs

winter range in early Feb. Arrives in southern CA early Feb., AZ in early Mar., IL in early Apr., and AK in mid-May. Departs after nestlings fledge, sometimes as early as late June. Peak is Aug.–early Sept., earlier in Southwest (July–early Aug.). May linger to early Nov. in East. WINTER: Grasslands, agricultural areas, near towns, and in marshes. S.A, from southern Argentina south to south-central Argentina. VAGRANT: Casual in Barbados in winter. Accidental to Wrangel I., Siberia, southern Greenland, and U.K.

Population Has expanded its range into the Great Plains and eastern N.A. in the past 150 years.

Cliff versus Cave Swallow in the East

Strong weather systems, characterized by prolonged strong west or southwest winds, sometimes bring Cave Swallows to the Atlantic and Great Lakes states late October through November. Cliff Swallows have typically left for their South American winter areas by then, but occasionally lingerers are recorded, presenting an identification challenge. The subspecies of Cave Swallow most likely occurring in the East during and following these weather events is thought to be the southwestern *pelodoma*, not the geographically closer *fulva*.

Adults of the eastern subspecies of Cliff Swallow *(pyrrhonota)* show a bright cream-colored forehead, unlike the Cave's chestnut forehead. Cliffs can be distinguished by their dark heads, including the throat,

Cave Swallow (NJ, Nov.)

Cliff Swallow (CA)

contrasting with whitish underparts. The Cave has a pale buff throat contrasting little with the breast.

Juvenile Cliffs typically have dark heads, but some have a few paler markings on the throat. Juvenile Caves are similar to adults; a small dark cap is relatively easy to see against pale buff cheeks and throat, even in flight. ∎

CAVE SWALLOW *Petrochelidon fulva*

juvenile

southwest
pelodoma

West Indies
fulva

This small, square-tailed, buff-rumped swallow has expanded its breeding range by utilizing man-made structures. Polytypic (3–6 ssp.; 3 in N.A.). L 5.5" (14 cm)
Identification ADULT: Square tail and orangish buff to russet-chestnut rump. Has a small blackish cap extending to the top of the eye, which gives the bird a somewhat masked look; broad pale buff collar, cheeks, and throat; chestnut forehead patch. Wings, tail, and uppertail coverts blackish; back is black with narrow white stripes. Underparts are whitish with pale buff flanks. JUVENILE: Similar to adult, but with less extensive forehead patch, variably paler chin and throat, browner back lacking distinct white stripes, and duller flanks. FLIGHT: Has a small black cap with pale buff collar and face visible at some distance. Glides frequently.

HYBRID: Rarely with the Barn Swallow, suspected with the Cliff Swallow.
Geographic Variation Subtle. Subspecies breeding in Florida *(fulva)* is slightly smaller, shows tawny-buff flanks, richer rufous-buff rump; subspecies breeding in southwestern U.S. *(pelodoma)* is slightly larger, shows grayish buff flanks, variable orange-buff rump. VAGRANT: Cuban subspecies *(cavicola)* probably not separable in the field from *fulva*.
Similar Species The Cliff Swallow, especially southwestern subspecies (see sidebar p. 438).
Voice CALL: Various chattering notes, including a short, clear *weet* or *che-weet*, ascending or descending in pitch. SONG: A complex squeaky twittering, slightly higher pitched and more prolonged than that of the Cliff Swallow.
Status & Distribution Locally common, but patchy in distribution. Migration little known, and wintering grounds of most U.S. breeding birds essentially unknown. BREEDING: Natural or man-made structure often near water. Has only recently expanded northward into the U.S.; first recorded nesting in TX in 1910, NM in 1930, and FL in 1987. Continues to expand in TX, but still fairly restricted in southern FL and NM. In colonies in twilight zone of caves, sinkholes, culverts, and under bridges (sometimes with Barn and Cliff Swallows), often high up and inaccessible

in caves. A crescent-shaped half bowl built entirely out of mud and saliva, sometimes with bat guano; 3–5 eggs (Apr.–Aug.). MIGRATION: Movements and routes little known. In spring, arrives mid-Feb.–early Mar. in NM. Departs from NM late Oct.–mid-Nov. Routes largely unknown, but has been reported from western Mexico, Curaçao, Costa Rica, and Panama (sight records). WINTER: Florida birds may winter in Caribbean. Winter range of Cave Swallows nesting in NM unknown. Texas birds move south to unknown areas, but since the 1980s hundreds have overwintered in southern TX, often along streams, rivers, or lakes. VAGRANT: Recent annual late fall invasions on eastern seaboard and in Great Lakes (see sidebar p. 438). A few spring records there as well. Casual to accidental in spring or summer in AZ, CA, central Great Plains, MS, AL, and NS. Cuban subspecies *(cavicola)* vagrant to southern FL.
Population Cave Swallows are potentially vulnerable to disturbance at nesting colonies, although populations appear stable. The species is expanding its breeding range to north and east using man-made bridges and culverts, most dramatically in Texas since the mid-1980s. Cave Swallows are vulnerable to temperature extremes and adverse weather conditions in New Mexico and Texas.

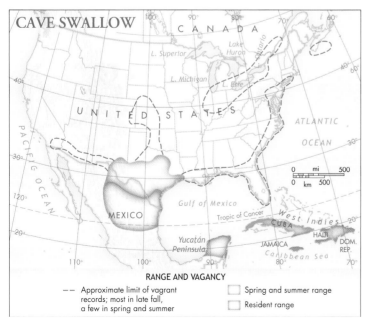

CAVE SWALLOW

CANADA

UNITED STATES

ATLANTIC OCEAN

MEXICO

Gulf of Mexico

Tropic of Cancer

CUBA

Yucatán Peninsula

JAMAICA

HAITI

DOM. REP.

West Indies

Caribbean Sea

PACIFIC OCEAN

0 mi 500
0 km 500

RANGE AND VAGANCY

– – Approximate limit of vagrant records; most in late fall, a few in spring and summer

☐ Spring and summer range

☐ Resident range

Genus Hirundo

BARN SWALLOW *Hirundo rustica*

This most widely distributed and abundant swallow in the world is familiar to birders and nonbirders. Polytypic (6–8 ssp.; *erythrogaster* breeds in N.A.). L 6.8"(17 cm)

Identification ADULT MALE: Deep iridescent blue crown, back, rump, and wing coverts; deeply forked tail with large white spots; rich buff to rufous forehead and underparts; iridescent blue patches on sides of breast, sometimes with very narrow connection in center. Wings and tail black. ADULT FEMALE: Similar to male but with paler underparts and less deeply forked tail. IMMATURE: Duller above than adults, with shorter but still deeply forked tail, buffy throat and forehead, whitish underparts. FLIGHT: Very pointy wings, deeply forked tail, and low zigzagging flight are distinctive. HYBRIDS: Rarely reported. Cliff and Cave Swallows in N.A., and Common House-Martin in Old World.

Geographic Variation Eurasian subspecies *(rustica),* casual in Alaska, has clean white underparts with broader dark breast band. East Asian subspecies

(gutturalis) similar to *rustica* but smaller, usually with incomplete blue breast band.

Similar Species No other swallow in North America shows such a deeply forked tail. Shorter-tailed juveniles in flight may suggest the Tree Swallow but will always show partial dark breast band and buff throat, white spots on tail.

Voice CALL: In flight repeats a high-pitched, slightly squeaky *chee-jit.* SONG: A long series of squeaky warbling phrases, interspersed with a nasal grating rattle.

Status & Distribution Common. BREEDING: In various habitats in lowlands and foothills with nearby open areas and water. Former natural nesting locales, including caves and cliff faces, have now mostly been abandoned in favor of a variety of man-made structures, including barns. A cup-shaped bowl made entirely of mud and the bird's saliva; 3–7 eggs (May–June). MIGRATION: In spring, arrives in extreme southern U.S. late Jan.–early Feb., peaking in mid-May in northeastern U.S. Early arrival in AK in mid-May. Departs northeastern U.S. as early as mid-July, peaking late Aug.–early Sept. Main routes through

C.A. and through Caribbean, but also a trans-Gulf migrant. WINTER: Often in fields and marshes mainly in lowlands; rarely in southern U.S. Uncommon from Mex. south through C.A. Most common throughout S.A. as far as central Chile and northern Argentina; breeding noted in Buenos Aires. VAGRANT: North American subspecies casual or accidental in western and northern AK and HI, southern Greenland, Tierra del Fuego, Falkland Is. Eurasian subspecies *(rustica)* casual in western AK, NT, NU, and southern Labrador. East Asian subspecies *(gutturalis)* casual in western AK and accidental in BC.

Population Common worldwide. In North America, the breeding range has been expanded by using man-made structures for nesting.

Eurasian rustica

dark

juvenile

adults

Genus Delichon

COMMON HOUSE-MARTIN *Delichon urbicum*

This Old World species is casual in migration in Alaska and on St. Pierre and Miquelon. Polytypic. L 5" (13 cm)

Identification ADULT MALE: Deep blue upperparts, white rump and underparts, forked tail, whitish underwing coverts. ADULT FEMALE: Similar to male; grayer underparts. JUVENILE: Duller upperparts, less deeply forked tail.

Geographic Variation Western European subspecies *(urbica)* shows dark uppertail coverts below white rump, forked

tail. East Asian subspecies *(lagopoda)* shows white uppertail coverts continuous with white rump, slightly less deeply forked tail.

Similar Species Tree and Violet-green Swallows lack white rump. Most similar is the Asian House-Martin *(D. dasypus),* not yet recorded from N.A., which shows duller upperparts, gray-brown underwing coverts, pale gray wash on throat and

undertail coverts, less deeply forked tail.

Voice CALL: A scratchy *prrit.* SONG: A soft twittering.

Status & Distribution BREEDING: Western Europe to eastern Siberia. VAGRANT: AK (1 specimen was tentatively identified as *lagopoda,* 7 sight records), St. Pierre and Miquelon Is. (1 sight record, likely *urbica*).

lagopoda

CHICKADEES AND TITMICE Family Paridae

Bridled Titmouse (AZ, May)

These lively sprites top many people's lists of favorite birds. The North American Paridae divides neatly into 2 groups: brightly patterned chickadees (7 sp.) and mostly drab titmice (5 sp.). They inhabit tundra, high mountains, desert scrub, old-growth forests, small woodland patches, urban parks, and suburban backyards. Nearly all are sedentary. The northernmost species can endure frigid winters, migrating only in intermittent irruptions south or moving short distances down-elevation for the winter when food is scarce. Among the most intensively studied North American birds, parids have provided immense knowledge and understanding of physiological adaptation, hybridization, vocalization, genetic variations and relationships, socialization, and many other aspects of avian behavior.

Structure Parids are small birds, either round-headed (chickadees) or prominently crested (titmice). Their relatively short, rounded wings and long tails are aerodynamically suited for agility in crowded habitats. Their short, sharply pointed bills are designed to grasp tiny arthropods and crack small seeds.

Behavior Acrobatic feeders, parids glean high and low, flitting from leaf to leaf and branch to branch in noisy chatter, nearly always easy to see and hear. Their vocal repertoires are exceedingly complex. Most species sing in clear whistles, and all have sputtering variations of *tsick-a-dee* or *chirr-chirr,* plus a seemingly endless array of gargles, twitters, and *zeets*—each sound used in a particular behavioral context. Parids eagerly visit bird feeders. All are cavity-nesters, and many use nest boxes.

Plumage The chickadee's standard features include a dark cap, white or partly gray cheeks, and a black bib; their body colors are various shades of gray or brown. Titmice are typically dull, unpatterned gray or brown, brightened only by rusty flanks in several species and by a brightly patterned face in one. The sexes in most species look alike, and juveniles differ little from adults.

Distribution The Paridae includes more than 60 species around the globe, with 12 occurring in North America. At distributional extremes, Black-capped and Boreal Chickadees span the continent, while only the northernmost Mexican Chickadees and Bridled Titmice and the easternmost Gray-headed Chickadees reach N.A. The family includes habitat generalists such as the Carolina Chickadee, at home in remote southeastern river bottomlands and crowded urban parks, as well as species with strong habitat preferences such as the Oak Titmouse, which relies heavily on the woodlands of its name.

Taxonomy The classification of North American chickadees has long been stable, but titmice have undergone considerable flux. The AOU divided the Plain Titmouse into Oak and Juniper species in 1997. Black-crested and Tufted Titmice, traditionally classified as separate species, were merged in 1976 and then separated again in 2002. The Black-capped Chickadee is the most variable of our parids, with at least 9 subspecies recognized in 3 geographic groups. The least geographically variable parid in N.A. is the Tufted Titmouse, which is monotypic.

Conservation Loss of habitat may be a potential threat to a few species, especially for the Oak Titmouse in California, where its favored oak woodlands are being destroyed for suburbs and agriculture. BirdLife International lists 1 species as threatened and 3 others as near threatened, none in North America. —*Paul Hess*

CHICKADEES Genus *Poecile*

Worldwide this Northern Hemisphere genus consists of 15 species, named chickadees in the New World and tits in the Old World, all of them formerly classified in the genus *Parus*. Seven of these species occur in North America, but the Mexican Chickadee and the Gray-headed Chickadee breed here only at the limits of their ranges.

MOUNTAIN CHICKADEE *Poecile gambeli*

This chickadee can be found above 12,000 feet, sometimes to timberline and beyond. It spends a lot of time in the postbreeding season caching conifer seeds for the winter. It forages higher in tall trees than most chickadee species, and it often spends the nonbreeding season foraging in flocks with Chestnut-backed and Black-capped Chickadees, as well as migrating passerines, including warblers and vireos. Polytypic. L 5.3" (13 cm)

Identification The white supercilium, which consists of white-tipped feathers, is unique among chickadees. Black cap, usually fronted by a white forehead that connects to the supercilium; black bib; white cheeks; grayish, brownish, or olive upperparts, depending upon the subspecies; greater wing coverts, secondaries, and tertials indistinctly edged with pale gray; dull white breast and belly; pale buff to drab gray, sometimes washed olive, sides and flanks.

Geographic Variation Four subspecies in N.A., plus another in Mexico—only 2 are field-identifiable. Nominate *gambeli* in the Rocky Mountains, the most wide-ranging subspecies, is tinged with buff or brownish olive on the back, has buffy sides and flanks, and has a prominent white supercilium. California's *baileyae* is entirely grayish on the back, sides, and flanks, sometimes with a slight olive tinge. It has a less distinct supercilium than *gambeli*. The other subspecies have various features intermediate between these two.

Similar Species When the supercilium is less conspicuous, as in the western subspecies, or when the feather tips are worn, a Mountain could be confused with its closest relative, the Black-capped. The latter sometimes has a hint of white in its superciliary area, but this condition is very rare. The wing edgings offer the most helpful distinction between the two: pale gray and inconspicuous on the Mountain, prominently white on the Black-capped. The Mountain's small bib should distinguish it from a Mexican Chickadee. A vagrant of the Rocky Mountain subspecies with a worn eyebrow might be troublesome in the westernmost Carolina Chickadee range, but the Mountain is noticeably larger, and its upperparts are brownish or olive in contrast to the Carolina's dull gray upperparts.

Voice CALL: A hoarse *chick-dzee-dzee-dzee,* as well as a variety of buzzes and chips. SONG: Typically a 3- or 4-note descending whistle, *fee-bee-bay,* or a *fee-ee-bee-bee* on 1 pitch, with many local dialects. The *fee-bee-bay* version has been compared to the melody of "Three Blind Mice." Some of its vocalizations are very similar to those of the Black-capped, and a good look may be necessary to ascertain the species.

Status & Distribution Common. BREEDING: Primarily found in montane coniferous forests and mixed woodlands, but locally in pinyon-juniper and desert riparian woodlands. Sometimes use nest boxes. WINTER: Some descend to lower elevations in foothills, riparian woodlands in valleys, and suburban areas, where it sometimes visits feeders. More or less regular to coastal CA; more rarely to southern AZ. VAGRANT: Casual, mostly in winter, east to SK, ND, SD, KS, NE, OK, and the TX Panhandle.

Population Breeding bird surveys show a long-term decline in many parts of the Mountain's range, but the causes have not been established.

Rockies *gambeli*

baileyae

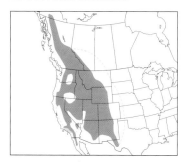

MEXICAN CHICKADEE *Poecile sclateri*

This Mexican species barely reaches the U.S. It calls frequently, and in the postbreeding season it forages among mixed-species flocks of as many as a hundred birds. Polytypic (4 ssp.; only *eidos* occurs north of Mexico). L 5" (13 cm)

Identification Black crown; the black bib, largest of any chickadee species, extends well down onto the breast; white cheeks; dark gray upperparts, sides, and flanks.

Similar Species Only chickadee within its limited U.S. range.

Voice CALL: Husky, nasal buzzes, such as *zhree;* various *tsip* or *chit* calls. SONG: A rapid, slightly buzzy warble, *chee-lee, chee-lee, chee-lee;* no clear whistled song.

Status & Distribution Uncommon to fairly common, but local, at high elevations. YEAR-ROUND: Mainly in montane coniferous forests to at least 9,000 feet at its northern range limits—the "sky islands" in the Chiricahua Mountains in southeast AZ and the Animas and Peloncillo (scarce) Mountains in southwestern NM. Some birds move to lower-elevation (±6,000 ft.) woodlands in the postbreeding season.

Population No trend data are available.

CAROLINA CHICKADEE *Poecile carolinensis*

The Carolina Chickadee is quite at home in cities and towns, readily using nest boxes and bird feeders. In fall and winter, the Carolina forages in mixed flocks with nuthatches, woodpeckers, warblers, and other woodland species. The only chickadee in the Southeast, the Carolina is smaller and duller than most other chickadee species. Polytypic. L 4.8" (12 cm)

Identification The cap and bib are black; the cheeks are white, usually tinged at rear with pale gray; the back and rump are gray, sometimes with an olive wash; the greater coverts are gray without pale edgings; the secondaries and tertials are indistinctly edged in dull white or pale gray; the flanks are pale grayish, tinged buffy when fresh in fall.

Geographic Variation Four subspecies—largest and palest on upperparts in western portions of the range; smallest and darkest in Florida. Differences are weak and clinal where ranges meet. Subspecies are not field-identifiable.

Similar Species The absence of white wing edgings on greater coverts and the grayish wash on flanks, even when slightly tinged with buff, help to separate it from the Black-capped. The

Carolina interbreeds extensively in some areas with the Black-capped along a belt from Kansas to New Jersey; the hybrid offspring are not easily identifiable (see sidebar below). Paler sides and flanks distinguish it from the Mountain Chickadee when the usually conspicuous white supercilium of the latter species is not visible.

Voice CALL: A fast and high-pitched *chick-a-dee-dee-dee*. Compare to Black-capped's call. SONG: A 4-note whistle, *fee-bee fee-bay*, the last note lowest in pitch. A Carolina may learn the Black-capped's 2- or 3-note song in areas where their ranges overlap, so do not identify by song alone at the contact zone.

Status & Distribution Common. YEAR-ROUND: Open deciduous forests, woodland clearings and edges, suburbs, and urban parks; in the Appalachians it prefers lower elevations than the Black-capped, but it has been recorded regularly as high as 6,000 feet. VAGRANT: Wanders casually short distances north; single records in MI and ON are extraordinary.

Population Apparently declining in some regions in recent decades, particularly in the Gulf Coast states, but its range has expanded northward along much of the contact zone with the Black-capped, particularly in Ohio and Pennsylvania.

Separating Black-capped and Carolina Chickadees

The differences between these two species are usually straightforward, except where the two species overlap and interbreed. Keep in mind the following:

1. Greater coverts. Brightly edged with white on the Black-capped, but inconspicuously bordered in dull whitish or gray on the Carolina.

2. Fringes of secondaries, tertials, and outer retrices. Prominently white on the Black-capped, but indistinctly dull whitish or grayish white on the Carolina.

3. Flanks. Pinkish tinged contrasting with pale gray breast and belly on the Black-capped, but dull grayish buff (and entirely grayish when worn) on the Carolina.

4. Wear of feather tips. The Black-capped's wing and tail edgings less bright in spring and summer, but still more conspicuous than those of the Carolina.

However, at the contact zone of the 2 species, a belt from Kansas to New Jersey, the hybrids or products of hybrid ancestry show a befud-

Black-capped Chickadee, fresh

Carolina Chickadee, fresh

dling combination of Black-capped and Carolina characteristics. Intermediacy in plumage features is also evident in the Appalachian Mountains, where the Black-capped and Carolina are found at higher and lower elevations respectively. Vocalizations are not particularly helpful here either. A bird that looks like one species may learn to sing the other's song or, bilingually, the songs of both species. Some sing aberrant songs that are not exactly representative of either species. The *chick-a-dee* calls (typically higher-pitched and faster for the Carolina) may be more reliable at the zone, but even these do not always exactly match the normal sounds or are confusingly intermediate. Other features frequently mentioned in field guides—for example, differences in the extent of white on the cheek and relative sharpness of the bib's lower edge—are little or no help as well.

Where these 2 species occur together, it is probably best to leave many of them unidentified. ∎

BLACK-CAPPED CHICKADEE *Poecile atricapillus*

fresh fall

worn summer

The most widespread, numerous, and geographically variable chickadee, this bird brightens winter days at bird feeders and eagerly takes advantage of nest boxes. It is curious, with little or no fear of humans, and it is famous for willingly, after a little "training," taking seeds and nuts from the hand. During fall postbreeding movements, its noisy little parties usually contain titmice, nuthatches, woodpeckers, and other species. The calls of a flock of Black-cappeds in the fall often signal the presence of migrant warblers and vireos. Polytypic. L 5.3" (13 cm)

Identification Black cap; white cheek; black bib; gray upperparts; greater coverts, secondaries, and tertials edged conspicuously white in fall and winter (less distinct in summer when the white fringes are worn off); sides and flanks buffy or pinkish when fresh, fading to pale buff by summer when worn; outer tail feathers edged prominently white.

Geographic Variation Three subspecies groups differ in several characters. A "northwestern" group is small and dark-backed, with narrow white wing edgings, and flanks heavily washed buffy tan. An "interior western" group is large and pale-backed, with broad white wing edgings, and pale buffy sides and flanks. An "eastern" group is variable, but its subspecies are generally intermediate between the other 2 groups in size, darkness of back, prominence of white wing edgings, and richness of buff wash on the flanks.

Similar Species Although the Mountain Chickadee is the Black-capped's closest relative, the Carolina Chickadee likely will cause the most trouble, especially in late spring and summer when the Black-capped's white wing edgings are worn. Where their ranges overlap, the 2 species resemble each other and they also hybridize, intergrading characters (see sidebar p. 443). Otherwise, the combination of bright white cheek, especially in fresh plumage, pure black cap and bib, gray upperparts, bright wing edgings, and pinkish sides and flanks should distinguish the Black-capped from other species.

Voice CALL: *Chick-a-dee-dee-dee,* lower and slower than Carolina. SONG: A clear, whistled 2-noted *fee-bee* or 3-noted *fee-bee-ee,* the first note higher in pitch. In the Pacific Northwest some birds sing *fee-fee-fee* with no change in pitch.

Status & Distribution Common. YEAR-ROUND: Deciduous and mixed woodlands, clearings, suburbs, and urban parks. Occurs in the Appalachians at higher elevations than the Carolina. FALL & WINTER: Makes irregular irruptions south, usually not far into the Carolina's range, but casually to southeastern MO, eastern KY, eastern VA, MD, more exceptionally as far south as AZ, OK, and TX.

Population Stable or increasing in nearly all regions, though its range may be contracting in areas where the Carolina is expanding.

CHESTNUT-BACKED CHICKADEE *Poecile rufescens*

The Chestnut-backed Chickadee is curious about humans, and spends the postbreeding and winter seasons foraging noisily in mixed-species flocks. Unlike other parids (except for the Mountain Chickadee), it forages high in the canopies of tall conifers. This species is the smallest chickadee in North America. One of the 3 "brown-backed" species (along with Boreal and Gray-headed), its nominate subspecies is the most richly colored parid. Polytypic. L 4.8" (12 cm)

Identification The chestnut color of the back is unique, but it varies in intensity. The cap is dark brown, shading to black at its lower edge from the bill through the eye; the cheek is white; the bib is black; the back and rump are rufous; the greater wing coverts are edged white; the breast and belly are whitish; the sides and flanks are bright rufous or dull brown, depending upon the subspecies; the tail is brownish gray.

Geographic Variation Three subspecies. The widely distributed *rufescens* is the most colorful, with a rich chestnut back, bright white edgings on the greater wing coverts, and extensively bright rufous flanks. The other 2 subspecies are restricted to coastal California; they differ notably on the underparts. In Marin County, the *neglectus* has reduced, pale chestnut flanks that do not contrast conspicuously with the whitish breast

coastal central California *barlowi*

rufescens

and belly; *barlowi,* found from San Francisco to northern Santa Barbara County, has grayish flanks, tinged with olive brown.

Similar Species The Boreal Chickadee also has a dark brown cap and rich brown sides and flanks, but it has predominantly grayish cheeks, lacks a rufous tint on the back and rump, and shows no white wing edgings.

Voice CALL: A hoarse, high-pitched, rapid *sik-zee-zee* or just *zee-zee;* also a characteristic sharp *chek-chek.* SONG: No whistled song is known.

Status & Distribution Common. YEAR-ROUND: Coniferous forests, especially of Douglas fir, and mixed and deciduous woodlands. DISPERSAL: Postbreeding movements have been noted to higher elevations in BC and to lower elevations in OR. VAGRANT: Wanders irregularly inland as far as southwestern AB and casually south of its usual range to southern CA.

Population Its range has expanded southward and eastward in recent decades from humid coastal regions to the drier eastern San Francisco Bay area and the forested Sierra Nevada in California. Numbers appear to be stable in the northern portion of the range, but recent declines in the interior expansion area have raised conservation concerns.

BOREAL CHICKADEE *Poecile hudsonicus*

This species is one of North America's largest chickadees and, like the Gray-headed Chickadee, it survives winters in the far north by hoarding large supplies of food. Unlike the Gray-headed, it sometimes makes long-distance irruptions southward, apparently in autumns when food is scarce, and to the delight of birders in central and mid-Atlantic states. The Boreal was sometimes called the Brown-capped Chickadee in older literature—an apt name, although the rest of the upperparts are brownish as well. Many observers comment on its tameness around humans in much of the year, but those who seek the Boreal during the breeding season know that it is exceedingly quiet and inconspicuous. Polytypic. L 5.5" (14 cm)

Identification The largely gray cheek is unique among chickadee species. The cap is dull brown; the bib is black; the back and rump are brownish in eastern portions of the range and grayer in western regions; the wings are plain brownish with no pale edges on the coverts or secondaries; the sides and flanks are extensively washed with dull chestnut, brown with a reddish tinge, or tawny, depending upon subspecies.

Geographic Variation Five subspecies are generally recognized in two groups: a grayish backed group (2 ssp.) in western Canada and the U.S. and a more colorful brown-backed group (3 ssp.) in central and eastern portions of the range. At their extremes the plumage differences are notable, but the characters vary clinally across the range, and the subspecies are not field-identifiable.

Similar Species The brown cap, plain wings, and dusky auriculars distinguish it easily from the Black-capped Chickadee. The dull wings and darker face also separate it from the Chestnut-backed and Gray-headed Chickadees. The relatively grayish northwestern Boreal could bring to mind the Gray-headed, but the wings and face differ enough to identify either species. The gray cheek is much darker and more conspicuous than the pale grayish area at the rear of a Carolina Chickadee's cheek.

Voice CALL: A wheezy, nasal, drawled *tseek-day-day;* also a characteristic single, high *see* or *dee.* SONG: A clear trill. No whistled song is known. It is usually less vocal than the Black-capped with which it shares much of its range.

Status & Distribution Fairly common. YEAR-ROUND: Prefers spruce and balsam fir forests, ranging north to the treeline on the taiga; to a lesser extent mixed woodlands. Its range overlaps widely with the ranges of the Gray-headed in AK and Chestnut-backed in BC, WA, ID, and MT, but no hybridization is known. MIGRATION: Regular short-distance movements southward have been reported within MN, SK, and MB. WINTER: Move slightly south of breeding range and have occurred casually as far south as IA, IL, IN, OH, WV, PA, VA, MD, DE, and NJ—but few, if any, records in recent years.

Population Trend data are unreliable because populations have not been surveyed in much of the range. Numbers increase greatly over short periods of years during spruce budworm outbreaks, then decline, making judgments about trends difficult. Numbers are considered stable in most regions but surveys suggest a gradual long-term decline in recent decades, particularly along the southern edge of the range in the northern tier of the U.S. Extensive logging in Canadian boreal forests poses a potentially serious threat.

GRAY-HEADED CHICKADEE *Poecile cinctus*

Known in Eurasia as a Siberian Tit, this species is one of North America's hardest-to-see breeding birds. It remains on its home territory through the Arctic winter, surviving on hoarded food supplies. The bird has a small head and long tail. Polytypic. L 5.5" (14 cm)

Identification Brownish gray cap; white cheek including auriculars; black bib, frayed at corners; brown back and rump with grayish tinge; greater coverts, secondaries, and tertials prominently edged white; buffy to cinnamon sides and flanks; whitish breast and belly. Ragged bib edges are usually a good field mark.

Geographic Variation Three subspecies in northern Eurasia; *lathami,* in North America. Differences are weak and clinal, although *lathami* averages paler and grayer overall, with slightly darker cinnamon flanks.

Similar Species The brownish tint of its cap and back differentiate it from the Black-capped Chickadee. Grayish northwestern Boreal Chickadees are possibly confusing, but the white auriculars and bright wing edgings of the Gray-headed are distinctive.

Voice CALL: A loud *deer deer deer* or *chi-urr chi-urr.* Apparently no clear, whistled song.

Status & Distribution Rare. YEAR-ROUND: Coniferous forests in Europe and Asia; mainly willows and stunted spruces along waterways in Brooks Range, east through the northern YK to Mackenzie in AK and northwest Canada. Distribution in N.A. is not well known; traditional locations in AK include Kelly Bar at the confluence of the Kelly and Noatak Rivers north of Kotzebue and the Canning River area in Arctic N.W.R. VAGRANT: Several winter records for Fairbanks (at feeders) are the only valid vagrant records.

Population The species is declining in much of its extensive Eurasian range.

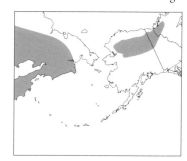

TITMICE Genus *Baeolophus*

All 5 species in this genus are New World titmice formerly classified in the genus *Parus.* Three breed almost entirely in North America, and 2 have substantial distributions in Mexico. Revisions to the taxonomy recently split the Plain Titmouse into Juniper and Oak species and separated the Black-crested Titmouse from the Tufted Titmouse.

OAK TITMOUSE *Baeolophus inornatus*

Once classified with the Juniper Titmouse as a subspecies of the aptly named Plain Titmouse, the Oak Titmouse is easily separable from other timice species except the Juniper. Its lack of field marks is, ironically, an important field mark. Polytypic. L 5" (13 cm)

Identification The bird is a drab brownish or grayish brown color overall, but is paler below. It has a short crest.

Geographic Variation Four subspecies, one restricted to Baja California; variation is weak and clinal. The northernmost subspecies, *inornatus,* from Oregon to south-central California, has medium brownish gray or olive-brown upperparts, pale gray underparts with pale brown tinge on flanks, and a short bill. The *affabilis* found in southwestern California is notably larger, has darker gray-brown or olive-brown upperparts, flanks washed in dusky brown, and a longer bill. The *mohavensis,* restricted to the Little San Bernardino Mountains in San Bernardino and Riverside Counties, is smaller, paler, and grayer than the *affabilis.*

Similar Species The closely related Juniper Titmouse is slightly larger, paler, and grayer, but similarly plain. The two are best separated by range; they are sedentary and are sympatric only in a small area of northern California. No other titmouse poses a problem; they can be identified by conspicuous differences in plumage on head or flanks.

Voice CALL: A hoarse *tsick-a-deer.* SONG: A series of clear, whistled sets of alternating high and low notes, such as *peter peter peter* or *teedle-ee teedle-ee,* with many variations.

Status & Distribution Common. YEAR-ROUND: Primarily oak and pine-oak woodlands on the Pacific slope. VAGRANT: Casually reported east of its usual limits in CA.

Population Declining in California because of losses in its preferred oak habitat, primarily by encroaching suburban and agricultural development, although disease could become a new threat with the appearance of Sudden Oak Death Syndrome.

affabilis

JUNIPER TITMOUSE *Baeolophus ridgwayi*

The Juniper Titmouse travels through woodlands in small family parties, does not habitually forage in mixed-species flocks, and will visit bird feeders. Formerly classified as a subspecies of Plain Titmouse, the Juniper has a much larger range than its close relative, the Oak Titmouse, yet its total population has been estimated at less than half that of the latter species. Polytypic. L 5.3" (13 cm)

Identification Sexes and ages similar. Drab medium-gray upperparts; grayish white underparts; short crest.

Geographic Variation Despite its wide distribution, the Juniper shows little geographic variation. Two or 3 subtly different subspecies are recognized,

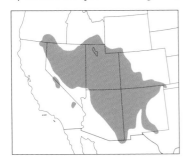

none of them identifiable in the field.

Similar Species The Juniper's utter lack of field marks sets it apart from all other titmice except for the Oak, which is slightly smaller, darker, and brownish tinted. To the eye, the differences appear slight, but genetic, morphological, ecological, and vocal characters set the species apart. They are best distinguished from each other by range; fortunately, they are quite sedentary, coming into contact only at the periphery of their ranges in a small area on the Modoc Plateau in northern California. Research at the contact zone indicates that there is little or no interbreeding and that physiological adaptations to temperature and precipitation differ significantly between the species.

Voice CALL: A hoarse, rapid *tsick-dee,* faster than the Oak, more like the Bridled Titmouse. SONG: A variety of long, rolling trills on a uniform pitch and 3-part groups of *wheed-leah,*

wheed-leah, wheed-leah. The male has a large repertoire of song types.

Status & Distribution Uncommon to fairly common. YEAR-ROUND: Primarily juniper and pinyon-juniper woodlands in the intermountain region and southward. It can be found at elevations up to 7,000–8,000 feet in AZ and NM.

Population Its relatively small numbers, low density, limited habitat preferences, and recent declines reported in the southern Rockies and the Colorado Plateau region have raised conservation concerns.

BRIDLED TITMOUSE *Baeolophus wollweberi*

Slightly smaller than other titmice, the Bridled sometimes behaves chickadee-like and at other times forages more slowly, more deliberately, and less noisily than other parids. Bridleds commune in substantial flocks, first as family groups and then, through fall and winter, in larger numbers of 2 dozen or more of their own species. They also form the nucleus of mixed-

species flocks, often including Mexican Chickadees and Juniper Titmice, which forage together flying from tree to tree. Polytypic. L 5.3" (13 cm)

Identification The Bridled's strikingly patterned face is an unmistakable field mark. ADULT: A black and white (the "bridle") face; a tall, dusty crest; a black throat, appearing as a small bib. The gray upperparts sometimes have an olive tint; the underparts are paler, washed with dull olive on the flanks; the belly sometimes has a yellow tint in fresh plumage. JUVENILE: The crest is shorter; the face pattern is duller; the bib is gray.

Similar Species The facial pattern and black throat separate it from all other titmice. The black bib might suggest a chickadee, when seen from below, but with a better look, the crest and face will easily eliminate that possibility.

Voice CALL: A rapid, high-pitched *tsic-ka-dee-dee* or a harsh *tzee-tzee-tzee-tzee,* similar to the Juniper. SONG: A rapid series of clear, whistled, identical *peet-peet* notes.

Status & Distribution Common. YEAR-ROUND: Oak, juniper, and sycamore

woodlands in mountains of southeastern AZ and southwestern NM, up to 7,000 feet. The main portion of its range is in Mexico. DISPERSAL: Flocks make local movements to riparian areas at lower elevations in winter. VAGRANT: Reports from TX have not been well documented.

Population The trend is uncertain because of insufficient monitoring, particularly in Mexico, but the Bridled's limited breeding range and the potential loss of its preferred habitats by logging and conversion to agriculture pose concern. The loss of oak woodlands has extirpated the species from some locations in Mexico.

TUFTED TITMOUSE *Baeolophus bicolor*

The active and noisy Tufted, North America's most widespread titmouse, is remarkably uniform morphologically, genetically, vocally, and behaviorally throughout its range. Besides gleaning trees and shrubs for arthropods, it spends more time on the ground searching leaf litter than do chickadees and most other titmouse species. The Tufted Titmouse does not usually associate with mixed-species flocks; after the breeding season it spends a lot of time in small foraging parties that typically consist of parents and their offspring. The Tufted Titmouse frequents well-vegetated urban and suburban areas, willingly uses nest boxes, and regularly visits bird feeders. Monotypic. L 6.3" (16 cm)

Identification ADULT: Gray crest; black forehead; gray upperparts; pale gray or whitish breast and belly; flanks prominently washed in rust or orange. JUVENILE: Gray forehead, rather than black; slightly paler crest than in the adult. HYBRID: Tufted and Black-crested Titmice interbreed in a north-south 30- to 60-mile–wide (50–100 km) belt extending from Oklahoma through central Texas, producing offspring with variably intermediate dusky crests and grayish foreheads that make identification near impossible.

Similar Species The only other titmouse likely found in its range is the Black-crested, which has a pale forehead. Juniper is much plainer and does not have brightly washed flanks.

Voice CALL: A harsh, scolding *zhee zhee zhee*. SONG: A loud, whistled *peto peto peto* or *wheedle wheedle wheedle*, often repeated monotonously.

Status & Distribution Common. YEAR-ROUND: Deciduous woodlands, suburbs, urban parks, wherever else trees are large enough to provide nest holes. DISPERSAL: Wanders casually north of its usual limits in fall and winter; records from SD, MN, QC, and NB.

Population The species is increasing in nearly every part of its range. Expansion northward has been under way for at least a century, and the movement continues through northern New England and southern Canada. The bird's extreme sedentary nature probably accounts for the slow progression.

BLACK-CRESTED TITMOUSE *Baeolophus atricristatus*

Except for its black crest, which no other titmouse has, and forehead, the Black-crested Titmouse could be a mirror image of the Tufted Titmouse in behavior and appearance. Throughout the summer, fall, and winter, this lively, noisy, and continually active bird forages in small family groups, searching trees and shrubs for insects, spiders, and their eggs. Confiding and curious, it shows little fear of humans and does not hesitate to use nest boxes. Polytypic. L 5.8" (15 cm)

Identification ADULT: Black crown and crest; dull white forehead; medium to dark gray upperparts, sometimes with a slight olive tinge; pale gray underparts with a cinnamon wash on the flanks. JUVENILE: Gray crest, sometimes washed with brown; dusky forehead. HYBRID: Black-crested and Tufted Titmice interbreed in a north-south 30- to 60-mile-wide (50–100 km) belt extending from Oklahoma through central Texas. The offspring show variably intermediate shades of dusky crests and gray or brownish foreheads, making it near impossible to assign them to a species.

Geographic Variation Three subspecies differ slightly in size and plumage coloration; they are not field-identifiable.

Similar Species Juveniles with gray crests may be difficult to distinguish from the Tufted or the Juniper Titmouse. Look for the juvenile Black-crested's whitish forehead and crown darker than upperparts.

Voice CALL: A harsh, scolding *jree jree jree*, sharper and more nasal than the Tufted. SONG: A series of slurred *chew chew chew* or *pe-chee-chee-chee* phrases, faster than the Tufted's similar vocalizations.

Status & Distribution Common. YEAR-ROUND: The Black-crested inhabits

oak and other deciduous woodlands along watercourses, open tracts with scattered trees, arid scrubby habitats, and urban and suburban areas west of the hybrid belt; east of the belt their preferred habitat is moister and denser woodlands.

Population No trend data exist, but fragmentation of oak-woodland habitats has raised concern. The Black-crested's return to full species status in 2002 has brought renewed attention to monitoring its numbers and its potential conservation needs.

PENDULINE TITS AND VERDINS Family Remizidae

Verdin (CA)

These are very small birds that generally resemble chickadees. All species have small, sharply pointed bills. Some species, like the Verdin, are rather solitary, while others are quite gregarious and nest in loose colonies. Nests of most species are a tightly woven bag or ball with a tubular side entrance.

Structure Most species are small-bodied, with a short tail. Although small, the Verdin of North America and the Penduline Tit of Eurasia, are notably larger and longer tailed than other family members. The bill is short and sharply pointed. The legs are long and slender.

Behavior They are acrobatic, easily moving through dense foliage and even hanging upside down while foraging. They often hold larger prey items under a foot while tearing it apart with the bill.

Plumage Most of the species in this family have nondescript plumage. They primarily have gray, olive, or yellow upperparts with pale, or white, underparts. One member of the family, the Penduline Tit, has rather ornate plumage.

Distribution The family reaches its greatest diversity in Africa. Singles species are found in North America and Europe; 2 are present in Asia.

Taxonomy Worldwide, there are 10 species in 5 genera. The Remizidae family is sometimes classified as a subfamily of the Paridae. A diverse assemblage of species and further research may result in 1 or more members moved to other families. The Penduline Tit is sometimes treated as a complex of up to 4 species.

Conservation No member of the family is considered of conservation concern, although 2 are considered rare, and many aspects of their biology are poorly known.
—*Mark W. Lockwood*

Genus *Auriparus*

VERDIN *Auriparus flaviceps*

juvenile

An acrobatic species, the Verdin is generally solitary away from nest sites. It is most easily detected by its surprisingly loud calls. Nest is an intricately woven ball of spiderwebs and small twigs. The male often builds several structures during the nesting season; both sexes roost in these year-round. Polytypic (4–6 ssp.; 2 in N.A.). L 4.5" (11 cm)

Identification Very small body size with a medium-length tail. Sexes similar. ADULT: Dull gray overall, darker on upperparts, with a yellow face and chestnut shoulder. Small though heavy bill with a straight culmen that is sharply pointed. JUVENILE: Similar to adult, but paler gray and lacking the yellow face and chestnut shoulder making them appear very plain. Juveniles also have a pale base to bill.

Geographic Variation Variation in the 2 North American subspecies is weak and clinal. Western birds *(acaciarum)* tend to have more brownish coloration on the upperparts than those found from southern New Mexico to central Texas *(ornatus)*.

Similar Species Yellow face and chestnut shoulder of adults distinguish them from other chickadee-like birds. Juvenile similar to Lucy's Warbler (particularly the female) but can be distinguished by its heavier bill with a pale base. The Bushtit has a longer tail and smaller bill with a curved culmen. Gnatcatchers have longer, black tails and prominent eye rings.

Voice CALL: A clear *tschep* and rapid *chip* notes. SONG: A plaintive 3-note whistle, *tee tyew too,* with the second note higher.

Status & Distribution Common; uncommon in UT and rare in OK and TX Panhandle. YEAR-ROUND: Resident in desert scrub and other brushy habitats, including mesquite woodlands.

Population Stable, although there is very little data concerning this species.

LONG-TAILED TITS AND BUSHTITS Family Aegithalidae

Bushtit, male (CA)

This family is characterized by very small birds with short wings and long tails. The small body size combined with rather loose contour feathers gives these birds the look of tiny fluff balls. **Structure** Small bodied; long tailed. All species have small black, conical bills; legs generally long and slender.

Behavior Sociable birds that live in small family groups during breeding season and congregate in larger flocks in nonbreeding season. Typically thought to be monogamous, but cooperative breeders and nest "helpers" recorded. **Plumage** In general, species in this family are gray or brown above and white below. Most have a black or brown mask, often combined with a black bib. Others are fairly uniform in color, such as the Bushtit. Sexes are similar in plumage, although juveniles are often distinctive. **Distribution** This family's greatest diversity is in the Himalaya and western China; single species in Europe and N.A. **Taxonomy** Sometimes included as a subfamily of Paridae; however, they differ in several important aspects, and DNA analysis confirms the distinctiveness of the family. The Bushtit is the only New World representative and is put in its own genus. It is a polymorphic species with 3 well-defined subspecies. These groups were formerly recognized as separate species; however, there is considerable intergradation in contact zone between these populations. Worldwide there are about 11 species in 4 genera, although taxonomic opinions vary. **Conservation** No member of the family is considered of conservation concern, but some Asian species are not well known. —*Mark W. Lockwood*

Genus Psaltriparus

BUSHTIT *Psaltriparus minimus*

This acrobatic species is most often encountered as a small- to medium-size flock moves through woodland. Its presence is usually announced by the almost constant calling between members of the groups as they move from tree to tree. Nest is an intricately woven hanging structure. Polytypic (10 ssp.; 5 in N.A.). L 4.5" (11 cm)

Identification Very small body size and long tail distinguish this species from other chickadee-like birds. ADULT: Pale gray overall, darker on upperparts, with very small bill. Interior birds have brown ear patch with a gray crown; coastal birds have a brown cap. Adult females have pale eyes. JUVENILE: Similar to adult except in Southwest, where juvenile males can show a black ear patch. Juvenile females develop pale eyes a few weeks after fledging.

Geographic Variation Subspecies in N.A. usually divided into 2 groups: brown-capped *(minimus)* of the Pacific coast and gray-capped *(plumbeus)* of the inter-mountain West. "Black-eared" Bushtit, from southeastern AZ eastward through central TX, was once considered a separate species but is a polymorphic variation mainly seen in juvenile males. There is evidence of an intergradation zone between gray-capped birds and the black-eared birds *(melanotis)* that occur through the remainder of the species range.

Similar species Immature Verdin more uniform in overall body plumage and has a shorter tail. Gnatcatchers have longer, black tails, prominent eye ring. **Voice** Sharp twittering *tsip* or *tseet*. **Status & Distribution** Common. YEAR-ROUND: Resident in a variety of woodland, scrub, and residential habitats; south to Guatemala. DISPERSAL: Some movement to lower elevation in northern part of range. VAGRANT: Very rare to western Plains. **Population** Populations appear to be stable in most of the United States.

interior ♂
plumbeus

interior ♀
plumbeus

"Black-eared
Bushtit"
juvenile ♂

coastal ♂

NUTHATCHES Family Sittidae

Pygmy Nuthatch (CO, Feb.)

Nuthatches are familiar acrobatic birds, with one or more species occurring throughout much of the U.S. and Canada. All but the Brown-headed Nuthatch are commonly seen at bird feeding stations. When not nesting, nuthatches frequently gather in mixed-species flocks that include chickadees, creepers, kinglets, and warblers. Experienced observers listen for nuthatch calls to try to detect other species. Identification is straightforward, except when a Brown-headed or Pygmy Nuthatch wanders far from its normal range.

Structure Nuthatches are small, chunky, and compact birds, with a short tail. They are well adapted to creeping about at all angles on tree trunks and branches with legs that are relatively short and with strong toes and claws. Their bills are rather long, straight, and pointed; their wings are short.

Behavior Nuthatches are usually seen on the surfaces of tree trunks and branches, climbing in any direction in pursuit of invertebrates and seeds. Unlike woodpeckers and creepers, they do not use their tail for support and may go down trees head first. The smaller species often forage among the outermost needles on branches. Occasionally they drop to the ground to feed. To open a seed, a nuthatch wedges it into a crevice and pounds on the seed with its bill. This behavior, known as *hacking*, likely gave rise to the family name. During fall and winter, nuthatches store nuts, seeds, and invertebrates in caches. The Brown-headed Nuthatch is one of few bird species known to use a tool: Individuals have been seen holding bark in their bill and using it to flake off another piece of bark. All nuthatches nest in cavities, mostly tree holes and cavities. Some Brown-headed and Pygmy Nuthatches are cooperative breeders. Most are vocal year-round, with their loud whistles, trills, and calls often belying their presence even before they are revealed by their active foraging style.

Plumage Nuthatches are blue-gray above, typically with black or brown markings on the head. The underparts are pale, sometimes washed with buff or rufous coloration. The sexes are similar or identical in all nuthatches; with good views, White-breasted and Red-breasted Nuthatches can be sexed in the field. Plumages are similar throughout the year with a prealternate (early spring) molt that is limited or absent. All species have a partial first prebasic (fall) molt. Under ideal field conditions, aging is possible by looking for worn, brownish colored wing coverts that contrast with the more blue-gray mantle on first-year birds. By late spring the worn appearance of adults makes aging very challenging, even in the hand.

Distribution Nuthatches are widely distributed throughout the Northern Hemisphere. They reach their greatest diversity in south Asia, where 15 species occur. Most nuthatches are nonmigratory, but in North America even the generally sedentary species are occasionally seen far from their normal range.

Taxonomy This is a relatively small family with roughly 25 species worldwide, 4 of which occur in North America. All but one species (the Wallcreeper, in its own subfamily Ticshodromadinae) belong to the genus *Sitta*. Species limits among the nuthatches continue to be debated. A recent study suggests that the subspecies of the Brown-headed Nuthatch found on Grand Bahama Island may be a separate species: the Bahama Nuthatch *(Sitta insularis)*. Work continues to determine whether the White-breasted may involve multiple species.

Conservation Habitat loss and degradation largely caused by shifts in cultivation, grazing, and timber harvesting pose the biggest threats to this family. Worldwide, the White-browed Nuthatch (western Myanmar) and the Algerian Nuthatch (northern Algeria) are considered endangered by BirdLife International; the Giant and Beautiful Nuthatches (Southeast Asia) are vulnerable. —*Christopher L. Wood*

Genus *Sitta*

RED-BREASTED NUTHATCH *Sitta canadensis*

The presence of this nuthatch is typically announced by its nasal calls. The Red-breasted Nuthatch has the unusual habit of smearing resin around the entrance hole to its nest, presumably to deter predators and competitors from entering the nest. During the breeding season, the Red-breasted is usually found in forests dominated by firs and spruces; during migration and winter, it is found in a variety of habitats. When not breeding, the Red-breasted can be seen in small flocks with other nuthatches, chickadees, kinglets, and Brown Creepers. Monotypic. L 4.5" (11 cm)

Identification Small, with a prominent supercilium that contrasts with darker crown and eye line. ADULT MALE: Bold face pattern: Inky black crown and nape; prominent white supercilium extending from sides of forehead to sides of nape and separating the crown from the very broad, black eye line. Upperparts otherwise a deep blue-gray. Wings are edged blue-gray. Whitish chin and throat blend into buff breast and rich buff belly, flanks, and undertail coverts. ADULT FEMALE: Similar to

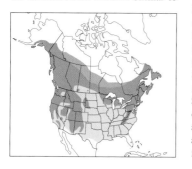

male, but black on head is paler, more lead-colored, often contrasting with blacker nape. Wings are edged dull gray with a brownish or olive tinge. Upperparts are duller gray; underparts are less richly colored. IMMATURE: Usually duller than adults of the same sex. Wings coverts, primaries, and secondaries are uniformly brownish gray without edging visible in adults. Many individuals not safely aged under normal field conditions, particularly by late spring when even bright adults have become quite worn. FLIGHT: Undulating and resembling a short-tailed woodpecker; white diagonal subterminal band on tail sometimes visible in flight.

Similar Species This is the only North American nuthatch with a broad white supercilium and contrasting broad dark eye line. The Chinese Nuthatch is found as close as southern Ussuriland (Rus.) but is unlikely to occur as a vagrant to North America. A vagrant Chinese Nuthatch would be differentiated by its ill-defined eye stripe, duller underparts, and lack of a diagonal white subterminal band on the tail.

Voice CALL: A nasal *yank* that is variable but typically repeated. Classically described as similar to a toy tin horn. Short versions are sometimes given in flight. Calls are higher and more nasal than the White-breasted Nuthatch's. SONG: A rapid, repeated series of *ehn ehn ehn* notes; reminiscent of calls.

Status & Distribution Common to abundant. BREEDING: Northern and subalpine conifers, particularly spruces and firs. Occasionally breeds south of mapped breeding range, usually in

conifer plantations or residential neighborhoods with conifers. MIGRATION: Irruptive; often moving in 2–3 year cycles but variable. Northernmost migrate annually; southernmost are generally resident. First detected away from breeding grounds as early as July (typically earliest in big flight years); peaks in Great Lakes Sept.–mid-Oct. Spring migration less pronounced, but migrants are seen through May in much of the lower 48 states. WINTER: Highest densities typically occur along the U.S.-Canada border (e.g., Northeast; MI-WI border; south-central BC and northwestern WA). VAGRANT: Casual in mainland north Mexico, north Baja California, and west AK; Bermuda (4 recs.); Iceland (1 rec.); England (1 rec.).

Population Bird Breeding Survey shows significant increase throughout the breeding range. In the East, resident range is expanding southward.

PYGMY NUTHATCH *Sitta pygmaea*

The endearing Pygmy Nuthatch is easily found, thanks to its hyperactive lifestyle and unremitting vocalizations. This is a very social species, even by nuthatch standards. The Pygmy is one of few cooperative breeding passerines: A third of breeding pairs are assisted by one to three male helpers, usually relatives. Pairs roost together, and juveniles roost with parents. In winter, congregations of a dozen or more birds may roost together: There are reports of more than 150 individuals roosting in a single tree. Pygmies usually forage well out on branches and tops of trees.

They regularly descend to the ground to feed. Polytypic. L 4.3" (11 cm)

Identification Tiny; found in long-needled pine forests in the West. ADULT: Dusky-olive crown; small pale nape spot, usually visible at close range. Lores, eye line may contrast darker. Rest of the upperparts blue-gray, not contrasting with bluish edges to wing coverts, primaries, and secondaries. Underparts pale, variably washed with buff on flanks. Sexes identical. IMMATURE: Average duller. Brownish gray wing coverts, secondaries, and primaries, contrast with blue-gray mantle. Aging difficult

in the field, particularly by spring. FLIGHT: Undulating and resembling that of a miniature short-tailed woodpecker; the white diagonal subterminal band on tail is at times visible in flight. **Geographic Variation** Three subspecies are found north of the U.S.-Mexico border (2 confined to Mex.). Widespread *melanotis* has blackish lores and eye line that contrast noticeably with the olive crown. Nominate *pygmaea* (coastal central CA) is smaller, with dusky lores and eye line that contrast only slightly with the crown. Flanks extensively washed buff. The subspecies *leuconucha* (montane San Diego County) is larger, with uniformly gray-olive crown, lores, and postocular; relatively large pale spot on nape; flanks only lightly washed buffy gray. **Similar Species** Best separated from the White-breasted and Red-breasted by face pattern; from the Brown-headed by range. Also note the Pygmy's more grayish olive crown, smaller pale nape spot, and buffier undertail coverts. The

Pygmy also has shorter primary projection (difficult to see on these active birds). Note vocalizations. **Voice** CALL: Rapid, clear, high-pitched notes usually given in a series of three or more notes: *bip-bip-bip* or *kit-kit-kit.* Calls vary in pitch and intensity, but are given almost incessantly. Calls of nominate *pygmaea* are very rapid. FLIGHT CALL: Similar but softer: *imp imp.* SONG: A rapid, high-pitched sequence of two-note phrases: *ki-dee, ki-dee, ki-dee,* similar to alarm calls. **Status & Distribution** Common. BREEDING: Long-needled pine forests of the West. Range essentially mirrors those of the Ponderosa Pine, Jeffrey Pine, and similar species. DISPERSAL: Irregularly disperses into lowlands during nonbreeding season (mostly late July–mid.-Dec.). In recent years, nearly annual in southeastern CO.

VAGRANT: Casual in southwestern BC, western KS, western OK, central MT. Accidental in eastern ND, IA, eastern KS, and eastern TX. **Population** It is a species of special concern in Idaho, Wyoming, and Colorado, where it is an indicator species of healthy Ponderosa pine forests. Threats include logging, fire suppression, and grazing.

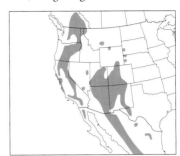

BROWN-HEADED NUTHATCH *Sitta pusilla*

This energetic, vocal species is generally more common and easier to find than the other two southeastern pine specialties (Red-cockaded Woodpecker and Bachman's Sparrow). Brown-headed Nuthatches spend most of their time foraging well out on branches and on treetops, frequently hanging upside down searching for insects and spiders, or feeding on cones. This species is perhaps better known for using tools than any other bird in N.A: An individual will take a bark scale, hold it in its bill, and use it as a wedge to pry off other bark scales as it searches for insects and spiders. Apparently, this behavior is more common in years of poor cone crops. Polytypic. L 4.3" (11 cm) **Identification** Tiny; found in pine forests in the Southeast. ADULT: Warm brown to chestnut crown and upper portion of the auriculars; relatively large whitish nape spot. By late winter, cap becomes more mottled; lores and eye line tend to contrast more with the crown. Underparts pale, washed with dull buff on flanks. Sexes identical. IMMATURE: On average slightly duller; outer wing coverts, secondaries, and primaries are brownish gray, contrasting slightly with blue-gray mantle. Base of lower mandible typically pale until November. Most very difficult to age in the field. FLIGHT: Subterminal tail band is grayish and limited to outer two pair of tail feathers, showing less contrast in the tail during flight than on other nuthatches. Flight style similar to the Pygmy's.

Geographic Variation Weak and clinal within the U.S. The subspecies *caniceps* (found in southern and central FL) may be smaller on average, with a larger bill and paler gray head; some doubt the validity of this subspecies. Recent work suggests highly endangered birds found on Grand Bahama Island constitute a separate species: the Bahama Nuthatch *(Sitta insularis).* **Similar Species** Easily separated from White-breasted and Red-breasted Nuthatches by face pattern and size; best separated from Pygmy by range. Also note Brown-headed's more brownish crown, larger pale nape spot, and less buff undertail coverts. Brown-headed has shorter primary projection, and its subterminal tail band is grayer and more limited, but this is difficult to see on these active birds. Note vocalizations, all of which tend to be lower pitched and less pure than the Pygmy's. **Voice** CALL: A repeated 2-part note like the squeak of a rubber duck, *KEW-deh.* At times, up to 10 or more notes may follow the first note. Feeding flocks also give a variety of twittering, chirping and talky *bit bit bit* calls. Flight calls similar. Differences between songs and calls poorly understood.

Status & Distribution Fairly common. BREEDING: Pine forests of the Southeast, particularly the loblolly-shortleaf in the upper Coastal Plain and the longleaf-slash association in the lower Coastal Plain. Favors mature open woodlands with dead wood (e.g., burn areas) but regularly found in young and medium-age pine stands. DISPERSAL: Very limited postbreeding dispersal. VAGRANT: Accidental southeastern WI, northern IN, northern IL, eastern KY, eastern OH, PA, and southern NJ. **Population** Declining throughout range; threatened by clear cutting and fire suppression, which degrade or destroy habitat. The species likely benefits from conservation efforts focused on the Red-cockaded Woodpecker, which occupies same range and habitat but is much more sensitive.

WHITE-BREASTED NUTHATCH *Sitta carolinensis*

Less gregarious than other nuthatches, the White-breasted Nuthatch is typically seen singly or in pairs. In fall and winter, it regularly forms small mixed-species flocks, but a single flock rarely includes more than 6 White-breasteds. Commonly seen at bird feeders, the White-breasted is often first detected by its calls, which it frequently gives year-round. Polytypic. L 5.8" (15 cm)

Identification The species has a black crown and nape that contrast with a white face and breast. ADULT MALE: It has a uniformly black crown and nape. Upperparts are blue-gray, similar in color to the blue-gray wing edging. FEMALES: They are duller than males; a paler crown often contrasts with a blacker nape; in the Southeast, the head pattern is more similar to the male's, but it is still duller overall on average. Also note the brownish or grayish edging to the wing feathers.

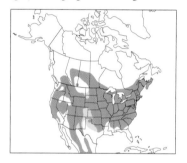

IMMATURE: It resembles the adult, but its primaries, secondaries, and most wing coverts are brownish gray and lack the edging found on the adult (and contrast with mantle). It is difficult to age and sex, particularly by early spring.

Geographic Variation See sidebar below.

Similar Species The white face with an isolated dark eye is distinctive; all other species of nuthatches in North America have a more extensive dark crown or dark eye line.

Voice CALL: Varies between subspecies, but all give short, soft high *inh* notes when foraging; see sidebar below. SONG: A series of repeated nasal whistles on one pitch: *whi-whi-whi-whi-whi-whi.* Similar in all populations.

Status & Distribution Fairly common. BREEDING: A variety of deciduous and mixed-forest habitats, generally preferring relatively open woods. DISPERSAL AND MIGRATION: Poorly known. Does not undertake large-scale irruptions (unlike the Red-breasted Nuthatch), but White-breasteds in the Rockies regularly move onto the Great Plains, and some northern birds disperse. Found in southeastern CO (where it does not breed) early Aug.–early May. VAGRANT: Casual Vancouver I., BC; Sable I., NS; and offshore CA (Santa Cruz Is. and the Farallones); 1 fall record for Bermuda.

eastern
carolinensis

Great Basin
♂ *tenuissima*

Population Increasing or stable throughout much of range; populations thought to have declined in the Southeast.

Variation in the White-breasted Nuthatch

There are 9 subspecies of the White-breasted Nuthatch in Mexico and North America, 5 of which occur north of the U.S.-Mexico border. All of the subspecies can be placed into 3 groups on the basis of plumage characteristics and calls. Songs appear to differ between the subspecies groups as well, but more study is needed. The 3 subspecies groups may constitute 3 separate species, but for now that question remains under review.

The "Eastern" (or *carolinensis*) group consists of the nominate *carolinensis,* and includes the formerly recognized subspecies *cookei.* This is the palest subspecies group. The centers of the tertials and wing coverts are sharply defined, deep black, and contrast distinctly with blue-gray upperparts. The crown stripe is broader, the bill is thicker and shorter, and the underparts are whiter than in either western group. Their nasal calls—*yank, yank*—are the classic, slow, low-pitched calls associated with most published descriptions of this species.

The "Interior West" (or *mexicana*) group consists of *nelsoni, tenuissima,* and *oberholseri;* and 3 additional subspecies in Mexico. This group provisionally includes the

birds from the Cape District of southern Baja California on the basis of their calls. It is the darkest subspecies group with much darker upperparts and more extensive dark coloration to the flanks, particularly when compared to "Eastern" group birds. Within this group there is a clinal variation with the darkest birds occurring in Mexico, where only the throat and sides of head are bright white. Their very short, rapid succession of high-pitched nasal calls—*nyeh-nyeh-nyeh-nyeh*—have a laughing quality about them, and are very different from the calls of "Eastern" or "Pacific" group birds.

The "Pacific" (or *aculeata*) group consists of *aculeata* and 1 other subspecies from northern Baja California. This group is somewhat intermediate in plumage between the "Interior West" and "Eastern" groups but more closely resembles "Interior West" birds. They are slightly paler overall, particularly on the mantle and flanks, and the paler centers of the tertials and wing coverts show little contrast with the rest of the upperparts. Their calls—*eeerh, eeerh*—resemble those of the "Eastern" group but are higher-pitched, longer, and harsher. ■

CREEPERS Family Certhiidae

Brown Creeper (OH, Feb.)

The Brown Creeper is the only certhiid found in the Americas.

Structure Creepers have short legs, long stiff tail feathers, long curved claws and toes, and relatively long and dense feathers.

Behavior Creepers are almost always found on trees, using their stiff tail as a prop. When foraging, they typically begin near the base of the tree and jerkily spiral upward, sometimes onto larger branches, until near the top, then fly to the base of the next trunk. In constant motion, they glean and probe for arthropods and insects. Creepers are vocal, but their high-pitched calls and songs may be difficult to hear. The nests of all but the Spotted Creeper are placed behind loose bark.

Plumage The upperparts are finely patterned with a mixture of white, rufous, brown, black, and buff markings. The underparts are pale. Males and females are apparently identical. Unlike other passerines, tree creepers retain the central rectrices until all others have been replaced. The first prebasic molt is incomplete, but all tail feathers are replaced. There is no prealternate molt.

Distribution Found in forested regions of the Northern Hemisphere, creepers reach their greatest diversity in the Himalaya.

Taxonomy There are 7 species in 2 genera. Some DNA comparisons suggest that creepers are part of a much larger family that includes nuthatches, chickadees, wrens, gnatcatchers, and gnatwrens. All but the unusual Spotted Creeper are in the genus *Certhia*.

Conservation Mature and old-growth forests, the species' prefered habitat, face increasing threats from logging and other forms of habitat destruction, deterioration, and fragmentation. —*Christopher L. Wood*

Genus *Certhia*

BROWN CREEPER *Certhia americana*

The Brown Creeper is quite vocal, but its high-pitched vocalizations are easily missed. It is generally solitary, but it sometimes migrates and winters with flocks of titmice, nuthatches, and kinglets. Polytypic (15 ssp.; 9 north of U.S.-Mexico border). L 5.3" (13 cm)

Identification Distinctive shape and foraging behavior. MALE AND FEMALE: Identical plumage; male larger. Cryptic upperparts streaked brown, buff, and black; underparts pale with warm wash on flanks; rump buff, tawny, or rufous. FLIGHT: Broad, pale wing stripe at base of flight feathers prominent in flight.

Geographic Variation Subspecies north of the U.S.-Mexico border divide into 3 groups: Western birds *(alascensis, occidentalis, stewarti, phillipsi, zelotes, montana)* are small, dark, and long billed; eastern birds *(americana, nigrescens)* are larger, generally paler, and shorter billed; the Mexican *albescens,* darker with white spotting that contrasts more, extends into southeast Arizona and southwest New Mexico. Rufous, brown, and gray morphs in several populations complicate identification.

Similar Species None; vaguely similar to some wrens, but shape and behavior very different.

Voice Very high-pitched. CALL: A soft, sibilant *see,* usually buzzier and doubled in western birds, *tseeesee.* FLIGHT CALL: A short, weak *tsf;* shorter and softer than Golden-crowned Kinglet and chickadees. SONG: Variable, but consists of several notes, *seee seeedsee sideeu.* Eastern songs more complex, quavering, and usually end on a high note; western songs more rhythmic and often end on a low note.

Status & Distribution Fairly common; uncommon or rare breeder in south-

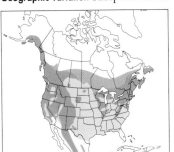

east portion of range. BREEDING: Coniferous, mixed, or swampy forests. Highest densities found in old-growth forest. Wider habitat variety during migration and winter. MIGRATION: Resident birds complicate detection of migrants in some areas. Peak late Mar.–mid-Apr. and Oct.–Nov. in Midwest/Northeast. WINTER: Much of N.A.

Population Populations thought to have declined throughout much of North America with the felling of old-growth forests. Breeding populations listed as endangered in Kentucky and as of special concern in some midwestern and eastern states.

WRENS Family Troglodytidae

Rock Wren (CA, Apr.)

North America's wrens are diverse (9 species in 7 genera) yet distinctive; members of Troglodytidae are rarely confused with species in other families. Our wrens are brown, and most have slender, decurved bills. Tail length and structure are variable; in many postures, however, wrens exhibit a characteristic cocked tail. With good views, sight identification is straightforward. Wrens are often found in dense cover, though, and can be fidgety. Song and microhabitat preferences are important for identification.

Structure In many situations, wrens strike a rotund, potbellied pose. When foraging or evading detection, they appear to flatten or prostrate themselves (in contrast to the upright postures of many flycatchers). The tail varies from very short to fairly long, but it is distinctive—typically cocked up and/or flipped about. Wrens have medium to very long, decurved, usually slender bills. Species in North America range in size from small to medium.

Behavior Wrens are often observed creeping about substrates close to or on the ground. Specialized microhabitat preferences are good cues to identification (e.g., Cactus Wrens within thorny shrubs, Rock Wrens about talus slopes). Songs are complex, variable, and distinctive, with several species (e.g., Winter and Canyon Wrens) among our finest vocalists). Birds of some species sing through the night (e.g., Marsh Wren) and/or during the winter (e.g., Carolina Wren). Several species build conspicuous "dummy nests" that are abandoned after construction.

Plumage All wrens of North America are largely brownish, darker above and paler below. Some species tend toward grayish or reddish tones, but these differences are usually of limited relevance to species-level identifi-

cation. Important marks to note include streaking and spotting on upperparts, barring and shading on underparts and tail, and the supercilium (strong, weak, or nearly absent). Below the species level, coloration is important in assigning individuals to different subspecies.

Distribution The wrens' center of diversity is Middle America, with more than 30 species in Mexico. All of the lower 48 host multiple wren species, but several do not range north to Canada, and only the Winter Wren is regularly found in Alaska. The Winter Wren is the only troglodytid that occurs in the Old World (recent research, however, indicates that the Eurasian Winter Wren comprises multiple species). Migratory strategies range from sedentary (e.g., Cactus Wren), to intermediate-distance migration (e.g., Sedge Wren). Long-term range shifts appear to be under way for several species.

Taxonomy The Troglodytidae are regarded by most authorities as a valid, monophylous taxon. Relationships among and within lower-order taxa are less clear-cut, however. For example, the genera *Salpinctes* and *Catherpes* are sometimes lumped, and the taxonomic affinities of *Troglodytes* are unclear. At the level of currently recognized species, future "splits" may be in the offing for House, Winter, and Marsh Wrens.

Conservation Most wren species in North America appear to be stable or increasing. Below the species level, population-change patterns are complex, as with the Bewick's Wren (eastern populations are in severe decline; several western populations are increasing and expanding). Habitat loss threatens local populations of Marsh and Sedge Wrens. Climate change may be implicated in the Carolina Wren's ongoing range expansion. —*Ted Floyd*

Genus Campylorhynchus

CACTUS WREN *Campylorhynchus brunneicapillus*

Calling to mind a small thrasher, the oversize Cactus Wren is a distinctive inhabitant of the thorn-scrub country of the desert Southwest. A good clue to this wren's presence is its characteristic dummy nest, placed conspicuously but inaccessibly amid chollas, acacias, etc. Polytypic. L 8.7" (22 cm)

Identification Large-proportioned, with bulky build, broad tail, relatively thick bill. ADULT: One molt a year; sexes similar. Plumage spotted and streaked all over; overall tones brown, black, and white. Note variable dark spotting on undersides and conspicuous white supercilium. In flight the rounded wings and tail are brown overall but heavily spotted and barred with white. JUVENILE: Similar to adult, but buffier overall, with spotting and barring more muted.

Geographic Variation Three subspecies in N.A., 4 others in Mex. The "San Diego" Cactus Wren *(sandiegense)*, resident in coastal southern CA, is distinguished from other subspecies by different pattern on underparts—black spotting is more uniform, and background color is more extensively white.

Similar Species Other wrens smaller and usually in other habitats, so confusion unlikely. Similar in certain respects to the Sage and Bendire's Thrashers.

Voice Most vocalizations low-pitched and grating. Species highly vocal, often singing through the hottest times of the day. CALL: Low, growling, clucking sounds, sometimes given in a loose series, *chut chut chut.* SONG: A distinctive, unmusical series of pulsing, chugging notes, reminiscent of an old car trying to start—*churr churr churr.*

Status & Distribution Locally common. southwestern U.S. and northern Mex.

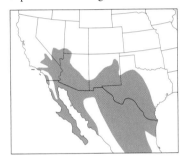

YEAR-ROUND: Towns, washes, and open desert with thorn scrub. VAGRANT: Very few records of wanderers.

Population "San Diego" subspecies threatened by habitat loss; species tolerant of humans. Local distribution limited by availability of nest sites.

Genus Salpinctes

ROCK WREN *Salpinctes obsoletus*

The well-named Rock Wren inhabits rocky and pebbly habitats of all sorts: from scree fields above timberline, to talus slopes and bajadas, to washes and road cuts in open desert. The nest site is indicated by a peculiar trail of pebbles. Polytypic. L 6" (15 cm)

Identification Usually seen creeping about the ground, but sometimes perches conspicuously and bobs up and down in exaggerated, jerky movements. ADULT: One molt a year; sexes similar. Brown and buff above. Tail pattern in flight distinctive, with broad buffy terminal band, broken at center. Underparts paler; throat and breast gray-white; belly pale buff. Upperparts spotted, with white; underparts streaked with black. Fresh birds (early fall) more contrastingly patterned than worn birds (midsummer). JUVENILE: Similar to adult, but less contrast.

Similar Species Structure and behavior generally wrenlike, but rarely confused with other species. Canyon Wren's habitat superficially similar, but tends more toward sheer, rock faces.

Voice Varied, but most vocalizations diagnostic. CALL: an emphatic *ch'-pweee,* with overall buzzy quality; softer twittering audible close-up. SONG: *Bweer bweer bweer, chiss chiss chiss, swee swee swee,* a repetitive complex of jangling series, suggesting a distant, weak-voiced Northern Mockingbird.

Status & Distribution Fairly common. south to Costa Rica. BREEDING: Arid country with sparse vegetation; usually in the immediate vicinity of loose, pebbly substrates. MIGRATION: Withdraws from northern portion of range; altitudinal withdrawal occurs throughout range. WINTER: Relative winter ranges of latitudinal versus altitudinal migrants poorly known. VAGRANT: Casual well east of core range (mostly fall and winter).

Population Little study, but populations thought to be secure.

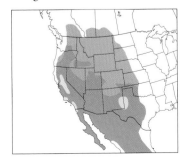

Genus *Catherpes*

CANYON WREN *Catherpes mexicanus*

The clear, sweet notes of the Canyon Wren are a characteristic sound of rimrocks and other mountainous country in western North America. The species can be difficult to see, but a good view reveals distinctive behavior, morphology, and plumage. Polytypic. L 5.9" (15 cm)

Identification Bill extremely long. Flattened profile perched and in flight. Rarely seen away from rock outcroppings or canyon walls; usually seen creeping or probing about crevices and rock faces. Behavior mouselike. ADULT:

One molt a year; sexes similar. White breast contrasts with reddish brown belly. Tail, wings, and back mainly reddish brown; head grayish. With close view, note spotting and barring on tail, wings, back, and belly. JUVENILE: Similar to adult, but with less spotting and barring.

Geographic Variation Four weakly differentiated subspecies north of Mexico; 4 others in Mexico.

Similar Species General structure and behavior call to mind other wrens, but plumage and song distinctive. Microhabitat preference often separates the Canyon from similar species. Can overlap with Rock Wrens, but these typically found in more pebbly and sandy environments (e.g., talus slopes, quarries).

Voice Vocalizations distinctive. CALL: shrill *beet,* given singly or repeatedly; year-round. SONG: Series of approximately 15 clear-whistled notes, often descending in pitch and slowing somewhat; usually ends with fewer than 5 rasping notes, audible at close range.

Audibility of song varies with terrain and orientation of observer; songs given fairly infrequently (interval less than 1 minute).

Status & Distribution Fairly common. South to Mexico. BREEDING: Canyons, rock faces, outcroppings. MIGRATION: Largely sedentary. WINTER: As breeding, with some wandering to lower elevations. VAGRANT: Casually to 100+ miles from area of regular occurrence.

Population Populations presumed to be secure, but little study; recreational climbing cited as possible threat.

Genus *Thryothorus*

CAROLINA WREN *Thryothorus ludovicianus*

The adaptable and highly vocal Carolina Wren is a familiar inhabitant of gardens and woodlands in the Southeast. Climate-related range shifts in the species are well documented. Polytypic. L 5.5" (14 cm)

Identification Active, inquisitive. In most of range, the most brightly colored wren in its habitat. ADULT: One molt a year; sexes similar. Upperparts bright reddish brown; breast and belly warm buffy-orange; throat whitish. White supercilium; long, conspicuous. JUVENILE: Overall tones duller.

Geographic Variation Six subspecies

north of Mexico; 4 others in Mexico and Central America. Populations fairly homogeneous north of about 32° N. More heterogeneous farther south, but field identification to subspecies is difficult.

Similar Species Where ranges overlap, Bewick's Wren may present confusion. Bewick's has colder colors and longer, white-corned tail. Songs different. Because of variability in song, beware of overlap with unrelated species (e.g., Tufted Titmouse, Kentucky Warbler, Northern Cardinal).

Voice Loud and frequent. CALL: Varied. One common note is a hollow, liquid *dihlip,* less sharp and harsh sounding than the Winter Wren's. Another sounds like a stick being run across a wire-mesh fence. SONG: Rich and repetitious. Most songs consist of short, repeated phrases; song may start and/or end with single notes—*chip mediator*

mediator mediator meep. Primitive antiphonal singing is sometimes heard: One bird begins with characteristic song; mate finishes with low rattle.

Status & Distribution Common. BREEDING: Dense vegetation, frequently near human habitation. MIGRATION: Largely sedentary. WINTER: As breeding. VAGRANT: Occasionally to 500+ miles from area of regular occurrence; apparent vagrants may be better thought of as vanguards in range expansion.

Population Northward range expansion is fairly sustained; westward expansion is erratic. Sudden range contractions follow harsh winters, but expansion resumes eventually. Tolerant of humans; projected beneficiary of global warming.

Genus *Thryomanes*

BEWICK'S WREN *Thryomanes bewickii*

Vocal and plumage variation in the Bewick's Wren is extensive, but all adults have a very long tail, tipped in white and flicked side to side. Eastern populations have disappeared from much of former range and are in continuing decline; conversely, western populations are stable or increasing and/or expanding. Polytypic. L 5.1" (13 cm)

Identification Long, mobile tail with attenuated body shape and active demeanor impart a lean look. ADULT: One molt a year; sexes similar. Plumage variable, but all subspecies gray-brown to rufous-brown above, gray-white below, with long, pale supercilium. White-tipped tail has black bands. JUVENILE: Plumage subtly paler than adult's.

Geographic Variation Complex, extensive. Variation in darkness of upperparts generally follows Gloger's Rule, with paler populations in the arid Southwest and intermontane West vs. darker populations in the East and Pacific Northwest. Some or all populations exhibit color polymorphisms, and random individual variation is extensive; 10 subspecies north of Mexico; 5 others in Mexico.

Similar Species In most of range distinctive tail and supercilium prevent confusion with other wrens. Where populations of the eastern subspecies-group overlap with Carolina Wren, confusion possible. However, Bewick's is not as brightly colored as Carolina, and the long, white-tipped, expertly maneuvered tail of Bewick's is diagnostic. Bill thinner than Carolina's.

Voice Varied. In many places in the West, the Bewick's Wren produces the local "mystery song." CALL: Variable, but many notes with raspy or buzzy quality, some quite loud. SONG: Most songs combine 1–5 short, breathy, buzzy, notes (sometimes run together in a short warble) with a longer, often loose, trill. Single buzzy or nasal notes may

be introduced. Overall rhythm and tone remind many observers of the Song Sparrow, but elements in the song of Bewick's are usually thinner, buzzier. Songs of birds in the interior subspecies-group *(eromophilus* group*)* are simpler than those from the far West or east of the Mississippi.

Status & Distribution Western populations are mainly uncommon to fairly common; locally common. Eastern subspecies-group (*bewickii* group) declining; *altus* subspecies ("Appalachian" Bewick's Wren), of questionable taxonomic validity, reduced to remnant populations; nominate *bewickii* subspecies, centered in Ozarks, declining. Abundance of any population may be underestimated by observers unfamiliar with song. BREEDING: Habitat types more variable than for most wrens, but shrubby vegetation always a requirement. Western individuals frequent arid juniper foothills, lush riparian corridors, residential districts, etc. Eastern subspecies-group formerly inhabited open woodlands; present habitat preferences are unclear. MIGRATION: Western populations largely sedentary. Eastern populations migratory, with general pattern of dispersal south and west following breeding.

WINTER: As breeding, with generally warmer and lower-elevation component. VAGRANT: Extralimital records difficult to assess. Apparent vagrants in the East may be remnants, natural migrants, or actual vagrants. Apparent vagrants in the West may refer to advance-guard birds involved in range expansions. In lower Missouri and Arkansas River Valleys, distinguish between potential vagrants of eastern versus western populations.

Population Several western populations are increasing (e.g., in OR, NV, and AZ). Subspecies *altus* once ranged northeast to NY and ON, but now limited to a few relict populations in the Ohio and Tennessee River Valleys. Competition with House Wren thought a major factor in the Bewick's decline, but direct evidence for long-term competitive exclusion not proven.

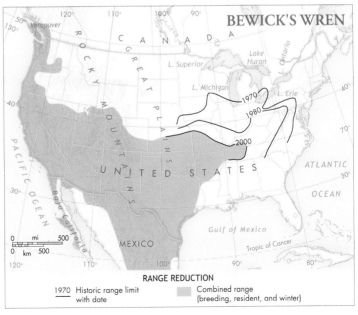

western interior
eremophilus

eastern
bewickii

BEWICK'S WREN

RANGE REDUCTION

1970 Historic range limit with date

Combined range (breeding, resident, and winter)

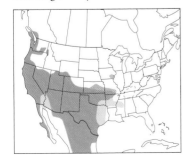

Genus Troglodytes

HOUSE WREN *Troglodytes aedon*

southeast Arizona
"Brown-throated Wren"

juvenile

eastern
aedon

western
parkmanii

Dull in appearance but notable for its effervescent song, the House Wren is a common summer inhabitant of scrublands and woodland edges throughout much of North America. Variation in plumage and call notes is extensive. Polytypic. L 4.7" (12 cm)
Identification A small wren with medium-length bill and tail, it responds readily to pishing. Overall jizz is of a plain, typical wren. ADULT: One molt a year; sexes similar. All populations brownish above, paler gray-brown or gray below. Supercilium, often indistinct, is paler than crown and auriculars. JUVENILE: Variable, but many differ from adults in having warmer buff and rufous tones, along with indistinct scalloping on throat and breast.
Geographic Variation Two widespread,

poorly differentiated subspecies in N.A.: Western *parkmanii* and eastern *aedon*. Eastern birds average more rufescent, western birds grayer. The *cahooni* subspecies, allied with Mexican *brunneicollis* ("Brown-throated Wren"), in mountains of southeastern AZ, shows warmer tones to the throat and breast; supercilium more distinct. Twenty-nine subspecies (possibly involving multiple species) occur south of N.A., ranging south to southern S.A.
Similar Species Main point of confusion is Winter Wren; it is smaller, shorter-tailed, more heavily barred on the flanks and crissum, and usually darker. Winter and House Wrens further distinguished by differences in song, call, timing of migration, microhabitat preferences, and foraging behavior.

VOICE Most vocalizations have a "dry" quality. CALL: Most given singly or in stuttering series. A scratchy, frequently heard call is similar to that of the Common Yellowthroat. Another note, which is raspy, resembles that of the Blue-gray Gnatcatcher. SONG: Loud, bubbly. Starts hesitantly, quickly erupts into a cascade of down-slurred dry trills. Usually easy to recognize, but due to considerable variation may be confused with certain non-troglodytids (e.g., Rufous-crowned Sparrow).
Status & Distribution Common. BREEDING: Most vegetated habitats, except for dense forests, open grassland, marshland, and desert. Favored microhabitats include clearings, edges, residential neighborhoods. MIGRATION: Most birds in N.A. migratory. Major spring movement follows that of the Winter Wren; major fall movement precedes that of the Winter. WINTER: Generally as breeding, but with greater tendency for dense cover. Not a hardy species; stragglers north of core wintering range uncommon. VAGRANT: Sometimes noted to offshore or peninsular locales from which otherwise absent.
Population Long-term population increases documented in many areas. Species is tolerant of humans and readily accepts nest boxes.

WINTER WREN *Troglodytes troglodytes*

The Winter Wren—tiny, nervous, and unforthcoming—breeds mainly in cool, shady forests and tangles at northern latitudes and higher elevations. Subspecific variation is pronounced and often field discernible. The Winter Wren's complex and striking song is frequently rated among the best among all North American birds. Polytypic. L 4" (10 cm)
Identification Diminutive in all respects.

Small bodied, stub tailed; bill short for a wren. Hides among dense shrubbery, tangled roots, etc. Surprisingly hard to glimpse, even when close. When seen, note constant twitching and jerking motions, with tiny tail held straight up. ADULT: One molt a year; sexes similar. All populations brown to dark brown, some tending toward grayer tones, others more rufescent. Dark barring on belly, flanks, and crissum prominent.

JUVENILE: Similar to adult, but with less distinct barring on belly and sometimes with faint breast-scalloping.
Geographic Variation Three subspecies-groups (comprising 12 ssp.) in N.A. show consistent differences, but overlap extensive. Eastern *hiemalis* group averages paler; western *pacificus* group darker, more reddish brown. Birds of the Aleutian Islands and other Bering Sea islands (*alascensis* group) noticeably

larger than individuals of continental populations. Widespread in Palearctic (29 additional ssp.).

Similar Species House Wren larger overall, with longer tail, plainer underparts, generally paler coloration. House Wren also less furtive, less fidgety.

Voice Distinctive. CALL: Sharp, slightly nasal, usually doubled *chimp chimp*. Calls of eastern birds sharper, reminiscent of those of the Song Sparrow; calls of western birds drier, more similar to those of the Wilson's Warbler. Agitated birds give stuttering series like that of the Ruby-crowned Kinglet.

SONG: Long-duration (up to 8 sec.) utterance of high-pitched trills, frequently changing pitch and tempo. Many song elements have tinkling or warbling quality; others sound tinny, lisping. Eastern birds sing more slowly, richly; song elements in western birds are buzzier, less musical.

Status & Distribution Fairly common; due to reclusive behavior, may be under-detected. BREEDING: Dense mesic forests, usually with a significant conifer component. MIGRATION: Eastern population more migratory than western. Main movements earlier in spring and later in fall than those of House Wren. Aleutian populations sedentary. WINTER: Thickets, streamsides, forests; usually near dense, dark cover. VAGRANT: Status of eastern vs. western vagrants

in fall and winter in intermontane West unclear. Records of western vagrants to East not well documented. Eastern birds have been found west to CA.

Population Breeding is concentrated in old-growth forests. Western logging and forest fragmentation have reduced numbers. Eastern populations may be increasing slowly with the regeneration of forest.

Aleutians

western
pacificus

eastern
hiemalis

Genus *Cistothorus*

SEDGE WREN *Cistothorus platensis*

Few North American birds show as much distributional complexity as the Sedge Wren. Nesting begins in the northern portion of the range in late spring and shifts southward by mid-summer. Although a weak flier, it is the only wren of North America. that withdraws completely from the breeding range in winter. Sedge Wrens are rarely detected on migration, but vagrants are recorded far from main routes. Highly disjunct and largely nonmigratory populations occur south

to islands off southern South America. Polytypic. L 4.5"(11.4 cm)

Identification Small. Bill short for a wren (species was formerly known as "Short-billed Marsh Wren"). In winter and migration can be difficult to glimpse, with most individuals staying under cover. Where locally common on breeding grounds easy to observe due to constant singing and frequent interactions. ADULT: Two molts a year (early spring, late summer); sexes similar. Buffy overall, subtly but extensively streaked and spotted. Note fine white streaks across brown crown, fairly coarse black-and-white steaks on buffy-orange back. Supercilium faint but discernible; buff-tinged. Unmarked underparts warm buff, brighter on breast and throat. Tail and wings broad, rounded; extensively but weakly barred with brown and buff. JUVENILE: More muted overall than adult; streaking on upperparts more subdued, and buffy tones on underparts weaker.

Geographic Variation One subspecies, *stellaris,* in N.A.; variation discrete and extensive (17 additional ssp.) farther south.

Similar Species Marsh Wren often treat-

ed as point of confusion, perhaps more because of taxonomic and nomenclatural affinities (both species were formerly known as "marsh wrens") than because of actual field-based characters. Marsh Wren differs in many respects, including darker colors and more contrast overall, solid brown crown, conspicuous white supercilium, and black back streaked with white. The 2 species rarely overlap on breeding grounds, with the Marsh in dense palustrine or estuarine cattail marshes, the Sedge in tall grasses in damp uplands.

Voice Most vocalizations sharp, chattering. CALL: Sharp *chap*, like introductory notes in song. Close-up, soft sputtering series, as given by other wrens. SONG: Several sharp notes followed by a short series of faster notes: *CHIP CHIP CHIP ch'ch'ch'ch'ch'ch'ch.*

Status & Distribution Complex. Locally common, but also scarce in or absent from many areas of seemingly suitable habitat. BREEDING: Loosely colonial in tall grasses; wet soil preferred, but extensive standing water a deterrent. Breeding in northern portion of range (upper Midwest, western Great

Lakes) occurs earlier than breeding farther south (central Great Plains). MIGRATION: Begins northward movement by early May. Many individuals retreat from northern breeding grounds in early summer to staging or breeding grounds farther south. Fall migration drawn out; late summer to mid-fall; bulk of records in Oct. WINTER: As breeding, but more general, with some individuals in wet marshes, others in drier scrub.

VAGRANT: Annually to hundreds of miles from area of regular occurrence; casual to West Coast. Most vagrants noted in fall.

Population In core range (western Great Lakes, upper Midwest), populations trending upward; populations to east may be declining. Local populations at risk to habitat alteration. Little conclusive long-term population data, given erratic, opportunistic, and likely unstable nature of all populations.

MARSH WREN *Cistothorus palustris*

The rambunctious and highly vocal Marsh Wren may be heard in cattail marshes throughout much of North America. all through the summer, at any time. Like most wrens, the Marsh is a recluse, but its densities are often high in favored breeding areas, and patient watching usually results in a good view. The ovoid dummy nests of the species are conspicuous. Vocal and plumage variation is extensive and often field-discernible, and population status is locally and regionally complex. Polytypic. L 5" (12.7 cm)

Identification Usually stays close to cover in dense cattails, even when singing. Glimpses tend to be brief, often of flying birds. In flight note rounded wings and tail, overall reddish brown coloration. Marsh Wrens are highly social and aggressive (both inter- and intraspecifically), and careful study may result in interesting behavioral observations. ADULT: Two molts a year (early spring, midsummer); sexes similar. Reddish brown above, with fairly high-contrast markings. Eastern birds are darker and more contrasting: Conspicuous supercilium is sharply set off against dark brown crown and gray-brown auriculars; black back

streaked with prominent white stripes; wings, tail, rump, and belly variably chestnut. Western birds basically similar, but colors more muted and contrast somewhat weaker. With close view, note spotting and barring on tail, wings, back, and belly. JUVENILE: More smudgy-looking, less contrastingly marked than adult, with few if any white streaks on back.

Geographic Variation Extensive (14 ssp. in N.A, 1 in Mexico), although clinal where populations meet. Major breakpoint involves eastern subspecies group *(palustris)* versus several western subspecies groups. Vocal differences between eastern and western Marsh Wrens are well studied, and full-species status has been proposed for the 2 populations. Zone of contact is in central Great Plains (e.g., central Nebraska), but complete details of range separation not fully worked out.

Similar Species See Sedge Wren.

Voice Geographic variation in songs extensive. CALL: Common call note a soft *chuck*, without the sharp, grating quality of the call notes of many other wren species. At close range, softer stuttering notes, more like those of other wren species, may be heard. SONG: All songs have a liquid or gurgling sound, more so than the dry, stuttering song of the Sedge Wren. Liquid quality is more pronounced in eastern birds than in western birds. General pattern is similar to that of the Sedge or House Wrens, with several well-spaced introductory notes followed by a more complex series: *Chik chik chu-u-u-u-u-u-u-u-rrr.*

Status & Distribution Locally common. BREEDING: All populations favor dense cattail marshes. Eastern birds most strongly concentrated in estuarine marshes fairly far inland, where conditions are less brackish. Eastern birds

also occur in large cattail marshes in association with large inland lakes and marshes. Western birds occur in similar situations, but are also frequently noted as nesters in very small cattail marshes (e.g., on golf courses), usually eschewed by eastern birds. MIGRATION: Complex. Some populations highly migratory, others partially migratory, others nonmigratory. Migration in general poorly detected, owing to reclusive behavior of migrants. Migratory populations usually back on breeding grounds by mid-May. Withdrawal to wintering grounds begins by midsummer, but most detections of migrants tend not to be until early fall, perhaps reflecting observer bias. Even on migration, most individuals are found in cattails and similar vegetation. WINTER: Cattail marshes generally favored, but a broader array of habitats is accepted. Dense cover almost always required. VAGRANT: Difficult to recognize as such, because migration occurs broadly across N.A.

Population Spatial and temporal variation extensive, and extrinsic vs. intrinsic causes thereof difficult to assess. General pattern is of increasing numbers in western populations vs. decreasing numbers in the East, possibly reflecting western birds' tendency to be more generalized in habitat selection. Destruction or alteration of wetlands, especially in the East, has caused local declines and extinctions.

DIPPERS Family Cinclidae

American Dipper (UT, June)

Few passerines are more specialized than the highly aquatic dippers. They spend their entire lives in the immediate vicinity of, and often actually in, rushing streams and rivers. Accordingly, details of their physiology and behavior are unique. There is one North American species, which is widespread in the West. Its absence from the Appalachians is reckoned by some experts as a biogeographic mystery.

Structure Portly overall, appearing bobtailed with strong legs and feet. The bill is short, compressed, and sturdy. Wings are short and rounded.

Behavior Highly distinctive foraging techniques. Often seen wading into rushing water, submerging head while looking for food—mostly aquatic larvae. Also swims on the surface for short distances, peering under water, while paddling with feet. Using its wings, a dipper can submerge completely and maneuver near stream bottoms by grasping the substrate—remaining under water for up to 30 seconds. When not in water, it stands on rocks and boulders, pumps its body up and down in highly stereotyped motion, and flashes white-feathered eyelids.

Plumage Dense and waterproof. All species exhibit significant brown or gray, some with white and/or chestnut. The American Dipper is one of the plainer species.

Distribution Found in large montane watershed complexes in the Americas, Europe, N. Africa, and Asia.

Taxonomy Worldwide, 5 closely-related species, all placed in a single genus. A close relationship with the wrens (Troglodytidae) has been posited, but some researchers have argued instead for a closer alliance with the mimic-thrushes (Mimidae).

Conservation Most dipper populations are naturally isolated and hence susceptible to local extinctions from habitat alteration and water pollution. *—Ted Floyd*

Genus *Cinclus*

AMERICAN DIPPER *Cinclus mexicanus*

One of the most charismatic species of the American West, the American Dipper is at home along rushing streams and rivers, from timberline to sea level. Although its attire is drab gray and brown, its behavior, physiology, and vocalizations are remarkable. Polytypic. L 7.5" (19 cm)

Identification Plump and monochromatic. Frequently bobs. Legs and feet pale; wings short; tail very short. ADULT: Slate gray with somewhat browner head; dark bill. One molt per year, in late summer. JUVENILE: May retain distinctive plumage into early winter; note paler tones overall, especially the throat; distinctive white scalloping to contour and wing feathers; yellowish bill. FLIGHT: Alcid-like: low over the water, buzzy.

Geographic Variation Five subspecies: 2 north of Mexico, 3 more from Mexico south to Panama. Variation weak and difficult to discern.

Similar Species Not likely to be confused with other species. Possible confusion with bobtailed Brewer's Blackbirds (feeding at waterways) in rectrix molt.

Voice CALL: Loud, sharp *bzeet,* given frequently by flushing birds; easily heard. On landing, may give fast series of these notes. SONG: Amazingly long (exceptionally to 5 mins.) series of repeated, varied, thrasher-like phrases. Song often ventriloqual; nearby birds may sound faint, far away.

Status & Distribution Fairly common. AK to Panama. BREEDING: Near rushing streams. Year-round resident where streams remain ice-free. MIGRATION: High-elevation breeders move to ice-free streams at lower elevations. Juveniles generally move to lower elevations than adults. VAGRANT: Occasionally to more than 100 miles from main range.

Population Overall population is stable but naturally fragmented; some local populations are at risk of extinction.

juvenile

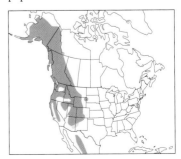

BULBULS Family Pycnonotidae

Red-whiskered Bulbul (Hong Kong)

Bulbuls are small, active passerines native to tropical areas of the Old World. Popular as cage birds, several escaped species have established naturalized populations in many regions of the world. In the United States, bulbuls are associated with parks and neighborhoods that are landscaped with exotic plants and trees that provide fruit and nectar year-round.

Structure Bulbuls are smallish and slim with long tails; some have small crests. The bill is short and moderately slender; the wings are short and rounded.

Plumage Commonly brown, olive, or gray, with red, yellow, or black markings. Many species have bold head patterns and brightly colored undertail coverts. Juvenile plumage generally resembles that of adult.

Behavior Highly gregarious during the nonbreeding season, most bulbuls forage and roost in large flocks. Primarily frugivorous, they feed on small fruits, along with leaves, flowers, buds, and nectar. Bulbuls also feed on insects, which are gleaned from foliage or captured in midair by flycatching or hawking. Many pairs of Red-whiskered Bulbuls in Florida are accompanied by a third adult, but cooperative breeding not documented.

Distribution Their native range extends from the western Palearctic to the Orient and to the Philippines. The Red-whiskered is found in North America as a result of escaped cage birds; another species is also naturalized in Hawaii.

Taxonomy A large family (±118–130 sp. in 14–22 genera), bulbuls are closely related to Old World warblers, kinglets, and swallows; they are only distantly related to silky-flycatchers (e.g., Phainopepla) and waxwings despite the physical resemblance.

Conservation The United States has banned further importation of Red-whiskereds because of their potential threat to crops, even though their bills are too small and weak to pierce the skins of most fruit. Other species, including the Red-vented Bulbul, which is widespread on Oahu, Hawaii, can still be imported. Most bulbuls are common in their native ranges. —*Bill Pranty*

Genus Pycnonotus

RED-WHISKERED BULBUL *Pycnonotus jocosus*

adult

juvenile

The Red-whiskered Bulbul is the sole representative of this Old World family in North America, although the Red-vented Bulbul (*P. cafer*) occurs in Hawaii. Bulbuls are popular cage birds, and U.S. populations formed from escapees. Polytypic (9 ssp.; *emeria* in FL; CA ssp. unknown). L 7" (18 cm)

Identification A small, slender songbird with a conspicuous crest and long tail, brown above and white below. Sexes similar. ADULT: Black forehead and crest, remainder of upperparts brown. Black eyes, bill, legs, and feet. Small red "whiskers" just below and behind eyes. Narrow black line separates white cheek from white throat and malar. White breast and belly, with blackish "spur" on sides of breast forming incomplete band. Flanks and vent washed with buff; red undertail coverts. Brown tail, broadly tipped with white on all but central rectrices. JUVENILE: Brown crown and crest, red "whiskers" lacking, buffy undertail coverts.

Similar Species Few other crested birds occur within narrow U.S. range. May be confused with Phainopeplas in California, which are wholly black or grayish, with white patches in the outer primaries. Bulbuls in Florida were originally confused with Tufted Titmice, which are casual to the Miami area.

Voice CALL: *Kink-a-jou* or *chip-pet-ti-grew; peet* given at roost or when alarmed. SONG: Rolling musical whistle *chee-purdee, chee-purdee-purdee.*

Status & Distribution Exotic in the U.S.; importation now banned. Common in native range from India to China and to the northern Malay Peninsula; ssp. found in FL native from India to Thailand. YEAR-ROUND: Nonmigratory. In U.S., restricted to CA (<100 in the San Gabriel Valley) and FL (perhaps a few hundred individuals at Kendall and Pinecrest, southwest of Miami). Florida birds nest Feb.–July in shrubs, palms, or small trees, usually those not native to the U.S.

Population In Florida, the range is stable or expanding slightly; in California, eradication efforts during the 1970s–1980s and increasing urbanization have reduced the population.

KINGLETS Family Regulidae

Golden-crowned Kinglet, female (NY, Oct.)

ican passerines. They have rounded bodies, medium-length tails, relatively short wings, and small, thin bills. **Plumage** Grayish or olive with bright olive-edged flight feathers, 2 white wing bars, concealed colorful crown patches. Like the Golden-crowned Kinglet, most species worldwide have boldly marked heads, particularly lateral black crown stripes. The Ruby-crowned Kinglet is unusually plain in this regard.

Behavior Frequently observed in feeding flocks in migration, in low shrubbery or canopy. Insectivorous and in winter feed on insects in buds and under bark, allowing them to winter farther north than other insectivores. When foraging, they tend to quiver or flick their wings in a manner unlike most other small songbirds. They often hover below leaves and branches to glean insects.

Distribution Six species worldwide: 2 in North America, 1 in Eurasia, 1 in Europe to North Africa, 1 endemic to the Canary Islands, and 1 endemic to Taiwan.

Taxonomy All species are in a single genus, *Regulus,* and were formerly classified with the Old World warblers (Sylviidae); recent genetic studies suggest they are not closely related. Current affinities are not known.

Conservation Generally common with healthy populations. Deforestation and wildfires may be the greatest threat in North America. —*Allen T. Chartier*

The 2 North American kinglet species are forest songbirds that are rather easily identified as they are among the smallest of our songbirds. Breeding in the upper canopy of boreal forest and near spruce bogs, kinglets are generally common in migration and in winter, and are usually encountered in small flocks.

Structure Kinglets are among the smallest of North Amer-

Genus *Regulus*

GOLDEN-CROWNED KINGLET *Regulus satrapa*

A tiny, thin-billed, wing-flicking insectivore, it has a conspicuously striped head. Polytypic. L 4" (10 cm)

Identification ADULT MALE: Dull grayish olive above, paler whitish below, head boldly marked with white supercilium, blackish lores and eye line. Yellow crown bordered broadly with black. Orange in center of yellow crown visible only during display, or when bird is agitated. Black at base of secondar-

ies, contrasting with white wing bar. ADULT FEMALE: Similar to male, no orange in crown. IMMATURE: Somewhat pointier tail feathers than adult; a few males may lack orange in crown.

Geographic Variation Western subspecies (*apache* and *olivaceus*) slightly smaller, somewhat brighter, with longer white supercilium, longer bill.

Similar Species Ruby-crowned Kinglet, readily distinguished by head pattern and call.

Voice CALL: When flocking, a very high, sibilant jingling, *tsii tsii tsii.* Also, a quiet, high single note, *tsit,* and a thin sibilant *seee* similar to call of the Brown Creeper. SONG: An extended version of the call, becoming louder and chattering toward the end; *tsii tsii tsii tsii tiii djit djit djit djit.*

Status & Distribution Common. BREEDING: Mainly boreal forests, a few in mixed or deciduous forests and conifer plantations. Also breeds in central Mexico and Guatemala. NEST: Upper crown of conifer near trunk, 8–9 eggs (May–June). SPRING MIGRATION: Spring and fall migration difficult to

detect in some areas with resident populations. Winter residents depart Gulf States before Apr. Peaks across continent late Mar.–late Apr. FALL MIGRATION: Begins mid-Sept. over much of range, peaking in East in Oct. and early Nov. WINTER: Many remain in breeding range through winter. Primarily south of Canada and north of Mexico in a wide variety of habitats. Numbers in southern CA and the Southwest vary from year to year.

Population Breeding range increasing in the East and the Midwest due to plantings of spruce and pine. Adversely affected by logging.

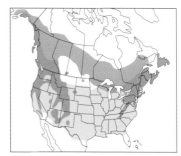

RUBY-CROWNED KINGLET *Regulus calendula*

This tiny, thin-billed, wing-flicking insectivore is grayish olive with a conspicuous broken white eye ring. Polytypic. 4.2" (11cm)

Identification ADULT MALE: Bright greenish gray above, paler below; broad, teardrop-shaped white eye ring, slightly broken at the top (especially) and bottom; lores olive. Ruby crown patch visible only during display, or when bird is agitated. Black at base of secondar-ies, contrasting with white lower wing bar. ADULT FEMALE: Similar to male, no ruby crown patch. IMMATURE: Somewhat pointier tail feathers than adult, a few males may have orange, yellow, or olive crown patch.

Geographic Variation Northwestern subspecies *(grinnelli)* slightly darker.

Similar Species Compare with Hutton's Vireo (see sidebar below).

Voice CALL: Most frequently heard is a husky 2-syllable *ji-dit.* SONG: Often heard in migration; begins with 2–3 very high-pitched notes, abruptly changing to a rich, and surprisingly loud warble: *tsii tsii tsii chew chew chew teedleet teedleet teedleet.*

Status & Distribution Common. BREEDING: Breeds in boreal spruce-fir forests, preferably near water and especially in black spruce bogs. Breeding begins immediately when females arrive in early May. NEST: High in conifer near trunk, 8–12 eggs (May–June) is largest clutch size of any passerine in N.A.. SPRING MIGRATION: As late as early May in Mexico. Mar. to early May, in southern U.S. Early Apr. to late May, peaking late Apr. to early May in central and northeastern U.S.

FALL MIGRATION: Begins mid-Sept.; peaks late Sept. to mid-Oct.; continuing through mid-Nov. Arrives as early as late Sept. in FL and Mex. WINTER: Not as hardy as the Golden-crowned, and winters farther south in a broad range of habitats. Primarily southern and western U.S. through Mex. to Guatemala. VAGRANT: Yucatán Peninsula of Mex., Bahamas, western Cuba, Jamaica (sight rec.), Greenland (2 recs.) and Iceland. Many records from ships off Atlantic coast, but no confirmed records from western Europe.

Population Breeding areas in the western United States may be adversely affected by logging and wildfire.

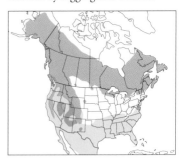

Ruby-crowned Kinglet and Hutton's Vireo

In winter Ruby-crowned Kinglets often join mixed-species flocks when foraging. Along the Pacific Coast and in southeastern Arizona, they may join with the nonmigratory, and superficially very similar Hutton's Vireo. In addition to plumage similarities, the Hutton's is unusual in that it also flicks its wings, very much like a kinglet. To distinguish these 2 similar species, focus on the following identification points:

1. Shape. The Ruby-crowned appears rather round-headed compared with the chunkier, thick-necked Hutton's.

2. Bill. Thin and pointed and black in the Ruby-crowned, it is thicker and paler in the Hutton's.

3. Facial pattern. The Ruby-crowned has olive lores with a teardrop-shaped eye ring more broken above than below, giving it a startled, wide-eyed appearance. The Hutton's has pale or whitish lores that join the whitish eye ring, broken above, giving it a paler-faced spectacled appearance.

Ruby-crowned Kinglet

Hutton's Vireo

4. Wing pattern. The Ruby-crowned shows 2 white wing bars, the front one very small, with olive between, and a distinct black area at the base of the secondaries, forming a distinct black bar below the larger wing bar. The Hutton's shows 2 distinct white wing bars, does not show this black bar on the secondaries, and tends to be darker between the 2 wing bars.

5. Feet. The Ruby-crowned has very thin black legs, with the soles of the feet yellowish, which is most easily seen on the inside of the hind toe on a perched bird. Hutton's has thicker bluish gray legs and feet.

6. Call notes. In winter the Ruby-crowned most often gives a husky *ji-dit,* quite different from the low *chit* or whining chatter of the Hutton's.

7. Behavior. The Ruby-crowned tends to be much more active and nervous, while the Hutton's is usually less active and somewhat more sluggish. Both species are noted for wing flicking. ∎

OLD WORLD WARBLERS & GNATCATCHERS Family Sylviidae

Middendorff's Grasshopper-Warbler (Japan, June)

The gnatcatchers, restricted to the New World, are the family representatives most likely encountered in North America.

Structure This family of songbirds is characterized by small size, delicate bill, and thin legs. Many species show prominent rictal bristles. They differ from New World warblers by having ten primaries with the tenth primary short, as opposed to 9 primaries in our wood-warblers. Sexes are generally of similar size.

Behavior The behavior varies somewhat by genus: Smaller leaf-warblers flit amongst leaves; brown, streaked *Locustella* often creep through grass and short shrubs; and gnatcatchers forage actively in trees and bushes. Those species that are not skulkers often use short, hovering flights to pick food off leaves. Most species that breed in more temperate northern areas are highly migratory, contrasting with many species in tropical latitudes that are nonmigratory. Songs vary from thin, wispy sounds to chattering notes, somewhat like wrens. Although territorial and antisocial during breeding season, most species in this family readily join mixed-species flocks during migration and winter.

Plumage Generally plain colored; little difference between sexes, except in some species of *Sylvia* warblers. Plumages generally alike throughout the year, except some Old World warblers are brighter in fall. Juveniles are generally similar to adults. There are significant identification challenges within some groups. For example, many *Phylloscopus* warblers share basic coloration, and patterns are identified only through subtle plumage differences. Complicating the matter further, plumage wear takes away color tones: Green plumages turn grayer, and, if present, streaks can be worn away. In the New World, this wear is less of a problem, although understanding variations in head patterns is important for identifying gnatcatchers.

Distribution A large, diverse family,with approximately 300 species and 15 genera, which is widespread in Europe, Asia, Africa, and the Americas. With the largely resident grass-warblers (genus *Cisticola*) and representatives from other genera, Sylviidae reach their greatest diversity in Africa. Habitats range from boreal forests to scrub and grasslands of the Old World, to a variety of woodlands and scrub habitats in the New.

Taxonomy Perhaps owing to the large size and tremendous diversity within this family, taxonomy is quite complex, with the likelihood that this taxonomic placement will change. The Old World warblers have been merged with Old World flycatchers (Muscicapidae) in the past, but recent molecular studies show Sylviinae, the Old World subfamily, is closest to babblers (Timaliidae), and are closely related to thrushes (Turdidae). Kinglets (and "crests" from the Old World) are sometimes included in Sylviidae, but most authors treat them as a separate family (Regulidae). Recent studies show that Polioptinae, the New World subfamily of gnatcatchers might be most closely related to wrens (Troglodytidae) or creepers (Certhiidae).

Conservation One gnatcatcher is threatened; population studies are needed on many Old World members of this family. Development or conversion of habitats for agriculture impact several species. —*Matthew T. Heindel*

OLD WORLD WARBLERS Genus *Locustella, Phylloscopus,* and *Sylvia*

These generally drab warblers are distinct from each other. *Locustella* are generally brown, with streaks, and, if not singing, skulk in grass or bushes. *Phylloscopus* usually have greenish upperparts and whitish underparts; a smaller number have primarily brownish upperparts. Identifications usually rely on exact shape of supercilium and the presence or absence of wing bars. Most *Phylloscopus* are leaf warblers, but a few species are found in lower shrubs and use the ground. *Sylvia* are slightly bulkier than most *Phylloscopus* and occupy lower- and mid-levels of small trees and shrubs; they are generally more colorful and patterned, and are sexually dimorphic. The following species are highly migratory.

MIDDENDORFF'S GRASSHOPPER-WARBLER *Locustella ochotensis*

If not singing from an exposed perch, this species, a vagrant from Asia, skulks in grasses and can be difficult to see. Monotypic (formerly conspecific with *L. pleskei* and *L. certhiola*). L 6" (15cm)
Identification A large, chunky, brown warbler with a relatively thick bill. The brown upperparts look more mottled than streaked; the rump and upper-tail coverts are lighter and warmer brown. A whitish supercilium is rather bold and offset by a dark eye line. The underparts are whitish, with buff flanks and sides of breasts, with streaks at the sides of the breast. The graduated tail is brown, with a dark subterminal mark and a whitish tip. As plumage wears, underparts become whitish and lose their streaks. FALL: Plumage more colorful when fresh, with much of underparts washed yellowish buff; supercilium buffy. FLIGHT: A frustrating species that is often flushed from underfoot, but otherwise not seen well as it dives back into

grass. In flight this is a large warbler, with an obviously warmer rump and tail; the tail looks wedge-shaped and has a pale tip.
Similar Species The other congener, the Lanceolated Warbler, is smaller, more obviously streaked above and below, and lacks the pale tip to the tail. There are no North American species that should be confused with a Grasshopper-warbler, although Pallas's Warbler, *L. certhiola,* from farther west in Asia, is very similar.
Voice CALL: An insectlike *trat-at-at-at.*
Status & Distribution An Asian breeder, winters primarily in the Philippines and vicinity. Casual migrant, primarily on the westernmost Aleutians in fall; also 4 spring records from islands off western AK.

fall

spring

LANCEOLATED WARBLER *Locustella lanceolata*

The Lanceolated is a vagrant from Asia. Quite secretive, it runs and walks on the ground; if it were not for the flicking wings that are often visible, the movement recalls that of a mouse. Singing birds perch up on grasses; otherwise unlikely to be seen much off the ground. Monotypic. L 4.5" (11 cm)
Identification A midsize warbler with black streaks on a brown crown, mantle, and rump. The wings are brownish and lack wing bars; the tertials are dark, with pale brown edges. There is a pale, thin supercilium on an otherwise streaked face. Below, the breast, flanks, and undertail coverts are streaked; ground color might be buff, or wears to whitish. The throat is usually white and generally unmarked.

Similar Species Somewhat similar to the larger Middendorff's Grasshopper-Warbler, but that species lacks extensive streaking above, including on the crown, and is streaked primarily on the sides of the breast. Also, the Middendorff's has a dark eye line, contrasting with the pale supercilium, and is larger. Finally, the tail of the Middendorff's has a pale tip and a dark subterminal patch. Otherwise, the plumage of a Lanceolated recalls a sparrow or pipit; the bill is too thin for a sparrow, and pipits have larger bills and are structurally different, with longer tails that have white.
Voice CALL: A distinctive, metallic *rink-tink-tink,* delivered infrequently; also an explosive *pwit* and excited rapid

adult

series of *chack* notes when disturbed. SONG: A thin, insectlike reeling sound, like line moving through a fishing reel.
Status & Distribution Up to 25 occurred on the Aleutian island of Attu during the spring and summer of 1984. Two more were found at Attu on June 2–6, 2000. It is accidental to CA, with 1 fall record: Sept. 11, 1995.

WILLOW WARBLER *Phylloscopus trochilus*

adult
yakutensis

The Willow Warbler is a vagrant from Asia. It occasionally wags its tail, usually immediately after landing. Polytypic. L 4.5" (11 cm)
Identification Uniform green to brownish olive above, without wing bars. A narrow, pale supercilium is offset by a thin, dark eye line. Below, whitish; some birds have pale yellow wash on the throat and breast. Legs are typically pale.
Geographic Variation The Siberian subspecies, *yakutensis,* can have very little green in the plumage and might have dark legs. Nominate *trochilus* and *acredula* from Europe, greener above and more yellow below.
Similar Species Most similar to the Chiffchaff *(collybita),* as of yet unrecorded in our area. The Siberian subspecies, *tristis,* is browner than the nominate Chiffchaff, and looks quite similar to the Siberian *yakutensis* of the Willow Warbler. The best character is the longer primary extension of the Willow, which is at least 75 percent of the length of the exposed tertials, compared to the shorter projection of the Chiffchaff, which is approximately 50 percent. Otherwise, the auriculars of the Chiffchaff are uniformly dark, whereas they are slightly paler on the Willow. The legs are usually paler in the Willow, but eastern birds can have dusky legs. The Tennessee Warbler has a different shape, more pointed bill, and contrastingly white undertail coverts.
Voice CALL: A disyllabic *hoo-eet.*
Status & Distribution Breeds in Eurasia, winters in Africa. One rec. from St. Lawrence I., AK (Aug. 25–30, 2002); thought to pertain to *yakutensis,* but it was rather green above.

WOOD WARBLER *Phylloscopus sibilatrix*

The Wood Warbler is a vagrant from Eurasia. Monotypic. L 5" (12.5 cm)
Identification Perhaps the most colorful of the leaf warblers, the Wood Warbler has bright green upperparts and no wing bars. The feather edges to the wing coverts are usually yellow, as are the dark-centered tertials. A bold yellow supercilium is offset by a dark eye line. Below, the throat and upper breast are a clear lemon yellow; the remainder of the underparts are cleanly white. Both the bill and legs are pale, usually pinkish.
Similar Species Not similar to the other potential *Phylloscopus,* as its throat and breast are distinctly yellow, contrasting with otherwise white underparts. The Arctic Warbler, the only likely congener, usually shows a wing bar and lacks the yellow throat and breast of the Wood Warbler.
Voice CALL: A plaintive *tew.*
Status & Distribution Breeds in Eurasia, but no further east than central Russia; winters in Africa. Two records from AK.: Oct. 9, 1978 on Shemya Island (Aleutians) and Oct. 7, 2004 on St. Paul Island. A few fall records from Japan suggest a weak pattern of dis-

fall adult

persal east of the breeding range during the fall.

DUSKY WARBLER *Phylloscopus fuscatus*

A vagrant from Asia, this brown *Phylloscopus* spends more time close to, or on, the ground, but will feed in trees on occasion. It works its way through low bushes or on the ground, flicking its wings and calling regularly. Monotypic. L 5.5" (14 cm)
Identification The upperparts of this warbler are dusky brown and rather uniform; this species lacks wing bars. The bill is short, thin, and dark; the legs are dark. The Dusky Warbler exhibits a subtle, but distinct face pattern: A dark eye line includes the lores and contrasts with a pale supercilium that is invariably dingy whitish in front of the eye. There is a faint but noticeable white eye ring. The underparts are dingy, darkest across the breast where it might be dusky, but otherwise creamy with buffy brown wash on the flanks and undertail coverts. Unlike that of most *Phylloscopus,* the tail is slightly rounded.
Similar Species The Arctic Warbler, the most likely *Phylloscopus* in our area, differs in several ways from the Dusky. The Arctic is green, has a wing bar on the greater coverts, has a thicker bill that is usually pale on the lower mandible, has pale mottling in the auriculars and has a different call. The Dusky is most similar to Radde's Warbler *(schwarzi),* which has not been recorded in our area. Radde's has a thicker bill that is noticeably pale on the lower mandible. The Radde's often has yellow or olive tones, which the Dusky lacks, and the undertail coverts of the Radde's are particularly contrasting and yellowish buff. The supercilium in front of the Radde's eye is more muted and yellowish. Finally, the calls of the 2 birds differ.
Voice CALL: A hard *tschik,* recalling the *chip* of the Lincoln's Sparrow.
Status & Distribution Asian species, casual on islands off western AK, and in fall, off south coastal AK and in CA; there are 2 fall records from Baja California.

YELLOW-BROWED WARBLER *Phylloscopus inornatus*

inornatus
1st fall

This bird is a vagrant from Asia. Polytypic (up to 3 ssp.; some authorities split nominate from polytypic Hume's Warbler). L 4.5" (11 cm)

Identification A small leaf warbler, greenish olive above, with an obvious supercilium and wing bars. The bill is small and thin. The greater coverts have a large wing bar; the median covert bar is smaller and less distinct, particularly when worn. The tertials are dark, with pale edges. There is a dark patch at the base of the secondaries, like that shown by the Ruby-crowned Kinglet.

Similar Species Boldly marked fall birds are distinguished by bold wing bars, unlike other expected *Phylloscopus*. The Arctic Warbler is larger, with a thicker bill, and has 1 thinner bar on the greater wing coverts.

Voice CALL: A high, ascending *swee-eet*.

Status & Distribution Breeds in Asia and winters in southern Asia, with a pattern of vagrancy to Europe and the Middle East. There are 2 fall records for Gambell, St. Lawrence I.

ARCTIC WARBLER *Phylloscopus borealis*

This Eurasian species breeds in Alaska. Polytypic. L 5" (13 cm)

Identification The long, yellowish white supercilium often curves upward behind the eye, and contrasts with a dark eye line. The auriculars are mottled, not uniform. The upperparts are olive, and the greater coverts have a thin, whitish wing bar. There is occasionally an indistinct wing bar on the median coverts; long primary extension. The underparts are whitish, with some brownish olive on the sides and

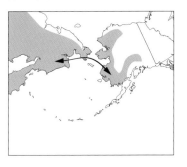

flanks; they might be more yellowish in fall. The bill is rather large and extensively pale; the legs and feet are straw-colored.

Geographic Variation Three subspecies, including nominate, which has paler underparts, and *xanthrodyas,* which is more yellow; both subspecies are larger, with larger bills than *kennicotti,* which breeds in Alaska.

Similar Species More olive than the Dusky Warbler, with a larger bill and at least 1 wing bar. Willow Warbler lacks a wing bar and has a thinner bill.

Voice CALL: A buzzy *dzik.* SONG: A long, loud series of toneless, buzzy notes.

Status & Distribution Eurasian species breeding east to AK. Fairly common in western and central AK; nonbreeding subspecies have occurred as migrants on western Aleutians. There are 2 fall records for coastal CA and an additional record for Baja California.

borealis

fall
ker

spring
kennicotti

LESSER WHITETHROAT *Sylvia curruca*

blythi
1st fall

The Lesser Whitethroat, a Eurasian species, is an accidental vagrant to Alaska. Polytypic. L 5.5" (14 cm)

Identification Slightly longer tailed than the leaf warblers in *Phylloscopus,* with

white in the outer rectrices. The crown is gray with a dark mask from the base of the bill to the auriculars. The wings and back are warm brown, with darker centers to the tertials, but otherwise unmarked. The tail is dark from above, and square. Below, the throat and undertail coverts are white; the flanks and sides have a tan-brown wash.

Geographic Variation Up to 5 subspecies, but an uncertain number of species; authorities have split the "northern" group from the "desert" group. The northern subspecies, *blythi* and *curruca,* have more well-defined face masks and more contrasting brown

wings compared to the Desert subspecies, (e.g., *minula* or *althaea*).

Similar Species While identification within the whitethroat complex is difficult, there are no challenges in separating this species from North American birds.

Voice CALL: A sharp *tik,* often repeated, and various chattering notes.

Status & Distribution Breeds in Eurasia and winters from Africa to southwest Asia. One record: Sept. 8–9, 2002, from St. Lawrence I., thought to pertain to the Northern complex. A few fall records from Japan and Korea suggest a weak pattern of vagrancy.

GNATCATCHERS Genus *Polioptila*

Gnatcatchers are small, long-tailed songbirds. They wave their graduated tails from side to side and cock them high above the body. They are generally gray above and white below, and identifications usually rest on head patterns and tail patterns. There are differences between the sexes, but these can be minor. Only 1 species is highly migratory.

BLUE-GRAY GNATCATCHER *Polioptila caerulea*

♀

breeding ♂

The Blue-gray Gnatcatcher is active, often foraging in trees or shrubs. Poly-typic.L 4.3"(11 cm)
Identification Thin and long tailed, with outer tail feathers almost entirely white (tail from below looks white). The bill is thin and pale gray. BREEDING MALE: Blue-gray above, including most of head and back. Crown has a black line at the forecrown that extends along the sides of crown; white eye ring contrasts with gray face. Wings brownish gray; tertials blackish, edged white. Underparts entirely white. NONBREEDING MALE: Black on crown absent, resulting in grayish

crown. FEMALE: Like nonbreeding male but grayer above.
Geographic Variation At least 7 sub-species; 3 north of Mexico. Nominate *caerulea* more extensively white tail; western *obscura* has a black base to the outer rectrices that extend beyond the undertail coverts. Western male slightly less blue on the back, with black forehead mark that is thicker, and less like a supraloral line found in nominate *caerulea.* Western females are dingier above; easterns are gray. A third subspecies, *deppei,* from south TX, is smaller and perhaps paler on average, but distinguishing these characteristics is likely impossible in the field.
Similar Species Most confusion is likely to occur with Black-tailed, and to a lesser extent, California Gnatcatcher. These species have different calls; California is also darker below. The best feature is the tail pattern. Blue-gray is almost entirely white on outer rectrices; Black-tailed and California have mostly black outer rectrices with white tips or edges. Be aware that in late summer gnatcatchers molt their tails. Blue-grays will look mostly dark from below when their outer rectrices are dropped. See Black-capped Gnatcatcher.
Voice CALL: A querulous *pwee* or various mewing calls. Western birds have lower, harsher notes, more like wrens; Easterns' common call slightly more

wiry, thin. SONG: thin, wiry notes; lower and harsher in western populations.
Status & Distribution Common. BREEDING: Various woodlands. MIGRATION: Spring migration begins in southern states in late Feb. Earliest migrants reach Great Lakes in late Mar., typically in early Apr. Peak late Apr. through early May, with stragglers to later in the month. Fall migration starts as early as late June or July, in southern states. Farther north migration starts mid-Aug., with peak mid-Sept. Small numbers seen into Oct. VAGRANT: Annual in fall in small numbers to Atlantic Canada, Aug.–Nov. Casual in spring to Atlantic Canada; to BC and Ottawa in spring and fall. WINTER: Southern U.S., south to Guatemala and Honduras.
Population Northward expansion in northeastern U.S. and southeastern Canada occurred in the 20th century.

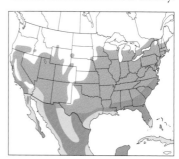

BLACK-CAPPED GNATCATCHER *Polioptila nigriceps*

This western Mexican species is rare in southeastern Arizona. Monotypic. L 4.3" (11 cm)
Identification The long bill is usually dark. The tail is strongly graduated, with the outer rectrices mostly white. BREEDING MALE: Black cap and lores; black extends below eye. Head and back blue-gray with indistinct white eye ring; face rather pale. Underparts whitish, with grayish wash on breast. NONBREEDING MALE: Black crown absent; dark line over the eye, or dark flecks. FEMALE: Like nonbreeding, but no black on crown.
Similar Species Separated from Blue-gray Gnatcatcher by more graduated

outer tail feathers, longer bill, and, in breeding males, more extensive black in the crown. From Black-tailed Gnatcatcher, in all plumages, the outer rectrices are mostly white and more graduated; in breeding plumage, the dark crown extends below the eye, and the eye ring, if present, is less distinct. In nonbreeding, note the different call and tail pattern of the Black-capped, as well as its obviously longer bill.
Voice CALL: A rising, then falling *mee-ur,* somewhat like the California Gnatcatcher. SONG: A jerky warble.
Status & Distribution Western Mexican species is very rare, most often recorded in spring and summer in south-

eastern AZ, but probably primarily resident there.
Population Stable.

♀

breeding ♂

CALIFORNIA GNATCATCHER *Polioptila californica*

breeding ♀

breeding ♂

A southern California and Baja California endemic, this gnatcatcher is restricted to coastal chaparral in our area. Formerly considered conspecific with the Black-tailed Gnatcatcher, it was split based on morphological and vocal differences. Polytypic (3–4 ssp.; only nominate in U.S.). L 4.3" (11 cm)
Identification A dark, rather dingy gnatcatcher with a dark tail. The black outer rectrices are edged white, including the tip, but the white does not extend noticeably inward from the tip. From below, the tail looks dark. Crown and upperparts dark gray, occasionally with blue tones. Wings decidedly brownish. Underparts are more grayish than whitish, and flanks have buffy wash.
BREEDING MALE: The crown is black to include slightly below the eye. The face and lores are paler; tertials are edged grayish. **NONBREEDING MALE:** The crown is gray, with black reduced to a streak over the eye. As greater wing coverts wear, they appear browner. **FEMALE:** Like nonbreeding male, but plumage browner, with brownish or grayish brown edges to tertials; flanks strongly washed with buff; lacks any black on the crown.
Similar Species Similar to Black-tailed, but with darker, dingier gray below. The tail of California is edged white, as opposed to the white tips of the outer tail feathers of Black-tailed, and California has a less distinct eye ring.

Ranges do not overlap in U.S.
Voice CALL: A rising and falling *zeeer*, rather kittenlike. SONG: A series of *jzer* or *zew* notes.
Status & Distribution Threatened. YEAR-ROUND: Local resident in sage scrub of southwest CA. Not known to migrate.
Population The northern nominate subspecies, which extends into northern Baja California to 30° N, is threatened by habitat destruction; only a few thousand pairs believed to remain in CA. Population of southern subspecies appears stable. The nominate is federally listed as threatened.

BLACK-TAILED GNATCATCHER *Polioptila melanura*

The Black-tailed is an inhabitant of desert thorn scrub, partial to washes. Although small, this feisty songbird will aggressively defend its nest against larger predators. Formerly considered conspecific with the California Gnatcatcher. Polytypic. L 4" (10 cm)
Identification Large white terminal spots on graduated tail feathers; short dark bill. **BREEDING MALE:** Glossy black cap extends past eye, contrasting with thin, white eye ring. Tertial edges usually whitish. **NONBREEDING MALE:** Like breeding male but dark cap is replaced by thin dark line over the eye. **FEMALE:** Like nonbreeding, but lacks dark line over the eye; back washed with brown.
Geographic Variation Three subspecies: One is from islands in the Gulf of California. In the U.S., *lucida,* which

breeds in the Sonoran and Mojave deserts (CA and AZ), has less white in the tail, a noticeably paler gray base to the mandible, and, in the female, a back with a rather brownish wash. Nominate *melanura,* which breeds in the Chihuahuan desert (NM and TX), has more white in the tail, a rather uniform dark bill with only slight paling at the base, and a lighter brown wash on the back of the female.
Similar Species Most likely confused with the Black-capped Gnatcatcher as birders search for the latter species in southeastern Arizona. Most easily distinguished by the white tips to the outer rectrices of the Black-tailed, compared to the extensive white undertail of the Black-capped. The tail of the Black-capped is also more graduated. Also note the Black-capped's longer bill and a more faint eye ring, usually limited to a crescent below the eye of breeding birds. In the nonbreeding Black-capped, note the pale face, including the auriculars, whereas the face of the Black-tailed is rather more uniform, and has the crown of the nonbreeding birds. See also the Blue-gray Gnatcatcher entry for separation

breeding ♀

breeding ♂

from that species.
Voice CALL: Rasping *cheeh* and hissing *ssheh;* in general, its vocalizations are rather wrenlike. SONG: A rapid series of *jee* notes.
Status & Distribution Fairly common. YEAR-ROUND: Resident in variety of arid habitats in the Southwest U.S., as well as in northern and central Mexico. This species moves very little, if at all. A specimen record from San Antonio, TX, is 1 of few records that might come from outside its known range. Any suspected Black-tailed Gnatcatcher outside its known range should be thoroughly documented.

OLD WORLD FLYCATCHERS Family Muscicapidae

Asian Brown Flycatcher (Singapore, Dec.)

Although these are upright perching birds and engage in sallying flights like New World tyrant flycatchers, the families are not closely related. Of 7 species recorded from North America, all records are from the western Aleutians or other Bering Sea islands in Alaska. Most are recorded in late spring, a few in summer and fall.

Structure Old World Flycatchers have rather flattened bills with a slight hook at the tip and well-developed rictal bristles at the base. Their tails are short and either square or slightly graduated, and the wings in most of the migratory species are long. They have 10 primaries. Their legs are short, and their feet are small.

Behavior Like tyrant flycatchers, they sally out after insects and return, often to the same perch. Most species are arboreal to one degree or another. Some use canopies of trees or exposed snags at the tops of trees for hunting perches (much as in some *Contopus* tyrant flycatch-

ers), while others forage lower in the undergrowth or from the ground. Many species engage in wing and tail flicking; others sit still after returning to a perch. They are solitary overall, and their songs tend to be not overly complex. Call notes can be important for identification but are infrequently heard away from breeding grounds in *Muscicapa* (more frequent in *Ficedula*).

Plumage In some genera the plumage is subdued, and all post-juvenal plumages look alike, while in others (e.g., *Ficedula*) there is strong sexual and sometimes seasonal and age variation. In Palearctic species there is a full molt after breeding and a partial molt prior to spring migration (though complete in the Spotted). Juveniles have a partial post-juvenal molt in Palearctic species; the molt is usually complete in tropical species.

Distribution Widespread in the Old World, mostly from Europe, Asia and Africa; greatest species diversity from tropical Asia.

Taxonomy A large family of about 114 species in 15 genera; 7 species and 2 genera have been recorded in North America. Based in large part on DNA-DNA hybridization analyses, many authorities place the Chats (also from the Old World and including such North American species as Bluethroat and Northern Wheatear) in this family, enlarging it to 275 species and 48 genera.

Conservation BirdLife International currently recognizes 15 species as threatened and another 17 species as near threatened (none of the 7 recorded for North America). *—Jon L. Dunn*

Genus *Ficedula*

This is a large genus of about (taxonomy dependent) 29 species, 3 of which have been recorded in North America. There is marked sexual, age, and in some cases seasonal dimorphism. Species in *Ficedula* often perch with their wings drooped. They nest in holes or cavities in trees or in nest boxes.

MUGIMAKI FLYCATCHER *Ficedula mugimaki*

A long-winged flycatcher that feeds from mid- to upper levels in the canopy of forests in eastern Asia; recorded only once in N.A. Monotypic. L 5.3" (13 cm)
Identification ADULT MALE: Blackish head and upperparts with bold, but short supercilium, white wing patch. Below, extensively orange from chin to belly. FEMALE: Grayish brown above, orangish on throat and breast, 2 thin wing bars. IMMATURE MALE: Overall closer to female; usually shows some indication of a supercilium.

Voice CALL: A rattled harsh *trrrt*.
SONG: A fast and musical warble.
Similar Species No confusion species in N.A.; Rufous-chested *(F. dumetoria)*, of lowland evergreen forests in southeast Asia, is plumaged similarly.
Status & Distribution Overall uncommon. BREEDING: Central and eastern Siberia and northeastern China in mature mixed forest. WINTER: In forests of Southeast Asia and east to Sulawasi. VAGRANT: Accidental. An accepted record from Shemya I., western Aleu-

1st year ♂

tians (May 24, 1985 supported by marginal photos); accidental in U.K.
Population Stable as far as is known.

NARCISSUS FLYCATCHER *Ficedula narcissina*

adult ♂

spring ♀

1st spring ♂

Adult males are 1 of the most stunning members of the Old World Flycatchers. Females and immatures are more subdued. The species has occurred only twice in North America, both events involved males on Attu Island, Alaska. Polytypic. L 5.3" (13 cm)

Identification *(narcissina)* ADULT MALE: Unmistakable with black head and upperparts, except for bold orange supercilum and rump and conspicuous white wing patch. Ventrally extensively orange. FEMALE: Brownish above with olive tinge on lower back and rump; whitish below with some mottling on sides of throat and breast and a grayish brown wash on the flanks; sometimes with pale yellow wash on

belly. IMMATURE MALE: Resembles female through winter but much more like adult males by spring, except for browner wings and patches of brown elsewhere on upperparts.

Geographic Variation Three subspecies. Subspecies *elisae,* with an isolated breeding range in northeast China and wintering primarily on the Malay Peninsula, is often split and recognized as its own species, the Green-backed Flycatcher. Adult males lack supercilium and are green dorsally; females are duller and

lack wing and rump patch, but are otherwise olive above with a contrasting rufous rump and tail and yellowish below. Another green-backed subspecies, *owstoni,* is resident on the southern Ryukyu Islands, Japan.

Similar Species The Yellow-rumped (tricolored) Flycatcher *(F. zanthopygia)* a possible stray to western Alaska; adult male resembles Narcissus but has an extended white spur from wing patch and white supercilium. Duller female has wing patch, spur and a yellow rump.

Voice CALL: *Tink-tink.* Song: A warble with repeated 3-syllable notes.

Status & Distribution BREEDING: Nominate *narcissina* breeds from Sakhalin, the Kuril Islands and Japan in deciduous, mixed, or coniferous woods with dense undergrowth; winters in forests of the Philippines, sparingly to Borneo. VAGRANT: Accidental, 2 specimen records, both from Attu Island, western Aleutians (May 20–21, 1989, and May 21, 1994).

Population Nominate *narcissina* stable as far as known. Subspecies *owstoni* has suffered severe declines; *elisae* no doubt vulnerable, but little data.

RED-BREASTED FLYCATCHER *Ficedula parva*

This Eurasian Flycatcher has a distinctive black tail, which is often flicked rapidly upward. White patches on outer tail feathers are best seen in flight. It often drops to catch prey on the ground. Polytypic. L 5.3" (13 cm)

Identification *(albicilla)* SUMMER ADULT MALE: Distinctive red throat; upperparts brownish, face and chest ashgrayish; whitish eye ring; underparts paler with buffy wash on sides and flanks. Black uppertail coverts and tail with white lateral patches, not usually visible on folded tail. FEMALE AND WINTER MALE: Plumage similar but red throat lacking and face and chest less grayish. Fall immatures show faint pale wing bars and tertial edges.

Geographic Variation Two distinctive subspecies, often now considered specifically distinct. Summer males of the more easterly *albicilla* subspecies, breeding from eastern European Russia east to Mongolia and Kamchatka and wintering from eastern India and through mainland Southeast Asia, have red restricted to the throat with gray band below that. On summer plumaged adult males of the more westerly nominate *parva* (breeds central and eastern Eur.,

southwest Siberia and to Iran and winters Pakistan and northern India), red extends to the chest. Females and immature males very similar, but in all *albicilla* the longest uppertail coverts are black (brown in nominate *parva*), breast is grayer, and bill is more uniformly dark. Differences in maturation, plumages of adult males (winter adult males of *parva* retain red throat and chest), song and calls, and apparently mitochondrial DNA, indicate that *albicilla* deserves full species status; both Red-throated and Taiga are used as English names. All Alaskan specimen records are of *albicilla* and probably all other Alaskan records are of that subspecies too.

Similar Species Summer males with red throat are unmistakable; distinctive on all birds is the black tail with white patches, which is rapidly raised.

Voice CALL: A brief and fast series of dry rattled notes, *trrrr;* a high-pitched *tzee.* SONG: The *albicilla* gives an Old World buntinglike song that lacks the clear descending notes of nominate *parva.*

Status & Distribution Eastern *albicilla* common in Asia in open woodland. VAGRANT: Casual to western Alaska

breeding adult ♂

1st fall

albicilla

♀

spring ♀

(mainly spring); 20+ records from western Aleutians; also recorded from Pribilof Is. and St. Lawrence I.; casual to northwest Europe.

Population Stable as far as is known.

Genus Muscicapa

This is a large genus of 23 species, 4 of which have reached western Alaska. Plumages are grayish to brownish, and males and females look alike (juveniles differ with pale spots dorsally). Nests are open, often placed in a tree fork.

DARK-SIDED FLYCATCHER *Muscicapa sibirica*

This Asian species, known previously as the Siberian Flycatcher, is not as regular to western Alaska as the Gray-streaked Flycatcher. Polytypic. In Asia it nearly always perches on conspicuous bare branches, often high in the canopy. Polytypic. L 6" (15 cm)

Identification ADULT: Grayish brown above with dark head and rather conspicuous white eye ring; whitish below with brownish wash on the sides and flanks and some diffuse to fairly obvious streaks on center of breast; whitish half-collar and rather pale buffy-brown supraloral spot; long primary projection that extends mostly or actually to tip of tail. JUVENILE: Darker above with pale buff spots/streaks. More streaking ventrally and with buff tips and edges to secondary coverts and tertials.

Geographic Variation Four subspecies are recognized. The Alaska specimens refer to the most migratory subspecies, nominate *sibirica,* which breeds in coniferous woodlands from central Siberia to Kamchatka, Japan, and northeast China and winters (in a variety of woodlands) in Southeast Asia, including western Indonesia and the Philippines. Three other sub-species—all shorter-distance migrants—breed in the Himalayan region; some winter south to the Malay Peninsula.

Similar Species Like the slightly larger and bigger-billed Gray-streaked, the Dark-sided is quite long winged, though usually is slightly shorter. It can be told from the Gray-streaked by more diffuse breast streaking against a more brownish rather than white background color. Note also the brownish cast to the supraloral spot and the white half-collar. The head is more uniformly dark, with no darker evident forehead streaks and the eye ring contrasts more. Though diagnostic on the Dark-sided, the dark markings on the undertail are often concealed. The stripes on the side of the face (malar and submustachial) are not as distinct as in the Gray-streaked. The Asian Brown Flycatcher has more distinctly bicolored lower mandible, is much paler ventrally, has a bolder eye ring, and has much shorter wings.

Voice CALL: Very high, short and rapid metallic trills and a single high downslurred note. SONG: A weak and subdued series of high thin notes followed

spring

1st fall

by musical trills and whistles.

Status & Distribution Uncommon to common. VAGRANT: Casual in spring (1 mid-Sept. record) to the western Aleutians and to St. Paul Island in the Pribilof Islands, Alaska, mainly from late May to mid-June.

Population Stable as far as is known.

GRAY-STREAKED FLYCATCHER *Muscicapa griseisticta*

1st fall

spring

Formerly called the Gray-spotted Flycatcher, the Gray-streaked is the most regularly occurring Old World flycatcher to North America (e.g., 27

recorded from Attu I. on June 2, 1999). Like the Dark-sided, the Gray-streaked perches conspicuously. Monotypic. L 6" (15 cm)

Identification ADULT: Moderately large and very long winged, the wing tips projecting nearly or actually to the tail tip. Distinct stripes on sides of throat and well defined dark ventral streaks against a white background color; grayish brown above with somewhat ill-defined eye ring and darker streaks visible on forehead. The undertail coverts are always whitish and unmarked. JUVENILE: Palely spotted with dark bars above.

Similar Species: Pattern of markings below distinctive from the Dark-sided Flycatcher (see that entry), though note that species is variable in this regard. Markings below are more distinctive than in the Spotted Flycatcher and note unmarked white throat and much longer wings. Crown of the Spotted more extensively streaked.

Voice CALL: A thin *seet* and a fairly loud *speet-teet-teet* have been described. SONG: Perhaps not described.

Status & Distribution Uncommon in a variety of woodland habitats. BREEDING: Southeastern Siberia to Sakhalin and southern Kamchatka. WINTER: From Philippines and northern Borneo to western New Guinea. MIGRANT: Eastern China, rarely Vietnam. VAGRANT: To western Aleutians and more recently small numbers from St. Paul in the Pribilof Is. Almost all records are for late spring (late May to mid-June); 3 Sept. recs. in 2004.

ASIAN BROWN FLYCATCHER *Muscicapa dauurica*

spring

1st fall

This accidental vagrant to western Alaska is vaguely suggestive of a Least Flycatcher in appearance. Unlike Spotted and Dark-sided Flycatcher adults, Asian Browns have a complete postbreeding molt on the breeding grounds rather than after reaching the winter grounds. This bird tends to perch somewhat more within the canopy of woodlands than other flycatchers.

Polytypic. L 5.3" (13 cm)
Identification ADULT: Grayish brown above with distinct white eye ring and supraloral line. Whitish below with grayish wash on sides of breast and, more rarely, diffuse streaks. Primary projection is relatively short, with wing tips falling to only base of tail. Distinct and sharply separated pale base to lower mandible on bill. JUVENILE: Distinct white spots on upper parts, bolder white markings on the wing, and some fine dark scaling on the breast.
Geographic Variation Complex. The 1 Alaskan specimen belongs to the most migratory, northerly *daurica*. Three to 4 other subspecies in Southeast Asia, 1 of which *(williamsoni)* is sometimes considered specifically distinct.
Similar Species This species is much less marked ventrally than the other *Muscicapa* flycatchers recorded from Alaska, especially the Dark-sided or Gray-streaked. Also the wing tips project far less down the tail in this species. Note, too, the distinctly pale-based lower mandible and the distinct white eye ring and supraloral line. The other *Muscicapa* are darker billed, and only

the Dark-sided has an eye ring that approaches the distinctness of the Asian Brown.
Voice CALL: Includes a series of high, thin, sharp notes, and a short, thin, and high-pitched *tzi.* SONG: Similar to Dark-sided but shorter and less pleasant, consisting of short trills, squawky notes and mixed with 2- to 3-note whistled phrases.
Status & Distribution Common and widespread in Asia. BREEDING: Nests in rather open mixed woodlands. Nominate subspecies breeds from south-central Siberia and northern Mongolia to northeast China, Sakhalin, and southern Kuril Islands south to the Himalaya. WINTER: Found in a variety of open woodlands, including parks and gardens, from India, southern China, and throughout mainland Southeast Asia and the Greater and Lesser Sundaes. Other races are less migratory and found in mainland Southeast Asia and northeast Borneo. VAGRANT: Two Alaska records, a specimen from Attu Island on May 25, 1985, and 1 photographed at Gambell, St. Lawrence I., on June 9, 1994.
Population Stable as far as is known.

SPOTTED FLYCATCHER *Muscicapa striata*

A familiar bird of Europe, this species has been recorded only once in North America. It tends to perch at mid-levels in vegetation, but is usually found on prominent perches. Polytypic. L 6" (15 cm)
Identification ADULT: Grayish brown above including head and face, and indistinct whitish eye ring. Fine dark streaking on crown and forecrown. Below, lacks distinct dark malar and pale submustachial (faint dark markings are present) stripes on sides of throat, but does show faint blurry streaks against a pale buffy background on the throat and across the chest. The bill is mainly dark. Although appearing long winged, the wing tips do not extend more than halfway down the tail. JUVENILE: Has prominent buff spotting above and dark mottling below. The fall immature has more prominent edges to the tertials and wing feathers and buff tips to the inner greater coverts, which form an ill-defined wing bar.
Geographic Variation Moderate, but differences are largely clinal. Five to 7 sub-

species are recognized, the closest to Alaska being the overall rather pale *neumanni.*
Similar Species Gray-streaked Flycatcher is much more prominently streaked below against a whiter background color, has streaking on crown restricted to forehead, and has wing tips that extend to about the tip of the tail. Asian Brown Flycatcher is cleaner underneath, has a more prominent whitish eye ring and supraloral line, and has a more extensive pale base to the lower mandible. Dark-sided Flycatcher is overall darker; it has darker sides and flanks with inverted whitish stripe up the midsection, a more prominent whitish eye ring and supraloral line, and has longer primary tip projection.
Voice CALL: Includes a thin and squeaky *zeeee,* a sharp *chick,* and a doubled note. SONG: Weak, high-pitched, somewhat squeaky and disjointed, often with long intervals between phrases.
Status & Distribution Breeds in a variety of rather open woodland environments from western Europe north

adult

to Scandinavia and south to northwest Africa, east to about Lake Baikal in central Siberia, and south to the Middle East and north and west Pakistan. WINTER: Africa south of the Sahara. VAGRANT: One photo-documented record from Gambell, St. Lawrence I. (Sept. 14, 2002) is surprising given the distance from the region of closest regular occurrence in central Siberia.

THRUSHES Family Turdidae

Hermit Thrush (OH, Oct.)

The thrush family houses some very distinctive species, with which few others can be confused, including some tough identification challenges. Chief among the latter group are the brown thrushes in the genus *Catharus,* though female bluebirds also cause their share of consternation. Relatively close and unobstructed views are required to identify the thrushes, as is strong experience in the variation, both individual and regional/subspecific, in plumages of the various species. All North American members of *Turdus* are called robins, though they are not related to the original recipients of that name (members of the genus *Erithacus*), and many wish to replace the group name "robin" with that of "thrush;" in fact, some field guides have made that change already.

Structure Thrushes are generally plumper, more compact than other similar-size birds, but generally have quite long wings; in fact, thrushes average among the longest-winged passerines relative to body size. There is relatively little variation in bill shape among the family, with all North American species possessing short- to medium-length and thin beaks. Many species are terrestrial and thus have long legs.

Plumage Although most thrushes are monomorphic in plumage (males and females appear similar), the family includes nearly the whole range of plumage variation from monomorphic to dimorphic. Some *Turdus* species exhibit sexual dimorphism, although in the American Robin this is confounded by individual and subspecific variation. The bluebirds are fairly dimorphic, with distinct male and female plumages, as are the assorted Old World chat-thrushes (e.g., Northern Wheatear and Siberian Rubythroat) that occur in North America. The forest-dwelling *Catharus* thrushes exhibit subtle- to not-so-subtle subspecific differences in plumage coloration. All North American

thrushes undergo a single annual molt after breeding; pre-alternate molts are absent or, at best, limited. The family is characterized by the typically spotted plumage of juveniles, a trait that few other families match. Upon completing their post-juvenal molt, young birds achieve the essentially adult plumage.

Behavior Flight style is strong and fairly uniform across the family, with quick, flicking wingbeats followed by very short glides with the wings held closed. This style produces a fairly level flight, unlike the flight of most other passerines, which tends to undulate. Some *Turdus* (e.g., the American Robin) forage in a very ploverlike manner, with short runs and stops when they search the ground for invertebrate prey. American Robins are purported to be able to hear earthworms (a staple for the species) under the surface of the ground, which may explain their common behavior of cocking their heads sideways—to better listen (or watch) for prey.

Distribution The thrushes make up one of the most widespread bird families, with the largest radiations in the Old World. In fact, 11 of the 29 species dealt with here are primarily birds of the Palearctic; another 6 are neotropical in origin. Half of the North American thrushes have wide distributions across the continent: 4 are primarily western species and 2 are eastern specialties. All species of thrush breeding in North America are at least partly migratory, with our Northern Wheatears having among the longest migration routes of any passerines in the world. Most of the true North American species are medium-distance migrants; 4 species of brown thrush regularly occur south of Mexico, and 2 of these winter solely in South America.

Taxonomy Except for the Gray-cheeked/Bicknell's Thrush complex, species-level taxonomy of North American thrushes has been amazingly stable over the past 3 decades, a period of widespread taxonomic change and uncertainty. At the family level, however, there is widespread disagreement on which groups are incorporated, with the chat-thrushes and Old World flycatchers being particularly controversial.

Conservation Of the North American breeding species, the Wood Thrush (and perhaps other brown thrushes) is threatened by habitat loss and fragmentation; it is particularly affected by the subsequent higher rates of nest predation and parasitism in forest fragments. BirdLife International classifies 37 species of thrush as vulnerable (including Bicknell's Thrush) and another 25 as near threatened. —*Tony Leukering*

Genus Luscinia

SIBERIAN RUBYTHROAT   *Luscinia calliope*

pink-throated adult ♀

adult ♂   1st fall ♂   ♀

Despite the male's distinctive ruby throat, this species of thrush can be quite difficult to see well, due to its skulking habits and its preference for dense, shrubby vegetation. Monotypic. L 6" (15 cm)

Identification The male is unmistakable. Its crown, nape, and back are grayish brown, with rump, upper-tail coverts, and tail being somewhat rustier. Bright white supercilia and malar stripes are bordered above and below by black, and the chin and the throat are a distinctive opalescent red, with a vague- black lower border. The gray ear-surround contrasts slightly with the browner auriculars. The chest and upper sides are gray, the lower sides and flanks are washed cinnamon, and the belly and vent area are white. The bill is somewhat long and black, and the legs are dark yellow. Females are similar in pattern, but are browner than males, with streaked auriculars and a white throat, some throats with varying amounts of red. Immature females have no red or pink on the throat.

Similar Species The immature Bluethroat and Red-flanked Bluetail are potentially confusing. The Bluethroat is distinguished by a distinct dark necklace and rufous tail base, and the Bluetail has distinct orange sides.

Voice CALL: A short, hard *chak;* a muffled, creaking *arrr;* and a whistling *ee-lyu.* FLIGHT NOTE: Unknown. SONG: A variable chatty and calm warbling, with a variety of high whistles and harder, lower notes, and often mimicry of other bird species.

Status & Distribution Uncommon. BREEDING: In dense thickets with or without overstory, from Kamchatka west to the Ural Mountains; winters in southeast Asia. VAGRANT: Accidental in Europe. In western Aleutians, rare in spring; rare to casual in fall. Casual spring and fall elsewhere in western Alaska (nearly annual on Pribilof Is.). One winter record from ON.

BLUETHROAT   *Luscinia svecica*

This species is a skulker, though singing males can be conspicuous. Polytypic (6 ssp. worldwide; nominate in N.A.). L 5.5" (14 cm)

Identification Runs along the ground, usually with tail cocked. MALE: Distinctive, though fall through winter extent of blue on throat is reduced by wide, white fringes to those feathers. FEMALE: Medium brown upperparts; distinct whitish supercilia bordered above by blackish lateral crown stripe; white malar stripes; black lateral throat stripes; and white throat. Black necklace crosses otherwise whitish underparts, though sides and flanks are washed buff. Bill black with yellowish base. JUVENILE: Darker than adult females, with cinnamon tipping to upperparts' feathers; some older immatures distinguished by thin cinnamon tips to outer-wing coverts and, in males in late spring and summer, white admixture in blue throat patch. FLIGHT: In all plumages, rufous patches at base of tail are distinctive and easily seen in flight.

Similar Species Similar to the Siberian Rubythroat in structure, in skulking,

1st fall ♀

♀

♀

breeding ♂

winter adult ♂

and in terrestrial habits.

Voice CALL: Common call a dry *tchak;* also a whistled *hiit* and a hoarse *bzru.* SONG: Strong, clear, and varied, usually beginning with metallic *ting* notes, speeding up and becoming a jumble of notes, often including imitations of other birds.

Status & Distribution Fairly common breeder from western Europe east through Siberia to northern AK and northern YT. BREEDING: Nests in willow riparian in U.S. and Canada; also in other soggy habitats in Old World. MIGRATION: Medium- to long-distance migrant. Spring: Arrives in western AK ±25 May. Fall: Most depart AK in Aug., but small numbers are still moving in Bering Strait area through early Sept. Winters primarily from northeastern Africa east through southeastern Asia. VAGRANT: Casual to Pribilof and western Aleutian Is.

Conservation Little apparent concern.

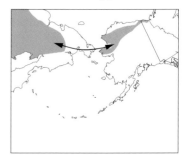

SIBERIAN BLUE ROBIN *Luscinia cyane*

The habitual, rapid tail-quivering behavior of this skulking, terrestrial species is distinctive. Monotypic. L 5.5" (14 cm) **Identification** MALE: Deep blue above; white underparts. FEMALE: Brownish olive above, buffy-white throat, and buff breast and flanks with darker scaling on throat and sides; some have blue in tail base. IMMATURES: Cinnamon tips to outer greater coverts. Immature males resemble adult females, but have dull blue uppertail coverts and usually have blue in the scapulars and some wing coverts. Immature females lack blue in tail.

Similar Species Vaguely resembles male Black-throated Blue Warbler. Female's olive-brown upperparts and bicolored bill might suggest a small *Catharus* thrush, but note shorter primary projection. See also Red-flanked Bluetail. **Voice** CALL: A hard *tuck* or *dak*. FLIGHT NOTE: Unknown. SONG: Loud, rapid, explosive *try try try* and *tjuree-tiu-tiu-tiu-tiu,* usually introduced by fine, spaced *sit* notes. **Status & Distribution** Uncommon coniferous-forest breeder, central Asia east through Kamchatka; winters southern China through S.E. Asia to Borneo.

adult ♀

VAGRANT: Accidental in Europe (2 recs. as of 2005) and Attu I. AK (May 21, 1985). One disputed report from YK. **Population** Declining due to habitat loss.

Genus *Tarsiger*

RED-FLANKED BLUETAIL *Tarsiger cyanurus*

♀ / adult ♂

This is one of many Siberian species that has occurred in North America, primarily in the western Aleutians. Polytypic (3 ssp.; nominate in N.A.). L 5.5" (14 cm)

Identification Spring male distinctive. Female similar in pattern, but head, back, and wings brownish gray; supraloral stripes indistinct and gray; well-defined, thin white eye ring, broken slightly in front by the black eye lines. White chin and throat contrast strongly with brownish chest. Most first-year males are not readily separable from females. **Similar Species** Siberian Blue Robin somewhat similar, but lacks orange sides and flanks and white supraloral stripes and has pinkish gray legs. Females have brown tails. Compare

with male Eastern Bluebird. **Voice** CALL: A whistled short *hweet* or *veet,* often repeated, and a hard, throaty *keck* or *trak,* usually doubled. FLIGHT NOTE: Unknown. SONG: Fast, clear, melancholy verse, *itru-churr-tre-tre-tru-truur,* repeated at length. **Status & Distribution** Common breeder in taiga and other coniferous forests in northern Asia, west through northwestern Russia to Finland; winters S.E. Asia. VAGRANT: Casual spring and fall in western Aleutians; 1 fall rec. on Pribilofs, 1 on Farallons (northern CA). Rare in Europe west of Finland.

STONECHATS Genus *Saxicola*

STONECHAT *Saxicola torquatus*

All North American records are attributable to the *maura* group of subspecies, split by some as Siberian Stonechat. Polytypic (21 ssp.; specimens from North America refer to *stejnegeri*). L 5.25" (13 cm) **Identification** Small size, short tail, thin bill, white patch on inner wing, contrastingly pale rump, and upright posture are unmistakable. MALE: Black head, back, wings, and tail; wide white ear surround; white belly, sides, and rump; and orange wash on chest. FEMALE: Pale brown head with indistinct paler supercilium, brown eye line, whitish throat, buffy-orange wash on chest and rump, and dark-centered back feathers. IMMATURES: Similar to

adult female, but males have traces of black in face. **Similar Species** Essentially unmistakable. **Voice** CALL: A shrill, sharp whistle; a throaty, clicking *vist trak-trak*. SONG: Short, high-pitched twittering, recalling the Horned Lark. **Status & Distribution** Common. BREEDING: In Old World. The Siberian Stonechat breeds in open scrubland and grassland with scattered shrubs in Asia and northeasternmost Europe; winters

fall adult ♂ / *maura* group / spring ♂ / 1st fall / spring ♀

from Japan south to southeastern Asia and west to northeast Africa. VAGRANT: Casual to various AK locations; 1 fall record from NB.

WHEATEARS Genus *Oenanthe*

NORTHERN WHEATEAR *Oenanthe oenanthe*

North American-breeding Northern Wheatears are among the longest-distance migrant passerines in the world. Polytypic. L 10" (25.5 cm)
Identification In nominate *oenanthe*, male has upperparts gray with contrasting white rump; white underparts with buff tinge to chest. Wide black eye line expands into auriculars. Wings blackish; tail pattern—black with large white basal corners— unique in North America. Female similar in pattern, but less contrasty and with strong buffy-brown cast. Males of *leucorhoa* similar, but a bit larger with richer buff on chest extending down sides to flanks; females browner. Adult males in fall and winter similar to females. JUVENILES: Distinctive; upperparts brownish with buff or cinnamon tipping; immatures have muted face pattern and cinnamon upperparts.
Geographic Variation Four subspecies worldwide, 2 in North America; *oenanthe* is widespread breeder in Eurasia; also Alaska, and northwesternmost Canada; *leucorhoa* breeds in Greenland and Nunavut; has bred in northern Newfoundland. Both winter in sub-Saharan Africa.
Similar Species Other wheatears are similar, particularly Isabelline (*isabellina*).
Voice CALL: A tongue-clicking *chack* and a short whistle, *wheet*. SONG: Scratchy warbling mixed with call notes and imitations of other birds; often given in flight.
Status & Distribution Common breeder across high-latitude Northern Hemisphere, through north-central Canada, wintering in sub-Saharan Africa. VAGRANT: Very rare along East Coast, primarily in fall; casual to accidental elsewhere south of North American breeding range; 1 wintered in LA. Determination to subspecies in fall is problematic, but probably both subspecies occur in the lower 48.

1st fall
leucorhoa

spring ♀
oenanthe

fall adult ♂
oenanthe

breeding adult
♂ *leucorhoa*

breeding adult
♂ *oenanthe*

BLUEBIRDS Genus *Sialia*

This is a strictly New World genus composed of 3 species. All are frugivorous (plucking small fruits from perches or while hovering) and insectivorous (sallying to the ground for prey). The Mountain Bluebird is noted for its hovering ability. Eastern and Mountain bluebirds hybridize; an apparent Eastern x Western bluebird has been found in Colorado.

EASTERN BLUEBIRD *Sialia sialis*

The Eastern bluebird is a species familiar to millions in eastern North America. Polytypic. L 7" (17.5 cm)
Identification MALE: Bright blue above, with orange throat, ear surround, chest, sides, and flanks. FEMALE: Differs in that upperparts are less blue (often grayish); has partial whitish eye ring, and whitish throat bordered by brown lateral throat stripes. JUVENILE: Very similar to Western Bluebird, but with tertials fringed cinnamon; immatures discernable with duller upperparts and browner primary coverts. Flight as in other bluebirds; pale wing stripe less obvious than in the Western Bluebird.
Geographic Variation Four subspecies in North America; compared with widespread and somewhat migratory, short-billed nominate *sialis,* resident *fulva* of southern Arizona slightly larger and paler, males with cinnamon-fringed scapulars; southern TX *nidificans* larger, more richly colored, with upperparts feathers edged with cinnamon; and southern Florida *grata* with longer bill.
Similar Species Male Western Bluebird with all-blue head, including chin and throat, and generally a deeper blue. Male Western also has at least some rufous on upperparts,

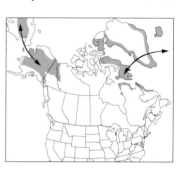

juveni[le]

♂ *sialis*

southwestern
♂ *fulva*

♀ *sialis*

particularly on scapulars.
See female bluebird sidebar
below.

Voice CALL: Musical, typically 2-noted *too-lee*. This call is also given in flight. SONG: Mellow series of warbled phrases; varied.

Status & Distribution Common in the eastern three-fifths of the lower 48 states and in southern Canada; uncommon and local in southeastern AZ. BREEDING: Nests in open woodland, second-growth habitats, and along the edges of fields and pastures, placing nest in cavity; readily accepts nest boxes. MIGRATION: Short- to medium-distance migrant. Spring: arrives Great Lakes ±25 Feb; southern SK ±1 April. Departs northernmost range during Oct. Usually migrates in flocks. WINTER: Almost always in flocks, often mixed with Yellow-rumped, Pine, and Palm Warblers and/or Dark-eyed Juncos; mainly central and southern U.S., but to south-central CO, central NM, and northeastern Mexico. VAGRANT: Casual west to AB and UT; recent local colonization in western CO.

Population Nest boxes have apparently helped reverse a decline.

Identifying Female Bluebirds

Many features provide clues to the identification of female bluebirds, and identification should be based on more than one. Except for the Mountain Bluebird, vagrancy in these species is quite rare, so range is a good first clue.

The Mountain Bluebird is usually the species most easily ruled in or out, as much about it is distinctive. The Mountain Bluebird has a distinctive structure, being longer-winged, longer-tailed, and longer-legged than the other 2 bluebirds; and its penchant for hovering while foraging is a further excellent identification feature. The female Mountain Bluebird's white eye ring is obvious on its otherwise bland face; both the Eastern and Western exhibit partial whitish eye rings (behind the eye). Eastern and Western bluebirds have darkish lateral throat stripes, with the Eastern's being darker than those on the Western (which can be quite vague) and contrasting more with the Eastern's white throat; the Western's throat is gray. The Eastern Bluebird has a distinctive orange ear surround. All 3 species can show gray backs, but the Western Bluebird often has at least a slight orange wash, particularly on the scapulars; the Eastern Bluebird can be quite blue-backed. The Mountain Bluebird has a more slender bill than do the other species.

The Mountain Bluebird typically has gray underparts, but a substantial minority have varying amounts of orange on the chest and, occasionally, the upper sides; this color does not extend to the flanks, which are a cold gray-brown and contrast sharply with the white undertail coverts. The Western Bluebird is usually orange on the chest, sides, and flanks; even duller females can nearly be matched by bright Mountains. The Eastern Bluebird is always orange on the chest, sides, and flanks, typically more so, even, than the Western. The bellies and vent areas on both the Mountain and the Eastern Bluebird are bright white, whereas the Western Bluebird is off-white to gray in this area, occasionally exhibiting some dark feather centers to the undertail coverts.

Though the differences in underwing pattern may be difficult to discern, this feature can be quite useful, particularly if the Eastern Bluebird can be excluded on other grounds. The Western Bluebird has the darkest underwing of the 3 species; thus it has, contrastingly. the brightest pale wing stripe. The Eastern Bluebird's wing stripe shows less contrast with other plumage than the Western's. Again, the Mountain Bluebird is relatively distinctive here, having the palest underwing with the least contrasting wing stripe. ∎

Eastern Bluebird, female (NC)

Western Bluebird, female (CA, Apr.)

Mountain Bluebird, female (CO, Oct.)

WESTERN BLUEBIRD *Sialia mexicanus*

This species typically prefers more wooded breeding habitats than does the Mountain Bluebird, though co-occurs widely with it. Polytypic. L 7" (17.5 cm)

Identification The Western Bluebird is shorter-winged and shorter-tailed than the Mountain Bluebird, producing similar wing/tail ratio, and different primary projection/tertial length ratio. MALE: Rich blue on head (including chin and throat), wings, and tail. FEMALE: Grayer head and back; paler orange underneath; at least partial whitish eye ring. JUVENILE: Similar to the Eastern Bluebird, being strongly spotted dark on underparts, whitish on

upperparts and wing coverts, but with tertials fringed grayish; immatures distinguishable by browner primary coverts, duller upperparts. Flight is level and typical of thrushes. Migrates diurnally in flocks, occasionally with Mountain Bluebirds, from which they can be distinguished by more obvious pale underwing stripe (created by darker wing linings and flight feathers) and, with experience, by shorter, rounder wings.

Geographic Variation Six subspecies, 3 in North America; Eastern *bairdi* (breeds western to central UT, southern AZ) larger; more extensive chestnut on upperparts than western *occidentalis; jacoti* of southeastern NM and trans-Pecos TX smallish, with extensive dark chestnut on upperparts.

Similar Species Unlike plumage of the Eastern Bluebird, male's head entirely blue; females confused with other bluebird species (see female bluebird sidebar p. 481).

Voice CALL: Similar to other bluebirds, but a more single-noted and harder *few,* though some calls are fairly strongly 2-noted; this call also given in flight. SONG: Consists of a series of call notes and is primarily heard at dawn.

Status & Distribution Uncommon to fairly common at mid- and low elevations

in western lower 48, extending north into Canada in BC. BREEDING: Nests in parklike, low-elevation pine and mixed forests, rich riparian bottomlands, and oak savanna. MIGRATION: Short-distance migrant that rarely strays far from nesting areas. Spring arrival central CO ±15 Mar.; eastern WA ±10 April. Fall: Most depart southern BC ±31 Oct.; northern CO ±30 Sept. WINTER: Primarily in southwestern U.S. and northern Mexico, but range to southern WA on Pacific slope; northern extent of wintering variable, dependent on food (juniper or mistletoe berries). VAGRANT: Casual east to ND, western KS, and eastern TX.

Population Populations depressed by alteration of pine habitats due to fire suppression.

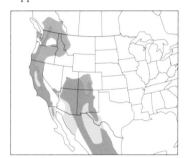

MOUNTAIN BLUEBIRD *Sialia currucoides*

The Mountain Bluebird often hovers above open country in a wide variety of western habitats. Monotypic. L. 7.25" (18.5 cm)

Identification The long-winged aspect, particularly the very long primary projection of the Mountain Bluebird, sets this species apart in all plumages. ADULT: The male's almost entirely sky-blue plumage is unique. Females are extensively gray underneath, though some, in fresh plumage, have orangish cast to the chest and upper sides. JUVENILE: Variably spotted white above,

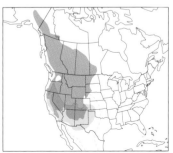

though nearly lacking in some, and vaguely spotted dark below; older immatures occasionally distinguished (at least through spring and into summer) by darker, drabber primary coverts and patchy retention of grayer body plumage. FLIGHT: Level and typically thrushlike. A flocking diurnal migrant, the female has translucent flight feathers; both sexes have long, pointed wings.

SIMILAR SPECIES Females, particularly orange-chested individuals, can be mistaken for other bluebird species (see sidebar p. 481), and grayer females for the Townsend's Solitaire (see that species account).

Voice CALL : A somewhat soft bluebird whistle, less 2-noted than that of the Eastern and softer, less single-noted than that of the Western. This call is also commonly given in flight. SONG: A series of notes similar to that of the call note, but more variable.

Status & Distribution Common and wide-

spread in western N.A. BREEDING: Nests in huge elevational and latitudinal range (grasslands through forests to alpine tundra), requiring nesting cavities or niches in proximity to open country for foraging; readily takes to bluebird boxes. MIGRATION: Short- to long-distance migrant. Arrivals or migrants apparent in spring starting ±15 Feb. in southerly areas, northern extreme of breeding range occupied ±1 May. Fall: Departs northernmost breeding areas ±30 Sept.; more southerly areas in Oct., though quite variable. WINTER: Mainly lower 48 states and northern Mexico, but extent and local occurrence of wintering high-ly variable and dependent on food resources (i.e., in CO, particularly juniper berries). Regularly found in flocks in agricultural fields, where hovering foraging behavior put to good use. VAGRANT: Numerous fall and winter records from east of the species' nor-mal range, to the Atlantic coastal states and Maritime provinces; found alone and in flocks of Eastern Bluebirds. **Population** Populations of the Mountain Bluebird have risen concomitant with a great increase in the provision of next boxes in the species' range.

SOLITAIRES Genus *Myadestes*

TOWNSEND'S SOLITAIRE *Myadestes townsendi*

The voice of the Townsend's Solitaire is often the first indication of its presence, and it is a characteristic sound in western coniferous forests. Polytypic (2 ssp.; nominate in N.A.). L 8.5" (21.5 cm)

Identification A long and slender, somewhat aberrant thrush, Townsend's Solitaire often perches conspicuously on the highest available perch. In some wintering situations, individuals hold territory with extensive supply of small fruits (e.g., juniper berries) defended by call note and, rare in North American birds, song. ADULT: Monomorphic. Entire head and body medium gray, though underparts can be slightly paler. Thin, but crisp, white eye ring; short, black bill; and short, black legs are distinctive. The central third of the long tail is bordered by black and with the outermost rectrix on each side mostly white. The wings are distinctive, being primarily gray with whitish fringes to the dark tertials and greater coverts with striking buffy-orange patches (but which are duller in some individuals). JUVENILE: Juveniles are heavily spotted throughout the body and wing coverts, with a less obvious wing pattern. Older immatures are virtually identical to adults, except that occasional birds retain a few juvenal wing coverts, as is typical in thrushes; at least through early spring, most should have more worn flight feathers. FLIGHT: It is really in flight that the Townsend's Solitaire is most distinctive, with floppier flight than is typical of thrushes, and a bold, buffy-orange wing stripe, more obvious from below than from above. The tail is often flicked open and closed in flight, with the bird resembling a long, thin junco.

juvenile

Similar Species The most common confusion is with the duller female Mountain Bluebirds, but they exhibit blue at least in their tail and wings. They have shorter tails and relatively longer wings and lack the solitaire's bold wing pattern. That wing pattern is surprisingly similar to that of the Varied Thrush, but nothing else about the species is. The Brown-backed Solitaire *(M. occidentalis),* a Mexican species of potential occurrence in southeastern Arizona, has a brown back and wings, a white malar stripe, and a long, absolutely distinctive song.

Voice CALL: A single *thnn,* similar to the toot of a pygmy-owl, usually repeated at intervals. FLIGHT NOTE: Unknown. SONG: A finch-like warble, at times quite long and disjointed, with occasional call notes interspersed and with no distinct pattern.

Status & Distribution Common. BREEDING: Nests in a wide variety of open conifer-dominated habitats, often with rock outcrops and/or cliffs on which the birds place their nests. MIGRATION: Short- to long-distance migrant, with a strong downslope aspect. Spring: Most birds have departed low-elevation winter areas by ±1 May, but some are still there in mid-May. Fall: Arrive at low elevations ±1 Sep., but general arrival there about ±25 Sept. WINTER: Throughout lower 48 breeding range, even at very high elevations (to 11,000 ft. in CO), and in lowlands adjacent to foothills and mountains; abandons all Canadian breeding range except for extreme southmost areas; winters to central Mexico. VAGRANT: Very rare, but regular fall and winter vagrant to the East, especially to the northern tier of states and southeastern Canada.

Population No current concern.

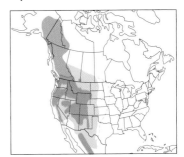

BROWN THRUSHES Genus *Catharus*

This terrestrial New World genus consists of 12 species; the 5 breeding north of Mexico have similar plumage patterns and retiring behaviors. Identification is complicated by subspecific variation. Boreal species exhibit a wide, pale wing stripe in flight. Two species of the neotropical radiation of this genus have occurred accidentally in southern Texas.

ORANGE-BILLED NIGHTINGALE-THRUSH *Catharus aurantiirostris*

This typically shy denizen of moist, high-elevation forests in Central and South America has found its way north of Mexico at least twice. Polytypic (up to 14 poorly-differentiated ssp. in the neotropics; 1 in N.A., presumably *clarus*). L 6.5" (16.5 cm)
Identification Orange-brown above with brighter uppertail coverts, wings, and tail. Underparts generally pale gray and whitish, with chest and flanks darkest. The bright orange bill, legs, and eye rings provide obvious field marks. In flight this species lacks the pale wing stripe typical of the boreal *Catharus*.

Similar Species Compared with the Orange-billed, the Black-headed Nightingale-Thrush is darker, more olive, on upperparts with distinctly blackish crown and face. The Russet Nightingale-Thrush *(occidentalis)* is less bright above, and has vague dark-ish spotting below and a black bill. **Voice** CALL: A nasal, Gray Catbird-like *meeer.* FLIGHT NOTE: Unknown. SONG: A jerky, short, scratchy warble of varied phrases.
Status & Distribution Fairly common inhabitant of montane understory. VAGRANT: This elevational migrant has occurred twice in the Lower Rio Grande Valley of TX (April 8, 1996, at Laguna Atascosa N.W.R.; May 28, 2004 at Edinburg).

BLACK-HEADED NIGHTINGALE-THRUSH *Catharus mexicanus*

A recent record in south Texas provided for this montane Middle American species' addition to the North American avifauna. Polytypic (3 ssp. worldwide; 1 in NA, presumably nominate *mexicanus*). L 6.5" (16.5 cm)
Identification Orange eye ring, bill, and legs are only bright parts of otherwise dark bird. Crown and face blackish with nape a bit paler; rest of upperparts and the wings olive. Chin, throat, and vent area whitish; rest of underparts gray. A skulker.
Similar species Orange-billed Nightingale-Thrush is similar in pattern and bright orange soft parts.
Voice CALL: Buzzy or petulant *mew, rreahr.* FLIGHT NOTE: Unknown. SONG: Similar to Orange-billed Nightingale-Thrush, but more melodious; 6–8 thin, high-pitched, flutey whistles and trills; some phrases repeated.
Status & Distribution Fairly common in humid montane forest; some suggestion of altitudinal migration. VAGRANT: Has occurred once in the lower Rio Grande Valley of TX (May 28–29 Oct. 2004).

VEERY *Catharus fuscescens*

western
salicicola

eastern
fuscescens

Among a retiring genus, the Veery is shy and relatively poorly known. Polytypic. L 7.3" (18 cm)

Identification For a *Catharus,* generally rather distinctive; less spotted below, brighter reddish above, and lacking eye rings. ADULT: Depending on subspecies, upperparts entirely dull reddish brown to bright rufous-brown, though small minority of western birds nearly gray-brown. Large, non-contrasting, pale grayish loral area and brown to reddish lateral throat stripes fairly weak; throat whitish to buffy. Chest washed buff, some pinkish buff, and vaguely to distinctly spotted with dull reddish brown on upper chest; any spotting on lower chest is grayish. Belly white, sides and flanks pale gray. Bill horn-colored with dark culmen. JUVENILE: Spotted whitish above, dark below; some older immatures distinguishable by presence of retained juvenal wing coverts with buffy shaft streak. FLIGHT: Wide, yellowish wing stripe typical of boreal *Catharus.*
Geographic Variation Five subspecies vary primarily in upperparts brightness and color and distinctness of chest spotting; subspecific identification in field problematic due to slight differences and individual variation; western *salicicola* has dullest upperparts (brown with reddish tinge) and distinct brownish spots; central Canadian and upper Midwest *levyi* (medium-dull reddish brown) and eastern Canadian *fuliginosus* (bright reddish brown) with distinct reddish brown spots;

northeastern U.S. *fuscescens* medium-bright reddish brown with indistinct reddish spots; southern Appalachian *pulichorum* dark reddish brown with moderately distinct brownishred spots.
Similar Species Other *Catharus* more spotted underneath, less reddish above. See "russet-backed" Swainson's Thrush.
Voice CALL: Abrupt, rough and descending *veer*; also a slow *wee-u* and a harsh chuckle; alarm call a sharp, low *wuck*. FLIGHT NOTE: Low *veer*. SONG: Flute-like, slow, somewhat mournful, downward-spiraling *veeerr veeerr veeerr*.
Status & Distribution Fairly common, but western birds restricted by limited

suitable riparian habitat. BREEDING: Most nest in deciduous and/or mixed forest but *salicicola* is primarily a shrubby willow riparian inhabitant. MIGRATION: Long-distance migrant; eastern birds trans-Gulf migrants, though many aspects of migration unknown. In spring, peaks on Gulf Coast ±25 Apr., southern Great Lakes ±15 May; casual-to-rare migrant in West, arrival in montane CO breeding areas ±25 May. In fall, Upper Midwest and Northeast peak ±10 Sept., though late migrants linger in northeastern U.S. into Oct. Winters solely at southern periphery, and a bit south, of Amazon

Basin. VAGRANT: Casual in CA, mainly in fall; accidental in montane SA, Eur.
Population Forest fragmentation may negatively impact populations.

BICKNELL'S THRUSH *Catharus bicknelli*

Bicknell's Thrush is basically a small version of the Gray-cheeked with a touch of the Hermit Thrush thrown in. Monotypic. L 6.8" (17 cm)
Identification Nearly indistinguishable from the Gray-cheeked, away from breeding areas. ADULT: Upperparts brown, usually with slight reddish cast; tail usually distinctly reddish. Compared to Gray-cheeked, wings are color of upperparts, except primaries fringed rufous, forming a more distinct wing panel; wings shorter; primary projection about equal to length of longest tertial. Pale loral area not contrasty; partial eye rings grayish; auriculars plain

grayish brown. Black lateral throat stripes contrast with auriculars and white throat. Chest spotting blackish, usually in a wash of buff; flanks olive-gray. Unmarked belly and vent white. Mandible mostly dull to medium yellow with dark tip; maxilla all dark. JUVENILE: Spotted buff above, blackish below; white throat. Some older immatures distinguishable by retained juvenal wing coverts with buffy shaft streak. FLIGHT: Wide, yellowish wing stripe typical of boreal *Catharus*.
Similar Species Gray-cheeked very similar, but larger, longer-winged, less distinct wing panel, and less rufous in tail.
Voice CALL: Similar to notes in song, single *wee-ooo;* also a sharper *shrip*. FLIGHT NOTE: Sharp, buzzy *peeez* or *cree-e-e* is higher, less slurred than that of Gray-cheeked. SONG: Similar to Gray-cheeked's, more even in pitch, beginning with low *chuck* notes; high-pitched phrases rise slightly toward end and terminate, after pause, with *shre-e-e*.
Status & Distribution Uncommon to rare and local. BREEDING: Mostly in dense stunted spruce and/or balsam fir forests

at tops of northeastern mountains; lower in eastern QC. MIGRATION: Medium-distance migrant, generally along Atlantic coastal plain; a Sept. specimen from northwestern OH. Typically arrives on breeding grounds ±25 May, slightly earlier in Adirondacks, slightly later in QC. Departs New England mid–late Sept.; probably peaks southern NJ late Sept.–early Oct. WINTER: Range of elevations, primarily on Hispaniola, but mostly in montane forests. VAGRANT: Accidental to Bermuda, Cuba.
Population Introduced exotic pests are killing trees of its habitat. Acid rain and global warming also major concerns.

How to Identify a *Catharus* Thrush

When viewing a *Catharus* thrush, one should discern as many features as circumstances allow and, particularly for a poorly-seen individual, be willing to let it go unidentified. First consider the time of year: All but the Hermit Thrush are exceedingly rare north of Mexico from November through March. The Hermit also has a distinctive tail-lifting behavior that, if observed, can help to eliminate other contenders. If the bird is in profile, concentrate on the precise facial pattern, the color of the lateral throat stripes, the color of the flanks, the presence and distinctness of a wing panel (primary fringes forming a block of rufous on the folded wing), the primary projection, and the color of the tail. From the front, consider the distinctness of the pale loral area, the color of the lateral throat stripes, and the color and distinctness of chest spotting. From behind, look for back/tail color contrast and note primary projection. Individuals in shadow can look quite different from those in dappled or strong light. ∎

GRAY-CHEEKED THRUSH *Catharus minimus*

1st fall
aliciae

aliciae

minimus

aliciae described. Newfoundland *minimus* upperparts and flanks grayish olive; breast lightly washed cream; and bill darker and duller, with yellow usually not extending beyond nostrils.

Similar Species Colder-colored than other *Catharus;* quite similar to the Bicknell's (see that entry).

Voice: CALL: Variable; downward-slurred *wee-ah,* higher, more nasal than that of the Veery; also a thin *pweep.* FLIGHT NOTE: *Che-errr,* which is similar to that of regular call note, but more nasal, stressing highest pitch in middle; ending more abruptly than that of the Bicknell's Thrush. SONG: A Veery-like descending spi-

ral, but thinner, higher, more nasal, and with a stutter.

Status & Distribution Uncommon. BREEDING: Nests in soggy areas, usually conifer bogs or willow or alder thickets; also in stunted spruce at high elevation. MIGRATION: Long-distance, trans-Gulf migrant. Spring: Gulf Coast peak ±1 May; arrival in western AK ±1 June, when some still migrating through LA. Fall: peak in eastern U.S. ±1 Oct. Winters at lower elevations in northwestern SA (south to eastern Ecuador). VAGRANT: Casual to accidental in West; annual in spring in eastern CO; casual to northern Europe (>45 to U.K.); accidental to Surinam.

Population As far as known, population stable, but bears watching.

Siberian breeders of this species are among the longest-distance passerine migrants. Polytypic. L 7.3" (18 cm)

Identification A cold gray-brown, long-winged *Catharus.* ADULT: Upperparts brownish olive; uppertail coverts and tail with slight reddish cast. Face quite plain with vague pale gray loral area and partial eye ring (particularly behind eye). Thin, buff to gray malar stripe and white throat contrast strongly with black lateral throat stripes. Chest spotting black and rounded, extending above and below cream wash on breast. Sides and flanks washed brown (with gray or olive cast). Belly and vent unmarked white. Wing panel slightly reddish and contrasting. Bill yellow, with dark culmen and tip; yellow usually extending beyond nostrils and contrasting with gray lores and white throat. JUVENILE: Spotted buff above, blackish below; some older immatures distinguishable by presence of retained juvenal wing coverts with buffy shaft streak.

Geographic Variation Two subspecies. Subspecific identification in field problematic due to slight differences and individual variation. Widespread

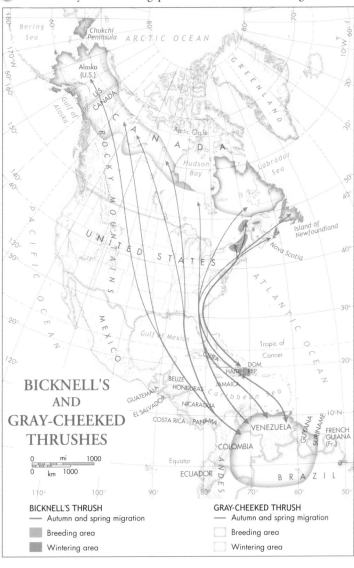

BICKNELL'S
AND
GRAY-CHEEKED
THRUSHES

0   mi   1000
0   km   1000

BICKNELL'S THRUSH
—— Autumn and spring migration
▨ Breeding area
▨ Wintering area

GRAY-CHEEKED THRUSH
—— Autumn and spring migration
☐ Breeding area
☐ Wintering area

HERMIT THRUSH *Catharus guttatus*

The Hermit Thrush is the only *Catharus* expected north of central Mexico in winter. Polytypic. L 6.8" (17 cm)

Identification The slow tail lift of the Hermit is distinctive in the genus. ADULT: In eastern *faxoni,* upperparts brown with moderate rufous wash. Eye ring whitish, occasionally not complete in front. Loral area darker than on other *Catharus* and not contrasting. Lateral throat stripes black, contrasting with white throat. Tail distinctly reddish, contrasting with upperparts. Distinct black spotting on generally white chest. Sides and flanks washed buffy-brown; brownish gray in other races. Wing panel rufous and moderately contrasting. Bill dark with pinkish base to mandible. JUVENILE: Spotted whitish to buff above, blackish below; some older immatures distinguishable by presence of retained juvenal wing coverts with buffy shaft streak; beware adults with cinnamon greater coverts tips in fresh plumage.

Geographic Variation Thirteen subspecies in 3 subspecies groups. Subspecific identification in field problematic due to slight differences and individual variation, but separation to group more likely. Lowland Pacific group includes *guttatus* (coastal southern AK to western BC), *nanus* (southern Alaska islands), *verecundus* (Queen Charlotte Is.), *vaccinius* (coastal southwestern BC and northwestern WA), *jewetti* (northwestern. WA to northwestern CA), *slevini* (interior south-central WA to west-central CA), *munroi* (central BC and western AB to northern MT), and *oromelus* (interior southern BC east to northwestern MT and south to northeastern CA). All with backs gray to brown and pale to dark, with little to no reddish aspect, and with richly-colored

tails. Interior Western Montane group includes *sequoiensis* (Sierra Nevada of CA), *polionotus* (eastern CA east to northwestern UT and AZ), and *auduboni* (southeastern WA east to southern MT, south to southern AZ and NM and western TX). All with pale, grayish brown backs and duller, less contrasting tails; the last subspecies having distinctive buff undertail coverts. Northern group includes *faxoni* (southern NT south to southern AB, east to NF and MD) and *euborius* (central AK and northern BC).

Similar Species Some similarity to Gray-cheeked, Bicknell's, and Swainson's thrushes (see entries).

Voice CALL: Soft, low blackbirdlike *chuck*; also a rising, whiny catbirdlike *wheeee.* FLIGHT NOTE: Clear, somewhat complaining *peew.* SONG: Flutelike; begins with long, clear whistle followed by series of rather clear phrases; successive songs often alternate pitch direction of song, rising then falling.

Status & Distribution Common. BREEDING: Typically in conifer-dominated forests, usually in areas of relatively little undergrowth; also in deciduous forests. MIGRATION: Medium- to long-distance migrant, with western montane breeders wintering farthest south (to southern Guatemala). Early migrant in spring, with southern Great Lakes peak ±25 Apr.; arrival in farthest reaches of breeding range ±10 May, though with stragglers still in West in early June. Fall: Western montane birds begin migration in early Sept., but *faxoni* and *guttatus* group peak in East ±15 Oct. Western subspecies winter in coastal states from WA south to southern Guatemala; *faxoni* group winters in Southeast (from southern NJ south), a few to southern Midwest, south to northeastern Mexico. VAGRANT: Regular to Bering Sea islands in migration and to Bermuda fall through spring; accidental north to northern AK and Canada, Greenland, Greater Antilles, and Europe.

Population Apparently more adaptable than other brown thrushes; there has been little expressed concern.

juvenile
faxoni

faxoni

adult
guttatus

auduboni

SWAINSON'S THRUSH *Catharus ustulatus*

swainsoni

This species is the most common migrant *Catharus* in much of N.A. Polytypic (2 ssp. groups: Olive-backed and Russet-backed). L 7" (17 cm)

Identification Typically bold, buffy eye ring and supraloral patch of most Swainson's Thrushes distinctive. ADULT: In "Olive-backed" group, upperparts olive-brown with slightly more reddish uppertail coverts. Strong, usually dark brown, lateral throat stripes contrast with buffy throat and malar stripes; ear surround usually buffy and obvious, but varies in

distinctness and color. Chest spots dark brown and round, often somewhat pointed on top, and usually entirely within buffy wash. Sides and flanks olive-gray. Tail similar in color to upperparts in eastern subspecies, more reddish in western races, often contrasting slightly with upperparts. Typically lacks contrasting wing panel. Bill dull yellow, with dark culmen and tip, not contrasting with face color. JUVENILE: Spotted buff above, dark gray-brown below, with white throat; some older

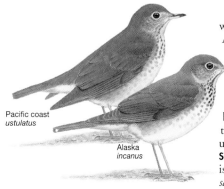

Pacific coast
ustulatus

Alaska
incanus

immatures distinguishable by presence of retained juvenal wing coverts with buffy shaft streak.

Geographic Variation Six subspecies, some of questionable validity; subspecific identification in field problematic due to slight differences and individual variation. Olive-backed group: Widespread *swainsoni* described; *appalachiensis* upperparts slightly darker and same color as uppertail coverts; *incanus* of western Alaska to northern British Columbia and north-central Alberta has upperparts paler and grayer, underparts whiter, and chest spotting nearly black. Russet-backed group: North-

western coastal *ustulatus* (southeastern AK to northwestern CA) and *phillipsi* (Queen Charlotte Is.) upperparts brown, tinged reddish, with breast washed brownish with indistinct spots, and flanks warm brown; and *oedicus* of rest of CA paler brown above with almost no reddish tinge; eye rings of western subspecies usually thinner, sometimes less buffy.

Similar Species Russet-backed subspecies is regularly confused with western *salicicola* Veery, but note differences in breast spotting, flank color, and facial pattern.

Voice CALL: Russet-backed gives a liquid *dwip,* Olive-backed a sharper *quirt;* also a rough, nasal chatter introduced by call note. FLIGHT NOTE: Clear, Spring Peeper-like *queep.* SONG: Flutelike, similar to Veery in spiraling pattern, but spiraling upward.

Status & Distribution Common, but in West restricted by limited suitable habitat. BREEDING: Mostly in deciduous and/or mixed forest; birds in western U.S. primarily nest in riparian habitat with combination of shrubby willow understory and deciduous or coniferous overstory. MIGRATION: Olive-backed group are trans-Gulf migrants; russet-backed birds migrate along Pacific coast and CA deserts. Peaks on Gulf Coast ±25 Apr., southern Great Lakes ±15 May; arrival in montane WY breeding areas ±25 May; spring migration continues into early June as far south as KS. In fall, most migrate Sept.–mid-Oct., arrival on CO plains ±25 Aug. Russet-backed winters from western Mexico to Panama; olive-backed birds winter in S.A. VAGRANT: Casual to accidental to northern AK and NT; casual to Europe.

Population Like other brown thrushes, forest fragmentation may negatively impact populations.

Genus *Hylocichla*

WOOD THRUSH *Hylocichla mustelina*

Formerly considered a member of *Catharus,* this species' large size and calls ally it also with *Turdus.* Monotypic. L 7.3" (18 cm)

Identification A chunky, well-marked brown thrush of eastern N.A. ADULT: Orange-brown upperparts, much brighter on rear crown and nape. Obvious white eye ring barely broken by dark gray eye line. Distinctive black-and-white striped auriculars and spotting on throat forming streaks. Underparts white with large and distinct, oval black spots extending onto lower belly and flanks, the latter washed warm brown. Bill grayish pink with

darker culmen. JUVENILE: Spotted whitish above, dark below; some older immatures distinguishable by flanks possibly less warm, and through fall by thin cinnamon tips to inner coverts forming very slight, partial wing bar. FLIGHT: Wide, pale wing stripe as in boreal *Catharus,* but wing base wider with pronounced secondary bulge.

Similar Species *Catharus* thrushes similar, but all smaller, less potbellied, less heavily spotted; most not as bright. Strong white eye ring not matched in *Catharus,* nor is auriculars pattern (though Gray-cheeked has vaguely-streaked auriculars). Brown and Long-billed thrashers also similar, but with much longer tail, bill; yellowish eyes.

Voice CALL: A rolling *popopopo* and a rapid, staccato *pit pit pit.* FLIGHT NOTE: Sharp, nasal *jeeen.* SONG: Beautiful, flutelike *eee-o-lay,* with last note accented and highest in pitch; this song usually introduced with quiet *po* notes, not audible at long distance, and ending with a buzzy or trilled whistle.

Status & Distribution Fairly common in East. BREEDING: Nests in deciduous forest. MIGRATION: Medium- to long-distance trans-Gulf migrant. Spring peaks Gulf Coast ±15 Apr.; southern Great Lakes ±15 May. In fall, some move early (late Aug.), but most still present near breeding grounds into Sept.; Gulf Coast peak in first half of Oct. Winters from eastern Mexico east and south to Panama. VAGRANT: Rare to accidental migrant in West and north to SK. Accidental in western Mexico, northern SA, Iceland, U.K., and Azores.

Population Forest fragmentation and resultant cowbird parasitism negatively impacts populations in parts of breeding and wintering ranges.

ROBINS Genus *Turdus*

Of the huge genus *Turdus* (as many as 66 species), North America north of southern Texas supports just a single breeding species, American Robin. However, 5 Old World species have occurred in N.A. Another 3 Mexican/neotropical species have occurred in the U.S., with the Clay-colored Robin recently adding south Texas to its breeding range.

EURASIAN BLACKBIRD *Turdus merula*

This all-dark *Turdus* is distinctive in North America, but similar to other blackish species in Middle and South America. Polytypic (15 ssp.; 1 in North America, presumably nominate *merula*). L 10.5" (26.5 cm)
Identification MALE: All black; orange-yellow eye ring and bill; dark legs. FEMALE: Browner; pale throat and dark-streaked chest; eye ring and bill duller.
Similar Species Unlike all other thrushes in northeastern North America where occurrence is most likely. A melanistic American Robin would be similar, but lacks the orange-yellow eye ring.
Voice CALL : Variable; a deep *pok* and a hard *chack-ack-ack*. FLIGHT NOTE: Quiet, rolling *srrri*. SONG: Similar to that of the American Robin.
Status & Distribution VAGRANT: 12 records from Greenland and 1 fully accepted record from NF (a specimen found dead 16 Nov. 1994). A few other Canadian records of uncertain origin.

EYEBROWED THRUSH *Turdus obscurus*

The Eyebrowed Thrush is a rare, but nearly annual, spring visitor to western Alaska. Monotypic. L 9" (22.5 cm)
Identification Superficially similar to the American Robin, but all plumages distinct. Head and throat of males are largely slaty gray with strong white supercilia, eye arcs, and chin, and black eye line; those of females are similar, but paler and browner with strong white malar stripe. Back, wings, and tail are brown, the latter without white tail corners. Sides and flanks are orange-rufous; belly and undertail coverts unmarked white. Bill yellowish with variably dusky tip. Legs yellowish brown to flesh.
Similar species Duller female American Robins somewhat similar, but easily identified by leg and upperparts colorations and precise head pattern.
Voice CALL: Variable; high, thin, penetrating *dzee*, a doubled *chack* or *tuck*, and a single *tchup*. FLIGHT NOTE: High *tseee*. SONG: Clear, whistled, mournful series of phrases of 2 or 3 syllables followed by a pause, and then a lower-pitched twittering; somewhat imitative of other birds.
Status & Distribution Rare spring migrant in western Aleutians, casual in fall; casual on Bering Sea islands; accidental elsewhere in western AK and north to Barrow. In some springs, groundings of migrants widespread in this area (e.g., 180 in May 1998). One late May record from southeastern CA is, presumably, of an individual that wintered in the New World.

DUSKY THRUSH *Turdus naumanni*

The 2 intergrading subspecies of this Siberian breeder have both occurred in N.A. Polytypic. L 9.5" (24 cm)
Identification Male blackish above; bright white supercilium; white lower eye arc connected to broad, white malar stripe, which is separated from white chin and throat by thin, patchy lateral throat stripe. Underparts blackish with variable extent of white fringing; wings mostly rufous. Female similar to male, but upperparts brown rather than black; face less white; wings brown. Whitish chest crescent on both sexes variable in extent, but distinctive.
Geographic Variation Dusky Thrush (*eunomus*) described; Naumann's Thrush (*naumanni*) rufous on head, where *eunomus* is white, and on belly, where *eunomus* is black; wings brown in both sexes.
Similar Species Varied Thrush vaguely similar, but head and wing patterns distinctive.
Voice CALL: Variable; series of *shack* notes; a chattering *kwaawag; kwet-kwet;* European Starling-like *spir*. FLIGHT NOTE: Thin *geeeh* or *shrree*, often repeated, or thin, high *huuit*. SONG: Flutey and melodious series of phrases, often ending in faint trill or *twitter, tryuuu-tvee—tryu*, with accent in first phrase.
Status & Distribution: Common breeder in north and central Siberia; winters primarily in eastern China, but also in Japan; a few to northern Thailand. VAGRANT: Very rare migrant in western Aleutians, accidental elsewhere. Recorded at St. Lawrence I. (Gambell) and twice in YK; has occurred in late fall or winter to southeastern AK, southern YK, and coastal BC. One or 2 sight recs. of "Naumann's Thrush" from western Aleutians.

FIELDFARE *Turdus pilaris*

The Fieldfare is a distinctive European and western Siberian breeder of casual occurrence in northeastern North America, where most occurrences follow large-scale, hard-weather movements out of northwestern Europe. Monotypic. L 10" (25 cm)

Identification The head is primarily medium gray with a black loral area; buffy-white to orange chin; throat with fine blackish streaking; and dark lateral throat stripe connected to black lower corner of auriculars. The bill varies from yellow to orange with a black tip of variable extent. Upper back, scapulars, and wing coverts are purplish brown; flight feathers are blackish. The lower back and rump are pale gray and contrast strongly with the rest of the upperparts; this feature is particularly noticeable in flight. The chest and sides are buffy to orange with blackish feather centers forming arrowhead-shaped spots, the lower ones typically larger. The belly and undertail coverts are white, the latter with dark centers or shaft streaks. The longish tail is black with vague gray corners. Legs are gray. Primary projection is about equal to length of longest tertial. In flight the bird's contrastingly white wing linings are obvious. Birds in first basic are a bit dingier, less contrasty, with a thin whitish lower wing bar and more extensive black on bill.

immature

Similar Species Vaguely similar to the American Robin, but brown upper back and wings, pale gray lower back and rump, and white wing linings of the Fieldfare are distinctive.

Voice CALL: Variable; *chack,* similar to the Dusky Thrush, is often doubled. FLIGHT NOTE: Thin, nasal *tseee* or *weeet.* SONG: Series of chattery or warbling notes with squeaky chuckles interspersed; without flutelike quality typical of genus. FLIGHT SONG: Chattering, more drawn out, and faster.

Status & Distribution Common breeder west from central Siberia through northern Europe and locally in southern Greenland. Winters primarily in southern Europe and southwestern Asia, but the species' fall migration has a strong facultative aspect, and many individuals continue only as far south as necessary to avoid snow. VAGRANT: Casual in late fall and winter in northeastern N.A.; accidental to ON and MN. Casual in western AK in late spring/early summer.

REDWING *Turdus iliacus*

A relatively small, short-tailed Old World *Turdus,* the Redwing has distinctive streaked underparts and reddish orange flanks and wing linings. The last feature gave the species its name. Polytypic. L 8.75" (21 cm)

Identification Upperparts from forehead to tail are medium grayish brown, with a strong face pattern of long white supercilium, black eye line, white-streaked auriculars, white malar stripe, black lateral throat stripe, and white chin and throat. Wings are colored as the back; tail is blackish. Chest and upper belly are white with extensive dark brown to blackish streaking. Streaking of the chest sides extends into reddish orange lower sides and flanks. The lower belly is unmarked white; the outer undertail coverts have dark centers.

Geographic Variation There are 2 poorly marked subspecies, with *coburni,* a breeder in Iceland, the Faroe Islands, and, recently, southern Greenland, being slightly larger and slightly darker in all plumage aspects. Which subspecies accounts for northeastern North American records is uncertain (though quite possibly *coburni*), but the recent record from Washington probably refers to nominate *iliacus.*

Similar Species The Redwing is unlikely to be confused with any other thrush in North America than a molting juvenile American Robin; however, the distinctive face pattern and lack of other juvenile traits (such as white upperparts spotting) should easily rule out that option. The Fieldfare is vaguely similar, but the distribution of orange underneath is quite different, as is the head pattern. Streaked underparts and strong black-and-white head pattern might cause confusion with one of the tropical streaked flycatchers, but behavior and underparts pattern are quite different. The Redwing might also recall a large pipit, with its streaked underparts and pink legs, but the extensive patch of reddish orange on the lower sides and flanks is distinctive. In flight, the Redwing's short-tail, triangular-wing shape recalls that of the European Starling, but that species has more pointed wing tip and appears chunkier.

Voice CALL: Variable; a nasal *gack;* a harsh *zeeh;* an abrupt *chup,* sometimes extended to *chidik.* FLIGHT NOTE: A long, somewhat hoarse *stoooof* or a thin, high *seeeh.* SONG: Quite variable across individuals, with tone and structure being more important than particular phrases; short phrases and squeaky twitters interspersed with long (up to 6 seconds) silent intervals.

Status & Distribution BREEDING: From eastern Siberia west to Iceland, with recent colonization of a small area in southern Greenland. Redwing winters primarily in southern Europe, northwest Africa, and southwest Asia. The species is a casual visitor, primarily in late fall and winter, to the rest of Greenland and to NF, and is accidental farther south in northeastern N.A. (to Long Island and eastern PA). Recent winter record in WA was the first in western N.A.

immature

CLAY-COLORED ROBIN *Turdus grayi*

Formerly just a wintering resident in southernmost Texas, this widespread tropical robin has recently been found breeding there. Polytypic (6 ssp. in New World; *tamaulipensis* in N.A.). L 10" (25 cm)

Identification A typical *Turdus,* the species is particularly common in Middle America and essentially replaces the American Robin there. ADULT: Lacks eye ring. Upperparts medium brown, underparts tan, with throat vaguely streaked brown and pale buff. The eyes are reddish orange, the bill is greenish yellow with a dark base, and the oddly-colored legs range from dull pink through greenish brown to gray. JUVENILE: Similar to adult but with pale buff shaft streaks on back feathers, scapulars, and median coverts, and with buff tips to median and greater coverts.

Similar Species This species is unlikely to be confused with anything else except the rarer White-throated Robin.

Voice CALL : Variable; a distinctive cat-like and rising *jerereee* (similar to a call of the Long-billed Thrasher) and some typical thrush notes, including doubled *tock.* FLIGHT NOTE: High, thin *siii,* weaker than that of the American Robin. SONG: Clear, whistled phrases recalling that of the American Robin, but with wider variety of phrases.

Status & Distribution Abundant in neotropics; uncommon to rare in U.S. BREEDING: Nests in areas similar to that of American Robin; in TX, usually in anthropogenic habitats. WINTER: Probably still some arrival in fall of wintering birds from Mexico that depart in spring. VAGRANT: Has occurred as far

tamaulipensis

north in TX as San Ygnacio and Huntsville, and west to Big Bend N.P. **Conservation** Strong adaptability and widespread distribution suggest little concern.

WHITE-THROATED ROBIN *Turdus assimilis*

This retiring tropical montane thrush is a casual winter visitor to southernmost Texas. Polytypic (10 ssp.; 1 in

suttoni

N.A., presumably nominate *assimilis*) L 10" (25 cm)

Identification The White-throated is a darkish *Turdus* of moist montane forests of Mexico, where it occupies the middle and canopy levels. This species can be difficult to see well due to its shy nature. Upperparts are dark brown; underparts dark tan, with the throat strongly streaked blackish and white, and undertail coverts somewhat paler. A distinctive white band on the upper chest can be difficult to see. Bold yellow-orange eye ring surrounds dark eyes; the bill is greenish brown, and the legs are dull pinkish brown.

Similar Species The White-throated Robin is unlikely to be confused with anything other than the Clay-colored Robin. Note upperpart color and presence or absence of eye ring.

Voice CALL: Quite variable; short, guttural *ep* or *unk*; nasal *rreuh*; whistled *peeyuu.* FLIGHT NOTE: Unknown. SONG: Similar to that of the American Robin, but with wider variety of phrases, and sometimes repeating phrases like a mimid.

Status & Distribution VAGRANT: The White-Throated Robin has occurred during 3 winters in the lower Rio Grande Valley of TX (8–10 recs. documented in winter 2004–2005).

RUFOUS-BACKED ROBIN *Turdus rufopalliatus*

The Rufous-backed is a Mexican robin with a distinctively orange bill. Grayson's Thrush *(graysoni)* is regarded by some authorities as a distinct species; it could possibly occur in the United States. Polytypic (2 ssp.; *rufopalliatus* in N.A.). L 9" (22 cm)

Identification Superficially similar to the American Robin, but all plumages distinct. Head and upper back are largely gray with variable extent (due to age?) of orangish brown on crown; lacks eye ring. Lower back and wing coverts bright orangy-rufous, contrasting with gray rump and tail. Black and white throat streaks extend onto upper chest; rest of underparts orange,

except for white central belly and undertail coverts. The legs are orangish pink, the eyes are orange, and the bill is dull to bright orange.

Similar Species Duller individuals might be mistaken for the American Robin, but bill and leg colors, plumage pattern, and lack of eye-ring distinctive.

Voice CALL: Variable; a typical *Turdus* throaty trebled *chok,* a plaintive, drawn-out, descending whistle, *peeeu-uuuu.* FLIGHT NOTE: High *sseep.* SONG: A leisurely, clear, low-pitched, warbled series of phrases with a repetitive pattern, recalling that of the American Robin.

rufopalliatus

Status & Distribution Rare but nearly annual fall and winter visitor to the southwestern U.S., primarily southern AZ, but with records scattered from southern TX to coastal southern CA.

AMERICAN ROBIN *Turdus migratorius*

This species' often confiding nature, distinctive plumage, pleasing song, and acceptance of human-dominated habitats make it one of the most beloved of N.A. birds. Polytypic. L 10" (25 cm) **Identification** A distinctive, potbellied bird. Forages on lawns and other areas of short vegetation for earthworms and other invertebrates in a run-and-stop pattern typical of terrestrial thrushes. ADULT: Depending on sex and subspecies, head, with white eye arcs, varies from jet black to gray, with white supercilia and throat, blackish lores and lateral throat stripe. Underparts vary, often in tandem with head color, from deep, rich reddish maroon to gray-scalloped, peachy orange. Males tend to be darker, females grayer, but overlap makes determining sex of many problematic. Throat streaked black and white; belly and undertail coverts white. Upperparts medium gray; tail blackish, with white corners. Bill color yellow with variable, season-dependent,

black tip. Legs dark. JUVENILE: Spotted dark on underparts; whitish on upperparts and wing coverts. Older immatures not distinguishable from adults; small percentage retain a few juvenal wing coverts or other feathers. FLIGHT: Quick, flicking wingbeats followed by short, closed-wing glides. Wing linings color of underparts; remiges blackish. **Geographic Variation** Seven subspecies, 5 in N.A.. Widespread taiga and northeastern *migratorius* described; north Pacific coastal *caurinus* and widespread western *propinquus* (larger, paler) with white tail corners small or lacking; Canadian maritime *nigrideus* dark brownish to blackish above, underparts deep rufous, medium-size tail corners; southeast U.S. *achrusterus* smaller, upperparts browner, smaller tail corners. **Similar Species** Duller females possibly mistaken for the Eye-

browed Thrush. Juveniles possibly confused with spotted thrushes. **Voice** CALL: Variable; low, mellow single *pup;* doubled or trebled *chok* or *tut;* shriller and sharper *kli ki ki ki ki;* high and descending, harsh *sheerr.* FLIGHT NOTE: Very high, trilled, descending *sreeel.* SONG: Clear, whistled phrases of 2 or 3 syllables *cheerily cheery cheerily cheery,* with pauses; lacks the burry quality of many tanagers; *Pheucticus* grosbeaks typically have different tempo. **Status & Distribution** Common and widespread. BREEDING: Wide variety of wooded or shrubby habitats with open areas. MIGRATION: Short to medium-distance migrant. Departs northerly winter-only areas by ±10 Apr.; arrival northern Great Lakes ±20 Mar.; central AK ±1 May. Strong facultative aspect (particularly in East) in fall, so variable timing; departs southern Canada ±20 Oct. WINTER: Mainly lower 48 and Mexico; also southernmost ON and BC, Bahamas (rare), northern Guatemala. VAGRANT: Widely in Europe; casual to Jamaica and Hispaniola.

Population Strong adaptability and widespread distribution suggest little concern.

juvenile

♀

♂

Genus *Ixoreus*

VARIED THRUSH *Ixoreus naevius*

This species' ethereal song is a distinctive aspect of wet northwestern forests. Polytypic. L 9.5" (25cm) **Identification** Orange legs and dark bill with yellow mandible base. MALE: Blue-gray above, orange below, with broad orange supercilia, black auriculars and chest band, complicated pattern of orange-on-black wings, and gray scalloping on flanks and lower belly. FEMALE: Similar but upperparts brown; auriculars mostly dark gray;

thinner, indistinct chest band gray; wings brown. JUVENILE: Similar to adult females, but chest heavily scalloped with dark gray-brown; central belly white. Older immatures similar to adults, though males less blue above, females browner; all have browner tails. FLIGHT: Similar to the American Robin, but orange-and-black wing linings and bold orange wing stripe. **Geographic Variation** Four subspecies in N.A. based on female plumages; north-

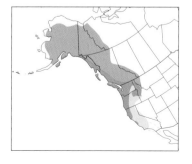

juvenile

♀

♂

ern *meruloides* paler;
north Pacific coastal *naevius* and *car-lottae* upperparts darker, tawny tinged, underparts orange; southern interior *godfreii* paler, upperparts reddish tinged. **Similar Species** American Robin has no wing pattern, lacks orange throat and supercilium and flank pattern of Varied Thrush. In flight Townsend's Solitaire's wing pattern quite similar, but species is thinner, with long, thin,

white-edged tail.
See Siberian Accentor.
Voice CALL: A low *tschook* similar to Hermit Thrush, but harder; a high *kipf;* a thin, mournful whistle, *woooeee.* FLIGHT NOTE: Short, humming whistle. SONG: Series of long, eerie whistles of 1 pitch,

with successive notes at different pitch and long inter-note intervals.
Status & Distribution Common. BREED-ING: Nests in moist, typically conifer-dominated, habitats in Northwest; in tall willow riparian north of treeline. MIGRATION: Short- to medium-distance migrant with some only moving altitudinally. Spring: Departs southern winter areas ±15 Mar., though some still there early May; arrives western AK ±30 Apr. Fall: Departs northern breeding areas ±15 Sept.; first arrivals in southern wintering areas ±10 Oct. WINTER: Coastal AK to southern CA and parts of northern Rockies; rare south and east of southern Rockies. VAGRANT: Subspecies *meruloides* rare, but regular fall and winter vagrant to East, particularly northern tier of states and southern Canada. Casual to Bering Sea islands; accidental to Iceland and U.K.
Population Logging in breeding range may be negatively impacting birds.

Genus *Ridgwayia*

AZTEC THRUSH   *Ridgwayia pinicola*

The Aztec Thrush is a Mexican visitor to the U.S. Southwest. Although by nature shy and inconspicuous, it is boldly patterned and distinctive. Monotypic. L 9" (22 cm)
Identification ADULT MALE: Blackish hood, browner on crown, face, and back; blacker on throat and chest, with blackish rump and tail. White uppertail coverts form a U-shaped band; tail tip is white. A dark brown vent strap separates white belly from white undertail coverts. The wings have an intricate pattern of black, white, and dark brown, with obvious white tertial and secondary tips. ADULT FEMALE: It is similarly patterned to the male, but all dark colors are paler and it has a more obvious streaked aspect to the head and chest; tips of the tertials and secondaries are gray. JUVENILE: Back, scapulars, and chest are streaked with buff; belly is creamy-colored and scaled with brown; and a dark eye line contrasts with a whitish, streaked supercilium. Some older immatures possibly distinguished by presence of retained juvenal wing coverts. FLIGHT: Bold pattern is distinctive; whitish wing stripe contrasts with blackish secondaries with white tips.

Similar Species Distinctive, but compare with juvenile Spotted Towhee.
Voice CALL: Harsh, slightly burry and whining *wheeerr* and a *whining,* slightly metallic *whein.* FLIGHT NOTE: Unknown. SONG: Probably a louder and steadily repeated variation of call note.
Status & Distribution Uncommon to rare. BREEDING: Pine forests in western and southern Mexico. MIGRATION: Northernmost breeders may be par-tially migratory, perhaps accounting for pattern of occurrence in U.S. Southwest. Winters primarily in breeding habitat and range, often joining mixed-species flocks of other frugivores (*Turdus* thrushes, Gray Silky-flycatchers). VAGRANT: Casual to southeastern AZ sky islands (mostly late summer and early fall) and Sierra Madre Oriental of Mexico (late fall, early winter); accidental to western and southern TX.

juvenile

♂

♀

BABBLERS Family Timaliidae

Wrentit (CA)

The Wrentit is the sole North American member of the babbler family, and of its genus. Identifying the Wrentit is straightforward, due to its habitat and skulking behavior.

Structure Babblers come in varied shapes and sizes, from large and jaylike laughing-thrushes to small titlike, or even wrenlike, species. Babblers tend to show loose and fluffy plumage. They have strong legs and feet and typically short, rounded wings. Tail lengths vary depending on the group, although the nearer relatives of the Wrentit show long, rounded tails.

Plumage Varied in appearance, babblers are mostly dull and brownish or olive, often with markings on the head and throat. Many are sexually monomorphic.

Behavior The social babbler lives in extended family groups, and even nests cooperatively. Wrentits are monogamous, long-lived, and territorial year-round. Pairs keep in close contact vocally. They perform allopreening and often roost together. Unusual for passerines, Wrentit males often help in building nests and in incubating eggs. The Wrentit is extremely sedentary.

Distribution The Wrentit is the only New World member of this Old World family with distribution throughout Europe, Africa, and Asia. A successful group, babblers have varied habitats and lifestyles. The Wrentit, is found west of the Cascades/Sierra mountain range, south along the coastal slope to northernmost Baja California.

Taxonomy There are 273 babblers classified under 50 genera. The taxonomic placement of the Wrentit as well as the limits of the babbler family have been controversial. Babblers have been considered a "catch-all taxon;" that is, the family may contain several unrelated groups because there is no better place for them. Recent molecular techniques suggest that the Wrentit is indeed a babbler, in a group that includes several Asian taxa, as well as the parrotbills and the genus Sylvia. The latter appears to be a babbler, rather than an Old World Warbler.

Conservation BirdLife International classifies 27 babblers as vulnerable, 6 as endangered, and another 40 as near threatened. —*Alvaro Jaramillo*

WRENTIT *Chamaea fasciata*

northern

southern

Wrentits are curiously long-tailed and ultra-skulking denizens of dense, non-forested chaparral on the West Coast. L 6.5" (17 cm)

Identification Recognized by distinctive round, fluffy body and long, round-tipped tail usually cocked at an angle. Is usually heard rather than seen. Whitish eye; short and stout bill; and lightly streaked buffy or cinnamon underparts are distinctive. Muted plumage is alike in all ages and sexes:

above brownish gray with darker tail, wings; below cinnamon to grayish buff with obscured darker streaking.

Geographic Variation Five subspecies recognized, but not clearly differentiated: Birds from northern, wetter areas darker, more cinnamon below; subspecies from southern dry sites grayish above, dull buffy-grey below.

Similar Species Wrentits are distinctive, not easily confused. The Bushtit shows a similar rotund body shape with a long tail, but is tiny and shows pale, unstreaked underparts.

Voice CALL: Wooden-sounding, rattled *churrrrrrr*, or longer *krrrrrrrrrrrr*. SONG: Male song a *pit-pit-pit-pit-pit-pit-trrrrrrrr*, which has a bouncing-ball quality as notes speed up into the trill. Female song similar, but lacks the trill, and the pit notes are spaced evenly.

Status & Distribution Common. YEAR-ROUND: Found in dense chaparral or Huckleberry-Salal thickets from sea level to 6,000 feet. Extremely site-tenacious and very unlikely to be found out of habitat or out of range.

Population Stable.

MOCKINGBIRDS AND THRASHERS Family Mimidae

Long-billed Thrasher (TX, Apr.)

Thrashers and mockingbirds, along with the Gray Catbird, constitute the Mimidae found in North America. Most of the species are known for their long, varied songs of repeated phrases; some, the Northern Mockingbird in particular, are well-known mimics of other birds. In general, the family reaches its highest diversity in the desert Southwest, where several species of thrasher coexist. They live in a variety of habitats, from wet thickets to desert washes and chaparral hillsides. Most are large, brown, ground-dwelling birds with long, decurved bills.
Structure Generally large for passerines, these birds have long tails and long, decurved bills used to probe for food items in leaf litter and holes in the ground. Their legs are rather long, with long toes used for running. Several species have distinctive yellow or orange eyes.
Behavior Most of the species are well adapted to their desert environment. They tend to be quite secretive, remaining well hidden during the heat of the day, but they often climb to the top of trees to sing. Members of the Mimidae family generally feed on insects and seeds, although several species take advantage of seasonal fruit production and feed on berries and cactus fruit, main-

ly in the fall and winter. Most are very territorial, defending both summer and winter territories. Some, particularly thrashers, form pairs that last multiple years. Most species are resident within their range. One species, the Gray Catbird, is a neotropical migrant, whereas some others (the Sage, Bendire's, and Brown Thrashers) move south seasonally and winter mainly in the southern United States. Some species (e.g., the Curve-billed Thrasher), although nonmigratory, disperse after the breeding season and have been detected well north and east of their breeding range.
Plumage Most of the thrasher species are brown, with varying amounts of streaking or spotting on the underparts. Some are concolor and characterized by their rusty crissums; others are heavily streaked underneath. The sexes are similarly plumaged in all species.
Distribution Mimidae comprises about 34 species in 11 genera worldwide. Ten species in 4 genera breed in North America. Two additional species are casual or accidental north of Mexico: the Blue Mockingbird, a vagrant from Mexico, and the Bahama Mockingbird, a vagrant from the Bahamas and West Indies. Except for the Gray Catbird, the Northern Mockingbird, and the Brown Thrasher, most species are found in desert environments in the Southwest.
Taxonomy The majority of the species are monotypic and show little, if any, geographical variation. Some, such as the Le Conte's and the Long-billed Thrashers, have additional subspecies father south in Mexico. The Curve-billed Thrasher can be divided into 2 distinct subspecies groups (possibly distinct species) that overlap in southeastern Arizona and southwestern New Mexico.
Conservation Several of the thrashers, in particular those species with local ranges (e.g., Le Conte's, California, Long-billed), are somewhat threatened by loss of natural habitat to urbanization and increased agriculture. The Northern Mockingbird, the Gray Catbird, and, to a lesser extent, the Bendire's Thrasher actually benefit from increase in disturbed habitats. —*Gary H. Rosenberg*

GRAY CATBIRD Genus Dumetella

The only member of this monotypic genus is the Gray Catbird, a neotropical migrant that is smaller and shorter billed than other members of the Mimidae family. With a uniform gray body, a black cap, and a rufous crissum, the Gray Catbird has a long, warbling song like other thrashers.

GRAY CATBIRD *Dumetella carolinensis*

This very distinctive mimid generally remains hidden in the understory of dense thickets in eastern woodlands and residential areas. It often cocks its longish, black tail, and it is usually detected by its harsh, downslurred *mew* call, reminiscent of a cat's *meow*. A chunky, medium-size bird, it is larger than *Catharus* thrushes yet smaller than other thrashers. No other North American bird has a uniform dark gray

plumage. Monotypic. L 8.5" (22 cm)
Identification Sexes similar. Body entirely dark gray, with black cap, black tail, and chestnut undertail coverts.
Similar Species Plumage unique. Its mimicking song resembles songs of other thrashers or the American Dipper, with which it overlaps in the western portion of its range. *Mew* calls can be confused with calls of the Hermit Thrush or the Spotted and Green-tailed Towhees.
Voice CALL: A nasal, catlike, downslurred *mew*. Also a *quirt* note and a rapid chatter alarm when startled. SONG: A variable mixture of melodious, nasal, and squeaky notes, interspersed with catlike *mew* notes. Some individuals are excellent mimics. Normally sings and calls from inside dense thickets.
Status & Distribution Common, but secretive. BREEDING: Nests in dense thickets along edge of mixed woodland. In the West, nests along willow- and alder-lined montane streams.

MIGRATION: Nocturnal migrant. Trans-Gulf and Caribbean migrant. Sometimes abundant during migratory fallouts along the Gulf Coast of TX and LA and in southern FL. Spring peak in TX mid-April–early May. WINTER: Mainly southeastern U.S., Mexico, northern C.A., and Caribbean islands. VAGRANT: Casual during fall and winter in the Southwest and along Pacific coast.
Population Western birds limited by loss of riparian habitats.

MOCKINGBIRDS *Genus Mimus*

Two members of this genus occur in North America; 7 others are neotropical. Generally medium-size with long tails and relatively straight bills, they have gray or brown coloration, with varying amounts of white in the wings and tail. Mockingbirds, widely known as great songsters that mimic other species, are territorial and often sing at night.

NORTHERN MOCKINGBIRD *Mimus polyglottos*

This very common, conspicuous mimid of the southern United States is known for its loud, mimicking song, often heard during spring and summer nights in suburban neighborhoods. Both sexes aggressively defend nesting and feeding territories. They flash their white outer tail feathers and white wing patches conspicuously during courtship and territorial displays. Seen often on wires and fences in towns, the Northern often feeds on berries during the winter. Monotypic. L 10" (25 cm)
Identification Sexes similar. ADULT: About the size of an American Robin, but thinner and longer tailed. Upper-

juvenile

parts gray, unstreaked; underparts grayish white, unstreaked; long black tail has white outer tail feathers; conspicuous white wing bars; white patch at the base of primaries contrasts with blacker wings. Black line through a yellow eye. Bill relatively short and straight. JUVENILE: Underparts can be heavily spotted; upperparts with pale edging give back and head a streaked appearance; black line through eye less distinct; eye darker.
Similar Species The Loggerhead Shrike is similarly colored, but note distinct shape differences, particularly in the bill; shrike lacks white wing bars and has more extensive black mask. (See Sage Thrasher.)
Voice CALL: A loud, sharp *check*. SONG: Long, complex song consisting of a mixture of original and imitative phrases, each repeated several times. Excellent mimic of other bird species. Often

sings at night.
Status & Distribution Common and conspicuous. BREEDING: Nests in a variety of habitats, including suburban neighborhoods. MIGRATION: Birds in the northern portion of range and at higher elevations migrate south during fall and winter. Birds in the southern portion of range are resident. VAGRANT: Birds are found casually north of mapped range.
Population Range is expanding as a result of urbanization and creation of disturbed habitats.

BAHAMA MOCKINGBIRD *Mimus gundlachii*

This Caribbean species occurs as a very rare vagrant to the south Florida mainland, the Florida Keys, and the Dry Tortugas. Generally more secretive than the Northern Mockingbird, the Bahama Mockingbird remains hidden in dense thickets. It behaves and looks more like a thrasher than a mockingbird, often running between thickets. It is also browner and more streaked above and below than the Northern Mockingbird. Polytypic (recs. in N.A. of nominate from Bahamas). L 11" (28 cm)

Identification Sexes similar. ADULT: Distinctive black streaks on a brown back extend up the neck onto the head; black streaking found on the lower belly, flanks, and undertail coverts. The wings have 2 relatively narrow white wing bars but no white at the base of the primaries. The tail has white tips to the outer feathers. Head has obvious black malar stripe and white eyebrow. Bill is longer and slightly more curved than the Northern Mockingbird's. IMMATURE: Less patterned than the adult, with less distinct streaking on the back and flanks. Dark malar is less pronounced.

Similar Species The immature Northern Mockingbird has spotting or streaks below, but this is more confined to breast, compared with the Bahama's streaked flanks. All plumages of the Bahama lack the white flash in primaries; all plumages also have white in tail confined to the tips of the outer feathers.

Voice CALL: A loud *chack* similar to the Northern Mockingbird's. SONG: More thrasher-like, with a complex mixture of phrases. Not known to mimic.

Status & Distribution Common resident in the Bahamas and in Jamaica. VAGRANT: Very rare visitor, primarily in spring, to parks with dense thickets along the coast of southern Florida, with most records from between West Palm Beach and Key West. Also recorded from the Dry Tortugas in spring.

Population Potential loss of breeding habitat due to development, and loss of habitat after hurricanes, may impact this species in the Bahamas.

Genus Oreoscoptes

SAGE THRASHER *Oreoscoptes montanus*

worn adult

This distinctive, small thrasher—characteristic of the open sagebrush plains of the montane West—is often seen singing atop sage bushes or along fence lines. It flies low from bush to bush and often runs on the ground with its tail cocked. On breeding grounds, the Sage is the only thrasher with heavily streaked underparts and a short, relatively straight bill. The Sage, which is smaller than other thrashers, is migratory, vacating breeding grounds during the winter. It can also often be found feeding in fruiting trees, particularly junipers and Russian olives. Monotypic. L 8.5" (22 cm)

Identification Sexes similar. ADULT: Generally gray-brown above, white below with heavy black streaking and a salmon-buff wash to the flanks. Wings with thin, distinct white wing bars. Tail long with white corners. Obvious black malar stripe, pale yellow iris, and short, relatively straight bill. LATE SUMMER ADULT: Can show virtually no streaking on the underparts when in very worn plumage. JUVENILE: Back and head streaked. Streaking on underparts reduced and not as black, especially on flanks. Eye darker.

Similar Species The Brown and Long-tailed Thrashers also have heavily streaked underparts, but they differ by having more rufescent upperparts and longer, more decurved bills. Worn adults can lack streaking and look very similar to the Bendire's Thrasher, but the Sage has a more contrasting head pattern and retains suggestion of white wing bars. Note difference in calls and song. (See juvenile Mockingbird.)

Voice CALL: Gives several calls, including a *chuck* and a high-pitched *churrr*. SONG: Long series of warbled phrases.

Status & Distribution Fairly common BREEDING: Restricted to specialized sagebrush habitat, mainly within and west of the Rocky Mountains. MIGRATION: In spring a very early migrant; in fall, most individuals leave breeding grounds by mid-Oct. Flocks occasionally detected during migration. Regularly found at desert oases in AZ and CA. WINTER: Mainly found in desert scrub habitat in the Southwest. VAGRANT: Disperses widely. Regular vagrant to coastal CA, casual east of breeding range, with numerous fall and winter records from many eastern states and provinces east to the Atlantic seaboard.

Population No threat known.

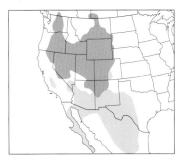

THRASHERS Genus *Toxostoma*

Seven species of *Toxostoma* thrasher are found in the United States (4 more endemic to Mexico). Generally large, brown, ground-dwelling birds of arid regions, most have long, decurved bills used for foraging in ground litter or holes. They often run with their long tail cocked in the air. Known for complex songs, some species mimic other species' songs.

BROWN THRASHER *Toxostoma rufum*

The widespread thrasher of eastern North America, the Brown Thrasher is generally a secretive bird of dense thickets and hedgerows. Often seen feeding on the ground, probing for insects with its long slender bill, the Brown Thrasher frequently sings from open exposed perches at the top of trees. Polytypic. L 11.5" (29 cm)

Identification Sexes similar. Similar in size to American Robin, but more slender, much longer tailed. Upperparts entirely bright rufous; underparts white to buffy-white, especially on flanks, with extensive black streaking. Wing coverts with black subterminal bar and white tips, forming 2 wing bars. Bill long and slender; little decurvature. Yellow eye.

Geographic Variation Western populations larger, paler, with less extensive streaking.

Similar Species Most similar to the Long-billed Thrasher of southern Texas, which is more grayish above and has a longer, more decurved bill; redder eye; and much shorter primary projection. Superficially similar in coloration to the Wood Thrush, but note very different size and shape, particularly the Brown's very long tail and its long and slender bill. Also, the Wood Thrush has more spotting on the underparts, compared to the Brown Thrasher's streaking.

Voice CALL: Most common calls include a low *churr* and a loud, smacking *spuck,* somewhat resembling the call note of a "Red" Fox Sparrow. SONG: A long series of varied melodic phrases, each phrase often repeated 2 or 3 times. Rarely mimics other bird species.

Status & Distribution BREEDING: Uncommon to dense thickets throughout the eastern U.S. MIGRATION: Birds from the northern portion of the breeding population migrate south in the fall, augmenting resident populations in the South. WINTER: Regularly winters across the southern U.S., extending into south-central TX. VAGRANT: Occasionally wanders west to AZ and CA. Casual to AK, BC, YK, NT, and NF. Casual in winter in northern Mexico.

Population Declines have been noted in the Northeast, probably as a result of habitat loss.

LONG-BILLED THRASHER *Toxostoma longirostre*

Superficially similar to the Brown Thrasher, the Long-billed replaces the Brown in south Texas and northeast Mexico. The Long-billed is found in dense thickets and in the understory of remaining natural woodland habitat in south Texas, particularly in the lower Rio Grande Valley. Habits similar to the Brown Thrasher's, particularly in feeding behavior and singing from exposed perches. Polytypic. L 11.5" (29 cm)

Identification Sexes similar. Coloration of upperparts grayish brown; very black streaking below; face quite gray, contrasting with browner head and back; wings with 2 white wing bars; bill black, long, and distinctly decurved; reddish eye.

Geographic Variation Two subspecies recognized; *sennetti* found in Texas.

Similar Species Most similar to the Brown, with which it barely overlaps in winter. The Long-billed has less rufous upperparts; a gray, contrasting face; and a distinctly longer, more decurved bill.

Voice CALL: Most common call is similar to the Brown Thrasher's loud smacking *spuck;* also known to give a mellow *kleak* and a loud whistle *cheeooep.* SONG: Similar to the Brown's long series of melodious phrases, yet the individual phrases are not duplicated as often. Song differs from the overlapping Curve-billed Thrasher's by being slower and more musical.

Status & Distribution Resident throughout breeding range in southern TX and northern Mexico. VAGRANT: Few extralimital records, but recorded casually in western TX; accidental in NM and CO.

Population Loss of most of the native brushland to agriculture in the lower Rio Grande Valley has likely had a serious impact on overall population.

CURVE-BILLED THRASHER *Toxostoma curvirostre*

juvenile
palmeri

palmeri

oberholseri

The Curve-billed Thrasher—the common thrasher of the rich, cactus-laden Sonoran Desert—can be very conspicuous, sitting up on saguaro or cholla cactuses, making its presence known by its loud 2- or 3-note call, *whit-wheet*. It often builds its nest within a cholla cactus. Its foraging behavior is similar to other desert thrashers, probing for critters in leaf litter or in holes in the ground, and it sometimes feeds on berries or cactuses fruit. Polytypic. L 11" (28 cm)

Identification Sexes similar. A largish, pale brown thrasher with uniform brown upperparts and round, somewhat blurry spots on the underparts. Wings have noticeable whitish wing bars, particularly in eastern birds. Tail has pale tips, the extent of which depends on sub-species. Bill is relatively long, black, and distinctly decurved. Eye is distinctly orange-yellow. JUVENILE: Recently fledged birds have less distinct spotting than do adults, and their bills are significantly shorter and less decurved.

Geographic Variation Subspecies *oberholseri* (southeastern AZ to south TX) has clearer spotting below, more distinct white wing bars, and more extensive white tips to the tail feathers. Western birds, *palmeri,* have less distinct breast spots and less conspicuous white tips to the tail feathers. Calls between the subspecies are slightly different.

Similar Species Adults distinctive; note different habitat and calls compared with the Bendire's Thrasher (see side-bar below). Juvenile Curve-billed easily confused with the Bendire's (esp. worn adult Bendire's and juvenile Curve-billed, which may overlap during late spring and early summer in southern AZ). Similar bill length and decurvature, but juvenile Curve-billed typically shows some pale flesh at the gape on the shortish bill. The Bendire's usually retains at least some fine dark streaking on the underparts, which is lacking on juvenile Curve-billed.

Voice CALL: Very distinctive loud *whit-wheet* or *whit-wheet-whit.* SONG: Long and elaborate, consisting of low trills and warbles, seldom repeating phrases. Quite different from Bendire's, but possibly confused with songs of the Crissal or the Le Conte's Thrasher.

Status & Distribution Common resident in desert habitats, particularly those rich in cholla and other cactuses. Particularly common in suburban neighborhoods that retain natural desert vegetation. Also found in mesquite-dominated desert washes. VAGRANT: Extralimital records mostly pertaining to *palmeri* from CA, NV, ID, and various states in the Midwest.

Population Although common, the species is experiencing habitat loss through urban development and increased agriculture in southern Arizona and southern Texas.

Curve-billed and Bendire's Thrashers

In southeastern Arizona and south-western New Mexico, Curve-billed and Bendire's Thrashers overlap in range and habitat. Although the Bendire's is very locally distributed, it can often be found with the more widespread Curve-billed. Adults in fresh plumage are more easily distinguished than worn adults. The larger Curve-billed has a longer, decurved bill; heavier, more blurry spotting on the underparts; and a distinctive, frequent 2-note *whit-wheet* call. The slightly smaller Bendire's has a relatively short, mostly straight bill (sometimes with slight decurvature)

Bendire's   Curve-billed

palmeri   oberholseri

and finer, more distinct arrow-shaped spotting on the underparts. Its call is a seldom-heard low *chuck.* Juveniles and worn adults pose a greater identification challenge: The juvenile Curve-billed has a shorter, straighter bill and, typically, a pale area along the gape. Both birds when worn have virtually no obvious spotting on the underparts, making structural differences and call more important. White-tips to the tail are much more reduced in the Bendire's in comparison with the Curve-billed's *oberholseri* but are virtually identical to the tail pattern of *palmeri*. ∎

BENDIRE'S THRASHER *Toxostoma bendirei*

fresh worn

Although locally distributed in the desert Southwest, the Bendire's is easiest to find during the late winter and early spring, when singing activity is at its peak. It is normally secretive, with its pale sandy brown coloration blending in nicely with the sparse desert environment it prefers (Feb.–May). Males sit up on shrubs, fences, power poles, and roofs to sing, making them more conspicuous. Like other thrashers, the Bendire's uses its longish bill

to probe for insects in holes on the ground and often runs with its tail cocked. Monotypic. L 9.8" (25 cm)

Identification Sexes similar. Easily confused with similar Curve-billed Thrasher, but slightly smaller. Overall plumage light brown above, slightly paler below; distinct arrow-shaped spots across the breast; buffy flanks and undertail coverts; relatively short, straight (or slightly decurved) bill, usually with pale at the base; pale yellow eye. Tail with narrow pale tips to the feathers. SUMMER ADULT: Late spring and summer adults in worn plumage show little or no spotting.

Similar Species Most commonly confused with juvenile Curve-billed Thrasher, which has a shorter, straighter bill than the adult. Note different habitat preference between the Bendire's and Curve-billed and their very different calls (see sidebar p. 499).

Voice CALL: A seldom heard low *chuck*. SONG: Different from the Curve-billed Thrasher's. A long series of warbling, melodic phrases, some with a harsh quality. Phrases often repeated 2 or 3 times each.

Status & Distribution Fairly common, but local in sparse brushy desert. BREEDING: Most common in the yucca-dominated Chihuahuan Desert and in the Sulphur Springs Valley in southeastern AZ. Rarer and more difficult to find at higher elevations across northern AZ and southern UT. A few nest in southeastern CA. WINTER: Birds from the northern portion of the range migrate to low-elevation desert in southern AZ and northern Sonora. Some birds move into suburban habitats. VAGRANT: Very rare visitor in fall and winter to coastal CA. **Population** The greatest threat to the Bendire's is the destruction of habitat due to intense urbanization in Arizona.

CALIFORNIA THRASHER *Toxostoma redivivum*

This is the characteristic thrasher of the chaparral foothills along the California coast and the Sierra Nevada, and it is the only large, uniform thrasher within its limited range. With habits similar to the Crissal Thrasher's, it is often detected by call or song, since it remains well hidden in dense vegetation on hillsides, except when it runs on the ground between thickets with its tail cocked in the air. In early spring, adult males sing from exposed perches at the tops of shrubs. Polytypic. L 12" (30 cm)

Identification Sexes similar. Dark overall, with long, black, decurved bill,

which is heavier than the bills of other thrashers. Tawny buff belly, flanks, and undertail coverts; paler than the Crissal's chestnut crissum. Dark brown breast; pale throat and eyebrow contrast with dark, patterned face; dark eye.

Geographic Variation The northern and southern California populations differ slightly.

Similar Species Only large, uniform brown thrasher within this range. Similar in coloration to Crissal Thrasher, but note non-overlapping ranges. Vagrant Curve-billed and Bendire's Thrashers potentially overlap, but note California's more uniform coloration and heavy, blacker bill. The California Thrasher does overlap with the California Towhee, which is chunky and similarly colored, but note the thrasher's much larger size and strongly decurved bill.

Voice CALL: A low, flat *chuck* and *chur-*

erp. SONG: Loud and sustained song made up of mostly guttural phrases, many repeated once or twice. Known to mimic other bird species and sounds.

Status & Distribution Fairly common resident on the chaparral hillsides and other dense brushy areas throughout most of coastal CA, the foothills of the Sierra Nevada, and northern Baja California. VAGRANT: Very sedentary, but has wandered north to southern OR.

Population The species has experienced losses in parts of its range due to development of preferred chaparral habitat.

CRISSAL THRASHER *Toxostoma crissale*

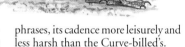

This normally secretive but distinctive thrasher often sings quietly from exposed dead branches that stick up from the tops of dense shrubs. Found in a variety of habitats, from brushy desert to juniper hillsides at higher elevation, it is very difficult to find when not singing. Sometimes it can be seen running on the ground with tail cocked, similar to other desert thrashers. The Crissal feeds by probing its long bill into ground litter or holes. Along with the California and the Le Conte's, it forms a complex of uniformly colored thrashers with long, black, decurved bills and chestnut crissums. Polytypic. L 11.5" (29 cm)

Identification Sexes similar. Uniformly dark grayish brown; often shows a

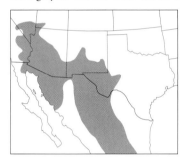

paler white throat, distinct black malar stripe, and chestnut undertail coverts. Worn individuals in late spring and early summer often lack the clear white throat, and the black malar stripe can appear quite faded. Yellow eye. Often detected by first hearing call or song. **Geographic Variation** Differences between 2 subspecies minor; eastern birds are slightly darker.

Similar Species The Crissal Thrasher is larger, darker, and more uniform than the Curve-billed and Bendire's Thrashers, with which it overlaps in desert washes in southern Arizona; all 3 can be found at the same locations. More similar in appearance to the California Thrasher, but note non-overlapping range. Overlaps with Le Conte's (sometimes found together at the same location), but note Le Conte's much paler overall color, smaller size, less-patterned malar and head, and lighter tawny undertail coverts. Note also different calls.

Voice CALL: A loud repeated *chideery* or *churry-churry-churry* or *toit-toit-toit.* SONG: Varied long series of musical phrases, its cadence more leisurely and less harsh than the Curve-billed's.

Status & Distribution Uncommon resident in the understory of dense mesquite and willows along streams; also ranging up to lower montane slopes at higher elevations. Very secretive, more so than other desert thrashers. Not known to wander like the Curve-billed does.

Population Local population threats due to conversion of habitat into agriculture and urbanization. Not as adaptable to such threats as either the Curve-billed or the Bendire's.

LE CONTE'S THRASHER *Toxostoma lecontei*

This attractive, pale thrasher—with a coloration matching the sparse, sandy desert environment it inhabits—is generally found in sparser desert than are other thrashers. The Le Conte's behavior is similar to that of the Crissal, with which it overlaps: It is secretive but is often seen running between shrubs with its tail cocked in the air; it sings from exposed perches but otherwise stays hidden; and it feeds by probing its long, decurved bill into ground litter or holes. Much paler than the Crissal, it too has unspotted underparts. Polytypic. L 11" (28 cm)

Identification Sexes similar. Generally pale grayish brown in coloration, with light tawny undertail coverts, thin black malar stripe, black lores, and a long, black decurved bill. Long, black tail contrasts with pale body. Dark eye. **Geographic Variation** Population in coastal Baja California considered distinct from nominate.

Similar Species The Le Conte's is unlike any other North American thrasher, but care should be taken where the Crissal overlaps in range. The Le Conte's is much paler overall, but lighting conditions can make it look darker. Note its contrasting dark eye and lores; its tawny undertail coverts are lighter than the Crissal's. It overlaps with the Curve-billed and Bendire's in southern Arizona but is more scarce and paler overall.

Voice CALL: Includes an ascending, whistled *tweeep* or *suuweep* and a shorter Crissal-like call. SONG: Very similar to the Crissal's, being loud, melodious, and consisting of numerous phrases, sometimes repeated. Little or no mimicry of other species. Heard mostly at dawn and dusk. May sing continuously for up to 20 minutes.

Status & Distribution Uncommon and local resident in sparse, sandy-soiled desert of southwestern AZ, southern CA, southern NV, and extreme southwestern UT. Also found in northeastern Sonora, Mexico, and Baja California. Not known to wander.

Population Populations generally declining due to urbanization and conversion of habitat into agricultural lands.

Genus Melanotis

BLUE MOCKINGBIRD *Melanotis caerulescens*

This fancy Mexican endemic, an accidental stray in the Southwest, is normally very secretive, remaining hidden low or on the ground under dense thickets in thorn forest. It is usually detected first by hearing 1 of its loud, varied calls. Monotypic. L 10" (25 cm)

Identification Larger than the Northern Mockingbird; more thrasherlike in shape and behavior. Dark slaty blue overall; black mask. ADULT: Appears to have paler blue streaking on head, throat, upper breast. Bill slightly

longer than a mockingbird's, with a slight decurvature. Red eye. IMMATURE: Grayer blue overall, less noticeable streaking; eye not as red.

Similar Species No other bird in N.A. is entirely blue with a black mask.

Voice CALL: Quite variable. Typical calls include a *chooo* or *chee-ooo*. Also a loud *wee-cheep* or *choo-leep*, a low *chuck*, and a sharp *pli-tick*. SONG: Mockingbird-like rich series of repeated phrases.

Status & Distribution Endemic to Mexi-

adult

co. Casual in AZ and TX; origin questioned only in CA. Known to move altitudinally in fall and winter.

STARLINGS Family Sturnidae

European Starling (IL, Apr.)

With their glossy plumages and sociable ways, it is not surprising that starlings and mynas have been popular with bird fanciers for generations. The approximately 114 species of Sturnidae are native to the Old World, but several species have been introduced across the globe. The 4 species treated here have had varying degrees of success in North America: The widespread European Starling is probably the most successful exotic, and the adaptable Common Myna is flourishing in south Florida; the Hill Myna is declining in Florida, and the Crested Myna has been extirpated.

Structure Most starlings are of medium size and medium build, with fairly thick, slightly decurved bills and sturdy feet. Mynas are on average larger, chunkier bodied, thicker billed, and shorter tailed than many starlings, and many species have ornate plumes or bare-part projections on the head and face.

Behavior Many species are gregarious, breeding colonially and gathering in immense numbers during the nonbreeding season. Social behavior is often advanced. Vocalizations are complex; many notes are coarse and unmusical, but several species are capable of a large array of sounds. Starlings and mynas adapt well to human-altered and human-inhabited landscapes, and introductions have succeeded in many regions.

Plumage Starlings vary in plumage, but many are largely black and iridescent, with patches of bright oranges, reds, and yellows on the feathers. Bare parts are frequently brightly colored. The species treated here are primarily black and iridescent with limited areas of white and bright yellow patches on some bare parts.

Distribution Ancestrally, starlings and mynas, which tend to be cavity nesters, were associated with woodlands in Africa, Southeast Asia, and their regional island complexes. For millennia, the family has been increasingly cosmopolitan in its range and generalist in its habitats. In North America, the European Starling is widely established; other established species are local, and the Crested Myna has been extirpated in North America.

Taxonomy Most authorities treat the Sturnidae family as a valid monophylous taxon. Where the Sturnidae family fall among the passerines, however, is unclear: Recent evidence points to affiliations with the Turdidae, Muscicapidae, and Mimidae. Within the Sturnidae, there may be a major break between the African and Asian taxa. The polyphyletic mynas belong to the Asian group, as does the European Starling.

Conservation Worldwide, the Sturnidae run the gamut from abundant nuisances to populations in danger of extinction. Habitat loss and capture for the cage-bird trade have been factors in the decline of several species. Sturnids are good candidates for captive breeding and other intensive conservation actions, but enthusiasm for their conservation has been fairly muted. Established or escaped populations in North America are sometimes targeted for control. —*Ted Floyd*

Genus *Sturnus*

EUROPEAN STARLING *Sturnus vulgaris*

Widespread and abundant in much of North America, the introduced European Starling is arguably and problematically the most successful bird on the continent. Often characterized as bold, this bird is actually fairly wary and can be difficult to approach. Polytypic. L 8.7" (22 cm)

Identification Stocky and short tailed, often seen strutting about lawns and parking lots. Flight profile distinctive: Buzzy in sustained flight, wings look triangular in more leisurely flight. In flight, wings appear translucent. ADULT: One molt per year, but fresh fall adults look very different from summer birds. On freshly molted birds, black plumage has white spots all over; by winter, spots start to disappear; and by spring, the birds are glossy black all over, with strong suffusions of iridescent pinks, greens, and ambers. Bill usually gray in fall and yellow by winter, but this character varies with diet. MALE: With good look, note blue-based bill. FEMALE: With good look, note pink-based bill, paler eyes. JUVENILE: Distinctive; dark gray-brown feathering all over. Birds begin a complete molt into adultlike plumage soon after

fall
winter
juvenile
breeding ♂

fledging, and briefly exhibit a striking mosaic of juvenal and adult feathers. **Geographic Variation** Apparently, only the nominate subspecies occurs here; 12 other subspecies in Old World.

Similar Species Structure distinctive, but sometimes confused with unrelated blackbirds, which often co-occur with starlings in large flocks. Blackbirds more slender bodied, with longer tails and less-pointy wings. Flight profile more like a waxwing's or a meadowlark's than blackbird's.

Voice Highly varied. CALL: Commonly heard calls include drawn-out, hissing *sssssheeeer* and whistled *wheeeeoooo*. SONG: Elaborate, lengthy (>1 min. long), with complex rattling and whirring elements, and overall wheezy quality; call notes may be incorporated into song. Imitates other species, especially those with whistled notes (e.g., Killdeer, Eastern Wood-Pewee). **Status & Distribution** Abundant. BREEDING: Needs natural or artificial cavities. Often evicts native species from nest holes. MIGRATION: Withdraws in winter from northern portion of range. WINTER: Gregarious, with largest concentrations around cities, feedlots. VAGRANT: Still expanding range in the Americas, and out-of-range individuals (e.g., on western Aleutians) are difficult to assess.

Population Successfully introduced in Central Park, New York, 1890–91; across continent by late 1940s. Population currently exceeds 200 million.

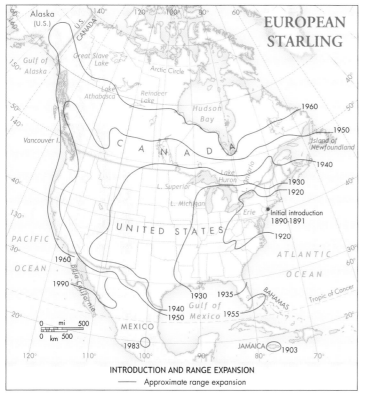

EUROPEAN STARLING

Initial introduction 1890-1891

INTRODUCTION AND RANGE EXPANSION
—— Approximate range expansion

Genera *Acridotheres* and *Gracula*

COMMON MYNA *Acridotheres tristis*

This Asian native is well established in south Florida. It is a popular cage bird (the "House Myna"), and escapees may be seen anywhere. Polytypic (2 ssp.). L 9.8" (25 cm)

Identification Chunky; often in loose interspecific or intraspecific flocks. ADULT: One molt per year. Molt schedule variable; Florida data lacking. Brown body; black head with yellow-orange bare patch around eye; yellow-orange bill; dull yellow-orange feet; white patches at base of primaries (conspicuous in flight), tail tip, and undertail coverts. JUVENILE: Duller overall.

Geographic Variation Populations in N.A. presumably of widespread nominate subspecies; more study needed.

Similar Species Resembles other *Acridotheres* mynas. Hybridizes with the Crested and other *Acridotheres* mynas, especially in introduced settings.

Voice Varied, but most vocalizations raucous; accomplished mimic. CALL: Loud, slurred whistles; short, grating notes. SONG: Long series of short notes, given by both sexes, with liquid, rolling syllables. Call notes often incorporated into song.

Status & Distribution First detected in FL in 1983; now common in southern FL. YEAR-ROUND: Warehouses, malls, fast-food restaurants, etc.; nests primarily in artificial cavities, especially signage. VAGRANT: Escapees possible anywhere.

Population Florida population has increased considerably; perhaps thousands of pairs currently breeding.

CRESTED MYNA *Acridotheres cristatellus*

The Crested Myna was introduced to Vancouver, British Columbia, in the 1890s. By the late 1920s, the population had swelled to 20,000 individuals, but it became extirpated there in February 2003. The species has been extirpated from Florida, too. Though rare, escapees from captivity are still seen in North America. Polytypic (3 ssp.). L 9.8" (25 cm)

Identification Chunky, dark. ADULT: One molt per year; sexes similar. Plumage largely black with white patches at base of primaries (conspicuous in flight) and tail tip. Vent area variable: black or barred black-and-white. Dull yellow bill, legs; orange eye.

Tuft of erect feathers at front of crown. JUVENILE: Browner; crest and white patches smaller or absent.

Geographic Variation Vancouver population was of the nominate subspecies.

Similar Species Hybridizes with other *Acridotheres* mynas, not treated here, which are possible escapees.

Voice Similar to the Common's. CALL: Whistled and grating notes; weaker, tinnier than Common's. SONG: Series of short whistled or chattering notes.

Status & Distribution Extirpated in N.A.; escapees possible anywhere. YEAR-ROUND: Urban, agricultural districts. VAGRANT: Individuals from extirpated BC population ranged south to WA;

1 strayed to Portland, OR.

Population No currently known breeding populations.

HILL MYNA *Gracula religiosa*

Even when judged by the overall standards of the myna clan's vocal excellence, the Hill is notable for its superior abilities as a songster and mimic. An established population in south Florida is waning. Polytypic (10 ssp. in S.E. Asia). L 10.6" (27 cm)

Identification Chunky. ADULT: One molt per year; sexes similar. Black overall; white primary bases, conspicuous in flight. Warty yellow nuchal and suborbital bare patches conspicuous. Dark eyes, orange bill, yellow-orange feet. JUVENILE: Plumage browner, duller; bare parts less colorful.

Geographic Variation Native to Southeast Asia. Florida subspecies is *intermedia*.

Similar Species Chunkier, marginally larger than *Acridotheres* mynas. Wings broader, more rounded. Tail tip not white, as in *Acridotheres*. The Hill Myna is usually found in trees; *Acridotheres* mynas are found on the ground.

Voice Varied; many vocalizations, especially of birds in captivity, have "human" qualities. CALL: Tremendously varied. Most are of short duration, some extremely loud. SONG: Complex; short to long series of chuckles and whistles. Song elements on average mellower than those of *Acridotheres* mynas.

Status & Distribution Uncommon around Miami, FL. YEAR-ROUND: Arboreal; nests primarily in natural cavities. VAGRANT: Escapees from captivity (not true vagrants) possible anywhere.

Population Remnant introduced population in Miami area currently numbers 25 to 100 breeding pairs.

ACCENTORS Family Prunellidae

Siberian Accentor (ID, Feb.)

The accentors are an Old World family, with 1 species vagrant to North America.

Structure Accentors are small passerines, similar in size and shape to sparrows although accentors have thin, warbler-like bills. The bill is thick at base and thins to a sharp tip. In general they are stocky with no outstanding unique structural features. The tail is of medium length and typically notched.

Plumage Accentors are brownish above, often with rufous tones, and streaked on the upperparts. Some species are largely grayish below while others are buffy or cinnamon below, some showing contrasting white or black throats. Many have a contrasting face pattern with a noticeable paler or warm-colored supercilium.

Behavior These ground foragers specialize on insects, but take seed in winter. Most are little known, but for the Dunnock. Drab in appearance, the Dunnock is colorful in its breeding behavior. Some pairs are monogamous, but many females mate and sire young from more than 1 male (polyandry) and sometimes several females and several males are involved (polygynandry). Males help at the nest roughly in proportion to mating success, so sometimes the 2 males are seen feeding the young.

Distribution Restricted to the Palearctic, from the British Isles to Japan, the family is confined to temperate latitudes as far south as North Africa and southern Asia. Several species are restricted to alpine or highland areas. One species has been introduced to South Africa and New Zealand.

Taxonomy There are 13 accentors, all in the genus *Prunella*. Thrushes may be closely related to accentors, but recent genetic studies have not adequately determined the placement of the accentors. Evidence places the accentors in the Passeridae, a group that includes finches and sparrows, tanagers, blackbirds, sunbirds, weavers, pipits and other taxa. Therefore, accentors appear to be distantly related to the thrushes, which are in an entirely different group. —*Alvaro Jaramillo*

Genus *Prunella*

SIBERIAN ACCENTOR *Prunella montanella*

The Siberian Accentor is a much-hoped-for vagrant in Alaska, due to its subtle but striking appearance and its being the 1 member of its family that visits N.A. Polytypic. L 5" (12 cm)

Identification A sparrow-like bird that forages on the ground, with hunched posture. Unlike a sparrow, it shows a thin warbler-like bill. The structure is otherwise like a sparrow, with a medium-length, notched tail. ADULT: Rufous brown above with diffuse streaking, contrasting with marked face and tawny-to-cinnamon underparts. Lacks bold wing bars. The thin, buffy lower wingbar is well formed. The head is dark, with a bold and contrasting tawny supercilium, as well as a diffuse tawny spot on the rear ear coverts, gray central crown stripe, and gray nape. Tawny throat contrasts with dark auriculars. Flanks are streaked rufous brown. Belly and vent are white. Legs are pink. Bill is dark, sometimes showing a paler horn base to the lower mandible. IMMATURE: Much like adult, duller in plumage with less grey on nape; some retain dark speckling on breast from juvenile plumage.

Geographic Variation Only 2 subspecies, the nominate in the north and west of the breeding range, and *badia* in eastern Siberia. Four Alaskan specimens refer to *badia,* the population closest to North America.

Similar Species The Siberian Accentor's bold, dark-and-tawny head pattern is distinctive for a small, ground-dwelling songbird. The Rustic Bunting, another Asian vagrant, shows a similar rusty brown plumage and bold face pattern. However, the bunting has a conical bill, whitish supercilium, and whitish throat. Similarly, the tawny-colored Smith's Longspur has a bold head pattern, but has a conical bill, white supercilium, and white face patch.

Voice CALL NOTES: High-pitched *tsee-ree-seee,* with the quality of Brown

Creeper calls. SONG: A squeaky, high-pitched warble, like Winter Wren, although slower and less complex.

Status & Distribution Breeds in Asia; winters in China and the Koreas. VAGRANT: Casual in southeastern AK. Unlike many Asian strays, the Siberian Accentor is more likely in fall. Winter and early spring records in BC, AB, MT, ID, WA, and southeastern AK suggest that this rare Asian vagrant has a tendency to winter in northwestern N.A. Most winter records have been at bird feeders. Vagrant in northern Europe.

Population Not a conservation concern; no population data available from Asia.

WAGTAILS AND PIPITS Family Motacillidae

Eastern Yellow Wagtail (AK, May)

Slender and highly migratory passerines from the Old World, wagtails and pipits have long tails and characteristic white outer tail feathers. Wagtails are typically black and white or yellow, while pipits are brown and streaked, blending more into their environment. Both share the distinctive behavior of walking on the ground and wagging their tails. They are generally found on or near the ground, usually in tundra habitats or near streams and rivers. Most species in North America are mainly found in the Arctic of western Alaska; 5 species (2 wagtails and 3 pipits) breed in North America, while 5 Eurasian species occasionally occur as migrants and vagrants.

Structure Pipits are generally small to medium-size, slender birds with long tails, except for the Sprague's Pipit, which has a relatively short tail. Their bills are also long and slender, and somewhat pointed. The pipits adapted long legs and toes, unusual for passerines, for walking on the ground. Wagtails are shaped similarly to pipits, but they have much longer tails.

Behavior Wagtails and pipits feed on the ground, walking and searching for insects. Usually both pipits and wagtails forage at the edge of streams and pools of water, often continuously wagging their tails as they walk, as well as bobbing their heads and necks like a chicken. Some species, the Sprague's Pipit in particular, rarely if ever wag their tails. During the spring and summer, wag-tails sing from exposed perches on shrubs, small trees, roofs, and even rusting machinery. Pipits have elaborate flight displays, but sometimes sing from the ground. Some pipits remain in flight singing for up to 20 minutes. Wagtails have a distinctive undulating flight, while pipits fly more directly, but both call often in flight; their species-specific calls aid in identification. The Sprague's Pipit, when flushed, rises gradually and then circles around before it plunges back to Earth, breaks its fall immediately above the ground, and disappears into the grass. Mostly diurnal migrants, wagtails and pipits use rivers and coasts as navigation aids (except the Sprague's, which migrates from the Great Plains to grasslands in the southern United States and northern Mexico). The American Pipit forms large single-species flocks in winter.

Plumage Wagtails are sexually dimorphic with several age, seasonal, and sex-related plumages—generally combinations of black, white, and yellow, with long tails and white outer tail feathers. Telling identification features include the extent of white in the wing, the color of the back, and the pattern of black on the underparts. Pipits are not sexually dimorphic, but some do have different winter plumages. Most are brown with plain or streaked backs, varying amounts of streaking on the underparts, and white outer tail feathers. Important features to notice include the degree of streaking on the back and underparts, the presence of buff on the underparts, and leg coloration.

Distribution North American wagtails breed almost exclusively in coastal arctic Alaska. Breeding species as well as vagrants have been regularly reported on offshore islands in the Bering Sea during migration, while some have been seen along the West Coast, rarely inland, in fall and winter. All wagtails winter in Southeast Asia. Pipits generally restrict themselves to arctic regions as well, breeding on rocky tundra; however, the American Pipit also breeds above treeline in the Rocky Mountains and Pacific states, and the Sprague's Pipit only breeds on the short-grass prairies of the Great Plains.

Taxonomy Worldwide there are at least 65 species in 5 genera. Recent genetic studies have influenced the determination of the species limit for some wagtails (White and Eastern Yellow) and pipits (American).

Conservation The motacillids are not threatened in North America; however, overgrazing and the introduction of non-native grasses are limiting the breeding and wintering grounds for the Sprague's Pipit. BirdLife International lists 4 species as threatened and 4 others as near threatened—all of them pipits. —*Gary H. Rosenberg*

WAGTAILS Genus *Motacilla*

Motacilla is mainly an Old World genus, with 2 breeding and 2 migrant species in North America, predominantly in the Arctic. Highly migratory, they winter in Asia, Europe, and Africa. They have distinctive calls and an undulating flight pattern. The immatures present the most trouble in terms of species identification.

EASTERN YELLOW WAGTAIL *Motacilla tschutschensis*

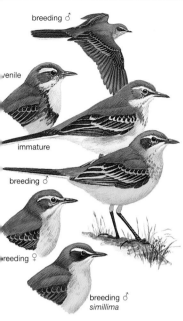

breeding ♂

juvenile

immature

breeding ♂

breeding ♀

breeding ♂
simillima

Formerly considered a subspecies of the Yellow Wagtail, the Eastern Yellow Wagtail is 1 of the more characteristic arctic passerines of western Alaska. Birders commonly see the bird singing from the tops of willows or feeding in the short, grassy tundra. The Eastern Yellow walks on the ground, where it searches for insects. Polytypic. L 6.5" (17 cm)

Identification The Eastern Yellow has a slender body with relatively long legs. BREEDING MALE: Quite distinctive. It generally is bright yellow underneath and green above with a gray crown and has a narrow white supercilium contrasting with dark gray cheeks. It has a relatively long black tail with white outer tail feathers; its wings have pale yellow edging to coverts and flight feathers, forming indistinct wing bars. FEMALE: She is slightly duller than the male and not as yellow underneath and is less dark on the cheek and less gray on the crown. JUVENILE: More pipitlike. Lacks yellow and is a dull grayish brown above, with narrow white supercilium, and grayish white below, with varying amounts of speckling on sides of breast and buffy flanks. It also has narrow white wing bars and a white throat with varying amount of dark malar. FIRST WINTER: Similar to juvenile, but it has less dark in the malar region.

Geographic Variation Two subspecies known from North America. The Alaska breeding nominate *tschutschensis* has a speckled breast band. The *simillima*, regular on the Aleutian and Pribilof Islands, is brighter yellow underneath and greener above, and typically lacks speckling on the sides of the breast.

Similar species Adults appear similar to the much rarer (in N.A.) Gray Wagtail female, but the Gray actually has blacker wings and a longer tail. The immature can be confused with the immature White Wagtail, but the Eastern Yellow is browner, has less distinct wing bars, and usually lacks dark on sides of breast. See also Citrine Wagtail.

Voice CALL: A loud *tsweep.* SONG: A series of high-pitched *tszee tszee tszee* notes.

Status & Distribution Common, but has a restricted range in N.A. BREEDING: Nests in willows in tundra along the Bering Sea in western and northern AK. MIGRATION: Trans-Beringian migrant; regular on islands in Bering Sea. Often seen migrating in large numbers in late summer along the Bering Sea. WINTER: Mainly S.E. Asia and Philippines. VAGRANT: Casual in fall and winter along West Coast of mainland U.S., with several recs. from coastal CA.

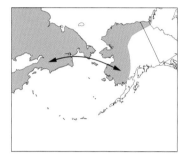

GRAY WAGTAIL *Motacilla cinerea*

This Eurasian wagtail is a rare spring migrant to North America. Almost always associated with water, the long-tailed Gray Wagtail typically walks on the ground, often at the edge of a stream or river. Like the White Wagtail, it is often detected in flight by a distinct 2-note call and its undulating flight pattern. Polytypic (*robusta* recorded in N.A.). L 7.8" (20 cm)

Identification ADULT MALE: Unmistakable. It is quite distinctive, with yellow below, gray above, a narrow white supercilium, an extensive black throat, and black wings. The wings have white tertial edging, and a white base to the secondaries forms a wing stripe that is visible in flight only. It also has pale flesh-colored legs. FEMALE: It does not have a black throat and is duller than the male, lacking much of the yellow on the underparts; it is brightest yellow on the undertail coverts. The most distinct field marks are its

very long tail, longer than other wagtail species, and lack of wing bars. JUVENILE: It is similar to the female, but browner overall, buffy across breast, and has 2 buffyish wing bars. It already has bright yellow undertail coverts.

Similar Species The combination of yellow underparts and black throat make the male unique. The female, however, looks similar to the Eastern Yellow Wagtail, but lacks wing bars and has grayer upperparts, a much longer tail, and duller underparts that contrast with brighter yellow undertail coverts. The Gray also has flesh-colored legs, whereas the Eastern Yellow's are black.

Voice CALL: A 2-note metallic *chink chink,* somewhat similar to the White's call, and very different from the single note call of the Yellow Wagtail.

Status & Distribution Eurasia. MIGRATION: Regular spring migrant to the western

breeding ♂

♀

breeding ♂

Aleutian Is., otherwise a casual late spring stray to islands in the Bering Sea (Pribilof Is. and St. Lawrence I.). VAGRANT: Accidental to CA and BC in the fall.

CITRINE WAGTAIL *Motacilla citreola*

winter
adult ♂

A rare vagrant to North America, the Citrine Wagtail is typically associated with water. It often mixes with Yellow and Eastern Yellow Wagtails on winter grounds in Southeast Asia and Europe. Polytypic (ssp. in N.A. suspected to be *citreola*). L 6.5" (17 cm)

Identification Resembles Eastern Yellow Wagtail in size and general proportions. BREEDING MALE: Unmistakable; brightly yellow on the head and underparts with a gray back and unique black nape. Wings have bold white tips and edges to coverts and tertials. FEMALE AND WINTER MALE: Note the hollow, grayish brown cheek surrounded by yellow, grayish back and crown, and white wing bars. FIRST-WINTER: Monochromatic; resembles the female, but lacks yellow in its plumage.

Similar Species Other than the breeding male, Citrines resemble Eastern Yellow Wagtails, but note the Citrine's much broader and encircling supercilium, more prominent white wing bars, gray upperparts, and pale lores.

Voice CALL: Very similar to the loud *tsweep* call of the Eastern Yellow Wagtail. SONG: Often given from atop a willow bush; resembles song of the White Wagtail.

Status & Distribution Locally common Eurasian species. Breeds in wet areas with low vegetation, open bogs, soggy riverbanks, and meadows. WINTER: Mainly in southern Asia; accidental in N.A. VAGRANT: One winter record from MS (Jan. 1992).

WHITE WAGTAIL *Motacilla alba*

Formerly considered 2 species (White and Black-backed Wagtails), the White generally prefers more disturbed habitats than the Eastern Yellow Wagtail. Birders frequently see it on beaches, in and around rocky breakwaters, around abandoned, rusting machinery, garbage dumps, or buildings. It sings from a high exposed perch and walks on the ground when feeding, usually near water. Birders can detect it in flight by its distinctive call notes and undulating flight. Polytypic. L 7.3" (18 cm)

Identification Sexually dimorphic with complicated age differences. Adults distinct, overall gray, black throat, black on hind crown, and white in wings; immatures more problematic. Tail black with white outer feathers. Separation of 2 subspecies complicated due to hybridization. BREEDING MALE: The *ocularis* has a gray back, black hind crown and nape, white forehead, black throat extending to bill, and a thin black line through eye. Wing coverts entirely white. The *lugens* has a black back, nape, and hind crown; black extending farther forward on crown. Black throat with white chin. Wider black line through eye. Entire wing, including flight feathers, mostly white. BREEDING FEMALE: The *lugens* has some gray in back. WINTER FEMALE: The *ocularis* has a gray back and the coverts have less white, forming more distinct wing bars. The *lugens* has some

breeding adult ♂

ocularis
breeding

lugens

adult breeding ♀

winter adult ♂

breeding adult ♂

immature

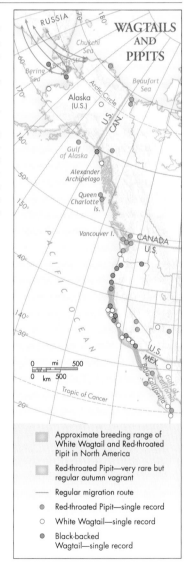

WAGTAILS AND PIPITS

RUSSIA

Chukchi Sea

Bering Sea

Bering Strait

Alaska (U.S.)

Arctic Circle

Beaufort Sea

U.S. CAN.

Gulf of Alaska

Alexander Archipelago

Queen Charlotte Is.

Vancouver I.

CANADA U.S.

PACIFIC OCEAN

U.S. MEX.

Baja California

Gulf of California

0 mi 500
0 km 500

Tropic of Cancer

Approximate breeding range of White Wagtail and Red-throated Pipit in North America

Red-throated Pipit—very rare but regular autumn vagrant

Regular migration route

● Red-throated Pipit—single record

○ White Wagtail—single record

● Black-backed Wagtail—single record

black on its scapulars and has mostly white wing coverts (patch). IMMATURE: Variable. Generally uniform gray above, whiter below, with varying amounts of black on the bib. Wing differences between subspecies generally as in females.

Geographic Variation The gray-backed subspecies *ocularis* is a more regular breeder on the Alaska mainland. The black-backed *lugens* is a casual summer visitor to the Aleutians and St. Lawrence Island. Separation of females and immatures between the subspecies is difficult. Subspecies hybridize when they come in contact. Nine other subspecies occur

across Europe and North Africa.
Similar Species The juvenile looks similar to the Eastern Yellow juvenile, but the White is grayer and has more distinct wing bars. Note different calls. **Voice** CALL: A distinctive 2-note *chizzik* given in flight; also a *chee-whee* given from the ground or an exposed perch. The vocalizations are identical between subspecies.
Status & Distribution Rare in extreme western AK. BREEDING: Nests sparsely in and around villages on Seward Peninsula and St. Lawrence I.; most breeding birds are *ocularis,* but mixed pairs with *lugens* or hybrids common.

WINTER: Mainly S.E. Asia. VAGRANT: Casual along CA coast, mainly in fall and winter. Accidental in AZ, MI, NC, NF, Sonora, and Baja California.

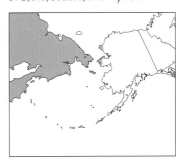

PIPITS Genus *Anthus*

Three breeding (mainly in Arctic tundra) and 3 migrant species occur in North America. They winter in grasslands and agricultural fields, where cryptic plumage protects them. The species exhibit little or no sexual dimorphism. Some species are very secretive; all are highly migratory. Individuals tend to be solitary, but may form large flocks during winter.

TREE PIPIT *Anthus trivialis*

Also known as the Brown Tree Pipit, this mainly western Palearctic species is an accidental visitor to North America. It will perch up in trees, but it also walks on the ground. It is more secretive than the American Pipit. Polytypic. 6" (15 cm)
Identification The sexes look similar. Overall brown, boldly streaked blackish above, with a necklace of fine streaking across the breast with underlying yellowish wash and faint streaking down the flanks. Median coverts with pale tips, forming 1 indistinct wing bar. Face pattern diffuse with short, nar-

row, pale eye line. Note unstreaked rump and uppertail coverts. Pale flesh-colored legs. JUVENILE: Like adult with buffier wash across breast.
Similar species The Olive-backed Pipit has a less streaked back and a bolder face pattern. The Pechora and non-adult Red-throated Pipits have bold white streaks on the back and bold black streaks down the flanks. **Voice** CALL: A thin, buzzy *teez,* similar to the Olive-backed and very different from the American.
Status & Distribution Common in Eurasia, where it breeds in a variety of forest-

ed habitats. VAGRANT: Three records (2 spring and 1 fall) in N.A. of nominate subspecies from northwestern AK from the northern Bering Sea region (Gambell and Wales).

OLIVE-BACKED PIPIT *Anthus hodgnosi*

This Eurasian pipit is a rare migrant to North America, where it mainly appears in western Alaska and treeless areas. The Olive-backed is usually more secretive than the American Pipit. It constantly pumps its tail when it walks on the ground. Polytypic (recs. in N.A. are of Siberian subspecies *yunnanensis*). L 6" (15 cm)
Identification The sexes look similar. The Olive-backed is a boldly patterned pipit with a relatively plain, faintly streaked grayish olive back and head, white underparts, rich buff breast, and boldly streaked black flanks. There's a rather large black mark on the side of the neck. The uniquely patterned face

has a buff line in front of the eye and a split white supercilium behind; there's also a distinctive blackish spot at the rear of the auriculars. Pale flesh-colored legs. Freshly molted birds are buffier and more boldly patterned.
Similar Species No other pipit has the same combination of white underparts, relatively plain olive back, rich buff wash on streaked breast, and unique face pattern.
Voice CALL: A high, thin, buzzy *tseee,* shorter and less descending than Red-throated Pipit call.
Status & Distribution Common species *yunnanensis* breeds in Siberia and winters in S.E. Asia. MIGRATION: Rare,

but regular migrant to the western Aleutians (e.g., Attu). VAGRANT: Casual stray in both spring and fall to islands in the Bering Sea (Pribilofs and St. Lawrence); accidental to CA and NV.

yunnanensis

PECHORA PIPIT *Anthus gustavi*

This very secretive Asian pipit remains hidden in grass and is often silent when flushed. It is slightly smaller than the more common Red-throated Pipit. Its call is very important in identification. Polytypic (nominate in N.A.). L 5.5" (14 cm)

Identification Sexes similar. Brown above with heavy streaks, contrasting white "braces" on sides of back, white underparts with rich buffy yellow wash across breast, breast and flanks heavily streaked black, 2 distinct white wing bars, face pattern very diffuse, rump streaked, pale flesh-colored legs. Note projecting primaries past tertials.

Similar Species First-winter or adult female Red-throated Pipit, which sometime lacks red coloration, looks similar. See the Red-Throated Pipit.

Voice CALL: A hard *pwit* or *pit,* but often silent. Very different than other pipits.

Status & Distribution Local breeder in Siberia; winters in the Philippines.

VAGRANT: Casual spring and fall migrant in western Aleutians (e.g., Attu). Several recent fall recs. from Gambell (St. Lawrence I.).

RED-THROATED PIPIT *Anthus cervinus*

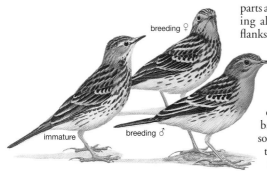

breeding ♀

immature breeding ♂

The Red-throated male is 1 of the more recognizable pipits in North America. Secretive, it hides in the grassy tundra, but it can be conspicuous while feeding in the open at the edge of small pools. It often calls when flushed, helping in the identification of females and immatures. In spring, the male sings from atop boulders or in a display flight. Monotypic. L 6" (15 cm)

Identification BREEDING MALE: Unmistakable. It has a unique bright tawnyred head, throat, and breast, which varies in intensity; the rest of the underparts are buffy white with streaking along sides of breast and flanks. ADULT FEMALE: It shows little or no red (if present it's mainly confined to the throat and upper breast) and has heavier black streaking on breast and sides. The back is heavily streaked, sometimes quite buffy, other times white. The crown is finely streaked, but the nape is unpatterned. It also has noticeable whitish wing bars, little or no primary projection, and pale legs. IMMATURE: It shows no red anywhere. The streaking (sometimes very white) above is heavy, and more so on the breast and sides.

Similar Species Adults in bright plumage do not look like any other pipit. Immatures and dull females can be confused with much rarer Pechora Pipit, but note the Red-throated's larger size, less intense buff wash across breast, unpatterned nape, unbroken eye ring, and lack of primary projection. The 2 species also have very different calls.

Voice CALL: Given in flight; a high, piercing *tseee* that descends at the end. SONG: A long, varied series of chirps, whistles, and buzzy notes, given from the ground or from a display flight.

Status & Distribution Common in Siberian tundra. BREEDING: Has bred in short, rocky tundra in western AK along the Bering Sea. MIGRATION: Regular spring and fall migrant to islands in the Bering Sea (mainly St. Lawrence); spring peak in early Jun.; fall peak in late Aug. VAGRANT: Casual along CA coast, mainly in Sept. and Oct.; accidental inland to AZ.

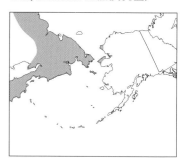

SPRAGUE'S PIPIT *Anthus spragueii*

In winter, the Sprague's Pipit is 1 of the more secretive grassland birds from the Southwest to eastern Texas, yet in summer its song is a characteristic sound of the western prairies, when displaying males give continuous varied song from high altitude. Female and wintering individuals are almost impossible to spot on the ground. When flushed, the bird calls alarmingly, rises to a great height while circling, plummets straight down with folded wings, opens its wings just before impact, and then disappears into the tall grass. However, it is usu-ally reluctant to flush, preferring to walk away rather than fly. Unlike other pipits, the Sprague's does not bob its tail. Monotypic. L 6.5" (17 cm)

Identification Sexes similar. It is stocky and rather short tailed for a pipit, heavily streaked on back and crown, rather buffy brown underneath, with fine streaking across breast, pale legs and base of mandible, and extensive white outer tail feathers. The very plain buffy face with large, dark eyes serves as the best field mark. JUVENILE: It is more scaled on the back and has bolder, white wing bars.

Similar Species The plumage of the immature Red-throated Pipit looks similar, but note the plainer face and lack of streaking on the flanks of the Sprague's; their flight call and behavior when flushed are also different. A juvenile Horned Lark may be confused with a Sprague's, but it has a different tail pattern, calls, and behavior. **Voice** CALL: A loud squeaky *squeet,* often given 2 or 3 times in succession. SONG: Given in flight; a series of descending *tzee* and *tzee-a* notes.

Status & Distribution Uncommon. BREEDING: Nests in grassy fields in open prairie. WINTER: Solitary. Found in tall patches of ungrazed grass in the southern U.S. to south Mexico. VAGRANT: Very rare in fall and winter to CA; accidental in the East.

Population Overgrazing and the introduction of non-native grasses are negatively affecting populations on both summer and winter grounds.

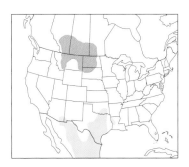

AMERICAN PIPIT   *Anthus rubescens*

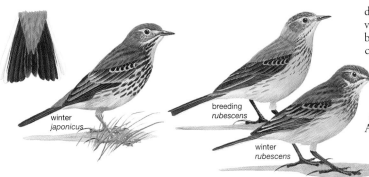

winter
japonicus

breeding
rubescens

winter
rubescens

Formerly known as the Water Pipit, this ground-dwelling species of high latitude and high elevation rocky tundra is widespread across North America's Arctic and mountaintops during summer, and it can be abundant in winter in agricultural fields, forming huge single species flocks across the southern United States. During migration and in winter, birders often see this pipit near water, particularly at sewage ponds, living up to its old name. Unlike other, more secretive pipits, the American forages out in the open, frequently bobbing its tail. Polytypic (3 distinct ssp. groups in N.A.). L 6.5" (17 cm)

Identification Sexes similar. Plumage highly variable, ranging from clear buffy underparts with no streaks, to whitish underparts with heavy streaks, depending upon subspecies and time of year. Upperparts generally gray to brown, unstreaked. Tail with white outer tail feathers. ADULT BREEDING: *A. r. alticola:* Pale gray above, unstreaked tawny-buff underparts, buffy auriculars with buffy supercilium, dark legs. *A. r. rubescens* (including *pacificus*): Darker gray above, buffy below, streaks across the breast that extend faintly down the flanks, gray auriculars with buffy supercilium, and dark legs. *A. r. japonicus:* Similar to *rubescens,* but with blacker streaking, a browner, slightly streaked back, and pale legs. ADULT WINTER: *A. r. alticola:* Pale overall with some faint streaking across breast, grayer auriculars, and buffy supercilium more prominent on grayer face. *A. r. rubescens:* Grayish brown above with faint streaking, whitish below, buffier on the flanks, heavy dark streaking across breast (amount variable, but always more than *alticola*), decidedly white supercilium, and dark legs (usually). *A. r. japonicus:* Boldly patterned. More streaking on the upperparts and thick black streaks on a white background on the underparts, prominent white wing bars, and pale legs.

Geographic Variation The North American subspecies divide into 3 main groups: the nominate *rubescens* group of the Arctic (of which there are 3 difficult-to-separate ssp.), the Rocky Mountain-breeding *alticola,* and the Asian *japonicus,* which occurs as a migrant, mainly in western Alaska.

Similar Species All other North American pipits are browner and more streaked on the upperparts, except the Olive-backed, which is somewhat similar to *japonicus,* but note distinct face pattern, buffy wash across breast, and different call. Leg color may be highly variable, with some North American birds appearing pale legged. This makes certain identification of *japonicus* more difficult, particularly away from the Bering Sea region.

Voice CALL: Given in flight; a sharp *pip-it.* Call of *japonicus* higher pitched, often single noted. SONG: A rapid series of *chee* or *cheedle* notes, typically given in flight display, lasting 15–20 seconds.

Status & Distribution Common. BREEDING: Widespread and scattered during the breeding season in rocky tundra across the Arctic *(rubescens),* high mountaintops in the Rocky Mountains and CA *(alticola),* and the Pacific Northwest *(pacificus).* WINTER: Abundant and widespread in agricultural areas and open country from southern U.S. south through Mexico. Rocky Mountain birds winter mainly in Mexico. Subspecies *rubescens* is more widespread and overlaps with *alticola.* MIGRATION: Found virtually anywhere in open country or by water across the U.S. Asian *japonicus* regular spring (early June) and fall (late Aug.–Sept.) visitor to islands in the Bering Sea, rarely (in fall) south to CA.

Population Winter birds are susceptible to the overuse of pesticides in agricultural areas.

WAXWINGS Family Bombycillidae

Bohemian Waxwing (MN, Jan.)

Finding waxwings is often feast or famine, particularly near the periphery of a species' range. They may be abundant one year, gone the next. Even during a single season, several different flocks may visit the same location, making it appear as though 1 flock is present all winter. Flocks are often quite tame and allow observers to approach closely, particularly when they are in a state of inebriation after consuming fermented fruits. Once waxwings are found, identifying them is straightforward: Differences in the wings, tail, and underparts between species are easily seen. Experienced birders often check flocks carefully in winter—stray waxwings often are found in flocks of the "other" waxwing species.

Structure Waxwings are relatively chunky birds with a pointed crest, which is conspicuous when the birds are perched. They have fairly long, pointed, and triangular wings and a short, square, or slightly rounded tail with very long undertail coverts. In flight this gives them an appearance similar to European Starlings. When perched, their distinctive silhouette makes them unlikely to be confused with other species. The short, broad bill is well adapted for grasping and gulping down large berries.

Behavior No other bird family in North America is more addicted to fruit than the Bombycillidae. From fall through early spring waxwings feed almost exclusively on sugary fruits; however, they will also consume developing fruits (flowers) and insects in springtime. Their fondness for fruit has led to their proclivity to form flocks. Except when nesting, waxwings are almost always seen in flocks. In winter flocks number in the hundreds, often even in the thousands. During these times they frequently forage in fruiting trees, sometimes with American Robins, bluebirds, and Pine Grosbeaks. Even during the breeding season, nesting pairs are often found in close proximity to each other, near an abundant food source. Lacking defended territories, waxwings evolved an unusual characteristic among passerines—they do not sing.

Plumage Waxwing plumages are characterized by a subtle yet elegant blend of soft and silky smooth browns and grays. Waxwings have dark throats and masks. The wings vary from the simple white edging on the inner edge of the tertials on the Cedar Waxwing, to the more elaborate patterns found in the Bohemian and Japanese Waxwings. Bombycillids have a modified basic molt strategy with a partial first prebasic molt where few wing coverts are replaced. While sexually dimorphic, differences between the sexes are subtle and may be challenging to see under most field conditions. Waxwings are named for the waxy droplets at the end of their secondaries, which are unique to the family. Synthesized from carotenoid pigments, these droplets form as extensions of the rachis that project beyond the feather veins. These may be lacking, or at least reduced on young birds, and most developed in adult males. The link between diet and feather color has been well studied in the Cedar. Typically, the Cedar only synthesizes yellow carotenoid from its diet, resulting in the classic yellow tail tip. In much of eastern North America, however, the introduction of exotic honeysuckle—with the red carotenoid pigment rhodoxanthin—has led to the Cedar molting in tail feathers with an orangish tip; the exact color depends upon how much honeysuckle the Cedar eats during the molt.

Distribution Waxwings are found only in the Northern Hemisphere. The Bohemian Waxwing is Holarctic, while the Japanese Waxwing inhabits eastern Asia, and the Cedar Waxwing resides only in North America.

Taxonomy There are only 3 waxwing species; all 3 belong to the genus *Bombycilla*. Waxwings are closely related to silky-flycatchers (Ptilogonatidae); some taxonomists merge the 2 families. Waxwings differ from silky-flycatchers in having pointed wings, a minute tenth primary, and waxy droplets at the tips of the secondaries. They lack the well-developed rictal bristles found in silky-flycatchers. The Palmchat *(Dulus dominicus)* of Hispaniola is also closely related. DNA-DNA hybridization suggests that bombycillids are closely related to dippers, Old World flycatchers, thrushes, and starlings.

Conservation Since waxwings congregate at berries near human habitations, they face a cornucopia of dangers posed by residential environments, particularly collisions with windows and cars and cat predation. The Japanese Waxwing is classified by BirdLife International as near threatened due to habitat loss and degradation. The populations of both North American species are thought to be increasing or stable. —*Christopher L. Wood*

BOHEMIAN WAXWING *Bombycilla garrulus*

The Bohemian Waxwing often winters in flocks of several hundred birds. In summer, it travels in pairs or small flocks and frequently perches on the top of black spruces. Stray individuals to the south are almost always found with Cedar Waxwings. Polytypic (3 ssp.; *pallidiceps* in N.A.). L 8.3" (21 cm)

Identification Starling-size; sleek crest; grayish overall with face washed in chestnut; rufous undertail coverts; tip of tail yellow. White primary tips make wing appear notched with white. Compared with female, the male has a larger throat patch that contrasts sharply with breast, broader yellow tip to tail, and more extensive waxy tips to secondaries. First-winter birds lack white tips to primaries and waxy tips reduced. JUVENILE:

Streaky below with white throat (June–Oct.). FLIGHT: White bases to primary coverts appear as contrasting white band in flight.

Geographic Variation Weak. The *centralasiae*, a vagrant from Asia to the western Aleutian and Pribilof Islands, is paler than the *pallidiceps* of N.A. It has little contrast between the forehead and the rest of head and is often darker on the undertail coverts.

Similar Species The Cedar Waxwing is similar but smaller, with a pale yellow belly, white undertail coverts, and plainer wings. In flight, European Starlings appear similar in shape and flight style.

Voice CALL: Commonly a high, sharply trilled *zeeee,* lower and distinctly more trilled than the Cedar Waxwing's (more rattlelike). Also a high, short, pure *tseew,* shorter than Cedar's analogous call. Does not sing.

Status & Distribution Uncommon to common locally. BREEDING: Open coniferous or mixed woodlands. MIGRATION: In fall departs interior AK in Sept. First arrivals in SK late Sept.; huge flocks arrive Dec. First arrivals in northern U.S. mid-Oct.–early Nov. In spring, most leave lower 48 by mid-Mar., but some

juvenile

Apr. WINTER: Largest concentrations occur across southern BC and AB and south-central SK. Irregular to the Northeast, usually in small numbers; annual in ME, Maritimes, and NF. VAGRANT: Rare and irregular to dashed line on map. Casual to southern CA, northwestern AZ, northern TX, northwestern AR, southern NJ, southern MD.

Population Stable or increasing. The spread of exotic fruiting plants and shrubs has likely affected migration and winter distribution. Increased risk of collisions (cars and windows) and pesticide poisoning in towns and cities.

CEDAR WAXWING *Bombycilla cedrorum*

The Cedar Waxwing is easily found in open habitat where there are berries. It times its nesting to coincide with summer berry production, putting it among the latest of North American birds to nest. It is highly gregarious; flocks of hundreds, occasionally thousands, are encountered during migration and winter. Polytypic. L 7.3" (8 cm)

Identification Smaller than the Bohemian Waxwing, with pale yellow belly and whitish undertail coverts. Tip of tail usually yellow, broadest in adult males, narrowest in immature females. Some birds (esp. immatures) have an orange tail tip, a result of consuming non-native honeysuckle fruit during molt. The male's chin has extensive amount of black that extends onto throat; the female's chin is dull or brownish black. First-winter males

and adult females can be similar. JUVENILE: Streaky below with white chin and bold malar stripe (June–Nov.).

Geographic Variation Two subspecies. Western *larifuga* averages paler with grayer (less reddish) breast than eastern *cedrorum,* but the differences are weak and clinal.

juvenile

Similar Species The Bohemian Waxwing is similar but larger, grayer, has rufous undertail coverts, white bar on primary coverts and chestnut wash on face. A juvenile Cedar can be separated from a Bohemian by its lack of white wing patches, and lack of any rufous on undertail coverts.

Voice CALL: Commonly a high trilled *zeeeee,* higher and less trilled than the Bohemian

Waxwing's. Also a long, high, pure *seeeee;* and a shorter descending *sweeew,* longer than analogous call of Bohemian. Does not sing.

Status & Distribution Common. BREEDING: Open woodlands and old fields. MIGRATION: In spring in much of east and central U.S. it peaks Feb.–Mar. and May–early June. Fall peak in northern U.S. Sept.–Oct.; in GA early Oct.–Dec. WINTER: Irregular. Southern U.S. to C.A., rarely to Panama.

Population Increasing, likely due in part to spread of exotic fruiting plants. VAGRANT: Central AK, YK, Iceland, U.K.

SILKY-FLYCATCHERS Family Ptilogonatidae

Phainopepla, male (AZ, May)

Members of this small Middle American family are often found in close proximity to fruit, although insects may also form a large percentage of silky-flycatchers' diet. The family's common name describes their soft, sleek plumage and agility in catching insects on the wing. They are not at all closely related to flycatchers, which has led some people to call them by the simpler name Silkies. Identification of all silky-flycatcher species is straightforward, with differences in coloration, structure, and patterning obvious.

Structure Silky-flycatchers are slender thrush-size birds with long tails and small bills. Short crests are standard. Their rounded wings help them make quick sallies from branches to catch insects.

Behavior Silky-flycatchers are seen in small flocks, pairs, or alone. They typically perch near the tops or edges of shrubs and trees. Most call frequently, making them easy to see. During the breeding season, they may form loose colonies when there is an abundance of fruit; during these times adults defend nests from other members of the same species but usually do not defend food supplies. They construct shallow cup nests placed in crotches of trees and shrubs.

Plumage Ptilogonatids have plumages characterized by black, gray, or pale brown, often with yellow or white highlights. The plumages are generally smooth and blended, without well-defined lines or distinct markings of color. Even juveniles lack spots, bars, streaks, or other distinctive markings. All species are sexually dimorphic, with males' plumage brighter or exhibiting more contrast. In Phainopepla there is a supplemental plumage (before the first prebasic molt). The first prebasic molt varies from partial to complete. There is no prealternate molt.

Distribution Silky-flycatchers are found from the southwestern United States to western Panama. Aside from the desert-loving Phainopepla, they primarily inhabit mountain ranges. Movements in Middle America require more study, but since these species feed heavily on fruit, it is likely all species stage at least local movements.

Taxonomy Ptilogonatidae breaks down into 3 genera with 4 species. The family is very closely related to waxwings and sometimes merged with that family. Silky-flycatchers differ from waxwings in having rounded wings and prominent rictal bristles; the tenth primary is also larger and the ninth primary is smaller. The monotypic genus *Phainoptila* (Black-and-yellow Silky-flycatcher found in the highlands of Costa Rica and western Panama) appears very different—much more thrush-like; however, unlike thrushes, the juvenal plumage is plain and unspeckled and the short tarsi are covered with broad transverse scales—both characteristics of silky-flycatchers.

Conservation Species populations are apparently stable. Habitat destruction and degradation pose the biggest threat to silky-flycatchers. Habitat fragmentation may not pose as great a threat as it does for many families since all silky-flycatchers are found to some degree in edge habitats. Some species are caught and kept in captivity. —*Christopher L. Wood*

SILKY-FLYCATCHERS Genus *Ptilogonys*

GRAY SILKY-FLYCATCHER *Ptilogonys cinereus*

This Middle American species is an accidental visitor to Texas; perhaps elsewhere in the Southwest. The Gray Silky-flycatcher feeds primarily on berries of mistletoe and other plants, as well as insects; it often perches conspicuously atop trees. Polytypic (2–4 ssp.). L 7.5" (20cm)

Identification Structurally similar to Phainopepla, but with a bushy crest that is not as wispy. ADULT MALE: Generally blue-gray overall, with orangey-yellow flanks and bright yellow undertail coverts. Wings and tail dark; tail has a broad white base to the outer tail feathers. Dark lores contrast with white eyering and paler forecrown. ADULT FEMALE: Similar to male, but coloration more subdued, with more brownish tones. Yellow often confined to undertail coverts. JUVENILE: Similar to adults, but duller overall.

Geographic Variation There is some discussion as to how much variation truly exists, as there are subtle differences in age and sex that have likely not been fully resolved. Records for the U.S. are presumably *otofuscus* from western Mexico or nominate *cinereus* from eastern and central Mexico.

Similar Species The Gray is unmistakable; note its structure, upright posture, bushy crest, eye ring, yellow at least on undertail coverts, and white patches in the long tail.

Voice CALL: Gives varied, chattering notes; flight calls and some calls given when perched may suggest call notes of *Piranga* tanagers.

Status & Distribution Accidental in TX: Laguna Atascosa N.W.R. (Oct. 21–Nov. 11, 1985) and El Paso (Jan.12–Mar. 5, 1995). Records from coastal southern CA controversial; natural occurrence questioned. BREEDING: Pine-oak and pine-evergreen forest in mountains of Mexico and Guatemala. MOVEMENTS: Largely resident, but occasionally nomadic; moves in large flocks, may move locally downslope in winter; possibly withdraws from northwestern Mexico. Potential for extralimital records pertaining to escapes complicates understanding natural distribution.

adult ♂

Genus *Phainopepla*

PHAINOPEPLA *Phainopepla nitens*

Phainopepla—Greek for "shining robe"—is the only ptilogonatid regularly found north of the U.S.–Mexico border. The Phainopepla is often solitary, but it may gather to feed on seasonally abundant crops. It feeds heavily on mistletoe berries in winter; its diet includes more insects at other seasons. It vigorously defends feeding territories, and excrement may pile several inches high under territorial perches. It perches upright, usually in the open on tops and sides of trees and shrubs. Polytypic. L 7.7" (20 cm)

Identification Slender thrush-size bird with a shaggy crest and long tail. Red eyes (both sexes). Males substantially larger than females. MALE: Shiny black; white wing patches very conspicuous in flight. FEMALE: Grayish; white edging on all wing feathers (less so on primaries and secondaries). White wing patches absent. JUVENILE: Similar to adult female but with buffy wing bars and brownish upperparts; dark eye. Immature male typically begins to acquire black feathers in fall, producing black patches. FLIGHT: Fluttery but direct; bold wing patches revealed on adult male.

Similar Species Waxwings are similar in shape, but they have shorter tails and much different coloration. The Northern Mockingbird has white wing patches, but a very different shape and horizontal posture. Mockingbirds are paler gray with darker wings and tail (the tail with white corners). The Gray Catbird has a different shape, contrasting dark crown, and rufous undertail coverts. Grackles, blackbirds, and starling have more horizontal postures and lack a crest.

Geographic Variation The smaller *lepida* (Southwest U.S. to Baja California and northwest Mexico) and larger *nitens* (southwest TX to central Mexico) differ in wing and tail length; they are not separable in the field.

Voice CALL: A distinctive, querulous, low-pitched, whistled *wurp?* May imitate other species (e.g., Red-tailed Hawk and Northern Flicker). SONG: A brief warble that includes a whistled *wheedle-ah;* infrequently heard.

Status & Distribution Common. BREEDING: Late winter–early spring in mesquite brushlands; in summer moves into cooler, wetter habitats and raises a second brood. Highest densities occur in riparian woodlands and dense mesquite thickets. MIGRATION: Short-distance migrant. Begins spring migration late Mar.–early Apr.; arrives northern CA early to mid-Apr. Fall return occurs Aug.–Nov. WINTER: Mostly lowlands from Sonoran Desert to central Mexico. VAGRANT: Casual in southern OR, CO, KS, south-central TX. Accidental to eastern N.A. with records for ON, WI, RI, and MA.

Population Apparently stable; potential threats include continued destruction of mesquite forests and riparian woodlands in the Southwest.

OLIVE WARBLER Family Peucedramidae

Olive Warbler, male (AZ)

Long considered an aberrant wood-warbler, the Olive Warbler was recently determined to be a distant relative, and placed in its own family with uncertain relationships.

Structure Olives are similar to *Dendroica* wood-warblers but have a slightly longer, thin bill, a slightly decurved culmen, a distinctly notched tail, and 10 primaries.

Plumage The adult male's tawny orange head coloration is unlike any wood-warbler, and a white patch at the base of the primaries is shared with only the Black-throated Blue Warbler.

Behavior Vocalizations consist of loud whistled notes (the females also sing). They flick their wings like kinglets. Olives allow their nestlings to soil the nests with droppings, a behavior unknown in wood-warblers.

Distribution Occurs in montane coniferous and mixed pine-oak forest from southeastern Arizona and southwestern New Mexico to extreme western Nicaragua. The northern subspecies is partially migratory, whereas the southern subspecies are sedentary.

Taxonomy On the basis of anatomy, Olives may be related to Old World warblers, but some behavioral differences and recent genetic evidence contradict this and suggest a closer relationship to the finches. More study will resolve the taxonomic position. Olives are generally considered to be more primitive than wood-warblers.

Conservation Although fairly common within its range, Olives could be negatively affected by logging activities.
—*Allen T. Chartier*

Genus *Peucedramus*

OLIVE WARBLER *Peucedramus taeniatus*

A distinctive warblerlike resident of southwestern pine forests, with a loud song and kingletlike wing flicking. Polytypic. L 5.2" (13 cm).

Identification ADULT MALE: Bright tawny orange head and upper breast with distinct black ear patch. Gray back, paler underparts. Two broad white wing bars and a white spot at base of primaries. Tail distinctly notched, with large white spots. ADULT FEMALE: Crown, nape, and back grayish. Ear patch mottled gray and black, surrounded by yellowish above eye and on sides of neck. Throat and breast yellowish, underparts pale gray. Wing bars narrower than male's, white spot at base of primaries smaller. IMMATURE MALE: Similar to adult male but duller, showing more mottled black and gray cheek patch, more yellowish head, including crown and upper breast. IMMATURE FEMALE: Similar to adult female but yellow on head duller and back more brownish. Wing bars very narrow and white spot at base of primaries very small or absent.

Geographic Variation Five subspecies worldwide. The northern *arizonae* in N.A. is larger, paler, and greener-backed than the 4 southern subspecies, and males show unique molt pattern, where breeding plumage is not attained until the second summer.

Similar Species Immatures are similar to an immature female Hermit Warbler, which lacks white at base of primaries and has an all yellow face, indistinctly notched tail, and different bill shape, calls, and songs.

Voice Very distinct. CALL: A soft, whistled *phew,* similar to the Western Bluebird. Also a hard *pit.* SONG: A loud *peeta peeta peeta peeta,* similar to the Tufted Titmouse.

Status & Distribution Fairly common in mountains of southeastern AZ and southwestern NM. BREEDING: Higher elevation pine and fir forests. NEST: High in conifer, far from trunk, 3–4 eggs (May–June). MIGRATION: Arrive in AZ early Apr. Departure schedule unknown. WINTER: Most move south of AZ; very few remain in breeding range, sometimes at slightly lower elevations. VAGRANT: West TX and portions of NM outside breeding range.

adult ♂

♀

1st spring ♂

1st fall

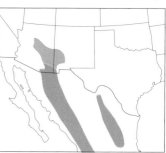

WOOD-WARBLERS Family Parulidae

Yellow-rumped Warbler (NJ, Oct.)

Wood-warblers include some of our most colorful birds. Most members of this exclusively New World family are neotropical migrants. In spring, birders eagerly anticipate their arrival. Most are fairly closely related, and a number of hybrids—even between genera—are known.

Structure Most are small songbirds with variable, colorful plumage in spring, sometimes more muted in fall, and 9 visible primaries. Some show rictal bristles, an adaptation to an insectivorous diet; others lack them.

Plumage Most species molt into a special breeding plumage, more colorful than their winter or nonbreeding plumage. Yellow, green, and olive figure prominently in many plumages, and some species have white and black on the head and underparts. Prominent wing bars are found on some species. Many species show extensive white on the outer tail feathers, which may appear as white spots.

Behavior All species in North America are generally insectivorous, but some feed on fruit or nectar in winter. Most species build a cup nest, placed on the ground or low to high in a shrub or tree; only 2 species nest in cavities. Many species have 2 song types: an often-accented primary song used for defending territory and an often-unaccented alternate song used in a variety of situations (e.g., near the nest when paired with a female). Songs are quite varied. Many eastern species undertake trans-Gulf migrations in spring and fall.

Distribution About 116 species (depending on taxonomy used) breed from Alaska to northern Argentina. Fifty-one species breed annually in North America (including 1 probably extinct), with the majority of those in the East; 6 additional species have been recorded as vagrants.

Taxonomy Wood-warblers are considered to be most close-ly related to the tanagers (Thraupidae), the honeycreepers (Coerebidae), and of course the Olive Warbler (Peucedramidae); but these relationships remain somewhat unresolved. Some recent DNA studies suggest that wood-warblers may actually be more closely related to the New World blackbirds (Icteridae) and Old World buntings (Emberizidae). About half of the world's wood-warblers are in 2 genera: 29 species in *Dendroica* and 24 species in *Basileuterus*. A number of species, many in N.A., are classified in their own genus, and their closest relatives within the family are uncertain. The Yellow-breasted Chat is perhaps the most aberrant family member; and an unusual tropical species, the Wrenthrush, is most likely also a member of the wood-warbler family.

Conservation Wood-warblers have experienced significant population declines in recent decades. Most North American wood-warblers migrate to the tropics, which puts them at risk not only through potential habitat destruction on both breeding and wintering grounds, but on their migration corridors as well. In particular, the hazardous, difficult trans-Gulf migration often results in high mortality. Many species' winter ranges are considerably smaller and more concentrated than their breeding ranges, which magnifies the effects of habitat destruction on their wintering grounds. Some species have restricted and specialized breeding ranges that, in some cases, are in conflict with human uses. Brown-headed Cowbird parasitism affects these rare species most dramatically, but as forests become fragmented, species depending on large tracts become more vulnerable. Worldwide, BirdLife International lists 14 species as endangered (including the probably extinct Bachman's and Semper's Warblers) and 7 as near threatened. —*Allen T. Chartier*

Genus *Vermivora*

This genus comprises a total of 9 species—1 of which is probably extinct—all occurring in North America. They can be recognized by their smaller size, shorter tails, and thin, pointed bills. Six species lack tail spots and conspicuous wing bars. All lack rictal bristles. Their vocalizations consist primarily of series of buzzes, chips, or trills.

BACHMAN'S WARBLER   *Vermivora bachmanii (E)*

adult ♀

1st spring ♂

adult ♂

This probably extinct warbler is a denizen of open areas in southern swamps. Monotypic. L 4.8" (12 cm)
Identification SPRING MALE: Thin, pointed, slightly decurved bill. Yellow forehead, supercilium, eye ring, chin, upper throat, and shoulders. Black crown and bib, gray nape. Dark olive back, wings, and tail. Yellow belly, white undertail coverts. White spots on the outer tail feathers. SPRING FEMALE: Duller than male. Gray crown, throat, and breast; yellow forehead; narrow white eye ring. IMMATURE: Male shows less black on crown and bib than adult male; smaller tail spots. Female duller than spring female.
Similar Species The Hooded has yellow undertail coverts and larger white tail spots; bill not decurved. The Golden-winged has a black cheek and yellow wing bars. Immature female similar to several species, but distinguished by pointed, decurved bill; complete white eye ring; and whitish undertail coverts.
Voice CALL: A buzzy *zip* or *zeep* given by both sexes. Little known. SONG: A rapid series of buzzy notes, similar in quality to alternate song of the Blue-winged and Golden-winged, delivered rapidly and on 1 pitch, sometimes ending with a sharp slurred note: *bzz-bzz-bzz-bzz-bzz-bzz-bzz-zip.*
Status & Distribution Probably extinct; last confirmed rec. was spring 1962, near Charleston, SC. Formerly a local breeder from MO to SC. Most recs. were migrants from southern FL, the western Keys, and southeastern LA. BREEDING: Probably open canebrakes in swamps and bottomlands. WINTER: Cuba and Isle of Pines in semideciduous forest, forested wetlands, and forested urban open space.
Population Degradation of breeding and wintering habitat is the most probable cause of decline.

BLUE-WINGED WARBLER   *Vermivora pinus*

A bright golden yellow bird with a distinct buzzy song, the Blue-winged warbler breeds in brushy fields. It nests on or near the ground at the base of a shrub or in a clump of grasses, laying 4–5 eggs (May–June). Monotypic. L 4.8" (12 cm)
Identification ADULT MALE: Bright yellow forehead, crown, and underparts contrast with greenish yellow nape and back; white undertail coverts. Bluish gray wings with 2 distinct white wing bars. Black lores with short black postocular line behind the eye. Large white spots on outer tail feathers. ADULT FEMALE: Duller than male, with yellow forehead blending into yellowish olive crown, nape, and back; whitish undertail coverts. Wing bars less distinct, sometimes tinged yellow. Lores and eye line slightly duller. IMMATURE: Duller, similar to adult female. HYBRIDS: Blue-winged x Golden-winged Warbler hybrids are well documented, and 2 types have been named; the "Brewster's" is more frequent, as all first-generation hybrids and some later-generation hybrids result in this type. A few back-crosses result in the rarer "Lawrence's." Some hybrids do not resemble these 2 types and combine characters of both parents. Hybrids usually sing the songs of one species or the other.
Similar Species The Yellow Warbler and the Prothonotary Warbler do not have black eye lines. The Pine Warbler is duller and also lacks an eye line, and its underparts are duller with diffuse olive streaks.
Voice CALL: Most-often heard call is a gentle *tsip,* identical to the Golden-winged Warbler's and similar to the

Field Sparrow's. FLIGHT CALL: A high, slightly buzzy *tzii*, often doubled. SONG: Primary song is typically a high-pitched, buzzy, inhaled-exhaled *beeee-bzzzz*. Alternate song is similar, but with a stuttering first note and a flatter second note: *be-ee-ee-ee-bttttt*.

Status & Distribution Locally common in brushy meadows and second-growth woodland edges; a trans-Gulf migrant. BREEDING: Overgrown old fields and brushy swamps, usually in early to mid-succession. MIGRATION: In spring, early Apr.–early May in TX; late Apr.–mid-May in OH, late Apr.–early June in MN. In fall, usually departs breeding grounds undetected. As early as late July in NJ, peaking in late Aug., a few to late Sept. Occasional Nov. recs. in Southeast, a few farther north. WINTER: Humid evergreen and semideciduous forest and edge from southern Mexico to Costa Rica, occasionally south to Pana-

ma and West Indies. VAGRANT: Casual in West, inc. SK, AB, WY, CO (approx. 40 recs.), NM (approx. 12 recs.), AZ (9 recs.), NV, WA, OR, and CA (30+ recs.). Rare north to Atlantic provinces

"Brewster's Warbler"

Blue-winged x Golden-winged hybrids

♀

♂

"Lawrence's Warbler"

♂

in fall; accidental in Iceland.

Population Expanding northward in Great Lakes into range of the Golden-winged Warbler, but declining due to reforestation of open habitats and urban sprawl in northeastern United States.

GOLDEN-WINGED WARBLER *Vermivora chrysoptera*

♀

♂

Boldly patterned with black, white, gray, and yellow, the Golden-winged Warbler is an active and acrobatic forager. It makes its nest on or near the ground at the base of a shrub or other leafy plants, laying 4 to 5 eggs (May–June). Monotypic. L 4.8" (12 cm)

Identification ADULT MALE: Gray upperparts with a bright yellow cap. Broad wing bars appear as a single large yellow patch. White underparts. Black cheek and throat contrast with white malar and supercilium. Large white spots on outer tail feathers. ADULT

FEMALE: Similar to male, but upperparts more olive-gray, cheek and throat gray, duller yellow cap blending in with gray nape; 2 yellow wing bars usually distinct, not forming a large yellow patch on the wing. IMMATURE: Duller than adult. Male more olive above, with duller yellow cap; black throat and cheek often slightly fringed with buff. Female more olive above with duller yellow cap contrasting little with grayish olive nape, paler gray throat and cheek patch. HYBRIDS: See the Blue-winged Warbler.

Similar Species Throat pattern and foraging behavior suggest the Black-capped Chickadee. The Black-throated Gray Warbler is similar when seen from below, but it shows distinct black streaking on sides.

Voice CALL: Most-often heard call is a gentle *tsip*, similar to the Field Sparrow's and identical to the Blue-winged Warbler's. FLIGHT CALL: A high, slightly buzzy *tzii*, often doubled. SONG: Primary song is a high-pitched, buzzy *zeee bee bee bee*, with a higher-pitched first note. Alternate song is indistinguishable from the Blue-winged Warbler's, with a stuttering first note and a flatter second note.

Status & Distribution Uncommon to rare

and declining; a trans-Gulf migrant. BREEDING: Wet shrubby fields, marshes, and bogs on edge of woodlands, most often restricted to early successional habitat. MIGRATION: In spring, peaks in early May in MI and PA, to late May in northern WI. In fall, often departs breeding grounds undetected during Aug., with latest dates in early to mid-Oct. WINTER: Woodlands and forest borders from southern Mexico to Panama. Casual in northern Colombia, Venezuela, and Caribbean. VAGRANT: Casual in West, recorded from most western states and provinces; 66 records from CA. One record from UK in winter.

Population Designated a species of special concern by the U.S. Fish and Wildlife Service. Population declining as the Blue-winged moves northward into its range, with greater frequency of hybridization.

TENNESSEE WARBLER *Vermivora peregrina*

breeding ♀

fall

fall

breeding ♂

This rather plain but common spruce-budworm specialist nests on the ground at base of small shrub or tree (3–8 eggs, June). Monotypic. L 4.8" (12 cm)

Identification SPRING MALE: Bright olive green upperparts, contrasting gray crown and nape, distinct white supercilium and underparts, distinct blackish eye stripe. Faint whitish wing bar. SPRING FEMALE: Duller than male, less contrasting crown and back, tinged yellow below. FALL ADULT: Duller than spring adult, usually some pale yellowish below, less contrasting nape and back. IMMATURE: Bright olive-green upperparts. Less distinct supercilium, buffy to pale yellowish; dusky eye line. Pale to bright yellowish underparts. Bright white undertail coverts,

sometimes tinged pale yellow.

Similar Species See sidebar below. Also, Philadelphia and Warbling Vireos have thicker bills with hooked tips.

Voice CALL NOTE: Sharp *tsit* when foraging. FLIGHT CALL: Thin, clear *see*. SONG: Loud, staccato series of *chip* notes, increasing speed in 2 or 3 distinct steps.

Status & Distribution Fairly common; mostly a trans-Gulf migrant. BREED-ING: Mainly mixed and coniferous forest and bogs in boreal zone. Arrives early Apr. on Gulf Coast. Bulk of migration in Great Lakes during mid- to late May. Adults depart breeding grounds very early, often in July. Peaks mid-Sept.–early Oct., a few to late Oct. WINTER: Open to semi-open second-growth forest from southern Mexico to Panama and northwestern S.A. Rarely in southeastern and coastal CA. VAGRANT: Small numbers annually in CA. Casual in OR and WA. Rare in AK, accidental northern Labrador Sea, southwestern Greenland, Iceland, UK.

Population Often abundant. Numbers vary with spruce budworm outbreaks.

Tennessee vs. Orange-crowned in Fall

In fall, distinguishing immature Tennessee Warblers and Orange-crowned Warblers requires careful observation. Tennessees begin migration earlier than many other warbler species, while Orange-crowned Warblers of the nominate (northern) subspecies begin migration latest. Greatest care should be taken August through mid-September. Focus on head pattern, underparts, shape, call notes, and behavior.

The Tennessee shows a long whitish or yellowish supercilium, sometimes indistinct, with a dusky eye line. The Orange-crowned shows a narrow whitish or yellowish split eye ring with an indistinct short yellowish supercilium.

Underneath, Tennessees are dull whitish to yellowish and unstreaked. The undertail coverts are usually bright white, sometimes tinged yellowish, but are always the whitest area of the underparts. Sometimes it can be difficult to see the blurry olive breast streaks on the Orange-crowned's dull yellowish underparts. The bright yellow undertail coverts are always the brightest yellow area of the underparts. Proportionately, the Tennessee's tail is much shorter and its primary extension is longer.

The Tennessee gives a sharp *tsit*, and the Orange-crowned gives a distinctive hard *stick* or *tik*. The Tennessee is a very nervous and active warbler, whereas the Orange-crowned is observed moving more deliberately. ∎

Orange-crowned Warbler (CA, Sept.)

Orange-crowned Warbler (CA, Apr..)

Tennessee Warbler (TX)

ORANGE-CROWNED WARBLER *Vermivora celata*

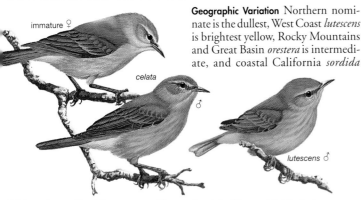

immature ♀

celata ♂

lutescens ♂

This rather yellowish green warbler, named for its least conspicuous character, forages lower than many species. It lays 4 to 5 eggs (Mar.–May in west, June in east) in its nest on or near the ground. Polytypic. L 5" (13 cm)

Identification ADULT MALE: Dusky olive green upperparts, grayer on crown and nape. Whitish or yellowish narrow broken eye ring, indistinct dusky eye line. Greenish yellow underparts with indistinct blurry streaks. Undertail coverts always brighter yellow than belly. **ADULT FEMALE:** Duller and grayer than male. **IMMATURE:** Duller, similar to adult female.

Geographic Variation Northern nominate is the dullest, West Coast *lutescens* is brightest yellow, Rocky Mountains and Great Basin *orestera* is intermediate, and coastal California *sordida* (mainly Channel Is.) is darkest green.
Similar Species Compare with Tennessee Warbler (see sidebar p. 520). In West, the Yellow and Wilson's Warblers are similar to *lutescens,* but both show plain faces with prominent dark eyes.
Voice CALL NOTE: Most frequent call a very distinctive, hard *stick* or *tik*. **FLIGHT CALL:** A high, thin *seet*. **SONG:** A high-pitched loose trill becoming louder and faster in the middle, weaker and slower at the end; faster in *lutescens.*
Status & Distribution Common in West, uncommon in East. **BREEDING:** Brushy deciduous thickets and second growth, from boreal forest in East to a great variety of habitats in West. In spring, northern subspecies takes a more westerly route up the Mississippi River Valley, mid-Apr.–late May. Western *lutescens* moves shorter distances, earlier peaking in late Mar.–early Apr. In fall, northern subspecies move later than other warblers, peaking in Oct. in much of northern U.S. Western subspecies moves earlier, mid-Aug.–early Oct. in AZ and CA. **WINTER:** Generally in thickets and shrubby areas from southeast U.S. and CA, through Mexico to Guatemala. Rarely lingers in northern U.S. **VAGRANT:** Bahamas (rare), Cuba, Jamaica, Cayman Is.
Population Reasonably stable, especially in West, with no significant threats identified.

NASHVILLE WARBLER *Vermivora ruficapilla*

The Nashville is a small olive-and-yellow warbler with a broad white eye ring and a gray head. The breeding ranges of the eastern and western subspecies do not overlap. In May–June, it lays 4 to 5 eggs in a nest on or near the ground, in thickets or bases of shrubs or small trees. Polytypic. L 4.8" (12 cm)

Identification ADULT MALE: Gray head contrasts with olive back, wings, and tail; bold white eye ring; yellow underparts. Small white area around vent. Rufous crown patch generally hidden. **ADULT FEMALE:** Duller than male, with more olive gray head. Smaller rufous crown patch. **IMMATURE:** Duller than adult female, with more brownish olive upperparts. Whitish throat.
Geographic Variation Western *ridgwayi* is brighter yellow-green on rump and brighter yellow on breast; has more white on vent; and often wags its longer tail.
Similar Species The Connecticut is much larger, with a gray hood, including the throat and upper breast. The Virginia's has less yellow below and is gray above. The Nashville is grayer above and always has olive-edged flight feathers.
Voice CALL: A distinctive sharp *tink*. **FLIGHT CALL:** A high, thin *tsip* or *seet*. **SONG:** A 2-part, loose series of sweet notes; the first part bounces, the second part is slightly faster: *see-bit, see-bit, see-bit, see see see see see.* The western subspecies has a similar but sweeter series of *see-bit* notes with less pattern.
Status & Distribution Common. **BREEDING:** Open deciduous or mixed forests, including spruce bogs in east. **MIGRA-**

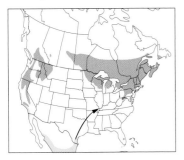

immature ♀

ruficapilla ♂

TION: Eastern birds are circum-Gulf migrants. Spring peak late Apr.–early May in much of eastern N.A.; much of fall migration late Aug.–late Oct. Western birds migrate through Southwest and along coast, most in Apr. in the West; in fall, somewhat earlier than the easterns. **WINTER:** Wooded areas in highlands and coastal areas, coastal CA (rare) through Mexico to Guatemala. **VAGRANT:** Very rare in fall and winter in Caribbean. Accidental in Greenland.
Population Stable populations in both breeding and winter range.

VIRGINIA'S WARBLER *Vermivora virginiae*

A tail-bobbing gray, white, and yellow warbler of our southwestern mountains, the Virginia's makes an open-cup nest of grasses on or near the ground in a clump of vegetation. It lays 3 to 5 eggs between May and June. Monotypic. L 4.8" (12 cm)
Identification SPRING MALE: Gray upperparts with yellowish green rump and uppertail coverts. Prominent white eye ring. Whitish underparts with a yellow patch on the breast and yellow undertail coverts. Extensive rufous crown patch often concealed. SPRING FEMALE: Like male, with less extensive yellow on breast and smaller rufous crown patch. FALL ADULT: Browner upperparts, buffy-tinged underparts. Yellow breast patch mixed

immat ♀

♂

with gray. Rufous crown patch obscured with gray. IMMATURE: Brownish gray upperparts, buffy underparts, yellow breast patch usually small or absent. Rufous crown patch very limited or absent. JUVENILE: Similar to immature, but with 2 pale buff wing bars.
Similar Species The Western subspecies of the Nashville Warbler also bobs its shorter tail, but it shows entirely yellow underparts, and its upperparts are greenish, not gray. The Colima Warbler is larger and browner, it lacks yellow on the breast, and its undertail coverts are not yellow.
Voice CALL: A high-pitched, hollow *chink.* FLIGHT CALL: A very high, clear *seet.* SONG: Similar to the song of the Nashville Warbler's western subspecies, but less structured and on 1 pitch: *s-weet, s-weet, s-weet, sweet-sweet-sweet.*
Status & Distribution Fairly common. BREEDING: Scrubby areas in steep-sloped pinyon-juniper and oak woodlands. MIGRATION: In spring, later than most other warblers, arriving in West late Apr.–mid-May, late Apr. in CO, and early May in WY. In fall, generally early Aug.–early Oct. in AZ

and NM. WINTER: Arid to semiarid scrub in highlands in southwest Mexico. Casual in southern TX and coastal southern CA. VAGRANT: During migration it has been recorded casually north to OR and coastal CA. Casual to accidental in southeastern TX, southwestern LA, ON, NS, Labrador, MI, NJ, NB, IL, MO, Belize, northern Guatemala, and Grand Bahama Is.
Population Populations on breeding grounds are apparently stable. The number of vagrants in CA may be declining.

COLIMA WARBLER *Vermivora crissalis*

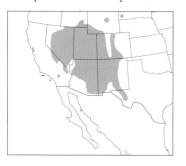

The Colima Warbler breeds only in the Chisos Mountains of west Texas and adjacent Mexico. The Colima nests on the ground in grasses, often those shaded by overhanging vegetation, and it produces 3 to 4 eggs between May and June. Monotypic. L 5.8" (15 cm)
Identification This is the largest and longest-tailed species in the genus *Vermivora.* ADULT: Grayish head,

brownish back, and yellowish olive rump. Whitish underparts with olive-brown sides on breast and flanks. Undertail coverts are tawny buff. Bold white eye ring. Partially concealed rufous crown patch. Females are slightly browner, but this is often not distinguishable. JUVENILE: Similar to the adult in plumage, but the juvenile is generally browner with paler underparts, brighter undertail coverts, and 2 obscure, pale buff wing bars. The juvenile also lacks the rufous crown patch.
Similar Species The Virginia's Warbler is smaller, shorter tailed, and grayer; it has no brown coloring. It has a distinct yellow patch on the breast, and it bobs its tail, unlike the Colima Warbler.
Voice CALL: A loud, sharp *plisk,* similar to the calls of the Nashville, Virginia's, and Lucy's Warblers. SONG: A simple musical trill in which the final 2 notes are downslurred, similar to the song of the Orange-crowned Warbler.

Status & Distribution Fairly common but very local. BREEDING: Montane areas of oak, pinyon, and juniper. Essentially unknown as a migrant. Arrives on breeding grounds as early as mid-Mar., with all birds arriving on territory by early May. All have departed the Chisos Mountains by mid-Sept. WINTER: Brushy areas of humid montane forests in southwestern Mexico.
Population The Chisos Mountains population is stable, with between 40 and 80 breeding pairs on censuses from 1960s to 1990s.

LUCY'S WARBLER *Vermivora luciae*

immature ♀

♂

A small gray bird of the arid southwest deserts, the Lucy's Warbler is 1 of only 2 species of cavity-nesting warblers. It makes its nest in a natural cavity, including crevices, under loose bark, or in an abandoned woodpecker hole. It produces 3 to 7 eggs between April and June. Monotypic. L 4.3" (11 cm)

Identification This very small warbler flicks its short tail. ADULT MALE: Pale gray upperparts, slightly darker wings and tail, white underparts. Dark eye stands out on the pale gray face, which shows white lores and an indistinct white eye ring. Chestnut crown patch and rump are both often concealed. Outer tail feather shows a small white spot near the tip. ADULT FEMALE: Similar to male, but paler face, smaller crown patch, and paler rump. IMMATURE: Similar to adult female, with pale buff cast on underparts. When fresh, immatures have 2 indistinct pale buffy wing bars.

Similar Species The Virginia's and Colima Warblers show yellowish on rump and undertail coverts, not chestnut. The Bell's Vireo has a thicker bill and wing bars. The juvenile Verdin has a much sharper, thicker-based bill and a longer tail. Females of the Yellow Warbler's desert subspecies *(sonorana)* always show some greenish on wings and tail as well as pale yellowish spots on tail.

Voice CALL: A sharp *chink,* similar to the call of the Virginia's Warbler. FLIGHT CALL: A weak *tsit.* SONG: A loud, lively, sweet song somewhat similar to the Yellow Warbler's: *tee-tee-tee-tee-tee-sweet-sweet-sweet.*

Status & Distribution Fairly common. BREEDING: Dense lowland riparian mesquite, cottonwood, and willow woodlands, mainly in the Sonoran Desert. MIGRATION: Earlier in spring than most migrants; arrives in southern AZ in early Mar. In fall, departs breeding grounds early, sometimes beginning as early as late July. Most gone from AZ by early Sept., with latest in early Oct. Rare on CA coast late Aug.–late Nov. WINTER: Thorn forest and riparian scrub in western Mexico. VAGRANT: Casual in southwestern CO. Accidental in ID, OR, LA, and MA.

Population Nests in unusually high densities for a noncolonial species. Declines due to the loss of riparian habitat from water projects, the cutting of mesquite trees, and increase in thickets of introduced tamarisks.

Genus *Parula*

The genus *Parula* comprises 4 species: 2 breed in N.A.; 1 breeds in Mexico and Central America and occurs as a vagrant in N.A.; and 1 species is endemic to the highlands of Costa Rica and Panama. All species are small with greenish or black patches on the back. They have slightly decurved bills with pale lower mandibles and buzzy songs.

CRESCENT-CHESTED WARBLER *Parula superciliosa*

This distinctive tropical species casually occurs north of Mexico and may actually be more appropriately classified in the genus *Vermivora.* Polytypic (6 ssp.; 2 poss. in N.A.). L 4.3" (11 cm)

Identification Blackish upper mandible; blackish lower mandible with flesh-colored base. ADULT MALE: Gray head with broad white supercilium and small white arc below eye; green back; yellow throat and breast with distinct crescent-shaped chestnut band on breast; whitish belly and undertail coverts. Gray wings and tail. ADULT FEMALE: Slightly paler than male, with smaller chestnut breast band. IMMATURE: Similar to female, but its breast band is much reduced or lacking.

Geographic Variation Very slight variation. The northernmost and palest subspecies *(sodalis)* likely has occurred in Arizona, while the slightly darker, brighter subspecies *(mexicana)* may have occurred in Big Bend, Texas (if rec. is correct).

Similar Species Both the Northern and the Tropical Parulas lack the white supercilium and have white wing bars. The Rufous-capped Warbler is rufous on crown and lacks chestnut breast band.

Voice CALL: A soft *sik,* similar to but softer than the Orange-crowned's. FLIGHT CALL: A high, thin *sip.* SONG: A short, flat buzz, reminiscent of a "Bronx cheer": *t-t-t-t-t-t-t-t-t.*

Status & Distribution Uncommon in montane pine-oak woodlands of Mexico to Nicaragua; casual vagrant to N.A. in spring, fall, and winter. BREEDING: Not in N.A. Montane pine-oak

immature ♀

adult ♂

and cloud forests from Mexico to Nicaragua. VAGRANT: Four confirmed records for AZ and 2 unconfirmed records for TX.

Population Mexican populations appear to be stable.

NORTHERN PARULA *Parula americana*

immature ♀

adult ♂

A small, short-tailed warbler, the Northern Parula inhabits mossy environments and is often found singing high in the treetops. It usually builds its nest in bunches of epiphytes (*Usnea* lichen in north, *Tillandsia* in south) on the end of a branch, ranging from low to high in a tree; it lays between 3 and 5 eggs from April to July. Monotypic. L 4.5" (11 cm)

Identification Bicolored bill: black upper mandible and yellow lower mandible. SPRING MALE: Blue-gray upperparts, including head and sides of throat, with greenish upper back; 2 broad, white wing bars; white eye ring broken at front and rear; black lores. Yellow throat and breast with reddish and black bands across breast; white belly and undertail coverts. Large white spots on outer tail feath-

ers. SPRING FEMALE: Similar to male, but duller blue-gray above; breast bands are much reduced or absent. IMMATURE: Similar to spring female, but duller with more greenish upperparts and smaller white tail spots.

HYBRIDS: The "Sutton's" Warbler is a very rare hybrid of the Northern Parula with the Yellow-throated Warbler. Its appearance is similar to the Yellow-throated Warbler, but it has the Northern Parula's green back patch, no white ear patch, and fewer side streaks.

Similar Species The Tropical Parula has a black face mask, but it lacks the black or chestnut bands on breast; it also lacks the white eye ring. The dullest immature female Magnolia Warblers show a complete eye ring, more extensive yellow coloring on the underparts, and white tail spots that form a band across the center of the tail.

Voice CALL: A sharp *tsip*. FLIGHT CALL: A high, weak, descending *tsif*. SONG: Primary song a rising trill with a terminal note that drops sharply. The song of western populations has a less emphatic, upslurred ending. Alternate song is more complex and wheezy: *b-zee-b-zee-b-zeee-zee-zee-zee-up*.

Status & Distribution Common breeding bird, typically departing the region entirely in winter. Eastern birds migrate through the Caribbean; western birds migrate through TX and Mexico. BREEDING: Moist decid-

uous, coniferous, or mixed woodlands in north; hardwood bottomlands along rivers and swamps. Almost always associated with epiphytic growth. MIGRATION: Arrives widely in southern U.S. late Mar.–early Apr., in northeastern U.S. in mid-May. Rare over much of the West. In fall, it departs breeding grounds in Aug., with migration peaking Sept.–mid-Oct. Rare in West (scarcer than spring). WINTER: In a wide variety of habitats, preferring undisturbed areas to disturbed areas. In Caribbean, most of Mexico south to El Salvador. Rare from Nicaragua to Panama. Casual in LA, NM, and SC, and a few in south TX and CA. VAGRANT: Casual or accidental in AK (sight rec. on Middleton I.), Greenland, Iceland, U.K. (more than 14 recs.), and France.

Population Due to habitat requirements, populations are locally variable. Long-term trends are stable, but recent shorter-term trends show declines.

TROPICAL PARULA *Parula pitiayumi*

This close relative of the Northern Parula—with which it is sometimes considered conspecific—only reaches North America in south Texas. From April to May, the Tropical Parula lays 2 to 5 eggs in a mass of *Tillandsia* on the outer branches of trees at low to moderate heights. Polytypic (14 ssp.). L 4.5" (11 cm)

Identification Black upper mandible, yellow lower mandible. SPRING MALE: Bright blue-gray upperparts, including head, with greenish upper back; 2 broad white wing bars, small black face mask. Yellow throat and belly, orange-yellow breast, white undertail coverts. Large square white spots on outer tail feathers. SPRING FEMALE: Similar to male, but duller above. The black face mask is lacking or

much duller; the breast shows little or no orange. IMMATURE: Similar to spring female, but more greenish above and duller yellow below.

Geographic Variation The east Mexican subspecies *(nigrilora)* breeds north to south Texas. The west Mexican subspecies *(pulchra)* is the probable vagrant to Arizona. It differs from the eastern subspecies by its larger size, longer tail, more white on greater wing covert tips, and more cinnamon on flanks. South American subspecies differ more subtly.

Similar Species The Northern Parula shows a broken white eye ring, and the blue-gray coloring extends to the sides of the throat. It has a white belly and less black on the face (lores only). Males show a breast band of black and

chestnut. The Tropical Parula may hybridize with the Northern Parula.

Voice CALL: A thin slurred *chip,* similar to the Northern Parula's call note.

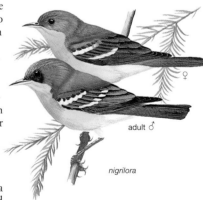

♀

adult ♂

nigrilora

SONG: The primary song is a rising trill that ends abruptly with a separate buzzy, downslurred terminal note. This song is unlike that of the Northern Parula's eastern populations, but it is similar to the song of the Northern Parula's western populations. The alternate song is quite variable and more complex, but it always has a buzzy quality.

Status & Distribution Uncommon in south TX, where it is partially migratory. BREEDING: In N.A., mainly in live-oak woodlands with abundant epiphytes, especially Spanish moss. MIGRATION: In spring, they arrive in south TX in mid-Mar. In fall, they depart south TX by Sept. WINTER: A few overwinter in the southern part of the breeding range (south TX). Some postbreeding dispersal to the north and east happens in fall and winter. Winter range of TX breeding birds uncertain. VAGRANT: West and central TX, southeastern AZ, MS, CO, and Baja California.

Population The southern Texas population declined significantly after a devastating freeze in the winter of 1951. Habitat destruction may have hindered the Tropical Parula's recovery. The species is common in most of its neotropical range.

Genus *Dendroica*

Dendroica is the largest and most diverse genus in the Parulidae family. It comprises 29 species: 21 in North America and 8 in the Caribbean. Most species show wing bars, white tail spots, streaking on the flanks, and patterning around the eyes. Most forage for insects on outer branches in the tops of trees or, less often, in low shrubbery. Their bills are not as pointed as those found on birds in the genus *Vermivora*, and generally their bills are not decurved. Most species lack obvious rictal bristles. Many species have distinctive songs, but these songs have notable individual variation.

CHESTNUT-SIDED WARBLER *Dendroica pensylvanica*

breeding adult ♀

breeding adult ♂

immature ♀

Commonly seen foraging low in small trees and shrubs with drooped wings and cocked tail, the Chestnut-sided Warbler lays 3 to 5 eggs in a nest among the shrubby understory, near the ground, between May and July. Monotypic. L 5" (13 cm)

Identification SPRING MALE: Bright yellow crown; black lores, eye line, and whisker; white cheek and underparts; extensive chestnut on sides. Wings with 2 pale yellow wing bars. SPRING FEMALE: Similar to male, with duller and less extensive crown, duller upperparts, less black on face, and less chestnut on sides. FALL ADULT: Distinctive; very different from spring adult. Bright lime green upperparts. Pale grayish cheek, throat, and upper breast. Whitish underparts. Conspicuous white eye ring. Less chestnut on sides than in the spring plumage. IMMATURE: Similar to fall adult, but all females and some males completely lack chestnut on sides.

Similar Species Fall adult and immature Chestnut-sided Warblers superficially resemble the Bay-breasted Warbler and the Blackpoll Warbler, but neither of these show bright green upperparts or a distinct white eye ring.

Voice CALL: A loud, sweet *chip,* like the Yellow Warbler's call note, but not in a series. FLIGHT CALL: A very burry, slightly musical *breeet.* SONG: The primary song is similar in quality to the Yellow Warbler's, but its phrasing is different, with variations similar to *please, please, pleased to meetcha.* The alternate song is rather nondescript and is more similar the to Yellow Warbler's song and to some songs of the American Redstart, with variations similar to *wee-weewee-wee-chi-tee-wee.*

Status & Distribution Fairly common breeder in early successional second growth. Medium-distance migrant to C.A. BREEDING: Northern hardwood and mixed woodland. MIGRATION: In spring, arrives in southern U.S. in early Apr. and in MN by mid-May. Common migrant along western Gulf Coast, rare and irregular in Caribbean. In fall, departs breeding grounds in Aug.; more easterly migration continues without a clear peak through Sept. and occasionally through mid-Oct. WINTER: Southern Mexico through Panama; most numerous in Costa Rica in a variety of forested and second-growth habitats. VAGRANT: All states (except HI) and all Canadian provinces except YK, NT, and NU. Rare in the West; has wintered in AZ and CA. Casual in northern S.A. Accidental in Greenland and Scotland.

Population The Chestnut-sided Warbler has benefitted from deforestation, which has opened up breeding habitat. Population declines since the 1960s are possibly related to urbanization as well as to reforestation and maturation of habitat.

YELLOW WARBLER *Dendroica petechia*

This very familiar and widespread warbler is often associated with willows. It builds its nest in an upright fork of a bush, sapling, or tree and lays 4 to 5 eggs (May–June). When the nest is parasitized by Brown-headed Cowbird, the Yellow Warbler is known to build a new nest on top of the old one. Polytypic (approx. 43 ssp.). L 5" (13 cm) **Identification** The only Wood-Warbler with yellow tail spots. Black bill. SPRING MALE: Entirely yellow, brightest on crown, face, and underparts; olive-yellow on nape, back, rump, and uppertail coverts. Forehead and crown sometimes tinged with chestnut. Conspicuous black eye on yellow face. Dusky wing feathers broadly edged with yellow. Broad chestnut streaks on breast and sides. SPRING FEMALE: Similar to male, but duller yellow on head and underparts. Breast streaking indistinct or absent. FALL ADULT: Similar to spring adult, but very slightly duller with less conspicuous streaking on breast and sides. IMMATURE: Similar to adult female, but duller and generally lacking chestnut breast streaks; its crown and face are more olive-yellow, as on the back. Sometimes very dull and grayish overall.

Geographic Variation The dozens of subspecies are often arranged into 3 main groups based on plumage characteristics and geographic distribution: the "Northern" *(aestiva),* "Golden" *(petechia),* and "Mangrove" *(erithachorides)* groups. The "Northern" group consists of 9 subspecies breeding across N.A.; they tend to be darker in the north and paler in the south; the southwestern subspecies *(sonorana)* is the most distinctive, showing minimal chestnut breast streaking. The "Golden" group

adult ♂
"Mangrove" *oraria*

adult ♂
"Golden" *gundlachi*

adult ♂
sonorana

immature
rubiginosa

immature
gundlachi

immature
aestiva

adult ♂

aestiva

♀

consists of 18 subspecies, mostly in the Caribbean. They are represented by a single subspecies *(gundlachi)* in N.A., which breeds in mangroves in south Florida and Cuba; it shows an extensively olive crown and shorter wings. The "Mangrove" group (16 ssp. found coastally from Mexico to Galápagos) is represented by a single subspecies *(oraria),* of which a small population has recently been found breeding in coastal southern Texas. This is the most easily identified of all the groups, for all the subspecies except *aureola* (from Galápagos) show an extensively chestnut head and throat.
Similar Species Generally distinctive, especially if the diagnostic yellow tail spots are seen. Duller immatures of northwestern *(rubiginosa),* Alaskan *(banksi),* and

south Florida *(gundlachi)* subspecies can be very grayish yellow, and they have occurred where confusion with the Orange-crowned, Chestnut-sided, Hooded, or Wilson's Warblers is possible. The Yellow Warbler can be recognized by its plain, unmarked face with a narrow yellow eye ring and by its yellow tail spots.
Voice CALL: A husky, downslurred *tchip* or a thinner *tsip.* FLIGHT CALL: A buzzy *zeet.* SONG: Primary song somewhat variable between individuals, usually most similar to *sweet sweet sweet sweeter than sweet.* Alternate songs are longer and more complex, lacking the accented upslurred or downslurred ending; sometimes similar to songs of the Chestnut-sided Warbler or the American Redstart.
Status & Distribution Common in second-growth and shrubby areas; a long-distance migrant to C.A., S.A., and southern Caribbean. BREEDING: Wet deciduous thickets and early successional habitats, usually those dominated by willows. MIGRATION: In East, mostly circum-Gulf or along western Gulf, arriving in southern U.S. by mid-Apr. and in Great Lakes in late Apr.–early May. In West, variable depending on subspecies, but generally by late Mar. in southern AZ, late Apr. in OR and WA, and late May in AK. In East, one of the earliest departing warblers in fall, with birds leaving the Great Lakes beginning in mid-July and rarely later than mid-Sept. Small numbers along the Gulf Coast into mid-Oct. Later in West, beginning in late July, peaking in late Aug. and early Sept., and extending into mid-Oct. WINTER: A variety of wooded and scrubby habitats from northern Mexico to northern S.A. to central Peru and northern Brazil. Rare in southern CA. VAGRANT: Accidental in fall in Europe: recorded from Greenland (2 recs.), Iceland, and Britain (4 recs.).
Population Widespread and common, population appears stable.

CAPE MAY WARBLER *Dendroica tigrina*

The Cape May is one of the most aggressive wood-warblers. Tiger-striped and chestnut-cheeked spring males make identification simple as they forage in the treetops, but fall birds, especially drab immature females, can be challenging. Their nests can be found near the top of a spruce or fir near the trunk, with 4 to 9 eggs (June). Monotypic. L 5" (13 cm)

Identification The slightly decurved bill is the most finely pointed in the genus (resembling *Vermivora*). Short tail. In all plumages, shows pale patch on side of neck behind darker ear coverts; indistinct in immatures. SPRING MALE: Yellow head sides with chestnut cheek patch, narrow black eye line. Olive crown and back with heavy black streaking. Faintly streaked yellowish rump. Yellow underparts with extensive black streaking on throat, breast, belly, and sides; whitish undertail coverts. Broad white wing bars, forming a nearly solid wing panel. SPRING FEMALE: Similar to male, but duller with paler yellow on face and underparts; lacks chestnut cheek patch; less boldly streaked; 2 narrow white wing bars. FALL ADULT: Male shows less chestnut in cheeks; duller crown and back. Female resembles spring female, but duller, with less olive upperparts and less distinct streaking. IMMATURE: Male similar to fall adult female, lacking chestnut in cheeks but with more white in wing. Female streaked above and below; very dull grayish with yellow on face; underparts very pale or absent.

Similar Species Immature female is similar to the "Myrtle" Yellow-rumped and Palm Warblers, which are larger and browner above, with heavier bills and longer tails; they lack the yellowish patch on sides of neck. The dull "Myrtle" has a contrasting bright yellow rump and lacks the eye line. The tail-pumping Palm has less streaking below and yellow undertail coverts.

Voice CALL: A high, sharp *tsip*. FLIGHT CALL: A soft buzzy *zeet*. SONG: Primary song a high-pitched penetrating *seet-seet-seet-seet-seet*. Alternate song lower pitched with several 2-syllable notes: *see-*

breeding adult ♀

breeding adult ♂

immature ♀

immature ♂

tee seetee seetee seetee seetee; similar to the Bay-breasted Warbler's.

Status & Distribution Fairly common boreal forest breeder. Long-distance migrant to Caribbean. BREEDING: Boreal coniferous forest and bogs with spruce and balsam fir. Favors areas with spruce budworm infestations. MIGRATION: In spring, more westerly route. Rare on western Gulf Coast. Arrives on FL coast in late Mar., peaks in late Apr. In Midwest, where more common than in the East, arrives early May, peaks in mid-May. In fall, more easterly route. Begins departing breeding areas in Aug. Peaks in Great Lakes and Northeast in mid-Sept., mid-Atlantic in late Sept., FL in late Sept.–mid-Oct. WINTER: In a variety of habitats, mainly in Caribbean, where it feeds substantially on nectar using its specialized semitubular tongue. Rare stragglers linger into Dec. and Jan. in eastern U.S. VAGRANT: To West, mostly late Sept.–early Oct. In CA, 200+ recs. Also recorded in OR, WA, and AK; 1 rec. from Scotland (June).

Population Variable depending on spruce budworm outbreaks. Little data on how spraying to control this insect affects breeding numbers.

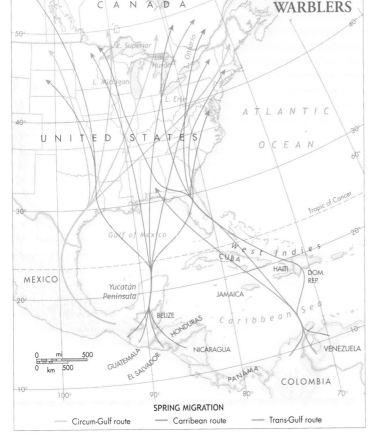

EASTERN WARBLERS

SPRING MIGRATION

— Circum-Gulf route   — Carribean route   — Trans-Gulf route

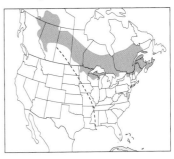

MAGNOLIA WARBLER *Dendroica magnolia*

Easily identified in all plumages by its unique black-and-white tail pattern, this boldly patterned warbler is very common. It nests low in dense conifer in June and lays 3 to 5 eggs. Monotypic. L 5" (13 cm)

Identification SPRING MALE: Gray crown with black mask and broad white line behind eye; black back and uppertail coverts; yellow rump. Yellow underparts with broad black streaks on breast and sides. White belly and undertail coverts. Broad white wing bars usually merged into a single patch. Black tail with broad white band across the middle. SPRING FEMALE: Variable; duller than male, with narrower wing bars and breast streaks, grayish mask, some greenish on back, less white in tail. FALL ADULT: Narrow white eye ring on grayish cheek. Male lacks black on head, shows greenish and black on back, has narrower wing bars and breast streaks; black uppertail coverts narrowly edged grayish. Female duller, with more greenish on back, less breast streaking, narrower wing bars. Uppertail coverts broadly edged grayish. IMMATURE: Similar to fall adult female, but duller, sometimes nearly lacking streaks on breast and sides (esp. female). Green back sometimes with narrow black streaks.

Similar Species Immature Prairie and Kirtland's Warblers are superficially similar, but the Magnolia shows a unique tail pattern and complete white eye ring on gray face, and it does not wag its tail. In particular, some first-spring female Magnolias are frequently confused with Kirtland's Warblers, but note their complete white eye ring.

Voice CALL: A unique nasal *enk,* most often heard in fall migration and on wintering grounds. Occasionally a subdued, high-pitched *chip.* FLIGHT CALL: A high, buzzy *zee.* SONG: Primary song is a variable short, musical *weeta weeta wit-chew,* accented on the final notes. Alternate song is an unaccented *sing sweet.*

Status & Distribution Fairly common to common breeding bird; very common in fall migration. Mainly a trans-Gulf migrant. BREEDING: Dense young coniferous or mixed woodland, usually fairly low to ground. MIGRATION: In spring, arrives on Gulf Coast in early Apr., peaks in northern U.S. in late May, arrives on breeding grounds in late May–early June. In fall, departs

1st spring ♀

breeding adult ♂

immature ♀

fall adult ♂

breeding grounds mid-Aug., peaks through Sept., and lingers as late as late Oct. (sometimes into Dec. and Jan. in LA and FL). WINTER: Shrubby second growth, wooded, and agricultural areas in Caribbean and from southern Mexico to Costa Rica. VAGRANT: Rare spring and fall migrant to Pacific states. Accidental in Barbados, Trinidad, Tobago, Venezuela, northern Colombia; 1 rec. from UK.

Population Stable or slightly increasing. Uses second growth. Parasitism by the Brown-headed Cowbird may be an increasing problem.

YELLOW-RUMPED WARBLER *Dendroica coronata*

"Myrtle Warbler"

breeding ♀

breeding ♂

fall ♀

These are probably the best known and most frequently encountered wood-warblers. Although variable, all Yellow-rumped Warblers possess a bright yellow rump, which is shared with only 2 other species. The Yellow-rumped's unique ability to digest the waxes in bayberries allows it to winter farther north than other warblers. Built in June on the fork of a horizontal conifer branch near the trunk at low to moderate height, the Yellow-rumped Warbler's nest contains 3 to 6 eggs. Polytypic (6 ssp.). L 5.3" (13 cm)

Identification SPRING MALE: Crown and back blue-gray streaked with black. Yellow crown patch, distinct rump patch, and patches at sides of breast. White or yellow throat. Black streaks on upper breast and side. White wing bars. White spots in outer tail feathers. SPRING FEMALE: Similar to male, but brownish above with smaller tail spots. FALL ADULT: Similar to spring adult, but generally browner above in both sexes with less black on breast. IMMATURE: Similar to spring female; some immature females very dull with indistinct streaking and much reduced yellow on sides of breast.

Geographic Variation Six subspecies in 2 groups that were formerly considered full species: "Myrtle" and "Audubon's." The "Myrtle" Warbler (nominate *coronata* over most of range and *hooveri* in Northwest) shows a white throat, black lores and ear coverts, a white line above lores and eye, 2 distinct white wing bars, a broken white eye ring, and large white spots on the outer 3 tail feathers. The

"Audubon's" Warbler (*auduboni* over most of range, similar *memorabilis* of the Rockies and Great Basin, *nigrifrons* of northwestern Mexico, and *goldmani* of Chiapas and Guatemala) shows a yellow throat, bluish gray sides of the head (inc. ear coverts), 2 broad white wing bars often forming a distinct patch, a broken white eye ring, and white spots

"Audubon's Warbler"

nwest breeding ♂

fall ♀

breeding ♂

on the outer 4 or 5 tail feathers. Some birds breeding in the southwestern mountains are intermediate between *auduboni* and darker-faced *nigrifrons*. Subspecific identification is more challenging in winter (see sidebar below).

Similar Species Compare to the Magnolia and Cape May Warblers, which have yellow rumps but also yellow underparts. The Palm Warbler shows yellow undertail coverts.

Voice CALL: The "Myrtle" gives a loud, husky, flat *chek;* the "Audubon's" gives a loud and richer *chep.* FLIGHT CALL: A high, clear *sip.* SONG: A variable, loosely structured trill, sometimes with 2 parts—the first higher pitched and the second lower and trailing off at the end: *chee chee chee chee wee wee wee we.* Louder and richer on breeding grounds than in migration. The "Audubon's" song is similar, but it is simpler and weaker.

Status & Distribution Common breeder in coniferous woodlands; very common short- to medium-distance migrant to central U.S. south to Caribbean and central Panama. BREEDING: Northern boreal and mixed forest, and montane conif-

erous woodland. MIGRATION: In spring, generally arrives earlier than other warblers, returning to northern breeding areas by late Apr. In fall, generally migrates later than other warblers, peaking in northern portions of nonbreeding range in late Sept.–mid-Oct. WINTER: A wide variety of habitats from central U.S. south through Caribbean to western Panama. VAGRANT: The "Audubon's" Warbler is casual in eastern North America. The "Myrtle" Warbler is casual or accidental to Attu I. (AK), Baffin I., Greenland, Iceland (7 recs.), Ireland, Great Britain (22 recs.), Madeira, the European mainland, and eastern Siberia (1 rec.).

Population Breeding and wintering populations appear stable.

Separating "Myrtle" and "Audubon's" in Winter

In winter, adult and immature birds of the 2 groups that compose the Yellow-rumped Warbler—the "Myrtle" and the "Audubon's" Warblers—become duller and more difficult to distinguish. In the West, the "Myrtle" and the "Audubon's" winter together in many areas, while in the East, the "Audubon's" is a possibility almost anywhere as a vagrant. The following points will help identify these subspecies groups in winter:

1. Overall color. The "Myrtle" is browner than the "Audubon's."

2. Throat color. The "Myrtle" always shows a whitish throat, whereas the "Audubon's" often shows a pale yellow throat. In a few dull immature female "Audubon's," however, the throat is sometimes pale buff or whitish.

3. Throat pattern. In the "Myrtle," the whitish throat extends part way around the rear of the ear coverts in a small curved point. In the "Audubon's," the yellowish or pale buff throat does not extend behind the ear coverts, and the line between the cheek and the throat is relatively straight.

4. Face pattern. The "Myrtle" shows darker ear

"Audubon's Warbler" (CO, Oct.)

coverts, a faint white supercilium, and a small white crescent below the eye. The "Audubon's" more uniform brown head shows a broken white eye ring (eye crescents).

5. Tail spots. This characteristic can also be useful in separating these birds. The "Myrtle" will usually show white spots on only the outer 2 or 3 tail feathers, with the outer being distinctly larger than the inner. The "Audubon's," however, will show more uniformly sized white spots on the outer 4 or 5 tail feathers.

6. Call notes. The "Myrtle" gives a flatter, softer *chek* or *chup,* and the "Audubon's" gives a richer *chep* or *chip.*

The photograph above shows a dull brownish "Audubon's" in the fall with very little yellow visible; the individual is probably an immature female. Although the throat appears whitish at first glance (perhaps suggesting "Myrtle"), the color is really pale buff and, importantly, it does not curl up behind the ear coverts. The face pattern is actually the best clue to this bird's identity. Note the broken eye ring and the lack of a whitish supercilium, both good field marks for the "Audubon's." ∎

BLACK-THROATED BLUE WARBLER *Dendroica caerulescens*

♀

♂

Appalachians ♂
cairnsi

The sexes of this species are strikingly different in plumage and easy to identify. Females lay 2 to 5 eggs in a June-built nest found in a fork of low shrub or sapling. Polytypic. L 5.3" (13 cm)

Identification ADULT MALE: Dark blue crown, back, shoulders. Black face, throat, flanks. White underparts. Large white wing patch at base of primaries. ADULT FEMALE: Greenish gray upperparts, buffy underparts. Dusky ear coverts, whitish stripe above the eye, narrow white crescent below eye. Small white wing spot at base of primaries. IMMATURE: Similar to adult; pale spot at base of primaries smaller

or absent. Male green-tinged above; black throat and breast feathers tipped with grayish white. Female duller above, buffy yellow below; eye stripe indistinct, yellowish.

Geographic Variation Males of the southern Appalachians *cairnsi* tend to have more black streaking on upperparts. **Similar Species** The female's head pattern resembles that of female and immature Yellow-rumped ("Myrtle") Warblers, but it lacks wing bars or yellow rump. **Voice** CALL: Popping *tuk*. FLIGHT CALL: Distinctive, prolonged *tseet*. SONG: Primary song a slow series of buzzy notes, rising at the end: *zhee zhee zhee zeeee;* sometimes faster (may resemble the

Cerulean Warbler's). Alternate song shorter: *zree zree zhrurrr*.

Status & Distribution Fairly common. Migrates mainly along the eastern seaboard. Vagrant, mostly in fall, in the West. BREEDING: Large tracts of deciduous and mixed woodland. MIGRATION: Arrives in Southeast mid-Apr., peaks in Great Lakes mid-May. Departs breeding grounds mid-Aug; peaks somewhat later than other warblers (late Sept.–early Oct.) in Great Lakes; occasionally lingers to Nov. WINTER: Forested areas of Greater Antilles; some Bahamas, a few in Yucatan Peninsula, Belize. VAGRANT: Iceland (1 rec.). **Population** Stable or increasing over most of its range; declining at southern edge.

BLACK-THROATED GRAY WARBLER *Dendroica nigrescens*

This boldly patterned warbler forms a superspecies group with the Golden-cheeked, Townsend's, Black-throated Green, and Hermit Warblers, sharing call notes and long tails with extensive white in the outer tail feathers. It nests on a horizontal branch (low to moderate height) in a deciduous or coniferous tree and produces 3 to 5 eggs (May–June). Polytypic. L 5" (13 cm)

Identification ADULT MALE: Black head, throat, breast, side streaks. Broad white supercilium, malar; tiny yellow spot on lores. Gray back with black streaks, 2 white wing bars. White underparts. ADULT FEMALE: Similar to male, but grayer head, white chin, black throat

patch mixed with white. IMMATURE: Similar to adult female; male with more restricted black on upper throat and crown; female with brownish gray on upperparts, buffy white underparts (chin to tail), with narrow streaks restricted to sides. **Geographic Variation** Southern *halseii* slightly larger and paler, with more white in tail and heavier side streaks. **Similar Species** The Townsend's has a green back and yellow underparts. The spring male Blackpoll has all-white cheek. The Black-and-white has a striped back, different foraging style. Immature male Ceruleans show bluish on upperparts, yellow on breast. **Voice** CALL: A dull *tip*. FLIGHT CALL: A high, clear *see*. SONG: Primary song is a series of 2-syllable buzzy notes, the second syllable louder and higher pitched, the final note falling: *buzz see buzz see buzz see buzz see wueeo*. Alternate song is longer, more complex, lacking the downward-inflected ending.

Status & Distribution Fairly common. Short- to medium-distance migrant. BREEDING: Open mixed or coniferous

adult ♂

♀

woodland with brushy undergrowth. MIGRATION: CA arrivals peak mid- to late Apr. in south, mid-Apr.–mid-May in north. In fall, migration in OR mid-Aug.–mid-Sept., rarely late Oct. In southern CA, good movement typically occurs Oct. 14–22. WINTER: A variety of forest, scrub, and thickets in Mexico from Baja California Sur to central Oaxaca. A few in central CA. Rare in LA, southern FL, southern AZ, southern TX. VAGRANT: Casual to accidental in migration east to NS, MA, NJ; north to MT.

Population Stable or slightly increasing.

GOLDEN-CHEEKED WARBLER *Dendroica chrysoparia* (E)

adult ♀

adult ♂

immature ♀

This aptly named warbler breeds only in central Texas and lays 3 to 4 eggs in a nest near the trunk of a 20- to 30-foot-tall Ashe Juniper, about two-thirds of the way up (Mar.–Apr.). Monotypic. L 5.3" (13 cm)

Identification Clear yellow cheeks, black line from eye to bill. ADULT MALE: Bright golden yellow sides of head, black line from bill to nape. Black crown, back, chin, throat, breast, broad side streaks. White belly, undertail coverts; 2 white wing bars. ADULT FEMALE: Duller than male; duller yellow face, black eye line

narrower. Black-streaked olive-green upperparts. Chin, throat mixed with yellow. Narrower streaks on sides. IMMATURE: Male similar to adult female. Female with white chin, throat; very restricted blackish patches on sides of breast; narrower side streaks.

Similar Species Black-throated Greens lack black crown, eye line, and back. Immature females do not show dark line through eye; have less extensive yellow face, pale yellow belly and undertail coverts. The Hermit is plainer, grayer.

Voice CALL: A *tsip,* similar to the Black-throated Green's. FLIGHT CALL: A high, thin *see.* SONG: A variable, short buzzy *dzeee dzweeee dzeezy see.* Alternate song simpler: *zee zee zee zee see.*

Status & Distribution Endangered; a medium-distance migrant. BREEDING: Mature juniper-oak woodlands of central TX. MIGRATION: Arrives breeding grounds early to mid-Mar.; departs as early as late June, but typically present to early Aug., stragglers until mid-Aug. WINTER: Montane pine-oak forests from

southern Mexico to Nicaragua. VAGRANT: Casual to accidental on upper TX coast, FL, CA, and Virgin Is.

Population Estimated 4,800–16,000 pairs in 1990, generally declining prior to that time. Prime habitat is relatively unfragmented old-growth juniper-oak woodlands, which have sometimes proven contentious to protect.

BLACK-THROATED GREEN WARBLER *Dendroica virens*

♀

ture ♀

adult ♂

A familiar bird of mixed and deciduous woodlands, the Black-throated Green Warbler is often detected by its buzzy, cheery song. It usually makes its nest low to moderately high in a conifer—away from the trunk—and nurtures 3 to 5 eggs (May–June). Polytypic. L 5" (13 cm)

Identification Yellow face, plain green back, pale yellow undertail coverts. ADULT MALE: Yellow sides of head with olive-yellow auriculars; greenish olive crown, back, and rump. Black chin, throat, breast, and broad side streaks.

Two white wing bars, whitish to pale yellowish belly and undertail coverts. ADULT FEMALE: Similar to male, but chin and upper throat mottled with (or entirely) whitish or pale yellowish; narrower side streaks. IMMATURE: Belly and undertail coverts more strongly tinged with yellow. Male similar to adult female. Female with whitish chin and throat (no black); very narrow side streaks.

Geographic Variation Smaller overall size and bill length of isolated southeastern coastal subspecies *waynei* probably not detectable in the field.

Similar Species The Golden-cheeked always shows a dark line from bill through eye to dark nape. Some hybrids of the Townsend's and Hermit can resemble the Black-throated Green Warbler.

Voice CALL: A soft, flat *tsip.* FLIGHT CALL: A high, sweet *see.* SONG: Primary song is variable with a whistled, buzzy quality; the last note is the highest: *zee-zee-zee-zoo-zee.* Alternate song a variable, more deliberate *zoo zee zoo zoo zee.*

Status & Distribution Common; primarily a trans- and circum-Gulf migrant, some move through FL to Caribbean. BREEDING: A wide variety of habitats: mainly coniferous and mixed forest, but sometimes deciduous. *Waynei*

breeds in cypress swamps. MIGRATION: Arrives in Gulf states in late Mar., in Midwest by late Apr., peaking in mid-May. Departs breeding grounds as early as late July, peaking mid- to late Sept. into late Oct.; stragglers widely recorded in North into Nov. WINTER: Mature montane forests from northeastern Mexico to Panama; wide variety of habitats in Caribbean. Small numbers winter in southern FL, southern TX. Rare in northern Colombia and western Venezuela. VAGRANT: Multiple recs. for most western states, most in fall and many (300+) in CA. Casual in coastal BC, southeastern AK, and NT. Accidental in Greenland, Iceland, and Germany (specimen from 1858).

Population Numerous and relatively stable, but some local trends indicate extended, slight declines.

TOWNSEND'S WARBLER *Dendroica townsendi*

This boldly patterned warbler of the Pacific Northwest gleans insects on its breeding grounds; on its wintering grounds, it will also exploit honeydew excreted by sap-sucking insects. Its well-concealed nest, host to 3 to 5 eggs, may be found at various heights in a conifer, from May to June. Monotypic. L 5" (13 cm)

Identification Dark auriculars surrounded by yellow, yellow on breast, extensive white on outer tail feathers, 2 white wing bars. ADULT MALE: Black cheek surrounded by yellow, with small yellow crescent below eye; black crown. Olive-green back streaked black. Black chin, throat, and broad side streaks. Yellow breast and sides; white belly and undertail coverts. ADULT FEMALE: Duller than male, with olive-green crown and auriculars; yellow chin and throat with limited black; narrower side streaks. IMMATURE: Male very similar to adult female. Female much duller, with no streaking on crown and back, no black on chin and throat, very narrow side streaks. HYBRIDS: The Townsend's frequently hybridizes with the Hermit where their ranges meet in Washington and Oregon. Most hybrids closely resemble the Hermit, especially in the face, which is often entirely yellow. The crown varies from black to yellow and the breast from yellow to white; flank streaks are extensive or absent; and the back is olive green or gray. Less frequently, hybrids show the Townsend's head pattern; a green or gray back with black streaks; and a breast with little or no yellow. Hybrids in Oregon sing like the Hermit, and hybrids in Washington sing like the Townsend's.

Similar Species The Black-throated Green is superficially similar to adult females and immatures, but it lacks the dark auricular and the yellow on throat and breast. The immature female Blackburnian shows less green and more streaking on back, including pale streaks on sides of back.

Voice CALL: A high, sharp *tsik*. FLIGHT CALL: A high, thin *see*. SONG: Primary song a variable, buzzy *weazy weazy weazy dzeee*. Alternate song a buzzy *zi-zi-zi-zi-zi-zi, zwee zwee*.

Status & Distribution Fairly common in coniferous forests of the Pacific Northwest. A medium- to long-distance migrant. BREEDING: Tall coniferous and mixed woodlands, preferring mature or old-growth forest. MIGRATION: Migrants from Central America arrive in southern CA in mid-Apr, peaking late Apr.–mid-May.

adult ♀

adult ♂

immature ♀

Arrives as early as late Apr. in AK, with most arriving in May. Departs AK by early Aug., lingering into early Oct. Peaks late Aug.–early Sept. in OR; peaks mid-Aug.–late Oct. in CA. WINTER: A variety of habitats in coastal Pacific Northwest and CA. Montane forests from northwestern Mexico to Costa Rica. VAGRANT: More than 90 records from east of Great Plains, from about half of the eastern states. Casual to accidental in Bermuda, Bahamas, northern AK, western Aleutians (to Shemya I.), and other Bering Sea islands.

Population May be expanding northward in Alaska. Stable to increasing in rest of range.

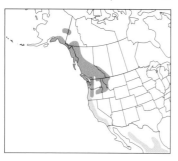

HERMIT WARBLER *Dendroica occidentalis*

immature ♀

adult ♀

adult ♂

Townsend's x Hermit hybrid adult ♂

This striking golden-headed warbler, named for its secretive behavior, is often difficult to see high in its conifer haunts. Between the bottom and middle of a tall conifer, it nests on a branch away from the trunk and produces 4 to 5 eggs between May and June. Monotypic. L 5.3" (13 cm)

Identification ADULT MALE: Yellow face, crown; black chin, throat, upper breast, lower nape. Gray back with black streaks. White underparts. Two white wing bars. Extensive white on outer tail feathers. ADULT FEMALE: Duller than male, with lower nape, small olive green throat patch, dull white to light gray sides, smaller tail spots; back without prominent streaks. IMMATURE: Male with olive on crown and ear coverts; chin and throat extensively mottled with olive green, yellow, and black. Dull whitish or grayish underparts. Female dullest, with extensive olive on crown and ear coverts; no black on back, nape, or throat; yellow face, throat, and narrow eye ring. Underparts tinged buffy.

Similar Species Female and immature Olive Warblers are similar to immature female, but show bright white patch at base of primaries and have much different voice. The Black-throated Green shows yellowish on underparts. See Townsend's for hybrids with Hermit.

Voice CALL: A flat *tip*, similar to the Black-throated Green's. FLIGHT CALL: A

high, clear *sip*. SONG: Primary song a variable *weezy weezy weezy weezy zee* (last note is highest in pitch). Alternate song is variable and more complex: *che che che che cheeo ze ze ze ze ze ze seet.* **Status & Distribution** Fairly common in mountain forests; a medium- to long-distance migrant. BREEDING: Montane coniferous forest. MIGRATION: Arrives in southern AZ and southern CA in mid-Apr., peaking late Apr.–mid-May. Departs breeding grounds early, some by mid-July, peaking mid-Aug.–early Sept., with some to mid-Oct. WINTER: Montane pine-oak and other forest from northwestern Mexico to Nicaragua. Also in live oak and coniferous woodland in coastal CA. VAGRANT: Casual to accidental central and eastern U.S. and Canada. Accidental to Panama. **Population** Stable, though competition and hybridization with the Townsend's may be reducing its range.

BLACKBURNIAN WARBLER *Dendroica fusca*

The fiery orange throat and head markings of the adult male Blackburnian Warbler are unique among wood-warblers. In June, the Blackburnian constructs a nest high in a conifer, on limbs well out from the trunk, and produces 3 to 5 eggs. Monotypic. L 5" (13 cm)

Identification In all plumages, the Blackburnian shows a dark cheek patch; a broad, pale supercilium connected to pale sides of the neck; pale stripes on sides of the back (braces). It is sometimes difficult to see. SPRING MALE: Black triangular cheek patch is surrounded by fiery orange, most conspicuous on the throat as bird is often viewed from below. Black crown with orange patch; black back with conspicuous pale yellowish stripes on each side of back (braces). Narrow black streaks on sides. Underparts pale yellow, shading to white on undertail coverts. Large white wing patch. Extensive white on outer tail feathers. SPRING FEMALE: Similar to male, but duller, with grayish cheek patch, crown, and side streaks; orange areas on head less intense and yellower; back striped brownish and olive with less prominent braces; less white in wing, forming 2 distinct wing bars. FALL ADULT: Male with duller orange coloring; its black areas are veiled with olive edges; and it has less white in wing, forming 2 wing bars. Female has yellower head markings than in spring; also has more olive upperparts. IMMATURE: The male is similar to a fall female, but with a black eye line above the grayish cheek patch; yellower throat and head markings; stronger back streaking; and blacker side streaks. The female immature has the dullest plumage, with throat and supercilium colored pale yellow to buffy and indistinct streaks on sides.

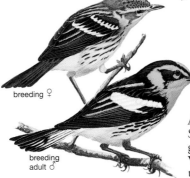

fall adult ♂

immature ♀

breeding ♀

breeding adult ♂

Similar Species An immature female Cerulean Warbler shows plainer greenish upperparts, a less conspicuous ear patch, and a shorter tail; its supercilium is not joined to the pale areas on sides of neck. Both the Bay-breasted Warbler and the Blackpoll Warbler lack pale stripes on back and show an inconspicuous supercilium. **Voice** CALL: A rich *tsip*. FLIGHT CALL: A buzzy *zzee*. SONG: The primary song is a very high-pitched, ascending series of notes, ending with an almost inaudible trill: *see-see-see-see-ti-ti-ti-siiii.* The alternate song begins at a high pitch and concludes with a lower-pitched ending: *tsee-tsee-tsiii-chi-chi.* **Status & Distribution** A common boreal forest breeder. A long-distance, mainly trans-Gulf migrant to S.A. BREEDING: Mature coniferous or mixed forests; also deciduous forests in the southern U.S. MIGRATION: In spring, it takes a more westerly route, arriving on the Gulf Coast in early Apr. and peaking in ON in mid-May. In fall, it takes a more easterly route, departing the breeding grounds early and arriving in the Great Lakes by early Aug., where it peaks in mid-Aug. It peaks in the south during Sept. and on through early Oct. Stragglers can be found into Nov. and Dec. WINTER: Most numerous in the montane forests of northern Andes, but also in Amazonia and northern S.A. A few winter in Costa Rica to Panama. VAGRANT: Recorded rarely or casually in all western states; more than 500 records from CA. Accidental in Greenland, Iceland, and U.K. **Population** Breeding populations are apparently stable, though the Appalachian breeding population is threatened by the loss of hemlock trees killed by introduced insect pests. The loss of preferred mature evergreen forests on wintering grounds is also a potential cause of declines.

YELLOW-THROATED WARBLER *Dendroica dominica*

yellow-lored
dominica ♂

white-lored
albilora ♂

The foraging behavior of this long-billed warbler, creeping along branches, is unusual among species in the genus *Dendroica*. It lays its eggs (3–5) in its nest high in canopy, often in clumps of Spanish moss or pine needles, between April and June. Polytypic. L 5.3" (13 cm)

Identification ADULT MALE: Gray forehead streaked with black; gray crown and upperparts; yellow throat and breast; black triangular ear patch, continuing along sides as bold black streaks; white supercilium, crescent below eye, patch at side of neck, belly, and undertail coverts; 2 white wing bars. ADULT FEMALE: Similar to male, but with less black on forehead and narrower side streaks. IMMATURE: Similar to adult, but with little black on forehead, brownish back and tertials, narrower side streaks, and duller black ear patch. Belly and undertail coverts washed with buff.

Geographic Variation Western subspecies *(albilora)* shows an entirely white supercilium (rarely yellow), including above the lores; more extensive black on forehead; often a small white spot at base of chin. Eastern subspecies *(dominica)* shows yellow above lores (rarely white) merging to white at front of eye; rarely shows a small white spot at base of chin. Subspecies in Florida panhandle and adjacent Alabama *(stoddardi)* with longer, narrower bill not field distinguishable from *dominica* population on Delmarva Peninsula. Endemic subspecies to Grand Bahama and Abaco in northern Bahamas *(flavescens)*, not yet recorded in North America, is distinctive and shows a noticeably longer bill with decurved culmen and straight lower mandible, little black on forehead, brownish gray upperparts, much narrower supercilium with yellow to rear of eye, much smaller white spot on side of neck, narrow streaks on whitish undertail coverts, and yellow extending to belly.

Similar Species The Grace's broad supercilium is more extensively yellow; it has much less black on cheek and face and a different foraging style. Immature male Blackburnians show streaked back and lack white in supercilium and on sides of neck. Bahaman subspecies superficially similar to the Kirtland's, which lacks white supercilium, has a different face pattern, shorter bill, and deliberate foraging style, and vigorously pumps its tail.

Voice CALL: A high, soft *chip*, similar to the Pine's, identical to the Grace's. FLIGHT CALL: A clear, high *see*. SONG: A somewhat variable series of clear, ringing, downslurred notes, rising and weaker at the end, similar to that of the Indigo Bunting or Louisiana Waterthrush: *tee-ew tee-ew tew tew tew tew wi*. Lacks an alternate song.

Status & Distribution Common woodland species, partial migrant. BREEDING: In South prefers cypress swamps and live-oak stands, especially those with large amounts of Spanish moss. In North, prefers bottomland with large sycamores or dry upland pine-oak forests. Pine woodlands in Bahamas. MIGRATION: Spring migration very early. Migrants reach FL by late Feb., southern breeding grounds by mid-Mar., and northern breeding grounds mid- to late Apr. Spring overshoots seen Great Lakes *(albilora)* and to NY and CT *(dominica?)*. Departs breeding grounds mid-Aug.–late Sept. in northernmost areas. A few remain well north into Dec. and Jan. WINTER: Swamps and more open areas in southeastern U.S. and semiopen woodlands, city parks, and gardens in Caribbean and northeastern Mexico to Costa Rica. VAGRANT: Rare in spring migration north of breeding range; rare in spring and fall in western states.

Population Stable, with breeding range expanding northward. In northwestern Florida, subspecies *stoddardi* is rare and declining.

PINE WARBLER *Dendroica pinus*

One of the most appropriately named warblers (it is closely tied to pines), the Pine has a drab plumage that makes identification challenging away from breeding areas. It is the only wood-warbler known to regularly feed on seeds, mainly in fall and winter. Between April and June, it builds a nest high in a pine on a horizontal limb, often at the end of a branch, and lays 3 to 5 eggs. Polytypic (4 ssp.; *pinus* and *florida,* not field identifiable, in N.A.). L 5.3" (13 cm)

Identification ADULT MALE: Olive green upperparts. Yellow throat, breast, and belly, extending to rear of olive cheeks; white lower belly and undertail coverts. Dull olive to blackish indistinct streaks on sides of breast. Indistinct broken yellow eye ring and supercilium. Two white wing bars; large white tail spots on outer tail feathers. ADULT FEMALE: Similar to male, but paler yellow, with streaks on sides, an eye ring, very indistinct supercilium, smaller tail spots. IMMATURE: Duller than adult; female often quite brownish and buffy with little or no olive or yellow.

Similar Species The Yellow-throated Vireo is larger and more sluggish and

adult ♀

adult ♂

has a thicker hooked bill, conspicuous yellow spectacles, and unstreaked underparts. In fall, Bay-breasteds and Blackpolls are similar. The Pine does not have streaking on upperparts, yellow on throat extending behind auriculars, longer tail extending well beyond undertail coverts, or shorter primary projection beyond tertials, and its wing bars contrast less with wings.

Voice CALL: A slurred *tsup*, similar to the Yellow-throated's and the Grace's. FLIGHT CALL: A slightly buzzy *zeet*.

SONG: A musical trill, most similar to the Chipping Sparrow's or the Dark-eyed Junco's but usually softer, more musical, and shorter, varying in speed. Occasionally 2-parted songs, with the second part being faster and higher pitched. Also similar to the Worm-eating's and Orange-crowned's.

Status & Distribution Common, occurring in N.A. year-round, with northern populations migratory (2 sedentary ssp. resident in Caribbean). BREEDING: A broad range of pine habitats. MIGRATION: One of the earliest spring migrant warblers in many areas: begins northward movement in late Feb., arriving by early Apr. in southern Great Lakes, mid-Apr. in New England, and late Apr.–early May in northernmost breeding areas. One of the latest fall migrant warblers: departs northernmost breeding areas as early as late Aug. but peaks late Sept.–mid-Oct., rarely into Nov. and with stragglers into Dec. and Jan. WINTER: Pine forests in southeastern

immature ♀

immature ♂

U.S., rarely to northern Caribbean. Sometimes forages on ground in fields and pastures near forest edges. VAGRANT: Rare, mainly in fall, in Atlantic Canada. Rare or casual in northern Great Plains and Prairie Provinces. Very rare in West, with most records (60+) from coastal southern CA in fall and winter. Casual in southern Caribbean in winter, accidental in fall in Greenland.

Population Stable or increasing.

GRACE'S WARBLER *Dendroica graciae*

This short-billed montane pine specialist of the Southwest is one of the least-known North American passerines. In the upper half of a conifer, well away from the trunk, it makes a nest for its 3 to 4 eggs between May and June. Polytypic. L 5" (13 cm)

Identification ADULT MALE: Gray upperparts with black streaks on crown and back. Yellow throat and breast, white belly and undertail coverts. Bold black

streaks on sides of breast and belly, yellow supercilium becoming white behind eye, small yellow crescent below eye, black lores and moustachial area. Two white wing bars, large white spots on outer tail feathers. ADULT FEMALE: Similar to male, but duller, with brownish gray back; finer streaks on crown, back, and sides; gray lores and moustachial area. IMMATURE: Male similar to adult female, with upperparts unstreaked and more brownish, duller yellow underparts, little black on crown and face, finer streaks on sides, buff wash on flanks. Female duller than immature male, lacking black on crown and face; more buff on flanks and belly.

Geographic Variation Slight and clinal, with back color brownest in northernmost subspecies, *graciae* (breeding in N.A.), to more blue-gray in 3 Central American subspecies; yellow of throat paler in north and deep orange-yellow in south.

Similar Species The Yellow-throated is larger with a bolder face pattern and different foraging style. The "Audubon's" Yellow-rumped shows yellow rump and dark cheek patch.

Voice CALL: A soft, slurred *chip*, iden-

tical to the Yellow-throated's. FLIGHT CALL: A very high, thin *sip*. SONG: An accelerating series of *chip* notes, most often 2-parted: *chew chew chew chew chew chew chee chee chee chee;* similar to the Virginia's and the "Audubon's" Yellow-rumped's.

Status & Distribution Uncommon to fairly common, short-distance migrant. BREEDING: Mainly montane open, parklike forests of tall pines. MIGRATION: Arrives on breeding grounds Apr.–early May. Departs breeding grounds as late as late Sept. WINTER: Pine forest to pine-oak woodland, from western Mexico to Nicaragua. VAGRANT: Casual on the central and especially southern CA coast (35 recs.). One recent record from IL is the only record from eastern N.A.

Population Range is increasing northward, but numbers may have declined in some areas.

KIRTLAND'S WARBLER *Dendroica kirtlandii (E)*

The rarest warbler in North America, the large Kirtland's forages lower than most warblers and persistently pumps its tail when foraging. Its nest can be found on the ground under the lowest branches of jack pines, where it mingles with ground vegetation; here it will deposit 3 to 6 eggs in June. Monotypic. L 5.8" (15 cm)

Identification ADULT MALE: Bluish gray upperparts, with black lores and black below eye; fine black streaks on crown, bolder on back. Yellow underparts with bold black streaks on sides, white undertail coverts. Broken whitish eye ring, indistinct wing bars. ADULT FEMALE: Similar to male, but duller, no black on face, less bold streaks on sides. Upperparts tinged brownish gray. IMMATURE: Male similar to adult female. Female more brownish above, with very indistinct side streaks and wing bars, less prominent back streaks, and less distinct broken eye ring.

Similar Species Adult male Canadas show complete eye ring, lack streaks on back, and have no wing bars or tail

spots. Adult female Magnolias are smaller; show green on back, yellow rump, more prominent wing bars, white band across middle of tail; and do not pump tail. The smaller Prairie wags its tail but has a yellow face pattern.

Voice CALL: A low, forceful *chip.* FLIGHT CALL: A thin, high *zeet.* SONG: A loud, deliberate, rich, throaty *chew chew chee chee wee wee,* suggesting the Northern Waterthrush.

Status & Distribution Endangered, but locally fairly common within its limited range and breeding habitat. Rarely observed in migration or on wintering grounds. May make entire migration in 1 "hop." BREEDING: Extensive, dense stands of young jack pine (7–15 yrs. old) on sandy soil in central MI. MIGRATION: Departure from winter grounds unknown, but possibly late Apr. or early May. Migrants rarely noted along route to breeding grounds, but a few reported typically in early to mid-May. Arrives on breeding grounds around May 12 (earliest May 3). Some leave as early as Aug., some linger as late as early Oct. Fewer reports of fall migrants along route than in spring. WINTER: Dense scrubby undergrowth mainly in central Bahamas; rarely observed. Recently found in moderate numbers on Eleuthera.

Population The extensive management of breeding habitat (through burning

or clear-cuts and replanting of jack pines, as well as removal of parasitic Brown-headed Cowbirds) has allowed the population to increase from a low of 167 singing males in 1974 and 1987 to more than 1,300 singing males (approx. 2,600 individuals) in 2003 and 2004. In addition to continually removing cowbirds, managing larger tracts of breeding habitat has proven to be more effective in increasing population than managing smaller tracts.

PRAIRIE WARBLER *Dendroica discolor*

This small tail-wagging warbler, often found in low scrub, has a distinctive, buzzy song. It builds its nest low to moderately high in the middle of a

small tree clump (over water in coastal FL) and lays 3 to 5 eggs (Apr.–June). Polytypic. L 4.8" (12 cm)

Identification Distinctive facial pattern: yellow supercilium, dark line through eye, broad pale crescent below eye, dark lower border to the cheek. Wags tail. ADULT MALE: Black and yellow face pattern; olive upperparts, usually with reddish spots on back; yellow underparts, paler on undertail coverts; bold black streaks on sides; distinct black spot on side of lower throat; yellowish wing bars. ADULT FEMALE: Similar to male, but dark olive and yellow face pattern, sometimes a little black on lower cheek. Less

distinct reddish spots on back and black streaks on sides. IMMATURE: Duller than adult. Male with very limited or no black on face, narrow side streaks. Female dullest, with indistinct face pattern showing no black, and yellow replaced by pale whitish, very indistinct side streaks.

Geographic Variation Nominate (most of range) and sedentary *paludicola* (coastal mangroves of FL) not field-separable. **Similar Species** The Pine is larger, shows no black on head or reddish on back, does not wag tail as habitually as the Prairie. The immature Magnolia shows yellow rump, white band across center of tail, complete white eye ring.

Voice CALL: A smacking *tsip,* or *tchick,* similar to the Palm's. FLIGHT CALL: A thin *seep.* SONG: Primary song a rapid or slower series of buzzy notes evenly ascending in pitch: *zee zee zee zee zee zee zee zee zee*. Alternate songs are more varied.

Status & Distribution Fairly common,

declining in some areas. Nominate is a medium-distance migrant to Caribbean. BREEDING: Not in prairie. Nominate in a variety of shrubby old fields, dunes, pine barrens, early successional habitats. MIGRATION: Arrives on Gulf Coast of FL mid-Mar, peaks in Apr.; arrives early to mid-May in Great Lakes. In fall, reaches FL and Bahamas mid- to late July; numbers reported on Gulf Coast by late July. Northern breeders depart early Aug.–early Oct., stragglers through Dec. WINTER: Second growth and forest edge, mangroves, gardens, other open habitats mainly in Caribbean and most of FL, rarely to coastal TX and NC. A few from coastal Yuca-

immature ♀

tan to El Salvador. VAGRANT: Rare but regular to CA in fall, casual to accidental through much of West in spring and fall (inc. southeastern AK). Rare to Atlantic Canada in fall.

Population Declining in parts of breeding range.

PALM WARBLER *Dendroica palmarum*

The most terrestrial *Dendroica*, the Palm wags its tail vigorously. Found in palms only in some areas of its winter range, it nests in sphagnum on the ground under a short conifer (4–5 eggs, May–June). Polytypic. L 5.5" (14 cm)

Identification SPRING MALE: Chestnut crown, olive-tinged and lightly streaked grayish brown back, yellow-olive rump. Yellow supercilium and submoustachial stripe, distinct dark eye line, narrow crescent below eye whitish. Bright yellow throat and undertail coverts contrast with whitish belly; thin dark chestnut malar streak and narrow streaks on breast and sides. SPRING FEMALE: Very similar to male; often not distinguishable. Tends to have less chestnut in crown, duller and paler yellow areas. FALL ADULT: Chestnut in crown reduced or lacking; dull whitish supercilium, submoustachial, and throat; less distinct breast and side streaks. Bright yellow undertail coverts (typically the only yellow at this season). IMMATURE: Very similar, often indistinguishable from adult. More pointed tail feathers.

Geographic Variation The more widespread "Western" Palm (nominate, described above) breeds from the Hud-

son Bay region west. The slightly larger "Yellow" Palm *(hypochrysea)* breeds east through Atlantic Canada and northern New England and shows entirely yellow underparts (chin to undertail coverts) with little or no contrast; yellowish narrow crescent below eye; yellow-green tinged upperparts; and broader, brighter chestnut breast and side streaks. The "Yellow" is duller in fall but still distinguishable; a "Western" can show yellow on belly, but always with contrastingly brighter undertail coverts and whitish supercilium. Intermediates can occur.

Similar Species Prairie and Kirtland's share tail-wagging habit but lack contrasting bright yellow undertail coverts. Similarly, female Cape May and fall Yellow-rumped lack bright yellow undertail coverts and do not wag their tails.

Voice CALL: A distinct, sharp *chick*. FLIGHT CALL: A high, light *seet* or *see-seet*. SONG: A somewhat buzzy or gravelly series of notes, uttered somewhat unenthusiastically and often more forcefully in the middle: *zwee zwee zwee zwee zwee zwee zwee.*

Status & Distribution Common, more easily observed in winter. BREEDING: Bogs in open coniferous boreal forest. MIGRA-

TION: In spring, earlier than most other wood-warblers: the "Western" migrates through Mississippi Valley to Canada, typically arrives in Upper Midwest mid- to late Apr., peaking in late Apr.–early May; the "Yellow" migrates northeast along the Atlantic coast, arrives by mid-Apr (NS) to early May (NF). In fall, later than most other wood-warblers: the "Western" takes a more easterly route than in spring, mainly arriving mid-Sept., peaking late Sept.–early Oct. through much of the East; the "Yellow" is rare west of the Appalachians, migrating slightly later. WINTER: A variety of woodland, second-growth, thickets, and open areas. The "Yellow" primarily along Gulf Coast (LA to FL); nominate throughout southeast (TX to NC, rarely farther north), Caribbean, and eastern coastal Mexico to Honduras. VAGRANT: Recorded in almost every western state and province. Rare annually in fall to coastal CA, sometimes in exceptional numbers. Casual in Costa Rica, Panama, northwestern Colombia, western Venezuela. One England rec.: a bird found dead on shoreline (1976).

Population Generally stable or increasing. Breeding grounds difficult to census, better data from wintering grounds.

breeding
hrysea

western breeding
palmarum

western fall
palmarum

BAY-BREASTED WARBLER *Dendroica castanea*

fall ♂

breeding ♀

breeding adult ♂

immature ♀

The male Bay-breasted's fall plumage presents identification challenges. It makes a nest for 4 to 7 eggs on a horizontal branch of dense conifer (June–July). Monotypic. L 5.5" (14 cm) **Identification** SPRING MALE: Black face; chestnut crown, throat, sides; cream neck patch; white belly; grayish olive back with blackish streaks; 2 broad white wing bars. Bluish gray soles of feet. SPRING FEMALE: Duller than male. Cheek mottled blackish; paler, less extensive chestnut on crown, throat, sides; buffy split eye ring. FALL ADULT: Sexes similar, female slightly duller. Crown, nape, and back more yellowish olive green, with indistinct black streaks; grayish rump, uppertail coverts. Pale olive face, indistinct pale supercil-

ium; buff throat, breast, belly, undertail coverts; some or little chestnut on flanks; dark legs, feet. IMMATURE: Similar to dullest fall adult female, but less conspicuous streaking on back; clear whitish buff underparts; much reduced (male) or absent (female) chestnut on flanks.

Similar Species In fall, the Pine lacks streaks on back, underparts; yellow of throat extends behind auriculars; wing bars contrast less with wings; longer tail extends well beyond undertail coverts; primary projection beyond tertials shorter. Blackpoll more similar (see sidebar below).

Voice CALL: Loud, slurred *chip*. FLIGHT CALL: Buzzy *zeet*. SONG: Variable series of very high-pitched lisping notes: *see-see-swee-see-see-swee-swee-see*.

Status & Distribution Fairly common, variable depending on spruce budworm outbreaks; mainly a trans-Gulf migrant, rarely through Caribbean. BREEDING: Boreal forest, mainly in mature dense, spruce-fir forests. MIGRATION: Arrives Gulf Coast mid- to late Apr., peaks Great Lakes last half of May. In fall, more easterly than in spring, departs late July; peaks eastern N.A. late Aug.–mid-Sept.; stragglers to late Oct., later on Gulf Coast. WINTER: Forest edges, second growth from Costa Rica through Panama to northwestern Colombia, northern Venezuela. Feeds mainly on fruit. VAGRANT: Casual to accidental to nearly all western states (rare in CA); sight rec. for central AK. Casual in Labrador, Greenland; accidental in U.K.

Population Spraying for spruce budworm has reduced breeding populations. Considered vulnerable on wintering grounds.

Separation of Bay-breasted and Blackpoll Warblers in Fall

These 2 species are perhaps the most difficult of the "confusing fall warblers." The Pine is often very similar too, but it can usually be distinguished by its different face pattern, shorter wings, and much longer tail projection. Adult Bay-breasteds and Blackpolls appear considerably different in fall than in spring but will often show enough similar plumage to be identifiable. Dull, fall immatures create the greatest confusion.

Both species show a similar face pattern, with a dark eye line and a pale broken eye ring. This tends to be better defined in the Blackpoll.

Both species have greenish olive backs with blackish streaks. Streaks tend to be more conspicuous on the Blackpoll and less so on the Bay-breasted, but this is somewhat variable. The Bay-breasted has a brighter yellowish olive on the crown, nape, and back. When noting wing bars, look for the Bay-breasted's often broader white wing bars.

Bay-breasted Warbler, immature (GA)

Blackpoll Warbler, immature (NY)

The Bay-breasted tends to be buffier from throat to undertail coverts, often buffiest on vent; it also has whitish undertail coverts and, sometimes, a little chestnut (or richer buff) on the flanks. The Blackpoll tends to be yellowish with contrastingly white (or occasionally yellow) undertail coverts. Unlike the Bay-breasted, it also usually shows narrow but conspicuous dark streaks on the sides of the breast and flanks.

Both species have white tail spots and long undertail coverts; however, the Blackpoll's undertail coverts tend to be longer and whiter, whereas the Bay-breasted's are slightly shorter and pale buff.

Foot color is also important. Although immatures of both species can show dark legs, the soles of the Bay-breasted's feet are bluish gray whereas the Blackpoll's are yellowish. Sometimes this yellowish color occurs narrowly up the rear of the tarsus. ∎

BLACKPOLL WARBLER *Dendroica striata*

The black-and-white males are easily identified in spring, but in fall much duller plumages make identification challenging. In June, Blackpolls place 3 to 5 eggs in their nest, which is built against the trunk of a tree, low to the ground. Monotypic. L 5.5" (14 cm)

Identification SPRING MALE: White cheek; black cap and malar stripe; black-streaked olive-gray back; bold black streaks on sides of white underparts. Two bold white wing bars, orange-yellow legs and feet, yellowish lower mandible. SPRING FEMALE: Much individual variation. Olive-gray upperparts, including cheeks, with dark streaks on back; crown sometimes heavily streaked. Face with dark eye line, broken buffy or whitish eye ring, dark streaking on malar. Bold or indistinct side streaks. Some more yellowish olive above and below, resembling fall birds. FALL ADULT: Upperparts dull olive with black streaks on back; underparts whitish or yellowish with narrow streaks on sides; white under-

breeding ♀

breeding ♂

fall

tail coverts. Face pattern similar to spring female's. Pale or dark legs, always with yellow on soles of feet. IMMATURE: Similar to fall adult, but usually greener above and yellower below with less streaking on sides. Sexes usually indistinguishable, but females slightly duller. Dark legs with yellow on soles of feet.

Similar Species In fall, the Pine lacks streaks on underparts and usually also on upperparts; it always has a longer tail and shorter primary projection. In fall, the Bay-breasted is very similar (see sidebar p. 538). The spring male is superficially similar to the Black-and-white Warbler, which has a dark cheek, a white median crown streak, and a different foraging style.

Voice CALL: A loud, sharp *chip*. FLIGHT CALL: A loud, sharp, buzzy *zeet*. SONG: A series of very high-pitched staccato notes, inaudible to some, usually louder in the middle: *tsit tsit tsit tsit tsit tsit tsit*.

Status & Distribution Common; undertakes extremely long nonstop overwater migrations. BREEDING: Boreal spruce forest and spruce-alder-willow thickets. MIGRATION: In spring, takes a more westerly route, through the Caribbean as far west as coastal TX; later than most other wood-warblers. Departs wintering areas in Apr. and arrives on breeding grounds mid-May–early June. Peaks in Midwest and mid-Atlantic states mid- to late May, with a few into early June. In fall, a more easterly route, including an overwater flight from northeastern coastal U.S. to northern S.A.; a few south through eastern Caribbean. Peak numbers through northeastern U.S. from mid-Sept. to early Oct., with some as late as Oct. and Nov. WINTER: A variety of wooded habitats in northern S.A. east of Andes south to northern Bolivia. VAGRANT: Recorded in nearly all western states, primarily in spring. Regular in fall on Pacific coast. Very rare in Costa Rica and Panama. Casual in fall to Greenland, Iceland, U.K., and islands off France.

Population Stable or slightly decreasing in recent years.

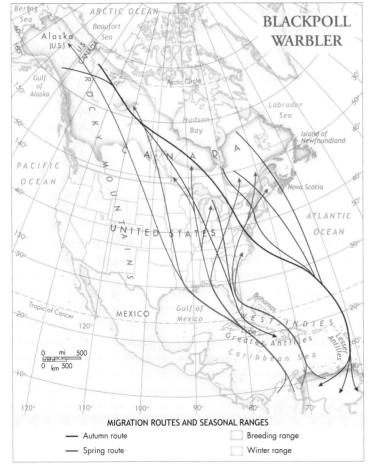

BLACKPOLL WARBLER

MIGRATION ROUTES AND SEASONAL RANGES
— Autumn route
— Spring route
☐ Breeding range
☐ Winter range

CERULEAN WARBLER *Dendroica cerulea*

immature ♀   adult ♂   adult ♀

This beautiful sky-blue warbler sings, forages, and nests higher in the treetops than most other species. It lays 2 to 5 eggs in a nest built on the limb of a tall deciduous tree (midstory or canopy) in June. Monotypic. L 4.8" (12 cm)

Identification Long wings, short tail. ADULT MALE: Cerulean upperparts, brightest on crown; black streaks on back; white underparts, narrow dark blue band across lower throat; bold dark blue streaks on sides. Whitish supercilium and reduced breast band in first-spring male. Two white wing bars. ADULT FEMALE: Bluish green crown, back, and rump; unstreaked back; whitish underparts variably washed with yellow; gray eye line, yellowish supercilium, white arc under eye; diffuse greenish streaks on sides, no breast band. Two white wing bars. IMMATURE: Similar to adult female. Male bluish gray above, streaked back, more prominent side streaks. Female dullest; greenish upperparts with little or no bluish tint; more yellow on underparts (esp. throat).

Similar Species Immature female Blackburnians are most similar to immature Ceruleans, but show dark auricular patch with yellow supercilium connected to yellow patch on sides of neck and more olive-gray upperparts with pale streaking on the sides of the back. Immature Black-throated Grays are similar, but never bluish or greenish.

Voice CALL: A slurred *chip*. FLIGHT CALL: A buzzy *zzee*. SONG: A variable, buzzy, accelerating, rising series of notes, the last note highest: *zhee zhee zhee zizizizizi zzzziiiii.* Similar to some songs of the Northern Parula, but the rising buzzy note at end is distinctive.

Status & Distribution Uncommon and declining; trans-Gulf migrant. BREEDING: Mature deciduous woods with open understory. MIGRATION: In spring, almost never in large numbers. Arrives on Gulf Coast early to mid-Apr.; arrives in Great Lakes early May, with latest migrants through end of May. In fall, departs breeding grounds very early and sometimes arrives on wintering grounds as early as Aug. Some linger on breeding grounds into Sept., rarely to Oct. in South. WINTER: Canopy and forest borders at middle and lower elevations on eastern Andean slopes from Colombia and Venezuela south to Peru, rarely to Bolivia. VAGRANT: Casual in West: recorded from CO, NM, AZ, NV, and CA (13+ recs.), as well as Baja California. Also casual in New England and Atlantic Canada, Bermuda, Bahamas, and Greater Antilles. Accidental in Iceland.

Population Formerly common and widespread, but with steep declines recently. Some expansion of range into northeastern U.S. Identified causes of declines include deforestation, fragmentation, management of forests for even-aged stands, and loss of some key tree species including oaks, elms, chestnuts, and sycamores.

Genus Mniotilta

BLACK-AND-WHITE WARBLER *Mniotilta varia*

This distinctive black-and-white striped warbler, which creeps along horizontal branches while foraging, is more like a nuthatch than most other wood-warblers. Between April and June, it nests on the ground against a shrub, tree, stump, rock, or log and produces 4 to 6 eggs. Monotypic. L 5.3" (13 cm)

Identification Long, slightly decurved bill; long hind claw grips tree trunks. SPRING MALE: Striped black and white overall, with black cheek and throat; black crown with white median stripe. First-spring males show much white, or all white, on chin and throat. SPRING FEMALE: Similar to male, but with grayish buff cheek, narrow black line behind eye, white chin and throat, narrower

immature ♀

bree adul

♀

streaks on sides. FALL ADULT: Male with chin and throat mottled with white (or nearly entirely white), smaller black cheek patch. Female very similar to spring, but sometimes with pale buffy wash on underparts. IMMATURE: Male similar to adult male, but with clear white cheek; female dullest, with rich-

er buff on flanks and undertail coverts; paler, blurry side streaks; buffy cheek patch.

Similar Species Spring male Blackpolls show white cheeks; Black-throated Grays lack white median crown stripe, have solid gray back, small yellow spot in front of eye. Yellow-throateds and Pines forage in a similar manner but show much yellow. Brown Creepers creep vertically and are striped with brown, not black.

Voice CALL: A dull *chip* or *tik*. FLIGHT CALL: A doubled *seet-seet*. SONG: Primary song a long, slightly variable, thin, rhythmic *weesee weesee weesee weesee weesee weesee,* sometimes described as sounding like a squeaky wheel.

Status & Distribution Common and widely distributed; a mid- to long-distance migrant, generally along a broad front. BREEDING: A variety of habitats, including deciduous and mixed woodlands, both mature and second growth. MIGRATION: In spring, arrives earlier than many warbler species, reaching central FL and TX in early Mar., PA and NJ by mid-Apr., New England by early May. Peaks in Great Lakes in early May. Departs breeding areas in late July; main migration from late Aug. through late Sept.; stragglers into Nov. WINTER: A wide variety of habitats, including mature forest, mangroves, and open areas, from coastal NC to FL and southern TX through C.A. and Caribbean to northern S.A., south to Ecuador (rare) and Peru (casual). VAGRANT: Rare but regular migrant through much of the West, also noted rarely in winter. Casual to accidental to OR, WA, and AK; accidental in fall to Iceland, Faeroes, U.K., and Ireland.

Population Appears stable, but may be negatively affected by severe forest fragmentation.

Genus Setophaga

AMERICAN REDSTART *Setophaga ruticilla*

This bird (closely related to *Dendroica*) is conspicuous in lower levels of vegetation as it frequently fans its tail, showing large tail spots, and as it sallies out to catch insects. It lays 1 to 5 eggs in its nest, built against the main trunk of a tree or woody shrub or, sometimes, on a horizontal branch away from the trunk (May–June). Monotypic. L 5.3" (13 cm)

Identification Flat, flycatcher-like bill with prominent rictal bristles. SPRING MALE: Largely black with conspicuous orange patches at sides of breast, on bases of wing feathers (forming broad wing stripe), and extensively at bases of outer tail feathers. White belly and undertail coverts. First-spring male sometimes nearly identical to spring female; most often with irregular black blotches on face, head, back, and underparts. SPRING FEMALE: Male's orange patches replaced with yellow (orange in some older females), light gray head, olive green back, white underparts. FALL ADULT: Male very similar to spring, but with narrow buffy edges on black body feathers. Female nearly identical to spring; more brownish back contrasts less with gray head. IMMATURE: Similar to adult female, often with narrower wing stripe. Sexes often indistinguishable; some males show orange-yellow patch on sides of breast.

Similar Species Slate-throated and Painted Redstarts similar in behavior, but only show white in tail.

Voice CALL: Thin *chip,* like the Yellow Warbler's. FLIGHT CALL: Penetrating, clear *seep.* SONG: Significantly variable, high-pitched series, sometimes with downslurred, slightly burry final note: *zee zee zee zee zweeah.* Some versions similar to songs of other warbler species.

Status & Distribution Common to locally abundant; migrates along a broad front. BREEDING: Wide variety of open wooded habitats. Usually arrives Gulf Coast first half of Apr., peaks mid-May through much of northern U.S. Departs breeding grounds July, peaks Upper Midwest late Aug.–mid-Sept., some into early Oct. WINTER: Forest, woodland, lower and middle elevations from southern FL and southern Mexico through Caribbean to northern S.A. south to Peru. VAGRANT: Accidental in Iceland, U.K., France, and near Azores.

Population Slight declines, significantly in northern New England; increases in Connecticut, Wisconsin, and Quebec.

♀

adult ♂

1st spring ♂

Genus Protonotaria

PROTHONOTARY WARBLER *Protonotaria citrea*

This is the only eastern wood-warbler that nests in natural and artificial cavities (3–7 eggs, Apr.–June). Monotypic. L 5.5" (14 cm)

Identification ADULT MALE: Bright golden yellow head, underparts; beady black eye; long black bill; greenish back; bluish gray wings, tail; white undertail coverts; large white tail spots; short tail. Flesh-colored lower mandible in fall.

ADULT FEMALE: Similar to male, but greenish olive wash on rear of crown, nape; smaller white spots on tail. IMMATURE: Male similar to adult female, with flesh-colored lower mandible. Female with extensive olive on crown, nape, cheek.

Similar Species The Blue-winged shows black eye line, whitish wing bars. The Yellow shows yellower wings, yellow tail spots, smaller bill.

Voice CALL: Loud, dry *chip,* like the Hooded's. FLIGHT CALL: Loud *seeep.* SONG: Simple, loud, ringing series of notes: *sweet sweet sweet sweet sweet sweet.*

Status & Distribution Fairly common, often local; mainly a medium-distance trans-Gulf migrant. Endangered in Canada. BREEDING: Larger wooded areas, mainly swamps and along rivers, always over water. MIGRATION: Arrives Gulf Coast mid-Mar., NJ mid-Apr., MN mid-May. Departs northern breeding areas Aug.; most by early Sept.; stragglers into Oct., rarely Nov. WINTER: Mangrove swamps, dry tropical forest, southern Mexico through C.A. (scarce north of Costa Rica) and Caribbean to extreme northern S.A. Casual southern FL, southern TX, and CA. VAGRANT: Rare to casual in western states.

Population Declining or stable. Sensitive to habitat fragmentation on breeding and wintering grounds.

adult ♂

Genus Helmitheros

WORM-EATING WARBLER *Helmitheros vermivorum*

This inconspicuous warbler feeds mostly on caterpillars by probing into suspended dead leaves. Its nest is found at the base of a sapling on a hillside or ravine, usually under dead leaves; it lays 4 to 6 eggs (May–June). Monotypic. L 5.3" (13 cm)

Identification Large bill; flesh-colored legs; short tail. ADULT: Rich buffy head with bold black lateral crown and eye stripes, buffy underparts, grayish olive upperparts. IMMATURE: Nearly identical to adult, with duller head stripes and rusty tips on tertials, greater and median wing coverts, which often wear off by fall.

Similar Species The Swainson's Warbler lacks bold head stripes and rich buff coloration.

Voice CALL: Includes a soft *chip.* FLIGHT CALL: A doubled *zeet-zeet,* also given at other times. SONG: A simple, dry, high-pitched trill similar to the Chipping Sparrow's, but drier and less staccato, and to the Pine Warbler's, but less musical. Note habitat of singer.

Status & Distribution Fairly common but often inconspicuous; migrates across a broad front. BREEDING: Large tracts where deciduous and mixed forests overlap with moderate to steep slopes. MIGRATION: In spring, arrives in FL and Gulf Coast in last half of Mar. continuing to early May; arrives in Midwest mid-Apr.–early-May. In fall, inconspicuous departure from breeding grounds mid-July–Aug. in northern areas, through Sept. in southern areas. WINTER: Forest and scrub habitats of eastern Mexico south to Panama and the northern Caribbean (inc. the Greater Antilles). VAGRANT: Rare to casual in West, including more than 92 records from CA, 33 from AZ, and 30 from NM. One record from Venezuela.

Population Probably stable; however, it is difficult to census populations accurately. The species is sensitive to forest fragmentation.

Genus *Limnothlypis*

SWAINSON'S WARBLER *Limnothlypis swainsonii*

This skulking warbler is very difficult to observe. It usually forages by shuffling through leaf litter (quivering its tail). Its well-hidden nest, in dense ground vegetation, hosts 2 to 5 eggs (Apr.–May). Monotypic. L 5.5" (14 cm)
Identification Large; heavy bodied; short tail; flat forehead. Long pointed bill, flesh-colored lower mandible; pinkish legs. ADULT: Rufous-brown crown, hind-neck; duller olive-brown back, wings; whitish or pale yellowish superciliary;

dark brown eye line; whitish or pale yellowish underparts, often grayish tinge on sides. IMMATURE: Identical to adult; no field-discernable differences.
Similar Species Worm-eating has conspicuous black stripes on head; Louisiana Waterthrush is streaked below.
Voice CALL NOTE: Distinctive *chip;* louder, sweeter than Prothonotary's. FLIGHT CALL: High, thin, slightly buzzy *swee* notes, sometimes doubled. SONG: Somewhat variable; loud, ringing *whee whee whee wee tu weeu.* Like Louisiana Waterthrush's, without sputtering notes.
Status & Distribution Uncommon; medium-distance migrant, mainly across eastern Gulf. BREEDING: Damp bottomland hardwoods, canebrakes, rhododendron thickets. MIGRATION: Arrives late Mar.–late Apr. Departs between mid-Sept. and mid-Oct., a few as early as mid-Aug., as late as mid-Nov. WINTER: Swamps and river floodplain forests in Yucatan, Belize, Guatemala, and west-

ern Caribbean. VAGRANT: Overshoots in spring, where recorded casually or accidentally north to WI, MI, OH, NJ, NY, MA, ON, NS; accidentally west to KS, NE, CO, AZ, and NM.
Population Trends are hard to discern because species is difficult to detect.

Genus *Seiurus*

All 3 species in this genus are large and have loud, ringing songs. Like miniature thrushes, they have spotted breasts and are very terrestrial; they can be seen walking (with pinkish legs), not hopping, on the forest floor. Waterthrushes habitually bob their tails, while the Ovenbird cocks its tail when alert or alarmed. All need large tracts of forest for breeding.

OVENBIRD *Seiurus aurocapilla*

A familiar voice from the forest, the Ovenbird spends nearly all of its time on or near the ground. Its domed, well-hidden nest, with its side entrance, is built on the ground and encloses 3 to 6 eggs in June. Polytypic. L 6" (15 cm)
Identification ADULT: Olive upperparts, black lateral crown stripes, bold white eye ring, hard-to-see orange crown patch. Underparts white; bold black streaks on breast, sides. IMMATURE: Similar to adult, with narrow rufous fringes on tertials, sometimes worn off by fall.
Geographic Variation Slight variation among 3 subspecies,

usually not evident in the field. Western *cinereus* is grayer and paler on the upperparts than eastern nominate; *furvior* (breeds NF) is slightly darker.
Similar Species Northern and Louisiana Waterthrushes are slimmer, brown backed; lack white eye ring. Waterthrushes habitually bob their tails.
Voice CALL: A loud, sharp *tsick,* often in a rapid series when alarmed. FLIGHT CALL: Thin, high *seee.* SONG: Primary song a loud, ringing *cher-TEE cher-TEE cher-TEE* or *TEA-cher TEA-cher TEA-cher* in a rising crescendo. Also an elaborate flight song.
Status & Distribution Common in mature forests, rare in the West. Migrates on a broad front in the East. BREEDING: Deciduous or mixed forests dominated by deciduous trees. MIGRATION: Arrives on the Gulf Coast late Mar.; in much of the South early Apr., peaks there mid-Apr.–early May; in the upper Midwest peaks mid-May. Departs as early as late July, earliest arrivals in the

South early Aug.; peaks in much of the East in mid-Sept., stragglers into Dec. (sometimes in northern states). WINTER: Primary and second growth forests from southern TX and coastal NC to southern FL south through C.A. and the Caribbean. VAGRANT: Recorded in all western states. Accidental in Ecuador, Greenland, and Great Britain.
Population Recent significant declines likely due to forest fragmentation on breeding grounds. Trends on wintering grounds unclear.

NORTHERN WATERTHRUSH *Seiurus noveboracensis*

The waterthrushes are appropriately named, as they are almost always found near water, and are on or near the ground, whether in migration or when breeding in northern forests. Often located by its loud song and calls, the Northern lays 1 to 5 eggs in a hollow of a fallen tree's root system or a streamside bank between May and June. Polytypic. L 5.8" (15 cm)

Identification Vigorously bobs tail up and down. Dull pink legs. ADULT: Olive-brown crown, back, wings, and tail; yellowish, buffy, or white supercilium (even width throughout); underparts whitish tinged with yellowish, or mainly whitish, with blackish spotting forming streaks on throat, breast, and sides. Usually very small, indistinct white spots on outer tail feathers. IMMATURE: Usually identical to adult; some with buffy or rusty tips on tertials or more pointed tail feathers, lacking any white on the outer tail feathers.

Geographic Variation Slight, clinal variation not well correlated with 3 named subspecies. Yellowest, in Northeast, has much variation throughout its range.

Similar Species Compare to the Louisiana Waterthrush (see sidebar below).

Voice CALL: Sharp, ringing, metallic *chink.* FLIGHT CALL: Buzzy *zeet.* SONG: Primary song is loud and ringing, rather staccato: *twit twit twit sweet sweet sweet chew chew chew.*

Status & Distribution Common; trans-Gulf, circum-Gulf, trans-Caribbean migrant; migrates on a broad front through the East. BREEDING: Wooded areas with slow-moving water (e.g., swamps, bogs, margins of lakes). MIGRA-TION: In spring, a slightly more westerly route: arrives on Gulf Coast early Apr., peaks late Apr.–early May; arrives in the Great Lakes and Northeast late Apr., peaks mid-May. In the West, smaller numbers late Apr.–early June. In fall, a slightly more easterly route: Departs breeding grounds in July, main arrival early Aug., peaks Sept. in northern U.S., few linger into Oct. WINTER: Mangroves, rain forest, second growth from coastal northern Mexico through C.A., Caribbean, and northern S.A. to northeastern Peru and northern Brazil. A few overwinter in southern FL, along Gulf Coast. VAGRANT: Casual in late spring to northern slope of AK, Wrangel I., Chukotski Peninsula; also Greenland, U.K., France.

Population Breeding areas appear stable and secure; wintering habitat (esp. mangroves) threatened with development.

Identification of Waterthrushes

The 2 species of waterthrush—Northern and Louisiana—are very similar in appearance, habits, and habitat. They can occur together during migration and in the overlap zone of their breeding grounds. Use the following points in combination to separate them.

Singing birds are easily identified by voice. See their species accounts for descriptions of their songs and calls.

Get a good look at head patterns. A Northern's supercilium is uniform in width and color (usually yellow, sometimes white). A Louisiana has a subtly bicolored supercilium, buffy above the lores and white behind, that broadens noticeably.

Compare the waterthrushes' throat pattern as well. Both species show a narrow malar streak. The Northern also shows small streaks

Northern Waterthrush (NJ, Sept.)

Louisiana Waterthrush (CA, Sept.)

on the throat, whereas the Louisiana usually shows a clean white throat or a very few streaks at most.

Underparts differ noticeably, too. The Northern most often shows yellowish uniformly colored underparts, though sometimes it may be white, with bolder darker streaking. The Louisiana shows white underparts, often with pinkish-buff flanks, and less-distinct streaking.

Note bill size. The Louisiana has a distinctly longer and heavier bill than the Northern.

Leg color is also helpful in identification. Generally, the Louisiana's legs are a brighter pink than the Northern's.

Finally, consider the bird's behavior. The Louisiana's tail bobbing is more exaggerated and more circular than the Northern's up-and-down bobbing. ∎

LOUISIANA WATERTHRUSH *Seiurus motacilla*

Larger and longer-billed than the Northern Waterthrush, the Louisiana has a distinctive ringing song. Between April and June, it will nest in a hollow of a fallen tree's root system or a streamside bank and lay 3 to 6 eggs. Monotypic. L 6" (15 cm)

Identification Bobs tail up and down, with some side-to-side motion. Large bill, bright pink legs. ADULT: Olive-brown crown, back, wings, tail. Two-tone supercilium: pale buff above lores; white, broader behind eye. White underparts usually with distinct pinkish buff on flanks, undertail coverts;

blackish spotting on breast, sides. Usually very small, indistinct white spots on outer tail feathers. IMMATURE: Usually identical to adult; some with buffy or rusty tips on tertials and more pointed tail feathers; lacks any white on the outer tail feathers.

Similar Species Compare to the Northern Waterthrush (see sidebar p. 544).

Voice CALL: Loud, rich *chik* or *chich,* less ringing or metallic than the Northern's. FLIGHT CALL: High *zeet.* SONG: Loud, rollicking primary song with clear slurred whistles ending in sputtering notes, like the Swainson's and Yellow-throated Warblers': *seeeu seeeu seeeu seewit seewit ch-wit it-chu.*

Status & Distribution Uncommon. BREEDING: Along streams in hilly deciduous forest, in cypress swamps and bottomland forest. MIGRATION: Arrives early, typically Gulf Coast in mid-Mar., peaks late Mar.–mid-Apr., reaches Great Lakes mid- to late-Apr. Migration generally complete by mid-May. Departs early, mostly by mid- to late July; migrates through

eastern N.A. during Aug., a few into early Sept., casually to early Oct., exceptionally later. WINTER: Rivers and streams in hilly or mountainous areas from coastal northern Mexico through C.A. and Caribbean to extreme northwestern S.A. Very rare southern FL, AZ. VAGRANT: Casually overshoots in spring migration to ND, QC, NS. Casual in West (inc. CA, NM, AZ, NV, CO, Baja California); 6 recs. from Venezuela.

Population Range is expanding in the Northeast; populations stable or slightly declining elsewhere.

Genus Oporornis

These 4 species tend to feed on or near the ground and are vocally similar. They share olive upperparts, yellow underparts, and pink legs. Their head markings include eye rings or other facial markings. They show no white in the tail. Of the 4 species, 3 show gray hoods—the Kentucky Warbler being the exception.

KENTUCKY WARBLER *Oporornis formosus*

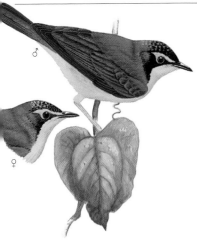

This skulking warbler is more often heard than seen. In May or June, it lays 3 to 6 eggs in a nest at the base of a small shrub. Monotypic. L 5.3" (13 cm)

Identification Chunky, short tail, pale pink legs. ADULT MALE: Olive-green upperparts, wings; black cap; yellow super-

cilium forming spectacles; black lores, triangular cheek patch (extends onto neck); bright yellow underparts. ADULT FEMALE: Similar to male, but less extensive black on crown, cheek. IMMATURE: Male similar to adult female. Female dullest; suggestion of face pattern; black mostly replaced by dark olive.

Similar Species Common Yellowthroats do not show yellow spectacles. Hooded Warblers have entirely yellow face and extensive white on outer tail feathers.

Voice CALL: Low, distinctive *chup,* similar to the Hermit Thrush's. FLIGHT CALL: Loud, buzzy *zeep.* SONG: Somewhat variable series of rich rolling notes, somewhat similar to the Carolina Wren's: *churree churree churree churree.*

Status & Distribution Fairly common, primarily a trans-Gulf migrant. BREEDING: Dense understory in deciduous or mixed woodlands, often near streams. MIGRATION: Arrives Gulf Coast late Mar.–early Apr., northern extreme of range early May. In fall, some take a more easterly

route than in spring. Departs early Aug., peaks late Aug.–early Sept., stragglers to late Sept. and (exceptional) early Oct. WINTER: Forested lowlands, second growth from northeastern Mexico to Panama and extreme northeastern Colombia and northwestern Venezuela. VAGRANT: Overshoots north in spring. Rare to casual in West. Casual in winter to FL, TX, and CA.

Population Generally stable; declining in some areas. Probably affected negatively by tropical deforestation.

CONNECTICUT WARBLER *Oporornis agilis*

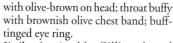

This secretive, skulking, very terrestrial denizen of northern spruce bogs is one of the most challenging wood-warblers for birders to add to a life list. Not surprisingly, its June-built nest is well concealed on or near the ground in thickets or at the base of a shrub (3–5 eggs). Monotypic. L 5.8" (15 cm)

Identification Large and chunky; short tail projection and long primary extension; habitually walks on or near ground. Pinkish legs; bill mostly pinkish with dusky brown culmen and tip. SPRING MALE: Gray head, throat, and upper breast form a distinct hood, paler on throat; prominent complete white eye ring, occasionally broken at rear; olive upperparts, pale yellow underparts. SPRING FEMALE: Similar to male, but with duller hood tinged brownish olive. FALL ADULT: Similar to spring, but washed with olive on head. IMMATURE: Similar to fall female, some duller; extensively washed with olive-brown on head; throat buffy with brownish olive chest band; buff-tinged eye ring.

Similar Species MacGillivray's and Mourning Warblers are smaller with longer tail projection; show dark lores with broken or absent eye rings; and hop instead of walk. The Nashville Warbler is much smaller and shows yellow on the throat and breast.

Voice CALL: A loud, nasal *chimp,* rarely heard. FLIGHT CALL: A buzzy *zeet,* also given when perched. SONG: Variable primary song loud, staccato, and more emphatic toward the end (similar in quality to the Northern Waterthrush's): *chuppa-cheepa chuppa-cheepa chuppa-cheep.*

Status & Distribution Uncommon; long-distance migrant. BREEDING: Boreal forest, spruce-tamarack bogs, muskeg, poplar woodlands, and deciduous forest. MIGRATION: In spring, through Caribbean to FL,

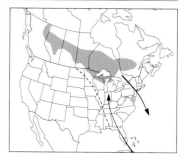

then northwest to breeding grounds; later than most other warblers. Arrives in FL early May–late May, peaks in Great Lakes in late May, stragglers into early June. More easterly route in fall, begins in late Aug., peaks in last half of Sept., stragglers to late Oct. on southern Atlantic coast. May fly nonstop across Atlantic to South America. WINTER: Most poorly known of all wood-warblers; woodlands, forest edge, and dense shrubby second growth. A few recorded south of Amazon in Pantanal of Brazil to Bolivia. VAGRANT: Casual in spring east of Appalachians and to LA, TX, and CA. Very rare to accidental in West, in fall most recs. along Pacific coast (90+ recs. from CA). Rare to casual in Atlantic Canada. Casual to northern Baja California, Honduras, Costa Rica, and western Panama.

Population Difficult to determine: some data suggest apparently stable or even increasing numbers, and other data suggest declines.

immature

adult ♀

adult ♂

MOURNING WARBLER *Oporornis philadelphia*

This skulking warbler arrives on its breeding grounds later than most warblers. Some can be very difficult to separate from the similar MacGillivray's and are best told by call. Built in June or July, its well-concealed nest is on or near the ground in tangles and shrubs (2–5 eggs). Monotypic. L 5.3" (13 cm)

Identification Chunky, short tailed. Flesh-colored legs, mostly pinkish bill somewhat dusky on upper mandible. Plumage somewhat variable. ADULT MALE: Blue-gray head and throat form a hood; black bib on upper breast sometimes extends onto throat; lores sometimes black; very rarely with thin, broken eye ring. Olive green back, wings, and tail. Bright yellow lower breast, belly, and undertail coverts. ADULT FEMALE: Similar to

male, but with paler gray hood and lacking black bib. Shows nearly complete, very thin eye ring in fall. IMMATURE: Similar to adult female, but with more olive-gray hood and incomplete olive-gray bib; yellowish throat, sometimes quite pale. Shows a thin, broken eye ring (thicker on some); some males may show limited black in bib.

Similar Species The adult male MacGillivray's has different song and calls, shows black lores and slaty mottling on throat; all ages and sexes also show distinct broadly broken eye arcs, above and below eyes, and longer tail projection. Connecticuts show distinct, complete eye rings and shorter tail projection; they walk instead of hop. Immature and female Common

adult ♂

adult ♀

Yellowthroats are longer tailed, lack gray on crown, have a smaller all-dark bill, and show no yellow on belly.

Voice CALL: A distinctive, sharp, scratchy *chit* or *jip.* FLIGHT CALL: A thin, sharp *seep.* SONG: Variable, most often 2-part, with first part louder and slightly burry, second part faster and lower: *curry churry churry chorry chorry.* Also, a 1-part song, somewhat similar to some songs of the Kentucky Warbler.

Status & Distribution Fairly common;

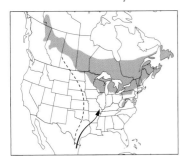

circum-Gulf migrant. BREEDING: Clearings in disturbed second growth, mixed forests. MIGRATION: In spring, a few arrive in southern TX as early as late Apr., peaking in Upper Midwest in late May–early June. Departs breeding grounds in early Aug., peaking late Aug.–early Sept., casually to late Oct., accidentally later. WINTER: Dense thickets, overgrown fields, shrublands, and other semi-open areas, often near water; southern Nicaragua to Ecuador. VAGRANT: In West mainly from CA, where rare: 110+ recs., most from fall. Casual in much of West. Accidental in fall to AK. Two recs. from Baja California, 3 specimens from Greenland, 2 exceptional winter records from CA.

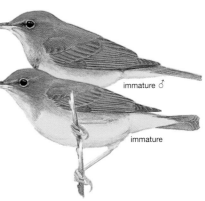

Population Stable; may be one of few species to benefit from human activities, especially from logging activities that create the openings it prefers.

MACGILLIVRAY'S WARBLER *Oporornis tolmiei*

A western version of the Mourning Warbler, the MacGillivray's Warbler is vocally distinct and breeds mainly in montane areas, where it makes a nest for 3–5 eggs on or slightly above the ground in dense shrubs or dense undergrowth between May and July. Polytypic. L 5.3" (13 cm)

Identification Pinkish legs, mostly pinkish bill somewhat dusky on upper mandible. ADULT MALE: Blue-gray head and throat form a hood; black lores; black and gray mottling on upper breast do not form a solid patch. Bold white crescents above and below eye. Olive-green back, wings, and tail.

Bright yellow lower breast, belly, and undertail coverts. ADULT FEMALE: Similar to male, but with paler gray hood, paler chin and throat, no black in lores, and narrower but distinct eye crescents. IMMATURE: Similar to adult female, but with more brownish olive hood. Most immatures show a complete grayish olive bib, which separates the yellow breast from the pale grayish, rarely yellowish, throat. Eye arcs are sometimes very narrow but distinct.

Geographic Variation The 2 subspecies are not detectable in the field. The nominate, *tolmei,* from the Pacific coast, is more yellow-olive on its upperparts and deeper yellow on its underparts than the interior subspecies, *monticola.*

Similar Species Mourning Warblers appear to be shorter tailed and have longer undertail coverts as well as a different song and calls. The adult male Mourning Warbler usually lacks black lores and usually shows an extensive black breast patch; white eye arcs are absent or very narrow. Immature Mourning Warblers show a yellowish throat and an incomplete breast band; the white around the eye, when present, is much thinner and often forms a nearly complete ring.

Voice CALL: A loud, sharp *tsik.* FLIGHT CALL: A penetrating *tseep.* SONG: Pri-

mary 2-part song, with a somewhat burry first part and a variable (higher- or lower-pitched) second part: *churry churry churry tree tree tree* or *sweet sweet sweet sweet peachy peachy.*

Status & Distribution Common; widespread migrant in the West. BREEDING: Open areas of montane mixed and coniferous forests, usually near rivers and streams. MIGRATION: In spring, arrives in southern AZ and southern CA in early Apr., peaking in mid-May in the Cascades, with stragglers to early June. In fall, departs breeding areas during Aug., peaking late Aug.–mid-Sept., with some into mid-Oct. and casually to mid-Nov. WINTER: A wide variety of densely vegetated habitats, from northwestern Mexico to central Panama. Casually in southern CA, AZ, and TX. VAGRANT: Casual in the East, recorded from ON, MN, IL, IN, TN, MO, GA, FL, MD, NJ, CT, and MA.

Population Stable population, probably benefitting from logging activities, which create the disturbed and second-growth habitat preferred by this species.

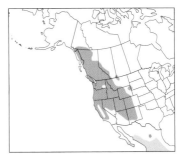

YELLOWTHROATS Genus *Geothlypis*

This rather distinctive group of skulking wood-warblers prefers wetland and marsh habitats. All species show black on the face, and all but 1 show extensive black on the ear coverts in adult males. All plumages possess yellow throats. Vocalizations are rhythmic and chanting. Currently 9 species are recognized, though taxonomy is unsettled.

COMMON YELLOWTHROAT *Geothlypis trichas*

adult ♀

immature ♂

adult ♂

immature ♀

southwestern
chryseola
adult ♂

Immature *Oporornis* warblers are larger, shorter tailed; typically with gray on head, all-yellow underparts.
Voice CALL: Includes husky *tschep;* rapid chatter similar to the Sedge Wren's song. FLIGHT CALL: Low, unmusical, buzzy *dzip.* SONG: A somewhat variable, loud, rolling *wichity wichity wichity wichity wich.*
Status & Distribution Common; a short- to long-distance migrant. BREEDING: Dense, low vegetation, from wetlands to prairie to pine forest. MIGRATION: Arrives Southeast late Mar.; southern CA, AZ late Feb.; peaks late Apr.–early May. Departs by mid-Aug., peaks in East Sept., in West late Sept.–early Oct. Stragglers late Oct. through much of range. WINTER: Dense vegetation, usually in or near wetlands, southern U.S. through C.A. to extreme northwestern S.A. and northern Caribbean. A few to Great Lakes. VAGRANT: Accidental Greenland, U.K.
Population Stable or slightly increasing. Vulnerable to loss of wetland habitats.

Heard more than seen, this skulking species nests on or near the ground in thick clumps of sedges and grasses (1–6 eggs, Apr.–July). Polytypic (15 ssp.; 11 in N.A.). L 5" (13 cm)
Identification Short wings, long tail; flesh-pink legs. Nominate described. ADULT MALE: Broad black face mask, pale gray border above, behind; olive upperparts. Bright yellow throat, undertail coverts; paler belly. ADULT FEMALE: Plain, like male, but black mask and grayish border replaced with brownish olive; cheeks contrast with yellow throat. IMMATURE: Like adult female; sexes often indistinguishable, but a few males may show some black feathers on face or in malar area, exceptionally on auriculars.
Geographic Variation Nominate in much of East; *ignota* (FL, east Gulf Coast) with rich buffy brown flanks; *chryseola* (western TX, southern AZ) largest and most distinct: underparts often entirely yellow, mask border tinged with yellow. Two dull, small, moderately dark subspecies along the Pacific coast with flanks washed with pale or dark olive.
Similar Species Kentucky Warblers have yellow spectacles. Gray-crowneds have thicker bill, no black on auriculars.

GRAY-CROWNED YELLOWTHROAT *Geothlypis poliocephala*

This species is the most aberrant in *Geothlypis.* Polytypic (6 ssp.; *ralphi* in N.A.). L 5.5" (14 cm)
Identification Moderately large; thick, bicolored bill, strongly curved culmen; long, graduated tail often cocked and waved. ADULT MALE: Gray crown and nape; black lores extend to below the eye; broken white eye ring; brownish olive upperparts and wings; grayish tail; bright yellow underparts, whitish on belly, brownish on flanks. ADULT FEMALE: Similar to male, but olive-gray crown and nape, slate-gray lores. IMMATURE: Similar to adult female, but buffier underparts, less distinct head pattern.
Similar Species The Common Yellowthroat has thinner all-dark bill, lacks strongly curved culmen. The larger, thicker-billed Yellow-breasted Chat has white spectacles. A possible Gray-crowned x Common hybrid was photographed in the Rio Grande Valley.
Voice CALL: Includes a distinctive, nasal *cheed-l-eet.* SONG: Primary song a rich, scratchy warble like a *Passerina* bunting's or the Blue Grosbeak's.

Status & Distribution Historically resident (through 1910) but now casual in extreme southern TX. At least 6 recs. in recent years.

Genus *Wilsonia*

HOODED WARBLER *Wilsonia citrina*

The Hooded is often seen only as a flash in open deciduous woodland. Its nest is placed low in a patch of shrub and holds 2 to 5 eggs (May–June). Monotypic. L 5.2" (13 cm)

Identification Opens and closes tail, revealing extensive white on outer tail feathers; large bill, eye. ADULT MALE: Black hood, throat; contrasting bright yellow forehead, cheeks, dark lores; olive-green upperparts; bright yellow underparts. ADULT FEMALE: Like male, but variable head pattern: most show only narrow black border; a few show nearly complete black hood. First-spring similar to immature. IMMATURE: Male similar to adult; hood feathers extensively tipped yellow and olive.

adult ♀

adult ♂

immature ♀

Female dullest; no black on throat, crown; indistinct yellow superciliary, throat; olive cheeks.

Similar Species The smaller, immature female Wilson's Warbler has smaller bill and eye; lacks dark lores, white tail spots. The Yellow Warbler has yellow tail spots.

Voice CALL: Loud *chink*. SONG: Clear and whistled, with emphatic ending: *ta-wee ta-wee ta-wee ta-wee tee-too*.

Status & Distribution Fairly common; primarily trans-Gulf migrant. BREEDING: Mixed hardwood forests in north; cypress-gum swamps in south, preferring larger woodlots. MIGRATION: Arrives Gulf Coast mid-Mar.; Midwest late Apr.; northern range early May. Slightly more easterly route in fall: earliest arrive FL mid-July; latest depart early Sept., small numbers in South into early Oct., casually into Nov. WINTER: Males lowland mature forest; females scrub, secondary forest, disturbed habitats. C.A.; rarely southern FL, northern Colombia, Venezuela. VAGRANT: Rare spring and fall to much of West, especially CA (has bred), AZ. Accidental in winter to southern states, inc. SC, CA, TX; 2 records from U.K.

Population Stable. May be sensitive to forest fragmentation.

CANADA WARBLER *Wilsonia canadensis*

Known as the "Necklaced" Warbler, in June the Canada builds a well-concealed nest for 2 to 6 eggs on or near the ground. Monotypic. L 5.3" (13 cm)

Identification Active; often cocks tail, flicks wings. Pink legs. ADULT MALE: Blue-gray upperparts (inc. wings, tail); black forehead, patch below eye; distinct complete white or yellow eye ring, yellow lores, forming spectacles; bright yellow underparts; rows of black spots across breast form a necklace; white undertail coverts. Black markings reduced in first-spring males. ADULT FEMALE: Duller than male, lacks black on face; less distinct dark necklace. IMMATURE: Male similar to spring female; more olive-gray above. Female duller; very indistinct necklace formed by grayish olive spots.

Similar Species Kirtland's streaked on back, sides (not breast); shows white tail spots; wags tail. Kentucky has olive upperparts, yellow undertail coverts, no black on yellow underparts.

Voice CALL: Sharp *tchup* or *tik*. FLIGHT CALL: High *zzee*. SONG: Primary song variable, staccato series of jumbled notes; often begins with loud *chip* note, then short pause: *chip … chupety swee-ditchety chip*.

Status & Distribution Common; mainly a circum-Gulf migrant. BREEDING: Cool, moist mixed forests with dense understory. MIGRATION: Late in spring; arrives southern TX after mid-Apr., Upper Midwest mid-May, continues into late May–early June. Departs early Aug., peaks in mid- to late Aug., continues into mid-Sept. Casual mid-Oct.–early Nov. WINTER: Dense montane undergrowth; from northern S.A. in Andes to central Peru. VAGRANT: Very rare to casual in West; casual in Caribbean.

Population Declining, likely from forest succession and loss of forested wetlands.

ure ♀

adult ♂

WILSON'S WARBLER *Wilsonia pusilla*

♀

♂

This small warbler feeds very actively, often fly-catching. Wilson's lay eggs (2–7) in a nest on or near the ground at the base of a shrub or small tree (Apr.–June).Polytypic. L 4.8" (12 cm) **Identification** Flips long tail up and down and in a circular motion. Nominate described and illustrated. ADULT MALE: Olive-green upperparts (inc. wings, tail, cheeks); solid shiny black cap; bright yellow forehead, lores, eye ring, broad superciliary, entire underparts. ADULT FEMALE: Similar to male, but smaller black cap, usually nearly absent or restricted to front half of crown (often mottled with olive). IMMATURE: Similar to adult; male with extensive olive mottling on black cap, female usually with olive crown, forehead; lacks black cap. **Geographic Variation** Nominate breeds through much of boreal Canada. The *pileolata* (AK, Rocky Mountains) has brighter yellow forehead and underparts. Pacific coast *chryseola* is brightest above and below: yellowish wash on cheeks, orange-tinged forehead. **Similar Species** Larger immature female Hoodeds have larger bill, dusky lores, white in tail. Shorter-tailed Orange-crowneds are drabber with diffuse breast streaks, dusky eye line, more pointed bill. Immature Yellow Warbler shows yellow tail spots, pale-edged wing feathers. **Voice** CALL: A somewhat nasal *timp*. FLIGHT CALL: A sharp, slurred *tsip*. SONG: Primary song short and chattering, dropping in pitch toward end: *chi chi chi chi chi chi chet chet*. Songs of *pileolata* and *chryseola* louder and faster. **Status & Distribution** Common; medium- to long-distance migrant, more common in West. BREEDING: Wet situations with dense ground cover, low shrubs. MIGRATION: Eastern birds are circum-Gulf migrants, arrive in southern TX late Apr., in Great Lakes late May. Pacific coast birds arrive in southern AZ late Feb., southwestern BC late Apr. In East, earliest fall migrants mid-Aug., peak late Aug.–mid-Sept., stragglers casually into Nov. Pacific coast birds depart mid-July. WINTER: Wide variety of habitats; northwestern Mexico to central Panama, rarely to extreme southeastern TX, southern LA, coastal southern CA. VAGRANT: Casual in winter to Colombia, northern Bahamas, Cuba, Jamaica. Accidental in Greenland, U.K. **Population** Declining (esp. in the West), possibly due to cowbird parasitism and loss of riparian habitats.

Genus **Cardellina**

RED-FACED WARBLER *Cardellina rubrifrons*

This strikingly plumaged southwestern mountain species is easily identified. In May–June, it constructs a nest in a depression on the ground, often on a slope at the base of woody plants and often with an overhang that helps conceal and protect the 4 to 6 eggs within. Monotypic. L 5.5" (14 cm) **Identification** Small bill; head appears peaked. Flips long tail around in a similar manner to a *Wilsonia*. ADULT MALE: Bright red face, upper breast, and sides of neck; black crown and cheeks; white nape spot, rump, and underparts; a single white wing bar on median coverts; gray upperparts. ADULT FEMALE: Nearly identical to male, but with duller, more orange-red face. IMMATURE: Similar to adult female, but with more brownish gray upperparts. Some males nearly as bright as adult males. **Similar Species** The Painted Redstart is the only other warbler with red in plumage (but not on face), and it shows large white patches in wings and tail. Chickadees are similarly gray above, and the Red-faced Warbler is sometimes similarly acrobatic, but once the red face is seen there can be no confusion. Also note that chickadees do not show white nape spots or white rumps. **Voice** CALL: A sharp *chup* or *tchip,* suggesting the Black-throated Gray. SONG: Primary song a series of assorted thinner notes with an emphatic ending: *wi tsi-wi tsi-wi si-wi-si-whichu*. **Status & Distribution** Fairly common; medium-distance migrant. BREEDING: Montane mixed and deciduous woodland. MIGRATION: Not often observed in spring migration; arrives late Apr.– late May. Departs as early as Aug., some into Sept. WINTER: Humid montane forest, pine-oak forest, riparian woodland from northwestern Mexico south to eastern Honduras. VAGRANT: Casual in TX (mostly Big Bend N.P.) and CA; accidental in CO, WY, and LA. **Population** Difficult to determine; possibly declining slightly. May be vulnerable to logging.

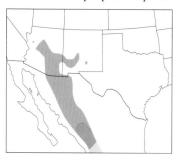

♂

WHITESTARTS Genus *Myioborus*

When it was first described, the Painted Redstart was thought to be closely related to the American Redstart, which was previously named mainly for its red tail patches. All 12 members of this mainly tropical genus show white tail patches, thus they are often called whitestarts, and only 2 species show any red in the plumage at all.

PAINTED REDSTART *Myioborus pictus*

With its bold black, red, and white coloration and its conspicuous wing- and tail-fanning behavior while creeping along branches, the Painted Redstart is unlikely to be confused with any other warbler species. It makes its nest on an embankment, often near water—well hidden under rocks, grasses, or roots—and lays 3 to 7 eggs in May. Polytypic (2 ssp.; nominate in N.A.). L 5.8" (15 cm)

Identification ADULT MALE: Mainly black with large white patches in wing, white on outer 3 tail feathers, and a small white crescent below eye. Red lower breast and belly; undertail coverts mixed slate and white. ADULT FEMALE: Nearly identical to male, with slightly paler red underparts, which can sometimes be determined only when both members of a pair are seen together. Females are known to sing. JUVENILE: Retains juvenal plumage later than most warblers, June–August. Similar to adult, but without red. Sooty lower underparts; undertail coverts mottled grayish and white. Red belly is acquired in late summer or early fall.

Similar Species The Slate-throated Redstart lacks the white wing patches and eye crescent, shows less white in tail, and has slaty (not black) upperparts.

Voice CALL: A unique, scratchy, whistled *sheu* or a richer *cheree*, similar to calls of the Pine Siskin. SONG: Primary song a somewhat variable series of rich, 2-part syllables, ending with 1 or 2 inflected notes: *weeta weeta weeta wee.*

Status & Distribution Common; a short-distance migrant. BREEDING: Pine-oak woodlands in foothills and mountains. MIGRATION: Arrives on breeding grounds mid- to late Mar. Departs breeding grounds in Sept., with some lingering into mid-Oct. WINTER: Pine-oak woodlands, sometimes at lower elevations than when breeding; from northwestern Mexico south to northern Nicaragua, where it mixes with sedentary subspecies. Casual in winter in breeding range. VAGRANT: Rare in fall and winter in southern CA (more than 100 recs.); casual in southwestern AZ, southwestern UT, southwestern CO, and southern TX. Accidental in Baja California, BC, MT, WI, MI, southern ON, OH, NY, MA, LA, MS, AL, and GA.

Population No evidence of declines; likely sensitive to deforestation.

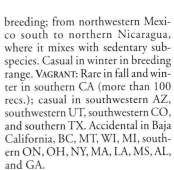

adult ♂

juvenile

SLATE-THROATED REDSTART *Myioborus miniatus*

adult ♂

An easily identified, flashy warbler, the Slate-throated Redstart occurs casually north of Mexico. Polytypic (12 ssp.; nominate in N.A.). L 6" (15 cm)

Identification The Slate-throated frequently fans its long, graduated tail. ADULT MALE: Slate-gray upperparts and wings; a blackish face, throat, and sides; a dark chestnut crown patch; a black tail with large white spots on outer tail feathers; red breast and belly; undertail coverts mottled white and slate gray. Central and South American subspecies show orange or yellow breast and belly. ADULT FEMALE: Nearly identical to the adult male, but with duller red underparts; a slate-gray face, throat, and sides; and smaller chestnut crown patch. JUVENILE: Similar to adult, but lacks red underparts; paler slaty coloring on breast and belly; undertail coverts mottled with cinnamon-brown.

Similar Species See Painted Redstart.

Voice CALL: A single, high *tsip,* similar to the call of the Chipping Sparrow. SONG: Primary song a variable series of *sweet s-wee* notes, often accelerating toward the end of the series. Although the pattern can suggest Painted Redstart, it is higher pitched and thinner, with slurred single notes rather than doubled ones. Some versions recall the songs of Yellow-rumped or Magnolia Warblers.

Status & Distribution Breeds in montane coniferous and mixed forest from northwestern and central Mexico south to northern S.A., south in Andes to central Bolivia. VAGRANT: Casual to accidental in spring (mostly Apr.–May) to southern AZ (5 recs.), southeastern NM (1 rec.), and western and southern TX (more than 5 recs.).

Population Little information is available, but this species is common and widespread in its home range.

Genus Euthlypis

FAN-TAILED WARBLER *Euthlypis lachrymosa*

adult

This unique, large warbler is similar in behavior to redstarts but is more secretive. The Fan-tailed is often seen near the ground or walking. Polytypic (3 ssp.; *tephra* in N.A.). L 5.8" (15 cm)

Identification Long, graduated white-tipped tail held open, swung up and down and side to side; long pink legs. ADULT: Distinct head pattern: blackish head with broken white eye ring, white supraloral spot, and yellow crown patch; gray upperparts, yellow underparts with tawny-orange wash on breast. IMMATURE: Very similar to adult,

with slightly duller black face.

Similar Species The Yellow-breasted Chat has less yellow on underparts and lacks yellow crown patch. The Slate-throated Redstart is red below, shows more white in tail, and has no white marks on head.

Voice CALL: A distinctive, high, thin *tsew* or a penetrating *schree*. SONG: Primary song a series of sweet notes ending in a sharp upslur or downslur: *che che che a-wee wee che-cheer*.

Status & Distribution Breeds in moist, shady, steep-walled ravines from Pacific slope of northwestern Mexico south

to Nicaragua, with a disjunct population in coastal east-central Mexico. VAGRANT: Casual from spring to early fall to southeastern AZ (7 recs.).

Genus Basileuterus

With 24 species, this mainly tropical genus—the second largest in the wood-warbler family—reaches its greatest diversity in South America. Only 2 species have been recorded in North America as vagrants. Most species are olive to gray above, yellow to whitish below, with some patterning on the crown or face.

GOLDEN-CROWNED WARBLER *Basileuterus culicivorus*

adult

The most widespread member of the genus, the Golden-crowned occurs only casually north of Mexico. Polytypic (13 ssp.; *brasherii* in N.A.). L 5" (13 cm)

Identification ADULT: Olive-gray upperparts; bright yellow underparts. Distinctive head pattern: yellow central crown patch, broad black lateral stripes, grayish olive auriculars, dull yellowish olive supercilium, gray loral spot, narrow broken yellow eye ring. IMMATURE: Very similar to adult; some show slightly less distinct head pattern.

Similar Species Orange-crowned and Wilson's are superficially similar, lack distinct crown stripes. Worm-eating is buffy, not yellow; has a larger bill.

Voice CALL: Often repeated, slightly

buzzy *tuck.* SONG: Several clear whistled notes, ending with a distinct upslur: *see-whew-whew-wee-see?*

Status & Distribution Disjunct populations from west-central and southeastern Mexico through much of C.A., northern S.A., the Guianas, and much of eastern Brazil to northern Argentina and Uruguay. VAGRANT: Casual, mainly in winter from Nov.–Mar. (1 rec. Oct.; 1 late Apr. rec.), to extreme southern TX (11 recs.). Accidental in spring to southern coastal TX and east-central NM.

RUFOUS-CAPPED WARBLER *Basileuterus rufifrons*

adult

Inhabiting dense brush in montane areas, the Rufous-capped has occurred north of Mexico casually and has even attempted to breed. Polytypic (8 ssp.). L 5.3" (13 cm)

Identification The Rufous-capped has a short, thick bill. It cocks and waves its long tail like a wren or gnatcatcher. ADULT: Distinct head pattern with rufous on crown and cheeks, broad white supercilium, dark lores; grayish olive upperparts; bright yellow throat and breast, white belly, grayish buff sides and flanks.

Geographic Variation Two northernmost subspecies recorded in North

America. The subspecies likely recorded from Texas *(jouyi)* is generally darker and more richly colored than the subspecies recorded from Arizona *(caudatus).*

Similar Species Unlike any other North American warbler.

Voice CALL: A hard *tik,* sometimes doubled or in a series. SONG: Primary song is a rapid, variable series of *chip* notes, chirps, and trills, usually changing in pitch and pace.

Status & Distribution From northern Mexico south to Panama and extreme northwestern S.A. VAGRANT: Casual from spring to fall to western and

central TX (16 recs.) and southeastern AZ (10 recs., inc. 1 attempted nesting in 1977).

Genus *Icteria*

Icteria, the most aberrant genus in the wood-warbler family, comprises only a single species—the Yellow-breasted Chat—which is characterized by its large size, exceptionally thick bill, long tail, and unique voice. In the past, some have suggested a closer relationship between *Icteria* and the tanagers (family Thraupidae) and, more recently, between *Icteria* and the mockingbirds (family Mimidae). However, DNA evidence places the Yellow-breasted Chat with the wood-warblers and supports the unique status of the genus.

YELLOW-BREASTED CHAT *Icteria virens*

western ♂
auricollis

eastern ♂
virens

eastern ♀
virens

The Yellow-breasted Chat is heard more often than it is seen: It is skulky and secretive in its brushy and often impenetrable habitat. In keeping with its secretive nature, the Yellow-breasted builds a well-concealed nest near to the ground in a dense thicket or shrub; here it lays 3 to 5 eggs from May to June. Polytypic. L 7.5" (19 cm)
Identification Very large—the largest of all wood-warblers—with a thick bill and a long tail. Nominate subspecies described. ADULT MALE: The bright yellow throat and breast sharply contrast with the white belly and undertail coverts and with the pale grayish flanks. The grayish olive head has white spectacles, black lores, and a very narrow white submoustachial stripe. The upperparts, wings, and tail are all olive green. The bill is black, with some gray at the base of the lower mandible. ADULT FEMALE: Very similar to the male, but the head is more olive and the lores are duller. It also shows yellowish pink at the base of the lower mandible and pale buffy on the flanks. IMMATURE: Similar to, but slightly duller than, the adult female.
Geographic Variation The variation between subspecies is subtle. The western subspecies (*auricollis*) is longer tailed (it is sometimes known as the "Long-tailed Chat"). It upperparts are more grayish olive; it has a broader white submoustachial stripe; and it shows richer orange-yellow on the

breast (though this can be affected by diet) than the nominate *virens*, described above.
Similar Species The Common Yellowthroat is much smaller, and it shows a prominent black mask. The Yellow-throated Vireo is also much smaller. It shows yellow spectacles and white wing bars, and it is much more arboreal than the Yellow-breasted Chat.
Voice CALL: The Yellow-breasted—though not often heard—gives a variety of calls, including a harsh *chough,* a nasal *air,* and a sharp *cuk-cuk-cuk.* SONG: It has an extensive repertoire, consisting of a series of irregularly spaced scolds, chuckles, mews, rattles, and other unmusical sounds. It often incorporates harsh *sheh sheh sheh sheh* calls and a higher-pitched *tu-tu-tu* series. Its songs are suggestive of mockingbirds or thrashers, especially given its tendency to mimic other birds. It is also known to sing in flight.
Status & Distribution Uncommon; a medium-distance migrant, both trans-Gulf and circum-Gulf. BREEDING: Low, dense vegetation with open canopy, including shrubby habitat in wetland areas and early second growth. MIGRATION: During spring migration in the East, it arrives on the

Gulf Coast in mid-Apr., reaching the Midwest by early May. In the West, it arrives in CA and southern AZ in mid-Apr., reaching northernmost breeding areas in Canada by late May. Its departure from the breeding grounds in fall is difficult to detect once singing stops in late summer. It moves mainly late Aug.–late Sept., with stragglers remaining into late Oct. WINTER: Shrub-steppe with dense, low cover of woody vegetation from northern Mexico south to western Panama. Rarely in southern U.S. and casually farther north. VAGRANT: Casual in spring migration north of the breeding range; regular in fall to Atlantic Canada; rare in fall to Bermuda; casual in fall and winter to Bahamas; very rare in Cuba and possibly Grand Cayman Is. Three specimens from Greenland.
Population Reports show precipitous declines throughout much of the Yellow-breasted Chat's range. There has been a near total withdrawal from southern New England. Populations are more stable in much of the West, but those in California and some adjacent areas are greatly reduced. Reasons for the declines are unclear but are probably due to reforestation and urbanization.

BANANAQUIT Family previously Coerebidae; now undetermined

Bananaquit (Bahamas, Mar.)

Formerly, the exclusively neotropical family Coerebidae included the honeycreepers, conebills, dacnises, and flower-piercers, which were assigned to other families (mainly Thraupidae, tanagers). The Bananaquit was not reassigned, and it remained the sole member of Coerebidae until the AOU removed this family from taxonomic status in 2005.

Structure The Bananaquit has a long, thin, decurved bill. Its tongue is specialized for feeding on nectar.

Plumage Variable, with a tendency toward dark hues. Many subspecies have a gray throat, and in the southern Caribbean some are almost entirely black. The amount of yellow on the underparts is also variable.

Behavior Though fairly social, the birds can be territorial especially at food sources, which include nectar, fruits, and berries. Sometimes they pierce the bases of larger flowers to gain access to nectar, and they often hang upside down when feeding. Their diet also includes small insects. They build untidy globular nests and use empty nests for roosting at night.

Distribution The Bananaquit is generally found in lowlands throughout the Caribbean except in Cuba, from southern Mexico south through Central America, and in South America south to northern Peru and southeastern Brazil. It is absent from a large area of the Amazon basin.

Taxonomy Genetic data have shown that the genus *Coereba* is related closely to various other species and does not warrant classification in a separate family. As of 2005, precise relationships of the genus were not clear; placement within another family was left undetermined pending further research. The formal term for this status is the Latin *incertae sedis,* meaning that the taxonomic position is uncertain.

Conservation The Bananaquit is common throughout its range and is well adapted to the presence of humans.
—*Allen T. Chartier*

Genus *Coereba*

BANANAQUIT *Coereba flaveola*

The Bananaquit is a small, short-tailed, warbler-like, black-and-white bird with a yellow breast and rump, and a thin, distinctly decurved bill. It feeds on nectar, often piercing through the bases of flowers. Polytypic (41 ssp.; *bahamensis* in N.A.). L 4.5" (11 cm)

Identification ADULT: Head black with long white supercilium and throat. Back, wings, and tail black, with small white tips on outer tail feathers and white patch at base of primaries. Breast yellow. Belly and undertail coverts white. Red gape corners. JUVENILE: Duller than adult, with yellowish supercilium and little or no yellow on dull white underparts. Has duller rump patch and duller gape.

Similar Species Adults are unlike any other North American bird. Juveniles may superficially resemble a Wood-Warbler, but are readily distinguished by their decurved bill.

Voice CALL NOTES: An unmusical *tsip.* Young birds give a *chit, chit, chit* similar to warblers. SONG: Several ticks followed by rapid clicking in Bahamas. Other subspecies give a thin, high-pitched, tumbling trill.

Status & Distribution Common in second growth and near human settlements. Resident throughout the Caribbean, except Cuba, from southern Mexico through Panama, and South American lowlands to southern Brazil. BREEDING: Related to rainfall, peaking in Feb.–Apr. in Bahamas. An untidy, globular nest

juvenile
bahamensis

adult
bahamensis

in the middle to top of shrub or small tree on outer branch (2–4 eggs). VAGRANT: Casual in southern FL (40+ recs.), mainly Jan.–Mar.

Population The Bananaquit is very common within its extensive range, and the bird seems to do well in gardens with abundant flowers.

TANAGERS Family Thraupidae

Scarlet Tanager, first-spring male (NJ, May)

Brightly plumaged male tanagers are some of the more recognizable songbirds found in North America, whereas females can be more challenging to identify. All the breeding tanagers in North America are members of the genus *Piranga* and are part of a widespread New World family of more than 250 species, which reaches its highest diversity in Central and South America. Identification marks to focus on include pattern and shade of the red plumage, presence or absence of white in the wings and tail, and bill shape and color. All breeding species are neotropical migrants.

Structure Considered part of the 9-primaried oscines, tanagers are relatively large songbirds, larger than warblers and more chunky than orioles. All have distinctive stocky bills, well adapted for feeding on fruit.

Behavior Mainly insectivorous during the spring and summer, tanagers switch to frugivorous in the late summer, fall, and winter. They are highly migratory, vacating breeding grounds in late summer and wintering from Mexico (as in Western) through Amazonia (as in Scarlet) and generally live in the canopy of forested habitats. Tanagers are usually found singly or in pairs during the breeding season but are known to migrate in small flocks. Songs of all species (except in the genus *Spindalis*) are similar, though calls are generally distinctive.

Plumage Bright male plumages are very distinctive, ranging from all red in the Summer, to bright red with black wings in the Scarlet, to black and yellow with a red head in the Western. Females are generally dull greenish yellow to grayish, some with white wing bars, others plain winged. It usually takes 2 years to acquire adult male plumage; first-spring males are often blotchy (esp. in the Summer Tanager) with some adult characteristics.

Distribution Of the 4 regularly breeding species, 1 nests exclusively in the East (Scarlet) and 1 is found in both the East and West (Summer), while the others (Western and Hepatic) are western species. The Flame-colored is mainly a Mexican species that is casual in Arizona during spring and summer; has nested recently. The Western Spindalis is a Caribbean species that is a casual visitor to south Florida and the Florida Keys.

Taxonomy Recent genetic studies of the *Piranga* suggest that our tanagers are actually more closely related to the Cardinalidae (cardinals, grosbeaks, and buntings) and may not be true tanagers after all. Of the North American breeding species, only the Summer and the Hepatic are polytypic.

Conservation In the East, the Scarlet Tanager has had its population decline due to forest fragmentation and negative effects from cowbird parasitism. Western populations of the Summer Tanager are declining due to loss of riparian habitats. Elsewhere in the New World, BirdLife International lists 22 species as threatened and 15 others as near threatened. —*Gary H. Rosenberg*

TANAGERS Genus *Piranga*

The 9 species, exclusively found in the Americas, include 4 regular breeding and 1 casual visitor in the ABA area. Males are mostly bright red in plumage; females are duller, greenish yellow. North American species are neotropical migrants. Recent genetic studies suggest *Piranga* are more closely related to cardinals and grosbeaks than to true tanagers.

SUMMER TANAGER *Piranga rubra*

Often taken for granted, the brightly plumaged male Summer Tanager is one of the more spectacular breeding birds of North America. The uniform blood-red feathers seen against a bright green background are quite a sight. The Summer feeds mainly on fruit, except during breeding season. Rather large and often sluggish, it usually sits still for long periods of time. Quite vocal, the Summer is often detected by its distinctive call. The bill is generally bulky and long and ranges from gray to pale horn in color. The head often shows a slight crested appearance. Polytypic. L 7.8" (20 cm)

Identification Sexually dimorphic. BREEDING MALE: The adult male is unmistakable—all bright red—and achieves its brightest plumage by the end of its second calendar year. BREEDING FEMALE: Generally mustard yellow-orange, with greener wings and upperparts. Some may have dull red mixed in the plumage or may lack orange tones, resembling quite closely immature female Scarlet Tanagers. FIRST-SPRING MALE: Mixture of red and greenish yellow, sometimes blotchy, sometimes with entirely red head and breast. FIRST-WINTER FEMALE: Can lack all mustard tones and look very similar to a Scarlet Tanager.

Geographic Variation Eastern birds *(rubra)* are slightly smaller, deeper red, with smaller bills. Western birds *(cooperi)* are larger, paler overall, with larger, paler bills.

Similar Species Adult males differ from the Scarlet Tanager by lacking black wings. The male Hepatic Tanager is more brick red in color and has a grayer bill, grayer flanks, and a dark grayish cheek patch. Also note difference in call notes. Females lacking all orange tones more problematic and can be confused with either female Scarlet or Hepatic Tanagers. Note yellow undersurface of tail in the Summer, lacking in the Scarlet. The Summer also has a

longer tail and longer bill than the Scarlet. Female Hepatics less uniform underneath, with brighter yellow throats contrasting with grayer underparts. **Voice** CALL: A distinctive *pi-tuck* or *pi-ti-tuck* or *ki-ti-tuck,* sometimes extended to several notes. SONG: An

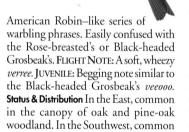

adult ♂

1st spring ♂

red morph ♀

rubra

♀

American Robin–like series of warbling phrases. Easily confused with the Rose-breasted's or Black-headed Grosbeak's. FLIGHT NOTE: A soft, wheezy *verree.* JUVENILE: Begging note similar to the Black-headed Grosbeak's *veeooo.*

Status & Distribution In the East, common in the canopy of oak and pine-oak woodland. In the Southwest, common

in cottonwood-willow habitats along permanent streams and rivers. BREEDING: Nesting birds arrive mid-Apr.–early May. MIGRATION: Nominate *rubra* is mainly a trans-Gulf migrant, common from along upper TX coast to coastal FL. Regular at the Dry Tortugas. WINTER: Mainly southern Mexico through C.A., uncommonly to northern S.A. Rare in winter in southern U.S. from FL to CA.

Population Western population threatened by loss of riparian habitats.

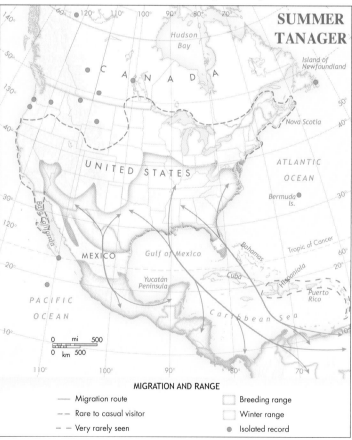

SUMMER TANAGER

MIGRATION AND RANGE

— Migration route
-- - Rare to casual visitor
- - Very rarely seen

Breeding range
Winter range
Isolated record

HEPATIC TANAGER *Piranga flava*

hepatica

adult ♂

Fairly common throughout the pine and pine-oak forests of the Southwest, the male Hepatic Tanager is often seen singing from exposed perches and is normally found in different habitat and at higher elevation than the similar, brighter Summer Tanager. Mainly insectivorous during summer, the Hepatic is known to eat fruit during fall and winter. Polytypic (15 ssp.). L 8" (20 cm)

Identification MALE: Entirely dark brick-red body, mixed with gray on the back and flanks. Auriculars are gray, and the bill is heavy and dark gray. FEMALE: Somewhat variable. Mostly greenish,

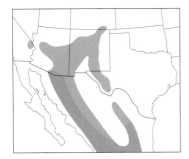

with strong gray overtones to the back, head, and flanks, contrasting with a bright yellow to yellow-orange throat and forehead. Bill similar to male's. IMMATURE MALE: Like female. JUVENILE: Similar to female, but more streaked above.

Geographic Variation In the United States, the subspecies *hepatica,* from southeastern California and southern Arizona, tends to be larger and duller than the *dextra,* from northern New Mexico to western Texas, with more extensive gray on auriculars and flanks.

Similar Species Males similar to the brighter red Summer, which lacks gray auriculars and grayish wash on the back and flanks and typically has paler bill. The female Hepatic's grayer overall plumage, contrasting with its bright yellow throat, is quite different from the uniform yellow-orange plumage of the female Summer. The female Western can be as gray as the Hepatic, but the larger Hepatic lacks wing bars. Note very different calls from other *Piranga.*

Voice CALL: A single low *chuck.* SONG: Robinlike and clearer than the West-

ern's; more similar to the song of the Black-headed Grosbeak, with which it overlaps.

Status & Distribution Fairly common in the Southwest's mixed coniferous forests (5,000–8,000 ft.), extending south through much of S.A. MIGRATION: Rather rare in lowlands, mainly in riparian areas, along streams. WINTER: Rare but regular winter resident on oak hillsides, mainly in the Patagonia-Nogales area of southeastern AZ. VAGRANT: Rare to coastal CA; accidental to IL, WY, and LA.

Population Populations in Texas and Arizona are susceptible to long-term drought.

SCARLET TANAGER *Piranga olivacea*

breeding adult ♂

fall adult ♂

The breeding male Scarlet Tanager is one of the easier North American birds to identify. Often seen in small flocks during migration, the Scarlet sings on the breeding grounds and feeds high in the canopy. It moves sluggishly and can be difficult to spot. Monotypic. L 7" (18 cm)

Identification Sexually dimorphic. Both sexes have whitish wing lining. BREEDING MALE: Unmistakable, brilliant red all over, with black wings and tail. The bill, somewhat short and stubby, is thick at the base. BREEDING FEMALE: Females are entirely yellow-green, with yellower throat and sides, dark wings and tail,

a thin eye ring, and wing coverts with greenish edging. Some adult females show weak wing bars. WINTER ADULT: Entirely greenish yellow, but retains black scapulars, wings, and tail. Late summer birds can be blotchy red. IMMATURE MALE: Resembles adult female but tends to be brighter yellow and has black scapulars and wing coverts. IMMATURE FEMALE: More problematic. Entirely greenish yellow with grayer wings and tail.

Similar Species Immature females are similar to some Summers that lack orange tones. Note the Scarlet's gray undersurface to tail, which is yellowish in the Summer. An adult female Western typically shows more distinct wing bars, a grayer back contrasting with yellower rump, and a longer, paler bill.

Voice CALL: A hoarse *chip* or *chip-burr,* unlike other tanagers. SONG: Robinlike but raspy. Very similar to Western Tanager's, a *querit queer querry querit queer.* FLIGHT NOTE: A whistled *puwi.*

Status & Distribution Commonly nests in deciduous forests in the eastern half of N.A. BREEDING: Arrives late

Apr.–mid-May. MIGRATION: Trans-Gulf migrant. WINTER: Mainly in Amazonia and the foothills of the Andes in S.A. VAGRANT: Casual west to CA coast, mainly in Oct. and Nov.

Population Sensitive to forest fragmentation and parasitism by Brown-headed Cowbirds.

1st spring ♂

1st fall ♂

WESTERN TANAGER *Piranga ludoviciana*

The striking black-and-yellow Western Tanager, with its bright red head, is one of the more characteristic summer species of western pine forests. Although brightly plumaged, it can be quite inconspicuous when feeding on insects high in the canopy or singing for long periods without moving. During migration, the Western often feeds on fruit and is more conspicuous. The Western is the only regular North American tanager with wing bars. Note its yellow underwing linings in flight. Its bill is small for a *Piranga*, larger in size than the Scarlet's, but smaller than other species' bills. Monotypic. L 7.3" (19 cm)
Identification Sexually dimorphic. BREEDING MALE: Plumage is un-mistakable. Bright yellow underparts, yellow rump, black back, and conspicuous wing bars contrast with black wings (yellow upper bar, lower white bar) and bright red head. BREEDING FEMALE: Duller, mostly greenish yellow below, grayish back and wings, with 2 thinner, pale wing bars. Underparts variable; some have brighter yellow belly and flanks, while others are quite gray. NONBREEDING ADULT MALE: Similar to breeding male, but loses red head. Duller red confined in varying amounts to forehead and chin. Black in plumage not as crisp, with some greenish edging to back. FIRST-FALL MALE: Generally yellow-green, yellower below with a yellow upper wing bar, and white lower bar. Bill noticeably pale. FIRST-FALL FEMALE: Can be very dull grayish yellow, still with 2 thin wing bars.

Similar Species Adult males unlikely to be confused with other tanagers. In southeastern Arizona, beware of confusing the Western with the Flame-colored Tanager, which has 2 white wing bars, a striped red-and-black back, white tips to the tertials, and white-tipped tail feathers. The Western has hybridized with the Flame-colored; the offspring has a mixture of Western and Flame-colored characteristics. The female Flame-colored has a streaked back, larger bill, and white tips to both its tertials and tail. Also note that some female Scarlets show pale wing bars, but female Westerns usually show a yellow upper bar. Also, some worn Westerns show little or no wing bars, but when compared to the Scarlet, the Western has a grayer back, a longer tail, and a larger bill.
Voice CALL: A *pit-er-ick,* with a noticeably rising inflection. Very different from both the Summer's and the Scarlet's, but indistinguishable from the Flame-colored's. SONG: Similar in tone and pattern to both the Scarlet's and Flame-colored's. FLIGHT NOTE: A whistled *howee* or *weet.*

Status & Distribution A common bird of western coniferous forests, although it breeds in deciduous riparian habitats as far north as southeast AK. MIGRATION: A common migrant throughout the lowlands of the West in spring (mid-Apr.–early June) and fall (mid-July–Sept.). WINTER: Found mainly from central Mexico south (rarely) to Costa Rica and Panama. Uncommon to rare in winter in southern coastal CA. VAGRANT: Very rare wanderer, mainly in fall, to eastern U.S.
Population Not threatened.

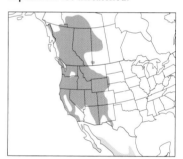

FLAME-COLORED TANAGER *Piranga bidentata*

A montane resident from Mexico to western Panama, the Flame-colored Tanager has become an increasingly regular summer visitor to the mountain canyons of southeastern Arizona, with several recent nesting records. It behaves much like other *Piranga* tanagers, mainly singing and feeding high up in cottonwoods and sycamores, with virtually all records from between 5,000 and 7,000 feet in elevation. Males are very striking in appearance. In Arizona, the Flame-colored Tanager occasionally forms mixed pairs with the similar-sounding Western Tanager. Its alternative name is Stripe-backed Tanager. Polytypic. L 7.3" (19 cm)

Identification Sexually dimorphic. ADULT MALE: Males are quite variable. Some have bright, flame orange-red heads and underparts, whereas others are duller. The characteristic feature of the male is the orange-red back streaked with black. The rump is also usually orange-red with black streaks. The Flame-colored has a distinctive darker cheek patch, normally with a blackish rear border. Its wings are blackish, contrasting with 2 distinct white wing bars and white tips to all the tertials. The flanks are grayer, and the blackish tail has white tips to the outer feathers, visible from underneath. The bill of the Flame-colored is rather

heavy and gray. ADULT FEMALE: Female is much different in color, being greenish yellow, but is similarly patterned with a streaked back, 2 white wing bars, and white tips to the tertials and outer tail feathers. FIRST-SPRING MALE: Yellower than typical adult male, its reddish orange coloring is confined to forehead and face. IMMATURE FEMALE: The back has less-distinct streaking.

Geographic Variation Males of the western Mexican subspecies *bidentata* are more orange than the eastern subspecies *sanguinolenta*, which tends to be redder.

Similar Species The Flame-colored Tanager overlaps with the similar-sounding Western Tanager in the mountains of Arizona, where the species have been known to form mixed pairs. Hybrids are well documented, with some resembling male Flame-coloreds, though they usually have some noticeable Western feature, such as a yellow upper wing bar, a yellow unstreaked rump, or intermediate white spotting on the tertials or tail tips. Hybrid females undoubtedly occur, but apparently they are more difficult to distinguish.

Voice CALL: A rising *pit-er-ick,* virtu-

ally indistinguishable from the rising call of the Western; also gives a huskier, low-pitched *prreck*. SONG: Similar to Western Tanager's.

Status & Distribution Rare-to-casual spring and summer visitor to montane canyons in southeastern AZ. BREEDING: Has nested several times in AZ. All nests have been in well-wooded mountain canyons in the Santa Rita, Huachuca, and Chiricahua Mountains of southeastern AZ, usually where sycamores occur. VAGRANT: Casual in the Chisos Mountains of western TX and along or near the lower Rio Grande River Valley.

Genus *Spindalis*

Generally distributed in the Bahamas and West Indies, the 4 species in this genus were previously considered 1 species —the Stripe-headed Tanager. Small tanagers with relatively short, stout bills. The male's plumage is a combination of black, white, and rich tawny; the female is very dull grayish green with a white spot in the wings.

WESTERN SPINDALIS *Spindalis zena*

Formerly named the Stripe-headed Tanager, this fancy West Indian tanager is a rare visitor from the Bahamas to coastal southeastern Florida and the Florida Keys. Typically found in fruiting trees, where it feeds sluggishly, the Western Spindalis sometimes sits motionless for long periods. Males have a striking plumage: a mixture of tawny brown, black, and white—unlike any other North American bird. Females are totally different and much duller. The Spindalis is smaller than other North American tanagers and has a very small bill. Polytypic. L 6.8" (17 cm)

Identification MALE: Plumage unmistakable. Most striking are the black-and-white stripes on the head. The Western's wings are black with entirely white greater coverts form-

ing a large white wing patch; most of the flight feathers have a white edging. Underparts are tawny with gray flanks; the lower belly and undertail coverts are white, and the back is black (or green in some subspecies), contrasting with tawny rump. The tail is black with white outer tail feathers. A white undersurface to tail is visible when viewed from underneath. In flight, the Western shows large white patches at the base of both primaries and secondaries. FEMALE: Much duller and completely different from male, the female's plumage is a drab grayish olive with darker auriculars, paler throat and malar. The wing coverts' narrow white edging and the primaries' white base together form a white tick visible on the folded wing, similar to that found

on the female Black-throated Blue Warbler.

Geographic Variation Black-backed birds from the central and southern Bahamas *(zena)* make up the bulk of the Florida reports. Green-backed birds from the northern Bahamas *(townsendi)* have been reported. Intergrades between the 2 Bahamian subspecies are possible. Also, an apparent recent record from Key West of the Green-backed Cuban subspecies *pretrei*.

Similar Species The males are unlikely to be confused with other species. The females, however, present more of a problem. They look most similar to female Black-throated Blue Warblers, which also show a white spot on the folded wing. Note that the Western Spindalis has a stout gray tanagerlike bill and white edging to wing coverts. It is also distinguished from the female Black-throated Blue Warbler by its very different behavior and larger size.

Voice CALL: A thin, high *tseee*, which is given singly or in a short series. SONG: Seldom heard in the U.S. In the Bahamas, a series of high thin notes ending in buzzy phrases.

Status & Distribution A common resident in the Bahamas and northern West Indies. A rare visitor to parks in coastal southern FL and the FL Keys, particularly found in fruiting trees. Most of the reports from spring, fall, and winter, with no summer records.

EMBERIZIDS Family Emberizidae

Baird's Sparrow (ND, June)

I n North America, the Emberizidae family is best represented by a bewildering array of sparrows, most of which are cryptically patterned with various shades of brown and are affectionately known to many birders as the quintessential LBJs: "Little Brown Jobs." While sparrow identification is one of the greater challenges for the beginning birder, familiarity with distinctive shapes of the genera, as well as with the habits and habitats of sparrows themselves, simplifies the process. **Structure** Emberizids are fairly small perching birds, ranging in size from very small seedeaters and grassquits to the much larger towhees. Their bills are conical, their wings are typically short and rounded, and their tails are often long.

Behavior Behavior is often quite skulking, particularly so in some species. The exception is during the breeding season, when males sing from elevated perches or perform skylarking flight songs. The songs can be faint and unremarkable, but more often they are quite complex and beautiful. Most species have several calls, which may include a simple chip and a high, thin lisping note. The latter note is often given as the flight note by nocturnal migrants (e.g., the White-throated Sparrow) but is used more frequently as a contact call when on the ground. **Plumage** Typically, the emberizid plumage is a dull collection of brown, gray, black, and white, but some species in North America have areas of bright yellow feathering or greenish color on the back and wings. In many species the sexes are similar, but a few species (e.g., grassquits, seedeaters, and certain towhees) show moderate to pronounced sexual dimorphism.

Distribution Emberizids occur worldwide, except in Australasia. They are most diverse in the New World, with just 42 Old World species, most of which are in the genus *Emberiza*. Although New World diversity is centered in the tropics, some 60 species are known north of Mexico. Preferred habitats are often open country, including fields, deserts, gardens, marshes, riparian areas, and wood edges; a few species prefer the forest interior. Most North American species are short-distance migrants, but some species inhabiting the southern United States are resident. Nests are typically an open cup that is placed on the ground or low in shrubbery. A typical clutch would include several eggs (2–5), which are often unmarked and whitish or pale blue, though occasionally they are patterned. The winter diet is primarily composed of seeds and other vegetable matter; in summer that diet is heavily supplemented by insects.

Taxonomy Emberizidae is currently the second largest passerine family in the world (second only to the tyrant flycatcher family Tyrannidae), comprising some 321 species in 71 genera. The taxonomic relationships of various groups within the family—specifically seedeaters, grassquits, and certain other neotropical genera—have been controversial, and these birds have not always been placed within Emberizidae.

Conservation These small birds are often fairly catholic in their habitat requirements, so most species have stable populations. However, certain species are less generalistic about their habitat, and some populations are severely depressed, endangered, or even extinct; habitat loss is almost always to blame. —*Marshall J. Iliff*

SEEDEATERS AND GRASSQUITS Genera *Sporophila* and *Tiaris*

These neotropical genera include 34 *Sporophila* species and 5 *Tiaris* species. All are small, with strong sexual dimorphism. *Sporophila* seedeaters have a distinctive "Roman nose" bill and a fairly long, rounded tail; *Tiaris* grassquits have a short, conical bill and a short, squared tail. Several other species known as grassquits are in different genera.

WHITE-COLLARED SEEDEATER *Sporophila torqueola*

sharpei

♀

1st winter ♂

adult ♂

During spring, males sing their cheery song from high perches. Females and nonbreeders can be secretive as they forage near the ground. Loosely colonial as nesters, White-collareds may form small flocks in the nonbreeding season. Polytypic. L 4.5" (11 cm) **Identification** Size, bill shape, and rounded tail are distinctive. ADULT MALE: Black cap and wings, white crescent below the eye, an incomplete buffy collar, white throat and breast washed with buff, narrow white wing bars, and white patch at base of primaries. IMMATURE MALE: Paler, browner, less distinctly marked. FEMALE: Brown overall; darker on wings with paler buffy color on breast; narrow wing bars. **Geographic Variation** Numerous subspecies in Middle America; Texas breeders are relatively indistinctly marked *sharpei*. Escapees in California are apparently the more boldly marked, buff-breasted western Mexican subspecies *torqueola* or *atriceps*. **Similar Species** Females can be confused with *Passerina* buntings or the Lesser Goldfinch; note the seedeater's smaller size, more arched bill, more rounded tail, different coloration, and distinctive calls. **Voice** CALL: Distinct, high *wink;* loud, whistled *chew;* and husky, rising *che*. SONG: A variable, clear-toned *sweet sweet sweet sweet cheer cheer cheer* that is pitched high, then low; recalls the American Goldfinch's song. **Status & Distribution** Mexico south to west Panama. YEAR-ROUND: Uncommon and local along Rio Grande in Starr, Zapata, and Webb counties, where it prefers stands of cane. Formerly occurred farther east along Rio Grande, but now casual there. EXOTIC: Rare but regular in urban southern CA, southeastern AZ, and southern TX; no established populations. **Population** Formerly more widespread, it lost ground in the U.S. due to habitat loss and possibly pesticide use. Small extant U.S. population is stable but vulnerable.

YELLOW-FACED GRASSQUIT *Tiaris olivaceus*

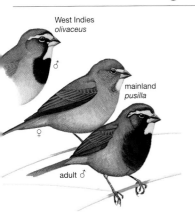

West Indies *olivaceus*

♂

mainland *pusilla*

♀

adult ♂

This bird feeds on grass seeds in vacant lots and weedy edges. Males sing from perches. Polytypic. L 4.3" (11 cm) **Identification** Very small; short tail; small, conical bill; straight culmen. ADULT MALE: Black head, breast, and upper belly; golden yellow eyebrow, throat, and crescent below eye; olive above. ADULT FEMALE AND IMMATURE MALE: Traces of same head pattern; olive above, lacking black below. **Geographic Variation** Five subspecies, 2 of which have reached the U.S. Subspecies *pusillus,* which has a more extensive black breast, occurs from Mexico to S.A. and accounts for Texas records; Florida records pertain to *olivaceus* of Cuba, Jamaica, and nearby islands. **Similar Species** Male distinctive; female nondescript with suggestion of the male face pattern, unlike female Black-faced Grassquit. Escaped Cuban Grassquits *(T. canorus)* found in southern Florida have a yellow frame around a black (male) or chestnut (female) face. **Voice** CALL: A high-pitched *sik* or *tsi.* SONG: Thin, insectlike trills. **Status & Distribution** Common. Resident. RANGE: Middle and S.A., Caribbean islands. VAGRANT: Casual in southern FL and accidental in southernmost TX. **Population** Stable.

BLACK-FACED GRASSQUIT *Tiaris bicolor*

Behavior like the Yellow-faced Grassquit's. Polytypic. L 4.5" (11 cm) **Identification** Very small; short tail; a small, conical bill and a straight culmen. ADULT MALE: Black face and upper breast, dark olive elsewhere; black bill. FEMALE: Extremely nondescript, pale gray below, gray-olive above; pale horn bill. IMMATURE: Like female. **Geographic Variation** Multiple island subspecies in Caribbean; Florida records pertain to the Bahama Islands subspecies, *bicolor.* **Similar Species** Male unmistakable; compare with Yellow-faced Grassquit. Sparrows and *Passerina* buntings are larger and are more patterned about the wings, breast, and face. **Voice** CALL: A lisping *tst.* SONG: A buzzing *tik-zeee.* **Status & Distribution** Common. Resident. West Indies (absent from Cuba). VAGRANT: Casual in southeastern FL (7 scattered records). **Population** Stable.

♀

♂

TOWHEES Genus *Pipilo*

The 9 *Pipilo* (6 in the U.S.) are large, chesty sparrows with fairly long, rounded tails. They feed on the ground, scratching noisily in leaf litter with both feet at once. Towhees fly low to ground with several quick flaps alternated with a short, flat-winged glide; flight recalls a thrasher more than a sparrow. Most species show no sexual dimorphism.

GREEN-TAILED TOWHEE *Pipilo chlorurus*

spring

fall

juvenile

This ground-loving bird emerges infrequently in the open to feed. In breeding season, males sing from exposed perches. Monotypic. L 7.3" (19 cm)
Identification Olive upperparts and tail; gray head and underparts, fading to whitish belly. Distinct head pattern with obvious reddish crown, white loral spot, distinct white throat, dark moustachial stripe, and white malar stripe. JUVENILE: Two faint wing bars, streaked plumage overall, olive-tinged upperparts. Lacks reddish crown.
Similar Species The Chipping Sparrow lacks the green back and tail, is drastically smaller and more arboreal, and has a notched tail. See the Olive Sparrow.
Voice CALL: Catlike *mew,* like the Spotted Towhee's but clearer and more 2-parted. Also a thin, high *tseeee* (poss. flight note) and varied chips when excited. SONG: Whistled notes beginning with *weet-chur* and ending in a raspy trill.

Status & Distribution Fairly common. Breeds south to northern Baja California. BREEDING: Dense brush and chaparral on mountainsides, high plateaus, and sage steppes. MIGRATION: Spring late Mar.–mid-May, most mid-Apr.–early May. Fall July–Oct., peaking Sept.–early Oct. Uncommon migrant generally, rare along West Coast. WINTER: South to central Mexico; favors brushy draws and desert thickets. VAGRANT: Casual in fall and winter throughout the East.
Population Has probably declined as sagebrush steppes have been converted to agricultural and grazing land.

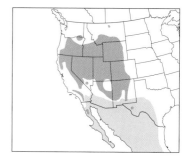

EASTERN TOWHEE *Pipilo erythrophthalmus*

juvenile

♀

Florida ♂
alleni

♂

erythrophthalmus   *alleni*

The Eastern behaves similarly to the Spotted Towhee. L 7.5" (19 cm)
Identification Conspicuous white corners on tail and white patch at base of primaries. MALE: Black upperparts, hood; rufous sides, white underparts. FEMALE: Black areas replaced by brown. JUVENILE: Brownish streaks below.
Geographic Variation Four subspecies show weak to moderate variation. Bird's overall size and the extent of white in its wings and tail decline from the northern part of the range to the Gulf Coast; bill, leg, and foot sizes increase. The large nominate subspecies (breeds in North) has red irides, most extensive white in tail. Smaller *alleni* of Florida paler and duller, with straw-colored irides. Intermediate southern subspecies *canaster* (west) and *rileyi* (east) have variably orange to straw-colored irides.
Similar Species See Spotted Towhee.

Voice CALL: Emphatic, upslurred *chewink;* in *alleni,* a clearer, even-pitched or upslurred *swee.* Also a high-pitched *szeeueet,* dropping in middle (poss. flight note). Various chips when agitated. SONG: Loud ringing *drink your tea,* sometimes with additional notes at beginning or shortened to *drink tea.* **Status & Distribution** Fairly common. BREEDING: Partial to second growth with dense shrubs and extensive leaf litter, coastal scrub or sand dune ridges, and mature southern pinelands. MIGRATION: Resident, except for partially migratory nominate subspecies. Migration primarily Oct. and Mar. VAGRANT: Casual to CO and NM. Accidental to AZ, ID, and Europe. **Population** Recent declines, especially in North, are due to urbanization. Southern populations more stable.

SPOTTED TOWHEE *Pipilo maculatus*

The Spotted and Eastern Towhees (formerly combined as the Rufous-sided Towhee) have a narrow hybrid zone in the central Great Plains. In general, a female Spotted differs less from a male than in the Eastern. L 7.5" (19 cm) **Identification** MALE: Plumage like Eastern Towhee's, except for white tips on median, greater coverts forming 2 white wing bars, variable white spotting on back and scapulars, lack of rectangular white patch at primary bases. FEMALE: Similar to male Spotted, but with a slate-gray hood (variable by ssp.). JUVENILE: Like juvenile Eastern, but lacks white primary patch. **Geographic Variation** Nine subspecies show weak to moderate variation. "Interior" birds have extensive white spotting above, prominent white tail corners; "Pacific" birds dark overall with white back spotting, reduced tail corners (variable). *Oregonus* is darkest; white increases southward to *megalonyx.* Within the "Interior" group, *arcticus* shows the most white spotting and most extensive white corners to the tail; other subspecies have less white, but are similar to one another. Females' head color varies as well. **Similar Species** Distinguished from the Eastern by white spotting on back, white wing bars, lack of patch at bases of primaries, and call. Hybrids occur in the Great Plains and winter to the south; often combine characteristics of both parents. **Voice** Song and calls also show great geographical variation. CALL: A descending and raspy mewing in *montanus;* an upslurred, questioning *queee* in *arcticus* and coastal subspecies. All subspecies also give a high, thin lisping *szeeueet* that drops in middle (poss. flight note), like the Eastern's call, and various chips when agitated. SONG: "Interior" group gives introductory notes, then a trill. "Pacific" birds sing a simple trill of variable speed. **Status & Distribution** Common. Some populations are largely resident; others are migratory. The most migratory subspecies is *arcticus.* Resident south to

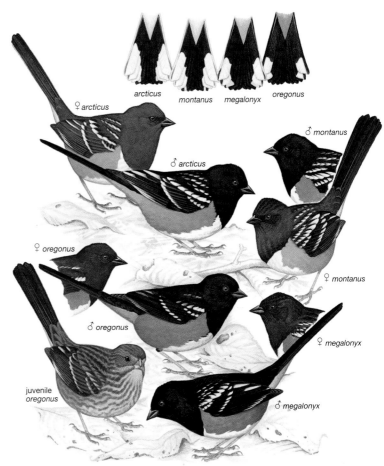

♀ *arcticus*

arcticus — *montanus* — *megalonyx* — *oregonus*

♂ *arcticus*

♂ *montanus*

♀ *oregonus*

♀ *montanus*

♂ *oregonus*

♀ *megalonyx*

juvenile *oregonus*

♂ *megalonyx*

Guatemala. Subspecies are *oregonus* (OR to BC), *falcifer* (coastal northwest CA), *megalonyx* (coastal central to southern CA), *clementae* (certain Channel Islands); *arcticus* (Great Plains), *montanus* (Rocky Mountains), *falcinellus* (south-central CA to OR), *curtatus* (primarily in Sierra Nevada), and *gaigei* (resident in mountains of southeastern NM and western TX). MIGRATION: Fall primarily Sept.–Oct.; spring Mar.–early May; earlier in Pacific states than interior. VAGRANT: Subspecies *arcticus* is casual to East. **Population** Stable in most areas. *Clementae* extirpated from San Clemente Island, one of California's Channel Islands, due to overgrazing by introduced goats; persists on Santa Catalina and Santa Rosa Islands. Another island subspecies from Guadalupe Island, off Baja California, is extinct.

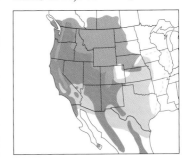

CANYON TOWHEE *Pipilo fuscus*

As its name implies, this species is common on shallow, rocky canyon slopes and rimrock in the Southwest. It is similar to the California, and the 2 were formerly considered the same species—the Brown Towhee. L 8" (20 cm)
Identification Plumage is pale gray-brown, fading to whitish on belly, with cinnamon-buff undertail coverts. Rufous-brown cap, buffy eye ring, buffy throat framed by necklace of black streaks typically forming black spot at base of throat. JUVENILE: Lacks rufous crown, has narrow buff wingbars, and is faintly streaked below.
Geographic Variation Three U.S. subspecies show weak and clinal variation in measurements, overall coloration, and prominence of the rufous cap. Two small, dark subspecies inhabit central and southwestern Texas *(texanus)* and the Sonoran and Chihuahuan Deserts of Arizona, New Mexico, and western Texas *(mesoleucus);* the more westerly subspecies has a much stronger rufous cap. Northern *mesatus* is large and pale, with a brown cap that is tinged rufous.
Similar Species The California Towhee has never been known to overlap in range, even as a vagrant. Compared to the California, the Canyon is paler, grayish rather than brown; it has a shorter tail and more contrast in the reddish crown, giving a capped appearance. The crown is sometimes raised as a short crest. The Canyon has a larger whitish belly patch with a diffuse dark spot at its junction with breast, a paler throat bordered by finer streaks, lores the same color as cheek, and a distinct buffy eye ring. Songs and calls are also very distinctive. See the Abert's Towhee.
Voice CALL: Shrill *chee-yep* or *chedup.* SONG: More musical, less metallic, than the California's; opens with a call note, followed by sweet slurred notes. Also gives duet of lisping and squealing notes, like the California.
Status & Distribution Common. Resident; no regular movements. YEAR-ROUND: Arid, hilly country; desert canyons. VAGRANT: Casual even a short distance out of range to southeastern UT and southwestern KS.
Population Stable.

CALIFORNIA TOWHEE *Pipilo crissalis*

juvenile

A widespread, abundant denizen of parks and gardens through most of coastal California, this species often occurs in pairs year-round, like the Canyon and the Abert's Towhees. The California and the similar Canyon were formerly conspecific, though they have never been known to overlap in range, even as vagrants. Polytypic. L 9" (23 cm)
Identification Brownish overall; crown slightly warmer brown than rest of upperparts. Buff throat bordered by a distinct broken ring of dark brown spots; no dark spot on breast, unlike the Canyon. Lores same color as throat, contrast with cheek; warm cinnamon undertail coverts . JUVENILE: Faint cinnamon wing bars; faint streaking below.
Geographic Variation Six subspecies in U.S. show weak and clinal variation in size and overall coloration. Generally, size decreases from north to south, with the 3 inland subspecies *(bullatus, car-olae, eremophilus)* averaging larger than the 3 coastal subspecies *(petulans, crissalis, senicula).* Coloration is generally darker to the north and paler to the south, but is fairly dark in *senicula* of coastal southern California.
Similar Species See Canyon and Abert's Towhees.
Voice CALL: Sharp metallic *chink* notes; also gives some thin, lispy notes and an excited, squealing series of notes, often delivered as a duet by a pair. SONG: Accelerating *chink* notes with stutters in the middle.
Status & Distribution Common. Resident; no known movements. YEAR-ROUND: Chaparral, coastal scrub, riparian thickets, parks, and gardens.
Population Stable, except for the federally threatened subspecies *eremophilus,* which is limited to Inyo County, California, and has declined due to degradation of its native riparian habitat; it may number fewer than 200 individuals.

ABERT'S TOWHEE *Pipilo aberti*

This towhee of the Southwest's low deserts can be fairly secretive inside thickets but is locally quite common, especially along the Colorado River and at the Salton Sea. It is similar to the Canyon and California Towhees, but its range does not overlap with the California, and the Canyon uses different habitats where it overlaps with the Abert's. Polytypic. L 9.5" (24 cm)

Identification A pale sandy, gray-brown, overall; black face (particularly the lores); warm brown upperparts, paler underparts; with cinnamon undertail coverts; tail contrastingly darker.

Geographic Variation The 2 subspecies are weakly defined and probably not separable in the field. The nominate occurs

in southeastern Arizona, extending barely into New Mexico. Subspecies *dumeticolus* occupies the rest of the range, including western Arizona, southeastern California (and northwestern Mexico) to southern Nevada and southwestern Utah. Compared to the nominate, it is paler, with a faint reddish tinge to the upperparts and underparts.

Similar Species The Canyon and California Towhees are similar, but only the former overlaps in range. The prominent black face, lack of streaking on the throat, and lack of a contrasting cap easily separate the Abert's from both species. Note also habitat differences: the Canyon is found on slopes and hills; the Abert's prefers moister, lower-lying areas, including mesquite thickets and riparian scrub.

Voice CALL: Piping or shrill *eeek*. Also high *seeep;* various chips when agitated. SONG: An accelerating series of *peek* notes, often ending in a jumble; frequently sings in a duet.

Status & Distribution Common. Resi-

dent; no known movements. Occurs south only to northern Sonora and Baja California. Inhabits desert woodlands, mesquite thickets, riparian growth, orchards, suburban yards. Found typically at lower altitudes than the similar Canyon.

Population The Abert's Towhee persists throughout its range, but it has declined rangewide due to the severe degradation of riparian habitat caused by the overuse of water in the Southwest, by grazing, and by the increase of invasive exotic plants. These impacts have been especially marked along the Colorado River.

Genus *Arremonops*

Of the 4 species in this genus, only the Olive Sparrow reaches the U.S.; the other species occur in Middle and South America. All are greenish on the back with head stripes; they tend to be fairly secretive, preferring dense brush where they forage on the ground. They are nonmigratory, typically occurring in pairs (sexes similar), and never form flocks.

OLIVE SPARROW *Arremonops rufivirgatus*

This fairly secretive sparrow stays close to dense cover, and it rapidly darts for the undergrowth when it is startled. Typically quite vocal, the Olive Sparrow can be heard calling often and singing at any season. Polytypic. L 6.3" (16 cm)

Identification The Olive's plumage is a dull olive above; underparts are an unmarked pale gray. A brown stripe is

juvenile

found on each side of the Olive's crown. JUVENILE: Buffier than the adult, with pale wing bars. The neck and breast are both faintly streaked.

Geographic Variation Of about 9 subspecies in Middle America, only *rufivirgatus* occurs in the United States.

Similar Species The Green-tailed Towhee is larger, and it has a distinct rufous cap. It also has a brighter greenish coloring on the back, wings, and tail, as well as a white throat.

Voice CALLS: A dry *chip,* given singly or repeated in a rapid series when agitated. Also a buzzy *speeee.* SONG: An accelerating series of dry *chip* notes.

Status & Distribution Common. Nonmigratory. Southern TX to Costa

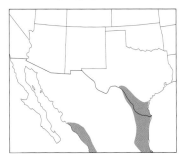

Rica. YEAR-ROUND: Dense undergrowth, brushy areas, mesquite thickets, live oak. VAGRANT: Occurs casually slightly north of mapped range.

Population Although still common in its native habitat, the Olive Sparrow has suffered significantly in the U.S. as mesquite thorn forest has given way to agriculture and residential uses, especially in the Lower Rio Grande Valley.

The Generic Approach to Sparrow Identification

Identifying sparrows uses somewhat different skills from those needed for the typical approach to bird identification. To identify a sparrow, consider first its shape, then its habitat and habits, and finally its field marks. Each genus has a distinctive silhouette; note especially tail length and shape. For example, *Ammodramus* has a flat head, big bill, and short tail, whereas *Spizella* is a round-headed, small-billed bird with a long, notched tail. Habitat is also useful: *Ammodramus* favors short-grass fields and marshes; *Melospiza* is found in brushy or weedy fields or tall grass. A hard-to-flush, skulking sparrow is likely an *Ammodramus* or *Aimophila*. Certain others (e.g., *Spizel-*

Le Conte's Sparrow (MN, June)

Chipping Sparrow (CA, Oct.)

la, Melospiza, Zonotrichia) are often conspicuous. Plumage characters to note include its appearance from below (streaky or plain), the tail pattern, and the exact face pattern (eye ring, malar stripes, and lateral or median crown stripes). ∎

Genus Aimophila

The 14 members of this genus include 6 that reach the United States; the balance occur in Middle America (6 species) and South America (2 species). During the breeding season, territorial males sing from exposed perches. At other seasons they are extremely secretive as they forage on the ground in dense grass. Individuals typically do not flock, but rather travel alone. Upon flushing, they usually fly directly away, low over the grass, diving back into dense cover; more rarely they will perch in a bush. They do not call in flight. Their songs are often loud and ringing, but they tend to be silent outside the breeding season. All have comparatively flat heads, large bills, and long rounded tails.

RUFOUS-WINGED SPARROW   *Aimophila carpalis*

juvenile

In the small corner of southeast Arizona where this species occurs, it is uncommon to fairly common. It sings from exposed perches, but even when it is not singing, it tends to be more conspicuous than other *Aimophila*. It often flies to the tops of bushes and fence lines when flushed. Polytypic. L 5.8" (15 cm)

Identification ADULT: Pale gray head with reddish eye line and cap; faint gray median crown stripe. Distinctive double whisker is the result of both black moustachial and malar stripes on face. Two-toned bill, with pale mandible. Gray-brown back, streaked with black; whitish underparts; 2 whitish wing bars.

Reddish lesser coverts distinctive but difficult to see. Grayish white underparts, without streaking. JUVENILE: Less-distinct facial stripes; buffier wing bars; darker bill; lightly streaked, whitish breast and sides; plumage can be seen as late as November.

Geographic Variation The larger *carpalis* is the U.S. subspecies; 2 additional Mexican subspecies are smaller.

Similar Species The small bill and body, long tail, and rufous cap could recall the Chipping Sparrow (or other *Spizella*), but note that the tail is rounded rather than notched. The color of the eye line also helps eliminate the Chipping, as does the double whisker mark.

See also the Rufous-crowned Sparrow.
Voice CALL: Distinctive, sharp, high *seep*. SONG: Two primary song types: an accelerating series of sweet *chip* notes lasting several seconds, and a shorter song consisting of 2–4 *chip* notes followed by fast trill, *tink tink tidleeeee.*

Status & Distribution Uncommon to fairly common, but local. No migration or vagrancy known. Occurs south to central Sinaloa in western Mexico. YEAR-ROUND: Rather level areas of desert grassland mixed with brush, shrubs, and cactus; often occurs along washes.

Population Heavy grazing has impacted the habitat of this species, and it is absent from many areas that it historically occupied. It is considered an indicator species for healthy grassland.

CASSIN'S SPARROW *Aimophila cassinii*

Its melodic song and skylarking display flight are distinctive. When not singing it is extremely secretive, flushing only when it is almost trod upon. When flushed it behaves like a typical *Aimophila*, flying low away from the observer and rarely showing itself again. Monotypic. L 6" (15 cm)

Identification A large, drab, grayish sparrow, with a large bill and fairly flat forehead. Long, rounded tail is dark gray-brown; outer tail feathers have indistinct white tips. Gray upperparts are streaked with dull black, brown, and variable amount of rust; underparts are grayish white, usually with a few short streaks on the flanks. JUVENILE: Streaked below; paler overall than juvenile Botteri's Sparrow.

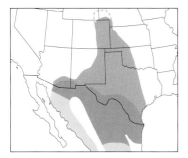

Similar Species Best identified by voice. The Botteri's Sparrow is generally browner, and it lacks the dark flank streaks and barred tail with pale tail corners. The Cassin's Sparrow has distinctive black crescents on its upper-tail coverts and scapulars (where the Botteri's Sparrow is streaked), its wings are more patterned, and its white-fringed tertials have black centers.

Voice CALL: High *stit* given when excited; also *psyit* call (poss. flight call). SONG: Often given in brief fluttery song flight, in which the bird rises to a height and then floats down. Song typically begins with a soft double whistle, a loud, sweet trill, a low whistle, and a final, slightly higher note; alternate versions include a series of chips ending in a trill or warbles. Also gives a trill of *pit* notes.

Status & Distribution Fairly common; variable abundance in response to rainfall. Occurs south to central Mexico.

juvenile

BREEDING: Breeds in grasslands with scattered shrubs, cactus, yucca, and mesquite. MIGRATION: Returns to breeding grounds in early Apr., departs Sept.–early Oct. VAGRANT: Casual to the Midwest, East, CA, and NV.

Population Loss of grasslands has caused declines rangewide.

BOTTERI'S SPARROW *Aimophila botterii*

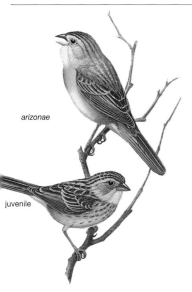

arizonae

juvenile

Behavior like the Cassin's, but does not skylark. Polytypic. L 6" (15 cm)

Identification Large and plain with large bill; fairly flat forehead; long, rounded, dusky-brown tail. Gray upperparts streaked with dull black,

rust, or brown; underparts unstreaked; whitish throat and belly; grayish buff breast and sides. JUVENILE: Buffy belly, broadly streaked breast, narrowly streaked sides.

Geographic Variation Nine subspecies (2, possibly 3, reach the U.S.) show marked variation in measurements and upperparts coloration. The subspecies *arizonae*, breeding in southeastern Arizona (and extreme southwestern New Mexico) and northern Mexico, is more reddish above and buff on the breast; *texana*, of extreme southern Texas and northeastern Mexico, is slightly grayer.

Similar Species Best identified by voice. See Cassin's and Bachman's Sparrows.

Voice CALL: Variable high *tsip* notes; also a high, piercing *seep* (poss. flight call). SONG: Several accelerating high *tsip* or *che-lik* notes, followed by 2 short trills and a longer series of notes accelerating into a trill, like a bouncing ball. A secondary song type (more prevalent in late summer) omits accelerating series. May perform perch-to-perch or perch-to-ground song flights, but does not skylark like the Cassin's does.

Status & Distribution Uncommon. Occurs south to Nicaragua. BREEDING: Fairly tall grasslands and prairies, often shrubby; also open grassy woodlands. Subspecies *arizonae* closely tied to tall, dense grasslands; *texana* found in coastal prairies. MIGRATION: Migrants return late Mar. *(texana)* or early May *(arizonae)*, depart by Oct. VAGRANT: Accidental breeder to western TX.

Population Both subspecies found in the United States have declined significantly because of degradation of their grassland habitat as a result of grazing, development, and the conversion to agriculture.

BACHMAN'S SPARROW *Aimophila aestivalis*

The Bachman's nonbreeding behavior is like the Cassin's. It sings in spring and summer from high perches, often an open pine branch. It does not perform song flights. Polytypic. L 6" (15 cm)
Identification This large sparrow has a large bill, a fairly flat forehead, and a long, rounded tail. It is gray above, heavily streaked with chestnut or dark brown; sides of head are buff or gray; belly whitish. JUVENILE: Distinct eye ring; streaked throat, breast, and sides, often into first winter.
Geographic Variation Three subspecies show moderate color variation. The *bachmani* breeds in the northeastern portions of the range and is very similar to the slightly richer-reddish *illinoensis* from the western portions of the breeding range. Southeastern *aestivalis* (SC to FL) is darkest and grayest.
Similar Species The Botteri's does not overlap in range and differs in voice. It also has richer coloration and more-patterned wings. Vagrant Cassin's and Bachman's might overlap. The Swamp Sparrow is similar in color but of entirely different shape, with a grayer face and darker back. Note voice differences.
Voice CALL: High *tsit.* SONG: One clear, whistled introductory note, followed by a trill or warble on a different pitch.

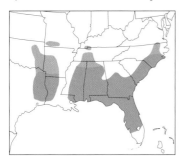

Pitch and speed of trill highly variable.
Status & Distribution Uncommon. Apparently extended its range north in the early to mid-1900s (probably because farm abandonment and logging created vast areas of early successional forest), occurring north to PA, MD, OH, IN, IL, and south ON; it has since greatly contracted its range. YEAR-ROUND: Inhabits dry, open, grassy woods, especially pines, and scrub palmetto. Also occupies regenerating pine forests that are 7–20 feet high. MIGRATION: Northern populations are migratory; timing is poorly known, and it is very rarely detected in migration. Returns to northern breeding grounds in Apr. or May; fall migration occurs early Aug.–mid-Oct. VAGRANT: Accidental to KS, MI, NJ, NY, and throughout its former range.
Population Considered "near threatened" by BirdLife International. Formerly common in open, old-growth pine forests, but that habitat has been

entirely lost to logging. Bachman's Sparrows currently persist in young pine stands (less than 15 years old) and what few older stands (more than 70 years old) remain in the Southeast. Fire suppression and cutting of pine stands favor shrubby undergrowth rather than the grass that the Bachman's prefers.

BACHMAN'S SPARROW

RANGE REDUCTION
— Approximate northern limit of range

RUFOUS-CROWNED SPARROW *Aimophila ruficeps*

Habitat is one of the best clues for this species: It is closely tied to dry, rocky slopes. The Rufous-crowned Sparrow feeds on the ground and might flush away from an observer into a bush or cactus, but it often sits up on rocks or bushes to survey the area. Its distinctive song and calls aid detection. This species, like most other *Aimophila*, is almost always found singly or in pairs and does not occur in flocks (though family groups may forage together in late spring and summer). It is con-

siderably less secretive, even when not singing, than other *Aimophila*. Polytypic. L 6" (15 cm)
Identification Gray head with dark reddish crown, distinct whitish eye ring, rufous line extending back from eye, and single black malar stripe on each side of face. Gray-brown above, with reddish streaks; gray-brown below; tail long, rounded. JUVENILE: Buffier above, with streaked breast and crown; may show 2 pale wing bars.
Geographic Variation Eleven subspecies

show moderate variation in size and coloration. Five U.S. subspecies fall into 2 groups: the small, warm-toned, Pacific coast group and the large, pale southwestern group. Birds of the Pacific coast group are small, with reddish upperparts; they include the northern *ruficeps*, which is smaller and somewhat warmer in color than the *canescens* of southern California; the subspecies *obscura* is similar to *canescens*, but is limited to California's Channel Islands. The southwestern

illinoensis

aestivalis

juvenile
illinoensis

group includes the pale gray *eremoeca,* which is found over much of the range's eastern interior, and the widespread southwestern subspecies *scottii,* which is pale and reddish.

Similar Species Similar to the smaller Rufous-winged, but the Rufous-crowned Sparrow has a larger bill, just 1 whisker mark, a contrasting white malar, and a bolder eye ring; it also lacks the Rufous-winged's rufous shoulder and pale mandible. The Chipping Sparrow and other *Spizella* are superficially similar, but the shape and behavior of the Rufous-crowned are distinctive.

Voice Song and calls are extremely helpful for detecting and identifying this species. CALL: A distinctive, sharp, *dear,* often given in a series; also drawn-

interior
eremoeca

coastal

coastal
juvenile

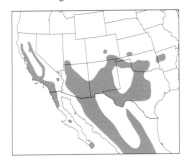

out *seep* notes (poss. flight note). SONG: A rolling, bubbly, series of rapid *chip* notes; can sound very similar to the House Wren's song, but note the Rufous-crowned's shorter duration and more explosive quality.

Status & Distribution Fairly common. Occurs south to southern Mexico. YEAR-ROUND: Strongly prefers rocky hillsides and steep grassy slopes with areas of open ground or bare rock. Largely resident, with some limited

local movements downslope. VAGRANT: Very rare or casual to central or southern Great Plains; accidental to WI.

Population Fire suppression and development have degraded the scrub habitats that this species prefers in Texas and, especially, in southern California *(canescens).* Some southern California populations occur in highly imperiled coastal sage-scrub habitat. Populations in Arkansas and eastern Oklahoma are small and isolated.

FIVE-STRIPED SPARROW *Aimophila quinquestriata*

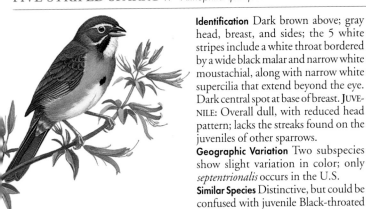

Extremely local in southernmost Arizona, the Five-striped Sparrow's first U.S. breeding was confirmed only in 1969. It has since been shown to be regular in small numbers in the U.S., but its populations appear to be somewhat cyclical or irruptive; only a few locations are occupied consistently. In non-breeding season it is apparently highly secretive; during breeding season territorial males can be found singing from the tops of bushes in the few canyons it occupies. Polytypic. L 6" (15 cm)

Identification Dark brown above; gray head, breast, and sides; the 5 white stripes include a white throat bordered by a wide black malar and narrow white moustachial, along with narrow white supercilia that extend beyond the eye. Dark central spot at base of breast. JUVENILE: Overall dull, with reduced head pattern; lacks the streaks found on the juveniles of other sparrows.

Geographic Variation Two subspecies show slight variation in color; only *septentrionalis* occurs in the U.S.

Similar Species Distinctive, but could be confused with juvenile Black-throated Sparrow. On the Five-striped, note gray sides, flanks, and breast with central spot; wide dark malar bordered by white throat; and thin white submoustachial.

Voice Best located by song. CALL: Gruff *churp;* also higher *pip* and *seet* notes when excited. SONG: Slow series of short, high, varied phrases, with chipping and trilled qualities; typical phrase is a *churp* followed by a short, variable trill; fairly long pauses between phrases.

Status & Distribution Uncommon. West Mexican species; locally west of the

Sierra Madre from Jalisco north to southeastern AZ, with seasonal movements in certain areas; U.S. range restricted to a few canyons in extreme southeastern AZ (e.g., California Gulch, Sycamore Canyon). BREEDING: Highly specialized habitat in the U.S.: favors tall, dense shrubs on rocky, steep hillsides and canyon slopes. MIGRATION: Status outside of breeding season poorly known; apparently rare in winter, and some may withdraw to Mexico. Most records late Apr.–late Sept.

Population The population in the U.S. is small and therefore vulnerable, but it is not threatened by human activity.

Genus *Spizella*

All 7 species in this genus occur north of Mexico. They are all distinctive in that they are fairly small, slender sparrows with small heads and small bills. Their proportionately long tails are distinctly notched. They typically feed in flocks on or near the ground, and they fly immediately up to a tree or bush if disturbed. Their flight is light, buoyant, and undulating, with frequent delivery of their flight call. Their songs vary from clear whistled phrases to dry buzzes and rattles.

AMERICAN TREE SPARROW *Spizella arborea*

winter   juvenile   breeding

One of the hardiest sparrows, this is the only one likely to winter in much of the far northern U.S. and southern Canada, where the Dark-eyed Junco can also be found. At that season it is frequently mistaken for the Chipping Sparrow, but the 2 rarely overlap in winter. The American Tree Sparrow often occurs in flocks of up to 50 birds. In habitat and behavior, they are much like Field Sparrows, but American Tree Sparrows are more frequent at bird feeders. Polytypic. L 6.3" (16 cm)

Identification Gray head and nape crowned with rufous; rufous stripe behind eye; gray throat and breast, with dark central spot; rufous-buff patches on sides of breast. Back and scapulars streaked with black and rufous. Outer tail feathers thinly edged in white on outer webs. Grayish white underparts with buffy sides. WINTER: More buffy; rufous color on crown sometimes forms a central stripe. JUVENILE: Streaked on head and underparts.

Geographic Variation Two subspecies show weak variation in measurements and overall coloration. The small, dark nominate subspecies breeds eastward from the eastern Northwest Territories and winters eastward from the central Great Plains. The western *ochracea* is larger and paler, and it winters from the central Great Plains west.

Similar Species See the Field Sparrow. The Chipping Sparrow rarely overlaps in range (except in certain areas in migration), has a distinct dark eye line in any plumage, and does not share the American Tree Sparrow's distinctly 2-toned bill.

Voice CALL: Sharp, high, bell-like *tink;* sometimes with a more lispy quality (poss. flight note). Flocks also give a musical *teedle-eet.* SONG: Usually begins with several clear notes followed by a variable, rapid warble.

Status & Distribution Fairly common. Uncommon to rare west of Rockies. BREEDING: Breeds along edge of tundra, in open areas with scattered trees, brush. WINTER: Weedy fields, marshes, groves of small trees. MIGRATION: One of the late-fall and early-spring migrants. Fall migration in U.S. typically mid- or late Oct.–late Nov.; spring migrants depart mid-Mar.–early Apr.; accidental in U.S. after early May (mid-Apr. in midlatitudes). VAGRANT: Casual to southern CA, central TX, and the Gulf Coast.

Population Possible declines in wintering population in East.

CHIPPING SPARROW *Spizella passerina*

breeding

Usually conspicuous, they may form sizable flocks during the nonbreeding seasons, often mixing with juncos, Lark or Clay-colored Sparrows, Pine or Palm Warblers, or bluebirds. They frequently give their distinctive flight note upon flushing, usually flying up to a tree or other elevated perch to survey the intrusion. Polytypic. L 5.5" (14 cm)

Identification All feature dark lores, gray nape and cheek, gray unstreaked rump, 2 white wing bars, and lack of a prominent malar stripe. BREEDING ADULT: Bright chestnut crown, distinct white eyebrow, black line from bill through eye to ear. WINTER ADULT: Browner cheek, dark lores, streaked crown with some rufous color. FIRST-WINTER: Similar to winter adult, but brownish crown; buff-tinged breast and sides. JUVENILE: Underparts prominently streaked; crown usually lacks rufous; may show slightly streaked rump. Plumage often held into October, especially in western subspecies.

Geographic Variation Seven subspecies (3 in N.A.) show moderate variation in color and measurements. Nominate eastern subspecies is small and fairly dark, with rich rufous upperparts. Western subspecies include the large, pale *arizonae* (breeds from Great Plains west) and the fairly small *stridula* (coastal BC to southern CA), which is intermediate in color.

Similar Species Clay-colored and Brewer's Sparrows differ from winter and immature Chippings by their pale lores, prominent malar and submoustachial stripes (particularly Clay-colored), and

winter

juvenile

1st winter

brownish rumps; lack chestnut on the cap. The Brewer's has a streaked nape and rump, and a duller face pattern with a more distinct eye ring; the Clay-colored is typically warmer buff-brown on the breast, especially in fall, and has a broader, pale supercilium and a more strongly contrasting gray nape.

Voice CALL: High *tsip;* sometimes a rapid twitter when excited. FLIGHT NOTE: High, sharp *tseet;* sharper at beginning of note than Brewer's or Clay-colored's.

SONG: Rapid trill of dry *chip* notes, all 1 pitch; speed can vary considerably.

Status & Distribution Common. Occurs south to Nicaragua. BREEDING: Lawns, parks, gardens, woodland edges, pine-oak forests. MIGRATION: Spring mid-Mar.–mid-May; fall late July–early Nov., peaking Sept.–late Oct. Rare in winter north of mapped range. VAGRANT: Casual to western AK.

Population Stable. Has largely benefited from human activities, including the clearing of forests and creation of open, grassy parks.

CLAY-COLORED SPARROW *Spizella pallida*

immature

breeding

juvenile

The Clay-colored's behavior is similar to the Chipping's. It may flock with that species or with Field Sparrows. Monotypic. L 5.5" (14 cm)

Identification Brown crown with black streaks and a distinct buffy white or whitish central stripe. Broad, whitish eyebrow; pale lores; brown cheek outlined by dark postocular and moustachial stripes; conspicuous pale submoustachial stripe. Gray nape; buffy brown back and scapulars, with dark streaks; rump not streaked and color does not contrast with back as in the Chipping. Adult in fall and winter is buffier overall. IMMATURE: Much buffier; gray nape and pale stripe on sides of throat stand out more. JUVENILE: Breast and sides streaked.

Similar Species Identification of fall *Spizella* can be quite challenging and

should focus on the details of head pattern. The Brewer's Sparrow is most similar, but it is duller overall and less distinctly marked. Its face pattern is indistinct, lacking the prominent white supercilium, whitish moustachial, and pale central crown stripe. The Brewer's nape is streaked and does not contrast with the head and breast, unlike the Clay-colored's. The Clay-colored usually shows a buffy wash across the breast, especially in fall, while the Brewer's is gray on the breast. The winter and immature Chipping are also similar but tends to be darker on the back, with chestnut tones rather than buff and tan. The Chipping's face is much more strongly marked, set off by a prominent dark eye line that extends through the lores. The Chipping typically does not have

the Clay-colored's prominent whitish supercilium and moustachial, and its usually grayish breast is unlike the Clay-colored's buff breast.

Voice CALL: High *tsik,* given repeatedly when excited. FLIGHT NOTE: A thin *sip,* like the Brewer's Sparrow's. SONG: A series of 3 to 4 long, insectlike buzzes; can recall the song of the Golden-winged Warbler.

Status & Distribution Fairly common. Winters south to southern Mex. BREEDING: Fairly common in brushy fields, groves, streamside thickets. WINTER: Primarily in Mexico, uncommonly in southern TX, rarely in southern FL and AZ. Casual in winter to both coasts. MIGRATION: Primarily through interior mid-Apr.–mid-May and late Aug.–late Oct. Rare in fall, casual in winter and spring to both coasts. VAGRANT: Casual in fall to AK, YK, and NF.

Population Stable.

BREWER'S SPARROW *Spizella breweri*

breweri

juvenile

This is a sparrow of the dry Great Basin desert, intermontane valleys, and mountain meadows. In winter and migration it is usually found in dry, sparse desert scrub; the similar Clay-colored Sparrow is more typically found in lusher, grassier habitats, though there is much overlap. The Brewer's may form flocks or mix with other sparrows, especially the White-crowned, in migration and winter. Polytypic. L 5.5" (14 cm)

Identification Brown crown with fine black streaks. Distinct whitish eye ring, grayish white eyebrow; overall indistinct face pattern. Pale brown ear patch with darker borders, pale lores, dark malar stripe. Buffy brown, streaked upperparts; buffy brown rump may be lightly streaked. Imma-ture, fall adults, and winter adults are somewhat buffy below. JUVENILE: Buffier overall, lightly *(breweri)* to prominently *(taverneri)* streaked on breast and sides.

Geographic Variation Two subspecies show moderate variation in measurements and overall color and pattern. The widespread nominate occupies the breeding range across most of the continent, where it nests primarily in sage steppe habitat. The other subspecies, *taverneri,* known as the "Timberline" Sparrow, has a largely disjunct breeding range and is thought by some to represent a different species. It breeds in the subalpine zone of the Canadian Rockies from northwestern Montana to east-central Alaska and is thought to winter in north-central Mexico. It has a slightly different song, a larger bill, heavier black streaking on the nape and upperparts, a stronger face pattern, and a darker gray breast that contrasts more with the belly. Juveniles are heavily streaked with blackish below. Despite these average differences, reliable field identification may not be possible (except by breeding range and habitat) due to variation within *breweri.*

Similar Species The Clay-colored Sparrow is most similar to the Brewer's. Note the Clay-colored's unmarked gray nape, which contrasts with the face and breast, and the more promi-nent facial pattern with a well-defined median crown stripe, whitish moustachial, and bold supercilium.

Voice CALL: High *tsik,* given repeatedly when excited. FLIGHT NOTE: A thin *sip,* like the Clay-colored Sparrow's. SONG: A series of varied, bubbling notes and buzzy trills at different pitches; entire song is often very long in duration.

Status & Distribution Common. Winters south to central Mexico. BREED-ING: Sage steppe habitats across the West, especially in extensive stands of big sagebrush. WINTER: Found in dry desert scrub, including saltbush and creosote; also weedy roadsides. MIGRATION: Spring Mar.–mid-May, peaking mid-Apr.–mid-May; fall early Aug.–early Oct., peaking in Sept. VAGRANT: Casual to Great Lakes. Accidental in fall to LA, MA, and NS; in spring to IL and ON; and in winter to IL.

Population The Breeding Bird Survey data show a gradual decline, presumably due to the loss of sage steppe habitats to grazing, agriculture, and the invasion of exotic plants.

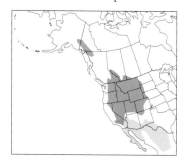

WORTHEN'S SPARROW *Spizella wortheni*

The type specimen of this poorly known Mexican species was taken in the United States, but it has not been found there since. In many respects it is similar to the Field Sparrow. Monotypic. L 5.5" (14 cm)

Identification It very closely resembles the Field Sparrow, differing primarily in its dark legs, rufous cap (restricted to the top of the crown), grayer plumage, different song, shorter tail, and lack of a gray median crown stripe.

Similar Species The Field Sparrow is extremely similar but has pinkish legs, a rufous cap that extends to the forehead, and a different song. Other similar sparrows do not have this combination of pink bill, eye ring, pale, unmarked malar region, and un-streaked breast.

Voice CALL: High, thin *tssip* (poss. flight note); probably also high chips when excited. SONG: Dry, chipping trill suggesting the Chipping Sparrow's song.

Status & Distribution Rare and local. Breeds on the Central Mexican Plateau, primarily in Coahuila and Nuevo Léon. BREEDING: Breeds in shrubby deserts, overgrown fields, grassy woodland edge. VAGRANT: One record from Silver City, NM (June 16, 1884); could have been a member of an isolated population that was quickly extirpated by overgrazing.

Population Considered endangered by

BirdLife International. Its population may be as small as several hundred birds. Decline is presumably a result of overgrazing, which degrades its breeding habitat.

FIELD SPARROW *Spizella pusilla*

western
arenacea

eastern juvenile
pusilla

eastern
pusilla

In migration and winter, the Field Sparrow forms small pure flocks (5–50 birds); it may also mix with other sparrows. It usually gives its flight call when flushed, typically employing a bounding flight to fly up ahead and drop back in the grass or fly into a hedgerow. Flocks will often gather in the same tree or bush to investigate a disturbance. Polytypic. L 5.6" (14 cm)
Identification Entirely pink bill is distinctive. Gray face with reddish crown, distinct white eye ring, and indistinct reddish eye line. Back is streaked except on gray-brown rump. Rich buffy-orange unstreaked breast and sides; grayish white belly; pink legs. JUVENILE:

Streaked below; buffy wing bars.
Geographic Variation Two subspecies show well-marked variation in measurements and overall coloration. The nominate breeds roughly east from the eastern Dakotas and eastern Texas; *arenacea* breeds to the west. The longer-tailed *arenacea* is larger, paler, and grayer; *pusilla* is especially rufous on the auriculars, buffier below, and richer above.
Similar Species The American Tree is most similar but has a 2-toned bill and a black central breast spot. The breeding-plumaged Chipping shares the rufous cap but has a dark eye line, is plain gray below without buff on the breast or flanks, has a dark bill, and lacks

the bold eye ring. See also the Worthen's.
Voice CALL: A high, sharp *chip,* similar to the call of the Orange-crowned Warbler. FLIGHT NOTE: High, loud *tseees.* SONG: A series of clear, plaintive whistles accelerating into a trill.
Status & Distribution Fairly common. Winters south to extreme northeast Mexico. MIGRATION: Spring mid-Mar.–early May, peaking mid-Apr; fall early Sept.–late Oct. Rare migrant in east CO and Maritimes. BREEDING: Open, brushy woodlands, power-line cuts, overgrown fields. WINTER: Prefers open fields with tall grass, often near hedgerows. VAGRANT: Casual to NF. Casual to accidental west of mapped range as far as CA.
Population Stable, but shrubby field habitat being developed.

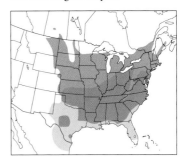

BLACK-CHINNED SPARROW *Spizella atrogularis*

breeding ♀

breeding ♂

juvenile

This attractive sparrow is typical of chaparral and brushy slopes, where its distinctive song may lead one to this small bird topping a high perch. Migrants are very rarely detected. In winter they may be found singly, in loose association with other sparrows, or in small flocks. Polytypic. L 5.6" (14 cm)
Identification Medium gray overall; rusty

back and scapulars, with black streaks; bright pink bill. BREEDING MALE: Black lores and chin; whitish gray lower belly. Long tail is all dark. FEMALE: Black chin is reduced or absent. WINTER: Lacks black chin. JUVENILE: Like winter, but may show faint streaks below.
Geographic Variation The 3 subspecies (2 in U.S.) show slight variation in overall coloration. Most of the U.S. range is occupied by *cana;* a slightly darker subspecies, *caurina,* breeds in central California (Marin to San Benito counties).
Similar Species The medium gray underparts and rufous back of the Black-chinned are distinctive; other *Spizella* are paler on the underparts. The Black-throated is sometimes confused with the Black-chinned, due mostly to their similar names.
Voice SONG: Plaintive song begins slowly and accelerates rapidly, like a bouncing ball. Begins with slow *sweet … sweet … sweet,* continuing in a rapid trill; somewhat like the song of the Field Sparrow, but accelerates much more rapidly and ends with a faster trill.

CALL: A high *tsik* is given when agitated; very similar to other *Spizella.* FLIGHT NOTE: High, thin *seep.*
Status & Distribution Uncommon to fairly common. BREEDING: Inhabits brushy arid slopes in foothills and mountains. MIGRATION: Rarely detected in migration; spring arrival seems to peak in early Apr.; most birds seem to be gone from breeding grounds by late Aug., with a very few individuals noted in Sept. VAGRANT: Casual to central TX and accidental to southern OR.
Population Stable in most areas, but may be declining in southern California due to development.

Genus *Pooecetes*

VESPER SPARROW *Pooecetes gramineus*

The Vesper Sparrow (monotypic genus) is a bird of open country often found feeding along roadsides or in open areas within the grassland. It often associates with Savannah, Brewer's, or Lark Sparrows. The Vesper flies up to a tree when disturbed and avoids thick brush. Polytypic. L 6.3" (16 cm)

Identification Large with a moderately long tail; distinctive white outer tail feathers best seen in flight; pale underparts marked with fine, distinct streaking, not contrastingly darker than that of the head and body; prominent white eye ring; dark ear patch bordered in white along lower and rear edges; supercilium indistinct. Chestnut lesser coverts distinctive but not easily seen.

Geographic Variation Four subspecies show moderate differences in measurements and overall coloration. Eastern nominate subspecies is smaller and slightly darker overall than the widespread *confinis*. Small, dark *affinis* breeds in coastal dunes of western Washington and Oregon; large, stout-billed *altus* breeds in the plateaus of the Four Corners states.

Similar Species The shorter-tailed Savannah Sparrow is smaller, has a less distinct eye ring, and lacks prominent white outer tail feathers. The Song Sparrow is larger and darker, has a rounded tail and blurrier streaking, and lacks white outer tail feathers. It also has different behavior and habitat.

Voice CALL: High chips when excited. FLIGHT NOTE: High, rising *pseeet;* calls less often in flight than does Savannah. SONG: Rich and melodious, 2 to 3 long, slurred notes followed by 2 higher notes, then a series of short, descending trills.

Status & Distribution Fairly common (uncommon in East). Winters south to southern Mexico. Breeds in dry grasslands, farmlands, open forest clearings, sagebrush. WINTER: Dry grasslands, grassy margins of agricultural fields, roadsides. Prefers shorter grass with open areas interspersed. MIGRATION: Spring late Mar.–early May, peaking in mid-Apr.; fall early Sept.–mid-Nov., peaking late Sept.–late Oct; fall migration is later in the East. VAGRANT: Casual to NF.

Population Moderate declines throughout its range are probably due to changes in farming practices and decline in quality of sage steppe habitat in the West.

Genus *Chondestes*

LARK SPARROW *Chondestes grammacus*

juvenile

This sparrow (monotypic genus) feeds on bare or sandy ground. When flushed, it flies to a high perch. Few other sparrows are likely to fly high overhead during daylight. They call both when flushing and when flying overhead; occur singly or in flocks up to 50. Polytypic. L 6.5" (17 cm)

Identification Largest open-country sparrow. Long, rounded tail with prominent white corners. ADULT: Distinctive harlequin face pattern of black, white, and chestnut. Bright white underparts marked only with dark central breast spot. JUVENILE: Duller face; fine, black streaks on breast, sides, and crown lost gradually through fall.

Geographic Variation Two subspecies show weak variation. Eastern *grammacus* darker overall with wider black back streaks than western *strigatus*.

Similar Species None.

Voice CALL: Sharp *tsik,* often a rapid series and frequently delivered in flight. High chips when excited. SONG: Begins with 2 loud, clear notes, followed by a series of rich, melodious notes and trills and unmusical buzzes. Sings one of the longest sparrow songs.

Status & Distribution Fairly common. Primarily west of the Mississippi; once bred as far east as NY and western MD. Rare migrant throughout the East, mainly in fall. Prairies, roadsides, farms, open woodlands, mesas. VAGRANT: Accidental to AK, northern Canada, and Europe.

Population Stable, though eastern populations are declining and it is extirpated from former breeding areas in the East.

Genus *Amphispiza*

The 2 species in this genus—the Sage and the Black-throated Sparrow—are of medium size, with medium-length, squared-off, blackish tails that they cock and flip about. Both sparrows, which are found in arid country, have tinkling call notes. They tend to be quite conspicuous, running through open areas and perching up on small bushes.

SAGE SPARROW *Amphispiza belli*

Forming small flocks in the nonbreeding seasons, the Sage flies with hesitant, irregular wingbeats (rarely far) when flushed and seems to hit the ground running. Often runs on ground with tail cocked up, like a miniature thrasher. When perching, may seem agitated, delivering a tinkling call and twitching its tail nervously. Polytypic. L 6.3" (16 cm)

Identification Gray head; white eye ring; white supraloral does not extend past eye; broad white submoustachial stripe; dark malar stripe. Whitish below with large, black central breast spot; buffy-brown wash, distinct streaks on flanks. Blackish tail with white outer tail feathers. JUVENILE: Duller, more streaked. **Geographic Variation** See sidebar below. **Similar Species** See juvenile Black-throated Sparrow.

Voice CALL: High, metallic, thin junco-like notes, delivered as a single note or as a twitter. SONG: A jumbled series of rising-and-falling phrases.

Status & Distribution Common (*nevadensis*) to uncommon (*belli*). South to northern Mexico. BREEDING: See below. MIGRATION: *Belli* is resident; *nevadensis* is migratory. Spring late Feb.–early May, probably peaking in late Mar.; fall late Sept.–late Oct. VAGRANT: "Bell's" accidental even a short distance from breeding grounds. "Interior" birds casual to plains states (e.g., SD, KS, NE) and accidental to NS.

Population Degradation of sage steppe habitats has negatively affected *nevadensis* rangewide; development in coastal CA has reduced available *belli* habitat.

coastal *belli*

interior *nevadensis*

interior juvenile *nevadensis*

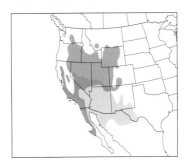

Sage Sparrow Subspecies

Four subspecies of the Sage Sparrow are currently recognized in the U.S. (an additional subspecies occurs on the central Baja Peninsula), and some consider the 2 groups ("Bell's" and "Interior") to constitute different species. The validity of *canescens* and *clementeae* has been disputed.

"Interior" birds are pale, with a weak malar, narrowly streaked back, white outer tail feathers, and strong contrast between the rump and tail;

"Bell's" Sage Sparrow (CA, Mar.)

Sage Sparrow, *nevadensis* (CA, June)

they breed in sagebrush and saltbush deserts and grasslands of the Great Basin and Mojave Deserts; and they winter in the Southwest. Most of that breeding range is occupied by *nevadensis*, but birds of California's Central Valley are *canescens*, which are slightly darker above and have a slightly more prominent malar than *nevadensis*, and thus tend toward *belli*.

"Bell's" birds include the coastal *belli*, which is dark-er and has a strong malar, an unstreaked brownish back, no white outer tail feathers, and reduced contrast between the rump and tail; it breeds in chaparral and coastal sage scrub of coastal California north to Humboldt County and also along the western slopes of the central Sierra Nevada. The Sage Sparrow on San Clemente Island is *clementeae*, which is larger billed and paler in juvenal plumage. ∎

BLACK-THROATED SPARROW *Amphispiza bilineata*

juvenile

The Black-throated Sparrow's behavior is similar to the Sage's, but the Black-throated is more confiding and less likely to flock. Polytypic. L 5.5" (14 cm) **Identification** In all ages, extent of white

on tail is greater than in Sage. ADULT: Black lores and triangular black patch on throat and breast contrast with white eyebrow, white submoustachial stripe, and white underparts. Upperparts plain brownish gray. JUVENILE: Plumage often held well into fall. Lacks black on throat; breast and back finely streaked. Note bold white eyebrow.

Geographic Variation Nine subspecies (3 in the U.S) show moderate but clinal variation in overall color and tail pattern. The nominate, breeding in central and southern Texas, is smallest, with a fairly dark back and more extensive white in the tail. Larger *opuntia* breeds west to southeastern New Mexico and southeast Colorado; *opuntia* and *deserticola*, which breed in the remaining western portions of the mapped range, are larger and paler and have reduced white in the tail.

Similar Species Juvenile similar to the Sage Sparrow; note the Black-throated's extensive white supercilium, its larger bill, and its lack of a malar stripe.

Voice CALL: Faint, high, metallic *tink;* also gives series of soft, metallic tinkling notes, especially when flushed. SONG: High pitched. Two clear notes followed by a trill.

Status & Distribution Fairly common. Resident south to central Mexico. Rare to casual migrant in coastal CA. A range of desert habitats, from fairly lush cactus forests, to dry stands of sagebrush, to rocky, sparsely vegetated slopes. VAGRANT: Casual to eastern N.A. in fall and winter.

Population Stable.

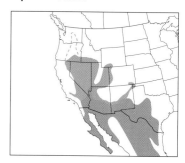

Genus *Calamospiza*

LARK BUNTING *Calamospiza melanocorys*

breeding ♂

early spring ♂

winter ♂

♀

A characteristic bird of fence lines and open prairie during summer, this species tends to form large flocks during the nonbreeding season. Flocks of other sparrows (with the exception of longspurs) are much looser: Birds flush individually even if the integrity of the flock is maintained. With the Lark Bunting, the entire flock seems to flush as one. In flight, it looks short and round-winged. Monotypic. L 7" (18 cm)

Identification Stocky, thick-necked and barrel chested for a sparrow, with a fairly short, squared-off tail and a thick, blue-gray bill. Males may migrate south in breeding plumage, which they often retain through August. BREEDING MALE: Entirely black with white wing patches; males in molt are a patchwork of brown and black. FEMALE: Brown above; pale below with regular sharp, brown streaking; buffy sides; brown primaries. WINTER MALE: Like female, but with black primaries, face, and throat. IMMATURE: Like female; males usually have some black on face, chin, or lores.

Similar Species Female and immature similar to some sparrows and *Carpodacus* finches. Note the diagnostic white or buffy-white wing patch

(sometimes concealed), the blue-gray bill, and its shape and behavior. Most finches do not spend as much time on the ground.

Voice FLIGHT NOTE: Distinctive, soft *hoo-ee*. SONG: A varied series of rich whistles and trills.

Status & Distribution Common. Winters south to central Mexico. BREEDING: Dry plains and prairies, especially in sagebrush. Annual shifts depending on precipitation. WINTER: Open grasslands, roadsides, dry, weedy fields. MIGRATION: Spring mid-Apr.–mid-May; fall early Aug.–mid-Oct. VAGRANT: Rare to West Coast. Casual to Pacific Northwest and to the East.

Population Apparently stable.

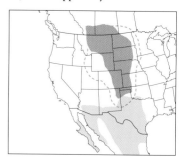

Genus Passerculus

SAVANNAH SPARROW *Passerculus sandwichensis*

The Savannah is distinguished by its small size and behavior. Among the most common sparrows of open country, Savannahs tend to be flighty: When flushed they usually fly up and away from the observer in an undulating or stair-step flight that is distinctive. Occasionally, they fly low over the grass more like an *Ammodramus*. When flushed, they will often assume an elevated perch to survey the intrusion; at other times they drop back to the grass. Their distinctive flight note is given frequently upon flushing, unlike *Ammodramus*, *Aimophila*, and certain other grassland sparrows. Polytypic. L 5.5" (14 cm)

Identification A fairly small sparrow with a short, square tail. Heavily streaked below; face pattern well marked with a supercilium, strong eye line, dark malar stripe, and pale moustachial; no eye ring. Most birds have distinctive yellow supraloral. Plumage otherwise highly variable by subspecies.

Geographic Variation Some 21 subspecies (14 north of Mexico) show marked variation in body and bill size and in overall color. They are divided into 4 distinct, field-identifiable groups. The "Typical" group (8 ssp.) is fairly small and small billed. Eastern birds are generally more richly colored (darker in the north), while western birds are generally paler and grayer; palest is the western interior breeding *nevadensis* and Arctic subspecies. Second, dis-

tinctive *princeps,* known as the "Ipswich Sparrow," breeds on Sable Island, Nova Scotia, and winters on East Coast beaches; it can be similar to *nevadensis,* but note its larger size, larger bill, and even paler plumage. Third, "Pacific" group birds are like "Typical" Savannahs in size and bill shape, but they are quite dark in plumage; they are increasingly darker from north to south, with the darkest being *beldingi* of southern California's salt marshes. Finally, the "Large-billed" Sparrow is a very distinctive complex involving several subspecies that breed in Mexican salt marshes; only *rostratus* reaches the U.S. Its bill is very large compared to other Savannahs, being especially thick at the base. It is pale brownish gray overall, and its underparts are marked with broad, blurry, reddish brown streaks.

Similar Species See Vesper Sparrow. The Savannah Sparrow is similar to the Baird's Sparrow, but it differs in structure, lacks double moustachial stripes and ochre crown stripe, and is rarely extensively orangish about head. The larger, browner Song Sparrow has a longer, rounded tail, lacks yellow above eye, and differs in behavior and habitat.

Voice All subspecies similar in voice, except for the "Large-billed." CALL: High *tip.* FLIGHT NOTE: A thin, descending *tseew;* in "Large-billed" a more metallic *zink.* SONG: Two or 3 *chip* notes, followed by a long, buzzy trill and a final *tip* note. Compare to that of Grasshopper Sparrow. "Large-billed" has short, high introductory notes, followed by about 3 rich, buzzy *dzeee's*; it usually does not sing in the U.S.

Status & Distribution Common. Occurs south to Guatemala. May be found in a variety of open habitats, usually with

nevadensis

"Ipswich Sparrow" *princeps*

beldingi

"Large-billed Sparrow" *rostratus*

short grass, including grasslands, airports, agricultural fields, salt marshes, and beaches. The "Large-billed" occurs exclusively in saline flats and shorelines of the Salton Sea and, more rarely, coastal southern CA; The "Ipswich" is found exclusively on East Coast beaches. MIGRATION: Timing varies, but generally in spring Mar.–mid-May, peaking in Apr.; and in fall mid-Aug.–early Nov., peaking in mid-Oct. "Large-billed" occurs in the U.S. primarily from mid-July–Feb.; it has not yet been found breeding at the Salton Sea. VAGRANT: Europe and Asia.

Population Most populations are stable. "Pacific" birds (e.g., *beldingi*) have declined drastically due to destruction of California salt marshes. The *princeps* subspecies is vulnerable due to its limited breeding area on a small, isolated island.

Genus Ammodramus

The 9 members of this genus (7 in N.A., 2 in S.A.) are notoriously difficult to observe, except during breeding season, when territorial males sing from exposed perches. At other seasons, they typically forage on the ground in dense grass and are usually seen only when flushed, at which point they may perch in the open. They are more difficult to flush than are other sparrows, often refusing to fly unless approached to 6 feet or less. Individuals typically do not flock, although they often occur near groups of other sparrows. Birds are silent when flushed (unlike the Savannah Sparrow); and their short flights are low to the ground and weak, ending with a sudden drop into the grass. All have comparatively flat heads; large bills; fairly short, sometimes spiky, tails; and wheezy or whispering songs. Several species migrate in juvenal plumage.

GRASSHOPPER SPARROW *Ammodramus savannarum*

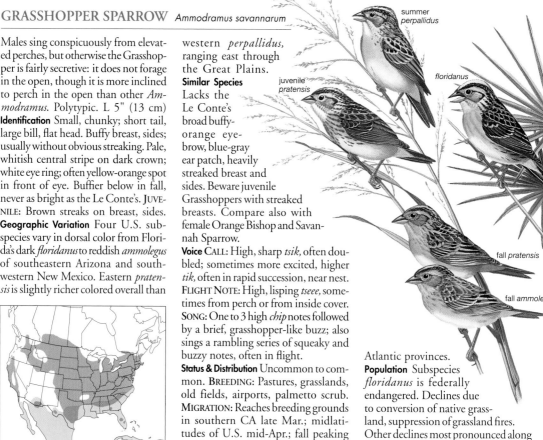

summer *perpallidus*

juvenile pratensis

floridanus

fall *pratensis*

fall *ammole*

Males sing conspicuously from elevated perches, but otherwise the Grasshopper is fairly secretive: it does not forage in the open, though it is more inclined to perch in the open than other *Ammodramus*. Polytypic. L 5" (13 cm) **Identification** Small, chunky; short tail, large bill, flat head. Buffy breast, sides; usually without obvious streaking. Pale, whitish central stripe on dark crown; white eye ring; often yellow-orange spot in front of eye. Buffier below in fall, never as bright as the Le Conte's. JUVENILE: Brown streaks on breast, sides. **Geographic Variation** Four U.S. subspecies vary in dorsal color from Florida's dark *floridanus* to reddish *ammolegus* of southeastern Arizona and southwestern New Mexico. Eastern *pratensis* is slightly richer colored overall than

western *perpallidus,* ranging east through the Great Plains. **Similar Species** Lacks the Le Conte's broad buffy-orange eyebrow, blue-gray ear patch, heavily streaked breast and sides. Beware juvenile Grasshoppers with streaked breasts. Compare also with female Orange Bishop and Savannah Sparrow. **Voice** CALL: High, sharp *tsik,* often doubled; sometimes more excited, higher *tik,* often in rapid succession, near nest. FLIGHT NOTE: High, lisping *tseee,* sometimes from perch or from inside cover. SONG: One to 3 high *chip* notes followed by a brief, grasshopper-like buzz; also sings a rambling series of squeaky and buzzy notes, often in flight. **Status & Distribution** Uncommon to common. BREEDING: Pastures, grasslands, old fields, airports, palmetto scrub. MIGRATION: Reaches breeding grounds in southern CA late Mar.; midlatitudes of U.S. mid-Apr.; fall peaking in Oct. VAGRANT: Very rare to BC,

Atlantic provinces. **Population** Subspecies *floridanus* is federally endangered. Declines due to conversion of native grassland, suppression of grassland fires. Other declines most pronounced along East Coast.

LE CONTE'S SPARROW *Ammodramus leconteii*

juvenile

Fairly common but secretive, the Le Conte's scurries through matted grasses like a mouse. Compared to the Grasshopper, it prefers lower-lying, often wet fields and marsh edges. When flushed, it flies away from the observer with a characteristically weak flight, flaring its narrow tail feathers upon landing. Monotypic. L 5" (13 cm) **Identification** White central crown stripe, becoming orange on forehead; chest-

nut streaks on nape; and straw-colored "cornrows" on the back distinguish the Le Conte's from sharp-tailed sparrows. Bright, broad, buffy orange eyebrow; grayish ear patch; thinner bill; and orange-buff breast and sides distinguish it from the Grasshopper Sparrow. Dark streaks on sides of breast and flanks. JUVENILE: Buffy; tawny crown stripe; breast heavily streaked. Some migrate in juvenal plumage, which can be retained through late Oct. **Similar Species** Nelson's and Saltmarsh Sharp-tailed Sparrows are most similar but have grayish central crown stripe; unstreaked gray nape; distinct white lines on back; larger bill; and more extensive gray face. Juveniles more similar, but the Le Conte's is paler, sandier, and streaked on the nape. See the Grasshopper Sparrow. **Voice** CALL: Sharp *tsit.* FLIGHT NOTE: High *tseeet,* like the Grasshopper Sparrow's. SONG: Short, high, insectlike buzz: *tsit-tshzzzzzzz.* **Status & Distribution** Fairly common. BREEDING: Wet grassy fields, bogs, marsh

edges. WINTER: High marsh and marsh edges, low-lying grassy fields, especially those with broomsedge or switchgrass components. MIGRATION: Commonly through Great Plains east to Mississippi River Valley; uncommon to rare east to Ohio River Valley. Mid-Sept.–mid-Nov.; spring Apr.–mid-May. VAGRANT: Casual to CA (about 35 recs.) and NM, and accidental to BC, WA, OR, and AZ. Occurs casually in migration along East Coast, primarily in fall; rare to casual in winter north to NJ and west to southeastern CO and western TX. **Population** Apparently stable.

BAIRD'S SPARROW *Ammodramus bairdii*

One of the rarer sparrows, this species is poorly known due to behavior and identification difficulties; migration and wintering areas incompletely known. The Baird's is secretive, especially away from breeding grounds. It looks more like Savannah than its congeners, as it is larger, with a more square tail, rounder head, and proportionately smaller bill. It typically flushes only at close range, silently flies short distances, and drops back into cover. This differs from the behavior of some Savannahs, which are more apt to flush at a distance, call in flight, rise to significant heights in flight, and perch in the open upon landing. Monotypic. L 5.5" (14 cm)

Identification Orange-tinted head (which is duller on worn summer birds); note

juvenile

especially 2 isolated dark spots behind ear patch, no postocular line. Double whisker (malar and moustachial) lines. Wide-spaced, short dark streaks on breast form a distinct necklace; chestnut on scapulars. JUVENILE: Head paler, creamier; central crown stripe finely streaked; white fringes give scaly appearance to upperparts; underparts more extensively streaked.

Similar Species See Savannah and Henslow's Sparrows.

Voice CALL: Excited *tink* or *tsip* notes near nest. FLIGHT NOTE: High, thin *tseee*. SONG: Two or 3 high, thin notes followed by a single warbled note and a low trill.

Status & Distribution Uncommon, local. BREEDING: Rolling short-grass prairies with scattered shrubs or weeds. WINTER: Large open grasslands, with clumps of grass interspersed with bare areas. MIGRATION: Rarely seen, through Great Plains (west KS to west MN, also north NM). Spring migration primarily in early May; fall Sept.–mid-Oct. Rare but probably overlooked in western TX and CO. VAGRANT: Casual breeder east

to west MN; accidental in summer to WI. Accidental in fall to East (NY and MD) and CA (4 recs.); winter to southern TX.

Population Significant declines throughout breeding range due to conversion of native prairie to agriculture, which is unsuitable for this species.

HENSLOW'S SPARROW *Ammodramus henslowii*

juvenile

On breeding grounds males deliver their songs from small shrubs or tall grass; at other times the Henslow's is very secretive, preferring to feed on or near the ground in fairly dense grass. After being flushed several times it may perch in the open for a few minutes before dropping back into cover. Polytypic. L 5" (13 cm)

Identification Large flat olive head; large gray bill; malar stripe; moustachial stripe; white eye ring; distinct streaking across pale breast, extending down flanks; rusty wings and back; narrow pale fringes to back feathers when fresh. JUVENILE: Paler, yellower, less streaking below; compare to adult Grasshopper.

Geographic Variation Two subspecies are weakly differentiated and not field separable: *susurrans* in East; smaller-billed, paler nominate in Midwest.

Similar Species Most similar to the Baird's, but greenish head, nape, and most of central crown stripe; wings extensively dark chestnut. Also confused with the Grasshopper; note the Henslow's greenish head and central crown stripe; malar and moustachial stripes; rusty wings and back; breast streaking. Beware juvenile Grasshopper with streaked breast.

Voice CALL: Sharp *tsik*. FLIGHT NOTE: High *tseee*, like Grasshopper's. SONG: Distinctive, short *tse-LICK*.

Status & Distribution Uncommon, local. BREEDING: Wet shrubby fields, weedy meadows, reclaimed strip mines. WINTER: Weedy old fields or wet second

growth, also understory of pine woods. Winters casually north to IL, IN; accidental to New England. MIGRATION: Poorly known; arrives at more southerly breeding areas by mid-Apr. VAGRANT: Accidental west of mapped range to ND, CO, and NM. Casual to New England, Maritimes, and coastal mid-Atlantic.

Population Formerly bred on mid-Atlantic coastal plain and in Northeast; now largely extirpated. Significant long-term declines due to loss of native grassland habitat. Recent management efforts have led to recovery in some areas.

NELSON'S SHARP-TAILED SPARROW *Ammodramus nelsoni*

subvirgatus

nelsoni

nelsoni

juvenile
nelsoni

Secretive and hard to find away from the breeding grounds, the Nelson's Sharp-tailed Sparrow's warm, soft colors make it distinctive once it is found. Its behavior is like the Le Conte's Sparrow's. Sometimes it responds to pishing, especially when forced to higher ground during a high tide. It has a somewhat smaller bill and rounder head than the Saltmarsh has, though this is less pronounced in the Atlantic coast subspecies *(subvirgatus)*.

Polytypic. L 4.8" (12 cm)

Identification Orange-buff triangle on indistinctly marked face; gray median crown stripe and nape; streaked buffy breast contrasts sharply with white belly; back marked with black and white stripes; wings tinged with rich rufous. Narrow, sharply pointed rectrices. JUVENILE: Fainter median crown stripe; duller nape; variably thicker eye line; less contrast above; lacks streaking across breast.

Geographic Variation Three subspecies with disjunct breeding ranges. Interior *nelsoni* is brightest, with rich orange on face and breast; distinct streaking on breast and flank; distinct white streaks on darker back. The *Subvirgatus* of the Maritimes and coastal Maine is duller overall (recalling the Seaside); has diffuse streaking below; grayer underparts; longer bill. In *alterus*, from James and Hudson Bays, brightness is intermediate, streaks blurred.

Similar Species See the Le Conte's and the Saltmarsh Sharp-tailed Sparrow.

Voice CALL: Sharp *tsik*. FLIGHT NOTE: A high, lisping *tsiis*, shorter and less strident than the Grasshopper's; regularly delivered from ground in cover. SONG: A wheezy *p-tshhhhhhh-uk*, ending on a lower note; flight display unlike the Saltmarsh's, with song delivered at zenith of a short vertical flight, followed by a slow descent.

Status & Distribution Fairly common. BREEDING: Fresh marshes, wet meadows, bogs *(nelsoni)*; salt marshes of James and Hudson Bays *(alterus)*; upper reaches of coastal salt marshes and coastal cranberry bogs *(subvirgatus)*. WINTER: Coastal salt marshes, in same habitats as the Saltmarsh Sharp-tailed, though may also occur in fresher upper reaches of marshes where Saltmarsh does not occur. No winter records for interior; very rare in winter in coastal CA. MIGRATION: Spring migration takes place during mid-May–late May; fall migration late Sept.–early Nov. Migration of *nelsoni* primarily through interior along Mississippi River Valley; rare inland migrant eastward. VAGRANT: Inland *nelsoni* is casual in migration to CA and CO. Accidental to AZ, NM, WY, and WA.

Population The diking and draining of salt marshes in the Maritimes and southern Maine has depressed the numbers of this species *(subvirgatus)*, and populations are showing a slight decline. Interior populations are probably stable.

SALTMARSH SHARP-TAILED SPARROW *Ammodramus caudacutus*

juvenile

This species and the Nelson's Sharp-tailed Sparrow were formerly treated together as the Sharp-tailed Sparrow. The Saltmarsh is restricted to salt and brackish marshes and is virtually unknown in freshwater. It hybridizes with the Nelson's *(subvirgatus)* where ranges overlap in Maine and New Hampshire. Its behavior is like the Nelson's, though it may be less secretive. It has a flat head and a fairly long, pointed bill. Its narrow tail is composed of narrow, sharply pointed rectrices. Polytypic. L 5" (13 cm)

Identification Orange face with extensive gray cheek; long dark postocular line; narrow dark malar stripe sets off white throat; gray nape and central crown stripe; reddish brown back with strong white stripes; indistinct buffy or whitish breast marked by extensive dark streaks across breast and along flanks. JUVENILE: Like juvenile Nelson's, but cheek, crown, nape, and back are darker; streaks below more widespread and distinct.

Geographic Variation Two subspecies differ subtly; not safely field separable. Nominate breeds from New Jersey to southern Maine; *diversus* breeds from New Jersey to northern North Carolina; smaller billed and duller on average. Winter ranges overlap.

Similar Species Similar to the Nelson's, but longer bill and flatter head; eyebrow streaked with black behind eye; orange-

buff face triangle contrasts strongly with paler, crisply streaked underparts; dark markings around eye and head more sharply defined. See also the Seaside (esp. juveniles).
Voice CALL: Like Nelson's. FLIGHT NOTE: Like the Nelson's; regularly delivered from ground in cover. SONG: Softer, more complex than the Nelson's. Flight display unlike Nelson's: song delivered in rapid, low flight over grass.
Status & Distribution Fairly common. BREEDING: Breeds in extensive coastal salt marshes (esp. those with a large component of saltmeadow cordgrass,

which forms short-grass pastures within drier portions of the marsh). WINTER: Less tied to saltmeadow cordgrass; frequently forages along dikes, ditches, pool edges, often in stands of taller smooth cordgrass or even shrubs during high tides. MIGRATION: Returns to breeding grounds between late Apr. and mid-May; most depart by early Nov; stragglers often linger north of wintering areas into Dec. VAGRANT: Accidental to PA (2 recs.), NS (1 rec.).
Population Diking and draining of salt marshes along Atlantic coast has depressed the numbers of this species,

but populations are probably stable. Considered near threatened by Bird-Life International.

SEASIDE SPARROW *Ammodramus maritimus*

This conspicuous *Ammodramus* can be seen taking long, low flights over marshes. Males sing from exposed perches or deliver flight songs (flying up from perch, then fluttering down as song is delivered). In winter, it is readily drawn into view by pishing. Fairly chunky, it has a flat head; long spikelike bill; and short, pointy tail. Polytypic. L 6" (15 cm)
Identification Distinct yellow supraloral patch; dark malar stripe; distinct whitish throat; broad, pale submoustachial. Breast varies (gray, whitish, or buffy), some streaking. Upperparts grayish with variable brown or olive coloration; variable reddish cast to wings; back variably streaked. JUVENILE: Warmer, paler, buffier than adult, especially on face and breast; breast streaking more distinct; may lack distinct yellow supraloral.
Geographic Variation The Seaside varies widely in overall color; forms 4 distinct groups: "Atlantic coast" *maritimus* (breeds from VA north, winters from NJ to FL) and *macgillivraii* (breeds NC to northeast FL) are dull grayish olive above, smoky gray on the breast with diffuse streaking. "Gulf Coast" (*sennetti* of southeast TX, *fisheri* from TX to northwestern FL, *peninsulae* of

western FL) has a buffier breast and face, more distinct breast and back streaking. "Cape Sable," the very localized *mirabilis*, inhabits a small area in the Everglades, with an olive cast to the back and nape, more distinct breast and back streaking. "Dusky" (*nigrescens*), the darkest, became extinct in June 1987. ("Cape Sable" and "Dusky" have been granted species status in the past.)
Similar Species Juvenile regularly confused with the Saltmarsh. Bigger Seaside has larger bill; longer, less spiky tail; flimsy, fresh juvenal feathering.
Voice CALL: Loud *tsup,* sometimes doubled. Rapid, high *tik* notes when excited on breeding grounds. SONG: Wheezy *tup zheee-errr,* like Red-winged Blackbird's, but softer, buzzier. Secondary song more complex, stuttering.
Status & Distribution Fairly common. Grassy tidal marshes; favors taller grass. MIGRATION: Resident (excl. *maritimus*); returns to breeding grounds between mid-Apr. and early May;

most departed by mid-Oct.; stragglers often linger north of wintering areas into Nov., Dec. VAGRANT: Accidental inland to PA, NC, and TX. Casual to the Maritimes.
Population Stable. Imperiled in New England and Florida; habitat limited, populations small. Only 4,000 to 6,000 "Cape Sable" birds remain. "Dusky" and population along St. John's River (sometimes given as a subspecies, *pelonotus*) are extinct; caused by diking of salt marshes and spraying of insecticides.

fisheri

maritimus

maritimus juvenile

nigrescens

mirabilis

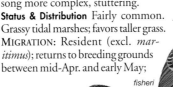

Genus Passerella

FOX SPARROW *Passerella iliaca*

iliaca

The Fox Sparrow feeds on the ground like a towhee. Pishing may bring the Fox into the open, but often it approaches cautiously from dense cover. Polytypic. L 7" (18 cm)

Identification This large, chunky sparrow has a medium-length tail, a large head, and a thick-based bill. Its plumage is highly variable by subspecies. Generally, it is dark above, with pale underparts that are heavily marked by dark triangular spots, which coalesce to form a central breast spot. Most subspecies have a reddish rump and tail; reddish coloring in the wings.

Geographic Variation See sidebar below.

Similar Species The "Red" Fox Sparrow is occasionally confused with the Hermit Thrush, but note the "Red" Fox's bill shape, streaked flanks, streaked back, and different behavior. The Lincoln's and Song Sparrows are both smaller, with thinner bills, sharper breast streaking and proportionately longer tails; and they are as likely

Fox Sparrow Subspecies Groups

Fox Sparrows comprise 4 fairly distinct subspecies groups that differ by consistent plumage traits, range, and voice. Some authorities consider these subspecies groups to be separate species. Identification to exact subspecies is rarely possible, given clinal variation, extreme similarity of certain subspecies, and the occurrence of intergrade populations. Key features of each group are overall upperparts coloration; color and extent of spotting below; presence of back streaking; bill size and color; and call note.

The "Red" Fox Sparrow includes the subspecies *iliaca* and the slightly duller, darker *zaboria;* it has bright reddish brown on its tail, rump, wings, and face; its back is gray with reddish brown streaks; its underparts are white with contrasting, blurry reddish brown streaks; and it often has narrow white wing bars. Breast spotting is also bright reddish brown; it is well defined on stark white underparts, converges into a distinct splotch in the center of the breast, and blurs together on the flanks, forming fairly dark streaks. The face pattern of the "Red" Fox Sparrow is particularly striking, with bright reddish brown crown and ear coverts prominent on the otherwise pale gray face. Juveniles of these subspecies have less distinct breast spotting and a brownish gray crown and back with no streaking. These birds breed in the boreal forests and taiga of the far north from the Seward Peninsula, Alaska, to Newfoundland and they winter in southeastern United States.

The "Sooty" is similar in pattern but lacks the wing bars, streaked back, and warm reddish brown tones of the "Red." The color of a "Sooty" varies from a cold blackish brown *(fuliginosa, townsendi, chilcatensis)* to a somewhat paler dark brown (e.g., *sinuosa, annectens, ridgwayi, unalaschensis*). The breast of the "Sooty" is so densely spotted that its central splotch extends across the entire breast and its flanks are more mottled than streaked. The base coloration of the underparts of the juvenile "Sooty" are a warm buff. These birds breed along the Pacific coast from the Alaska Peninsula to northwestern Washington and they winter south to southern California.

Some in the "Sooty" group show gray on the head like the "Slate-colored" birds, and are tinged with brown on the wings, rump, and tail. Breast spotting is heavy and dense, often forming a checkerboard-like pattern. The "Slate-colored" has a medium gray head, nape, and unstreaked back, with contrasting dull red-brown wings, rump, and tail. Subspecies differ subtly, from the *olivacea,* with a reddish cast to the head and back; to the *schistacea* and the *swarthi,* with more gray-brown on the head and back; to the intermediate *canescens,* with less brown on the back and a larger bill (tending toward the "Thick-billed"). Markings below, while generally like those of the "Red," are a much darker brown and are more sharply defined. A problematic subspecies of northwestern Canada, *altivagans,* is intermediate between the "Slate-colored" and "Red" groups but lacks the rich reddish tones of "Red." Look closely for its very faintly streaked gray back. "Slate-colored" birds breed across much of the Rocky Mountains and winter in California, Arizona, and New Mexico.

The "Thick-billed" has a consistently large, very thick-based bill; its plumage is similar to the "Slate-colored." It typically has a gray mandible (as does the "Slate-colored"), but its bill can be yellowish or orangish (as on the "Red" or "Sooty"); bill color may vary seasonally. Bill size varies from the smaller-billed *megarhyncha* (OR to northern CA) to the *brevicauda* (northwestern CA) and the southern *stephensi* (central and southern CA mountains), which have especially large bills. Breast spotting is most distinct and blackest in the "Thick-billed." Both the "Slate-colored" and the "Thick-billed" can sometimes show very faint whitish wingbars.

"Red" and "Slate-colored" birds give a *tchewp* call note; this is slightly less downslurred in the "Sooty," which has a smacking *tschup;* "Thick-billed" birds and some *canescens* have a distinctive *chink,* similar to the California Towhee's. Song differences are subtle and complex, but "Red" birds tend to sing sweeter, clearer notes; others use more buzzes and trills. ∎

to be found in grassy or weedy areas than in wooded thickets.

Voice CALL: Large-billed Pacific subspecies give a sharp *chink* call, like the California Towhee's; others give a *tschup* note, similar to but louder than the Lincoln's Sparrow's, and similar to but softer than the Brown Thrasher's. FLIGHT NOTE: High, rising *seeep*, given commonly on ground and in thickets. SONG: Sweet, melodic, warble composed of 7 or more phrases:

for example, *too-weet-wiew too-weet tuck-soo-weet-wiew*. Sweeter in the northern reddish subspecies; includes harsher or buzzy trills in other subspecies.

Status & Distribution Common. Winters south to northwest Mexico; the "Thick-billed" breeds in northern Baja California. BREEDING: Dense willow and alder thickets ("Red"); montane willow and alder thickets ("Slate-colored") or coastal forests and thickets ("Sooty"); montane thickets and chaparral ("Thick-billed"). WINTER: Undergrowth and dense thickets in coniferous or mixed woodlands, chaparral. MIGRATION: Fall migration late Sept.–late Nov.; Spring migration mid-Feb.–late Apr. "Red" migrates several weeks earlier in the spring and later in the fall than western groups do.

Population Stable.

schistacea

stephensi

unalaschcensis

fuliginosa

Genus *Melospiza*

All 3 species are of medium size, with fairly long, rounded tails. Favoring brushy areas along streams, pond edges, bogs, swales, or marshes, they may feed on the ground or in rank grasses. Their tails are usually pumped in flight, flipped upon landing, and cocked when perched. Secretive but inquisitive, they are responsive to pishing. All are quite vocal.

LINCOLN'S SPARROW *Melospiza lincolnii*

juvenile

This sparrow stays in or close to dense cover, flushing away from the observer with its short tail flipped on landing. It often raises its slight crest when disturbed. Polytypic. L 5.8" (15 cm)

Identification Buffy wash and fine streaks on breast and sides contrast with whitish, unstreaked belly. Note broad gray eyebrow, whitish chin, and eye ring. Briefly held juvenal plumage is

paler overall than juvenile Swamp Sparrow's. Distinguished from juvenile Song Sparrow by it s shorter tail, slimmer bill, and thinner malar stripe, often broken.

Geographic Variation The 3 subspecies show weak, clinal variation in measurements and general coloration. The nominate breeds in the northern portion of the breeding range (AK to the Maritimes), *alticola* breeds in the montane west, and *gracilis* breeds in the Pacific Northwest. Generally, *alticola* is largest and *gracilis* is smallest and darkest.

Similar Species The Song is larger with a longer, rounded tail; it lacks an eye ring, and streaking on the underparts looks as if it were painted with a broad brush. The Lincoln's has pencil-thin streaks, is grayer on the face (esp. supercilium), and has a buffy wash to the breast that the Song lacks, but beware a juvenile Song with a buffy breast and finer breast streaking. The similar-size Savannah is found more often in open fields and often flies high when flushed. (The Lincoln's almost never does.) The Savannah also lacks the gray face, rich reddish brown back and wings, and buffy wash on breast. See also the some-

times streak-chested juvenile Swamp.

Voice CALL: A hardy flat *tschup*, repeated in a series as an alarm call. FLIGHT NOTE: Sharp, buzzy *zeee*, similar to that of the Swamp but sharper; given commonly on ground and in thickets. SONG: A rich, loud, series of rapid bubbling notes, ending with a trill.

Status & Distribution Common in West, uncommon in East. Winters south to Central America. BREEDING: Bogs, mountain meadows, wet thickets. WINTER: Thickets, overgrown fields, dense brush, cutover woods. MIGRATION: Spring migration Mar.–mid-May; fall migration Sept.–Nov.

Population Stable.

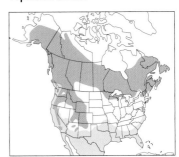

SONG SPARROW *Melospiza melodia*

Probably the most widespread sparrow, Song Sparrows commonly visit feeders and are responsive to pishing. In winter they may form small flocks, often with other sparrows, including the Lincoln's, Swamp, or *Zonotrichia*. Polytypic. L 5.8–7.5" (15–19 cm)

Identification Distinctive long, rounded tail, often flipped in flight and when landing. Broad, grayish eyebrow; broad, dark malar stripe; whitish throat. Upperparts usually streaked. Underparts whitish; streaking on sides, breast, often converge in central spot. Pinkish legs, feet. JUVENILE: Buffier; fine streaking.

Geographic Variation Depending on the taxonomy, 20 to more than 30 subspecies occur in the U.S. and Canada (with at least 4 more in Mex.). Extensive, marked variation in measurements, overall color, pattern. Identification to individual subspecies almost never possible in the field, but easy to recognize the larger geographic trends. Here they are separated into 5 subspecies groups.

Perhaps most distinctive is the "Alaska Island" group: 4 subspecies resident on the Aleutian Island chain and southern Alaska east to Kodiak Island, all of which are very large (close to Fox's size), large-billed, and generally sooty-colored. No other subspecies groups approach them in size; the subspecies from the western Aleutians (e.g., *maxima*) are largest. The "Pacific Northwest" group is fairly large and dark sooty or dark rusty colored; streaking on the breast and flanks often has a dusky background. "California" birds (inc. *heermanni* and those resident on the Channel Islands) are small and dark, with distinctly marked rich reddish wings, very gray faces; sharp blackish streaking below contrasts markedly with the upperparts. "Southwestern" birds (e.g., *fallax*) are quite pale reddish brown with well-defined breast streaking, contrasting little with the back and wings. Typical of the "Eastern" group is the nominate, which is medium-size and

fairly brown-backed with moderate contrast in breast streaking.

Similar Species See the Lincoln's, Swamp, Savannah, Fox, and Vesper.

Voice CALL: A nasal, hollow *chimp;* also high chips when excited. FLIGHT NOTE: A clear, rising *seeet.* SONG: Three or 4 short clear notes followed by a buzzy *tow-wee,* then a trill.

Status & Distribution Common. Winters south to northern Mexico; isolated resident population in central Mexico. BREEDING: Brushy areas, especially dense streamside thickets. Also occurs in lush beach vegetation, marsh edges. WINTER: Migratory populations tend to winter primarily in brushy areas, rank weedy fields, swampy woods; often with the Swamp and Lincoln's. In the West, the Song is more closely tied to ponds or streams with lush growth. MIGRATION: Most populations are migratory; Pacific and southwestern populations generally resident. Spring early Mar.–late Apr., peaking late Mar.; fall mid-Sept.–mid-Nov., peaking late Oct. VAGRANT: Europe.

Population Stable in most portions of range. Resident populations extirpated from 2 of the Channel Islands, due to overgrazing. Degradation of salt marsh habitats around the San Francisco Bay and desert riparian habitats in the Southwest has also negatively affected certain populations.

SWAMP SPARROW *Melospiza georgiana*

Sometimes abundant, Swamp Sparrows do not form a cohesive flock in winter; in rank brush or tall grass they may cluster with Song and Lincoln's. They can be brought into view with other sparrows by pishing. They deliver a loud, metallic call note when excited and at dawn and dusk, when marshes and brushlands are filled with their chorus of *chip* notes. A Swamp often flies away, straight and low, when flushed,

and may flip its long tail (esp. when landing). It typically does not call in flight, but often calls upon landing. Polytypic. L 5.8" (15 cm)

Identification Gray face; white throat; rich rufous wings contrast with upperparts; reddish brown back streaked with black. BREEDING ADULT: Reddish crown, gray breast, whitish belly. WINTER ADULT AND IMMATURE: Buffier overall, especially on flanks; duller crown streaked,

divided by gray central stripe. JUVENILE: Briefly held plumage usually even buffier; darker overall than the juvenile Lincoln's or Song; redder wings and tail.

Geographic Variation Three subspecies show moderate variation. The nominate and *ericrypta* divide the breeding range roughly at the Canadian border (nominate south, *ericrypta* north). Both small-billed and warm; nominate slightly warmer flanks and cap, grayer back.

The local *nigrescens* (breeds in brackish marshes from NJ to MD) has poorly known winter range, longer bill, darker back, black streaking in the crown, no buff tones to the flanks.

Similar Species The Song and Lincoln's are similar but heavily streaked below. Juvenile and first-winter Swamp can be streaked lightly, but never as prominently as the Lincoln's or Song. Unlike the Lincoln's, the Swamp lacks an eye ring; also has a somewhat longer tail and richer red-brown wings, with gray chest.

Voice CALL: Hard, metallic *chip*, somewhat similar to the Eastern's or Black Phoebe's. FLIGHT NOTE: A prolonged, buzzy *zeee*, similar to the Lincoln's, but

softer. SONG: A slow, single-pitched musical trill. Some deliver a faster trill.

Status & Distribution Common. Winters south to central Mexico. BREEDING: Nests in dense, tall vegetation in marshes, bogs, alder swales, wet hay fields. WINTER: Tall grass marshes, brushy fields, wet open woodland, esp. cutover forest. Rare in migration and winter in the West. MIGRATION: Spring mid-Mar.–early May, peaking mid-Apr.; fall mid-Sept.–mid-Nov., peaking mid-Oct. VAGRANT: Casual to AK, Europe.

Population Most populations stable; mid-Atlantic subspecies *nigrescens* sharply declined recently (reasons poorly known).

breeding
winter adult
juvenile
immature

Genus *Zonotrichia*

This genus comprises 5 species (4 breed in Canada and the northern U.S.; 1 in the highlands of C.A.). Adults are distinctive, with strong face patterns; immatures are more indistinctly marked. Songs are loud whistled phrases, often simple but melodic. They typically feed in flocks along dense cover, darting for safety at once when danger approaches.

WHITE-THROATED SPARROW *Zonotrichia albicollis*

tan-striped morph
white-striped morph
juvenile

Note fairly common morph: some adults with tan supercilium and median crown stripe; difficult to distinguish from first-winter plumage. FIRST-WINTER: Tan supercilium and median crown stripe; ill-defined white throat patch, often prominent malar stripe. JUVENILE: Grayish eyebrow, throat; breast, sides heavily streaked.

Similar Species See White-crowned Sparrow.

Voice CALL: A sharp *pink*, like the White-crowned's but higher. Flocking birds give husky chatter. FLIGHT NOTE: Drawn-out, lisping *tseep*. SONG: Thin whistle, generally 1 to 2 single notes, followed by 3 to 4 long notes, sometimes tripled: *Pure sweet Canada Cana-*

da Canada. Often sings in winter.

Status & Distribution Common. Some winter south to northern Mexico. WINTER: Common in woodland undergrowth, brush, gardens. BREEDING: Clearings in deciduous or evergreen forests, bogs. MIGRATION: Spring late Mar.–mid-May, peaking mid-Apr.; fall mid-Sept.–early Nov., peaking mid-Oct. Rare but regular in migration and winter in the West. VAGRANT: Casual to northern AK.

Population Stable.

This woodland sparrow of the East frequents feeders or feeds along woodland edges, darting for cover if disturbed. It may reemerge in response to pishing and can occur in large flocks (up to 150) in winter. Monotypic. L 6.8" (17 cm)

Identification Conspicuously outlined white throat; mostly dark bill; dark crown stripes, eye line. Broad yellow eyebrow in front; remainder white. Upperparts rusty brown; underparts grayish, sometimes diffuse streaking.

HARRIS'S SPARROW *Zonotrichia querula*

breeding

winter adult

winter adult

immature

The behavior of this sparrow is much like that of the White-throated. Regularly occurring in medium-size flocks, it mixes sometimes with the White-throated, White-crowned, or other sparrows. Monotypic. L 7.5" (19 cm)
Identification Large sparrow, larger than other *Zonotrichia*. Bright pink bill; black crown, face, and bib variable by age and plumage; all show postocular spot. BREEDING ADULT: Extensive black from crown to throat; gray face. WINTER ADULT: Buffy cheeks; throat all black or with white flecks or partial white band. IMMATURE: Resembles winter adult with less black; white throat bordered by dark malar stripe.
Similar Species Only other sparrows with black face are the otherwise dissimilar Black-throated and Black-chinned. The male House (not a true sparrow; see p. 456) has the same black throat, but is smaller, has bolder wing bars and a chestnut crown, does not have the bright pink bill, and behaves totally unlike an Emberizid sparrow.
Voice CALL: Loud *wink*. Flocking birds give a husky chatter. FLIGHT NOTE: A drawn-out *tseep*. SONG: Series of long, clear wavering whistles, often beginning with 2 notes on 1 pitch followed by 2 notes on another pitch.
Status & Distribution Uncommon to fairly common. BREEDING: Stunted boreal forest. WINTER: Open woodlands, brushlands, hedgerows. MIGRATION: Spring late Mar.–late May; fall early Oct.–early Nov. VAGRANT: Rare to casual east and west of narrow range.
Population Stable.

GOLDEN-CROWNED SPARROW *Zonotrichia atricapilla*

juvenile

immature

breeding

winter adult

The adults of this Pacific species are distinctive, but the immatures are the plainest-faced *Zonotrichia*. The bird prefers denser brush than the White-crowned, and its behavior is similar to the White-throated. Monotypic. L 7" (18 cm)
Identification Brownish back streaked with dark brown; breast, sides, and flanks grayish brown. Bill dusky above, pale below. ADULT: Yellow patch tops black crown; less distinct in winter. IMMATURE: Less-distinct yellow patch on brown crown. JUVENILE: Dark streaks on breast and sides. Plumage briefly held.
Similar Species White-crowned Sparrows have distinct head striping at all ages; the Golden-crowned has a plainer, brown face, with almost no contrast, darker underparts, and dusky bill. The yellow crown is usually present as a trace of color on the forecrown and above the eyes.
Voice CALL: A flat *tsick*. Flocking birds give a husky chatter. FLIGHT NOTE: A soft *tseep*. SONG: A series of 3 or more plaintive, whistled notes, often with each on a descending note: *oh dear me*.
Status & Distribution Fairly common. Winters south to northern Baja California. BREEDING: Stunted boreal bogs and in open country near tree line, especially in willows and alders. WINTER: Dense woodlands, tangles, brush, chaparral. MIGRATION: Spring migration mid-Mar.–mid-May, peaking mid-Apr; fall migration mid-Sept.–early Nov., peaking mid-Oct. VAGRANT: Casual to the East.
Population Stable.

WHITE-CROWNED SPARROW *Zonotrichia leucophrys*

One of the most common winter sparrows, the White-crowned typically occurs in flocks, which may involve more than 100 birds. They feed in short grass or open areas adjacent to woodlands, hedgerows, or brush piles. They may pop out in response to pishing and raise their crown feathers when agitated. Polytypic. L 7" (18 cm)

Identification For bill color, see sidebar below; whitish throat; brownish upperparts; mostly pale gray underparts. ADULT: Black-and-white striped crown. IMMATURE: Tan and brownish head stripes. JUVENILE: Brown and buff head; streaked underparts.

Geographic Variation See sidebar below.

Similar Species The White-throated Sparrow has a dark bill, prominent

adult
gambelii

juvenile
gambelii

adult
nuttalli

adult
leucophrys

immature
leucophrys

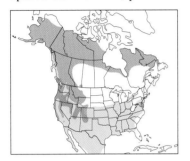

white throat, and yellow supraloral. Immature similar to immature Golden-crowned, but note the latter's dark gray bill, indistinct head pattern, and dingy underparts.

Voice CALL: Loud, metallic *pink*. Flocking birds give a husky chatter. FLIGHT NOTE: Sharp *tseep*. SONG: One or more thin, whistled notes followed by a variable series of notes. (See sidebar below.)

Status & Distribution Common in the West, uncommon in East, rare in the Southeast. Winters south to central Mexico. BREEDING: Clumps of bushes or stunted trees on taiga and tundra; coastal scrub, chaparral for "Pacific" group birds. WINTER: Hedgerows, desert scrub, brushy areas, wood edges, and feeders. MIGRATION: Spring mid-Mar.–mid-May, peaking early to mid-Apr.; fall early Sept.–mid-Nov., peaking mid-Oct. VAGRANT: Europe and Asia.

Population Stable.

White-crowned Sparrow Subspecies

The White-crowned Sparrow is divided into 3 well-defined subspecies groups: "Dark-lored" (Rocky Mountain *oriantha* and eastern *leucophrys*), "Pacific" (northern *pugetensis* and southern *nuttalli*), and "Gambel's" (western *gambelii*). Individual subspecies are often not identifiable in the field. The region around the lores gives the best first clue. The median crown stripe meets the eye line at the base of the maxilla in the "Dark-lored" birds; the supercilium is pinched off and the supraloral region is black. In "Pacific" and "Gambel's," the white supercilium meets the gray lores and the supercilium is not pinched off. Judge the bill color carefully, too: yellow in "Pacific," orange in "Gambel's," and pink in "Dark-lored." "Pacific" birds often show a prominent malar stripe, rare in the others. Note as well that the primary extension is comparatively short in "Pacific," longest in "Gambel's," and intermediate to longish in "Dark-lored." "Pacific" lacks gray striping on its back, showing only dark brown and tan; gray striping is fairly prominent on the back of "Gambel's" and "Dark-lored." "Pacific" also has more brownish coloration to its breast and flanks. First-winter birds show a distinctive difference that can be very hard to spot in the field: the first-winter "Pacific" has a small patch of yellow feathers right at the bend of its wing; on "Dark-lored" and "Gambel's," this patch is white.

Songs differ somewhat: rising and falling *zuuuu zeee jeee jeee zee* for "Gambel's"; clearer and more rapid with different introductory note and more trills (esp. last 2 notes) for "Pacific"; song of "Dark-lored" is inconsistent between the 2 subspecies. Even within subspecies though, individual variations and local permutations can occur. Call notes are flatter in "Pacific" and *oriantha*. Another behavioral distinction is that "Pacific" birds place their nests in low bushes, while "Dark-lored" and "Gambel's" birds place it directly on leaf litter.

Subspecies *leucophrys* of the "Dark-lored" group breeds mainly in the east Canadian tundra. In the same group, *oriantha* breeds in the Rocky Mounatins and in the higher elevations of the Sierra-Cascade Range. Subspecies *pugetensis* and *nuttalli* of the "Pacific" group reside along the Pacific coast from southern British Columbia to southern California. The *gambelii* breeds from western Alaska to Hudson Bay. Winter ranges are not nearly so differentiable, but comprise much of the southern United States and northern Mexico. "Pacific" *pugetensis* is casual inland in southern California, rare south of Los Angeles County; "Gambel's" is rare to casual in the East; "Dark-lored" is very rare during migration in coastal California. Intermediate birds may represent intergrades, not uncommon in areas of overlap (esp. "Gambel's" x "Dark-lored" and "Gambel's" x "Pacific"). ∎

Genus *Junco*

This genus includes 3 species (or, according to some authors, 4 or more), 2 of which occur north of Mexico. These birds are shades of gray above and white below, with pink bills and prominent white outer tail feathers. Their behavior (often feeding on the ground singly or in groups; flying up suddenly to a tree) may recall *Spizella* sparrows.

DARK-EYED JUNCO   *Junco hyemalis*

"Oregon" *thurberi*

"Slate-colored" ♂

"Slate-colored" *hyemalis*

juvenile

Dark-eyed Juncos are unique sparrows that nest on or near the ground in forests. In winter, they typically form flocks and often associate with other species, including Chipping Sparrows, Pine and Palm Warblers (in the southeastern U.S.), and bluebirds. When disturbed the entire flock suddenly flies up to a tree, usually perching in the open and calling in aggravation at the intrusion. Polytypic. L 6.3" (16 cm)

Identification A fairly lean sparrow with a long notched tail and a small pinkish or horn-colored bill (bicolored in *dorsalis*). Two prominent white outer tail feathers in most subspecies; 3 outermost in the "White-winged." Most subspecies have a gray or brown head and breast sharply set off from a white belly. Otherwise highly variable. (See Geographic Variation.) MALE: Typically darker with sharper markings. FEMALE: Typically browner with more indistinct markings. JUVENILE: Heavily streaked, often with a trace of adult pattern.

Geographic Variation The 12 subspecies show marked variation and fall into 5 major groups: "White-winged" (1 ssp.), "Slate-colored" (2 subtle ssp., plus *cismontanus*), "Oregon" (5 subtle ssp.), "Pink-sided" (1 ssp.), and "Gray-headed" (2 distinctive ssp.). The groups have at times been considered separate species. The "White-winged" Junco is the most local, breeding exclusively in the Black Hills region and wintering

along the eastern edge of the Rockies; it is casual to accidental in western Texas, Arizona, and southern California. The "Slate-colored" is the most widespread and the only form found regularly in the East. It breeds throughout the species' range east of the Rockies and in the northern region; it winters mainly in the East and is uncommon to rare in the West. The "Oregon" Junco breeds in the West Coast states north to southern Alaska and east to central Nevada and western Montana; it winters throughout the West and Great Plains and is casual to the East. The "Pink-sided" breeds in the northern Rockies, centered on Yellowstone and ranging from northern Utah to southernmost Alberta and Saskatchewan; it winters in the southern Rockies, Southwest, and western Great Plains, rarely to the West Coast, and is accidental to the East. The "Gray-headed" is the subspecies of the southern Rockies, breeding through much of Nevada, Utah, and Colorado south to central Arizona and western Texas; it winters in the southwest and southern

Rockies states and is rare to the West Coast and accidental to the East.

The distinctive "White-winged Junco," *aikeni*, is mostly pale gray above, usually with 2 thin white wing bars; it is also larger, with more white on its tail. It is most similar to the "Slate-colored" (which can rarely have narrow wingbars) but is larger and paler, with contrasting blackish lores and more extensive white in the tail. The male "Slate-colored Junco" has a white belly contrasting sharply with a dark gray hood and upperparts, usually with very little contrast between the hood and back; immatures can have some brown wash on the back and crown. In the female, the amount of brown on the head and at the center of the back varies; it's more extensive in immatures. The "Slate-colored Junco" comprises 2 subspecies: the widespread nominate and the larger, bluer-billed *carolinensis*, which is resident in the Appalachians from Pennsylvania to northern Georgia. An additional subspecies, *cismontanus*, is often grouped with the "Slate-colored." It breeds from the Yukon to central British Columbia and Alberta and may winter throughout the West; it is casual to the East. *Cismontanus* is intermediate between the "Slate-colored" and the "Oregon," with males showing a blackish hood that contrasts with a usually grayish back (occasionally with some brown). Females and immatures are very similar to the "Oregon" Juncos, but are less distinctly hooded. The male "Oregon" Junco has a slaty to blackish hood, contrasting sharply with its rufous-brown to buffy-brown back and sides; the female has duller hood color. Of the 5 "Oregon" subspecies, the more southerly subspecies

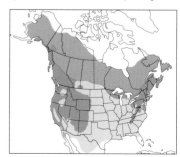

are paler. The "Pink-sided" Junco, *mearnsi,* has broad, bright pinkish cinnamon sides, a blue-gray hood, a poorly defined reddish brown back and wings that do not contrast markedly with the flanks, and blackish lores. Females duller, but retain basic pattern; they can resemble "Oregon" females closely. In the "Gray-headed" Junco, the pale gray head and dark lores resem-

"White-winged" *aikeni* ♂

"Pink-sided" *mearnsi*

"Gray-headed" races

dorsalis

caniceps

ble the head pattern of the "Pink-sided," but the flanks are gray rather than pinkish, and the back is marked by a very well-defined patch of reddish hue that does not extend to the wings and that contrasts sharply with the rest of the body. A distinctive subspecies, *dorsalis,* is sometimes known as the "Red-backed" Junco and is resident from northwestern Arizona through New Mexico to the Guadalupe Mountains of western Texas. It differs from the more widespread, migratory, northerly breeding *caniceps* in having an even paler throat and a larger, bicolored bill that is black above and bluish below. Intergrades between some subspecies are frequent. Common intergrades are: "Pink-sided" x "Oregon" and "Pink-sided" x "Gray-headed." *Cismontanus* may be a broad intergrade population of "Oregon" x "Slate-colored" Juncos. Identification to sub-

species group thus requires caution to eliminate the possibility of an intergrade; for intergrades, look for intermediate characteristics: For example, a darker, more contrasting hood on a "Pink-sided" indicates the influence of "Oregon" genes; reduced pink sides and a well-defined reddish back on a "Pink-sided" indicate "Gray-headed" parentage.

Similar Species See Yellow-eyed Junco.
Voice Songs and calls among the subspecies are generally similar, but songs and calls of the "Gray-headed" *dorsalis* are more suggestive of the Yellow-eyed Junco. CALL: Sharp *dit.* FLIGHT NOTE: A rapid twittering. SONG: A musical trill on 1 pitch; often heard in winter.
Status & Distribution Common. Breeds south to northern Baja California; winters south to northern Mexico. BREEDING: Breeds in coniferous or mixed woodlands. WINTER: Found in a wide variety of habitats, the Dark-eyed Junco tends to avoid areas of denser brush; it especially favors feeders, parks, and open forest without an understory. MIGRATION: Withdraws from wintering areas during Apr., typically early–mid-Apr. Fall arrivals first appear in late Sept., peaking in late Oct. VAGRANT: Southern FL and Europe.
Population Stable.

YELLOW-EYED JUNCO *Junco phaeonotus*

juvenile

This distinctive bird, with piercing yellow eyes, replaces the Dark-eyed Junco in certain mountain ranges adjacent to the Mexican border. It behaves much like the Dark-eyed, but it rarely forms large flocks. Polytypic. L 6.3" (16 cm)
Identification Bright yellow eyes, black lores. Bicolored bill with dark maxilla, pale mandible. Pale gray above; bright rufous back; rufous-edged greater coverts and tertials; pale gray underparts. JUVENILE: Similar to juveniles in the Dark-eyed's "Gray-headed" subspecies, but with rufous wing panel like the

adult; eye is brown, becoming pale before changing to yellow of adult.
Geographic Variation Five subspecies show marked variation; only *palliatus* occurs north of Mexico.
Similar Species The "Gray-headed" group of the Dark-eyed is most similar. The Yellow-eyed differs not only in eye color, but also in the rich rufous on the wings. (Beware "Gray-headed" x "Pink-sided" intergrades, which may show dull rufous on the wings.) Note also that only the *dorsalis* subspecies ("Gray-headed" group) has the bicolored bill.

Voice CALL: Sharp *dit,* softer than the Dark-eyed's. FLIGHT NOTE: A high, thin *seep,* similar to the Chipping Sparrow's call, lower than the Dark-eyed's; also rapid twitter as in the Dark-eyed. SONG: A variable series of clear, thin whistles and trills.
Status & Distribution Fairly common. Breeds in mountains south to Guatemala. In the U.S., found only in southeastern AZ and southwestern NM. Coniferous and pine-oak slopes, generally above 6,000 feet. Some move to lower altitude in winter. VAGRANT: Casual to western TX.
Population Stable.

LONGSPURS Genus *Calcarius*

The behavior of the 4 *Calcarius* species (3 endemic to N.A.; 1 widespread, circumpolar) resembles that of the *Plectrophenax* buntings: they occur in open areas and use trees or bushes only for song perches. In winter they occur in large flocks, often with other species. They call often when flushed and while in their strong, undulating flight.

LAPLAND LONGSPUR *Calcarius lapponicus*

winter ♂
winter ♀
buffy fall ♀
juvenile
breeding ♂
breeding ♀

Sometimes found singly or in single-species flocks, Laplands are also often found amid flocks of Horned Larks and Snow Buntings. Look for the Lapland's darker overall coloring and smaller size. It may flock with other longspurs as well. Polytypic. L 6.3" (16 cm)

Identification Outer 2 tail feathers on each side of tail are partly white, partly dark; reddish edges on the greater coverts and on the tertials, which are also indented. BREEDING ADULT MALE: Black, well-outlined head and breast; a broad white or buffy stripe extends back from eye and down to sides of breast; reddish brown nape. BREEDING ADULT FEMALE: Duller version of male. WINTER: Bold, dark triangle outlining plain buffy ear patch; dark streaks (female) or patch (male) on upper breast; dark streaks on side; broad buffy eyebrow and buffier underparts; belly and undertail are usually white. JUVENILE: Buffy and heavily streaked above and on breast and sides.
Geographic Variation Six subspecies (3 in N.A.) show weak variation in coloration. Eastern *subcalcaratus* breeds from north-central Northwest Territories to Labrador and winters west to

Texas; the remainder of the North American range is occupied by *alascensis,* which is comparatively much paler. Asian *coloratus* is dark and bright compared to *alascensis,* and it has occurred as a rare or casual breeder on islands in Alaska's Bering Sea.
Similar Species See sidebar p. 591.
Voice CALL: A musical *tee-lee-o* or *tee-dle.* FLIGHT NOTE: A dry rattle distinctively mixed with whistled *tew* notes; other longspurs do not include the *tew* notes with their rattle, but the Snow Bunting does; the Lapland's rattle is more distinct. SONG: Rapid warbling, frequently given in short flights; only on breeding grounds.
Status & Distribution Common. Circumpolar distribution. BREEDING: High arctic tundra. WINTER: Grassy fields, grain stubble, airports, beaches. MIGRATION: Spring late Feb.–early Apr.; fall early Sept.–late Nov, peaking late Oct.–early Nov. in most of the United States.
Population Stable.

SMITH'S LONGSPUR *Calcarius pictus*

winter ♂

Habitat provides a good initial clue for this species, as it is very faithful in winter to areas of ankle-high grass or alfalfa, where it can be extremely secretive, with whole flocks virtually invisible until they are flushed. This behavior is similar to that of the Chestnut-collared Longspur, but it is generally unlike that of the Lapland and the McCown's, which usually prefer more open areas and behave less secretively. The Smith's sometimes flocks with Laplands; identification is often easiest by strong buff underparts and by call, since all long-

spurs call when flushed and when in flight. Monotypic. L 6.3" (16 cm)
Identification Outer 2 tail feathers on each side of tail are almost entirely white. Bill thinner than other longspurs'. Note long primary projection, a bit shorter than the Lapland's, but much longer than the Chestnut-collared's or the McCown's; shows rusty edges to greater coverts and tertials. BREEDING ADULT MALE: Bold black-and-white head pattern; rich buff nape and underparts; white patch on shoulder, often obscured. BREEDING ADULT

breeding ♂

breeding ♀

FEMALE: Duller, crown streaked, chin paler. Dusky ear patch bordered by pale buff eyebrow; pale area on side of neck often breaks through dark rear edge of ear patch. Underparts pale buff with thin reddish brown streaks on breast and sides. Much less white on lesser coverts than males. WINTER AND IMMATURE: Like female.

Similar Species See sidebar below.

Voice CALL: Short, nasal *tseu*. FLIGHT NOTE: Dry, ticking rattle, harder and sharper than the call of the Lapland and the McCown's. SONG: Rapid, melodious warbles, ending with a vigorous *wee-chew*. Heard in spring migration and on the breeding grounds; delivered only from the ground or a perch.

Status & Distribution Uncommon. BREEDING: Open tundra and damp, tussocky meadows. WINTER: Open, ankle-high grassy areas. MIGRATION: Spring late Mar.–late May in U.S.; arrives on breeding grounds late May–early June; fall early Sept.–mid-Nov. Typically migrates earlier in fall and later in spring than the Lapland. Regular spring migrant in the Midwest, east to western IN; rare migrant in western Great Lakes. VAGRANT: Casual to both coasts.

Population Stable.

Winter Longspurs

Winter longspurs present one of the greater challenges among North American Emberizids, in part because the shifting flocks can be quite furtive on the ground, making viewing difficult. Details of plumage, shape, and tail pattern are useful, but identification is always aided by a consideration of call notes, habitat, and behavior. The Lapland most resembles the Smith's; the Chestnut-collared is most like the McCown's. The bird's tail pattern provides a good starting point and is best seen in flight, especially as the tail is flared upon landing. The Lapland and the Smith's have white outer tail feathers (whiter in the Smith's). The Chestnut-collared and the McCown's have largely white tails with differing patterns of black: a black triangle in the Chestnut-collared and a black inverted "T" in the McCown's. On the ground, the Smith's and the Lapland have a long primary extension, while the McCown's and the Chestnut-collared have a comparatively short primary extension. When on the ground, the Smith's is best told from the Lapland by its wing panel, which is a contrasting chestnut color in the Lapland and noncontrasting buffy in the Smith's. Also note the Smith's smaller, slimmer bill; finer, sparser streaking below; often broken rear border to the facial frame; and white (adult male) or white-edged lesser coverts. All Smith's are extensively buffy below, but this can be matched by rare Laplands. The McCown's is large and pale, with a large pinkish bill and distinctive dull face pattern (recalling female House Sparrow); sometimes its chestnut median coverts are shown. The Chestnut-collared is shaped more like the Lapland or the Smith's but tends to be plainer gray-brown, is more evenly colored overall with a less distinct face pattern, and has a grayish rather than a pinkish bill. All 4 species' flight calls are distinctive when learned and invaluable to identification. Focus on the Lapland's dry rattle, interspersed with *tew* or *jit* notes; the Smith's slower, clicking rattle; the McCown's softer, more abrupt rattle, interspersed with a distinctive *pink* note; and the Chestnut-collared's unique *kittle* call. Habitat, while not diagnostic, can be an important clue. The McCown's prefers the most open country (heavily grazed grasslands, plowed fields, flat dirt areas). The Lapland similarly prefers open areas that are mostly lacking in vegetation, but it may be slightly more regular in short grass areas (e.g., airports) than the McCown's. Both the Chestnut-collared and the Smith's are found in short grass areas, typically in ankle-high grass. The Chestnut-collared is often found in areas that have some patches of bare ground interspersed; the Smith's is usually in denser, more complete areas of grass. The 2 denser-grass species are also more furtive and often flush from almost underfoot; the Lapland and the McCown's are more likely to flush at a distance. ∎

McCown's Longspur, winter

Lapland Longspur, winter

Smith's Longspur, winter

Chestnut-collared Longspur, winter

MCCOWN'S LONGSPUR *Calcarius mccownii*

breeding ♂

breeding ♀

winter ♀

winter ♂

juvenile

This species generally favors more barren country than do other longspurs (except the Lapland) and flocks most often with Horned Larks. Look for the McCown's chunkier, shorter-tailed shape and slightly darker plumage, its mostly white tail, its thicker bill, and its undulating flight. On breeding grounds it is easily separated from the Chestnut-collared by its unique display flight. Monotypic. L 6" (15 cm)

Identification The McCown's white tail is marked by a dark inverted T-shape. Note also the stouter and thicker-based bill than found on other longspurs. Its primary projection is slightly longer than the Chestnut-collared's; in a perched bird, the wing extends almost to the tip of the short tail. BREEDING ADULT MALE: Black crown, black malar stripe, black crescent on breast; gray sides. Upperparts streaked with buff and brown, with gray nape and rump; chestnut median coverts form con-

trasting crescent. BREEDING ADULT FEMALE: Streaked crown; may lack black on breast and show less chestnut on wing. WINTER ADULT: Large pinkish bill with a dark tip; feathers edged with buff and brown. Winter adult female paler than female Chestnut-collared, with fewer streaks on underparts and a broader buffy eyebrow. Some winter males have gray on rump and variable blackish on breast; retain the chestnut median coverts. JUVENILE: Streaked below; pale fringes on feathers give upperparts a scaled look; paler overall than juvenile Chestnut-collared.

Similar Species See the Chestnut-collared Longspur for identification of juveniles. See also sidebar p. 591.

Voice FLIGHT NOTE: A dry rattle, a little softer and more abrupt than the Lapland's. A unique *pink* note is especially useful for identification; it may recall a soft Bobolink or Purple Finch flight note. SONG: Heard only on

breeding grounds; a series of exuberant warbles and twitters, generally given in a distinctive song flight, unlike that of the Chestnut-collared. The McCown's rises to a considerable height and then delivers its song as it floats slowly back to the ground with its wings held in a sharp dihedral. The appearance recalls a falling leaf or a floating butterfly.

Status & Distribution Uncommon to fairly common, but range has shrunk significantly since the 19th century. Winters south to northern Mexico. BREEDING: Dry shortgrass prairies. WINTER: Dry shortgrass prairies and fields, also plowed fields, airports, and dry lake beds. Very rare visitor to interior CA and NV. MIGRATION: Spring migration early Mar.–mid-May; fall migration mid-Sept.–late Nov. Migrates primarily through western Great Plains. VAGRANT: Casual in coastal CA and southern OR; accidental to the East Coast.

Population Breeding range drastically reduced since the 1800s; for example, the species formerly bred in Oklahoma, South Dakota, and western Minnesota. Contraction in range and overall decrease in population is due to land management practices that have greatly reduced shortgrass prairie. Conversion to large-scale agriculture is especially to blame.

CHESTNUT-COLLARED LONGSPUR *Calcarius ornatus*

breeding males

The fairly secretive Chestnut-collared Longspur favors denser grass in migration and in winter than does either the McCown's Longspur or the Lapland Longspur. Flocks of Chestnut-collared Longspurs flush from underfoot and can vanish again into ankle-high grass. The Chestnut-collared mixes less frequently with other longspurs, and it very rarely wanders into the open (unlike the Lapland Longspur and the McCown's

Longspur). Its *kittle* call, given upon flushing, is the easiest way to identify it. Monotypic. L 6" (15 cm)

Identification The white tail is marked with a blackish triangle. Primary projection is short; primary tips barely extend to base of tail. Fall and winter birds have grayish, not pinkish, bills. BREEDING ADULT MALE: Black-and-white head, buffy face, and black underparts are distinctive; a few have chestnut on underparts. Whitish

lower belly and undertail coverts. Upperparts are black, buff, and brown, with chestnut collar, whitish wing bars. WINTER MALE: Paler; feathers are edged in buff and brown, partially obscuring black underparts. Male has small white patch on shoulder, often hidden; compare to the Smith's Longspur. BREEDING ADULT FEMALE: Usually shows some chestnut on nape. WINTER FEMALE: Like breeding female, but paler. JUVENILE: Pale feather fringes give upperparts a scaled look.
Similar Species Juvenile is best distin-

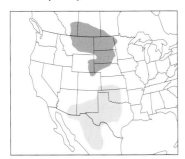

guished from juvenile McCown's Longspur by its tail pattern and bill shape. See sidebar page 591.
Voice FLIGHT NOTE: Distinctive 2-syllable *kittle,* repeated 1 or more times. Also gives a soft, high-pitched rattle and a short *buzz* call. SONG: Pleasant rapid warble, given in song flight or from a low perch; heard only on breeding grounds.
Status & Distribution Fairly common. Winters south to northern Mexico. BREEDING: Nests in moist upland prairies and typically prefers moister areas with taller, lusher grass than does the McCown's Longspur. MIGRATION: Spring migration mid-Mar.–mid-Apr.; fall migration Sept.–mid-Nov. Migration is primarily through western and central Great Plains. Male Chestnut-collared Longspurs may wander during mid-summer. Rare in CA in migration and winter. VAGRANT: Casual during migration to eastern North America and the Pacific Northwest. Accidental in winter and mid-summer to the East Coast.

winter ♂

winter ♀

Population Like the McCown's Longspur, the Chestnut-collared Longspur has suffered due to the destruction of native prairies by overgrazing and the conversion to large-scale agriculture. Formerly, the Chestnut-collared Longspur bred in Kansas, and it was more widespread throughout its current range.

Genus Emberiza

The 39 species in this Old World genus make it the largest in the Emberizidae. *Emberiza* buntings are typically small to medium in size and are sexually dimorphic, with males often being quite boldly marked with black, white, brown, chestnut, or yellow coloration. Several species have white outer tail feathers. They feed on the ground, much like juncos, and fly up to a tree when disturbed. All are vagrants to North America, though the Rustic Bunting is annual on the westernmost Aleutians. Details of plumage pattern, as well as call notes, are important for identification.

PINE BUNTING *Emberiza leucocephalos*

fall
adult ♂

Two fall records of the Pine Bunting from Attu Island (the most western island of the Aleutian Islands) are the sum of its North American occurrences. This species is very unlikely to be found by North American birders. Polytypic. L 6.5" (17 cm)
Identification A largish, fairly long-tailed bunting with a medium bill. MALE:

Distinctive white cheek is unique. In breeding plumage, the male is rusty about the face and throat, and it has a white median crown stripe. In winter plumage, the rust is replaced by gray-brown and the median stripe is lost. FEMALE: Rusty supercilium; underparts are whitish and finely streaked; white cheek is less prominent than on the male; rusty rump. IMMATURE: Like the female, but often duller and lacking the white cheek patch entirely, though it has a white spot (at least) at the rear auriculars, similar to that found on the Rustic Bunting.
Geographic Variation The Pine Bunting comprises 2 subspecies, but only *leucocephalos* has been found in North America.
Similar Species The white cheek patch is distinctive on adults. Immatures could be confused with either the Rus-

tic Bunting or the Little Bunting. Note, however, that the Pine Bunting's weak malar; its lack of both a strong eye ring and a crest; and its dull or whitish cheek, which is never chestnut like that found on the Little Bunting. FEMALE AND IMMATURE: The Yellow-breasted Bunting is also similar to the Pine Bunting; however, the Yellow-breasted always shows some tint of yellow on the face or underparts.
Voice CALL: Abrupt *spit* or *tic,* often doubled, *spi-tit;* also a hoarse *jeeit.* SONG: Long and variable, repetitious warbling phrases.
Status & Distribution The Pine Bunting breeds across northern Russia; winters south to central-south Asia. VAGRANT: Accidental to Attu I., AK, where there are 2 records: Nov. 18–19, 1985, and Oct. 6, 1993. Casual in western Europe.

LITTLE BUNTING *Emberiza pusilla*

immature

breeding ♂

First recorded in Alaska in 1970, this species had only 3 records between 1970 and 1990. Since then it has been found repeatedly in fall at Gambell (St.

Lawrence I.), and it may prove annual with continued coverage. Monotypic. L 5" (13 cm)

Identification Small, with short legs, a short tail, and a small triangular bill; bold creamy white eye ring, chestnut ear patch, and 2 thin pale wing bars. Whitish and heavily streaked underparts; white outer tail feathers. BREEDING ADULT: Chestnut crown stripe bordered by black stripes; many males have chestnut on chin. IMMATURE AND WINTER ADULT: Chestnut crown, tipped and streaked with buff and black.

Similar Species Female Rustic may be confused with the Little Bunting. Note the Rustic Bunting's larger size, heavier bill with pink lower mandible, diffuse rusty streaking below, and lack of eye ring.

Voice CALL: Sharp *tsick*. SONG: Short, variable series of rising and falling notes.

Status & Distribution Common. Breeds from Scandinavia to eastern Siberia; winters from Nepal and India to S.E. Asia. Rare in western Europe. VAGRANT: Casual to St. Lawrence I. in fall (late Aug.–early Oct.); accidental elsewhere in western AK (3 recs.) and CA (2 recs., Sept.–Oct.).

RUSTIC BUNTING *Emberiza rustica*

A regular migrant in extreme western Alaska, this attractive bunting is also the most regular *Emberiza* south of Alaska. Polytypic. L 5.8" (15 cm)

Identification Has a slight crest, whitish nape spot, and a prominent pale line extending back from eye; white outer tail feathers. BREEDING MALE: Black head; prominent white supercilium; upperparts bright chestnut, with buff and blackish streaks on back; white underparts, with chestnut breast band and streaks on sides. FEMALE: Brownish head pattern, with pale spot at rear of ear patch. IMMATURE AND WINTER MALE: Similar to female.

Geographic Variation Slight; only *latifascia* recorded from N.A.

Similar Species The Lapland Longspur is similar to the Rustic Bunting, but its behavior is different (e.g., the longspur is unlikely to perch in a bush). Among

other plumage differences, the Lapland lacks the pale ear spot, crested appearance, and rufous streaking below. The Rustic differs from the female and immature Reed Bunting and from the Pallas's Bunting in its crested appearance; its stronger face pattern, pale median crown stripe, and small pale nape spot; the extensive rufous streaking on breast and flanks; and its more prominent wing bars. See also the Little Bunting.

Voice CALL: Hard, sharp *jit* or *tsip,* lower and sharper than the Little Bunting's call. SONG: A soft bubbling warble.

Status & Distribution Common. Eurasian species; breeds from northern Scandinavia east to Kamchatka and north-

♀

breeding ♂

ern Sakhalin I. (Russia). It winters primarily in eastern China, Korea, and Japan. Rare in western Europe. MIGRATION: Uncommon spring migrant on western Aleutians, rare in fall; very rare on other islands in Bering Sea. VAGRANT: Casual in fall and winter on West Coast from southern AK south to CA.

GRAY BUNTING *Emberiza variabilis*

This is a large bunting with a heavy, pinkish bill. It shows no white in its tail. Monotypic. L 6.8" (17 cm)

Identification Bill is pinkish at base. BREEDING MALE: Gray overall, prominently streaked with blackish on back and wings. WINTER AND IMMATURE MALE: Broadly edged with buff on upperparts, paler below. Immature plumage is largely held through first spring. ADULT FEMALE: Patterned

breeding ♂   immature ♂   ♀

like male but brown instead of gray; chestnut rump and tail is conspicuous in flight.

Similar Species The male Gray could be confused with the "Slate-colored" Junco, but it has a gray belly and lacks white in the tail. Female Gray is like other *Emberiza*, only large, with a thick bill and a distinctive rusty rump and tail, without white outer tail feathers.

Voice CALL: Sharp *zhii*. SONG: Warbling series of loud notes.

Status & Distribution Breeds in east Asia; winters primarily in Japan. VAGRANT: Three records from western Aleutian Islands, AK: May 18, 1977; late May 2005 (Shemya Is.); and May 19, 1980 (Attu I.).

YELLOW-THROATED BUNTING *Emberiza elegans*

♂

This bird has generated only 1 record in North America, in western Alaska. Polytypic. L 6" (15 cm)
Identification Adults prominently crested. MALE: Black auriculars; supercilium white at front, yellow at rear; black crest over yellow crown; yellow throat; brown, streaked back; whitish breast with brownish streaking. FEMALE AND IMMATURE: Duller version of male; auricular brownish.

Geographic Variation Three subspecies; the Alaska record is probably *elegans*.
Similar Species The Yellow-throated's crested appearance is distinctive among *Emberiza*.
Voice CALL: Sharp *tzick*. SONG: Long series of sweet rollicking phrases.
Status & Distribution Breeds in eastern Asia; winters in coastal eastern Asia. VAGRANT: One record: Attu I., AK (May 25, 1998).

YELLOW-BREASTED BUNTING *Emberiza aureola*

This bright bunting has appeared a few times in western Alaska. Males are distinctive; females and immatures are subtle. Polytypic. L 6" (15 cm)
Identification White outer tail feathers. BREEDING MALE: Rufous-brown upperparts, black face, bright yellow underparts, white patch on lesser and median wing coverts. WINTER ADULT MALE: Usually shows features of breeding plumage. FEMALE: Striking head pattern: median crown stripe; ear patch with dark border and pale spot in rear; yellowish underparts with sparse streaking; unmarked belly; brown lateral crown stripes with internal black streaking; whitish median crown stripe. IMMATURE: Like female, often paler yellow.
Geographic Variation Two subspecies; only *ornata* has occurred in N.A.
Similar Species The Pine, Reed, and Pallas's all lack yellow wash, striking face.
Voice CALL: Sharp *tzip,* similar to the Rustic's. FLIGHT NOTE: Flat *stuck.*
Status & Distribution Breeds Scandinavia to Siberia; winters mainland S.E. Asia. Rare in western Europe. VAGRANT: Casual in AK May–June. Records from St. Lawrence I. and western Aleutians.

♀

breeding ♂

PALLAS'S BUNTING *Emberiza pallasi*

♀

reeding ♂

A vagrant from Asia, the Pallas's often flicks its tail when perched. Polytypic. L 6" (13 cm)
Identification White outer tail feathers. Like Reed, but smaller; shorter tail; smaller, straighter 2-toned bill with pink base (black in breeding male); grayish lesser coverts. BREEDING MALE: Like breeding male Reed, but lacks all rust. FEMALE AND IMMATURE: Like female Reed, but mostly unmarked below, lacks median crown stripe, has less distinct eyebrow and lateral crown stripe, browner rump.
Similar Species Female, immature Reed separated by call. See Identification.
Voice CALL: Loud *cheeep,* recalling House Sparrow's, very unlike Reed's call.
Status & Distribution Breeds in north-central and eastern Siberia; winters primarily in coastal eastern Asia. VAGRANT: Three spring AK records (1968, 1973, 1993); the specimen in Barrow was *polaris.* Accidental in British Isles.

REED BUNTING *Emberiza schoeniclus*

Like the Pallas's Bunting, the Reed is a casual visitor to western Alaska. Polytypic. L 6" (15cm)
Identification The Reed has solid chestnut lesser wing coverts. Note also its gray bill with curved culmen; cinnamon wing bars; dark lateral crown stripes; and paler median crown stripe. BREEDING MALE: Black head, throat; broad white submoustachial stripe; white nape; upperparts streaked black and rust; gray rump. White underparts with thin reddish streaks alongside and flanks. FEMALE: Pale buffy rump, broad buffy-white eyebrow. IMMATURE: Like female, but more buff.
Geographic Variation Fifteen subspecies; U.S. records are east Asian *pyrrhulina.*
Similar Species See Pallas's and Rustic.
Voice CALL: A falling *seeoo.* FLIGHT NOTE: A hoarse *brzee.*
Status & Distribution Common. Widespread Eurasian species. VAGRANT: Casual on westernmost Aleutians in late spring; accidental in fall to St. Lawrence I.

fall adult ♂

♀

breeding ♂

Genus *Plectrophenax*

SNOW BUNTING *Plectrophenax nivalis*

The Snow's breeding and flocking behaviors are similar to the Lapland Longspur's. Polytypic. L 6.8" (17 cm)
Identification Long black-and-white wings; breeding plumage acquired by end of spring, largely by wear. Bill black (summer) or orange-yellow (winter). Males usually show more white (esp. wings). JUVENILE: Grayish, streaked; buffy eye ring. First-winter plumage (premigratory) darker than adult's.
Geographic Variation Four subspecies (2 in U.S.): larger, whiter, bigger-billed *townsendi* breeds and winters on western Alaskan islands; nominate occurs throughout rest of range.
Similar Species See McKay's. Sometimes confused with albinistic sparrows. Note plumage, behavior.

Voice CALL: Often given in flight. Sharp, whistled *tew;* short buzz; and musical rattle or twitter. Rattle and *tew* notes like the Lapland's (rattle softer, *tew* clearer). SONG: Loud, high-pitched musical warbling, only on breeding grounds.
Status & Distribution Fairly common. BREEDING: Tundra, rocky shores, talus slopes. WINTER: Shores, weedy fields, grain stubble, plowed fields, roadsides. MIGRATION: Fall late Oct.–early Dec.; spring early Feb.–late Mar. VAGRANT: Casual to northern CA, TX, and FL; accidental to southern CA.
Population Stable.

MCKAY'S BUNTING *Plectrophenax hyperboreus*

This is one of the rarest breeding birds in North America. Monotypic. L 6.8" (17 cm)
Identification Like the Snow, but comparable plumage more white in tail, primaries. BREEDING: Male mostly white, including back (black in the Snow), with less black on wings and tail. Female like the Snow, but white panel on greater coverts. WINTER: Edged with rust or tawny brown; male whiter overall than the Snow. JUVENILE: Like juvenile Snow.

Similar Species Snow is very similar, not safely separable in all plumages; beware hybrids. Male McKay's more extensively white; black limited to feather tips. Female McKay's whiter in tail and primaries than male Snow. Juveniles very similar.
Voice Calls and song identical to Snow's.
Status & Distribution Uncommon. McKay's is known to breed regularly

only on Hall and St. Matthew Is. in the Bering Sea. A few often present in summer on the Pribilofs, and it has bred there; sometimes present in migration on St. Lawrence I. Rare to uncommon in winter along west coast of AK from Kotzebue south and west to Cold Bay; casual in winter southward, in interior of AK and on Aleutians. VAGRANT: Accidental south along Pacific coast to BC (1 rec.), WA (3 recs.), and OR (2 recs.).
Population Stable, but vulnerable, given its restricted range on 2 small islands.

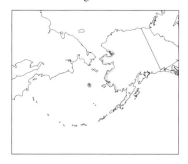

CARDINALS, SALTATORS, AND ALLIES Family Cardinalidae

Pyrrhuloxia, male (AZ)

I n North America, the Cardinalidae is a hodgepodge family represented by some of the region's brightest and most striking species, such as the Northern Cardinal and Indigo Bunting. Members of the family share similar bill characteristics, are all sexually dimorphic, and males of the species require up to 2 years to achieve breeding plumage. Males are typically uniquely colored and unmistakable; yet females, and in some cases immature males, are duller and more challenging to identify. Important features used to identify similarly looking females of closely related species include bill size and shape, overall color, and presence or absence of wing bars. All breeding species except the Northern Cardinal are nocturnal neotropical migrants. The Rose-breasted Grosbeak and Indigo Bunting are among the more common species seen during migratory fallouts along the Gulf Coast.

Structure Considered part of the 9-primaried oscines, members of the Cardinalidae family are variable in size, with cardinals and grosbeaks relatively large for passerines (about the size of a tanager) and buntings relatively small (about the size of a sparrow). All have distinctly shaped conical bills adapted for eating seeds and fruit. Some species have disproportionately large bills (Yellow Grosbeak). Genus *Cardinalis* is unique in the family, characterized by long, pointed crest.

Behavior They mainly feed on a combination of insects (breeding season), seeds, and fruit (fall and winter). Grosbeaks in particular switch to almost exclusively fruit beginning in late summer. Some are conspicuous singers during the breeding season (Northern Cardinal and Blue Grosbeak); others sing from inside dense vegetation

(Painted Bunting). Songs are mostly similar across the family: a series of paired phrases, somewhat robin-like. Males and females of some species (Northern Cardinal and Black-headed Grosbeak) sing. Calls usually consist of sharp single notes, often metallic in quality and difficult to differentiate within genus. Members of the genus *Passerina* (buntings and Blue Grosbeak) are known for tail-twitching behavior. Except for the Northern Cardinal, all are medium- to long-distance nocturnal migrants, wintering from Mexico into northern South America. At least 1 species, Pyrrhuloxia, disperses northward during the nonbreeding season.

Plumage Bright male plumages make these some of the most distinctive and recognizable species in North America. Females are equally famous for their dull brown plumages and difficult identifications. Males attain adult plumage by their second winter, normally with distinct first-summer plumage. Immature males typically resemble adult females and are well known to establish territories and sing. Winter adult males usually have brown edging to body feathers, obscuring bright plumage.

Distribution Members of the genus *Cardinalis* are generally resident, while all other North American cardinalids vacate their breeding grounds and migrate south for winter. Cardinalids are generally more prevalent south of the U.S., with no fewer than 30 additional species found exclusively in Central and South America. Ten species breed in North America and 3 occur as vagrants from Mexico. The Crimson-collared Grosbeak and the Blue Bunting are both casual in the Rio Grande Valley, while the Yellow Grosbeak is casual in southeastern Arizona. Species that breed in N.A. are found in a variety of habitats, from deciduous forest canopies to arid brushy hillsides. Several species are associated with streams and rivers.

Taxonomy The affinities of the Cardinalidae remain unresolved. Recent genetic studies suggest a close relationship to the Emberizidae and Thraupidae. In fact, members of the tanager genus *Piranga* may be more closely related to cardinalids than to true tanagers. Many of the species are monotypic, others have weakly differentiated subspecies, and some show distinct geographical variation. Some species, Painted and Varied Buntings in particular, have isolated breeding populations. Closely related species in the genera *Pheucticus* and *Passerina* hybridize when they come in contact. Dickcissel, in the genus *Spiza,* is sometimes aligned with the icterids, but genetic studies place it with the cardinalids.

Conservation As most species are found in a variety of disturbed and semidisturbed habitats, they are generally considered common and not threatened at present. Some species frequent riparian habitats in the West, the reduction of which may impact population numbers. Pesticide use in the neotropics may adversely impact Dickcissel populations on the wintering grounds. BirdLife International considers 4 neotropical species as near threatened. —*Gary H. Rosenberg*

Genus Rhodothraupis

CRIMSON-COLLARED GROSBEAK *Rhodothraupis celaeno*

adult ♀

adult ♂

This uniquely colored grosbeak is endemic to northeastern Mexico but wanders casually north to southern Texas, mainly in fall and winter. The winter of 2004–2005 was exceptional, with at least 15 individuals found. Usually associated with fruiting trees, particularly mulberries, this grosbeak is occasionally seen feeding on the ground, where it sometimes raises and lowers its crown feathers. No other North American bird has the color combination of an adult male Crimson-collared Grosbeak. Monotypic. L 8.5" (22 cm)

Identification Sexually dimorphic. ADULT MALE: Pinkish red underparts and collar contrast with the black hood and bib. It is mostly blackish above, with 2 thin pinkish wing bars. ADULT FEMALE: Females have a similar pattern, with pinkish red replaced by greenish yellow, and a heavyish, stubby dark gray bill. IMMATURE MALE: Like immature female. Can show pinkish red blotches. IMMATURE FEMALE: Like adult female, but less black in hood and bib.

Similar Species Males unmistakable. Female superficially similar in body, head, and bib color to the adult male Audubon's Oriole, but note the oriole's different shape, particularly bill length and shape, and its white wing bars.

Voice CALL: A penetrating, rising and falling *seeiyu*. SONG: A varied warble.

Status & Distribution Endemic to northeastern Mexico. Casual fall and winter visitor to southern TX, mainly to well-vegetated parks and refuges in the Lower Rio Grande Valley. Some individuals remain until spring.

CARDINALS Genus *Cardinalis*

The Northern Cardinal and the Pyrrhuloxia are characterized by long, pointed crests and stout, conical bills. They are mainly resident within their home range. Males are brightly plumaged; females and immatures are duller. Cardinals feed mainly on seeds and fruit and commonly come to seed feeders.

NORTHERN CARDINAL *Cardinalis cardinalis*

The bright red male Northern Cardinal, with its conspicuous crest, is one of the most recognizable birds in N.A. It is found abundantly through virtually all of the eastern United States in a variety of habitats, including suburban gardens. Although the cardinal can be secretive and remain hidden in thickets, males usually sing from exposed perches. The species is commonly attracted to feeders and open areas with birdseed. Its thick, reddish cone-shaped bill is specialized for cracking seeds. Polytypic. L 8.8" (22 cm)

Identification Sexually dimorphic. ADULT MALE: Plumage unmistakable. Males are uniquely colored, with a bright red body, a black face, and an obvious, pointed crest. ADULT FEMALE: Females are similarly shaped, but are buffy brown in coloration, with a reddish tinge on wings, tail, and crest. JUVENILE MALE: Similar to adult female, but it is generally browner overall and has a bill with less reddish coloration. JUVENILE FEMALE: Lacks reddish tones in wings and tail.

Geographic Variation Four subspecies described north of Mexican border.

juvenile ♂

Size and coloration varies clinally from east to west, with the eastern birds *(cardinalis)* being smaller, shorter crested, and duller red than the western birds *(superbus)*. The other 2 subspecies, *canicaudus* and *magnirostris,* are intermediate.

Similar Species In the East, the Northern Cardinal is not really confused with any other species. Note that the adult male Summer Tanager is also bright red, but it lacks both the crest and the black face. In the Southwest, the Northern Cardinal overlaps with the very similarly shaped Pyrrhuloxia, but note their color differences. Female and immature Pyrrhuloxias are very similar to female and immature cardinals. The Pyrrhuloxia has a noticeably yellow bill that has a distinct downward curve to the culmen, whereas the cardinal has a distinctly straighter culmen as well as a pointier, reddish bill. The plumage of the female Pyrrhuloxia is grayer with very little red.

Voice CALL: A sharp, somewhat metallic *chip*. SONG: Variable. A liquid, whistling *cue cue cue*, or *cheer cheer cheer*, or *purty purty purty*. Both sexes sing virtually all year, though females sing less frequently than the males do. **Status & Distribution** Very common. BREEDING: Throughout the East, found in a variety of habitats, including woodland edges, swamps, streamside thickets, and suburban gardens. In the West, restricted mainly to southwestern TX, southern NM, and southern AZ, where it is common in mesquite-dominated habitats, usually near water. Very rare along the Colorado River in southern CA. Generally nonmigratory. **Population** Cardinals generally expanded their range northward in the 20th century.

PYRRHULOXIA *Cardinalis sinuatus*

This bird's coloration and bill distinguish it from the cardinal. It often sings from exposed perches, particularly power lines. It also frequents birdseed feeders. Polytypic. L 8.8" (22 cm)

Identification Sexually dimorphic. ADULT MALE: Unmistakable. Plumage consists of a pearly gray body and blood-red face, bib, center to the breast and belly, and tip of crest. Thick yellow bill and curved culmen. Red-edged primaries and tail

feathers. ADULT FEMALE: Duller, lacks most of the red coloration. JUVENILE: Lacks red tones in wings and tail. Bill not as yellow as adult's.

Similar Species Females and juveniles easily confused with female and juvenile Northern Cardinal. Distinguished by more curved culmen, yellower bill, fewer red tones, and spikier crest.

Voice CALL: A *chink*, like the cardinal's, but decidedly more metallic. SONG: Reminiscent of, but thinner and shorter than, the cardinal's liquid whistles.

Status & Distribution Fairly common. BREEDING: Thorny brush and mesquite thickets in Southwest lowland desert; more arid environments than cardinal. Often in brushy borders near houses. WINTER: More widespread, north from breeding areas in AZ, NM, and TX. VAGRANT: Casual, mainly in fall and winter to southern CA, as well as the Great Plains. Accidental to ON.

Population Still common, but potentially threatened by loss of natural desert habitats in the Southwest.

GROSBEAKS *Genus Pheucticus*

Two species breed in N.A.; 1 is a vagrant from Mexico. These large passerines feature brightly plumaged males and duller females and immatures. Males attain breeding plumage after 2 years. With generally large, conical bills, they feed on insects during the breeding season and fruit during fall and winter. They are known to frequent seed feeders.

YELLOW GROSBEAK *Pheucticus chrysopeplus*

A resident of the thorn-forest and riparian areas north through western Mexico, the Yellow Grosbeak is usually quite conspicuous, owing to its large size and bright yellow coloration. Monotypic. L 9.3" (24 cm)

Plumage ADULT MALE: Bright yellow with black-and-white wings: white median coverts, white-tipped greater coverts, and white-based primaries form a white patch on the folded wing. White tips to the tertials. Black tail with white inner webs. ADULT FEMALE: Duller yellow and more streaking on upperparts. Wings and tail browner. IMMATURE MALE: Like female, with a yellower head. It achieves adult male plumage by its second winter.

Similar Species The Evening Grosbeak has a massive bill and white in the wing but is more gold in color and usually travels in flocks. The Black-headed Grosbeak female is more buffy underneath and has a more patterned head and a smaller bill.

Voice CALL: A *Pheucticus*-type *eek*, like the Black-headed's. SONG: Rich and warbled, similar to the Black-headed's.

Status & Distribution Primarily a Mexican species. Casual late spring and early summer to riparian areas in the lowlands and canyons of southeastern AZ.

ROSE-BREASTED GROSBEAK *Pheucticus ludovicianus*

breeding
adult ♂

winter adult ♂

breeding
adult ♂

1st fall ♂

♀

1st spring ♂

The striking Rose-breasted Grosbeak is a common bird of wooded habitats across much of eastern and midwestern North America. Singing from the canopy of a deciduous forest, even a brightly colored male can be difficult to locate. Late in the summer and during migration, it often feeds in fruiting trees. Monotypic. L 8" (20 cm)

Identification Sexually dimorphic. Takes more than a year to acquire adult plumage. ADULT MALE: Unique in N.A. Its black head, throat, back, wings, and tail contrast with gleaming white underparts and rump. Gets its name from a conspicuous bright rosy pink patch on the breast. Note the white wing bar and patches on black wing, and rose-red wing linings. Large, pinkish bill. ADULT FEMALE: Mainly brown above with streaks, paler below with extensive dark streaking. Yellow wing linings. WINTER MALE: Molts into winter plumage before migrating. Brown-edged head and upperparts, barred rump, and dark streaks on sides and flanks. Wings as in adult. FIRST-FALL MALE: Has buffy wash with fine streaks across breast, usually with some pink feathers visible on sides of breast. FIRST-SPRING MALE: Similar in pattern to adult male, but all of the black plumage is tinged brown, particularly the head, wings, and tail.

Similar Species Males in most plumages unmistakable. Plumage of females and first-fall males is very similar to plumage of female Black-headed Grosbeak (see sidebar below).

Voice CALL: A sharp *eek,* squeakier than the Black-headed's. SONG: A robinlike series of warbled phrases, but shorter. Songs are similar to those of the Black-headed Grosbeak.

Status & Distribution Common. BREEDING: Nests commonly in deciduous forest habitats, mainly in eastern U.S., but ranging northwest to northeastern BC. WINTER: Mainly Mexico, C.A., and rarely Cuba; casual in southern U.S., including coastal CA. MIGRATION: Peak spring migratory period in eastern U.S. mid-Apr.–mid-May; peak fall migratory period mid-Aug.–mid-Oct. Often seen in flocks during migratory fallouts. VAGRANT: Regular during late spring and fall in the Southwest. Casual, mainly in Oct., to U.K. and Europe.

Population Possible decline due to forest fragmentation.

Identification of Female *Pheucticus* Grosbeaks

One of the more difficult identification challenges among the Cardinalidae involves telling the female and immature *Pheucticus* grosbeaks apart. Although the breeding ranges of the Rose-breasted and the Black-headed Grosbeaks rarely overlap, both species have a tendency to wander, particularly during the fall, often including females and immatures. Characteristics to focus on are the extent of streaking and amount of buff on the underparts and the coloration of the bill.

Determining the age and sex of the grosbeak is usually a good first step in identifying it to species. The female Rose-breasted is generally whitish underneath and more heavily streaked. In addition, the streaks are made bolder by the near or sometimes complete absence of any buff coloration on the breast, nape, and chin. The female Black-headed in comparison tends to be quite buffy underneath with little or no streaking. The very worn female Black-headed can be quite white underneath, but it will still show little or no streaking. The female Rose-breasted usually has a pale, pinkish bill, whereas the Black-headed's bill is bicolored: dark gray above, light gray below. Females of both species have yellow underwing linings, although the Black-headed's is brighter yellow.

The first-fall male Rose-breasted has a buff wash across the breast and can look very similar to the female Black-headed. Typically, however, the first-fall male Rose-breasted has more streaking on the center of its breast, which the female Black-headed lacks altogether, and it usually has some pink feathers visible on the sides of its breast. The immature male Rose-breasted has pink wing linings, compared to yellow wing linings on the female Black-headed. Also beware of hybrids, particularly in the Great Plains, where the 2 species some-

BLACK-HEADED GROSBEAK *Pheucticus melanocephalus*

breeding
adult ♂

1st fall ♂

♀

The handsome Black-headed Grosbeak is the western counterpart to the East's Rose-breasted Grosbeak, and the 2 even occasionally hybridize where they come into contact in the western Great Plains. Singing males are generally easy to see in a variety of habitats, from open coniferous forests to montane riparian areas. The Black-headed is insectivorous during the nesting season and then mainly frugivorous, particularly during late summer. Like the Rose-breasted, it is a neotropical migrant. Males are striking; females and immatures are duller. The bill is large and conical, typically bicolored; the wing linings are yellow in both sexes. Polytypic (the 2 N.A. subspecies are poorly differentiated; the coastal birds have shorter wings, smaller bills, and a tawnier supercilium than the interior birds). L 8.3" (21 cm)

Identification ADULT MALE: Plumage is striking: a cinnamon-colored body including collar, with entirely black head, mostly black back with narrow streaks, black wings with bold white wing bars, white tips to tertials, and white patch at the base of primaries. Center to lower belly yellow. ADULT WINTER: Similar to adult male, but head less black, supercilium and crown strip cinnamon, and streaks on back more prominent. FIRST-SUMMER MALE: Like adult winter male, but wings less black. FIRST-WINTER MALE: Like female, but underparts more cinnamon without streaking, and underside of tail gray. ADULT FEMALE: Mainly dull brown, with streaked back, buffy-white nape and supercilium. Underparts variable, from buffy to almost white, with varying amount of streaking on the sides of the breast and flanks.

Similar Species The adult male not confused with other species. The female and first-winter male confused with the female and first-winter male Rose-breasted. Note the different amount of streaking on the underparts and the color of the bill (see sidebar below).

Voice CALL: A sharp *eek*, similar to the Rose-breasted's, but decidedly less squeaky. SONG: Robinlike series of warbled phrases, like Rose-breasted's. Virtually indistinguishable from the Hepatic Tanager's song, where the 2 species overlap.

Status & Distribution Common throughout entire West. BREEDING: Nests in a variety of habitats, from mixed coniferous forest to montane riparian. Arrives on breeding ground from mid-Apr. (in south) to mid-May (in north). MIGRATION: Migrates in spring singly or in small groups, unlike the Rose-breasted, which sometimes migrates in large flocks. In fall, not uncommon to see several in a fruiting tree. Adults begin migrating south by mid-July. Juveniles migrate later, through Oct. WINTER: Mainly Mexico. VAGRANT: Casual or accidental wanderer, mainly in fall and winter, to virtually all eastern states and provinces. Spring overshoots known from AK and NT.

Population No known threats.

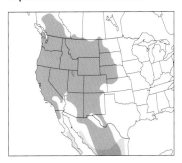

Black-headed Grosbeak, female

Rose-breasted Grosbeak, female

Rose-breasted Grosbeak, 1st-fall male

times come together and interbreed. A hybrid can show characteristics passed down from each of its parents, such as a bright yellow underwing lining coupled with a pale, pinkish bill.

Voice also plays a role in identification. Although the calls of both species are similar, the Rose-breasted's is a noticeably higher-pitched, squeakier *eek*. Of the 3 birds above, only the first-fall male Rose-breasted sings. ■

Genus Cyanocompsa

BLUE BUNTING *Cyanocompsa parellina*

adult ♂

This Middle American endemic is a rare, irregular visitor to southern Texas. Reminiscent of a small Blue Grosbeak, it is typically more secretive and remains hidden in brushy thickets and fields. Most records are from feeders in the Lower Rio Grande Valley. Polytypic (4 ssp.). L 5.5" (14 cm)

Identification Sexually dimorphic. ADULT MALE: Blackish blue body with brighter blue crown, cheeks, shoulder, and rump. Lacks wing bars. IMMATURE MALE: Like adult male, but with brownish cast to wings. FEMALE: Uniformly rich, buffy brown, lacking streaks or wing bars. Stout dark bill with curved culmen.

Similar Species Male Blue Grosbeak is much larger and heavier billed, with more blue overall and rufous wing bars. Female is larger with buffy wing bars. Female Varied Bunting, also plainly colored, has less rusty brown and is smaller billed, with a bluish tint to primaries and tail.

Voice CALL: A metallic *chink,* similar to the Hooded Warbler's. SONG: A series of high, clear warbled phrases, usually beginning with 2 separate notes.

Status & Distribution Casual to rare, mainly in winter, in brushy areas in the Rio Grande Valley of southern TX. VAGRANT: Accidental to upper TX coast and southwestern LA in winter.

BUNTINGS Genus *Passerina*

These birds are relatively small-bodied with small, conical bills. Males are very brightly plumaged; females are very dull brown or green, some with wing bars, some without. All have the characteristic behavior of twitching the tail while perched. They feed mainly on insects during breeding season, seed during fall and winter. They are nocturnal neotropical migrants.

BLUE GROSBEAK *Passerina caerulea*

breeding adult ♂

♀

immature

1st spring ♂

Closely related to the North American buntings, the larger Blue Grosbeak is a bird of the southern United States. Found in overgrown fields, along brushy roadsides, or in riparian habitats, it usually stays low in the brush but is often seen singing from an exposed perch. Like buntings, it has the distinctive behavior of twitching and spreading its tail. It feeds mainly on seeds. Polytypic (4 ssp. north of Mexico; eastern birds slightly smaller and larger billed than western birds). L 6.8" (17 cm)

Identification Highly sexually dimorphic. ADULT MALE: The large male is deep blue and has bright chestnut wing bars. Also note the black in face and chin and the indistinct blackish streaking to the upperparts. ADULT FEMALE: Females very different: pale grayish brown body overall. Buffy brown median coverts, lighter lower wing bar, indistinct streaking on back, some blue tinge to scapulars and tail. Note the large, massive bill. FIRST-SUMMER MALE: A mixture of male and female plumage, favoring the female with a mostly blue head, some blue patches on breast, and more blue tinge to primaries and tail. Chestnut in wings more extensive than in female. FIRST-WINTER MALE AND FEMALE: Similar. Overall richer rufous brown than adult female, with chestnut wing bars. No streaking on underparts.

Similar Species Males similar to male Indigo Bunting, but note larger size, larger bill, and chestnut wing bars. Females more problematic. Very similar to female Indigo Buntings, but more rufescent in the fall and winter. Wider and more rufescent upper wing bar. The Indigo Bunting always with faint to moderate streaking on underparts (variable) and much smaller bill. Calls and song very different.

Voice CALL: A loud, explosive *chink.* SONG: A series of rich, rising and falling warbles.

Status & Distribution Common. BREEDING: Found in a variety of brushy habitats, often near water, all across the southern U.S. MIGRATION: Arrives on the southern breeding grounds by early to mid-Apr., northern range by mid-May. Eastern population trans-Gulf migrants. WINTER: Both eastern and western populations winter in Mexico and C.A. south to Panama. Rare in Cuba and Bahamas. VAGRANT: Rare in fall north to New England and Atlantic provinces. Casual or accidental as far north as AK.

LAZULI BUNTING *Passerina amoena*

breeding adult ♂

1st spring ♂

♀

A western counterpart to the Indigo Bunting, the Lazuli Bunting is found in a variety of habitats, and its blue, white, and rich buff plumage makes it one of the more attractive songbirds of the West. It is quite similar to other *Passerina* buntings in behavior: frequents brushy borders to fields and roads, seen sometimes in single-species flocks, and often twitches and spreads its tail while perched. Occasionally it hybridizes with the Indigo Bunting. Monotypic. L 5.5" (14 cm)
Identification Highly sexually dimorphic.

Achieves adult plumage by second winter. ADULT MALE: The distinctive male is bright turquoise blue above and on the throat with a rich cinnamon-buff wash across the breast; white on the belly with a thick white upper wing bar. WINTER MALE: As in the Indigo Bunting, blue plumage obscured by buffy-brown edging to feathers, with blue visible on head and throat. ADULT FEMALE: Very different, duller, resembling the female Indigo Bunting. Note the drab grayish brown coloration with buffy wash across the breast, 2 narrow white wing bars, and lack of streaking on underparts. WINTER FEMALE: Like breeding female but with warmer buff wash on breast, grayer throat, and buffier wing bars. FIRST-SUMMER MALE: Like adult male with some brown feathers intermixed with blue. JUVENILE: Like female, but with distinct fine streaking across breast.
Similar Species Male unmistakable. Females confused with female Indigo and Varied Buntings and with female Blue Grosbeak. Note overall grayer plumage, warm buff wash across breast, lack of streaking on underparts (except in juvenile, which has finer, less blur-ry streaks), and more distinct narrow white wing bars.
Voice CALL: A dry, metallic *pik,* similar to the Indigo's. SONG: A series of varied phrases, sometimes paired, but faster and less strident than the Indigo's.
Status & Distribution Fairly common. BREEDING: Found in open deciduous or mixed woodland and in chaparral, particularly along streams and rivers. MIGRATION: Congregates during migration in the Southwest (late July–Nov.), where molting occurs, before continuing migration to Mexico. WINTER: Mainly western slope of Mexico. Rare in southeastern AZ. VAGRANT: Casual, mainly in spring and late fall north and east of breeding range.

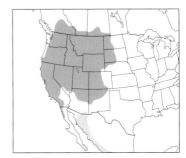

INDIGO BUNTING *Passerina cyanea*

The male Indigo Bunting is commonly seen as a breeding species and at migration hot spots. In the spring, the Indigo may be present in large flocks, particularly during migratory fallouts, and is often seen in brushy habitat or along weedy margins of fields and roads, where it sits up and twitches its tail. It sometimes hybridizes with the Lazuli Bunting. Monotypic. L 5.5" (14 cm)
Identification Highly sexually dimorphic. SUMMER MALE: Plumage unmistakable, entirely bright blue. WINTER MALE: Blue obscured by brown and buff edging; mottled brown and blue early in winter. SUMMER FEMALE: Dull brown, usually with 2 faint wing bars

and indistinct streaking on underparts. Whitish throat, small conical bill with straight culmen, relatively long primary projection. IMMATURE AND WINTER FEMALE: More rufescent overall than breeding female, with blurry streaking on breast and flanks.
Similar Species Males smaller than the male Blue Grosbeak, but lack chestnut wing bars, black on face, and dark streaks on back; also has smaller bill. Females similar to other female *Passerina* buntings (see sidebar p. 604).
Voice CALL: A dry, metallic *pik.* SONG: A series of sweet, varied phrases, usually paired.
Status & Distribution Common. BREEDING: Found in brushy borders to mainly deciduous woodland throughout eastern U.S. In the Southwest, mainly found in riparian habitats. WINTER: Mainly Mexico through C.A., rarely to northern S.A. Also on Caribbean

♀

fall

winter adult ♂

1st spring ♂

breeding adult ♂

islands. Rare along Gulf Coast and southern FL. MIGRATION: Mainly nocturnal. Arrives on breeding grounds mid-Apr.–early June. In fall, mainly mid-Sept.–mid-Oct. VAGRANT: Rare to Pacific states and Atlantic provinces.
Population Western birds may be limited by decrease in riparian habitats.

VARIED BUNTING *Passerina versicolor*

winter
adult ♂

♀

breeding
adult ♂

One of the more colorful of the buntings, this Southwest specialty appears uniformly dark in poor light. Found in more arid habitats than other buntings, it is often seen in desert washes or on cactus-laden hillsides of canyons. Similar in behavior to other *Passerina* buntings and an inhabitant of dense mesquite thickets, the Varied Bunting is usually difficult to see, but it often sings from exposed perches. Males are stunning in good light; females are extraordinarily dull. Polytypic. L 5.5" (14 cm)

Identification Highly sexually dimorphic. SUMMER MALE: Quite colorful, but colors difficult to see. Striking are the bright red nape, deep blue head and rump, and dark purplish body. Bill is rather small, with distinctive curved culmen. SUMMER FEMALE: Extremely

dull and featureless: almost entirely grayish brown, with very faint suggestion of wing bars, but no obvious pale edging to tertials. Note curved culmen. WINTER MALE: As in other *Passerina* buntings, its color is obscured by brownish edging to many feathers. WINTER FEMALE: Similar to summer female, but slightly more rufescent overall. FIRST-SPRING MALE: Like adult female, but with varying amounts of purple on forehead; often sings like adult male and defends breeding territory.

Geographic Variation Nominate subspecies *versicolor* from southeastern New Mexico and southern Texas has duller red nape, purple throat with reddish tinge, and pale blue rump. Subspecies *pulchra* (including *dickeyae*) from southeastern Arizona (and Baja) has brighter red nape, purple throat with no red tones, and purplish blue rump. Females grayer in Arizona. Baja subspecies very isolated and may represent separate species.

Similar Species Males unmistakable in good light. Females more of a challenge. Lack of distinguishing characteristics actually an identifying feature of female Varied. Female Lazuli has distinct pale wing bars and a buff wash across breast. Female Indigo is dark-

er, always with some streaking on underparts. First-year female Painted Buntings can be very drab but are still greenish above. Note distinctive curved culmen in the Varied.

Voice CALL: A loud, rich *chip,* similar to other buntings. SONG: A series of rich, sweet, unrepeated phrases, very similar to the Painted Bunting's and hard to differentiate in areas of overlap in Texas.

Status & Distribution Common, but local. BREEDING: In summer, inhabits dense, thorny thickets in desert washes, canyon hillsides, and sometimes along streams and rivers. Mostly found at lower elevations. MIGRATION: Most of the North American breeding population migrates south in winter. Population in extreme south TX may be resident. TX breeding population arrives mid-Apr.; AZ population very late arriving, mostly late May–early June (very rare before mid-May). WINTER: Western Mexico, mainly Sonora to Oaxaca. Casual in southwestern TX. VAGRANT: Accidental to CA (late fall and winter) and ON (spring).

Identification of Female *Passerina* Buntings

Although male *Passerina* buntings are some of the easier species to identify in North America, the females present several challenges. There are 5 species in this genus in North America, many of which overlap distributionally: the Indigo, Lazuli, Varied, and Painted Buntings and the Blue Grosbeak. Key characteristics include overall coloration, especially of the underparts; presence or absence of streaking below; presence or absence of wing bars; length of primary extension; and bill shape. Be aware that in some species, 1-year-old males look very much like females, but they sing. Also, fresh birds in fall are usually warmer brown in color.

The Indigo is probably the most common and widespread. Females are drab brown and whiter on the throat, and always have at least some streaking on the underparts. The wings typically show faint wing bars.

In the fall, females are brighter cinnamon. The Lazuli female can be similar, but always has a warmer buff wash across the breast with no streaking, more prominent wing bars, and a grayer, less contrastive coloration to the throat. While the female Indigo has only a hint of blue coloration to its tail feathers, on the female Lazuli a drab blue will often extend from the tail onto the rump, especially during spring and summer. The Varied is generally much drabber, with more uniform underparts, no streaking, and very faint wing bars. Note the Varied's distinctive curved culmen and very short primary extension. Fresh fall birds can be quite cinnamon in color. The Painted is generally easier to identify, as it is always green on the upperparts and dull yellowish below. Immature females and very worn adults can lose much of their coloration, but still retain at least some green color to the back. The female Blue Grosbeak is

PAINTED BUNTING *Passerina ciris*

adult ♂

juvenile

♀

Found across the South in 2 discrete populations, the male Painted Bunting, with its incongruous combination of red, blue, and green, can be considered North America's gaudiest songbird. Despite its bright plumage, it can be amazingly difficult to see, often singing from inside dense thickets. Females look very different, lacking the bright colors. The Painted regularly comes to seed feeders during the nonbreeding season. Polytypic. L 5.5" (14 cm)
Identification Sexually dimorphic. ADULT MALE: Unmistakable. Bright red underparts and rump, lime-green back, dark wings with green edging, and dark blue head (except for red chin and center to throat), red eye ring, dark tail. ADULT FEMALE: Very different, lacking any bright coloration. Upperparts lime green, dull yellowish below. Greenish edging on wings and tail. FIRST-WINTER MALE: Resembles female. FIRST-SUMMER MALE: Also like female, but often shows some blue on head or some

red on breast. Achieves adult plumage by second winter. FIRST-FALL FEMALE: Trickiest plumage to identify. Very drab, lacking much of the adult female's green tones. Upperparts are greener than plain underparts.
Geographic Variation Although the variation in plumage between the eastern nominate subspecies *ciris* and the western *pallidior* is slight, migratory and molt patterns differ. Eastern birds molt on the breeding grounds and then winter in Florida and Caribbean, while western birds molt at migratory staging grounds or on the winter grounds in Mexico and Central America.
Similar Species The adult male is unlike any other North American bird. Green upperparts of the immature male and all female plumages separate the Painted from all other buntings. The female Varied Bunting, particularly when worn in late summer, can look very similar, but it lacks any green tones above.
Voice CALL: A loud *chip*, sweeter than

other *Passerina* buntings' calls. SONG: A rapid series of varied phrases, thinner and sweeter than the Lazuli Bunting's, but surprisingly similar to the Varied's.
Status & Distribution Locally common. BREEDING: Often secretive in brushy thickets and woodland borders, often along streams and rivers, along the southeast coast (NC, SC, GA, FL) and much of the south-central U.S., west to western TX and southeastern NM. WINTER: Mainly Mexico south to Costa Rica and Panama; also southern FL, Bahamas, and Cuba. MIGRATION: Spring migration relatively early (early Apr.–early May). Fall migrations differ by population; eastern birds mainly late Sept.–Oct. and western birds late July–early Oct. Western birds have interrupted migration where they molt out of breeding plumage, mainly in Sonora, Mexico, but rarely to southeastern AZ. VAGRANT: Rare to casual, primarily in spring and fall north and west of mapped breeding range.
Population The Atlantic coast breeding population is limited and affected by loss of habitat.

Indigo Bunting, female (TX, Apr.)   Lazuli Bunting, female (CA)   Varied Bunting, female (AZ)

considerably larger than other *Passerina* buntings and has prominent buffy wing bars, a larger bill, and even some blue coloration on its shoulders. Although not a *Passerina*, the female Blue Bunting can be similar in size and overall appearance, but is a rich cinnamon red-

dish brown, and has plain wings and a thick, dark bill with a distinct curved culmen.

Hybridization can further complicate matters, resulting in variable intermediate plumages and sometimes making exact identification almost impossible. ∎

Genus *Spiza*

DICKCISSEL *Spiza americana*

The Dickcissel, a sometimes abundant migrant and breeding bird of the central United States, gets its name from the verbal interpretation of the male's song. Usually found in open prairie or weedy agricultural fields, its numbers and breeding distribution vary from year to year. Males often sing while sitting up on a tall weed, shrub, or wire. In migration, the Dickcissel is usually detected when flying over, giving a distinctive, flat call. Large flocks congregate during migration and on the winter grounds. Sometimes the Dickcissel is found with House Sparrows at feeders in the East. Monotypic. L 6.3" (16 cm)
Identification Sexually dimorphic. ADULT MALE: Distinctively patterned; grayish brown and sparrow-like. Underparts with a black bib surrounding white chin, yellow breast, whitish lower belly and undertail coverts. Grayish back, boldly streaked black, and gray rump, unstreaked. Wings with bright chestnut shoulder patch. Gray nape. Complex face pattern: gray auriculars; yellow eyebrow above and in front of the eye, white behind the eye; yellow malar, widening to white neck mark. Bill rather long and conical. WINTER ADULT MALE: Similar to breeding male, but

browner overall and with a less-distinct black bib. ADULT FEMALE: Similar to male but duller and browner. Varying amount of black speckling instead of black bib. Eyebrow duller, buffy behind the eye. IMMATURE: Males similar to adult female. Females very dull: Have fine streaking on breast and flanks and bold streaking on back, but lack any chestnut on shoulders.
Similar Species Immatures, which lack the chestnut shoulder and have no yellow on the underparts, can resemble female or juvenile House Sparrows. Note the distinct white upper wing bar and lack of any streaking on the underparts of the House Sparrow. Note also the House Sparrow's shorter bill and the Dickcissel's much longer primary projection.
Voice CALL: A flat *bzrrrrt,* often given in flight. SONG: A variable *dick dick dickcissel.*
Status & Distribution Common, sometimes locally abundant. Numbers fluctuate annually outside core breeding range. BREEDING: Nests in open, weedy meadows, in agricultural fields, and in prairie habitats. WINTER: Mainly the Llanos in Venezuela; very rare in northeastern U.S. and Atlantic provinces in winter, usually at feeders,

breeding ♂

breeding ♀

winter adult ♂

immature ♂

immature ♀

and in the southern portion of breeding range. MIGRATION: Mainly a nocturnal migrant, but large flocks are seen migrating during the day. Flocks coalesce, sometimes reaching numbers in the thousands. Spring period mid-Apr.–mid-May; fall period mid-Aug.–mid-Oct. VAGRANT: Rare, mainly in fall to East and West Coasts.
Population Large-scale conversion of native grasslands to agriculture in the main breeding areas has likely had a negative impact on population size.

DICKCISSEL

0 mi 1000
0 km 1000

BREEDING AND WINTER RANGES

– – Rare, irregular winter range

▢ Breeding range

▢ Winter range

BLACKBIRDS Family Icteridae

Altamira Oriole (TX, Feb.)

Contrary to popular thought, blackbirds are not all black. In fact, the family name, Icteridae, refers to their yellow color. So really these are the "yellow birds."

Structure Blackbirds are sturdy and large songbirds. They all have strong bills, ranging from short and finch-like, to sharp, to stout and heavy. The culmen is flattened and straight. Blackbirds have strong legs, particularly the species which feed terrestrially. Overall, blackbirds are stocky, but some orioles are slim, while the meadowlarks are rotund and stocky. Tail length in most species is medium, extremes being the short tails of the meadowlarks and the long and keel-shaped tails of the grackles. In the tropics, other groups, such as the caciques and oropendolas, are found, and the latter are amongst the largest neotropical passerines.

Plumage Generally blackbirds show some black, yellow, orange, or red on the plumage. Females of some species are brownish and streaked. Many of the blackbirds and grackles have largely or fully black plumages, often with blue or green iridescence. Flash colors may be present as red on epaulet (shoulder) or yellow on head. The black species often show bright yellow eyes. The meadowlarks' upperparts are streaked and patterned for adequate camouflage; however, their underparts are bright yellow with a distinctive black V on the breast. Orioles are the brightest blackbirds: Their plumages are a mix of yellow, orange, or chestnut with black. Several species have black hoods, while others have a black face mask and black bib, contrasting with a yellow or orange head and underparts. Female orioles vary depending on the species: Some are dull and yellowish, lacking the strong patterns

of the adult male, while others are like adult males in plumage. Young males may look similar to females. The tropical blackbirds include some very showy species, but the presence of bright yellow, orange, or red flash colors is typical.

Behavior All blackbirds share special musculature that allows them to open their bill with great force, allowing them to insert the bill tips in the ground or a crevice and then open the bill with strength, creating an opening for them from which to extract food. This "gaping" is characteristic of blackbirds and shared by the starling family. Other common behaviors include "bill tilting," in which an individual will point its bill up toward the sky. This aggressive signal often is given to a nearby individual during feeding and in territorial disputes. During territorial singing, blackbirds make the flash colors obvious, flaring red epaulets, exposing yellow breasts, or twisting yellow heads. In display, the grackles deeply keel the tail, ruffle the plumage, and drop the wings. Blackbirds have interesting mating systems. Orioles tend to be largely monogamous; some of the resident southern species defend territories year-round, with a great deal of female involvement. More migratory species show duller female plumages, and most territorial defense is performed by the male. Larger grackles and marsh-nesting blackbirds have polygamous (many mates) unions. Usually a male defends a large, high-quality habitat and several females settle in his territory and mate with him. Among the grackles, the females congregate in a breeding colony and the largest and most aggressive male defends the "harem." Defending a harem is a behavior nearly unknown in birds. Cowbirds lay their eggs in the nests of other species, doing away with parental care altogether. Many territorial species are highly social during the nonbreeding season, forming large mixed-species flocks. The Tricolored Blackbird is also highly social and colonial during the summer. It is the only strictly colonial land bird extant in North America.

Distribution Restricted to the New World, blackbirds successfully exploit habitats from grasslands and urban areas to forests and shrublands from Alaska to Tierra del Fuego. The most migratory species breed in North America, with the Bobolink showing the longest and most impressive migration.

Taxonomy There are nearly 100 species of blackbirds in 5 main family lineages. North American blackbirds fit into 3 of these groups: the orioles, the blackbird-grackle group, and the meadowlark and allies. Interestingly, the Bobolink and Yellow-headed Blackbird are part of the meadowlark allies!

Conservation The Tricolored Blackbird and Rusty Blackbird are of conservation concern, as their populations have drastically declined in the last few decades. Eleven species outside of North America are listed as threatened or near threatened. —*Alvaro Jaramillo*

Genus Dolichonyx

BOBOLINK *Dolichonyx oryzivorus*

summer ♀

breeding ♂

early spring ♂

fall

The Bobolink is a charismatic, attractive bird with a black and white plumage that suggests a tuxedo. Monotypic. L 7" (18 cm)

Identification A small blackbird with a short and sparrow-like bill. Stocky and very long winged, with pointed tail feathers. SUMMER MALE: Black, with buffy nape and large white patches on scapulars and lower back to uppertail coverts. Early in the season, brown tips to face and underparts, brown streaking on back and brown edging on wings. SUMMER FEMALE: Streaked and sparrow-like, with pink-based bill and pinkish legs. Dark crown with crisp white median stripe, buffy face, a short but obvious postocular stripe broadens above ear. Above brown, with yellowish buff streaking. Below pale buff to whitish when worn, with crisp streaking restricted to breast sides and flanks. FALL: Similar to summer female, but warmer yellowish below.

Similar Species The adult male Bobolink is distinctive. The male Lark Bunting is black with white on wings, but not on nape or body. Females and fall plumage are superficially sparrow-like, but note the Bobolink's larger size and bright pink legs. Also, the streaking is crisp and restricted to the flanks, while the head shows a dark crown with a buff central stripe, a short postocular stripe, and pale lores. LeConte's Sparrows are much smaller, streaked on breast, white on belly, brighter orange-buff on face, and short winged.

Voice CALL AND FLIGHT NOTE: A loud and sharp *pink*. SONG: A euphoric, complex bubbling and gurgling that gives the bird its name, *bob-o-link bob-o-link blink blank blink*. Usually the song is given during an aerial display.

Status & Distribution Common. BREEDING: Old fields. MIGRATION: Arrive in FL in mid-Apr., and in the Northeast

early May, after breeding congregates in marshes to molt, then heads south Aug.–late Sept., lingerers to Oct. Mostly a migrant through FL, fewer in Gulf Coast states. Many appear to take a

nonstop overwater route to S.A. WINTER: In south-central S.A. VAGRANT: Rare, primarily in fall on West Coast. **Population** Surveys suggest a general decline in numbers.

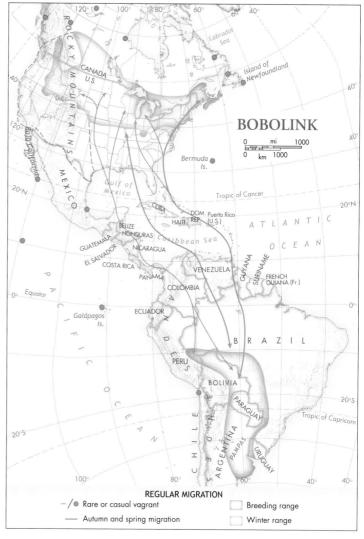

BOBOLINK

REGULAR MIGRATION
− /● Rare or casual vagrant
— Autumn and spring migration
☐ Breeding range
☐ Winter range

BLACKBIRDS Genus *Agelaius*

The 5 species belonging to this genus are restricted to North America, Central America, and the Caribbean. A group of similar South American species were previously included. Largely black plumages; bright red, tawny, or yellow "epaulets" or shoulder patches; and unmusical and screechy songs characterize the males.

TAWNY-SHOULDERED BLACKBIRD *Agelaius humeralis*

The Tawny-shouldered is an accidental vagrant from Cuba and Haiti. Polytypic (2 ssp.). L 8" (20 cm)
Identification Like a small and slim Red-winged Blackbird, but plumage entirely black with tawny lesser coverts, median coverts tawny with yellowish tips. Bill slim and sharply pointed.
Similar Species The Red-winged Blackbird is larger and bulkier, with a red epaulet and a wider yellow border. The Tawny-shouldered is more arboreal and has a different song.
Voice CALL: A *chuck* note typical of blackbirds. SONG: A muffled buzzy drawn-out *zwaaaaaaaa,* lasting just over a second in length.
Status & Distribution Accidental. YEAR-ROUND: Arboreal, preferring open woods, edge, and parklike settings. VAGRANT: Two visited the Key West Lighthouse (Feb. 27, 1936).

adult ♂

RED-WINGED BLACKBIRD *Agelaius phoeniceus*

adult ♀

immature ♀

1st year ♂

"Bicolored Blackbird"

♀

adult ♂

adult ♂

This species is one of the most widely distributed, abundant, well-known, and well-named birds in North America. Polytypic. L 8.7" (22 cm)
Identification Usually sits in an obvious place or is found in flocks, feeding on ground. A medium-size passerine with a sharply pointed, strong bill, somewhat upright posture. SUMMER MALE: Black, including soft parts, with bright red shoulder patch or "epaulet," bordered by yellow in most subspecies. WINTER MALE: As summer male, but shows warm brown feather tips throughout the body. FEMALE: Well streaked throughout, with whitish supercilium. Above brown and streaked. Face and underparts pale with dense streaking, broadly on breast and upper belly. Peachy wash on chin and throat. Dull reddish edges to lesser coverts create a poorly developed reddish epaulet. Soft parts blackish. IMMATURE MALE: As winter male, but heavily edged and fringed rusty, brown or buffy above, often showing buff supercilium. Epaulet shows black spotting. IMMATURE FEMALE: As adult female, but epaulet not developed and throat lacks peachy wash.
Geographic Variation Approximately 26 subspecies recognized, 14 in North America. Most are poorly defined, but the California Bicolored group *(californicus, mailliardorum)* are characterized by dark females appearing solidly blackish brown above and on lower breast to vent and show no or a poorly developed supercilium. Males show black median coverts, so the red epaulet lacks a yellow border.

Similar Species The male Tricolored Blackbird has a thinner, more pointed bill, a white epaulet border, colder gray-buff upperpart markings in winter, and a different voice. See sidebar page 610 to separate Tricolored females.
Voice CALL: *Chuk.* SONG: A hoarse, gurgling *konk-la-ree;* variable but gurgled start and trilled ending characteristic.
Status & Distribution Abundant. YEAR-ROUND: Open or semi-open habitats, closely associated with farmland. BREEDING: Usually in cattail marsh, but also in moist open, shrubby habitats. MIGRATION: Southern populations resident; northern ones short-distance migrants, which arrive in Northeast late Feb.–Mar. and leave by Nov.

VAGRANT: Casual to Arctic AK, Greenland, and Iceland.
Population One of the most abundant birds in North America, the Red-winged's count was estimated at 190 million in the mid-1970s. Populations are stable.

TRICOLORED BLACKBIRD *Agelaius tricolor*

breeding ♂

♀

The Tricolored is very similar in appearance, but not in behavior, to the Red-winged Blackbird. The great majority is restricted to California. Monotypic. L 8.7" (22 cm)

Identification This medium-size passerine with a sharply pointed, strong bill is seldom alone, breeding in colonies and wintering in medium- to large-size flocks. SUMMER MALE: Black with slight blue iridescence, including soft parts, with dark red shoulder patch or "epaulet." The epaulet is bordered by white. WINTER MALE: As summer male, but shows gray-buff feather tips throughout the body, and the epaulet border is creamy white. FEMALE: Dark, but streaked, most strongly on throat and breast; poorly developed paler supercilium. Above brown; below whitish on breast and throat with brown streaks, solidly brown on belly and vent.

Dull reddish edges to the lesser coverts create a poorly developed epaulet. Soft parts blackish. IMMATURE MALE: As winter male, but more heavily edged and fringed and often showing buff supercilium. Epaulet shows black spotting.

Similar Species Red-winged Blackbird males have thicker-based bills and a yellow or no epaulet border, warmer cinnamon or buff upperpart markings in winter, and a different voice. See sidebar below to separate Red-winged females.

Voice CALL: *Kuk,* lower in pitch than similar Red-winged Blackbird call. SONG: A nasal, drawn-out *guuuaaaak* or *kergwuuuuaaaa,* lasting 1–1.5 seconds. Apart from its frog-like nasal quality, the song differs from the Red-winged's by lacking the accented final trill.

Status & Distribution Fairly Common. YEAR-ROUND: Open or semi-open habitats, closely associated with farmland. BREEDING: Highly colonial, traditionally in large CA marshes, more recently in dense thickets of introduced Himalayan blackberry. Colonies are tightly synchronized while nesting, presumably an adaptation for overwhelming predators in the historically huge colonies. MIGRATION: After breeding, many move toward the coast, starting in mid-July. WINTER: Closely associated with rangeland, dairy operations. VAGRANT: Previously vagrant to WA, OR, and NV, but has now bred in isolated small colonies in those states. Casual to southeastern CA.

Population Currently the population is estimated at 230,000 birds. Once a single colony in Glenn County, California, held more than 200,000 birds, and many colonies had more than 100,000. Habitat change and colonial nesting make it a vulnerable species. A survey detected a potential 37 percent decrease in numbers between 1994 and 1997! California lists it as a species of special concern.

Identification of Female Red-winged and Tricolored Blackbirds

The separation of female Red-winged and Tricolored Blackbirds in California, where their ranges overlap, is one of the toughest field identification challenges for bird-watchers. Birders tend to ignore the females and concentrate on the males, which is a valid way to identify the species, but really not that useful when one comes across a lone female or a vagrant. In order to make an adequate separation one needs to look at the bill shape, wing structure, and tones and colors on the upperparts in fresh plumage.

Compared to the strongly dark-streaked female Red-winged Blackbirds from most of North America, the females of many California Red-winged subspecies are largely dark, and when worn can look largely solidly blackish above and unstreaked and solidly blackish on the belly and vent, with dark streaks on a pale background restricted to the throat and upperbreast. This plumage coloration is generally the same pattern shown by female Tricolored Blackbirds.

Structurally, these species do differ somewhat. Tricolored Blackbirds show thinner-based and longer bills than most California Red-winged Blackbirds, but note that the subspecies breeding in the Kern River Valley *(aciculatus)* is characterized by its long and slender bill. The Tricolored has a more pointed wing shape, which can be looked for on the perched bird. The outer primary, P9, is shorter than P6 on the Red-winged but longer on the Tricolored. In addition, on the folded wing, the distance between the longest primary (P8) and the next (P7) is noticeable on a Tricolored but minimal in a Red-winged.

In fresh plumage (during fall and early winter), a Red-winged Blackbird is edged with rufous, golden, and warm buffy edges on the upperparts, while these same areas are cold gray-buff on a Tricolored Blackbird. Often on a Red-winged there are 2 obviously paler, more

Genus Xanthocephalus

YELLOW-HEADED BLACKBIRD *Xanthocephalus xanthocephalus*

The Yellow-headed Blackbird is a beautiful marsh-dwelling blackbird of the prairies and the West. Monotypic. L 9.5" (24 cm)

Identification Large and bulky; males noticeably larger than females. ADULT MALE: Black with a bright yellow head (darker in winter), accented by a triangular black mask. White primary coverts create obvious wing patch in flight. Yellow around vent, difficult to see in the field. Bill, eyes, and legs blackish. ADULT FEMALE: Brownish, with yellow supercilium and breast. Whitish throat with dark lateral stripes and yellow malar stripes above them. IMMATURE MALE: Like female, but substantially larger, more extensive yellow on head and neck, black lores; noticeable white on the primary coverts, although not a fully formed patch. JUVENILE: Cinnamon head, contrasting with whitish throat and brownish body. Two whitish wing bars and cinnamon fringes to the tertials.

Similar Species No other bird in North America looks like the male Yellow-headed Blackbird. Duller females are identified by being brown, unstreaked, and having a contrasting yellow breast.

Voice CALL: A rich, liquid *check*. SONG: Two song types, both with a mechanical, unpleasant, or at least unusual, sound that renders them unmistakable. The primary song, *kuk, koh-koh-koh ... waaaaaaaa*, lasts 4 seconds; the final nasal scraping sound is separated from the introductory notes, accompanied by an asymmetrical display where neck and head are bent to one side. The second song, a croaking *kuuk-ku, WHAAA-kaaaa*, lasts 2 seconds, accompanied by a symmetrical display.

Status & Distribution Common. BREEDING: Deepwater wetlands of cattail, rushes, or Phragmites; it forages in adjacent grasslands or farmland. MIGRATION: First southbound birds in July, but most move Aug.–late Sept., in spring males arrive 1–2 weeks before females, arriving mid-Apr.–mid-May. A diurnal migrant, usually moving in single-sex flocks. WINTER: A few birds in agricultural areas in border states from CA to southern TX. Most in Mexico. Females winter farther south than males. VAGRANT: Casual in AK and NT. Accidental in Europe.

Population There was a general increase in population during the 1970s. Local droughts can greatly alter their numbers.

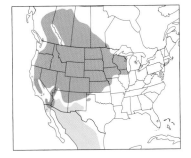

spring adult ♂

immature ♂

♀

juvenile

spring adult ♂

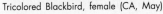

Tricolored Blackbird, female (CA, May)　　Red-winged Blackbird, female (IL)　　Red-winged Blackbird, *aciculatus*, female (CA)

yellowish lines of streaks on the back, like suspenders. The white tips to the median coverts (upper wing-bar) are broader and more noticeable on a Tricolored. Finally, some adult female Red-wingeds show a peachy or pinkish wash to the throat, absent in Tricoloreds.

Worn summer females, which by this point lack the paler feather tips on the upperparts, may by unidentifiable if not studied closely, although a Tricolored usually shows a stronger white bar on the median coverts. ■

MEADOWLARKS Genus *Sturnella*

The meadowlarks are open-country blackbirds, with a distinctive rotund and short-tailed starling-like shape. They fly with an odd flight style, using shallow fluttery wingbeats. The 2 North American species are yellow below, with a black V on the breast; most of the 7 species in this genus are red breasted.

WESTERN MEADOWLARK *Sturnella neglecta*

The song of the Western Meadowlark is emblematic of the West. Polytypic. L 9.5" (24 cm)

Identification Rotund, stocky, medium-size blackbird with a long bill, short tail, strong legs, and pointed tail feathers. SUMMER ADULT: Cryptically patterned above; bright yellow below with a bold black V on breast. Crown brown with white median crown stripe, pale face accented by bold dark postocular stripe, yellow supralores. Yellow on throat invades the malar area. Gray-buff flanks crisply streaked brown, vent and undertail coverts whitish, streaked vent. Back feathers edged white, but have complicated pattern of buff, and darker brown in centers. Fresh birds appear scaly due to complete pale fringing of feathers, but worn individuals look pale streaked as pale tip wears. Coverts pale brown with separate thin dark bars that remain separate to center of shaft. Similarly, central tail feathers are pale brown with discrete narrow dark brown bars. White on outer 3 tail feathers, a small brown strip remains on outer corner of outer 2 rectrices, but next one in (R4) largely dark with only a white wedge on inner vane. Bill gray with darker culmen and tip, legs dull pink, eyes dark. WINTER ADULT: Pale tips cloud black V on breast. Slightly more buffy yellow underparts; more scaly looking upperparts. JUVENILE: Similar to winter adult, but duller face pattern, paler yellow below, and breast streaked in a V, not solid.

Geographic Variation Subspecies *confluenta* of the Pacific Northwest is darker, and it shows dark bars on tail feathers and coverts that widen at center of each feather and join up with adjacent dark bars, like the Eastern Meadowlark.

Similar Species The Eastern Meadowlark is extremely similar and sometimes not separable. The southwestern form of Eastern Meadowlark (known as the "Lilian's") is even more similar to the Western than the more widespread eastern forms due to its pale plumage. To separate these look-alikes one needs to concentrate on the voice, extent of yellow of throat, plumage patterns, and tail pattern. Some vocalizations are diagnostic, such as the blackbird-like call of the Western. The 2-parted song is lower in frequency and lacks the ascending whistles of the Eastern (including the "Lilian's") song; however, the song is learned, and in rare cases the meadowlarks can learn each other's songs—this is not the case for the call. The Western shows more yellow on the throat; it extends to the malar area, and this can be surprisingly easy to see in a scope view. The Western is generally paler than the Eastern, but similar to the "Lilian's," showing a pale gray-brown overall color, rather than the warmer, more saturated brown of the Eastern. The Western shows pale gray-buff flanks, like the "Lilian's," and the Eastern has darker, midtone buff flanks with stronger streaks. The wing coverts show up as a grayish brown panel with narrow dark bars on the Western, while on the Eastern they are warm brown to cinnamon brown, with wider dark bars. The Western shows largely white outer 2 tail feathers, while the Eastern shows largely white outer 3 tail feathers.

Voice CALL: A low *chupp* or *chuck*. Females give a dry rattle, males

a slower rolling note. FLIGHT NOTE: A sweet whistled *weeet*. SONG: Males have melodious and flute-like song lasting approximately 1.5 seconds. Two phrases, starting with several clear whistles, and a terminal phrase which is more gurgled, bubbling and complex, *tuuu-weet-tooo-TWLEEDLOoo*.

Status & Distribution Common. BREEDING: Dry grasslands, agricultural areas. MIGRATION: Diurnal migrant; northern populations migratory, southern ones resident. Eastern breeders are also easternmost in winter. Spring arrival dependent on snow melt, usually Mar.–Apr., fall movements peak Sept.–Oct. WINTER: Dry grassy sites. VAGRANT: Casual in AK, NT, and Hudson and James Bays. Casual to East Coast from NS to GA.

Population Slowly declining in last 20 years.

spring
neglecta

spring
confluenta

fall
neglecta

juvenile
neglecta

EASTERN MEADOWLARK *Sturnella magna*

The sweet, whistled song betrays the presence of this ground-loving blackbird. Polytypic. L 9.5" (24 cm)

Identification Rotund, stocky medium-size icterid with a long bill, short tail, strong legs, and pointed tail feathers. SUMMER ADULT: Cryptically patterned above; bright yellow below with bold black V on breast. Crown dark brown with white median crown stripe, dark postocular stripe, otherwise yellow supraloes stand out on the paler face. Warm buff flanks crisply streaked brown. Back feathers edged white, but have complicated pattern of buff, and darker brown in centers. Fresh birds have a scaly look due to complete pale fringing of feathers. Coverts warm brown with dark bars that widen and meet adjacent dark bars at the feather shaft. Similarly, central tail feathers show confluent dark bars along shaft. Outer 3 tail feathers largely or entirely white. Bill gray with darker culmen and tip, legs dull pink, eyes dark. WINTER ADULT: Pale tips cloud the black V on breast. Slightly more buffy yellow underparts; scaly upperparts. JUVENILE: Similar to winter adult, but paler yellow below and breast V streaked.

Geographic Variation Fifteen subspecies recognized, 4 in North America. The most distinct, and perhaps a good species, is *lilianae,* the "Lilian's." Found in the desert Southwest, it is smaller, has longer wings and legs, and is generally paler than typical Easterns. It shows pale gray-brown plumage, like a Western Meadowlark, and separate and narrow bars on tail and greater coverts. It has extensive white on the tail, with the outer 3 rectrices entirely white, and the next in with substantial white. Although the calls are the same as for the Eastern, the song of the "Lilian's" is slightly more complex and lower in pitch, somewhat reminiscent of a Western.

Similar Species The Western Meadowlark is very similar; see that account. The call of the Eastern is diagnostic; the higher-pitched chatter is unlike the dry rattle of a Western. The Eastern lacks yellow on the malar and is generally darker than a Western, showing a saturated brown overall color. The Eastern shows largely white outer 3 tail feathers, white is even more extensive on the "Lilian's" Meadowlark. The "Lilian's" shows the pale plumage and discrete, separate barring as in Western, but it lacks streaking on the pale, thus showing a great deal of contrast with the dark eye line and crown, and whitish supercilium and cheeks.

Voice CALL: A buzzy *dzert;* also a chatter given by both sexes, higher pitched than rattle of the Western Meadowlark. FLIGHT

NOTE: A sweet whistled *weeet.* SONG: Three to 5 or more loud, sliding, descending whistles lasting approximately 1.5 seconds, *tsweee-tsweee-TSWEEEOOO.*

Status & Distribution Common. BREEDING: Grasslands and old field habitats; where sympatric with Western, takes moister grassland and shrubby edge habitats. "Lilian's" in desert grassland. MIGRATION: Diurnal migrant; northern birds move >620 miles, southern ones resident. Spring arrival dependent on snow melt, usually Mar.–Apr., fall movements peak Sept.–Oct. WINTER: Farmland, grasslands, and rangelands. VAGRANT: Casual to NF, ND, CO, southwestern AZ, and MB.

Population General declines have been detected from the 1960s to the 1990s due to habitat loss.

juvenile
magna

fall
magna

spring
magna

spring
lilianae

spring
hoopesi

spring
argutula

BLACKBIRDS Genus *Euphagus*

The 2 species in *Euphagus* are closely related to the grackles and the neotropical genus *Dives*. They resemble grackles in having ruff-out displays that accompany the song: the tail is cocked, the wings are drooped, the body is ruffled, and often the pale eyes are prominent. Unlike the grackles, *Euphagus* have standard-shaped tails.

RUSTY BLACKBIRD *Euphagus carolinus*

The Rusty is a nondescript blackbird of swampy forests, adorned with rusty in the winter. Polytypic. L 9" (23 cm)
Identification A slim blackbird lacking any striking structural features. SUMMER MALE: All black; in good light shows a dull greenish gloss. Black bill and legs; bright yellow eyes. WINTER MALE: Black with wide cinnamon, buff, or warm edges. In fall and early winter edging wide and bold, breast and back appear largely rusty. Buff supercilium and malar. Coverts and tertials tipped rusty; rump blackish. As winter progresses edging wears, revealing black plumage. SUMMER FEMALE: Blackish gray with darker wings, tail, and lateral throat stripes. Bill black, legs black, and eyes yellow. WINTER FEMALE: Widely edged rusty and buff. Similar to winter male, but paler and even more rusty, and rump grayish.
Geographic Variation Two subspecies; *nigrans,* which breeds in the Maritimes and Newfoundland, is not field identifiable.
Similar Species The Brewer's Blackbird is similar, but it has a shorter bill and curved culmen. In winter, the wide rusty edging on the Rusty's plumage is distinctive, although immature male Brewer's can show some dull buff on breast and upperparts. Brewer's never show rusty edges to tertials. Male Rusty in summer blackish, lacking strong gloss

of Brewer's; its iridescence is dull green and even throughout body. Summer female Rusty more grayish than Brewer's, and shows yellow eye. A small percentage of Brewer's females also show yellow eyes, but female Brewer's more brownish. Common Grackle has a long, graduated tail often held in a deeply keeled shape. Common Grackles show more complex and brighter iridescence patterns than the Rusty Blackbird.
Voice CALL: A *chuck,* not as deep as that of a grackle. SONG: A squeaky, sweet, rising *kush-a-lee* or *chuck-la-weeeee.* A secondary song begins with 2 or 3 musical notes followed by a harsher long note. Females sing a weaker version.
Status & Distribution Fairly Common. BREEDING: Bogs in boreal forest. MIGRATION: Diurnal migrant; arrives

southern Canada by late Mar., southbound late Sept.–Nov. WINTER: Wet open woodlands, or fields near wetlands. VAGRANT: Casual on Pacific from BC to CA, casual on Pribilofs Is.
Population Numbers have declined precipitously since 1960, with some sources estimating a 90 percent drop between the 1960s and 1990s.

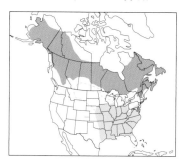

BREWER'S BLACKBIRD *Euphagus cyanocephalus*

A common and widespread ground-dwelling icterid of the West, the Brewer's in some ways replaces the Common Grackle ecologically. Monotypic. L 9" (23 cm)

Identification A slim blackbird lacking striking structural features. MALE: Basically black with bright yellow eyes. Strongly iridescent, with a bright blue or purplish blue sheen on the head, while the body is greenish. Bill and legs black. FEMALE: Dull brownish gray and unstreaked, with darker wings and tail. Slightly paler supercilium; dark eyes. IMMATURE MALE: Some young males exactly as adults, others show some buffy feather tips on breast and warmer buff tipping on back.
Similar Species A summer Rusty Blackbird is similar, but it has a more slender pointed bill. The male Brewer's is more strongly glossy, showing blue on head and green on body. In winter some young male Brewer's' show buff tipping on breast, head, and upperparts, but tertials are always entirely black. The female Brewer's is

immature ♂

darker and browner, with dull green gloss on the wings, than the female Rusty, which has grayish color, particularly the rump. Female Brewer's typically show a dark eye, although a few show yellowish eyes. Common Grackle has a long, graduated tail often held in a deeply keeled shape. Common Grackles show more complex and brighter iridescence patterns than the Brewer's, with a characteristic abrupt break in color from the head iridescence to that of the body.

Voice CALL: A *chak*, or *chuk* similar to that of a Rusty or Red-winged Blackbird. When alarmed, it gives a whistled *teeeuuuu* or *sweeee*. SONG: Often

gives a faint and unappealing raspy *schlee* or *schrrup* during the ruff-out display; both sexes sing and display.

Status & Distribution Common. YEAR-ROUND: Varied habitats, inc. urban areas, golf courses, agricultural lands, open shrubby areas, forest clear-cuts, and riparian forest edges. Requires open ground for foraging and some dense vegetation or edge for nesting. Farther east, where sympatric with the Common Grackle, it takes more open sites than the grackle. MIGRATION: Poorly understood, easternmost populations more migratory. Extent of movements correlated with snowcover. Wintering groups somewhat nomadic. VAGRANT:

Casual to central and northern AK, NT, and northeastern VA.

Population Breeding Bird Survey has detected a general decline in this species, at a rate of 2.1 percent per year.

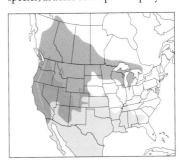

GRACKLES Genus *Quiscalus*

There are 7 grackle species worldwide, 1 of which is now extinct. The males have a glossy black plumage and often have yellowish eyes. During breeding displays, the strongly graduated tail is held deeply keeled, giving a V-shaped cross section. The larger species show a great size difference between males and females.

COMMON GRACKLE *Quiscalus quiscula*

The Common Grackle is a common and often urban blackbird of eastern North America. Polytypic. L 12.6" (32 cm)

Identification A large blackbird with strong legs and a long, graduated tail that is held in a deep keeled shape during the breeding season. ADULT MALE: Entirely black with noticeable iridescence in good light. Widespread form (see Geographic Variation) shows bronze gloss to body, blue head, and purple or blue iridescence on wings and tail. The iridescence of the head is different from that of the body, and changes abruptly; this applies to all forms of Common Grackle. Eyes are bright yellow, while legs and bill are black. ADULT FEMALE: Smaller and duller than male and does not hold tail in deep keel shape. JUVENILE: Brown, with dark eyes and faintly streaked on breast.

Geographic Variation Three subspecies. The Bronzed Grackle *(versicolor)*, found northwest of the Appalachians, has bronze iridescence on body, a blue head, and pur-

plish tail and wings. The Purple Grackle *(stonei)*, found southeast of the Appalachians, has a purplish body and head, with a blue or greenish glossed tail. The Florida Grackle *(quiscula)*, ranging from Florida to southern Louisiana and South Carolina, has a greenish iridescence on its back.

Similar Species Brewer's and Rusty Blackbirds lack the long, graduated tail of Common Grackle, and they never hold it in a keeled shape. Boat-tailed and Great-tailed Grackles are much larger, with even more striking tails. Common Grackles show a clear, abrupt division between the gloss color of the head and body.

Voice CALL: A loud and deep *chuck*. SONG: A mechanical, squeaky *readle-eak*. Both sexes sing.

Status & Distribution Abundant. YEAR-ROUND: Open and edge habitats, urban areas, agricultural lands, golf courses, swamps, and marshes. MIGRATION: Diurnal migrant; southern popu-

lations resident. Arrive at breeding areas mid-Feb.–mid-Mar. and early Apr. in northernmost sites. Begins southward movements as early as late Aug., peaking Oct.–early Nov. VAGRANT: Casual to far north, AK, YK, NT, and Churchill, MB. Also casual in Pacific states and BC.

Population Populations have boomed due to human alteration of habitat and spilled grain, but in the last 30 years the numbers have decreased significantly in the East. In the Northwest, populations and range are increasing.

juvenile

bronze ♂
versicolor

purple ♂
quiscula

BOAT-TAILED GRACKLE *Quiscalus major*

The Boat-tailed Grackle inhabits coastal marshes of the Atlantic and Gulf Coasts. Polytypic. L 15–16.5" (38–42 cm)

Identification A large grackle with a moderate-size bill, a rounded crown, and a steep forehead. ADULT MALE: Entirely black with obvious blue iridescence, becoming violet on head. Eyes yellow to dull yellowish or even honey brown; bill and legs black. Long, deeply keeled tail. ADULT FEMALE: Smaller than male. Brown above; warm tawny on head and below, becoming darker brown on belly and vent. Eyes usually dark. Does not hold tail in deep keel. IMMATURE

MALE: Like adult male, but smaller with shorter tail, dull iridescence, and browner wings. JUVENILE: Like female, but paler and duller below.

Geographic Variation The 4 subspecies vary primarily in eye color, some having yellow eyes, others brown. They are not field identifiable other than by breeding range.

Similar Species The very similar Great-tailed Grackle was once conspecific. The Boat-tailed shows a steeper forehead, rounder crown, and smaller bill; this is more obvious on males than on females. A male Boat-tailed often shows dark eyes, violet gloss on head,

and blue-green lower back, abdomen, and flanks. The song differs between the species; the display where the wings are flipped high over the back is characteristic of a Boat-tailed. The *kle-teet* call of a female Boat-tailed is diagnostic. A female Boat-tailed is warmer colored than a Great-tailed and usually has dark eyes; its dark lateral throat stripes are absent or indistinct.

Voice CALL: A low *clak* or a *kle-teet*. SONG: A continuous, long, harsh trilling song interspersed with other notes, *jeeb-jeeb-jeeb tireeet chrr chrr chrr chrr tireet tireet tireet tireet*. Wing-flipping display accompanies lower *chrr* notes.

Status & Distribution Common. YEAR-ROUND: Coastal marshes, but various open habitats in FL, incl. agricultural and urban. MIGRATION: Resident, but some birds wander south in winter. VAGRANT: Casual in New England.

Population Stable, but the species has been expanding its range since the 1890s.

juvenile ♀

immature ♂

adult ♂

western Gulf coast

♀

Subspecies of Great-tailed Grackle

Eight Great-tailed Grackle subspecies are recognized, but only 3 are found in North America. These northern subspecies are *prosopidicola*, found in the east of the Great-tailed's range west to central Texas; *monsoni*, found from central Arizona east to western Texas; and *nelsoni*, found in California and western Arizona. All 3 subspecies of the Great-tailed are spreading northward in the United States. For the most part, there is little information regarding which subspecies have spread to which areas, therefore the range descrip-

Great-tailed Grackle, female (AZ, Feb.)

tions given above are tentative. And some intergradation may be occurring now that these subspecies are coming widely into contact.

The males of these subspecies are similar, differing mainly in size, with *prosopidicola* and *monsoni* being large subspecies while *nelsoni* is noticeably smaller. With regards to plumage, a male *monsoni* shows on average more of a purplish gloss, but this is variable. Differences in plumage are much more marked in females. In general, *monsoni* females are darkest below, *nelsoni* palest, and *prosopidicola* intermediate, although

GREAT-TAILED GRACKLE *Quiscalus mexicanus*

This huge blackbird is hard to ignore due to its boisterous nature. Polytypic. L 15–18" (38–46 cm)

Identification Long, deeply keeled tail. Large, thick bill, with nearly straight culmen. Flat crown; shallow forehead. ADULT MALE: Entirely black with obvious violet-blue iridescence. Eyes yellow; bill and legs black. ADULT FEMALE: Smaller than male. No keeled tail. Brown above with dull iridescence on wings and tail; buffy on head and below, becoming darker brown on belly and vent. Dark lateral throat stripes usually obvious. Eyes yellow. IMMATURE MALE: Smaller than the adult male, with shorter tail, dull iridescence, browner wings, and frequently dark eyes. JUVENILE: Like female, but paler and shows diffuse streaking below.

Geographic Variation See sidebar p. 616.

Similar Species The very similar Boat-tailed Grackle overlaps with the Great-tailed Grackle in southwestern coastal Louisiana and eastern Texas. See the Boat-tailed Grackle.

Voice CALL: A low *chut;* males may give a louder clack. Eastern males give a striking ascending whistle *twoooeeeeeeee!* SONG: The eastern bird sings a 4-part song beginning with harsh notes similar to the breaking of twigs, then an soft undulating *chewechewe,* and then twig-breaking notes and finally several loud 2-syllable *cha-wee* calls, *crrrk crrrk chewechewe crrk cha-wee cha-weewlii.* Subspecies *nelsoni* sings a repeated series of notes, ending in a more accented

note *chk-chk-chk-chap-chap-chap-chap-CHWEEE,* often interspersed with various other repeated notes.

Status & Distribution Abundant. YEAR-ROUND: Open habitats with dispersed trees, from agricultural to urban. MIGRATION: Not well understood; more are wintering farther north now. VAGRANT: Casual to the north of its range, from BC east to NS.

Population The species has experienced a great range and population increase in the United States, showing a 3.7 percent annual increase from 1966 to 1998.

---

closer to *monsoni.* In fact, *nelsoni* females may be pale grayish below with a nearly white throat; this coloration is strikingly different from the buff to warm brown underparts of *prosopidicola* and *monsoni.* The pale plumage combined with the small size sets *nelsoni* well apart from *prosopidicola* and *monsoni.*

Historically, the mountains of central Mexico divided the general population of Great-tailed Grackles into an eastern and central group and a western group. The "Western" Great-tailed Grackles—from *nelsoni* in the north, to coastal forms

Great-tailed Grackle, female (TX, Nov.)

in west Mexico south to Guerrero—are small, they have a noticeably different song than the more eastern populations, and there are genetic differences. However, with the opening of more grackle-friendly habitats throughout the area due to agricultural and urban development, this previously isolated population has come into contact with eastern Great-tailed Grackles. In Arizona intergradation between *nelsoni* and *monsoni* appears to be common, and birds that have *monsoni* mitochondrial DNA are by measurements small and like *nelsoni.* ∎

COWBIRDS Genus Molothrus

The true cowbirds, of which there are 5 species, are all obligate brood parasites, laying their eggs in the nests of other species. Parental care is performed entirely by the hosts. Unlike many cuckoos, cowbirds are generalists, using various host species. They have stocky bodies and short tails. Male plumage shows glossy black; females are duller.

SHINY COWBIRD Molothrus bonariensis

The Shiny Cowbird is a recent invader to the Southeast, from South America via the Caribbean. It is one of the few brood parasites in North America. Polytypic. L 7.5" (19 cm)

Identification A smallish, stocky blackbird very similar in shape to the Brown-headed Cowbird, but longer billed and perhaps with a longer tail and slimmer body. ADULT MALE: Entirely black with violet-blue iridescence on head and anterior part of body, becoming less violet and more pure blue toward posterior parts of body. Eyes dark; legs and bill black. ADULT FEMALE: Dull brownish throughout, with paler supercilium and darker wings and tail. Legs and bill black. JUVENILE: Similar to female, but obscurely streaked below.

Geographic Variation Of the 7 subspecies recognized, only the northern South American and Caribbean *minimus* is known from North America.

Similar Species The male Shiny's strong gloss and violet head separate it from the Brown-headed Cowbird. Male is similar in color to a Brewer's Blackbird, but the Shiny is smaller and stockier, and has a dark eye and thicker bill. A female Shiny is extremely similar to a Brown-headed. The Shiny is generally darker, lacking white throat, but with a stronger face pattern with a noticeably paler supercilium, a longer and slimmer body, and a longer, shiny black bill. A female Brown-headed shows a paler bill with a horn or yellowish base to lower mandible. On the closed wings, the secondaries do not show obvious pale fringes on the Shiny. Finally, the Shiny has shorter, more rounded wings; the outermost primary (P9) is equal in length to P7 or P6 but noticeably shorter than P8, the second outermost primary.

Voice CALL: A soft *chup;* females give a chatter. SONG: Primary song strange sounding, liquid and bubbling, lasting 2–3 seconds. It begins with several purring bubbly notes and then a screechy series of high-pitched notes, *blurr-glurr-glurr-pt-tcheeeEEE.* Males also give a flight whistle, which may be considered a secondary song rather

than a call. It is a more complicated and long series of short whistles, and it shows a great deal of geographic variation. The whistle is given both in flight and while perched.

Status & Distribution Rare in FL. BREEDING: Open and edge habitats; agricultural areas for foraging and forest edge habitats for finding host species. MIGRATION: Not studied, but new arrivals from farther south appear Mar.–Apr. WINTER: Open sites, agricultural areas, feeders. VAGRANT: Casual north of FL, records from NB, ME, OK, TX (2 recs.), LA (several), AL (many), MS (several), TN (1 rec.), VA (1 rec.), NC (several), SC (several), GA (several). Most records away from FL have occurred in the spring.

Population A recent arrival to North America, the species was first detected in Florida in 1985. After a flurry of observations in the late 1980s and early 1990s, sightings have decreased.

BRONZED COWBIRD Molothrus aeneus

The largest of our cowbirds, the Bronzed has a rather sinister appearance thanks to the male's typically hunchbacked look and bloodred eye. It gives an odd hovering display that is unique. Polytypic. L 8.7" (22 cm)

Identification A thick-set cowbird with a large and deep black bill. Males in particular may look proportionately small headed, especially when ruffling the nape feathers in display. Legs black. ADULT MALE: Entirely black with bronzed body iridescence, becoming blue-green on wings and tail. Eyes bright red. ADULT FEMALE: Varies geographically, see below. More widespread east-

ern subspecies has a black female plumage, lacking strong gloss, with browner wings and tail. Eyes red. JUVENILE: Similar to female but dark brown.

Geographic Variation Four subspecies recognized, 2 in North America: the more widespread *aeneus,* found from south-central Texas eastward, and *loyei* from New Mexico to California. Males are similar, but females black in *aeneus* and grayish brown in *loyei.*

Similar Species The Bronzed is larger than other cowbirds, and adults show bright red eyes and thick bills. Juveniles could be mistaken for female Brown-headed Cowbirds, but note

their larger size, larger bulk, and thick bill. There is no black bird with red eyes on the continent other than the very different Phainopepla, which is slim

southwestern
♀ *loyei*

aeneus

juvenile

♀

♂

and crested, with white wing patches.
Voice CALL: A rasping *chuck*. Females
give a rattle. SONG: A series of odd
squeaky gurgles, *gluup-gleeeep-
gluup-bloooop*. Flight whistle highly geographically variable, given in
flight and while perched. About 4 seconds long, it is a series of long sliding
or vibrating whistles. Three general
dialects in North America: "Arizona"
(CA to westernmost TX), "Big Bend"
(Big Bend, TX), and "South Texas"
(east of Big Bend).
Status & Distribution Uncommon to fairly common. YEAR-ROUND: Open shrub-
land, forest edge, and agricultural areas
(esp. those associated with livestock).
BREEDING: Brood parasite, specializes

on sparrows and orioles.
MIGRATION: Not well known.
Spring movements in TX in Mar.,
southbound movements in Sept. Small
but increasing numbers winter in FL.
WINTER: In flocks, particularly in agricultural areas. VAGRANT: Accidental in

NS, MO, and MD.
Population The range and
population of this species
began a marked expansion in the
1950s, but presently the population
appears stable. It has recently spread
to Florida and the Gulf states.

BROWN-HEADED COWBIRD *Molothrus ater*

juvenile

♀

♂

The common Brown-headed Cowbird is the most widespread brood
parasite in North America. Polytypic.
L 7.5" (19 cm)
Identification A smallish, compact and
stocky blackbird with a short and
thick-based bill, almost finchlike. Foraging birds are commonly seen on the
ground with the tail cocked. ADULT
MALE: The glossy black body, with a
greenish iridescence, contrasts with a
brown head. The eyes are dark; the bill
and legs are black. ADULT FEMALE: Dull
brownish throughout, with darker
wings and tail. The secondaries show
crisp pale fringes. The face has a beady-
eyed look due to dark eyes; the lores
are pale, as is the area below the eyes.
The whitish throat contrasts with the
darker face; the underparts are obscurely streaked. The bill is dark, but shows
a pale or horn-colored base to the
lower mandible; the legs are black.
JUVENILE: It resembles the female, but
is more strongly streaked below, and
upperparts are often scaly-looking due

to pale feather fringes.
Geographic Variation The 3 subspecies, differing mainly in size
and darkness of females, are not
field identifiable.
Similar Species The male's combination of glossy black body
and brown head is diagnostic.
The female is extremely similar to
the vagrant Shiny Cowbird female.
However, the Brown-headed is paler
overall, showing a whitish throat and
a pale face with a beady-eyed look.
The Shiny has a more marked dark
eye line and paler supercilium, giving it a more striking face pattern.
Compared to a Shiny, the Brown-
headed is more compact, with a shorter tail and bill. The Brown-headed's
dark bill shows a pale or horn base to
the lower mandible; on the Shiny,
the bill is shiny black. On the closed
wings the secondaries show obvious
pale fringes on the Brown-headed.
Finally, the Brown-headed has a
longer and more pointed wing, and
the outermost primary (P9) is equal
in length or longer than the second
outermost primary (P8).
Voice CALL: A soft *kek*. Females give a
distinctive dry chatter, while males
may give a single modulated whistle,
particularly just after taking off. SONG:
Primary song is a series of liquid,
purring, gurgles followed by a high
whistle, *bub ko lum tseeee or glug glug
glee*. The song of the Brown-headed
has the highest frequency range of any
species in North America. Males also
give a flight whistle, which may be
considered a secondary song rather
than a call. It is a geographically vari-

able series of 2 to 5 whistles, often frequency modulated. The flight whistle
is given both in flight and while
perched. Note that primary songs
appear to be hardwired, while flight
whistles are learned; this accounts for
why "dialects" are found in the latter
but not in the former.
Status & Distribution Common. BREED-
ING: Open and edge habitats. MIGRA-
TION: A short-distance diurnal
migrant; northbound mostly mid-
Mar.–mid-Apr., southbound late
July–Oct. WINTER: Open sites, agricultural areas, feeders.
Population The Brown-headed Cowbird increased its range and population greatly during the early 1800s,
when the eastern forests were cleared.
Commonly it is said that the Brown-
headed was restricted to the Great
Plains, where the buffalo herds were,
and they spread east and west from
there. However, there are multiple subspecies, suggesting the range of the
species was more widespread and primarily that an expansion in abundance
occurred. More recently, Brown-
headed Cowbird numbers have been
on a decline.

ORIOLES Genus *Icterus*

The most colorful icterids, largely orange, yellow, or chestnut, orioles are generally slim and long tailed with sharply pointed bills. They weave a characteristic nest that looks like a hanging basket. Plumage patterns are plastic, and species with very similar patterns (e.g., Hooded and Altamira, Baltimore and Orchard) are quite distantly related. In addition, sexual dichromatism is heavily influenced by the role females have in territorial defense and migratory tendency. More migratory orioles show a greater degree of difference in plumage, while in tropical, resident species the female may be as brightly plumaged as the male. Immature male plumage is retained for at least a year.

BLACK-VENTED ORIOLE *Icterus wagleri*

The striking Black-vented Oriole is a vagrant from Mexico. Polytypic L 8.7" (22 cm)
Identification Slim and long-tailed; blue-gray legs; thin, downcurved bill with basal third of lower mandible blue-gray. ADULT: Entirely black above, including the hood down to the mid-breast. Below bright orange-yellow with black crissum. Black breast separated from the yellow underparts by a narrow chestnut area. Black wings with bright yellow shoulders; tail entirely black. IMMATURE: Variable. Olive above, obscurely streaked on back, and yellow-orange below; wings gray-brown with greenish shoulder patch. Black on the face and breast varies from black lores and chin with scatted black feath-

ers on throat to black face and extensive black bib with irregular border and scattered black feathers on the head.
Geographic Variation Two subspecies. Presumably *castaneopectus* is the vagrant to the U.S.
Similar Species The wings of the Black-vented Oriole show no wing bars, or white fringes on the flight feathers; this separates it from all adult North American orioles. Black vent is diagnostic. In addition the peachy-yellow underparts are not matched by any of the similarly patterned orioles. Immatures may be confused with Hooded Oriole; however,

1st spring

adult

Black-vented lack wing bars, have a messy black bib (when present), and are streaked on the back.
Voice CALL: A nasal *nyeh;* also a mechanical chatter. SONG: A series of nasal notes and squeaky whistles.
Status & Distribution Accidental vagrant. YEAR-ROUND: Open forest and edge from northern Mexico to Nicaragua. VAGRANT: Accidental to western and southern TX (2 recs.) and southeastern AZ (1 rec.).

ORCHARD ORIOLE *Icterus spurius*

1st spring ♂

♀

breeding adult ♂

This smallest oriole is common in the East and Midwest. Polytypic (3 ssp.; *spurius* in N.A.). L 7" (18 cm)
Identification A small oriole, may recall a warbler due to small size. Bill slightly downcurved, thicker at base with basal third of lower mandible blue-gray. ADULT MALE: Black hood and back; chestnut below and on rump. Wings black with chestnut shoulder, white lower wing bar, and white edging to flight feathers. Tail entirely black. ADULT FEMALE: Olive above; bright yellow below. Two crisp white wing bars and white edging to flight feathers. IMMATURE MALE: Similar to female, but by first spring shows a neat black

bib and lores, often some chestnut spotting on face or especially on breast.
Similar Species Widely sympatric with the Baltimore Oriole; however, the male Orchard is chestnut below, and immatures and females are bright yellow below, not orange or orange-yellow as in the Baltimore. Female and immature Hooded Orioles are similar to an Orchard, although a Hooded is slimmer and longer tailed, shows more tail graduation, and has a longer, more downcurved bill (but caution is needed with a short-billed juvenile Hooded). An Eastern Hooded is more orange than an Orchard; the similar Western Hooded is not as bright yellow below and has less well defined wing bars. An immature male Orchard has a more restricted black bib than corresponding Hooded plumage. The *chuck* call of an Orchard is deeper and huskier than a similar call rarely given by young Hoodeds; the *wheet* call of the Hooded is not given by the Orchard.

Voice CALL: A sharp *chuck,* often in a series. SONG: A musical, springy, and rapid warbled song interspersed with raspy notes.
Status & Distribution Fairly common to common. BREEDING: Open woodlands, urban parks, and riparian woodlands particularly in the west of range. MIGRATION: Trans-Gulf migrant in spring with arrival in north late Apr.–early May, moves south as early as mid-July, but most head south in Aug. WINTER: From Mexico to northern S.A., in open forests and edge where flowering trees are found. VAGRANT: Rare west to CA, AZ, and Maritimes. Casual to OR, accidental to southeastern AK.

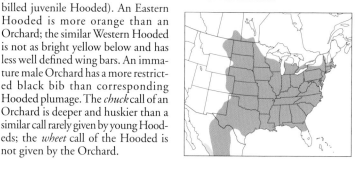

HOODED ORIOLE *Icterus cucullatus*

This slim oriole has a fondness for palms. Polytypic. L 8" (20 cm) **Identification** Long, strongly graduated tail. Thin, noticeably downcurved bill, blue-gray on the basal half lower mandible. ADULT MALE: A crisp black bib, face, and back contrasting with the orange or yellow-orange lower back and rump. Black wings, with black shoulders, 2 white wing bars, crisp white fringes on flight feathers. Tail black. ADULT FEMALE: Olive above; yellowish or dull orange below, with dusky wash on flanks and belly. Two dull wing bars per wing, white fringes on flight feathers. IMMATURE MALE: Like female, but by spring shows a neat black bib and lores. **Geographic Variation** Five subspecies in 2 groups: the *cucullatus* group, including *sennetti,* from Big Bend east, is more orange, with a shorter bill and more

black on forehead; the *nelsoni* group, found in New Mexico and west, shows yellow-orange, with a longer, more downcurved bill.
Similar Species The male is

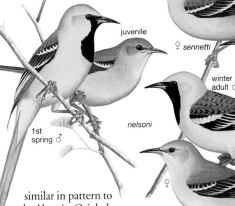

breeding adult ♂ *sennetti*

juvenile

♀ *sennetti*

winter adult ♂

nelsoni

1st spring ♂

breeding adult ♂

♀

similar in pattern to the Altamira Oriole, but slimmer, with a slenderer bill, and a black shoulder and white upper wing bar. Also see the Orchard Oriole.
Voice CALL: A whistled *wheet* and a short chatter. Also a *chut,* usually by juveniles, similar to call of the Orchard Oriole. SONG: A quick and abrupt series of springy, nasal, or whiny notes, lacking the sweet whistled sounds of other orioles.
Status & Distribution BREEDING: Open areas with scattered trees, riparian areas,

and suburban and park settings. MIGRATION: Arrives during Mar., departs in Aug. WINTER: Mainly in Mexico. VAGRANT: Casual to BC and WA, annual in OR; accidental in ON and southern YK.
Population The species is expanding north in California, but populations have decreased in southern Texas.

STREAK-BACKED ORIOLE *Icterus pustulatus*

This Mexican oriole has the characteristic streaked back of orioles. Polytypic. L 8.3" (21 cm) **Identification** This mid-size oriole has a thick-based, straight, pointed bill. ADULT MALE: The body is bright orange; the head is reddish orange. Restricted black is found on the lores and narrow bib; entirely black tail. The back is streaked black, and the black wings are densely edged with white, forming a nearly solid white panel on the closed secondaries and primaries. There are bold white wing bars. FEMALE AND IMMATURE: They resemble the adult male; however, the body plumage is dull yellowish, becoming more orange around face; the back and tail are greenish. The wings have less extensive white edging than on male.
Geographic Variation Six subspecies in 3 groups. Only *microstictus,* known as

microstictus

1st fall ♀

1st fall ♀

♂

the "Scarlet-headed" Oriole, occurs in our area.
Similar Species The male's streaked back, extensive white on wings, and reddish orange head together are diagnostic. The female Streak-

backed is similar to an immature male Bullock's Oriole, but her streaked back and white on wings also identify the Streak-backed. The Bullock's also shows a largely blue-gray bill with black culmen, while the entire upper mandible of the Streak-backed is black.
Voice CALL: A low *wrank,* also a sweet *chuwit* like a House Finch, a dry chatter. SONG: Melodious whistled song similar to that of a Bullock's Oriole, but with a stop and start pattern.
Status & Distribution Vagrant, has bred in southeastern AZ. Found from northern Mexico to Costa Rica, on Pacific slope. YEAR-ROUND: Open woodlands, forest edge. VAGRANT: Casual mainly in fall to CA and AZ; accidental to OR, NM, eastern TX, and WI.

SPOT-BREASTED ORIOLE *Icterus pectoralis*

The Central American Spot-breasted was introduced to the Miami, Florida, area. Polytypic (4 ssp.; nominate in N.A.). L 9.5" (24 cm)

Identification A large oriole with a sturdy bill that shows a slight curve to the culmen. ADULT: Bright orange body with a black back. A small face mask and narrow bib are black; the rows of black spots immediately below the bib are distinctive. Black wings show an orange shoulder, a white spot at the base of the folded primaries, and a white wedge on the folded tertials. The tail is entirely black. IMMATURE: Less intensely orange than adult, with olive green back and tail, as well as duller pattern on wings. JUVENILE: Duller than immature and lacking black lores and bib; bill may show pinkish base to lower mandible.

Similar Species The spotted breast is diagnostic; no other oriole with a large white wedge on folded tertials is found in North America. In Florida, an immature Orchard Oriole shows a similar black face and bib but is yellowish, not orange. Also, an immature Spot-breasted already shows the diagnostic white wedge on the tertials and is much larger than an Orchard.

Voice CALL: A nasal *nyeh,* also a sharp *whip* and a short chatter. SONG: A lengthy, repetitive yet pleasing set of warbled whistles, some of which are delivered slowly and clearly. One song style more repetitive, another more variable; often songs start with a note repeated twice. Female's song less complex than that of the male.

Status & Distribution Uncommon in south FL; native to C.A. YEAR-ROUND: Parks and urban habitats in FL; open shrubby woodlands in native range.

Population The Spot-breasted was first found nesting in Florida in 1949. The population has oscillated since the introduction but is now on a decline. Its range in the U.S. has correspondingly grown and shrunk.

ALTAMIRA ORIOLE *Icterus gularis*

A Lower Rio Grande specialty bird, this oriole makes an absurdly long hanging nest. Polytypic. L 10" (25 cm)

Identification The Altamira is the largest and stockiest oriole in North America; in addition, the bill is very thick at the base. The bill is black, with only the extreme base of the lower mandible grayish. The legs are blue-gray. ADULT: Bright orange body, with deeper orange face and bold black mask and narrow bib. Back black, contrasting with orange lower back, rump, and uppertail coverts. Wing black, with an orange shoulder, a well-marked white lower wing bar, and white fringes on tertials and secondaries. (On primaries, most of white restricted to a bold white patch at their base.) Tail entirely black on male; often a variable amount of olive on female tail. IMMATURE: Similar to adult, but duller orange and back and tail olive. Wings blackish, lacking orange shoulder and white edging greatly restricted. JUVENILE: Duller still, with buffy wing bars and no black on lores or bib.

Geographic Variation Six subspecies recognized. They vary in minor ways in size and saturation of color. Only *tamaulipensis* is found in Texas.

Similar Species The Hooded Oriole is similar to an adult Altamira in pattern, but the Altamira is much bigger and thicker billed. In addition, the Altamira shows an orange shoulder patch. Immatures are also separable by size and bill, but note the thinner bib on the Altamira.

Voice CALL: Contact call is a nasal *ike,* or *yehnk,* often repeated. SONG: A series of loud musical whistles, often interspersed with harsher notes. Songs are repeated several times before switching to a different song type. The song is easily imitated by a human whistler.

Status & Distribution Uncommon nonmigratory resident. YEAR-ROUND: Open woodlands, particularly mesquite and riparian willows. Often places nest in a mimosa, and close to an aggressive species such as the Great Kiskadee or the Couch's Kingbird.

Population The Altamira is threatened in Texas, but the population appears reasonably stable.

AUDUBON'S ORIOLE *Icterus graduacauda*

The secretive Audubon's Oriole stays low in the understory. Polytypic (4 ssp.; *audubonii* in TX). L 9.5" (24 cm)
Identification This bird is a thick-set, large oriole with a moderately thick, straight bill. The basal half of the lower mandible is blue-gray; the legs are also blue-gray. ADULT: The black hood contrasts with greenish yellow back and lemon yellow underparts. The black wings have a yellow shoulder, a white lower wing bar, and white fringes on

tertials and on secondaries, but fringes do not reach to base of secondaries, creating a dark bar there. The tail is black. Female shows a duller, more greenish back. JUVENILE: Lacks the black hood of the adult and is greener above; wings dull blackish, and tail greenish.
Similar Species This oriole is the only one with an isolated black hood. All our other hooded orioles have black backs. A juvenile may be confused with a juvenile Altamira Oriole, but the Audubon's is yellowish, not orange, and shows a duller, grayish head color. A juvenile Hooded Oriole is also similar, but smaller, much slimmer, and slimmer billed, with clear buffy white to white wing bars.
Voice CALL: A nasal *nyyyee;* and a high-frequency buzz. SONG: A long song of melancholy, tentative, and slow whis-

tles. The whistles sound flat and in the same pitch. Both sexes sing.
Status & Distribution Uncommon; a nonmigratory resident. YEAR-ROUND: A variety of wooded habitats, but they all share dense low and mid-stories. Found in mesquite thickets to riparian thickets. DISPERSAL: May wander north of regular breeding range in winter.
Population Appears to be stable, but neither the range or population in Texas is extensive or large.

SCOTT'S ORIOLE *Icterus parisorum*

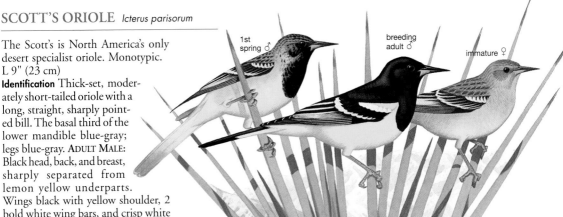

The Scott's is North America's only desert specialist oriole. Monotypic. L 9" (23 cm)
Identification Thick-set, moderately short-tailed oriole with a long, straight, sharply pointed bill. The basal third of the lower mandible blue-gray; legs blue-gray. ADULT MALE: Black head, back, and breast, sharply separated from lemon yellow underparts. Wings black with yellow shoulder, 2 bold white wing bars, and crisp white fringes on all flight feathers. Tail black with yellow bases to outer rectrices. ADULT FEMALE: Olive above, with obscure streaking on back and finer streaking on crown and nape; few with black on throat. Below olive-yellow, with gray wash on throat and upper breast, face also grayish. Wings blackish with white wing bars and white

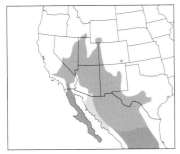

fringes on flight feathers. Tail olive-yellow. IMMATURE MALE: Similar to female, and some not separable, but back more densely marked and underparts brighter yellow. Typically black bib and face, and variable black spotting on crown and sides of head.
Similar Species The Audubon's and Scott's Orioles are the only yellow orioles in N.A. A black back, 2 white wing bars, and yellow on tail identify the Scott's. A Scott's female is much more olive and generally muddier colored than other orioles; its obscurely streaked back may suggest a female Streak-backed Oriole, but the Scott's lacks the orange on face and the black mask and bib, and has a thinner-based bill.

Voice CALL: A harsh *chuck* or *shack* and a scolding *cheh-cheh*. SONG: A fluty warbled set of whistles; the low pitch and richness of the notes resemble the song of a Western Meadowlark at times. Songs usually last under 2 seconds. Females sing a softer and weaker song than the males.
Status & Distribution Common. BREEDING: Desert, particularly at interface of low desert to higher elevation. Often in yucca or agave as well as juniper. MIGRATION: In spring arrive late Mar.–early Apr., leave in fall late July–mid-Sept. WINTER: Retreats mainly to Mexico. VAGRANT: Casual north of range in Great Basin, MN, and to LA. Accidental to WI and ON.

BULLOCK'S ORIOLE *Icterus bullockii*

breeding adult ♂

♀

1st spring ♂

immature ♀

The Bullock's Oriole is the widespread and common oriole of the West. Polytypic. L 8.7" (22 cm)

Identification Long wings; relatively short tail; straight, sharply pointed largely blue-gray bill with a blackish culmen; blue-gray legs. ADULT MALE: Black eye line, crown, nape, and back. Bright orange supercilium. Bright orange on underparts and rump. Very narrow black bib. Wings black with very extensive white wing patch on coverts; flight feathers also widely fringed white. Black tail with an orange base to outer rectrices. FEMALE: Orange to orange-yellow on head and breast, showing a ghost pattern of male face pattern, with darker eye line and brighter yellowish supercilium. Back gray, below pale whitish gray with darker flanks, white or sometimes yellowish vent. Blackish wings with 2 bold white wing bars, crisp white fringes to flight feathers. Tail grayish yellow. First-fall females slightly duller, more yellowish on breast. IMMATURE MALE: Like female, but by spring shows black lores and bib as well as brighter orange breast. JUVENILE: Much duller than female, bill pink or orange-pink at base. Wings duller, brownish black with buffier and less well-developed wing bars.

Geographic Variation The 2 subspecies are poorly differentiated and thus not field identifiable.

Similar Species The orange supercilium, black eye line, and solid white wing patch are diagnostic for the adult male Bullock's. The female and the immature can be confused with a dull Baltimore Oriole (see sidebar below). Female and immature Hooded Orioles are entirely yellow below, slimmer, and longer tailed and have a thin, down-curved bill. Hybrids with Baltimore Orioles show features intermediate between the species.

Voice CALL: A short rattle, given by both sexes; also a sweet but faint *kleek,* or *pheew.* SONG: A musical, lively series of whistles ending in a sweeter note: *kip, kit-tick, kit-tick, whew, wheet.* In comparison to the Baltimore Oriole's songs, the songs are shorter, not as melodic, and a lot less variable.

Status & Distribution Common. BREEDING: Mainly open woodlands and riparian areas, esp. fond of cottonwoods. MIGRATION: Spring arrival in south Mar.–Apr., crosses into Canada by early to mid-May. Adult males southbound beginning early July, females and immatures Aug.–mid-Sept. WINTER: Most retreat to Mexico, but a few in coastal urban habitats in southernmost CA. VAGRANT: Casual to the East, particularly in fall and winter.

Population Survey data showed a gradual and slow decline between the 1960s and 1980s, particularly in the far west of the range.

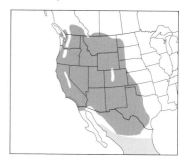

Baltimore Oriole versus Bullock's Oriole in Winter

Two identification issues exist when attempting to separate a Baltimore Oriole from a Bullock's Oriole in winter. First, these species hybridize commonly in a narrow zone in the Great Plains; and second, a dull immature Baltimore is similar in plumage and pattern to a female Bullock's. These issues may be related, as it is impossible to know if some of the Baltimores showing Bullock's-like plumages may in fact be hybrids. Adult male hybrids are easy to identify as they show a mix of features intermediate between the species, but female and immature hybrids may not always be readily identifiable. Fortunately the area where hybridization is common is a narrow zone, and hybrids are a small

Baltimore Oriole, immature (NJ, Aug.)

proportion of the population of these 2 oriole species.

The tricky identification issue lies in separating the duller fall/winter Baltimore Orioles from the Bullock's Orioles. These dull Baltimores are grayish above and yellowish on the throat and breast, with a grayish lower breast and belly as in the Bullock's. However, in comparison to the Bullock's, these dull Baltimores tend to have more extensive yellow on the underparts and often show an orange tone. The yellow of the throat and upper breast blends into the grayer belly, usually on the Bullock's this change is more abrupt.

The Bullock's Oriole tends to have a face pattern that mirrors that of the adult male Baltimore, with

maximum black
spring adult ♀

breeding
adult ♂

1st
spring ♀

fall
immatures

fall immature ♂

BALTIMORE ORIOLE *Icterus galbula*

The Baltimore Oriole is the common oriole throughout much of the East. Monotypic. L 8.7" (22 cm)

Identification Long wings; relatively short tail; straight, sharply pointed largely blue-gray bill with a blackish culmen; blue-gray legs. ADULT MALE: Orange, with black hood and back. Wings black with orange shoulder, white lower wing bar, crisp white fringes to flight feathers. Tail black with black-based orange outer rectrices. FEMALE: Variable. Some like male, but usually lack solid black head and have greenish orange tail. Typical female orange below, with brownish orange face and back, spotted or blotched dark on back and crown. Wings blackish with 2 white wing bars (upper 1 wider), white fringes to flight feathers. IMMATURE MALE: Variable. Like female, but no black on face, more extensively orange below, bill often with pinkish or orange tone. JUVENILE: Duller than immature, olive face lacking streaking, and dull, narrow buffy wing bars. Pink tone to bill obvious.

Similar Species The male Orchard and Scott's Orioles are similar to a male Baltimore; however, they lack orange below and on the distal portion of the outer tail feathers. A female Scott's, yellowish below with a characteristic greenish gray color on face and upper-breast, somewhat resembles typical female and immature Baltimores, which show a darker face contrasting with orange or yellow malar and throat and dusky spotting or blotching on upperparts. A dull Baltimore is very similar to a Bullock's Oriole (see sidebar p. 624). A female Orchard Oriole is yellow below and greenish above, slimmer, and smaller; an immature male has a crisp black bib.

Voice CALL: A whistled *hew-li* and a dry chatter. SONG: A series of musical, sweet whistles; quite variable.

Status & Distribution Common. BREEDING: Deciduous forest, forest-edge parkland, riparian forest. MIGRATION: Northbound along Gulf Coast, but many are trans-Gulf migrants. Arrive Gulf Coast by early Apr., and Canada by early May. Southbound late July–early Aug., peaking late Aug.–early Sept. in north, and mid-Sept.–mid-Oct. on Gulf Coast.

WINTER: From southern Mexico to northern S.A. in moist forest and shade coffee plantations. A small number in the U.S. South and FL, largely in urban settings. VAGRANT: Rare in NF and CA; casual to Pacific Northwest and western Europe.

Population Despite a small decline from the 1980s to the mid-1990s, the species is not of conservation concern.

---

extensive yellow on the auriculars and supercilium that contrasts with a darker eye line. These areas are a darker olive-gray, contrasting with the yellow throat, on the Baltimore Oriole; the separation of a darker face from yellow malar and throat can be quite abrupt. The Bullock's does not show an abrupt change in color here, the yellow of the face being continuous with that of the throat and malar.

On the upperparts, the Baltimore Oriole usually shows darker centers to the mantle feathers; those of the Bullock's Oriole are nearly or entirely unmarked gray. As well, the rump of the Baltimore Oriole has a yellowish wash, while the Bullock's Oriole shows a grayish rump. The undertail coverts of

Bullock's Oriole, immature (CA, Sept.)

a dull Baltimore is usually (possibly always) yellow, whereas they are often gray, sometimes yellow, on a Bullock's. Gray undertail coverts and rump are good identifying features for a Bullock's, as opposed to a dull Baltimore.

The wing bars on the Baltimore Oriole are separate, while they are often connected by pale greater covert edges in the Bullock's Oriole. Additionally, the Bullock's tends to show an upper wing bar with intruding dark "teeth" on each white median covert, although this feature is variable and can be matched by some Baltimores. The calls of these species are very similar, but the Baltimore has a drier, more stuttering rattle. ■

FRINGILLINE AND CARDUELINE FINCHES Family Fringillidae

Pine Siskin (CA, Oct.)

Fringillid songbirds range in size from 4 to 8 inches and have characteristic conical-shaped bills used for feeding on seeds. Some are dainty with tiny bills, while others are chunky with large bills, but nearly all have short, notched tails. Most species have undulating flights with distinctive flight call notes. Several species occur in boreal or montane habitats and are widespread, while others stay in very restricted ranges, mainly in western North America. Some fringillids are arboreal and prefer coniferous forests, while others are terrestrial and live in tundra habitats or above tree line. Many are attracted to seed feeders in the winter.

Structure All species share the conical or finchlike bill, although its size varies considerably—from tiny in the Hoary Redpoll to massive in the Hawfinch. The size and shape of the bill greatly aids birders in separating closely related species, as with redpolls and *Carpodacus* finches. In addition, the crossbills have uniquely shaped bills with crossed tips, specialized for extracting seeds from pinecones. Fringillids usually have deeply notched tails that are typically short for songbirds; their wings, however, vary in shape. Many fringillids are long-distance migrants, and thus evolved elongated primaries, but some less migratory species (e.g., the House Finch and the Lesser Goldfinch) have shorter, rounder wings.

Behavior All North American fringillids are at least partially migratory in winter, vacating breeding areas in search of fluctuating food supply. Many fringillids are very erratic in their dispersal and are often irruptive—being present in areas in very large numbers some years, only to be absent other years; redpolls and crossbills are famous for this behavior. The rosy-finches and a few others vacate higher elevations during the winter in search of food. Most species feed on seeds, finding seed feeders very attractive. All species share a distinctive undu-

lating flight, but each can be easily recognized in flight by its species-specific flight call. In most species, the song is not as important as group contact calls; the Evening Grosbeak, however, rarely, if ever, sings.

Plumage All species are highly sexually dimorphic, the males being brightly colored, as in goldfinches and *Carpodacus* finches, and females duller, browner, and often streaked. Some species, such as the Brambling and the Pine Grosbeak, take longer than 1 calendar year to achieve adult breeding plumage, usually molting into it during the second winter. Some species—the American Goldfinch for instance—have a distinct winter plumage, while most have a distinct first-winter plumage duller than adult breeding birds. Many species have combinations of wing bars and white in the tail, both more conspicuous in flight.

Distribution The Fringillidae family consists of about 150 species in 32 genera worldwide. In North America, there are 23 species in 8 genera, of which 16 breed and 7 occur as vagrants. Several species generally are found in coniferous forests across the boreal zone in Canada and northern United States, as well as in pine and spruce-fir forests in the mountainous west. A number of species (e.g., goldfinches and the Pine Siskin) are widespread during the breeding season, but then form gregarious single-species flocks in the winter that can be found virtually anywhere. Other species (e.g., the Lawrence's Goldfinch and the Brown-capped Rosy-Finch) have very restricted breeding ranges with limited dispersal.

Taxonomy Fringillidae members are considered aligned with other 9-primaried oscines and are most closely related to the Emberizidae and Cardinalidae families. Taxonomists sometimes further divide the family into 2 subfamilies, the Fringillinae, which includes the Brambling and the Common Chaffinch, and Carduelinae, which includes all other North American finches. Our knowledge of taxonomic relationships within the family is an evolving process. For instance, recent studies of the Red Crossbill suggest that as many as 9 species may be involved, based on differences in bill size, distribution, and flight call notes.

Conservation Certain species that breed in coniferous forests may be adversely affected by clear-cutting and thinning of old-growth forest. Some species (e.g., the House Finch and the Evening Grosbeak) are expanding their range, while others (e.g., the Purple Finch) have ranges that are contracting. BirdLife International lists 8 species as threatened and 4 more as near threatened.
—*Gary H. Rosenberg*

OLD WORLD FINCHES Genus *Fringilla*

Of this highly migratory Old World genus, only the Brambling and the Common Chaffinch occur in North America as rare migrants or vagrants. Medium-size birds, the males are generally colorful, while the females appear drabber and browner. They usually feed on the ground.

COMMON CHAFFINCH *Fringilla coelebs*

This Palearctic finch, one of the more common songbirds in Europe, is a casual visitor to North America's northeast. Found on a variety of breeding ground habitats, the Common Chaffinch is highly migratory, making it an excellent candidate for vagrancy. It often feeds on seeds on the ground. It has an undulating flight. The white markings on its

wings and tail are very conspicuous. Polytypic (up to 17 ssp., with nominate from mainland Europe or *gengleri* from the British Isles most likely to appear in N.A.). L 6" (15 cm)

Identification The Common Chaffinch is highly sexually dimorphic. MALE: A pale gray crown and nape surround a brown face. The back is brown; the underneath is pinkish. The very conspicuously marked wings are black with white lesser coverts; each has a white wing bar and a white base to the primaries. The flight feathers have noticeable pale edges. The tail is dark with white outer feathers. The conical bill is somewhat long. FALL MALE: He resembles the summer male, but many feathers are edged in brown, which wears off by late winter. FEMALE AND JUVENILE: Both birds are much duller than the male—mostly brown,

darker above and buffier below. A conspicuous gray area surrounds a brown cheek. The wing markings appear as in male, but the coloration is slightly browner overall.

Similar Species No other species in North America resembles a male Chaffinch. The winter female American Goldfinch is somewhat similar to the female Chaffinch, but the Chaffinch is noticeably larger and uniformly buffier brown underneath and has a much larger bill and a different distribution of white in the wings.

Voice CALL: A metallic *pink-pink* or *hweet.*

Status & Distribution Casual or accidental vagrant from Eurasia to northeastern N.A., mainly in fall and winter. Accepted records from NF, NS, ME, and MA. Additional reports from the western U.S., as well as several other states in the East, are usually considered to be escaped cage birds.

BRAMBLING *Fringilla montifringilla*

The Brambling, a highly migratory Eurasian finch, is a regular vagrant to western Alaska, sometimes occurring in small flocks. The male is strikingly patterned in black, white, and rufous. The Brambling often forages on the ground. It has a very undulating flight, and its characteristic white rump is best observed just when the bird takes flight. Monotypic. L 6.3" (15 cm)

Identification The Brambling is sexually dimorphic. BREEDING MALE: In spring, the adult male has a black head and back; bright tawny-orange throat, breast, and shoulders; and white lower belly with dark spotting on flanks. The tail is black and deeply notched. The wings are black with white lesser wing coverts, a buffy lower wing bar, and white bases to the primaries that form a small white patch on the folded wing. The rump is white, but it is often covered by folded wings. The conical bill is relatively small. WINTER MALE: Similar to the breeding male, but the black plumage is overlaid by a brown edging that

wears off throughout winter, revealing the striking plumage underneath. FEMALE: Browner overall, the head is grayish brown, with a grayer face and lateral black stripes on the sides of the nape, and the brown back has blackish scaling. The underparts are a duller rufous and have less distinct spotting on the flanks than the male. The wings have a more rufous edging on greater coverts and tertials. The rump is white.

Similar species No other species has the same color combination and all-white rump. The female Brambling could be somewhat suggestive of a Harris's Sparrow, but note the Brambling's white rump and lack of black on breast.

Voice CALL: A nasal *check-check-check;* often given in flight. Also a nasal *zwee.*

Status & Distribution Fairly common but irregular migrant to islands in the central and western Aleutians. Rare on islands in the Bering Sea (St. Lawrence and Pribilofs), more regular in late spring

(early June), when small groups ocasionally form. Casual in fall and winter to Canada and northern U.S., and western states south to central CA and NV.

breeding ♂

fall ♂

♀

ROSY-FINCHES Genus *Leucosticte*

Characterized by their bright rose-pink bellies and wings, the 3 North American members of this genus were formerly considered 1 species. They are usually found in the Arctic or above tree line in the West's high mountains, preferring the tundra often seen at the edge of snowfields. During winter they disperse to lower elevations in flocks.

GRAY-CROWNED ROSY-FINCH *Leucosticte tephrocotis*

Pribilofs winter
♂ *umbrina*

tephrocotis
group

juvenile

"Hepburn's"
winter ♂
littoralis

breeding ♂

The Gray-crowned Rosy-Finch is the most widespread of the rosy-finches; it comprises several identifiable subspecies. Found in alpine and rocky coastal areas in extreme northwest North America, it frequents steep rocky cliffs during the breeding season. Birders often see it at the edge of snowfields. Some sedentary subspecies inhabit the Aleutian and Pribilof Islands, while other subspecies migrate. Migratory Gray-crowneds frequently form mixed flocks with other rosy-finch species during the winter at higher elevations in the interior west. The Gray-crowned typically feeds on the ground, but it will visit seed feeders. The Gray-crowned stands out best against snow-covered ground, but it can be easily spotted searching for seeds along the sides of roads. Polytypic. L 6" (15 cm)
Identification In general, the Gray-crowned is a chunky ground-dwelling brown finch with bright rosy-pink tinting its lower belly, rump, lesser wing coverts, and edging to wing feathers. Both sexes have blackish bills in summer and yellowish bills in winter. All subspecies have a distinctive black forecrown and pale gray hindcrown. MALE: The belly and wings are a brighter rosy-pink. FEMALE: Overall, she is a paler brown than the male; there's also less pink on the underparts and a lighter pink edging to the wing feathers. JUVENILE: It is entirely gray-

ish brown with pale edging to wing coverts and flight feathers, and a darker forecrown. The bill is darker and not as yellow as the winter bird's.
Geographic Variation As a species (current taxonomy), the Gray-crowned can be divided into "gray-cheeked" *(littoralis)* and "brown-cheeked" *(tephrocotis)* groups. The main difference between them is the distribution of gray on the head, with *littoralis* having a pale gray hind crown that wraps around and encompasses the cheeks and malar region, while on the *tephrocotis* the gray stops abruptly at the eye and the cheeks are distinctly brown. The *littoralis* group consists of 3 subspecies: The *umbrina* from the Pribilof Islands is very large, has a black throat, darker brown underparts, and a darker back; the *griseonucha* found in the Aleutian Islands is also very large but it has a duskier throat and is not as dark overall as the *umbrina*; *littoralis* ("Hepburn's Rosy-Finch") is more coastal in distribution, is much smaller, has a smaller bill, and has a dark throat contrasting with warmer brown underparts. Of the 3 subspecies in the *littoralis* group, only the "Hepburn's" is migratory; the other 2 are sedentary. The brown-cheeked *tephrocotis* group, found mainly in the Rocky Mountains, divides into at least 3 subspecies as well, but separation in the field is more subtle and problematic.

Similar Species The unmistakable gray-cheeked Gray-crowned does not overlap with other rosy-finches during the breeding season. The head pattern of the brown-cheeked Gray-crowned and the Black Rosy-finch look similar, but the Black is always much blacker or a charcoal gray. The female Brown-capped Rosy-Finch could also be mistaken for an immature female Gray-crowned.
Voice CALL: A high, chirping *chew*, sometimes given in repetition and often given in flight. SONG: A series of descending *chew* notes; sometimes given in flight display. It is seldom heard.
Status & Distribution Fairly common. BREEDING: Resident in the Aleutian *(griseonucha)* and Pribilof *(umbrina)* Islands, where it frequents coastal cliffs and rocky tundra. Migratory *littoralis* mainly found in coastal mountains from AK south to WA, OR, and northern CA. Interior subspecies *tephrocotis* group mainly found above tree line throughout the northern Rocky Mountains, north into AK and south to ID; also in Sierra Nevada. WINTER: Both migratory subspecies *(littoralis* and *tephrocotis)* winter south of breeding range, mostly at higher elevations throughout the interior west, south to CO, UT, northern NM, and northern CA. Both can be found in the same flocks at wintering locations in CO and NM. The winter distribution is somewhat erratic, with species invading farther south some years in search of food. VAGRANT: Casual in AZ and various states and provinces east of breeding and wintering range. Accidental in ME, QC, and ON.

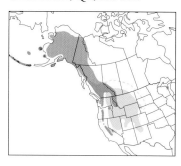

BLACK ROSY-FINCH *Leucosticte atrata*

breeding ♀

breeding ♂

The Black Rosy-Finch is restricted to the central Rocky Mountains in the interior west. It frequents rocky tundra above tree line, often feeding on the ground at the edge of snowfields. During winter, it will join with other Blacks to form large single-species flocks. Some years the Black invades farther south in moderate numbers and frequents steep rocky ledges and cliffs. It's been known to sometimes visit seed feeders. Monotypic. L 6" (15 cm)
Identification The Black is much darker than the similarly patterned *tephro-*

cotis Gray-crowned Rosy-Finch. Both sexes have blackish bills in summer and yellowish bills in winter. MALE: The almost entirely black body has some grayish edging to the breast and back feathers. The pale silvery gray of the hind crown extends down to the level of the eye, forming a gray headband. A pink blush extensively covers the lower belly and upper tail coverts. Obvious pink coverts form a pink wing patch on each of the blackish wings. BREEDING FEMALE: She is patterned similar to male, but she is more of a charcoal gray color than black. The whitish lower belly has little or no pink. The pink wing coverts are much lighter than the male's. FIRST-WINTER FEMALE: The head pattern is less distinct and the body a grayish color. JUVENILE: The body is uniformly gray with 2 buffy-cinnamon wing bars and a pale eye ring. The bill is pale.
Similar Species The Black Rosy-Finch is much blacker than any other rosy-finch. Similar head patterns could cause it to be confused with an "interior" Gray-crowned Rosy-Finch, but the Black is blacker or grayer bodied. The Black juvenile looks similar to other rosy-finch juveniles, but it is grayer overall.

Voice CALL: A high chirping *chew;* often given in series and while in flight. It is similar to the Gray-crowned Rosy-Finch's call. It is difficult to discern single call notes out of large, noisy flocks.
Status & Distribution Fairly common within its limited range. BREEDING: It is found in high-elevation rocky tundra, usually above tree line in the central Rocky Mountains from southern MT and ID to southeastern OR, NV, and northern UT, where it occurs on top of isolated high mountains. WINTER: It forms large flocks that move down to lower elevations and south to northern NM. Casual to northern AZ (sometimes occurring in large single-species flocks) and eastern CA.

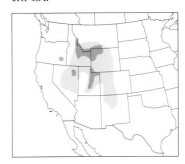

BROWN-CAPPED ROSY-FINCH *Leucosticte australis*

Limited to Colorado and Wyoming, the Brown-capped Rosy-Finch has a much more restricted breeding range than the Gray-crowned and Black Rosy-Finches. Birders easily recognize the Brown-capped from other rosy-finches by the lack of gray on the hind crown or nape. It behaves much like other rosy-finches, breeding above tree line in rocky tundra and often feeding on the ground at the edge of snow patches. Like the "interior" Gray-crowned and Black, the Brown-capped migrates to lower elevations during the winter and frequents seed feeders. Monotypic. L 6" (15 cm)

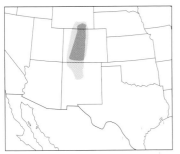

Identification Unlike other rosy-finches, the Brown-capped lacks gray on its head. Both sexes have blackish bills in summer and yellowish bills in winter. MALE: Body almost entirely rich brown with a darker, almost blackish crown. The lower belly is bright reddish pink, while wing coverts and rump are extensively edged in pink. BREEDING FEMALE: Much drabber than male, with a uniformly darker brown body and little or no pink on the belly, rump, or wing coverts. IMMATURE FEMALE: Distinguished by a pale grayish brown body, more blended head pattern, light pink wing coverts, and no pink on belly.
Similar species The Brown-capped is generally browner and paler than any plumage of the Black Rosy-Finch. Some individuals have varying amounts of gray on the hind crown, making a field identification from the Gray-crowned difficult or impossible.
Voice CALL: A high, chirping *chew;* usually given in flight. It is similar to other rosy-finch calls.
Status & Distribution Fairly common in proper habitat. BREEDING: Like other

breeding ♀

breeding ♂

rosy-finches, it prefers high-elevation rocky tundra, but it has a more limited breeding range, which is restricted to above tree line in the eastern Rocky Mountains of CO and southern WY. Most often seen in Rocky Mountain National Park in summer. WINTER: Moves to lower elevations and joins mixed-species flocks with other rosy-finches. Recorded regularly south to northern NM. It has not been recorded farther west in AZ or CA, like the other 2 rosy-finch species. Often visits seed feeders.

Genus *Pinicola*

PINE GROSBEAK *Pinicola enucleator*

The large, plump Pine Grosbeak is one of the more characteristic and sought-after finches of the North American boreal forest. Birders often see it singing from the top of spruce trees; its loud, melodic song carries for a great distance. Typically found in singles or in pairs, the Pine Grosbeak frequently forms small groups during the nonbreeding season that feed in fruiting trees or on young spruce buds. It is often unwary and approachable. Migratory. Polytypic. L 9" (23 cm)

Identification Generally, the Pine Grosbeak is a large, chunky, long-tailed finch with a stubby, curved bill. ADULT MALE: He has a mostly rich pinkish-red body with dark wings and 2 white wing bars. Depending on the subspecies, there are varying amounts of gray on the underparts, particularly on the flanks and belly, as well as varying amounts of dark centers to the back feathers. A dark eye line and pale area usually shows above and below the eye. ADULT FEMALE AND IMMATURE MALE: They are mostly gray overall with 2 distinct white wing bars and a variably yellowish olive wash to the head, back, and rump. Similar to the adult male, they also show a dark eye line and are pale around the eyes. VARIANT: Some females and immature males are quite russet on the head and rump.

Geographic Variation Of 11 subspecies, 6 occur in N.A; 2 are resident (the *car-* *lottae* in coastal British Columbia and the *californicus* from eastern California), the others are migratory. The coastal Pacific *flammula* shows less gray on flanks and more dusky centers to back feathers than the western interior *montanus,* which tends to be very gray on the belly and flanks. The northern boreal *leucurus* has more distinct dark markings on its back, and only a little gray on the flanks. This subspecies has irruptive migrations in the East.

Similar Species The male Pine Grosbeak could be confused with the male White-winged Crossbill, but the latter is much smaller and has a distinctive bill shape.

Voice CALL: Geographically variable. Includes a whistled *pui pui pui* or *chii-vli.* SONG: A short musical warble.

Status & Distribution Fairly common in coniferous forest. WINTER: May move into deciduous woods and orchards. Irruptive winter migrant, mostly in the east *(leucurus)* and interior West *(montanus).*

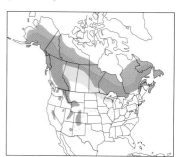

"RED" FINCHES Genus *Carpodacus*

In North America, 3 breeding species and 1 Eurasian vagrant make up this highly sexually dimorphic genus. The males are bright red or pink; the females are brown and streaked. To help separate the similar-looking species, focus on the bill size and shape, the degree of streaking on flanks and undertail coverts, and distinctive calls.

COMMON ROSEFINCH *Carpodacus erythrinus*

This Eurasian species is a very rare migrant in western Alaska, where other "red" finch species are less likely to occur. Virtually all reports are from offshore islands in the Aleutians and in the Bering Sea. It is typically found in singles, but it does occur in small groups. Birders usually see it feeding on the ground; it mainly eats seeds. It is more likely to be found during the spring, when most of the records pertain to bright males. Polytypic (at least 5 ssp. recognized; *grebnitskii* likely to occur in N.A.). L 5.8" (15 cm)

Identification Knowing the ranges of the *Carpodacus* finches will help in the identification of this species. MALE: The head, breast, back, and rump are a pinkish red. The back is marked with indistinct dark streaking, while the flanks and lower underparts have little or no diffuse streaking. It lacks distinct eyebrows. The bill is finchlike, but it has a strongly curved culmen. The wings have 2 indistinct pinkish wing bars. FEMALE AND IMMATURE: Both are a very drab brown with diffuse streaking above and below, except on paler throat.

Similar Species This is the most likely *Carpodacus* finch to occur in the Aleutian and Bering Sea islands. The male differs from the Purple Finch in having a more uniform face and no distinct eyebrows. In addition, the Purple's culmen is decidedly straight, making it appear more pointed. The House Finch has browner cheeks and back, and more prominent streaking on a paler belly. The Common Rosefinch female looks similar to the female House, but she is noticeably drabber, with more diffuse streaking overall. The throat of the female House is usu-ally streaked, whereas it is plain in the Common Rosefinch. Note again the distinctly curved culmen in the Common Rosefinch, although the House female also has curved culmen. **Voice** CALL: A soft, nasal *djuee.*

Status & Distribution The Common is a casual spring migrant (late May–early June) on the western Aleutians (e.g., Attu, Shemya) and islands in the Bering Sea (e.g., St. Paul and St. Lawrence). It is rarer in the fall, when sightings mostly pertain to females or immatures.

grebnitskii

adult ♂

HOUSE FINCH *Carpodacus mexicanus*

typical ♂

variant ♂

The attractive House Finch is one of the more common and recognizable species throughout the United States. Originally a "western" species of semi-arid environments, it was introduced in the East in the 1940s; it has now expanded its range and spread to virtually every state, as well as a multitude of habitats. It has become very common in suburban areas and is easily attracted in large numbers to seed feeders. Polytypic. L 6" (15 cm)
Identification The House is a relatively small *Carpodacus* finch with a longish, slightly notched tail, short wings, and a distinctly small bill with a curved culmen. MALE: The breast, rump, and front of the head are typically red, but the color can vary to orange or occasionally yellow. The red breast is clearly demarcated from a whitish belly with dark streaks. The top of crown and auriculars are brown. Back is brown and noticeably streaked. The wings have 2 pale indistinct wing bars each. FEMALE: She is much drabber, lacking the all-red coloration of the male. The brown body has distinct, blurry streaking above and below. She lacks the distinct pale eyebrow found on the male.

Geographic Variation Of the at least 13 described subspecies, 4 occur in North America north of Mexico. Clinal variation where populations come together, as well as individual variation and effects of diet on plumage coloration complicate the separation of different subspecies. Subspecies *frontalis,* the most widespread throughout the U.S., sports a generally more orange-red to yellow breast and has less distinct streaking on the belly. Both the *clementis* from the Channel Islands in California and the *potosinus* from central Texas are brighter red, with bolder streaking on a whiter belly.
Similar Species Identifying the male and female House from other *Carpodacus* finches requires care. The male House differs from the male Purple Finch not only by having a smaller, more curved bill, but also by lacking a distinct eyebrow, having a brown cap and auricular patch, and being heavily streaked on belly. Told from male Cassin's Finch by brown cap and eyebrow and curved bill. Other tell-tale differences between the species include the Cassin's pink cheek and pinkish tone on its back, and on female and immature Cassin's, the much finer and crisp streaks on its belly. The male Common Rosefinch is more rose-pink overall and lacks distinct streaking on its belly. The female finches are more problematic. The female House has a very plain face, unlike the Purple and Cassin's, which both show distinct eyebrows. The female House tends to have browner underparts than the 2 as well, with blurry streaks below. Also note the House's smaller, more curved bill. The female Common Rosefinch looks similar, but she is drabber, with less distinct streaking below.
Voice CALL: Most commonly a whistled *wheat.* SONG: Lively and high-pitched, consisting of varied 3-note phrases that usually end in a nasal *wheeer.*
Status & Distribution Very common, often abundant resident throughout much of the U.S., extending north into much of extreme southern Canada and south into Mexico. Both western and introduced eastern populations appear to be spreading. MIGRATION: Some northern populations appear to be migratory, moving south in winter.
Population The human modification of natural habitats, particularly the increase of seed feeders throughout the East, greatly benefits the House Finch populations. Only natural island populations appear to be threatened.

PURPLE FINCH *Carpodacus purpureus*

♀ *californicus*

Pacific coast
adult ♂
californicus

♀ *purpureus*

eastern adult ♂
purpureus

This migratory rose red (not purple) finch is fairly common throughout much of the Northeast, Canadian provinces, and much of the Pacific coast. Generally found in less disturbed habitats than House Finch. Polytypic (2 ssp.). L 6" (15 cm)

Identification A rather chunky *Carpodacus* finch with a shortish, strongly notched tail. MALE: Body mostly rose red, brightest on the head and rump. Back brownish with noticeable streaks and pinkish ground color. Head rather bright, with distinct paler pink eyebrow contrasting with a darker cheek. Two indistinct pinkish wing bars on each wing. Lower belly whitish with varying amounts of wide blurry streaks.

Undertail coverts clean white. Bill rather large, conical, with a straight culmen. FEMALE: Underparts whitish with heavy dark brown streaking that does not extend to the white undertail coverts. Head boldly patterned with whitish eyebrow and submoustachial stripe that contrast with a dark brown cheek and malar stripe. Crown and back have pale streaks. Pacific birds buffier below overall with more diffuse streaking.

Geographic Variation Range and plumage differences delineate 2 distinct subspecies. Nominate *purpureus* resides in the Northeast and the boreal forests of southern Canada; the male has longer wings and is brighter overall, the female has a bolder head pattern and whiter underparts. The Pacific coast *californicus* male is less bright and has a brownish wash on its back and sides; the female is much buffier underneath with a less bold face pattern and more blurred back streaking.

Similar Species Males and females most similar to Cassin's Finch, which do not overlap with each other in the East, but are more confusing in the West. Male Cassin's is lighter pink, particularly on the underparts and eyebrow. To separate the female Purple from the female Cassin's, see the sidebar below.

Voice CALL: A musical *chur-lee,* and a sharp *pit* given in flight. SONG: A rich warbling; shorter than the Cassin's and lower pitched and more strident than the House Finch. Songs of nominate subspecies more complex.

Status & Distribution Fairly common. BREEDING: Inhabits open coniferous forests and mixed woodland in the East and North, and montane coniferous forest and oak canyons in the West. WINTER: Eastern birds migrate south to lower latitudes, sometimes irrupting with major invasions south to the southern U.S. Western birds move to lower elevations. Rare throughout much of the interior West.

Identification of Female Purple and Cassin's Finches

One of the more challenging identification problems in the West involves separating adult female Purple and Cassin's Finches. The females (and immature males) of both species are basically brown with coarse dark streaking on whitish underparts. Both species also have similar face patterns with a pale eyebrow, a pale submoustachial streak, and a darkish malar stripe. Further complicating the identification, the Purple Finch has 2 distinct subspecies that differ just enough to be problematic. Visible differences between the 3 are subtle, and perhaps best used in combination with each other; however, note that each has different call notes. The Purple Finch gives a quick, musical *chur-lee* when perched and a sharp *pit* in flight. The calls of the eastern *purpureus* race are clearer and higher-pitched. The Cassin's call when perched can be similar to the Purple's, but in flight it gives a distinctive high-pitched *kee-up* or, the longer version, *tee-dee-yip.*

The female Eastern Purple Finch *(purpureus),* overall the bolder patterned of the species, has a very bold face pattern, with a broad eyebrow, a whiter submoustachial stripe, and a prominent black malar streak. The underparts are white with very dark streaking and a slight buffy wash on the flanks. The white, unstreaked undertail coverts are a critical field mark. The bill is relatively long, with a slightly curved culmen.

The face pattern on the Western Purple Finch *(californicus)* resembles the face pattern on the Cassin's; the former, however, appears more washed-out. The underparts on *californicus* look more like those on a House Finch, with very blurry streaks. Again note that the undertail coverts are white and unstreaked. The bill has a slightly curved culmen.

The Cassin's Finch is slightly larger than either

CASSIN'S FINCH *Carpodacus cassinii*

The attractive Cassin's Finch of the montane west is slightly larger and longer winged than the similar Purple Finch, which it occasionally overlaps with during winter. It is often seen in small flocks, mainly in pine forest, but it is known to occasionally invade into lowland deciduous areas during the winter. It occasionally joins the more common House Finch at seed feeders in winter. Polytypic. L 6.3" (16 cm)

Identification Highly sexually dimorphic with males pink and females brown. Generally lighter pink than other *Carpodacus* finches, with distinctive fine streaking on the undertail coverts. MALE: A bright pinkish-red crown contrasts sharply with a brown streaked nape. The back is heavily streaked and washed pink. The fairly wide eyebrow and submoustachial stripe are both pale pink. The light pink throat and breast blends into the white on the lower belly. Varying amounts of fine black streaking cover the flanks and undertail coverts. The bill is longer and more pointed than other *Carpodacus* finches. FEMALE: The upperparts are brown and streaked, while the underparts are white with fine, crisp streaking, which is heaviest on the breast and flanks. The undertail coverts are also finely streaked. The rather diffuse face pattern has a noticeable pale eyebrow and submoustachial stripe.

Geographic Variation Two described subspecies show subtle plumage and size differences, with birds of the Sierra Nevada and Cascades slightly darker and with longer bills than those of the Rocky Mountains.

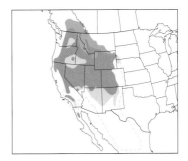
adult ♂
♀

Similar Species The male is most similar to the male Purple Finch, but there is only limited overlap in range during the breeding season. The Cassin's eyebrow and streaking on back tend to be wider and frostier; it usually has fine streaking on the flanks and undertail coverts as well. The primary projection is noticeably longer in the Cassin's, as is the bill. Note the different flight calls between the 2. Distinguishing a female Cassin's from a female Purple can be more of a challenge (see sidebar below). The Cassin's and House overlap more, with the Cassin's typically found in coniferous forest and the House in the lowlands, but they might overlap in winter when Cassin's populations irrupt to the lowlands. Note the Cassin's pink eyebrow, finer black streaking on the flanks, frostier upperparts, longer primary projection, and longer bill with a straight culmen.

Voice CALL: In flight gives a dry *kee-up* or *tee-dee-yip*. SONG: A lively, varying warble, longer and more complex than the Purple or House Finches'.

Status & Distribution Fairly common in montane coniferous forests. BREEDING: Found throughout much of the Rocky Mountains, west into the Cascades in WA and OR, and the Sierra Nevada and southern mountain ranges in CA. WINTER: Unpredictable. Often stays in breeding range, but periodically drops to lower elevations. Winters as far south as the mountains of central Mexico. More common in the lowlands of the interior west than is Purple Finch. VAGRANT: Casual to eastern CO, NE, and KS; northern TX; AK; and CA coast.

"Eastern" Purple Finch, female (NJ, Jan.)

"Western" Purple Finch, female (CA, Jul.)

Cassin's Finch, female (CA, Feb.)

Purple. It has very white underparts with finer black streaking, particularly on the flanks, and the streaking extends to the undertail coverts. The face pattern, similar to that of *californicus*, often shows a pale eye ring.

The long bill has a straight culmen. At close range, note the Cassin's longer, less evenly spaced primary extensions and the more distinct white edging to its flight and tail feathers. ∎

CROSSBILLS Genus *Loxia*

Found in coniferous forests, crossbills use their highly specialized bills with crossed tips to extract seeds from pinecones. Highly nomadic, the species disperse great distances in search of food. The taxonomy is complicated; in North America, only 2 species are recognized, but variable populations with different bill sizes and calls suggest more.

RED CROSSBILL *Loxia curvirostra*

variant ♂
juvenile
northern minor ♀
typical ♀
typical ♂
southwestern stricklandi ♂

Because they specialize in pinecones, the Red Crossbill is found almost exclusively in coniferous forests across the boreal zone of Canada and in the montane west. Dependent upon the local pinecone crop, it moves around both seasonally and annually. An invasive and irruptive species, it often becomes abundant in an area only to remain a few weeks or months, then vanish when the cones are depleted. Polytypic. L 6.3" (16 cm)

Identification Highly sexually dimorphic. Chunky, medium-size bird with a shortish notched tail, large head, and a stout, uniquely crossed bill. MALE: It typically is entirely brick red with darker, unmarked wings (some show narrow whitish wing bars). The back usually has some dark scaling, while the undertail coverts are whitish with black chevrons. FEMALE: Entire body is a dull yellowish olive, while the unmarked wings are dark and the throat gray. May show some patches of red on the body. JUVENILE: Mostly brown, but paler below with heavy dark streaking. Varying narrow white wing bars (usually with upper bar thinner than the lower). FIRST-YEAR MALE: Resembles female, but is more orange.

Geographic Variation Very complicated. The Red Crossbill subspecies are referred to as "types," differentiated mainly by range, overall size, bill size, and most important, flight call notes. As many as 9 different types have been identified so far in N.A. (potentially another 13 in Europe and Asia). Several potential separate species may be involved. The identification of different types is very difficult in the field. Given that many of the types can turn up in virtually any part of the Red's range and that different types sometimes flock together, a certain identification to type is very problematic. Only broad extremes will be covered here (for more information refer to technical literature). The smallest and small-billed crossbills have been put into *minor* (type 3); they generally are found farther north (into AK), but they are very widespread. The largest Red is the *stricklandi* (type 6), with a relatively huge bill; it is restricted to southeastern Arizona. Two populations that have very restricted ranges include the *percana* (type 8) found in Newfoundland and an unnamed subspecies (type 9) in southern Idaho. The remaining types (1, 2, 4, 5, and 7) are generally put into the *pusilla*. They are medium-size birds with medium-size bills; some are restricted to the west, others are more widespread.

Similar Species The White-winged Crossbill is the only other crossbill in N.A., and in all plumages it has a distinctive patterned wing with all-white lesser coverts (forming a wider upper wing bar) and a prominent lower wing bar. A male White-winged is generally pinker than the brick-red male Red. Use wing patterns to separate females and juveniles. Some Reds have narrow wing bars, but note different pattern. Flight notes are also different.

Voice CALL: Generally a *kip-kip* or *chip-chip* usually given in double notes, but sometimes difficult to discern individual calls as multiple individuals call simultaneously. Given in flight and vary between types. Identification of different calls to different types not safely done in the field. SONG: Begins with several 2-note phrases, ending in a warbling trill; often given from the top of a conifer.

Status & Distribution Fairly common. BREEDING: Irregular breeder anywhere there are pine or spruce-fir forests, as far south as GA, and north to AK and NF. Different subspecies appear to form single-species flocks and may have non-overlapping breeding ranges, but more study is needed. MIGRATION: Wander greatly in search of food. Known to "invade" the lowlands in the West, sometimes turning up in ornamental pines in parks and cemeteries. Casual, mainly in winter, to Southeast.

Population Logging in old-growth coniferous forests may affect food supplies; trees generally produce cones only once they reach 60 years old. In Newfoundland, the population is also threatened by introduced red squirrels, which outcompete the Reds for pinecones, and loss of breeding habitat.

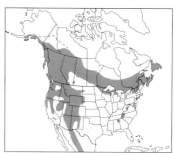

WHITE-WINGED CROSSBILL *Loxia leucoptera*

juvenile

♀

winter
adult ♂

immature ♂

The White-winged Crossbill is one of 2 species in North America with a distinctive finchlike bill that crosses at the tip; its cousin, the Red Crossbill, is the other. The White-winged inhabits the northern boreal forest from Newfoundland to Alaska; highly nomadic, its populations move around both seasonally and annually because of fluctuating spruce cone crops. It forms large single-species flocks during the nonbreeding season. It is also an irruptive migrant, but it is generally found farther north than the Red. Polytypic (nominate in N.A.). L 6.5" (17 cm)

Identification Boldly patterned black wings, with very contrasting white lesser coverts (often covered by the scapulars), bold white wing bar, and white tips to the tertials, identify this species in all plumages. ADULT MALE: Pink body. Grayish flanks and undertail coverts. Black scapulars and lores. Dark on rear portion of auricular forms a crescent on side of head. WINTER MALE: Paler pink overall. FEMALE: Brownish olive body, with very indistinct streaking on the underparts. Pale yellow rump. Dark lores. Auricular patch more distinct. IMMATURE MALE: Like adult male, but yellow with patches of orange. JUVENILE: Brown with heavy streaks all over. Wings have thinner white wing bars than adult.
Similar Species The Red Crossbill is the only other North American species

with a bill distinctly crossed at the tip; however, the White-winged male is pinker and all plumages have a bolder wing pattern. Know that some Reds show narrow white wing bars. The Pine Grosbeak, which has white wing bars and is red overall, lacks the crossed bill and is a third again larger.
Voice CALL: A rapid series of dry *chet* notes and a double or triple *chik-chik;* given in flight. Generally softer than a Red's call. SONG: A series of mechanical trills and whistles, usually rising in pitch; given from a treetop or in flight display.
Status & Distribution Fairly common, but erratic. BREEDING: Frequents northern boreal forests, but irregular and nomadic. Present at locations one year, absent the next. Timing and success dependent upon spruce cone produc-

tion. WINTER: Generally south of normal breeding areas, but inconsistent year to year. Regular in the northern states; casual to NM, TX, and FL.
Population As with the Red Crossbill, logging practices in coniferous forests may significantly affect populations; it takes nearly 60 years for mature forests to produce cones.

GOLDFINCHES, REDPOLLS, AND SISKINS Genus *Carduelis*

These highly recognizable, generally very small birds have small bills and short, notched tails. The redpolls, found in the high Arctic and boreal Canada in the summer, winter in the northern United States, periodically invading farther south in search of food. The more widespread goldfinches and siskins frequent brushy roadsides and fields.

ORIENTAL GREENFINCH *Carduelis sinica*

A casual spring migrant in the outer Aleutians, this Asian finch sometimes occurs in small groups. No other finch in N.A. is brown with large yellow wing patches. Polytypic. L 6" (15 cm)
Identification Small, stocky brown finch with a deeply notched tail; short, stubby bill; and a large yellow wing patch in the primaries. ADULT MALE: Uniformly olive-brown, with greener face and rump; dark gray nape and crown; white patch on tertials and tips of primaries visible on folded wing. Yellow undertail coverts and base of tail feathers. ADULT FEMALE: Duller, lacks the gray crown and nape. JUVENILE: Simi-

lar to female, but finely streaked below.
Similar Species The female Oriental looks a little like the female Lawrence's Goldfinch, but the wing patterns are different. A juvenile resembles a Pine Siskin, but it is unstreaked above, and has more yellow in wing.
Voice CALL: Includes a twittering rattle and a nasal *zweee.*
Status & Distribution Asian species; southern Russia to Japan. VAGRANT: Casual (ssp. *kawarahiba*) in outer Aleutians; 1 Bering Sea island rec. (St. Paul).

adult ♀

adult ♂

juvenile

kawarahiba

COMMON REDPOLL *Carduelis flammea*

juvenile   breeding ♀   breeding ♂   winter ♀

flammea   winter ♂

Common and Hoary Redpolls are 2 closely related finches of the boreal forest and Arctic tundra scrub. The Common is the more widespread species of the 2, usually inhabiting subarctic forest during the summer and frequenting seed feeders in southern Canada and northern United States during the winter, when they form large flocks. Adults have characteristic red cap or "poll." Polytypic. L 5.3" (13 cm)

Identification The Common is generally a relatively small, streaked finch with a small, pointed bill; short, deeply notched tail; 2 white wing bars; black chin; red cap; and varying amounts of red underneath. BREEDING MALE: The cap is bright red. The upperparts are brown with distinct streaking. The bright rosy red of the throat and breast extends onto the cheeks. The white flanks and undertail coverts have fine black streaking; the paler rump has distinctive streaking. BREEDING FEMALE: She lacks the red breast of the male and

has variable amounts of streaking underneath, usually confined to sides. WINTER MALE: Duller. Buffy wash on sides and rump. WINTER FEMALE: Also buffier on sides. IMMATURE: First-year birds resemble an adult female, but they tend to be buffier. JUVENILE: Brown and streaked, it acquires the red cap in the late summer molt.

Geographic Variation Two breeding subspecies in N.A. The small-billed and smaller *flammea* has less coarse streaking and is widespread across Canada to Alaska; the large-billed and larger *rostrata* has coarser streaking underneath and is found on Baffin Island and Greenland. Both overlap during winter, but the clinal variation makes identification problematic.

Similar Species Great care is needed to separate the Common from the very similar-looking Hoary. The breeding adult male Hoary is a very frosty white above, and white below with a very pale pink blush on breast. Females and immatures are much more difficult;

rely on the differences in bill size and shape, the presence or absence of streaking on the rump, the quality of the streaking on the flanks and undertail coverts, and to a lesser degree, location (see sidebar below). The juvenile Common can resemble a juvenile Pine Siskin, but it lacks yellow in the wing. The extent of interbreeding between Common and Hoary Redpolls is unknown.

Voice CALL: When perched, gives a *sweee-eet;* flight call a dry rattling *jid-jid-jid-jid.* SONG: A lengthy series of trills and twittering rattles.

Status & Distribution Common. BREEDING: Found in the subarctic forests and tundra across northern Canada and much of AK. The *rostrata* breeds in tundra scrub, where it overlaps with the Hoary. WINTER: Forms large flocks. Irruptive migrant south through much of Canada to northern U.S. Generally winters farther south than Hoary. VAGRANT: Casual or accidental anywhere in southern U.S.

Redpoll Identification

The task of identifying Common Redpolls from Hoary Redpolls ranges from very easy to virtually impossible. Usually, a single field character is not enough to nail down an identification—use a suite of characters. Critical field marks include the overall color of the bird, the color of the streaking on the upperparts, the color of the pink or red on the underparts, the amount and quality of the streaking on the flanks, and whether or not the streaking extends onto the undertail coverts. Pay particular attention to whether or not the rump is streaked. Also focus on the length of the bill. The songs and calls of these 2 birds are virtually indistinguishable in the field, so not all individuals are identifiable. Also keep in mind

Common Redpoll, female (NH)

that these 2 species often mix together into the same foraging flock.

Identifying adult males in breeding plumage is fairly straightforward. The Common is generally much darker overall than the Hoary, with extensive rosy-red on much of the underparts and very dark streaking on the back. The bold streaking on its flanks extends to the undertail coverts. The Hoary, however, is very pale overall and has very frosty streaking on the back, faint streaking on the flanks, and no streaking on the undertail coverts. The pink on its breast is more of a pale blush. In general, the main character difference between the 2 species is the color or pattern on the rump: The Common's is darker and more heavily streaked, the Hoary's

HOARY REDPOLL *Carduelis hornemanni*

The Hoary Redpoll is very similar to its sister species, the Common Redpoll, but it is generally found farther north in tundra habitats during the breeding season. The adults have the characteristic red cap or "poll" and are generally white or frosty above and below. During the nonbreeding season, the Hoary forms large flocks and winters mainly in Canada, though it sometimes mixes with Common Redpolls at seed feeders in the northern United States. Polytypic. L 5.5" (14 cm)

Identification The Hoary is a relatively small finch with a short, notched tail and a very short, stubby bill. Like the Common, it sports a distinctive red cap in all plumages except the juvenile. BREEDING MALE: Very frosty white with contrasting red cap and pale pinkish blush on the breast. Wings with rather bold wing bars and white edging on the secondaries. Rump white, usually unstreaked. Flanks with fine black streaking, undertail coverts usually clean white, or with a hint of streaking. Bill very short. BREEDING FEMALE: Generally pale overall. Typically white below with fine black streaking on sides and flanks. Rump white with little or no streaking. Back streaking quite white. WINTER ADULT: Buffier overall on sides. IMMATURE: Streaking more prominent on sides. JUVENILE: Lacks the red cap. Pale brown overall with streaking above and below.

Geographic Variation Two subspecies breed in N.A. Nominate *hornemanni*, found in Baffin Island and Greenland,

winter ♀
exilipes

winter ♂
exilipes

winter ♂
hornemanni

is larger, larger billed, and overall paler than the more widespread *exilipes*.

Similar Species The Hoary Redpoll is most confused with the very similar Common Redpoll. Separating adult males is fairly easy; the whiter (frostier) Hoary has a pale pinkish blush on its breast, while the Common's breast is rose red. Females and immatures present more of a problem. Main characteristics used to separate the 2 include size and shape of bill, presence or absence of streaking on the rump, degree of streaking on the flanks and undertail coverts, and to a lesser extent, location (see sidebar below). The juvenile Hoary could be confused with a juvenile Pine Siskin, but the Pine has yellow in the wings.

Voice CALL & SONG: Very similar to Common Redpoll, essentially indistinguishable in the field.

Status & Distribution Common in tundra scrub. BREEDING: Found across

the high Arctic, generally above tree line, or in willows and alders, across northern Canada and northern AK. Generally (at least for *exilipes*) found farther north in nonforested habitats as compared to the Common Redpoll. WINTER: Forms large flocks that migrate south across much of Canada, rarely into extreme northern U.S. Casual into northern tier states, usually associated with Commons coming to seed feeders.

---

is whiter and unstreaked. In another character difference, the Common has a longer, more pronounced bill, while the Hoary has a tiny, insignificant bill. This lends the face of the Hoary an even more "pushed in" look than that of the Common, whose longer bill stands out more distinctly from the dark patches surrounding it.

Separating the females and immatures of the species can be quite challenging. In general, the female Hoary is paler and has less coarse streaking on the sides, whiter (typically) unstreaked undertail coverts, bolder, often broader, wing bars, paler streaking on the back, whiter (usually) unstreaked rump, and shorter, pug bill. The female and immature Hoary also tend to show a

Hoary Redpoll, female (NH)

greater amount of white edging to their flight feathers, which is evident on their greater coverts in flight.

Both species of Redpoll have distinct subspecies that reside in Greenland, but sometimes wander to eastern Canada in winter. The Greenland subspecies of Common Redpoll is darker than that of the mainland, with a larger patch of black on the throat and a greater amount of brown overall. The Greenland subspecies of Hoary Redpoll is paler overall than its continental counterpart, with less streaking on the sides, a frostier back, and very little pink on the breast of the breeding male. These birds are easier to differentiate between species, but may prove problematic when narrowing down to subspecies. ■

LESSER GOLDFINCH *Carduelis psaltria*

psaltria
black-backed
adult ♂

hesperophila
green-backed
adult ♂

immature ♂

pale ♀

This very common carduelid finch of the Southwest breeds in a variety of habitats at different elevations. It is often seen in small flocks feeding along brushy roadsides, particularly where thistle grows. Northern populations migrate south in winter, augmenting resident populations from southern California to southern Texas. It is often detected by its distinctive flight calls. Polytypic. 4.5" (11 cm)

Identification A relatively small, sexually dimorphic finch with a short, notched tail and a small, dark, conical bill. BREEDING MALE: Differs greatly depending on subspecies. In the "green-backed" *hesperophila,* the bright yellow underparts and black cap contrast with an olive-green back that can show some fine dark streaking. Nar-

row pale tips to the lesser coverts and wider white tips to the greater coverts form 2 distinct wing bars on a black wing. The white at the base of the primaries forms a white "tick" on the folded wing. The tertials are broadly edged in white. The mostly white bases to the outer tail feathers form distinctive white tail patches visible from underneath or when in flight. In the "black-backed" *psaltria* (*mexicanus* of some authors), bright yellow underparts contrast with entirely black upperparts. The wings and tail are similar to the *hesperophila.* FEMALE: More uniform yellow-green, often yellower below and greener above, but less contrasting. The head does not have a black cap. The wings are similarly patterned to male, but they are decidedly duller. A distinctive white at base of primaries is present. Some females very dull and drab, mostly gray with some yellowish green wash to body; wings duller, but still with white "tick." IMMATURE MALE: It lacks the full black cap of the adult, but it still has black on the forehead *(hesperophila)* or has some black intermixed with green on the back and crown *(psaltria).*

Geographic Variation There are 2 distinct subspecies in N.A. The green-backed *hesperophila* is more widespread in the

Southwest, with black-backed *hesperophila* breeding from Colorado to southern Texas. Intergradation occurs clinally between Texas and Colorado.

Similar Species Males are very distinct from other goldfinch species. The female American Goldfinch is larger and has white undertail coverts, a wide buffy lower wing bar with very little white at the base for the flight feathers, and a pale pinkish bill. A very pale female Lesser can show whitish undertail coverts, but it has a different wing pattern than all Americans and is always greener than the female Lawrence's.

Voice CALLS: Includes a plaintive, kittenlike *tee-yee.* SONG: Very complex jumble of musical phrases, often mimicking other species.

Status & Distribution Very common. BREEDING: A variety of habitats at different elevations from arid lowlands to high pine forests, often found near water. WINTER: Northern and high elevation populations migrate to southern U.S. and Mexico, augmenting resident populations there. VAGRANT: Casual north and east of mapped range in Great Plains. Accidental in the East.

LAWRENCE'S GOLDFINCH *Carduelis lawrenci*

The subtle combination of gray, yellow, and black makes the male Lawrence's Goldfinch one of the more striking carduelids in North America. Largely restricted during the breeding season to the foothills and montane valleys in California, it has a unique irregular dispersal pattern some winters to the southwestern United States. Often seen in small groups, it frequents brushy areas, preferring those found along riparian corridors. Like other goldfinches, it favors feeding on thistle plants. Monotypic. L 4.8" (12 cm)

Identification A relatively small goldfinch with a longish, deeply notched tail and short, stubby bill. BREEDING MALE:

Very sharp plumage. Mostly gray body; lighter gray cheeks; black front of crown, face, and chin; and yellow breast. Black wings with extensive yellow forming 2 broad wing bars and yellow edging to the flight feathers. Yellow rump. Distinct circular white tail spots. BREEDING FEMALE: Much duller than male. Grayish body, brownish gray above with more contrasting gray cheek. No black on head. Reduced amount of yellow on breast. Two prominent yellowish wing

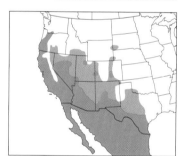

winter ♀

winter ♂

breeding ♂

juvenile

bars, with yellow edging to the primaries. WINTER MALE: Like breeding male, but much browner above and duller below. WINTER FEMALE: Like breeding female, but much browner. JUVENILE: Streaked; unlike other goldfinches.

Similar Species The breeding male is unlike any other goldfinch. The female could be confused with very dull Lesser Goldfinch female, but it has whiter undertail coverts and more prominent wing bars. The Lesser typically also shows a greenish yellow tone to the body that the Lawrence's lacks. The adult winter American goldfinch is larger, with bold buffy wing bars. Note very different call notes among the goldfinch species.

Voice CALL: A very distinctive, rather soft bell-like *tink-ul.* SONG: A series of jumbled musical twittering, often interjecting *tink* notes, and mimicking other species like Lesser Goldfinch.

Status & Distribution Rather uncommon and local. BREEDING: Prefers drier interior foothills and montane valleys of CA and northern Baja. Some populations resident, while others highly migratory. Has bred casually in central AZ. Breeding areas not consistent from year to year. WINTER: Irregular fall and winter movement to the southwestern U.S., occasionally wintering in moderate numbers in southeastern AZ and northern Mexico, casual to southern NM and west TX. AZ wintering birds begin arriving by mid-Oct. Some years the

wintering grounds remain largely unknown. VAGRANT: Casual to northern AZ and NM, and to central OR.

Population The loss of oak and chaparral habitats in California may have an adverse effect on the already low population size.

AMERICAN GOLDFINCH *Carduelis tristis*

The brightly colored male American Goldfinch is especially recognizable. The American regularly visits seed feeders, particularly in the East. It is often very gregarious, especially during the nonbreeding season, when it flocks to roadsides and brushy fields to feed on thistle and sunflowers. It is often heard in flight, giving distinct flight calls. Polytypic (4 named ssp.; differences slight). L 5" (13 cm)

Identification A relatively large carduelid. BREEDING MALE: Unmistakable. Body entirely bright lemon yellow with white undertail coverts. Jet black cap. Black wings with yellow lesser coverts and narrow white tips to greater coverts, forming 2 white wing bars along with white edging to the tertials. White inner webs to most of the tail feathers. Pink, conical bill. BREEDING FEMALE: Very different from male. Underparts very yellow with white undertail coverts, while upperparts, including head, olive green. Lower wing bar buffy and quite wide. Tail feathers with white tips and inner webs. Bill pinkish. WINTER MALE: Cinnamon brown above and on breast and flanks, with white lower belly and undertail coverts, yellowish wash on throat and face, and muted black on forehead. Wings more boldly patterned. Yellow lesser coverts. Wide, whitish lower wing bar. Bill darker than in breeding season. WINTER FEMALE: Mostly drab gray body with black wings and 2 bold buffy wing bars. White undertail coverts and edging to tail feathers. Dark bill. IMMATURE MALE: Black on forehead reduced or lacking. Lesser

coverts duller. JUVENILE: Resembles adult female. Unstreaked.

Similar Species The male is unlike any other finch in N.A; the Wilson's Warbler is the only other bright yellow species with a black cap, but it does not have the finchlike bill or the bold wing pattern of the American. All other plumages can be separated from the Lesser Goldfinch by their bolder wing pattern and white undertail coverts. The female Lawrence's Goldfinch is gray like a nonbreeding adult female American, but note the American's wider, buffier wing bars and different pattern of white in tail. The call notes of the American are very distinct from those of the Lesser and the Lawrence's.

Voice CALL: Various, including *per-chik-o-ree* or a descending *ti-di-di-di;* given mainly in flight. SONG: A long series of musical phrases, often repeated randomly; similar to the Lesser. Not known to mimic other species.

Status & Distribution Common throughout much of U.S. and southern Canada. BREEDING: A variety of habitats, from weedy fields to open second growth woodland, and along riparian corridors, particularly in the West. Does not breed over much of southern third of U.S. WINTER: Populations from northern third of breeding range migrate to southern U.S. and Mexico, augmenting resident populations throughout middle section of the U.S.

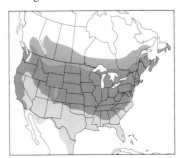

EURASIAN SISKIN *Carduelis spinus*

fall adult ♂

The habits of this Eurasian species are similar to the Pine Siskin. Monotypic. L 4.8" (12 cm)

Identification Shaped like a Pine Siskin, but looks like a cross between a siskin and a goldfinch. MALE: Fairly olive above and heavily streaked. Black forecrown and chin. Yellow throat and breast, blending to white on flanks and belly. Prominent black streaking on flanks. Olive auriculars surrounded by yellow. Two bold yellow wing bars; extensive yellow edging on flight feathers and at base of tail. Yellow rump. FEMALE: No black on crown or chin. Yellow on underparts restricted to sides of breast, wash on face, eyebrow, and rump. JUVE-NILE: Brown streaked above, whitish below, with heavy black streaking.
Similar Species Males unlike other carduelids in N.A. Female and especially juvenile very similar to female or juvenile Pine Siskin, but note blacker wing coverts on Eurasian.
Voice CALL: A 2-note whistled *ti-lu* or a short rattle.
Status & Distribution Eurasian species. Accidental in spring in outer Aleutians. Casual in northeast N.A., with records from ON, ME, MA, NJ, and off NF, but origin of these questioned.

PINE SISKIN *Carduelis pinus*

A widespread and conspicuous breeding species of coniferous forest across the boreal zone of Canada and northern United States, as well as in mountainous areas of the west, the Pine Siskin is an irregular and less predictable winter visitor virtually anywhere in the U.S. It forms large flocks during the nonbreeding season and is commonly attracted to seed feeders. Polytypic (3 ssp. in N.A. weakly differentiated by size, quality of streaking on underparts, and extent of yellow

in wing). Polytypic (nominate in N.A.). L 5" (13 cm)
Identification It is entirely brown and streaked and has prominent yellow in the wing, a short deeply notched tail, long wings, and a longish, pointed bill. MALE: Brown and streaked above, below whitish with coarse dark streaking. Two prominent wing bars, the lower one extensively yellow. Distinct yellow edging to flight feathers and tail, conspicuous in flight and on folded wing. Some males very yellowish with reduced streaking. FEMALE: Similar to male, but yellow in wings and tail greatly reduced. JUVENILE: Is quite buffy yellow, but fades by late summer.
Similar Species It is the only carduelid that is entirely brown and streaked. All of the *Carpodacus* finches are considerably larger with thicker bills and lack the yellow flash in the wing characteristic of siskins.
Voice CALL: Most commonly a buzzy, rising *zreeeeee*; also gives a harsh,

adult ♂

juvenile

adult ♂

descending *chee* in flight. SONG: A lengthy jumble of trills and whistles similar to that of the American Goldfinch, but more huskier.
Status & Distribution Common and gregarious. BREEDING: Found in coniferous forests of the north and mountainous west. WINTER: Range erratic from year to year, likely due to fluctuating food supply; can be found virtually anywhere. Often associates with goldfinches.

Genus *Pyrrhula*

EURASIAN BULLFINCH *Pyrrhula pyrrhula*

cassinii

♂

♀

The bright pink male of this striking Eurasian species is one of the more recognizable species to occur in North America. Sometimes occurs in small flocks. Polytypic (*cassinii* occurs in N.A.). L 6.5" (17 cm)
Identification A chunky finch with a very short, stubby bill. MALE: Intense reddish pink underparts and cheeks contrast with black crown and chin. Gray back contrasts with black wings (one prominent white wing bar) and tail and distinct white rump and undertail coverts. FEMALE: Similarly patterned, but brown where the male is pink. JUVENILE: Resembles female, but has a brown cap.
Similar Species No other North American bird has this color combination.
Voice CALL: A soft, piping *pheew.*
Status & Distribution Eurasian species. Casual in spring (late May–early June) to the outer Aleutians and St. Lawrence I. (Gambell). Casual in winter to AK mainland.

EVENING GROSBEAK AND HAWFINCH Genus *Coccothraustes*

Both species in this finch genus are large with very short tails, striking black-and-white wing patterns, and very large bills. The Evening Grosbeak breeds in North America, whereas the Hawfinch occurs as a vagrant from Asia. Both form flocks during the nonbreeding season that feed in fruiting trees.

EVENING GROSBEAK *Coccothraustes vespertinus*

breeding ♂

vespertinus

juvenile ♀

breeding ♂

This noisy finch is relatively secretive during the breeding season, yet forms large, gregarious flocks during the winter. It is found during summer mainly in coniferous forests across boreal Canada and in the Rocky Mountains; its winter movements are both erratic and irruptive, likely due to fluctuating food supply. Polytypic. L 8" (20 cm) **Identification** A large, stocky, boldly patterned finch with a very short tail and heavy bill. MALE: Uniquely patterned, the body is a rich golden brown, becoming darker brown on head and black on crown. Both the forehead and eyebrows are bright golden yellow. The tail and wings are black; the latter has contrasting pure white secondaries and tertials. The pale yellowish green bill is large for a finch. FEMALE: The body is grayish brown above, buffier on

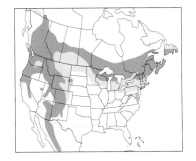

underparts, collar, and rump. The throat is almost whitish and has a distinctive dark malar stripe. Like the male, the wings are black, but the secondaries are not as pure white and have a dark edging, and a white base to the primaries forms a white patch visible in a folded wing. There are large white spots at the end of the tail. The wing and tail pattern are conspicuous in flight. JUVENILE: The male looks like an adult male, only the body is a duller uniform brown and the eyebrows are a dull yellow. The female looks like the adult female. **Geographic Variation** Three subspecies in N.A. The eastern *vespertinus* tend to have shorter bills and broader yellow eyebrows than the southwestern *montanus*. Western *brooksi* is also long

billed. Flight calls different. **Similar Species** Only the Hawfinch has a similar pattern. **Voice** CALL: Flight calls of eastern birds a ringing *clee-ip* or *peer;* western birds give a clear, whistled *tew,* similar to the Olive Warbler but louder. SONG: Seldom heard and poorly described. **Status & Distribution** BREEDING: Coniferous forest and mixed woods, mainly in mountains in the west. WINTER: Sometimes common at lower elevations and south of breeding range. Often seen in flocks at seed feeders. Rare to casual in southern states. VAGRANT: Casual in spring north to AK.

HAWFINCH *Coccothraustes coccothraustes*

breeding ♂

breeding ♂

This Eurasian species related to the Evening Grosbeak is a rare migrant to the outer Aleutians, and has been recorded from islands in the Bering Sea. Typically it is much more wary than the Evening Grosbeak, with many reports of fly-by individuals. It sometimes occurs in small groups, but it tends to be elusive. When on the ground, it walks with a parrotlike waddle. Polytypic (at least 5 ssp. across Europe and Asia; *japonicus* in N.A.). L 7" (18 cm) **Identification** A large, stocky, short-tailed finch with a massive bill. BREEDING MALE: The body is yellowish brown above and pinkish brown below, while the head is a more golden brown. The throat and lores are black; the nape and

collar are gray. The black wings have white secondaries and bases to the primaries that form a conspicuous white band on the folded wing and make a striking black-and-white pattern in flight. The tail feathers have broad white tips. Bill is blue-black in the spring and turns yellowish in the fall. FEMALE: Overall, she is duller than the male and has grayer wing patches. **Similar Species** No other finch looks like a Hawfinch, **Voice** CALL: A loud, explosive *ptik.* **Status & Distribution** A rare but regular spring migrant in the outer Aleutians (e.g., Attu), with a maximum annual count of 30+ in 1998. Elsewhere a casual spring visitor to western AK islands in Bering Sea.

OLD WORLD SPARROWS Family Passeridae

House Sparrows, female and male (IL, Oct.)

With about 34 species in 3 genera, Old World sparrows are widespread in Africa and the Palearctic. Two species have been successfully introduced to North America, with different results: The House Sparrow is ubiquitous to about 60° N, whereas the Eurasian Tree Sparrow is more restricted in range. Our 2 introduced species are found in small flocks in human-dominated landscapes.

Structure Old World sparrows are small, with medium to slender builds. Most species have short legs and short, thick bills. Proportions of the wings and tail are unremarkable in all species.

Behavior Most Old World sparrows are seen on or near the ground, where feeding typically occurs. Many species are gregarious, and some are abundant. Several passerid species have flourished in human-influenced environments, and many are tame and approachable.

Plumage Old World sparrows are mainly clad in browns, grays, and russets. In many species, there are marked differences between juveniles and adults, as well as between the sexes. Seasonal variation can be pronounced, too.

Distribution The genus *Passer* (to which both N.A. species belong) is the most speciose, the most widespread, and the most diverse in its habitat preferences. Two other genera, not introduced to North America, are more specialized: Widespread *Petronia* (rock sparrows) is restricted mainly to warm, arid climes; *Montifringilla* (snowfinches), centered around the Tibetan Plateau, occurs in barren habitats at high elevations.

Taxonomy Old World sparrows are not closely related to New World sparrows in the family Emberizidae. Instead, their closest alliance is with the family Ploceidae, in which they were formerly placed. Taxonomists differ in the division of species between the 2 families.

Conservation Especially in the genus *Passer,* many species enjoy commensal relationships with humans. The House Sparrow, however, long regarded as a textbook example of a beneficiary of human activity, is currently in sharp decline in parts of its native range. —*Ted Floyd*

Genus Passer

HOUSE SPARROW *Passer domesticus*

The cheery and sociable House Sparrow is more closely associated with humans than any other widely established North American exotic. Introduced to New York City in 1851, the species today flourishes in both large cities and remote agricultural outposts—just so long as there is some trace of human influence. It aggressively defends nest cavities, possibly to the detriment of native species. It is more gregarious in winter. Polytypic. L 6.3" (16 cm)

Identification Tame; gregarious. Flight more direct, often higher, than native sparrows. Bill thick, conical; legs short; stocky build. One molt per year, but seasonal variation pronounced. ADULT MALE: Worn (breeding) male con-

fall ♂

breeding ♂

♀

trastingly marked; throat and breast black, postoccipital and nuchal regions chestnut, wings russet. On a freshly molted bird, the blackish and reddish regions are obscured by gray feather tips. Bill black in summer; yellowish base to lower mandible in winter. ADULT FEMALE: Mainly gray-tan. Buffy eye stripe; gray-brown crown and auricu-

lars. Bill more yellowish than male's; tip, culmen are dusky. JUVENILE: Variable. Plain overall. Resembles adult female.

Geographic Variation The North American population (nominate ssp.)

exhibits extensive geographic variation, with clinal variation: larger birds with shorter appendages in colder climes, darker plumages in more-humid environments.

Similar Species Males distinctive; plainer females and juveniles present a combination of structural and plumage characters that separate them from native sparrows. Flight more resembles the House Finch than native sparrows. A female Orange Bishop may be passed off as female House Sparrow by observers unfamiliar with the former.

Voice All vocalizations simple. CALL: Varied, but 3 notes are prevalent: throaty *jigga*, usually given by agitated birds; soft *chirv*, often heard in flight; honest-to-goodness *chirp*, given in various settings. SONG: Short series of pleasant *chirp* notes.

Status & Distribution Locally abundant. YEAR-ROUND: Cities, farms, and other human-transformed environments. VAGRANT: Several recs. for western

Canada and AK, outside current range. **Population** Some Palearctic populations are in sharp decline, possibly due to changing land-use patterns.

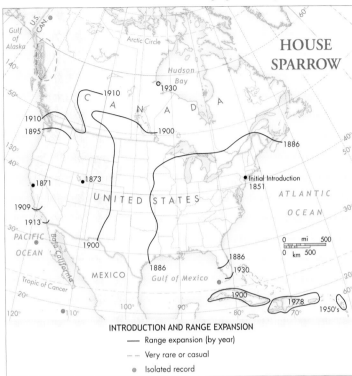

HOUSE SPARROW

INTRODUCTION AND RANGE EXPANSION
— Range expansion (by year)
-- Very rare or casual
• Isolated record

EURASIAN TREE SPARROW *Passer montanus*

Like the House Sparrow, the Eurasian Tree Sparrow was deliberately introduced to North America (St. Louis, 1870). Unlike the House Sparrow, its range has not expanded greatly. The 2 species differ substantially in details of sexual and seasonal plumage variation. Polytypic. L 5.9" (15 cm)

Identification Usually in small flocks. ADULT: One molt per year; seasonal variation weak. Sexes similar. Key mark is white cheek with large black spot. Crown and nape chestnut; neck collar white; throat black. Wings extensively russet; flanks suffused with pale rufous.

On worn plumage (spring, early summer), russet and chestnut regions browner, duller. JUVENILE: Resembles adult; buffier, duller overall; bill straw-yellow.

Geographic Variation None in North America. Our subspecies is nominate *montanus;* there are 8 other subspecies in the Old World.

Similar Species The white neck collar, black cheek spot, and chestnut-brown across entire crown separate a Eurasian Tree Sparrow from a House Sparrow. Size differences are minor, but overall impression is that the Eurasian Tree is a slighter, smaller bird than the House.

Voice Varied; all notes simple. CALL: Monosyllabic utterances, sharper and more metallic than the House Sparrow's, typically without the pleasing, liquid qualities: *chet, kip,* etc. SONG: Series of sharp monosyllabic notes, interspersed with more liquid, disyllabic notes.

juvenile

adult

Status & Distribution Locally common. Occupies an area of about 10,000 sq. mi., mainly in west-central IL. YEAR-ROUND: Near human habitation. VAGRANT: Generally northward. Out-of-range individuals difficult to establish as vagrants; some may be at vanguard of range expansion, others may be escapes. Presumed vagrants noted MN, WI, ON, MB. Presumed escapes or ship-assisted birds have been observed along West Coast.

Population The range in N.A. is expanding slowly, generally northward. Competition with the House Sparrow may be restricting the expansion, but there's little proof for this hypothesis.

WEAVERS Family Ploceidae

Orange Bishop, breeding male (AZ, July)

Known for their elaborate, suspended nests woven from grass and other plant fibers, the weavers are a large family of finchlike birds, primarily of the African tropics. Their colorful plumage makes them popular captives, resulting in naturalized populations in many regions of the world. **Structure** They are small to medium size with conical bills;

most have relatively short tails, short, rounded wings, and short but strong legs. Breeding male widowbirds *(Euplectes)* and whydahs *(Vidua)* grow stunning tails that are 3 to 4 times their body length.

Plumage Breeding males are brightly colored—red, orange, or yellow bodies, often with contrasting black faces or masks—in many species. Nonbreeding males resemble females, which resemble sparrows.

Behavior Many species are highly colonial, foraging and roosting in large flocks; some are colonial nesters. Weavers are largely sedentary, making only local or seasonal movements, but some species are migratory. They feed primarily on seeds and grain, although some species also take insects, fruit, or nectar.

Distribution They are found primarily in Africa, but some species are also in Eurasia, Australia, and Oceania.

Taxonomy Authorities vary on taxonomy (±118-124 sp. in ±16-17 genera in at least 4 subfamilies). The passerids and the estrildid finches are the ploceids' closest kin.

Conservation BirdLife International lists 1 species as critical, 6 as endangered, 7 as vulnerable, and 3 as near threatened. Some species are serious crop pests in their native ranges and are killed in large numbers; populations of others have been reduced by capture for the pet trade. —*Bill Pranty*

BISHOPS Genus *Euplectes*

This genus comprises 9 species known as bishops and 8 as widowbirds. Breeding male bishops are brightly colored with short tails, while breeding male widowbirds are less showy but grow spectacular tails that are shed after breeding. All species are endemic to Africa, but many occur elsewhere as a result of escaped or released captives.

ORANGE BISHOP *Euplectes franciscanus*

The Orange Bishop is the only weaver found in numbers in North America. Polytypic (2 ssp.; presumably nominate in N.A.). L 4" (10 cm)
Identification Small finches with stout bills and short tails that are often flicked open. BREEDING ADULT MALE: Orange upperparts with black crown and face. Black eyes and bill; pink legs and feet. Black wings and tail with brown feather edges. Black breast and belly; orange undertail coverts obscure undertail. FEMALE, IMMATURE, AND NONBREEDING MALE: Sparrowlike. Head buffy with pale supercilium, grayish brown auriculars, and streaked crown and nape. Black eyes prominent on pale face; pink bill, legs, and feet. Brown upperparts heavily streaked with black. Breast and sides of neck buffy with dark streaking. Remainder of underparts white or buffy with dark streaking. **Similar Species** The breeding male Red

Bishop *(E. orix)*, occasionally seen in N.A., is very similar but it has a black throat and chin. Females and nonbreeding males resemble sparrows (esp. the Grasshopper Sparrow), but note the stout, wholly pink bill, short tail, and pattern of black streaking on the upperparts.
Voice CALL: Includes a sharp *tsip* and a mechanical *tsik-tsik-tsk.* SONG: High-pitched and buzzy.
Status & Distribution Exotic in U.S. Native to sub-Saharan Africa. YEAR-ROUND: Nonmigratory. In southern CA (mostly Los Angeles and Orange Cos.), ±500 found in flood control basins and channeled rivers. About 15 birds found in Phoenix, AZ.
Population Declining in California due to unfavorable land management. The population in Phoenix has persisted since 1998 but remains quite small.

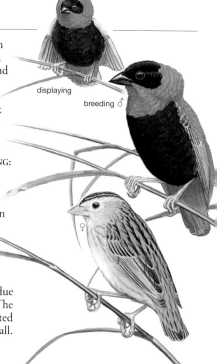

displaying

breeding ♂

♀

ESTRILDID FINCHES Family Estrildidae

Nutmeg Mannikin (CA, Feb.)

A large family (± 140 sp. in 28 genera), Estrildids are found in tropical regions of the Old World, primarily in the African tropics. They are typically open-country birds. Several species are common in aviculture, and some have established exotic populations in many regions of the world, including North America.

Structure They range from tiny to small, and have pointed tails, short, rounded wings, and proportionately large, conical bills.

Plumage Most estrildids are brightly colored, while most *Lonchura* are brown, black, or white. They exhibit no seasonal variation. The bill is often brightly colored, azure in many *Lonchura*. Some species show marked sexual dimorphism; in others, the sexes look similar.

Behavior Many species are highly colonial outside the breeding season, but most breed solitarily. Estrildids feed chiefly on the ground or in low vegetation, primarily on seeds and grain with some fruit or insects taken.

Distribution They are found in Africa, Asia, Australia, and on South Pacific islands.

Taxonomy The taxonomy is confusing and undergoing extensive revision as a result of DNA studies. Generally, there are 3 main groups: the waxbills of the African tropics; the grassfinches and allies of Australasia and the western Pacific; and the mannikins/munias and allies of Africa and Australasia. Estrildids are closely related to weavers (Ploceidae) and sparrows (Passeridae).

Conservation Most estrildids are common to abundant in their native ranges, however, BirdLife International does list 3 species as critical and 8 as vulnerable. —*Bill Pranty*

Genus *Lonchura*

The members (±41 sp.) of this genus are known by several names: mannikin (generally those from Africa or New Guinea), munia (generally those from Asia), silverbill, or sparrow. All are small, pointed-tailed granivorous finches, usually found in flocks. Many naturalized populations are found around the world, including 1 in North America.

NUTMEG MANNIKIN *Lonchura punctulata*

The Nutmeg Mannikin, the only munia found in numbers in N.A., is largely restricted to southern California, where flocks feed on grass seeds in weedy river channels and residential areas. It is known by several names, including Scaly-breasted Munia/Mannikin and Spice Finch/Bird. Polytypic (12–13 ssp.; apparently only nominate in N.A.). L 4.5" (11 cm)
Identification ADULT: Sexes similar. Rufous face and breast, remainder of head brown. Red eyes; black bill; gray legs and feet. Brown back and wings. Yellow-orange uppertail coverts and brown uppertail. Feathers on lower breast and flanks are white, bordered with black, giving underparts a scaly appearance. Remainder of underparts buff, with black chevrons on undertail coverts. JUVENILE: Upperparts wholly light brown. Auriculars and underparts peach, with paler throat and undertail coverts. Dark eyes; gray bill.

Similar Species A juvenile is indistinguishable from other *Lonchura* species that occur in North America, such as the Chestnut Munia *(L. atricapilla)* or Tricolored Munia *(L. malacca)*. Told from an immature bunting by smaller size and thinner tail.
Voice CALL: *Beee* or *ki-BEE,* repeated frequently. SONG: High pitched and quiet; nearly inaudible.
Status & Distribution Exotic in the U.S. Native from India to China and much of the Orient. Birds in CA from Indian subcontinent; provenance of birds in FL unknown. YEAR-ROUND: Nonmigratory, but movements of more than 20 miles noted in CA based on banding recoveries. In U.S., restricted to CA (thousands; primarily Los Angeles and Orange Cos., but locally in small numbers to San Francisco and to San Diego)

adult

juvenile

and FL (a few; Pensacola and Miami).
Population The population is increasing in California. It is not protected in the U.S. because it is an exotic.

ADDITIONAL READING

Bird books offer essential reference and guidance. Following is a short list of recommended sources, arranged by general interest and family. The National Geographic's *Field Guide to the Birds of North America,* 4th edition, is the essential, portable field guide for birders of every stripe. Tapes and CDs of bird songs and calls are available from a variety of commercial sources.

Nationwide status and distribution information is supplied quarterly by the journal *North American Birds,* published by the American Birding Association. Numerous state and regional guides (including breeding bird atlases) are available and are useful in detailing local status and distribution. To guide readers to the best local birding areas, site guides exist for all regions of the country. Popular birding magazines and ornithological journals round out the printed record.

Electronically, Web sites (and telephone hotlines) are the preferred source for keeping track of current sightings and rare bird information. Specialty Web sites exist for most groups of birds and most types of birding interest. As a starting point, we include a few of the main Internet portals below.

GENERAL

American Ornithologists' Union [AOU]. *Check-list of North American Birds,* 7th ed. AOU, 1998. Standard taxonomic authority for North American birds.

Cramp, Stanley, and K. E. L. Simmons, eds. *The Birds of the Western Palearctic,* Volumes 1-9. Oxford University Press, 1977-1994. Standard reference to European birds; updated version available as CD-ROM.

del Hoyo, Josep, Andrew Elliot, Jordi Sargatal, and David Christie, eds. *Handbook of the Birds of the World.* Volumes 1-10. Lynx Ediciones, 1992-2005. Comprehensive treatment of all bird species, five additional volumes planned.

Dickinson, Edward C. *The Howard and Moore Complete Checklist of the Birds of the World,* 3rd ed. Princeton, 2003. Up-to-date checklist with subspecies and ranges.

Elphick, Chris, John B. Dunning, Jr., and David Allen Sibley. *The Sibley Guide to Bird Life and Behavior.* Alfred A. Knopf, 2001. North American bird families.

Howell, Steve N. G., and Sophie Webb. *A Guide to the Birds of Mexico and Northern Central America.* Oxford University Press, 1995. Most complete guide to Mexican birds.

Mullarney, Killian, Lars Svensson, Dan Zetterström, and Peter J. Grant. *The Complete Guide to the Birds of Europe.* Princeton University Press, 2000. Exceptional field guide to European birds.

Poole, A., and F. Gill, eds. *The Birds of North America.* The Academy of Natural Sciences and The American Ornithologists' Union, 1992-2002. Accounts of all North American breeding birds, including Hawaii. Published individually by species; available online (access fee).

Pyle, Peter, with Steve N.G. Howell, David F. DeSante, Robert P. Yunick, and Mary Gustafson, *Identification Guide to North American Birds, Part I.* Slate Creek Press, 1997. In-depth, banders' guide to North American passerines and near-passerines; extensive treatment of subspecies and molt.

Raffaele, Herbert, et al. *A Guide to the Birds of the West Indies.* Princeton, 1998. Up-to-date field guide to the region.

WEB SITES

American Birding Association. http://americanbirding.org/
American Bird Conservancy. http://www.abcbirds.org/
Birding on the Net. http://www.birdingonthe.net/index.html
Birds of North America. http://bna.birds.cornell.edu/BNA/
Cornell Laboratory of Ornithology. http://birds.cornell.edu/
Frontiers of Identification. http://www.birdingonthe.net/mailinglists/FRID.html
Handbook of the Birds of theWorld.

http://www.hbw.com/index.html

DUCKS, GEESE, AND SWANS

Bellrose, Frank C. *Ducks, Geese and Swans of North America.* Stackpole Books, 1976.

Blomdahl, Anders, Bertil Breife, and Niklas Holmstrom. *Flight Identification of European Seabirds.* Christopher Helm, 2003.

Madge, Steve, and Hillary Burn. *Waterfowl: An Identification Guide to the Ducks, Geese, and Swans of the World.* Houghton Mifflin Co., 1988.

Ogilvie, Malcolm, and Steve Young. *Photographic Handbook of the Wildfowl of the World.* New Holland, 1998.

CURASSOWS AND GUANS

Delacour, Jean, and Dean Amadon. *Curassows and Related Birds.* Lynx Ediciones, 2004.

PARTRIDGES, GROUSE, AND TURKEYS / NEW WORLD QUAIL

Johnsgard, Paul A. *Grassland Grouse and Their Conservation.* Smithsonian Books, 2002.

Madge, Steve, and Phil McGowan. *Pheasants, Partridges, & Grouse.* Princeton University Press, 2002.

GREBES

Ogilvie, Malcolm, and Chris Rose. *Grebes of the World.* Bruce Coleman, 2002.

Konter, André. *Grebes of Our World: Visiting All Species on Five Continents.* Lynx Ediciones, 2001.

ALBATROSSES / SHEARWATERS AND PETRELS / STORM-PETRELS

Brooke, Michael. *Albatrosses and Petrels of the World.* Oxford University Press, 2004.

Enticott, Jim, and David Tipling. *Seabirds of the World.* Stackpole, 1997.

Harrison, Peter. *Seabirds: An Identification Guide.* Houghton Mifflin Co., 1983.

Stallcup, Rich. *Ocean Birds of the Nearshore Pacific.* Point Reyes Bird Observatory, 1990.

Tickell, W. L. N. *Albatrosses.* Yale University Press, 2000.

Warham, John. *The Petrels: The Behavior, Population Biology and Physiology of the Petrels.* Academic Press, 1996.

BOOBIES AND GANNETS

Nelson, J. Bryan. *The Sulidae: Gannets and Boobies.* Oxford University Press, 1978.

PELICANS / CORMORANTS / DARTERS

Johnsgard, Paul A. *Cormorants, Darters, and Pelicans of the World.* Smithsonian Institution Press, 1993.

BITTERNS, HERONS, AND ALLIES

Hancock, James, and James Kushlan. *The Herons Handbook.* Harper & Row, 1984.

HAWKS, KITES, EAGLES, AND ALLIES

Dunne, Pete, et al. *Hawks in Flight.* Houghton Mifflin Co., 1988.

Wheeler, Brian K. *Raptors of Eastern North America.* Princeton University Press, 2003.

Wheeler, Brian K. *Raptors of Western North America.* Princeton University Press, 2003.

Wheeler, Brian K., and William S. Clark. *A Photographic Guide to North American Raptors.* Academic Press, 1995.

RAILS, GALLINULES AND COOTS

Ripley, S. Dillon. *Rails of the World.* Godine, 1977.

Taylor, Barry. *Rails: A Guide to the Rails, Crakes, Gallinules and Coots of the World.* Yale University Press, 1998.

THICK-KNEES / LAPWINGS AND PLOVERS / OYSTERCATCHERS / STILTS AND AVOCETS / JACANAS / SANDPIPERS, PHALAROPES, AND ALLIES / PRATINCOLES

Hayman, Peter, John Marchant, and Tony Prater. *Shorebirds:*

ADDITIONAL READING

An Identification Guide to the Waders of the World. Croom Helm Ltd., 1986.

Paulson, Dennis. *Shorebirds of North America: The Photographic Guide.* Princeton University Press, 2005.

Paulson, Dennis. *Shorebirds of the Pacific Northwest.* University of British Columbia Press, 1993.

Rosair, David, and David Cottridge. *Photographic Guide to the Shorebirds of the World.* Facts on File, 1995.

SKUAS, GULLS, TERNS, AND SKIMMERS /
AUKS, MURRES, AND PUFFINS

Gaston, Anthony J., and Ian L. Jones. *The Auks.* Oxford University Press, 1998.

Grant, P. J. *Gulls: A Guide to Identification,* 2nd ed. Buteo Books, 1986.

Olsen, Klaus Malling, and Hans Larsson. *Terns of Europe and North America.* Princeton University Press, 1995.

Olsen, Klaus Malling, and Hans Larsson. *Gulls of North America, Europe and Asia.* Princeton University Press, 2004.

PIGEONS AND DOVES

Gibbs, David, Eustance Barnes, and John Cox. *Pigeons and Doves.* Yale University Press, 2001.

PARAKEETS, MACAWS, AND PARROTS

Juniper, Tony, and Mike Parr. *Parrots: A Guide to Parrots of the World.* Yale University Press, 1988.

CUCKOOS, ROADRUNNERS, AND ANIS

Payne, Robert B. *The Cuckoos.* Oxford University Press, 2005.

OWLS

Duncan, James R. *Owls of the World: Their Lives, Behavior and Survival.* Firefly Books, 2003.

Johnsgard, Paul A. *North American Owls: Biology and Natural History.* Smithsonian Books, 2002.

Karalus, Karl E., and Allan W. Eckert. *The Owls of North America (North of Mexico).* Doubleday & Company, Inc., 1974.

König, Claus, Friedhelm Weick, and Jan-Hendrik Becking. *Owls: A Guide to the Owls of the World.* Yale University Press, 1999.

Voous, Karel H. *Owls of the Northern Hemisphere.* The MIT Press, 1988.

NIGHTHAWKS AND NIGHTJARS

Cleere, Nigel. *Nightjars: A Guide to the Nightjars, Nighthawks and Their Relatives.* Yale University Press, 1998.

Holyoak, David. *Nightjars and Their Allies.* Oxford University Press, 2001.

SWIFTS

Chantler, Phil, and Gerald Driessens. *Swifts: A Guide to the Swifts and Treeswifts of the World,* 2nd ed. Yale University Press, 2000.

HUMMINGBIRDS

Howell, Steve N. G. *Hummingbirds of North America: The Photographic Guide.* Academic Press, 2002.

Williamson, Sheri L. *Hummingbirds of North America.* Houghton Mifflin Co., 2001.

KINGFISHERS

Fry, C. Hilary, Kathie Fry, and Alan Harris. *Kingfishers, Bee-eaters and Rollers.* Princeton University Press, 1992.

WOODPECKERS AND ALLIES

Short, Lester L. *Woodpeckers of the World.* Delaware Museum of Natural History, 1982.

Winkler, Hans, David A. Christie, and David Nurney. *Woodpeckers: A Guide to the Woodpeckers of the World.* Houghton Mifflin Co., 1995.

SHRIKES

Harris, Tony. *Shrikes and Bush-Shrikes.* Princeton University Press, 2000.

Lefranc, Norbert. *Shrikes: A Guide to the Shrikes of the World.* Yale University Press, 1997.

JAYS AND CROWS

Madge, Steve, and Hilary Burn. *Crows & Jays.* Princeton University Press, 1994.

SWALLOWS

Turner, Angela, and Chris Rose. *Swallows & Martins: An Identification Guide and Handbook.* Houghton Mifflin Co., 1989.

CHICKADEES AND TITMICE / PENDULINE TITS AND VERDINS
LONG-TAILED TITS AND BUSHTITS / NUTHATCHES /
CREEPERS

Harrap, Simon, and David Quinn. *Chickadees, Tits, Nuthatches & Treecreepers.* Princeton University Press, 1996.

Smith, Susan M. *The Black-capped Chickadee: Behavioral Ecology and Natural History.* Cornell University Press, 1991.

WRENS / DIPPERS / MOCKINGBIRDS AND THRASHERS

Brewer, David. *Wrens, Dippers, and Thrashers.* Yale University Press, 2001.

THRUSHES

Clement, Peter. *Thrushes.* Princeton University Press, 2000.

STARLINGS

Feare, Chris, and Adrian Craig. *Starlings and Mynas.* Princeton University Press, 1999.

WAGTAILS AND PIPITS

Alström, Per, and Krister Mild. *Pipits and Wagtails of Europe, Asia and North America.* Princeton University Press, 2003.

WOOD-WARBLERS

Curson, Jon, David Quinn, and David Beadle. *Warblers of the Americas: An Identification Guide.* Houghton Mifflin Co., 1994.

Dunn, Jon L., and Kimball L.Garrett. *A Field Guide to Warblers of North America.* Houghton Mifflin Co., 1997.

Mayfield, H. F. *The Kirtland's Warbler.* Cranbrook Institute of Science, 1960.

TANAGERS

Isler, Morton L., and Phyllis R. Isler. *The Tanagers.* AC Black, 1999.

EMBERIZIDS

Byers, Clive, Jon Curson, and Urban Olsson. *Sparrows and Buntings: A Guide to Sparrows and Buntings of North America and the World.* Houghton Mifflin Co., 1995.

Rising, James, and David Beadle. *A Guide to the Identification and Natural History of the Sparrows of the United States and Canada.* Academic Press, 1996.

Rising, James, and David Beadle. *Sparrows of the United States and Canada: The Photographic Guide.* Academic Press, 2002.

Zimmer, Kevin J. *Birding in the American West.* Cornell University Press, 2000.

BLACKBIRDS

Jaramillo, Alvaro, and Peter Burke. *New World Blackbirds: The Icterids.* Princeton University Press, 1999.

FRINGILLINE AND CARDUELINE FINCHES /
OLD WORLD SPARROWS

Clement, Peter. *Finches and Sparrows: An Identification Guide.* Princeton University Press, 1993.

ILLUSTRATIONS CREDITS

Jonathan Alderfer: pages 32-eider heads, 33-Labrador Duck, 46-Greater Sage-Grouse displaying, 47-Gunnison Sage-Grouse, 52-Sharp-tailed Grouse displaying, 65 grebe heads, 67-70, 73, 77-Hawaiian Petrel, 78-Bulwer's Petrel, 80, 81-except right two Greater Shearwaters, 82-left bird and head of Short-tailed Shearwater, 83-head, 84, 85-except upper two Manx Shearwater, 89-Black-bellied Storm-Petrel, 97-Blue-footed Booby, 98-100, 105-7, 178, 180, 207-Marbled Godwit, except in flight, 208, 209-Hudsonian Godwit, 211-Black Turnstone in flight, 223-Stilt Sandpiper, except in flight, 226-9, 230-American Woodcock, 281-in flight winter Dovekie, 283-Great Auk, 286-Long-billed Murrelet, 290-Parakeet Auklet, 291-2, 293-Crested Auklet and Rinoceros Auklet in flight, 299-Oriental Turtle-Dove (with Schmitt), 300-302 (with Schmitt), 303-Passenger Pigeon, 303-Mourning Dove (with Schmitt), 309-Carolina Parakeet, 381-Tufted Flycatcher , 398-Social Flycatcher, 400-1, 402-except 1st fall and worn summer adult Thick-billed Kingbird, 405, 435-Mangrove Swallow, 471-Blue-Gray Gnatcatcher female tailfeathers, 502, 504-Common Myna, 515-Gray Silky-flycatcher. **David Beadle:** pages 74-Great-winged Petrel, 168-except Purple Swamphen, 175, 297-Scaly-naped Pigeon, 340-Gray Nightjar, 346-Antillean Palm-Swift, 356-Bumblebee Hummingbird, 380, 385-91, 414, 416-Yucatan Vireo, 434, 461-Winter Wren western *pacificus,* 484-except Veery, 523-Crescent-chested Warbler, 538-fall male Bay-breasted Warbler, 550-Red-faced Warbler, 572-Worthen's Sparrow, 609-Tawny-shouldered Blackbird. **Peter Burke:** pages 112-American Bittern, 120-1, 123-Glossy Ibis, except in flight, 124, 384, 395-7, 398-Piratic Flycatcher, 399-Variegated Flycatcher, 408, 410-Gray Vireo, 491-White-throated Robin, 548-Gray-crowned Yellowthroat, 552-3, 556-8, 561-adult White-collared Seedeater and Yellow-faced Grassquit, 562-5, 598-Crimson-collared Grosbeak, 618-Shiny Cowbird, 620-5. **Mark R. Hanson:** pages 72, 75-Mottled Petrel, 77-Cook's Petrel, 78-Stejneger's Petrel, 79, 81-right Greater Shearwater, 82-except left bird head of Short-tailed Shearwater, 83-birds in flight, 85-upper two Manx Shearwater, 86, 88-Wilson's Storm-Petrel, 89-White-faced Storm-Petrel, 90-93, 163-171. **Cynthia J. House:** pages 3-5, 6-Snow Goose, 7-13, 14-except immature Whooper Swan, 15-except flying Muscovy Duck, 16-17, 18-except female head American Black Duck, 19-31, 32-except eider heads, 34-41, 42-except Egyptian Goose. **H. Jon Janosik:** pages 62-4, 65-breeding birds, 94-5, 97-Northern Gannet, 101-4, 108, 109-Magnificent Frigatebird, 189, 191-92. **Donald L. Malick:** pages 127-8, 131-except adult Osprey in flight, 132-Bald Eagle, except third year, 133-White-tailed Eagle, 134, 135-Mississippi Kite, 136-Swallow-tailed Kite, 137-9 except birds in flight, 141-Harris's Hawk perched, 142- Zone-tailed Hawk perched, 145- Short-tailed Hawk perched, 146, 148-9, 151, 154-Crested Caracara, 155-except flying adult American Kestrel, 156- Eurasian Kestrel perched, 157-Merlin perched, 158-Aplomado Falcon perched, 159-61, 304-6, 320, 322-Flammulated Owl, 323-8, 329-Burrowing Owl, 330-1, 332-Long-eared Owl, 333-4, 361-2, 364-74, 375-Black-backed Woodpecker,

376-8. **Killian Mullarney:** pages 177, 181-Lesser Sand-Plover not in flight, 186-except Killdeer in flight, 187, 202-Upland Sandpiper, 220-except birds in flight, 224-Ruff, except in flight, 225-Buff-breasted Sandpiper, except in flight, 231-2. **Michael O'Brien:** pages 74-except Great-winged Petrel, 75-Fea's Petrel, 76. **John P. O'Neill:** pages 359, 360-Eared Quetzal, 430-1, 442-50, 494. **Kent Pendleton:** pages 44, 45-except Chukar, 46-except Greater Sage-Grouse displaying, 47-Ruffed Grouse, 48-51, 52-except Sharp-tailed Grouse displaying, 53-7, 131-adult Osprey in flight, 133-Golden Eagle, 135-except Mississippi Kite, 136-Snail Kite, 152-Northern Harrier. **Diane Pierce:** pages 111, 112-Great Egret, 113, 115-Snowy Egret, 116-8, 119-Green Heron, 122, 123-Glossy Ibis in flight and White Ibis, 125-6, 129, 173-4, 381-Olive-sided Flycatcher, 566-71, 572-Brewer's Sparrow, 573, 574-Lark Sparrow, 575-7, 578-Grasshopper Sparrow, 579, 581-7, 588-9 except Dark-Eyed Junco in flight, 590-92, 593-Chestnut-collared Longspur, 594, 595-Pallas's Bunting and Reed Bunting, 596, 598-Northern Cardinal, 599-606, 627-39, 640-except Eurasian Siskin, 641. **John C. Pitcher:** pages 182-Snowy Plover, 183-5 except birds in flight, 194-except birds in flight, 196-Spotted Redshank, 197-Wood Sandpiper, 198-9 except birds in flight, 200-1, 202-Terek Sandpiper, 210, 211-Surfbird, 214-Semipalmated Sandpiper, 215-Western Sandpiper not in flight, 216, 217-except Temminck's Stint, 218-9 except birds in flight, 221 except birds in flight, 223-Spoonbilled Sandpiper, 224-Broad-billed Sandpiper. **H. Douglas Pratt:** pages 297-Rock Pigeon, 298, 299-Band-tailed Pigeon, 315-9, 348-except immature Green Violet-ear, 349-Broad-billed Hummingbird, 350-except Xantus's Hummingbird, 351-Buff-bellied Hummingbird, 352, 353-except Lucifer Hummingbird, 354-except Black-chinned Hummingbird wing feathers, 355, 356-Calliope Hummingbird, 357-8, 381-Olive-sided Flycatcher side view, 382-3, 392-3, 398-Great Kiskadee, 399-Sulphur-bellied Flycatcher, 402-Thick-billed Kingbird 1st fall and worn summer adult, 403-4, 407, 409, 410-Black-capped Vireo, 411-3, 415, 416-Yellow-green Vireo, 418-20, 421-Florida Scrub-Jay, 422, 423-Mexican Jay juvenile head, Pinyon Jay, 424-9, 433, 435-Tree Swallow ,436-9, 440-Barn Swallow, 452-60, 461-except Winter Wren western *pacificus,* 462-6, 468-Middendorff's Grasshopper-Warbler, 469-Dusky Warbler, 470-Arctic Warbler, 471-Blue-gray Gnatcatcher, except female tail feathers, 472, 480-Eastern Bluebird, 482-3, 489-except Eurasian Blackbird , 491-except White-throated Robin, 492-3, 496, 497-Bahama Mockingbird, 498, 503, 504-except Common Myna, 507, 408-White Wagtail, 510-Red-throated Pipit, Sprague's Pipit tail-feathers, 511-3, 515-Phainopepla, 516, 518-22, 523-Lucy's Warbler, 524-5, 527-37, 538-except fall male Bay-breasted Warbler, 539-45, 548-Common Yellowthroat, 549, 550-Wilson's Warbler, 551, 554, 561-White-collared Seedeater, Black-faced Grassquit, 609-Red-winged Blackbird, 610-11, 614-7, 618-Bronzed Cowbird, 619. **David Quinn:** pages 6-Lesser White-fronted Goose, 58-61, 88-European Storm-Petrel, 114, 115-Western Reef-Heron, 119-Chinese Pond-Heron, 168-Purple Swamphen, 181-Greater Sand-Plover, 182-

PHOTOGRAPHY CREDITS

Collared Plover, 188, 190, 196-Marsh Sandpiper, 197-Common Redshank, 206-Slender-billed Curlew,230-Eurasian Woodcock, 233, 243-Gray-hooded Gull, 276-Whiskered Tern, 351-Cinnamon Hummingbird, 360-Eurasian Hoopoe, 363, 375-Great Spotted Woodpecker, 406, 440-Common House-Martin, 468-Lanceolated Warbler, 469-except Dusky Warbler, 470-except Arctic Warbler, 473-9, 480-Northern Wheatear, 489-Eurasian Blackbird, 490, 505, 508-Citrine Wagtail, 509, 510-Pechora Pipit, Sprague's Pipit, 593-Pine Bunting, 595-Yellow-breasted Bunting and Yellow-throated Bunting, 640-Eurasian Siskin. **Chuck Ripper:** pages 281-except in flight winter Dovekie, 282, 283-Thick-billed Murre, 284-5, 286-Marbled Murrelet, 287-89, 290-Cassin's Auklet, 293-Rinoceros Auklet not in flight, 294-5, 336-9, 340-Whip-poor-will, excluding lower tail feathers. **N. John Schmitt:** pages 14-immature Whooper Swan, 15-flying Muscovy Duck, 18-female head American Black Duck, 42-Egyptian Goose, 43, 45-Chukar, 132-Steller's Sea-Eagle and third year Bald Eagle, 136-9 birds in flight, 140, 141-birds in flight, 142-Zone-tailed Hawk in flight, 143-4, 145-except perched Short-tailed Hawk, 147, 150, 155-adult flying American Kestrel, 156-except perched Eurasian Kestrel, 157-except perched Merlin, 158-Aplomado Falcon in flight, 203-Little Curlew, 205-adult Bristle-thighed Curlew, 207-adult Eurasian Curlew, 299-Oriental Turtle-Dove (with Alderfer), 300-302 (with Alderfer), 303-Mourning Dove (with Alderfer), 308, 309-except Carolina Parakeet, 310-13, 342-5, 346-White-throated Swift, 421-Island Scrub-Jay, 423-Mexican Jay, 497-Sage Thrasher, 499-501, 574-Vesper Sparrow, 578-Le Conte's Sparrow, 580, 588-Dark-eyed Junco in flight, 642-5. **Thomas R. Schultz:** pages 109-except Magnificent Frigatebird, 142-Roadside Hawk, 152-Crane Hawk, 154-Collared Forest-Falcon, 158-Red-footed Falcon, 213-except Red Knot in flight, 214-Sanderling not in flight, 222-except birds in flight, 235-42, 243-Bonaparte's Gull, 244-8, 250-75, 276- White-winged Tern, 277-9, 322-Oriental Scops-Owl, 329-Mottled Owl, 332-Stygian Owl, 484-Veery, 485-8, 526-Yellow Warbler, 546-7, 559, 608, 612-3. **David S. Smith:** pages 181-Lesser Sand-Plover in flight, 182-6 birds in flight, 194-9 birds in flight, 202-Upland Sandpiper in flight, 203-Eskimo Curlew, 204, 205-except adult Bristle-thighed Curlew, 206-Long-billed Curlew, 207-birds in flight, 209-Bar-tailed Godwit in flight, 213-birds in flight, 217-Temminck's Stint not in flight, 218-25 birds in flight. **Sophie Webb:** pages 340-Whip-poor-will lower tail-feathers, 348-immature Green Violet-ear, 349-Green-breasted Mango, 350-Xantus's Hummingbird, 353-Lucifer Hummingbird, 354-Black-chinned Hummingbird wing feathers.

PHOTOGRAPHY CREDITS
Abbreviations: t-top, b-bottom, c-center, l-left, r-right.
2, Richard Crossley; 5, Michael S. Peters; 10, Kevin Karlson; 13 (l-r) Rob Curtis, Bob Steele, Tom Vezo; 21 (t) Brian Small, (b) Larry Sansone; 28, Larry Sansone; 29, Brian Small; 43, S. Holt/VIREO; 44, Richard Day/Daybreak Imagery; 54, Tom Vezo; 58, Kevin Karlson; 62, Tom Vezo; 66, 71, Mike Danzenbaker; 79 (both) George L. Armistead; 83 (t) Larry Sansone, (b) Mike Danzenbaker; 87, M. Hale/VIREO; 93, Tom Ulrich; 96, P. Robles Gil/ VIREO; 100, Larry Sansone; 102, Richard Crossley, 104 (t) Kevin Karlson, (b) Make Danzenbaker; 107, Kevin Karlson; 108, K. Schafer/VIREO; 110, 121, 125, Kevin Karlson; 126, Doug Wechsler/VIREO; 128, Kevin Karlson; 130, Tom Vezo; 138, Kevin Karlson; 139, Larry Sansone; 148 (both) Brian K. Wheeler; 149 (both) Brian K. Wheeler; 153, Richard Crossley; 162, Tom Vezo; 166 (t) Brian Small, (b) Rob Curtis; 171, J. Schumacher/ VIREO; 172, Tom Vezo; 175, R. & N. Bowers/VIREO; 176, Tom Vezo; 177 (t) Richard Crossley, (b) Mike Danzenbaker; 184, Richard Crossley; 185, Richard Crossley; 188, Tom Vezo; 190, Maslowski Photos; 192, K. Schafer/VIREO; 193, Richard Crossely; 199 (l) Tom Vezo, (r) Brian Small; 212 (l) Richard Crossley, (r) Larry Sansone; 215 (both) Richard Crossley; 233, Mike Daznebaker; 234, Richard Crossley; 238, Ran Schols; 239 Brian Small; 249, Richard Crossley, (t) Richard Crossley, (b); 251 (t) Larry Sansone, (b) Mike Danzenbaker; 268 (t) Brian Small, (b) Monte Taylor; 280, Art Wolfe; 296, Maslowski Photos; 307, Rob Curtis; 314, Tom Ulrich; 320, Taxi/Getty Image; 321, Brian Small; 327 (both) Brian Small; 333 (t) Jeff Nadler, (b) Steve Metz; 335, S. Holt/VIREO; 341, Alan G. Nelson/Animals Animals; 347, Brian Small; 348 (both) Brian Small; 359, R. & N. Bowers/VIREO; 360, H. & J. Eriksen/VIREO; 361, Brian Small; 363, J. Schumacher/VIREO; 379, Rob Curtis; 384 (all) Brian Small; 394 (all) Brian Small; 406, Maslowski Photo; 408, Richard Day/Daybreak Imagery; 412 (both) Brian Small; 417, Brian Small; 430, Brian Small; 432, Mike Danzenbaker; 438 (l) Mike Danzenbaker, (r) Richard Crossley; 441, Maslowski Photos; 443 (both) Kevin Karlson; 449, B. Steele/VIREO; 450, B. Steele/VIREO; 451, Maslowski Photos; 455, Maslowski Photos; 456, Brian Small; 463, Alan Fuchs; 464, M. Hale/VIREO; 465, Kevin Karlson; 466 (t) Brian Small, (b) Richard Crossley ; 467, Mike Danzenbaker; 473, M. Strange/VIREO; 477, Maslowski Photo; 481 (l-r) J. Culbertson/VIREO, Bob Steele, Brian Small; 494, B. Steele/VIREO; 495, Tom Vezo; 502, Richard Day/Daybreak Imagery; 505, Larry Sansone; 506, Maslowski Photos; 512, Brian Small; 514, Maslowski Photos; 516, R. & N. Bowers/VIREO; 517, Richard Crossley; 520 (l-r) Brian Small, Brian Small, B. Schorre/VIREO; 528, Larry Sansone; 538 (t) Giff Beaton, (b) Tom Vezo; 544 (t) Kevin Karlson, (b) Brian Small; 554, Kevin Karlson; 555, Kevin Karlson; 560, Brian Small; 566, Brian Small; 575 (both) Brian Small; 591 (l) Larry Sansone, (c-l) Brian Small, (c-r) Brian Small (r) Larry Sansone; 597, J. Cancalosi/VIREO; 601, Brian Small; 605 (all) Brian Small; 607, Mike Danzenbaker; 611 (l-r) Brian Small, Tom Vezo, Bob Steele; 617 (l) Brian Small, (r) Kevin Karlson; 624, Kevin Karlson; 625, Brian Small; 626, Bob Steele; 633 (l-r) Kevin Karlson, Brian Small, Brian Small; 637 (both) G. McElroy/ VIREO; 642, Rob Curtis; 644, Tom Gatz; 645, Kimball Garrett.

INDEX

INDEX

INDEX

INDEX

INDEX

INDEX

INDEX

INDEX

INDEX

INDEX

INDEX

INDEX

INDEX

INDEX

COMPLETE BIRDS OF NORTH AMERICA
Edited by Jonathan Alderfer

PUBLISHED BY THE NATIONAL GEOGRAPHIC SOCIETY

John M. Fahey, Jr.	*President and Chief Executive Officer*
Gilbert M. Grosvenor	Chairman of the Board
Nina D. Hoffman	*Executive Vice President*

PREPARED BY THE BOOK DIVISION

Kevin Mulroy	*Senior Vice President and Publisher*
Kristin B. Hanneman	*Illustrations Director*
Marianne R. Koszorus	*Design Director*
Carl Mehler	*Director of Maps*
Barbara Brownell Grogan	*Executive Editor*

STAFF FOR THIS BOOK

Barbara Levitt	*Editor*
Jon L. Dunn	*Associate Editor*
Jane Sunderland	*Lead Text Editor*
Toni Eugene, Jennifer Seidel	*Text Editors*
Kate Griffin	*Illustrations Editor*
Megan McCarthy	*Art Director*
Carol Farrar Norton	*Bird Program Art Director*
Paul Lehman	*Chief Map Researcher/Editor*
Matt Chwastyk	*Chief of Map Production*
Sven M. Dolling Greg Ugiansky	*Map Research and Production*
Daniel O'Toole	*Contributing Writer*
Gary Colbert	*Production Director*
Rick Wain	*Production Project Manager*
Teresa Neva Tate	*Illustrations Specialist*
Francis Koszorus Lauren Pruneski	*Editorial Assistants*

MANUFACTURING AND QUALITY CONTROL

Christopher A. Liedel	*Chief Financial Officer*
Phillip L. Schlosser	*Managing Director*
John T. Dunn	*Technical Director*
Vincent P. Ryan	*Manager*
Clifton M. Brown	*Manager*

Founded in 1888, the National Geographic Society is one of the largest nonprofit scientific and educational organizations in the world. It reaches more than 285 million people worldwide each month through its official journal, NATIONAL GEOGRAPHIC, and its four other magazines; the National Geographic Channel; television documentaries; radio programs; films; books; videos and DVDs; maps; and interactive media. National Geographic has funded more than 8,000 scientific research projects and supports an education program combating geographic illiteracy.

For more information, please call 1-800-NGS LINE (647-5463) or write to the following address:

National Geographic Society
1145 17th Street, N.W.
Washington, D.C. 20036-4688 U.S.A.

Log on to nationalgeographic.com;
AOL Keyword: NatGeo.

Library of Congress Cataloging-in-Publication Information available upon request.

ISBN Regular: 0-7922-4175-4
Deluxe: 0-7922-4482-6
Mail: 0-7922-4239-4

SPECIAL CONTRIBUTORS
Art: John Anderton, Britt Griswold

Birding Consultants: Paul Lehman, Paul Hess, Matthew T. Heindel

Editing: Suzanne Crawford, Lee Hassig, Karen Kinney, Judy Klein, Rebecca Lescaze, Mary BethOelkers-Keegan

Layout: Sanaa Akkach, Robert Rose

ACKNOWLEDGMENTS

The editors wish to thank the following individuals and institutions for their valuable assistance in the preparation of this volume.

George Armistead, Philadelphia, PA; Louis R. Bevier, Fairfield, ME; Edward S. Brinkley, Cape Charles, VA; Jamie Cameron, Stella, NC; Richard A. Erickson, Irvine, CA; Tom Gatz, Phoenix, AZ; Daniel D. Gibson, Fairbanks, AK; Shawneen Finnegan, Tucson, AZ; Nancy Gobris, Estes Park, CO; Robert A. Hamilton, Long Beach, CA; Floyd Hayes, Hidden Valley Lake, CA; Tom and Jo Heindel, Big Pine, CA; Greg Lasley, Austin, TX; Paul Lehman, Cape May, NJ; Bruce Mactavish, St. John's, NL; Curtis Marantz, Ithaca, NY; Ian A. McLaren, Halifax, NS; Steven Mlodinow, Everett WA; Michael O'Brien, Cape May, NJ; Michael A. Patten, Bartlesville, OK; J. Brian Patteson, Hatteras, NC; Grayson Pearce, Chesapeake, VA; Peter Pyle, Bolinas, CA; Van Remsen, Baton Rouge, LA; Bill Schmoker, Longmont, CO; Willie Sekula, San Anto- nio, TX; Larry Semo, Westminster, CO; Debra Shearwater, Hollister, CA; Douglas Stotz, Chicago, IL; Giles Timms, Vermillion, SD; Bill Tweit, Olympia, WA; Phil Unitt, San Diego, CA; Nick Ward, Vermillion, SD; Angus Wilson, New York, NY; Sherrie York, Salida, CO; Archbold Biological Station, Venus, FL; Burke Museum, University of Washington, Seattle; Cornell Laboratory of Ornithology, Ithaca, NY; Field Museum of Natural History, Chicago, IL; Museum of Natural Science, Louisiana State University, Baton Rouge; Museum of Vertebrate Zoology, University of California, Berkeley; Natural History Museum of Los Angeles County, Los Angeles, CA; PRBO Conservation Science, Stinson Beach, CA; pullUin software, Vermillion, SD; San Diego Natural History Museum, San Diego, CA; Wings, Tucson, AZ.